Tuscarora-English / English-Tuscarora Dictionary

Twenty-five years ago, when Blair Rudes first began his research, there were still some fifty individuals who had learned Tuscarora as a first language and spoke it fluently. Rudes, who had the benefit of working with many of these speakers, has based his dictionary on their teachings. In addition, he draws from the extensive documentation of the language that dates back some three hundred years.

Tuscarora is an Iroquoian language originally spoken by inhabitants of the Carolinas. Forced to flee northward in the early eighteenth century, the Tuscaroras are centered today in two main localities: the Six Nations Reserve at Grand River, Ontario, and the Tuscarora Indian Nation Resevation near Lewiston, New York. Only four or five Turcaroras now remain who can speak their language fluently.

The dictionary is designed for use by the Tuscaroran people in reclaiming their language, and by anthropologists, historians, teachers, and linguists.

BLAIR A. RUDES is Senior Associate with Development Associates, Inc., and Adjunct Professor at American University in Washington, D.C.

BLAIR A. RUDES

Tuscarora-English / English-Tuscarora Dictionary

UNIVERSITY OF TORONTO PRESS
Toronto Buffalo London

© Blair A. Rudes, Tuscarora Indian Nation Council, and Tuscarora Band Council 1999
Toronto Buffalo London
www.utppublishing.com
Printed in the U.S.A.

Reprinted in paperback 2015

ISBN 978-0-8020-4336-8 (cloth)
ISBN 978-1-4426-2880-9 (paper)

Printed on acid-free paper

Library and Archives Canada Cataloguing in Publication

Rudes, Blair A.
Tuscarora-English, English-Tuscarora dictionary / Blair A. Rudes.

Includes bibliographical references and index.
ISBN 978-0-8020-4336-8 (bound). – ISBN 978-1-4426-2880-9 (pbk.)

1. English language – Dictionaries – Tuscarora.   2. Tuscarora language –
Dictionaries – English.   I. Title

PM2501.Z5R82 1999   497'.55   C989-32678-0

Financial support of this publication has been provided by the Government of
Ontario through the Ministry of Education and Training.

University of Toronto Press acknowledges the financial assistance to its publishing
program of the Canada Council for the Arts and the Ontario Arts Council, an agency
of the Government of Ontario.

University of Toronto Press acknowledges the financial support for its publishing
activities of the Government of Canada through the Canada Book Fund.

Contents

Preface

Over one hundred years ago, Erminnie A. Smith began work on a Tuscarora-English dictionary. In the late 1870s Smith was engaged by the U.S. Bureau of Ethnology (later renamed the Bureau of American Ethnology [BAE]) to carry out research on the cultures, languages, and native literatures of the Six Nations of the Iroquois, one product of which was a Tuscarora version of the Indian Language Schedule developed by the BAE's director, Major Powell (BAE ms. 375). She was aided in her work to complete the schedule by a young Tuscarora man named John Napoleon Brinton (J. N. B.) Hewitt. The material obtained to complete the schedule was organized into file slips as a prelude to a dictionary of the language. Upon the death of Smith in 1883 Hewitt was hired to complete the dictionary.

Hewitt's employment at the Bureau lasted more than fifty years, during which time he continued work on the dictionary and collected voluminous materials relating to the culture, history, language, and literature of the Iroquois and other Indian nations. However, Hewitt published very little during his lifetime and the dictionary begun by Smith (BAE ms. 2850) never appeared in print. Upon Hewitt's death in 1967 the file slips for the dictionary were found among the unpublished manuscripts in his office at the BAE and preserved in the National Anthropological Archives of the Smithsonian Institution in Washington, D.C.

In 1974 I began working with Tuscarora speakers to update Hewitt's material and make it more widely available. The first product of the research was a two-volume collection of texts in Tuscarora and English (Rudes and Crouse 1987). That work was soon followed by the publication of a lexicon, *Tuscarora Roots, Stems and Particles: Toward a Dictionary of Tuscarora* (Rudes, 1987), which presented the contents of my Tuscarora field notes through 1985. In the decade that has passed since these works appeared in print I have acquired much additional data on the language. For the present work I have re-elicited all of the data contained in the nearly 3,000 file slips of Smith and Hewitt's manuscript dictionary as well as the Tuscarora data contained in Hewitt's other unpublished papers. In addition every attempt was made to include all information about the Tuscarora language ever recorded by others. Material recorded prior to the mid-1900s was uniformly re-elicited, as were data collected later that were considered unreliable. The present dictionary includes all of the data presented in Rudes (1987), as well as all of the additional data from Hewitt's papers and other researchers' work. Nevertheless, I make no claim that the material I have included in this dictionary reflects all of the lexical resources of the Tuscarora language. Some roots or stems do not appear in the dictionary simply because they did not occur in the lexical and textual materials that were consulted.

In compiling the data on the Tuscarora language into a dictionary, many questions had to be answered in order to decide how to present the information. The first and undoubtedly most important question was, for whom is the dictionary intended? I determined that the main audience is the Tuscarora people. A second important audience comprises those individuals—anthropologists, historians, language teachers, and linguists—who are assisting the Tuscarora people in the development of instructional materials and reference works intended to aid in the reinforcement and continuation of the culture and language. Each of these two audiences has very different expectations of a dictionary.

The Tuscarora people are mainly interested in knowing the words of their language, although English, not Tuscarora, is now the primary language spoken by the Tuscarora people. In searching for a Tuscarora word most Tuscaroras will look up the English word to identify the Tuscarora equivalent in the English-Tuscarora section. If additional information about the word is desired, they will then turn to the Tuscarora-English section. These preferences dictated that the English-Tuscarora word index comprise English glosses (words and phrases) that approximated as closely as possible the meaning of the Tuscarora words listed under the glosses. Parenthetical references to entries providing fuller discussion of each word in the Tuscarora-English section follow each Tuscarora word.

On the other hand, scholars working to develop pedagogical materials and reference works want to know not only the existing words of the Tuscarora language but also the constituent parts (morphemes) that make up the words and that can be productively combined to form new words in the language. To serve the needs of this audience, a more technical format has been used in the Tuscarora-English section of the dictionary. Entries consist of roots, stems, and grammatical morphemes, as well as idiosyncratic words and particles. In addition an English-Tuscarora morpheme index is provided to aid scholars in locating relevant forms in the dictionary.

It has become common when writing in English, especially for professonals, to avoid the use of pronouns and nouns marked for a particular gender unless the referent of the word is clearly of the specified gender. Thus, for example, a sentence that ten years earlier might have read, "A policeman knows he must uphold the law," would, by authors sensitive to gender bias in language, be rendered as something like, "Police officers know they must uphold the law."

Every attempt has been made to embrace such gender-neutral usage in the text of this dictionary. However, the reader should be aware that there are important cultural and historical reasons why gender-neutral language is not employed everywhere in the dictionary.

First, much of the Tuscarora data and the corresponding English translations were recorded in the nineteenth and early twentieth centuries, long before awareness of gender bias in language had become widespread. This fact is perhaps most clearly demonstrated in the Tuscarora data contained in Smith and Hewitt's manuscript dictionary. With few exceptions, all of the verb forms with human subjects or objects in that database are inflected with a masculine pronominal prefix, which in Tuscarora can refer only to a male, and are thus glossed with the pronouns *he* or *him*. To have engaged in editing the language of Smith and Hewitt and other early researchers to achieve gender-neutrality would, I believe, have been an act of unwarranted historical revisionism and have destroyed the empirical value of the material presented. As should be clear from the archaic flavor of many glosses for Tuscarora words, these glosses are direct citations of the original authors' words.

However, the dictionary also contains much data that I personally collected and some glosses for these data are gender-marked. In part, the lack of gender-neutrality in these cases results from two considerations. First, the speakers of Tuscarora with whom I worked had nearly all passed their fiftieth birthday and had not been sensitized to issues of gender bias. Thus, they occasionally gave glosses for words in texts that specified gender unnecessarily. A second and clearly more important reason, however, is that I began my work with speakers of the Tuscarora language in the early 1970s, when I myself was only beginning to become aware of gender bias in English. Thus, some gender-biased glosses may result from my insensitivity at the time.

Some gender bias in English glosses also results from fundamental differences between the Tuscarora and Euro-American cultures. The Tuscarora culture is matrilineal (i.e., kinship and property are traced through the mother's rather than the father's lineage) and, at least in part, matriarchal (i.e., leading women within each clan [clan mothers] appoint the political leaders [chiefs] who are males). Similarly, the neutral gender in Tuscarora is the feminine rather than the masculine as in English. In the spirit of gender-neutral usage I have generally translated the feminine pronoun with the English indefinite pronoun *one* except where the referent is clearly female.

Finally, I feel a few words are needed on my choice of English orthography. Given that the final stages of the preparation of the dictionary were supported through a generous grant from the Province of Ontario and that the work has been published by a Canadian press, it would be reasonable to expect that the orthographic conventions of Canada, in the main the conventions used in the *Oxford Dictionary of the English Language*, would be followed. However, I have not done so and have instead used the orthographic conventions of *Webster's Unabridged Dictionary*, the standard for the United States of America. I have not made this choice lightly. As noted earlier, much of the material in the dictionary comes from information recorded by earlier researchers. With the sole exceptions of John Lawson, whose vocabulary dates from the late seventeenth century, and Frans Olbrechts, who wrote in Dutch, all of the earlier researchers were U.S. citizens and used Webster's orthography. To have edited the English orthography throughout the dictionary to Canadian standards would have distorted the authenticity of glosses. Thus, with apologies to Canadian readers, I have chosen to retain Webster's orthography for the dictionary.

Acknowledgments

In a very real sense every investigator who has worked to record the Tuscarora language and all of the Tuscarora speakers who have shared their knowledge of the language with researchers have materially contributed to this work. The names of these individuals appear on pages xv-xvi.

I am particularly grateful for the encouragement and support of the Chiefs Council of the Tuscarora Indian Nation and the leadership of the Tuscarora Band on the Six Nations Reserve for production of this dictionary. I also extend to Francene Patterson, the designated language specialist of the Tuscarora Chiefs Council, my sincerest thanks for her tireless assistance in gathering additional data, checking forms, serving as liaison with the Council, and proofreading earlier version of the dictionary. In addition I wish to express my appreciation to the staff of the National Anthropological Archives of the Smithsonian Institution in Washington, D.C., for assistance over the years in locating and obtaining copies of manuscripts by Albert S. Gatschet and J.N.B. Hewitt, and to the staff of the American Philosophical Society in Philadelphia, Pennsylvania, for providing copies of Anthony F.C. Wallace's field notes. Thanks are also due to Floyd G. Lounsbury and Michael K. Foster, who provided copies of their Tuscarora field work. In addition, I wish to acknowledge a debt to Michael K. Foster, Karin Michelson, and Hanni Woodbury for helping to shape my ideas about how to present Tuscarora data in the dictionary; Barbara Graymont for input on the history of the Tuscarora nation; and Kenneth Wentzel for developing the fonts used in the production of this dictionary.

Financial support for this work has been provided by the Government of Ontario through the Ontario Ministry of Education and Training (OMET). I thank John Stanley of OMET and the staff of the Woodland Cultural Centre in Brantford, Ontario, in particular the director—Joanna Bedard—for assistance in the administration of the grant.

Introduction

The first mention of the Tuscarora people in historical records appears in the mid-1600s when contacts between European settlers along the Carolina coast and inland tribes are noted in the *Colonial Records of the Carolinas* (Saunders, 1886-1980). However, significant details about the culture and language of the Tuscaroras did not appear until the writings of John Lawson, an English explorer, were published in 1701. Included in his description of the interior of the Carolinas was a vocabulary of the Tuscarora language.

Not long after Lawson compiled his vocabulary, troubles began between the European colonists and the Tuscaroras, troubles that escalated into the Tuscarora Wars of 1711-13. Following defeat in these wars the residents of the more southerly Tuscarora towns were forced to flee the area, while the residents of the more northerly towns remained.

In 1717 the Tuscaroras from the northern towns moved to a reservation in present-day Bertie County, North Carolina. Meanwhile, the fragmented peoples of the southern towns migrated northward and found their way to New York State. There they settled between the territories of the Onondagas and Oneidas, where they formed the Tuscarora Indian Nation and were adopted as the Sixth Nation of the Iroquois Confederacy sometime between September 1722 and May 1723.

Following the U.S. War for Independence, in which most of the Tuscaroras sided with the victors, the majority of the Tuscarora Indian Nation moved from Oneida territory to the general area of the present-day reservation at Niagara Landing. However, some 130 Tuscaroras who had sided with the colonists loyal to the British Crown relocated to Upper Canada (present-day Ontario). Later, in the early nineteenth century, religious factionalism erupted on the Tuscarora Reservation at Niagara Landing between converts to Christianity and adherents of traditional Tuscarora beliefs. Ultimately the non-Christians left the reservation and joined the Tuscaroras already living on the Six Nations Reserve.

Back in North Carolina relations between the Tuscaroras who had remained and their neighbors deteriorated and, in 1801, a delegation from the Tuscarora Nation in New York was dispatched to negotiate the sale of Tuscarora lands to the State. At the conclusion of the sale in 1804 most of the Tuscarora who had remained in North Carolina joined the negotiators in returning to the Tuscarora Indian Nation Reservation in New York. Thus, by 1804, the Tuscarora people were living in two main localities: the Tuscarora Indian Nation Reservation near Lewiston, New York, and the Six Nations Reserve in Upper Canada.

The fragmentation of the Tuscarora people between 1711 and 1804 had major repercussions on the language. However, several events that occurred at the outset of the twentieth century had even more profound consequences.

Up to the late 1800s nearly all members of the Nation, whether resident in the States of North Carolina and New York or the Province of Ontario, spoke Tuscarora as their first language. Beginning in the late 1800s many Tuscarora children were sent off-reservation to schools where they were forbidden to use their native language. The punishments for using their language were severe and left a lasting impression on the children. At the same time, the economic life of reservation residents became more closely intertwined with that of the surrounding non-Indian communities and there was a growing need to speak English. Given their experience as children at boarding schools and the economic necessities of the times, most Tuscaroras chose not to teach their children the language. Rather, they emphasized the learning of English. As a result, use of the language in the daily affairs of the Nation rapidly declined.

By the middle of this century both Anthony Wallace and Floyd Lounsbury found only a small number of fluent speakers on the Tuscarora Indian Nation Reservation, and in only a few families was the Tuscarora language in daily use. Twenty years later, when I began my work, there were around forty fluent speakers at the Tuscarora Indian Nation and another ten on the Six Nations Reserve. Now, around twenty-five years later, only one or two fluent speakers remain, although there are a number of individuals both in New York and Ontario who retain a limited facility with the language.

Language History

A great deal of information about the Tuscarora language has been recorded. Beginning with Lawson's late seventeenth century vocabulary, more than sixteen investigators have worked with more than twenty-seven speakers to record and preserve the language. This work has resulted in hundreds of pages of texts, vocabularies, grammatical notes, and even a manuscript dictionary. A chronological summary of this work is provided on the next page.

The vocabularies recorded in the early nineteenth century, when compared with vocabularies from other languages of North America, early made researchers realize that the Tuscarora language was most similar to the languages spoken by the Five Nations Iroquois (the Cayuga, Mohawk, Oneida, Onondaga, and Seneca) and the Huron. Subsequent research, most notably by the Tuscarora scholar J.N.B. Hewitt, revealed that these languages share striking similarities with the language spoken by the Cherokee.

Dates	Location	Speakers	Researcher
1700	Carolina Frontier	Unknown	John Lawson
1816	Tuscarora Nation	David Cusick	Thomas Jefferson
1836	Tuscarora Nation	Unknown	Thomas Parish
1848, 1960	Tuscarora Nation	William Chew	Gilbert Rockwood
1880-1883	Tuscarora Nation	Cornelius Cusick others	Lewis Henry Morgan
1883	Tuscarora Nation	J.N.B. Hewitt John Mt. Pleasant others	Erminnie A. Smith
1883-1912	Tuscarora Nation	John Gansworth Joseph Henry Lucinda Thompson George Williams Joseph Williams others	J.N.B. Hewitt
1929	Tuscarora Nation	Unknown	Frans Olbrechts
1948, 1949	Tuscarora Nation	Nellie Gansworth Jonas Green David Hewitt William Mt. Pleasant Denny Printup Clinton Rickard Edgar Rickard Daniel Smith	Anthony F.C. Wallace
1952, 1954	Tuscarora Nation	Nellie Gansworth	Floyd G. Lounsbury

Dates	Location	Speakers	Researcher
1964	Tuscarora Nation	Nellie Gansworth Martin Johnson	Joan G. Fickett
1966-1985	Tuscarora Nation	Nellie Gansworth Elias Johnson Clinton Rickard William Rickard	Barbara Graymont
1970-present	Tuscarora Nation Six Nations Reserve	Shirley Chew Elton Greene Eunice Hill Howard Hill Ellen Jacobs Robert Mt. Pleasant	Marianne Mithun
1972	Six Nations Reserve	Percy Cayuga	Michael K. Foster
1973-present	Tuscarora Nation	Paul Bissell Birdie Crogan Dorothy Crouse Louise Henry Eunice Hill Howard Hill David Patterson Kenneth Patterson Marjorie Printup Amelia Williams Ted Williams	Blair A. Rudes
1995-present	Tuscarora Nation	Eunice Hill Howard Hill	Francene Patterson

This group of languages has since come to be referred to as the Iroquoian language family.

By comparing the grammar and vocabulary from the various Iroquoian languages, researchers have learned much about the prehistory of the Iroquoian languages. For example, it is clear that all of these languages developed from a common parent language, Proto-Iroquoian, which was spoken about 3,500 years ago or around 1,500 B.C. (Lounsbury, 1961). About this time individual groups of Iroquoian speakers moved away from one another and developed separate dialects that became distinct languages. The first group to develop a separate language was the Cherokees.

Compared to Cherokee, all of the other Iroquoian languages — collectively known as Northern Iroquoian languages — are very similar; however, there are important differences. The largest number of differences are those found between the southernmost languages, Tuscarora and Nottoway, and the others. At the same time, the Tuscarora and Nottoway languages themselves are quite similar to one another (Rudes, 1981), which suggests that they developed from a common dialect that separated from the parent language around 100 B.C.

As noted earlier, the first substantial documentation of the Tuscarora language was the word list prepared by John Lawson at the end of the seventeenth century. Comparison of the Tuscarora words written down by Lawson with their modern equivalents reveals that the language has undergone very little change in pronunciation and grammar since the late 1600s, although there have been substantial changes in vocabulary. Lawson's vocabulary also provides the earliest recorded case of a loan word from English, namely, the word for *a horse* which Lawson gives as «A hots» (modern áha·θ). Nearly continuous contact with speakers of English since the late seventeenth century has resulted in other loan words as well. A representative sample of such loans that appear in this dictionary are kà·winar *governor*, yé·-suhs *Jesus*, pè·rih *barley*, lí·li· *lily*, spì·nič *spinach*, ú·č *oats*, pí·kak *peacock*, kwè·-nihs *cents, pennies*; *copper*, čí·hs *cheese*, káhwih *coffee*, lè·mun *lemon*, píhskit *biscuit, roll*, pì·ye⁷ *beer*, réhse·n *raisin*, ré·ti·θ *radish*, sá·iter *cider*, winí·ker *vinegar*, θútar *soldier*, stà·č *starch*, kà·nar *colonel*, krú·si⁷ *grocery store*, mę̀·nit *minute*, mę́·teh *Monday*, mí·ryę *billion*, sà·w *saw*, and stúw *stove*. It is noteworthy, however, how few such loan words there are. In all of the materials recorded on the Tuscarora language only around thirty English loan words have been found. And of these, the majority occur only in records from the twentieth century, when the use of the Tuscarora language had declined dramatically in favor of English.

Following the defeat of the Tuscaroras by the colonists and their Indian allies in the wars of 1711-1713, the historical records are mute as regards the language until the early nineteenth century, when Thomas Jefferson and other intellectuals of the period became interested in determining the relationships among the native peoples of the Americas through their languages. To this end they obtained vocabularies of Indian languages from knowledgeable sources. For the Tuscarora language the vocabularies include one by David Cusick, prepared for Thomas Jefferson (1817); one by William Chew, recorded for Henry Rowe Schoolcraft (1846); and one by Thomas Parish, collected for Albert Gallatin (1836). All of these vocabularies were recorded from speakers living in New York State. Later in the century, Lewis Henry Morgan visited the Tuscaroras and recorded several place names that appear in Morgan (1851). In addition he obtained a kinship schedule for the Tuscarora language from "a Tuscarora woman with Isaac Doctor (Seneca) as interpreter and a partial schedule from Cornelius Cusick" (1871).

The most copious sources of data on modern Tuscarora date from the late 1800s. These include the manuscript dictionary prepared by Smith and Hewitt, data gathered by Albert S. Gatschet, and materials compiled by Hewitt. These works record the Tuscarora language at a time when it was last learned as a first language and used as the daily medium of conversation.

The Tuscarora language recorded by Smith and Hewitt is noteworthy for its lack of variation from one speaker to the next. In part this results from the fact that all of their data were collected from speakers living in New York State, and there is little evidence in their works of any of the features that distinguish the Western dialect. The material gathered during the same time period by Albert S. Gatschet, however, shows nearly all of the features that characterize the modern Western dialect, although Gatschet collected his data from residents of the Tuscarora Nation in New York State. This may be due to the fact that the speaker with whom Gatschet worked most, Elias Johnson, was born in Canada and came to New York State at an early age. However, it may also reflect a tendency on Hewitt's part to normalize his transcription of Tuscarora and to eliminate divergent features. Corroborating evidence is provided by stray notes in Hewitt's manuscripts that show he was aware of the dialectal differences.

Twentieth-century scholars who have worked with Tuscarora speakers to record their language include Joan Fickett, Michael Foster, Floyd Lounsbury, Marianne Mithun, Frans Olbrechts, Francene Patterson, Anthony Wallace, and me.

Language Contact

In their historic homeland in the Carolinas the Tuscaroras were in direct contact with two other nations that spoke Northern Iroquoian languages, the Nottoway of southeastern Virginia (Rudes, 1981) and the Meherrin on the Virginia-Carolina border (Landy, 1978; Rudes, 1984). Little is known about the language of the Meherrin, but the information on the Nottoway language shows it to be fairly similar to Tuscarora. The similarities are such that any influence of one of these languages upon the other would be difficult if not impossible to identify.

When large portions of the Tuscarora people fled the Carolinas after the fall of Fort Neoheroka in 1713, many first sought refuge near the Susquehannock in Pennsylvania, another nation that spoke a Northern Iroquoian language (Mithun, 1981). However, given the meager data available on the Susquehannock language, it is impossible to determine what if any influence it had on Tuscarora. It was upon contact with the member nations of the Five Nations Iroquois and adoption as the Sixth Nation that major changes in Tuscarora vocabulary can be discerned.

As a result of membership in the Iroquois Confederacy, the Tuscaroras adopted wholesale the political and judicial procedures of the Confederacy and the words necessary to describe this new approach to government. Among the vocabulary items borrowed to talk about judicial and political matters was the verb stem –ne–.–ya[?]turehT–, which occurs in such words as nekakheya[?]tù·reht *I will judge them*; nehraya[?]turéhtha[?] *judge, magistrate* (compare Oneida tehaya[?]tolétha[?] *he judges her, judge* [Christjohn and Hinton, 1996: 508]). Also borrowed was the root –yan(e)(r)–, which occurs in such words as ruyà·ner *lord, Confederate Chief, Jesus Christ* (compare Mohawk royá·ner *he is noble, he is a confederate chief* [Michelson, 1995: 75]).

The move northward from the Carolinas also brought the Tuscaroras to a somewhat different terrain with geographic features, as well as flora and fauna, that were not common further south. For many of these features the Tuscaroras adopted words from other members of the Six Nations. Among the unfamiliar geographic features were lakes. The coastal plain of the Carolinas is characterized by many rivers flowing from the Appalachian Mountains to the Atlantic Ocean, but few bodies of water large enough to be called lakes. (Lakes that appear on modern maps of the area are nearly all reservoirs created by damming rivers.) New York, on the other hand, has numerous lakes. Thus, the Tuscaroras adopted the word unyá·tareh (compare Mohawk onyá·tara⁷ *lake* [Michelson, 1974: 86]).

Furthermore, while there are islands in many of the larger rivers of the Carolina coastal plain, few of them are large and most are transient, being covered over by the river during the rainy season. The islands found in the lakes of New York, on the other hand, are both larger and more permanent. The need to refer to these resulted in the adoption of the word yuhwè·nu⁷ (compare Oneida yohwé·note⁷ *island* [Christjohn and Hinton, 1996: 607]). The adoption of this word was most likely further influenced by the role that it plays in the formation of political terminology. The Iroquoian Cosmology teaches that the world is an island that was formed on the back of a turtle in the primordial sea (Hewitt, 1903, 1928; Rudes and Crouse, 1987).

Under the influence of this teaching, the root for island has taken on the meaning *continent, country*. This is seen in the following words: kahwené·tih *congress, legislature* (lit., "it makes islands"); rahwenętihú⁷y *Senator* (lit., "great island maker"); and uhwenętíhsteh *congress, continent, council, legislature, realm, reign, seat of government, the area of governmental representation* (lit., "that which makes islands"), as well as Ha⁷ Kę·nę⁷ Yuhwè·nu·⁷ *America*.

Numerous species of plants and animals that were rare or unknown on the Carolina coastal plain were encountered by the Tuscaroras in New York. Rather than create new words, the Tuscaroras frequently borrowed the terms in use by other member nations of the Iroquois Confederacy. New types of evergreens included hemlock (Tuscarora unę̇⁷teh—compare Oneida onv́·ta⁷ *hemlock* [Christjohn and Hinton, 1996: 602]) and tamarack (Tuscarora kanę̇⁷tęhs—compare Oneida kanvtv́·sa *tamarack* [Christjohn and Hinton, 1996: 650]). Deciduous trees not familiar to the Tuscaroras included birch (both yellow and white) (Tuscarora uná·kyeh—compare Oneida ona·ké· *birch* [Christjohn and Hinton, 1996: 567]) and black ash (Tuscarora kahęwè·ya⁷—compare Oneida kahuwe·· yá· *black ash* Christjohn and Hinton, 1996: 567]). Other plants common in New York but not in the Carolinas included apple trees and their fruit (Tuscarora θwahyù·wa⁷—compare Oneida sewahyo·wáne⁷ *apple* [Christjohn and Hinton, 1996: 562]), a species of corn adapted to the colder northern climate, a type of white or flour corn (Tuscarora kanęhakę̇·rat—compare Seneca onę̇ǫkę·ęt *white corn* [Chafe 1967 #1155]), and pigweed (Tuscarora θkanatanę̇hwe⁷–

compare Oneida skanuʔtanu·wé· [Christjohn and Hinton, 1996: 626]).

Unfamiliar fauna of New York for which the Tuscaroras borrowed names included the loon (Tuscarora aʔù·węʔ— compare Oneida aho·wv́ *loon* [Christjohn and Hinton, 1996: 614]), the moose (Tuscarora θkaʔnyę́hseh—compare Oneida skaʔnyúhsaʔ *moose* [Christjohn and Hinton, 1996: 619]), the muskrat (Tuscarora anúʔkwyę—compare Mohawk anò·tyv *muskrat* [Michelson, 1974: 28]), and the mullet (Tuscarora θkarihstù·waʔ—compare Seneca káisto·wa·ʔ *mullet* [Chafe 1967 #797]).

The climate of New York differed from that of the Carolinas in degree rather than kind. That is, the Tuscarora were already familiar and had words for all of the different aspects of weather encountered in New York, e.g., hail, rain, sleet, snow, cold, cool, hot, warm, wind, lightning, thunder. For the most part, these words were cognate with those used by the other five of the Six Nations. However, because the colder aspects of weather were more noticeable in New York, certain conditions resulting from cold weather were new to the Tuscarora. For example, it is rare for enough snow to accumulate on the coastal plain for slush to form during warmer weather. Thus, when the Tuscarora encountered slush in New York, they borrowed a word (Tuscarora yunyataná·wę·) from Oneida or Mohawk to refer to it.

Less than twenty years elapsed between the initiation of direct contact and trade between the Tuscaroras and Europeans in the Carolinas and their flight north. Furthermore, the last five or so years of this time were characterized by intermittent aggression leading to full-scale war. As a result, the Tuscaroras did not fully become accustomed to or adopt the European approaches to commerce until they arrived north. There, the Five Nations were thoroughly knowledgeable about the European notions of buying and selling, and the use of currency. These concepts the Tuscaroras learned from their Iroquois neighbors. This is reflected by the fact that two of the roots most central to the European approach to commerce are borrowed from other Northern Iroquoian languages, viz., the roots meaning *sell* (Tuscarora –atęhninę– as in ękayętęhninę́hek *they will be selling things* and utęhninę́hsteh *a shop* [compare Mohawk katvhní·nus *I sell* [Michelson, 1974: 53]) and the root meaning *money* (Tuscarora –hwihst– as in uhwíhstaʔ *cash, money* and yuhwíhstuʔ *lucrative*—compare Mohawk ohwístaʔ *metal, bell, money* [Michelson, 1974: 58]). Furthermore, in addition to a native root meaning *buy* (Tuscarora –tyaʔk–), a borrowed root (Tuscarora –hninę– as in ranęhsnahnì·nęh *he buys grain*, ranęθahnì·nęh *he buys potatoes*—compare Mohawk khní·nus *I buy* [Michelson, 1974: 53]) is used. With the use of currency came the knowledge that one could be without it. To describe this condition the Tuscarora borrowed the root seen in rutę́htaʔ *he's poor* (compare Oneida lotv́thaʔ *he's poor* [Christjohn and Hinton, 1996: 223]).

Most historians date the rise of Christianity among the Tuscaroras to the arrival on the Tuscarora Reservation of Reverend Elkanah Holmes of the New York Missionary Society in 1800. This was not, however, the Tuscaroras' first brush with this religion. The records show that attempts were made to bring Christianity to the Tuscaroras who stopped at the Freiedenhaus settlement in

Pennsylvania on their way north, albeit with apparently little success. Also, the Tuscarora would have been at least exposed to Christianity while they resided in Oneida territory as the result of early missionary work among the Oneida, as well as the neighboring Mohawks and Onondagas, and the conversion of some to this faith. Whatever the cause, Christianity came to the Tuscaroras after they had fled the Carolinas and joined their northern relatives. This is amply demonstrated by the fact that much of the vocabulary of Christianity in use among the Tuscaroras is borrowed from other Northern Iroquoian languages. Identifiable loan words include rawęnì·yu⁹ *God* and kayeręhya⁹kyehrù·nę⁹ *angels* (compare Mohawk rawvní·yo *God* [Michelson, 1974: 119] and eruhya⁹kehró·nu *angels* [Michelson, 1974: 100]); the root seen in ru⁹nęčhu·t *he is kneeling* and ra⁹nęčhú·tha⁹ *he kneels*, and the phrase ha⁹ ru⁹nęčhu·t *genuflection* (compare Oneida tehatutsótha⁹ *he is kneeling* [Christjohn and Hinton, 1996: 139]; and the root seen in wahratrę̀·nayę⁹ *he prayed* (compare Mohawk aterv́·nayv *prayer* [Michelson, 1974: 96]). Also here belongs the personal name of the famous Seneca prophet *Handsome Lake*, Ɵkanyatarí·yu· (compare Mohawk skanyatarí·yo *Handsome Lake* [Michelson, 1974: 86]). It may also be the case that the loan word uhyatę́hsteh *book, paper* (compare Mohawk kahyatúhsera⁹ *book, paper* [Michelson, 1974: 59]) belongs here, originally borrowed to refer to the Bible, although subsequently the more specific term uhyatęhstatukę́hti (lit. "holy book"), consisting of two borrowed roots, came to be used for the Bible.

As illustrated above, there are good reasons why the Tuscaroras borrowed most of the words that are foreign to the language. However, there remain a few words of foreign origin for which no good reason for borrowing can be found. For example, despite the existence of several native words for *rock, stone*, including the word uhrę́⁹neh, the Tuscaroras borrowed the word učtę́hreh from either Oneida or Mohawk (compare Mohawk otstv̀·ra⁹ *rock* [Michelson, 1974: 64]) and this has become the everyday word. Similarly, there is plenty of evidence from early written records as well as other vocabulary in the Tuscarora language that they knew how to and in fact did hunt while in the Carolinas. Nevertheless, the Tuscaroras borrowed a root for *hunt* from another Northern Iroquoian language, probably Oneida, seen for example in ratú·ra·č *he hunts: hunter* (compare Oneida lato·láts *he hunts* [Lounsbury, 1953: 86]).

Tuscarora Dialects

The historical records of the Tuscarora language show that there always has been variation in pronunciation and vocabulary among speakers. This variation continues among contemporary speakers of the language. Some differences appear to be unique to individuals. Most, however, are shared by groups of speakers and serve to distinguish the major dialects of the language.

Two major dialects of modern Tuscarora may be distinguished: the Western dialect, spoken on the Six Nations Reserve in Canada, and the Eastern dialect, spoken on the Tuscarora Indian Reservation in the United States. The major differences between the Western and Eastern dialects concern vocabulary and pronunciation. Living among members of the other nations of the Six Nations Confederacy at Grand River, speakers of Western Tuscarora were subject to greater influence from the other Northern Iroquoian languages. This is particularly noticeable in vocabulary. However, not all of the differences between the two dialects result from borrowing from other languages. Rather, some differences are the result of independent innovations to name items new to the culture, and still others reflect different treatments of inherited words. The list below illustrates the differences through a comparison of words taken from a vocabulary of the Western dialect (Cayuga, 1972) and the equivalent words as they appear in the Eastern dialect.

Six Nations	Tuscarora Nation	Translation
u'ę̇·'neh	unáčreh	*bow*
utrá'neh	awętrá'neh	*horn*
u'áhsę	uhá'θeh	*neck*
u'áhneh	uturáčreh	*ribs*
u'téhareh	u'téheh	*sand*
učí·steh	u'nihsę̇·reh	*star*
utenę̇hstreh	híhne'?	*sun*
uhwíhsneh	uyęhwíθneh	*wing*
wakye'tawá'kę	wakwá'kę	*I hold it*
wá·kwahst	wákwahst	*it is good*
ì·wes	tiwe·θ'ú'y	*it is long*

The most noticeable difference in pronunciation between the Eastern and Western dialects is the loss of the distinction between *s* and *θ* in the Western dialect, where both are pronounced as *s*. Thus, for example, the contrast seen in Eastern srihwíhs'ahs *you promise* and θrihwíhs'a· *promise!* is reduced to a difference between srihwíhs'ahs *you promise* and srihwíhs'a· *promise!* in the Western dialect. The loss of the difference between *s* and *θ* is not unique to the Western dialect of Tuscarora; the same change is found in all of the other modern Northern Iroquoian languages, although the distinction between the two fricatives found today only in the Eastern dialect of Tuscarora is also found in the early records of Onondaga, Huron, and Wyandot (Rudes, 1992).

A second distinctive feature of the Western dialect is the consonant cluster *hstr*, which corresponds to Eastern *hst*. For example, the word for *year* in the Eastern dialect is awúhsteh, whereas this word appears as awúhstreh in the Western dialect. Comparative evidence shows that the pronunciation found in the Western dialect is older, since Western *hstr* and Eastern *hst* correspond to *hsr* in Cayuga and *sl* in Oneida. These correspondences indicate that the cluster was originally **hsr*. In early Tuscarora a *t* was inserted as a transitional consonant between the *s* and the *r*. In the Eastern dialect the *r* was later dropped.

Another feature of the Western dialect, which it shares with certain other Six Nation languages, is the loss of *w* from *wy* clusters, as seen in Western uyáhseh and Eastern uwyáhseh, both meaning *cross*. The consonant cluster *wy* is preserved in the Eastern dialect and by some Oneida speakers, broken up by an epenthetic vowel in Mohawk (*wey*) and Cayuga (*way*), and simplified to *y* in Onondaga and Seneca, as well as by some speakers of Oneida.

The Western dialect also exhibits a distinctive epenthesis of the vowel *i* between a pronominal prefix and a verb root or stem that begins with the consonant cluster *ʔn*. For example, whereas one finds wáʔtknę*ʔ I fly* (root –ne –.–ʔnę– *fly*) in the Eastern dialect, the Western dialect has waʔtkí·ʔnę*ʔ I fly* (with regular penultimate accent and vowel length).

The Western dialect also shares several changes that distinguish subdialects within Eastern Tuscarora. These include the loss of vowel length in some word-final syllables, pronunciation of some instances of *t* and *k* after vowels as the clusters *ʔt* and *ʔk*, the change of syllable-final *r* to *s*, and loss of some instances of word-final *w*.

While there were likely differences in the speech of different members of the Tuscarora community on the Six Nations Reserve in Ontario, no evidence of these differences has survived. On the Tuscarora Indian Reservation, on the other hand, there is abundant evidence of differences in pronunciation among speakers. The following discussion of dialect variation among speakers of Eastern Tuscarora is based on information recorded between 1948 and the present from ten speakers. The speakers

and the researchers were previously listed on pages xv-xvi. The major dialect differences among these speakers, and how their speech compares to the Western dialect and to the late 1800s speech of George Williams (Eastern dialect) and Elias Johnson (Western dialect), are shown on the next page.

The most obvious pronunciation difference within the Eastern dialect is between speakers who pronounce syllable-final *r* in čír *dog* and urhá·ʔnakęw *in the forest* as a voiceless trill [r] and those speakers who pronounce syllable-final *r* as a distinctively long, tense *s* [s·]. Speakers with the first pronunciation include Amelia Williams, Dan Smith, Louise Henry, Birdie Crogan, and Elton Greene. Speakers with the second pronunciation include Dorothy Crouse, Percy Cayuga, Nellie Gansworth, Martin Johnson, Clinton Rickard, and Marjorie Printup. The data recorded in 1883 by Albert S. Gatschet and a few notations in manuscripts left by J.N.B. Hewitt indicate that this dialect feature was already present in the late 1800s.

Many speakers who pronounce syllable-final *r* as *s* also have a distinctive pronunciation of syllable-final *y*, as in Uyhęha·kt *Lewiston, New York*. While most speakers' pronunciation of syllable-final *y* is similar to the pronunciation of *ch* in German ich *I* and Milch *milk*, for some speakers syllable-final *y* is pronounced like *sh* in English fish.

Another difference in the pronunciation of different speakers of Tuscarora is the articulation of word-final clusters of *y* and *ʔ*. For the majority of speakers whose speech was documented in the 1900s, the consonants *y* and *ʔ* occur in the order *ʔy* when final in a word as in wahrꞓheʔy *he died* and unꞓhsehúʔy *big*

Speaker	r > s	y > š	yʔ > ʔy	V· > V	hstr > hst	θ > s
George Williams	-	-	-	-	+	-
Louise Henry	-	-	-	-	+	-
Elton Greene	-	-	+	-	+	-
Amelia Williams	-	-	+	+	+	-
Birdie Crogan	-	-	+	-	+	-
Kenneth Patterson	+	+	+	-	+	-
Nellie Gansworth	+	+	+	-	+	-
Marjorie Printup	+	+	+	-	+	-
Martin Johnson	+	+	+	+	+	-
Dorothy Crouse	+	+	+	+	+	-
Elias Johnson	+	+	+	-	-	+
Percy Cayuga	+	+	(> ʔ)	+	-	+

house. For a few speakers, however, these consonants occur in the order *yʔ*, in particular in the augmentative enclitic. Thus, for these speakers, the word for *big house* is pronounced unęhsehúyʔ. Evidence from texts recorded by J.N.B. Hewitt suggests that this latter pronunciation is older, since he consistently wrote the augmentative enclitic «u-wiʼ» as in «u-něⁿ-se-hu-wiʼ».

There is great variation in the pronunciation of syllable-final *w*. (For fuller discussion, see chapter 1 of Rudes, 1976.) The variation results from two changes. First, as in the case of *r* and *y*, some speakers change the pronunciation of syllable-final *w* from a voiceless resonant [w] to an obstruent in certain environments. This obstruent may be either a bilabial fricative [φ] or labiodental fricative [f]. Thus, wáʔkhaʔw *I brought*

it may be pronounced with a final [w], [φ], or [f]. Second, syllable-final *w* is completely eliminated by some speakers, in particular when it follows the consonant *k*. For example, while some speakers pronounce wáʔtkatkw *I danced* as [wáʔ-t'gɑtkw], others pronounce it as if there were no final *w*, saying [wáʔ-t'gɑtk]. When a word-final *w* is eliminated, the preceding vowel is lengthened. Thus, while some speakers pronounce unęhsakęw *in the house* as [ù·-nęh-sa-Gęf], others pronounce this word [ù·-nęh-sa-Gę·].

For some speakers of Tuscarora, the obstruent stops *t* and *k* are preglottalized, that is, pronounced extra strong in certain environments. For *k*, this occurs whenever the consonant follows a vowel as in ukyéʔweh *hair* [u-'G·yǽʔ-wæh] and ękíʔręʔ *I will set* [ę-'G·íʔ-ręʔ]. The consonant *t* is preglottalized (strong) in the same environments; however, there is a special restriction on *t*. Only certain instances of *t*, namely, those that derive historically from Proto-Northern Iroquoian **t* show this pronunciation. Those *t*'s that result from the change of Proto-Northern Iroquoian **n* to Tuscarora *t* do not. Thus, one finds that the *t* of útkę*ʔ inherent power*, from Proto-Northern Iroquoian *ótkę*ʔ*, shows preglottalization ([ú·'tgę*ʔ*]), whereas the *t* of ká·tkę*ʔ blood, gore*, from Proto-Northern Iroquoian *kánkǫ*ʔ* ([gá·-tgę*ʔ*]), does not. This restriction on the preglottalization of *t*, together with other evidence (see Rudes, 1981), indicates that the feature arose early in the history of the Tuscarora language. Other speakers (e.g., Amelia Williams) preserve the preglottalization of *t*, but do not preglottalize *k* at all. Still other speakers (e.g., Dorothy Crouse and Percy Cayuga) have reinterpreted some cases of preglottalized *t* as clusters of *ʔ* plus *t*, but have otherwise completely lost the feature.

A distinctive feature of the Tuscarora, Seneca, and Cayuga languages, as compared with other Northern Iroquoian languages, is the presence of a contrast between long and short vowels in word-final syllables. This is seen, for example, in the difference between waʔkíʔrę*ʔ I was at home*, with a short final vowel, and waʔkíhrę·*ʔ I said*, with a long final vowel. The evidence indicates that this contrast is old and has been lost in the other languages (Rudes, 1995). Based on the data from researchers who heard and recorded the contrast of vowel length at the end of words in Tuscaora, the following situation appears to have prevailed. The older contrast of long and short vowels in final syllables was fully preserved in the speech of Birdie Crogan, Nellie Gansworth, Elton Greene, Louise Henry, and Marjorie Printup. Amelia Williams preserved the distinction everywhere except before final laryngeals (*h*, *ʔ*), where the contrast was usually lost in favor of the short vowel. For Percy Cayuga and Dorothy Crouse, the contrast was lost completely before a word-final consonant or consonant cluster, but preserved when no consonant followed.

Guide to Using the Dictionary

Most dictionaries of Iroquoian languages published in the twentieth century have been concerned with listing the morphemes of the languages, as well as uninflected particles. As a result, the majority of entries in these dictionaries have comprised root morphemes. (See, for example, Chafe, 1967; Michelson, 1974; Feeling, 1978; Rudes, 1987.) However, comments by Iroquois speakers and other dictionary users, as well as researchers, most notably Michael Foster, Karin Michelson, and Hanni Woodbury (1988), indicate that this approach has failed to describe adequately the lexical resources of these languages.

Words in the Tuscarora language can be defined in terms of phonological and morphological characteristics. In phonological terms a word in Tuscarora is a unit of speech that, when spoken in isolation, has only one word-stress, which may fall on the ultimate, penultimate, or antepenultimate syllable (Rudes, 1995). However, in connected speech comprising two or more words, the word-stress may be lost on simple words that carry grammatical meaning (particles).

In morphological terms words in Tuscarora are defined by restrictions on possible initial and final morphemes. In this regard, Tuscarora words must be divided into two classes: those which are morphologically simple and those which are morphologically complex. Simple words have no internal structure; that is, they cannot be subdivided further into smaller meaningful parts (morphemes). Complex words, on the other hand, have internal structure. That is, they are built from roots with the addition of other roots and affixes (prefixes and suffixes). A detailed discussion of the morphological composition of Tuscarora words and the distributional restrictions on initial and final morphemes is provided in Williams (1974).

Separate main entries are provided for simple words as well as the constituents of complex words, namely roots and affixes. In addition, there are many combinations of roots with other roots or with affixes (stems) that have come to have idiomatic meanings that cannot be derived from the meanings of the individual morphemes (roots, affixes) from which they are built. Such stems are also listed as main entries in the dictionary. Phrases that have become fixed expressions with idiomatic meanings and enclitics (i.e., lexical forms that appear sometimes as simple words and other times as suffixes on preceding words) are also given separate main entries.

All of the different types of main entries share certain common elements. For example, they all begin with the main entry given in **bold** typeface followed by the English gloss (i.e., approximations of the meaning of the entry). It also is important to note that many main entries have more than one English gloss for one or another of the following reasons.

Speakers of a language may develop specialized meanings for certain roots, stems, and words, which at the same time retain the basic meaning. Thus, a word that originally had one meaning may come to be polysemous, i.e., have several meanings. An example of this phenomenon in English is provided by the word root, as in root (of a tree), root (of a problem), and root (of a word). In the dictionary specialized meanings are separated from one another and the more general meaning by semicolons, as in the main entry −nȩhs− *cage, cottage, house, hut; umbrella; hut or lodge of an animal such as a beaver or muskrat.*

A more frequent explanation for multiple English glosses for Tuscarora words is the fact that there can be significant differences in the ways in which speakers of two different languages talk about the world around them. Such cultural differences can, in turn, be reflected in the range of meaning of words in the two languages. This phenomenon can easily be illustrated using the English and French languages. In French an

obligatory distinction is made between a large flow of water *towards* a lake, ocean, or sea (une fleuve) and a large flow of water *away* from a lake, ocean, or sea (une rivière). In English, on the other hand, a large flow of water is called a river, regardless of whether it flows toward or away from an ocean or sea. Thus, in a bilingual English-French dictionary, the word river would be glossed by both French fleuve and rivière. An example involving Tuscarora and English is the Tuscarora root −nȩT−, which means both *hill* and *mountain.*

Finally, a Tuscarora main entry may have several glosses in English for purely arbitrary reasons. For example, in the early days of contact between the Tuscarora people and the English colonists, the Tuscaroras learned that the English used the word bear to refer to the animal that they called uhčíhrȩ?. Later, the Tuscarora people were introduced to a fruit that the European colonists called a pear. Since the Tuscarora language does not distinguish between voiced and voiceless consonants, the word pear sounded just like the word bear and, therefore, the word uhčíhrȩ? *bear* was used to name the pear as well (Fickett, 1967).

Returning to the discussion of the common features of main entries in this dictionary, the gloss(es) of the main entry is (are) followed by an abbreviation that states the specific nature of the entry (e.g., verb root, noun root). Where necessary, this abbreviation is followed by a note that explains any unexpected features of the entry.

There is one last common feature of all of the main entries in the dictionary that should be noted. For every word (as opposed to root, stem, or affix) cited in main entries, an abbreviated reference to the earliest published or unpublished source, i.e., book, article, or manuscript, is provided in parentheses following the word. The abbreviations consist of the last name or initials of the authors, followed where necessary by the page number in the source where the word appears. (The abbreviation used for each source is provided following the citation for the reference under *Sources of Tuscarora Words*.) Furthermore, since words and phrases cited in the dictionary are often taken from sentences in published texts, I have typically not provided additional example sentences for words or phrases here.

The remaining information in each main entry differs according to the specific type of entry involved. In general, entries for simple words contain the least additional information, while entries for noun roots contain more information and entries for verb roots contain the most.

Simple Words

Words that have no internal structure, that is, that are not created from roots or stems through the addition of prefixes and/or suffixes, are called here simple words and appear as main entries in the dictionary. Simple words may be distinguished by the role that they play in forming sentences in the language. By far the largest number of simple words are particles, that is, words that carry various adjectival, adverbial, and grammatical meanings such as kęˀ *where*, né·kti· *two*, ahskę̀·nęˀ *slow, peaceful,* and tíhsnęˀ *and*. In addition, there are a handful of nouns and verbs that occur as simple words. A typical entry for a particle is shown in the first example below, a typical entry for a

noun is shown in the second example, and a typical entry for a verb is shown in the third example.

Particle

áhsę three (RC 23:2) [Lawson «Ohs-sah» '3']. *part.* −ahsę̧hst −: uhsę́hsteh ‹three-'ness› *patrimony, inheritance from one's father* (HS); áhsę ę́·či −raku −: áhsę ę́·či ękará·kuˀ ‹three one prediction-it-choose› *one third* (AG); áhsę ti −. −ahθhę −: áhsę tiwáhθhę· ‹three so-it-is ten› *thirty* (R) [Lawson «Ossa tewartsau» '30'].

Noun

čárhuˀ tobacco *(Nicotiana angustifolia)* [Lawson «Char-ho» 'tobacco'] [Gallatin «charhouh»]. *n.* n-poss., inc. Requires the increment −n − when incorporated. −čarhuˀn̲atyaˀT −: wahračarhúˀnatyaˀt ‹fact-he-tobacco-bought› *he bought tobacco* (R); −čarhuˀnahrihr −: ęyečarhuˀnáhrir ‹prediction-one-tobacco-scatter› *one will scatter tobacco* (RC 16:1).

Verb

kíˀah listen! (R). *v.*

Main entries for simple words, be they particles, nouns, or verbs, include the following information:
1. The word, written in phonemic transcription in **bold** letters.
2. The English gloss(es) for the word.
3. For words referring to plants or animals, the genus and species (in *italics*) are provided where known.

4. An indication in parentheses of the published or unpublished source of the word. Where a word occurs in multiple sources, reference is to the earliest, beginning with Smith and Hewitt's dictionary.

5. For words documented in eighteenth- and early nineteenth-century sources, the following information is provided in square brackets: the name of the author of the source, the Tuscarora word found in the source enclosed in double-angled brackets («»), and its gloss(es).

6. An abbreviated specification of whether the entry is a noun (*n*.), a particle (*part*.), or a verb (*v*.).

7. An indication of any important idiosyncrasies about the morphology, semantics, or use of the word.

8. Additional stems or words that are derived from the main entry, either by means of enclitics or through compounding. For each derived stem, the following information is provided:

a. The stem, written in morphophonemics, or the word, written in phonemics, printed in **bold**.

b. A rough morpheme-by-morpheme translation in single angle brackets (‹›) followed by the gloss in *italics* and all of the same information described in (1-5).

c. For stems, a Tuscarora word containing the stem is provided, written in phonemics.

d. Following the Tuscarora word, all of the same information described in (b) is provided.

e. Additional words containing the stem follow.

Roots

The simplest type of complex word is one composed of a root plus one or more prefixes or suffixes. There are two types of roots in the language, verb roots and noun roots, distinguished by the meanings that they carry and the prefixes and suffixes with which they occur.

Verb Roots. The most complex types of main entries in the dictionary are verb roots. The example below provides a partial dictionary entry for a typical transitive verb root. (Not all of the stems formed from the root are listed here. See the actual entry in the dictionary.) Each

---

–**ahrihr** – scatter, sow. *v.r.-t.* hab: -s, pnt: -ɸ, stat: -, prog: -, prp: -, dst: -, caus: -, rvs: -, dat: -, inc.-ɸ-pat. ráhrihč *he sows* (HS), ęhráhrir *he will sow* (HS); –**yah** –. –**ahrihr** –: yahwahráhrir ‹thither-fact-he-scattered› *he threw it there* (RC 14:3); –**čarha̱ʔnahrihr** –: ęyečarha̱ʔnáhrir ‹prediction-one-tobacco-scatter› *one will scatter tobacco* (RC 16:1); –**nęhsnahrihr** –: ranęhsnáhrihč ‹he-seed-scatters› *he sows the grain; spills the grain* (H 2484); –**ʔwah** = **θrahrihr** –: raʔwahθráhrihč ‹he-drop-scatters› *he sprinkles* (HS).

---

entry for a verb root presents minimally the following information:

1. The root, given in morphophonemic transcription and written in **bold** letters.

2. The English gloss(es) for the root.

3. An abbreviated specification of the type of verb root, that is:

- verb root-transitive (*v.r.-t.*)
- verb root-active intransitive (*v.r.-a.i.*)
- verb root-stative intransitive (*v.r.-s.i.*)
- verb root-kin term (*v.r.-k.*).

4. A list of the lexically determined allomorphs of the suffixes that have been

observed with the root, in the following order:
- habitual aspect (hab:)
- punctual aspect (pnt:)
- stative aspect (stat:)
- progressive (prog:)
- purposive (prp:)
- distributive (dst:)
- causative (caus:)
- reversive (rvs:)
- dative (dat:).

The dative suffix itself occurs in three series, each with distinctive forms before different verbal aspects (Williams, 1974: 75).

	I	II	III
Habitual/ stative	-ʔθe-	-ati-	-ati-
Punctual/ imperative	-ʔθ-	-ahθ-	-ę-

These series are abbreviated {dative I}, {dative II}, and {dative III}, respectively.

A hyphen following any one of the suffix labels indicates that the root has not been documented with that morpheme. If the root has been found with two or more different forms of one of these morphemes, the alternatives are listed in order of frequency and separated by a tilde (~). (The habitual aspect and punctual aspect do not occur with stative intransitive verbs and are thus not noted for such entries. Similarly, none of these suffixes occurs with verb roots denoting kin terms for relations who are the same age or youn-ger than the speaker and, thus, all are omitted.)

5. An indication of whether the root accepts incorporated noun roots (incorporating [inc.], non-incorporating [n-inc.]) and, if it does, an indication of the form of the empty noun root that occurs when no noun root is incorporated (ɸ indicates that the root does not require an empty noun root). If more than one empty noun root occurs with the entry, they are listed in order of frequency and separated by a tilde (~). Also provided is an indication of whether the verb root incorporates only noun roots representing the patient of the verb (-pat.), only noun roots representing the agent of the verb (-ag.), or both (-ag./pat.).

6. An indication of any important idiosyncrasies about the morphology, semantics, or use of the root.

7. The presentation of words containing the entry follows the information described in (1) and (6). Words are cited in the following standard format:

a. The word, written in phonemic transcription.

b. The English gloss(es) (in *italics*).

c. For words referring to plants or animals, the genus and species (in *italics*) are provided.

d. An indication in parentheses of the source of the word. Where a word may be found in multiple sources, preference is given to the earliest, beginning with the dictionary by Smith and Hewitt.

e. For words documented in eighteenth- and early nineteenth-century sources, the following information appears in square brackets ([]): the name of the author of the source, the Tuscarora word found in the source enclosed in double-angled brackets («»), as well as its gloss(es).

8. Following the information described in (7) are listed stems derived from the main entry. They are presented in the following order: stems composed of the root plus one or more suffixes, stems composed of the root plus one or more prepronominal prefixes, stems composed of the root plus one or more suffixes and

one or more prepronominal prefixes, and stems composed of two or more roots or roots and particles, with or without suffixes and/or prepronominal prefixes, which result in lexical items composed of more than one word. For each derived stem, the following information is provided:

a. The stem, written in morphophonemic transcription and printed in **bold**.

b. A Tuscarora word containing the stem, written in phonemic transcription.

c. A rough morpheme-by-morpheme translation of the word enclosed in single-angled brackets (‹›).

d. Following the morpheme-by-morpheme translation all of the same information described in (7b) through (e) is provided.

e. Additional words containing the stem follow.

For each example, all of the same information described in (b) through (d) is provided.

Noun Roots. The next most complex types of entries are those for noun roots. The following example provides a partial entry for a typical noun root. (Not all of

---

-**ahry**- bait, fishing gear, fishing line, fishhook. *n.r.* aln.: akáhryayę[?] *my fishing gear, tackle* (R), inc., n.sfx.: -eh. úhryeh *bait, fishing gear, fishing line, fishhook, tackle* (R); -**ahryu**-: ráhryuh ‹he-fishing gear-is in water› *he fishes* (HS).

---

the stems derived from the root are listed here. See the actual listing in the dictionary.) Each entry for a noun root provides minimally the following information:

1. The root, given in morphophonemic transcription and written in **bold**.

2. The English gloss(es) for the root.

3. A notation that the entry is a noun root (*n.r.*).

4. An indication of whether the possessibility of the root is unknown, the root is unpossessible (i.e., cannot be inflected to indicate the possessor [n-poss.]), can be inflected to indicate inalienable possession (inaln.), can be inflected to indicate alienable possession (aln.), or can be inflected both to indicate alienable and inalienable possession. If the root can be inflected either for alienable or inalienable possession, or both, one or more examples of the inflected root, together with the English gloss(es) and an indication as to source, are provided.

5. An indication of whether the incorporability of the root is unknown, the root is unincorporable (n-inc.), or the root can be incorporated (inc.) into appropriate verb roots and stems.

6. A specification of which form(s) of the simple noun suffix (n.sfx.) occur with this root. If the root occurs with more than one simple noun suffix, but one is considered older or archaic, this is noted as well. Also, if there are differences in the meaning of the root when it occurs with different simple noun suffixes, this is noted.

7. An indication of any important idiosyncrasies about the morphology, semantics, or use of the root.

8. The presentation of words containing the entry begins following the information described in (1) and (7). Words are cited in the following format:

a. The word, written in phonemic transcription with initial capital letters for proper names.

b. The English gloss(es) for the word, written in *italics*.

c. For words referring to plants or animals, the genus and species (in *italics*) are provided.

d. An indication of the source of the word is given in parentheses. Where a word may be found in multiple sources, preference is given to the earliest, beginning with the dictionary by Smith and Hewitt.

e. For words documented in eighteenth- and early nineteenth-century sources, the following information is provided in square brackets ([]): the name of the author of the source, the Tuscarora word found in the source enclosed in double-angled brackets («»), and its gloss(es).

9. Following the information described in (8) are listed stems that are derived from the main entry. For each derived stem, the following information is provided:

a. The stem, written in morphophonemic transcription in **bold** letters.

b. A Tuscarora word containing the stem, written in phonemic transcription.

c. A rough morpheme-by-morpheme translation enclosed in single-angled brackets (‹›).

d. Following the morpheme-by-morpheme translation all of the same information described in (8b) through (e) is provided.

e. Additional words containing the stem follow. For each example, all of the same information described in (b) through (d) above is provided.

Stems

Stems in Tuscarora are built from roots through the addition of other roots, derivational suffixes, or certain prefixes. In the case where a stem contains a prefix, the stem may be considered discontinuous since inflection for pronominal person, gender, and number appears between the prefix and the rest of the stem. This is indictated in main entry by the symbols (-.-) placed between the prefix and the rest of the stem.

Also, any stem formed with the dative suffix is considered discontinuous since aspect suffixes may occur between the dative and the other part of the stem. Therefore, the symbol (-) separates the dative from the rest of the stem.

Many stems in Tuscarora are transparent in meaning; that is, the meaning of the stem can be derived from the meaning of the roots and affixes from which it is constructed. For example, the stem **-nęhsahwaryakę**- in unęhsahwaryá·kę? *white house* is easily derived from the meaning of the roots **-nęhs**- *house* and **-ahwaryakę**- *white*. Such stems are listed under the main entry for the noun and verb roots from which they are built.

A number of stems, however, have developed idiomatic meanings that can no longer be determined from the meanings of the constituents. Such stems appear both as entries under the roots from which they are constructed and as separate main entries. There are also a number of stems that, while transparent in meaning, exhibit unexpected sound changes or different inflectional affixes than the roots from which they are built. Such stems are listed as separate main entries and as entries under the roots from which they are built.

Three types of stems appear as main entries: noun stems, deverbal noun stems, and verb stems. Noun stems are built from noun roots and function as nouns. Deverbal noun stems are built from verb roots but function as nouns. Verb stems are derived from verb roots and function as verbs. The following three sample entries illustrate dictionary entries for these three types of stems.

Noun Stem

–her–.#ẹwe Timothy (grass). *n.s.* uherehẹ̀·we ‹green-genuine› *Timothy (grass) (Phleum pratense)* (HS).

Deverbal Noun Stem

–atkẹhsa'nẹ'ʔθahnẹ– tattoo marks. *dv.n.s.* watkẹhsaʔnẹʔθáhnẹh ‹it-itself-face-writes-much› *tattoo marks* (SH 375).

Verb Stem

–ahθharaku– snatch. *v.s.-t.* rahθhará·kwahs ‹he-handful-chooses› *he snatches it* (HS).

The entry for a stem includes the following information:
1. The stem, given in morphophonemic transcription and written in **bold** letters.
2. The English gloss(es) for the stem.
3. A notation that the entry is a noun stem (*n.s.*), deverbal noun stem (*dv. n.s.*), or a verb stem and, if the latter, the type of verb stem, that is:
- verb stem-transitive (*v.s.-t.*)
- verb stem-active intransitive (*v.s.-a.i.*)
- verb stem-stative intransitive (*v.s.-s.i.*)
- verb stem-kin term (*v.s.-k.*).
4. An indication of any important idiosyncrasies about the morphology, seman-

tics, or use of the stem. If the stem requires different inflectional suffixes than its final constituent root, a situation found only with a very few verb stems (see, for example, the entry for the verb stem –**athẹhnaT**– *listen*), these suffixes are listed in the main entry for the stem as they would be for a root. In other cases, the reader is referred to the main entry for the last root of the stem for specification of inflectional information.
5. Words containing the entry. Words are cited in the following standard format:
   a. The word, written in phonemic transcription with initial capital letters for proper names.
   b. A rough morpheme-by-morpheme translation of the word in single-angle brackets (‹›).
   c. The English gloss(es) for the word in *italics*.
   d. For words referring to plants or animals, the genus and species (in *italics*) are provided.
   e. An indication of the source of the word, given in parentheses. Where a word may be found in multiple sources, preference is given to the earliest, beginning with the manuscript dictionary by Smith and Hewitt.
   f. For words documented in eighteenth- and early nineteenth-century sources, the following information is provided in square brackets ([]): the name of the author of the source, the Tuscarora word found in the source, enclosed in double-angled brackets («»), and its gloss(es).

Affixes

There are ten types of affixal morphemes: nominal root prefixes, verbal root prefixes, noun prefixes, verb pre-fixes, nominal root suffixes, verbal root suffixes, noun suffixes, verbal suffixes, nominal increments, and verbal incre-ments. Nominal and verbal root prefixes attach directly to the root or stem, while noun and verb prefixes attach in front of nominal or verbal root prefixes. Sim-ilarly, nominal and verbal root suffixes are affixed directly to the root or stem, while noun and verb suffixes are affixed to nominal or verbal root suffixes.

Increments are forms that have no meaning and are suffixed to a nominal root or stem or prefixed to a verbal root or stem in composition. Nominal incre-ments occur when a noun root or stem is incorporated or takes certain suffixes; verbal increments occur when no noun root has been incorporated.

Entries for grammatical morphemes, with the exception of verbal root suf-fixes, have the same structure. A typical main entry for an affix is given below.

---

a(r)(a)‒ optative mode. *v.pfx.* The optative mode prefix is used to indicate that, as far as the speaker is concerned, the event described by the verb has never occurred and may never occur. Its gloss in this dic-tionary is "unknown". The form **ara‒** occurs when word-accent falls on this prefix; the form **ar‒** occurs before pro-nominal prefixes that begin with the consonants *w* or *y*; the form **a‒** occurs elsewhere.

Such entries include the following infor-mation:
1. The morpheme, in morphophonemic transcription in **bold** letters.

2. The grammatical label for the mor-pheme.
3. An abbreviated specification of the type of grammatical morpheme.
4. An indication of any important idio-syncrasies about the morphology, seman-tics, or use of the affix.

In addition to the information pro-vided for other grammatical morphemes, entries for verbal root suffixes specify the forms of the following suffixes that occur after the entry:
- habitual aspect (hab:)
- punctual aspect (pnt:)
- stative aspect (stat.)
- progressive (prog:)
- purposive (prp:)
- distributive (dst:)
- causative (caus:)
- reversive (rvs:)
- dative (dat:).

The following example provides a typ-ical main entry for a verbal root suffix.

‒(a)hθ‒ dative. *v.r.s.* pnt: -h- ~ -ф, prog: -, prp: -, dst: -, caus: -, rvs: -. Member of dative series II that occurs in the punctual aspect and the im-perative; the form **‒ahθ‒** occurs following certain roots and stems that end in a consonant.

Enclitics

Enclitics are lexical items that appear sometimes as independent words and other times suffixed to the preceding word. Suffixation is reflected by the loss of stress on the preceding word and, for enclitics that begin with a vowel, inser-tion of *ʔ* or *h* between the preceding word and the enclitic. The following example illustrates a typical main entry for an enclitic in the dictionary.

#kȩheʔ ex-, deceased, former (decessive). *enc.* When present with words denoting living entities the decessive functions to indicate that the entity no longer exists in the named state, as in –**kuwan**–.**#kȩheʔ**: rakuwanȩkȩheʔ ‹he-is chief-deceased› *the former chief* (R). When present with stative verbs, it denotes past tense as in –**hsa̱ʔk**–**#kȩheʔ**: ráhsaʔk kȩheʔ ‹he-is useful-deceased› *he was useful* (HS).

Phrases

Expressions that consist of two or more words and carry idiomatic meaning, i.e., meaning that cannot be predicted from the meaning of the constituent words, are treated like stems. They are given separate main entries and are classified as noun stems, deverbal nouns stems, or verb stems according to the main entry type of the most salient constituent of of the construction. For example, in the phrase urȩ́hyeh tiwahθuhkúʔnȩ· *azure*, the first word, a noun meaning *sky*, carries the greatest weight in determining the meaning of the construction. Thus, the entry for the phrase is classified as a noun stem. A typical main entry for a phrase in the dicationary is given below.

–rȩhy– **ti–.–ahθuhkuʔnȩ–** azure. *n.s.* urȩ́hyeh tiwahθuhkúʔnȩ· ‹sky so-it-color-instrument-is a kind of› *azure* (HS).

Using the English-Tuscarora Dictionary

The content of the English-Tuscarora dictionary differs in important respects from the Tuscarora-English dictionary. The Tuscarora-English dictionary contains entries for all Tuscarora simple words, roots, affixes, enclitics, and idiomatic or idiosyncratic stems and phrases noted by researchers over the past three centuries. Many of these entries are archaic or unknown to speakers of the language today. Such entries include words for occupations that are infrequently practiced today (e.g., blacksmith, farrier), objects that have fallen out of use (e.g., crupper, draughthead), and place names for early Tuscarora settlements that have no contemporary correspondence. Such entries are not cross-referenced in the English-Tuscarora dictionary.

The format of the English-Tuscarora dictionary also differs from that of the Tuscarora-English dictionary. The primary difference is that much less information is provided about individual entries. I assume that the majority of users of the English-Tuscarora dictionary, including the Tuscaroras themselves, are already fluent or at least proficient in English. Therefore, less detailed grammatical information is provided for English entries than is given for Tuscarora entries. Also, it is likely that readers will use the English-Tuscarora dictionary for two related, but different, purposes. Many readers will use the dictionary as a means to locate the equivalent Tuscarora word for an English word, while other readers will employ the English-Tuscarora dictionary as an index to the fuller entries in the Tuscarora-English dictionary. The format of the English-Tuscarora section has been

chosen with these different purposes in mind. Each entry heading is an English word cited in **bold**. The heading is followed by an abbreviation in *italics* for the grammatical category of the word:
- adjective (*adj.*)
- adverb (*adv.*)
- conjunction (*conj.*)
- interjection (*interj.*)
- noun (*n.*)
- preposition (*prep.*)
- intransitive verb (*v.i.*)
- transitive verb (*v.t.*).

The grammatical abbreviation is followed by a Tuscarora word or words equivalent in meaning to the heading. In the case of verbs, the Tuscarora is fully inflected for pronominal subject and other obligatory grammatical categories. Following the Tuscarora word is an English gloss in *italics*. For most words except verbs, the gloss and heading are identical.

The English gloss is followed by a citation in parentheses of the root or stem of the Tuscarora word that cross-references the entry in the English-Tuscarora dictionary to the appropriate entry in the Tuscarora-English dictionary. For some entries in the English-Tuscarora dictionary, additional Tuscarora words that are full or partial translations for the English heading may follow the parenthetical cross-reference. Each additional Tuscarora word is followed by the same information as the first listing in the entry, as discussed above.

Using the Index of Proper Names

A separate index to proper names of individuals, ethnic groups, and communities follows the English-Tuscarora dictionary. Entries consist of the proper name in English, followed by an indication of whether the entry is an adjective (*adj.*) or a noun (*n.*), and the full form of the Tuscarora word with its English gloss. The English gloss is followed by the entry (in parentheses) under which the word can be found in the Tuscarora-English dictionary.

Using the Index of Interjections and Expressive Vocabulary

The index of proper names is followed by an index to interjections and expressive vocabulary, that is, words that express extra-linguistic meanings, such as imitative noises (barf, cluck, gulp), speaker emotions (aw, uh, yow), exclamatory comments (alas!, oh nuts!), or implicit directions (hush!, listen!, look there!, stop it!). In Tus-carora such words are always unin-flected particles. Entries consist of the English gloss followed by the Tuscarora word with the gloss repeated. The English gloss is followed by the entry (in parentheses) under which the word can be found in the Tuscarora-English dictionary.

Using the Index to Grammatical Morphemes

An index to Tuscarora grammatical morphemes cited in the Tuscarora-English dictionary follows the index of interjections and expressive vocabulary. Each entry in the index consists of the accepted linguistic label for the morpheme followed by an abbreviation (in *italics*) of the positional class of the morpheme:
- enclitic (*enc.*)
- increment (*inc.*)
- prefix (*pfx.*)
- suffix (*sfx.*).

The form of the morpheme cited in the heading to the entry in the Tuscarora-English dictionary follows the abbreviation.

Symbols Used in Writing Tuscarora

The consonantal phonemes of Tuscarora are *t k ʔ č s θ h n r y w* and the vocalic phonemes are *i e a u ę*. The marginal phonemes *a l m o p* occur in loan words and expressive vocabulary. In addition, there is a phoneme of length (·) associated with vowels, and two phonemic pitch accents: one a high-pitch accent (´) and one a low-pitch accent (`). These are the symbols used to write Tuscarora words in this dictionary.

In addition, certain special symbols are used to represent abstract phonological segments (morphophonemes) of morphemes and morpheme boundaries that have different phonological realizations when they occur in different environments. The symbols used in entries are the following. Underlining of a vowel, i.e., *i, e, ę, a, u*, indicates that the vowel in question behaves exceptionally with respect to stress placement. If it occurs in the penultimate syllable, and is not preceded by another underlined vowel, it is skipped over by the stress, which instead falls on the antepenultimate syllable; if it occurs in a penultimate syllable and is preceded by another underlined vowel, then it receives the stress.

A vowel enclosed in parentheses, i.e., *(i), (e), (ę), (a)*, is sometimes present and sometimes absent. Where the factors conditioning the absence and presence of the vowel are known, they are specified in a note at the beginning of the entry.

The vowel *ę* followed by a superscript *o* (*ęᵒ*) indicates that, although the vowel always appears as *ę*, it conditions the same changes in preceding segments as does the vowel *u*; that is, it causes a preceding *w* to be dropped and the selection of the pronominal forms -**yak**- *third-person singular feminine/indefinite agent* and -**kayak**- *third-person plural agent* .

The symbol *ī* indicates a vowel that appears as *i* in some environments and as *e* in others. The specific environments are specified in a note at the beginning of the entry.

The vowel *u* preceded by a superscript *n* (*ⁿu*) indicates that, although the vowel always appears as *u*, it conditions the selection of dual pronominal prefixes ending in *n* (as would be found before the vowel *ę*) instead of *t* (as would be found elsewhere before *u*).

The symbol N indicates that the consonant appears as *n* before the nasal vowel *ę*, the consonants *ʔ* and *h*, and at the end of a word, and appears elsewhere as *t*.

The symbol T indicates that the consonant appears as *t* before the consonants *k, h*, and *ʔ* and at the end of a word; appears as *ʔ* before the consonants *t, č*, and *r* unless word-initial, where it is dropped before *t, č*, and *r*; appears as *ʔn* before the consonants *w* and *y* and before any vowel, unless word-initial, in which case it appears simply as *n*; and, merges with the consonants *θ* or *s*, or a cluster of *θ* or *s* preceded by *h*, and appears as *čh* before a vowel and *č* before a consonant. The cluster *ʔn* that appears before *w*, *y*, and vowels behaves exceptionally with respect to tonic length. Although it is phonetically a cluster, it behaves like a single consonant and permits lengthening of a preceding stressed vowel.

The consonant *n* preceded by an apostrophe (*'n*) indicates that, although this segment is always realized as the cluster *ʔn*, it behaves like a single consonant and permits lengthening of a preceding vowel.

The symbol k^w indicates that, although this segment is always realized as the cluster *kw*, it behaves like a single consonant and permits lengthening of a preceding stressed vowel under appropriate circumstances.

A dash (-) is used to represent a morpheme boundary. A sequence of a dash followed by a period, followed by another dash (-.-) indicates that the forms on either side of this boundary are parts of a discontinuous stem.

The symbol # represents the boundary between a word and a following enclitic. Where an enclitic remains a separate word, this boundary is realized merely as a syllable division. When an enclitic is joined with the preceding word, the boundary is realized as: (1) a syllable boundary before an enclitic that begins with a consonant, (2) a *ʔ* between a word that ends in a non-laryngeal consonant and an enclitic that begins with a vowel, (3) an *h* between a word that ends in a vowel and an enclitic that begins with a vowel, and (4) nothing (i.e., is simply lost) between a word that ends in a laryngeal consonant and an enclitic that begins with a vowel.

Guide to Pronunciation

The pronunciation of Tuscarora differs between the Six Nations Reserve, where the Western dialect is spoken, and the Tuscarora Nation, where the Eastern dialect is spoken. The phonemic orthography used in this dictionary is based on the Eastern dialect. It is also adequate, athough not ideal, for the Western dialect. I describe here first the pronunciation of the symbols used in the Eastern dialect, after which I note the ways in which the pronunciation of these symbols differs in the Western dialect. (The abbreviation IPA stands for the International Phonetic Alphabet.)

Vowels in the Eastern Dialect. Vowels in Tuscarora can be either long, in which case they are followed by a raised dot (·), or short. The pronunciation of the nasal vowel (ę) varies from speaker to speaker. For some it may sound more like English "in" in **hint** (IPA [ɨ̃]) or more like "un" in **hunt** (IPA [ɜ̃]). Sometimes the nasal quality is absent and the vowel sounds like "i" in **hit** (IPA [ɨ]).

Symbol	IPA	Tuscarora Examples	Translation	English Equivalent
i	[i]	čír	*dog*	pizza
		wísk	*five*	
i·	[iː]	uwì·reh	*infant*	spaghetti
		wí·sę·t	*strawberry*	
e	[ɛ]	séher	*besides*	bet
		ukyéʔweh	*hair*	
		teʔ	*what?*	
e·	[ɛː]	né·kti·	*two*	bed
		kyè·wę	*today*	

a	[ɔ]	yučá'tuh	*it is cool*	hawk
		áhsę	*three*	
		wáhθhę·	*ten*	
a·	[ɔ:]	á·thu'	*cold*	law
		hà·ne'	*that is*	
u	[u]	tú'ks	*cranberry*	tune
		awúhsteh	*year*	
u·	[u:]	awú·kę'	*blister*	rude
		utù·reh	*corn husk*	
		kanù·rę'	*it is precious*	
ę	[ɨ]	učę́heh	*fire*	hint
		unę́hseh	*house*	
ę·	[ɨ:]	ę́·kweh	*human being*	wind
		urę́·teh	*magic*	

Vowels in the Western Dialect. The major difference between vowels in the Eastern and Western dialects involves the pronunciation of stressed versus unstressed short vowels. In the Eastern dialect the pronunciation of short vowels remains essentially the same whether they are stressed or not. However, in the Western dialect most of the short vowels are pronounced somewhat differently depending on stress. Long vowels are pronounced the same in both dialects.

Symbol	IPA	Tuscarora Examples	Translation	English Equivalent
í	[i]	uhčíhrę'	*bear*	pizza
i	[ɪ]	kihswę́'kye	*my back*	bit
é	[æ]	u'éhneh	*hand*	bat
e	[ɛ]	yú'neks	*it is burning*	bet
á	[ɔ]	wáhsęh	*it is ugly*	hawk
a	[a]	účareh	*door*	hot
ú	[u]	úhyeh	*fruit*	tune
u	[o]	uhę́hneh	*ear*	sofa
ę́	[ɜ]	u'kę́hreh	*ashes*	hunt
ę	[ɪ]	kę́·čęh	*fish*	hint

Consonants in the Eastern Dialect. The pronunciation of Tuscarora consonants varies depending on their position in a word. The consonants *t*, *k*, *r*, *n*, *y*, and *w* are voiceless (sound like English *t*, *k*, *s*, *hn*, *sh*, *f*) at the end of a word and before another consonant except *y* and *w*. Before the consonants *y* and *w* or before a vowel, *t*, *k*, *r*, *n*, *y*, and *w* are voiced (sound like English *d*, *g*, *r*, *n*, *y*, *w*). The pronunciation of ', *č*, *h*, *θ*, and *s* does not vary by position.

Symbol	IPA	Tuscarora Examples	Translation	English Equivalent
t	[t]	wí·sę·t	*strawberry*	take
		rútkę'	*wizard*	
	[d]	tú'ks	*cranberry*	date
		utù·reh	*corn husk*	
		tyà·re'	*first*	
k	[k]	ęhrá·ri·k	*he will bite it*	kale
		né·kti·	*two*	
	[g]	ukáhreh	*eye*	gale
		ę́·kweh	*human being*	
		ukyé'weh	*hair*	
'	[']	u'áhseh	*breast*	unh-unh
		ráhs'ahs	*he is finishing*	
		učí'reh	*spark*	
č	[tʃ]	učí'reh	*spark*	cheese
		učę́heh	*fire*	
		učtę́hreh	*stone*	
s	[s]	wí·sę·t	*strawberry*	sale
		Skarù·rę'	*Tuscarora*	
θ	[θ]	θáhe'	*bean*	thought
		Nyuθrù·rę'	*Buffalo, N.Y.*	
		áha·θ	*horse*	
h	[h]	hà·ne'	*that is*	house
		θáhe'	*bean*	
		wa'úrhę'	*daytime*	
r	[r]	utù·reh	*corn husk*	butter
		khrirù·rę'	*whiteman*	
		ká·ryu·'	*wild animal*	
	[s]	čír	*dog*	hiss
		wa'úrhę'	*daytime*	
		ur'ęhsę́·te	*clan*	
n	[n]	né·kti·	*two*	no
		ahskę̀·nę'	*peace*	
		Nyuθrù·rę'	*Buffalo, N.Y.*	
	[n]	kę́nhe'	*I am alive*	inhale
		u'nhę́hseh	*egg*	
		θhré·n	*cut it!*	
w	[w]	wáhθhę·	*tenlike*	way
		uwyáhseh	*cross*	
	[f]	unę́hsakęw	*in house*	puff
		wá'kha'w	*I carried it*	

y	[y]	yučáʔtuh	*it is cool*	you
		Ruyà·ner	*Lord*	
	[ʃ]	ękíheʔy	*I will die*	dish
		ú·ʔy	*other*	
		Uyhę́ha·kt	*Lewiston, N.Y.*	

Both the consonants *t* and *k* may be pronounced somewhat more "strongly" by some speakers and may sound like the "t" and "d" of English **it does** or the "t" and "g" of English **let go** when said quickly. The pronunciation of these two consonants may be further "strengthened" and result in *t* and *k* sounding like the consonant clusters ʔt and ʔk.

Consonants in the Western Dialect. The consonants in the Western dialect are pronounced the same as in the Eastern dialect, with the following exceptions. The consonants *t* and *k* always undergo the extra strengthening noted above and appear as the consonant clusters ʔt and ʔk. The distinction between the consonants θ and *s* has been lost and both appear as *s*. Finally, where the consonants *y* and *w* would be pronounced voiceless in the Eastern dialect, and sound like English *sh* and *f*, respectively, they are frequently dropped from the word in the Western dialect, that is, not pronounced at all.

Syllable Division and Hyphenization

For written English there are well-established rules of hyphenization that are employed when a word extends across more than one line of text. For Tuscarora no such rules exist. I have adopted here the practice of dividing Tuscarora words according to the divisions between syllables that occur in the spoken language.

Tuscarora words are syllabified as follows.

1. If a word contains a vowel followed by a single consonant, the syllable boundary falls between the vowel and the consonant, e.g., u-há-heh *path*, á-θeʔ *when*, ra-wę-nì·-yuʔ *God*.

2. If a word contains a vowel followed by a consonant other than *h* or ʔ followed by *r*, *w* or *y*, the syllable boundary falls between the vowel and the consonant, e.g., wá-kwahst *it is good*, ká·-ryu·ʔ *wild animal*.

3. If a word contains a vowel followed by a consonant other than *t* or *k* and another consonant, the syllable boundary falls between the first and second consonant, e.g., uʔ-tyę́h-seh *nose*, uč-tę́h-reh *stone*, uh-nę́h-weh *upper shoulder*, ra-nę́s-neʔ *he likes it*.

4. If a word contains a vowel followed by the consonants *t* or *k* and another consonant other than ʔ, the syllable boundary falls between the vowel and the *t* or *k*, e.g., ká·-tkęʔ *blood*, ú-khęh *soup*.

5. If a word contains a vowel followed by any consonant followed by the consonant ʔ, the syllable boundary falls between the first consonant and the ʔ, e.g., wa-kít-ʔuhs *I am sleeping*, ya-wé·k-ʔę *it tastes good*, ye-ká·θ-ʔah *child, girl*, rah-θáw-ʔahs *he begins*.

It has also been necessary on occasion to divide Tuscarora stems and roots at the end of a line in the dictionary. Where this has occurred I have followed the syllabification rules used for hyphenating whole words; however, I have used the symbol (=) rather than a hyphen to avoid confusion with the dashes that occur at the beginning and end of roots and stems.

Sources of Tuscarora Vocabulary

Cayuga, Percy. 1972. Canadian Tuscarora Vocabulary and Texts. Recorded by Michael K. Foster at the Six Nations Reserve. (Partially transcribed by Blair A. Rudes, 1989.) Hull, Quebec: Canadian Ethnological Service, Canadian Museum of Civilization. (PC)

Fickett, Joan G. 1967. The Phonology of Tuscarora. *Studies in Linguistics* 19: 33-57. (F)

Gallatin, Albert. 1836. A Synopsis of the Indian Tribes within the United States East of the Rocky Mountains, and in the British and Russian Possessions in North America. *Archaeologia Americana, Transactions of the American Antiquarian Society* 2:1-422. (Gallatin)

Gatschet, Albert S. 1883. Tuskarora Notebook. Ms. 372-b. Washington, D.C.: National Anthropological Archives, Smithsonian Institution. (AG)

Greene, Elton. 1969. *The Tuscarora Language*. Murfreesboro, N.C.: Johnson Publishing. (G)

Hewitt, J.N.B. n.d. The Cheroki an Iroquoian Language. A critical Study & Comparison of Etymologies, words, sentence-words, phrase-forms & conjugations common to the Cherokian & Iroquoian tongues to Establish their common origin. Bureau of American Ethnology Manuscript No. 447. Washington, D.C.: National Anthropological Archives, Smithsonian Institution. (H 447)

Hewitt, J.N.B. n.d. Tuskarora Paradigms. Bureau of American Ethnology Manuscript No. 2484. Washington, D.C.: National Anthropological Archives, Smithsonian Institution. (H 2484)

Hewitt, J.N.B. n.d. Miscellaneous Iroquois Grammatical Notes. Bureau of American Ethnology Manuscript No. 3518. Washington, D.C.: National Anthropological Archives, Smithsonian Institution. (H 3518)

Hewitt, J.N.B. n.d. Words, Roots, and Other Linguistic Material. Bureau of American Ethnology Manuscript No. 3483. Washington, D.C.: National Anthropological Archives, Smithsonian Institution. (H-notebook)

Hewitt, J.N.B. 1897. Predicative Function in Iroquoian Speech as Exemplified in the Tuscarora. Bureau of

American Ethnology Manuscript No. 2892. Washington, D.C.: National Anthropological Archives, Smithsonian Institution. (H 2892)

Hewitt, J.N.B. 1918-1923. Law Prohibiting Tyrannical Conduct on the Part of Federal Chiefs. Bureau of American Ethnology Manuscript No. 469. Washington, D.C.: National Anthropological Archives, Smithsonian Institution. (Tyranny)

Hewitt, J.N.B. 1910. Tuscarora. In: Fredrick Webb Hodge, ed. *Handbook of American Indians North of Mexico*. Bureau of American Ethnology Bulletin No. 20, Part 2. Washington, D.C.: Government Printing Office (H-Handbook)

Jefferson, Thomas. 1817. A Manuscript Comparative Vocabulary of Several Indian Languages. Ms. no. 497/J35. Philadelphia, Penn.: American Philosophical Society. (Jefferson)

Lawson, John. 1709. *A New Voyage to Carolina*. Originally published as part of *A New Collection of Voyages and Travels: With Historical Accounts of Discoveries and Conquests in All Parts of the World*, collected by John Stevens. London: 1708-1711. [1714 edition reprinted as *Lawson's History of North Carolina*, 1937, edited by F.L. Hariss, for the North Carolina Society of the Colonial Dames of America. Richmond, Va.: Garrett and Massie.] (Lawson)

Lounsbury, Floyd G. 1952, 1954. Tuscarora Notes. Ms. East Haven, Conn.: Author. (L)

Mithun, Marianne. 1970-1996. Tuscarora Field Notes. Santa Barbara, Calif.: Author. (M)

Mithun, Marianne. 1984. The Proto-Iroquoians: Cultural Reconstruction from Lexical Materials. In Michael K. Foster, Marianne Mithun, and Jack Campisi (eds.), *Extending the Rafters: Interdisciplinary Approaches to Iroquoian Studies*. Albany, N.Y.: State University of New York. (M 84)

Mithun, Marianne. 1987. Handout. Renssaelerville, N.Y.: Conference on Iroquoian Research. (M 87)

Mithun, Marianne and Elton Greene. 1980. The Dinosaur, The Wart. In Marianne Mithun and Hanni Woodbury (eds.), *Northern Iroquoian Texts*. International Journal of American Linguistics-Native American Texts Series, pp. 104-109, 156-157. Chicago, Ill.: University of Chicago. (GM)

Morgan, Lewis Henry. 1851. *League of the Ho-de´-no-sau-nee, or Iroquois*. Rochester, N.Y.: Sage & Brother. (Morgan, League)

Morgan, Lewis Henry. 1870. *Systems of Consanguinity and Affinity of the Human Family*. Smithsonian Contributions to Knowledge 17. Washington, D.C.: Smithsonian Institution. (Morgan, Systems)

Olbrechts, Frans. 1929. De pronominale prefixen in het Tuscarora. Donum natalicium Schrijnen; verzameling van opstellen door oudleeringen en bevriende vakgenooten opgedragen aan mgr. prof. dr. Jos. Schrijnen bij gelegenheid van zijn zestigsten verjaardag, 3 Mei 1929, pp. 154-161. Nijmegen-Utrecht: N.V. Dekker and Van de Vegt.

Printup, Marjorie. 1980. *Exegesis on Noah's Ark*. Gospel Recordings. (MP)

Rudes, Blair A. 1973-1997. Tuscarora Field Notes. Washington, D.C.: Author. (R)

Rudes, Blair A. 1981. A Sketch of the Nottoway Language from a Historical-Comparative Perspective. *International Journal of American Linguistics* 47:28-51. (Rudes 1981)

Rudes, Blair A., and Dorothy Crouse. 1987. *The Tuscarora Legacy of J.N. B. Hewitt: Materials for the Study of the Tuscarora Language and Culture.* 2 Vols. Mercury Series Paper No. 108. Hull, Quebec: Canadian Museum of Civilization. (RC)

Saunders, William L. (ed.). 1886-1980. *The Colonial Records of North Carolina.* 10 Vols. (Colonial Records)

Smith, Erminnie A., and J.N.B. Hewitt. n.d. Tuskarora Dictionary. Bureau of American Ethnology Manuscript No. 2850. Washington, D.C.: National Anthropological Archives, Smithsonian Institution. (HS)

Smith, Erminnie A., and J.N.B. Hewitt. 1880. Tuscarora Version of Major Powell's Indian Language Schedule. Bureau of American Ethnology Manuscript No. 375. Washington, D.C.: National Anthropological Archives, Smithsonian Institution. (SH 375)

Wallace, Anthony F.C. 1948, 1949. Field Notes to Accompany Tuscarora Language Recordings. Philadelphia, Penn.: A-merican Philosophical Society. (AW)

Williams, Marianne Mithun. 1974. A Grammar of Tuscarora. Unpublished PhD dissertation. New Haven, Conn.: Yale University. (W 74)

Williams, Ted. 1976. *The Reservation.* Syracuse, N.Y.: Syracuse University Press. (TW)

Abbreviations

adj.	adjective	pat.	patient
adv.	adverb	*pfx.*	prefix
ag.	agent	*prep.*	preposition
aln:	alienable	*pro.*	pronoun
caus:	causative	pnt:	punctual aspect
dat:	dative	prog:	progressive
dst:	distributive	prp:	purposive
dv.n.r.	deverbal noun root	*r.sfx.*	root suffix
dv.n.s.	deverbal noun stem	rvs:	reversive
East.	Eastern dialect	stat:	stative aspect
enc.	enclitic	*v.*	verb
hab:	habitual aspect	*v.r.pfx.*	verbal root prefix
inaln:	inalienable	*v.r.sfx.*	verbal root suffix
inc.	increment	*v.i.*	intranstive verb
inc.	incorporable/incorporating	*v.inc.*	verbal increment
interj.	interjection	*v.pfx.*	verbal prefix
n.	noun	*v.r.-a.i.*	verb root-active intransitive
n.r.pfx.	nominal root prefix	*v.r.-k.*	verb root-kin term
n.r.sfx.	nominal root suffix	*v.r.-s.i.*	verb root-stative intransitive
n.r.	noun root	*v.r.-t.*	verb root-transitive
n.s.	noun stem	*v.s.-a.i.*	verb stem-active intransitive
n.sfx.	noun suffix	*v.s.-s.i.*	verb stem-stative intransitive
n-inc.	non-incorporating	*v.s.-t.*	verb stem-transitive
n-poss.	unpossessible	*v.t.*	transitive verb
part.	particle	*West.*	Western dialect

TUSCARORA-ENGLISH DICTIONARY

A

á stop it! (HS). *part.* Used only with children. **á.#hči:** áhči ‹stop it-very› *stop it now!* (HS).

á· ah (HS), aw (L 53). *part.* **á· tha –. –ihey –:** á· thahsíhe'²y ‹aw unusual-unknown-you-die› *aw, you might as well die* (L 53).

á.#hči stop it now!. *part.* áhči ‹stop it-very› *stop it now!* (HS).

–(a)čęh – fire; immediate (nuclear) family. *n.r.,* inaln: kčę́heh *my family* (R), inc., n.sfx. -eh. učę́heh *fire* (R) [Lawson «Utchar» 'fire']; **–(a)čęhakari –:** ęyakučęhakà·ri'² ‹prediction-one-family-devour› *one will consume family* (RC 15:10); **–(a)čęhakęhyaT –:** tiwačęhakę́hya·t ‹so-it-fire-extends from› *so it extends from fire* (RC 12:21); **–(a)čę=hakT –:** učę́hakwt ‹fire-next to› *hearth* (HS); **–(a)čęhaktha'nye'² –:** učęhakwthá·'²nye'²θ ‹fire-next to-going along› *going along next to fire* (RC 12:25); **–(a)čęhayę(T) –:** yečę́hayę'² ‹one-fire-lays› *family* (RC 16:1), wakčę́hayę'² ‹I-fire-laid› *I am in council* (H 3567); **–(a)čęhuka'²nahkw –:** wa'²kayečęhuká'²nahkw ‹fact-they-fire-blister-caused-instrument› *they used it to start fire* (RC 6:14); **–(a)čęhuhkw –:** učęhúhkweh ‹fire-cover-instrument› *type of fire-witch, flickering-light witch* (RC 7:8); **–(a)čęhuryahnę –:** ęhsčęhuryáhnę·'² ‹prediction-you-fire-stir-much› *you will poke up the fire* (R); **–(a)čęhuri'²=**thę –: račęhuri'²thęh ‹he-fire-stir-causes-much› *he pokes the fire, he stirs the fire* (HS); **–ne –. –(a)čęhak"ekT –:** nekakučęhakwé·kę ‹two-they-fire-closed› *whole family* (RC 13:10); **–ne –. –(a)čę=hatekę –:** neyękyačęhaté·kę· ‹we two-fire-join› *my neighbor* (R); **–ne –. –(a)=čęhatekęhrę –:** nekačęhatekę́hręh ‹two-it-fire-joins-many› *among members of a family* (R), neyękwačęhatekę́hręh ‹two-we-fire-join-many› *neighbors* (HS); **–ne –. –(a)čęhahkw –:** nekačęháhkhwa'² ‹apart-it-fire-picks up› *jack-o'-lantern* (AG); **–ne –. –(a)čęhuhkwahkw –:** neyečęhuhkwáhkhwa'² ‹apart-one-fire-cover-instrument-picks up› *she will witch around* (RC 23:10); nekačęhuhkwáhkhwa'² ‹apart-it-fire-cover-instrument-picks up› *jack-o'-lantern* (AG); **–ne –. –(a)čęhihar –:** neyečęhíha'²r ‹two-one-fire-hung› *the two of them formed a family* (RC 35:1).

–(a)čęhakT – hearth. *n.s.* učę́hakwt ‹fire-next to› *hearth* (HS).

–(a)čęhayę(T) – family. *dv.n.s.* yečę́hayę'² ‹one-fire-lays› *family* (RC 16:1).

–(a)čęhuhkw – type of fire-witch, flickering-light witch. *n.s.* učęhúhkweh ‹fire-cover-instrument› *type of fire-witch, flickering-light witch* (RC 7:8).

–ačętrahT – growl. *v.r.-a.i.* hab: -ha'², pnt: -, stat: -, prg: -, prp: -, dst: -, caus: -, rvs: -, dat: -, n-inc. wačętráhtha'² *it growls* (HS).

–ačhakwahsnahnę – arrange. *v.s.-t.* račhakwahsnáhnęh ‹he-X-is good-much› *he arranges it* (HS).

-ačhakwahsT - fix, make good again, make ready, prepare. *v.s.-t.* ęhsačhákwahst ‹prediction-you-yourself-X-be good› *you will fix it, you will make it good again* (RC 35:5), račhakwáhstha⁷ ‹he-himself-X-is good› *he puts it in order, he disposes of it, he makes it good* (HS), ękayęčhákwahst ‹prediction-they-themselves-X-be good› *they will make it ready, they will prepare it* (L 35); -ačhakwahsnahnę -: račhakwahsnáhnęh ‹he-himself-X-is good-much› *he arranges it* (HS); -(a)ha= hačhakwahsT -: rahahačhakwáhstha⁷ ‹he-path-self-X-is good› *he repairs, is repairing the road; he repairs roads* (H 2484); -hehnačhakwahsT -: rahehnačhakwáhstha⁷ ‹he-field-self-X-is good› *he causes the field to look well, puts the field in order and trim* (H 2484); -nęhsnačhakwahsT -: ranęhsnačhakwáhstha⁷ ‹he-seed-self-X-is good› *he cares for the grain, is getting it ready to house or to put into the barn, as curing it and binding it, etc.* (H 2484); -či-.-ačhakwahsT -: θhračhakwáhstha⁷ ‹again-he-self-X-is good› *he repairs it* (HS), čučhákwahst ‹again-fact-it-X-was good› *reparable* (HS); kwęhs -či-.-ačhakwahsT -: kwęhs ęθayučhakwáhsnęk ‹no unknown-again-it-X-be good› *it is irreparable, it is incorrigible* (HS).

-ačhakʷaraʔnihr - bawl. *v.s.-a.i.* ručhakwaraʔníhrę ‹he-himself-clamor-stood› *he bawls* (HS).

-ačhakʷaraʔnihT - clamor. *v.s.-a.i.* račhakwaraʔníhtha⁷ ‹he-himself-clamor-stand-causes› *he clamors* (HS).

-ačhayaʔT - delay. *v.s.-a.i.* račhayáʔtha⁷ ‹he-himself-make slow-causes› *he delays* (HS).

-ačherhar - live in a hut. *v.s.-a.i.* račhérhar ‹he-himself-bark covering-hangs› *he lives in a hut* (HS).

-ačheʔnaku - dismount. *v.s.-t.* račheʔnáˑkwahs ‹he-himself-be carried on someone's shoulders-cause-undoes› *he dismounts it* (H-notebook).

-ačheʔT - mount. *v.s.-t.* račhéʔtha⁷ ‹he-himself-be carried on someone's shoulders-causes› *he mounts* (H-notebook).

-ačhę -{dative I} be enemies, hate one another. *v.s.-t.* neyęčhę́ʔθeh ‹two-one-themselves-are ugly-for› *the two of them are enemies, the two of them hate each other* (HS).

-ačhęnar - sign, subscribe to. *v.s.-t.* račhę̀ˑnar ‹he-himself-name-is in› *he signs it, he subscribes to it* (HS).

-ačhęnęti - be happy. *v.r.-a.i.* hab: -h, pnt: -ʔ, stat: -ę, prg: -, prp: -ahte-, dst: -, caus: -aʔT-, rvs: -, dat: -, n-inc. waʔęčhęnę́ˑtiʔ *one was happy* (RC 3:26); -ačhęnętyahte -: yęčhęnętyáhteʔ ‹one-be happy-is going to› *one is pleased* (RC 3:49); -ačhęnętyaʔčr -: učhęnętyáʔčreh ‹be happy-'ness› *delight* (HS); -ačhęnętyaʔT -: učhęnę́ˑtyaʔt ‹be happy-cause› *bliss, happiness* (HS), kakučhęnę́ˑtyaʔt ‹they-be happy-causes› *it pleases them* (RC 12:1).

-ačhęnyaʔT - be pleased. *v.r.-a.i.* hab: -, pnt: -ɸ, stat: -, prg: -, prp: -, dst: -, caus: -, rvs: -, dat: -, n-inc. This entry and -ačhętyaʔT -{dative II}, below, both derive from earlier * -ačhęnyaʔt -, the latter showing the regular change of earlier *n to *t in Tuscarora, whereas the entry above retains the original *n. waʔthračhę́ˑnyaʔt *he was pleased* (RC 6:9).

-ačhęryuhkwaʔnihr - exhale. *v.s.-a.i.* wačhęryuhkwáʔnihč ‹it-itself-smell-cover-instrument-stands up› *it exhales* (H-notebook).

-ačhętyaʔT -{dative II} please, make

happy. *v.r.-t.* hab: -, pnt: -, stat: -, prg: -, prp: -, dst: -, caus: -, rvs: -, dat: II (-ati-/-ahθ), n-inc. See: −ačhęnya?T −. ękheyačhętyá?thahθ *I will please them* (RC 4:5).

−ačhęwati − be smooth. *v.s.-s.i.* yučhęwá·tye? ‹it-itself-smoothed› *it is smooth* (HS).

ačhíharahk pennyroyal (*Hedoma pulegioides*) (H-notebook). *n.* Archaic. Modern: hačhíharahst.

−ačhuhkwh(e)r − boy (10-15 years old). *dv.n.s.* ručhúhkhwer ‹he-himself-flesh-hangs› *male adolescent* (RC 35:43), *boy (10-15 years old)* (AG), kakučhuhkhrá·wę· ‹they-themselves-flesh-hang-many› *boys* (AG).

−ačhuhkwętihT − shave. *v.s.-t.* yęčhuhkwę́·tiht ‹one-oneself-flesh-make-causes› *one shaves it* (R), wa?kayęčhuhkwę́·tiht ‹fact-they-themselves-flesh-make-caused› *they shaved it* (R).

−ačhukaręhnahkw − razor. *dv.n.s.* yęčhukaręhnáhkhwa? ‹one-oneself-beard-fall-causes-instrument› *razor* (HS).

−ačhukaręhT − shave. *v.s.-a.i.* wa?kačhú·karęht ‹fact-I-myself-beard-fall-caused› *I shaved* (R), račhukaręhtha? ‹he-himself-beard-fall-causes› *he shaves* (HS).

−ačhuri − eat. *v.r.-a.i.* hab: -h, pnt: -?, stat: -·, prg: -, prp: -ehe-, dst: -, caus: -a?T-, rvs: -, dat: -, n-inc. ačhù·rih *eatable* (HS), wačhù·rih *it eats* (RC 15:5); *it assimilates* (HS), ęhračhù·ri? *he will eat* (RC 12:4), wakačhú·ri· *I have eaten* (RC 2:6); −ačhurya?T −:

yęčhuryá?tha? ‹one-eat-causes› *kitchen* (R), wačhuryá?tha? kačhè·nę? ‹it-eat-causes it-is domestic animal› *manger* (HS); −ačhurya?nahkw −: wačhurya?náhkhwa? ‹it-eat-causes-instrument› *pasture land* (HS); yęčhurya?náhkhwa? ‹one-eat-causes-instrument› *refectory* (HS); −ačhuryehe −: ękačhuryéhe? ‹prediction-I-eat-be going to› *I am going to eat* (HS); −ačhurya?T − −chenę −: wačhuryá?tha? kačhè·nę? ‹it-eat-causes it-is domestic animal› *manger* (HS).

−ačhuri − eatable. *part.* ačhù·rih ‹eat› *eatable* (HS).

−ačhurya?nahkw − pasture land, refectory. *dv.n.s.* wačhurya?náhkhwa? ‹it-eat-causes-instrument› *pasture land* (HS); yęčhurya?náhkhwa? ‹one-eat-causes-instrument› *refectory* (HS).

−ačhurya?T − kitchen. *dv.n.s.* yęčhuryá?tha? ‹one-eat-causes› *kitchen* (R).

−ačhurya?T − −chenę − manger. *dv.n.s.* wačhuryá?tha? kačhè·nę? ‹it-eat-causes it-is domestic animal› *manger* (HS).

−ačhu?kuw − be rich. *v.r.-s.i.* stat: -·, prg: -, prp: -, dst: -, caus: -, rvs: -, dat: -, inc.-ɸ-pat. arękwačhú?ku·k *that I were rich* (R); −ačhu?kuwahčr −: učhu?kuwáhčreh ‹be rich-'ness› *affluence, riches* (HS); −ačhu?kuwahčratkęha −: ručhu?kuwahčratkę́hę ‹he-be rich-'ness-arise› *he is magnificent* (HS); −ačhu?kuwahčręti −: račhu?kuwahčrę́·tih ‹he-be rich-'ness-makes› *he enriches it* (HS); −nęhsačhu?kuw−: unęh-

---

Tuscarora Pronunciation Key:
/a/ l<u>a</u>w; /e/ h<u>a</u>t; /i/ p<u>i</u>zza; /u/ t<u>u</u>ne; /ę/ h<u>i</u>nt; /č/ <u>ch</u>eese; /h/ <u>h</u>oe; /m/ <u>m</u>other; /s/ <u>s</u>ame; /t/ <u>d</u>o (before a vowel y, or w), <u>t</u>oo (elsewhere); /k/ <u>g</u>ale (before a vowel y or w), <u>k</u>ale (elsewhere); /n/ i<u>n</u>hale (before a consonant or word-final), <u>n</u>ote (elsewhere), /r/ hi<u>ss</u> (before a consonant or word-final), <u>r</u>un (trilled as in Italian, elsewhere); /w/ cu<u>ff</u> (before a consonant other than y or word-final), <u>w</u>ay (elsewhere); /y/ fi<u>sh</u> (before a consonant or word-final), <u>y</u>ou (elsewhere), /θ/ <u>th</u>ing; /?/ (the sound between the vowels in unh-unh); /·/ long vowel, /´/ high pitch; /`/ low pitch.

sačhú꞉ʔku· ‹house-is rich› *it is a richly furnished house* (HS).

-ačhuʔkuwahčr – affluence, riches. *n.s.* učhuʔkuwáhčreh ‹be rich-'ness› *affluence, riches* (HS).

-ačhuʔkuwahčratkęha – be magnificent. *v.s.-a.i.* ručhuʔkuwahčratkę́hę ‹he-be rich-'ness-self-raised› *he is magnificent* (HS).

-ačhuʔkuwahčręti – enrich. *v.s.-t.* račhuʔkuwahčrę́·tih ‹he-be rich-'ness-makes› *he enriches it* (HS).

-ačinatę – sleep together, sleep with spouse. *v.r.-a.i.* hab: -h, pnt: -ʔ, stat: -·, prg: -, prp: -, dst: -, caus: -, rvs: -, dat: -, n-inc. The meaning of the root carries with it the notion of sexual activity taking place. ęči·natęʔ *it slept with its spouse* (R); ti–.–**ačinatę**–: thwaʔnyęčì·natęʔ ‹so-fact-they two-slept together› *the two of them slept together so many times* (RC 3:61).

-ačkahręwuhar – gargle. *v.s.-a.i.* račkahręwúhar ‹he-himself-mouth-washes› *he gargles* (HS).

-ačkaruręʔ be Tuscarora. *v.s.-s.i.* kayęčkarù·ręʔ ‹they-themselves-are Tuscaroras› *they are Tuscaroras* (R).

-ačkęʔr – bones, skeleton. *n.s.* učkę́ʔreh ‹self-bone› *bones, skeleton* (R).

-ačkʷaʔnetyęku – squirm. *v.s.-a.i.* račkwaʔnetyę́·kwahs ‹he-himself-snake-many-picks up› *he squirms* (HS).

-ačnahkw – use for. *v.s.-t.* ęyęčnáhkwaʔ ‹prediction-one-oneself-use-instrument› *one will use it for* (RC 6:15).

-ačnęhsnaʔči come down. *v.s.-a.i.* nęčnęhsnáʔči ‹hither-fact-it-descended-very› *it came down* (RC 32:12).

-ačnęhT –/–ačnęhsT – descend, get down. *v.r.-a.i.* hab: -haʔ, pnt: -ɸ, stat: -ę, prg: -, prp: -, dst: -, caus: -, rvs: -, dat: -, n-inc. The form **–ačnęhsT –** occurs whenever an enclitic follows. The form **–ačnęhT –** occurs elsewhere. θáčnęht *get down!* (RC 26:23), yučnę́hnę *it got down: descent* (HS), ęʔnyę́čnęht *one will get down there* (RC 26:26); –t–.–**ačnęhsT –.#hči**: nęčnęhsnáʔči ‹hither-fact-it-descended-very› *it came down* (RC 32: 12).

-ačnęhT – descent. *dv.n.s.* yučnę́hnę ‹it-got down› *descent* (HS).

-ačnyuʔθręhT – molt. *dv.n.s.* wačnyuʔθrę́htha ‹it-itself-scruff-fall-causes› *it (animal, reptile) molts* (H-notebook).

-ačrayayęʔθk – tuberculosis. *dv.n.s.* yęčrayayę́ʔθkę ‹one-oneself-fresh-lay-easily› *tuberculosis* (AW 98).

-ačriʔrarurę – shrivel up, wrinkle. *v.s.-a.i.* wačriʔrarù·ręh ‹it-itself-wrinkle-contributes› *it shrivels up, it wrinkles* (HS).

-ačT – use. *v.s.-t.* ę̀·yęčt ‹prediction-one-oneself-use› *one will use it* (RC 5:9), wáčthaʔ ‹it-itself-uses› *it uses it* (RC 12:15).

-ačT – weapon. *dv.n.s.* yę́čthaʔ ‹one-oneself-uses› *weapon* (HS).

-(a)čtehrihT –/–(a)čtehrihsT – become involved with. *v.r.-t.* hab: -haʔ ~ -ɸ, pnt: -ɸ, stat: -ę, prg: -, prp: -, dst: -, caus: -, rvs: -, dat: -, n-inc. The form **–ačtehrihsT –** occurs with the habitual marker **–ha ʔ** and the stative marker **–ę**; the form **–ačtehrihT –** occurs with the punctual aspect marker **–ɸ**. (However, Lounsbury [p. 46] also cites a form [wætstæ̀·rihst] (= wečtéhrihst) *she took care of it*, which shows the form ending in *hst* in the punctual aspect.) The forms beginning in *č* occur after the semireflexive morpheme **–aT –**. waʔkačtéhriht *I got involved* (R), račtehríhsthaʔ *he manages it, he cares for it* (R), węčtehríhsnę *she has taken care of it* (L 46 = [watstæ̀·ríhsnə̄h]); **–aʔčtehrihsT –**: kaʔčtehríhsthaʔ ‹I-myself-become involved with› *it bothers me* (R); **íhskah -a'čtehrihsT -:** íhskah wa'kačtéhriht ‹not fact-I-become involved with› *I ignored it* (R), íhskah wa'kheyačtéhriht ‹not fact-I=another-become involved with› *I left another alone, I did not bother another* (R); **kwęhs -a'čtehrihsT -:** kwęhs wahračtéhrihst ‹no fact-he-become involved with› *he was inadvertent* (HS).

-ačtkę'ne - be ill with tuberculosis or other respiratory disease. *v.r.-s.i.* stat: -', prg: -, prp: -, dst: -, caus: -, rvs: -, dat: -, n-inc. wačtkę·'ne' *it is deathly ill* (RC 35:2), tiθačtkę·'ne' *you are deathly ill* (RC 35:24).

-ačtur - hurry. *v.s.-a.i.* ručtù·re' ‹he-himself-is fast› *he hurries* (RC 36:1).

ačú·· brr (sound made after touching something very cold) (R). *part.*

-ač'a - die. *v.s.-a.i.* kayę́č'ahs ‹they-themselves-are finishing› *they are dying* (H-notebook).

-ač'a - dead. *dv.n.s.* ha' kakúč'ę ‹the they-themselves-finished› *the dead* (HS).

-ač'ahT - drip. *v.s.-a.i.* wač'áhnę ‹it-itself-finish-caused› *it drips* (HS).

#áh little (diminutive). *enc.* The boundary # is automatically realized as *h* following a vowel, ' following a non-laryngeal consonant, and φ following a laryngeal consonant. The principal function of the diminutive is to note that an object is small in size (e.g., **-hehn -.#áh:** uhehneháh ‹field-little› *the field is small, it is a small field, a little field* (H 2484)). Often, the meaning of nouns with the diminutive is to a greater or lesser extent opaque or idiomatic (e.g., **aha·θ.#áh:** aha·θ'áh ‹horse-small› *colt* (R), **-ę'raks -.#áh:** wę'raksęháh ‹it-fur-is bad-little› *lamb* (AG), **-ę°k"e -.#áh:** ękweháh ‹human-little› *mannequin* (R), **-hęwarahT -.#áh:** yehęwarahtha'áh ‹one-tube-cause-little› *fife* (HS)). The diminutive is also used with kinship terms to denote certain distinctions. For example, when affixed to the words meaning mother and father the constructions signify maternal aunt and paternal uncle, respectively (e.g., **-hri'ę.#áh:** akhri'ęháh ‹I-be father to-little› *my paternal uncle* (R)). When it occurs with words meaning brother or sister the derived forms mean step-brother or step-sister (e.g., **-hči'.#áh:** akči'áh ‹I-have as older sister-little› *my older step-sister* (R)). The diminutive is also used to constrain the meaning of attributive predicates (e.g., **ti -. -(a)haheθ -.#áh:** tiwahahe·θ'áh ‹so-it-path-is long-little› *the road is short or the row is not long* (H 2484)). In addition, the diminutive has several other, more specialized uses. It may be used to form adjectives from nouns (e.g., **athu'.#áh:** athu'áh ‹cold-little› *boreal, northerly* (HS), **-ręhyakęw.#áh:** uręhyakęw'áh ‹sky-in-little› *celestial* (HS), **-ta'nakęw.#áh:** uta'nakęw'áh ‹settlement-in-little› *urbane* (HS)). It is also used to emphasize the

Tuscarora Pronunciation Key:

/a/ l<u>a</u>w; /e/ h<u>a</u>t; /i/ p<u>i</u>zza; /u/ t<u>u</u>ne; /ę/ h<u>i</u>nt; /č/ <u>ch</u>eese; /h/ <u>h</u>oe; /m/ <u>m</u>other; /s/ <u>s</u>ame; /t/ <u>d</u>o (before a vowel y, or w), <u>t</u>oo (elsewhere); /k/ <u>g</u>ale (before a vowel y or w), <u>k</u>ale (elsewhere); /n/ i<u>n</u>hale (before a consonant or word-final), <u>n</u>ote (elsewhere), /r/ hi<u>ss</u> (before a consonant or word-final), <u>r</u>un (trilled as in Italian, elsewhere); /w/ cu<u>ff</u> (before a consonant other than y or word-final), <u>w</u>ay (elsewhere); /y/ fi<u>sh</u> (before a consonant or word-final), <u>y</u>ou (elsewhere), /θ/ <u>th</u>ing; /'/ (the sound between the vowels in unh-unh); /·/ long vowel, /´/ high pitch; /`/ low pitch.

diminutive sense of attributive verbs and particles (e.g., **áhči?.#áh**: ahči?áh ‹scant-little› *a little* (RC 3:54), **–ę°k"ehčayę(T)–.#áh**: ękwehčayęháh ‹human-be of no account› *person of no account* (RC 28:1)). In addition, the diminutive may occur with intransitive verbs to indicate that the duration of the activity is shortened (e.g., **ti+či–. –ę°nhe–.#áh**: tiθkęnhehs?áh ‹so-again-I-am living-little› *my life is coming to an end/is short* (L 4)). Finally, in many cases the meaning of constructions containing the diminutive has become so idiomatic that no specific meaning can be attributed to the enclitic (e.g., **–nę?takęw.#áh**: unę?takęw?áh ‹hemlock-in-little› *second Wolf Clan ("under-the-pine")* (L 47), **tha–. –eka·t–.#áh**: thyakyekatha?áh ‹unusual-one-liquid-stands-little› *lobelia, great lobelia (Lobelia sp.)* (H-notebook), **–či–. –hne?reθ–.#áh**: čuhne?re·θ?áh ‹again-it-root-is long-little› *sarsaparilla* (HS).

#ah little (diminutive). *enc.* See: **#áh**. This form occurs in some dialects and shows regularization of accent to the penultimate syllable, i.e., the syllable preceding the suffix. The boundary # is automatically realized as *h* following a vowel, ? following a non-laryngeal consonant, and ɸ following a laryngeal consonant.

–(a)hah– aisle, journey, lobby, path, road, track. *n.r.* n-poss., inc., n.sfx. –eh. The conditioning factor(s) that determine(s) the occurrence of **–ahah–** versus **–hah–** are unknown. uháheh *aisle, journey, lobby, path, road, track* (HS); **–(a)hah–.#keha·?**: uhaha?kyéha·? ‹path-customary› *plantain (Plantago sp.)* (AG); **–(a)hahačhakwahsT–**: rahahačhakwáhstha? ‹he-path-X-is good›

he repairs, is repairing the road, he repairs roads (H 2484); **–(a)hahahkw–**: yuhaháhkwę· ‹it-road-picked up› *rut* (HS); **–(a)hahahkwi?T–**: rahahahkwí?tha? ‹he-path-moves away› *he switches the road (railroad)* (H 2484); **–(a)hahahrahT–**: uhaháhraht ‹path-put up-cause› *it is an awful road, a road to be feared* (H 2484); **–(a)hahahra?–**: rahaháhra?θ ‹he-path-put up-begins› *he dreads the road (either on account of its condition or on account of its being infested by beasts or robbers)* (H 2484); **–(a)hahahsęwati–**: kahahahsęwá·tih ‹it-path-smoothes› *it smoothes the road (this is the name for a road-scraper)* (H 2484); **–(a)ha = hahsthu–**: wahaháhsthę ‹it-path-is small› *the road is narrow* (H 2484); **–(a)hahahsthu?T–**: rahahahsthú?tha? ‹he-path-be small-causes› *he makes the road narrower, he narrows the road* (H 2484); **–(a)hahahtir–**: yuhahahtì·rę ‹it-path-is durable› *the road is hard, firm* (H 2484); **–(a)hahahti?r–**: yuhahahtí?rę ‹it-path-be durable-began› *the road has become hard* (H 2484); **–(a)hahakaręhw–**: rahahakà·ręws ‹he-path-goes around› *he turns back, he retraces his way; he puts a turn in the road* (H 2484); **–(a)ha = hakarę?rahT–**: rahahakarę?rahč ‹he-path-be sloped-causes› *he inclines the road (its surface to one side)* (H 2484); **–(a)hahakęw**: uháhakęw ‹path-in› *in the road* (H 2484); **–(a)ha = hakęw?ahči**: uhahakęw?áhči ‹path-in-very› *in the very road, in the very middle of the road* (H 2484); **–(a)ha = hakhahsi–**: nęyehahakháhsi? ‹two-prediction-one-path-put together-undo› *the two of them will go separate ways* (RC 35:39); **–(a)hahaks–**: wahahá·ksę· ‹it-path-is bad› *it is a bad road, a dirty*

road, a poor road, or way (H 2484);
–(a)hahaks –.#ha'nę': wahahaksęhá'-nę' ‹it-path-is bad-many› *the roads are bad, poor: they are bad, poor roads* (H 2484); –(a)hahaksę'T –: wahahaksę'tha' ‹it-path-be bad-causes› *it makes the road bad or difficult* (H 2484); –(a)hahakT –: uháhakwt ‹path-next to› *beside, near the road* (H 2484); –(a)hahaktha'nye' –: uhahakwthá·'nye' ‹path-next to-going along› *alongside of the road, path or way* (H 2484); –(a)hahakwahsT –: wahahákwahst ‹it-path-is good› *(it is) a good, fine road* (H 2484), wahahakwáhstha' ‹it-path-is good› *it renders the road fine or good* (H 2484); –(a)hahak͏ʷek –: kaháhakweks ‹it-path-closes› *it closes the road (as a fallen tree or drifted-snow in winter)* (H 2484), raháhakweks ‹he-path-closes› *he obstructs a road* (HS); –(a)hahakwe'niyu –: wahahakwe'nì·yu' ‹it-path-be principal› *principal path* (RC 26:3), *(it is) the main, principal road; it is the highway, public way* (H 2484); –(a)hahakerhu –: yuhahakyérhę ‹it-path-climbed up› *an ascending-way, a stairway, a pair of stairs* (H 2484); –(a)haharaku –: rahahará·kwahs ‹he-path-be in-undoes› *he turns it off the road or track, as a train or cart, or other things* (H 2484); *he averts it* (HS), nathahará·kwahs ‹one=another-path-be in-undoes› *one puts another out of the road, one misleads another* (HS); –(a)hahara' –: raháhara'θ ‹he-

path-be in-begins› *he reaches, he gets on the road* (H 2484); –(a)haharurę=ku –: wahaharurę́·kwahs ‹it-path-contribute-undoes› *it undoes the road, it destroys the road (said of the weather in winter when a warm spell thaws the snow and thereby spoils the sleighing)* (H 2484); –(a)hahaθkwi' –: ruhaháθkwi'θ ‹he-path-blots out› *it blots out his path or road (said of a path in the snow or sand that disappears by the action of the weather)* (H 2484); –(a)hahaT –: kaháha·t ‹it-path-stand› *(it is) a road contained in something, as in a valley or ravine* (H 2484); –(a)hahatihsthu –: wahahatíhsthę ‹it-path-are small› *roads are small* (H 2484); –(a)hahaturę –: ruhahatù·ręh ‹he-path-put away› *the road is too difficult for him, too hard for him to use* (H 2484); –(a)hahayę'ner –: kayehahayę'nè·rih ‹they-path-know› *they know the path* (RC 32:2); –(a)haha'=ke: uhahá'kye ‹path-on› *on the road, path, way* (H 2484); –(a)haha'ne –: wahahá·'ne' ‹it-path-is present› *there is a road (lit. the road is present, stands forth, projects)* (H 2484) [Lawson «Wauh-hauhne» 'A Path']; –(a)haha'ni: uháha'ni ‹path-at edge of› *at the edge of path* (RC 33:8); –(a)haha'riye –: yuhaha'rì·ye' ‹it-path-entangled› *(it is) a blind-road, a road overgrown by weeds or shrubs from non-use (this term is applied to a road which is lost in a forest or to one that is no longer in use and has become*

Tuscarora Pronunciation Key:
/a/ law; /e/ hat; /i/ pizza; /u/ tune; /ę/ hint; /č/ cheese; /h/ hoe; /m/ mother; /s/ same; /t/ do (before a vowel y, or w), too (elsewhere); /k/ gale (before a vowel y or w), kale (elsewhere); /n/ inhale (before a consonant or word-final), note (elsewhere), /r/ hiss (before a consonant or word-final), run (trilled as in Italian, elsewhere); /w/ cuff (before a consonant other than y or word-final), way (elsewhere); /y/ fish (before a consonant or word-final), you (elsewhere), /θ/ thing; /'/ (the sound between the vowels in unh-unh); /·/ long vowel, /́/ high pitch; /̀/ low pitch.

overgrown by weeds or shrubs) (H 2484); –(a)**haha?θ** –: waháha·ˀθ ‹it-path-be of a size› *the roads are large or broad* (H 2484); –(a)**haha̠?tirah** = **rahT** –: uhahaˀtiráhraht ‹path-X-put up-cause› *it is a fearful, terrifying road* (H 2484); –(a)**hahehke**: uhahéhkye ‹path-at› *at the road, at the place of the road* (H 2484); –(a)**haheθ** –: wahá-he·θ ‹it-path-is long› *it is a long road, path, or row or line of inanimate things* (H 2484); –(a)**haheθę** –: wahahé·θęh ‹it-path-is long-many› *the paths or roads are long* (H 2484); –(a)**hahęhawi** –: rahahęhà·wiˀ ‹he-path-brought-X› *guide* (HS); –(a)**hahęhT** –: rahahę́hneˀ ‹he-path-fall-causes› *he is on the road, is following the road* (H 2484); –(a)**hahęti** –: rahahę́·tih ‹he-path-makes› *he makes, is making a road or path* (H 2484); –(a)**hahę?ke**: uhahę́ˀ-kye ‹path-on› *on or against the road, or stairway* (H 2484); –(a)**hahihar** –: wahahíheˀr ‹it-path-hangs› *(it is) a road upon something (as on a ledge or hill)* (H 2484); –(a)**hahihę**: uhahíhę ‹path-in middle of› *in the middle of the road, path or way* (H 2484); –(a)**hahiyu** –: wahahí·yu· ‹it-path-be great› *great path* (RC 26:3); –(a)**hahi** = **yuhT** –: rahahiyúhthaˀ ‹he-path-be great-causes› *he enlarges, is enlarging, widens road* (H 2484); –(a)**hahu** = **kęhsT** –: yuhahukę́hsthęˀ ‹it-path-be forked-caused-much› *the road is divided in branches or forks* (H 2484); –(a)**hahya?k** –: kaháhyaˀks ‹it-path-break› *it obviates it: difficulty (concrete)* (HS), raháhyaˀks ‹he-path-breaks› *he prevents it (by cutting off its path, lit. he cuts or breaks off its road)* (H 2484), *he intercepts* (HS); –(a)**hahyenę?** –: ruhahyè·nęˀθ ‹he-path-grab-begins› *the road falls on him*

(this means that one's way has failed him, that he has, in fact, died by the way; so that it may be rendered as well, he died by the way) (H 2484); –(a)**hahyęti** –: wahahyę́·tiˀ ‹it-path-extends› *the path, road lies extended away* (H 2484); –(a)**hahyętiha'nye?** –: wahahyętihá·ˀnyeˀ ‹it-path-extend-going along› *the road extends along, meanders* (H 2484); –(a)**hahyętihę** –: wahahyętíhęˀ ‹it-path-extends-many› *the rows extend away (said of rows of hills of corn, etc., trees, or cocks of grain, etc.)* (H 2484); –**athaha̠hkw** –: kakuthahahkę́heˀ ‹they-themselves-path-picked up-remote› *they had been walking* (AW 56); –**athaha̠r** –: rutháhaˀr ‹he-himself-path-is in› *he lays in wait* (RC 25:4), *he keeps watch, he patrols* (HS); –**athaha̠r** –{**dative III**}: akatháhręˀ ‹unknown-I-myself-path-am in-for› *that I join* (RC 13:6); –**athaha̠rahkw** –: yuthaharáhkwę ‹it-itself-path-collected› *it is out of the way* (H 2484); –**athaha̠raku** –: wathahará·kwahs ‹it-itself-path-be in-undoes› *it gets off the track or road* (H 2484); –**athaha̠ruhčrę** –: yuthaha-rúhčręˀ ‹it-itself-path-gathers› *crossroads* (HS); –**athaha̠yę?na'nye?** –: ru-thahayęˀná·ˀnyeˀ ‹he-himself-path-lays-going along› *he is traveling along* (H 2484); –**athaha?riye** –: wathahaˀ-rì·yehs ‹it-itself-path-entangled› *it wears away the road* (HS); –**athahiN** –: rathahì·nęhs ‹he-himself-path-proceeds› *he travels* (HS), rathahí·teˀ ‹he-himself-path-proceed-ed› *he is traveling* (H 2484); –**či** –. –**athaha̠karęhw** –: θakayęthahakà·ręw ‹again-they-them-selves-path-went around› *they turned this road about, they returned* (RC 12:11); –**ne** –. –(a)**haha̠hkw** –: waˀtkaye-háhahkw ‹fact-they-path-picked up›

they walked on a path (RC 32:2);
-ne -. -(a)hah<u>a</u>hskanek<u>e</u>T -: neyuha-
hahskané·k<u>e</u>·t ‹apart-it-path-is strange›
it is a peculiar, curious road or way
(H 2484); -ne -. -(a)hah<u>a</u>kh<u>a</u>hsi -:
n<u>e</u>yehahakháhsi^ʔ ‹two-prediction-one-
path-divide-undo› *the two of them
will go separate ways* (RC 35:39);
-ne -. -(a)hahaw<u>e</u>r<u>e</u>h -: neyuhahaw<u>è</u>·r<u>e</u>hθ
‹apart-it-path-diminishes› *the road
cramps it, is too narrow for it* (H
2484); -ne -. -(a)hahaw<u>e</u>r<u>e</u>T -: newaha-
haw<u>e</u>r<u>é</u>·tha^ʔ ‹apart-it-path-diminishes›
*it takes up a part of the road (said of
an obstruction on a road, lit. it encroaches upon the road, it makes the
road too small, is a free rendering of
this)* (H 2484); -ne -. -(a)hahiθ -: nehra-
hahí·θahs ‹apart-he-path-meets› *he
meets it* (H 2484), nehrahahíθhe^ʔ
‹apart-he-path-meet-is going to› *he is
about to meet it* (H 2484); -ne -.
-(a)hahya^ʔk -: nehraháhya^ʔks ‹apart-
he-path-breaks› *he crosses the road* (H
2484); -ne -. -athah<u>a</u>hkw -: nehrutha-
háhk<u>e</u> ‹he-himself-path-picks up› *he is
walking* (L 13), nehruthahahk<u>e</u>há·^ʔ-
nye^ʔ ‹he-himself-path-took-going
along› *he is walking along* (L 13);
-ne -. -athah<u>a</u>hkwa^ʔT -: neyuthahah-
kwá^ʔtha^ʔ ‹apart-it-it-self-path-pick up-
causes› *ground, baked, white corn (a
provision traditionally taken along on
a trip)* (R); -ne -. -athah<u>a</u>tek<u>e</u> -: neyu-
thahaté·k<u>e</u>· ‹two-it-itself-path-put together› *the two roads are side by side*
(H 2484); ti -. -(a)haheθ -: tiwaháhe·θ
‹so-it-path-is long› *as long as is the
road* (H 2484); ti -. -(a)haheθ -.#áh:
tiwahahe·θ^ʔáh ‹so-it-path-is long-little›
*the road is short or the row is not
long* (H 2484); ti -. -(a)haheθ -.#<u>e</u>tíh:
tiwahaheθ^ʔ<u>e</u>tíh ‹so-it-path-is long-
many little› *the rows are short* (H
2484); -yah -. -athah<u>a</u>kuhsi -: wa^ʔθatha-
hakúhsi ‹thither-you!-yourself-path-
take-undo› *straighten out your path
there!* (RC 3:44); -yah+ne -. -(a)hahiθ -:
ya^ʔn<u>e</u>θwaháhi·θ ‹thither-you-path-
meet› *you will wait there* (RC 33:4);
ti+yah+ne -. -(a)hahiθ -: tyahwa^ʔnye-
háhi·θ ‹so-thither-fact-they two-path-
met› *they two met there* (RC 30:40);
ti+yah+ne -. -(a)hahiθ<u>e</u> -: tyah<u>e</u>θahru-
hahí·-θ<u>e</u>^ʔ ‹so-thither-again-fact-he-
path-met-for› *where he returned to
his own path* (RC 31:3); k<u>e</u>^ʔ -atha=
h<u>a</u>ruhčr<u>e</u> -: k<u>e</u>^ʔ yuthaharúhčr<u>e</u>^ʔ ‹where
it-itself-path-gathered› *where the roads
are collected (this is another name for
the four-corners or crossroads of high-
ways)* (H 2484); k<u>e</u>^ʔ -athah<u>a</u>yahθ(e)r -:
k<u>e</u>^ʔ yuthahayáhθe^ʔr ‹where it-itself-
path-crossed› *where the roads are
folded one on the other, or are tiered
(this is the term applied to the four
corners at the juncture of roads or
where one crosses the other)* (H
2484); na^ʔ ti -. -(a)hahu^ʔn<u>e</u> -: na^ʔ tyu-
hahú^ʔn<u>e</u>· ‹much so-it-path-is a kind
of› *course* (HS).
-(a)hah -.#keha·^ʔ plantain. *n.s.* uha-
ha^ʔkyéha·^ʔ ‹path-customary› *plantain
(Plantago sp.)* (AG).

Tuscarora Pronunciation Key:
/a/ l<u>a</u>w; /e/ h<u>a</u>t; /i/ p<u>i</u>zza; /u/ t<u>u</u>ne; /<u>e</u>/ h<u>i</u>nt; /č/
<u>ch</u>eese; /h/ <u>h</u>oe; /m/ <u>m</u>other; /s/ <u>s</u>ame; /t/ <u>d</u>o
(before a vowel y, or w), <u>t</u>oo (elsewhere); /k/ <u>g</u>ale
(before a vowel y or w), <u>k</u>ale (elsewhere); /n/
i<u>n</u>hale (before a consonant or word-final), <u>n</u>ote
(elsewhere), /r/ hi<u>ss</u> (before a consonant or word-
final), <u>r</u>un (trilled as in Italian, elsewhere); /w/ cu<u>ff</u>
(before a consonant other than y or word-final),
<u>w</u>ay (elsewhere); /y/ fi<u>sh</u> (before a consonant or
word-final), <u>y</u>ou (elsewhere), /θ/ <u>th</u>ing; /^ʔ/ (the
sound between the vowels in unh-unh); /·/ long
vowel, /ʹ/ high pitch; /ˋ/ low pitch.

-(a)**hahačhakwahsT** - repair road. *v.s.-a.i.* rahahačha-kwáhstha⁷ ‹he-path-X-is good› *he repairs, is repairing the road, he repairs roads* (H 2484).

-(a)**hahahkw** - rut. *dv.n.s.* yuhaháhkwę· ‹it-road-picked up› *rut* (HS).

-(a)**hahahkwi⁷T** - railroad. *dv.n.s.* rahahahkwí⁷tha⁷ ‹he-path-moves away› *he switches the road (railroad)* (H 2484).

-(a)**hahahra⁷** - dread the road. *v.s.-a.i.* rahaháhra⁷θ ‹he-road-put up-begins› *he dreads the road (either on account of its condition or on account of its being infested by beasts or robbers)* (H 2484).

-(a)**hahahsęwati** - road-scraper. *dv.n.s.* kahahahsęwá·tih ‹it-path-smoothes› *it smoothes the road (this is the name for a road-scraper)* (H 2484).

-(a)**hahahsthu** - be narrow road. *v.s.-s.i.* wahaháhsthę ‹it-path-is small› *the road is narrow* (H 2484).

-(a)**hahakaręhw** - turn back, retrace way. *v.s.-a.i.* rahahakà·ręws ‹he-path-goes around› *he turns back, he retraces his way: he puts a turn in the road* (H 2484).

-(a)**hahakhahsi** - go separate ways. *v.s.-a.i.* nęyehahakháhsi⁷ ‹two-prediction-one-path-put together-undo› *the two of them will go separate ways* (RC 35:39).

-(a)**hahak"ek** - close road, obstruct road. *v.s.-a.i.* kaháhakweks ‹it-path-closes› *it closes the road (as a fallen tree or drifted-snow in winter)* (H 2484), raháhakweks ‹he-path-closes› *he obstructs a road* (HS).

-(a)**hahakwe⁷niyu** - principal path; the main, principal road; it is the highway, public way. *dv.n.s.* wahahakwę⁷nì·yu⁷ ‹it-path-is principal› *principal path* (RC 26:3), *(it is) the main, principal road: it is the high-*

way, *public way* (H 2484).

-(a)**hahakerhu** - ascending-way, stairway, pair of stairs. *dv.n.s.* yuhahakyérhę ‹it-path-put up-caused› *an ascending-way, a stairway, a pair of stairs* (H 2484).

-(a)**hahęhawi** - guide. *dv.n.s.* rahahęhà·wi⁷ ‹he-path-brings› *guide* (HS).

-(a)**hahya⁷k** - obviate, prevent. *v.s.-t.* kaháhya⁷ks ‹it- path-break› *it obviates it* (HS), raháhya⁷ks ‹he-path-breaks› *he prevents it (by cutting off its path, lit. he cuts or breaks off its road)* (H 2484).

-(a)**hahya⁷k** - difficulty (concrete). *dv.n.s.* kaháhya⁷ks ‹it -path-breaks› *difficulty (concrete)* (HS).

-(a)**hahyenę⁷** - die by the way. *v.s.-a.i.* ruhahyè·nę⁷θ ‹he-path-grasp-begins› *the road falls on him (this means that one's way has failed him, that he has, in fact, died by the way, so that it may be rendered as well, he died by the way)* (H 2484).

áha·θ horse *(equus caballus)* (R) [Lawson «a hots» 'a horse']. *n.* aha·θ. **#áh:** aha·θ⁷áh ‹horse-small› *colt* (R); **áha·θ -a⁷netyahstawę -:** áha·θ yu⁷netyahstà·węh ‹horse it-itself-get dressed-'ness-possesses› *horse's harness* (HS); **áha·θ -e⁷wihshar -:** áha·θ re⁷wíhsher ‹horse he-saddle-hangs› *he saddles a horse* (HS); **áha·θ -ęnęh = kwa⁷t -:** áha·θ ręnęhkwáhkwa⁷t ‹horse he-cure-causes› *farrier* (HS); **áha·θ -hęhneθę -:** áha·θ kahęhné·θęh ‹horse it-ear-is long-much› *ass* (HS); **-hęh = neθę - áha·θ:** kahęhné·θęh áha·θ ‹it-ear-is long-much horse› *mule* (HS); **áha·θ -nęwę -:** áha·θ unę̀·wę⁷ ‹horse female› *mare* (HS); **áha·θ -⁷nhęh = sukę⁷:** áha·θ u⁷nhęhsú·kę⁷ ‹horse egg-less› *gelding* (HS); **áha·θ -ne -. -arah = suθ -:** áha·θ nehrarahsú·θe⁷ ‹horse apart-he-shoe-covered› *he shoed a* *horse* (HS).

aha·θ.#áh colt. *n*. aha·θ·ʔáh ‹horse-small› *colt* (R).

áha·θ -aʔnetyahstawę – horse's harness. *n.s.* áha·θ yuʔnetyahstà·węh ‹horse it-itself-get dressed-'ness-possesses› *horse's harness* (HS).

áha·θ -eʔwihshar – saddle horse. *v.s.-a.i.* áha·θ reʔwíhsher ‹horse he-saddle-hangs› *he saddles a horse* (HS).

áha·θ -ęnęhkwaʔT – farrier. *n.s.* áha·θ ręnęhkwáʔthaʔ ‹horse he-cure-causes› *farrier* (HS).

áha·θ -hęhneθę – ass. *n.s.* áha·θ kahęhné·θęh ‹horse it-ear-is long-much› *ass* (HS).

áha·θ -ne -. -arahsuθ – shoe a horse. *v.s.-a.i.* áha·θ nehrarahsú·θeʔ ‹horse apart-he-shoe-covers› *he shoes a horse* (HS).

áha·θ -nęwe – mare. *n.s.* áha·θ unę̀·weʔ ‹horse female› *mare* (HS).

áha·θ -ʔnhęhsukęʔ gelding. *n.s.* áha·θ uʔnhęhsú·kęʔ ‹horse egg-less› *gelding* (HS).

-(a)haʔkęhw – raise head, extend neck. *v.s.- a.i.* aręháʔkęw ‹unknown-it-neck-be around mouth› *that it raise its head* (RC 30:46); **-athaʔkęhw -:** ruthaʔkę́hę ‹he-himself-neck-was around mouth› *he has his neck up* (RC 30:21).

aháʔneʔ but (R). *part.*

-ahč – fist. *n.r.*, *n-poss.*, *inc.*, *n.sfx.* -eh. úhčeh *fist* (R); **-ahčarę -:** waʔnyę́hčaręʔ ‹fact-they two-fist-added› *the two of them pushed* (RC 25:13); **-ahčaT -{dative II}:** ęyęhčá·thahθ ‹pre-

diction-one-fist-stand-for› *one will point out* (RC 15:9); **-ahčir -{dative I} -hrę -:** naʔnahčiraʔθéhręh ‹one= another-fist-moves through-for-much› *one insults another* (HS); **-ahčuhčr -:** uhčúhčreh ‹fist-cover-'ness› *glove, mitten* (R), ruhčúhčręʔ ‹he- fist-cover-'ness-possesses› *he is wearing gloves* (HS); **-ne -.-ahčakʷek -:** nehruhčakwekęhá·ʔnyeʔ ‹he-fist-closed-going along› *he was carrying in his clenched fists* (RC 3:90); **-ne -.-ahčaʔnihr -:** waʔthrahčáʔnir ‹fact-apart-he-fist-stood› *his fists stood apart* (RC 24: 10); **-ne -.-ahčaʔnihrhę -:** neyuhčaʔnírhę· ‹apart-it-fist-stood-much› *pot* (HS); **-yah -.-ahčaT -:** yęwahčá·ʔneʔ ‹thither-prediction-it-fist-be present› *it will point there* (RC 30:28); **-ihn - -ahčakewaʔT -:** úhneh yęhčakyewáʔthaʔ ‹cloth one-fist-wipe-causes› *napkin* (HS).

-ahčarę – push. *v.s.-t.* waʔnyę́hčaręʔ ‹fact-they two-fist- added› *the two of them pushed it* (RC 25:13).

-ahčaT -{dative II} point out. *v.s.-t.* ęyęhčá·thahθ ‹prediction-one-fist-stand-for› *one will point it out* (RC 15:9).

-ahčaʔnahkw – corrode, mutilate, pervert, ruin, spoil. *v.r.* -t. hab: -haʔ, pnt: -ɸ, stat: -ę, prog: -, prp: -, dst: -ahnę-, caus: -, rvs: -, dat: -, inc.-ɸ-pat. wahčaʔnáhkhwaʔ *it corrodes it, it spoils it* (HS), rahčaʔnáhkhwaʔ *he mutilates it, he perverts it, he ruins it, he spoils it* (HS); **-ahčaʔnahkwahnę -:** wahčaʔnah-

---

kwáhnęh ‹it-spoils-much› *it destroys* (R); **-nęθahča[?]nahkw** –: ranęθahča[?]náhkhwa[?] ‹he-potato-spoils› *he is wasting potatoes, he is destroying potatoes* (H 2484); **-a'nahča[?]nahkę = ha'nye[?]** –: yu[?]nahča[?]nahkęhá·[?]nye[?] ‹it-itself-spoiled-going along› *it is rotting* (RC 8:24); **kwęhs** –a'nahča[?]nahkw –: kwęhs aryu[?]nahča[?]náhkęk ‹no un-known-it-itself-spoil› *unspoiled* (HS).

-ahča[?]nahkwahnę – destroy. *v.s.-t.* wahča[?]nahkwáhnęh ‹it-spoils-much› *it destroys it* (R).

-ahčę[?]wahT – destroy, end, quit, stop. *v.r.-t.* hab: -ha[?], pnt: -ϕ, stat: -, prog: -, prp: -, dst: -, caus: -, rvs: -, dat: -, n-inc. rahčę[?]wáhtha[?] *he quits it* (HS), ęwahčę[?]waht *it will destroy it* (RC 22:2), ęhčę[?]waht *it ended, the end* (R), ę[?]nyahčę[?]waht *you and I must stop it* (RC 3:39), wa[?]kahčę[?]waht *I quit it* (R); **-či** –. **-ahčę[?]wahT** –: ęθwahčę[?]waht ‹prediction-again-it-destroy› *it will destroy it again* (RC 16:3); **sè·nę[?]** **-a[?]nahčę[?]wahT** –: sè·nę[?] arę[?]nahčę[?]-wáhthek ‹never unknown-it-itself-destroy› *it is unending* (HS).

-(a)hčh – nominalizer. *v.r.s.* See **-(a)hčr** –; the form **-ahčh** – occurs following certain roots and stems that end in a consonant or *i* preceding roots that begin with *y*, the *y* being dropped; the form **-hčh** – occurs following certain roots and stems that end in a consonant and roots and stems that end in a vowel, preceding roots that begin with *y*, the *y* being dropped.

-ahčir –{dative I} **-hrę** – insult. *v.s.-t.* na[?]nahčira[?]θéhręh ‹one=another-fist-moves through-for-much› *one insults another* (H).

áhči[?] little, less, meager, scant, small (HS). *part.* **áhči[?].#áh**: ahči[?]áh ‹scant-little› *a little* (RC 3:54) [Gallatin «ah-tcheeah» 'Small, Little'].

áhči[?].#áh a little. *part.* ahči[?]áh ‹scant-little› *a little* (RC 3:54) [Gallatin «ah-tcheeah» 'Small, Little']; **séher kwęhs ęwę·ru[?] áhči.#áh**: séher kwęhs ęwę·ru[?] ahčí[?]ah ‹also no at most a little› *not even a little* (RC 3:55).

-(a)hčr – nominalizer. *v.r.s.* The main use of the nominalizer is to make a noun out of a verb root (e.g., **unęhwákčreh** ‹ache-'ness› *illness, sickness*). The form **-ahčr** – occurs following certain roots and stems that end in a consonant or *i*; the form **-hčr** – occurs elsewhere, with the initial *h* being dropped if preceded by a consonant.

-ahčuhčr – glove, mitten. *n.s.* uhčúhčreh ‹fist-cover-'ness› *glove, mitten* (R).

-ahčuhčrę – wear gloves. *v.s.-a.i.* ruhčúhčrę[?] ‹he-fist-cover-'ness-possesses› *he is wearing gloves* (HS).

-(a)h(e)r – add to, impose, put onto, put on top, put up. *v.r.-t.* hab: -ϕ ~ -ha[?], pnt: -a[?], stat: -[?], prog: -, prp: -, dst: -awę-, caus: -ahT-, rvs: -aku-, dat: -, inc.-ϕ ag./pat. ráher *he imposes it, he puts it onto something, he puts it on top, he adds to it* (HS); **-(a)hraku** –: rahrá·kwahs ‹he-put up-undoes› *he takes off a thing* (HS); **-(a)hrawę** –: ęhsrà·wę[?] ‹prediction-you-put up- sev-eral› *you will put around* (R), kahrà·węh ‹it-put up-several› *it puts around* (RC 3:64); **-(a)hrawęku** –: θwahrawę·kuh ‹you-put up-several-undo› *you take it down* (RC 3:61); **-(a)hra[?]** –: yuhrá[?]ę ‹it-put up-began› *it has gotten on it* (L 53); **tha** –. **-(a)h(e)r** –: thękáhra·k ‹unusual-prediction-it-put up› *it will be put there* (RC 3:22); **-(a)ha = hahrahT** –: uhaháhraht ‹path-put up-cause› *it is an awful road, a road to be feared* (H 2484); **-(a)hahahra[?]** –: ra-haháhra[?]θ ‹he-path-put up-begins› *he* *dreads the road (either on account of its condition or on account of its being infested by beasts or robbers)* (H 2484); –či⁷ehnahrahT –: uči⁷ehnáhraht ‹claw-put up-cause› *the claw is awful, its claw is awful* (H 2484); –hču⁷= kwahrawę –{dative I}: wahrahču⁷-kwahrà·wę⁷θ ‹fact-he-portion of meat-put up-much-for› *he placed portions of meat* (RC 12:2); –hehnahrahT –: uhehnáhraht ‹field-put up-cause› *it is an awful field, a field to be feared, on any account whatsoever* (H 2484); –hnawahrahT –: wahrahnawahráhnahk ‹fact-he-current-put up-caused› *he went against the current* (RC 12:29); –hnyahrahT –: uhnyáhraht ‹news-put up-cause› *awful news, awful story* (L 13); –hskanenahrahT –: uhskanenáhraht ‹countenance-put up-cause› *awfulness* (RC 28:9), *ferocious* (HS), *how awful, how terrible* (R); –hstihrawęku –: wa⁷-kayehstihrawę́·ku⁷ ‹fact-they-bark-put up-several-undid› *they took down bark* (RC 3:63); –(i)⁷nyuhkwahrahT –: u⁷-nyuhkwáhraht ‹crowd-put up-cause› *multitude* (HS); –khwah(e)r –: yakwa-khwáher ‹we-food-put up› *we make a feast* (L 34); –kθraku –: θekθrá·ku ‹you!-dish-put up-undo› *take the dishes off!* (L 54); –kθrawę –: ęhse-kθrà·wę⁷ ‹prediction-you dish-put up-several› *you will set the table, you will put dishes around* (R); –nęha= h(e)r –: ranęháhrę ‹he-corn-puts up› *he sets, places corn grains (in the ground), hence, he plants corn* (H 2484); –nęhahrę⁷ke: kanęharę́⁷kye ‹it-corn-puts up-at› *at corn-planting (a subaudition of the word for time), this is the name of the month of April(?)* (H 2484); *March* (R); –nęhsahrahT –: unęhsáhraht ‹house-put up-cause› *it is a great, massive house; it is an awful house* (H 2484); –nęth(e)r –: yunę́·ther ‹it-hill-puts up› *peak* (HS), *hill* (PC) [Gallatin «younunthehr» 'Hill']; –nę= th(e)r –.#ha·⁷: Akunętherę́ha·⁷ ‹one-hill-put up-characterized by› *Turtle Clan* (AG), ranętherę́ha·⁷ ‹he-hill-put up-characterized by› *he is of the Turtle Clan* (AG); –nęth(e)r –.#ke: unę-thrá⁷kye ‹hill-puts up-at› *top of mountain* (AG); –nęth(e)r –.#ú⁷y: yunęther-⁷úy⁷ ‹it-hill-puts up-great› *mountain* (PC); –nhurahrahT –: unhuráhraht ‹disease- put up-cause› *it is a tough, serious disease* (RC 16:3); –ręhyah(e)r –: wahraręhyáhra⁷ ‹fact-he-sky-put up› *he "climbed the sky" (i.e., traveled from horizon to zenith)* (RC 12:19); –rę⁷karah(e)r –: wa⁷karę⁷karáhrę⁷ ‹fact-it-finger span-put up› *to reach, span the fingers, extend, etc.* (AG); –rihwahrahT –: urihwáhraht ‹matter-put up-cause› *crime* (HS), *terrible thing* (R); –θwętahrahT –: ruθwętáhraht ‹he-??-put up-caused› *he is rude* (HS); –tahskwahrahT –: utahskwáhraht ‹slave-put up-cause› *annoyance* (R); –takwthrawę'nye⁷ –: katakwthrawę́·⁷-nye⁷ ‹it-bed-put up-several-going along› *beds were put around* (RC 3:5); –te⁷wahrahT –: ute⁷wáhraht ‹??-

---

put up-cause› *something terrible* (RC 3:56), yute'wáhraht ‹it-'?-put up-cause› *it is frightful* (HS); **-te'wah = rahT -{dative II}**: na'te'wahrahná·tih ‹one=another-'?-put up-cause-for› *one frightens another* (HS); **-ye'tuhrahT -**: ruye'túhraht ‹he-rat-put up-cause› *mythic strong creature* (AW 53); **-wetahrahT -**: uwetáhraht ‹word-put up-cause› *terrible noise* (RC 28:7); **-či -. -htawh(e)r -**: θakahtáwhra' ‹again-fact-it-stream of water-put up› *stream of water again gushed up* (RC 6:9); **-t -. -htawah(e)r -**: nakahtawáhra' ‹hither-fact-it-stream of water-put up› *stream of water gushed up* (RC 6:9); **ti -. -čewahrawe -**: neθwačewrà·we' ‹so-prediction-you-burial pole-put up-several› *you will put burial poles around* (RC 3:22); **-ath(e)r -**: éthra·k ‹prediction-it-itself-put up› *it put itself* (RC 12:10); **-athrahthar -**: wa'keyathráhtha'r ‹fact-I=you-self-put up-cause-hung› *I scolded you* (AG), wa'na'nathráhtha'r ‹fact-one=another-self-put up-cause-hung› *she scolded (the boy)* (AG), wahsheyathráhtha'r ‹fact-you=another-self-put up-cause-hung› *you scolded (the boy)* (AG); **-a'nekhwa = h(e)r -**: ra'nekhwáher ‹he-himself-food-puts up› *he takes his meal* (HS), ehra'nekhwáhre' ‹prediction-he-himself-food-put up› *he will take his meal* (HS); **-a'nekhwahrahčr -**: u'nekhwahráhčreh ‹self-food-put up-'ness› *table* (R); **-a'nekhwahruhT -**: ye'nekhwahrúhtha' ‹one-oneself-food-put up-cover-causes› *tablecloth* (HS).

-(a)he - many, much (distributive). *v.r.s.* hab: -h, pnt: -·', stat: -·, prog: -, prp: -, caus: -, rvs: -ku-, dat: -. The distributive is used to indicate either that the action of the verb is spread over time or that the object of the verb is distributed over an area (e.g., **wahraturá·the·'** ‹fact-he-hunted-many› *he hunted several (animals scattered about the forest)* or *he hunted several times*). The form **-ahe -** occurs following certain stems that end in a consonant or *i*; the form **-he -** occurs elsewhere, with loss of initial *h* following fricatives.

-(a)he'n - clearing, field, grassy plot, meadow, pasture, sward. *n.r.* n-poss., inc., n.sfx. -eh. The factors conditioning the choice of **-ahe'n -** versus **-he'n -** are unknown. uhé'neh *clearing, field, grassy plot, meadow, pasture, sward* (R); **-(a)he'nahnine -**: rahe'nahnì·neh ‹he-clearing-buys› *he buys the field* (H 2484); **-(a)he'nah = nine'T -**: rahe'nahniné'tha' ‹he-clearing-buy-causes› *he buys the field with it* (H 2484); **-(a)he'nahsthu -**: wahe'náhsthe ‹it-clearing-is small› *the meadow is small* (H 2484); **-(a)he' = nakew**: uhé'nakew ‹clearing-in› *in the meadow* (H 2484); **-(a)he'naks -**: wahe'ná·kse· ‹it-clearing-is bad› *poor clearing* (H 2484); **-(a)he'nakT -**: uhé'nakwt ‹clearing-next to› *next to clearing* (RC 25:1); **-(a)he'na = kwahsT -**: wahe'nákwahst ‹it-clearing-is good› *it is a good clearing* (RC 25: 1); **-(a)he'nara' -**: rahe'nara'θ ‹he-clearing-be in-begins› *he reaches, arrives at the meadow* (H 2484), wa'ehé'nara' ‹fact-one-clearing-be in-began› *one was in a clearing* (RC 25:5); **-(a)he'natehnine -**: rahe'natehnì·neh ‹he-clearing sells› *he sells the field* (H 2484); **-(a)he'nath -**: yuhe'ná·the ‹it-clearing-is dry› *the meadow is dry* (H 2484); **-(a)he'na = tihsthu -**: wahe'natíhsthe ‹it-clearing-are small› *the meadows are small* (H 2484); **-(a)he'nawe -**: ruhé'nawęh ‹he-clearing-possesses› *the meadow belongs to him, it is his meadow* (H 2484); –(a)hę^ˀnawę'na'nehsT –: yuhę^ˀ-nawę́·^ˀna^ˀnehst ‹it-clearing-is pleasant› *it is a pleasant meadow* (H 2484); –(a)hę^ˀnawihsi –: rahę^ˀnawíhsyęhs ‹he-clearing-give-undoes› *he takes the meadow out (of a difficulty) (said of a person who saves a meadow from loss by debt or other cause)* (H 2484); –(a)hę^ˀnaya^ˀk –: rahę^ˀnaya^ˀks ‹he-clearing-breaks› *he cuts the meadow (i.e., the crop growing on the meadow)* (H 2484); –(a)hę^ˀnayę(T) –: kahę́^ˀnayę^ˀ ‹it-clearing-lay› *the meadow lies, is, exists: there is a meadow* (H 2484), wahę́^ˀnayę^ˀ ‹it-clearing-lay› *grotto* (HS); –(a)hę^ˀna^ˀke: uhę^ˀná^ˀkye ‹clearing-at› *on, on the surface of the meadow* (H 2484); –(a)hę^ˀna^ˀθ –: wahę́^ˀna^ˀθ ‹it-clearing-is of a size› *the meadow is large* (H 2484); –(a)= hę^ˀnehke: uhę^ˀnéhkye ‹clearing-at› *at,in the meadow or grassy plot of ground* (H 2484); –(a)hę^ˀneθ –: wahę́^ˀ-ne·θ ‹it-clearing-is long› *the meadow is long* (H 2484); –(a)hę^ˀnęti –: ruhę^ˀ-nę́·ti· ‹he-clearing-made› *he made a clearing* (RC 25:1); –(a)hę^ˀnę^ˀke: u-hę^ˀnę́^ˀkye ‹clearing-at› *on or in the meadow as a part of its surface* (H 2484); –(a)hę^ˀnihę: uhę^ˀníhę ‹clearing-in middle of› *in the middle of the meadow, in the very center of the meadow* (H 2484); –(a)hę^ˀnihs^ˀa –: rahę^ˀníhs^ˀahs ‹he-clearing-finishes› *he completes, he finishes the meadow*

(i.e., the work he has to do on it, as gathering the hay, plowing or harrowing it, etc.) (H 2484); –(a)hę^ˀniyu –: wahę^ˀní·yu· ‹it-clearing-is great› *the meadow is large* (H 2484); –(a)hę^ˀ = nu^ˀ –: wahę́^ˀnu^ˀθ ‹it-clearing-be in water-begins› *the meadow is subject to overflow (from some stream of water), the meadow customarily becomes inundated* (H 2484); –(a)hę^ˀ = nuči –: kahę^ˀnú·či^ˀ ‹it-clearing-is cuneate› *sharp point of land, land pointing into the water* (AG); –(a)hę^ˀnyęti –: wahę^ˀnyę́·ti^ˀ ‹it-clearing-extends› *the meadow lies, extending hence* (H 24 84); –athę^ˀnę^ˀneT –: rathę^ˀnę^ˀné·tha^ˀ ‹he-clearing-goes alongside of› *he follows the edge of the meadow* (H 2484); –ne –. –athę^ˀna'naθ(e) –: nehra-thę^ˀna^ˀná·θehs ‹apart-he-himself-clearing-goes around› *he goes around the meadow* (H 2484), nehrathę́^ˀna^ˀ-na·č ‹apart-he-himself-clearing-goes around› *he goes around the meadow, either within or on the outside of the meadow* (H 2484); –yah –. –(a)hę^ˀ = na'ne –: wewahę^ˀná·^ˀne^ˀ ‹thither-it-clearing-be present› *there is a clearing there* (RC 25:2).

–ahę^ˀnayę(T) – grotto. *dv.n.s.* wahę^ˀnayę^ˀ ‹it-clearing- lay› *grotto* (HS).

–(a)hę^ˀnęha'nye^ˀ – frontward, onward. *n.s.* uhę^ˀnęhá·^ˀnye^ˀ ‹front-going along› *frontward, onward* (HS).

–(a)hę^ˀnuči – sharp point of land, land pointing into the water. *dv.n.s.* kahę^ˀ-nú·či^ˀ ‹it-clearing-is cuneate› *sharp*

Tuscarora Pronunciation Key:
/a/ l<u>a</u>w; /e/ h<u>a</u>t; /i/ p<u>i</u>zza; /u/ t<u>u</u>ne; /ę/ h<u>i</u>nt; /č/ <u>ch</u>eese; /h/ <u>h</u>oe; /m/ <u>m</u>other; /s/ <u>s</u>ame; /t/ <u>d</u>o (before a vowel y, or w), <u>t</u>oo (elsewhere); /k/ gale (before a vowel y or w), <u>k</u>ale (elsewhere); /n/ i<u>n</u>hale (before a consonant or word-final), <u>n</u>ote (elsewhere), /r/ hi<u>ss</u> (before a consonant or word-final), <u>r</u>un (trilled as in Italian, elsewhere); /w/ cu<u>ff</u> (before a consonant other than y or word-final), <u>w</u>ay (elsewhere); /y/ fi<u>sh</u> (before a consonant or word-final), <u>y</u>ou (elsewhere), /θ/ <u>th</u>ing; /^ˀ/ (the sound between the vowels in unh-<u>u</u>nh); /·/ long vowel, /ˊ/ high pitch; /ˋ/ low pitch.

*point of land, land pointing into the
water* (AG).

-(a)hę꞉T- front. *n.r.* inaln: rahę́꞉ne꞉
leader, he is in front, he precedes
(HS), inc., n.sfx. -ę. uhę́꞉nę *in front
of* (RC 25:16); -(a)hę꞉nęha'nye꞉-:
uhę꞉nęhá·꞉nye꞉ ‹front-going along›
frontward, onward (HS); -(a)hę꞉thę-:
wahę́꞉thę ‹it-front-in middle of› *in the
middle of* (RC 25:12); -athę꞉ne꞉T-:
yuthę꞉né꞉nę ‹it-itself-front-caused›
priority (HS); -(a)hę꞉T- -a'nę꞉T-:
uhę́꞉nę ru꞉nę́꞉nę ‹in front of he-is in
a line› *the head one* (AW 55), *leader*
(M 87); -(a)hę꞉T- -a'nę-: uhę́꞉nę
rá·꞉nęh ‹in front of he-says› *he presides* (HS); -(a)hę꞉T- kę꞉ná꞉kę: uhę́꞉-
nę kę꞉ná꞉kę ‹in front of side› *anterior*
(HS); -(a)hę꞉T- -yah-. -(ę)hawi-:
uhę́꞉nę yękahá·wi·t ‹in front of
thither-prediction-it-brings› *henceforth*
(HS).

-(a)hę꞉T- -a'nę- preside. *v.s.-a.i.* uhę́꞉nę
rá·꞉nęh ‹in front of he-says› *he presides* (HS).

-(a)hę꞉T- -a'nę꞉T- head one, leader.
dv.n.s. uhę́꞉nę ru꞉nę́꞉nę ‹in front of
he-is in a line› *the head one* (AW 55),
leader (M 87).

-(a)hę꞉T- kę꞉ná꞉kę anterior. *n.s.* uhę́꞉nę
kę꞉ná꞉kę ‹in front of side› *anterior*
(HS).

-(a)hę꞉T- -yah-. -(ę)hawi- henceforth.
n.s. uhę́꞉nę yękahá·wi·t ‹in front of
thither-prediction-it-brings› *henceforth* (HS).

-(a)hę꞉thę- in the middle of. *n.s.* wahę́꞉-
thę ‹it-front-in middle of› *in the
middle of* (RC 25:12).

-(a)hk stative factual. *v.r.s.* The stative
factual indicates that a state of being
existed in the past (e.g., rahę́sčihk ‹he-
was black› *he was black*). The form
-hk- occurs after roots and stems that

end in a vowel; the form -ahk- occurs
after roots and stems that end in a
consonant.

-(a)hkar- green bark, slice, timber,
wood, yoke. *n.r.* n-poss., inc., n.sfx.
-eh. úhkareh *green bark* (RC 9:2),
slice, timber, wood, yoke (HS); -(a)h=
karahtręha'nye꞉-: ruhkarahtręhá·꞉nye꞉
‹he-bark-tied-going along› *bark is tied
to him* (RC 32:10); -(a)hkarakęhey-:
yuhkarakęhè·yę ‹it-bark-is dead› *bark
has been dead* (RC 26:3); -(a)hka=
rawihsi-: rahkarawíhsyęhs ‹he-bark-
give-undoes› *he unbars a gate* (HS);
-(a)hkarayę(T)-{dative II}: ruhka-
rayę́·tih ‹he-bark-laid-for› *he laid
down bark for* (RC 12:2); -(a)hkara=
'ne-: yuhkará·꞉ne꞉ ‹it-bark-is present›
it is bitter, it is brackish (RC 10:1);
-(a)hkara꞉nihr-: rahkará꞉nihč ‹he-
bark-stands up› *he taps a tree* (HS);
-(a)hkaręti-: rahkarę́·tih ‹he-bark-
makes› *he chips it, he makes chips*
(HS); -(a)hkarętihT-: rahkarętíhtha꞉
‹he-bark-make-causes› *he cuts slices*
(HS); -(a)hkariyu-: yuhkarí·yu· ‹it-
bark-is great› *it is pliant, it is limber*
(HS), ruhkarí·yu· ‹he-bark-is great› *he
is agile, he is limber, he is spry, he is
supple* (HS); -(a)hkarur-: ráhkaruč
‹he-bark-covers› *he panels it* (HS),
ruhkarù·rę ‹he-bark-covered› *he paneled it* (HS); -a'nehkarur-: yu꞉nehka-
rù·rę ‹it-itself-bark-covered› *paneling*
(HS); -ne-. -(a)hkarayę'nahkw-: neyęh-
karayę꞉náhkhwa꞉ ‹apart-one-bark-
lays-instrument› *draught-head* (HS);
-ne-. -(a)hkaręhnahnę-: neyuhkaręh-
náhnę· ‹apart-it-bark-fall-cause-much›
it is square (HS); -ne-. -(a)hkarstraku-:
nehrahkarstrá·kwahs ‹apart-he-bark-
'ness-collects› *he unyokes* (HS), neh-
ruhkarstrá·kwę ‹apart-he-bark-'ness-
collected› *he un-yoked* (HS); -ne-.

-(a)h<u>ka</u>rurT -: neyuhkarúrne'' ‹apart-it-bark-cover-causes› *wild geranium (Geranium maculatum)* (H-notebook); tha+ne -. -(a)hk<u>a</u>r<u>e</u>hT -: tha'newáhkar<u>e</u>ht ‹unusual-apart-it-bark-fall-cause› *it is an unusual kind of square* (RC 23:2); ti -. -(a)hkar<u>a</u>či'tkwahna = y<u>e</u>(T) -: tiwahkarači'tkwáhnay<u>e</u>' ‹so-it-bark-yellow-lays› *yellow oak (Quercus sp.)* (R); ti+ne -. -(a)hk<u>a</u>r<u>e</u>hnahn<u>e</u> -: thwa'thrahkar<u>e</u>hnáhn<u>e</u>'‹so-fact-apart-he-bark-fall-caused-much› *he made them square* (RC 12:2).

-(a)hk<u>a</u>rak<u>e</u>hey - bark is dead. *v.s.-s.i.* yuhkarak<u>e</u>hè·y<u>e</u> ‹it-bark-is dead› *bark has been dead* (RC 26:3).

-(a)hk<u>a</u>rawihsi - unbar a gate. *v.s.-a.i.* rahkarawíhsy<u>e</u>hs ‹he-bark-give-un-does› *he unbars a gate* (HS).

-(a)hk<u>a</u>ray<u>e</u>(T) -{dative II} lay down bark. *v.s.-a.i.* ruhkaray<u>é</u>·tih ‹he-bark-laid-for› *he laid down bark for* (RC 12:2).

-(a)hk<u>a</u>ra'ne - be bitter, be brackish. *v.s.-s.i.* yuhkará·'ne' ‹it-bark-is present› *it is bitter, brackish* (RC 10:1).

-(a)hk<u>a</u>ra'nihr - tap a tree. *v.s.-a.i.* rahkará'nihč ‹he-bark-stands up› *he taps a tree* (HS).

-(a)hk<u>a</u>r<u>e</u>ti - chip, make chips. *v.s.-t.* rahkar<u>é</u>·tih ‹he-bark-makes› *he chips it, he makes chips* (HS).

-(a)hk<u>a</u>r<u>e</u>tihT - cut slices. *v.s.-a.i.* rahkar<u>e</u>tíhtha' ‹he-bark-make-causes› *he cuts slices* (HS).

-(a)hk<u>a</u>riyu - be agile, be limber, be pliant, be spry, be supple. *v.s.-s.i.* yuhka-rí·yu· ‹it-bark-is great› *it is limber, it is pliant* (HS), ruhkarí·yu· ‹he-bark-is great› *he is agile, he is limber, he is spry, he is supple* (HS).

-(a)hk<u>a</u>rur - panel. *v.s.-t.* ráhkaruč ‹he-bark-covers› *he panels it* (HS), ruhka-rù·r<u>e</u> ‹he-bark-covered› *he paneled it* (HS).

-ahk(e)T - go and return, go back and forth. *v.r.-a.i.* hab: -<u>e</u>hs, pnt: ()-, stat: -<u>e</u>, prog: -, prp: -he-, dst: -h<u>e</u>-, caus: -a'T-, rvs: -, dat: -, n-inc. -ahkn<u>e</u>h<u>e</u> -: sahkn<u>é</u>h<u>e</u>hs ‹you-go back and forth-much› *you call on someone, you court someone* (R); -či -. -ahk(e)T -: θahráhkye·t ‹again-fact-he-went back and forth› *he turned back* (L 79), θwáhkn<u>e</u>hs ‹again-it-goes back and forth› *it reverts* (HS); -ne -. -ahk(e)T -: nehrúhkn<u>e</u>hs ‹apart-he-goes back and forth› *he folds it* (HS), n<u>e</u>hrúhkye·t ‹apart-prediction-he-go back and forth› *he will fold it* (HS); -ne+t -. -ahk(e)T -: n<u>e</u>'n<u>é</u>hkye·t ‹apart-hither-it went back and forth› *it returned there* (RC 26:29), n<u>e</u>'nahráhkye·t ‹apart-prediction-hither-he-go back and forth› *he will return there* (RC 11:3); -yah -. -ahk(e)T -: wewáhkn<u>e</u> ‹thither-it went back and forth› *it goes and returns* (RC 34:12); -yah -. -ahkn<u>e</u>he -: wewahkn<u>é</u>he' ‹thither-it-went back and forth-going to› *it was going and coming* (RC 28:5); -yah -+ -č -. -ahk(e)T -: y<u>e</u>čháhkye·t ‹thither-prediction-again-you-go back and forth› *you will go back there again* (R); -a'nahkna'na =

Tuscarora Pronunciation Key:
/a/ l<u>a</u>w; /e/ h<u>a</u>t; /i/ p<u>i</u>zza; /u/ t<u>u</u>ne; /<u>e</u>/ h<u>i</u>nt; /č/ <u>ch</u>eese; /h/ <u>h</u>oe; /m/ <u>m</u>other; /s/ <u>s</u>ame; /t/ <u>d</u>o (before a vowel y, or w), <u>t</u>oo (elsewhere); /k/ <u>g</u>ale (before a vowel y or w), <u>k</u>ale (elsewhere); /n/ i<u>n</u>hale (before a consonant or word-final), <u>n</u>ote (elsewhere), /r/ hi<u>ss</u> (before a consonant or word-final), <u>r</u>un (trilled as in Italian, elsewhere); /w/ c<u>uff</u> (before a consonant other than y or word-final), <u>w</u>ay (elsewhere); /y/ fi<u>sh</u> (before a consonant or word-final), <u>y</u>ou (elsewhere), /θ/ <u>th</u>ing; /'/ (the sound between the vowels in unh-unh); /·/ long vowel, /´/ high pitch; /`/ low pitch.

'**nye** –: ru'nahkna'ná·'nyc' ‹he-him-self-go and return-caused-going along› *he struts* (HS).

–**ahknęhę** – call on, court. *v.s.-t.* sahknę-hęhs ‹you-go back and forth-much› *you call on someone, you court some-one* (R).

–**ahkθen** – be taken. *v.r.-a.i.* hab: -, pnt: -, stat: -, prog: -ę'nye'-, prp: -, dst: -, caus: -, rvs: -, dat: -, n-inc. –**a'nah** = **kθenę'nye'** –: wa'nahkθenę·'nye' ‹it-itself-is taken-going along› *things being carried* (RC 8:3).

–**(a)hkw** – instrumental. *v.r.s.* hab: -ha', pnt: -ɸ, stat: -ę°, prog: -, prp: -, dst: -, caus: -T-, rvs: -, dat: -. The main use of the instrumental is to form nouns that refer to instruments or tools from verbs (e.g., **yęchukaręhnáhkhwa'** ‹one-oneself-beard-fall-cause-instru-ment› *razor*). The form –**ahkw** – occurs following certain roots and stems that end in a consonant; the form –**hkw** – occurs elsewhere, with loss of initial *h* following a consonant.

–**ahkwa'T** – wrap up; yearn for. *v.r.-t.* hab: -hs, pnt: -, stat: -ę, prog: -, prp: -, dst: -, caus: -, rvs: -, dat: -, n- inc. –**či** –.–**ahkwa'T** –: čęhkwa''č ‹again-one-wraps up› *one wraps oneself up* (RC 34:22); –**yah** –.–**ahkwa'T** –: wehrah-kwá'nę ‹thither-he-yearned for› *he yearns for* (RC 34:3); –**ne** –.–**ekah** = **kwa'nahT** –: newekáhkwa'nahč ‹apart-it-liquid-wrap up-causes› *it eddies* (HS).

–**ahkweθ** – partridge, ruffled grouse. *n.r.* n-poss., inc., n.sfx. -ę. uhkwé·θę *par-tridge, ruffled grouse (Bonasa umbel-lus)* (RC 11:22) [Jefferson «oh-qua-sen» 'partridge'] [Gallatin «ohquasen» 'Partridge']; –**ahkweθa'θ** –: wahkwé·-θa'θ ‹it-partridge-is of a size› *drum-ming of partridges* (AG); –**ahkwe** =

θa'θ –.**#ke.#aka·'**: wahkweθa'θkye-há·ka·' ‹it-partridge-is of a size-at-characterized by› *the St. Regis tribe* (AG), *residents of Ahkwesahsne Re-serve* (R).

–**ahkweθa'θ** – drumming of partridges. *dv.n.s.* wahkwé·-θa'θ ‹it-partridge-is of a size› *drumming of partridges* (AG).

–**ahkweθa'θ** –.**#ke.#aka·'** the St. Regis tribe, residents of Ahkwesahsne Re-serve. *dv.n.s.* wahkweθa'θkyehá·ka·' ‹it-partridge-is of a size-at-character-ized by› *the St. Regis tribe* (AG), *resi-dents of Ahkwesahsne Reserve* (R).

áhkwir doe (RC 7:3). *n.*

–**ahnahkw** – Indian shoe, moccasin. *n.r.*, aln: akahnáhkwayę' *my moccasin* (R), inc., n.sfx. -a'. uhnáhkwa' *Indian shoe, moccasin* (RC 30:59) (also: ahnáhkwa' (R)); –**ahnahkw** –.**#ęwe**: uhnahkwehę̀·we ‹Indian shoe-genuine› *moccasins* (AG), –**ahnahkwęti** –: rah-nahkwę́·tih ‹he-Indian shoe-makes› *shoemaker* (HS).

–**ahnahkw** –.**#ęwe** moccasin. *n.s.* uhnah-kwehę̀·we ‹Indian shoe-genuine› *moc-casins* (AG).

–**ahnahkwęti** – shoemaker. *dv.n.s.* rahnah-kwę́·tih ‹he-Indian shoe-makes› *shoe-maker* (HS).

–**ahnahn** – pieces. *n.r.*, n-poss., inc. This root has been found only incorporated. thwa'kayęhnahnę'ę́·tih ‹so-fact-they-pieces-fell-many little› *lots of little piles fell* (RC 6:15), thwahrahnah-nę'ę́·tih ‹so-fact-he-pieces-fell-many little› *he made the pieces small* (RC 12:2).

–**ahnę** – disappear. *v.r.-a.i.* hab: -h, pnt: -', stat: -·, prog: -ha'nye'-, prp: -, dst: -, caus: -a'T-, rvs: -, dat: -, inc.-ɸ-ag./pat. wáhnęh *it disappears* (R); –**ahnę'T** –: rahnę́'tha' ‹he-disappear-causes› *he abolishes it, he blots it out, he destroys it; he purloins it* (HS), *he spends it* (HS), wa'kayę'na'náhnę't ‹fact-they=another-disappear-caused› *they destroyed them* (RC 12:7); **tha –**. **-ahnę –**: thęwáhnę' ‹unusual-it-disappears› *it will disappear* (RC 15:1); **ti+yah –**. **-ahnęha'nye' –**: tyahwa'uhnęhá·'nye' ‹so-thither-it-disappears-going along› *so it went along disappearing there* (RC 5:14); **-yah –**. **-ahnę'ęha'nye' –**: yahwa'uhnę'ęhá·'nye' ‹thither-fact-it-disappeared-going along› *it receded* (HS); **-(ę)'tikęh = rahnę –**: wahra'tikęhráhnę' ‹fact-he-mind-disappeared› *he fainted, he lost consciousness* (RC 24:9), ra'tikęhráhnęh ‹he-mind-disappears› *he is lethargic* (HS); **-(ę)'tikęhrahnę'T –**: na'tikęhrahné'tha' ‹one=another-mind-disappear-causes› *one stuns another* (HS), ra'tikęhrahné'tha' ‹he-mind-disappear-causes› *he stupefies it* (HS); **-rihwahnę'T –**: rarihwahné'tha' ‹he-matter-disappear-causes› *he pardons* (HS), yurihwáhnę't ‹it-matter-disappear-caused› *pardonable* (HS); **-yahstahnę –**: wa'kyahstáhnę' ‹fact-I-individual-disappeared› *I got lost* (RC 3:40); **-yahstahnę'nye' –**: rayahstahnęhá·'nye'θ ‹he-individual-disappears-going along› *he wanders* (HS); **-yahstahnę'T –**: ęyę'na'nyahstáhnę't ‹prediction-one=another-individual-disappear-causes› *one will murder another* (HS); **-a'rihwahnę'T –**: yu'rihwáhnę't ‹it-itself-matter-disappeared› *(it is) pardonable* (HS); **kwęhs -a'rih = wahnę'T –**: kwęhs arę'rihwahné'thek ‹no unknown-it-itself-matter-disappear-cause› *it is inexcusable* (HS); **kwęhs -či –. -a'rihwahnę'T –**: kwęhs ęθę'rihwahné'thek ‹no unknown-again-it-itself-matter-disappear-cause› *it is inexplicable, it is irremissible* (HS).

-(a)hnę – many, much (distributive). *v.r.sfx.* hab: -h, pnt: -·', stat: -·, prog: -, prp: -, dst: -, caus: -, rvs: -, dat: -. The distributive is used to indicate either that the action of the verb is spread over time or that the object of the verb is distributed over an area (e.g., **wa'kaye'tikwáhnę·'** ‹fact-they-sewed-many› *they sewed (several garments)*). The form **-ahnę –** occurs following roots and stems that end in a consonant or *i*; the form **-hnę –** occurs elsewhere.

-ahnę'T – abolish, blot out, destroy, purloin, spend. *v.s.-t.* rahné'tha' ‹he-disappear-causes› *he abolishes it, he blots it out, he destroys it; he purloins it, he spends it* (HS), wa'kayę'na'náhnę't ‹fact-they=another-disappear-caused› *they destroyed them* (RC 12: 7).

-(a)hrahT – be awful, be terrible. *v.s.-s.i.* Requires an incorporated noun root. **-(a)hahahrahT –**: uhaháhraht ‹path-put up-cause› *it is an awful road, a road to be feared* (H 2484); **-či'ehnah = rahT –**: uči'ehnáhraht ‹claw-put up-cause› *the claw is awful, its claw is* *awful* (H 2484); **-hehnahrahT** -: uhehnáhraht ‹field-put up-cause› *it is an awful field, a field to be feared, on any account* (H 2484); **-hnawahrahT** -: wahrahnawahráhnahk ‹fact-he-current-put up-caused› *he went against the current* (RC 12:29); **-hnyahrahT** -: uhnyáhraht ‹news-put up-cause› *awful news, awful story* (L 13); **-hskane = nahrahT** -: uhskanenáhraht ‹countenance-put up-cause› *awfulness* (RC 28: 9), *ferocious* (HS), *how awful, how terrible* (R); **-(i)ʔnyuhkwahrahT** -: uʔnyuhkwáhraht ‹group-put up-cause› *multitude* (HS); **-nęhsahrahT** -: unęhsáhraht ‹house-put up-cause› *it is a great, massive house; it is an awful house* (H 2484); **-nhurahrahT** -: unhuráhraht ‹disease-put up-cause› *it is a tough, serious disease* (RC 16:3); **-rih = wahrahT** -: urihwáhraht ‹matter-put upcause› *crime* (HS), *terrible thing* (R); **-θwętahrahT** -: ruθwętáhraht ‹he-ʔʔ-put up-caused› *he is rude* (HS); **-tah = skwahrahT** -: utahskwáhraht ‹slave-put up-cause› *annoyance* (R); **-teʔwah = rahT** -: uteʔwáhraht ‹ʔʔ-put up-cause› *something terrible* (RC 3:56), yuteʔwáhraht ‹it-ʔʔ-put up-cause› *it is frightful* (HS); **-teʔwahrahT** - {dative II}: naʔteʔwahrahná·tih ‹one=another-ʔʔ-put up-cause-for› *one frightens another* (HS); **-wętahrahT** -: uwętáhraht ‹word-put up-cause› *terrible noise* (RC 28:7).

-(a)hraku - take off. *v.s.-t.* rahrá·kwahs ‹he-put up-undoes› *he takes off a thing* (HS).

-ahrar - be a hole. *v.r.-s.i.* stat: -ę, dst: -, caus: -, rvs: -, dat: -, inc.-ɸ-pat. yúhrarę *it is a hole* (RC 25:2); **-ahrarak** -: ráhrara·ks ‹he-be a hole-eats› *he bores, he perforates* (HS); **-ahrarakT** -: yęhraráktha? ‹one-be a hole-eat-

causes› *auger, bore* (HS); **-aʔwnah = rar** -: yuʔwnáhrarę ‹it-earth-is a hole› *cave* (HS); **-čtęhrahrar** -.#úʔy: yučtęhrahraręhúʔy ‹it-stone-was a hole-great› *large hole in stone* (RC 11:1); **-ęteh = stahrar** -: yawętehstáhrarę ‹it-dirt floor-is a hole› *it is a hole in the ground* (RC 3:73), *cave* (HS); **-hstwahrar** -: uhstwáhrarę ‹fuzz-be a hole› *caterpillar (said to mean "hole with hair around it"; if so, then the word shows haplology from* *uhstwahráhrarę*)* ; **-nęčhahrarak** -: naʔnęčháhrara·ks ‹one= another-arm-be a hole-eats› *one inoculates another* (HS); **-nęhsahrar** -: yunęhsáhrarę ‹it-house-is a hole› *window* (R); **-nęʹnahrar** -: yunęʔnáharę ‹it-hill-is a hole› *cave, cavern* (AG); **-nę = ʹnahrarahsthę** -: yunęʔnaharáhsthę· ‹it-hill-be a hole-causes-many› *caves, caverns* (AG); **-ręʔahrar** -: neyuręʔáhrarę ‹two-it-tree-is a hole› *two trees with holes in them* (RC 25:2); **-ręʔ = ahrarak** -: raręʔáhrara·ks ‹he-tree-be a hole-eats› *he mortises* (HS); **-ręʔahra = rakT** -: yęręʔahraráktha? ‹one-tree-be a hole-eat-causes› *carpenter's (large) bore* (HS); **-ręʹnahrar** -: uręʔnáhrareh ‹log-be a hole› *ladder* (HS).

-ahrarak - bore, perforate. *v.s.-t.* ráhrara·ks ‹he-be hole- eats› *he bores it, he perforates it* (HS).

-ahrarakT - auger, bore. *dv.n.s.* yęhraráktha? ‹one-be hole-eat-causes› *auger, bore* (HS).

-(a)hrawę - put around. *v.s.-t.* ęhsrà·węʔ ‹prediction-you-put up-many› *you will put it around* (R), kahrà·węh ‹it-put up-many› *it puts it around* (RC 3:64).

-(a)hrawęku - take down. *v.s.-t.* θwahrawę́·kuh ‹you-put up-many-undo› *you take it down* (RC 3:61).

-(a)hraʔ - get on. *v.s.-a.i.* yuhráʔę ‹it-put up-began› *it has gotten on it* (HS).

-ahrę̨ʔn- hear, listen. *v.r.-t.* hab: -, pnt: -a·t, stat: -eʔ, prog: -, prp: -, dst: -, caus: -, rvs: -, dat: -, n-inc. This root always takes the completive suffix -(a)·t where the punctual aspect marker might otherwise be expected. ruʔnahrę̨ʔneʔ *he hears it* (HS), waʔkayę̨ʔnahrę̨ʔna·t *they listened to another* (RC 26: 8).

-ahrihr- scatter, sow. *v.r.-t.* hab: -s, pnt: -ɸ, stat: -, prog: -, prp: -, dst: -, caus: -, rvs: -, dat: -, inc.-ɸ-pat. ráhrihč *he sows it* (HS), ęhráhrir *he will sow it* (HS); **-yah-.-ahrihr-**: yahwahráhrir ‹thither-fact-he-scattered› *he threw it there* (RC 14:3); **-čarhuʔnahrihr-**: ęyečarhuʔnáhrir ‹prediction-one-tobacco-scatter› *one will scatter tobacco* (RC 16:1); **-nę̨hsnahrihr-**: ranę̨hsnáhrihč ‹he-seed-scatters› *he sows the grain: spills the grain* (H 2484); **-ʔwahθrahrihr-**: raʔwahθráhrihč ‹he-drop-scatters› *he sprinkles* (HS).

-ahrihskę̨- be together. *v.r.-a.i.* hab: -, pnt: -ʔ, stat: -, prog: -, prp: -, dst: -, caus: -, rvs: -, dat: -, n-inc. ęyakyahríhskęʔ *we two must be together* (RC 30:6).

-ahruyę̨ʔ- ask, inquire, question. *v.r.-t.* hab: -, pnt: -ɸ, stat: -, prog: -, prp: -, dst: -, caus: -, rvs: -, dat: -, n-inc. ęhsahrù·yęʔ *you will ask* (RC 30:28); **-a'nahruyę̨ʔ-**: wahraʔnahrù·yęʔ ‹fact-he-himself-inquired› *he asked of someone* (RC 12:18), raʔnahrù·yęʔ ‹he-himself-inquires› *he interrogates, he questions* (HS).

-ahry- bait, fishing gear, fishing line, fishhook, tackle. *n.r.* aln.: akáhryayęʔ *my fishing gear* (R), inc., n.sfx. -eh. úhryeh *bait, fishing gear, fishing line, fishhook, tackle* (R); **-ahryu-**: ráhryuh ‹he-fishing gear-is in water› *he fishes* (HS); **-ahryuhkw-**: yę̨hryúhkweh ‹one-fishing gear-be in water-instrument› *fishline* (SH 375).

-ahryu- fish. *v.s.-a.i.* ráhryuh ‹he-fishing gear-is in water› *he fishes* (HS).

-ahryuhkw- fishline. *dv.n.s.* yę̨hryúhkweh ‹one-fishing gear-be in water-instrument› *fishline* (SH 375).

-(a)hθ- dative. *v.r.sfx.* pnt: -h- ~ -ɸ, prog: -, prp: -, dst: -, caus: -, rvs: -. Member of dative series II that occurs in the punctual aspect and the imperative; the form **-ahθ-** occurs following certain stems that end in a consonant. (Stems that end in *t* typically insert an *h* between the stem and this suffix.) The form **-hθ-** occurs elsewhere.

-ahθ- empty noun root. *v.inc.* See: **-kenha-** *strive.*

-ahθawę̨hr- desire. *v.r.-t.* hab: -, pnt: -, stat: -eʔ, prog: -, prp: -, dst: -, caus: -aʔT-, rvs: -, dat: -, n-inc. wahθawę̨hreʔ *it desires it* (RC 35:41); **-ahθawę̨hraʔT-**: rahθawę̨hraʔč ‹he-desire-causes› *he cautions, he denies, he forbids* (HS), kakuhθawę̨hráʔnę̨ ‹they-desire-caused› *they forbid it* (H-Tyranny), wahθawę̨hráʔnę̨ ‹it-desire-caused› *it is forbidden* (HS); **-ahθa=wę̨hraʔT-{dative III}**: waʔę̨hθawę̨hráʔnę̨ ‹fact-one-desire-caused-for› *one* *forbade it* (H-Tyranny); −(ę)nęhθa=węhraʔT −: ahręnęhθawęhraʔt ‹unknown-he-himself-desire-cause› *that he be forbidden* (H-Tyranny).

−ahθawęhraʔT − caution against, deny, forbid. *v.s.-t.* rahθawęhraʔč ‹he-desire-causes› *he cautions against it, he denies it, he forbids it* (HS), kakuhθawęhráʔnę ‹they-desire-caused› *they forbid it* (H-Tyranny), wahθawęhráʔnę ‹it-desire-caused› *it is forbidden* (HS).

−ahθawęhraʔT −{dative III} forbid. *v.s.-t.* waʔęhθawęh-ráʔnęʔ ‹fact-one-desire-caused-for› *one forbade it* (H-Tyranny).

−ahθathu − be dark. *v.r.-a.i.* hab: -, pnt: -ʔ, stat: -ę, prog: -, prp: -, dst: -, caus: -, rvs: -, dat: -, n-inc. yuhθáʔthę *it is dark, night* (RC 5:34), waʔuhθáʔthuʔ *evening* (RC 10:3) [Lawson «Oosottoo» 'Night'], ęyuhθáʔthuʔ *it will be evening* (RC 6:18); −ahθathu −.#áh: waʔuhθathuʔáh ‹fact-it-was dark-little› *twilight* (RC 27:20); néʔktiʔ −ahθathu −: néʔktiʔ ęyuhθáʔthuʔ ‹two prediction-it-be dark› *the day after tomorrow* (H 447).

−ahθathu − evening, night. *dv.n.s.* yuhθáʔthę ‹it-is dark› *night* (RC 5:34), waʔuhθáʔthuʔ ‹fact-it-was dark› *evening* (RC 10:3) [Lawson «Oosottoo» 'Night'], ęyuhθáʔthuʔ ‹prediction-it-be dark› *it will be evening* (RC 6:18).

−ahθathu −.#ah twilight. *dv.n.s.* waʔuhθathuʔáh ‹fact-it-was dark-little› *twilight* (RC 27:20).

−ahθawʔ − begin. *v.r.-t.* hab: -ahs, pnt: -aʔ, stat: -ɸ ~ -ę, prog: -, prp: -, dst: -, caus: -, rvs: -, dat: -, inc.-ɸ-ag. rahθáʔwʔahs *he begins* (R), ruhθáʔwʔę *he began* (HS), wahrahθáʔwʔaʔ *he began* (RC 21:8), wahęhθáʔwʔaʔ *it began* (MP); −či −. −ahθawʔ −: θhrahθáʔwʔahs ‹again-he-begins› *he re-*

sumes (HS); −t −. −ahθawʔ −: nyúhθaʔʔw ‹hither-it-began› *it began there* (RC 28:13); −či −. −rihwahθawʔ −: θhrurihwáhθaʔʔw ‹again-he-matter-began› *he repeats it* (HS); −aʔnwętahθawʔahsT −: yuʔnwętahθáʔwʔahst ‹it-itself-word-begin-caused› *it is legible* (HS); −t −. −aʔrihwahθawʔ −: nyuʔrihwáhθaʔʔw ‹hither-it-itself-matter-began› *rudiments* (HS); −ne+t −. −aʔrihwahθawʔ −: nęʔnyuʔrihwáhθaʔʔw ‹apart-hither-it-itself-matter-began› *the practice is begun* (RC 8:50).

−(a)hθeʔ − going to (purposive). *v.r.s.* hab: -θ, pnt: -ɸ, stat: -ɸ, prog: -, prp: -, dst: -, caus: -, rvs: -, dat: -. The purposive is used to indicate that the speaker is expressing a logical assumption based on available evidence but has not witnessed the event first hand (e.g., ręʔnhéʔkwθeʔ ‹he-plays a game-going to› *he is going to play a game (at least, that is what he told me he was planning on doing)*. The form −ahθeʔ − occurs following certain roots or stems that end in a consonant; the form −hθeʔ − occurs elsewhere, with loss of initial *h* following a consonant.

−ahθehT − hide, sequester. *v.r.-t.* hab: -haʔ, pnt: -ɸ, stat: -ę, prog: -, prp: -, dst: -, caus: -, rvs: -, dat: I (-ʔθe-/-ʔθ-), inc.-ɸ-ag./pat. kahθéhthaʔ *I am hiding it* (R), waʔkáhθeht *I hid it* (R), ęhráhθeht *he will sequester it* (HS); −a'nahθehT −: yuʔnahθéhnę ‹it-itself-hid› *it is occult* (HS); −a'nahθehnęʔke: uʔnahθehnęʔkye ‹self-hide-at› *in concealment, in secret, stealthily, stealth, secretly, underhanded* (HS); −rih=wahθehT −: rurihwahθéhnę ‹he-matter-hid› *he doesn't tell* (HS), rarihwahθéhthaʔ ‹he-matter-hides› *he keeps it secret* (HS), yurihwahθéhnę ‹it-matter-is hidden› *it is a mystery, a secret*

(HS), na'rihwahθéhtha' ‹one=another-matter-hides› *one entrusts another with a secret* (HS); **-ne -.-ahθęhT -** {dative I}: wa'nwakahθéhnę'θ ‹fact-apart-I-hid-for› *I fainted* (AG), nęwakahθéhnę'θ ‹prediction-I-hide-for› *I will faint* (AG); **-a'nętakʷnahθehT -:** yu'nętakwnahθéhnę ‹it-itself-room-hid› *arcanum* (HS).

-(a)hθę - many, much (distributive). *v.r.s.* hab: -h, pnt: -·', stat: -·, prog: -, prp: -, dst: -, caus: -, rvs: -, dat: -. The distributive is used to indicate either that the action of the verb is spread over time or that the object of the verb is distributed over an area (e.g., **wahrę'nhé·kwθę·'** ‹fact-he-play a game-much› *he played games (at different times or in different locations)*. The form **-ahθę -** occurs following certain roots and stems that end in a consonant; the form **-hθę -** occurs elsewhere, with loss of initial *h* following a consonant.

-ahθęT - become dark. *v.r.-a.i.* hab: -, pnt: -ɸ, stat: -e', prog: -a'nye'-, prp: -, dst: -, caus: -, rvs: -, dat: -, n-inc. This is etymologically the same root as **-ahθęT -** *darkness*, given below. **-ahθę'narhu -:** rahθę'nárhuhs ‹he-become dark-mixes› *he blackens it, he darkens it* (HS); **-ahθę'na'na'nye' -:** wahθę'na'ná·'nye' ‹it-be-come dark-causes-going along› *it is getting dark* (RC 3:61); **tha+ne -.-ahθęT -:** tha'newáhθę·t ‹unusual-apart-it-becomes dark› *midnight* (RC 5:31); **ti+yah -.**

-ahθęT -: thwewahθę·'ne' ‹so-thither-it-becomes dark› *it is dark* (RC 33: 10); **-t -.-ahθę'nayę(T) -:** wa'nwahθę'nayę·'na' ‹fact-hither-it-become dark-laid› *it got dark* (RC 3:65); **ti -.-ahθę = 'nę'ni -{dative III}:** thwahrahθę'né·'nyę' ‹so-fact-he-become dark-threw-for› *he becomes puzzled* (SH 375); **tha+ne -.-ahθę'neθę -:** tha'newahθę'né·θę ‹unusual-apart-it-become dark-is long-much› *equinox* (HS).

-ahθęT - darkness, blackness, a speck. *n.r.* n-poss., n-inc., n.sfx. -eh. This is etymologically the same root as **-ahθęT -** *become dark*, given above. As a noun root, **-ahθęT -** is irregular in that it takes the verbal distributive suffix, **-hę -**, and a unique form of the customary enclitic, **-yeha·'**. Note also that it does not take a pronominal prefix if a suffix (other than the simple noun suffix *-eh*) is present. uhθę́·'neh *darkness, blackness, a speck* (R) [Gallatin «autsonneah» 'Night']; **-ahθęthe -:** ahθę́·the' ‹darkness-be going to› *before* (R); **-ahθęthę -:** ahθę́·thę' ‹darkness-much› *at night* (RC 4:5) [Lawson «Oosottoo» 'Night']; **-ahθę'nyeha·':** ahθę'nyéha·' ‹darkness-customarily› *nocturnal* (RC 3:2), *moon* (short for ahθę'nyéha·' híhte' *nocturnal celestial orb*) (R) [Jefferson «au-senk-nih-han» 'moon'] [Gallatin «(heetay,) ahtsuhnyyaihau» 'moon']; **-ahθę'nyęnęthu -:** rahθę'nyęnę́·thuhs ‹he-dark-ness-??› *he benights, he makes it dark as night* (H-notebook); **-t -.-ahθę'nar -:** ę'nyuh-

---

θέ·ʾnaraʾ ‹prediction-hither-it- dark-ness-be in› *it will be dark* (RC 8:13); –či –. **–ahθęʾnaT** –: θwahθέ·ʾna·t ‹again-it-dark-ness-stands› *night* (HS); –či –. **–ahθęʾnaʾr** –: čuhθέ·ʾnaʾr ‹again-it-dark-ness-is much› *speck, black spot* (RC 8:39).

ahθέ·theʾ ‹darkness-be going to› *before* (R). *part.*

ahθέ·thęʾ ‹darkness-much› *at night* (RC 4:5) [Lawson «Oosottoo» 'Night']. *n.*

–(a)hθęʾn(e)r – (archaic)/**–(a)hθęʾr** – (modern) *hang down. v.r.-a.i.* hab: ()-φ (archaic)/-haʾ (modern), pnt: -ęʾ, stat: -φ, prog: -, prp: -, dst: -awę-, caus: -, rvs: -aku-, dat: -, n-inc. The archaic form of the root is recoverable from Hewitt & Smith's habitual form. Apparently, the regular form of this root with following suffixes beginning with a vowel (e.g., the future form given by Hewitt & Smith) was generalized everywhere in modern Tuscarora. kahθέʾrhaʾ *it hangs down* (R); **–(a)h**= **θęʾr** –: uhθέʾreh ‹hang down› *graft, joint, knuckle, link* (HS); **–ne** –. **–(a)h**= **θęʾn(e)r** –: neyúh-θęʾr ‹apart-it-hung down› *it is spliced, it is grafted* (R), nehrahθέʾner ‹apart-he-hangs down› *he grafts it, he joins it, he splices it, he lengthens it* (HS), nęhrahθέʾreʾ ‹apart-prediction-he-hang down› *he will fasten it end-to-end, he will splint it* (R), neyuhθέʾner ‹apart-it-hangs down› *joint (of bones)* (SH 375); **–ne** –. **–(a)hθęʾrawę** –: neyuhθęʾrà·węʾ ‹apart-it-hang down-much› *two things are connected together* (RC 30:45); **–ne** –. **–aʾnahθęʾraku** –: nehraʾnahθęʾrá·kwahs ‹apart-he-himself-hang down-undoes› *he succeeds, he follows another* (HS), newaʾnahθęʾrá·kwahs ‹apart-it-it-self- hang down-undoes› *it luxates, it dislocates* (HS).

–ahθęʾnarhu – blacken, darken. *v.s.-t.* rahθęʾnárhuhs ‹he-become dark-mixes› *he darkens it, he blackens it* (HS).

ahθέ·ʾnyeʾ last night (AG). *part.*

ahθęʾnyéha·ʾ ‹darkness-customarily› nocturnal (RC 3:2). *part.*

ahθęʾnyéha·ʾ moon (short for ahθęʾnyéha·ʾ híhteʾ *noctural celestial orb*) [Jefferson «au-senk-nih-han» 'moon'] [Gallatin «(hee-tay,) ahtsuhnyyaihau» 'moon']. *part.*

–ahθęʾnyęnęthu – benight, make dark as night. *v.s.-t.* rahθęʾnyęnέ·thuhs ‹he-darkness-??› *he benights it, he makes it dark as night* (H-notebook).

–(a)hθęʾr – graft, joint, knuckle, link. *n.s.* uhθέʾreh ‹hang down› *graft, joint, knuckle, link* (HS).

–ahθh – handful. *n.r.* n-poss., inc. n.sfx. -eh. úhθheh *handful* (R); **–ahθharaku** –: rahθhará·kwahs ‹he-handful-chooses› *he snatches it* (HS); **–ahθharętyęku** –: rahθharętyέ·kwahs ‹he-handful-scratch-undoes› *he claws, he scratches* (HS); **–ahθhęhaw** –: rahθhέhaʾw ‹he-handful-carries› *he has a handful* (H-notebook); **–ne** –. **–ahθhahkw** –: waʾ-thráhθhahkw ‹fact-two-he-handful-picked up› *he picked up two handfuls* (RC 14:3); **–ne** –. **–ahθhake** –: newahθhá·kye· ‹two-it-handful-is in number› *two handfuls* (RC 16:1); **–ne** –. **–ahθharati** –: waʾthrahθhará·tyeʾ ‹fact-two-he-handful-rubbed› *he rubbed two handfuls together* (RC 14:3); **–yah** –. **–ahθhęʾni** –: yahęhθhέ·ʾniʾ ‹thither-fact-it-handful-threw› *it threw a handful there* (RC 11:22).

–ahθharaku – snatch. *v.s.-t.* rahθhará·kwahs ‹he-handful-chooses› *he snatches it* (HS).

–ahθharętyęku – claw, scratch. *v.s.-t.* rahθharętyέ·kwahs ‹he-handful-scratch-undoes› *he claws it, he scratches it* (HS).

-ahθhę- be ten. *v.r.-s.i.* stat: -· prog: -ha'nye'-, dst: -, caus: -, rvs: -, dat: -, n-inc. The root may actually be a stem, derived from -ahθh- *handful* plus -ę- *fall*. In the word *dozen* the expected pronominal prefix is unaccountably absent. The word may result from folk etymology of the English loan word táhsę *dozen*. wáhθhę· *ten* (RC 9:2) [Lawson «Wartsauh» 'Ten']; -ahθhę-.#ha'nę't: wahθhęhá'nę't ‹it-is ten-'th› *tenth* (RC 12: 10); -ahθhęha'nye'-: wahθhęhá·'nye' ‹it-is ten-going along› *ten apiece* (HS); -ne-.-ahθhę-: newáhθhę· ‹two-it-is ten› *twenty* (R); -ne-.-hęwah= θhę-: Nekahęwáhθhę· ‹two-it-boat-is ten› *Twenty-Canoes (Chief of the Beaver Clan)* (H-Handbook); tha-.-ahθhę-: tháhθhę· ‹unusual-ten› *dozen* (R); ti-.-ahθhę-: tiwáhθhę· ‹so-it-is ten› *'-ty* (in decades above twenty, as in áhsę tiwáhθhę· *thirty*) (R); -ahθhę-ti-.-rihwake-: wáhθhę· tyurihwá·kye· ‹ten so-it-matter-is in number› *decalogue, Ten Commandments* (HS); -ah= θhę-ti-.-yahsti-na' -yahst-: wáhθhę· tikayáhstih na' uyáhsteh ‹ten so-it-individual-is a group much individual› *million* (HS).

-ahθhę-ti-.-rihwake- decalogue, Ten Commandments. *n.s.* wáhθhę· tyurihwá·kye· ‹ten so-it-matter-is in number› *decalogue, Ten Commandments* (HS).

-ahθhę-ti-.-yahsti-na' -yahst-million. *n.s.* wáhθhę· tikayáhstih na' uyáhsteh ‹ten so-it-individual-is a group much individual› *million* (HS).

-ahθhę-.#ha'nę't tenth. *dv.n.s.* wahθhęhá'nę't ‹it-is ten-'th› *tenth* (RC 12: 10).

-ahθhęha'nye'- ten apiece. *dv.n.s.* wahθhęhá·'nye' ‹it-is ten-going along› *ten apiece* (HS).

-ahθkenha- compete for, fight for. *v.s.-t.* rahθkyénha' ‹he-X-strove› *he is fighting for it, he is competing for it* (HS).

-ahθkenha- competitor. *dv.n.s.* ha' rahθkyénhahs ‹the he-X-strives› *competitor* (HS).

-ahθkenha-{dative I} be greedy. *v.s.-s.i.* ruhθkyenhá'θe· ‹he-X-strove-for› *he is greedy* (HS).

-ahθkenha'- avarice, avidity, covetousness, greediness. *n.s.* uhθkyenhá'ę ‹X-strive-begin› *avarice, avidity, covetousness, greediness* (HS).

-ahθkw- fade. *v.r.-t.* hab: -ahs, pnt: -, stat: -ę, prog: -, prp: -, dst: -, caus: -, rvs: -, dat: -, n-inc. wáhθkwahs *it fades it* (H-notebook); kwęhs -a= 'nahθkw-: kwęhs aryu'náhθkwęk ‹no unknown-it-itself-fade› *it is unfaded* (HS), kwęhs aryu'nahθkwáhshek ‹no unknown-it-itself-fade› *it is unfading* (HS).

-ahθkwarihT- be parent. *v.r.-a.i.* hab: -ha', pnt: -, stat: -, prog: -, prp: -, dst: -, caus: -, rvs: -, dat: -, n-inc. This root has been found only in the

---

habitual aspect. kahθkwaríhtha·ˀ *I am parent* (HS), yęhθkwaríhtha·ˀ *mother* (R), rahθkwaríhtha·ˀ *father* (RC 3:37), naˀ'nahθkwaríhtha·ˀ *one's parents* (HS).

-ahθr- empty noun root. *v.inc.* See: -tekę- *join*.

-(a)hθreˀ- going to (purposive). *v.r.s.* hab: -θ, pnt: -φ, stat: -φ, prog: -, prp: -, dst: -, caus: -, rvs: -, dat: -. The purposive is used to indicate that the speaker is expressing a logical assumption based on available evidence but has not witnessed the event first hand (e.g., **kiheyęhθreˀ** ‹I-die-going to› *I am going to die*. The form -ahθreˀ- occurs after certain roots and stems that end in a consonant; the form -hθreˀ- occurs elsewhere, with loss of initial *h* following a consonant.

-(a)hθrę- many, much (distributive). *v.r.sfx.* hab: -h, pnt: -·ˀ, stat: -·, prog: -, prp: -, caus: -, rvs: -, dat: -. The distributive is used to indicate either that the action of the verb is spread over time or that the object of the verb is distributed over an area (e.g., **yurhęˀθręh** ‹it-be day-begins-many› *days*). The form -ahθrę- occurs after roots and stems that end in certain consonants. The form -hθrę- occurs elsewhere with loss of **h** following another consonant.

-ahθu(h)- color, paint. *v.r.-t.* hab: -h ~ ()-ahs ~ ()-θ, pnt: -ˀ ~ ()-aˀ, stat: -ę, prog: -, prp: -, dst: -, caus: -hT-, rvs: -ku-, dat: II (-ati-/-hθ-), inc.-φ-pat. -ahθuh- is the archaic form of the root found in the examples cited in Hewitt & Smith, while -ahθu- is the modern form. yúhθwę *it was colored* (R), wahráhθuˀ *he painted it* (R), rahθúhahs *he paints* (HS), ęhrahθúhaˀ *he will paint* (HS), rahθúhahs

painter (HS), yúhθuhθ *it is colored, it is stained* (HS); -ahθuhkw-: uhθúh-kweh ‹color-instrument› *color, paint* (R); -ahθuhkwahęsči-: wahθuh-kwahęsči ‹it-color-is black› *brown* (HS); -ahθuhkwakaˀne-: yuhθuhkwa-káˀneˀ ‹it-color-instrument-is much› *having many colors* (AG); -ahθuh= wakwahsT-: wahθuhkwákwahst ‹it-color-instrument-is good› *purple* (SH 375); -či-.-aˈnahθuhkw-: θwaˀnahθúh-kwahs ‹again-it-itself-color-takes› *purple* (HS); -ne-.-ahθuhkwayer-: newahθuhkwayè·rę ‹apart-it-color-instrument-did› *it varigates, it changes color* (HS); ti-.-ahθuhkuˀnę-: tiwahθuh-kúˀnę· ‹so-it-color-instrument-is a kind of› *it is colored* (RC 2:1); -aˈnah= θuku-: raˀnahθú·kwahs ‹he-himself-color- undoes› *he blanches* (HS); -atkęhsahθuh-: ratkęhsahθúhahs ‹he-himself-face-colors› *he paints his face* (HS); -čhikuˀrahθuhahT-: yečhikuˀ-rahθuháhtaˀ ‹one-shoe-color-causes› *shoe polish* (HS); -nęhsahθuh-: ranęh-sahθúhahs ‹he-house-colors› *he paints the house, he paints houses, he is painting the house* (H 2484); -čiˀči-ti-.-ahθuhkuˀnę-: číˀčiˀ tiwahθuh-kúˀnę· ‹liverwort flower so-it-color-instrument-is a kind of› *violet (color)* (HS); -ręhy-ti-.-ahθuhkuˀnę-: urę́h-yeh tiwahθuhkúˀnę· ‹sky so-it-color-instrument-is a kind of› *azure* (HS).

-ahθuh- painter. *dv.n.s.* rahθúhahs ‹he-paints› *painter* (HS).

-ahθuh- be colored, be stained. *v.s.-a.i.* yúhθuhθ *it is colored, it is stained* (HS).

-ahθuhkw- color, paint. *n.s.* uhθúhkweh ‹color-instrument› *color, paint* (R).

-ahθuhkwahęsči- brown. *dv.n.s.* wahθuh-kwahęsči ‹it-color-is black› *brown* (HS).

-**ahθuhkwakwahsT** – purple. *dv.n.s.* wah-θuhkwákwahst ‹it-color-instrument-is good› *purple* (SH 375).

-**(a)hs** habitual aspect. *v.r.sfx.* The form -**ahs** occurs following certain roots and stems that end in a consonant or *i*; the form -**hs** occurs elsewhere, with loss of *h* following a consonant. Following a root or stem that ends in *h* or *ʾ*, the *s* of the habitual becomes θ. The *s* of the habitual combines with the final *t*, θ or *r* of a preceding root or stem to become *č*.

-**ahs** – foot, paw. *n.r.* inaln.: káhseh *my foot* (R), inc., n.sfx. -eh. This root conditions a unique form of the semi-reflexive morpheme, -**ar**-, in certain constructions. úhseh *foot* (R) [Gallatin «uhseh» 'Feet (sing.)']; -**ahsuhsku** –: ruhsúhskę ‹he-foot-picked off› *he is barefooted* (HS), ruhsuhskęhá·ʾnyeʾ ‹he-foot-picked off-going along› *he is barefoot* (HS), wakahsúhskę ‹I-foot-picked off› *I am barefoot* (R); -**arah**=**sęthu** –: waʾkarahsę́·thuʾ ‹fact-I-my-self-foot-conclude-caused› *I kicked it* (R), kheyarahsę́·thuhs ‹I=another-my-self-foot-conclude-cause› *I kick someone* (HS); -**arahskaręhw** –: warahskà·-ręws ‹it-itself-foot-goes around› *it paws* (HS); -**aʹnahsarahkw** –: wahraʾ-náhsarahk ‹fact-he-himself-foot-gathered› *he put his feet together* (RC 25:13); -**aʹnahsawak** –: raʾnahsà·waks ‹he-himself-foot-shakes› *he shakes the dust from his feet* (H-notebook); -**a**=**ʹnahsaweθhę** –: wahraʾnahsawé·θhę·ʾ ‹fact-he-himself-foot-chopped› *he smashed his foot* (RC 36:title); -**aʹnah**=**sawiʾnahkw** –: yęʾnahsawiʾnáhkhwaʾ ‹one-oneself-foot-give-causes-instrument› *slipper* (HS); -**aʹnahsuhči** –: raʾnahsuhčę́hęʾ ‹he-himself-foot-removed-much› *he is going kicking it* (RC 25:13); -**či** –. -**ahsaT** –: θwáhsa·t ‹again-it-foot-stands› *one foot* (RC 25: 2); -**ne** –. -**ahsęt**: neyúhsę·t ‹two-it-foot-possesses› *biped* (HS); -**ne** –. -**ah**=**sęʾke**: neyęhsę́ʾkye ‹two-one-foot-at› *(on) the two of their feet* (RC 25:13); -**ne** –. -**ahsukę** –: neyuhsú·kęʾ ‹two-it-foot-is forked› *cloven foot, pronged foot: it is ungulate* (HS); ti –. -**ahsake** –: tiwahsá·kye· ‹so-it-foot-is in number› *so many feet* (R); -**yah**+**ne** –. -**ahsayę** –: yahwaʾthráhsayęʾ ‹thither-fact-two-he-foot-lay› *his two feet lay there* (RC 3:50); -**ne** –. -**arahsarkęheʾ**: neyurah-sarkę́heʾ ‹apart-it-itself-foot-is abundant-dead› *it used to be a brace* (R); -**ne** –. -**arahstahkw** –: neyurahstáhkę ‹apart-it-itself-foot-collected› *it is kicked to pieces, it is stomped on, it is trampled on* (RC 32:13), nehrarah-stáhkhwaʾ ‹apart-he-himself-foot-collects› *he overruns it, he stamps on it* (HS); -**yah** –. -**aʹnahsanęʹnaknahnę** –: yahwaʾę́ʾnahsanęʾnaknáhnęʾ ‹thither-one-oneself-foot-fastened-many› *one fastened one's feet there* (RC 11:23); -**aʹnahsawiʾnahkw** – -**eʾwihsę́ʾke**: yę́ʾ-nahsawiʾnáhkhwaʾ aweʾwihsę́ʾkye ‹one-oneself-foot-give-causes-instrument saddle-at› *stirrup* (HS).

***ahsé·tha?** yesterday [Lawson «Oousotto»]. *part.* Obsolete; attested only in the Lawson vocabulary. A number of other Northern Iroquoian languages show related words meaning *yesterday*, namely, Huron-Wyandot «achitek», Onondaga ahsé·teh, Susquehannock «shehaitah». It appears that the word was originally found in Tuscarora, but was subsequently replaced by modern thé·?nę? *yesterday* and lost entirely from the language.

áhsę three (RC 23:2) [Lawson «Ohs-sah» '3']. *part.* **-ahsęhst -:** uhsę́hsteh ‹three-'ness› *patrimony, inheritance from one's father* (HS); **áhsę ę́·či -raku -:** áhsę ę́·či ękará·ku? ‹three one prediction-it-choose› *one third* (AG); **áhsę -či -. -(i)har -:** áhsę θkáhe?r ‹three again-it-hung› *thirteen* (R); **áhsę ti -. -ahθhę -:** áhsę tiwáhθhę· ‹three so-it-is ten› *thirty* (R) [Lawson «Ossa tewartsau» '30']; **áhsę ti+či -. -hterhę -:** áhsę tičuhtérhę ‹three so-again-it-X-is day› *Wednesday* (R); **áhsę ti -. -?ęhręT -:** áhsę tyu?ę́hrę·t ‹three so-it-leaf-possesses› *clover (Trifolium* sp.*)* (HS).

-ahsę - be bad, be evil, be ugly. *v.r.-s.i.* stat: -·, prp: -he?-, dst: -Nyę-, caus: -hT-, rvs: -, dat: II (-ati-/-ę-), inc.-φ- pat. wáhsę· *it is bad, it is evil, it is ugly: vice* (R); **-ahsęhčr -:** uhsę́hčreh ‹be evil-'ness› *malice* (R); **-ahsęhe? -:** rahsę́he? ‹he-be evil-is going to› *he hates* (R); **-ahsęhT -:** úhsęht ‹be evil-cause› *animosity, hate, rancor, resentment, spite* (HS); **-ahsęnyęhT -:** yuhsę́·nyęht ‹it-be evil-much-caused› *it is detestable* (HS); **-ahsę? -:** wáhsę?θ ‹it-be evil-begins› *it deteriorates* (HS); **-činę?therahsę -{dative II}:** račinę?therahsę́·tih ‹he-curl-is evil-for› *he rejects, repudiates the curl, or curly-haired person* (H 2484); **-ne+ci -. -a =**

'**nwętahsęhnahnę -:** ne?nahra?wętahsęhnáhnę? ‹apart-again-he-himself-word-be evil-caused-many› *he scolded it again* (RC 31:10); **ha? -ahsę -:** ha? wáhsę· ‹the it-is evil› *turpitude* (HS); **-ahsę - -yu?nehkw -:** wáhsę· ruyu?néhkę ‹it-is evil he-worked-instrument› *malefactor* (HS); **-yahskahT - -ahę?θrę -:** kayáhskaht wahsę́?θreh ‹it-follows it-be evil-begins-much› *it becomes worse* (HS).

-ahsę - vice. *dv.n.s.* wáhsę· *vice* (R).

-ahsę - turpitude. *n.s.* ha? wáhsę· ‹the it-is evil› *turpitude* (HS).

áhsę -či -. -(i)har - thirteen. *dv.n.s.* áhsę θkáhe?r ‹three again-it-hung› *thirteen* (R).

áhsę ę́·či -raku - one third. *dv.n.s.* áhsę ę́·či ękará·ku? ‹three one prediction-it-choose› *one third* (AG).

áhsę ti -. -ahθhę - thirty. *dv.n.s.* áhsę tiwáhθhę· ‹three so-it-is ten› *thirty* (R) [Lawson «Ossa tewartsau» '30'].

áhsę ti -. -?ęhręT - clover. *dv.n.s.* áhsę tyu?ę́hrę·t ‹three so-it-leaf-possesses› *clover (Trifolium* sp.*)* (HS).

áhsę ti+či -. -hterhę - Wednesday. *dv.n.s.* áhsę tičuhtérhę ‹three so-again-it-X-is day› *Wednesday* (R).

-ahsę - -yu?nehkw - malefactor. *dv.n.s.* wáhsę· ruyu?néhkę ‹it-is evil he-worked-instrument› *malefactor* (HS).

-ahsęhčr - malice. *n.s.* uhsę́hčreh ‹be evil-'ness› *malice* (R).

-ahsęhe? - hate. *v.s.-a.i.* rahsę́he? ‹he-be evil-is going to› *he hates* (R).

-ahsęhst - patrimony, inheritance from father. *n.s.* uhsę́hsteh ‹three-'ness› *patrimony, inheritance from one's father* (HS).

-ahsęhT - animosity, hate, rancor, resentment, spite. *n.s.* úhsęht ‹be evil-cause› *animosity, hate, rancor, resentment, spite* (HS).

ahsę·nę average, center, half, mean, middle (HS) *part*. See: **tha⁷ahsę·nę**. **ahsęnęháh** ‹center-little› *central* (HS); **ahsęnęteháh** ‹center-'ever-little› *central* (HS).

ahsęnęháh ‹center-little› central (HS). *part*.

ahsęnęteháh ‹center-'ever-little› central (HS). *part*.

–**ahsęnyęhT** – be detestable. *v.s.-a.i.* yuhsę́·nyęht ‹it-be evil-much-caused› *it is detestable* (HS).

–**ahsęT** – paw; stocking. *n.r.* inaln.: wahsę́·⁷neh *its paw* (R), aln.: ruhsę́·⁷neh *his stockings* (R), inc., n.sfx. -eh. uhsę́·⁷neh *paw: stocking* (R), wahsę́·⁷neh *stocking* (R) [Lawson «Way haushe» 'Stockings'] (also: yuhsę́·⁷nę⁷ (HS)); –**ahsę'nawę** –: yuhsę⁷nà·wę⁷ ‹it-paws-many› *paws* (RC 28:1).

–**ahsę⁷** – deteriorate. *v.s.-a.i.* wáhsę⁷θ ‹it-be evil-begins› *it deteriorates* (HS).

–**(a)hsh** – nominalizer. *v.r.sfx.* See –**(a)hst** –. The form –**ahsh** – occurs after roots and stems that end in a consonant or *i* and preceding certain bases that begin with *y*, the *y* being dropped; the form –**hsh** – occurs after other roots and stems and preceding certain roots that begin with *y*, the *y* being dropped.

–**(a)hshek** habitual aspect. *v.r.sfx.* The form –**ahshek** occurs following certain roots and stems that end in a consonant or *i* when the construction is inflected for mode; the form –**hshek** occurs following certain other roots and stems that end in a consonant or a vowel when the construction is inflected for mode, with loss of initial *h* following a consonant.

–**(a)hsi** – undo (reversive). *v.r.sfx.* hab: -ęhs, pnt: -⁷, stat: -ę, prog: -, prp: -, dst: -, caus: -a⁷T-, dat: -. The main use of the reversive is to indicate that the action of the verb is undone or reversed (e.g., **wa⁷ętkyehnáhsi⁷** ‹fact-one-oneself-fasten on back-undid› *one unfastened one's backpack*). The form –**ahsi** – occurs following certain roots and stems that end in a consonant or *i*; the form –**hsi** – occurs elsewhere, with loss of initial *h* following a consonant. For both forms, the final *i* automatically becomes *y* when followed by a suffix that begin with a vowel.

–**ahsku** – Auburn, New York. *n.* Áhsku·⁷ ‹bridge-be in water› *Auburn, New York* (R) [Morgan, League «Ah´-sko» 'Auburn'].

–**ahskw** – bridge, hard ground, porch, prepared field. *n.r.* aln.: rúhskwayę⁷ *his porch* (R), inc., n.sfx. -eh. úhskweh *bridge, hard ground* (R); –**ahsku** –: Áhsku·⁷ ‹bridge-be in water› *Auburn, New York* (R) [Morgan, League «Ah´-sko» 'Auburn']; –**ahskuha⁷T** –: wa⁷kayęhskúha⁷t ‹fact-they-bridge-put in water-cause› *they put bridge in water* (RC 24:7); –**ahskwakęw**: áhskwakęw ‹bridge-in› *in the porch* (RC 27:2), úhskwakęw ‹bridge-in› *under*

Tuscarora Pronunciation Key:
/a/ law; /e/ hat; /i/ pizza; /u/ tune; /ę/ hint; /č/ cheese; /h/ hoe; /m/ mother; /s/ same; /t/ do (before a vowel y, or w), too (elsewhere); /k/ gale (before a vowel y or w), kale (elsewhere); /n/ inhale (before a consonant or word-final), note (elsewhere), /r/ hiss (before a consonant or word-final), run (trilled as in Italian, elsewhere); /w/ cuff (before a consonant other than y or word-final), way (elsewhere); /y/ fish (before a consonant or word-final), you (elsewhere), /θ/ thing; /⁷/ (the sound between the vowels in unh-unh); /·/ long vowel, /´/ high pitch; /`/ low pitch.

the bridge (R); –**ahskwaʔke**: uhskwáʔ-kye ‹bridge-at› *at the bridge, at solid ground* (RC 24:10); –**ahskwihsʔa** –: wahrahskwíhsʔa·ʔ ‹fact-he-field-finished› *he finished (preparing) field* (RC 5:21).

–**ahskwihsʔa** – finish (preparing) field. *v.s.-a.i.* wahrahskwíhsʔa·ʔ ‹fact-he-field-finished› *he finished (preparing) field* (RC 5:21).

–**(a)hst** – nominalizer. *v.r.sfx.* Basic form in the Eastern dialect. The main use of the nominalizer is to make a noun out of a verb root (e.g., **uʔę̃hsteh** ‹be mother to-'ness› *maternity*). The form –**ahst** – occurs following certain roots and stems that end in a consonant; the form –**hst** – occurs elsewhere, with loss of initial *h* following a consonant.

–**(a)hsT** – causative. *v.r.sfx.* The causative is used to form verbs that overtly express the cause of an event or activity and to form nouns of causality or instruments from verbs (e.g., **yęthe = rahwanháhsthaʔ** ‹one-oneself-green-encircle-causes› *bracelet made of woven grass*). The form –**ahsT** – occurs with certain roots and stems that end in a consonant; the form –**hsT** – occurs elsewhere.

–**ahsthu** – be petty, be slender, be small, be tiny. *v.r.-s.i.* stat: -ę̃°, prog: -ęha'nyeʔ-, prp: -, dst: -haʔnęʔ-, caus: -ʔT-, rvs: -, dat: -, inc.-ɸ-ag./pat. This root shows a special form with plural patients, –**atihsthu** –. wáhsthę *it is small* (R), *it is petty, it is slender, it is tiny* (HS) [Lawson «Wausthanocha» 'I will sell you Goods very cheap' = wáhsthę áhčiʔ *it is small, scant*], yę́hsthę *the youngest* (RC 29:22); –**ah = sthuʔT** –: wahsthúʔnę ‹it-be small-caused› *it is lessened* (HS); rahsthúʔ-thaʔ ‹he-be small-causes› *he dimin-*

ishes it, he lessens it, he narrows it, he reduces it (HS); –**yah** –.–**ahsthu** –: wehráhsthę ‹thither-he-is small› *he is the smallest* (RC 13:1); –**t** –.–**ahsthuʔę = ha'nyeʔ** –: ęʔnyuhsthuʔęhá·ʔnyeʔ ‹prediction-hither-it-be small-begin-going along› *it will grow to be less* (RC 3:20); **ti+yah** –.–**ahsthuʔ** –: thweyuhsthúʔę ‹so-thither-it-is small› *it grew small there* (RC 35:14); –**(a)hahah = sthu** –: wahaháhsthę ‹it-path-is small› *the road is narrow* (H 2484); –**(a)ha = hahsthuʔT** –: rahahahsthúʔthaʔ ‹he-path-be small-causes› *he makes the road narrower, he narrows the road* (H 2484); –**(a)hahatihsthu** –: wahahatíhsthę ‹it-path-are small› *roads are small* (H 2484); –**(a)hęʔnahsthu** –: wahęʔnáhsthę ‹it-clearing-is small› *the meadow is narrow* (H 2484); –**(a)hę'natihsthu** –: kahęʔnatíhsthę ‹it-field-are small› *the meadows are small* (H 2484); –**činęʔ = therahsthu** –: kačinęʔtheráhsthę ‹it-curl-is small› *the curl is small; it is a small curl* (H 2484); –**čiʔenatihsthu** –: kačiʔe-natíhsthę ‹it-claw-are small› *its claws are small, the claws are small* (H 24 84); –**(ę)tahsnahsthu** –: katahsnáhsthę ‹it-stick-is small› *a small stick* (L 78); –**hsęnahsthu** –: rahsęnáhsthę ‹he-name-is small› *he is inferior in rank* (HS); –**kweniʔtahsthu** –: kakweniʔtáhsthę ‹it-penny-is small› *a few pennies* (L 73); –**nęhahsthu** –: kanęháhsthę ‹it-corn-is small› *the corn grain is small* (H 2484); –**nęhsahsthu** –: kanęhsáhsthę ‹it-house-is small› *it is a small house or umbrella* (H 2484); –**nęhsahwaθah = sthu** –: kanęhsahwaθáhsthę ‹it-house-breadth-is small› *it is a narrow house or room, the house or room is narrow* (H 2484); –**nęhsatihsthu** –: kanęhsatíh-sthę ‹it-house-are small› *the houses are small* (HS); –**nęhsahsthu** –.**#háʔnęʔ**:

kanęhsahsthęhá''nę' ‹it-house-is small-many› *small houses* (HS); –nęhsnah = sthu –: kanęhsnáhsthę ‹it-seed-is small› *the corn grain is small* (H 2484); –nęθahsthu –: kanęθáhsthę ‹it-potato-is small› *small potato* (H 2484); –rih = wahsthu –: yurihwáhsthę ‹it-matter-is small› *frivolous* (HS); –'ęyahsthu'T –: ra'ęyahsthú'tha' ‹he-cost-be small-causes› *he depreciates* (HS); –'nhę = hahsthu –: ra'nhęháhsthę ‹he-urine-is small› *his urine is scanty, he makes but a small quantity of urine* (H 24 84); ha' ti –. –ęhrahsthu –: ha' tika-kawęhráhsthę ‹the so-they-sort-are small› *paucity* (HS).

–ahsthu'T – lessen. *v.s.-t.* wahsthú'nę ‹it-be small-caused› *it is lessened* (HS), rahsthú'tha' ‹he-be small-causes› *he lessens it* (HS).

–(a)hstr – nominalizer. *v.r.sfx.* Basic form in the Western dialect. The form –ah = str – occurs following certain roots and stems that end in a consonant; the form –hstr – occurs elsewhere, with loss of initial *h* following a consonant.

–ahsuhsku – be barefoot. *v.s.-s.i.* wakah-súhskę ‹I-foot-picked off› *I am barefoot* (R), ruhsúhskę ‹he-foot-picked off› *he is barefooted* (HS), ruhsuh-skęhá·'nye' ‹he-foot-picked off-going along› *he is barefoot* (HS).

–(a)hT – causative. *v.r.sfx.* hab: -ha', pnt: -ɸ, stat: -ę, prog: -, prp: -, dst: -, rvs: -, dat: -. The causative is used to form verbs that overtly express the cause of an event or activity (e.g., ranęhsiyúh-tha' ‹he-house-be great-causes› *he builds an addition on the house*) and to form nouns of causality or instruments from verbs (e.g., yečarhúhtha' ‹one-smoke tobacco-causes› *pipe*). The form –ahT – occurs following certain roots and stems that end in a consonant; the form –hT – occurs elsewhere, with loss of initial *h* following a consonant.

–(a)hte' – going to (purposive). *v.r.sfx.* hab: -θ, pnt: -ɸ, stat: -ɸ, prog: -, dst: -, caus: -, rvs: -, dat: -. The purposive is used to indicate that the speaker is expressing a logical assumption based on available evidence but has not witnessed the event first hand (e.g., ye-wirayęhte' ‹one-infant-lays-going to› *she is going to have a baby (at least, that is what it looks like from the size of her belly)*). The form –ahte' – occurs following certain roots and stems that end in a consonant; the form –hte' – occurs elsewhere, with loss of initial *h* following a consonant.

–ahtki'yę – defecate, excrete. *v.r.-a.i.* hab: -h, pnt: -', stat: -·, prog: -, prp: -, dst: -, caus: -, rvs: -, dat: -, n-inc. rah-tkí'yę· *he excreted, he defecated* (R), aręhtki'yęhek *that it excrete* (RC 15: 5); –ahtki'yę'T –: rahtki'yę'nęhs ‹he-excretes-moving› *he goes to excrete* (HS), rahtki'yę'the' ‹he-excretes-moving-going to› *he will go to excrete* (HS); –nęhs –.#áh –ahtki'yęhkw –: unęhseháh yęhtki'yęhkhwa' ‹house-little one-excretes-instrument› *out-*

Tuscarora Pronunciation Key:
/a/ l<u>a</u>w; /e/ h<u>a</u>t; /i/ p<u>i</u>zza; /u/ t<u>u</u>ne; /ę/ h<u>i</u>nt; /č/ <u>ch</u>eese; /h/ <u>h</u>oe; /m/ <u>m</u>other; /s/ <u>s</u>ame; /t/ <u>d</u>o (before a vowel y, or w), <u>t</u>oo (elsewhere); /k/ <u>g</u>ale (before a vowel y or w), <u>k</u>ale (elsewhere); /n/ i<u>n</u>hale (before a consonant or word-final), <u>n</u>ote (elsewhere); /r/ hi<u>ss</u> (before a consonant or word-final), run (trilled as in Italian, elsewhere); /w/ cu<u>ff</u> (before a consonant other than y or word-final), <u>w</u>ay (elsewhere); /y/ fi<u>sh</u> (before a consonant or word-final), <u>y</u>ou (elsewhere), /θ/ <u>th</u>ing; /'/ (the sound between the vowels in unh-unh); /·/ long vowel, /´/ high pitch; /`/ low pitch.

house, privy (HS); **-sheręt- -ahtki⁷yę-**: ushé·rę·t yuhtkí⁷yę· ‹cow it-defecated› *cow dung, manure* (AG).

-ahtki⁷yę⁷T- go to excrete. *v.s.-a.i.* rahtki⁷yę́⁷nęhs ‹he-excretes-moving› *he goes to excrete* (HS), rahtki⁷yę́⁷the⁷ ‹he-excretes-moving-going to› *he will go to excrete* (HS).

-aht⁷ehsT- stumbling block. *dv.n.s.* yakuht⁷éhstha⁷ ‹one-X-strike-causes› *stumbling block* (HS).

-aht⁷e(k)- stumble, trip. *v.s.-a.i.* rúht⁷ehs ‹he-X-strikes› *he stumbles, he trips* (HS).

-ahwara̱'nehT- be pale, be whitish. *v.r.-s.i.* stat: -ɸ, prog: -, prp: -, dst: -, caus: -, rvs: -, dat: -, inc.-ɸ-pat. yuhwà·ra⁷neht *it is whitish* (R) (also, through contamination from uhwaryá·kę⁷ *white*: yuhwà·rya⁷neht (R)); **-ę⁷= rahwara̱⁷nehT-**: yawę⁷rahwà·ra⁷neht ‹it-nut-is whitish› *almond* (HS); **-a'nahwara̱'nehT-**: ru⁷nahwà·ra⁷neht ‹he-himself-is whitish› *he is pale, he is fair, he is light-skinned* (HS).

-ahwaryakę- white. *n.r.* inaln: ruhwaryá·kę⁷ *he is white* (RC 12:20), n.-inc., n.sfx. -⁷. uhwaryá·kę⁷ *white* (RC 12:18) [Lawson «Ware-occa» White] [Gallatin «ohwaruryaukuh» White], ruhwaryá·kę⁷ *he is white* (RC 12:20), rahwaryá·kę⁷ í·kę· *he is white* (H 2892), ruhwaryá·kę⁷ kę́he⁷ *he was white* (H 2892); **-čiręhrahwaryakę-**: učiręhrahwaryá·kę⁷ ‹brown-be white› *light brown* (R); **-iθnahwaryakę-**: uθnahwaryá·kę⁷ ‹scale-be white› *shad (Alosa sp.)* (HS); **-nęhahwaryakę-**: unęhahwaryá·kę⁷ ‹corn-be white› *white corn, the corn is white, it is white corn* (H 2484); **-nęhsnahwaryakę-**: unęhsnahwaryá·kę⁷ ‹seed-be white› *the grain is white* (H 2484); **-hwih= sta̱nurę- -ahwaryakę-**: kahwihstanù·-

rę⁷ uhwaryá·kę⁷ ‹it-metal-is precious white› *silver* (HS); **-ne-. -(ę)nęhrya⁷k- -ahwaryakę-**: newęnę́hrya⁷ks uhwaryá·kę⁷ ‹two-it-scalp-breaks white› *Canada violet* (HS).

-ahwa⁷nę⁷ be niece, be nephew. *v.r.-k.* kheyahwá⁷nę⁷ *my niece, my nephew (lit. 'my brother's daughter/son')* (R).

-(a)hwihsT-/-(a)hwihsh- be heavy, be onerous (of inanimates); be strong, be powerful (of animates and inanimates). *v.r.-s.i.* stat: -e⁷ ~ -ę, prog: -, prp: -, dst: -, caus: -a⁷T-, rvs: -, dat: -, inc.-ɸ-pat. The form **-(a)hwihsh-** occurs before the causative suffix and as the first element in compound verbs. wahwíhsne⁷ *it is heavy* (H 2892), *it is onerous* (HS), kahwíhsne⁷ *it is strong, it is powerful* (H-notebook), khwíhsne⁷ *I am strong* (R), rahwíhsne⁷ *he is strong or powerful* (H 2892); **-(a)h= wihsha⁷T-**: rahwihshá⁷tha⁷ ‹he-be strong-causes› *he overloads it, he tires it* (HS); **-(a)hwihshęheyahT-**: nathwihshęheyáhtha⁷ ‹one=another-be strong-die-causes› *one tires another* (HS); **-athwihshę(T)- {dative III}**: rathwihshę́·tih ‹he-himself-be strong-lays-for› *he forces it* (HS); **-ne-. -(a)hwihshę= hey-**: nehruhwihshęhé·yę· ‹apart-he-be strong-died› *he is tired, he is fatigued* (R); **-ne-. -(a)hwihshęhęyahT-**: neyuhwihshęhè·yaht ‹apart-it-be strong-die-causes› *it is fatiguing* (HS); ti-. **-(a)h= wihsT-**: tikahwíhsne⁷ ‹so-it-is strong› *it is strong* (RC 28:6); **-nęčahwihsT-**: ranęčahwíhsne⁷ ‹he-arm-is strong› *his arm is strong* (RC 24:9); **-wyę= nahwihsT-**: kawyęnahwíhsne⁷ ‹it-preparation-is strong› *strong preparation* (RC 17:3); **-(a)hwihsT- #kęhe⁷**: kahwíhsne⁷ kę́he⁷ ‹it-is strong deceased› *it was strong or powerful* (H 2892).

-(a)hwihsha⁷T- overload, tire. *v.s.-t.*

rahwihshá·'tha·' ‹he-be strong-causes›
he overloads it, he tires it (HS).
-(a)hwihshęheyahT - tire. *v.s.-t.* nathwih-
shęheyáhtha·' ‹one=another-be strong-
die-causes› *one tires another* (HS).
-(a)hy - berry, fruit. *n.r.* aln: akáhyawęh
my fruit (R), inc., n.sfx. -eh. Factors
conditioning the choice of -ahy - versus -hy - are unknown. úhyeh *berry,*
fruit (R); -(a)hyak -: wa·'kayehyá·khe·'
‹fact-they-fruit-ate-going to› *they were*
going eating fruit (RC 11:17); -(a)h =
yakęre -: wahyakę̀·re·' ‹it-fruit-is
scarce› *berries are, fruit is, scarce* (H
2892); -(a)hyarih -: yuhyà·rih ‹it-fruit-
boiled› *ripe fruit: mellowness* (HS);
-(a)hyaT -: wáhya·t ‹it-fruit-stands›
fruit is in it, it contains fruit, there is
fruit in it (H 2892); -(a)hya'θharar -:
yuhyá·'θhara·'r ‹it-fruit-is prickly›
gooseberry (Ribes sp.*), wild goose-*
berry (Grosularia cynosbati) (H-notebook); -(a)hyaratyę -: θahyá·tyę· ‹you!-
fruit-grab-much› *pick fruit!* (L 45),
ruhyá·tyę· ‹he-fruit-grabbed-much› *he*
has picked fruit (L 45), rahyá·tyęh
‹he-fruit-grabs much› *he picks fruit* (L
45), wahrahyá·tyę·' ‹fact-he-fruit-
grabbed-much› *he picked fruit* (L 45);
-(a)hyęti -: wahyę́·tih ‹it-fruit-makes› *it*
bears fruit, it fructifies (HS); -(a)hyę =
tyahnę -: yuhyętyáhnę· ‹it-fruit-makes-
much› *it is fruitful* (HS); -(a)hyęy -:
yúhyęy ‹it-fruit-hangs down› *hanging*
fruit (R); -(a)hyu -: yúhyu·' ‹it-fruit-is
in water› *berry or fruit is imbedded,*
set, or are, in swampy land (said of

cranberry patches) (H 2892); -a'nah =
yarihT -: ru·'nahyaríhnę ‹he-himself-
fruit-boil-caused› *he waits for her to*
ripen (said of an old man waiting for
a young girl to mature so he can mar-
ry her) (R); -či -. -(a)hyeθ -: θhúhye·θ
‹again-it-fruit-is long› *haw, mulberry*
(H-notebook); -či -. -(a)hyeθa'ke: čuh-
yeθá·'kye ‹again-it-fruit-be long-at›
February (AG), *April* (R) (HS: June
15-July 15); -či -. -ihnaks - -(a)hyak -:
θkęhná·ksę·' wáhyaks ‹wolf it-fruit-
eats› *false Solomon's seal (Smilacina*
sp.*)* (H-notebook); čír -(a)hyak -: čír
wáhyaks ‹dog it- fruit-eats› *nightshade*
(Solanum sp.*)* (H-notebook); -hs =
kwa'n - -(a)hyak -: úhskwa·'neh wáhyaks ‹snake it- fruit-eats› *partridge*
vine, partridge berry (Mitchella re-
pens) (H-notebook); loanword from
another Northern Iroquoian language
containing -(a)hy -: θwahyù·wa·' *apple*
(Malus sp.*)* (R); -(a)hy- -tkwat'ahsT -:
úhyeh katkwat'áhsnę ‹fruit it-stomach-put in-caused› *fruit pie* (HS);
kwęhs -(a)hyęti -: kwęhs aręhyętíhek
‹no unknown-it-fruit-make› *it is un-*
fruitful (HS).
-(a)hyaratyę - pick fruit. *v.s.-a.i.* θahyá·-
tyę· ‹you!-fruit-grab-much› *pick fruit!*
(L 45), ruhyá·tyę· ‹he-fruit-grabbed-
much› *he has picked fruit* (L 45),
rahyá·tyęh ‹he-fruit-grabs much› *he*
picks fruit (L 45), wahrahyá·tyę·'
‹fact-he-fruit-grabbed-much› *he picked*
fruit (L 45).
-(a)hyarih - mellowness. *dv.n.s.* yuhyà·rih

‹it-fruit-boiled› *mellowness* (HS).

-(a)hya̱ʔθha̱rar – gooseberry, wild gooseberry. *dv.n.s.* yuhyá'ʔθhara'ʔr ‹it-fruit-is prickly› *gooseberry (Ribes* sp.*), wild gooseberry (Grosularia cynosbati)* (H-notebook).

-(a)hyęti – bear fruit, fructify. *v.s.-a.i.* wahyę́·tih ‹it-fruit-makes› *it bears fruit, it fructifies* (HS).

-(a)hyętyahnę – be fruitful. *v.s.-a.i.* yuhyętyáhne'ʔ ‹it-fruit-made-much› *it is fruitful* (HS).

-(a)·k stative aspect. *v.r.sfx.* The form –a·k occurs following certain roots and stems that end in a consonant when inflected for future or optative mode; the form –·k occurs following other roots and stems inflected for the future or optative mode.

ak–/akʷ– my (first person singular inalienable). *n.r.pfx.* The form akʷ– occurs before roots and stems that begin with the vowel *a.* The form ak– occurs elsewhere with insertion of "epenthetic" e before roots and stems that begin with certain consonant clusters.

ak–/e– one's, her (third person feminine/indefinite inalienable). *n.r.pfx.* The form ak– occurs before roots and stems that begin with the vowel *u* or the morphophoneme {ę°}. The form e– occurs before roots and stems that begin with consonants; the vowels *a* and certain cases of *i,* which vowels are dropped; the vowel *e* with which the vowel of the prefix coalesces to yield –ę–; and the vowel ę which causes the *e* of the prefix to be dropped.

-(a)karęʔr – be inclined, be sloped. *v.r.-a.i.* hab: -e'ʔ, pnt: -, stat: -e'ʔ, prog: -, prp: -, dst: -, caus: -hT-, rvs: -, dat: -, inc.-ɸ-pat. wakarę́'ʔre'ʔ *it is a slope, it is inclined: inclination* (HS); -(a)ka= rę'ʔr –: ukarę́'ʔreh ‹be sloped› *downhill, incline* (PC); -(a)karęʔrahT –: rakarę́'ʔrahč ‹he-be sloped-causes› *he inclines it, he leans it, he slopes it* (HS); -t-. -(a)karę'ʔr –: nakakarę́'ʔrę'ʔ ‹hither-unknown-it-be sloped› *that it disturb its position* (RC 3:22); -(a)hahakaręʔ= rahT –: rahahakarę́'ʔrahč ‹he-path-be sloped-causes› *he inclines the road (its surface to one side)* (H 2484); -(ę)'ʔ= tikęhkaręʔrahT –:   u'ʔtikęhkarę́'ʔraht ‹mind-be sloped-cause› *commotion* (HS); -nęhsakarę'ʔr –: kanęhsakarę́'ʔrę'ʔ ‹it-house-is sloped› *the house is inclined, i.e., is out of plumb* (H-notebook); -ne-.-(ę)'ʔtikęhkarę'ʔr –: nęθa'ʔtikęhkarę́'ʔrę'ʔ   ‹apart-prediction-you-mind-be sloped› *you will be bothered by it* (HS).

-(a)karęʔr – inclination, downhill, incline. *n.s.* wakarę́'ʔreh ‹it-slopes› *inclination* (HS), ukarę́'ʔreh ‹be sloped› *downhill, incline* (PC).

-(a)karęʔrahT – incline, lean, slope. *v.r.-t.* rakarę́'ʔrahč ‹he-be sloped-causes› *he inclines it, he leans it, he slopes it* (HS).

-(a)kaθn – be heavy (of inanimates); be strong. *v.r.-s.i.* See: -aθn-.

Akawęčʔá·ka·ʔ Meherrin (Rudes 1984). *n.*

-akayę – be old (of inanimates). *v.r.-s.i.* stat: -·'ʔ, prog: -, prp: -, dst: -, caus: -, rvs: -, dat: -, inc.-ɸ-ag. waká·yę·'ʔ *it is old* (R); -rihwakayę –: urihwaká·yę·'ʔ ‹matter-be old› *olden times; old ways, traditions; culture* (RC 9:1); -rihwaka= yęʔčrakęw: urihwakayę́'ʔčrakęw ‹matter-be old-in› *in antiquity* (RC 3:1).

#aka·ʔ characterizer. *enc.* The boundary # automatically becomes *h* after a vowel, 'ʔ after a non-laryngeal consonant, and ɸ after laryngeal consonants. The primary function of the characterizer is to denote an individual or group that is distinguished from other individuals or groups by the named feature (e.g., –aturaT –.#aka·ʔ: raturač-ʔá·ka·ʔ ‹he-hunts-characterized by› *professional hunter* (R), –(ę)ʔteyanę –.#aka·ʔ: raʔteyanęʔá·ka·ʔ ‹he-crowd-guard-characterized by› *shepherd* (HS), –hnęw –.#aka·ʔ: rahnęwʔá·ka·ʔ ‹he-be related to through one's mother-characterized by› *people of his mother's relations* (HS)). Often, such constructions are used to label social groups such as tribes (e.g., –ahkwe= θaʔθ –.#ke.#aka·ʔ: wahkweθaʔθkye-há·ka·ʔ ‹it-partridge-is of a size-at-characterized by› *the St. Regis tribe* (AG), *residents of Ahkwesahsne Reserve* (R)). More rarely, the characterizer is found in deverbal noun stems that do not refer to individuals or groups of individuals (e.g., –ne –.–are=ruhsT –.#aka·ʔ: nekayęreruhsthaʔá·ka·ʔ ‹apart-they-run-cause-characterized by› *runners: snowsnake* (R), –ęˊrihst –.#a=ka·ʔ: awęrihstʔá·ka·ʔ ‹breathe-'ness-characterized by› *breath* (R)).

–ake – be in number, be of such a number. *v.r.-s.i.* stat: -·, prog: -haʔnyeˊ-, prp: -, dst: -, caus: -, rvs: -, dat: -, inc.-ɸ-pat. Used primarily in constructions where a definite number of entities is being specified. One of four prepronominal prefixes is always present: the dualic –ne – (if two things are being enumerated), the partitive ti – (if more than two things are being enu-merated), the contrastive tha – (if an unusual quantity of something is being enumerated), or the generic čwe – (if all existing examples of something are being enumerated). In referring to quantities that existed in the past, the root usually occurs with the completive suffix –(a)·t, although the stative aspect marker –·k is used if the entities referred to continue to be present in the same quantity. čwe –.–ake –: čwewá·kye· ‹all kinds of-it-is in number› *all kinds of* (AG); ti –.–ake –: tiwá·kye· ‹so-it-is in number› *it is so many* (RC 6:6); čwe –.–čikʔęwarake –: čwekačikʔęwará·kye· ‹all kinds of-it-bug-is in number› *all kinds of bugs* (RC 15:1); čwe –.–čikʔęwarčrake –: čwekačikʔęwarčrá·kye· ‹all kinds of-it-bug-'ness-is in number› *all kinds of bugs* (RC 30:56); čwe –.–čiʔnęʔčrake –: čwekačiʔnęʔčrá·kye· ‹all kinds of-it-bird-'ness-is in number› *all kinds of birds* (RC 11:14); čwe –.–ęʔrake –: čwewęʔrá·kye· ‹all kinds of-it-nut-is in number› *all kinds of nuts* (RC 11:6); –ne –.–ahθhake –: newahθhá·kye· ‹two-it-handful-is in number› *two handfuls* (RC 16:1); –ne –.–(ę)ʔtikęhke –: nehruʔ-tikęhkye· ‹two-he-mind-is in number› *he is dubious, he wavers* (HS); –ne –.–nęhsake –: nekanęhsá·kye· ‹two-it-house-is in number› *there are two houses (modern)* (H 2484), nekanę́h-skye· ‹two-it-house-is in number› *there are two houses (archaic)* (H 2484); ti –.–ahsake –: tiwahsá·kye· ‹so-

Tuscarora Pronunciation Key:
/a/ l<u>a</u>w; /e/ h<u>a</u>t; /i/ p<u>i</u>zza; /u/ t<u>u</u>ne; /ę/ h<u>i</u>nt; /č/ <u>ch</u>eese; /h/ <u>h</u>oe; /m/ <u>m</u>other; /s/ <u>s</u>ame; /t/ <u>d</u>o (before a vowel y, or w), <u>t</u>oo (elsewhere); /k/ gale (before a vowel y or w), <u>k</u>ale (elsewhere); /n/ in<u>h</u>ale (before a consonant or word-final), <u>n</u>ote (elsewhere), /r/ hi<u>ss</u> (before a consonant or word-final), <u>r</u>un (trilled as in Italian, elsewhere); /w/ cu<u>ff</u> (before a consonant other than y or word-final), <u>w</u>ay (elsewhere); /y/ fi<u>sh</u> (before a consonant or word-final), <u>y</u>ou (elsewhere), /θ/ <u>th</u>ing; /ʔ/ (the sound between the vowels in unh-unh); /·/ long vowel, /ˊ/ high pitch; /ˋ/ low pitch.

it-foot-is in number› *so many feet* (R); **ti –. -akwę⁷črake –**: tiwakwę⁷črá·kye· ‹so-it-pound-is in number› *so many pounds* (W 74); **ti –. -arihstake –**: tiwarihstá·kye· ‹so-it-minute-is in number› *so many minutes* (R); **ti –. -ęhrake –**: tyawęhrá·kye· ‹so-it-sort-is in number› *it is so many* (RC 6:7), nęyawęhrá·kye·k ‹so-prediction-it-sort-be in number› *it will be so many kinds* (RC 9:5); **ti –. -ę'nake –**: nęwę⁷ná·kye·t ‹so-prediction-it-day-be in number› *it will be so many days* (RC 15:3); **ti –. -heh = nake –**: tikahehná·kye· ‹so-it-field-is in number› *the fields number as many as* (H 2484); **ti –. -hsu⁷kwake –**: tikahsu⁷kwá·kye· ‹so-it-finger-is in number› *so many fingers* (RC 17:2); **ti+yah –. -ake –**: thwewá·kye· ‹so-thither-it-is in number› *it is assorted* (R); **ste⁷ ti –. -ake –**: ste⁷ tiwá·kye· ‹some so-it-is in number› *several* (HS); **-yahsti – ti –. -uhstake –**: kayáhstih tiwuhstá·kye· ‹it-individual-is a group so-it-year-is in number› *century* (HS).

-akerhu – climb up. *v.r.-a.i.* hab: -h, pnt: -⁷, stat: -ę, prog: -, prp: -, dst: -, caus: -, rvs: -, dat: -, inc.-φ-pat. **-yah –. -akerhu –**: yahwa⁷ękyérhu⁷ ‹hither-fact-one-climbed up› *one climbed up there* (RC 3:62); **-(a)hahakerhu –**: yuhahakyérhę ‹it-path-climbed up› *an ascending-way, a stairway, a pair of stairs* (H 2484).

-akew – wipe. *v.r.-t.* hab: -ahs, pnt: -⁷, stat: -ę, prog: -, prp: -, dst: -ahnę-, caus: -a⁷T-, rvs: -, dat: -, inc.-r-pat. wa⁷krá·kye⁷w *I wiped it* (R), rarakyè·wahs *he wipes it* (HS); **-kθakewa⁷T –**: yekθakyewá⁷tha⁷ ‹one-dish-wipe-causes› *washcloth* (HS); **-kwęhna = kew –**: rakwęhnakyè·wahs ‹he-rust-wipes› *he wipes off rust* (HS); **-rake = wahnęha'nye⁷ –**: yurakyewahnęhá·⁷-

nye⁷ ‹it-X-wiped-much-going along› *it is being worn away* (RC 15:2); **-či –. -tak"nakyew –**: θkatakwnakyè·wę ‹again-it-bed-wiped› *bed is again empty* (RC 29:18); **-ihn – -ahča = kewa⁷T –**: úhneh yęhčakyewá⁷tha⁷ ‹cloth one-fist-wipe-causes› *napkin* (HS) **kwęhs -a⁷rakew –**: kwęhs arę⁷rakyewáhshek ‹no unknown-it-itself-X-wipe› *it is ineffaceable* (HS); **-rake = wahnę – -kč –**: ęhsrakyewáhnę·⁷ ú·kθeh ‹prediction-you-X-wipe-much   dish› *you'll wipe the dishes* (L 80).

-akęhyaT – extend from. *v.r.-s.i.* stat: -φ, prog: -a'nye⁷-, prp: -, dst: -, caus: -, rvs: -, dat: -, inc.-φ-pat. **-akęhyathu –**: rakęhyá·thuhs ‹he-extend from-causes› *he wanders to* (HS); **ti –. -akęhyaT –**: tiwakęhya·t ‹so-it-extends from› *its edge* (H-notebook), ha⁷ tiwakęhya·t ‹the so-it-extends from› *the coast, the limit* (HS); **kę⁷ ti –. -akęhya'na'nye⁷ –**: kę⁷ tiwakęhya⁷ná·⁷nye⁷ ‹where so-it-extend from-going along› *the coast, the edge* (HS); **-nęhskęhyaT –**: kanęhskęhya·t ‹it-house-extends from› *the bounds of the house; hence, at the very side of the house* (H 2484); **ti –. -(a)čęhakęhyaT –**: tiwačęhakęhya·t ‹so-it-fire-extends from› *so it extends from the fire* (RC 12:21); **ti –. -(i)hsa⁷ = nęhkwakęhyaT –**: tikahsa⁷nęhkwakęhya·t ‹so-it-bury-instrument-extends from› *at side of grave pit* (RC 3:70); **ti –. -nę⁷yečkwakęhyaT –**: tikanę⁷yečkwakęhya·t ‹so-it-nest-extends form› *nest extends from* (RC 17:2).

-akęhyathu – wander to. *v.s.-a.i.* rakęhyá·thuhs ‹he-extend from-causes› *he wanders to* (HS).

-akęre – be scarce, be seldom. *v.r.-a.i.* hab: -⁷, pnt: -, stat: -⁷, prog: -, prp: -, dst: -, caus: -, rvs: -, dat: -, inc.-φ-pat. wakę·re⁷ *it is seldom* (H 2892); *it is* *scarce: dearth* (HS); –(a)hyak**ę**re –: wahyak**ę̀**·re⁷ ‹it-fruit-is scarce› *berries are, fruit is, scarce* (H 2892); –**ę̊k**ʷeh = stak**ę**re –: w**ę**kwehstak**ę̀**·re⁷ ‹it-human-'ness-is scarce› *persons, men, are scarce* (H 2892); –**hwihstak**ę**re** –: kahwihstak**ę̀**·re⁷ ‹it-money-is scarce› *money is scarce* (H 2892); –**n**ę**hsnak**ę**re** –: kan**ę**hsnak**ę̀**·re⁷ ‹it-seed-is scarce› *the grain is scarce, not plentiful* (H 2484); –**n**ę**θak**ę**re** –: kan**ę**θak**ę̀**·re⁷ ‹it-potato-is scarce› *potatoes are scarce* (H 2892); –**θahe⁷rak**ę**re** –: kaθahe⁷rak**ę̀**·re⁷ ‹it-bean-is scarce› *beans are scarce* (H 2892), kaθahe⁷rak**ę̀**·rehk ‹it-bean-was scarce› *beans were scarce* (H 2892), **ę**kaθahe⁷rak**ę́**·re·k ‹prediction-it-bean-be scarce› *beans will be scarce* (H 2892).

–**ak**ę**re** – dearth. *dv.n.s.* wak**ę̀**·re⁷ ‹it-is scarce› *dearth* (HS).

akę́**·su⁷r** soft maple, red maple *(Acer rubrum)* (RC 12:2). *n.* Also: **hak**ę́**hsu·⁷θ** *soft maple* (M 84).

–**ak**ę**w** internal locative. *n.r.sfx.* The primary function of the internal locative is to indicate location within or under the named entity (e.g., –(a)hahak**ę**w: uháhak**ę**w ‹path-in› *in the road* (H 24-84), –(a)h**ę**⁷nak**ę**w: uh**ę**⁷nak**ę**w ‹clearing-in› *in the meadow* (H 2484), –**ah** = skwak**ę**w: úhskwak**ę**w ‹bridge-in› *under the bridge* (R)). More rarely, it serves to create adjectives from nouns (e.g., –a⁷wnak**ę**w: ú⁷wnak**ę**w ‹earth-in› *subterranean* (HS), –thekwnak**ę**w: uthékwnak**ę**w ‹sweat-in› *sweaty* (HS)).

Occasionally, the English gloss for words containing the internal locative obscures the locational meaning of the suffix (e.g., –**čisnuhku** – –**kahrak**ę**w**: yučisnúhku⁷ ukáhrak**ę**w ‹it-spot-cover it-eye-in› *pupil (of the eye)* (HS), –**hnawak**ę**w**: uhnà·wak**ę**w ‹current of water-in› *swamp* (R), –**r**ę**hyak**ę**w**: ur**ę́**hyak**ę**w ‹sky-in› *Heaven (modern)* (R), *Sky Land (archaic)* (RC 3:3)). With the progressive suffix, the internal locative indicates motion inside the named entity (e.g., –**hnawak**ę**wha** = 'nye⁷ –: uhnawak**ę**whá·⁷nye⁷ ‹current of water-in-going along› *going along in the swamp* (RC 33:8), –**n**ę**'nak**ę**w** = ha'nye⁷ –: un**ę**⁷nak**ę**whá·⁷nye⁷ ‹hill-in-going along› *going along in hill* (RC 33:3), –**nyatarak**ę**wha'nye⁷** –: unyatarak**ę**whá·⁷nye⁷ ‹lake-in-going along› *going into lake* (RC 26:34)).

–**ak**ę**w** – lie within. *v.r.-a.i.* hab: -, pnt: -ɸ, stat: -, prog: -, prp: -, dst: -h**ę**-, caus: -, rvs: -, dat: -, inc.-ɸ-pat. This root is archaic. It is almost certainly the source of the internal locative suffix –**ak**ę**w**. –**yah** –. –**ak**ę**wh**ę** –: wehrak**ę́**wh**ę**h ‹thither-he-lies within-much› *he lies inside it* (RC 3:73); –**t** –. –(a)č**ę**huhkwa = k**ę**w –: n**ę**kač**ę**húhkwak**ę**w ‹hither-prediction-it-fire-cover-instrument-lie within› *fire witch will be inside* (RC 7:12); kw**ę**hs –**ak**ę**wa⁷T** –: kw**ę**hs aryuk**ę**wá⁷n**ę**k ‹no unknown-it-lie within-cause› *it is unique* (HS).

–**ak**ę**w⁷ahči** internal locative+intensive. *n.r.sfx.*

-akraθ smell. *v.r.-s.i.* stat: -ɸ, prog: -, prp: -, dst: -, caus: -, rvs: -, dat: -, inc.-ɸ-ag. wá·kra·θ *it smells* (HS); **-hskęnakraθ** -: yehskęná·kra·θ ‹one-ghost-smells› *one smells of death* (R); **-kerhakraθ** -: kakyerhá·kra·θ ‹it-body-smell› *goat* (R), skyerhá·kra·θ ‹you-body-smell› *you have body odor* (R); **-yęwakraθ** -: kayęwá·kra·θ ‹it-treeless plot of ground-smells› *horsemint, monarda (Monarda* sp.) (R); **-ʔnhęhsu = kraθ** -: kaʔnhęhsú·kra·θ ‹it-egg-juice-smells› *it emits the foul smell of urine (said of animals)* (shortened from *kaʔnhęhsukrá·kra·θ) (H 2484).

-akriʔ liquid. *n.r.sfx.* This suffix is used to indicate a liquid containing or derived from the named entity (e.g., **-čikheʔnakriʔ**: učikheʔná·kriʔ ‹salt-liquid› *brine* (HS), **-hseharakriʔ** uhsehará·kriʔ ‹lye-liquid› *lye* (HS), **-ręʹna = kriʔ**: uręʔná·kriʔ ‹tree-liquid› *sugar* (R), **-ʔwahrakriʔ**: uʔwahrá·kriʔ ‹meat-liquid› *gravy, meat juices* (HS)).

-aks- be bad. *v.r.-a.i.* hab: -, pnt: -ęʔ, stat: -ę·, prog: -ęʹnyeʔ-, prp: -, dst: -, caus: -hT-, rvs: -, dat: -, inc.-ɸ-pat. wá·ksę· *it is bad* (R); **-(a)hahaks** -: wahahá·ksę· ‹it-path-is bad› *it is a bad road, a dirty road, a poor road, or way* (H 2484); **-(a)hahaks -.#háʔnęʔ**: wahahaksęháʔnęʔ ‹it-path-is bad-many› *the roads are bad, poor: they are bad, poor roads* (H 2484); **-(a)hahaksęʔT** -: wahahaksęʔthaʔ ‹it-path-be bad-causes› *it makes the road bad or difficult* (H 2484); **-(a)hęʔnaks** -: wahęʔná·ksę· ‹it-clearing-is bad› *poor clearing* (H 2484); **-atkęhčraks** -: utkęhčrá·ksę· ‹inherent power-'ness-be bad› *evil spirit from whom all witches get their power* (HS); **-atkęhčraks -.#úʔy**: utkęhčraksęhúʔy ‹inherent power-'ness-be bad-great› *Satan, Apollyon* (HS); **-aʔw =**

naks -: waʔwná·ksę· ‹it-earth-is bad› *badlands, sterile land* (HS); **-čhaʔ = raks** -: ručhaʔrá·ksę· ‹he-anger-is bad› *he is cross, he is intemperate, he is peevish* (HS), *he is mad* (L 21); **-či = nęʔtheraks** -: yečinęʔtherá·ksę· ‹one-curl-is bad› *she has poor, ill-looking curly hair; her curls are not fine nor beautiful* (H 2484); **-čiʔruraks** -: kačiʔrurá·ksę· ‹it-medicine stick-is bad› *bad medicine stick* (RC 30:53); **-ę°kʷeh = staks** -: sękwehstá·ksę· ‹you-human-'ness-is bad› *you are a bad person* (R); **-ę°kʷehstaks -.#háʔnęʔ**: kayakękwehstaksęháʔnęʔ ‹they-human-'ness-is bad-several› *bad humans* (RC 27:31); **-ę°kʷehstaksęʔ** -: rękwehstá·ksęʔθ ‹he-human-'ness-be bad-begins› *he deteriorates* (HS); **-(ę)tičhaʔraksęʔ** -: rutičhaʔraksęʔę ‹he-himself-anger-be bad-began› *he raves* (HS); **-ęʹnaks** -: węʔná·ksę· ‹it-day-is bad› *stormy* (HS); **-ęʹnaksaʔT** -: węʔnaksáʔthaʔ ‹it-day-be bad-causes› *storm* (HS); **-(ę)ʔtikęh = raks** -: Kaʔtikęhrá·ksę· ‹it-mind-is bad› *Bad Mind (one of the primordial twins), evil spirit* (R); **-(ę)ʔtikęhraks -** {dative II}: waktikęhrá·ksęhθ ‹I-mind-am bad-for› *I am unhappy* (R); **-(ę)ʔtikęhraksaʔT** -: yuʔtikęhrá·ksaʔt ‹it-mind-be bad-causes› *lamentable, mournful* (HS), naʔtikęhraksáʔthaʔ ‹one=another-mind-be bad-causes› *one vexes another* (HS); **-ęʔraks** -: węʔrá·ksę· ‹it-fur-is bad› *lamb, mutton, sheep* (R); **-ęʔraks -.#áh**: węʔraksęháh ‹it-fur-is bad-little› *lamb* (AG); **-heh = naks** -: kahehná·ksę· ‹it-field-is bad› *the field is poor, unproductive; the field or garden is bad in shape, is ill-formed, is difficult to till* (H 2484); **-hsyaks** -: kahsyá·ksę· ‹it-X-is bad› *it is mean* (RC 24:2), rahsyá·ksę· ‹he-X-is bad› *he is unkind* (HS); **-hsya =**

ksę'nye⁷ –: rahsyaksę·'⁷nye⁷ ‹he-X-is bad-going along› *he is unkindly* (RC 24:2); –**kerhaks** –: skyerhá·kse· ‹you-body-is bad› *you have body odor* (R); –**nęči⁷theraks** –: kanęči⁷therá·ksę· ‹it-curl-is bad› *the curl of hair is of poor quality, is ill-looking; the curl looks frowsy* (H 2484); –**nęhaks** –: kanęhá·ksę· ‹it-corn-is bad› *the corn is bad (as to quality)* (H 2484); –**nęhsnaks** –: kanęhsná·ksę· ‹it-seed-is bad› *it is bad, poor grain, it is a bad or poor grain* (H 2484); –**nęθaks** –: kanęθá·ksę· ‹it-potato-is bad› *the potato is bad, unfit for use, ill-favored* (H 2484); –**ręh**=**saks** –: raręhsá·ksę· ‹he-leg-is bad› *his leg is bad* (H 2484); –**rihwaksa⁷T** –: rarihwaksá⁷tha⁷ ‹he-matter-be bad-causes› *he profanes, he swears* (HS); –**rihwaksa⁷T**–{dative II}: na⁷rihwaksa⁷ná·tih ‹one=another-matter-be bad-causes-for› *one damns another, one vilifies another* (HS); –**θręhnaksę⁷** –: ruθręhnaksę́⁷ę ‹he-sleep-be bad-began› *his dream* (HS), raθręhná·ksę⁷θ ‹he-sleep-be bad-begins› *he dreams* (HS), ękθręhná·ksę⁷ ‹fact-I-sleep-be bad-began› *I dreamt (had a bad dream)* (AW 50); –**tahkwaks** –: katahkwá·ksę· ‹it-marriage-is bad› *mismarriage* (HS); –**tra⁷θwaks** –: θatra⁷θwá·ksę· ‹you-luck-is bad› *you have bad luck* (R); –**tra⁷θwaksa⁷T** –: yutra⁷θwá·ksa⁷t ‹it-luck-be bad-causes› *it is disastrous, it causes ill-fortune* (HS); –**tra⁷θwa**=**ksę⁷** –: yutra⁷θwaksę́⁷ę ‹it-luck-be bad-began› *misfortune* (HS); –**wętaks** –: ra-wętá·ksę· ‹he-word-is bad› *he has coarse speech* (HS); –**wyęnaks** –: rawyęná·ksę· ‹he-preparation-is bad› *he is uncivil* (HS); –**či** –. –**kahraksę** –: θkakahrá·ksę⁷ ‹again-it-eye-is bad› *pickerel* (H 3518); ti –. –**(a)hahaks** –: tiwahahá·ksę· ‹so-it-path-is bad› *such a bad path* (RC 13:7); ti –. –**(ę)⁷tikęh**=**raks** –: thwa⁷ka⁷tikęhrá·ksę⁷ ‹so-fact-it-mind-was bad› *it was so unhappy* (RC 35:29); ti –. –**yeraks** –: tikayerá·ksę· ‹so-it-smell-is bad› *it smells bad* (RC 33:11); –**a⁷rihwaksę⁷T** –: ra⁷rihwaksę́⁷-tha⁷ ‹he-himself-matter-be bad-causes› *he quarrels* (HS); –**a⁷rihwaksę⁷**=**na⁷T** –: ru⁷rihwaksę⁷ná⁷ne⁷ ‹he-himself-matter-be bad-caused-moving› *he is quarrelsome* (HS); loanword from another Northern Iroquoian language containing –**aks** –: θkęhná·ksę⁷ *fox (Vulpes sp.)* (R); ha⁷ –**a⁷rihwaksę⁷** –: ha⁷ ru⁷rihwaksę́⁷ę ‹the he-himself-matter-be bad-began› *his quarrel* (HS).

–**akT** next to (lateral locative). *n.r.sfx.* This suffix optionally, but frequently, appears as –**akwt** – in word-final position or when followed by a suffix that begins with a consonant. This is the result of an old rule of assimilation that caused the stops *t k* to develop rounding when they were the first member of a cluster of two or more obstruents and were preceded by *a* or *u*. The suffix is clearly derived from the verb root –**akT** – *be next to, be near.* Its primary function is to indicate location next to or near the

---

named entity (e.g., –(a)hahakT: uháhakwt ‹path-next to› *beside, near the road* (H 2484), –(a)hẹˀnakT: uhẹˀnakwt ‹clearing-next to› *next to clearing* (RC 25:1), –hehnakT: uhéhnakwt ‹field-next to› *beside, alongside of the field, garden or lot* (H 2484)). Occasionally, the English gloss obscures the locative meaning of the suffix (e.g., –(a)čẹhakT: učẹhakwt ‹fire-next to› *hearth* (HS), –čatakT: učá·takwt ‹brightness-next to› *seaside, strand, waterside* (HS), –ẹ'nakT: awẹ·ˀnakwt ‹day-next to› *Saturday* (R)).

–akT– be next to, be near. *v.r.-t.* hab: -, pnt: -ɸ, stat: -ẹ, prog: -ha'nyeˀ-, prp: -, dst: -, caus: -, rvs: -, dat: -, inc.ɸ-pat. –akT–: ú·kwt ‹be next to› *beside* (RC 23:2), *near* (HS); –aktha'nyeˀ–: ukwthá·ˀnyeˀ ‹be next to-going along› *about, around, sidelong, round* (HS), *alongside* (R); –akT–.#kẹˀnaˀkẹ: ukwtkẹˀnáˀkẹ ‹be next to-side› *lateral* (HS); –t–.–akT–: naˀá·ktakwt ‹hitherwe-be next to› *that the two of us be near one another, that I replace another* (R); –(i)yhakT–: akẹyhakwt ‹unknown-it-river-be next to› *that it be next to river* (RC 26:19); –ne–.–a'niy= hakT–: neyuˀniyháknẹ ‹two-it-itselfriver-be next to› *it is next to both sides of river, it lays across river* (RC 26:16).

–akT– beside, near. *n.s.* ú·kwt ‹be next to› *beside* (RC 23:2), *near* (HS).

–akT–.#kẹˀnaˀkẹ– lateral. *n.s.* ukwtkẹˀnáˀkẹ ‹be next to-side› *lateral* (HS).

–aktha'nyeˀ– about, alongside, around, side-long, round. *n.s.* ukwthá·ˀnyeˀ ‹next to-going along› *about, around, sidelong, round* (HS), *alongside* (R).

–(a)ku– undo (reversive). *v.r.sfx.* hab: -ẹhs, pnt: -ˀ, stat: -ẹ, prog: -, prp: -, dst: -, caus: -aˀT-, dat: -. The main

use of the reversive is to indicate that the action of the verb is undone or reversed (e.g., **wahrayẹthwá·kuˀ** ‹facthe-plant-undid› *he harvested*). The form –aku– occurs following certain roots and stems that end in a consonant; the form –ku– occurs elsewhere. For both forms, the final *u* automatically becomes *w* when followed by a suffix that begin with a vowel.

Á·kuks name of a mythic species of crow-like birds (see: RC 12). *n.*

Akunẹhsyẹ·niˀ League of the Iroquois, Iroquois Confederacy, the Six Nations (AG). *n.*

Akutrẹ·we name of a mythic, anthropomorphic creature (see: RC 24 and RC 25). *n.*

akʷ– deer, white tail deer. *n.r.* n-poss., inc., n.sfx. –eh. á·kweh *deer* (RC 3: 61), *white tail deer (Odocolleus virginianus)* (R) [Lawson «Ocques» 'Buckskin']; **akʷ–.#kẹha̲ˀnẹˀ**: akwakẹhaˀnẹˀ ‹deer-many› *deer (distributive plural)* (RC 12:4); **akʷ–.#keha·ˀ**: akwehkyéha·ˀ ‹deer-customarily› *cervine* (HS).

akʷ–.#keha·ˀ cervine. *n.s.* akwehkyéha·ˀ *cervine* (HS) ‹deer-customarily›.

–akwahsT– be good. *v.r.-a.i.* hab: -haˀ, pnt: -ɸ ~ -aˀ, stat: -ɸ, prog: -ha'nyeˀ-, prp: -, dst: -ahnẹ-, caus: -, rvs: -, dat: -, inc.-ɸ-ag./pat. The punctual aspect is marked by the suffix –aˀ whenever a prepronominal prefix such as the repetitive or a derivational suffix such as the dative is present; elsewhere, the punctual aspect, like the stative aspect, is not overtly marked on this verb root. When the semireflexive and the empty noun –hsy– are present, giving the meaning *make good, fix*, the punctual aspect is always unmarked. wákwahst *it is good* (R) [Gallatin «wauquast» 'Good'], arękwahst *that it be good, that it be possible* (RC 31:2), ęwakwáhsnęk *it will be good* (R); -či -. -akwahsT -: θękwáhsna⁷ ‹again-fact-it-was good› *again it was good* (RC 12:30); -ačhakwahsnahnę -: račhakwahsnáhnęh ‹he-himself-X-is good-much› *he arranges it* (HS); -ačha= kwahsT -: ęhsačhákwahst ‹prediction-you-yourself-X-be good› *you will fix it, you will make it good again* (RC 35:5), račhakwáhstha⁷ ‹he-himself-X-is good› *he puts it in order, he disposes of it, he makes it good* (HS), ękayęčhákwahst ‹prediction-they-themselves-X-be good› *they will make it ready, they will prepare it* (L 35); -či -. -ačhakwahsT -: ęθwačhákwahst ‹prediction-again-it-itself-X-be good› *it will make it good again* (RC 7: 11); -(a)hahakwahsT -: wahahákwahst ‹it-path-is good› *(it is) a good, fine road* (H 2484), wahahakwáhstha⁷ ‹it-path-is good› *it renders the road fine or good* (H 2484); -(a)hę⁷nakwahsT -: wahę⁷nákwahst ‹it-clearing-is good› *it is a good clearing* (RC 25:1); -ahθuh= kwakwahsT -: wahθuhkwákwahst ‹it-color-instrument-is good› *purple* (SH 375); -činę⁷therakwahsT -: yečinę⁷therákwahst ‹one-curl-is good› *her curls are pretty, nice-looking, good; her curl is pretty, nice-looking, good* (H 2484); -ę°kʷehstakwahsT -: kękwehstákwahst ‹I-human-'ness-am good› *I am good, I am a good person* (R); -(ę)⁷tikęhra= kwahsT -: Ka⁷tikęhrákwahst ‹it-mind-

is good› *Good Mind (one of the primordial twins): good spirit, benevolence* (HS); -hsyakwahsT -: rahsyákwahst ‹he-X-is good› *he has good taste* (HS); -hehnakwahsT -: kahehnákwahst ‹it-field-is good› *the field, soil or crop is good, looks well, is productive or easy to till* (H 2484); -kah= kwahsT -: rakáhkwahst ‹he-eye-is good› *he is sharp-sighted* (HS); -nę= či⁷therakwahsT -: kanęči⁷therákwahst ‹it-curl-is good› *the curl of hair is of good quality, looks well, is fine-looking* (H 2484), yenęči⁷therákwahst ‹one-curl-is good› *her curls are fine-looking, she has a fine head of curly hair, her curly locks are beautiful* (H 2484); -nęhakwahsT -: kanęhákwahst ‹it-corn-is good› *the corn is good, it is good corn* (H 2484); -nęhsakwahsT -: kanęhsákwahst ‹it-house-is good› *it is a good house or room (in the latter sense, it means the parlor of a modern house)* (H 2484); -nęhsnačhakwahsT -: ranęhsnačhakwáhstha⁷ ‹he-seed-self-X-is good› *he cares for the grain, is getting it ready to house or to put into the barn, as cutting it and binding it, etc;* (H 2484); -nęhsnakwahsT -: kanęhsnákwahst ‹it-seed-is good› *it is good grain; the grain is good, fine* (H 2484); -nęθakwahsT -: kanęθákwahst ‹it-potato-is good› *good potato* (H 24 84); -rihwakwahsT -: rurihwákwahst ‹he-matter-is good› *he is beneficent* (HS); -rihwakwahsT -{dative III}: wa⁷kakurihwakwáhsnę⁷ ‹fact-they-

Tuscarora Pronunciation Key:
/a/ l<u>a</u>w; /e/ h<u>a</u>t; /i/ p<u>i</u>zza; /u/ t<u>u</u>ne; /ę/ h<u>in</u>t; /č/ <u>ch</u>eese; /h/ <u>h</u>oe; /m/ <u>m</u>other; /s/ <u>s</u>ame; /t/ <u>d</u>o (before a vowel y, or w), <u>t</u>oo (elsewhere); /k/ <u>g</u>ale (before a vowel y or w), <u>k</u>ale (elsewhere); /n/ i<u>n</u>hale (before a consonant or word-final), <u>n</u>ote (elsewhere); /r/ hi<u>ss</u> (before a consonant or word-final), <u>r</u>un (trilled as in Italian, elsewhere); /w/ cu<u>ff</u> (before a consonant other than y or word-final), <u>w</u>ay (elsewhere); /y/ fi<u>sh</u> (before a consonant or word-final), <u>y</u>ou (elsewhere), /θ/ <u>th</u>ing; /⁷/ (the sound between the vowels in unh-unh); /·/ long vowel, /´/ high pitch; /`/ low pitch.

matter-were good-for⟩ *they believed it to be true* (RC 26:8); -yęrakwahs(T) - {dative I}: wakyęrakwáhsθeh ⟨I-odor-is good-for⟩ *I like the smell of it* (L 76); -ʔęyakwahsnaʔ -: yuʔęyakwáhsnaʔθ ⟨it-cost-be good-begins⟩ *it is cheap, the price falls, the price becomes good* (HS); -či-. -ihnakwahsT -: θakęhnakwáhsnaʔ ⟨again-fact-it-skin-was good⟩ *skin was good (strong) again* (RC 11:28); kwęhs -akwahsT -: kwęhs arękwahst ⟨no unknown-it-be good⟩ *it is impracticable* (HS); sè·nęʔ -yah-. -akwahsT -: sè·nęʔ yayukwáhsnęk ⟨never thither-unknown-it-be good⟩ *it is an impossibility* (HS).

-akʷek - close, make whole. *v.s.-t.* See: -kʷek -.

-akwęʔčr - pound. *n.r.* aln: rukwę́ʔcrayęʔ *his pound* (R), inc., n.sfx. -eh. ukwę́ʔčreh *pound* (R); ti -. -akwęʔčrake -: tiwakwęʔčrá·kye· ⟨so-it-pound-is in number⟩ *so many pounds* (W 74); ka = yáhsti ti -. -akwęʔčrake -: kayáhsti tiwakwęʔčrá·kye· ⟨hundred so-it-pound-be in number⟩ *hundred weight* (HS).

-akwęʔnh(e)r - be too short. *v.r.-s.i.* stat: -ʔ, prog: -, prp: -, dst: -, caus: -ahT-, rvs: -, dat: -, inc.-ɸ-pat. Hewitt (2892) notes that, "this [root] is only used when speaking of a thing with regard to a stated or standard length. With the exception of the inanimate or zoic pronoun wa 'it' no pronoun may be prefixed directly to this term." wakwę́ʔnheʔr *it is too short, it is not long enough* (HS), wakwęʔnhrahk *it was short or not long enough* (H 28 92), ęwakwę́ʔnhra·k *it will be short, etc.* (H 2892); -akwęʔnhrahT -: rakwę́ʔnhrahč ⟨he-be too short-causes⟩ *he abbreviates it, he shortens it* (HS); -akwęʔnhraʔ -: ęwakwę́ʔnhraʔ ⟨prediction-it-be short-begin⟩ *it will become*

short (H 2892); -čiʔehnakwęʔnh(e)r -: kačiʔehnakwę́ʔnheʔr ⟨it-claw-is too short⟩ *the claw is short; it is a short claw* (H 2484); -aʔwnakwęʔnh(e)r -: yuʔwnakwę́ʔnheʔr ⟨it-earth-is too short⟩ *tract (a spot of ground)* (HS).

-akwęʔnhrahT - abbreviate, shorten. *v.s.-t.* rakwę́ʔnhrahč ⟨he-be too short-causes⟩ *he abbreviates it, he shortens it* (HS).

-akwęʔnhraʔ - become short. *v.s.-a.i.* ęwakwę́ʔnhraʔ ⟨prediction-it-be short-begin⟩ *it will become short* (H 2892).

akyá ouch! (TW). *part.*

-akʔu - free, let go, release. *v.r.-t.* hab: -hs, pnt: -ʔ, stat: -ę, prog: -, prp: -, dst: -ʔθrę-, caus: -, rvs: -hsi-, dat: -, inc.-ɸ-pat. -akʔuhsi -: rakʔúhsyęhs ⟨he-release-undoes⟩ *he unfolds* (HS); -aˈnak = ʔu -: naʔnaʔná·kʔuhs ⟨one=another-oneself-releases⟩ *one sets another free (e.g., releases a prisoner)* (HS); raʔ-ná·kʔuhs ⟨he-himself-releases⟩ *he cedes, he gives up, he lets go* (HS); -či-. -aˈnakʔu -: θhraʔná·kʔuhs ⟨again-he-himself-releases⟩ *he releases it, he lets it go again* (HS); -ęθrakʔuʔθrę -: ręθrakʔúʔθrę· ⟨he-taste-releases-much⟩ *he relishes it* (HS); -rihwakʔuhsi -: rarihwakʔúhsyęhs ⟨he-matter-release-undoes⟩ *he authenticates, he justifies* (HS), karihwakʔúhsyęhs ⟨it-matter-release-undoes⟩ *decisive* (HS); -riʔwak = ʔuhsi -: rariʔwakʔúhsyęhs ⟨he-bedding-release-undoes⟩ *he unfurls it* (HS); -θręhnakʔu -: ruθręhná·kʔę ⟨he-dream-released⟩ *he likes sleep* (R); -aʔrih = wakʔuhsi -: ruʔrihwakʔúhsyę ⟨he-himself-matter-release-undid⟩ *upright (sober) man* (RC 12:1), *he is pious* (HS); -či-. -ačhęnaʔnakʔu -: θhračhęnaʔná·kʔuhs ⟨again-he-himself-name-self-releases⟩ *he abdicates* (HS); pì·yeʔ -ęθrakʔu -{dative I}: pì·yeʔ rawęθrak-

ʔúʔθe· ‹beer he-taste-released-for› *he likes the taste of beer* (HS).

-akʔuhsi – unfold. *v.s.-t.* rakʔúhsyęhs ‹he-release-undoes› *he unfolds it* (HS).

-(a)nę – be mellow, be soft, be tender; be generous, be liberal, share. *v.r.-s.i.* stat: -·, prog: -, prp: -, dst: -, caus: -ʔT-, rvs: -, dat: -, inc.-ɸ-pat. Hewitt & Smith give both ká·nę· (stem -nę-) and wá·nę· (stem -anę-) for *it is mellow, it is soft, it is tender*. ká·nę· *it is mellow, it is soft, it is tender* (HS), wá·nę· *it is mellow, it is soft, it is tender* (HS), rú·nę· *he is generous, he shares, he is liberal* (HS); –ʔwahranę–: kaʔwahrá·nę· ‹it-meat-is soft› *it is tender meat* (HS); –(a)nęʔT–: ranęʔthaʔ ‹he-be soft-causes› *he softens it* (HS).

-anęhtr – top of head. *n.r.* inaln: kanęhtręʔkye *on top of my head* (R), inc., n.sfx. -eh. unęhtreh *top of head* (R); **-anęhtriθ** –: waʔnyęnęhtri·θ ‹fact-two-one-top of head-joined› *the two of them butted heads* (RC 30:40).

-anęhtriθ – butt heads. *v.s.-a.i.* waʔnyęnęhtri·θ ‹fact-two-one-top of head-joined› *the two of them butted heads* (RC 30:40).

anęhsnači sassafras *(Sassafras albidum)* (H-notebook). *n.*

anęnù·ręk esteem, honor (HS). *n.*

-anęwhęrhę – peck. *v.r.-a.i.* hab: -h, pnt: -, stat: -, prog: -, prp: -, dst: -, caus: -, rvs: -, dat: -, n-inc. wanęwhęrhęh *it pecks* (R).

anę́·ʔnyaʔ red cedar *(Juniperus virginiana)* (H-notebook). *n.*

-(a)nęʔT – soften. *v.s.-t.* ranęʔthaʔ ‹he-be soft-causes› *he softens it* (HS).

-(a)nha – fill. *v.r.-t.* hab: -hs, pnt: -ʔ, stat: -ę, prog: -, prp: -, dst: -hθę-, caus: -, rvs: -, dat: -, inc.-ɸ-pat. The form **-anha** – occurs when an incorporated noun root is present. The form **-nha** – occurs elsewhere. kánhę *it is full* (RC 2:4), ránhahs *he fills it* (HS), waʔkakúnhaʔ *they were full* (RC 12:14); **-(a)nhahčr** –: unháhčreh ‹fill-'ness› *fullness, satiety* (HS); **-(a)nhahθę** –: kanháhθęh ‹it-fills-many› *they are filled* (RC 3:66); **-kahkweʔranha** –: kakahkweʔránhę ‹it-eye-circles-is full› *it is full of eye-circles (said of a place, thicket, or other thing full of game that are at bay and looking out)* (HS); **-nęhsnanha** –: kanęhsnánhę ‹it-seed-fills› *it is full of grain (said of a barn or bin, or bag; it is applied in this sense to grain yet in the straw)* (H 24 84); **-yahkwanhahsi** –: naʔnyahkwanháhsyęhs ‹one=another-girth-be full-undoes› *one unswathes another, one unwraps another* (HS); **-yahkwanhah**=**sthę** –: naʔnyahkwanháhsthęh ‹one=another-girth-be full-causes-much› *one swaddles another* (HS); **-yęhsawanh** –: kayęhsawánhę ‹it-rubbish-filled› *it is full of rubbish; discord* (H-notebook); **-yetanhahθę** –: kayetanháhθęh ‹it-grease-fills-much› *it is filling with oil* (RC 7:24); **-či** –. **-(a)nha** –: čúnhę ‹again-it-is full› *herring* (H 3518); **haʔ** **-(a)nhahkw** –: haʔ yunháhkę ‹the it-filled-instrument› *secretion* (HS);

kwẹhs -(a)nha-: kwẹhs akánhẹk ‹no
unknown-it-fill› *it is unfilled* (HS);
-(a)nha- -ʔne-hahT-: kánhẹ uʔnéhaht
‹it-is full shame› *shameful* (HS).

-(a)nha- -ʔnehahT- shameful. *dv.n.s.*
kánhẹ uʔnéhaht ‹it-is full shame›
shameful (HS).

-(a)nhahčr- fullness, satiety. *n.s.* unháhčreh ‹fill-'ness› *fullness, satiety* (HS).

-(a)nhahkw- secretion. *dv.n.s.* haʔ yun-
háhkẹ ‹the it-filled-instrument› *secretion* (HS).

anúʔkwyẹ muskrat *(Ondatra zibethica)*
(R). *n.*

-ar- semireflexive. *v.r.pfx.* A rare, lexically determined form that occurs
preceding the root -ahs- *foot.*

a(r)(a)- optative mode. *v.pfx.* Glossed
"unknown" in this dictionary, the
optative mode is used to indicate that
the verb to which it is attached refers
to an activity or state that has never
happened and may never happen as
far as the speaker knows. The form
ara- occurs whenever the prefix receives word accent; if this form is followed by a pronominal prefix that begins with the sequence *wa*, the final
vowel contracts with the sequence to
give **arẹ**-. The form **ar**- occurs when
the prefix is unaccented before pronominal prefixes that begin with the
glides *w* or *y*. The form **a**- occurs
elsewhere.

-ara-/-(h)a·- grab, seize. *v.r.-t.* hab: -hs,
pnt: -ʔ, stat: -ʔ, prog: -, prp: -, dst:
-hẹ-, caus: -hT- ~ -hw-, rvs: -, dat: -,
inc.-ɸ-pat. The form -ara- occurs
word-medial when followed by another verb root; the form -a·- occurs
elsewhere after vowels and the consonants *y w r n h* ʔ; the form -ha·-
occurs elsewhere after *t k c s* θ. If the
ʔ of the stative and punctual suffixes

is immediately followed by a morpheme that begins with *h*, an *r*
appears after the root. -yah+či-.
-athara-: wečẹ·tha·ʔ ‹thither-again-
one-oneself-grabs› *one has frequented*
(RC 5:26); -ẹhraʔrhẹ-: yawẹhráʔrhẹ·
‹it-dirt-grabbed-much› *it is touching
ground, it touched ground* (H-notebook); -hseʔyuhčrahT-: yehseʔyuhčráhthaʔ ‹one-cork-'ness-grab-causes›
corkscrew (HS); -nẹčiʔtherara-: ranẹ-
číʔtherahs ‹he-curl of hair-grabs› *he
seizes the curl of hair, the head of
curly hair, the person having the head
of curly hair* (H 2484); -tkuʔθrara-:
waʔktkúʔθra·ʔ ‹fact-I-baby-grabbed› *I
received a baby* (L 32); -tkwarahw=
hẹ-: katkwaráwhẹh ‹it-blood-grab-
causes-much› *floods of blood* (H-notebook); -aʔnẹchara-: waʔnyẹʔnẹčha·ʔ
‹fact-they two-themselves-arm-grab-
bed› *the two of them grabbed one
anothers' arms* (RC 30:21); -či-.-hneʔ=
rahwhẹ-: θkahneʔráwhẹ· ‹again-it-
root-grab-causes-many› *it clings to
roots* (RC 5:17); -ne-.-hshẹwara-:
waʔtkahshẹ·wa·ʔ ‹fact-apart-it-hollow-
grabbed› *it grabbed hollow (log)* (RC
8:5); -a'narahtʔehsnahnẹ-: waʔnyẹʔ-
naʔnarahtʔehsnáh-nẹʔ ‹fact-two-one=
another-grab-cause-strike-caused-
many› *one grabbed and cuffed another
around* (RC 27:32).

-arahsẹthu- kick. *v.s.-t.* waʔkarahsẹ·thuʔ
‹I-myself-foot-conclude-caused› *I
kicked it* (R), kheyarahsẹ·thuhs ‹I=an-
other-self-foot-conclude-cause› *I kick
someone* (HS).

-arahskarẹhw- paw. *v.s.-a.i.* warahskà·-
rẹws ‹it-itself-foot-goes around› *it
paws* (HS).

-arahsT- be mirthful, be sprightly. *v.r.-
s.i.* stat: -ɸ, prog: -, prp: -, dst: -,
caus: -, rvs: -, dat: -, n-inc. wà·rahst *it*

is mirthful, it is sprightly (HS); –a=rahsT– –ęti–: wà·rahst rawę́·ti· ‹it-is mirthful he-made› *he refreshes* (HS); –arahsT– –ętyahT–: wà·rahst yawę́·tyaht ‹it-is mirthful it-make-caused› *recreation* (HS).

–arahsT– –ęti– refresh. *v.s.-t.* wà·rahst rawę́·ti· ‹it-is mirthful he-made› *he refreshes it* (HS).

–arahsT– –ętyahT– recreation. *dv.n.s.* wà·rahst yawę́·tyaht ‹it-is mirthful it-make-caused› *recreation* (HS).

–arahsu– shoe. *n.r.* aln: ruráhsuyę̓ *his shoe* (R), inc., n. sfx. –̓. Possibly a compound of –ahs– *foot* with the semireflexive prefix –ar– and the verb root –ur– *cover* as suggested in Mithun (1984); however, speakers are no longer aware of this derivation. uráhsu̓ *shoe* (R) [Lawson «Oo-ross-soo» 'Shoes']; –arahsuhči–: wahrarahsúhči̓ ‹fact-he-shoe-remove› *he took off his shoes* (R); –ne+či–. –arahsuθ–: neθhrarahsú·θe̓ ‹apart-again-he-shoe-covered› *he shoed it again* (HS), neθhraráhsu·č ‹apart-again-he-shoe-covers› *he shoes it again* (HS); áha·θ –ne–. –arahsuθ–: áha·θ nehrarahsú·θe̓ ‹horse apart-he-shoe-met› *he shoed a horse* (HS).

–arahsuhči– take off shoes. *v.s.-a.i.* wahrarahsúhči̓ ‹fact-he-shoe-remove› *he took off his shoes* (R).

–arasči– be gay, be happy, be jovial. *v.r.-s.i.* stat: –·, prog: –, prp: –, dst: –, caus: –, rvs: –, dat: –, n-inc. warásči· *it is gay, it is happy, it is jovial* (HS).

–ara̓ brother-in-law (lit. 'husband's brother'); cousin's husband (lit. 'mother's sister's daughter's husband'). *n.r.* aln: akà·ra̓ *my brother-in-law* (R), n-inc., n.sfx. –. akà·ra̓ *my brother-in-law, my cousin's husband* (R).

–ara̓áh sister-in-law (lit. 'one's husband's sister'); cousin's (same or different clan) wife. *n.r.* aln: akara̓áh *my sister-in-law* (R), n-inc., n.sfx. –. akara̓áh *my sister-in-law, my cousin's wife* (R).

–ara̓θe̓ cousin (archaic). *n.r.* aln: rurá̓θe̓ *his cousin* (H-notebook), n-inc., n.sfx. –. Found only in Hewitt & Smith and in Hewitt's notebook. Comparative evidence points to –ara̓θe̓ as the expected Tuscarora form of the root. The modern form –ara̓se̓ may have resulted from contact with other Northern Iroquoian languages. neyę̨rá̓θe̓ *the two of them are cousins* (HS), rurá̓θe̓ *his cousin* (H-notebook); –ara̓θehčr–: ura̓θéhčreh ‹be cousin-'ness› *cousin* (HS); –ara̓θehst–: ura̓θéhsteh ‹be cousin-'ness› *cousin* (HS); –ara̓θe̓shę(T)–: rura̓θé̓shę̓ ‹he-be cousin-'ness-lays› *he has a cousin* (HS).

–ara̓θehčr– cousin. *n.s.* ura̓θéhčreh ‹be cousin-'ness› *cousin* (HS).

–ara̓θehst– cousin. *n.s.* ura̓θéhsteh ‹be cousin-'ness› *cousin* (HS).

–ara̓θe̓shę(T)– have a cousin. *v.s.-s.i.* rura̓θé̓shę̓ ‹he-be cousin-'ness-lays› *he has a cousin* (HS).

–ara̓se̓ cousin (modern). *n.r.* aln: akya-

---

rá'se' *my cousin* (R), n-inc., n. sfx. -.
See: **-ara'θe'**. akyará'se' *the two of
us are cousins, my cousin (lit. 'mother's brother's child, father's sister's
child')* (R).

-ar(e)ku – go away, leave, move on. *v.r.-
a.i.* hab: -()ęha' ~ -()ahs, pnt: -', stat:
-()ę·, prog: -ęha'nye'-, prp: -, dst: -hę-,
caus: -'T-, rvs: -, dat: -, inc.-ɸ-ag.
Hewitt (notebook) makes the following comment with regard to the combination of this verb with the repetitive prefix, "With the verb move it
[the repetitive] also has a very peculiar force. One being in a certain place
other than home says "ăⁿ-ç-kăr´ku',"
[ęθkárku'] lit. *I will again move*, but
meaning *I will go home*. Without the
repetitive sign the verb signifies *I
willmove on*." The variation in the
form that occurs with the serial aspect
ap-pears to be a dialectal or idiolectal
trait. waré·kwę· *it has left* (RC 27:16),
ruré·kwę· *he is absent, he is gone* (R),
ahruré·kwę·k *that he has gone* (R),
warekwęha' *it goes to* (RC 34:12),
waré·kwahs *it goes away* (RC 8:20),
wahrárku' *he went* (RC 26:2) [Law-
son «Its Warko» 'go you']; **-ar(e)=
kwęha'nye'** –: rurekwęhá·'nye' ‹he-
moves on-going along› *he makes progress* (HS); yurekwęhá·'nye' ‹it-
moves on-going along› *progressively*
(HS); **-či –. -ar(e)ku** –: θęrku' ‹again-
fact-it-moved on› *it returned home*
(RC 26:29), θhraré·kwahs ‹again-he-
moves on› *he retires to his home* (H-
notebook); **-t –. -ar(e)ku** –: nwaré·kwę·
‹hither-it-moves on› *it comes from*
(RC 34:12); **-rihwarekwa'T** –: rurihwarekwá'nę ‹he-matter-moves on-
caused› *he officiates* (HS).

arekwéhu'y *lizard* (AW 58). *n.* Also:
rukwéhu *newt* (R), *mythic lizard* (RC

10:19), rukwéhu'y *lizard* (AW 58).

-ar(e)kwęha'nye' – make progress. *v.s.-
a.i.* rurekwęhá·'nye' ‹he-moves on-
going along› *he makes progress* (HS),
yurekwęhá·'nye' ‹it-moves on-going
along› *progressively* (HS).

-ar(e)kwęha'nye' – progressively. *dv.n.s.*
yurekwęhá·'nye' ‹it-moves on-going
along› *progressively* (HS).

-areręti – set (of the sun). *v.r.-a.i.* hab: -
ęhs, pnt: -', stat: -ę·, prog: -, prp: -,
dst: -, caus: -, rvs: -, dat: -, n-inc.
yurerę́·tyę· *sunset* (HS); **-yah** –. **-arerę=
ti** –: wewarerę́·tyęhs ‹thither-it (sun)
sets› *west, it is setting* (HS); **-yah** –.
-areręti – kę'náhkę: wewarerę́·tyęhs
kę'náhkę ‹thither-it (sun) sets side›
western (HS).

-areręti – sunset. *dv.n.s.* yurerę́·tyę· *sunset*
(HS).

-areru – run. *v.r.-a.i.* hab: -ha' ~ -hs, pnt:
-', stat: -·, prog: -, prp: -he-, dst: -,
caus: -'T-, rvs: -, dat: -, n-inc.
karerúha' *I am running* (R), kayę-
rè·ruhs *they run* (L 57); **-areruhehθę** –:
kayęreruhéhθęh ‹they-run-much› *they
run around* (L 57); **-yah** –. **-areruhe** –:
yahęrerúhe·t ‹thither-fact-it-ran-going
to› *it was going running there* (RC 2:
10); **-ne+t** –. **-areruhe** –: nęthrarerúhe·t
‹apart-prediction-hither-he run-going
to› *he will be going running there*
(RC 6:7); **-ne** –. **-areruhsT** –.#aka·'**:
nekayęreruhstha'á·ka·' ‹apart-they-
run-cause-characterized by› *runners;
snowsnake* (R).

-arethu – pour in. *v.r.-t.* hab: -h, pnt: -',
stat: -ę°, prog: -, prp: -, dst: -, caus: -,
rvs: -, dat: -, n-inc. Encountered only
with the translocative; however, the
meaning of the construction suggests
that it could occur without the translocative as well. **-yah** –. **-arethu** –: yahę-
ré·thu' ‹thither-fact-it-poured in› *it*

poured it in there (RC 10: 15).

à·rę about, approximately (RC 26:2). *part.* à·rę na? ú?nę? ‹about much on the other side› *on the other side* (AW 57); à·rę the? kyè·nę ? ‹about no this› *is this yours?* (R); à·rę ukę́? ‹about or› *around or about, in or near* (RC 4:4).

à·rę na? ú?nę? ‹about much on the other side› on the other side (AW 57). *part.*

à·rę the? kyè·nę ? ‹about no this› is this yours? (R). *part.*

à·rę ukę́? ‹about or› around or about, in or near (RC 4:4). *part.*

–(a)rę?naT– blow air on. *v.r.-t.* hab: -s, pnt: -ɸ, stat: -ę, prog: -, prp: -, dst: -, caus: -, rvs: -, dat: -, n-inc. The initial *a* is absent before the semireflexive morpheme and present elsewhere. The meanings *fortune teller* and *soothsayer* for the deverbal noun given below derive from the practice of telling fortunes by holding small twigs in one's hand, blowing into them and causing them to scatter on the ground, and then reading the fortune from the patterns formed by the fallen twigs. wahrarę́?na·t *he blew air on it* (RC 14:7); –a?rę?naT–: ra?rę́?na·č ‹he-himself-blows air on› *he blows air on it: fortune teller* (RC 6:1), *he prophesizes: clairvoyant* (HS), wahra?rę́?na·t ‹fact-he-himself-blew air on› *he devined* (RC 27:27), *soothsayer* (HS), θa?rę́?na·t ‹you!-yourself-blow air on› *blow air on it!* (R); čha? –(a)rę?naT–: čha? warę́?na·č ‹there at it-blows air on› *bellows* (HS); ha? –a?rę?naT–: ha? ru?rę?ná·?nę ‹the he-himself-blew air on› *his prophecy* (HS).

–arę?nęw– snort. *v.r.-a.i.* hab: -s, pnt: -?, stat: -, prog: -, prp: -, dst: -θę-, caus: -, rvs: -, dat: -, n-inc. rarę́?nęws *he snorts* (HS), ęhrarę́?nę?w *he will snort* (HS); –yah–. –arę?nęw–: yahwa?ęrę́?nę?w ‹thither-fact-one-snorted› *there she blew* (M 87); kwískwis –arę?nęw= θę–: kwískwis warę?nę́wθęh ‹pig it-snorts-much› *pig is grunting* (AG).

–arh– empty noun root. *v.inc.* See: -a'ni- /-ę'ni- *throw*.

–arhak paternal aunt. *n.r.* aln: akwárhak *my paternal aunt* (R), n-inc., n.sfx. -. kúrhak *my paternal aunt (vocative, i.e, used in addressing one's aunt)* (R), akwárhak *my paternal aunt (referential, i.e., used in referring to one's aunt)* (R), rúrhak *his paternal aunt* (R).

–arihst– minute. *n.r.* poss. ?, inc. Found only incorporated in the following construction. ti –. –arihstake–: tiwarihstá·kye· ‹so-it-minute-is in number› *so many minutes* (R).

–aryeh sister-in-law (lit. 'brother's wife [woman speaking]'). *n.r.* aln: akyá·ryeh *my sister's-in-law* (R), n-inc., n.sfx. -. akyá·ryeh *my sister's-in-law* (R).

–aθa– optative mode+repetitive. *v.pfx.*

–aθahnęhst– bucket. *dv.n.r.* n-poss., n-inc., n.sfx. -. The verb root from which this noun is derived is otherwise unattested. yęθahnę́hstha? *bucket (she dips with thing)* (HS).

á·θe·ʔ new, green, raw, unripe. *part.* aθe·ʔ.#hči: aθéʔči ‹new-very› *newly* (HS); **-ęˇkʷehstaθe·ʔ**: awękwehstá·θe·ʔ ‹human-'ness-new› *youth* (HS); **-hih = teʔčraθe·ʔ -**: yuhihteʔčrá·θe·ʔ ‹it-sun-'ness-new› *new moon* (R); **-hnyaθe·ʔ -**: uhnyá·θe·ʔ ‹news-new› *new news* (L 12); **-hseʔyuhčraθe·ʔ**: uhseʔyuhčrá·θe·ʔ ‹cork-'ness-new› *new stopper* (RC 15:8); **-nęθaθe·ʔ -**: unęθá·θe·ʔ ‹potato-new› *new potato, new potatoes* (H 2484); **-rihwaθe·ʔ -**: urihwá·θe·ʔ ‹matter-new› *new fashioned, modern* (RC 21:2), *innovation, novelty* (HS); **-ta'naθe·ʔke**: Utaʔnaθé·ʔkye ‹village-new-at› *Geneva, New York* (R) [Morgan, League «O-tä-nä-sä´-ga» 'Geneva']; **-tkwaraθe·ʔ -.#hči**: utkwaraθéʔči ‹blood-new-very› *new blood* (RC 21:11); **-uhstaθe·ʔ -**: awuhstá·θe·ʔ ‹year-new› *New Year's Day* (R).

aθe·ʔ.#hči newly. *n.s.* aθéʔči ‹new-very› *newly* (HS).

áθę when (RC 3:2). *part.* áθę hà·neʔ ‹when that is› *finally* (RC 3:38); áθę theʔ ‹when not› *not yet* (RC 23:2).

áθę hà·neʔ ‹when that is› finally (RC 3:38). *part.*

áθę theʔ ‹when not› not yet (RC 23:2). *part.*

aθęhkęhči at that time (RC 8:37), while at first or while at the beginning (H 2892). *part.*

-aθhęʔru - howl. *v.r.-a.i.* hab: -h, pnt: -, stat: -, prog: -, prp: -, dst: -, caus: -, rvs: -, dat: -, n-inc. waθhęʔruh *it howls* (AG).

-aθhu - smell. *v.r.-t.* hab: -, pnt: -ʔ, stat: -, prog: -, prp: -, dst: -, caus: -, rvs: -, dat: -, inc.-rę-pat. Forms recorded by Lounsbury (p. 76) indicate a root with a medial glottal stop (i.e., **-ręʔθhu -**) that is not present either in the forms that I recorded or those cited by Hew-

itt. **-nęhsnaθhu -**: yunęhsnáθhwahs ‹it-seed-smells› *it smells the grain* (H 2484); **-ręθhu -**: ękrę́θhuʔ ‹fact-I-X-smelled› *I smelled it* (R), weθarę́θhuʔ ‹fact-you-X-smelled› *you smelled it* (R); **-ręʔθhu -**: ękréʔθhuʔ ‹fact-I-X-smelled› *I smelled it* (L 76), waʔkarȩ́ʔθhuʔ ‹fact-one-X-smelled› *she smelled it* (L 76), wahruréʔθhuʔ ‹fact-he-X-smelled› *he smelled it* (L 76); **-ręθhwahT -**: rarę́θhwáhthaʔ ‹he-X-smell-causes› *he smells* (HS); **-yęʔ = kwaraθhu -**: waʔuyęʔkwaráθhuʔ ‹fact-it-smoke-smelled› *it smelled of smoke* (RC 32: 11).

-aθkwar - lips. *n.r.* inaln: kaθkwarȩ́ʔkye *on my lips* (R), inc., n.sfx. -eh. úθkwareh *lips* (HS); **-aθkwarakarati -**: wakwaθkwarakará·tyęʔ ‹I-lip-rubbed› *I whoop* (AG), wahraθkwarakará·tyęʔ ‹fact-he-lip-rubbed› *(he) made the whoop (war whoop) by vibrating hands to mouth repeatedly* (AG); **-a = θkwaruha -**: raθkwarúhahs ‹he-lips-puts in water› *he sips* (HS); **-aθkwa = rur -**: wáθkwaruh ‹it-lip-covers› *string of beads* (RC 30:43); **-aθkwaruʔT -**: uθkwarúʔneh ‹lip-stand› *bead* (R); **-aθkwarʔe(k) -**: raθkwárʔehs ‹he-lips-strikes› *he shouts, he whoops* (HS); **-ne -.-aθkwaraw -**: nehráθkwaraws ‹apart-he-lips-gives› *he opens his mouth* (H-notebook); **-ne -.-aθkwaru = 'narhę -**: nehraθkwaruʔnárhęh ‹apart-he-lip-hooks-much› *he embroiders* (HS).

-aθkwarakarati - make a war whoop. *v.s.-a.i.* wakwaθkwarakará·tyęʔ ‹I-lip-rubbed› *I whoop* (AG), wahraθkwarakará·tyęʔ ‹fact-he-lip-rubbed› *(he) made the whoop (war whoop) by vibrating hands to mouth repeatedly* (AG).

-aθkware - be a swine. *dv.n.r.* waθkwà·-

reh *swine* (R) [Lawson «Watsquerre» 'Swine'].

-aθkwaruha- sip. *v.s.-t.* raθkwarúhahs ‹he-lips-puts in water› *he sips* (HS).

-aθkwarur- string beads. *dv.n.s.* wá-θkwaruh ‹it-lip-covers› *string of beads* (RC 30:43).

-aθkwaruʔT- bead. *n.s.* uθkwarúʔneh ‹lip-cover-cause› *bead* (R).

-aθkwarʔe(k)- shout, whoop. *v.s.-a.i.* raθkwárʔehs ‹he-lips-strikes› *he shouts, he whoops* (HS).

-aθkwiʔ- blot out. *v.r.-t.* hab: -θ, pnt:-, stat: -, prog: -, prp: -, dst: -, caus: -, rvs: -, dat: -, inc.-ϕ-pat. Found only in the construction cited below. -(a)ha= haθkwiʔ-: ruhaháθkwiʔθ ‹he-path-blots out› *it blots out his path or road (said of the weather in winter when a warm spell thaws the snow and thereby spoils the sleighing)* (H 2484).

-aθn-/-(a)kaθn- be heavy (of animates); be hard, be strong. *v.r.-s.i.* stat: -eʔ, prog: -, prp: -, dst: -, caus: -, rvs: -, dat: -, inc.-ϕ-pat. The form -aθn- occurs only following the root -(i)ʔ=θh- *power*. The form -akaθn- occurs when no incorporated noun is present and with a few (mostly recently) incorporated noun roots; the form -ka=θn- occurs with the majority of incorporated noun roots. raká·θneʔ *he is heavy* (R), waká·θneʔ *it is hard, it is strong* (R) [Lawson «Wau-cots ne» 'Hard or heavy']; -erihkaθn-: rawerih-ká·θneʔ ‹he-breath-is strong› *he is suffering, he is patient* (R); -hsyuʔ=

kaθn-: rahsyuʔká·θneʔ ‹he-grip-is strong› *his grip is strong* (R); -(i)ʔ=θhaθn-: uʔθhá·θneh ‹power-be strong› *authority, power, strength* (R), yuʔ-θhá·θneh ‹it-power-is strong› *acrid, cogent, strength* (HS), weʔθhá·θneʔ ‹it-power-is strong› *it is enduring, it lasts* (HS), kaʔθhá·θneʔ ‹it-power-is strong› *it is potent* (HS), *it is powerful* (RC 28:7), reʔθhá·θneʔ ‹he-power-is strong› *he is enduring* (HS); -(i)ʔθha=θnęhčr-: uʔθhaθnę́hčreh ‹power-be strong-'ness› *authority, power, strength* (R); -(i)ʔθhaθnęhst-: uʔθhaθnę́hsteh ‹power-be strong-'ness› *prerogative, right* (HS); -(i)ʔθhaθnęhčrayę(T)-: wakyeʔθhaθnę́hčrayęʔ ‹I-power-be strong-'ness-lay› *I am strong* (R); -(i)ʔθhaθnęhstakʷek-: raʔθhaθnęhsta-kwé·kę ‹he-power-be strong-'ness-is whole› *he is almighty* (HS), ęhsiʔθha-θnęhstakwé·kęk ‹prediction-you-power-be strong-'ness-be whole› *you will have the authority* (RC 23:3); -kah=kaθn-: rakahká·θneʔ ‹he-eye-is strong› *his eye is strong, he has good vision* (R); -nęhakaθn-: kanęhaká·θneʔ ‹it-corn-is strong› *flint corn* (HS); ti-. -erihkaθn-: tiwerihká·θneʔ ‹so-it-breath-is strong› *as much as it can tolerate* (RC 19:2); haʔ -erihkaθn-: haʔ rawerihká·θneʔ ‹the he-breath-is strong› *patience* (HS).

-aθnar- cry, weep. *v.r.-a.i.* hab: -ϕ, pnt: -ʔ, stat: -ę, prog: -, prp: -ahteʔ-, dst: -, caus: -, rvs: -, dat: III (-ati-/-ę-), n-inc. Unless another prepronominal prefix is present, the dualic prefix must be present with this verb root. -či-. -aθnarahte?-: θhraθnaráhte? ‹again-he-cries-going to› *he is going crying again* (RC 11:2); -ne-. -aθnar-: neká·θnar ‹apart-I-cry› *I am crying* (R), wa?tká·θna?r ‹fact-apart-I-cried› *I cried* (R); -ne-. -aθnar-{dative III}: wa?thraθnà·rę? ‹fact-apart-he-cried-for› *he cried for it* (RC 11:4); -ne-. -aθnarahte?-: nehraθnaráhte?θ ‹apart-he-cries-going to› *he is going crying for it* (RC 11:4); -ne-. -aθnarčrakar-: newaθnárčrakar ‹apart-it-cry-'ness-makes a noise› *it sobs* (HS).

áθneh outside (RC 27:6). *part.* aθneh. #áh: aθneháh ‹outside-little› *gopher, mole* (AG).

aθneh.#áh: aθneháh ‹outside-little› gopher, mole (AG). *n.*

aθnéhte exterior, outside (H-notebook), outward (HS). *part.*

-aθnerhęhčihę- finish completely. *v.s.-t.* waθnerhęhčíhę· ‹it-finished-very-much› *it had completely finished it* (RC 5:29).

-aθnerhu- accomplish, finish. *v.r.-t.* hab: -hs, pnt: -?, stat: -ę°, prog: -, prp: -, dst: -, caus: -, rvs: -, dat: -, n-inc. Because of the meaning of the root, it is rarely encountered in aspects other than the punctual. θaθnérhu *finish it!* (L 55), waθnérhę *it has finished* (RC 5:35), raθnérhuhs *he accomplishes it* (HS), *he finishes it* (L 55), wa?nyęθnérhu? *the two of them finished* (RC 5:30), ęθnérhu? *it finished* (R), wa?kaθnérhu? *I finished* (R); -aθnerhu-. #ęwe: raθnerhuhs?è·we ‹he-finishes-genuine› *he perfects it* (HS); -aθner=hęhčihę-: waθnerhęhčíhę· ‹it-finished-very-much› *it had completely finished* (RC 5:29); -aθnerhu-ha? ti-. -a?rih=wayę(T)-{dative II}: raθnérhuhs ha?

tihru?rihwayę́·tih ‹he-finishes the so-he-himself-matter-lays-for› *he does his duty* (HS).

-aθnerhu-ha? ti-. -a?rihwayę(T)-{dative II} do duty. *v.s.-a.i.* raθnérhuhs ha? tihru?rihwayę́·tih ‹he-finishes the so-he-himself-matter-lays-for› *he does his duty* (HS).

-aθnerhu-.#ęwe perfect. *v.s.-t.* raθnerhuhs?è·we ‹he-finishes-genuine› *he perfects it* (HS).

-aθnę- dry up, evaporate, run dry, shrivel. *v.r.-a.i.* hab: -hs, pnt: -?, stat: -·, prog: -, prp: -ahte-, dst: -, caus: -hT-, rvs: -, dat: -, n-inc. Apparently ę́θnęhs *it dried up, it shriveled up* (RC 22:1) is a blend or back formation from the expected habitual form wá·θnęhs *it runs dry* and the expected factual form ę́θnę? *it ran dry, it evaporated.* yúθnę· *it is dry, it dried up* (R), wáθnęhs *it runs dry, it evaporates* (R); -aθnęhT-: raθnę́htha? ‹he-dry up-causes› *he condenses it, he dries it, he simmers it* (HS); -aθnę?-: yuθnę́?ę ‹it-dry up-began› *inanition, emptiness, exhaustion (from lack of food)* (HS).

-aθnęhT- condense, dry, simmer. *v.s.-t.* raθnę́htha? ‹he-dry up-causes› *he condenses it, he dries it, he simmers it* (HS).

-aθnę?- inanition, emptiness, exhaustion (from lack of food). *dv.n.s.* yuθnę́?ę ‹it-be dried up-began› *inanition, emptiness, exhaustion (from lack of food)* (HS).

-aθnę?kw- animal droppings, bunch, bundle, burden, cluster, dumplings, lump, mass, package, skein. *n.r.* aln: ruθnę́?kwayę? *his bundle* (R), inc., n.sfx. -eh. uθnę́?kweh *animal droppings, bunch, bundle, burden, cluster, dumplings, lump, mass, package, skein* (R); -aθnę?kw-.#hči: uθnę?-

kwéhči ‹bunch-very› *bunchy* (HS); –a'naθnę̨ʔkwęti –: ra'ʔnaθnę̨ʔkwę́·tih ‹he-himself-bundle-makes› *he muffles himself up, he bundles himself up* (HS); –a'naθnę̨ʔkwihsʔa –: wa'ę̨'na- θnę̨ʔkwíhsʔa·' ‹fact-one-oneself-bun- dle-finished› *one finished bundle, one finished packing* (RC 3:39).

–aθnę̨ʔkw –.#hči bunchy. *n.s.* uθnę̨ʔkwéh- či ‹bunch-very› *bunchy* (HS).

–aθT(e)k – vomit. *v.r.-a.i.* hab: -ęhs, pnt: ()-ɸ, stat: -ę, prog: -, prp: -ęhe-, dst: -, caus: -aʔT-, rvs: -, dat: -, inc.-ɸ-pat. wáθtkęhs *it vomits: vomit* (RC 33:11), yę́θtkęhs *one vomits* (RC 20:1), ęwá·- θne·k *it will vomit* (RC 27:17), ę́·- θne·k *it vomited* (RC 33:11); –a= θtkaʔT –: yúθtkaʔt ‹it-vomit-caused› *it is disgusting, it is emetic, it is filthy* (HS); rúθtkaʔt ‹he-vomit-caused› *he is disgusting* (HS), akęyáθtkaʔt ‹un- known-I=you-vomit-cause› *that I make you vomit* (RC 30: 51), naʔ'- naθtká'ʔnę· ‹one=another-vomit-caus- ed-for› *one made another vomit* (RC 30:68); –aθtkaʔčr –: uθtká'ʔčreh ‹vomit- 'ness› *vomit* (L 79); –aθtkaʔnahkw –: yęθtka'ʔnáhkhwa' ‹one-vomit-cause- instrument› *emetic* (HS); –aθtkęhe –: ęhraθtkę́he' ‹prediction-he-vomit-be going to› *he will be going vomiting* (RC 20:1); –nęhsaθtkaʔT –: unęhsá- θtkaʔt ‹it-house-vomit-cause› *it is a filthy house* (H 2484).

–aθT(e)k – vomit. *dv.n.s.* wáθtkęhs *vom- it* (RC 33:11).

–aθtkaʔčr – vomit. *n.s.* uθtká'ʔčreh ‹vomit- 'ness› *vomit* (L 79).

–aθtkaʔnahkw – emetic. *dv.n.s.* yęθtka'ʔ- náhkhwa' ‹one-vomit-cause-instru- ment› *emetic* (HS).

–aθtkaʔT – be disgusting, be emetic, be filthy. *v.s.-a.i.* yúθtkaʔt ‹it-vomit- caused› *it is disgusting, it is emetic, it is filthy* (HS), rúθtkaʔt ‹he-vomit- caused› *he is disgusting* (HS).

–aθtkaʔT – make vomit. *v.s.-t.* akęyá- θtkaʔt ‹unknown-I=you-vomit-cause› *that I make you vomit* (RC 30:51), naʔ'naθtká'ʔnę· ‹one=another-vomit- caused-for› *one made another vomit* (RC 30:68).

–asθę̨ – be fat. *v.r.-a.i.* hab: -h, pnt: -·', stat: -·, prog: -, prp: -, dst: -, caus: -, rvs: -, dat: -, n-inc. yúsθę̨· *it is fat* (R), rúsθę̨· *he is fat* (HS), kásθę̨h *I am fat* (R), wa'ʔkásθę̨·' *I was fat* (R), ęhrúsθę̨·k *he will be fat* (HS).

–asθę̨r be a widower. *v.r.-k.* rúsθę̨r *he is a widower* (HS).

–asθhar – care for, provide, support. *v.r.-t.* hab: -ɸ, pnt: -a', stat: -', prog: -a'nye'-, prp: -, dst: -, caus: -, rvs: -, dat: -, n-inc. kayę'na'násθha'r *one cared for them* (RC 9:3), kheyásθhar *I am caring for another* (R), na'nás- θhar *one supports another* (HS), rús- θhar *he provides for it, he cares for it* (HS), ęwásθhara' *it will care for it* (RC 11:11), kayeθásθharahk *they had cared for you* (RC 11:27), wa'ʔkheyás- θhara' *I defend somebody* (AG), ęka- yę'na'nasθhará·'nye' *in defending themselves (lit., they will be defend-*

ing themselves) (AG); –(i)tǫhT – –as =
θha̱r –: yakú·tǫht wásθhar ‹one-is poor
it-cares for› *alms house* (HS), *homeless shelter, poor house* (R).
–(a)·t completive. *v.r.sfx.* The completive
occurs in place of the punctual aspect
marker with verbs of motion to indicate that a goal has been reach (e.g.,
yahwáhre·t ‹thither-fact-he-went-com-
plete› *he went there*). It also occurs in
place of the stative aspect marker to
indicate a maximum (e.g., **áhsǫ nǫka =
nǫhsá·kye·t** ‹three so-prediction-it-
house-be in number-complete› *there
will be three (and only three) houses*).
The form –a·t occurs after roots and
stems that end in a consonant; the
form –·t occurs after roots and stems
that end in a vowel.
–aT– be, be in, be present, be upright,
stand. *v.r.-a.i.* hab: -ɸ, pnt: -e·ʔ, stat: -
ǫ, prog: -, prp: -he-, dst: -, caus: -,
rvs: -, dat: II (-ati-/-ahθ), inc.-ɸ-ag./
pat. The stem –athǫhnaT – shows a
divergent set of aspect markers, suggesting that this stem has been lexicalized as a unit. ì·wa·t *it (inanimate)
is in* (H 2892); –(a)hahaT –: kaháha·t
‹it-path-stands› *(it is) a road contained
in something, in a valley or ravine* (H
2484); –ahčaT –{dative II}: ǫyeh-
čá·thahθ ‹prediction-one-fist-stand-for›
one will point out (RC 15:9); –(a)h =
yaT –: wáhya·t ‹it-fruit-stands› *fruit is
in it, it contains fruit, there is fruit in
it* (H 2892); –athǫhnaT –: rathǫhna·č
‹he-himself-ear-stands› *he listens* (RC
30:29), wakathǫhná·ʔneʔ ‹I-myself-
ear-stand› *I am listening* (R); –(ǫ)ʔti =
kǫhraT –: yuʔtikǫhra·t ‹it-mind-stands›
animal (as opposed to vegetable) (R),
ruʔtikǫhra·t ‹he-mind-stands› *he has
discretion* (HS); –hnekaT –: kahné·ka·t
‹it-liquid-stands› *there is sap in it, it*

contains sap (H 2892); –kahrat –.#hči:
nakwakahratáhči ‹you!=us-eye-stand-
very› *share our vision!* (R); –kǫhraT –:
ukǫhrá·ʔnǫ ‹disdain-stand› *derision,
humility* (HS); –kǫhraT – {dative II}:
rukǫhraʔná·tih ‹he-disdain-stands-for›
he disdains it, he holds it common
(HS); –nǫhaT –: unǫha·t ‹corn-stand›
pip (HS); –nǫhraʔsaT –: unǫhráʔsa·t
‹udder-stand› *it has milk in it: cow*
(HS); –nǫhsnaT –: kanǫhsna·t ‹it-seed-
stands› *there is grain in it, it contains
grain or a grain* (H 2892); –nǫθaT –:
kanǫ·θa·t ‹it-potato-stands› *it contains
a potato, or other vegetable bulbs:
there are potatoes or there is a potato
in it* (H 2892); –terhyaʔčraT –: kater-
hyáʔčra·t ‹it-shovel-stands› *there is a
spade or shovel in it, it contains a
shovel* (H 2892); –či –.–ahsaT –: θwáh-
sa·t ‹again-it-foot-stands› *one foot* (RC
25:2); –či –.–ǫ'naT –: θwǫ·ʔna·t ‹again-
it-day-stands› *one day* (RC 21:7); –či –.
–hihteʔčraT –: θkahihtéʔčra·t ‹again-it-
sun-'ness-stands› *one month* (R); –či –.
–hθaT –: θkáhθa·t ‹again-it-width of
flexible material-stands› *one pace (of
3 feet), yard* (AG); –či –.–hwihstaT –:
θkahwíhsta·t ‹again-it-metal-stands›
one dollar (HS); –či –.–nǫhsaT –: θka-
nǫhsa·t ‹again-it-house-stands› *one
house* (R); –či –.–nǫhsnaT –: θkanǫh-
sna·t ‹again-it-seed-stands› *one seed*
(RC 23:6); –či –.–uhstatha'nyeʔ –: θwuh-
stathá·ʔnyeʔ ‹again-it-year-stands-going along› *yearly* (HS); –či –.–yahstaT –:
θhrayáhsta·t ‹again-he-individual-
stands› *one male, an individual man*
(RC 1:8); –či –.–yahstatha'nyeʔ –: θka-
yeyahstathá·ʔnyeʔ ‹again-they-individual-stand-going along› *one-by-one*
(RC 3:81); ti –.–a'newyaT –: thwaʔné·-
wya·t ‹so-it-itself-armspan-stands›
measure as long as the arms extend

from tip of one hand to the other (AG); **ti** –. –**hečhathe** –: tyuhečhá·the⁷ ‹so-it-buttocks-stands-going to› *exposed buttocks* (H-notebook); –**yah** –. –**ahčaT** –: yęwahčá·⁷ne⁷ ‹thither-prediction-it-fist-stand› *it will point there* (RC 30:28); –**nęhsn** – –**nęhaT** –: unę́hsneh yunę́ha·t ‹seed it-corn-stands› *grain, it has seed in it (this is the name of any grain used or intended to be used for planting)* (H 2484).

–**atahw** – be frayed. *v.r.-s.i.* stat: -ɸ, prog: -, prp: -, dst: -, caus: -ahT-, rvs: -, dat: -, inc.-ɸ-pat. Found only in the following construction. –**či⁷ruratah** = **waht**: uči⁷ruratáhwaht ‹medicine stick-be frayed-cause› *frayed medicine stick* (RC 19:11).

–**aT(e)** – semireflexive. *v.r.pfx*. The form –**at** – occurs before roots and stems that begin with the consonants *k*, *⁷*, or *h* and combines with the initial consonant(s) of roots and stems that begin with *hs*, *s* or *θ* to yield –**ačh** –, the final *h* of which is lost if a consonant other than a glide follows. The form –**a'n** – occurs before roots and stems that begin with a vowel. The form –**a⁷** – occurs before roots and stems that begin with the consonants *t*, *č* or *r* and before some roots and stems that begin with *n*. The form –**a'ne** – occurs before roots and stems that begin with a consonant cluster that conditions the appearance of "epenthetic" e. The form –**a'nę** – occurs before roots and stems that begin with *hn* or *ht* and most roots and stems that begin with *n*.

–**aT** –. –**ętiyeT** –/–**a'nętiyeT** – convey, send. *v.r.-t.* hab: -ha⁷, pnt: -ɸ, stat: -ę, prog: -, prp: -, dst: -, caus: -, rvs: -, dat: -, inc.-ɸ-pat. The form –**aT** –. –**ętiyeT** – occurs whenever an incorporated noun root is present. Elsewhere, the form –**a'nętiyeT** – occurs. This stem is clearly derived through the addition of the semireflexive to a root * –**ętiyeT** – which, however, is not otherwise attested in the language. ra⁷nętiyé·tha⁷ *he conveys, he sends* (HS); –**yah** –.- –**a'nętiyeT** –: yęka⁷nętí·ye·t ‹thither-prediction-I-myself-send› *I will send there for one* (RC 3:61), yahwahsa⁷nętí·ye·t ‹thither-fact-you-yourself-sent› *you sent it there* (R), wehru⁷nętiyé·⁷nę ‹thither-he-himself-sent› *he has sent it there* (R); –**yah** –. –**a⁷rihwę** = **tiyeT** –: yahwahra⁷rihwętí·ye·t ‹thither-fact-he-himself-matter-sent› *he sent word* (R).

–**aT** –. –**ę⁷neT** –/–**a'nę⁷neT** – go alongside of, hide behind. *v.r.-t.* hab: -ha⁷, pnt: -, stat: -, prog: -, prp: -, dst: -, caus: -, rvs: -, dat: -, inc.-ɸ-pat. The form –**aT** –. –**ę⁷neT** – occurs whenever an incorporated noun root is present. Elsewhere, the form –**a'nę⁷neT** – occurs. This stem is clearly derived through the addition of the semireflexive to a root * –**ę⁷neT** – which, however, is not otherwise attested in the language. ra⁷nę⁷né·tha⁷ *he hides behind it* (HS); –**a'nę⁷ne'nahkw** –: yę⁷nę⁷ne⁷náhkhwa⁷

‹one-oneself-hide behind-instrument›
defender, shield (HS); –at⁷ęyę⁷neT –:
rat⁷ęyę⁷né·tha⁷ ‹he-himself-enclosure-
hides behind› *he goes alongside the
fences* (H-notebook); –a'nęnęhsę⁷neT –:
ra⁷nęnęhsę⁷né·tha⁷ ‹he-himself-house-
hides behind› *he goes alongside of the
house, he hides behind the house* (H
2484).

–atęhninę – betray, sell. *v.r.-t.* hab: -h,
pnt: -, stat: -, prog: -, prp: -, dst: -,
caus: -ahT-, rvs: -, dat: I (-⁷θe-/-⁷θ-),
inc.-ɸ-pat. Comparison with the verb
root –hninę – *buy* shows that both roots
are borrowed from another Northern
Iroquoian language, since expected
changes of *t to ⁷n and *n to t are
absent. The initial *atę* of the root
meaning *sell* is undoubtedly the semireflexive morpheme (Tuscarora –a'nę –)
as it would appear in any of the other
Northern Iroquoian languages. ękayę-
tęhninéhek *they will be selling things*
(W 74), na⁷natęhnì·nęh *one betrays
another* (HS); –atęhninę –{dative I}:
yękhiyatęhniné⁷θe· ‹one=us-sold-for›
one sold it to us (RC 26:12); –atęh =
ninęhst –: utęhninéhsteh ‹sell-'ness› *a
shop* (HS); –(a)hę⁷natęhninę –: rahę⁷-
natęhnì·nęh ‹he-field-sells› *he sells the
field* (H 2484); –či –. –atęhninę – θhra-
tęhnì·nęh ‹again-he-sells› *he resells it*
(HS); –athyatęhstatęhninę –: rathyatęh-
statęhnì·nęh ‹he-himself-paper-sells›
stationer (HS); ti –. –aθrę'nye⁷ –.#áh
–atęhninę –: tiwaθrę⁷nye⁷áh ratęhnì·-
nęh ‹so-it-is so big-going along-little
he-sells› *he sells retail* (HS).

–atęhninę –{dative I} sell to. *v.s.-t.* yę-
khiyatęhniné⁷θe·   ‹one=us-sold-for›
one sold it to us (RC 26:12).

–atęhninęhst – shop. *n.s.* utęhninéhsteh
‹sell-'ness› *a shop* (HS).

–ath – be dry. *v.r.-s.i.* stat: -ę, prog: -,

prp: -a⁷θe-, dst: -hę-, caus: -a⁷T-, rvs:
-, dat: I (-a⁷θe-/-a⁷θ-), inc.-hsn-pat.
yuhsná·thę *it is dry*, aryahsná·thęk *that
it have been dry* (RC 7:1), –hsnath –
{dative I}: yuhsnathá⁷θe· ‹it-X-is dry-
for› *it is arid* (HS); –hsnatha⁷T –: kah-
snathá⁷nę ‹it-X-be dry-caused› *they
were dried* (RC 3:61); –hsnathę⁷ –:
kahsná·thę⁷θ ‹it-X-be dry-begins› *it
dries* (HS); –(a)hę⁷nath –: yuhę⁷ná·thę
‹it-field-is dry› *the meadow is dry* (H
2484); –nęhath –: kanęhá·thę ‹it-corn-is
dry› *dry, seasoned corn* (H 2484), yu-
nęhá·thę ‹it-corn-is dry› *the corn is
dry or seasoned corn* (H 2484); –nęha =
tha⁷T –: ranęhathá⁷tha⁷ ‹he-corn-be
dry-causes› *he is drying, seasoning,
the corn* (H 2484); –nęhsathę⁷ –: ka-
nęhsá·thę⁷θ ‹it-house-be dry-begins›
the house is drying, is becoming dry
(H 2484); –nęhsnath –: yunęhsná·thę
‹it-seed-is dry› *the grain is dry or
seasoned* (H 2484); –nęθathę⁷ –: kanę-
θá·thę⁷θ ‹it-potato-be dry-begins›
*potato is (or are) drying, potato is (or
are) become dry* (H 2484); –nu =
rathę⁷ –: wa⁷kanurá·thę⁷ ‹fact-it-string
of corn-be dry-began› *string of corn
dried* (RC 5:33); –tehwatha⁷nahnę –:
wa⁷nyetehwatha⁷náhnę⁷   ‹fact-they
two-skin-dry-caused-many› *they two
dried skins* (RC 30:64); ha⁷ –hsnathę –:
ha⁷ yuhsná·thę ‹the it-is dry-much›
aridity (HS).

–athahahkw – walk. *v.s.-a.i.* kakuthahah-
kéhe⁷ ‹they-themselves-path-picked
up-remote› *they had been walking*
(AW 56).

–athahar – keep watch, lay in wait, patrol.
v.s.-a.i. rutháha⁷r ‹he-himself-path-
was in› *he lays in wait* (RC 25:4), *he
keeps watch, he patrols* (HS).

–athahar –{dative III} join. *v.s.-a.i.* akatháhrę⁷ ‹that-I- myself-path-be in-for›

that I join (RC 13:6).

-athaharahkw – be out of the way, put out of the way. *v.s.-a.i.* yuthaharáhkwę ‹it-itself-path-collected› *it is out of the way* (HS), rathaharáhkwahs ‹he-himself-path-collects› *he deviates, he turns aside* (HS).

-athaharuhčrę – crossroads. *dv.n.s.* yuthaharúhčrę⁷ ‹it-itself-path-gathers› *crossroads* (HS).

-athahiN – travel. *v.s.-a.i.* rathahì·nęhs ‹he-himself-path-proceeds› *he travels* (HS), rathahí·te⁷ ‹he-himself-path-proceeded› *he is traveling* (H 2484).

-athahsęhnahkw – watch, wristwatch. *dv. n.r.* Probably composed of the semireflexive **-at-** and an unidentifiable root **-hahsę-** followed by the causative and instrumental suffixes. Occurs only in the following construction. yęthahsęhnáhkhwa⁷ *watch, wristwatch* (HS).

-atharhu – be introvenient. *v.s.-a.i.* wathárhuhs ‹it-itself-hang-causes› *it is introvenient* (HS).

-athečrahkw – chair, seat, stool. *n.s.* uthečráhkweh ‹self-buttocks-gather-instrument› *chair, seat, stool* (R), yęthečráhkhwa⁷ ‹one-oneself-buttocks-gathers-instrument› *one uses it to support his buttocks* (Hewitt 1893).

-athečrahkw- -i⁷rę- chairman. *n.s.* uthečráhkweh ré⁷rę⁷ ‹self-buttocks-gather-instrument he-sets› *chairman* (HS).

-athehnuri – scarecrow. *dv.n.s.* rathehnù·rih ‹he-himself-field-stirs› *(he is a) scarecrow* (H 2484).

-athehtrak – be affable, be elegant, be estimable, be genteel. *v.r.-s.i.* stat: -ɸ, prog: -, prp: -, dst: -, caus: -, rvs: -, dat: -, n-inc. ruthéhtrak *he is affable, he is genteel: he is ruler* (R), yuthéhtrak *it is elegant* (HS), akuthéhtrak *she is estimable, she is a lady* (HS); **-a= thehtrakčr-**: uthehtrákčreh ‹be affable-'ness› *majesty* (HS).

-athehtrakčr – majesty. *n.s.* uthehtrákčreh ‹be affable-'ness› *majesty* (HS).

-ath(e)r – put oneself. *v.s.-a.i.* ęthra·k ‹fact-it-itself-put up› *it put itself* (RC 12:10).

-atherahwanhahsT – bracelet. *dv.n.s.* yętherahwanháhstha⁷ ‹one-oneself-green-wind-causes› *bracelet (originally made from braided grass)* (R).

-athe⁷ – pound. *v.r.-t.* hab: -θ, pnt: -ɸ, stat: -ɸ, prog: -, prp: -, dst: -, caus: -, rvs: -, dat: -, n-inc. Rarely encountered as a verb. wa⁷ká·the⁷ *I pounded it* (R), kayę́·the⁷θ *they are pounding it* (R); **-athe⁷čr-**: uthé⁷čreh ‹pound-'ness› *powder, flour* (RC 32:1); **-athe⁷čra⁷r-**: yuthé⁷čra⁷r ‹it-pound-'ness-is much› *powdery* (HS); **-či-**. **-athe⁷čręti-**: ęčęthe⁷črę́·ti⁷ ‹prediction-again-one-pound-'ness-make› *one will make powder again* (RC 15:10); **-athe⁷črih= s⁷a-**: wa⁷ęthe⁷čríhs⁷a·⁷ ‹fact-one-pound-'ness-finished› *one finished powder* (RC 3:54); **tha-**. **-athe⁷čru⁷nę-**: thahęthe⁷črú⁷nę· ‹unusual-fact-it-pound-'ness-was a kind of› *it was an unusual kind of powder* (RC 15:8).

-athe⁷čr – flour, powder. *n.s.* uthé⁷čreh ‹pound-'ness› *flour, powder* (RC 32:

1).

-athe⁷čra⁷r - powdery. *dv.n.s.* yuthé⁷čra⁷r ‹it-pound-'ness-is much› *powdery* (HS).

-athẹhn - obey. *v.r.-s.i.* stat: -e⁷, prog: -, prp: -, dst: -, caus: -, rvs: -, dat: -, n-inc. yuthẹ́hne⁷ *it obeys* (RC 30:29).

-athẹhnačk - be docile. *v.s.-a.i.* ruthẹhnáčkẹ· ‹he-himself-ear-stands-easily› *he is docile* (HS).

-athẹhnačT - audience. *dv.n.s.* ha⁷ kakuthẹhnáčtha⁷ ‹the they-themselves-earstand-for› *audience* (HS).

-athẹhnaT - listen. *v.s.-a.i.* hab: -s, pnt: -φ, stat: -e⁷. rathẹ́hna·č ‹he-himself-earstands› *he listens* (RC 30: 29), wakathẹhná·⁷ne⁷ ‹I-myself-ear-stand› *I am listening* (R).

-athẹhsuri - disquiet, disturb. *v.s.-a.i.* rathẹhsù·rih ‹he-himself-ear-stirs› *he disquiets himself so as not to hear something disagreeable, he is disturbed* (HS).

-athẹkarya⁷k - volunteer. *v.s.-a.i.* ruthẹkaryá⁷kẹ ‹he-himself-volunteer-broke› *he volunteered* (HS), rathẹká·rya⁷ks ‹he-himself-volunteer-breaks› *he volunteers* (HS); *volunteer* (R).

-athẹkarya⁷k - volunteer. *dv.n.s.* rathẹká·rya⁷ks ‹he-himself-volunteer-breaks› *volunteer* (R).

-athẹwanẹ'nakT - land a boat. *v.s.-a.i.* wa⁷akyathẹwa-nẹ́·⁷nakt ‹fact-another and I-boat-attach-caused› *the two of us landed a boat* (HS).

-athẹwa'nehT - dock, quay, pier, port. *dv.n.s.* wathẹwa⁷néhtha⁷ ‹it-itselfboat-be present-causes› *dock, quay, pier, port* (HS).

-athẹwuha - go by boat, go by water. *v.s.-a.i.* rathẹwúhahs ‹he-himself-boatputs in water› *he goes by water, he goes by boat* (HS).

-athẹ⁷ne⁷T - be a priority. *v.s.-a.i.* yuthẹ⁷né⁷nẹ ‹it-itself-be in frontcaused› *priority* (HS).

-athnekahninẹ - inn. *dv.n.s.* yẹthnekahnì·nẹh ‹one-oneself-liquor-buys› *inn* (HS).

-athnẹ - play ball. *v.r.-t.* hab: -hst-ha⁷, pnt: -⁷, stat: -·, prog: -, prp: -, dst: -, caus: -, rvs: -, dat: -, n-inc. Requires the the dualic prefix in verbal constructions. -athnẹhst -: uthnẹ́hsteh ‹play ball-'ness› *(game) ball; setting* (R); -athnẹhstẹti -: rathnẹhstẹ́·tih ‹heplay ball-'ness-makes› *he winds it into a ball (e.g., yarn)* (R); -ne -.-athnẹ -: nehráthnẹ ‹apart-he-played ball› *he plays ball* (RC 25:title), nehrathnẹ́hstha⁷ ‹apart-he-plays ball› *he plays ball* (RC 25:3), wa⁷thráthnẹ⁷ ‹factapart-he-played ball› *he played ball* (R); tha+ne -.-atkwe⁷nẹti - hané⁷či -a= thnẹhst -: tha⁷neyutkwe⁷nẹ́·ti· hané⁷či uthnẹ́hsteh‹unusual-apart-it-itself-arcmade that is-very play ball-'ness› *globular (round like ball)* (AG).

-athnẹhst - ball; setting sun. *n.s.* uthnẹ́hsteh ‹play ball-'ness› *(game) ball: setting sun* (R).

-athnẹhstẹti - wind into a ball. *v.s.-t.* rathnẹhstẹ́·tih ‹he-play ball-'ness-makes› *he winds it into a ball (e.g., yarn)* (R).

-athnẹhu'narhuhst - suspenders. *dv.n.s.* rathnẹhu⁷narhúhstha⁷ ‹he-himself-upper shoulder-hook-cause-causes› *his suspenders* (HS).

-athnẹhwa'niha - sprain one's shoulder. *v.s.-a.i.* rathnẹhwa⁷níhahs ‹he-himselfupper shoulder-sprains› *he sprains his shoulder* (HS).

-athnẹhwa'niha - sparrow hawk. *dv.n.s.* wathnẹhwa⁷níhahs ‹it-itself-upper shoulder-sprains› *sparrow hawk* (R).

-athrahthar - scold. *v.s.-t.* wa⁷kẹyathráhtha⁷r ‹fact-I=you-self-put up-causehung› *I scolded you* (AG), wa⁷na⁷-

nathráhtha⁷r ‹fact-one=another-self-put up-cause-hung› *she scolded (the boy)* (AG), wahsheyathráhtha⁷r ‹fact-you=another-self-put up-cause-hung› *you scolded (the boy)* (AG).

-athra⁷nęhT – molt, shed feathers. *v.s.-a.i.* wathra⁷nęhtha⁷ ‹it-itself-feather-fall-causes› *it (bird) molts, it sheds its feathers* (HS).

-athre⁷ – be blamable. *v.s.-a.i.* ruthré⁷ahs ‹he-himself-blames› *he is blamable* (HS).

-athre⁷ahst – censure. *dv.n.s.* yuthré⁷ahst ‹it-itself-blame-caused› *censure* (HS).

-athręhwaku – turn around, turn about. *v.s.-a.i.* wahrathręhwá·ku⁷ ‹fact-he-himself-put up-cause-undid› *he turned around* (L 79), rathręhwá·kwahs ‹he-himself-put up-cause-undoes› *he turns about* (HS).

-athręhwakuhę – revolve. *v.s.-a.i.* wathręhwakúhęh ‹it-itself-put up-causes-much› *it revolves* (HS).

-athriya⁷k – precipice. *dv.n.s.* yuthriyá⁷kę ‹it-itself-spill-broke› *precipice* (RC 8: 10).

-athriya⁷k – extremity. *dv.n.s.* ha⁷ yuthriyá⁷kę ‹the it-itself-spill-broke› *extremity* (HS).

-athriya⁷k-.#ú⁷y abyss. *dv.n.s.* yuthriya⁷kęhú⁷y ‹it-itself-spill-broke-great› *abyss* (HS).

-athuhku – bunch, clump, sheaf, tuft. *n.r.* n-poss., inc., n.sfx. -eh. uthúhkweh · *bunch, clump, sheaf, tuft* (R); **-athuh=kwęti** –: rathuhkwę́·tih ‹he-sheaf-makes› *he makes sheaves* (HS); **-a=**

thuhkwętyahnę –: ęhsathuhkwętyáhnę·⁷ ‹prediction-you-sheaf-make-many› *you will make clumps, you will make sheaves* (RC 30:34); ti –. **-athuhkwa⁷θrę** –: nęwathuhkwá⁷θrę·k ‹so-prediction-it-bunch-be so big› *clump will be so big* (RC 30:34); ti –. **-athuhkuha** –: nęyęthuhkúha⁷ ‹so-prediction-one-bunch-put in water› *one will put bunch of it in water* (RC 18: 11).

-athuhkwęti – make sheaves. *v.s.-a.i.* rathuhkwę́·tih ‹he-sheaf-makes› *he makes sheaves* (HS), ęhsathuhkwętyáhnę⁷ ‹prediction-you-sheaf-make-many› *you will make clumps, you will make sheaves* (RC 30:34).

-athukęhsT – be astride. *v.r.-a.i.* hab: -, pnt: -, stat: -ę, prog: -, prp: -, dst: -, caus: -, rvs: -, dat: -, n-inc. ruthukę́hsnę *he is astride* (HS).

-athurahT – be eldest, be senior. *dv.n.s.* rathuráhtha⁷ ‹he-himself-grow old-causes› *oldest male* (RC 13:3), *senior* (HS), yęthuráhtha⁷ ‹one-oneself-grow old-causes› *eldest* (RC 29:2).

á·thu⁷ cold (R) [Gallatin «authooh» 'Cold']. *part.* **athu⁷.#áh**: athu⁷áh ‹cold-little› *boreal, northerly* (HS); **athu⁷.#ke**: athú⁷kye ‹cold-at› *north* (R) [Lawson «Ho-thooka» 'Northwest wind']; **á·thu⁷ -r(i)yu** –: á·thu⁷ wakrì·yuhs ‹cold I-kill› *I am cold* (R); **-nęh=sathu⁷**: yunęhsá·thu⁷ ‹it-house-cold› *the house is cold, is subject to cold, is not built warm* (H 2484).

á·thu⁷ -r(i)yu – be cold (of humans). *v.s.-*

a.i. á·thu⁷ wakrì·yuhs ‹cold I-kill› *I am cold* (R).

athu⁷.#áh boreal, northerly. *n.s.* athu⁷áh ‹cold-little› *boreal, northerly* (HS).

athu⁷.#ke north. *n.s.* athú⁷kye ‹cold-at› *north* (R) [Lawson «Hothooka» 'Northwest wind'].

-athu⁷seryę(T) -{dative I} have a cold. *v.s.-a.i.* ruthu⁷seryę́⁷θe· ‹he-himself-cold-is laying-for› *he has a cold* (HS).

-athwarit - backpack, belongings, body. *n.s.* uthwarí·teh ‹self-backpack› *backpack, belongings, body (as a physical container for the non-corporal spirit)* (R).

-athwaritę'ni - leave body. *v.s.-a.i.* ęwakathwaritę̇·⁷ni⁷ ‹prediction-I-myself-backpack-throw› *my spirit will leave my body in death* (RC 11:24).

-athwari'nęti - pack up. *v.s.-a.i.* rathwari⁷nę́·tih ‹he-himself-backpack-makes› *he packs up* (HS).

-athwe⁷nęti - charge. *v.s.-a.i.* ęthwe⁷nę́·ti⁷ ‹fact-it-itself-furrow-made› *it (animal) charged* (AW 57).

-athwe⁷nętyęha'nye⁷ - push forward. *v.s.-a.i.* ruthwe⁷nętyęhá·⁷nye⁷ ‹he-himself-furrow-makes-going along› *he pushes forward* (R).

-athwęhs - liver. *n.r.* inaln: kathwęhsę́⁷kye *my liver (organ of my body)* (R), inc., n.sfx. -eh. uthwę́hseh *liver* (R); -⁷wahrawę – -athwęhs -: wak⁷wáhrawęh uthwę́hseh ‹I-meat-possess liver› *my liver (e.g., to eat)* (R).

-athwęr - deserve, earn, be worthy of. *v.r.-t.* hab: -e·θ, pnt: -ɸ, stat: -ę, prog: -, prp: -, dst: -, caus: -, rvs: -, dat: -, n-inc. ruthwę̀·rę *he is worthy of it, he has earned it* (HS), rathwę́·re·θ *he deserves it* (HS), ęhrá·thwęr *he will be worthy of it* (HS); kwęhs –athwęr –: kwęhs ahruthwę̀·ręk ‹no unknown-he-deserve› *he is undeserving* (HS).

-athwę⁷nak⁷u - bloat. *v.s.-a.i.* rathwę⁷ná·k⁷uhs ‹he-him-self-distended stomach-releases› *he bloats* (HS).

-athwę⁷r - lung. *n.r.* inaln: kathwę⁷rę́⁷kye *my lung* (R), inc., n.sfx. -eh. Anthony F.C. Wallace (p. 76) cites the form uthwę́⁷seh from Nellie Gansworth, a speaker of the s-dialect of Eastern Tuscarora, although the *r* is not syllable-final here. uthwę́⁷reh *lung* (H-notebook).

-athwihshęti - force. *v.s.-t.* rathwihshę́·tih ‹he-himself-be strong-extends› *he forces it* (HS).

-athwihstarahkw - ravish, violate. *v.s.-t.* rathwihstaráhkhwa⁷ ‹he-himself-be strong-collects› *he ravishes* (HS), wa⁷kayęthwíhstrarahk ‹fact-they-themselves-money-collected› *they violated (females)* (AG).

-athwihstarahkw -{dative III} violate. *v.s.-t.* wa⁷kheyathwihstraráhkę⁷ ‹fact-I=another-myself-money-collected-for› *I violated (it)* (AG), kęyathwihstrarahkwá·tih ‹I=you-myself-money-collect-for› *I am violating (you)* (AG).

-athwihstętyahT - be money-making, be profitable. *v.s.-a.i.* yuthwihstę́·tyaht ‹it-itself-metal-make-causes› *(it is) money-making, (it is) profitable* (HS).

-athyatęhstatęhninę - stationer. *dv.n.s.* rathyatęhstatęhnì·nęh ‹he-himself-paper-sells› *stationer* (HS).

-(a)ti - dative. *v.r.sfx.* hab: -h, stat: -·, prog: -, prp: -, dst: -, caus: -, rvs: -. Member of dative series II and of dative series III that occurs in the habitual and stative aspects; the form -ati - occurs following roots and stems that end in a consonant or *i*, the form -ti - occurs elsewhere.

-atihar - hang (plural patient). *v.s.-t.* yučaratiharáhkę ‹it-door-are hung-instrument› *hinge* (HS); yuhseyatihará·wę·

‹it-ear of corn-are hanging-many› *ears of corn are hanging around* (RC 2:6); ranɛhsatíhar ‹he-house-are hanging› *he makes an addition to the house* (H 24 84).

–atihyečkna²nahnɛ – acrobat. *dv.n.r.* The constituent parts of this root/stem are uncertain, although it is clearly connected to the root of –ɛnɛhyečkn – somersault. ratihyečkna²náhnɛh *acrobat* (R).

–atihsthu – be small (plural patient). *v.s.- s.i.* wahahatíhsthɛ ‹it-path-are small› *roads are small* (H 2484); kahehnatíhsthɛ ‹it-field-are small› *the fields are small* (H 2484); kahɛ²natíhsthɛ ‹it-clearing-are small› *the meadows are small* (H 2484); kači²enatíhsthɛ ‹it-claw-are small› *its claws are small, the claws are small* (H 2484); kanɛhatíhsthɛ ‹it-corn-are small› *the corn grains are small* (H 2484); kanɛhsatíhsthɛ ‹it-house-are small› *the houses are small, diminutive* (H 2484).

–atiyɛ²k͏ʷ – shoot (plural patient). *v.s.-t.* Attested only in the cited construction. wa²karɛ²atiyɛ²khrɛ²ú²y ‹fact-it-tree-X-shot-many-great› *it shot many trees* (RC 5: 41).

–atkahči²ra²niha – squint. *v.s.-a.i.* ratkahči²ra²níhahs ‹he-himself-blink-sprains› *he squints* (HS).

–atkahkeθku – raise eyes. *v.s.-a.i.* wa²kayɛtkahkyé·θku² ‹fact-they-themselves-eye-raised› *they raised their eyes* (RC 3:77).

–atkahna²nahkw – raspberry. *dv.n.s.* The composition of this stem is uncertain. The initial –at – is apparently the semireflexive. watkahna²náhkwahs ‹it-itself-??› *raspberry (Rubus sp.)* (HS).

–atkahnɛ – cook. *v.s.-a.i.* ratkáhnɛh ‹he-himself-cooks› *he cooks* (HS).

–atkahnɛhkw – flints, something to start a fire. *dv.n.s.* yɛtkahnɛ́hkhwa² ‹one-oneself-cooks-instrument› *flints, something to start fire with* (RC 8:13).

–atkahnɛhw – wake up. *v.r.-a.i.* hab: -, pnt: -ɸ, stat: -, prog: -, prp: -, dst: -, caus: -, rvs: -, dat: -, inc.-ɸ-pat. -t+či –. –atkahnɛhw –: nɛθkayɛtkáhnɛw ‹hither-prediction-again-they-wake up› *they will wake up again* (RC 8:3).

–atkahnɛti –{dative III} build a fire, kindle. *v.s.-a.i.* wa²ɛtkahnɛ́·tyɛ² ‹fact-one-oneself-cook-made-for› *one built a fire* (RC 3:39).

–atkahrahtrɛ – be blindfolded. *v.s.-a.i.* ratkahráhtrɛhs ‹he-himself-eye-ties› *he is blindfolded* (HS).

–atkahrat²ahsT – telescope. *dv.n.s.* yɛtkahrat²áhstha² ‹one-oneself-eye-be filled-causes› *telescope* (HS).

–atkahri – tell. *v.r.-a.i.* hab: -ɛhs, pnt: -e², stat: -ɛ, prog: -, prp: -, dst: -hɛ-, caus: -e²T-, rvs: -, dat: I (-²θe-/-²θ-), inc.-ɸ-pat. Forms cited by Floyd Lounsbury show a different set of primary aspects, namely, hab: -e·, pnt: -e·², stat: -eh, suggesting that the root had been analogically remodeled to –atkahrye – by the speakers with whom he worked. In their manuscript dictionary, Hewitt & Smith also show an ir-

regular habitual form. **ratkáhrih** *he warns*. rutkáhrye· *he has told* (L 21), ratkáhryeh *he tells* (L 21), wahratkáhrye·ʔ *he told* (L 21), ęhsatkáhryeʔ *you will tell* (RC 3:61), wahratkáhryeʔ *he told* (RC 6:3); **–atkahri –** {**dative I**}: ahskwatkahríʔθek ‹unknown-you=me-tell-for› *that you had told me* (R), naʔnatkahríʔθeh ‹one=another-tells-for› *one informs another* (HS), kęyatkahríʔθeh ‹I=you-tell-for› *I am telling you* (R), waʔnaʔnatkáhriʔθ ‹fact-one=another-told-for› *one told another* (RC 35:29); **–atkahrye= hętyę –**: kayętkahryehętyéhahk ‹they-told-much-much-had› *they had told* (RC 3:1); **–atkahryeʔčr –**: utkahryéʔčreh ‹tell-'ness› *story* (HS); **ti –**. **–atkah= ryeʔruʔnę –**: tiwatkahryeʔčrúʔnę· ‹so-it-tell-'ness-is a kind of› *such is the kind of account or report* (R); **kwęhs –atkahryeʔT –**: kwęhs aryutkahryéʔnek ‹no unknown-it-tell-cause› *it is inexpressible* (HS); **haʔ –atkahri –**: haʔ rutkáhryeʔ ‹the he-told› *testimony* (HS).
–atkahri – testimony. *dv.n.s.* haʔ rutkáhryeʔ ‹the he-told› *testimony* (HS).
–atkahri –{**dative I**} tell. *v.s.-t.* ahskwatkahríʔθek ‹unknown-you=me-tell-for› *that you had told me* (R), naʔnatkahríʔθeh ‹one=another-tells-for› *one informs another* (HS), kęyatkahríʔθeh ‹I=you-tell-for› *I am telling you* (R), waʔnaʔnatkáhriʔθ ‹fact-one=another-told-for› *one told another* (RC 35:29).
–atkahryeʔčr – story. *n.s.* utkahryéʔčreh ‹tell-'ness› *story* (R).
–atkahthu – look at. *v.r.-t.* hab: -hs, pnt: -ʔ, stat: -ę, prog: -, prp: -, dst: -, caus: -hT-, rvs: -, dat: -, inc.-ɸ-pat. With the translocative prefix the meaning of this root becomes *watch*. ratkáhthuhs *he looks* (R), θwatkáhthu *look at it!* (RC 3:76), waʔkayętkáhthuʔ *they*

looked at it (RC 7:7); **–atkahthuhT –**: ęhskwatkahtúhthek ‹prediction-you=me-look at-cause› *you will use it to remember me by* (RC 35:16); **–yah+ či –.–atkahthu –**: yahęθętkáhthuʔ ‹thither-prediction-again-you-look at› *again it watched there* (RC 26:34).
–atkahrʔu – blink, wink. *v.s.-a.i.* -t-. **–atkahrʔu –**: nahratkárʔuʔ ‹hither-he-himself-eye-exhibited› *he blinked, he winked* (RC 26:28); **haʔ –atkahrʔu –**: haʔ ratkárʔuhs ‹the he-himself-eye-exhibits› *nystagmus* (HS).
–atkahrʔu – nystagmus. *dv.n.s.* haʔ ratkárʔuhs ‹the he-himself-eye-exhibits› *nystagmus* (HS).
–atkahthuhT – use to remember. *v.s.-t.* ęhskwatkahthúhthek ‹prediction-you=me-look at-cause› *you will use it to remember me by* (RC 35:16).
–atkanęnyaht luxury. *n.r.* poss. ?, n-inc., n.sfx. -. This root is ultimately a stem derived with the causative suffix –hT– from a verb root that is otherwise unattested. utkanę·nyaht *luxury* (R), yutkanę·nyaht *luxury* (HS).
–atkarayę'nahkw – pledge. *v.s.-a.i.* ratkarayęʔnáhkhwaʔ ‹he-himself-debt-lays-instrument› *he pledges* (HS).
–atkaraʔw – be rough. *v.r.-s.i.* stat: -ę, prog: -, prp: -, dst: -, caus: -, rvs: -, dat: -, inc.-ɸ-pat. yutkaráʔwę *it is rough* (HS).
–atkaręhw – turn. *v.s.-a.i.* yutkaręhę ‹it-itself-went around› *it has turned* (HS), ratkà·ręws ‹he himself-goes around› *he turns (out or away)* (HS).
–atkaręhw – turn. *dv.n.s.* yutkaręhę ‹it-itself-went around› *turn* (HS).
–atkaręniʔ – damned. *dv.n.s.* haʔ kakutkaręníʔę ‹the they-themselves-damage-began› *the damned* (HS).
–atkaruharT – indemnity. *dv.n.s.* yutkaruhárnę ‹it-itself-debt-wash-caused› *in-*

demnity (HS).

–atk<u>a</u>rut owe. *v.s.-t.* yękyátkaru·t ‹we two-ourselves-debt-stand› *I owe another or you. another or you owe me* (SH 375).

–atk<u>a</u>rya^ʔk – pension. *dv.n.s.* ratkaryá^ʔki ‹he-himself-debt-broke› *his pension* (HS).

–atkehnahsi – unfasten and remove from back. *v.s.-t.* wa^ʔętkyehnáhsi^ʔ ‹fact-one-oneself-fasten on back-undid› *one unfastened it and took it off one's back* (RC 3:41).

–atkehnaT – carry a burden. *v.s.-a.i.* yętkyéhna·č ‹one-oneself-fastens on back› *one carries a burden* (R).

–atkehnawek take shape. *v.r.-a.i.* hab: -, pnt: -ɸ, stat: -, prog: -, prp: -, dst: -, caus: -, rvs: -, dat: -, n-inc. ętkyehná·we·k *it took shape* (RC 26:33).

–atkehr – be heaped, be piled, be stacked. *v.s.-s.i.* yutkyéhrę^ʔ ‹it-itself-piled› *they are heaped, they are piled, they are stacked (applicable to a collection of inanimate objects)* (H 2892).

–atkehr – lump, tumor. *n.s.* utkyéhreh ‹self-pile› *lump, tumor* (HS).

–atkerh<u>a</u>nę – protect oneself. *v.s.-a.i.* a-ryętkyérhanę·t ‹unknown-one-oneself-body-guard-complete› *that one protect oneself* (RC 17:2).

–atkerh<u>a</u>r –{dative III} draw. *v.s.-t.* wa^ʔ-katkyerhà·rę^ʔ ‹fact-I-myself-body-was in-for› *I drew myself* (R).

–atkerh<u>a</u>raku – remove, take away. *v.s.-a.i.* ętkyerhará·ku^ʔ ‹fact-it-itself-body-collect› *it took itself away* (RC 2:8).

–atkerha^ʔne^ʔku – pull back, withdraw. *v.s.-a.i.* ęhsatkyerha^ʔné^ʔku^ʔ ‹prediction-you-yourself-body-flee› *you will pull back, you will withdraw* (RC 3: 54).

–atkerhihs^ʔa – grow to adulthood. *v.s.-a.i.* wa^ʔętkyerhíhs^ʔa·^ʔ ‹fact-one-oneself-body-finished› *one grew to adulthood* (RC 3:37).

–atkeyu – feel bad. *v.r.-s.i.* stat: -^ʔ, prog: -, prp: -, dst: -, caus: -, rvs: -, dat: -, n-inc. wakatkyè·yu^ʔ *I don't feel well* (R).

–atke^ʔθr<u>a</u>rurę – scowl. *v.s.-a.i.* ratkye^ʔθrarù·ręh ‹he-himself-frown-donates› *he scowls* (HS).

–atke^ʔθręti – scowl. *v.s.-a.i.* ratkye^ʔθrę́·tih ‹he-himself-frown-makes› *he scowls* (HS).

–atke^ʔth(e)r – go to visit. *v.r.-t.* hab: -()ɸ, pnt: -a^ʔ, stat: -()^ʔ, prog: -, prp: -, dst: -, caus: -, rvs: -, dat: -, n-inc. The epenthetic (e) at the end of this root is present whenever no other vowel follows the root and absent otherwise. ratkyé^ʔther *he visits (the sick)* (R), kayę^ʔna^ʔnatkyé^ʔther *they go to visit another* (RC 5:38); –či–. –atke^ʔth(e)r – {dative III}: ęθkęyatkyé^ʔthrę^ʔ ‹prediction-again-I=you-go to visit-for› *I will return to visit you* (RC 35:18).

–atke^ʔwraku – wig. *dv.n.s.* yętkye^ʔwrákhwa^ʔ ‹one-oneself-hair-collects› *wig* (HS).

–atkę – inherent power; sorcerer, witch. *n.r. inaln:* rútkę^ʔ *his inherent power; sorcerer* (RC 13:commentary), inc., n.

sfx. -ʔ. The gloss given here and elsewhere for this root is but an approximation of the meaning. The root refers to a type of power that all objects in nature—animate and inanimate— possess. This power may be latent or overt. When exercised, it may be beneficial or malevolent in nature. Probably under the influence of the recent (mid-l9th century) Christianization of the Tuscarora, the root is also used to refer to spirits, especially evil or bad spirits. útkęʔ *inherent power* (RC 11:20), kakútkęʔ *witches* (RC 13:commentary); **-atkęhT** -: útkęht ‹inherent power-cause› *witchcraft* (RC 30:70); **-atkęhčraks** -: utkęhčrá·ksę· ‹it-inherent power-'ness-be bad› *evil spirit from whom all witches get their power* (HS)ʹ; **-atkęhčraks** -.**#úʔy**: utkęhčraksęhúʔy ‹it-inherent power-'ness-be bad-great› *Satan, Apollyon* (HS); **-a =ʹnatkęhčręʹnahkw** -:ruʔnatkęhčręʔnahkęheʔ ‹he-himself-inherent power-'ness-end-instrument-had› *it had knocked the evilness out of him* (RC 30: 56); **čwe** -. **-atkęʔčrake** -: čwewatkęʔ- črá·kye· ‹all kinds of-it-inherent power-'ness-is in number› *all kinds of monsters* (AG).

-atkęh be brother. *v.s.-k.* kayętkęh ‹they- themselves-are brothers› *brothers* (AW 55).

-atkęh - be rancid, be rotten. *v.r.-a.i.* hab: -θ, pnt: -ɸ, stat: -ɸ, prog: -, prp: -, dst: -, caus: -T-, rvs: -, dat: -, inc.-ɸ-pat. Lounsbury gives [yú:tʼgɜ·ʔ] *rot* (L 75) (= yú·tkę·ʔ) and [yurɜʔá:tʼgɜ·ʔ] *the tree is rotten* (L 75) (= yuręʔá·tkę·ʔ). yú·tkęh *it is rotten* (R), waʔú·tkęh *it got rotten* (RC 21:3); **-ekatkęh** -: ya- weká·tkęhθ ‹it-liquid-is rotten› *stagnant water* (HS); **-ęhratkęh** -: yawęh- rá·tkęh ‹it-dirt-is rotten› *fallow* (HS);

-hskęʔratkęh -: yuhskęʔrá·tkęhθ ‹it- bone-is rotten› *carries, tooth decay* (HS); **-keʔčatkęhnahkw** -: yekyeʔča- tkęhnáhkhwaʔ ‹one-dough-be rotten- causes-instrument› *one leavens it* (HS); **-ʔtyęhsatkęh** -: kaʔtyęhsá·tkęhθ ‹it-nose-is rotten› *catarrh* (HS).

-atkęha - arise, get out of bed. *v.s.-a.i.* θatkę́ha ‹you!-yourself-raise› *get up!, get out of bed!* (R), ratkę́hahs ‹he- himself-raises› *he rises, he gets up* (HS), wahratkę́haʔ ‹fact-he-himself- raised› *he arose* (RC 5:19).

-atkęhčraks - evil spirit. *n.s.* utkęhčrá·ksę· ‹it-inherent power-'ness-be bad› *evil spirit from whom all witches get their power* (HS).

-atkęhčraks -.**#uʔy** Satan, Apollyon. *n.s.* utkęhčraksęhúʔy ‹it-inherent power- 'ness-be bad-great› *Satan, Apollyon* (HS).

-atkęheyęʔnayęʹnahkw - hospital, infirmary. *dv.n.s.* yętkęheyęʔnayęʔnáhkhwaʔ ‹one-oneself-die-cause-lays-instrument› *hospital, infirmary* (HS).

-atkęheyęʔnęhawiʔnahkw - litter, stretcher. *dv.n.s.* yętkęheyęʔnęhawiʔnáh- khwaʔ ‹one-oneself-die-cause-carry- causes-instrument› *litter, stretcher* (HS).

-atkęhθr - purulence, pus, rot, slime; leather wood. *n.r.* n-poss., inc., n.sfx. -eh ~ -iʔ. utkę́hθreh *purulence, pus, rot, slime* (R), utkę́hθriʔ *leather wood (Dirca palustris)* (H-notebook); **-a = tkęhθrak** -: ętkę́hθra·k ‹fact-it-rot-ate› *it ate pus* (RC 21:10); **-atkęhθra = rahkw** -: yutkęhθraráhkę ‹it-rot-collec- ted› *it collects pus* (RC 21:11); **-a = tkęhθraʔθ** -: watkę́hθraʔθ ‹it-rot-is of a size› *fetid, it smells of rot* (HS); **-atkęhθrur** -: ętkę́hθruʔ ‹fact-it-rot-cov- ered› *it gets pustular* (R); **-atkęhθrur** -. **#úʔy**: ętkęhθruʔúʔy ‹fact-it-rot-covered-great› *it was covered greatly with pus* (RC 21: 3); tha–. **–atkęhθrạrahkw –:** thahętkę́hθrarahk ‹unusual-fact-it-rot-collected› *the pus was in it* (RC 21:6).

–atkęhθraʔθ – fetid; smell of rot. *v.s.-s.i.* watkę́hθraʔθ ‹it-rot-is of a size› *fetid, it smells of rot* (HS).

–atkęhθru – get pustular. *v.s.-a.i.* ętkę́hθruʔ ‹fact-it-rot-covered› *it gets pustular* (R).

–atkęhsahθuh – paint face. *v.s.-a.i.* ratkęhsahθúhahs ‹he-himself-face-paints› *he paints his face* (HS).

–atkęhsayataʔT – grimace. *v.s.-a.i.* ratkęhsayatá́ʔthaʔ ‹he-himself-face-pouts› *he makes grimaces* (H-notebook), ratkęhsayataʔnáhnęh ‹he-himself-face-pouts-much› *he makes grimaces, he grimaces* (H-notebook).

–atkęhsạ'nęʔθahnę – tattoo marks. *dv.n.s.* watkęhsaʔnęʔθáhnęh ‹it-itself-face-writes-much› *tattoo marks* (SH 375).

–atkęhst – brother. *n.s.* utkę́hsteh ‹self-be younger sibling-'ness› *brother (very rare)* (HS).

–atkęhsuhči – unmask oneself. *v.s.-a.i.* ratkęhsúhčęhs ‹he-himself-face-removes› *he unmasks himself* (HS).

–atkęhsurę – False Face, mask. *n.s.* utkęhsù·rę ‹self-face-cover› *False Face, mask* (HS), yutkęhsù·rę ‹it-itself-face-cover› *mask* (AW 46).

–atkęhsu'narhuhsT – halter. *dv.n.s.* watkęhsuʔnarhúhsthaʔ ‹it-itself-face-hooks-for› *halter* (HS).

–atkęhT – witchcraft. *n.s.* útkęht ‹inherent power-cause› *witchcraft* (RC 30:70).

–atkęhy – lust. *n.r.* n-poss., n-inc., n.sfx. -eh. utkę́hyeh *lust* (HS).

–atkęnihsʔa – hold council. *v.s.-a.i.* eθwatkęníhsʔa·ʔ ‹unknown-you-yourselves-excel-finish› *that you hold council* (R), kakutkęníhsʔę ‹they-themselves-excel-finished› *they counseled* (RC 12:8); ratkęníhsʔahs *councilman* (AG); **–atkęnihsʔaʔT –:** yętkęnihsʔáʔthaʔ ‹one-oneself-excel-finish-causes› *council house* (R); **–atkęnihsʔa –.#úʔy:** waʔkayętkęnihsʔa·ʔúʔy ‹fact-they-themselves-excel-finished-great› *they had a great council* (RC 12:16).

–atkęnihsʔa – councilman. *n.s.* ratkęníhsʔahs *councilman* (AG).

–atkęnihsʔaʔT – council house. *dv.n.s.* yętkęnihsʔáʔthaʔ ‹one-oneself-excel-finish-causes› *council house* (R).

–atkęryaʔkhę – grizzly bear. *dv.n.s.* yutkęryáʔkhę· ‹it-it-self-cut a crease around-much› *grizzly bear (Ursus horribilis)* (HS).

–atkętyęyaʔT – cling. *v.s.-a.i.* rutkętyęyáʔnę ‹he-himself-hump-hang down-caused› *he clung* (R).

–atkę'netyaʔT – be changeable, be mutable. *v.s.-s.i.* yutkęʔnetyáʔnę ‹it-itself-change-caused› *it is changeable, it is mutable* (HS).

–atkęʔθe – examine, investigate, view, watch. *v.s.-t.* ratkę́ʔθeh ‹he-himself-sees-going to› *he examines, he investigates, he views* (HS), kayętkę́ʔθeh ‹they-them-selves-see-going to› *they are watching* (R).

–atkęʔθe – spectator. *dv.n.s.* haʔ ratkę́ʔ-

θeh ‹the he-himself-see-going to›
spectator (HS).

–atkę ͐θehstaw – come to look at. *v.s.-t.*
kayętkę ͐θéhstaws ‹they-themselves-
see-going to-'ness-come› *they come to
look at* (RC 5:37).

–atkę ͐θrahkw – be a foundation, be a
support. *v.s.-s.i.* yutkę ͐θráhkę ‹it-it-
self-supported-instrument› *it is supported by: foundation* (HS).

–atkę ͐θrur – form matter. *v.s.-a.i.* watkę ͐-
θru ͐ ‹it-itself-support-covers› *it forms
matter* (HS).

–atkiwaT – be the worst. *v.r.-a.i.* hab: -
ha ͐, pnt: -, stat: -, prog: -, prp: -, dst:
-, caus: -, rvs: -, dat: -, n-inc.
ratkiwá·tha ͐ *he is the worst* (H-notebook).

–atkrenęT – bray. *v.r.-a.i.* hab: -s, pnt: -,
stat: -, prog: -, prp: -, dst: -, caus: -,
rvs: -, dat: -, n-inc. ratkrè·nęč *he brays*
(HS).

–atkręhT – blubber, flab, fat, obesity. *n.s.*
utkrę́hneh ‹be corpulent› *blubber, flab,
fat, obesity* (HS).

–atkręhT – be corpulent, be fat. *v.r.-s.i.*
stat: -e ͐, prog: -, prp: -, dst: -, caus: -,
rvs: -, dat: -, n-inc. ratkrę́hne ͐ *he is
corpulent* (HS); –atkręhT –: utkrę́hneh
‹be corpulent› *blubber, flab, fat, obesity* (HS).

–atku – rob, take away, usurp. *v.s.-a.i.*
rá·tkwahs ‹he-himself-gets› *he robs,
he usurps, he takes away* (HS), rú·t-
kwę ‹he-himself-got› *he usurped* (HS),
ęhrá·tkwa ͐‹prediction-he-himself-get›
he will usurp (HS).

–atku – usurpation. *dv.n.s.* ha ͐ rú·tkwę
‹the he-himself-got› *usurpation* (HS).

–atkuhkw – be bloated, be large. *v.r.-s.i.*
stat: -e ͐, prog: -, prp: -, dst: -, caus: -,
rvs: -, dat: -, n-inc. ratkúhkwe ͐ *he is
bloated, he is large* (HS); –atkuhkwi =
yu –: ratkuhkwì·yuh ‹hc-be bloated-is

great› *he is bloated, he is large* (HS).

–atkuhkwiyu – be bloated, be large. *v.s.-
a.i.* ratkuhkwì·yuh ‹he-be bloated-is
great› *he is bloated, he is large* (HS).

–atkuwihsT – be reserved. *v.r.-s.i.* stat: -ę,
prog: -, prp: -, dst: -, caus: -, rvs: -,
dat: -, n-inc. rutkuwíhsnę *he is reserved* (HS).

–atku ͐čęnya ͐T – beautify oneself. *v.r.-a.i.*
hab: -ha ͐, pnt: -ɸ, stat: -ę, prog: -,
prp: -, dst: -, caus: -, rvs: -, dat: -, n-
inc. yętku ͐čęnyá ͐tha ͐ *one beautifies
oneself* (RC 17:4), ęyętku ͐čę́·nya ͐t
one will beautify oneself (RC 17: 4).

–atkwahčr – dance. *n.s.* utkwáhčreh ‹self-
pick up-'ness› *dance* (HS).

–atkʷahnahkw – be abrupt. *v.s.-s.i.* yutkwahnáhkę ‹it-it-self-cut off-instrument *it is abrupt* (HS).

–atkʷahnaku – have success. *v.s.-a.i.* ra-
tkwahná·kwahs ‹he-himself-cut off-
cause-undoes› *he has success* (HS).

–atkwahnę – wiggle. *v.r.-a.i.* hab: -h, pnt:
-, stat: -, prog: -, prp: -, dst: -, caus: -,
rvs: -, dat: -, n-inc. ratkwáhnęh *he
wiggles* (R).

–atkʷahT – be brittle; be stopped. *v.s.-a.i.*
watkwáhtha ͐ ‹it-itself-cuts off› *it is
brittle* (HS), ęwátkwaht ‹prediction-it-
itself-cut off› *it will stop* (RC 3:20).

–atkwariha ͐T – hurry up. *v.s.-a.i.* θatkwa-
ríha ͐t ‹you!-yourself-hurry› *hurry up!*
(R), rutkwarihá ͐nę ‹he-himself-hur-
ried› *he is hurrying* (R).

–atkwatihčayęhst – embolden. *v.s.-a.i.*
ratkwatihčayę́hstha ͐ ‹he-stomach-is
cowardly-causes› *he emboldens himself* (H-notebook).

–atkwa ͐naku – prosper. *v.r.-a.i.* hab: -ahs,
pnt: -, stat: -, prog: -, prp: -, dst: -,
caus: -, rvs: -, dat: -, n-inc. ratkwa ͐-
ná·kwahs *he prospers* (R).

–atkwehawek – be full of maggots, be
eaten by vermin. *v.r.-a.i.* hab: -s, pnt:

-, stat: -, prog: -, prp: -. dst: -, caus: -, rvs: -, dat: -, n-inc. rutkwéhaweks *he is maggoty, he is eaten by vermin* (H-notebook).

-atkweni – win. *v.s.-a.i.* rutkwé·nyę ‹he-himself-was able› *he has won* (L 40), ratkwé·nyęhs ‹he-himself-is able› *he wins* (HS), wa'kayętkwè·ni' ‹fact-they-themselves-were able› *they won* (R).

-atkwerih – covet, desire. *v.r.-t.* hab: -θ, pnt: -ɸ, stat: -ę, prog: -, prp: -, dst: -, caus: -, rvs: -, dat: -, inc.-ɸ-pat. rutkweríhę *he coveted it, he desired it* (HS), ratkwè·rihθ *he covets it, he desires it* (HS); **–činę'theratkwerih** –: račinę'theratkwè·rihθ ‹he-curl-covets› *he longs for the curl: he longs for the curly-headed person—for curly hair* (H 2484); **–hehnatkwerih** –: rahehnatkwè·rihθ ‹he-field-covets› *he longs for the field, desires fondly to own the field* (H 2484); **–nęhatkwerih** –: ranęhatkwè·rihθ ‹he-corn-covets› *he fondly wants the corn, desires the corn with longing* (H 2484).

-atkweru'nawyęhę – be artful, be crafty. *v.s.-a.i.* rutkweru'nawyęhęh ‹he-himself-X-knows-much› *he is artful, he is crafty* (HS).

-atkwe'nęti – move. *v.s.-a.i.* ratkwe'nę́·tyę ‹he-himself-movement-made› *he moved* (RC 24:10); ti –. **–atkwe'nęti** –: tiwatkwe'nę́·tyę ‹so-it-itself-movement-made-for› *it has moved* (RC 15:7).

-atkwęnyęhsnęha'nye' – decently. *dv.n.s.* yutkwęnyęhsnęhá·'nye' ‹it-itself-treated with respect-going along› *decently* (HS).

-atkwęnyęhsT – civility, decency, politeness. *dv.n.s.* yutkwę́·nyęhst ‹it-itself-treats with respect› *civility, decency, politeness* (HS).

-atkwęnyęhsT – respectability. *dv.n.s.* ha' yutkwę́·nyęhst ‹the it-itself-treats with respect› *respectability* (HS).

-(a)tkwir – branch. *n.r.* n-poss., inc., n.sfx. -eh. utkwì·reh *branch* (R); **–(a)=tkwira'ke**: utkwirá·'kye ‹branch-at› *on branch* (RC 15:2); **–ne –. –(a)tkwira'ne** –: newatkwirá·'nę' ‹two-it-branch-is present› *picnic* (HS); **–ne –. –(a)tkwira'neh=te'** –: wa'tkatkwira'néhte' ‹fact-two-it-branch-was present-going to› *picnic* (R); **–yah –. –(a)tkwira'ne** –: wekatkwirá·'ne' ‹thither-it-branch-is present› *crown of tree* (AG), *end of branch* (RC 4:1); **–ne –. –atkwiru'y(e)** –: nehratkwirú'yęhs ‹two-he-himself-branch-bends› *he bends the sapling to himself* (H-notebook).

-atkwi'T – move away. *v.s.-a.i.* ęwátkwi't ‹prediction-it-itself-move away› *it will move away* (RC 23:4).

-atr – beam, column, pole. *n.r.* n-poss., inc., n.sfx. -eh. ú·treh *beam, column, pole* (R); **–atrayę(T)** –: wá·trayę' ‹it-pole-lays› *post (lying down on ground)* (AG); **–atra'nihr** –: watra'níhrę ‹it-pole-stands up› *upright beam, column, pole* (R); **–ne –. –atre'rukę** –: nęyutre'rú·kę·k ‹apart-prediction-it-pole-be forked› *it will be a forked*

---

pole (R), neyutre'rukȩ́hsthȩ' ‹apart-it-pole-is forked-many› *it is "V" shaped* (RC 6:11); –t–. –**atrahrȩhwatyȩ** –: tkaku-trahrȩhwá·tyȩ' ‹hither-they-pole-put up-cause-many› *they put poles around* (RC 6:12).

–**atra'θw** – luck. *n.r.* n-poss., inc., n.sfx. -. Found only incorporated. –**atra'** = **θwaks** –: θatra'θwá·ksȩ· ‹you-luck-is bad› *you have bad luck* (R); –**atra'** = **θwaksa'T** –: yutra'θwá·ksa'ʔt ‹it-luck-be bad-causes› *it is disastrous, it causes ill-fortune* (HS); –**atra'θwak** = **sȩ'** –: yutra'θwaksȩ́'ȩ ‹it-luck-be bad-began› *misfortune* (HS); –**atra'θwiyu** –: θatra'θwí·yu· ‹you-luck-is great› *you have good luck* (R), čhiyatra'θwí·yu·k ‹you all!-luck-is great› *prosper!* (AG), wakatra'θwí·yu· ‹I-luck-is great› *I prosper* (AG).

–**atra'θwaks** – have bad luck. *v.s.-s.i.* θatra'θwá·ksȩ· ‹you-luck-is bad› *you have bad luck* (R).

–**atra'θwaksa'T** – be disastrous, cause ill-fortune. *v.s.-s.i.* yutra'θwá·ksa'ʔt ‹it-luck-be bad-causes› *it is disastrous, it causes ill-fortune* (HS).

–**atra'θwaksȩ'** – misfortune. *dv.n.s.* yutra'θwaksȩ́'ȩ ‹it-luck-be bad-began› *misfortune* (HS).

–**atra'θwiyu** – have good luck, prosper. *v.s.-s.i.* θatra'θwí·yu· ‹you-luck-is great› *you have good luck* (R); čhiyatra'θwí·yu·k ‹you all!-luck-is great› *prosper!* (AG), wakatra'θwí·yu· ‹I-luck-is great› *I prosper* (AG).

–**atrȩnayȩ** – pray. *v.r.-a.i.* hab: -, pnt: -', stat: -, prog: -, prp: -, dst: -, caus: -, rvs: -, dat: -, n-inc. wahratrȩ̀·nayȩ' *he prayed* (R), ȩkatrȩ̀·nayȩ' *I will pray* (R); –**atrȩnayȩ** –{dative II}: nekheyatrȩ-nayȩ́·tih ‹two-I=another-pray-for› *I marry him to her* (AG); –**atrȩnayȩta'** = čr– utrȩnayȩtá'čreh ‹pray-X-'ness›

prayer (HS); –**yan(e)(r)** – –**atrȩnayȩta'** = **črawȩ** –: Ruyà·ner Rutrȩnayȩta'črà·wȩh ‹he-rules he-pray-lay-'ness-possesses› *Lord's Prayer* (HS).

–**atrȩnayȩ** –{dative II} marry. *v.s.-t.* nekheyatrȩnayȩ́·tih ‹two-I=another-pray-for› *I marry him to her* (AG).

–**atrȩnayȩta'čr** – prayer. *dv.n.s.* utrȩna-yȩtá'čreh ‹pray-X-'ness› *prayer* (HS).

–**aturaT** – hunt. *v.r.-t.* hab: -hs, pnt: -, stat: -ȩ, prog: -ȩha'nye'-, prp: -he'-, dst: -hȩ-, caus: -, rvs: -, dat: -, n-inc. The fact that intervocalic *t* is preserved unchanged shows that this root is borrowed from another Northern Iroquoian language. However, in all dialects of Tuscarora, the final consonant of this root undergoes the uniquely Tuscarora alternation of *t* and *'n*, showing that it has been at least partially nativized. ratú·ra·č *he hunts: hunter* (RC 12:4), kayetú·ra·č *hunters* (RC 24:2); –**aturaT** –.**#aka·'**: raturač'á·ka·' ‹he-hunts-characterized by› *professional hunter* (R); –**aturathe'** –: raturá·the'θ ‹he-hunts-going to› *he is going hunting* (RC 12:2), raturá·the' ‹he-hunted-going to› *he is going hunting, he has gone hunting: amateur hunter* (RC 24:1), ȩhsaturá·thek ‹prediction-you-hunt-going to› *you will hunt* (RC 30:28); –**aturathȩ** –: raturá·thȩhs ‹he-hunts-many› *he goes hunting for some* (RC 12:2); ti –. –**atura'nȩha'nye'** –: tihru-tura'nȩhá·'nye' ‹so-he-hunted-going along› *he was going along hunting* (RC 5:2).

–**aturaT** – hunter. *dv.n.s.* ratú·ra·č *hunter* (RC 12:4), kayetú·ra·č *hunters* (RC 24:2)

–**aturaT** –.**#aka·'** professional hunter. *n.s.* raturač'á·ka·' ‹he-hunts-characterized by› *professional hunter* (R).

–**aturathe'** – amateur hunter. *dv.n.s.* raturá·the⁷ ‹he-hunted-going to› *amateur hunter* (RC 24:1).

-(a)tyę- many, much (distributive). *v.r.sfx.* hab: -h, pnt: -·⁷, stat: -·, prog: -, prp: -, caus: -, rvs: -, dat: -. The distributive is used to indicate either that the action of the verb is spread over time or that the object of the verb is distributed over an area (e.g., **wahraturá·tyę·⁷** ‹fact-he-swim-much› *he swam all over the place*). The form **-atyę-** occurs after certain roots and stems that end in a consonant or *i*, the form **-tyę-** occurs elsewhere.

-(a)t⁷a-/-(a)t⁷ah- put in. *v.r.-t.* hab: -hs, pnt: -·⁷, stat: -ę, prog: -, prp: -, dst: -, caus: -, rvs: -, dat: -, inc.-φ-ag./ pat. The forms **-at⁷ah-** and **-t⁷ah-** occur in the imperative. The forms beginning with *t* occur following the feminine/ indefinite agent and the third person plural agent pronominal prefixes. The forms beginning with *a* occur elsewhere. In the stative aspect this root has the idiomatic meaning of *be full, be satisfied*, the subject being marked by a patient pronominal prefix. With the reflexive and the empty noun root **-r-** the stem means *get in*. waká·t⁷ę *I am full, I am satisfied* (R), nęyé·t⁷a·⁷ *the two of them will put it in* (RC 15:6); **-yah+či-.-(a)t⁷a-:** yahęčé·t⁷a·⁷ ‹thither-fact-again-one-put in› *one put it back in there* (RC 15:8); **-či-.-a'nę⁷= teyat⁷a-:** čę⁷nę⁷teyá·t⁷a·⁷ ‹again-fact-one-oneself-crowd-put in› *crowd got back in* (R); **-(ę)⁷tikęhrat⁷a-:** ru⁷tikęh-rá·t⁷ę ‹he-mind-put in› *he advises* (HS), na⁷tikęhrá·t⁷ahs ‹one=another-mind-puts in› *one advises another* (HS); **-kerhat⁷a-:** ęhskwakyerhá·t⁷a·⁷ ‹prediction-you=me-body-put in› *all of you will put me in it* (RC 3:22); **-tkwat⁷a-:** katkwá·t⁷ę ‹it-stomach-put in› *pie, pudding* (R); **-tkwat⁷a⁷T-:** ękayetkwat⁷á⁷ne·⁷ ‹prediction-they-stomach-put in-moving› *they will make pies* (L 36); **-⁷wahrat⁷a-:** ra⁷-wahrá·t⁷ahs ‹he-meat-puts in› *he stuffs it* (HS); **-a⁷rat⁷a-:** wa⁷kayę⁷rá·t⁷a·⁷ ‹fact-they-themselves-X-put in› *they got in* (RC 27:13), ra⁷rá·t⁷ahs ‹he-himself-X-puts in› *he gets in* (L 55), ru⁷rá·t⁷ę ‹he-himself-X-put in› *he has gotten in* (L 55), θa⁷rá·t⁷ah ‹you!-yourself-X-put in› *get in!* (L 55), ča⁷rá·t⁷ah ‹you two-yourselves-put in› *get in, you two!* (RC 27:13); **-či-.-a⁷rat⁷a-:** θka⁷rá·t⁷ahs ‹again-I-my-self-X-put in› *I embark again* (HS); **-atkahrat⁷ahsT-:** yętkahrat⁷áhstha⁷ ‹one-oneself-eye-put in-causes› *telescope* (HS); **-(a)hy- -tkwat⁷ahsT-:** úhyeh katkwat⁷áhsnę ‹fruit it-stomach-put in-caused› *fruit pie* (HS); **ha⁷ -(ę)⁷tikęhrat⁷a-:** ha⁷ ru⁷tikęhrá·t⁷ę ‹the he-mind-put in› *counsel* (HS); **-te⁷kwakęw -(a)t⁷a-:** ruté⁷kwakęw rá·t⁷ahs ‹he-bag-in he-puts in› *he put in his purse* (HS).

-(a)t⁷a-/-(a)t⁷ah- be full, be satisfied. *v.s.-s.i.* waká·t⁷ę ‹I-put in› *I am full, I am satisfied* (R).

-at⁷ahsęya⁷T-.#ú⁷y giantess. *dv.n.s.*

nwat⁷ahsẹya⁷nẹhú⁷y ⟨hither-it-itself-breast-hang-caused-great⟩ *giantess* (RC 11:5).

-at⁷ehnakewahT – towel. *dv.n.s.* ha⁷ yẹt⁷ehnakyewáhtha⁷ ⟨the one-oneself-hand-wipe-causes⟩ *towel* (HS).

-at⁷ehnakwẹhnar – slap. *v.s.-t.* rat⁷ehnakwẹ́hnar ⟨he-himself-hand-turns down⟩ *he slaps it* (HS), rut⁷ehnakwẹhnà·rẹ ⟨he-himself-hand-turned down⟩ *he has slapped it* (HS), ẹhrat⁷ehnakwẹ́hna⁷r ⟨prediction-he-himself-hand-turn down⟩ *he will slap it* (HS).

-at⁷ẹhrẹy⁷T – quaking aspen, poplar. *dv. n.s.* wat⁷ẹhrẹ́⁷ytha⁷ ⟨it-itself-leaf-hang-causes⟩ *quaking aspen, poplar (Populus sp.)* (R).

-at⁷ẹyayẹ(T) – fort. *dv.n.s.* wat⁷ẹ̀·yayẹ⁷ ⟨it-itself-enclosure-goes into⟩ *fort* (HS).

-at⁷ẹyayẹ(T) – fortify oneself. *v.s.-a.i.* rat⁷ẹ̀·yayẹhs ⟨he-himself-enclosure-goes into⟩ *he fortifies himself* (HS).

-at⁷ẹya⁷nẹr – arrears. *dv.n.s.* yut⁷ẹya⁷nẹ̀·rẹ ⟨it-itself-cost-self-remained⟩ *arrears* (HS).

-at⁷ẹyityẹ⁷T – run into debt. *v.s.-a.i.* rat⁷ẹyityẹ́⁷tha⁷ ⟨he-himself-cost-arrive-causes⟩ *he runs into debt* (HS).

-at⁷ihsT – arrogate, be egotistic. *v.s.-a.i.* rat⁷íhstha⁷ ⟨he-himself-I-causes⟩ *he arrogates, he is egotistic* (HS), rut⁷íhsnẹ ⟨he-himself-I-caused⟩ *he was egotistic* (HS).

-at⁷ihsT – egotism. *dv.n.s.* ha⁷ rat⁷íhstha⁷ ⟨the he-himself-I-causes⟩ *his egotism* (HS).

-at⁷nahkw – dislocate, get out of place. *v.r.-a.i.* hab: -ahs, pnt: -, stat: -, prog: -, prp: -, dst: -, caus: -, rvs: -, dat: -, n-inc. wat⁷náhkwahs *it dislocates, it gets out of place* (HS).

-at'nẹht⁷ahsT – womb. *dv.n.s.* yẹt⁷nẹh-t⁷áhstha⁷ ⟨one-oneself-bury-begin-causes⟩ *womb* (R).

-at'niha – be disproportionate, differ. *v.s.-a.i.* neyut⁷níhẹ ⟨two-it-itself-sprained⟩ *disproportionate: the two of them differ* (HS).

-at⁷nihahsT – tomboy. *dv.n.s.* wat⁷niháhsnẹ ⟨it-itself-be male-caused⟩ *tomboy* (HS).

-at⁷wa – elude, escape. *v.r.-a.i.* hab: -h, pnt: -·⁷, stat: -, prog: -, prp: -, dst: -, caus: -hT-, rvs: -, dat: I (-⁷θe-/-⁷θ-), inc.-ɸ-pat. nyá·t⁷wa·⁷ *you and I escape* (R); **-at⁷wa**–{dative I}: yẹkwat⁷wá⁷θe⁷ ⟨we-escaped-for⟩ *it escaped us* (RC 29:16), na⁷nat⁷wá⁷θeh ⟨one=another-escapes-for⟩ *one eludes another* (HS), rá·t⁷wa⁷θ ⟨he-escapes-for⟩ *he deserts* (HS); **-či–**. **-at⁷wa–**: ẹθẹ́·t⁷wa·⁷ ⟨prediction-again-it-escape⟩ *it will reescape* (RC 17:1), θahrá·t⁷wa·⁷ ⟨again-fact-he-escaped⟩ *he escaped again* (RC 26:36); **kwẹhs –at⁷wahT –**: kwẹhs ahrat⁷wáhthek ⟨no unknown-he-escape-cause⟩ *he is infallible* (HS).

-at⁷wa–{dative I} desert, elude, escape. *v.s.-t.* yẹkwat⁷wá⁷θe⁷ ⟨we-escaped-for⟩ *it escaped us* (RC 29:16), na⁷nat⁷wá⁷θeh ⟨one=another-escapes-for⟩ *one eludes another* (HS), rá·t⁷wa⁷θ ⟨he-escapes-for⟩ *he deserts* (HS).

-aw – give to, hand to, present; infect. *v.r.-t.* hab: -s ~ -ẹhs, pnt: -a⁷, stat: -i, prog: -, prp: -, dst: -, caus: -i⁷T- ~ -ahsT-, rvs: -ihsi-, dat: -, inc.-ɸ-ag./pat. With the punctual aspect marker -a⁷ and the causative suffix -ahsT- the root contracts according to the general Tuscarora rule by which sequences of *awa* or *a⁷wa* become ẹ. The imperative form of this root is irregular. Also note that Hewitt & Smith give the form ráws *he presents, gives to* for expected *íhraws. The likely reason for the failure of prothetic *i* to occur here is to avoid homophony with íhraws *he comes* (see: −aw−/−u−). The regular habitual aspect marker is −s; the marker −ęhs has been found only in na'nà·węhs *one infects another* and račihskwà·węhs *he besmears it, he putties it.* ná·kwę *give me!* (R), ráws *he presents, he gives* (HS), rú·wi· *he presented, he gave* (HS), na'nà·węhs *one infects another* (HS), na'ná·'nę' *one handed it to another* (R), wahrà·wę' *he was given* (R); −awihsi−: ęwawíhsi' ‹prediction-it-give to-undo› *it will extract* (RC 10:1); −awi'T−: rawí'tha' ‹he-give to-causes› *he inserts, he puts in* (HS); −(a)hę'na=wihsi−: rahę'nawíhsyęhs ‹he-clearing-give to-undoes› *he takes the meadow out (of a difficulty) (said of a person who saves a meadow from loss by debt or other cause)* (H 2484); −(a)h=karawihsi−: rahkarawíhsyęhs ‹he-bark-give to-undoes› *he unbars a gate* (HS); −čihskwaw−: račihskwà·węhs ‹he-mush-gives to› *he besmears it, he putties it* (HS); −čtęhrawi'nahnę−: wahračtęhrawi'náhnę·' ‹fact-he-stone-give to-caused-many› *he put in many rocks* (RC 11:3); −(ę)ta'rawi'T−: ruta'rawí'nę ‹he-head-give to-caused› *it penetrated his head* (RC 30:2); −(ę)tu'θawihsi−: ratu'θawíhsyęhs ‹he-tooth-give to-undoes› *he draws teeth, he extracts teeth, he pulls out teeth* (HS); −hne'rawihsi−: rahne'rawíhsyęhs ‹he-root-give-undoes› *he uproots it* (HS); −hsęnaw−: rahsę̀·naws ‹he-name-gives to› *he titles it* (HS); −hsnahręwawihsi−: wahrahsnahręwawíhsi' ‹fact-he-marrow-give to-undid› *he extracted marrow* (RC 8:25); −hsu'kwaw−: ękęhsú'kwę' ‹prediction-I=you-finger-give› *I will give you finger* (RC 30:28); −hwihstaw−: ękayę'nathwíhstę' ‹prediction-they=another-metal-give to› *they will give money (to another)* (L 35); −(i)'-θhaθnęhstaw−: ra'θhaθnę́hstaws ‹he-power-be strong-'ness-gives to› *he authorizes it* (HS); −nęhaw−: wa'na'na'néhę' ‹fact-one=another-corn-gave to› *one handed another corn (to announce a marriage contract)* (R); −nęhsnawihsi−: ranęhsnawíhsyęhs ‹he-seed-give-undoes› *he pulls out a grain, grain* (H 2484); −nęθawihsi−: ranęθawíhsyęhs ‹he-potato-give-undoes› *he pulls out potatoes, as from a cache or pit* (H 2484); −nęθawi'T−: ranęθawí'tha' ‹he-potato-give-causes› *he inserts potato(es), sets potato(es)* (H 2484); −nę'nahstaw−: ranę'nahsáhstaws ‹he-feed-'ness-gives› *he gives it to eat* (RC 18:23); −rihwaw−: raríhwaws ‹he-matter-gives to› *he attributes* (HS), na'ríhwaws ‹one=another-matter-gives to› *one imputes* (HS); −rihwęhsT−: rarihwę́hstha' ‹he-matter-give-causes› *he inculcates* (HS); −takwnaw−: wa'kayę'na'tákwnę' ‹fact-they=another-space-gave› *they gave them a place* (AW 102); −ya'rawihsi−: na'nya'rawíhsyęhs ‹one=another-intestine-

---

Tuscarora Pronunciation Key:
/a/ l<u>a</u>w; /e/ h<u>a</u>t; /i/ p<u>i</u>zza; /u/ t<u>u</u>ne; /ę/ h<u>i</u>nt; /č/ <u>ch</u>eese; /h/ <u>h</u>oe; /m/ <u>m</u>other; /s/ <u>s</u>ame; /t/ <u>d</u>o (before a vowel y, or w), <u>t</u>oo (elsewhere); /k/ <u>g</u>ale (before a vowel y or w), <u>k</u>ale (elsewhere); /n/ i<u>n</u>hale (before a consonant or word-final), <u>n</u>ote (elsewhere), /r/ hi<u>ss</u> (before a consonant or word-final), <u>r</u>un (trilled as in Italian, elsewhere); /w/ c<u>u</u>ff (before a consonant other than y or word-final), <u>w</u>ay (elsewhere); /y/ fi<u>sh</u> (before a consonant or word-final), <u>y</u>ou (elsewhere), /θ/ <u>th</u>ing; /'/ (the sound between the vowels in unh-unh); /·/ long vowel, /´/ high pitch; /`/ low pitch.

give-undoes› *one disembowels another*
(HS); –**yeraw**–: yeyerà·węhs ‹one-
flesh-gives› *goldplate, silverplate*
(HS), rayerà·węhs ‹he-flesh-gives› *he
soils it, he taints it* (HS); –**yetaw**–:
rayetà·węhs ‹one-grease-gives› *he
greases it, he oils it* (HS); –**yeta**=
wihsi–: ęyeyetawíhsi⁷ ‹prediction-one-
grease-give-undoes› *one will extract
grease* (RC 11: 23); –⁷**ahθraw**–: wa⁷-
nat⁷áhθrę⁷ ‹fact-one=another-basket-
gave to› *one gave another a basket*
(R); –⁷**tuhsaw**–: na⁷tuhsà·wi ‹one=an-
other-clam (shell)-gave to› *one gave
another clam(shell)* (RC 35:23);
–**ne**–.–**aw**–: nehrá·⁷na⁷naws ‹apart-he=
another-gives to› *he barters, he
reciprocates* (HS); –**t**–.–**aw**–: tkę̀·yaws
‹hither-I=you give to› *I give it to you*
(R), čkà·wi ‹hither-you=me-give to›
you handed it to me (R); –**či**–.
–**hseharawihsi**–: ęθkahseharawíhsi⁷
‹prediction-again-it-lye-give to-undo›
it will extract lye (RC 10:1); –**či**–.
–**čtęhrawihsyęku**–:čečtęhrawihsyę́·ku⁷
‹again-one-stone-give to-undo-picked
up› *one removed the stone by picking
it up* (RC 11:8); –**a⁷nahsawi⁷nahkw**–:
yę⁷nahsawi⁷náhkhwa⁷ ‹one-oneself-
foot-give to-causes-instrument› *slipper*
(HS); –**a⁷tu⁷θawihsya⁷T**–: yę·⁷tu⁷θa-
wihsyá⁷tha⁷ ‹one-oneself-tooth-give
to-undo-causes› *forceps* (HS); –**(ę)ti⁷**=
rhwęθawihT–: ręti⁷rhwęθawíhtha⁷
‹he-himself-tail-give to-causes› *he is
sheepish; sycophant* (HS); –**yah**–.
–**atkahrawi⁷T**–: weyutkahrawí·⁷nę
‹thither-it-itself-eye-give to-caused› *it
was peaking* (RC 8:35).

aw–/**u**– noun prefix. *n.r.pfx.* The form
aw– occurs before roots and stems
that begin with the vowels *i, e, u,* or
ę. The form **u**– occurs before roots
and stems that begin with a consonant

or the vowel *a.*

aw–/**u**– its (third person singular neuter
alienable). *n.r.pfx.* The form **aw**–
occurs before roots and stems that
begin with the vowels *i, e, u,* or ę.
The form **u**– occurs before roots and
stems that begin with a consonant or
the vowel *a.*

–**aw**–/–**u**– arrive, come. *v.r.-a.i.* hab: -s,
pnt: -⁷, stat: -·, prog: -, prp: -⁷θe-, dst:
-, caus: -hsT-, rvs: -, dat: I (-⁷θe-/-⁷θ-
), n-inc. The form –**aw**– occurs with
third person agent pronominal prefixes
and in compounds; the form –**u**–
occurs elsewhere. rá·wu· *he has come*
(H-notebook), íhraws *he arrives* (HS),
he comes (H-notebook), ę́·⁷w *it came*
(RC 30:24), ę̀·wa⁷w *it will come* (RC
27:18); –**aw**–{**dative I**}: wa⁷kakà·wu⁷θ
‹fact-they-came-for› *it came to them*
(RC 12:7), rawú⁷θeh ‹he-came-for› *he
receives it, it comes to him* (R); –**tah**=
sahstaw–: wa⁷kayetahsáhsta⁷w ‹fact-
they-assail-'ness-came› *they attacked,
they came looking for a fight* (RC
33:2), ękayetahsáhsta⁷w ‹prediction-
they-assail-'ness-come› *they will attack, they will come looking for a
fight* (RC 33:3); –**či**–.–**aw**–: θá·ku⁷
‹again-fact-I-came› *I came back* (RC
30:33); –**či**–.–**aw⁷θe**–: θhráw⁷θeh
‹again-he-comes-going to› *he is about
to return* (HS); –**yah**–.–**aw**–: wehrá·wu·
‹thither-he-came› *he arrived there* (RC
12:23), yahwá⁷ę⁷w ‹thither-fact-one-
came› *one came there* (RC 33:9),
yę́hsu⁷ ‹thither-prediction-you-come›
you will come there (RC 30:33); **ti**+
yah–.–**aw**–: tyáhę⁷w ‹so-thither-fact-it-
came› *it came to that point* (RC 1:5);
–**atkę⁷θehstaw**–: kayętkę⁷θéhstaws
‹they-themselves-see-going to-come›
they come to look at (RC 5:37); **ha⁷**
–**či**–.–**aw⁷θe**–: ha⁷ θhrawú⁷θe· ‹the

again-he-came-going to› *remorse* (HS).

-aw -{dative I} come to, receive. *v.s.-t.* wa?kakà·wu?θ ‹fact-they-came-for› *it came to them* (RC 12:7), rawú?θeh ‹he-came-for› *he receives it, it comes to him* (R).

-awak - shake. *v.r.-t.* hab: -s, pnt: -ɸ, stat: -, prog: -, prp: -, dst: -, caus: -, rvs: -, dat: -, inc.-ɸ-pat. rà·waks *he shakes it* (HS); **-(a)hyawak** -: rahyà·waks ‹he-fruit-shakes› *he knocks down fruit* (HS); **-(ę)terawak** -: węterà·waks ‹it-roe-shakes› *it spawns* (HS); **-a'nahsawak** -: ra?nahsà·waks ‹he-himself-foot-shakes› *he shakes the dust from this feet* (H-notebook); **-a'ne?nawak** -: wahra?ne?nà·wak ‹fact-he-himself-??-shook› *he shook free of (things clinging to him)* (H-notebook).

awehnú?ę water-logged rotten wood, wet driftwood (HS). *n.*

-awehθayę - darken. *v.s.-a.i.* See: **-eh= θayę** -.

-awerhu - cover. *v.r.-t.* hab: -hs, pnt: -?, stat: -ę, prog: -, prp: -, dst: -, caus: -, rvs: -, dat: -, inc.-ɸ-pat. θawérhu *cover it!* (R), rawérhuhs *he covers it* (R); **-awerhuhčr** -: uwerhúhčreh ‹cover-'ness› *cover, lid* (R); **-awerhuhsi** -: rawerhúhsyęhs ‹he-cover-undoes› *he uncovers it* (HS); **-a?wnawerhu** -: yu?wnawérhę ‹it-earth-covered› *it covers land* (RC 1:1); **-hehnawerhu** -: kahehnawérhuhs ‹it-field-covered› *it covers, over-spreads the field* (H

2484); **-nęθawerhu** -: ranęθawérhuhs ‹he-potato-covers› *he covers, is covering potato* (H 2484); **-?ahθrawerhu** -: wahra?ahθrawérhu? ‹fact-he-basket-covered› *he fastened the basket shut* (RC 30:14); **à·wę? -a?wnawerhu** -: à·wę? wa?wnawérhę ‹water it-earth-covered› *flood* (MP).

-awerhuhčr - cover, lid. *n.s.* uwerhúhčreh ‹cover-'ness› *cover, lid* (R).

-awerhuhsi - uncover. *v.s.-t.* rawerhúhsyęhs ‹he-cover-undoes› *he uncovers it* (HS).

-aweryuh brother-in-law. *n.r.* aln: akawé·ryuh *my brother-in-law* (R), inc., n.sfx. -. akawé·ryuh *my brother-in-law (sister's husband)* (R).

-aweryuháh brother-in-law, sister-in-law. *n.r.* aln: akaweryuháh *my bother-in-law, my sister-in-law* (R). akaweryuháh *my bother-in-law (wife's brother), my sister-in-law (wife's sister)* (R).

-aweθhę - chop, cut up fine, smash. *v.r.-t.* hab: -h, pnt: -·?, stat: -?, prog: -, prp: -, dst: -tyę-, caus: -, rvs: -, dat: -, inc.-ɸ-pat. wawé·θhęh *it is cut* (RC 26:1), rawé·θhęh *he chops it* (HS), ruwé·θhę? *he chopped it* (HS), ęhrawé·θhę·? *he will chop it* (HS); **-(ę)ta?raweθhętyę** -: akęta?raweθhé·tyę? ‹unknown-I-you-head-chop-much› *that I smash up your head* (RC 31:6); **-a'nahsaweθhę** -: wahra?nahsawé·θhę? ‹fact-he-himself-foot-chopped› *he smashed his foot* (RC 36:title); **-t** -. **-aweθhę** -: nwawé·θhę? ‹hither-it-

Tuscarora Pronunciation Key:
/a/ l<u>a</u>w; /e/ h<u>a</u>t; /i/ p<u>i</u>zza; /u/ t<u>u</u>ne; /ę/ h<u>i</u>nt; /č/ <u>ch</u>eese; /h/ <u>h</u>oe; /m/ <u>m</u>other; /s/ <u>s</u>ame; /t/ <u>d</u>o (before a vowel y, or w), <u>t</u>oo (elsewhere); /k/ <u>g</u>ale (before a vowel y or w), <u>k</u>ale (elsewhere); /n/ i<u>nh</u>ale (before a consonant or word-final), <u>n</u>ote (elsewhere), /r/ hi<u>ss</u> (before a consonant or word-final), <u>r</u>un (trilled as in Italian, elsewhere); /w/ cu<u>ff</u> (before a consonant other than y or word-final), <u>w</u>ay (elsewhere); /y/ fi<u>sh</u> (before a consonant or word-final), <u>y</u>ou (elsewhere), /θ/ <u>th</u>ing; /?/ (the sound between the vowels in unh-unh); /·/ long vowel, /ˊ/ high pitch; /ˋ/ low pitch.

chopped⟩ *it is cut there* (RC 26:2);
–ne+t–. –aweθhę̣ –: nę̣ʔnwawé·θhę̣hk
⟨apart-hither-fact-it-chopped⟩ *it had
been cut* (RC 26:1).
–**awethu** – swallow. *v.r.-t.* hab: -, pnt: -,
stat: -ę̣°, prog: -, prp: -, dst: -, caus: -,
rvs: -, dat: -, n-inc. nyę̣wé·thę̣k *one
swallowed it* (RC 17:3).
–**(a)wę** – many, much (distributive). *v.r.
sfx.* hab: -h, pnt: -·ʔ, stat: -·, prog: -,
prp: -, caus: -, rvs: -, dat: -. The distributive is used to indicate either that
the action of the verb is spread over
time or that the object of the verb is
distributed over an area (e.g., **wahrak =
θhrá·wę·ʔ** ⟨fact-he-dish-put up-many⟩
*he set the table (lit., he put dishes
around*). The form –**awę** – occurs after
roots and stems that end in a consonant; the form –**wę** – occurs after roots
and stems that end in a vowel.
awę̣háh small (PC). *part.*
–**awę̣hte** – be between two things. *v.r.-s.i.*
stat: -ʔ, prog: -, prp: -, dst: -, caus: -,
rvs: -, dat: -, inc.-φ-pat. Found only
with an incorporated noun root. –**heh =
nawę̣hte** –: kahehnawę̣hteʔ ⟨it-field-is
between two things⟩ *a field is between
(two others)* (H 2484); –**ihnawę̣hte** –:
yuhnawę̣hteʔ ⟨it-cloth-is between two
things⟩ *a piece of cloth (skin) is between (two others)* (H 2892); –**nę̣hsa =
wę̣hte** –: yunę̣hsawę̣hteʔ ⟨it-house-is
between two things⟩ *it is a house
between (two others)* (H 2892), Ka-
nę̣hsawę̣hteʔ ⟨it-house-is between two
things⟩ *House-In-Between (male proper name)* (H 2484); –**ʔnę̣wawę̣hte** –:
yuʔnę̣wawę̣hteʔ ⟨it-pot-is between two
things⟩ *the/a pot is infixed between
(two others)* (H 2892), *a small kettle
put in the space made by two larger
and the back log* (H-notebook).
–**awę̣ri** – stir. *v.r.-t.* hab: -h, pnt: -eʔ, stat:

-eʔ, prog: -, prp: -, dst: -, caus: -, rvs:
-, dat: -, inc.-φ-ag. Requires the dualic
in the meaning *stir* or the semireflexive in the meaning *travel*, unless
an incorporated noun is present. When
both the dualic and semireflexive are
present, the construction may mean
stir or *travel* depending on the con-
text. –**a'nę̣hrawę̣ri** –: raʔnę̣hrawę̣·rih
⟨he-himself-dirt-stirs⟩ *he dirties it, he
soils it* (HS); –**(ę̣)ʔtikę̣hrawę̣ri** –: naʔti-
kę̣hrawę̣·rih ⟨one=another-mind-stirs⟩
one bewilders another (HS); –**hsya =
wę̣ri** –: rahsyawę̣·rih ⟨he-palm-stirs⟩ *he
handles it* (HS); –**nę̣ʔrarawę̣ri** –: ranę̣ʔ-
rarawę̣·rih ⟨he-pollution-stirs⟩ *he pollutes it* (HS); –**tuwę̣hnawę̣ri** –: ratuwę̣h-
nawę̣·rih ⟨he-tell a lie-cause-stirs⟩ *he
belies* (HS), ę̣hratuwę̣hnawę̣·riʔ ⟨pre-
diction-he-tell a lie-cause-stir⟩ *he will
belie* (HS); –**yerawę̣ri** –: rayerawę̣·rih
⟨he-flesh-stirs⟩ *he begrimes it, he tarnishes it* (HS); –**ne** –. –**awę̣ri** –: neka-
wę̣·rih ⟨apart-I-stir⟩ *I stir it* (R), waʔ-
nyę̣wę̣·ryeʔ ⟨fact-apart-one-stirred⟩ *one
stirred it* (RC 5:18); –**a'nawę̣ri** –: raʔ-
nawę̣·rih ⟨he-himself-stirs⟩ *he rambles
about, he travels around* (R), waʔkaʔ-
nawę̣·ryeʔ ⟨fact-I-myself-stirred⟩ *I was
traveling* (R); –**athnekawę̣ryaʔT** –: wa-
thnekawę̣·ryaʔč ⟨it-itself-liquid-stir-
causes⟩ *liquid roils; something unusual happens to liquid* (RC 6:9);
–**a'nyerawę̣ri** –: raʔnyerawę̣·rih ⟨he-him-
self-flesh-stirs⟩ *he soils himself* (HS);
–**ne** –. –**a'nawę̣ri** –: nehruʔnawę̣·ryeʔ
⟨apart-he-himself-stirred⟩ *he stirred
himself, he went from place to place*
(RC 12:15).
awę̣·te thing (RC 2:4). *part.* See also:
thaʔawę̣·te *anything*, **staʔawę̣·te** *something*, and **sawę̣·te** *nothing*, all of
which probably derive from the root
–**ę̣te** – *be a certain* with the neuter third

singular patient pronominal prefix -(y)aw-.

awę́·te –ira'ne– muddy, soiled, turbid. *n.s.* awę́·te kęrá·ʔneʔ ‹thing it-grain-is present› *muddy, soiled, turbid* (HS).

à·węʔ water (RC 17:4) [Lawson «Awoo» 'Water'] [Jefferson «auwen» 'water'] [Gallatin «auwuh» 'Water']. *n.* awęʔ. **#hči**: awę́ʔči ‹water-very› *watery (of food)* (HS); **awęʔ.#ke**: awę́ʔkye ‹water-at› *watery (of roads)* (HS); **awęʔ. #keha·ʔ**: awęʔkyéha·ʔ ‹water-customarily› *aquatic, of the water* (RC 3:76), *fond of water* (H-notebook); **à·węʔ čikheʔ.#hči**: à·węʔ čikhéʔči ‹water salt-very› *briny* (HS); **à·węʔ –aʔwna=werhu–**: à·węʔ waʔwnawérhę ‹water it-land-covered› *flood* (MP); **à·węʔ –tiʔkaręwe–**: à·węʔ naʔtiʔkarę̀·weh ‹water one=another-injects› *one injects* (HS).

à·węʔ čikheʔ.#hči briny. *n.s.* à·węʔ čikhéʔči ‹water salt-very› *briny* (HS).

à·węʔ –aʔwnawerhu– flood. *dv.n.s.* à·węʔ waʔwnawérhę ‹water it-land-covered› *flood* (MP).

awęʔ.#hči watery (of food). *n.s.* awę́ʔči ‹water-very› *watery (of food)* (HS).

awęʔ.#ke watery (of roads). *n.s.* awę́ʔkye ‹water-at› *watery (of roads)* (HS).

awęʔ.#keha·ʔ aquatic, of the water, fond of water. *n.s.* awęʔkyéha·ʔ ‹water-customarily› *aquatic, of the water* (RC 3:76), *fond of water* (H-notebook).

–awę'na'nehsT– make pleasant. *v.r.-t.* See: –ę'na'nehsT–.

–awihsi– extract, pull out. *v.s.-t.* ęwa-wíhsiʔ ‹prediction-it-give to-undo› *it will extract it* (RC 10:1).

–awiʔT– insert, put in. *v.s.-t.* rawíʔthaʔ ‹he-give to-causes› *he inserts it, he puts it in* (HS).

–ayaʔnerę– harm, injure, wound. *v.r.-t.* hab: -h, pnt: -ʔ, stat: -·t, prog: -, prp: -, dst: -, caus: -, rvs: -, dat: -, inc.-ɸ-pat. rayaʔnè·ręh *he harms it, he injures it, he wounds it* (HS), yuyaʔné·ręt *it is harmful, it is injurious, it is nocent, it is pernicious* (HS), ęyaʔnè·ręʔ *it is wounded* (R); **–ayaʔnerę–**: uyaʔné·ręt ‹harm› *harm, hurt* (HS); **–ičayaʔnerę–**: waʔkičayaʔnè·ręʔ ‹fact-I-fish-harmed› *I wounded fish* (R).

–ayaʔnerę– harm, hurt. *n.s.* uyaʔné·ręt ‹harm› *harm, hurt* (HS).

–(a)ʔ punctual aspect. *v.r.sfx.* The form -aʔ occurs after certain roots and stems that end in an obstruent; the form -ʔ occurs after roots and stems that end in a vowel or a resonant.

-aʔ simple noun suffix. *n.r.sfx.* Rare.

–(a)ʔ– begin (inchoative). *v.r.sfx.* hab: -θ, pnt: -ɸ, stat: -ę, prog: -, prp: -, dst: -, caus: -, rvs: -, dat: -. The inchoative is used to indicate that the activity described by the base is just beginning. The form -aʔ– occurs after certain verb roots and stems that end in a consonant; the form -ʔ– occurs elsewhere.

á·ʔ, á·ʔ, á·ʔ caw, crow's call (RC 12:24). *n.*

á·ʔa·ʔ crow *(Corvus americanus)* (RC 12:5) [Jefferson «auh-au» 'crow']. *n.*

aʔaʔ.#kẹha̱ʔnẹʔ: aʔaʔkẹhaʔnẹʔ ‹crow-many› *crows* (RC 12:4).

–aʔča̱rakẹhčrẹ – knock at a door. *v.s.-a.i.* waʔkayẹʔčarakẹ́hčrẹ·ʔ ‹fact-they-them-selves-door-mistreated› *they knocked at the door* (MP).

–aʔča̱ranẹ – Door-Keepers (Seneca Nation). *dv.n.s.* Kayẹʔčarà·nẹh ‹they-themselves-door-guard› *Door-Keepers (official title within the Iroquois Confederacy of the Seneca Nation from their responsibility as guardians of the western fringe [the western door] of the Confederacy)* (AG).

–aʔčaʔtuh – be cold. *v.s.-a.i.* kaʔčáʔtuh ‹I-myself-am cool› *I am cold* (PC).

–aʔčaʔtuhsnahkw – fan. *dv.n.s.* yẹʔčaʔtuh-snáhkhwaʔ ‹it-itself-be cool-causes-instrument› *fan* (HS).

–(a)ʔčh – nominalizer. *v.r.sfx.* See: –(a)ʔčr –. The form –aʔčh – occurs after roots and stems that end in a consonant or *i* and preceding certain roots and stems that begin with *y*, the *y* being dropped; the form –ʔčh – occurs after roots and stems that end in a vowel other than *i* when preceding certain roots and stems that begin with *y*, the *y* being dropped.

–aʔčiʔerhar – blush. *v.s.-a.i.* raʔčiʔérher ‹he-himself-scar-let-hangs› *he blushes* (HS).

–(a)ʔčr – nominalizer. *v.r.sfx.* The form –aʔčr – occurs following roots and stems that end in a consonant or *i*; the form –ʔčr – occurs elsewhere.

–aʔčtehrihsT – bother. *v.s.-t.* kaʔčtehríh-sthaʔ ‹I-myself-become involved with› *it bothers me* (R).

–aʔčunẹti – strip, remove all clothes. *v.s.-a.i.* waʔẹʔčunẹ́·tiʔ ‹fact-one-oneself-naked body-made› *one stripped, one removed all one's clothes* (RC 3:55).

–aʔčunuhsku – take clothes off, make naked. *v.s.-a.i.* θaʔčunúhskẹ ‹you!-yourself-naked body-bare› *take your clothes off!, make yourself naked!* (RC 3: 54).

–aʔk – dig. *v.r.-t.* hab: -haʔ, pnt: -ɸ, stat: -, prog: -ẹha-'nyeʔ-, prp: -, dst: -hẹ-, caus: -, rvs: -, dat: -, inc.-t-pat. ratáʔkhaʔ *he is digging it* (L 72), wáʔktaʔk *I dug it* (R); –taʔkẹha'nyeʔ –: kataʔkẹhá·ʔnyeʔ ‹it-digs-going along› *trench* (HS); –taʔkhẹ –: waʔktáʔkhẹ·ʔ ‹I-dug-many› *I dug (some)* (L 72); –yah –.-taʔk –: yahwaʔé·taʔk ‹thither-fact-one-dug› *one dug there* (RC 34: 10); –čihẹhraʔk –: račihẹhráʔkhaʔ ‹he-coal-digs› *he mines coal* (HS); –ẹh=raʔk –: rẹhráʔkhaʔ ‹he-dirt-digs› *he burrows, he roots* (HS); –hwihstaʔk –: rahwihstáʔkhaʔ ‹he-money-digs› *he mines gold* (HS); –nẹθaʔk –: ranẹθáʔ-khaʔ ‹he-potato-digs› *he digs potatoes* (H 2484).

–aʔkẹhr – ashes, dust; gray. *n.r.* n-poss., inc., n.sfx. -eh. uʔkẹ́hreh *ashes, dust: gray* (R); –aʔkẹhr –.#hči: ukẹhréhči ‹dust-very› *dusty* (HS); –aʔkẹhra̱rih=nahkw –: yẹʔkẹhrarihnáhkhwaʔ ‹one-ashes-boil-causes-instrument› *lime kiln* (HS); –aʔkẹhra̱rihT –: waʔkẹhra-ríhnẹ ‹it-ashes-boil-caused› *cement, lime* (HS); –aʔkrẹhreθ –: yuʔkẹ́hre·θ ‹it-dust-is long› *the dust lies deep* (AG); –aʔkẹhrẹhT –: raʔkẹhrẹ́hthaʔ ‹he-dust-fall-causes› *he dusts* (HS); –a='naʔkẹhraʔnihr –: yuʔnaʔkẹhraʔníhrẹ ‹it-itself-dust-stood up› *it is flying dust* (H-notebook), *it is dusty (e.g. a road)* (AG); íhskah –aʔkẹhr –: íhskah uʔkẹ́hreh ‹no dust› *there is no dust* (AG).

–aʔkẹhr –.#hči dusty. *n.s.* uʔkẹhréhči ‹dust-very› *dusty* (HS).

–aʔkẹhra̱rihnahkw – lime kiln. *dv.n.s.* yẹʔkẹhrarihnáhkhwaʔ ‹one-ashes-boil-causes-instrument⟩ *lime kiln* (HS).

-aʔkẹhrạrihT – cement, lime. *dv.n.s.* waʔkẹhraríhnẹ ⟨it-ashes-boil-caused⟩ *cement, lime* (HS).

-aʔkẹhrẹhT – dust. *v.s.-t.* raʔkẹhrẹ́hthaʔ ⟨he-dust-fall-causes⟩ *he dusts it* (HS).

-aʔkwar – be covered over. *v.r.-s.i.* stat: -ʔ, prog: -, prp: -, dst: -, caus: -, rvs: -, dat: -, inc.-ɸ-pat. Found only in the cited construction. -(ẹ)taʔraʔkwar-. #úʔy: yawẹtaʔraʔkwaʔrhúʔy ⟨it-head-is covered over-great⟩ *its great head is covered over* (RC 28:2).

-aʔke on, on top of (simple noun suffix+external locative). *n.r.sfx.* From the examples given by Hewitt (H 2484) it appears that this combination of suffixes had the consistent meaning of "on top of" in his time, as compared to combinations of the external locative with other forms of the simple noun suffix, which meant "at the place of" and "on the surface of". See: -ehke and -ẹʔke. -(a)hẹʔnaʔke: uhẹʔnáʔkye ⟨clearing-at⟩ *on, on the surface of the meadow* (H 2484); -ahskwaʔ = ke: uhskwáʔkye ⟨bridge-at⟩ *at the bridge, at solid ground* (RC 24:10); -(a)tkwiraʔke: utkwiráʔkye ⟨branch-at⟩ *on branch* (RC 15:2); -aʔwnanẹhaʔke: uʔwnanẹhá·ʔkye ⟨earth-be old-at⟩ *in the old country* (L 61); -aʔwnaʔke: aʔwnáʔkye ⟨earth-at⟩ *on earth* (RC 12:19); -či -. -(a)hyeθaʔke: čuhyeθáʔ-kye ⟨again-it-fruit-be long-at⟩ *April* (R) (HS: June 15-July 15); -činẹʔ = theraʔke: učinẹʔtheráʔkye ⟨curl-at⟩ *on

curled hair: on a curl of hair, hence, strewed with curled hair (H 2484); -čiʔehnaʔke: učiʔehnáʔkye ⟨claw-at⟩ *on, on top of the claw, talon* (H 24 84); -čtẹhraʔke: učtẹhráʔkye ⟨stone-at⟩ *stoniness* (HS); -ẹ°hraʔke -: ẹhráʔkye ⟨dirt-at⟩ *on dirt* (RC 3:41); -hehnaʔke: uhehnáʔkye ⟨field-at⟩ *on the field (that is, on its surface)* (H 2484); -hnawaʔ = ke: kahnawáʔkye ⟨it-current of water-at⟩ *Sault St. Louis* (HS); *Kahnawake (Mohawk) Reserve* (R); -hsutaʔke: Rahsutáʔkye ⟨he-be ancestor to-at⟩ *King Blunt's Town (a village on the Tuscarora Reservation of 1717 in North Carolina)* (Colonial Records); -hswẹʔnaʔke -: uhsweʔnáʔkye ⟨rotted out log-at⟩ *at hollow (log)* (RC 30:9); -kẹnhaʔke: kẹnháʔkye ⟨season-at⟩ *(in the) summer* (HS); naʔ -rihwaʔke: naʔ urihwáʔkye ⟨much matter-at⟩ *concerning* (HS); -nẹčiʔtheraʔke: unẹčiʔthe-ráʔkye ⟨curl of hair-at⟩ *on, on the top of the curl of hair* (H 2484); -nẹhaʔ = ke: unẹháʔkye ⟨corn-at⟩ *on, on the top of the corn, either a single grain or on a heap of ears or grains* (H 2484); -nẹhsaʔke: unẹhsáʔkye ⟨house-at⟩ *on, on the top of the house or umbrella* (H 2484); *roof* (HS); -nẹhsnaʔke: unẹhsnáʔkye ⟨seed-at⟩ *on, on the top of the grain or seed; literally, on grain, meaning that the ground or floor is covered with grain* (H 2484); -nẹhsnaʔke.#úʔy: unẹhsnaʔkyehúʔy ⟨seed-at-great⟩ *on much grain; that is, much grain lies on the ground or floor

(H 2484); **–nęhsuhara^ʔke**: unęhsuhará^ʔkye ‹house-tip-at› *on the top of the house, on the summit of the house* (H 2484); **–nęθa^ʔke**: unęθá^ʔkye ‹potato-at› *on (on the top of) the potato, or tuber* (H 2484); **–nę'na^ʔke**: unę^ʔná^ʔkye ‹hill-at› *on, at hill* (R); **–nę'nuhara^ʔ = keha'nye^ʔ –**: unę^ʔnuhara^ʔkyehá·^ʔnye^ʔ ‹hill-tip-at-going along› *going along at the summit of hill* (RC 33:5); **–rih = wa^ʔke**: urihwá^ʔkye ‹matter-at› *in regard to, official* (HS); **–t –.–(ę)^ʔ = tya^ʔke**: nyu^ʔtyá^ʔkye ‹hither-it-bay-at› *France* (R); **tha –.–hręhwa^ʔke**: tha^ʔθahręhwá^ʔkye ‹unusual-you-put up-cause-at› *at your leisure* (R); **–tkwara^ʔke**: utkwará^ʔkye ‹blood-at› *sanguinary* (HS); **–yanręhsta^ʔke**: uyanręhstá^ʔkye ‹rule-'ness-at› *legal, legitimate* (HS); **–ya^ʔθra^ʔke**: uya^ʔθrá^ʔkye ‹cross-at› *on a cross* (R); **–yęwa^ʔke**: uyęwá^ʔkye ‹treeless plot of ground-at› *a treeless tract at times surrounded by woods* (H 3518); **–^ʔehna^ʔke**: s^ʔehná^ʔkye ‹you-hand-at› *on your hand* (RC 30:28); **–^ʔnhęha^ʔke**: u^ʔnhęhá^ʔkye ‹urine-at› *on urine, on the top of urine* (H 2484); **–^ʔnhęhsukra^ʔke**: u^ʔnhęhsukrá^ʔkye ‹egg-rubbish-at› *on foul urine* (H 24 84); **–^ʔθkwehsa^ʔke**: u^ʔθkwehsá^ʔkye ‹cutting block-at› *on cutting block* (RC 30:28); **–^ʔteha^ʔkye**: u^ʔtehá^ʔkye ‹sand-at› *it is sandy (said of a place with deep sand, or where you have put sand)* (AG), *on sand, sandy* (HS); **–^ʔtehęwa^ʔke**: u^ʔtehęwá^ʔkye ‹loam-at› *loam* (HS).

–a^ʔn – bow, gun. *n.r.* n-poss., inc., n.sfx. -eh. á^ʔneh *bow, gun* (R) [Lawson «Auk-noc» 'Gun', «Ou-kn» 'Gun powder']; **–a^ʔn –.#ęwe**: a^ʔnahę̀·we ‹bow-genuine› *prickly ash (Xanthoxylun sp.)* (AG); **–a^ʔn –.#ú^ʔy**: a^ʔnahú^ʔy ‹gun-great› *cannon, mortar* (HS);

–a^ʔnaturę –: wa^ʔka^ʔnatù·rę^ʔ ‹fact-I-gun-stored› *I put away my gun, I stored my gun* (R); **–a^ʔnu^ʔy(e) –**: u^ʔnú^ʔyeh ‹gun-bend› *ramrod* (HS); **ti –.–a^ʔna^ʔθ –**: tiwá^ʔna^ʔθ ‹so-it-gun-is of a size› *so gun was in size* (RC 24:2); **ti –.–a^ʔneθ –.#áh**: tiwa^ʔne·θ^ʔáh ‹so-it-gun-is long-small› *pistol* (HS); **–a^ʔn –.#ú^ʔy –a^ʔtawę –**: a^ʔnahú^ʔy ú^ʔtawęh ‹gun-great projectile-belong to› *cannon ball* (HS).

–a^ʔn –.#ęwe prickly ash. *n.s.* a^ʔnahę̀·we ‹bow-genuine› *prickly ash (Xanthoxylum sp.)* (AG).

–a^ʔn –.#ú^ʔy cannon, mortar. *n.s.* a^ʔnahú^ʔy ‹gun-great› *cannon, mortar* (HS).

–a^ʔn –.#ú^ʔy –a^ʔtawę – cannon ball. *n.s.* a^ʔnahú^ʔy ú^ʔtawęh ‹gun-great projectile-belong to› *cannon ball* (HS).

–a^ʔnačT – works. *dv.n.s.* Found only in the two cited constructions. **–wenę – –a^ʔnačnahnę –**: uwè·nę^ʔ yu^ʔnačnáhnę· ‹iron it=another-used-much› *ironworks* (HS); **–wenę – –a^ʔnačT –**: uwè·nę^ʔ yu^ʔnáčnę ‹iron it=another-used› *iron-works* (HS).

–a'nahča^ʔnahkęha'nye^ʔ – be rotting. *v.s.-s.i.* yu^ʔnahča^ʔnahkęhá·^ʔnye^ʔ ‹it-itself-spoiled-going along› *it is rotting* (RC 8:24)

–a^ʔnahka^ʔr – affray, clamor, confusion, uproar. *n.r.* n-poss., inc., n.sfx. -eh. u^ʔnáhka^ʔreh *affray (rare), clamor, confusion, uproar* (HS); **–a^ʔnahka^ʔ = rayę(T) –**: yu^ʔnahka^ʔrà·yę^ʔ ‹it-affray-lays› *affray, carousal, tumult, uproar* (HS); **–a^ʔnahka^ʔrayę'na'nye^ʔ –**: yu^ʔnahka^ʔrayę^ʔná·^ʔnye^ʔ ‹it-affray-lay-going along› *tumultuously* (HS).

–a^ʔnahka^ʔrayę'na'nye^ʔ – tumultuously. *dv. n.s.* yu^ʔnahka^ʔrayę^ʔná·^ʔnye^ʔ ‹it-affray-lay-going along› *tumultuously* (HS).

–a^ʔnahka^ʔrayę(T) – affray, carousal, tumult, uproar. *dv.n.s.* yu'ʔnahka'ʔrà·yę'ʔ ‹it-affray-lays› *affray, carousal, tumult, uproar* (HS).

-a'nahkna'ʔna'nye'ʔ – strut. *v.s.-a.i.* ru'ʔnahkna'ʔná·'ʔnye'ʔ ‹he-himself-go and return-caused-going along› *he struts* (HS).

-a'nahkθenę'nye'ʔ be being carried. *v.s.-a.i.* wa'ʔnahkθenę́·'ʔnye'ʔ ‹it-itself-is taken-going along› *things being carried* (RC 8:3).

-a'nahku – take out. *v.r.-t.* hab: -ahs, pnt: -'ʔ, stat: -ę, prog: -, prp: -, dst: -, caus: -, rvs: -, dat: -, n-inc. ra'ʔnáhkwahs *he takes out* (HS), ęhra'ʔnáhku'ʔ *he will take out* (HS), ru'ʔnáhkwę *he took out* (HS).

-a'nahruyę'ʔ – ask of, interrogate. *v.s.-t.* wahra'ʔnahrù·yę'ʔ ‹fact-he-himself-asked› *he asked of someone* (RC 12: 18), ra'ʔnahrù·yę'ʔ ‹he-himself-asks› *he asks, he interrogates* (HS).

-a'nahθehnę'ʔke in concealment, in secret, secretly, stealthily, underhanded; stealth. *n.s.* u'ʔnahθehnę́'ʔkye ‹self-hide-at› *in concealment, in secret, secretly, stealthily, underhanded: stealth* (HS).

-a'nahθehT – be occult. *v.s.-s.i.* yu'ʔnahθéhnę ‹it-itself-hid› *it is occult* (HS).

-a'nahθkenha – bustle, defend, hasten, hurry, push oneself harder, strive for, struggle to help. *v.s.-a.i.* wahra'ʔnahθkyénha'ʔ ‹fact-he-himself-X-strove› *he pushed himself harder, he struggled to help* (RC 36:2), ru'ʔnahθkyénhę ‹he-himself-X-strove› *he bustles, he defends, he hastens, he hurries, he strives for* (HS); ha'ʔ -a'nahθkenha-: ha'ʔ ru'ʔnahθkyénhę ‹the he-himself-X-strove› *his ardor* (HS).

-a'nahθkenha – ardor. *dv.n.s.* ha'ʔ ru'ʔnahθkyénhę ‹the he-himself-X-strove› *his ardor* (HS).

-a'nahθkw – tarnish. *v.r.-a.i.* hab: -ahs, pnt: -, stat: -, prog: -, prp: -, dst: -, caus: -, rvs: -, dat: -, n-inc. wa'ʔnáhθkwahs *it tarnishes* (HS).

-a'nahθuku – blanch. *v.s.-a.i.* ra'ʔnahθú·kwahs ‹he-himself-color-undoes› *he blanches* (HS).

-a'nahsawak – shake the dust from feet. *v.s.-a.i.* ra'ʔnahsà·waks ‹he-himself-foot-shakes› *he shakes the dust from his feet* (H-notebook).

-a'nahsaweθhę – smash foot. *v.s.-a.i.* wahra'ʔnahsawé·θhę·'ʔ ‹fact-he-himself-foot-chopped› *he smashed his foot* (RC 36:title).

-a'nahsawi'ʔnahkw – slipper. *dv.n.s.* yę'ʔnahsawi'ʔnáhkhwa'ʔ ‹one-oneself-foot-give-causes-instrument› *slipper* (HS).

-a'nahsawi'ʔnahkw – **-e'ʔwihsę'ʔke** stirrup. *dv.n.s.* yę'ʔnahsawi'ʔnáhkhwa'ʔ awe'ʔwihsę́'ʔkye ‹one-oneself-foot-give-causes-instrument saddle-at› *stirrup* (HS).

-a'nahsi – expose. *v.r.-t.* hab: -ęhs, pnt: -, stat: -, prog: -, prp: -, dst: -, caus: -, rvs: -, dat: -, n-inc. ru'ʔnáhsęhs *he exposes it* (H-notebook).

-a'nahsuhči – kick. *v.s.-t.* ra'ʔnahsuhčę́hęh ‹he-himself- foot-removed-much› *he is*

---

going kicking it (RC 25: 13).

-a'nahwara̱ʔnehT - be pale, be fair, be light-skinned. *v.s.-s.i.* ruʔnahwà·raʔ-neht ‹he-himself-is whitish› *he is pale, he is fair, he is light-skinned* (HS).

-a'nahya̱rihT - wait for someone to mature. *v.s.-t.* ruʔnahyaríhnę ‹he-himself-fruit-boil-caused› *he waits for her to ripen (said of an old man waiting for a young girl to mature so he can marry her)* (HS).

-aʔnakhwerȩti - carouse, debauch. *v.r.-a.i.* hab: -h, pnt: -ʔ, stat: -·, prog: -, prp: -, dst: -, caus: -, rvs: -, dat: -, n-inc. This "root" may be an old compound of the semireflexive, a noun root -akhwer - of uncertain meaning, and the verb -ȩ°ti - *make.* raʔnakhwerȩ·tih *he debauches himself, he carouses* (HS).

-a'nakʔu - cede, give up, let go, release, set free. *v.s.-t.* raʔná·kʔwahs ‹he-himself-releases› *he cedes, he gives up, he lets go* (HS), naʔnaʔná·kʔuhs ‹one=another-oneself-releases› *one sets another free (e.g., releases a prisoner)* (HS).

-aʔnarȩʔT - have colic, have a stomachache from overeating. *v.r.-s.i.* stat: -eʔ, prog: -, prp: -, dst: -, caus: -, rvs: -, dat: -, n-inc. ruʔnarȩʔneʔ *he has colic, he has a stomachache from overeating* (R).

-a'narhȩ'ni - spring. *v.s.-a.i.* raʔnarhȩ·ʔ-nyȩhs ‹he-himself-X-throws› *he springs* (HS).

-a'narhwek - have a fever. *v.r.-a.i.* hab: -s, pnt: -, stat: -, prog: -, prp: -, dst: -, caus: -, rvs: -, dat: -, n-inc. wakaʔ-nárhweks *I have a fever* (R), ruʔnár-hweks *he has a fever* (HS); -a'nar=hwekčr -: uʔnarhwékčreh ‹have a fever-'ness› *fever* (HS).

-a'narhwekčr - fever. *n.s.* uʔnarhwékčreh

‹have a fever-'ness› *fever* (HS).

-aʔnarih - be warm, be hot. *v.r.-s.i.* stat: -ȩ·, prog: -, prp: -, dst: -, caus: -, rvs: -, dat: -, inc.-ɸ-ag./pat. yuʔnaríhȩ· *it is warm, it is hot* (R) [Gallatin «younaureehuh» 'Warm, hot'], wakaʔnaríhȩ· *I have a fever* (R); -rihwaʔnarih -: rurihwaʔnaríhȩ· ‹he-matter-is warm› *he is ardent* (HS); -aʔnarihaʔT -: waʔnarihá·ʔtha· ‹it-be warm-causes› *calefacient* (HS); -aʔnarihȩhst -: uʔnarihȩ́hsteh ‹be warm-'ness› *heat* (HS); -či -. -aʔnarihaʔT -: θhraʔnarihá·ʔtha· ‹again-he-be warm-causes› *he reheats it* (HS); -aʔwnaʔnarihuʔT -: ȩkaʔwnaʔ-naríhuʔt ‹prediction-I-earth-be warm-cause› *I will heat up the earth* (RC 4:5); haʔ ti -. -aʔnarih -: haʔ tyuʔnaríhȩ· ‹the so-it-is hot› *the temperature* (HS); kwéʔyȩ· ti -. -aʔnarih -: kwéʔyȩ· tyuʔ-naríhȩ· ‹barely so-it-is hot› *tepid* (HS); ti -. -tkwa̱rayȩ(T) - ti -. -aʔnarih -: tika-tkwarà·yȩʔ tyuʔnaríhȩ· ‹so-it-blood-lays so-it-is hot› *red-hot* (HS).

-aʔnarih - have a fever. *v.s.-s.i.* wakaʔ-naríhȩ· *I have a fever* (R).

-aʔnarihaʔT - calefacient. *dv.n.s.* waʔnarihá·ʔtha· ‹it-be warm-causes› *calefacient* (HS).

-aʔnarihȩhst - heat. *n.s.* uʔnarihȩ́hsteh ‹be warm-'ness› *heat* (HS).

-a̱ʔnaθ(e) - encircle, go around. *v.r.-t.* hab: ()-hs ~ -s, pnt: ()-·ʔ, stat: -, prog: -, prp: -, dst: -, caus: -, rvs: -, dat: -, inc.-kw-~-hw-pat. Requires either the translocative or the dualic prefix except in proper names. Hewitt gives two different habitual aspect forms in the same manuscript. -nȩʔnaʔna·θ -: Yenȩʔná·ʔna·č ‹one-mountain-encircles› *Mohawk Valley* (AG); -yah -. -a̱ʔnaθ(e) -: yahwahrakwaʔná·θe·ʔ ‹thither-fact-he-X-encircled› *he went around it* (HS); -yah+či -. -a̱ʔnaθ(e) -:

yahęθahrakwaʔná·θe·ʔ ‹thither-fact-again-he-X-encircled› *he went around the same side* (HS); –ne –. –athę**ʔna**ʔ = na**θ(e)** –: nehrathęʔnaʔná·θehs ‹apart-he-himself-field-encircles› *he goes around the meadow* (H 2484); nehrathę́ʔnaʔna·č ‹apart-he-himself-field-encircles› *he goes around the meadow, either within or on the outside of the meadow* (H 2484); –ne –. –athwa**ʔ**naθehę –: neyęthwaʔnaθéhęh ‹apart-one-oneself-X-encircles-much› *spiral* (HS).

–a'naθnę**ʔ**kwęti – bundle oneself up, muffle. *v.s.-a.i.* raʔnaθnęʔkwę́·tih ‹he-himself-bundle-makes› *he muffles, he bundles himself up* (HS).

–a'naθnę**ʔ**kwihsʔa – finish packing. *v.s.-a.i.* waʔęʔnaθnęʔkwíhsʔa·ʔ ‹one-oneself-bundle-finished› *one finished packing* (RC 3:39).

–a'naT(e) – reflexive. *v.r.pfx.* The form –a'nat – occurs preceding verb roots and stems that begin with *k h ʔ*. The form –a'naʔ – occurs preceding verb roots and stems that begin with *t, č, r* or *n*. The form –a'na'n – occurs preceding roots and stems that begin with the glides w or y or any vowel. The form –a'na'ne – occurs before verb roots and stems that begin with consonant clusters that condition "epenthetic" e.

–a'natkę**ʔ**črę**ʔ**nahkw – knock the evil out of. *v.s.-t.* ruʔnatkęʔčręʔnahkę́heʔ ‹he-himself-inherent power-'ness-end-instrument of-had› *it had knocked the evil out of him* (RC 30:56).

–a'natihar – fasten to (plural patient). *v.s.-t.* raʔnatíhar ‹he-himself-hangs› *he fastens to them* (HS).

–a'natkweni – be independent. *v.s.-a.i.* ruʔnatkwé·nyę ‹he-himself-is able› *he is independent* (HS).

–a'natkwęnyęhsT – respect oneself. *v.s.-a.i.* raʔnatkwęnyę́hstha ʔ ‹he-himself-treats with respect› *he respects himself* (HS).

–a**ʔ**nawę – swim, bathe. *v.r.-a.i.* hab: -s, pnt: -ʔ, stat: -·, prog: -, prp: -, dst: -, caus: -, rvs: -, dat: -, n-inc. kaʔnà·węhs *I am swimming (as an amusement), I am bathing* (R).

–a'nawę – possess. *v.s.-t.* ruʔnà·węh ‹he-himself-belongs to› *he possesses it* (RC 24:8).

–a'nawęri – ramble about, travel around. *v.s.-a.i.* raʔnawę̀·rih ‹he-himself-stirs› *he rambles about, he travels around* (R), waʔkaʔnawę́·ryeʔ ‹fact-I-myself-stirred› *I was traveling* (R).

–a'nawst – be decrepit. *v.r.-s.i.* stat: -eʔ, prog: -, prp: -, dst: -, caus: -, rvs: -, dat: -, n-inc. raʔnáwsteʔ *he is decrepit* (HS).

–a'naʔčwen – be forlorn. *v.r.-s.i.* stat: -ʔ, prog: -, prp: -, dst: -, caus: -, rvs: -, dat: -, n-inc. ruʔnáʔcweʔn *he is forlorn* (HS).

–a'naʔkęhraʔnihr – be dusty. *v.s.-s.i.* yuʔnaʔkęhraʔníhrę ‹it-itself-dust-stood up› *it is flying dust* (H-notebook), *it is dusty (e.g. a road)* (AG).

–a'naʔnihraʔT – make whole. *v.s.-a.i.*

ęyę'na'níhra't ‹prediction-one-one-self-stand up-cause› *it will make one whole* (RC 7:11).

–a'na'ner– be presumptuous. *v.s.-a.i.* ra'na'nè·rih ‹he-himself-wants› *he is presumptuous* (HS).

–a'na'nęr– extra one, leftover. *dv.n.s.* yu'na'nę̀·rę ‹it-itself-left behind› *extra one, leftover* (R).

–a'na'nęr– left(side). *dv.n.s.* yu'na'nę̀·rę ‹it-itself-left behind› *left(side)* (R).

–a'na'nęr– leavings, remainder, remains. *dv.n.s.* ha' yu'na'nę̀·rę ‹the it-itself-left behind› *leavings, remainder, remains* (HS).

–a'na'nętiha'nye'– make into. *v.s.-t.* yu'na'nętihá·'nye' ‹it-itself-made-going along› *it is making itself into it* (RC 9:6).

–a'na'nihra'T– make one whole. *v.s.-a.i.* ęyę'na'níhra't ‹prediction-one-one-self-stand up-cause› *it will make one whole* (RC 7:11).

–a'na'nyęwahT– be lavish, spend lavishly. *v.s.-a.i.* ra'na'nyęwáhtha' ‹he-himself-sacrifices› *he is lavish, he spends foolishly* (HS).

–a'na'rar– be abreast of. *v.r.-t.* hab: -ɸ, pnt: -, stat: -, prog: -, prp: -, dst: -, caus: -, rvs: -, dat: -, n-inc. newa'ná'rar *the two of them are abreast of one another* (R).

–a'na'wya'k– limp. *v.s.-a.i.* ra'ná'wya'ks ‹he-himself-back-breaks› *he limps* (HS), ra'na'wya'khę'ú'y ‹he-himself-back-breaks-much-great› *he, the big one, is limping along* (RC 25:13).

–(a)'ne– be visible, be present, project, protrude, stick out. *v.r.-s.i.* stat: -', prog: -, prp: -, dst: -tyę-, caus: -hT-, rvs: -ku-, dat: -, inc.-ɸ-ag. wá·'ne' *it protrudes, it sticks out* (H 2892), wá·'nehk *it protruded, it stuck out* (H

2892); –(a)'nehT–: ka'néhnę ‹it-be present-caused› *it offered* (RC 6:12), ra'néhtha' ‹he-be present-causes› *he offers* (R), yú·'neht ‹it-be present-caused› *it is shrill, it is sharp* (HS); –(a)'nehT–{dative II}: wa'kayę'nat-'néhtha'θ ‹fact-they=another-be present-caused-for› *they offered one* (AW 98); –t–. –(a)'ne–: nwá·'ne' ‹hither-it-is present› *it looms, it projects, it protrudes* (HS); tha–. –(a)'netyę–: thika'né·tyę' ‹unusual-it-is present-many› *others (used like cetera or alia in et cetera, et alia)* (AG); ti–. –(a)'ne–: tihrá·'ne' ‹so-he-is present› *he is another person (not the one meant, an outsider), he is somebody else (i.e., he is an odd one, in the sense of projecting or protruding beyond the complement of persons)* (H 2892), *some other male* (RC 3:83), tiká·'ne' ‹so-it-is present› *another, a different, besides* (HS); –yah–. –(a)'ne–: wewá·'ne' ‹thither-it-is present› *tip top, top, summit* (HS); –(a)haha'ne–: wahahá·'ne' ‹it-path-is present› *there is a road (lit., the road is present, stands forth, projects)* (H 2484); –(a)h=k̲ara'ne–: yuhkará·'ne' ‹it-bark-is present› *it is bitter, brackish* (RC 10:1); –čata'nehT–: yučatá·'neht ‹it-brightness-be present-caused› *it is shiny* (HS); –(ę)ta'ra'ne–: rata'rá·'ne' ‹he-head-is present› *his head sticks out* (H 2892); –(ę)tu'θa'ne–: katu'θá·'ne' ‹it-tooth-is present› *a tooth sticks out* (H 2892); –e'ra'ne–: aryawe'rá·'nek ‹unknown-it-hair-be present› *that hair be present* (R); –ę'wa=ˈnehT–: rawę'wá·'neht ‹he-back-be present-caused› *he is active* (HS); –herara'ne–: yuherará·'ne' ‹it-green-be in-is present› *nettles* (HS); –hna=wa'nehT–: yuhnawá·'neht ‹it-currentbe present-caused⟩ *it is a sharp current* (RC 12:29); **-khwa'nehT** –: rukhwá·ʔ-neht ⟨he-food-be present-caused⟩ *he is hungry* (HS); **-nę̄hsa'ne** –: kanę̄hsá·ʔneʔ ⟨it-house-is present⟩ *house protrudes, house stands out* (H 2892); **-tenę̄hsta= 'nehT** –: yutenę̄hstá·ʔneht ⟨it-be sunny-'ness-be present-causes⟩ *sunny* (HS); **-the̱'nehT** –: yú·the̱ʔneht ⟨it-X-be present-caused⟩ *it is piquant* (HS); **-wisa= 'ne** –: waʔuwisá·ʔneʔ ⟨fact-it-ice-was present⟩ *hail* (R); **-či** –. **-(ę)taʔra'ne** –. **#áh:** θhrataʔraʔneʔáh ⟨again-he-head-is present-little⟩ *a little of his head is present* (RC 24:10); **-ne** –. **-rę̄ʔna'ne** –: waʔnyerę̄ʔná·ʔneʔ ⟨fact-two-one-log-was pre-sent⟩ *one overlapped ends of logs* (RC 30:27); **tha** –. **-nę̄hsa'ne** –: thikanę̄hsá·ʔneʔ ⟨unusual-it-house-is present⟩ *it is another, is a different house* (H 2892); **tha** –. **-nę̄θa'ne** –: thyunę̄θá·ʔneʔ ⟨unusual-it-potato-was present⟩ *potatoes lie scattered about, lie about or around* (H 2484); **tha** –. **-rihwa'netyę** –: thyurihwaʔé·tyęʔ ⟨unus-ual-it-matter-is present-much⟩ *other things* (AG); **-yah** –. **-(a)hę̄'na'ne** –: wewahę̄ʔná·ʔneʔ ⟨thither-it-field-is present⟩ *there is a field* (RC 25:2); **-yah** –. **-(a)tkwira-'ne** –: wekatkwirá·ʔneʔ ⟨thither-it-branch-be present⟩ *crown of tree* (AG) *at end of branch* (RC 4:1); **-athę̄wa'nehT** –: wathę̄waʔnéhthaʔ ⟨it-itself-boat-be present-causes⟩ *dock, quay, pier, port* (HS); **-aʔrihwa'ne** –: yuʔrihwá·ʔneʔ ⟨it-itself-matter-is present⟩ *account* (HS); **-aʔrihwa'neku** –:

raʔrihwaʔné·kwahs ⟨he-himself-mat-ter-be present-undoes⟩ *he dissembles* (HS); **-ne** –. **-atʔęya'ne** –: nekakutʔę-yá·ʔneʔ ⟨two-they-themselves-enclosed area-is present⟩ *they had enclosed in barricade* (RC 33:11); **haʔ** **-(a)'ne** –: haʔ wá·ʔneʔ ⟨the it-is present⟩ *summit* (HS); **haʔ** **-rihwa'ne** –: haʔ yurihwá·ʔ-neʔ ⟨the it-matter-is present⟩ *chore* (HS).

-(a)'ne – summit. *dv.n.s.* haʔ wá·ʔneʔ ⟨the it-is present⟩ *summit* (HS).

-a'nečharhu – be enclosed. *v.s.-s.i.* yuʔ-nečhárhę ⟨it-itself-closed door⟩ *it is enclosed* (HS).

-a'nečharhuhsT – prison. *dv.n.s.* yę̄ʔ-nečharhúhsthaʔ ⟨one-oneself-close door-causes⟩ *prison* (HS).

-a'nečhari – open. *v.s.-a.i.* waʔnečhá·ryęhs ⟨it-itself-opens door⟩ *it opens* (HS).

-aʔneha'ʔT – cause; abash, shame. *v.r.-t.* hab: -haʔ, pnt: -, stat: -ę, prog: -, prp: -, dst: -, caus: -, rvs: -, dat: -, n-inc. waʔnehá·ʔnę *it caused it* (RC 26:1), waʔnehá·ʔthaʔ *it causes it* (RC 33:10), raʔnehá·ʔthaʔ *he abashes it, he shames it* (HS).

-a'nehka̱rur – paneling. *dv.n.s.* yuʔnehka-rù·rę ⟨it-itself-bark-covered⟩ *paneling* (HS).

-aʔnehskT – be antiquated, be senile, be superannuated. *v.r.-a.i.* hab: -haʔ, pnt: -ɸ, stat: -ę, prog: -, prp: -, dst: -, caus: -, rvs: -, dat: -, n-inc. kaʔnéhskthaʔ *I am senile* (R), waʔnéhskthaʔ *it is superannuated* (HS), yuʔnéhskwnę *it is antiquated* (HS).

Tuscarora Pronunciation Key:
/a/ l**a**w; /e/ h**a**t; /i/ p**i**zza; /u/ t**u**ne; /ę/ h**i**nt; /č/ **ch**eese; /h/ **h**oe; /m/ **m**other; /s/ **s**ame; /t/ **d**o (before a vowel y, or w), **t**oo (elsewhere); /k/ **g**ale (before a vowel y or w), **k**ale (elsewhere); /n/ i**nh**ale (before a consonant or word-final), **n**ote (elsewhere), /r/ hi**ss** (before a consonant or word-final), **r**un (trilled as in Italian, elsewhere); /w/ c**uff** (before a consonant other than y or word-final), **w**ay (elsewhere); /y/ fi**sh** (before a consonant or word-final), **y**ou (elsewhere), /θ/ **th**ing; /ʔ/ (the sound between the vowels in unh-unh); /·/ long vowel, /ˊ/ high pitch; /ˋ/ low pitch.

–(a)'nehT – offer. *v.s.-a.i.* ka²néhnę ‹it-be present-caused› *it offered* (RC 6:12), ra²néhtha² ‹he-be present-causes› *he offers* (R).

–(a)'nehT – be shrill, be sharp. *v.s.-a.i.* yú·²neht ‹it-be present-causes› *it is shrill, it is sharp* (HS).

–a'nehuT – exhibit, prove, show. *v.s.-a.i.* ęθwa²nehú·²nę² ‹prediction-you-your-selves-show› *you will show yourselves* (RC 33:8), ę²nehú·²nę² ‹it-it-self-showed› *it proved it* (R), ra²ne-hú·tha² ‹he-himself-shows› *he exhibits himself* (HS).

–a'nehu'nahkw – sign. *dv.n.s.* yu²nehu²-náhkę ‹it-itself-showed-instrument› *sign* (HS).

–a'nehwati – look. *v.r.-a.i.* hab: -, pnt: -, stat: -ę, prog: -, prp: -ęhte²-, dst: -, caus: -, rvs: -, dat: -, n-inc. ka²-nehwá·tyę *I have looked* (AW 52); –či -. –a'nehwati –: ęθwa²nehwatyęhte² ‹prediction-again-it-look-going to› *it will again be looking for* (AW 53).

–a'nehyahr – be virtuous. *v.s.-s.i.* ra²neh-yáhrę ‹he-himself-remembered› *he is virtuous* (HS).

–a'nehyahręhčr – adulthood, character, civilization, conscience, coyness, good manners, knowledge, manhood, memory, memory-of-self, self-respect, virtue. *n.s.* u²nehyahręhčreh ‹self-remember-'ness› *adulthood, character, civilization, conscience, coyness, knowledge, manhood, memory-of-self, self-respect, virtue* (HS), yu²nehyahręhčreh ‹it-itself-remember-'ness› *good manners, memory* (HS).

–a'nehyahrhuhkw –{dative III} use to remind. *v.s.-t.* ękayę²na²nehyarhúhkę² ‹prediction-they-themselves-remember-cause-instrument-for› *they will use it to remind themselves* (R).

–a'nekayę(T) –{dative II} dropsy. *dv.n.s.* yaku²nekayę́·tih ‹one-oneself-liquid-lay-for› *dropsy* (RC 18:title).

–a'nekęr – dregs, residue. *n.s.* u²nekę̀·reh ‹self-liquid-leave behind› *dregs, residue* (HS).

–a'nekhwah(e)r – take a meal. *v.s.-a.i.* ra²-nekhwáher ‹he-himself-food-puts up› *he takes his meal* (HS), ęhra²ne-khwáhrę² ‹prediction-he-himself-food-put up› *he will take his meal* (HS).

–a'nekhwahrahčr – table. *n.s.* u²nekhwah-ráhčreh ‹self-food-put up-'ness› *table* (RC 17:5).

–a'nekhwahruhT – tablecloth. *dv.n.s.* yę²-nekhwahrúhtha² ‹one-oneself-food-put up-cover-causes› *tablecloth* (HS).

–a'nekhwihsakT – pasturage. *dv.n.s.* wa²-nekhwihsáktha² ‹it-itself-food-seek-causes› *pasturage* (HS).

–a'nekrirurę – whiteman's. *dv.n.s.* yu²ne-krirù·rę² ‹it-it-self-is whiteman› *whiteman's* (HS), u²nekrirù·rę² ‹self-white-man› *whiteman's* (HS).

–a'nekrirurę – θáhe² peas. *dv.n.s.* yu²ne-krirù·rę² θáhe² ‹it-itself-whiteman bean› *peas* (HS); θáhe² u²nekrirù·rę² ‹bean self-whiteman› *peas* (HS).

–a²nekskru – assault, harm by force, hurt, inflict upon, maltreat, play a trick on. *v.r.-t.* hab: -h, pnt: -, stat: -, prog: -, prp: -, dst: -, caus: -, rvs: -, dat: -, n-inc. ra²nékskruh *he is assaulting it, he is harming it by force, he is hurting it, he is inflicting upon it, he is maltreating it, he is playing a trick on it* (HS); *sorcerer* (RC 24:11).

–a²nekskru – sorcerer. *dv.n.s.* ra²nékskruh ‹he-maltreats› *sorcerer* (RC 24:11).

–a'nek²u – raise, swell. *v.s.-a.i.* wa²né·k-²uhs ‹it-itself-rises› *it is raising, it is swelling (of dough)* (R); –či -. –a²nek=²uhsi –: θwa²nek²úhsyęhs ‹again-it-it-self-rise-undoes› *it springs up again* (H-notebook).

–a'**nenha** – command, hire out, serve. *v.s.-a.i.* ra'nénha'θ ‹he-himself-employs› *he commands, he hires out, he serves* (HS), wa'ę'nénha' ‹fact-one-oneself-employed› *one ordered another* (RC 27: 31).

–a'**nerkęhw** – be abundant. *v.s.-s.i.* yu'nerkę́hę ‹it-itself-have plenty-caused› *it is abundant* (HS).

–a'**ner'ęhsęti** – flourish, propagate. *v.s.-a.i.* čhiya'ner'ęhsę́·ti ‹you all!-yourselves-clan-make› *propagate!* (AG), wa'ka'ner'ęhsę́·ti' ‹fact-I-myself-clan-made› *I flourish, I propagate* (AG).

–a'**ne θnęri** – break open a healing sore, hurt. *v.r.-a.i.* hab: -ęhs, pnt: -, stat: -, prog: -, prp: -, dst: -, caus: -, rvs: -, dat: -, n-inc. ra'neθnę́·ryęhs *he hurts himself, again he breaks open a sore* (H-notebook).

–a'**ne θwek** – want. *v.r.-t.* hab: -, pnt: -ę', stat: -ih, prog: -, prp: -, dst: -, caus: -T, rvs: -, dat: -, n-inc. ru'neθwé·kih *he wants it* (RC 1:8), waka'neθwé·kih *I want it* (R), akaku'neθwekíhek *that they were willing* (L 64), ęhru'neθwé·kę' *he will want* (HS); –a'ne = θwekT –: yu'né·θwekt ‹it-want-caused› *it is urgent, it is necessary, it needs, it wants* (HS), ru'né·θwekt ‹he-want-caused› *it behooves him* (HS).

–a'**ne θwekT** – behoove; be necessary, be urgent. *v.s.-a.i.* yu'né·θwekt ‹it-want-caused› *it is urgent, it is necessary, it needs, it wants* (HS), ru'né·θwekt ‹he-want-caused› *it behooves him* (HS).

–a'**neti(y)** – get dressed. *v.s.-a.i.* wa'ę'né·ti' ‹fact-one-oneself-produced› *one got dressed* (R).

–a'**netkę'** – rise. *v.r.-a.i.* hab: -θ, pnt: -ɸ, stat: -ɸ, prog: -, prp: -, dst: -, caus: -, rvs: -, dat: -, n-inc. yu'nétkę' *risen (of bread), it has risen* (L 34); –t –. –a'netkę' –: nwa'nétkę'θ ‹hither-it-rises› *east: it rises there* (RC 4:1).

–a'**netkwahtręhsT** – belt. *dv.n.s.* wa'netkwahtrę́hstha' ‹it-itself-stomach-ties-for› *belt* (HS).

–a'**netyahčihę** – be ready, be fully dressed. *v.s.-a.i.* ru'netyahčíhę· ‹he-himself-produced-very-much› *he is ready, he is fully dressed* (R), yu'netyahčíhę· ‹it-itself-produced-very-much› *all ready* (R).

–a'**netyahčr** – clothes, raiment. *n.s.* u'netyáhčreh ‹self-produced-'ness› *clothes, raiment* (HS).

–a'**netyahst** – attire, clothes, dress, harness, raiment. *n.s.* u'netyáhsteh ‹self-produced-'ness› *attire, clothes, dress, harness, raiment* (HS).

–a'**newrękuhT** – draft of air. *n.s.* yu'newrękúhnę ‹it-itself-air-went through› *draft of air* (AG).

–a'**newyęhsT** – retain knowledge. *v.s.-a.i.* ra'newyę́hstha' ‹he-himself-know how-causes› *he retains (knowledge)* (HS).

–a'**newyęhw** – be adroit, be crafty, be ingenious, be skillful. *v.s.-a.i.* ra'newyę́hę ‹he-himself-know how-caused› *he is adroit, he is crafty, he is ingenious, he is skillful* (HS).

–a'**newyęhw** – carpenter. *v.s.-a.i.* ra'ne-

---

wyę́hę ‹he-himself-know how-caused›
carpenter (HS).
-a'newyęnęT – finish preparations. *v.s.-
a.i.* wahra'newyęnę́·'na' ‹fact-he-him-
self-preparations-concluded› *he finished his preparations* (RC 12:3).
-a'newyęnęti – create. *v.s.-t.* ra'newyę-
nę́tih ‹he-himself-preparations-makes›
he creates it (HS).
-a'ne'ku – flee, run away. *v.r.-a.i.* hab: -
ahs, pnt: -', stat: -ę, prog: -ęha'nye',
prp: -he-, dst: -'θę-, caus: -ahT-, rvs:
-, dat: -, inc.-φ-ag. yu'né'kwę *it had
run away* (RC 2:10), ra'né'kwahs *he
flees* (HS), wa'kayę'né'ku' *they ran
away* (RC 24:9); **-a'ne'kuhe'θę -**: waka'nekuhé'θę·' ‹I-fled-going to-much›
I avoided another (R); **-a'ne'kwah =
shę(T) -**: ra'ne'kwáhshęhs ‹he-flee-
'ness-lays› *he takes refuge* (HS); **-a' =
ne'kwahshę'nahkw -**: yę'ne'kwahshę'náhkhwa' ‹one-flee-'ness-lays-instrument› *refuge* (HS); **-a'ne'kwęha =
'nye' -**: ęhru'ne'kwęhá·'nye' ‹predic-
tion-he-flee-going along› *he will be
running away* (RC 6:7); **-či -. -a' =
ne'ku -**: či'nya'né'ku ‹again-we-flee›
let us two run away again (RC 30:17);
ęθę'né'ku' ‹prediction-again-it-flee› *it
will get away* (RC 7:3); **-yah -. -a'ne' =
kuhe'T -**: wekaku'ne'kuhé'nę ‹thither-
they-flee-going to-caused› *it is making
them run there* (RC 11:16); **-yah -.
-a'ne'kwahT -**: yahwahra'né'kwaht
‹thither-fact-he-flee-caused› *he ran
over there* (RC 31:4); **-atkerha'ne' =
ku -**: ęhsatkyerha'né'ku' ‹prediction-
you-yourself-body-flee› *you will pull
back, you will withdraw* (RC 3:54).
-a'ne'kuhe'θę – avoid. *v.s.-t.* waka'ne'-
kuhé'θę·' ‹I-fled-going to-much› *I
avoided another* (R).
-a'ne'kwahshę(T) – take refuge. *v.s.-a.i.*
ra'ne'kwáhshęhs ‹he-flee-'ness-lays›

he takes refuge (HS).
-a'ne'kwahshę'nahkw – refuge. *dv.n.s.*
yę'ne'kwahshę'náhkhwa' ‹one-flee-
'ness-lays-instrument› *refuge* (HS).
-a'ne'nawak – shake free of. *v.s.-t.* wahra'ne'nà·wak ‹fact-he-himself-X-
shook› *he shook himself free of
(things clinging to him)* (H-notebook).
-a'nę – become. *v.r.-t.* hab: -h, pnt: -',
stat: -', prog: -, prp: -, dst: -, caus: -,
rvs: -, dat: -, inc.-φ-ag. ká·'nęh *I
become, I am becoming* (H 2892),
wá·'nęh *it becomes* (H 2892), ę́·'nę'
it became (RC 25:3), wahrá·'nę' *he
became* (R); **-a'nę -.#ęwe.{dative I}**:
θa'nęhę̀·we'θ ‹you!-become-genuine-
for› *behave yourself!* (R); **-a'nę' -**:
yu'nę́'ę ‹it-become-began› *it became,
it had become* (RC 30:8), neyu'nę́'ę
‹two-it-become-began› *two became
one* (RC 26:21); **-(ę)tera'nę -**: rute-
rá·'nę' ‹he-conception-be-comes› *he
is subject* (HS); **-θrahkwa'nę -**: ęh-
sθrahkwá·'nę' ‹prediction-you-coagu-
lation-become› *you will can it, you
will preserve it* (R); **-a'nę'ęha'nye' -**:
yu'nę'ęhá·'nye' ‹it-become-began-
going along› *it is becoming, it is
changing into* (RC 21:10); **-ne -. -ya' =
ta'nę -**: neyuya'tá·'nę' ‹apart-it-body-
becomes› *it is becoming, it becomes
it, it is appropriate, it is appropriate to
it, it is seemly* (HS); **á·thu' -a'nę -**:
á·thu' wá·'nęh ‹cold it-becomes› *it is
becoming cold* (H 2892), á·thu' ę́·'nę'
‹cold fact-it-became› *it became cold*
(H 2892), á·thu' ęwá·'nę' ‹cold pre-
diction-it-become› *it will become cold*
(H 2892); **-atkę - -a'nę -**: útkę' ká·'nęh
‹inherent power I-be-come› *I am becoming a witch* (H 2892); **-či'yu -
-a'nę -**: ruči'yúha' yú·'nę' ‹he-nausea-
covers it-became› *he is enervated, he
became feeble* (HS); **ę́·či -a'nę -**: ę́·či

wá·ˀnęˀ ‹one it-becomes› *it coalesces* (HS); ę́·či -ne -. -a'nę -: ę́·či nehrá·ˀnęˀ ‹one two-he-becomes› *he unites* (HS); -hčihrę - -a'nę -: uhčíhręˀ wakaˀnę́ˀę ‹bear I-become-began› *I have become a bear* (H 2892); kwęhs -yaˀta'nę -: kwęhs ahruyaˀtá·ˀnęk ‹no unknown-he-body-become› *he is unbecoming* (HS); -yahstiyu - -a'nę -: ruyahstí·yu· wá·ˀnęˀ ‹he-individual-is great it-becomes› *his decline of years* (HS).

-a'nę -/-ę -/-ihrę - affirm, assert, say. *v.r.-a.i.* hab: (-aˀnę)-h, pnt: (-ihrę)-·ˀ, stat: (-ę)-·, prog: -, prp: -hteˀ-, dst: -, caus: -, rvs: -, dat: -, n-inc. One of the very few truly suppletive verbs in Tuscarora. -a'nę -: yę́·ˀnęh *she says* (RC 26:26), sá·ˀnęh *you say* (RC 3:18), rá·ˀnęh *he affirms* (HS), kayę́ˀnęhahk *they said* (R); -a'nę -: haˀ rá·ˀnęh ‹the he-says› *his affirmation* (HS); -a'nęh = teˀ -: raˀnę́hteˀθ ‹he-said-going to› *he is going to say* (RC 12:24); tú ˀks -a = 'nę -: tú ˀks wá·ˀnęh ‹doo'ks it-says› *cranberry (Vaccinium* sp.*)* (R); -ę -: rá·wę· *he asserted* (HS), *he said* (R), wá·kę· *I have said* (R), í·θę· *you have said* (R); -ę -: haˀ rá·wę· ‹the he-said› *his assertion* (HS); -t -. -ę -: nahrá·wę· ‹hither-he-said› *he replied* (R); -ihrę -: číhrę· *say it!* (R), wahrę́hrę·ˀ *he said* (RC 1:8), waˀkíhrę·ˀ *I said* (R); -či -. -ihrę -: čaíhrę·ˀ ‹again-one-said› *one repeated* (RC 26:25); -t -. -ihrę -: nahréhrę·ˀ ‹hither-he-said› *he replied* (RC 12:19); teˀ -ihrę -: teˀ číhrę· ‹what you!-say› *I guess so, whatever you say* (R).

-a'nę - affirmation. *dv.n.s.* haˀ rá·ˀnęh ‹the he-says› *his affirmation* (HS).

-a'nę -.#ęwe.{dative I} behave. *v.s.-a.i.* θaˀnęhę̀·weˀθ ‹you!-become-genuine-for› *behave yourself!* (R).

-a'nęčhuT - genuflect, kneel. *v.r.-a.i.* hab: -haˀ, pnt: -, stat: -ɸ, prog: -, prp: -, dst: -, caus: -, rvs: -, dat: -, n-inc. ruˀnę́čhu·t *he is kneeling* (HS), raˀnęčhú·thaˀ *he kneels* (HS), *he genuflects* (R); haˀ -a'nęčhuT -: haˀ ruˀnę́čhu·t ‹the he-knelt› *genuflection* (HS).

-a'nęčhuT - genuflection. *dv.n.s.* haˀ ruˀnę́čhu·t ‹the he-knelt› *genuflection* (HS).

-a'nęhkaryaˀk - starve. *v.r.-a.i.* hab: -s, pnt: -ɸ, stat: -, prog: -, prp: -, caus: -, rvs: -, dat: -, n-inc. kayęˀnęhká·ryaˀks *they starve* (L 62), waˀkayęˀnęhká·ryaˀk *they starved* (L 61); -a'nęhka = ryaˀk -: uˀnęhkaryáˀkę ‹starve› *famine, hunger, starvation* (HS).

-a'nęhkaryaˀk - famine, hunger, starvation. *dv.n.s.* uˀnęhkaryáˀkę ‹starve› *famine, hunger, starvation* (HS).

-a'nęhkwaru'narihsi - unbridle. *v.s.-t.* raˀnęhkwaruˀnaríhsyęhs ‹he-himself-bridle-fasten-undoes› *he unbridles it* (HS).

-a'nęhkʷek - suffocate. *v.s.-a.i.* raˀnęhkweks ‹he-himself-X-closes› *he is suffocating* (HS).

-a'nęhniha - lend, rent. *v.r.-t.* hab: -hs, pnt: -ˀ, stat: -ę, prog: -, prp: -dst: -, caus: -, rvs: -, dat: -, n-inc. raˀnęhníhahs *he lends it, he rents it* (L 61), wahra⁷nẹhníha⁷ *he lent it* (L 61), ru⁷nẹhníhẹ *he lent it* (L 61), θa⁷nẹhníha *lend it!* (L 61).

–a'nẹhnyayẹ – beg. *v.r.-a.i.* hab: -, pnt: -⁷, stat: -, prog: -, prp: -, dst: -, caus: -, rvs: -, dat: -, n-inc. wa⁷kayẹ⁷nẹhnyà·yẹ⁷ *they begged* (RC 6:16).

–a'nẹhrar – be dirty. *v.s.-s.i.* This root also has the form –a'nẹ⁷rar – for some speakers of modern Tuscarora. yu⁷néhra⁷r ‹it-itself-dirt-is in› *it is dirty*; –a'nẹhrar –: u⁷néhrareh ‹self-dirt-be in› *dirt, filth* (HS); –a'nẹhrar –.#hči: u⁷nẹhraréhči ‹self-dirt-be in-very› *dirty* (HS); –nẹhsa'nẹhrar –: unẹhsa⁷néhrareh ‹house-self-dirt-is in› *it is a dirty house* (H 2484); –tahskwa'nẹhrar –: yutahskwa⁷néhra⁷r ‹it-domestic animal-self-dirt-is in› *animals are dirty* (R).

–a'nẹhrar – dirt, filth. *n.s.* u⁷néhrareh ‹self-dirt-is in› *dirt, filth* (HS).

–a'nẹhrar –.#hči dirty. *n.s.* u⁷nẹhraréhči ‹self-dirt-be in-very› *dirty* (HS).

–a'nẹhrarawẹri – dirty, soil. *v.s.-t.* ra⁷nẹhrarawẹ·rih ‹he-himself-dirt-stirs› *he dirties it, he soils it* (HS).

–a'nẹhruha – dive, plunge. *v.s.-a.i.* ra⁷nẹhrúhahs ‹he-himself-scalp-puts in water› *he dives in, he plunges* (HS).

–a'nẹhruha – diver. *dv.n.s.* ra⁷nẹhrúhahs ‹he-himself-scalp-puts in water› *diver* (HS).

–a'nẹhruhar – be diverted. *v.s.-a.i.* ru⁷nẹhrúhar ‹he-himself-scalp-washes› *he is diverted* (HS).

–a⁷nẹhskẹ⁷θrahkw – basis. *dv.n.s.* ha⁷yu⁷nẹhskẹ⁷θráhkẹ ‹the it-itself-house-supported-instrument› *basis* (HS).

–a'nẹhsku⁷yeT – be surreptitious. *v.s.-s.i.* yu⁷nẹhsku⁷yé·⁷nẹ ‹it-itself-stole-moving› *it is surreptitious* (HS).

–a'nẹhstahkw – foundation. *dv.n.s.* yu⁷nẹhstáhkẹ ‹it-itself-house-gathered› *foundation* (HS).

–a'nẹhtir –{dative III} be hardy. *v.s.-a.i.* ẹ⁷nẹhtì·rẹ⁷ ‹fact-it-itself-was durable-for› *it was hardy* (RC 26:34).

–a'nẹhtira⁷T – dare, hazard. *v.s.-a.i.* ra⁷nẹhtirá⁷tha⁷ ‹he-himself-be durable-causes› *he dares, he hazards (e.g., a guess)* (H-notebook), ra⁷nẹhtì·ra⁷č ‹he-himself-be durable-causes› *he dares, he hazards (e.g., a guess)* (H-notebook), ra⁷nẹhtirá⁷nẹ ‹he-himself-be durable-caused› *he dared* (H-notebook).

–a'nẹhwati – search; cheat. *v.r.-a.i.* hab: -, pnt: -, stat: -ẹ·, prog: -, prp: -hte⁷-, dst: -, caus: -ẹ⁷T-, rvs: -, dat: -, n-inc. ka⁷nẹhwá·tyẹ *I searched* (AW 52), kaku⁷nẹhwá·tyẹ· *they cheated* (MP); –a'nẹhwatyẹhte⁷ –: ẹkheya⁷nẹhwatyẹ́hte⁷ ‹prediction-I=another-cheat-going to› *I will be going to cheat another* (RC 27:17); kwẹhs –a'nẹhwatyẹ⁷T –: kwẹhs aryu⁷nẹhwatyẹ́⁷nek ‹no unknown-it-cheat-cause› *it is unsearchable* (HS).

–a'nẹkuhnahkw – passage. *dv.n.s.* yẹ⁷nẹkuhnáhkhwa⁷ ‹one-oneself-go through-causes-instrument› *passage* (HS).

–a'nẹkuhnahnẹ – escape, traverse. *v.s.-a.i.* ru⁷nẹkuhnáhnẹ· ‹he-himself-go through-caused-much› *he traversed* (HS), wa⁷kayẹ⁷nẹkuhnáhnẹ⁷ ‹fact-they-themselves-go through-caused-much› *they escaped* (AW 102).

–a'nẹkuhT – pass through, surpass. *v.s.-t.* ẹwa⁷nẹ́·kuht ‹prediction-it-itself-go through-cause› *it will pass through it* (RC 15:4), wa⁷kayẹ⁷nẹ́·kuht ‹fact-they-themselves-go through-caused› *they passed through it* (RC 26:15), ẹka⁷nẹ́·kuht ‹prediction-I-myself-go through-cause› *I will pass through it* (RC 11:23), wa⁷nẹkúhtha⁷ ‹it-itself-go through-causes› *it is transient* (HS), ra'nękúhtha'? ‹he-himself-go through-causes› *he passes it by, he surpasses it* (HS).

–a'nękuhT – bygone. *dv.n.s.* yu'nękúhnę ‹it-itself-go through-caused› *bygone* (HS).

–a'nękuhT – past. *dv.n.s.* ha'? yu'nękúhnę ‹the it-itself-go through-caused› *the past* (HS).

–a'nękʷehstawęniyu – be a man-god, be theandric. *v.s.-s.i.* ra'nękwehstawęnì·- yu'? ‹he-himself-human-'ness-is god› *he is a man-god, he is theandric* (HS).

–a'nękʷehstihs'a – enter the prime of life, mature. *v.s.-a.i.* ra'nękwehstíhs'ahs ‹he-himself-human-'ness-finishes› *he matures* (HS), ru'nękwehstíhs'ę ‹he-himself-human-'ness-finished› *he is in the prime of life* (HS).

–a'nęna·hyęhsT – ally oneself, associate oneself. *v.s.-a.i.* ra'nęnahyéhstha' ‹he-himself-ally-causes› *he allies himself, he associates himself* (HS).

–a'nęnawayę'nahkw – storehouse. *dv.n.s.* yę'nęnawayę'náhkhwa' ‹one-oneself-goods-lays-instrument› *storehouse* (HS).

–a'nęnayehsT – make proud. *v.s.-a.i.* ra'?- nęnayéhstha' ‹he-himself-be proud-causes› *he makes himself proud* (HS).

–a'nęnayę – hide. *v.r.-a.i.* hab: -, pnt: -'?, stat: -, prog: -, prp: -, dst: -, caus: -, rvs: -, dat: -, n-inc. wahra'nęnà·yę' ‹fact-he-himself-concealed› *he hid himself* (RC 3:70).

–a'nęne'ner – be execrable, be mean, be odious, be vile. *v.r.-s.i.* stat: -ϕ, prog: -, prp: -, dst: -, caus: -, rvs: -, dat: -, n-inc. yu'nęné'ner *it is execrable, it is mean, it is odious, it is vile* (HS), ru'- nęné'ner *he is mean* (HS); –a'nęne'? = nerčrakęw: u'nęne'nerčrá·kęw ‹be mean-'ness-in› *meanly* (HS); ha'? –a'? = nęne'ner –: ha'? yu'nęné'ner ‹the it-is mean› *meanness* (HS).

–a'nęne'ner – meanness. *dv.n.s.* ha'? yu'- nęné'ner ‹the it-is mean› *meanness* (HS).

–a'nęne'nerčrakęw meanly. *n.s.* u'nęne'- nerčrá·kęw ‹be mean-'ness-in› *meanly* (HS).

–a'nęnęheratęhT – meritorious. *dv.n.s.* yu'nęnęherá·tęht ‹it-itself-thank-caus- ed› *meritorious* (HS).

–a'nęnęhkar – be shorn. *v.s.-s.i.* yu'nęnęh- karę ‹it-itself-cut hair› *it is shorn* (HS).

–a'nęnęhsę'neT – go alongside of the house, hide behind the house. *v.s.-a.i.* ra'nęnęhsę'né·tha' ‹he-himself-house-hides behind› *he goes alongside of the house, he hides behind the house* (HS).

–a'nęnęhskwahčrakęw stealth. *n.s.* u'nę-nęhskwáhčrakęw ‹self-steal-'ness-in› *stealth* (HS).

–a'nęnęhskwahT – go stealthily. *v.s.-a.i.* ra'nęnęhskwáhtha' ‹he-himself-steal-causes› *he goes stealthily* (HS).

–a'nęnęhskwahT – stealth. *v.s.-a.i.* u'nę-nęhskwaht ‹self-steal-cause› *stealth* (HS).

–a'nęnęhstahkw – foundation. *dv.n.s.* yu'-

Tuscarora Pronunciation Key:
/a/ l<u>a</u>w; /e/ h<u>a</u>t; /i/ p<u>i</u>zza; /u/ t<u>u</u>ne; /ę/ h<u>in</u>t; /č/ <u>ch</u>eese; /h/ <u>h</u>oe; /m/ <u>m</u>other; /s/ <u>s</u>ame; /t/ <u>d</u>o (before a vowel y, or w), <u>t</u>oo (elsewhere); /k/ <u>g</u>ale (before a vowel y or w), <u>k</u>ale (elsewhere); /n/ i<u>nh</u>ale (before a consonant or word-final), <u>n</u>ote (elsewhere), /r/ hi<u>ss</u> (before a consonant or word-final), <u>r</u>un (trilled as in Italian, elsewhere); /w/ cu<u>ff</u> (before a consonant other than y or word-final), <u>w</u>ay (elsewhere); /y/ fi<u>sh</u> (before a consonant or word-final), <u>y</u>ou (elsewhere), /θ/ <u>th</u>ing; /'?/ (the sound between the vowels in unh-unh); /·/ long vowel, /´/ high pitch; /`/ low pitch.

nęnęhstáhkę ‹it-itself-house-collected› *foundation (of building)* (HS).

−a'nęnęhwakT − pretend to be sick. *v.s.-a.i.* ru'nęnęhwá·knę ‹he-himself-ached› *he pretended to be sick* (HS).

−a'nęnęhwaru'yehsT − be licentious, fornicate. *v.s.-a.i.* ra'nęnęhwaru'yéhstha' ‹he-himself-brain-bend-causes› *he fornicates, he is licentious* (HS).

−a'nęnęhweči − spend the night. *v.s.-a.i.* nę'nęnęhwé·či' ‹so-fact-it-itself-spent the night› *it spent so many nights* (RC 30:18).

−a'nęnę'yahsT − caper, gambol, get drunk, make merry. *v.s.-a.i.* ra'nęnę'yáhstha'‹he-himself-alcohol-uses› *he gets drunk* (RC 3:70), *he capers, he gambols, he makes merry* (HS).

−a'nęnę'yaksę'T − be unruly. *v.s.-a.i.* ra'nęnę'yaksę'tha' ‹he-himself-alcohol-be bad-causes› *he is unruly* (HS).

−a'nęnhahnę − be imperious. *v.s.-a.i.* ru'nęnháhnę· ‹he-himself-commanded-much› *he is imperious* (HS).

−a'nęnhatuhsT − be chilled, shiver. *v.s.-a.i.* ru'nęnhatúhsnę ‹he-himself-be alive-froze› *he is chilled, he shivers* (HS).

−a'nęnha'nę'-{dative I} mourn. *v.s.-a.i.* ęθa'nęnhá·'nę'θ ‹prediction-you-yourself-be alive-became› *you will mourn, it will deaden your life (said when one wantonly kills a bird, snake, brute, or insect)* (H-notebook).

−a'nęnhehkčr − life. *n.s.* u'nęnhéhkčreh ‹be alive-instru-ment-'ness› *life* (HS).

−a'nęnhehkčrukę' lifeless. *n.s.* u'nęnhehkčrú·kę' ‹be alive-instrument-'ness-less› *lifeless* (HS), ra'nęnhehkčrú·kę' ‹he-himself-be alive-instrument-'ness-less› *he is inanimate* (HS).

−a'nęnhehkT − life, soul. *n.s.* u'nęnhehkt ‹self-be alive-instrument-cause› *life* (HS), *soul* (AG), akwa'nęnhehkt ‹I-myself-be alive-instrument-cause› *my*

life substance (RC 3:19).

−a'nęnhehkT −.#keha·' spiritual. *n.s.* u'nęnhehktkyéha·' ‹self-be alive-instru-ment-cause-customarily› *spiritual* (HS).

−a'nęnhęT − beseech, complain, invoke. *v.s.-a.i.* ra'nęnhę́·tha' ‹he-himself-be alive-concludes› *he beseeches, he complains, he invokes* (HS).

−a'nęnhihsakT − occupation, trade. *dv.n.s.* yę'nęnhihsáktha' ‹one-oneself-be alive-seek-causes› *occupation, a trade* (HS).

−a'nęnhihT − abjure, evade, renounce, reprobate. *v.s.-t.* ra'nęnhíhtha' ‹he-himself-ignore-causes› *he abjures it, he evades it, he renounces it, he reprobates it* (HS).

−a'nęnhihT −{dative II} be embarrassed. *v.s.-a.i.* ru'nęnhihná·ti· ‹he-himself-ignore-caused-for› *he is embarrassed* (HS).

−a'nęnhuθnę be an orphan. *v.r.-k.* wa'nęnhú·θnę *orphan* (HS).

−a'nęnhwiyę − do penance. *v.r.-a.i.* hab: -h, pnt: -, stat: -, prog: -, prp: -, dst: -, caus: -, rvs: -, dat: -, n-inc. ra'nęnhwì·yęh *he does penance* (HS).

−a'nęniharhu − intermeddle. *v.r.-a.i.* hab: -hs, pnt: -, stat: -ę°, prog: -, prp: -, dst: -, caus: -, rvs: -, dat: -, n-inc. ra'nęnihárhuhs *he intermeddles* (HS); −ne−. −a'nęniharhu −: nehru'nęnihárhę ‹apart-he-intermeddled› *he interferes* (HS).

−a'nęnitęhT − humble. *v.s.-a.i.* ra'nęnitę́htha' ‹he-himself-is poor› *he humbles himself* (HS).

−a'nęnur close relatives, lovers, friends, in-laws. *n.r.* aln: akya'nę̀·nur *my sister, my brother* (AG)/inaln: ra'nę̀·nur *his friends* (RC 27:25), n-inc., n.sfx: -. ra'nę̀·nur *his friends* (RC 27: 25), akya'nę̀·nur *my sister (said by* brother), *brother (said by sister)* (AG) [Gallatin «eanunnoor» 'Sister'], nyę'-nę·nur *one's close relatives* (RC 6:6), neyę'nę·nur *the two of them are close relatives: lovers* (RC 3:9); −a'nęnurčr −: u'nęnúrčreh ‹be close relatives-'ness› *sister, sisterhood* (HS).

−a'nęnurčr − sister, sisterhood. *n.s.* u'-nęnúrcreh ‹be close relatives-'ness› *sister, sisterhood* (HS).

−a'nęr − be slight. *v.s.-s.i.* ra'nę·rih ‹he-himself-left behind› *he is slight (small in stature)* (HS).

−a'nęrhw − cloud, get cloudy. *v.s.-a.i.* hab: -, pnt: -a·t, stat: -, prog: -, prp: -, dst: -, caus: -, rvs: -, dat: -, n-inc. Takes the completive suffix wherever the punctual aspect would be expected. ę'nęrhwa·t *it got cloudy* (R); −a'nęrhw −: u'nęrhweh ‹cloud› *cumulus cloud, nimbus cloud, storm cloud, thundercap* (R); −t −. −a'nęrhwitkę −: nę'nęrhwí·tkę' ‹hither-it-cloud-came forth› *clouds came forth there* (RC 36:1); kwęhs −a'nęrhw −: kwęhs aryu'-nęrhwek ‹no unknown-it-cloud› *it is unclouded* (HS).

−a'nęrhw − cumulus cloud, nimbus cloud, storm cloud, thundercap. *n.s.* u'nęr-hweh ‹cloud› *cumulus cloud, nimbus cloud, storm cloud, thundercap* (R).

−a'nęri − breathe. *v.s.-a.i.* ka'nę·ryęhs ‹I-myself-breath› *I breathe* (RC 3:20), ra'nę·ryęhs ‹he-himself-breaths› *he breathes* (HS), neyę'nę·ryę ‹two-one-themselves-breathed› *the two of them breathed* (RC 3:14), wa'ka'nę·ri'

‹fact-I-myself-breathed› *I breathed* (R).

−a'nęri −.#ú'y sigh. *v.s.-a.i.* ra'nęryęhs-'ú'y ‹he-himself-breath-great› *he sighs* (HS), ęhra'nęri'ú'y ‹prediction-he-himself-breath-great› *he will sigh* (HS).

−a'nęrihshę(T) − rest. *v.s.-a.i.* ra'nęríhshęh ‹he-himself-breath-'ness-lays› *he is resting* (L 22), ru'nęrihshę·'nahk ‹he-himself-breath-'ness-laid› *he has rested* (L 22), ru'nęríhshę· ‹he-himself-breath-'ness-lay› *he has (gone to) rest* (L 22), wahra'nęríhshę' ‹fact-he-him-self-breath-'ness-laid› *he rested* (L 22).

−a'nęrihshę'nahkw − resting place. *dv.n.s.* yę'nęrihshę'náhkhwa' ‹one-oneself-breath-'ness-lays-instrument› *resting place* (HS).

−a'nęrihstiya'k − expire. *v.s.-a.i.* ra'nę-rihstì·ya'ks ‹he-himself-breath-'ness-breaks› *he expires* (H-notebook).

−a'nęrihstuhar − din. *dv.n.s.* yu'nęrih-stúhar ‹it-itself-breath-'ness-wash› *din* (HS).

−a'nęru' close relatives, lovers, friends. *n.r.* inaln: ra'nę·ru' *his good friend* (R), n-inc., n.sfx. -. ra'nę·ru' *his good friend* (R), nya'nę·ruhk *you and I have been friends* (RC 25:16), wa'-nyę'nę·ru' *the two of them became friends* (M 87); −a'nęru'.#kęha'nę': ra'nęru'kęha'nę' ‹he-is close friends-many› *his close friends* (RC 14:6); −a'nęru'čhę(T) −: wa'nęrú'čhę' ‹it-be good friend-'ness-lays› *her close friend, boyfriend, lover* (RC 34:38);

–a'nęru'čr –: u'nęrú'čreh ‹be good friends-'ness› *mistress* (HS); –a'**nęru'** = **čręti** –: ra'nęru'črę̇·tih ‹he-be good friends-'ness-makes› *he befriends* (HS).

–a'**nęru'čhę(T)** – be a close friend, be a boyfriend, be a lover. *v.s.-s.i.* wa'nęrú'čhę' ‹it-be good friend-'ness-lays› *her close friend, boyfriend, lover* (RC 34:38).

–a'**nęru'čr** – mistress. *n.s.* u'nęrú'čreh ‹be close friends-'ness› *mistress* (HS).

–a'**nęru'čręti** – befriend. *v.s.-t.* ra'nęru'črę̇·tih ‹he-be good friends-'ness-makes› *he befriends* (HS).

–a'**nęryehT** – gills. *dv.n.s.* wa'nęryéhtha' ‹it-itself-breathe-causes› *gills (of fish)* (SH 375).

–a'**nęθratyę'nę** – taste. *v.s.-t.* ra'nęθra-tyę́'nę ‹he-himself-taste-tries› *he tastes it* (HS).

–a'**nęθrętya'T** – fondle. *v.s.-t.* ra'nęθrę-tyá'tha' ‹he-himself-be so much-make-causes› *he fondles it* (HS).

–a'**nęθriyuhT** – be contumacious. *v.s.-a.i.* ru'nęθriyúhnę ‹he-himself-be so much-be great-caused› *he was contumacious* (HS), ra'nęθriyúhtha' ‹he-himself-be so much-be great-causes› *he is contumacious* (HS).

–a'**nęt** – take along food. *v.r.-a.i.* hab: -, pnt: -ɸ, stat: -, prog: -, prp: -, dst: -, caus: -a'T-, rvs: -, dat: -, n-inc. –a'**nętahčr** –: u'nętáhčreh ‹take along food-'ness› *provisions (food for a journey or work)* (HS); –a'**nęta'T** –: wa'kayę'nę́·ta't ‹fact-they-take along food caused› *they took something to eat* (RC 32:1); –**ne** –. –a'**nęt** –: wa'tka-yę́·'nę·t ‹fact-apart-they-took along food› *they entertained* (RC 36:title).

–a'**nętahčr** – provisions. *n.s.* u'nętáhčreh ‹take along food-'ness› *provisions (food for a journey or work)* (HS).

–a'**nętaknahθehT** – arcanum. *dv.n.s.* yu'-nętakwnahθéhnę ‹it-itself-room-hid› *arcanum* (HS).

–a'**nęt(a')** – lament, mourn, suffer. *v.r.-a.i.* hab: -()θ, pnt: -()ɸ, stat: -ę, prog: -, prp: -, dst: -, caus: -, rvs: -, dat: -, n-inc. yę'nę́·'nę *one lamented* (RC 34:11), ra'nę́·ta'θ *mourner* (HS), kayę'-nę́·ta'θ *they are compatient, they suffer together, they lament together* (HS), ęhra'nę́·ta' *he will mourn* (HS), yę'nę́·ta'θ *one laments for it* (RC 3:26).

–a'**nęt(a')** – Condolence Ceremony. *dv.n.s.* Kayę'nę́·ta'θ ‹they-lament-for› *Condolence Ceremony* (R).

–a'**nęta'nurahst** – quench thirst. *v.r.-a.i.* hab: -ha', pnt: -, stat: -, prog: -, prp: -, dst: -, caus: -, rvs: -, dat: -, n-inc. ra'nęta'nuráhstha' *he quenches his thirst, he slakes his thirst, he wets his thirst* (HS).

–a'**nęta'T** – take something to eat. *v.s.-a.i.* wa'kayę'nę́·ta't ‹fact-they-took along food-caused› *they took something to eat* (RC 32:1).

–a'**nęte** – be a certain one. *v.s.-s.i.* wa'-nę́·te' ‹it-itself-is a certain› *it is a certain one* (RC 9:5).

–a'**nętenęhsT** – bask in the sun. *v.s.-a.i.* ru'nętenę́hsnę ‹he-himself-be sunny-caused› *he basks in the sun* (HS).

–a'**nęti** – be born. *v.s.-a.i.* ra'nę́·tih ‹he-himself-makes› *he is born* (HS), wah-ra'nę́·ti' ‹fact-he-himself-made› *he was born* (L 32).

–a'**nętihyę** – provide for oneself, save for oneself, save up. *v.r.-t.* hab: -hs, pnt: -', stat: -, prog: -, prp: -, dst: -, caus: -, rvs: -, dat: -, n-inc. ra'nętíhyęhs *he provides himself with it, he stores it for himself* (R), wa'kayę'nętíhyę' *they saved some for themselves* (RC 3:67), ęča'nętíhyę' *that you save up*

(RC 29:12), wa'nętíhyęhs *it stores it* (MG 88).

–a'nętikahT – chase, pursue closely. *v.s.-t.* ra'nętikáhne' ‹he-himself-chases› *he chases it* (RC 25:14), *he pursues it closely* (HS), wahra'nętí·kaht ‹fact-he-himself-chased› *he chased* (RC 25:10).

–a'nętu'θęti – teethe. *v.s.-a.i.* ra'nętu'-θę́·tih ‹he-himself-tooth-makes› *he teethes* (HS).

–a'nę' – become. *v.s.-t.* yu'nę́'ę ‹it-become-began› *it became it, it had become it* (RC 30:8), neyu'nę́'ę ‹two-it-become-began› *two became one* (RC 26:21).

–a'nę'na'nehsT – enjoy oneself. *v.s.-a.i.* ra'nę'na'néhstha' ‹he-himself-is pleasant› *he enjoys himself* (HS).

–a'nę'kʷek – smolder. *v.s.-a.i.* yu'nę'-kwé·kę ‹it-itself-X-closed› *it smolders* (HS).

–a'nę'ne'nahkw – defender, shield. *dv.n.s.* yę'nę'ne'náhkhwa' ‹one-oneself-hide behind-instrument› *defender, shield* (HS).

–a'nę'nu'kT –{dative II} have time come to an end. *v.s.-a.i.* wa'aku'nę'nú'-kthahθ ‹fact-one-oneself-day-ended-for› *one's time came to an end* (RC 3:39).

–a'nę'θr – be restive. *v.r.-s.i.* stat: -ę, prog: -, prp: -, dst: -, caus: -, rvs: -, dat: -, n-inc. yu'nę́'θrę *it is restive* (HS).

–a'nę'T – be in a line, be the n-th one. *v.r.-a.i.* hab: -ha', pnt: -, stat: -ę, prog: -, prp: -, dst: -, caus: -, rvs: -, dat: -, n-inc. Related to the enclitic #ha'nę't used to form ordinal numbers. wa'-nę'tha' *it forms a line* (RC 15:4); –(a)hę'T – –a'nę'T –: uhę́'nę ru'nę́'nę ‹in front of he-is in a line› *the head one* (AW 55), *leader* (M 87).

–a'nę'tahkra'nihr – blaze, flame. *v.s.-s.i.* yu'nę'tahkra'níhrę ‹it-itself-flame-stands up› *it blazes, it flames* (HS).

–a'nę'tikęhkęni – be illusory. *v.s.-s.i.* yu'-nę'tikęhkę́·nya·t ‹it-itself-mind-excelled› *it is illusory* (HS).

–a'nę'tikęhrahręhw – anticipate. *v.s.-t.* ru'nę'tikęhráhręw ‹he-himself-mind-put up-caused› *he anticipates it* (HS).

–a'nę'tikęhrar – be prudent. *v.s.-a.i.* ra'-nę'tikę́hrar ‹he-himself-mind-is in› *he is prudent* (HS).

–a'nę'tikęhrar –{dative III} beware. *v.s.-a.i.* θa'nę'tikę́hrarę ‹you!-yourself-mind-be in-for› *beware!* (HS).

–a'nę'tikęhrihsak – search mind. *v.s.-a.i.* ra'nę'tikęhríhsa·ks ‹he-himself-mind-searches› *he searches his mind* (HS).

–a'nę'tikęhrurihT – amuse oneself. *v.s.-a.i.* yę'nę'tikęhruríhtha' ‹one-oneself-mind-stir-causes› *one amuses oneself* (RC 31:4).

–a'nę'tiranhe – assistant, helper. *dv.n.s.* ha' ra'nę'tiránheh ‹the he-himself-X-aids› *assistant, helper* (HS).

–a'nę'traku – aim be off. *v.s.-a.i.* ę'nę'-trá·ku' ‹fact-it-itself-aim-picked up› *its aim was off* (RC 24:9).

–a'nę'tyati'T – be tardy. *v.s.-a.i.* ru'nę'-tyá·ti't ‹he-himself-be a long time-causes› *he is tardy* (HS).

-a'nę̓tyę̓'nęh – try. *v.s.-t.* θa'nę̓'tyę̓·'nęh ‹you!-yourself-measure› *try it!* (R), wahra'nę̓'tyę̓·'nęh ‹fact-he-himself-measured› *he tried it* (RC 27:21), ęka'nę̓'tyę̓·'nęh ‹prediction-I-myself-measure› *I will try it* (RC 11:17).

-a'nhęhsę – lay eggs. *v.s.-a.i.* See: -'nhęhsę -.

-(a̱)'ni at edge of (peripheral locative). *n.r.sfx.* The form –a̱'ni follows roots and stems that end in a consonant; the form –'ni follows roots and stems that end in a vowel. The suffix is probably derived historically from the verb root –a'ni – *abandon, throw away*. The primary function of the suffix is to indicate location at the periphery or behind the named entity (e.g., –(a)ha=ha̱'ni: uháha'ni ‹path-at edge of› *at the edge of path* (RC 33:8), –ča̱ra'ni: učará·'ni ‹door-at edge of› *at edge of door, next to door, other side of door* (R), –ka'na'ni: uká'na'ni ‹ring-at edge of› *at edge of circle* (RC 31:3)). In combination with the particle na' *some* the suffix is used to form directionals (e.g., ę̓'nyéhči na' –. –a̱'ni: ę̓'nyéhči na'ú·'ni ‹noon some it-at edge of› *meridional (noon-side)* (HS), –'tehsnakT na' –. –(a)'ni: u'téhsnakwt na'ú·'ni ‹back much-it-at the edge of› *backward, reverse* (HS)).

-a'ni –/–ę'ni – abandon (thing), lose, throw, throw away. *v.r.-t.* hab: -ęhs, pnt: -', stat: -, prog: -, prp: -, dst: -hnę- ~ -ahθę-, caus: -, rvs: -, dat: II (-ati-/-ahθ-) ~ III (-ati-/-ę-), inc.-ɸ-pat. The form –ę'ni – occurs with the semi-reflexive morpheme and in most cases when an incorporated noun root is present. The form –a'ni – occurs elsewhere. ęwakwá·'ni' *I will lose it* (R), rú·'nyęhs *he abandons (thing)* (HS), ęθá·'ni' *you will throw* (AW 58),

wahrú·'ni' *he threw* (AW 56), ęhrú·'ni' *he will lose it; he will throw it, he will pitch it (ball)* (R) [Lawson «Oon est nonne it quost» 'Don't lose it' = ù·nę θa'né·'ni, kwęhs *now throw it away, no*]; –a'ni –{dative II}: rú·'nyahθ ‹he-threw-for› *he loses it, he leaves it; he casts (a mold)* (R); –t-. –a'ni –: kaθá·'ni ‹hither-you-throw› *throw it to me!* (R); –yah-. –a'ni –: yahwahę́·'ni' ‹thither-fact-one-threw› *one threw it there* (R), yahwahrú·'ni' ‹thither-fact-he-threw› *he threw it there* (RC 14:7); –yah -. –a'ni –{dative II}: wehrú·'nyehθ ‹thither-he-threw-for› *he throws* (HS); –yah-. –a'nyehθę –: yahwa'kaku'nyáhθę' ‹thither-fact-they-threw-many› *they threw some there* (RC 9:4); –a'narhę'ni –: ra'narhę́·'nyęhs ‹he-himself-X-throws› *he springs* (R); –a'tę'ni –: ru'tę́·'nyęhs ‹he-arrow-throws› *he shoots arrows* (HS); –či'rę'ni –: yuči'ré·'nyęhs ‹it-ember-throws› *meteor* (SH 375); –hwaritę'ni –: wa'uhwaritę́·'ni' ‹fact-it-backpack-threw› *one left behind backpack* (RC 11:24); –(i)'θrehčrę'ni –{dative III}: wahru'θrehčrę́·'nyę' ‹fact-he-ride-'ness-threw-for› *he lost a car* (R); –nęhsę'ni –: runęhsę́·'nyęhs ‹he-house-throws› *he leaves the house (habitually) (said of one who leaves his house daily)* (HS); –tu'krę'ni –: wa'ktu'kré·'ni' ‹fact-I-saliva-throw› *I spit* (HS); –wisę'ni –: yuwisę́·'nyęhs ‹it-ice-throws› *sleet* (HS); –yahstę'ni –: rayahstę́·'nyęhs ‹he-individual-throws› *he abandons (person)* (HS); –ne -. –athunęhya'nihnę –: neyuthunęhya'níhnę· ‹apart-it-itself-sinew-threw-many› *it throws apart sinews* (RC 28:9); ti -. –ahθę'nę'ni –{dative III}: thwahrahθę'né·'nyę' ‹so-fact-he-become dark-threw-for› *he becomes puzzled* (SH

375); -yah-.-ahθhę'ni-: yahęhθhę́·'ni' ‹thither-fact-it-handful-threw› *it threw handful there* (RC 11:22); -yah-. -a'narhę'ni-: yahwahra'narhę́·'ni' ‹thither-fact-he-himself-X-threw› *he threw himself off there* (RC 26:27); -yah-.-a'nę'ni-: yahwahru'nę́·'ni' ‹thither-fact-he-himself-threw› *it threw him there* (RC 6:9); -yah-.-kθę'ni-: yahwa'kakθę́·'ni' ‹thither-fact-it-dish-threw› *it threw dish there* (RC 11:22); -yah-.-'ahθrę'ni-: yahwa'u''ahθrę́·'ni' ‹thither-fact-it-basket-threw› *basket is thrown away* (RC 10:5).

-a'ni-{dative II} loosen, leave; cast. *v.s.-t.* rú·'nyahθ ‹he-threw-for› *he loosens it, he leaves it; he casts (a mold)* (R).

-a'nihęthu- pull. *v.r.-t.* hab: -hs, pnt: -', stat: -, prog: -, prp: -, dst: -hθrę-, caus: -, rvs: -, dat: -, n-inc. In the Western dialect this root requires the dualic prefix. wa'ka'nihę́·thu' *I pulled it* (R); -a'nihęthuhθrę-: wa'nihęthúhθrę·' ‹it-pulled-much› *pulling power* (AW 53); -'tyęhkra'nihęthu-: wahra'tyęhkra'nihę́·thu' ‹fact-he-snot-pulled› *he sniffed* (R); -ne-.-a'ni=hęthu-: neka'nihę́·thuh ‹apart-I-pull› *I pull it* (PC), ętka'nihę́·thu' ‹prediction-apart-I-pull› *I will pull it* (PC); -ne-.-a'ne'nihęthu-: newa'ne'nihę́·thuhs ‹apart-it-itself-pulls› *elastic* (AG); -t-.-a'nihęthu-: nyaku'nihę́·thuhs ‹hither-one-pulls› *one is attracted there* (RC 25:5), thra'nihę́·thuhs ‹hither-he-pulls› *he withdraws* (R); ha? -a'nihęthu-: ha' wa'nihę́·thuhs ‹the it-pulls› *whooping cough* (HS).

-a'nihęthu- whooping cough. *dv.n.s.* ha' wa'nihę́·thuhs ‹the it-pulls› *whooping cough* (HS).

-a'nihęthuhθrę- pulling power. *dv.n.s.* wa'nihęthúhθrę·' ‹it-pulled-much› *pulling power* (AW 53).

-a'nihnyahsT- stole. *dv.n.s.* yę'nihnyáhstha' ‹one-oneself-wear around neck-causes› *stole* (HS).

-a'nih(r)- stand up. *v.r.-a.i.* hab: ()-s, pnt: ()-ɸ, stat: ()-ę, prog: -, prp: -θe'-, dst: ()-hę-, caus: -θT- ~ ()-a'T-, rvs: -, dat: I (-'θe-/-'θ-), inc.-ɸ-ag./pat. This verb requires an animate subject; the form -a'nih- occurs before the causative -θT-, the dative, and the purposive suffixes; elsewhere, the form -a'nihr- occurs. The unusual form of the causative (-θT-) perhaps results from an assimilation of the cluster -hrhT-. (Note the phonetic realization of the similar cluster -'rhw- in u'rhwę́·θeh [u'.ð^{θw}ɔ́·.θæh] *tail*.) wahra'ná'nir *he stood up* (RC 23:3); -a'na'nihra'T-: ęyę'na'níhra't ‹prediction-one-oneself-stand up-cause› *it will make one whole* (RC 7:11); -t-. -a'na'nihr-: thra'ná'nihč ‹hither-he-himself-stands up› *he arises (from a sitting position)* (HS); ti+yah-.-a'=nihr-: thwehru'na'níhrę ‹so-thither-he-stood up› *he is standing up there* (RC 31:10); -ačhakʷara'nihr-: ruchakwara'níhrę ‹he-himself-clamor-stood up› *he bawls* (HS); -ačhakʷara'nihT-: ra-

Tuscarora Pronunciation Key:
/a/ law; /e/ hat; /i/ pizza; /u/ tune; /ę/ hint; /č/ cheese; /h/ hoe; /m/ mother; /s/ same; /t/ do (before a vowel y, or w), too (elsewhere); /k/ gale (before a vowel y or w), kale (elsewhere); /n/ inhale (before a consonant or word-final), note (elsewhere), /r/ hiss (before a consonant or word-final), run (trilled as in Italian, elsewhere); /w/ cuff (before a consonant other than y or word-final), way (elsewhere); /y/ fish (before a consonant or word-final), you (elsewhere), /θ/ thing; /'/ (the sound between the vowels in unh-unh); /·/ long vowel, /´/ high pitch; /`/ low pitch.

čhakwaraʔníhthaʔ ‹he-himself-clamor-stand up-causes› *he clamors* (HS); –ačhęryuhkwaʔnihr –: wačhęryuhkwáʔnihč ‹it-itself-savor-cover-instrument-stands up› *it exhales* (H-notebook); –(a)hkara̲ʔnihr –: rahkaráʔnihč ‹he-bark-stands up› *he taps a tree* (HS); –atraʔnihr –: watraʔníhrę ‹it-pole-stood up› *upright beam, column, pole* (R); –čiʔraʔnihr –: θčiʔráʔnir ‹you!-ember-stand up› *turn on the lights!* (HS), račiʔráʔnihč ‹he-ember-stands up› *he sets it on fire* (HS), kačiʔraʔníhrę ‹it-ember-stood up› *it is lit* (HS); –čtęhraʔnihr –: kačtęhraʔníhrę ‹it-stone-stood up› *tombstone* (HS); –(ę)ʔtahkraʔnihθk –: yawęʔtahkraʔníhθkę· ‹it-flame-stands up-easily› *inflammable* (HS); –(ę)ʔtikęhraʔnihr –: ruʔtikęhráʔnihč ‹he-mind-stands up› *it interests him* (HS), ruʔtikęhraʔníhrę ‹he-mind-stood up› *his sympathy* (HS); –hsę=waʔraʔnihr –: rahsęwaʔráʔnihč ‹he-nail-stands up› *he hammers, he rivets* (HS); –hskwehtaʔnihr –: yuhskwehtaʔníhrę ‹it-tree stump-stood up› *standing tree stump* (RC 26:1); –hstraʔnihr –: kahstraʔníhrę ‹it-stature-stands up› *it is sitting up* (RC 5:37), ruhstraʔníhrę ‹he-stature-stood up› *he is sitting* (L 15); –hstraʔnihθne –: naʔ-nihstraʔníhθneh ‹one=another-stature-stands up-going to› *one seats another* (HS); –hstraʔnihr – –ręʔaʔke: kahstráʔnihč uręʔáʔkye ‹it-stature-stands up tree-on› *perch* (HS); –nęhaʔnihr –: kanęháʔnihč ‹it-corn-stands up› *it sets corn (grains), said of corn ears when the grain buds begin to appear* (H 2484); –nęhsaʔnihθT –: yenęhsaʔníhθthaʔ ‹one-house-stand up-causes› *the house one erects (this is the descriptive name of an umbrella)* (H 2484); –nękwaruʔnaʔnihr –: ranękwa-

ruʔnáʔnihč ‹he-pin-stands up› *he sets a pin, he strikes a pin* (HS); –nęʔ=araʔnihr –: yunęʔaraʔníhrę ‹it-climbing vine-stood up› *climbing vine stands* (RC 7:5); –ręhθaʔnihr –: yuręhθaʔníhrę ‹it-leg-stood up› *its leg* (RC 24:8); –rhahstaʔnihr –: waʔerhahstáʔnir ‹fact-one-cradleboard-stood up› *one stood up cradleboard* (RC 30:4); –riʔwaʔ=nihr –: rariʔwáʔnihč ‹he-sheet-stands up› *he hoists a sail* (HS); –riʔwaʔ=nihrhę –: rariʔwaʔnírhęh ‹he-sheet-stands up-much› *he sails* (HS); –riʔ=waʔnihθT –: yeriʔwaʔníhθthaʔ ‹one-sheet-stand up-causes› *she raises a flag* (HS); –taʔyaʔnihr –: rutaʔyaʔníhrę ‹he-??-stood up› *he is squatting* (HS); –teʔkwaʔnihr –: kateʔkwáʔnihč ‹he-bag-stands up› *it bags it* (HS), kateʔkwaʔníhrę ‹it-bag-stood up› *circus* (HS); –tkwaʔnihr –: yutkwaʔníhrę ‹it-stomach-stood up› *it bulges, it is convex* (HS); –tuka̲raʔnihr –: waʔktukaráʔnir ‹fact-I-point-stood up› *I sharpened it (e.g., pencil)* (HS); –turaʔnihr –: yuturaʔníhrę ‹it-husk-stood up› *it has a husk* (RC 7:5); –yęhwiθnaʔnihr –: yuyęhwiθnaʔníhrę ‹it-wing-stood up› *it wing stands* (M 87); –yętaʔnihr –: rayętáʔnihč ‹he-brush-stands up› *he piles it up* (HS); –ʔčiraʔnihr –: raʔčiráʔnihč ‹he-sting-stands up› *he stings* (HS); –ʔęyaʔnihr –: kaʔęyaʔníhrę ‹it-enclosure-stands up› *corncrib* (AG); –ʔnahkwaʔnihrhę –: kaʔnahkwaʔnírhęh ‹it-box-stood up-many› *boxes standing upright* (RC 11:16); –atʔęyaʔnihθnę=heʔ: kakutʔęyaʔnihθnę́heʔ ‹they-themselves-enclosure-stood up-caused-had› *they were setting up enclosure* (RC 24:11); –aʔnęʔtahkraʔnihr –: yuʔnęʔtahkraʔníhrę ‹it-itself-flame-stood up› *it blazes, it flames* (HS); –ne –. –ahčaʔ=nihr –: waʔthrahčáʔnir ‹fact-apart-he-fist-stood up⟩ *he fell on his face* (RC 24:10); –ne –. -ahča?nihrhę –: neyuhča?nírhę· ⟨apart-it-fist-stood up-much⟩ *pot* (HS); –ne –. -a'na?nihr –: nehru?na?níhrę ⟨apart-he-himself-stood up⟩ *he strives* (HS); –ne –. -a'na?nihrhę –: nehru?na?nírhęh ⟨apart-he-himself-stands up-much⟩ *rival* (HS); –ne –. -atkahra?nihr –: wa?nwatkahrá?nir ⟨fact-two-it-itself-eye-stood up⟩ *it opened its eyes* (RC 8:22); –ne –. -tkwa?nihθT –: neyutkwa?níhθnę ⟨two-it-stomach-stand up-caused⟩ *convex-o-convex (shaped like a lens or a magnifying glass)* (HS); -t –. -rihwa?nihθT –: nyurihwa?níhθnę ⟨hither-it-matter-stand up-caused⟩ *principal* (HS); -t –. -(ta)?čuhkwa?nihr –: nyuta?čuhkwa?níhrę ⟨hither-it-heap-stood up⟩ *there is a great heap* (R); -t –. -yęta?nihr –: nahrayęta?níhrę ⟨hither-fact-he-pile-stood up⟩ *he piled up brush* (RC 7:4); tha –. -nęčha?nihrhę –: thayunęčha?nírhęk ⟨unusual-it-arm-stood up-much⟩ *he had arms on* (AG); ti –. -trahna?nihr –: nęyutrahna?níhręk ⟨so-prediction-it-leaf-stand up⟩ *so many leaves will be standing* (RC 23: 2); –yah –. -hstra?nihr –: wehruhstra?níhrę ⟨thither-he-stature-stood up⟩ *he is sitting over there* (L 15); –yah –. -?či = ra?nihrhę –: wekaku?čira?nírhę· ⟨thither-they-sting-stand up-many⟩ *they were stung* (RC 26:10); –ne –. -a?čih = skęhkara?nihr –: wa?tka?na?čihskęh kará?nir ⟨fact-apart-I-myself-self-fin gernail-stood up⟩ *I pinched myself* (AG), wa?nyakya?čihskęhkará?nir

⟨fact-apart-the two of us-ourselves-fin gernail-stood up⟩ *we pinched each other* (AG), wa?tkheya?čihskęhkará? nir ⟨fact-apart-I=another-self-finger nail-stood up⟩ *I pinched him/her* (AG); –yah –. -a'na?nihr –: wewa?na? níhrę ⟨thither-it-itself-stood up⟩ *it stands up there* (RC 3:41); –yah –. -a'na?nih -{dative I}: wa?čhiya?ná? nihθ ⟨thither-you!-yourself-stand up-for⟩ *stand someone else up!* (RC 3: 25); –yahsti – ti –. -?ęhra?nihr –: kayáhsti tika?ęhrá?nihč ⟨it-individual-is a group so-it-leaf-stands up⟩ *centifolious* (HS).

-a'nihθkawęhsT – commix, commingle. *v.r.-a.i.* hab: -, pnt: -, stat: -ę, prog: -, prp: -, dst: -, caus: -, rvs: -, dat: -, n-inc. yu?nihθkawéhsnę *commixture; promiscuity, it is promiscuous* (HS); čwe –. -ake – –ne –. -a'nihθkawęhsT –: čwewá·kye· neyu?nihθkawéhsnę ⟨all kinds of-it-is in number two-it-com mixed⟩ *medley* (HS); ha? –ne –. -a'nih θkawęhsT –: ha? neyu?nihθkawéhsnę ⟨the two-it-commixed⟩ *commixture* (HS).

-a'nihθkawęhsT – commixture; promiscu ity. *dv.n.s.* yu?nihθkawéhsnę ⟨it-com mixed⟩ *commixture; promiscuity* (HS).

-a?nihθku – pick. *v.r.-t.* hab: -, pnt: -?, stat: -, prog: -, prp: -, dst: -, caus: -a?T-, rvs: -, dat: -, inc.-ɸ-pat. wah ra?níhθku? *he picked it* (RC 7:6), arye?níhθku? *that one pick it* (RC 23:1); –čara?nihθku –: ahračara?níh θku? ⟨unknown-he-door-pick⟩ *that he pick off door* (RC 27:24); –nęčha? =

---

nihθku –: wa'na'nęčha'níhθku' ‹fact-one=another-arm-picked› *she picked the arms out* (AG); –rę'a'nihθku –: ękayerę'a'níhθku' ‹prediction-they-tree-pick› *they will pick off, uproot tree* (RC 3:70); –tura'nihθku –: ęye-tura'níhθku' ‹prediction-one-stalk-pick› *one will pick off stalk* (RC 20: 1); kwęhs –a'nihθkwa'T –: kwęhs aryu'nihθkwá'nęk ‹no unknown-it-pick-cause› *it is impregnable, it is invulnerable* (HS).

–a'nihsuh(e)r – hide. *v.r.-a.i.* hab: ()-φ, pnt: -ę', stat: ()-', prog: -, prp: -, dst: -awę-, caus: -, rvs: -, dat: -, n-inc. ru'nihsúhe'r *he was hiding* (RC 8:35), wahra'nihsúhrę' *he hid* (AW 57), yu'nihsúhe'r *it is hidden* (HS), wa'-kayę'nihsuhrá·wę·' *they hid* (AW 102); –a'nihsuh(e)r –: yę'nihsúher ‹one-hides› *hide & seek (game)* (HS); –a'nihsuhrahkw –: yę'nihsuhráhkhwa' ‹one-hides-instrument› *hiding places, refuge* (HS).

–a'nihsuh(e)r – hide & seek (game). *dv. n.s.* yę'nihsúher ‹one-hides› *hide & seek (game)* (HS).

–a'nihsuhrahkw – hiding places, refuge. *dv.n.s.* yę'nihsuhráhkhwa' ‹one-hides-instrument› *hiding places, refuge* (HS).

–a'nihtręhsT – poultice. *dv.n.s.* yę'nih-trę́hstha' ‹one-oneself-ties-for› *poultice* (HS).

–a'nikęhkari – starve. *v.r.-a.i.* hab: -ahs, pnt: -, stat: -, prog: -, prp: -, dst: -, caus: -, rvs: -, dat: -, n-inc. ra'nikęh-ká·ryahs *he starves* (HS).

–a'niθtur – grow fast. *v.r.-a.i.* hab: -, pnt: -, stat: -e', prog: -a'nye', prp: -, dst: -, caus: -, rvs: -, dat: -, n-inc. yu'-niθtù·re' *it was growing fast* (RC 5: 22); –a'niθtura'nye' –: wa'niθturá·'-nye' ‹it-grows fast-going along› *it is growing fast* (RC 3:35); ti –. –a'niθtur –: tiwa'niθtù·re' ‹so-it-grows fast› *it grew so fast* (RC 3: 25).

–a'ni'nęr – be compassionate, be gracious, be pitiful. *v.s.-s.i.* ru'ni'nę̀·rę ‹he-him-self-pitied› *he is compassionate, he is gracious, he is pitiful* (HS).

–a'ni'nęrahsk – be merciful, be prone to pity. *v.s.-s.i.* ru'ni'nęráhskę ‹he-him-self-pities-easily› *he is merciful, he is prone to pity* (HS).

–a'ni'nęrahT – be pitiable. *v.s.-a.i.* yu'ni'-nę̀·raht ‹it-itself-pity-causes› *it is pitiable* (HS).

–a'ni'nęręhčr – charity, grace, mercy, pity. *n.s.* u'ni'nęręhčreh ‹self-pity-'ness› *charity, grace, mercy, pity* (HS).

–a'ni'nęręhčrukę' pitiless. *n.s.* ru'ni'nę-ręhčrú·kę' ‹he-himself-pity-'ness-less› *he is pitiless* (HS).

–a'ni'rę – be fixed in place. *v.s.-s.i.* yu'-ní'rę' ‹it-itself-set› *it is fixed in place* (HS).

–a'ni'θhahnęhT – relent. *v.s.-a.i.* ra'ni'-θhahnę́htha' ‹he-himself-power-dis-appear-causes› *he relents* (HS).

–a'ni'θhęni – defeat, master, overcome, overpower, prevail. *v.s.-t.* ra'ni'θhę́·-nyęhs ‹he-himself-defeats› *he masters it, he overcomes it, he overpowers it, he prevails* (HS), ęyakwa'ni'θhè·ni' ‹prediction-we-ourselves-defeat› *we will defeat another* (RC 33:8).

–a'ni'θkuhar – bathe. *v.s.-a.i.* ra'ni'θkú-har ‹he-himself-X-washes› *he is bathing, he bathes* (R).

–a'ni'θkuha'T – bath. *dv.n.s.* ha' yę'ni'-θkuhá'tha' ‹the one-oneself-X-put in water-causes› *bath* (HS).

–a'nuhnę – swell. *v.r.-a.i.* hab: -h, pnt: -', stat: -·', prog: -, prp: -, dst: -, caus: -, rvs: -, dat: -, n-inc. wa'núhnęh *it swells (as of a bruise, a sore, or a part of the body)* (HS), yu'núhnę·' *it is swollen* (HS).

–a**'nuhsner** – be of same age. *v.r.-s.i.* stat: -ɸ, prog: -, prp: -, dst: -, caus: -, rvs: -, dat: -, n-inc. neyę**'**núhsner *twins, the two of them are of the same age* (RC 13:2).

–a**'nuhsner** – twins. *dv.n.s.* neyę**'**núhsner ‹two-one-is of the same age› *twins* (RC 13:2).

–a**'nuhstę** – hibernate, winter. *v.s.-a.i.* ra**'**núhstęh ‹he-himself-year-falls› *he hibernates, he winters* (HS).

–a**'nuka'T** – inflame, ulcerate. *v.s.-a.i.* wa**'**nuká**'**tha**'** ‹it-itself-blister-causes› *it inflames, it ulcerates* (HS).

a**'**nú·kę**'** ax (R) [Lawson «Au-nuka»]. *n.*

–a**'nukʷatyę** – cause a relapse of sickness, hurt oneself. *v.s.-a.i.* ra**'**nukwá·tyęh ‹he-himself-spreads out-much› *he hurts himself or causes a relapse of sickness* (H-notebook).

–a**'nuri** – drive. *v.s.-a.i.* ra**'**nù·rih ‹he-himself-stirs› *he drives* (HS), wa**'**ka**'**nù·ri**'** ‹fact-I-myself-stirred› *I drove* (R).

–a**'nuryahnę** – make an attempt, struggle. *v.s.-a.i.* wahra**'**nuryáhnę**'** ‹fact-he-himself-stirred-much› *he struggled* (RC 7:2), ru**'**nuryáhnę· ‹he-himself-stirred-much› *he made an attempt* (RC 8:21).

–a**'nuwharhę** – partition (of a building). *dv.n.s.* yu**'**nuwhárhę· ‹it-??-hang-much› *partition (of a building)* (HS).

–a**'nu'knakęwke** ultimate. *n.s.* u**'**nu**'**kna-kęwkye ‹self-come to an end-in-at› *ultimate* (HS).

–a**'nu'krahkw** – float. *v.s.-a.i.* ra**'**nu**'**kráh-khwa**'** ‹he-himself-floats› *he floats* (HS), yu**'**nu**'**kráhkę ‹it-itself-floated› *he is floating* (HS).

–a**'nu'krakwahte'** – float up. *v.s.-a.i.* wa**'**-nu**'**krakwáhte**'** ‹it-itself-floats-going to› *it is floating up* (RC 3:76).

–a**'nu'kT** – come to an end, end, run out of, terminate. *v.s.-a.i.* yú·**'**nu**'**kt ‹it-itself-came to an end› *it came to an end* (RC 2:15), nę**'**nú**'**knę**'** ‹hither-fact-it-itself-came to an end› *it ended* (RC 15:6), wa**'**kayę**'**nú**'**knę**'** ‹fact-they-themselves-came to an end› *they ran out of it* (R), wa**'**nú**'**ktha**'** ‹it-itself-comes to an end› *it terminates* (HS).

–a**'nu'kT** – end. *dv.n.s.* yú·**'**nu**'**kt ‹it-it-self-came to an end› *the end* (RC 2:15).

–a**'nu'narhę** – avoid. *v.s.-t.* ra**'**nu**'**nárhę· ‹he-himself-hooked-much› *he avoids it* (HS).

–a**'nu'narihsi** – disengage oneself. *v.s.-a.i.* ra**'**nu**'**naríhsyęhs ‹he-himself-hook-undoes› *he disengages himself* (HS).

–a**'nu'nę** – calve, give birth to (of animals). *v.r.-a.i.* hab: -h, pnt: -·**'**, stat: -**'**, prog: -, prp: -, dst: -, caus: -, rvs: -, dat: -, n-inc. wa**'**nú**'**nęh *it calves, it gives birth (of animals)* (HS), yu**'**nú**'**-nę**'** *it calved* (HS), ęwa**'**nú**'**nę·**'** *it will calve* (HS); –a**'nu'nę'**: waka**'**nú**'**-nę**'** ‹I-gave birth to› *my child, my daughter, my niece (sister's daughter) (referential, lit. it is my child)* (R) [Lawson «Woccanookne» 'A child'], kęya'nú'nę' ‹I=you-gave birth to› *my child, my daughter, my niece (direct address, lit. I have you as child)* (RC 27:22), kheya'nú'nę' ‹I=another-gave birth to› *my child (indirect address, lit. I have one as my child)* (RC 30:6), ru'nú'nę' ‹he-gave birth to› *his child* (RC 1:2); –a'nu'nę'–.#áh: ka'nu'nę'-áh ‹I-gave birth to-little› *my niece, my nephew (same clan, i.e., mother's side of family)*; ha? –a'nu'nę': ha' wa'-nú'nę' ‹the it-gave birth to› *interest (e.g., on borrowed money)* (HS); –'ni = ha – –a'nu'nę': ra'níha· waka'nú'nę' ‹he-is male I-gave birth to› *my son, my nephew (sister's son)* (R).

–a'nu'nę' have as one's child. *v.s.-k.* waka'nú'nę' ‹I-gave birth to› *my child, my daughter, my niece (sister's daughter) (referential, lit. it is my child)* (R) [Lawson «Woccanookne» 'A child'], kęya'nú'nę' ‹I=you-gave birth to› *my child, my daughter, my niece (direct address, lit. I have you as child)* (RC 27:22), kheya'nú'nę' ‹I=another-gave birth to› *my child (indirect address, lit. I have one as my child)* (RC 30:6), ru'nú'nę' ‹he-gave birth to› *his child* (RC1:2); –a'nu'nę'–.#áh: ka'nu'nę'áh ‹I-gave birth to-little› *my niece, my nephew (same clan, i.e., mother's side of family)* (R); –'niha – –a'nu'nę': ra'níha· waka'nú'-nę' ‹he-is male I-gave birth to› *my son, my nephew (sister's son)* (R).

–a'nu'nę' interest. *dv.n.s.* ha' wa'nú'nę' ‹the it-gave birth to› *interest (e.g., on borrowed money)* (HS).

–a'nu'nę'–.#áh be niece, be nephew. *v.s.-k.* ka'nu'nę'áh ‹I-gave birth to-little› *my niece, my nephew (same clan, i.e., mother's side of family)* (R).

–a'nu'r – shrink. *v.r.-a.i.* hab: -s, pnt: -φ, stat: -ę, prog: -, prp: -, dst: -, caus: -,

rvs: -, dat: -, n-inc. yu'nú'rę *it shrank* (HS), wá·'nu'č *it shrinks* (HS).

–a'nu'y(e) – ramrod. *n.s.* u'nú'yeh ‹gun-bend› *ramrod* (HS).

–a'nwakanyęku – stammer. *v.r.-a.i.* hab: -ahs, pnt: -, stat: -, prog: -, prp: -, dst: -, caus: -, rvs: -, dat: -, n-inc. ra'nwa-kanyę́·kwahs *he stammers* (HS).

–a'nwaksę'T – swagger. *v.r.-a.i.* hab: -ha', pnt: -, stat: -, prog: -, prp: -, dst: -, caus: -, rvs: -, dat: -, n-inc. ra'nwa-ksę́'tha' *he swaggers* (HS).

–a'nwatkę'T – prate. *v.r.-a.i.* hab: -, pnt: -, stat: -ę, prog: -, prp: -, dst: -, caus: -, rvs: -, dat: -, n-inc. ru'nwatkę́'nę *he prates* (HS).

–a'nwa'kw – be a premonition. *v.r.-s.i.* stat: -ih, prog: -, prp: -, dst: -, caus: -, rvs: -, dat: -, n-inc. wa'nwá'kwih *it is a premonition* (L 4).

–a'nwehaks – talk nonsense. *v.s.-a.i.* ru'-nwehá·ksę· ‹he-himself-talk-is bad› *he talks nonsense* (HS).

–a'nwenę'nanę'naknahkw – ice skates. *dv. n.s.* yę'nwenę'nanę'naknáhkhwa' ‹one-oneself-iron-fastens to-instrument› *ice skates* (HS).

–a'nwenę'nuha – be at anchor *v.s.-s.i.* yu'nwenę'núhę ‹it-itself-iron-put in water› *it is at anchor* (HS).

–a'nwęniyu – be free. *dv.n.s.* ka'nwę-nì·yu' ‹I-myself-am god› *I am free* (AG).

–a'nwęniyuhsT – rebel. *dv.n.s.* ra'nwęni-yúhstha' ‹he-himself-be god-causes› *rebel* (HS).

–a'nwęniyu' – be freed, be set free, free from slavery. *v.s.-a.i.* ra'nwęnì·yu'θ ‹he-himself-is god-for› *he is set free, he is freed* (HS), ru'nwęniyú'ę ‹he-himself-be god-began› *he is free from slavery* (HS).

–a'nwęθkęri – mumble, talk through teeth. *v.r.-a.i.* hab: -h, pnt: -, stat: -, prog: -, prp: -, dst: -, caus: -, rvs: -, n-inc. ra'nwę̆θkę̀·rih *he mumbles, he talks through his teeth* (HS).

–a'nwętahęˀT – propose. *v.s.-t.* ra'nwętáhę'č ‹he-himself-word-is in front› *he proposes it* (HS).

–a'nwętahθaw'ahsT – be legible. *v.s.-a.i.* yu'nwętahθá·-w'ahst ‹it-itself-word-begin-caused› *it is legible* (HS).

–a'nwętahsa'nę – be monotonous. *v.s.-s.i.* ru'nwętahsá'nę' ‹he-himself-word-buried› *he is monotonous* (HS).

–a'nwętahsęhT – boast, mock. *v.s.-a.i.* ra'nwętahsę́htha' ‹he-himself-word-be evil-causes› *he boasts, he mocks* (HS).

–a'nwętahskanekęt – allegory. *dv.n.s.* yu'nwętahskané·kę·t ‹it-itself-word-is strange› *allegory* (HS).

–a'nwętakara'naT – interpret. *v.s.-a.i.* ra'nwętakará'na·č ‹he-himself-word-?› *he interprets* (HS).

–a'nwętakeθku – raise voice. *v.s.-a.i.* ra'nwętakyé·θkwahs ‹he-himself-word-raises› *he raises his voice* (HS).

–a'nwętanh – be responsible. *v.s.-s.i.* wahsa'nwętánhek ‹fact-you-yourself-word-aided› *you are responsible* (HS).

–a'nwętanh – responsibility. *dv.n.s.* ha' ru'nwętánhę ‹the he-himself-word-aided› *his responsibility* (HS).

–a'nwętarahkw – be obedient, be obliging, obey. *v.s.-a.i.* ru'nwę́·tarahkw ‹he-himself-word-collected› *he is obedient, he is obliging* (HS), ra'nwętaráhkhwa' ‹he-himself-word-collects› *he obeys* (HS), na'na'nwętaráhkhwa' ‹one=another-oneself-word-collects›

one follows another's command, one obeys another (MP); kwęhs –a'nwę=tarahkw –: kwęhs ahru'nwętaráhkęk ‹no unknown-he-himself-word-collect› *he disobeys, he is disobedient* (HS).

–a'nwętayerik – realize promise, fulfill promise. *v.s.-a.i.* ra'nwętayè·riks ‹he-himself-word-fills up› *he realizes his promise, he fulfills his promise* (HS).

–a'nwętayęˀT – speak ill of. *v.s.-t.* ra'nwętayę́'tha' ‹he-himself-word-go into-causes› *he speaks ill of it* (HS).

–a'nwętayęhT – invective. *n.s.* u'nwę́·tayęht ‹self-word-go into-cause› *invective* (HS).

–a'nwętaT – hum, intone. *v.s.-a.i.* yu'nwę́·ta'ne' ‹it-itself-word-is present› *it hums, it intones* (HS); –a'nwęta='nahT –: ra'nwę́·ta'nahč ‹he-himself-word-be present-causes› *he intones* (HS); –a'nwęta'na'nye' –: yu'nwęta'ná·'nye' ‹it-itself-word-is present-going along› *it goes by humming* (HS); –a'nwęta'netyę –: yu'nwęta'né·tyę' ‹it-itself-word-is present-much› *there is noise* (RC 26:7).

–a'nwęta'nahT – intone. *v.s.-a.i.* ra'nwę́·ta'nahč ‹he-himself-word-be present-causes› *he intones* (HS).

–a'nwętęˀT – spare. *v.r.-t.* hab: -ha', pnt: -, stat: -, prog: -, prp: -, dst: -, caus: -, rvs: -, dat: -, n-inc. ra'nwętę́'tha' *he spares it* (HS).

–a'nwętuhnę – be hoarse. *v.s.-a.i.* ra'nwętúhnęh ‹he-himself-word-swells› *he is hoarse* (HS).

–a'nwę'erę – play a musical instrument,

Tuscarora Pronunciation Key:
/a/ law; /e/ hat; /i/ pizza; /u/ tune; /ę/ hint; /č/ cheese; /h/ hoe; /m/ mother; /s/ same; /t/ do (before a vowel y, or w), too (elsewhere); /k/ gale (before a vowel y or w), kale (elsewhere); /n/ inhale (before a consonant or word-final), note (elsewhere), /r/ hiss (before a consonant or word-final), run (trilled as in Italian, elsewhere); /w/ cuff (before a consonant other than y or word-final), way (elsewhere); /y/ fish (before a consonant or word-final), you (elsewhere), /θ/ thing; /'/ (the sound between the vowels in unh-unh); /·/ long vowel, /´/ high pitch; /`/ low pitch.

make music. *v.r.-a.i.* hab: -h, pnt: -ʔ, stat: -, prog: -, prp: -, dst: -, caus: -, rvs: -, dat: II (-ati-/-ahθ-), n-inc. raʔ-nwęʔè·ręh *he plays a musical instrument, he sings: musician* (RC 26:10); −a'nwęʔerę −{dative II}: waʔkayęʔnwęʔè·ręhθ ‹fact-they-played a musical instrument-for› *they played music with it* (RC 7:7); −a'nwęʔeręhkw −: yęʔnwęʔerę́hkhwaʔ ‹one-plays a musical instrument-instrument› *organ* (HS); −a'nwęʔeręʔčr −: uʔnwęʔerę́ʔčreh ‹play a musical instrument-'ness› *music* (R); −a'nwęʔeręʔčrakwahsT −: waʔnwęʔeręʔčrákwahst ‹it-make music-'ness-is good› *good music* (RC 26:7); −a'nwęʔeręʔčrukęʔ: raʔnwęʔeręʔčrú·kęʔ ‹he-make music-'ness-less› *he is songless, he is tuneless* (HS).

−a'nwęʔeręhkw − organ. *dv.n.s.* yęʔnwęʔerę́hkhwaʔ ‹one-plays a musical instrument-instrument› *organ* (HS).

−a'nwęʔeręʔčr − music. *n.s.* uʔnwęʔerę́ʔčreh ‹play a musical instrument-'ness› *music* (R); −a'nwęʔeręʔčra= kwahsT −: waʔnwęʔeręʔčrákwahst ‹it-make music-'ness-is good› *good music* (RC 26:7); −a'nwęʔeręʔčrukęʔ: raʔnwęʔeręʔčrú·kęʔ ‹he-make music-'ness-less› *he is songless, he is tuneless* (HS).

−a'nwęʔeręʔčrukęʔ songless, tuneless. *n.s.* raʔnwęʔeręʔčrú·kęʔ ‹he-make music-'ness-less› *he is songless, he is tuneless* (HS).

−a'nwiranę − care for a child, nurse. *v.s.-a.i.* raʔnwì·ranęh ‹he-himself-infant-guards› *he cares for a child, he nurses* (HS).

−a'nwiraraku − adopt a child. *v.s.-a.i.* waʔkaʔnwirará·kuʔ ‹fact-I-myself-infant-collected› *I adopted child* (R).

−a'nwirarakwaʔ − Adoption Ceremony. *dv.n.s.* yakwaʔnwirará·kwaʔθ ‹we-ourselves-infant-collect-begin› *Adoption Ceremony* (R).

−a'nwirayę(T) − give birth. *v.s.-a.i.* waʔnwì·rayęhs ‹it-itself-infant-lays› *it gives birth* (RC 7:11).

−a'nwiręčT − be sterile. *v.s.-s.i.* ruʔnwirę́čnę ‹he-himself-infant-conclude-caused› *he is sterile* (HS).

−a'nwiręti − procreate. *v.s.-a.i.* raʔnwirę́·tih ‹he-himself-infant-makes› *he procreates* (HS).

−a'nyahkwayę(T) − expose for sale. *v.s.-t.* ruʔnyáhkwayęhs ‹he-himself-girth-lays› *he exposes it for sale* (HS).

−a'nyahkwayę(T) − prostitute. *dv.n.s.* waʔnyáhkwayęʔ ‹it-itself-girth-laid› *prostitute* (HS).

−a'nyahkwayę'nahkw − market. *dv.n.s.* yęʔnyahkwayęʔnáhkhwaʔ ‹one-one-self-girth-lays-instrument› *market* (HS).

−a'nyahkwhar − oscillate, swing. *v.s.-a.i.* yuʔnyáhkhwar ‹it-itself-girth-hangs› *it oscillates, it swings* (HS), raʔnyáhkhwar ‹he-himself-girth-hangs› *he swings* (HS).

−a'nyahkwiN − peddle goods, sell. *v.s.-a.i.* raʔnyahkwì·nęhs ‹he-himself-girth-proceeds› *he peddles goods, he sells* (HS).

−a'nyake − urinate. *v.r.-a.i.* hab: -h, pnt: -ʔ, stat: -·, prog: -, prp: -, dst: -, caus: -, rvs: -, dat: -, n-inc. ruʔnyá·kye· *he urinated* (RC 2:12), waʔnyá·kye· *it urinated* (RC 2:12); ti −. −a'nyake −: tiθaʔnyá·kye· ‹so-you-urinated› *you urinated* (RC 30:9).

−a'nyarutarhu − pilot a ship. *v.r.-a.i.* hab: -hs, pnt: -, stat: -, prog: -, prp: -, dst: -, caus: -, rvs: -, dat: -, n-inc. raʔnyarutárhuhs *he pilots a ship* (HS).

−a'nyataʔT − be poison. *v.s.-s.i.* yuʔnyatáʔnę ‹it-itself-sulked› *it is poison* (RC 2:14).

–a'nyatur– hurry, speed. *v.r.-s.i.* stat: -ę̧, prog: -, prp: -, dst: -, caus: -ahT-, rvs: -, dat: -, n-inc. yu'nyatù·rę̧ *it hurries* (RC 28:7), ru'nyatù·rę̧ *he speeds* (R); –a'nyaturahT–: ra'nyatù·rahč ‹he-hurry-causes› *he hastens on* (HS); –či–. -a'nyatur–: θahra'nyatù·rę̧ ‹again-he-hurried› *again he hurries* (RC 26: 3).

–a'nyaturahT– hasten. *v.s.-a.i.* ra'nyatù·rahč ‹he-hurry-causes› *he hastens on* (R).

–a'nya'karę̧'ni– canter, gallop. *v.s.-a.i.* ra'nya'karę́·'-nyę̧hs ‹he-himself-upper part of body-throws› *he canters, he gallops* (HS).

–a'nya'θrawę̧– be tiered. *v.s.-a.i.* yu'nya'θrà·wę̧' ‹it-it-self-crossed-much› *it is tiered* (HS).

–a'nya'tahstę̧nya'T– ornament. *dv.n.s.* yę̧'nya'tahstę̧nyá'tha' ‹one-oneself-body-adorn-causes› *ornament* (HS).

–a'nya'takwe'niyuhsT– monopolize. *v.s.-a.i.* ra'nya'takwe'niyúhstha' ‹he-himself-body-be principal-causes› *he monopolizes* (HS).

–a'nyenę̧– catch. *v.s.-t.* ra'nyè·nę̧hs ‹he-himself-grabs› *he catches it* (R).

–a'nyenę̧– wrestle. *v.s.-t.* ra'nyè·nę̧hs ‹he-himself-grabs› *he wrestles* (R).

–a'nyenę̧– policeman. *dv.n.s.* ra'nyè·nę̧hs ‹he-himself-grabs› *policeman* (R).

–a'nyerawę̧ri– soil oneself. *v.s.-a.i.* ra'nyerawę̧·rih ‹he-himself-flesh-stirs› *he soils himself* (HS).

–a'nyerę̧– have an unexpected experience. *v.r.-a.i.* hab: -, pnt: -, stat: -, prog: -'nye'-, prp: -, dst: -hθrę̧- ~ -Nyę̧-, caus: -hT-, rvs: -, dat: II (-ti-/-hθ-), n-inc. –a'nyerę̧hnyę̧–{dative II}: ru'nyerę̧hnyę́·tih ‹he-have an unexpected experience-cause-goes into-for› *it appears to him (supernatural)* (HS); –ne–. -a'nyerę̧hnahkw–: nyu'nyerę̧hnáhkę̧ ‹apart-it-have an unexpected experience-cause-picked up› *firstly* (HS); –ne–. -a'nyerę̧hnyę̧–: newa'nyerę́hnyę̧' ‹apart-it-have an unexpected experience-cause-went into› *it is haunting: spirit is going around, mysterious movements* (L 83), wa'nwaka'nyerę́hnyę̧' ‹fact-apart-I-have an unexpected experience-cause-went into› *it disturbs me* (RC 32:11), nehru'nyerę́hnyę̧' ‹apart-he-have an unexpected experience-cause-went into› *he is a prodigy, he is deformed* (HS); –ne–. -a'nyerę̧hnyę̧–{dative II}: wa'thru'nyerę́hnyę̧'θ ‹fact-apart-he-have an unexpected experience-cause-went into-for› *he foretold a bad experience* (RC 26:22); –ne–. -a'nyerę̧nyę̧–: neyu'nyerę́·nyę̧· ‹apart-it-had an unexpected experience-much› *monster (lit., it is deformed), monstrous* (HS); –ne–. -a'nyerę̧'nyę̧–: nehra'nyerę́·'nyę̧' ‹apart-he-has an unexpected experience-going along› *he is acting, he acts (as in a circus)* (HS); –t–. -a'nyerę̧hT–: nahra'nyè·rę̧ht ‹hither-he-have an unexpected experience-caused› *he made it happen* (RC 3:84), nę̧'nyè·rę̧ht ‹hither-fact-it-have an unexpected experience-caused› *first time* (RC 6:6),

---

nę²nyeręhnahk ‹hither-fact-it-have an unexpected experience-caused› *first time* (RC 6:7); ti –. –a'nyeręhči –: thwahra²nyeręhči² ‹so-fact-he-had an unexpected experience-very› *he was quite surprised* (R); ti –. –a'nyeręhθrę –: thwa²kaku²nyeręhθrę² ‹so-fact-they-had an unexpected experience-much› *accidents happened to them* (RC 32:1); tha+ne –. –a'nyeręhnyę –: tha²neyu²nyeręhnyę² ‹unusual-apart-it-have an unexpected experience-cause-go into› *it happens for the first time* (RC 7:7); ha² –a'nyerę² –: ha² yu²nyeré²ę ‹the it-have an unexpected experience-began› *accident, happening, incident* (HS).

–a'nyeręhnyę –{dative II} appear to. *v.s.-t.* ru²nyeręhnyé·-tih ‹he-have an unexpected experience-cause-goes into-for› *it appears to him (supernatural)* (HS).

–a'nyeręti –{dative II} have visions. *v.s.-a.i.* ru²nyerętyá·tih ‹he-himself-flesh-makes-for› *he has visions* (R).

–a'nyerętihnahkw – sign, symbol. *dv.n.s.* yu²nyerętihnáhkę ‹it-itself-flesh-make-caused-instrument› *sign, symbol* (HS).

–a²nyerętihnęha'nye² – apparently. *dv.n.s.* yu²nyerętihnęhá·²nye² ‹it-itself-flesh-make-caused-going along› *apparently* (HS).

–a'nyerę² – accident, happening, incident. *dv.n.s.* ha² yu²nyeré²ę ‹the it-have an unexpected experience-began› *accident, happening, incident* (R).

–a'nyerę²narahkw – assimilate. *v.s.-a.i.* wa²nyerę²naráhkhwa² ‹it-itself-flesh-collects› *it assimilates* (HS).

–a'nyeruruhčę²ke loin. *n.r.* n-poss., n-inc., n.sfx. -. u²nyeruruhčę́²kye *loin (over the kidneys)* (HS).

–a'nyeθa²T – be profligate, squander. *v.s.-a.i.* ra²nyeθá²-tha² ‹he-himself-curses› *he is profligate, he squanders* (HS).

–a'nyetawa²k – receipt. *dv.n.s.* yu²nyeta-

wá²kę ‹it-itself-grease-grabbed› *receipt* (HS).

–a'nyethar – cream. *dv.n.s.* wa²nyé·ther ‹it-itself-grease-hangs› *cream* (HS).

–a'nye²t – be plentiful. *v.r.-s.i.* stat: -i, prog: -, prp: -, dst: -, caus: -, rvs: -, dat: -, n-inc. yu²nyé²ti *it is plentiful* (H-notebook).

–a'nyęhskwe²T – smile. *v.s.-a.i.* ru²nyęhskwé²nę ‹he-himself-laugh-caused› *he smiles* (HS), ru²nyęhskwe²nę́he² ‹he-himself-laugh-caused-remote› *he had smiled* (HS).

–a'nyękʷakar – snore. *v.r.-a.i.* hab: -φ, pnt: -, stat: -, prog: -, prp: -, dst: -, caus: -, rvs: -, dat: -, n-inc. ra²nyę́·kwakar *he snores* (HS).

–a'nyękwirukarę – split wood. *dv.n.s.* yu²nyękwiruká·rę· ‹it-itself-wood-is broken up› *split wood* (HS).

–a'nyętaręhkw – breastplate. *dv.n.s.* yę²nyętaréhkhwa² ‹one-oneself-pile-adds-instrument› *breastplate* (HS).

–a'nyęwahnęhkw – altar. *dv.n.s.* ha² yę²nyęwahnę́hkhwa² ‹the one-oneself-sacrifice-causes-instrument› *altar* (HS).

–a'nyęwahnęti – make votive offerings. *v.s.-a.i.* ra²nyęwahnę́·ti· ‹he-himself-sacrifice-cause-made› *he made votive offerings* (RC 12:6).

–a'nyęwahT – bless, immolate, sacrifice (by fire), waste. *v.s.-t.* ru²nyęwáhnę ‹he-himself-sacrifice-caused› *he sacrificed, he immolated* (HS), na²nyęwáhtha² ‹one=another-sacrifice-causes› *one blesses another* (HS), ęhra²nyęwáhnę·² ‹prediction-he-himself-sacrifice-cause› *he will immolate* (HS).

–a'nyęwnarę² – allow to happen, come to ruin, come to disaster. *v.r.-a.i.* hab: -θ, pnt: -, stat: -, prog: -ęha'nye²-, prp: -²θre²-, dst: -, caus: -, rvs: -, dat: -, n-inc. ru²nyę́wnarę²θ *he allows it to happen, he comes to ruin, he comes to*

disaster (HS), ruˀnyęwnaręˀˀęhá·ˀnyeˀ
he progresses harmed (H-notebook),
ruˀnyęwnaręˀˀθreˀ *he is going to get
harmed* (H-notebook).

-aˈnyęˀkwaˀnihr – smoke. *v.s.-a.i.* yuˀ-
nyęˀkwaˀníhrę ‹it-itself-smoke-stood›
it smokes (e.g., a gun) (HS).

-aˈnyęˀkwih – belt oneself, put on belt;
encircle. *v.s.-a.i.* raˀnyęˀkwihs ‹he-
himself-belts› *he belts himself, he puts
on his belt* (HS), ruˀnyęˀkwih ‹he-
himself-belted› *it encircled him* (RC
32:10).

-aˈnyuhčr – brother-in-law, sister-in-law.
n.r. n-poss., inc., n.sfx. -eh. uˀnyúh-
čreh *brother-in-law, sister-in-law* (HS).

-aˈnyuháh husband of a cousin belonging
to a different clan. *n.r.* aln: akaˀnyuháh *my cousin's husband* (R), inc.,
n.sfx.-. akaˀnyuháh *my cousin's (of a
clan other than my own) husband* (R).

-(a)ˀr – be much. *v.r.-s.i.* stat: -ɸ, prog: -,
prp: -, dst: -, caus: -, rvs: -, dat: -, n-
inc. The form -ˀr – occurs immediately
following the third person singular
neuter agent prefix ka-. Elsewhere,
-aˀr– occurs. ti+yah+ či-.-(a)ˀr-:
thwé·θkaˀr ‹so-thither-again-it-was
much› *there is again so much there*
(RC 25:2); -eˀraˀr-: yawéˀraˀr ‹it-
hair-is much› *much hair* (RC 6:11);
rawéˀraˀr ‹he-hair-is much› *he is hair-
y* (HS); -hraˀkwaˀr-: yuhráˀkwaˀr ‹it-
quill-is much› *tail feather* (RC 12:5);
-kwiraˀr-: yukwì·raˀr ‹it-tree-is much›
there are some trees (H-notebook);
-nhuraˀnaˀr-: yunhuráˀnaˀr ‹it-dis-

ease-caused-much› *epidemic* (HS);
-ręryuhkwaˀr-: yuręryúhkwaˀr ‹it-ray-
is much› *it has a halo* (HS); -rętaˀr-:
rurę́·taˀr ‹he-magic-is much› *wizard*
(RC 6:1); -ręˈnakriˀčraˀr-: yuręˀna-
kríˀčraˀr ‹it-tree-liquid-ˈness-is much›
cake (R); -tahskwaˀr-: kakutáhskwaˀr
‹they-domestic animal-are much› *it
plagues them* (RC 2:2); -wisaˀr-: yu-
wí·saˀr ‹it-ice-is much› *icy* (HS); -ˀę =
waˀr-: kaˀę̀·waˀr ‹it-tray-is much›
small "hill" of plants (H 3518); -či-.
-ahθęˈnaˀr-: čuhθę́·ˀnaˀr ‹again-it-be
dark-is much› *black spot* (RC 8:39);
-aˀ ręˀkaraˀr-: waˀ ręˀ́karaˀr ‹it-itself-
finger span-is much› *geometrical caterpillar* (AG).

-aˀračę – rent, tear. *dv.n.s.* haˀ yuˀrá·čęˀ
‹the it-itself-tore› *rent, the tear* (HS).

-aˀračęku – the tearing, ripping noise of
thunder. *dv.n.s.* waˀračę́·kwahs ‹it-it-
self-tear-undoes› *the tearing, ripping
noise of thunder* (AG).

-aˀrakarerahsT – noisemaker, rattle. *dv.
n.s.* yęˀrakareráhsthaˀ ‹one-oneself-
sound-be in-causes› *noisemaker, rattle*
(HS).

-aˀrakęri – roll around. *v.r.-a.i.* hab: -h,
pnt: -, stat: -, prog: -, prp: -, dst: -ehę-
, caus: -, rvs: -, dat: -, n-inc. kaˀra-
kę̀·rih *I roll around* (RC 30:9); -aˀra =
kęryehę-: θaˀrakęryéhę· ‹you!-roll
around-much› *roll around!* (R).

-aˀraku – keep to oneself, secede. *v.s.-a.i.*
raˀrá·kwahs ‹he-himself-be in-undoes›
he keeps to himself, he secedes (HS).

-aˀ ranęˈnahsi – come off. *v.s.-a.i.* ę̀ˀranę꞉ʔnáhsiʔ ‹fact-it-itself-X-fasten-un-did› *it came off* (RC 26:27).

-aʔrathe?T – ascend. *v.s.-a.i.* ruʔrathéʔnę ‹he-himself-climbed-moving› *he ascended* (HS).

-aʔratʔa – get in (a conveyance). *v.s.-a.i.* kaʔrá·tʔahs ‹I-myself-X-put in› *I get into a conveyance* (H-notebook), raʔrá·tʔahs ‹he-himself-X-puts in› *he gets in* (L 55), θaʔrá·tʔah ‹you!-yourself-X-put in› *get in!* (L 55), waʔkayęʔrá·tʔa·ʔ ‹fact-they-themselves-X-put in› *they got in* (RC 27:13), čaʔrá·tʔah ‹you two-yourselves-X-put in› *get in, you two!* (RC 27:13).

-aʔraʔkar – depend on, lean against. *v.r.-a.i.* hab: -φ, pnt: -, stat: -eʔ, prog: -, prp: -, dst: -, caus: -ʔT-, rvs: -, dat: -, n-inc. ruʔráʔkareʔ *he leans against* (HS), raʔráʔkar *he leans against, he depends on* (HS); -aʔraʔkaraʔT –: raʔráʔkaraʔč ‹he-lean against-causes› *he leans* (HS), ruʔraʔkaráʔnę ‹he-lean against-caused› *he leaned* (HS), ęhraʔráʔkaraʔt ‹prediction-he-lean against-cause› *he will lean* (HS).

-aʔraʔkaraʔT – lean. *v.s.-a.i.* raʔráʔkaraʔč ‹he-lean against-causes› *he leans* (HS), ruʔraʔkaráʔnę ‹he-lean against-caused› *he leaned* (HS), ęhraʔráʔkaraʔt ‹prediction-he-lean against-cause› *he will lean* (HS).

-aʔraʔnaku – disembark, get out of (a conveyance). *v.s.-a.i.* raʔraʔná·kwahs ‹he-himself-X-put in-undoes› *he gets out, he disembarks* (HS).

-aʔreh/ -aʔreʔ have as grandchild, have as grandniece, have as grandnephew, have as great grandchild. *v.r.-k.* The form -aʔreh occurs in the vocative and in terms of direct address; the form -aʔreʔ occurs in referential terms. kęyá·ʔreh *my grandchild, my grandniece, my grandnephew, my great grandchild (direct address)* (RC 11:5), kwá·ʔreh *my grandchild, my grandniece, my grandnephew, my great grandchild (vocative)* (RC 26:31), sheyá·ʔreʔ *your grandchild, your grandniece, your grandnephew, your great grandchild (referential)* (RC 30:11); -aʔreʔ.#kęhaʔnęʔ: sheyaʔreʔkęhaʔnęʔ ‹you=another-have as grandchild-many› *your kin (referential)* (RC 23:2); -aʔreʔčhę(T) –: wakaʔré·čhęʔ ‹I-be grandparent-'ness-lays› *my grandchildren* (R).

-aʔreʔ.#kęhaʔnęʔ be kin. *v.s.-k.* sheyaʔreʔkęhaʔnęʔ ‹you=another-have as grandchild-many› *your kin (referential)* (RC 23:2).

-aʔreʔčhę(T) – have as grandchildren. *v.s.-k.* wakaʔré·čhęʔ ‹I-be grand-parent-'ness-lays› *my grandchildren* (R).

-aʔrę – abuse. *v.r.-t.* hab: -, pnt: -ʔ, stat: -, prog: -, prp: -, dst: -, caus: -, rvs: -, dat: -, n-inc. waʔnaʔnáʔręʔ *one abused another* (RC 24:2).

-aʔręhyakęʔT – toil. *v.s.-a.i.* raʔręhyakęʔthaʔ ‹he-himself-suffer-causes› *he toils* (HS), ruʔręhyakęʔnę ‹he-himself-suffer-caused› *he is toiling* (HS).

-aʔręnęti – make magic, put in a state of enchantment. *v.s.-a.i.* waʔęʔręnę́·tiʔ ‹fact-one-oneself-magic-made› *one made magic* (RC 3:41), waʔkayęʔręnę́·tiʔ ‹fact-they-themselves-magic-made› *they put it in a state of enchantment* (RC 35:11).

-aʔręnęti – magician, wizard. *dv.n.s.* ruʔręnę́·ti· ‹he-himself-magic-made› *magician, wizard* (RC 14:2).

-aʔręr – bewail, long for. *v.r.-t.* hab: -φ, pnt: -, stat: -, prog: -, prp: -, dst: -, caus: -, rvs: -, dat: -, n-inc. naʔnáʔręr *one bewails, one longs for another* (HS).

-aʔręθhwahT – scent, smell. *v.s.-t.* raʔ-

ręθhwáhtha[?] ‹he-himself-X-smell-causes› *he scents it, he smells it* (HS).

-a[?]ręwa[?]nihr – stand on end, rear (e.g., horse). *v.s.-a.i.* yu[?]ręwa[?]níhrę ‹it-itself-stature-stood› *it stands on end* (HS), wa[?]ręwá[?]nihč ‹it-itself-stature-stands› *it rears (e.g., horse)* (HS).

-a[?]rę[?]ačhęwati – sycamore, buttonwood tree. *n.s.* wa[?]rę[?]ačhęwá·tih ‹it-itself-tree-self-smoothes› *sycamore or buttonwood tree (Alcer pseudoplatanus, Ficus sycamorus)* (AG).

-a[?]rę[?]kara[?]r – geometrical caterpillar. *dv. n.s.* wa[?]ŕę[?]kara[?]r ‹it-itself-finger span-is much› *geometrical caterpillar* (AG).

-a[?]rę[?]kuhw – lurch, stagger, swag, sway, totter. *v.r.-a.i.* hab: -, pnt: -, stat: -ę, prog: -, prp: -, dst: -, caus: -, rvs: -, dat: -, n-inc. ru[?]rę[?]kúhę *he lurches, he staggers, he swags, he sways, he totters* (HS).

-a[?]rę[?]naT – divine, prophesy. *v.s.-a.i.* ra[?]rę́[?]na·č ‹he-himself-blows air on› *he prophesies* (HS), wahra[?]rę́[?]na·t ‹fact-he-himself-blew air on› *he divined* (RC 27:27).

-a[?]rę[?]naT – clairvoyant, fortune teller, prophet. *dv.n.s.* ra[?]rę́[?]na·č ‹he-himself-blows air on› *clairvoyant* (HS), *fortune teller, prophet* (RC 6:1).

-a[?]rę[?]naT – prophecy. *dv.n.s.* ha[?] ru[?]rę[?]ná·[?]nę ‹the he-himself-blew air on› *his prophecy* (HS).

-a[?]rhew – fan, sift, winnow. *v.s.-t.* ka[?]rhè·wahs ‹I-myself-sift› *I fan it, I sift it* (H-notebook), waka[?]rhè·wę ‹I-myself-sifted› *I fanned it, I sifted it, I winnow it* (SH 375), ęká[?]rhe[?]w ‹prediction-I-myself-sift› *I will fan it, I will sift it, I winnow it* (SH 375).

-a[?]rihęt have as business. *v.s.-a.i.* ru[?]ríhę·t ‹he-himself-matter-possesses› *he has it as his business* (RC 26:35).

-a[?]rihęt officer. *dv.n.s.* ru[?]ríhę·t ‹he-himself-matter-possesses› *officer* (HS).

-a[?]rihęti –{dative III} read. *v.s.-a.i.* ra[?]rihętyá·tih ‹he-himself-matter-makes-for› *he reads* (HS).

-a[?]rihęti –{dative III} pupil, student. *dv. n.s.* ha[?] ra[?]rihętyá·tih ‹the he-himself-matter-makes-for› *pupil, student* (HS).

-a[?]rihęti –{dative III} –[?]T – be studious. *v.s.-a.i.* ru[?]rihętyatí[?]ne[?] ‹he-himself-matter-made-for-moving› *he is studious* (HS).

-a[?]rihętya[?]T – origin. *n.s.* wa[?]rihętyá[?]tha[?] ‹it-itself-matter-make-causes› *origin* (HS).

-a[?]rihę'na'nye[?] – delegate. *v.s.-a.i.* ru[?]rihę[?]ná·[?]nye[?] ‹he-himself-matter-possess-causes-going along› *he delegates* (HS).

-a[?]rihuk^wahT – be audacious, be boastful, be haughty, be impertinent, be impudent. *v.s.-a.i.* ra[?]rihú·kwaht ‹he-himself-matter-spread out-causes› *he is haughty, he is impertinent, he is impudent* (HS), ru[?]rihukwáhnę ‹he-himself-matter-spread out-caused› *he is audacious, he is boastful* (HS).

-a[?]rihurya[?]T – abuse, bother, make nasty, spoil, stultify, trifle with. *v.s.-t.* arę[?]rihú·rya[?]t ‹unknown-it-itself-matter-stir-cause› *that it bother it, that it spoil it, that it make it nasty* (RC 3:22), ra⁷rihuryá⁷tha⁷ ‹he-himself-matter-stir-causes› *he abuses, he stultifies, he trifles with it* (HS), na⁷na⁷na⁷rihuryá⁷tha⁷ ‹one=another-self-matter-stir-causes› *one is abusing another, one is teasing another* (HS), nęyę⁷-na⁷na⁷na⁷rihú·rya⁷t ‹two-prediction-one=another-self-matter-stir-cause› *one will mistreat another two* (RC 27:31).

-a⁷rihwahnę⁷T - be pardonable. *v.s.-a.i.* yu⁷rihwáhnę⁷t ‹it-itself-matter-disappear-caused› *(it is) pardonable* (HS).

-a⁷rihwahstęni - amend. *v.s.-t.* ra⁷rihwahstę̀·nih ‹it-itself-matter-adorns› *he amends it* (HS).

-a⁷rihwaksę⁷ - quarrel. *n.s.* ha⁷ ru⁷rihwaksę́⁷ę ‹the he-himself-matter-be bad-began› *his quarrel* (HS).

-a⁷rihwaksę⁷na⁷T - be quarrelsome. *v.s.-a.i.* ru⁷rihwaksę⁷ná⁷ne⁷ ‹he-himself-matter-be bad-caused-moving› *he is quarrelsome* (HS).

-a⁷rihwaksę⁷T - quarrel. *v.s.-a.i.* ra⁷rihwaksę́⁷tha⁷ ‹he-himself-matter-be bad-causes› *he quarrels* (HS).

-a⁷rihwak⁷uhsi - upright, sober man. *dv.n.s.* ru⁷rihwak⁷úhsyę ‹he-himself-matter-release-undid› *upright, sober man* (RC 12:1).

-a⁷rihwanęt(a⁷) - forgive. *v.s.-t.* nakwa⁷rihwanę́·ta⁷θ ‹you!=us-ourselves-matter-lament› *forgive us!* (MP), yękwa⁷rihwanę́·ta⁷ ‹we-ourselves-matter-lament› *we forgive it* (MP).

-a⁷rihwarurękʷahT - revocable. *dv.n.s.* yu⁷rihwarurę́·kwaht ‹it-itself-matter-contribute-undo-causes› *revocable* (HS).

-a⁷rihwatet⁷ - notary. *dv.n.s.* ra⁷rihwaté·t-⁷ahs ‹he-himself-matter-lines› *notary* (HS).

-a⁷rihwatiheθ -{dative III} be trusting.

v.s.-a.i. wa⁷ka⁷rihwatihé·θę⁷ ‹fact-I-myself-matter-was dependent-for› *I am trusting* (AG).

-a⁷rihwatukęhT - recapitulate. *v.s.-a.i.* ra⁷rihwatukę́htha⁷‹he-himself-matter-??-causes› *he recapitulates* (HS).

-a⁷rihwaya⁷θrakʷahT - expiatory. *dv.n.s.* yu⁷rihwaya⁷θrá·kwaht ‹it-itself-matter-cross-undo-caused› *expiatory* (HS).

-a⁷rihwa'ne - account. *dv.n.s.* yu⁷rihwá·⁷ne⁷ ‹it-itself-matter-is present› *account* (HS).

-a⁷rihwa'neku - dissemble. *v.s.-a.i.* ra⁷rihwa⁷né·kwahs ‹he-himself-matter-be present-undoes› *he dissembles* (HS).

-a⁷rihwa⁷tikęhrya⁷khę - inconvenience. *v.s.-t.* ra⁷rihwa⁷tikęhryá⁷khęh ‹he-himself-matter-mind-breaks-much› *he inconveniences* (HS).

-a⁷rihwharhu - be a difficulty. *v.s.-s.i.* yu⁷riwhárhę ‹it-itself-matter-hang-caused› *it is a difficulty* (R).

-a⁷rihwharhu - difficulty. *dv.n.s.* wa⁷riwhárhuhs ‹it-itself-matter-hang-causes› *difficulty (abstract)* (HS).

-a⁷rihwihs⁷a - bargain, contract, plot, promise, stipulate. *v.s.-a.i.* ra⁷rihwíhs⁷ahs ‹he-himself-matter-finishes› *he bargains, he contracts, he stipulates* (HS), kaku⁷rihwíhs⁷ę ‹they-themselves-matter-finished› *they plotted, they promised* (RC 24:8); -a⁷rih=wihs⁷a-: yu⁷rihwíhs⁷ę ‹it-itself-matter-finished› *behest* (HS); -a⁷rihwihs⁷a-. {dative III}: ra⁷rihwihs⁷á·tih ‹he-himself-matter-finishes-for› *he makes a resolution* (HS); ti-. -a⁷rihwihs⁷a-: ti-yakya⁷rihwíhs⁷ahs ‹so-we two-ourselves-matter-finish› *we two promised one another* (RC 30:23).

-a⁷rihwihs⁷a - behest. *dv.n.s.* yu⁷rihwíhs-⁷ę ‹it-itself-matter-finished› *behest* (HS).

-a⁷rihwihs⁷a -{dative III} make a resolution. *v.s.-a.i.* raʔrihwihsʔá·tih ‹he-himself-matter-finishes-for› *he makes a resolution* (HS).

-aʔrihwiyuhsT - pretend to be religious. *v.s.-a.i.* raʔrihwiyúhsthaʔ ‹he-himself-matter-be great-causes› *he pretends to be religious* (HS).

-aʔriyu - fight. *v.s.-a.i.* waʔkaʔrì·yuʔ ‹fact-I-myself-killed› *I fought* (R).

-aʔriyuʔčr - fighting, war. *n.s.* uʔriyúʔ-čreh ‹self-kill-'ness› *fighting, war* (HS).

-aʔriyuʔčraręʔnhaʔ - war. *v.s.-a.i.* raʔ-riyuʔčrarę́ʔnhaʔθ ‹he-himself-kill-'ness-is accustomed to› *he wars* (HS).

-aʔriyuʔT - be a fighter. *v.s.-s.i.* wakaʔ-riyúʔneʔ ‹I-myself-kill-moving› *I am a (professional) fighter* (R).

-aʔriʔruhči - peel off. *v.s.-a.i.* ęwaʔriʔ-rúhčiʔ ‹prediction-it-itself-peel-remove› *it will peel off* (R).

-aʔruhčrę - assembly. *dv.n.s.* waʔrúhčręh ‹it-itself-gathers› *assembly* (HS).

-aʔruhčręhkw - assembly, meeting room. *dv.n.s.* yęʔruhčrę́hkhwaʔ ‹one-oneself-gathers-instrument› *assembly, meeting room* (HS).

-aʔruhčręhkw -.#ke church, at church. *dv.n.s.* yęʔruhčręhkhwáʔkye ‹one-oneself-gathers-instrument-at› *church, at church* (R).

-aʔruhčręhT - go to church. *v.s.-a.i.* wah-raʔruhčrę́htheʔ ‹fact-he-himself-gather-caused-going to› *he is going to church* (L 25), ruʔruhčrę́hnę· ‹he-himself-gather-caused› *he's gone to church* (L 25), raʔruhčrę́hnęhs ‹he-himself-gath-

er-causes› *he goes to church* (L 25), θaʔruhčrę́hthe ‹you!-yourself-gather-going to› *go to church!* (L 25).

-aʔruręku - ravel, unravel. *v.s.-a.i.* waʔru-rę́·kwahs ‹it-itself-contribute-undoes› *it (un)ravels* (HS).

-aʔθ - empty noun root. *v.inc.* See: -ę-*fall*.

-(a)ʔθ dative. *v.r.sfx.* pnt: -ɸ, prog: -, prp: -, dst: -, caus: -, rvs: -. Member of dative series II that occurs in the punctual aspect and the imperative; the form -aʔθ - follows roots and stems that end in a consonant; the form -ʔθ - follows roots and stems that end in a vowel.

-aʔθ - be of a size, be large. *v.r.-s.i.* stat: -ɸ, prog: -, prp: -, dst: -, caus: -, rvs: -, dat: -, inc.-ɸ-ag./pat. Requires the partitive or, more rarely, the combination of the contrastive and the dualic, except in the idiomatic usage noted in the first several examples. -(a)hahaʔθ -: waháhaʔθ ‹it-path-is of a size› *the roads are large or broad* (H 2484); -(a)hęʔnaʔθ -: wahę́ʔnaʔθ ‹it-field-is of a size› *the meadow is large* (H 2484); -atkęhθraʔθ -: watkę́hθraʔθ ‹it-rot-is of a size› *fetid, it smells of rot* (HS); -čiʔehnaʔθ -: kačiʔéhnaʔθ ‹it-claw-is of a size› *the claws are large, it is a large claw* (H 2484); -hehnaʔθ -: kahéhnaʔθ ‹it-corn-is of a size› *the fields are large* (H 2484); -hskęʔraʔθ -: kahskę́ʔraʔθ ‹it-bone-is of a size› *they are large bones* (H 24 84); -nęhaʔθ -: kanę́haʔθ ‹it-corn-is of

Tuscarora Pronunciation Key:
/a/ la̱w; /e/ ha̱t; /i/ pi̱zza; /u/ tu̱ne; /ę/ hi̱nt; /č/ cheese; /h/ ho̱e; /m/ mo̱ther; /s/ sa̱me; /t/ do̱ (before a vowel y, or w), to̱o (elsewhere); /k/ ga̱le (before a vowel y or w), ka̱le (elsewhere); /n/ inha̱le (before a consonant or word-final), no̱te (elsewhere), /r/ hi̱ss (before a consonant or word-

final), ru̱n (trilled as in Italian, elsewhere); /w/ cu̱ff (before a consonant other than y or word-final), wa̱y (elsewhere); /y/ fi̱sh (before a consonant or word-final), yo̱u (elsewhere), /θ/ thi̱ng; /ʔ/ (the sound between the vowels in unh-unh); /·/ long vowel, /´/ high pitch; /`/ low pitch.

a size› *the corn grains are large (no singular form)* (H 2484); -nęhsaʔθ -: kanę́hsaʔθ ‹it-house-is of a size› *the houses are large (an idiomatic use of the ending)* (H 2484); -nęhsnaʔθ -: kanę́hsnaʔθ ‹it-seed-is of a size› *the grains are large* (H 2484); -yaʔθaʔθ -: kayáʔθaʔθ ‹it-track-is of a size› *mud sleigh* (H 3518); ti -. -aʔθ -: tì·waʔθ ‹so-it-is of a size› *it is of a size* (RC 12:15), *so it is large, as large as it is* (H 2892) [Lawson «Ut-tewots» 'How many'], nęwáʔθhek ‹so-will-it-be of a size› *it will be of a size* (RC 33:6); ti -. -aʔθ -.#áh: tiwaʔθʔáh ‹so-it-is of a size-little› *it is small* (R) [Gallatin «teewautsah» 'Small, Little']; ti -. -aʔθ -.#úʔy: tiwaʔθʔúʔy ‹so-it-is of a size-great› *it is big* (R); ti -. -aʔnaʔθ -: tiwáʔnaʔθ ‹so-it-gun-is of a size› *so gun was in size* (RC 24:2); ti -. -aʔ=taʔθ -.#úʔy: tiwaʔtaʔθʔúʔy ‹so-it-projectile-is of a size-great› *large projectiles* (RC 24:2); ti -. -ęhraʔθ -: tikakawę́hraʔθ ‹so-they-sort-are of a size› *they are large in number* (R); ti -. -hehnaʔθ -.#áh: tikahehnaʔθʔúʔy ‹so-it-field-is of a size-little› *the field is small, diminutive* (H 2484); ti -. -heh=naʔθ -.#úʔy: tikahehnaʔθʔúʔy ‹so-it-field-is of a size-great› *the field is very large* (H 2484); ti -. -hweθnaʔθ -.#úʔy: tikahweθnaʔθʔúʔy ‹so-it-belly-is of a size-great› *it has a big belly* (RC 2:4); ti -. -nęhaʔθ -.#úʔy: tikanęhaʔθʔúʔy ‹so-it-corn-is of a size-great› *the corn grain is very large* (H 2484); ti -. -nęhsaʔθ -.#úʔy: tikanęhsaʔθʔúʔy ‹so-it-house-is of a size-great› *it is a great large house* (H 2484); ti -. -nęh=snaʔθ -.#úʔy: tikanęhsnaʔθʔúʔy ‹so-it-seed-is of a size-great› *the grains are very large* (H 2484); ti -. -takwnaʔθ -.#áh: tikatakwnaʔθʔáh ‹so-it-room-is of a size-little› *cell* (HS); ti -. -tyaʔnaʔθ -.#úʔy: tikatyaʔnaʔθʔúʔy ‹so-it-puffed-up-bag-is of a size-great› *large hornet's nest* (RC 26:5); ti -. -wętaʔθ -.#áh: tihrawętaʔθʔáh ‹so-he-word-is of a size-little› *he has a small, thin voice* (AG); ti -. -ʔnhęhaʔθ -.#áh: tihraʔnhęhaʔθʔáh ‹so-he-urine-is of a size-little› *his urine is small in quantity* (H 2484); ti -. -athwaritaʔθ -.#áh: tiwathwaritaʔθʔáh ‹so-it-itself-back-pack-is of a size-little› *small backpack* (RC 26:17); tha+ne -. -aʔθ -: thaʔnè·waʔθ ‹unusual-apart-it-is of a size› *it is as much as, it is of equal size (things), it is coordinate* (HS); tha+ne -. -rihwaʔθ -: thaʔneyuríhwaʔθ ‹unusual-apart-it-matter-is of a size› *they are equivalent* (H-notebook); haʔ ti -. -aʔθ -: haʔ tì·waʔθ ‹the so-it-is of a size› *its size* (HS); haʔ ti -. -ʔęyaʔθ -: haʔ tyuʔę̀·yaʔθ ‹the so-it-enclosure-is of a size› *cost, the price of it* (HS).

-(a)ʔθe - dative. *v.r.sfx.* hab: -h, stat: -·, prog: -, prp: -, dst: -, caus: -, rvs: -. Member of dative series I that occurs in the habitual and stative aspects; the form -aʔθe - follows roots and stems that end in a consonant; the form -ʔθe - follows roots and stems that end in a vowel.

-aʔθęhT - drop, knock off, remove. *v.s.-t.* waʔkáʔθęht ‹fact-I-X-fall-caused› *I dropped it* (R), yęyéʔθęht ‹thither-prediction-one-X-fall-cause› *one will drop it there* (RC 12:2); raʔθę́hthaʔ ‹he-X-fall-causes› *he knocks off, he removes it* (HS).

-aʔθk - empty noun root. *v.inc.* See: -ęhsę- *parch*, -rih- *boil*.

-aʔθkarihT - scald. *v.s.-t.* raʔθkaríhthaʔ ‹he-X-boil-cau-ses› *he scalds it* (HS).

-aʔθkęhsę - parch. *v.s.-t.* aryęʔθkę́hsęʔ ‹unknown-one-X-parch› *that one parch *it* (RC 21:2).

-aʔθr – adze, ax, hatchet, tomahawk; aim, marksmanship. *n.r.* n-poss., inc., n.sfx. -eh. úʔθreh *adze, ax, hatchet, tomahawk; aim, marksmanship* (R); -aʔ= θranęT –: waʔkayę́ʔranę·t ‹they-hatchet-gave to eat› *they made an alliance* (R); -aʔθrarehsT –: ruʔθraréhsthaʔ ‹he-aim-stretches› *he is excessive, he is outrageous, he overdoes it* (HS), yúʔ-θrarehst ‹it-aim-stretched› *excessively, extravagant, outrageous* (HS); -aʔ= θriharhuhsT –: yęʔθriharhúhsthaʔ ‹one-hatchet-hang-cause-causes› *tomahawk* (R).

-aʔθranęT – make an alliance. *v.s.-a.i.* waʔkayę́ʔranę·t ‹they-hatchet-gave to eat› *they made an alliance* (R).

-aʔθrarehsT – be excessive. *v.s.-a.i.* ruʔ-θraréhsthaʔ ‹he-aim-stretches› *he is excessive, he is outrageous, he overdoes it* (HS), yuʔθráhrehst ‹it-aim-stretched› *it is exceeding; excessively, extravagant, outrageous* (HS).

-aʔθrarehsT – excessively, extravagant, outrageous. *dv.n.s.* yuʔθrà·rehst ‹it-aim-stretched› *excessively, extravagant, outrageous* (HS).

-(a)ʔθreʔ – going to (purposive). *v.r.sfx.* hab: -θ, pnt: -ɸ, stat: -ɸ, prog: -, dst: -, caus: -, rvs: -, dat: -. The purposive is used to indicate that the speaker is expressing a logical assumption based on available evidence but has not witnessed the event first hand (e.g., ya= kuwirayęʔnáʔreʔ ‹one-infant-lays-going to› *she is going to give birth (or so it appears from the size of her belly)).* The form -aʔθreʔ – follows roots and stems that end in a consonant; the form -ʔθreʔ – follows roots and stems that end in a vowel.

-(a)ʔθrę – many, much (distributive). *v.r.sfx.* hab: -h, pnt: -ʔ, stat: -·, prog: -, prp: -, caus: -, rvs: -, dat: -. The distributive is used to indicate either that the action of the verb is spread over time or that the object of the verb is distributed over an area (e.g., ękahríʔθręʔ ‹prediction-it-spill-much› *it will spill all over).* The form -aʔ= θrę – follows roots and stems that end in a consonant; the form -ʔθrę – follows roots and stems that end in a vowel.

-aʔθręn – be chaste, be clean, be pure. *v.r.-s.i.* stat: -ɸ, prog: -, prp: -, dst: -, caus: -, rvs: -, dat: -, inc.-ɸ-pat. There is a widespread tendency to eliminate the final *n* of this root, i.e., to treat it as if it were -aʔθrę –. This tendency dates back at least to Hewitt's time, since he cites the form ráʔθręhs *he cleans*, which is unusual not only because the final *n* of the root is dropped before the habitual aspect marker, but also because the root is treated as if it were active intransitive. yúʔθręn *it is chaste, it is clean, it is pure* (HS); -t-. -aʔθręnęhT –: nayuʔθrę̀·nęht ‹hither-fact-it-be clean-caused› *it cleaned it* (RC 6:10); -nęhaʔθręn –: yunęháʔθręn ‹it-corn-is clean› *the corn is clean, free from dirt* (H 2484); -nęhsaʔθręn –:

---

yunęhsáʔθręn ⟨it-house-is clean⟩ *the house is clean* (H 2484).

-aʔθriharhuhsT – tomahawk. *dv.n.s.* yęʔ-θriharhúhsthaʔ ⟨one-hatchet-hang-cause-causes⟩ *tomahawk* (R).

áʔθruʔ thorn apple *(Crataegus puntata)* (H-notebook). *n.* Archaic. See: háʔ-θruʔ.

-aʔθwahnahkw – fire extinguisher. *n.s.* raʔθwahnáhkhwaʔ ⟨he-extinguish-causes-instrument⟩ *fire extinguisher* (R).

-aʔθwahT – extinguish, blow out, put out. *v.s.-t.* yuʔθwáhnę ⟨it-extinguish-caused⟩ *it put out fire* (RC 32:13), raʔ-θwáhthaʔ ⟨he-extinguish-causes⟩ *he extinguishes it* (R), waʔkáʔθwaht ⟨fact-I-extinguish-caused⟩ *I blew it out* (W 74).

-aʔθwaʔ – extinguish, blow out, put out. *v.r.-t.* hab: -θ, pnt: -, stat: -ę, prog: -, prp: -, dst: -, caus: -hT-, rvs: -, dat: -, n-inc. yuʔθwáʔę *it is out* (W 74), uʔθwáʔę *dead coals* (H 447); -aʔ=θwahT -: yuʔθwáhnę ⟨it-extinguish-caused⟩ *it put out fire* (RC 32:13), raʔθwáhthaʔ ⟨he-extinguish-causes⟩ *he extinguishes it* (R), waʔkáʔθwaht ⟨fact-I-extinguish-caused⟩ *I blew it out* (W 74); -aʔθwahnahkw -: raʔθwahnáh-khwaʔ ⟨he-extinguish-causes-instrument⟩ *fire extinguisher* (HS); -či -. -aʔ=θwaʔ -: θwáʔθwaʔθ ⟨again-it-extinguishes⟩ *it is extinguished* (RC 13:9); kwęhs -aʔθwahT -: kwęhs aryuʔθwáhnęk ⟨no unknown-it-extinguish-cause⟩ *it is unquenchable* (HS).

-aʔθwaʔ – dead coals. *dv.n.s.* uʔθwáʔę ⟨extinguished⟩ *dead coals* (H 447).

-(a)ʔT – causative. *v.r.sfx.* hab: -haʔ ~ -s, pnt: -ɸ, stat: -ę, prog: -, prp: -, dst: -, rvs: -, dat: -. The causative is used to form verbs that overtly express the cause of an event or activity and to form nouns of causality or instruments from verbs (e.g., waʔkayęʔnaʔnáhnęʔt ⟨fact-they=another-disappear-caused⟩ *they destroyed him/her/them*). The form -aʔT- occurs after most roots and stems that end in a consonant; -ʔT- occurs after bases that end in a vowel and certain roots and stems that end in a consonant.

-aʔt – arrow, bullet, dart, projectile. *n.r.* n-poss., inc., n.sfx. -eh. Probably to be seen nominalized in Lawson's «Oo-teste» 'Gun-lock', from *uʔtáhsteh. áʔ-teh *arrow, bullet, dart, projectile* (R), úʔteh *arrow, bullet, dart, projectile* (R); -aʔtę'ni -: ruʔtę́·ʔnyęhs ⟨he-projec-tile-throws⟩ *he shoots arrows* (HS); -aʔtętyahnę -: wahraʔtętyáhnę·ʔ ⟨fact-he-projectile-made-many⟩ *he made some projectiles* (RC 6:5); ti -. -aʔ=taʔθ -.#úʔy: tiwaʔtaʔθʔúʔy ⟨so-it-pro-jectile-is of a size-big⟩ *large projec-tiles* (RC 24:2); ti -. -aʔtęhawi -: tihraʔ-tęhà·wiʔ ⟨so-he-projectile-carried⟩ *he carried so many projectiles* (RC 24:2); aʔnahúʔy -aʔtawę -: aʔnahúʔy úʔtawęh ⟨gun-great projectile-belong to⟩ *can-non ball* (HS).

-aʔtahs – assail. *v.s.-t.* waʔkayęʔnáʔtahs ⟨fact-they-them-selves-assaulted⟩ *they assailed them* (RC 12:7).

-aʔtaʔrahtręhsT – wreath. *dv.n.s.* yęʔta-rahtrę́hstaʔ ⟨one-oneself-head-tie-causes⟩ *wreath* (HS).

-aʔtaʔrahwanhahsT – wreath. *dv.n.s.* yęʔ-taʔrahwanháhstaʔ ⟨one-oneself-head-wind-causes⟩ *wreath* (HS).

-aʔtehwatęhninęʔT – peltry. *dv.n.s.* yęʔ-tehwatęhninę́ʔthaʔ ⟨one-oneself-skin-sell-causes⟩ *peltry, selling of pelts* (HS).

-aʔtewnaʔ – reach. *v.r.-t.* hab: -t, pnt: -ɸ, stat: -ę, prog: -, prp: -, dst: -, caus: -, rvs: -, dat: -, n-inc. ruʔtewnáʔę *he reached it* (HS), ra'téwna'ʔt *he reaches it* (HS), ęhra'ʔtéwna'ʔ *he will reach it* (HS).

-a'ʔtę'ni - shoot arrows. *v.s.-a.i.* ru'ʔ-té·'ʔnyęhs ‹he-projectile-throws› *he shoots arrows* (HS).

-a'ʔtikhuręhkw- implements for mending; needle, awl, thread. *dv.n.s.* yę'ʔtikhu-réhkhwa'ʔ ‹one-oneself-sew-splits-instrument› *implements for mending: needle, awl, thread* (RC 8:3).

-a'ʔtuwęhT - tell a lie. *v.s.-a.i.* ęka'ʔtù·węht ‹prediction-I-myself-lie-cause› *I will tell a lie* (RC 30:19).

-a'ʔtyakę - get better. *v.r.-a.i.* hab: -, pnt: -ɸ, stat: -, prog: -, prp: -, dst: -, caus: -hw-, rvs: -, dat: -, n-inc. -a'ʔtya= kęhw -: ahru'ʔtyá·kęw ‹unknown-he-get better-cause› *that it cure him* (RC 21: 5); -a'ʔtyakęhwst -: yu'ʔtyá·kęwst ‹it-get better-cause-caused› *curable* (HS); -či -. -a'ʔtyakę -: θahra'ʔtyá·kę'ʔ ‹again-fact-he-got better› *he got better again* (RC 21:10); -či -. -a'ʔtyakęhw -: čaku'ʔ-tyá·kęw ‹again-one-get better-causes› *it cures again* (RC 21:11).

-a'ʔtyakęhw - cure. *v.s.-t.* ahru'ʔtyá·kęw ‹unknown-he-get better-cause› *that it cure him* (RC 21:5).

-a'ʔtyakęhwsT - curable. *dv.n.s.* yu'ʔtyá·kęwst ‹it-get bet-ter-cause-caused› *curable* (HS).

-a'ʔu - be a path. *v.r.-s.i.* stat: -· prog: -, prp: -, dst: -, caus: -, rvs: -, dat: -, n-inc. wá'ʔu· *path; it is a path* (R); ti+ yah -. -a'ʔu -: thwewá'ʔu· ‹so-thither-it-is a path› *there is a path* (R).

a'ʔù·wę'ʔ loon *(Gavia* sp.*)* (RC 3:76). *n.*

-a'ʔw - back. *n.r.* See: -ę'ʔw -.

-a'ʔwnahrar - cave. *dv.n.s.* yu'ʔwnáhrarę ‹it-earth-is a hole› *cave* (HS).

-a'ʔwnakaręhrę - *dv.n.s.* wa'ʔwnakahréhrę'ʔ ‹it-earth-goes around-much› *earthquake* (R).

-a'ʔwnakęw subterranean. *n.s.* ú'ʔwnakęw ‹earth-in› *subterranean* (HS).

-a'ʔwnaks - badlands, sterile land. *dv.n.s.* wa'ʔwná·ksę· ‹it-land-is bad› *badlands, sterile land* (HS).

-a'ʔwnakwę'ʔnh(e)r - tract (a spot of ground). *dv.n.s.* yu'ʔwnakwę́'ʔnhe'ʔr ‹it-land-is too short› *tract (a spot of ground)* (HS).

-a'ʔwnanęha'ʔ - Asia, Old World. *n.s.* u'ʔwnanęha'ʔ ‹earth-be old› *Asia, Old World* (HS).

-a'ʔwnarawę - atlas. *dv.n.s.* yu'ʔwnarà·wę'ʔ ‹it-land-is in-much› *atlas* (HS).

-a'ʔwnaya'ʔk - abroad, desert, strange land, waste. *n.s.* u'ʔwnayá'ʔkęh ‹earth-be broken› *abroad, desert, strange land, waste* (HS).

-a'ʔwT - earth, land, territory; farm. *n.r.* n-poss., inc., n.sfx. -eh. Shows an abridged form of the characterizer morpheme, -ha'ʔ, for usual -keha·'ʔ following the medial locative. á'ʔwneh *earth, land* (R); *farm* (HS), ú'ʔwneh *earth, land* (R); *farm* (HS); -a'ʔw-nahrar -: yu'ʔwnáhrarę ‹it-earth-is a hole› *cave* (HS); -a'ʔwnakaręhrę -: wa'ʔwnakahréhrę'ʔ ‹it-earth-goes a-round-much› *earthquake* (R); -a'ʔw= nakęw: ú'ʔwnakęw ‹earth-in› *subter-*

---

ranean (HS); –aˀwnaks –: waˀwná·ksę· ‹it-land-is bad› *badlands, sterile land* (HS); –aˀwnakwęˀnh(e)r –: yuˀwnakwę́ˀnheˀr ‹it-land-is too short› *tract (a spot of ground)* (HS); –aˀwnarawę –: yuˀwnarà·węˀ ‹it-land-is in-much› *atlas* (HS); –aˀwnanęha·ˀ –: uˀwnanęha·ˀ ‹earth-be old› *Asia, Old World* (HS); –aˀwnanęhaˀke: uˀwnanęhá·ˀkye ‹earth-be old-at› *in the old country* (L 61); –aˀwnatawęhT –: ękaˀwnatà·węht ‹prediction-I-earth-be warm-cause› *I will warm earth* (RC 4:5); –aˀwna=werhu –: yuˀwnawérhuˀ ‹it-earth-covered› *it covers land* (RC 1:1); –aˀw=ayaˀk –: uˀwnayáˀkęh ‹earth-be broken› *abroad, desert, strange land, waste* (HS); –aˀwnayę(T) –: wáˀwnayęˀ ‹it-earth-lay› *there is land* (RC 3:38) [Jefferson «waugh-ni-yen» 'earth']; –aˀwnaˀke: aˀwnáˀkye ‹earth-at› *on earth* (RC 12:19) [Gallatin «aufnawkeh» 'Earth, Land']; –aˀwnaˀnari=huˀT –: ękaˀwnaˀnaríhuˀt ‹prediction-I-earth-be warm-cause› *I will heat up the earth* (RC 4:5); –aˀwnaˀwthęhaˀ: uˀwnaˀthęhaˀ ‹earth-earth-in middle of-customarily› *of the wilds, from the wilderness* (RC 18:1); –aˀwT –.#ke=ha·ˀ: aˀwnaˀkyéha·ˀ ‹earth-customarily› *carnal, worldly, of the earth* (HS); –aˀwthę: áˀwthę ‹earth-in middle of› *waste, a wild* (HS); –aˀwthę=haˀ: aˀwthęhaˀ ‹earth-in middle of-customarily› *it is uncivilized, it is untamed, it is wild* (R); –aˀwthęhaˀ.#úˀy: aˀwthęhaˀúˀy ‹earth-in middle of-customarily-great› *great wilds* (RC 8:1); –aˀnaˀwnakehnaT –: ęhraˀnaˀwnakyéhna·t ‹prediction-he-himself-earth-carry on back› *he will bear the earth on his back* (RC 3:79); –aˀnaˀwnuri –: waˀnaˀwnù·rih ‹it-itself-earth-stirs› *it drives earth* (RC 12:15); –ne –. –aˀwna=

kwarihęˀ –: waˀnyuˀwnakwaríhęˀ ‹fact-apart-it-earth-hasten-began› *land trembled, earthquake* (RC 28:6); –ne –. –aˀwnihyaˀkθę –: nehruˀwnihyáˀkθę· ‹apart-he-earth-cross over-much› *he traverses* (HS); ti –. –aˀnaˀwnakahrę=waˀT –: nęwaˀnaˀwnakahręwáˀneˀ ‹so-prediction-it-itself-earth-be an opening-moving› *it will create an opening in the land* (RC 3:70); à·węˀ –aˀwnawerhu –: à·węˀ waˀwnawérhę ‹water it-earth-covered› *flood* (MP); –aˀwthęhaˀ tahuré·tik: aˀwthęhaˀ tahuré·tik ‹earth-in middle of-customarily chicken› *pheasant* (L 35); tahuré·tik –aˀwthęhaˀ: tahuré·tik aˀwthęhaˀ ‹chicken earth-in middle of-customarily› *pheasant* (L 35); kwęhs tha –. –aˀnaˀwnyeriha –: kwęhs tharyuˀnaˀwnyeríhęk ‹no unusual-unknown-it-itself-earth-straighten› *it is uneven (earth)* (HS).

–aˀwT –.#keha·ˀ carnal, worldly. *n.s.* aˀwnaˀkyéha·ˀ ‹earth-customarily› *carnal, worldly, of the earth* (HS).

áˀwthę ‹earth-in middle of› waste, a wild (HS). *n.*

aˀwthęhaˀ ‹earth-in middle of-customarily› untamed, wild (R). *n.*

Č

–čahnihčr – assiduity, smartness. *n.s.* učahníhčreh ‹be assiduous-'ness› *assiduity, smartness* (HS).

–čahnihT – be assiduous, be industrious, be smart. *v.r.-s.i.* stat: -ɸ, prog: -, prp: -, dst: -, caus: -, rvs: -, dat: -, n-inc. ručáhniht he is *assiduous, industrious, smart* (HS); –čahnihčr –: učahníhčreh ‹be assiduous-'ness› *assiduity, smartness* (HS).

-čahskwir – ankle. *n.r.* inaln: kčahskwì·reh *my ankle* (R), inc. ?, n.sfx. -eh. učahskwì·reh *ankle* (H 447).

čá··hu hel-lo! is anybody there? (yelled in the woods to see if anyone else is there) (R). *part.*

-čaN – badge; shore; brightness, smoothness. *n.r.* n-poss., inc., n.sfx. -eh. učá·teh *shore (of sea, lake, river, etc.), edge of brightness* (AG), *badge: brightness, smoothness* (HS); –ča=nęhT –: račanę́htha? ‹he-brightness-drops› *he polishes it* (HS); –čanęti –: račanę́·tih ‹he-brightness-makes› *he scours it, he smoothes it, he polishes it* (HS); –čatakT –: učá·takwt ‹brightness-next to› *seaside, strand, waterside* (HS); –čatakT –ne –. -tehuharęhw –: učá·takwt neyutehúharęw ‹it-brightness-next to apart-it-sand-cover-hang-cause› *beach* (HS); –čataktha'nye?: učatakwthá·?nye? ‹brightness-next to-going along› *on the shore* (AG); –ča=ta?ke: učatá?kye ‹brightness-at› *on the surface of the water* (AG); –čata='nehT –: yučá·ta?neht ‹it-brightness-be present-causes› *it is shiny* (HS); –ča=tuka?T –: kačatuká?tha? ‹it-bright-ness-blister-causes› *it shines, is glossy* (HS).

-čanęhT – polish. *v.s.-t.* račanę́htha? ‹he-brightness-drops› *he polishes it* (HS).

-čanęti – burnish, polish, scour, smooth. *v.s.-t.* račanę́·tih ‹he-brightness-makes› *he burnishes it, he polishes it, he scours it, he smoothes it* (HS).

-čar – door, gate. *n.r.* n-poss., inc., n.sfx. -eh. ú·čareh *door* (R); –čar –.#áh: učareháh ‹door-little› *wicket* (HS); –čara=nę –: račarà·nęh ‹he-door-guards› *door-man, usher* (HS); –čaranę'nakhę –: yučaranę?ná·khę? ‹it-door-is attached-many› *doors were affixed* (RC 3:6); –čaraktihar –: yučaraktíhar ‹it-door-be next to-hangs› *port, portal, door of a ship* (MP); –čarake?ihar –: ručarakye?íhar ‹he-door-at-hangs› *he opens the door a crack* (HS); –čaratiha=rahkw –: yučaratiharáhkę ‹it-door-are hanging-instrument› *hinge* (HS); –čara'ni: učará·?ni ‹door-at edge of› *at edge of door, next to door, other side of door* (R); –čara?nihθku –: ahračara?níhθku? ‹unknown-he-door-pick off› *that he pick off door* (RC 27:24); –čaruhči –: račarúhčęhs ‹he-door-removes› *he is taking the door off its hinges, he unhinges door* (HS); –a?=čarakęhčrę –: wa?kayę?čarakę́hčrę? ‹fact-they-themselves-door-mistreated› *they pounded on door* (R); –a?čaranę –: Kayę?čarà·nęh ‹they-themselves-door-guard› *Door-Keepers (Seneca) (title within the Iroquois Confederacy of the Senecas from their responsibility as guardian of the western edge of the Confederacy)* (AG).

-čar –.#ah wicket. *n.s.* učareháh ‹door-little› *wicket* (HS).

-čarake?ihar – open door a crack. *v.s.-a.i.* ručarakye?íhar ‹he-door-at-hangs› *he opens the door a crack* (HS).

-čaraktihar – port, portal, door of a ship. *dv.n.s.* yučaraktíhar ‹it-door-be next

to-hangs› *port, portal, door of a ship* (MP).
–**čaranę** – doorman, usher. *dv.n.s.* rača·rà·nęh ‹he-door-guards› *doorman, usher* (HS).
–**čaratiharahkw** – hinge. *dv.n.s.* yučaratiharáhkę ‹it-door-are hanging-instrument› *hinge* (HS).
–**čarhu** – smoke tobacco. *v.r.-a.i.* hab: -hs, pnt: -φ, stat: -φ, prog: -, prp: -, dst: -, caus: -hT-, rvs: -, dat: -, n-inc. sčárhuhs *you smoke* (R), θčárhu *smoke!* (R); –**čarhuhT** –: yečarhúhtha⁷ ‹one-smoke tobacco-causes› *pipe* (R).
–**čarhuhT** – pipe. *dv.n.s.* yečarhúhtha⁷ ‹one-smoke tobacco-causes› *pipe* (R).
čárhu⁷ tobacco *(Nicotiana angustifolia)* [Lawson «Char-ho» 'tobacco'] [Gallatin «charhouh»]. *n.* n-poss., inc. Requires the connective suffix –n– when incorporated. **čarhu⁷.#ęwe** čarhu⁷ę̀·we ‹tobacco-genuine› *ritual tobacco (Nicotiana rustica)* (R); –**čarhu⁷natya⁷T** –: wahračarhú⁷natya⁷t ‹fact-he-tobacco-bought› *he bought tobacco* (R); –**čar=hu⁷nahrihr** –: ęyečarhu⁷náhrir ‹prediction-one-he-tobacco-scatter› *one will scatter tobacco* (RC 16:1).
čarhu⁷.#ęwe ritual tobacco *n.* čarhu⁷ę̀·we ‹tobacco-genuine› *ritual tobacco (Nicotiana rustica)* (R).
·–**čaruhči** – unhinge door. *v.s.-a.i.* račarúhčęhs ‹he-door-removes› *he is taking the door off its hinges, he unhinges door* (HS).
–**čatakT** – seaside, strand, waterside. *n.s.* učá·takwt ‹brightness-be next to› *seaside, strand, waterside* (HS).
–**čatakT** – –**ne** –. –**tehuharęhw** – beach. *dv.n.s.* učá·takwt neyutehúharęw ‹it-brightness-be next to apart-it-sand-cover-hang-cause› *beach* (HS).
–**čata⁷ke** on the surface of water. *n.s.* učatá⁷kye ‹bright-ness-at› *on the sur-*

face of the water (AG).
–**čata̱'nehT** – be shiny. *v.s.-a.i.* yučá·ta⁷neht ‹it-brightness-be present-cause› *it is shiny* (HS).
–**čatuka⁷T** – shine, be glossy. *v.s.-a.i.* kačatuká⁷tha⁷ ‹it-brightness-blister-causes› *it shines, it is glossy* (HS).
čà·wak thwump (sound of a spear entering water) (TM). *interj.*
čaweryahskáhrę ‹again-it-heart-is an opening› elderberry (H-notebook). *n.*
–**čayę(T)** – be of little value, be of little use. *v.r.-s.i.* stat: -, prog: -, prp: -, dst: -, caus: -, rvs: -, dat: -, inc.-φ-pat. –**či** –. –**čayę(T)** –: ęθahručayę̇·⁷nak ‹unknown-he-be of little value› *that he have had a bad habit* (RC 30:71); –**ę̓k̓ehčayę(T)** –.#**áh**: ękwehčayęháh ‹human-is of little value-little› *person of no account* (RC 28:1); **the⁷** –**ačha=yę(T)** –: the⁷ aryučhayę̇·⁷nak ‹not unknown-it-itself-be of little value› *not mischievous, faulty, i.e., it was gentle* (L 33).
ča⁷kawì·nę otter *(Lutra canadensis)* (RC 3:84) [Lawson «Chackauene» 'Min(k)']. *n.*
–**ča⁷kr** – wet, wetness. *n.r.* n-poss., inc., n.sfx. -a⁷. učá⁷-kra⁷ *wet, wetness* (HS); –**ča⁷kręti** –: rača⁷kṛ́·tih ‹he-wetness-makes› *he wets it* (HS).
–**ča⁷kręti** – wet. *v.s.-t.* rača⁷kṛ́·tih ‹he-wetness-makes› *he wets it* (HS).
čá·⁷nahk seven (R) [Lawson «Chauhnoc» 'Seven']. *part.* **čá·⁷nahk** –**či** –. –**(i)har** –: čá·⁷nahk θkáhe⁷r ‹seven again-it-hangs› *seventeen* (R); **čá·⁷=nahk ti** –. –**ahθhę** –: čá·⁷nahk tiwáhθhę· ‹seven so-it-is ten› *seventy* (R).
čá·⁷nahk –**či** –. –**(i)har** – seventeen *dv.n.s.* čá·⁷nahk θkáhe⁷r ‹seven again-it-hangs› *seventeen* (R).
čá·⁷nahk ti –. –**ahθhę** – seventy *dv.n.s.* čá·⁷nahk tiwáhθhę· ‹seven so-it-is ten›

seventy (R).

–čaˀnarih – boil. *v.s.-s.i.* yučaˀnarihęhθéhahk ‹it-X-is hot-was going to› *it has boiled* (L 50).

–čaˀnarihaˀT – boil. *v.s.-t.* θčaˀnaríhaˀt ‹you!-X-be hot-cause› *boil it!, let it boil!* (L 50), waˀučaˀnaríhaˀt ‹fact-it-X-be hot-caused› *it boiled* (L 50).

–čaˀnarihę? – boil. *v.s.-s.i.* yučaˀnaríhęˀθ ‹it-X-be hot-begins› *it is boiling* (L 50), yučaˀnarihę́ˀę ‹it-X-be hot-began› *it has boiled* (L 50).

Čaˀnúhskye Sandusky, Ohio (R). *n.*

–čaˀr – fried cakes, pancakes. *n.r. n-poss., inc., n.sfx.* -eh. učáˀreh *fried cakes, pancakes* (R).

–čaˀtuh – be cool; be cold (of things). *v.r.-a.i.* hab: -θ, pnt: -, stat: -ɸ, prog: -, prp: -, dst: -, caus: -sT-, rvs: -, dat: -, inc.-ɸ-pat. yučáˀtuh *it is cool* (R), ęwakčáˀtuh *I will be cool to the touch* (RC 3:19); **–čaˀtuh** –: yučáˀtuhθ ‹it-is cool› *peppermint (Mentha piperita)* (H-notebook); **–čaˀtuhst** –: učaˀtúhsteh ‹be cool-'ness› *well; coolness* (HS); **–čaˀtuhsT** –: račaˀtúhsthaˀ ‹he-be cool-causes› *he cools it* (HS), kačaˀtúhsthaˀ ‹it-be cool-causes› *it is cooling* (HS); **–čaˀtuhst –.#keha·?**: učaˀtuhstaˀkyéha·ˀ ‹be cool-'ness-customarily› *spring of water* (RC 16:1); **–čaˀtuh = stitkęhw** –: yučaˀtuhstitkéhę· ‹it-is cool-'ness-issues forth-caused› *source, water gushing* (AG), *coolness comes forth* (RC 12:29); **–aˀčaˀtuh** –: kaˀčaˀtuh ‹I-myself-am cool› *I am cold* (PC); **–aˀčaˀtuhsnahkw** –: yęˀčaˀtuh-

snáhkhwaˀ ‹it-itself-is cool-instrument› *fan* (HS); **–ekačaˀtuh** –: ęyawekačáˀtuh ‹prediction-it-liquid-be cool› *liquid will cool* (RC 18:3); **–nęhsa = čaˀtuh** –: yunęhsačáˀtuh ‹it-house-is cool› *the house is cool, chilly; the house is cold: said of a house that is so poorly built that it is difficult to keep it warm in winter or cold weather* (H 2484); **–wračaˀtuh** –: yuwračáˀtuh ‹it-air-is cool› *cool breeze* (R).

–čaˀtuh – peppermint. *dv.n.s.* yučáˀtuhθ ‹it-is cool› *peppermint (Mentha piperita)* (H-notebook).

–čaˀtuhst – well; coolness. *n.s.* učaˀtúhsteh ‹be cool-'ness› *well; coolness* (HS).

–čaˀtuhsT – cool. *v.s.-t.* račaˀtúhsthaˀ ‹he-be cool-causes› *he cools it* (HS), kačaˀtúhsthaˀ ‹it-be cool-causes› *it is cooling* (HS).

–čaˀtuhst –.#keha·? spring of water. *n.s.* učaˀtuhstaˀkyéha·ˀ ‹be cool-'ness-customarily› *spring of water* (RC 16:1).

–čaˀtuhstitkęhw – source (of water). *dv. n.s.* yučaˀtuhstitkéhę· ‹it-is cool-'ness-issues forth-caused› *source, water gushing* (AG), *coolness comes forth* (RC 12: 29).

čaˀúhshę? almost, nearly (RC 30:19). *part.* **čaˀúhshę?** –t –. **–atkʷahT** –: čaˀúhshęˀ nyutkwáhnę ‹almost hither-it-itself-cut off› *third quarter of moon* (SH 375).

čaˀúhshę? –t –. **–atkʷahT** – third quarter of moon. *dv.n.s.* čaˀúhshęˀ nyutkwáhnę ‹almost hither-it-itself-cut off› *third*

---

quarter of moon (SH 375).

-čaˀw- bald, a bare spot. *n.r.* n-poss., n-inc., n.sfx. -eh. učáˀweh *bald, a bare spot (of any kind)* (HS).

čé come now! (HS). *v.*

čé··n boo! (said with hands splayed like lion's claws) (R). *part.*

-čę- get water, dip for water. *v.r.-a.i.* hab: -hs, pnt: -ˀ, stat: -·, prog: -heˀ-, prp: -he-, dst: -, caus: -ˀT-, rvs: -, dat: -, inc.-ɸ-pat. rá·čęhs *he dips for water* (R), rú·čę· *he has dipped for water* (R); -čęheˀ-: wahračęheˀ ‹fact-he-dip for water-was going to› *he was going dipping for water* (RC 12:29); -čęˀT-: kačę́ˀthaˀ ‹it-dip for water-causes› *dipper* (R), yakučę́ˀthaˀ ‹one-dip for water-causes› *scoop* (HS).

čęčúhner first quarter of moon (SH 375). *n.*

-čęh- fire; immediate (nuclear) family. *n.r.* See: -(a)čęh-.

-čęhakT- hearth. *n.s.* See: -(a)čęhakT-.

-čęhayę(T)- family. *n.s.* See: -(a)čęha̲=yę(T)-.

-čęhuhkw- type of fire-witch, flickering-light witch. *n.s.* See: -(a)čę=huhkw-.

-čęhuryaˀT- poker. *n.s.* See: -(a)čęhu=ryaˀT-.

čę́htkwęˀ flower-nosed mole (R). *n.*

čè·riˀ wild cherry (*Prunus virginiana*; *Prunus serotina*) (H-notebook). *n.*

-čęw- burial pole, lever, stake. *n.r.* n-poss., inc., n.sfx. -eh. učę̀·weh *burial pole, lever, stake* (HS); -t-.-čęwaˀnihrhę-: tkakučęwaˀnírhęˀ ‹hither-they-burial pole-stand up-many› *they stand up burial poles* (RC 3:13); ti-.-čęwaˀnihrhę-: nęθwačęwaˀnírhęˀ ‹so-prediction-you-burial pole-stand up-many› *you will put around burial poles* (RC 3:22); -aˀčęwhrawę-: çθwaˀčęwhrà·węˀ ‹prediction-you-

yourselves-burial pole-put up-many› *you will put burial poles around* (RC 3:22).

-čęˀT- dipper, scoop. *dv.n.s.* kačę́ˀthaˀ ‹it-dip for water-causes› *dipper* (R), yakučę́ˀthaˀ ‹one-dip for water-causes› *scoop* (HS).

-čęˀw- crispness, crumb, crust, dried thing. *n.r.* n-poss., inc., n.sfx. -eh. učę́ˀweh *crispness, crumb, crust, dried thing* (RC 30:44); ti-.-čęˀwaˀθrę-: tikačę́ˀwáˀθręˀ ‹so-it-crispness-is so big› *big dried things* (RC 30:43).

Čhakyéha·ˀ Delaware Indians (AG). *n.*

-čharhu- close a door. *v.r.-a.i.* hab: -hs, pnt: -ˀ, stat: -ę, prog: -, prp: -, dst: -, caus: -, rvs: -, dat: -, n-inc. wahračhárhuˀ *he closed door* (R), ručhárhę *he has closed door* (R), račhárhuhs *he encloses it* (HS); -čharhu-: naˀnečhárhuhs ‹one=another-closes a door› *one imprisons another* (HS); -a'ne=čharhu-: yuˀnečhárhę ‹it-itself-closed a door› *it is enclosed* (HS); -a'nečhar=huhst-: yęˀnečharhúhsthaˀ ‹one-oneself-closes a door-causes› *prison* (HS).

-čharhu- imprison. *v.s.-t.* naˀnečhárhuhs ‹one=another-imprisons› *one imprisons another* (HS).

-čhari- open a door. *v.r.-a.i.* hab: -ęhs, pnt: -ˀ, stat: -ę, prog: -, prp: -, dst: -, caus: -, rvs: -, dat: III (-ati-/-ę-), n-inc. račhá·ryęhs *he opens the door* (HS), waˀečhà·riˀ *one opened door* (RC 35:10), θečhà·ri *open the door!* (MP); -čhari-{dative III}: nakyečhá·ryę ‹you!=me-open a door-for› *open the door for me!* (RC 35:9); -či-.-čhari-: θhračhá·ryęhs ‹again-he-opens a door› *he reopens it* (HS); -a'nečhari-: waˀnečhá·ryęhs ‹it-itself-opens a door› *it opens (itself)* (HS).

čhaˀ there at (RC 3:3). *part.* čhaˀ -(a)rę'naT-: čhaˀ warę́·ˀna·č ‹there at it-blows air on› *bellows* (HS); čhaʔ -(a)'ni: čhaʔ ká·ʔni ‹there at it-at the edge of› *one side* (L 39).

čhaʔ -(a)rę'naT - bellows. *n.s.* čhaʔ warę·ʔna·č ‹there at it-blows air on› *bellows* (HS).

čhaʔ -(a)'ni one side. *n.s.* čhaʔ ká·ʔni ‹there at it-at the edge of› *one side* (L 39).

-čha̱'n - fog, mist. *n.r.* n-poss., inc., n.sfx. -eh. učhá·ʔneh *fog, mist* (HS), yú-čhaʔneh *mist* (R); -ne-. -čha̱'nayę(T) -: neyučhá·ʔnayęʔ ‹apart-it-fog-lay› *it is foggy, it is misty* (R).

-čhaʔn - gall. *n.r.* n-poss., inc., n.sfx. -eh. Lounsbury's ['uts'áhnæh] *bile* (p. 81) may contain the same root, with medial *h* an error for ʔ. učháʔneh *gall* (R); -ne-. -čhaʔnahrihT - ti -. -čhaʔruri -: nehračhaʔnáhriht tihručhaʔrú·ri· ‹apart-he-gall-breaks so-he-anger-stirred› *he is so angry his gall is bursting* (H-notebook).

-čhaʔnur - be difficult. *v.r.-s.i.* stat: -ɸ, prog: -, prp: -, dst: -, caus: -hT-, rvs: -, dat: III (-ati-/-ę-), inc.-ɸ-pat. yúčhaʔnur *it is difficult* (HS); -čhaʔnur -: učhaʔnú·ręʔ ‹be difficult› *difficulty* (R); -čhaʔnur -{dative III}: ručhaʔnurá·tih ‹he-is difficult-for› *it is difficult for him* (H-notebook); -yuʔnęhsta̱-čhaʔnur -: yuyuʔnęhstačháʔnur ‹it-work-'ness-is difficult› *it is laborious* (HS); -ne-. -čha̱ʔnuhT -: nekačhaʔnúhthaʔ ‹apart-it-be difficult-causes› *it "sweats", it exhales* (H-notebook).

-čhaʔnur - difficulty. *n.r.* n-poss., n-inc., n.sfx.: -ę·ʔ. učhaʔnú·ręʔ ‹be difficult› *difficulty* (R).

-čha̱ʔnur -{dative III} be difficult for. *v.s.-t.* ručhaʔnurá·tih ‹he-is difficult-for› *it is difficult for him* (H-notebook).

-čhaʔr - anger, choler, madness, wrath. *n.r.* n-poss., inc., n.sfx. -eh. učháʔreh *anger, choler, madness, wrath* (R); -ne-. -čhaʔrhu -: nehručháʔrhuʔ ‹apart-he-anger-caused› *he is sullen* (HS); -čhaʔrahęhθahkw -: račhaʔrahęhθáhkę ‹he-anger-throat-picked up› *he is passionate, quick to anger* (HS); -čaʔ=raks -: ručhaʔrá·ksę· ‹he-anger-is bad› *he is cross, he is intemperate, he is peevish* (HS), *he gets mad* (L 21); -čhaʔręti -: naʔčhaʔré·tih ‹one=another-anger-makes› *one angers another* (R), račhaʔré·tih ‹he-anger-makes› *he offends* (HS); -čhaʔrętyahT -: yučhaʔrę·tyaht ‹it-anger-make-cause› *offensive* (HS); -čhaʔruri -: wakčhaʔrú·ri· ‹I-anger-stirred› *I am mad* (R) [Lawson «Cotcheroore» 'Angry'], ručhaʔrú·ri· ‹he-anger-stirred› *he raves* (HS), ručhaʔruríhahk ‹he-anger-has stirred› *he was angry* (R), waʔučhaʔrù·riʔ ‹fact-it-anger-stirred› *it got mad* (RC 31:10); -čhaʔruriʔ -: aryękchaʔruríʔęk ‹unknown-one=me-anger-stir-begin› *that one have gotten me mad* (R); -(ę)ti=čhaʔraksęʔ -: rutičhaʔraksę́ʔę ‹he-himself-anger-be bad-begins› *he raves* (HS); -(ę)tičhaʔrakʷek -: rętičháʔrakwe·ks ‹he-himself-anger-is whole› *he is in a frenzy* (HS); -(ę)tičhaʔręti -:

rętička^ʔrę́·tih ‹he-himself-anger-makes› *he gets mad* (R); –(ę)tička^ʔ=ruhθ(e)r –: rętička^ʔrúhθręhs ‹he-himself-anger-strips off› *passion* (R); ha^ʔ–ne–. –(ę)tička^ʔruhθ(e)r –: ha^ʔ nehrętička^ʔrúh-θręhs ‹the apart-he-himself-anger-strips off› *his rage* (HS).

–ča^ʔrah̨ęhθahkw – be passionate, be quick to anger. *v.s.-s.i.* rača^ʔrah̨ęh-θáhkę ‹he-anger-throat-picked up› *he is passionate, he quick to anger* (HS).

–ča^ʔraks – be cross, be intemperate, be peevish. *v.s.-a.i.* rucha^ʔrá·ksę· ‹he-anger-is bad› *he is cross, he is intemperate, he is peevish* (HS), *he gets mad* (L 21).

–ča^ʔręti – anger, incense, offend. *v.s.-t.* na^ʔčha^ʔrę́·tih ‹one=another-anger-makes› *one angers another* (R), rača^ʔrę́·tih ‹he-anger-makes› *he incenses, he offends* (HS).

–ča^ʔrętyahT – offensive. *dv.n.s.* yucha^ʔrę́·tyaht ‹it-anger-make-cause› *offensive* (HS).

–ča^ʔruri – be angry, be mad, rave. *v.s.-a.i.* akcha^ʔrú·ri· ‹I-anger-stirred› *I am mad* (R) [Lawson «Cotcheroore» 'Angry'], rucha^ʔrú·ri· ‹he-anger-stirred› *he raves* (HS), rucha^ʔuríhahk ‹he-anger-has stirred› *he was angry* (R), wa^ʔucha^ʔrù·ri^ʔ ‹fact-it-anger-stirred› *it got mad* (RC 31:10).

–ča^ʔruri^ʔ – get mad. *v.s.-a.i.* aryękcha^ʔrurí^ʔęk ‹unknown-one=me-anger-stir-begin› *that one have gotten me mad* (R).

–čenę – be a domestic animal, be a pet, be a slave. *v.r.- s.i.* stat: -^ʔ, prog: -, prp: -, dst: -, caus: -, rvs: -, dat: -, n-inc. kačhè·nę^ʔ *(it is a) domestic animal, slave, pet* (R), akčhè·nę^ʔ *my slave* (R), θtičhè·nę^ʔ *you two (are) slaves* (RC 3:56); –čenę –.#kwę́: kačhenę^ʔkwę́ ‹it-be a domestic animal-

like› *brutal* (HS); –čhenę^ʔčrayę(T) –: akčhenę́^ʔčrayę^ʔ ‹I-be a domestic animal-lays› *I have a domestic animal* (H 447).

–čhenę –.#kwę́ brutal. *dv.n.s.* kačhenę^ʔkwę́ ‹it-be a domestic animal-like› *brutal* (HS).

–čheyar – be coy, be modest, be retiring. *v.r.-s.i.* stat: -ę, prog: -, prp: -, dst: -hę-, caus: -, rvs: -, dat: -, n-inc. rucheyà·rę *he is coy, he is modest, he is retiring* (HS); –čheyar –: učhè·ya^ʔr ‹be modest› *modesty* (R) (archaic: učheyá·rę·^ʔ *modesty* (HS)); –če=yarhę –: rucheyárhę· ‹he-is coy-much› *he is shy, he is bashful* (R).

–čheyar – modesty. *n.r.* n-poss., n-inc., n.sfx. -^ʔ (archaic: -ę·^ʔ). učhè·ya^ʔr ‹be modest› *modesty* (R) (archaic: učheyá·rę·^ʔ *modesty* (HS)).

–čheyarhę – be bashful, be shy. *v.s.-a.i.* rucheyárhę· ‹he-is coy-much› *he is shy, he is bashful* (R).

–če^ʔ – bottle, gourd, jug. *n.r.* n-poss., inc., n.sfx. -h. účheh *bottle, gourd, jug* (M 84).

čhé^ʔru^ʔr gourd bowl (RC 27:17). *n.*

–če^ʔw – gourd, melon, pumpkin, squash, yam; bottle. *n.r.* n-poss., inc., n.sfx. -eh. učhé^ʔweh *bottle, gourd, melon, pumpkin, squash, yam* (RC 7:5) [Lawson «U-tchaawa» 'A Gourd or Bottle']; –če^ʔw –.#áh: učhe^ʔweháh ‹bottle-little› *phial* (HS); –če^ʔw –.#ęwe: učhe^ʔwehę̀·we ‹gourd-genuine› *true gourd (as opposed to, for example, a melon or cucumber which could also be referred to as a type of učhé^ʔweh)* (R); –ne+či –. –če^ʔwęhaw –: nęθahrache^ʔwę́ha^ʔw ‹two-fact-a-gain-he-squash-carried› *he took back two squash* (RC 7:6); –t –. –če^ʔwękuh –: nayuche^ʔwę́·kuh ‹apart-fact-it-gourd-went through› *it is through the gourd*

(RC 15:4); **ti –. –čhe⁷węt**: tyučhé⁷wę·t ‹so-it-gourd-possesses› *it has squash* (RC 7:5).

–čhe⁷w –.#ah phial. *n.s.* učhe⁷weháh ‹bottle-little› *phial* (HS).

–čhe⁷w –.#ęwe true gourd. *n.s.* učhe⁷wehę̀·we ‹gourd-genuine› *true gourd (as opposed to, for example, a melon or cucumber which could also be referred to as a type of učhé⁷weh)* (R).

–čhe⁷wa⁷k – bottle-holder. *dv.n.s.* yučhe⁷wá⁷kę ‹it-bottle-hold› *bottle-holder* (HS).

čhę⁷ just, just now, new, newly, only, recently (R). *part.* ha⁷ čhę⁷ **–herya⁷k –**: ha⁷ čhę⁷ kaheryá⁷kę ‹the just it-green-broke› *stubble* (HS).

čhę⁷ –herya⁷k – stubble. *dv.n.s.* ha⁷ čhę⁷ kaheryá⁷kę ‹the just it-green-broke› *stubble* (HS).

–čhiku⁷r – manufactured shoe, commercial shoe. *n.r.* n-poss., inc., n.sfx. –eh. učhikú⁷reh *manufactured shoe, commercial shoe* (R); **–čhiku⁷ręti –**: račhiku⁷rę́·tih ‹he-shoe-makes› *he makes shoes, shoemaker* (R); **–čhiku⁷rahθu = hahT –**: yečhiku⁷rahθuháhtha⁷ ‹one-shoe-color-causes› *shoe polish* (HS); **–čhiku⁷r – –(i)htręhst –**: učhikú⁷reh yehtrę́hstha⁷ ‹shoe one-tie-causes› *shoelace* (HS).

–čhiku⁷r – –(i)htręhst – shoelace. *dv.n.s.* učhikú⁷reh yehtrę́hstha⁷ ‹shoe one-tie-causes› *shoelace* (HS).

–čhiku⁷rahθuhahT – shoe polish. *dv.n.s.* yečhiku⁷rahθuháhtha⁷ ‹one-shoe-color-causes› *shoe polish* (HS).

–čhiku⁷ręti – shoemaker. *dv.n.s.* račhiku⁷rę́·tih ‹he-shoe-makes› *shoemaker* (R).

–čhi(y) – you all! (second person non-singular imperative). *v.r.pfx.* The form –čhi– occurs before verb roots and stems that begin with a consonant; the form –čhiy– occurs before verb roots and stems that begin with a vowel. Archaic.

–či – again (repetitive). *v.pfx.* The form či– occurs before the consonants θ or t, or the clusters ⁷n or ⁷t. The form č– occurs before the consonant y and the y is dropped. The form θ– occurs elsewhere. The repetitive, in ninety percent of cases, carries the meaning of recurrence. With verbs of motion it typically carries the meaning of movement toward point of origin. Its usual English translation is *again* (or *back* with verbs of motion) and its gloss in this dictionary is ‹again›. With a number of verb roots and stems, however, the meaning of the repetitive is more opaque. Where this is the case, the repetitive is considered a discontinuous part of the root or stem. Below are listed all those cases that have been encountered in the data base from which this dictionary has been constructed where the repetitive is opaque in meaning and forms part of a root or stem.

–či –. –ačhakwahsT – repair. *v.s.-t.* θhračhakwáhstha⁷ ‹a-gain-he-X-is good› *he repairs it* (HS).

–či –. –ačhakwahsT – reparable. *dv.n.s.* ču-

čhákwahst ‹again-fact-it-X-was good›
reparable (HS).
–či –. –a**čhekwahsT** – reform. *v.s.-t.* θhra-
čhekwáhstha[,] ‹again-he-?'?› *he re-
forms it* (HS).
–či –. –a**čhęna**ʔ**nak**ʔ**u** – abdicate. *v.s.-a.i.*
θhračhęna[,]ná·k-[,]uhs ‹again-he-himself-name-self-releases› *he abdicates*
(HS).
–či –. –a**hk(e)T** – revert, turn back. *v.s.-a.i.*
θahráhkye·t ‹again-fact-he-go and re-
turn› *he turned back* (L 79), θwáh-
knęhs ‹again-it-goes and returns› *it
reverts* (HS).
–či –. –a**hθaw**ʔ – resume. *dv.n.s.* θhrah-
θá·w[,]ahs ‹again-he-begins› *he resumes* (HS).
–či –. –a**hθę'nat** night. *dv.n.s.* θwahθę·[,]na·t
‹again-it- darkness-be one› *night* (HS).
–či –. –a**hθę'na**ʔ**r** – speck, dark spot. *dv.n.s.*
čuhθę·[,]na[,]r ‹again-it-darkness-be
much› *speck, black spot* (RC 8: 39).
–či –. –(a)**hyeθ** – haw, mulberry. *dv.n.s.*
θhúhye·θ ‹again-it-fruit-is long› *haw,
mulberry (Morus sp.)* (R).
–či –. –(a)**hyeθa**ʔ**ke** February, April. *dv.n.s.*
čuhyeθá[,]kye ‹again-it-fruit-is long-at›
February (AG), *April* (HS: June 15-
July 15).
–či –. –a**kna**ʔ**T** – drive back, thrust back.
v.r.-t. hab: -ha[,], pnt: -, stat: -, prog: -,
prp: -, dst: -, caus: -, rvs: -, dat: -, n-
inc. θhrakná[,]tha[,] ‹again-he-thrusts› *he
drives it back, he thrusts it back* (HS).
–či –. –(a)**nha** – herring. *dv.n.s.* čúnhę
‹again-it-is full› *herring (Clupea ha-
rengus)* (H 3518).
–či –. –a**r(e)ku** – return home, retire to
home. *v.s.-a.i.* θhraré·kwahs ‹again-he-
moves on› *he retires* (HS), θę́rku[,]
‹again-fact-it-moved on› *it returned
home* (RC 26:29).
–či –. –a**t** be one. *v.s.-a.i.* Requires that an
incorporated noun root be present.

θwáhsa·t ‹again-it-foot-stands› *one
foot* (RC 25:2), θwę́·[,]na·t ‹again-it-
day-stands› *one day* (RC 21:7),
θkahtkwí·ra·t ‹again-it-spoon-stands›
spoonful (HS), θkahwíhsta·t ‹again-it-
metal-stands› *one dollar* (HS), θka-
nę́hsa·t ‹again-it-house-stands› *one
house* (H 2484), θkanę́hsna·t ‹again-it-
seed-stands› *one seed* (RC 23:6), ču-
rę́[,]kara·t ‹again-it-finger span-stands›
one stretch/reach of fingers (AG),
θhrayáhsta·t ‹again-it-individual-
stands› *one male, one individual man*
(RC 1:8).
–či –. –a**tęhninę** – resell. *v.s.-t.* θhratęhnì·
nęh ‹again-he-sells› *he resells it* (HS).
–či –. –a**thahakarę(w)** – return, turn back.
v.s.-a.i. θakayęthahakà·ręw ‹again-
fact-they-themselves-path-went   a-
round› *they turned this road about,
they returned* (RC 12:11).
–či –. –a**tkęha** – –(i)**hey** – raise the dead.
v.s.-a.i. čę[,]natkę́hahs węhè·yę ‹again-
one=another-raises it-died› *one raises
the dead* (HS).
–či –. –a**tkęha**ʔ**θe** – resurrection. *dv.n.s.* ha[,]
ęčętkęhá[,]θe[,] ‹the unknown-again-one-
oneself-raise-going to› *resurrection*
(HS).
–či –. –a**tkehr** – be a pile. *v.s.-s.i.* čutkyéh-
re[,] ‹again-it-itself-piled› *it is a pile*
(R).
–či –. –a**tkeθku** – recover. *v.s.-a.i.* θhra-
tkyé·θkwahs ‹again-he-himself-raises›
he recovers (HS).
–či –. –a**w** – return. *v.s.-a.i.* θhrá·wu·
‹again-he-came› *he returns* (R).
–či –. –a**w**ʔ**θe**ʔ – remorse. *dv.n.s.* ha[,] θhra-
wú[,]θe[,] ‹the again-he-came-going to›
remorse (R).
–či –. –a**'nahθuhkwahsT** – purple. *dv.n.s.*
θwa[,]nahθúhkwahst ‹again-it-itself-
color-be good› *purple* (HS).
–či –. –a**'nak**ʔ**u** – let go, release. *v.s.-t.*

θhraʔná·kʔuhs ‹again-he-himself-releases› *he lets it go, he releases it* (HS).

-či-. -a'narihaʔT - reheat. *v.s.-t.* θhraʔnariháʔthaʔ ‹again-he-be hot-causes› *he reheats it* (HS).

-či-. -a'na'nęr - be the exception. *v.s.-a.i.* θhraʔná·ʔnęr ‹again-he=another-leaves behind› *he was the exception* (RC 13:3).

-či-. -a'netihstihsʔa - finish dressing. *v.s.-a.i.* čęʔnetyahstíhsʔa·ʔ ‹again-fact-it-itself-produce-finished› *one finished dressing* (RC 3:59).

-či-. -a'neti(y) - put clothes back on. *v.s.-a.i.* θaθʔané·ti ‹again-you!-yourself-produce› *put your clothes back on!* (RC 3:58), čęʔné·tiʔ ‹again-fact-it-itself-produced› *one put one's clothes back on* (RC 3:59).

-či-. -a'newyat - fathom. *dv.n.s.* θwaʔné·wya·t ‹again-it-itself-wingspan-stands› *(one) fathom* (R).

-či-. -a'niʔθęni - reconquer. *v.s.-t.* θhraʔniʔθę·nyęhs ‹again-he-himself-defeats› *he reconquers it* (HS).

-či-. -a'nuhči - pay up, repay, retaliate. *v.s.-a.i.* θhraʔnúhčęhs ‹again-he-himself-removes› *he pays up, he repays, he retaliates* (HS).

-či-. -a'nuhsar - be enervated by women. *v.s.-a.i.* θhraʔnúhsar ‹again-he-himself-is enervated by women› *he is enervated by women* (H-notebook).

-či-. -a'nwętak - retract. *v.s.-t.* θhraʔnwę́·ta·ks ‹again-he-himself-word-eats› *he retracts it* (HS).

-či-. -a'nwętar - revoice. *v.s.-t.* θhraʔnwę́·tar ‹again-he-himself-word-is in› *he revoices it* (HS).

-či-. -a'nwiręhT - abortion (by choice). *dv.n.s.* θwaʔnwirę́hnę ‹again-it-itself-infant-fall-caused› *abortion (by choice)* (HS).

-či-. -a'nwiriʔθ(e)r - take infant home. *v.s.-a.i.* nęčęʔnwiríʔθeʔr ‹two-prediction-again-one-oneself-infant-drag› *the two of them will take the infant home* (RC 11:15).

-či-. -a'nyaʔtakʔuhsi - resume (speed). *v.s.-a.i.* θhraʔnyatakʔúhsyęhs ‹again-he-himself-body-release-undoes› *he resumes (his speed)* (HS).

-či-. -a'nyaʔθrę - retrace steps. *v.s.-a.i.* θhraʔnyáʔθręh ‹again-he-himself-step-falls› *he retraces his steps* (HS).

-či-. -a'nyerę - resemble. *v.s.-t.* θwaʔnyé·rę· ‹again-it-itself-flesh-fell› *it resembles it* (HS).

-či-. -a'nyerętihnahkw - vestige. *dv.n.s.* čuʔnyerętihnáhkę ‹again-it-itself-flesh-make-caused-instrument› *vestige* (HS).

-či-. -a'nyę - abdicate. *v.s.-t.* θhrá·ʔnyęhs ‹again-he-himself-lays› *he abdicates* (HS).

-či-. -aʔθwaʔ - extinguish. *v.s.-t.* θwáʔθwaʔθ ‹again-it-extinguishes› *it is extinguished* (RC 13:9).

-či-. -čari - reopen. *v.s.-t.* θhračá·ryęhs ‹again-he-opens door› *he reopens it* (HS).

-či-. -ehyahraʔ - remember. *v.s.-a.i.* θahrehyáhraʔ ‹again-fact-he-had on his mind› *he remembered* (RC 31:3);

Tuscarora Pronunciation Key:
/a/ law; /e/ hat; /i/ pizza; /u/ tune; /ę/ hint; /č/ cheese; /h/ hoe; /m/ mother; /s/ same; /t/ do (before a vowel y, or w), too (elsewhere); /k/ gale (before a vowel y or w), kale (elsewhere); /n/ inhale (before a consonant or word-final), note (elsewhere), /r/ hiss (before a consonant or word-final), run (trilled as in Italian, elsewhere); /w/ cuff (before a consonant other than y or word-final), way (elsewhere); /y/ fish (before a consonant or word-final), you (elsewhere), /θ/ thing; /ʔ/ (the sound between the vowels in unh-unh); /·/ long vowel, /ˊ/ high pitch; /ˋ/ low pitch.

θhrehyáhra'θ ‹again-he-has on his mind› *he remembers, he recollects* (HS).

-či-. -ehyahrhuhkw -{dative III} be reminded, memorize. *v.s.-s.i.* θhrawehyarhuhkwá·tih ‹again-he-think about-causes-instrument-for› *he is reminded, he memorizes* (R).

-či-. -ekaT - dose. *dv.n.s.* θwé·ka·t ‹again-it-liquid-stand› *dose* (HS).

-či-. -ekaT - window sash. *dv.n.s.* θwé·ka·t ‹again-it-liquid-stand› *window sash* (HS).

-či-. -ekęti - wild honeysuckle. *dv.n.s.* čawekę́·tye' ‹again-it-liquid-makes› *wild honeysuckle (Lonicera sp.)* (H-notebook).

-či-. -eti(y) - redress, remake, revest. *v.s.-t.* θhretì·yahs ‹again-it-makes› *he redresses it, he remakes it, he revests it* (HS).

-či-. -e' - return. *v.s.-a.i.* íθhre'θ ‹again-he-go-begins› *he returned* (HS).

-či-. -e'θ - walk around. *v.s.-a.i.* ęθawé'θhek ‹again-unknown-it-be in a location› *that it be walking around* (RC 7:9).

-či-. -ęhnęθhar - reembrace. *v.s.-t.* θhręhnę́θhar ‹again-he-embraces› *he reembraces it* (HS).

-či-. -ęhnęθaraT - armful. *dv.n.s.* θwęhnę́θhara·t ‹again-it-embrace-stands› *armful* (HS).

-či-. -ęnęhkwa'T - cure. *v.s.-t.* ęθkakawęnę́hkwa'twa ‹prediction-again-they-medicine-cause› *it will cure them* (AW 51).

-či-. -ęnehyahrhuhkw -{dative III} commemorate. *v.s.-t.* θhręnehyarhuhkwá·tih ‹again-he-himself-think about-causes-instrument-for› *he commemorates it* (HS).

-či-. -ę°nhahkT - bring back to life, raise the dead, revive. *v.s.-t.* θhrę́nhahkt ‹again-he-be alive-instrument-caused› *he brings it back to life, he raises the dead, he revives it* (HS).

-či-. -ę°nhehkw - liveforever. *dv.n.s.* čawęnhéhkę ‹again-it-is alive-instrument› *liveforever (Sedum triphylum, S. purpureum)* (H-notebook).

-či-. -ętihrečhę'ni - retreat. *v.s.-a.i.* θhrętihrečhę́·'nyęhs ‹again-he-backside-throws› *he retreats* (HS).

-či-. -ę'nahtir - be refreshed. *v.s.-a.i.* θhrawę́·'nahtič ‹again-he-day-is durable› *he is refreshed* (HS).

-či-. -(ę)'teyhaw - bus. *dv.n.s.* θká'teyhaws ‹again-it-crowd-brings› *bus* (R).

-či-. -(ę)'tikęhraT -{dative III} give an idea to. *v.s.-t.* čęktikęhrá·'nę' ‹again-fact-one=me-mind-stood-for› *one gives me an idea* (RC 6:18).

-či-. -(ę)'tikęhritkę' - come to, revive. *v.s.-a.i.* θhra'tikęhrí·tkęhθ ‹again-he-mind-issue-begins› *he comes to, he revives* (HS).

-či-. -hne'ra·'whę - cling to roots. *v.s.-a.i.* θkahne'rá·'whęh ‹again-it-root-grabs-many› *it clings to roots* (RC 5:17).

-či-. -hne'reθ - spikenard. *dv.n.s.* čuhné're·θ ‹again-it-root-is long› *spikenard (Aralia racemosa)* (HS).

-či-. -hne'reθ -.#áh sarsaparilla. *dv.n.s.* čuhne're·θ'áh ‹again-it-root-is long-little› *sarsaparilla (Smilax sp.)* (HS).

-či-. -hne'reθ -.#ú'y wild sarsaparilla. *dv.n.s.* čuhne're·θ'ú'y ‹again-it-root-is long-great› *wild sarsaparilla (Aralia nudicaulis)* (HS).

-či-. -hnyęhawi - report. *v.s.-a.i.* θhrahnyęhà·wi' ‹again-he-news-brings› *he reports* (HS).

-či-. -hraT - renumerate. *v.s.-t.* θhráhra·č ‹again-he-counts› *he renumerates it* (HS).

-či-. -hθaT - one pace, yard (unit of measurement). *dv.n.s.* θkáhθa·t ‹again-it-width of flexible material-stands› *one pace (of 3 feet), yard* (AG).

-či-. -hstra?nihr – reseat. *v.s.-t.* θhrahstrá?nihč ‹again-he-X-stands up› *he reseats it* (HS).

-či-. -hsu?kw<u>a</u>kanęt – red squirrel. *dv.n.s.* čuhsu?kwaká·nę·t ‹again-it-finger-licked› *red squirrel (Tamiasciurus hudsonicus)* (AG).

-či-. -hterhę – morning. *dv.n.s.* θuhtérhę ‹again ?-it-X-is day› *morning* (RC 4:7).

-či-. -hterhę.#áh morning. *dv.n.s.* θuhterhę?áh ‹again ?-it-X-is day-little› *morning* (HS).

-či-. -hterhę.#ke in the morning, forenoon. *dv.n.s.* θuhterhę́·kye ‹again ?-it-X-is day-at› *forenoon* (HS), *in the morning* (H 447).

-či-. -hterhę- -a'nekhwah(e)r – breakfast. *dv.n.s.* θuhtérhę yę?nekhwáher ‹again ?-it-X-is day one-oneself-food-puts up› *breakfast* (HS).

-či-. -hwečręti – refold. *v.s.-t.* θhrahwečrę́·tih ‹again-he-??› *he refolds it* (HS).

-či-. -ič<u>a</u>nę – dogfish. *dv.n.s.* θkę́·čanęh ‹again-it-fish-guards› *dogfish* (H 35 18).

-či-. -ihnaks – fox. *dv.n.s.* θkęhná·ksę? ‹again-it-hide-is bad› *fox* (R).

-či-. -ihnaks- -(a)hy<u>a</u>k – false Solomon's seal. *dv.n.s.* θkęhná·ksę? wáhyaks ‹again-it-hide-is bad it-fruit-eats› *false Solomon's seal (Smilacina sp.)* (H-notebook).

-či-. -ihrę – repeat. *v.s.-a.i.* čaíhrę·?

‹again-fact-one-said› *one repeated* (RC 26:25).

-či-. -i?rę – readjust, reset. *v.s.-t.* θhrę́?ręhs ‹again-he-sets› *he readjusts it, he resets it* (HS).

-či-. -kahraks – pickerel. *dv.n.s.* θkakahrá·ksę? ‹again-it-eye-is bad› *pickerel* (H 3518).

-či-. -keθku – reestablish, reordain. *v.s.-t.* θhrakyé·θkwahs ‹again-he-raises› *he reestablishes it, he reordains it* (HS).

-či-. -ku?čęri – recover. *v.s.-t.* θhraku?čę́·ryęhs ‹again-he-finds› *he recovers it* (HS).

-či-. -nęhw<u>a</u>riyu – catfish, sucker (fish). *dv.n.s.* čunęhwarí·yu· ‹again-it-brain-is great› *catfish, sucker (fish) (Esox sp.)* (H 3518).

-či-. -nyatariyu – Handsome Lake. *dv.n.s.* Θkanyatarí·yu· ‹again-it-lake-is great› *Handsome Lake* (R).

-či-. -nyatarati.#aka·? Nanticokes. *dv.n.s.* Θkanyataratihá·ka·? ‹again-it-lake-??-characterized by› *Nanticokes* (probably "near the ocean") (AG).

-či-. -nyatarati?ku-.#aka·? Europeans. *dv.n.s.* Θkanyatarati?ku?á·ka·? ‹again-it-lake-??-characterized by› *Europeans* (HS).

-či-. -rakar(e) – resound. *v.s.-s.i.* čurá·kar ‹again-it-sounds› *it resounds* (HS).

-či-. -rihuri – make fun of. *v.s.-t.* θakayę?na?rihú·rye? ‹again-fact-they=another-matter-stirred› *they made fun of him* (AW 56).

-či-. -rihwahθaw? – repeat. *v.s.-t.* θhrurihwáhθa?w ‹again- he-matter-began› *he*

Tuscarora Pronunciation Key:
/a/ l<u>a</u>w; /e/ h<u>a</u>t; /i/ p<u>i</u>zza; /u/ t<u>u</u>ne; /ę/ h<u>in</u>t; /č/ <u>ch</u>eese; /h/ <u>h</u>oe; /m/ <u>m</u>other; /s/ <u>s</u>ame; /t/ <u>d</u>o (before a vowel y, or w), <u>t</u>oo (elsewhere); /k/ <u>g</u>ale (before a vowel y or w), <u>k</u>ale (elsewhere); /n/ i<u>n</u>hale (before a consonant or word-final), <u>n</u>ote (elsewhere), /r/ hi<u>ss</u> (before a consonant or word-final), <u>r</u>un (trilled as in Italian, elsewhere); /w/ c<u>u</u>ff (before a consonant other than y or word-final), <u>w</u>ay (elsewhere); /y/ fi<u>sh</u> (before a consonant or word-final), <u>y</u>ou (elsewhere), /θ/ <u>th</u>ing; /?/ (the sound between the vowels in unh-unh); /·/ long vowel, /´/ high pitch; /`/ low pitch.

repeats it (HS).

-či-. -rihwahtinę – beg. *v.s.-a.i.* θahrarih-
wahtì·nę² ‹again-fact-he-matter-begged› *he begged* (AW 56).

-či-. -rihwakę²neti – alter resolution. *v.s.-
a.i.* θhrarihwakę²né·tyęhs ‹again-he-
matter-changes› *he alters his resolution* (HS).

-či-. -rihwayahθraku – reply. *v.s.-a.i.* θhra-
rihwayahθrá·kwahs ‹again-he-matter-
cross-undoes› *he replies* (HS).

-či-. -rihwa²nihethu – revoke. *v.s.-t.* θhra-
rihwa²nihę́·thuhs ‹again-he-matter-
pulls› *he revokes it* (HS).

-či-. -takęhku – purple. *dv.n.r.* čutakę́hku²
‹again-it-is purple› *purple* (R).

-či-. -ta'nyę – revisit. *v.s.-t.* θhratá·²nyę²
‹again-he-town-goes into› *he revisits it*
(HS).

-či-. -tenę²ke Where-The-Sun-Shines. *dv.
n.s.* Čutenę́²kye ‹again-it-sunshines-at›
*Where-The-Sun-Shines (place where
the Tuscarora stopped on route north
from the Carolinas)* (AG).

-či-. -thwęhętyę – heal. *v.s.-a.i.* čuthwę-
hę́·tyę· ‹again-it-cure-much-much› *(it)
had healed* (AW 98).

-či-. -tkwara'nehT – cardinal, any reddish-
colored bird. *dv.n.s.* čutkwará·²neht
‹again-it-be red-stand-causes› *cardinal,
any reddish-colored bird* (R).

-či-. -uhstatha'nye – yearly. *dv.n.s.* θwuh-
stathá·²nye² ‹again-it-year-stand-is going along› *yearly* (HS).

-či-. -u²knęku – refold. *v.s.-t.* θhru²knę́·
kwahs ‹again-he-come to an end-un-
does› *he refolds it* (HS).

-či-. -we²rke January. *dv.n.s.* θkawé²rkye
‹again-it-air-at› *January* (R) (HS:
February 15-March 15).

-či-. -wętęhawihT – Bringer-of-Language.
dv.n.s. Čewętęhawíhtih ‹again-one-
word-bring-causes› *Bringer-of-Language (mythic bird, said to have

brought language from God to man)*
(See RC:text 2).

-či-. -wiraT – brood. *dv.n.s.* θkawí·ra·t
‹again-it-off-spring-stands› *a brood*
(HS).

-či-. -wirę² – miscarry. *v.s.-a.i.* čewì·rę²θ
‹again-one-infant-fall-begins› *one miscarries* (HS).

-či-. -wirę² – abortion, miscarriage, premature birth. *dv. n.s.* θkawirę́²ę ‹a-
gain-it-infant-fall-began› *abortion (by
accident), miscarriage, premature birth*
(HS).

-či-. -wiθraT – snowflake. *dv.n.s.* θkawí·
θra·t ‹again-it-snow-stands› *snowflake*
(R).

-či-. -yahstatha'nye – one-by-one. *dv.n.s.*
θkayeyahstathá·²nye² ‹again-they-individual-stand-going along› *one-by-one*
(RC 3:81).

-či-. -yahsti – hundred. *dv.n.s.* θkayáhsti·
‹again-it-individual-is a group› *hundred* (L 13).

-či-. -yenę – retake. *v.s.-t.* θhrayè·nęhs
‹again-he-grabs› *he retakes it, he takes
it back* (HS).

-či-. -yerik(T) – fill back up, restore. *v.s.-
t.* θhrayè·riks ‹again-he-fills up› *he
fills it back up, he restores it* (HS),
θhruyerí·knę ‹again-he-filled up› *he
filled it back up, he restored it* (HS),
ęθhrayè·rikt ‹prediction-again-he-fill
up› *he will fill it back up, he will restore it* (HS).

-či-. -yę – eclipse. *v.s.-a.i.* θkà·yęh ‹again-
it-goes into› *it goes into eclipse, it is
wont to be in eclipse; eclipse* (H-notebook), čù·yę² ‹again-it-went into› *it is
in eclipse* (H-notebook).

-či-. -yę – reenter. *v.s.-a.i.* θhrà·yę² ‹a-
gain-he-went into› *he reenters* (HS).

-či-. -yę(T) – abdicate, replace. *v.s.-t.*
θhrà·yęhs ‹again-he-lays› *he abdicates,
he replaces it* (HS).

-či-. -yęthu - replant. *v.s.-t.* θhrayę́·thwahs ‹again-he-plants› *he replants it* (HS).

-či-. -yę'ner - recognize. *v.s.-t.* θhrayę́·'ner ‹again-he-knows› *he recognizes it* (HS), θhruyę'nè·rę ‹again-he-knew› *he recognized it* (HS).

-či-. -'ęyuhar - reimburse, repay, revenge. *v.s.-a.i.* θhra'ęyúhar ‹again-he-debt-washes› *he reimburses, he repays, he revenges* (HS).

-či-. -'θkęhnakuhę - redeemer. *dv.n.s.* čękhi'θkęhnakúhę' ‹again-fact-one=us-fall-cause-pick up-many› *redeemer* (HS).

-či-. -'tyakę' - recover (from an illness). *v.s.-a.i.* θhra'tyá·kę'θ ‹again-he-get better-begins› *he recovers (from an illness)* (HS).

číčhu small fox, lynx *(Lynx* sp.*)* (RC 27:22) [Lawson «Che-chou» 'Fox-skin']. *n.* Also: **kačíčhu** (M 87).

-čihę - whisper. *v.r.-a.i.* hab: -h, pnt: -·', stat: -·, prog: -, prp: -, dst: -tyę-, caus: -, rvs: -, dat: II (-ati-/-hθ-), n-inc. račíhęh *he whispers* (R); -čihę -{dative II}: wa'na'číhęhθ ‹fact-one=another-whispered for› *one whispered to another* (RC 29:20); -čihętyę -: kačihę́·tyęh ‹it-whisper-much› *they twitter (of birds)* (HS); -yah+ne-. -čihę -: yahwa'nyečíhę·' ‹hither-fact-apart-one-whispered› *one leaned over and whispered* (RC 34:9); -čihęhstači-: račihę́hstačih ‹he-whisper-'ness-very› *curé, minister, priest* (HS); -čihę= hstači- -ne-. -a'newya'ręht - račihę́hstačih nehra'newya'réhtha' ‹he-whisper-

'ness-very apart-he-himself-know how-settle-causes› *Jesuit* (HS); -čihęh= stači-.#ú'y: račihęhstačihú'y ‹he-whisper-'ness-very-great› *Pontiff, Pope* (HS).

-čihęhr - black, coal. *n.r.* n-poss., inc., n.sfx. -eh. učihę́hreh *black* (R), *coal* (PC); -čihęhra'k -: račihęhrá'kha' ‹he-coal-digs› *he mines coal* (HS).

-čihęhstači - curé, minister, priest. *dv.n.s.* račihę́hstačih ‹he-whisper-'ness-very› *curé, minister, priest* (HS).

-čihęhstači - -ne-. -a'newya'ręht - Jesuit. *dv.n.s.* račihę́hstačih nehra'newya'réhtha' ‹he-whisper-'ness-very apart-he-himself-know how-settle-causes› *Jesuit* (HS).

-čihęhstači -.#ú'y Pontiff, Pope. *dv.n.s.* račihęhstačihú'y ‹he-whisper-'ness-very-great› *Pontiff, Pope* (HS).

-čihętyę - twitter. *v.s.-a.i.* kačihę́·tyęh ‹it-whisper-much› *they twitter (of birds)* (HS).

čihkù·weh land turtle (H 3518), mud turtle *(Kinosternon* sp.*)* (H 447). *n.*

-čihkw - club, fist, hammer, knot of a tree, locomotive, mallet; turnip. *n.r.* n-poss., inc., n.sfx. -eh (*club, fist,* etc.)/-a' (*turnip*). učíhkweh *club, fist, hammer, knot of a tree, locomotive, mallet, fist* [Lawson «Chinqua» 'A stick'], učíhkwa' *turnip (Brassica* sp.*)* (R); -čihkw -.#hči: učihkwéhči ‹knot-very› *knotty* (HS); -čihkwęhawihθę -: wa'kayečihkwęhawíhθę' ‹fact-they-club-brought-many› *they carried clubs* (RC 24:6); -čihkwętyahnę -: račihkwętyáhnẹh ‹he-fist-makes-much› *he makes fists* (HS).

číhkw louse (R) [Lawson «Cheecq» 'A Louse']. *n.* **čihkw.#hči:** číhkwči ‹louse-very› *lousy* (HS); **–čihkwna͟ = wẹ –:** učíhkwnawẹh ‹it-louse-possess› *its louse* (RC 27:8); **–čihkwna͟k –:** kačíhkwna·ks ‹it-louse-eats› *monkey* (R); **–čihkwna͟k –.#ú ˀy:** kačihkwnaks-ˀúˀy ‹it-louse-eats-big› *ape* (R); **–čih = kwnihsak –:** nakčihkwníhsa·k ‹you!= me-louse-seek› *seek my lice!* (RC 27: 3), waˀnaˀčihkwníhsa·k ‹fact-one= another-louse-sought› *one sought another's lice* (RC 27:4).

číhkw.#hči lousy. *n.s.* číhkwči ‹louse-very› *lousy* (HS).

–čihkw –.#hči knotty. *n.s.* učihkwéhči ‹knot-very› *knotty* (HS).

čihkwé·kẹh grasshopper (R). *n.*

–čihkwẹtyahnẹ – make fists. *v.s.-a.i.* račihkwẹtyáhnẹh ‹he-fist-makes-much› *he makes fists* (HS).

–čihkwna͟k – monkey. *dv.n.s.* kačíh-kwna·ks ‹it-louse-eats› *monkey* (R).

–čihkwna͟k –.#ú ˀy ape. *dv.n.s.* kačih-kwnaksˀúˀy ‹it-louse-eats-great› *ape* (R).

–čihs – False Face, mat, anything made of corn husks. *n.r.* n-poss., n-inc., n.sfx. -eh. učíhseh *False Face, mat, anything made of corn husks* (R).

čí·hs cheese (L 8). *n.*

–čihsẹw – empty vessel; a fruit-berry (such as an apple, pumpkin, squash). *n.r.* n-poss., n-inc., n.sfx. -eh. učih-sẹ·weh *empty vessel: fruit-berry (such as an apple, pumpkin, squash)* (R).

–čihskẹhkar – claw, fingernail. *n.r.* inaln: kčihskẹhkareh my claw, my fingernail (R), inc., n.sfx. -eh. učihskẹhkareh *claw, fingernail* (R); **ti –.–čihskẹhka͟ = reθẹ –.#ú ˀy:** tikačihskẹhkareθẹhúˀy ‹so-it-claw-is long-much-great› *great,*

long claws (RC 28:1); **–ne –.–a ˀčih = skẹhka͟raˀnihr –:** waˀtkaˀnaˀčihskẹhka-ráˀnir ‹fact-apart-I-myself-self-finger-nail-stood up› *I pinched myself* (AG), waˀnyakyaˀčihskẹhkaráˀnir ‹fact-a-part-the two of us-ourselves-finger-nail-stood up› *we pinched each other* (AG), waˀtkheyaˀčihskẹhkaráˀnir ‹fact-apart-I=another-self-fingernail-stood up› *I pinched him/her* (AG).

čihskẹ̀·kẹ· katydid *(Platyphyllum conca-vum)* (R). *n.*

–čihskẹnyaˀčr – crown of the head. *n.* učihskẹnyáˀčreh *crown of the head* (SH 375).

čihskẹhrè·weh slug, snail (AG). *n.*

čihskú·ku robin *(Merula migratoria: Turdus migratorius)* (R) *n.* Also: **čih-skúˀkuˀ** (R).

čihskúˀuˀ robin *(Merula migratoria; Turdus migratorius)* (R) *n.* Also: **čih-skú·ku** (R).

–čihskw – glue, gum, mud, mush. *n.r.* n-poss., inc., n.sfx. -eh *(mush)*/-aˀ *(glue, gum, mud).* učíhskweh *mush* (R), učíhskwaˀ *glue, gum, mud* (R), yučíhskwaˀ *soggy, muddy* (HS); **–čih = skwa͟rihẹ ˀ –:** yučihskwaríhẹˀθ ‹it-mush-boil-begins› *it cooks mush* (RC 3:55); **–čihskwaw –:** račihskwà·wẹhs ‹he-mush-gives to› *he besmears it, he putties it* (HS); **–čihskwẹti –:** θčihskwẹ́·ti ‹you!-mush-make› *make mush!* (RC 3:52); **ti –.–a ˀčihskukuhẹ –:** nẹwaˀčih-skukú-hẹˀ ‹so-prediction-it-itself-mush-pick up-many› *mush will splatter* (RC 3:54).

–čihskwaw – besmear, putty. *v.s.-t.* račih-skwà·wẹhs ‹he-mush-gives to› *he besmears it, he putties it* (HS).

Číhstuh Rabbit (male proper name) (H 447). *n.*

číhtkẹr chestnut *(Castanea dentata)* (RC 11:16). *n.*

čikahkwarè·reh sunfish (H 3518). *n.*

–čikęw – fiddle, violin. *n.r.* n-poss., inc., n.sfx. -eh. učikę̀·weh *fiddle, violin* (R); –čikęwakarati –: račikęwakà·ratih ‹he-fiddle-rubs against› *he is playing the fiddle* (R).

–čikęwakarati – play the fiddle. *v.s.-a.i.* račikęwakà·ratih ‹he-fiddle-rubs against› *he is playing the fiddle* (R).

číkheʔ salt (R) [Lawson «Cheek-ha» 'Salt']. *n.* Requires the stem increment –n – when incorporated. čikhéʔkye ‹salt-at› *salty* (AG), *ocean* (HS); –čikheʔnakriʔ: učikheʔná·kriʔ ‹salt-liquid› *brine* (HS); –čikheʔnuhar –: račikheʔnúhar ‹he-salt-washes› *he freshens it* (HS); –čikheʔnuku –: račikheʔnú·kwahs ‹he-salt-be in water-undoes› *he freshens it* (HS).

čikhéʔkye ‹salt-at› *salty* (AG), *ocean* (HS). *n.*

–čikheʔnakriʔ brine. *n.s.* učikheʔná·kriʔ ‹salt-liquid› *brine* (HS).

–čikheʔnuhar – freshen. *v.s.-t.* račikheʔnúhar ‹he-salt-washes› *he freshens it* (HS).

–čikheʔnuku – freshen. *v.s.-t.* račikheʔnú·kwahs ‹he-salt-be in water-undoes› *he freshens it* (HS).

–čikheʔt – sugar maple tree *(Acer saccharinum).* *n.r.* n-poss., n-inc., n.sfx. -aʔ. učikhéʔtaʔ *sugar maple tree (Acer saccharinum)* (R) (alternative: yučikhéʔtaʔ (M 87)).

–čikuhs – hoof. *n.r.* n-poss., n-inc., n.sfx. -eh. učikúhseh *hoof* (HS); –čikuh = sukęʔ: učikuhsú·kęʔ ‹hoof-less› *hoof-*

less (HS).

–čikuhsukęʔ hoofless. *n.s.* učikuhsú·kęʔ ‹hoof-less› *hoofless* (HS).

–čikʔęwar – beetle, bug, wood louse; lock. *n.r.* n-poss., inc., n.sfx. -ɸ. In the Western dialect the elicitation form is učikʔę̀·weh (PC) with replacement of the final vowel and consonant of the root with the simple noun suffix -eh. učikʔę̀·war *beetle, bug* (RC 15:8); *wood louse; lock* (HS); –čik = ʔęwar –.#kęhaʔnęʔ: ručikʔęwarkę́haʔnęʔ ‹he-bugs-many› *bugs* (R); čwe –. –čikʔęwarake –: čwekačikʔęwará·kye· ‹all-it-bug-is in number› *all kinds of bugs* (RC 15:1); čwe –. –čikʔęwar = črake –: čwekačikʔęwarčrá·kye· ‹all-it-bug-'ness-is in number› *all kinds of bugs* (RC 30:56).

čì·nahs big wheel, pompous important person (HS). *n.*

–činęhnu – be lousy. *v.r.-a.i.* hab: -h, pnt: -, stat: -, prog: -, prp: -, dst:-, caus: -, rvs: -, dat: , n-inc. račinę́hnuh *he is lousy* (HS), θačinę́hnuh *you've got head lice* (R).

–činęʔther – curl of hair. *n.r.* inaln: kčinęʔtheráʔkye *my curl of hair* (R), inc., n.sfx. -eh. učinęʔthereh *curl of hair* (H 2484); –činęʔtheraʔke: učinęʔtheráʔkye ‹curl-at› *on curled hair; on a curl of hair, hence, strewed with curled hair* (H 2484); –činęʔtheręʔke: učinęʔtherę́ʔkye ‹curl-at› *on (as a part of) the curl* (H 2484); –činęʔtherakęw: učinęʔtherá·kęw ‹curl-in› *in, among curls* (H 2484); –činęʔtherakęwʔahči:

učinę^ʔtherakęw^ʔáhči ‹curl-in-very›
deep in or among curls (H 2484); –**či**=
nę^ʔtherakT: učiné^ʔtherakwt ‹curl-next
to› *beside the curl or curled hair* (H
2484); –**činę^ʔtherahsę** –{dative II}:
račinę^ʔtherahsę́·tih ‹he-curl-is evil-for›
*he rejects, repudiates the curl, or
curly-headed person* (H 2484); –**činę^ʔ** =
therahsthu –: kačinę^ʔtheráhsthę ‹it-curl-
is small› *the curl is small: it is a small
curl* (H 2484); –**činę^ʔtheraks** –: yeči-
nę^ʔtherá·ksę· ‹one-curl-is bad› *she has
poor, ill-looking curly hair: her curls
are not fine nor beautiful* (H 2484);
–**činę^ʔtherakwahsT** –: yečinę^ʔtherá-
kwahst ‹one-curl-is good› *her curls
are pretty, nice-looking, good: her curl
is pretty, nice-looking, good* (H 2484);
–**činę^ʔtheratkwerih** –: račinę^ʔthera-
tkwè·rihθ ‹he-curl-covets› *he longs for
the curl: he longs for the curly-headed
person—for curly hair* (H 2484); –**či**=
nę^ʔtherayę(T) –: račinę^ʔtherà·yę^ʔ ‹he-
curl-lays› *he has, possesses a curl, or
a curly-headed person* (H 2484);
–**činę^ʔthereθ** –: kačiné^ʔthere·θ ‹it-curl-
is long› *the curl is long: it is a long
curl* (H 2484), yečiné^ʔthere·θ ‹one-
curl-is long› *her curls are long: she
has long curls: she has a long curl* (H
2484); –**činę^ʔtheręti** –: račinę^ʔtherę́·tih
‹he-curl-make› *he makes himself
curly-headed: lit. he makes himself a
curl (i.e., he causes himself to become
a curl or curly-headed person)* (H
2484); –**činę^ʔtherihsak** –: račinę^ʔthe-
ríhsa·ks ‹he-curl-looks for› *he is
looking for a curl: he is looking for a
curly-headed person* (H 2484); –**či**=
nę^ʔtheriyu –: yečinę^ʔtherí·yu· ‹one-
curl-is great› *she has a large head of
curly hair: her hair is abundant,
luxuriant* (H 2484).

čír dog *(Canus sp.)* (RC 11:20) [Lawson

«Cheeth» 'Dog'] [Gallatin «tcheerr»
'Dog']. *n.* **čir.#kéha·^ʔ** čirkyéha·^ʔ ‹dog-
customarily› *canine* (HS); **čir.#ú^ʔy**
čir^ʔú^ʔy ‹dog-great› *bulldog* (HS); **čír**
–**(a)hyak** –: čír wáhyaks ‹dog it-fruit-
eats› *nightshade (Solanum* sp.*)* (H-
notebook); –**hęhneθę** – **čír**: kahęhné·θęh
čír ‹it-ear-is long dog-much› *hound*
(HS).

čír –**(a)hyak** – nightshade *(Solanum* sp.*)*
n.s. čír wáhyaks ‹dog it-fruit-eats›
nightshade (Solanum sp.*)* (H-notebook).

čir.#kéha·^ʔ canine. *n.s.* čirkyéha·^ʔ ‹dog-
customarily› *canine* (HS).

čir.#ú^ʔy bulldog *n.* čir^ʔú^ʔy ‹dog-great›
bulldog (HS).

čiráhsa^ʔ hornbeam *(Carpinus caroliniana)*, ironwood (H-notebook). *n.*

čirá·kare·θ skunk cabbage *(Symplocarpus
foetidus)* (R). *n.*

–**čiręhr** – brown. *n.r.* n-poss., n-inc., n.sfx.
-eh. učiréhreh *brown* (R); –**čiręhrah** =
waryakę –: učiręhrahwaryá·kę^ʔ ‹brown-
is white› *light brown* (R).

–**čirurę** – incite, irritate, provoke, urge on.
v.r.-t. hab: -h, pnt: -, stat: -, prog: -,
prp: -, dst: -, caus: -, rvs: -, dat: -, n-
inc. račirù·ręh *he incites it, he irritates
it, he provokes it, he urges it on* (HS);
ha^ʔ –**čirurę** –: ha^ʔ račirù·ręh ‹the he-
provokes› *aggressor* (HS).

–**čirurę** – aggressor. *dv.n.s.* ha^ʔ račirù·ręh
‹the he-provokes› *aggressor* (HS).

Čiru^ʔęhá·ka·^ʔ Nottoway Nation, Nottoway Indian (term of abuse on the
Tuscarora Reservation in New York
State during the early twentieth century) (R) (see the Nottoway self-designation «Cheroohoka», «Tcheroha-
ka'» cited by Hewitt 1910 [Handbook,
p. 87]). *n.*

–**čirwę** – strangle. *v.r.-t.* hab: -h, pnt: -^ʔ,
stat: -·, prog: -, prp: -, dst: -, caus:

-hsT-, rvs: -, dat: -, inc.-ɸ-pat. ęyc-
čí·rwę⁷ *one will strangle it* (RC 19:2);
-čirwęhsthę -: wahračirwęhstę·⁷ ‹fact-
he-strangle-cause-much› *he wrings it
out* (R); ti -.-čirwęhsthę -: nęyečir-
węhstę·⁷ ‹so-prediction-one-strangle-
cause-much› *one will squeeze it out*
(RC 20:1); -ha⁷čirwę -: wa⁷kęha⁷-
čí·rwę⁷ ‹fact-I=you-neck-strangled› *I
strangled you* (R); -ke⁷čačirwę -:
rakye⁷čačí·rwęhs ‹he-dough-strangles›
he kneads (HS).

-čirwęhsthę - wring out. *v.s.-t.* wahračir-
węhstę·⁷ ‹fact-he-strangle-cause-much›
he wrings it out (R).

-čisn - female genitals, vagina. *n.r.* n-
poss., n-inc., n.sfx. -eh. učísneh *female genitals, vagina* (R).

-či·sn - ember, glowing coal, spark. *n.r.*
n-poss., inc., n.sfx. -eh. učí·sneh *ember, glowing coal, spark* (R) [Jefferson
«ojisneh» 'fire']; -čisnakęw: učí·sna-
kęw ‹ember-in› *in the coals* (RC 28:
11); -čisnakwe⁷niyu -: Kayečisnakwe⁷-
nì·yu⁷ ‹they-ember-are principal›
*Onondaga sachems, Keepers-of-the-
Fire* (R); -čisnayę(T)-: kačí·snayę⁷ ‹it-
ember-lays› *court of justice* (HS);
-čisnęti -: kakučisnę́·ti· ‹they-ember-
made› *they counsel, they deliberate*
(RC 12:26); -čisnuka⁷T -: kačisnu-
ká⁷tha⁷ ‹it-spark-blister-causes› *it
sparkles* (HS); -ne -.-čisnahkwa'nę -:
nekačisnahkwá⁷nę⁷ ‹apart-it-spark-in-
strument-fly› *falling star* (PC); -ne -.
-čisnuhrarakT -: neyečisnuhráráktha⁷
‹two-one-ember-press-causes› *tongs*

(HS).

-čisnakwe⁷niyu - Onondaga sachems,
Keepers-of-the-Fire. *dv.n.s.* Kayeči-
snakwe⁷nì·yu⁷ ‹they-ember-are principal› *Onondaga sachems, Keepers-of-
the-Fire* (R).

-čisnayę(T) - court of justice. *dv.n.s.* ka-
čí·snayę⁷ ‹it-ember-lays› *court of justice* (HS).

-čisnęti - counsel, deliberate. *v.s.-a.i.* ka-
kučisnę́·ti· ‹they-ember-made› *they
counsel, they deliberate* (RC 12: 26).

-čisnuhkw - comma, speck, spot. *n.r.* n-
poss., inc., n.sfx. -eh. učísnuhkweh
comma, spot (R) [Jefferson «o-jes-no-
qua» 'star'] [Gallatin «otcheesnooh-
quay» 'Star']; -čisnuhkw -.#ú⁷y: učis-
nuhkwehú⁷y ‹spot-great› *clown* (HS);
-čisnuhkwar -: yučisnúhkwa⁷r ‹it-spot-
is in› *note (of music)* (HS); -čisnuh=
kwahrawę -: yučisnuhkwahrà·wę⁷ ‹it-
spot-puts up-many› *speckled, spotted*
(HS), račisnuhkwahrà·węh ‹he-spot-
puts up-many› *he speckles it, he spots
it* (HS); -čisnuhkw - -kahrakęw: yučisnúhku⁷ ukáhrakęw ‹it-spot-covers it-
eye-in› *pupil (of the eye)* (HS);
kęhreks -čisnuhkw -: kęhreks učísnuhkweh ‹mountain lion spot› *leopard*
(HS).

-čisnuhkw - -kahrakęw pupil (of the eye).
dv.n.s. yučisnúhku⁷ ukáhrakęw ‹it-
spot-cover it-eye-in› *pupil (of the eye)*
(HS).

-čisnuhkw -.#ú⁷y clown. *n.s.* učisnuh-
kwehú⁷y ‹spot-great› *clown* (HS).

-čisnuhkwar - note (of music). *dv.n.s.*

---

yučisnúhkwaʾr ‹it-spot-is in› *note (of music)* (HS).

–čisnuhkwahrawę – speckle, spot. *v.s.-t.* yučisnuhkwahrà·węʾ ‹it-spot-puts up-many› *speckled, spotted* (HS), račisnuhkwahrà·węh ‹he-spot-puts up-many› *he speckles it, he spots it* (HS).

–čisnukaʾT – sparkle. *v.s.-a.i.* kačisnukáʾthaʾ ‹it-spark-blister-causes› *it sparkles* (HS).

–čistu – star. *n.r. West.* n-poss., n-inc., n.sfx. –h. Occurs only in the Western dialect where it is almost certainly a loan word from Mohawk. učí·stuh *star* (PC).

čitipápat put put put (sound of the engine of an old car) (R). *part.*

–čiwak – become bitter, become sour, turn rancid, turn sour. *v.r.-a.i.* hab: -s, pnt: -, stat: -ę, prog: -, prp: -, dst: -, caus: -, rvs: -, dat: -, inc.-ɸ-pat. yučì·wakę *it is bitter, it is rancid, it is sour* (R), yučì·waks *it sours, it turns sour* (HS); **–čiwakčr** –: učiwákčreh ‹become bitter-'ness› *bitterness* (HS); **–čiwakst** –: učiwáksteh ‹become bitter-'ness› *asperity, bitterness, sourness* (HS); **–kerhačiwak** –: yukyerhačì·wakę ‹it-body-is bitter› *bitter hickory* (R); **–nęhsnačiwak** –: yunęhsnačì·wakę ‹it-seed-is bitter› *black pepper (Piper nigrum)* (R); **–ʾęhračiwak** –: yuʾęhračì·wakę ‹it-leaf-is bitter› *sorrel* (HS), kaʾęhračì·wakę ‹it-leaf-is bitter› *smartweed* (R).

–čiwakčr – bitterness. *n.s.* učiwákčreh ‹become bitter-'ness› *bitterness* (HS).

–čiwakst – asperity, bitterness, sourness. *n.s.* učiwáksteh ‹become bitter-'ness› *asperity, bitterness, sourness* (HS).

–čiyę – pour. *v.r.-t.* hab: -, pnt: -ʾ, stat: -, prog: -, prp: -, dst: -, caus: -hw-, rvs: -, dat: -, n-inc. **–čiyęhw** –: račì·yęws ‹he-pour-causes› *he spills liquid* (HS),

ručiyę́hę ‹he-pour-caused› *he has spilled liquid* (HS); **–čiyęʾ** –: kačì·yęʾθ ‹it-pour-begins› *it leaks, it spills* (HS); **–yah** –. **–čiyę** –: yahwahračì·yęʾ ‹hither-fact-he-poured› *he poured it* (RC 12: 29).

–čiyęhw – spill liquid. *v.s.-a.i.* račì·yęws ‹he-pour-causes› *he spills liquid* (HS), ručiyę́hę ‹he-pour-caused› *he has spilled liquid* (HS), ęhračì·yęw ‹prediction-he-pour-cause› *he will spill liquid* (HS).

–čiyęʾ – leak, spill. *v.s.-a.i.* kačì·yęʾθ ‹it-pour-begins› *it leaks, it spills* (HS).

–čiʾčęti – make a ruffle, plait. *v.s.-a.i.* račiʾčę́·tih ‹he-ruffle-makes› *he makes a ruffle, he plaits* (HS).

–čiʾči – fringe, ruffle; liverwort flower. *n.r.* n-poss., inc., n.sfx. –eh *(fringe, ruffle)*/ –ʾ *(liverwort flower)*. učíʾčeh *fringe, ruffle* (R), učíʾčiʾ *liverwort flower* (HS); **–čiʾčęti** –: račiʾčę́·tih ‹he-ruffle-makes› *he plaits, he makes a ruffle* (HS); **–čiʾčihręhw** –: račiʾčihrę́whaʾ ‹he-ruffle-put up-cause› *he puts on fringe* (HS); **–čiʾči** – **ti** –. **–ahθuhkuʾnę** –: číʾčiʾ tiwahθuhkúʾnę· ‹liverwort flower so-it-color-instrument-is a kind of› *violet (color)* (HS).

–čiʾči – **ti** –. **–ahθuhkuʾnę** – violet (color). *dv.n.s.* číʾčiʾ tiwahθuhkúʾnę· ‹liverwort flower so-it-color-instrument-is a kind of› *violet (color)* (HS).

–čiʾčihręhw – put on fringe. *v.s.-a.i.* račiʾčihrę́whaʾ ‹he-ruffle-put up-cause› *he puts on fringe* (HS).

–čiʾčihskę – blossoms. *dv.n.s.* yučiʾčihskę́heʾ ‹it-flower-see-is going to› *blossoms, many flowers* (RC 3:38).

–čiʾčihskęhw – bloom. *v.s.-a.i.* kačiʾčíhskęws ‹it-flower-see-causes› *it is blooming* (R).

–čiʾčihs(t) – flower. *n.r.* n-poss., inc., n.sfx. –eh. The form **–čiʾčihs** – occurs before suffixes or stems that begin in *k*; the form –či⁷čihst– occurs elsewhere. uči⁷číhsteh *flower* (R); –či⁷= čihskę –: yuči⁷čihskę́he⁷ ‹it-flower-see-is going to› *blossoms, many flowers* (RC 3:38); –či⁷čihskęhw –: kači⁷číhskęws ‹it-flower-see-causes› *it is blooming* (R); –či⁷čihsta⁷nihrhę –: yuči⁷čihsta⁷nírhę⁷ ‹it-flower-stand up-many› *flowers stood up* (RC 3:38); –či⁷čihstuhsku –: wa⁷kči⁷čihstúhskę⁷ ‹fact-I-flower-picked off› *I picked flowers* (R), rači⁷čihstúhskwahs ‹he-flower-picks off› *he deflowers it* (HS); –či⁷čihstuhri⁷ –: yuči⁷čihstuhrí⁷ę ‹it-flower-ruined› *wilted flower* (R); –či⁷= čihstyeriha –: rači⁷čihstyeríhahs ‹he-flower-straightens› *he strews flowers* (HS).

–či⁷čihstuhsku – deflower, pick flowers. *v.s.-a.i.* wa⁷kči⁷čihstúhskę⁷ ‹fact-I-flower-picked off› *I picked flowers* (R), rači⁷čihstúhskwahs ‹he-flower-picks off› *he deflowers it* (HS).

–či⁷čihstuhri⁷ – wilted flower. *n.s.* yuči⁷čihstuhrí⁷ę ‹it-flower-ruined› *wilted flower* (R).

–či⁷čihstyeriha – strew flowers. *v.s.-a.i.* rači⁷čihstyeríhahs ‹he-flower-straightens› *he strews flowers* (HS).

–či⁷ehn – claw, paw, talon. *n.r.* n-poss., inc., n.sfx. -eh. uči⁷éhneh *paw, claw* (HS); –či⁷ehn –.#áh: uči⁷ehneháh ‹claw-little› *the claw is small; its claw is small* (H 2484); –či⁷ehnahrahT –: uči⁷ehnáhraht ‹it-claw-put up-caused› *the claw is awful; its claw is awful* (H

2484); –či⁷ehnak͈ahT –: rači⁷ehnakwáhtha⁷ ‹he-claw-cuts off› *he cuts off its claw* (H 2484); –či⁷ehnakwę⁷n = h(e)r –: kači⁷ehnakwę́⁷nhe⁷r ‹it-claw-is too short› *the claw is short; it is a short claw* (H 2484); –či⁷ehnatihsthu –: kači⁷ehnatíhsthę ‹it-claw-are small› *its claws are small, the claws are small* (H 2484); –či⁷ehna⁷ke: uči⁷ehná⁷kye ‹claw-at› *on, on top of the claw, talon* (H 2484); –či⁷ehna⁷θ –: kači⁷éhna⁷θ ‹it-claw-is of a size› *the claws are large; its claws are large* (H 2484); –či⁷ehnehke: uči⁷ehnéhkye ‹claw-at› *at, at the place of the claw* (H 2484); –či⁷ehneθ –: kači⁷éhne·θ ‹it-claw-is long› *its claw is long; it is a long claw; the claw is long* (H 2484); –či⁷ehnę⁷ke: uči⁷ehnę́⁷kye ‹claw-at› *on (as a fixture of) the claw* (H 2484); –či⁷ehniyu –: kači⁷ehní·yu· ‹it-claw-is great› *the claw is large; its claw is large* (H 2484); –či⁷ehnu –: ruči⁷éhnu⁷ ‹he-claw-is in water› *he has a claw (or claws) seething* (H 2484); –ne –. –či⁷ehnya⁷k –: nehrači⁷éhnya⁷ks ‹a-part-he-claw-breaks› *he breaks the claw; he breaks its claw* (H 2484); ti –. –či⁷ehnatkwarayę –: tikači⁷ehnatkwarà·yę⁷ ‹so-it-claw-is red› *the claw is red; its claws are red* (H 2484).

–či⁷eniči –iye – castor oil. *n.s.* uči⁷ení·či kę̀·ye⁷ ‹?? oil› *castor oil* (HS).

–či⁷er – brown, scarlet. *n.r.* n-poss., inc., n.sfx. -eh. učí⁷ereh *scarlet* (HS), *brown* (R); –či⁷eraku –: či⁷erá·kwę ‹scarlet-picked up› *lobster (Homarus*

Tuscarora Pronunciation Key:
/a/ l**a**w; /e/ h**a**t; /i/ p**i**zza; /u/ t**u**ne; /ę/ h**i**nt; /č/ **ch**eese; /h/ **h**oe; /m/ **m**other; /s/ **s**ame; /t/ **d**o (before a vowel y, or w), **t**oo (elsewhere); /k/ **g**ale (before a vowel y or w), **k**ale (elsewhere); /n/ i**n**hale (before a consonant or word-final), **n**ote (elsewhere), /r/ hi**ss** (before a consonant or word-

final), **r**un (trilled as in Italian, elsewhere); /w/ cu**ff** (before a consonant other than y or word-final), **w**ay (elsewhere); /y/ fi**sh** (before a consonant or word-final), **y**ou (elsewhere), /θ/ **th**ing; /⁷/ (the sound between the vowels in unh-unh); /·/ long vowel, /´/ high pitch; /`/ low pitch.

sp.*)* (AG); −a⁷či⁷**ęrhar** −: ra⁷či⁷érher ‹he-himself-scarlet-hangs› *he blushes* (HS).

−či⁷**ęraku** − lobster. *dv.n.s.* či⁷erá·kwę ‹scarlet-picked up› *lobster (Homarus sp.)* (AG).

−či⁷**newar** − red flannel, striped. *n.r.* poss. ?, inc., n.sfx. −eh. uči⁷nè·wareh *red flannel* (HS), *striped* (AG); −či⁷**newa** = **ra**yę(T) −: kači⁷newarà·yę⁷ ‹it-striped-lay› *she lay all streaked and dirty* (R).

čí⁷**nęhs** compassion, mercy (R). *n.*

čí⁷**nę⁷** bird (RC 10:6) [Lawson «Chee-nuh» 'Bird']. *n.* (*West.* čí·⁷nę⁷ (PC) with long accented vowel.) či⁷nę⁷ #eθu⁷.#kęha⁷nę⁷.#u⁷y: čí⁷nę⁷ heθu⁷-kęha⁷nę⁷ú⁷y ‹bird-great many-many-great› *very many large birds* (RC 12:5); −či⁷nę⁷: učí⁷nę⁷ ‹bird› *female genitals (euphemistic)* (R); čwe −. −či⁷ = nę⁷**črake** −: čwekači⁷nę⁷črá·kye· ‹all kinds of-it-bird-'ness-is in number› *all kinds of birds* (RC 11:14).

−či⁷**nę⁷** female genitals. *n.s.* učí⁷nę⁷ ‹bird› *female genitals (euphemistic)* (R).

−či⁷**r** − candle, ember, flash of light, lamp, light, spark, taper. *n.r.* n-poss., inc., n.sfx. −eh. učí⁷reh *candle, ember, flash of light, lamp, light, spark, taper* (HS) [Gallatin «stire» 'Fire']; −či⁷**rak** −: yučí⁷ra·ks ‹it-ember-eats› *one eats em-bers* (RC 28:12); −či⁷**rak**ᵂ**ahnahkw** −: yeči⁷rakwahnáhkhwa⁷ ‹one-ember-cut off-instrument› *candle snuffer* (HS); −či⁷**rak**ᵂ**ahT** −: rači⁷rakwáhtha⁷ ‹he-em-ber-cuts off› *he snuffs out a candle* (HS); −či⁷**ra⁷nihr** −: θči⁷rá⁷nir ‹you!-ember-stand up› *turn on the lights!* (R), rači⁷rá⁷nihč ‹he-ember-stands up› *he sets it on fire* (HS), kači⁷ra⁷níhrę ‹it-ember-stood up› *it is lit* (HS); −či⁷ = **ręhaw** −: rači⁷ręhà·wi⁷ ‹he-ember-brings-X› *Lucifer* (HS); −či⁷**ręhsę** −:

ruči⁷ręhsę· ‹he-ember-parch› *he bic-kers* (HS); −či⁷**rę'ni** −: yuči⁷ręˑ⁷nyęhs ‹it-ember-throws› *meteor* (SH 375); −či⁷**ri⁷θrehT** −: yeči⁷ri⁷θréhtha⁷ ‹one-ember-drag-causes› *lantern* (HS); −**ne** −. −či⁷**rahkw** −.#ú⁷y: wa⁷tkači⁷rahkw⁷ú⁷y ‹fact-apart-it-ember-picked up-much› *a big flash of light appeared* (RC 9:9); −**t** −. −či⁷**rę** −: nakačí⁷ręh ‹hither-fact-it-ember-fall› *fire fell down* (R).

−či⁷**rak**ᵂ**ahnahkw** − candle snuffer. *dv.n.s.* yeči⁷rakwahnáhkhwa⁷ ‹one-ember-cut off-instrument› *candle snuffer* (HS).

−či⁷**rak**ᵂ**ahT** − snuff out a candle. *v.s.-a.i.* rači⁷rakwáhtha⁷ ‹he-ember-cuts off› *he snuffs out a candle* (HS).

čí⁷**raręh** fawn. *n.* či⁷raręh.#ah.#kęhe⁷: či⁷raręhahkę́he⁷ ‹fawn-little-deceased› *deceased little fawn* (RC 7:2); či⁷ = **raręh**. −**k**ᵂ**ahT** −: či⁷rarę́hkwaht ‹fawn-cut off› *tag alder (Alnus serrulata)* (H-notebook).

či⁷**raręh**. −**k**ᵂ**ahT** − tag alder. *n.s.* či⁷rarę́h-kwaht ‹fawn-cut off› tag alder *(Alnus serrulata)* (H-notebook).

−či⁷**ra⁷nihr** − light, turn on lights, set on fire. *v.s.-a.i.* θči⁷rá⁷nir ‹you!-ember-stand up› *turn on the lights!* (R), ra-či⁷rá⁷nihč ‹he-ember-stands up› *he sets it on fire* (HS), kači⁷ra⁷níhrę ‹it-ember-stood up› *it is lit* (HS).

čí⁷**re⁷** opossum *(Didelphis virginiana)* (H 3518). *n.* či⁷re⁷.#áh: či⁷re⁷áh ‹opos-sum-little› *opossum (Didelphis virgin-iana)* (H 3518).

či⁷**re⁷**.#**áh** opossum. *n.s.* či⁷re⁷áh ‹opos-sum-little› opossum (H 3518).

−či⁷**ręhaw** − Lucifer. *dv.n.s.* rači⁷ręhà·wi⁷ ‹he-ember-brings-X› *Lucifer* (HS).

−či⁷**ręhsę** − bicker. *v.s.-a.i.* ruči⁷ręhsę· ‹he-ember-parch› *he bickers* (HS).

−či⁷**rę'ni** − meteor. *dv.n.s.* yuči⁷ręˑ⁷nyęhs ‹it-ember-throws› *meteor* (SH 375).

−či⁷**ri⁷θrehT** − lantern. *dv.n.s.* yeči⁷ri⁷-

θréhthaʔ ‹one-ember-drag-causes› *lantern* (HS).

–čiʔrur– medicine stick, whip. *n.r.* n-poss., inc., n.sfx. –eh. This root most likely refers specifically to the branch of a willow (*Salix* sp.), which would function equally well as a source of salicylic acid, a pain-killer and a major component of aspirin, and a whip. učíʔrureh *medicine stick* (HS), *whip* (RC 30:42); –čiʔrurakethę̨–: ęyečiʔrurakyé·thę̨ʔ ‹prediction-one-medicine stick-scratch-many› *one will scrape the bark from a medicine stick* (RC 19:2); –čiʔruraks–: kačiʔrurá·ksę̨· ‹it-medicine stick-is bad› *bad medicine stick* (RC 30:53); –čiʔruratahwahT–: učiʔruratáhwaht ‹medicine stick-fray-cause› *frayed medicine stick* (RC 19:11); –čiʔruryaʔk–: wahračiʔruryáʔkheʔ ‹fact-he-medicine stick-broke› *he was going along breaking a medicine stick* (RC 30:53); ti–. –čiʔruratkwarayę̨(T)–: tikačiʔruratkwarà·yę̨ʔ ‹so-it-medicine stick-is red› *rose willow (Salix purpurea)* (RC 6:6).

–čiʔtkwahn– yellow. *n.r.* n-poss., inc., n.sfx. –eh. učiʔtkwáhneh *yellow* (R); –čiʔtkwahn–: ručiʔtkwáhnahs ‹he-yellow› *he is bilious* (HS); –čiʔtkwah=nuri–{dative III}: wakčiʔtkwahnuryá·ti·k ‹I-yellow-stirred-for› *I am feeling bilious* (L 80); –čiʔtkwahnut: kačiʔtkwáhnu·č ‹it-yellow-is in an upright position› *it grows yellow* (HS); ti–. –čiʔtkwahnayę̨(T)–: tikačiʔtkwáhnayę̨ʔ ‹so-it-yellow-lays› *gold* [Galla-

tin «ticot-tcheet kwaunaugeh» 'Yellow']; ti–. –čiʔtkwahnayę̨(T)–.#ę̨tíh: tikačiʔtkwahnayę̨ʔę̨tíh ‹so-it-yellow-lays-many little› *yellow jackets, hornets (Vespa maculata)* (R); ti–. –(a)hkaračiʔtkwahnayę̨(T)–: tiwahkaračiʔtkwáhnayę̨ʔ ‹so-it-bark-yellow-lays› *yellow oak (Quercus sp.)* (H-notebook).

–čiʔtkwahn– be bilious. *v.s.-a.i.* ručiʔtkwáhnahs ‹he-yellow› *he is bilious* (HS).

–čiʔtkwahnuri–{dative III} feel bilious. *v.s.-a.i.* wakčiʔtkwahnuryá·ti·k ‹I-yellow-stirred-for› *I am feeling bilious* (L 80).

–čiʔtkwahnut grow yellow. *v.s.-a.i.* kačiʔtkwáhnu·č ‹it-yellow-is in an upright position› *it grows yellow* (HS).

číʔtkwar bile, yellow stuff (R). *n.* čiʔ=tkwar.#úʔy: čiʔtkwarʔúʔy ‹bile-great› *jaundice, great amount of bile* (RC 20:1); –čiʔtkwaryaʔk–: yučiʔtkwaryáʔkę̨ ‹it-yellow stuff-breaks› *it is sprouting leaves (said of a forest or tree that has just burst its buds)* (R).

čiʔtkwar.#úʔy jaundice, great amount of bile. *n.* čiʔtkwarʔúʔy ‹bile-great› *jaundice, great amount of bile* (RC 20:1).

–čiʔtkwaryaʔk– sprout leaves. *v.s.-a.i.* yučiʔtkwaryáʔkę̨ ‹it-yellow stuff-breaks› *it is sprouting leaves (said of a forest or tree that has just burst its buds)* (R).

–čiʔy– anemia, nausea, condition of being run-down. *n.r.* n-poss., inc., n.sfx. –eh. učíʔyeh *anemia, nausea,*

condition of being run-down (R);
–čiʔyu –: ručiyúhaʔ ‹he-nausea-covers›
*he is enfeebled, he is impotent, he is
infirm* (HS), ručíʔyu· ‹he-nausea-cov-
ered› *he is feeble* (HS); –čiʔyuh =
črakęw: učiʔyúhčrakęw ‹it-nausea-cov-
er-'ness-in› *feebly* (HS); –čiʔyuhčręti –:
waʔučiʔyuhčrę́·tiʔ ‹fact-it-nausea-cov-
er-'ness-made› *it made it nauseous*
(RC 30:43), račiʔyuhčrę́·tih ‹he-naus-
ea-cover-'ness-makes› *he enervates,
weakens it* (HS), ručiʔyuhčrę́·ti· ‹he-
nausea-cover-'ness-made› *it makes
him weak* (HS); –čiʔyu – –a'nę –: ručiʔ-
yúhaʔ yú·ʔnęʔ ‹he-nausea-covers it-
became› *he is enervated, he became
feeble* (HS).
–čiʔyu – be feeble. *v.s.-a.i.* ručíʔyu· ‹he-
nausea-covered› *he is feeble* (HS).
–čiʔyuhčrakęw feebly. *n.s.* učiʔyúhčrakęw ‹it-nausea-cover-'ness-in› *feebly*
(HS).
–čiʔyuhčręti – enervate, make nauseous,
weaken. *v.s.-t.* waʔučiʔyuhčrę́·tiʔ
‹fact-it-nausea-cover-'ness-made› *it
made it nauseous* (RC 30:43), račiʔ-
yuhčrę́·tih ‹he-nausea-cover-'ness-
makes› *he enervates, he weakens it*
(HS), ručiʔyuhčrę́·ti· ‹he-nausea-cover-
'ness-made› *it makes him weak* (HS).
–čkerh – beech tree, beechnut. *n.r.* n-
poss., n-inc., n.sfx. -aʔ. učkyérhaʔ
*beech tree (Fagus grandifola, Fagus
sp.), beechnut* (H-notebook).
–čkr(ęʔn) – gonorrhea, pox, syphilis, any
venereal disease. *n.r.* n-poss., inc.,
n.sfx. -eh (archaic: -ęʔ). účkreh *gonorrhea, pox, syphilis, any venereal
disease* (R), úč-kręʔ *gonorrhea, pox,
syphilis, any venereal disease* (HS),
učkrę́ʔneh *gonorrhea, pox, syphilis,
any venereal disease* (HS); –čkręʔn –.
#hči: učkręʔnéhči ‹gonorrhea-very›
smutty (HS).

–čkreʔn –.#hči smutty. *n.s.* učkręʔnéhči
‹gonorrhea-very› *smutty* (HS).
–čtehrihT –/–čtehrihsT – become involved
with. *v.r.-t.* See: –(a)čtehrihT –/–(a)č =
tehrihsT –.
–čtęhr – stone; cliff. *n.r.* n-poss., inc.,
n.sfx. -eh. učtę́hreh *stone* (RC 2:10),
yučtę́hreh *cliff on land or in water*
(AG); –čtęhr –.#hči: učtęhréhči ‹stone-
very› *stony* (HS); –čtęhrahrar –.#úʔy:
yučtęhrahraręhúʔy ‹it-stone-is a hole-
great› *large hole in stone* (RC 11:1);
–čtęhranę –: račtę́hranęh ‹he-stone-
guards› *mason* (HS); –čtęhrawiʔ =
nahnę –: wahračtęhrawiʔnáhnę ʔ ‹fact-
he-stone-give-caused-much› *he put in
many rocks* (RC 11:3); –čtęhrayęʔkʷ –:
račtę́hrayęʔkws ‹he-stone-shoots› *he
stones it* (HS); –čtęhraʔke: učtęhráʔ-
kye ‹stone-at› *stoniness* (HS); –čtęh =
raʔnihr –: kačtęhraʔníhrę ‹it-stone-stood
up› *tombstone* (HS); –čtęhręhT –: naʔ-
nečtęhréhthaʔ ‹one=another-stone-fall-
causes› *one throws another down
headlong* (HS); –čtęhręθkar –: račtęh-
rę́θkar ‹he-stone-lays in a certain way›
he paves (HS), kačtęhrę́θkar ‹it-stone-
lays in a certain way› *pavement* (HS);
–čtęhręti –: kačtęhré·tih ‹it-stone-
makes› *it petrifies* (HS), račtęhrę́·tih
‹he-stone-makes› *sculptor* (HS); –čtęh =
rih(e)r –: kačtęhríher ‹it-stone-put up›
on top was a·stone (AW 45); –čtęh =
riyu –: kačtęhrí·yu· ‹it-stone-is great› *a
large stone* (AW 45); –či –.–čtęhra =
wihsyęku –: čečtęhrawihsyę́·kuʔ ‹again-
fact-he-stone-give-undo-undid› *one removed the stone by picking it up* (RC
11:8); –ne –.–čtęhrut –: nekačtę́hru·t
‹apart-it-stone-is in an upright position› *masonry* (HS); **tha+ne –.–čtęh =
rukenę –**: thaʔnekačtęhrukyé·nę· ‹unusual-apart-it-stone-divided› *between the
stones* (AG); **ti –.–čtęhraʔθ –.#úʔy**: ti-

kačtęhra'θ'ú'y ‹so-it-stone-be of a size-great› *large stone, boulder* (RC 25:12); ha' –ne –. –čtęhraT –: ha' nekačtęhra'nę ‹the apart-it-stone-stood› *wall* (HS); –čtęhr – –a'nę' –: učtęhreh wá·'-nę' ‹stone it-becomes› *it petrifies* (HS); –hrę'na'nihrahT – –čtęhr –: yehrę'na'nihráhtha' učtęhreh ‹one-stone-stand up-causes stone› *marble* (HS).

–čtęhr –.#hči stony. *n.s.* učtęhréhči ‹stone-very› *stony* (HS).

–čtęhranę – mason. *dv.n.s.* račtęhranęh ‹he-stone-guards› *mason* (HS).

–čtęhrayę'kʷ – stone. *v.s.-t.* račtęhrayę'kws ‹he-stone-shoots› *he stones it* (HS).

–čtęhra'ke stoniness. *n.s.* učtęhrá'kye ‹stone-at› *stoniness* (HS).

–čtęhra'nihr – tombstone. *dv.n.s.* kačtęhra'níhrę ‹it-stone-stood up› *tombstone* (HS).

–čtęhręθkar – pave. *v.s.-t.* račtęhréθkar ‹he-stone-lays in a certain way› *he paves it* (HS).

–čtęhręθkar – pavement. *dv.n.s.* kačtęhréθkar ‹it-stone-lays in a certain way› *pavement* (HS).

–čtęhręti – petrify. *v.s.-a.i.* kačtęhrę·tih ‹it-stone-makes› *it petrifies* (HS).

–čtęhręti – sculptor. *dv.n.s.* račtęhrę·tih ‹he-stone-makes› *sculptor* (HS).

čúhe' pin oak *(Quercus palustris)* (R). *n.*

čuha'θ'á·ka·' ‹again-it-neck-characterized by› gull, sea gull *(Larus sp.)* (R). *n.*

čuhkúhnę' balsam *(Abies balsamea)* (H-notebook). *n.*

čuhkwá·tę·t Cayuga; witch (R). *n.*

čúhner first half of moon (SH 375). *n.*

čuhryú'kę chipmunk (R). *n.*

čuhstekyerhyá'kę buffalo, bison *(Bison bison)* (R). *n.* Also: čuhtekyerhayá'kę (R). čuhstekyerhyá'kę –tehwęte: čuhstekyerhyá'kę utehwę́·te ‹buffalo hide-a certain one› *buffalo robe* (HS).

čuhstekyerhyá'kę –tehwęte buffalo robe. *n.s.* čuhstekyerhyá'kę utehwę́·te ‹buffalo hide-a certain one› *buffalo robe* (HS).

čuhtekyerhyá'kę buffalo, bison *(Bison bison)* (R) [Jefferson «chu-ta-ga rayau-goon» 'buffalo']. *n.* Also: čuhstekyerhayá'kę (R).

čuhtíčhe·θ wampum (RC 3:31) [Lawson «Chu-teche» 'Peak', «Katichhei» 'Thief or Rogue']. *n.*

–čun – a dressed hog or beef, bare, naked, naked body, torso. *n.r.* inaln: sčunę́'kye *on your naked body* (RC 3:54), inc., n.sfx. –eh. učù·neh *a dressed hog or beef, bare, naked* (HS), *naked body, torso* (RC 30:63); –čunawa'k –: ručunawa'kę́he' ‹he-naked body-held-had› *it had held his body* (RC 30:56); –čunę'ke: učunę́'kye ‹naked body-at› *on its naked body* (RC 30:44); –čunu = har –{dative III}: wa'na'čunuhà·rę' ‹fact-one=another-torso-washed-for› *one washed another's torso* (RC 11:28); –čunu'awi –: Čunu'awíhθę' ‹naked body-float-many› *Naked-Bodies-Floating (woman's proper name)* (RC 34:7); –a'čunęti –: wa'ę́'čunę́·ti' ‹fact-

Tuscarora Pronunciation Key:
/a/ law; /e/ hat; /i/ pizza; /u/ tune; /ę/ hint; /č/ cheese; /h/ hoe; /m/ mother; /s/ same; /t/ do (before a vowel y, or w), too (elsewhere); /k/ gale (before a vowel y or w), kale (elsewhere); /n/ inhale (before a consonant or word-final), note (elsewhere), /r/ hiss (before a consonant or word-final), run (trilled as in Italian, elsewhere); /w/ cuff (before a consonant other than y or word-final), way (elsewhere); /y/ fish (before a consonant or word-final), you (elsewhere), /θ/ thing; /'/ (the sound between the vowels in unh-unh); /·/ long vowel, /´/ high pitch; /`/ low pitch.

one-oneself-naked body-made› *one stripped, one removed all one's clothes* (RC 3:55); –aʔčunuhskę –: θaʔ-čunúhskę ‹you!-yourself-naked body-pick off› *make yourself naked!, take your clothes off!* (RC 3:54).

Čunahstí·yu· Andaste, Susquehannock (AG). *n.*

–**čunaʔtiyu** – be great hunter. *v.r.-s.i.* hab: -, pnt: -, stat: -·, prog: -, prp: -, dst: -, caus: -hw-, rvs: -, dat: -, n-inc. ękčunaʔtí·yu·k *I will be a great hunter* (R), računaʔtí·yu· *he is a great hunter* (RC 12:1).

čunaʔtáhčre·θ field mouse, mole (R). *n.*

Čunehstí·yu· Genesee River (AG). *n.*

čunęwahskrì·yuʔ common milkweed *(Asclepias sp.)* (H-notebook). *n.*

–**čunuʔawi** – Naked-Bodies-Floating. *dv. n.s.* Čunuʔawíhθęʔ ‹naked body-float-many› *Naked-Bodies-Floating (woman's proper name)* (RC 34:7).

čuranuháh marten *(Delichon urbica)* (H-notebook). *n.*

čurù·ruθ bluebird *(Sialia sialis)* (R). *n.*

čutakę́hku scarlet, deep red (HS). *n.*

čuteθęwará·θę hummingbird (AG). *n.*

čutráθnakar barn swallow *(Hirundo rustica)* (SH 375). *n.*

čuʔkwakweʔnę́·ni· black walnut *(Juglans nigra)* (RC 11: 16). *n.*

čúʔnakęʔ beaver *(Castor canadensis)* (RC 3:89) [Lawson «Chaunoc» 'Otter']. *n.*

–**čuʔriθ** – pierce, prick, stab, stick. *v.r.-t.* hab: -ahs, pnt: -ɸ, stat: -ɸ, prog: -, prp: -, dst: -, caus: -, rvs: -, dat: -, n-inc. waʔkčú·ʔri·θ *I stabbed it (as stabbing an animal, putting a fork into a potato, or spearing a fish)* (L 78), θčú·ʔri·θ *pierce it!* (R), waʔakučú·ʔri·θ *one was stuck by it* (RC 2:4), račuʔ-rí·θahs *he pricks it, he thrusts it* (HS).

čuʔwahrù·waʔ elk *(Alces alces)* (R), wapiti *(Cervus canadensis)* (HS). *n.*

čúʔyę girl (pet name) (H-notebook). *n.*

čwe – all kinds of (generic). *pfx.* The primary function of the generic prefix is to indicate that reference is to all instances or the entire class of the named entity. Its usual translation in this dictionary is *all kinds of.* It typically cooccurs with the verb root –ake- *be in number.* čwe –. –čikʔęwar = črake –: čwekačikʔęwarčrá·kye· ‹all-it-bug-'ness-is in number› *all kinds of bugs* (RC 30:56), čwe –. –čiʔnęʔčrake –: čwekačiʔnęʔčrá·kye· ‹all kinds of-it-bird-'ness-is in number› *all kinds of birds* (RC 30:56).

čwe –. –ake – all kinds of. *v.s.-s.i.* čwe-wá·kye· ‹all kinds of-it-is in number› *all kinds of* (AG).

čwé·ʔkye again, once again (RC 27:14). *part.* haʔ čwé·ʔkye ‹the once again› *the next* (HS).

čwé·ʔkye the next. *part.* haʔ čwé·ʔkye ‹the once again› *the next* (HS).

čwé·ʔn again, still; hello. *part.* čwé·ʔn ahskę̀·nę hę ‹again unknown-be at peace ?› *hello* (RC 3:2); čwé·ʔn haʔ íhsʔę ‹again the more› *moreover* (R).

čwé·ʔn ahskę̀·nę hę ‹again unknown-be at peace ?› hello (RC 3:2). *part.*

čwé·ʔn haʔ íhsʔę ‹again the more› moreover (R). *part.*

E

–**e** – go on foot, go. *v.r.-a.i.* hab: -ʔθ, pnt: -ʔ, stat: -ʔ, prog: -, prp: -, dst: -, caus: -hT-, rvs: -, dat: -, n-inc. Without a mode marker, this verb means to *go on foot, walk*; with a mode marker, it means simply *go.* The form –ę – occurs with, and overlaps, the third person feminine/indefinite agent prefix and the third person plural agent prefix. The form -e- occurs elsewhere. The completive aspect marker -·t occurs whenever the translocative or the combination of the partitive plus the cislocative is present. The third person singular neuter agent has the form -h- in the factual mode. í·kye² *I am walking* (R), ì·yę² *one walks* (RC 3:49), kà·ye² *they are walking* (R), wá²ę² *one went* (RC 3:49), ę́·kye² *I will go* (R) [Lawson «Unta hah» 'Will you go along with me' = ę́²te² hę *will you and I go?*], íhse *go! (said to the dog)* (L 51); -či-. -e-: íθhre²θ ‹again-he-goes› *he returned* (HS); -t-. -e-: ę́čhę² ‹prediction-hither-you-go› *you will come* (R), ę́tkye² ‹prediction-hither-I-go› *I will come* (R), náhre² ‹hither-he-goes› *he is absent* (HS), *he is coming* (R); -t-. -ehnahte-: nahrehnáhte² ‹hither-he-go-caused-going to› *he is coming by degrees* (H-notebook); ti-. -e-: tì·we² ‹so-it-goes› *so it walks* (RC 31:7); -yah-. -e-: yahwáhe·t ‹thither-fact-it-gone-complete› *it went there* (RC 8:35), wá²θe ‹thither-you!-go› *go!* (L 13); -ne+t-. -e-: nę́²nyę·t ‹apart-prediction-hither-one-go-complete› *one comes out from there* (RC 11:5), nę́thre² ‹apart-prediction-hither-he-go› *he will come* (R); ha² -t-. -e-: ha² nà·we² ‹the hither-it-goes› *future* (HS); ha² -yah-. -e-: ha² yę̀·we² ‹the thither-prediction-it-go› *eternity, forever* (HS).

-eh simple noun suffix. *n.r.sfx.*

-eh- little. *n.r.* n-poss., inc., n.sfx. -a².awéha² *little* (HS); -ehak-: awé·ha·k ‹little-eats› *facetious, garrulous: a wit, buffoon, jester* (HS); -ehar-: awé·-hareh ‹little-be in› *scurf, itch* (HS); -ehčrukr-: awehčrú·kri² ‹little-'ness-rubbish› *stuff, trifles* (HS); tha-. -e-.#ęwe: tha²awehę̀·we ‹unusual-it-little-genuine› *a simpleton* (HS), thah-rawehę̀·we ‹unusual-he-little-genuine› *he is a simpleton* (HS).

-ehak- facetious, garrulous; a wit, buffoon, jester. *n.s.* awé·ha·k ‹little-eats› *facetious, garrulous: a wit, baffoon, jester* (HS).

-ehar- itch, scurf. *n.s.* awé·hareh ‹little-be in› *itch, scurf* (HS).

-ehčrukr- stuff, trifles. *n.s.* awehčrú·kri² ‹little-'ness-rubbish› *stuff, trifles* (HS).

-ehę- many, much (distributive). *v.r.sfx.* Rare, lexically determined form, see: -(a)hę-.

-ehke simple noun suffix+external locative. *n.r.sfx.* From the examples given by Hewitt (H 2484) it appears that this combination of suffixes had the consistent meaning of "at the place of" in his time, as opposed to combinations of the external locative with other forms of the simple noun suffix which meant "on top of" and "on the surface of". See -a²ke and -ę²ke. -(a)= hahehke: uhahéhkye ‹path-at› *at the road, at the place of the road* (H 2484); -(a)hę²nehke: uhę²néhkye ‹clearing-at› *at, in the meadow or grassy plot of ground* (H 2484);

–či^ʔehnehke: uči^ʔehnéhkye ‹claw-at› *at, at the place of the claw* (H 2484); –hehnehke: uhehnéhkye ‹field-at› *at the field* (H 2484); –nęhehke: unęhéhkye ‹corn-at› *at the corn, at the place of corn* (H 2484); –nęhsehke: unęhséhkye ‹house-at› *at the house or at the place of the house* (H 2484); –nęhsnehke: unęhsnéhkye ‹seed-at› *at the seed or pit, at the place of the seed or pit* (H 2484); –ʔnhęhehke: uʔnhęhéhkye ‹urine-at› *at the place of urine, at the urine* (H 2484).

ehnáhkę below (R), lower (AG). *part.* kę·ne^ʔ ehnáhkę ‹here below› *here below* (HS); ehnáhkę –(ę)hawihT –: ehnáhkę rahawíhtha^ʔ ‹below he-bring-X-causes› *he abases* (HS); ehnáhkę –ę°ti –: ehnáhkę rę́·tih ‹below he-makes› *he abases* (HS).

ehnáhkę –(ę)hawihT – abase. *v.s.-a.i.* ehnáhkę rahawíhtha^ʔ ‹below he-bring-X-causes› *he abases* (HS).

ehnáhkę –ę°ti – abase. *v.s.-a.i.* ehnáhkę rę́·tih ‹below he-makes› *he abases* (HS).

ehnú·kęw mankind; pieces of cloth (for the rag bag), rags (HS). *n.*

–ehr – drink. *v.r.-a.i.* See: –ïhr –.

–ehraʔT – water (animals). *v.r.-a.i.* See: –ïhraʔT –.

–ehθayę –/–aweθayę – be dark. *v.r.-a.i.* hab: -hs-, pnt: -ʔ, stat: -ʔ, prog: -, prp: -, dst: -, caus: -hsT-, rvs: -, dat: -, inc.-ɸ-ag. The form –awehθayę – occurs with incorporated noun roots. The form –ehθayę – occurs elsewhere. yawéhθayę^ʔ *it is dark* (RC 11:2), *it got dark* (HS), réhθayęhs *he darkens, he obscures* (HS); –ehθayęhsT –: rehθayę́hstha^ʔ ‹he-be dark-causes› *he darkens it* (HS), rehθayę́hsnę ‹he-be dark-caused› *he darkened it* (HS), ęhréhθayęhst ‹prediction-he-be dark-cause› *he will darken it* (HS); –(ę)ʔ = tikęhrawehθayę –: ruʔtikęhrawéhθayę^ʔ ‹he-mind-is dark› *his is dark-minded* (HS); –rihwawehθayę –: yurihwawéhθayę^ʔ ‹it-matter-is dark› *abstruse, enigma* (HS).

–ehθayęhsT – darken. *v.s.-t.* rehθayę́hstha^ʔ ‹he-be dark-causes› *he darkens it* (HS), rehθayę́hsnę ‹he-be dark-caused› *he darkened it* (HS), ęhréhθayęhst ‹prediction-he-be dark-cause› *he will darken it* (HS).

–ehs – log. *n.r.* n-poss., inc., n.sfx. -eh. awéhseh *log*; –ehsahręhw –: wehsáhręw ‹it-log-put up-causes› *there is a log* (RC 3:43); –ehsu –: wéhsu·^ʔ ‹it-log-is in water› *crosspiece* (AG); ti –. –ehsuʔ = nę –: tiwehsúʔnę· ‹so-it-log-is a kind of› *that kind of log* (RC 3:47).

–ehsak – search for, seek. *v.r.-t.* See: –ïhsak –.

–ehsayę – common, low, vulgar. *n.r.* n-poss., inc., n.sfx. -ʔ. awéhsayę^ʔ *common, low, vulgar; it is of small value* (HS); –ękwehsayę –: ękwéhsayę^ʔ ‹human-vulgar› *dwarf: Little People (mythic)* (R); –rihwehsayę –: yurihwéhsayę^ʔ ‹it-matter-vulgar› *frivolous* (HS).

–ehsu – crosspiece. *dv.n.s.* wéhsu·^ʔ ‹it-log-is in water› *crosspiece* (AG).

–ehuT – show. *v.r.-t.* hab: -ha^ʔ, pnt: -ę^ʔ, stat: -·t, prog: -a'nye^ʔ, prp: -, dst: -, caus: -, rvs: -, dat: III (-ati-/-ę-), n-inc. yawehuʔná·ʔnye^ʔ *it is going along showing* (RC 3:69), rehú·tha^ʔ *he shows it, he exhibits it* (R), rawéhu·t *he has shown it* (R), wahrehú·ʔnę^ʔ *he showed it* (R), waʔakyehú·ʔnę^ʔ *one showed it* (RC 3:54); –ehuT –{dative III}: yękwehuʔná·ti· ‹one=me-showed-for› *one showed me* (AW 99); –ehuʔ = nawę –: rehuʔnà·węh ‹he-shows-much› *he describes it* (HS); –a'nehuT –: ra^ʔ-

nehú·tha⁷ ‹he-himself-shows› *he exhibits himself* (HS), ęθwa⁷nehú·⁷nę⁷ ‹prediction-you-yourselves-show› *you will show yourselves* (RC 33:8), ę⁷nehú·⁷nę⁷ ‹fact-it-itself-shown› *it proved it* (R); –a'nehu⁷nahkw –: yu⁷nehu⁷náhkę ‹it-itself-showed-instrument› *sign* (HS).

–ehu⁷nawę – describe. *v.s.-t.* rehu⁷nà·węh ‹he-shows-much› *he describes it* (HS).

–ehwaya⁷θ – be single (of humans). *v.r.-a.i.* hab: -s, pnt: -ɸ, stat: -, prog: -, prp: -, dst: -, caus: -, rvs: -, dat: -, n-inc. yakyéhwaya⁷č *eligible male* (RC 35:2), wahréhwaya⁷θ *he was single* (RC 35:2).

–ehyahr – have on mind, think about, remind of. *v.r.-t.* hab: -ɸ ~ -ahstha⁷, pnt: -a⁷, stat: -ɸ, prog: -a'nye⁷, prp: -, dst: -, caus: -, rvs: -, dat: -, n-inc. réhyar *he remembers it* (HS), kęyehyahrá·⁷nye⁷ *I am thinking about you* (RC 35:9); –či –. –ehyahra⁷ –: θahrehyáhra⁷ ‹again-fact-he-have on his mind-began› *he remembered* (RC 31:3), θhrehyáhra⁷θ ‹again-he-have on his mind-begins› *he remembers, he recollects* (HS); –a'nehyahr –: ra⁷nehyáhrę ‹he-himself-thought about› *he remembers himself, he is virtuous* (HS); –a'nehyahręhčr –: u⁷nehyahrę́hčreh ‹self-think about-'ness› *adulthood, civilization, conscience, good manners, manhood, memory, memory-of-self, self-respect, virtue* (HS); –a'na = 'nehyahrhuhkw –{dative III}: ękayę⁷na⁷nehyarhúhkę⁷ ‹prediction-they-themselves-think about-cause-instrument-for› *they will use it to remind themselves* (R); –či –. –ehyahrhuhkw –{dative III}: θhrawehyarhuhkwá·tih ‹again-he-think about-causes-instrument- for› *he is reminded, he memorizes* (R); –či –. –ęnehyahrhuhkw –{dative III}: θhręnehyarhuhkwá·tih ‹again-he-himself-think about-causes-instrument-for› *he commemorates* (HS); ha⁷ –ehyahr –: ha⁷ rehyahráhstha⁷ ‹the he-has on his mind› *(his) memory* (HS).

–ehyahr – memory. *n.s.* ha⁷ rehyahráhstha⁷ ‹the he-has on his mind› *(his) memory* (HS).

–ek – liquid; glass, looking glass, mirror, speculum, window. *n.r.* n-poss., inc., n.sfx. –eh (archaic: -ę⁷). In the absence of modifiers, the liquid referred to by this root is assumed to be water. awé·kyeh *liquid; glass, looking glass, mirror, speculum, window* (HS), awé·kę⁷ *liquid* (HS); –ekača⁷tuh –: ęyawekačá⁷tuh ‹prediction-it-liquid-be cool› *liquid will cool* (RC 18:3); –ekakt: awé·kakwt ‹liquid-next to› *next to liquid, next to mirror* (R); –ekanę = 'nak –: yawekanę⁷ná·kę ‹it-liquid-is attached› *window* (R); –ekaθe?: aweká·θe⁷ ‹it-liquid-new› *fresh water* (AG); –ekaθray –: awekaθrà·yeh ‹liquid-fresh› *fresh liquid, fresh water* (RC 19:2); –ekatkęh –: yaweká·tkęhθ ‹it-liquid-is rotten› *stagnant water* (HS); –ekęT –{dative II}: wekę́·⁷nahθ ‹it-liquid-close-for› *water subsides* (HS); –ekę =

ti –: aryakyekę́·ti ‹unknown-one-liquid-make› *that one steep it* (RC 23:7), wekę́·tih ‹it-liquid-makes› *decoction, wine* (HS); –ekitkęhw –: wekí·tkęws ‹it-liquid-issue forth-causes› *press (e.g., for wine, cider)* (HS), ęyakyekí·tkęw ‹prediction-one-liquid-issue forth-cause› *one will draw liquid out* (RC 19:2); –ekitkę^ʔ–: yawekitkę́^ʔę ‹it-liquid-issue forth-began› *juice* (HS), wekí·tkę^ʔθ ‹it-liquid-issue forth-begins› *it distills* (HS); –eku –: yawé·ku^ʔ ‹it-liquid-is in water› *a fluid or liquid is imbedded (in it) (said of water in a blister or serum in a sore)* (H 2892); –či –.–ekaT –: θwé·ka·t ‹again-it-liquid-stands› *window sash; dose* (HS); –či –.–ekęT –{dative II}: θwekę́·^ʔnahθ ‹again-it-liquid-closes-for› *water settles back down again* (HS); –či –.–ekęti –: čawekę́·tye^ʔ ‹again-it-liquid-makes› *wild honeysuckle (Lonicera* sp.*)* (H-notebook); –ne –.–ekah = kwa^ʔnahT –: newekáhkwa^ʔnahč ‹apart-it-liquid-wrap up-causes› *it eddies* (HS); –ne –.–ekanę –: newé·kanęh ‹apart-it-liquid-guards› *casement of a window*; –t –.–ekę –: nyawé·kę^ʔ ‹hither-it-liquid-fell› *mouth of river* (AG); –t –.–eku^ʔnętyę –: naweku^ʔnę́·tyę^ʔ ‹hither-it-liquid-was a kind of-much› *blister* (RC 3:57); tha –.–eka·t –.#áh: thyakyekatha^ʔáh ‹unusual-one-liquid-stands-little› *lobelia, great lobelia (Lobelia* sp.*)* (H-notebook); ti –.–eku^ʔ = nę –: thwahekú^ʔnę^ʔ ‹so-fact-it-liquid-been a kind of› *it became such a liquid* (RC 12:29); –a'nekayę(T) –{dative II}: yaku^ʔnekayę́·tih ‹it-itself-liquid-lay-for› *dropsy* (RC 18:title); –a'nekęr –: u^ʔnekę̀·reh ‹self-liquid-leave behind› *dregs, residue* (HS); –ek –.–ę°ti –: awé·kę^ʔ rę́·tih ‹liquid he-makes› *he liquifies* (HS); ha^ʔ –ekarahkwahT –

–ekanurę –: ha^ʔ yakyekarahkwáhtha^ʔ wekanù·ręh ‹the one-liquid-be in instrument-causes it-liquid-is precious› *decanter* (HS).

–ek –.–ę°ti – liquify. *v.s.-t.* awé·kę^ʔ rę́·tih ‹liquid he-makes› *he liquifies it* (HS).

–ekanę'nak – window. *dv.n.s.* yawekanę^ʔná·kę ‹it-liquid-is attached› *window* (R).

–ekarahkwahT – –ekanurę – decanter. *dv.-n.s.* ha^ʔ yakyekarahkwáhtha^ʔ wekanù·ręh ‹the one-liquid-be in-instrument-causes it-liquid-is precious› *decanter* (HS).

–ekaθe^ʔ fresh water. *n.s.* aweká·θe^ʔ *fresh water* (AG).

–ekatkęh – stagnant water. *dv.n.s.* yaweká·tkęhθ ‹it-liquid-is rotten› *stagnant water* (HS).

–ekęti – steep. *v.s.-t.* aryakyekę́·ti^ʔ ‹unknown-one-liquid-make› *that one steep it* (RC 23:7).

–ekęti – decoction, wine. *dv.n.s.* wekę́·tih ‹it-liquid-makes› *decoction, wine* (HS).

–ekitkęhw – press. *dv.n.s.* wekí·tkęws ‹it-liquid-issue forth-causes› *press (e.g., for wine, cider)* (HS).

–ekitkę^ʔ – distill. *v.s.-a.i.* wekí·tkę^ʔθ ‹it-liquid-issue forth-begins› *it distills* (HS).

–ekitkę^ʔ – juice. *dv.n.s.* yawekitkę́^ʔę ‹it-liquid-issue forth-began› *juice* (HS).

–ek^ʔ – be savory, be sweet, intoxicate, taste good. *v.r.-s.i.* stat: -ę, prog: -, prp: -, dst: -, caus: -, rvs: -, dat: -, n-inc. yawé·k^ʔę *it tasted good* (RC 21:15), *it is delicious* (HS), wakyé·k^ʔę *I am a drunkard* (R), rawé·k^ʔę *he is intemperate* (HS), *he is a drunkard* (R); ha^ʔ –ek^ʔ –: ha^ʔ rawé·k^ʔę ‹the he-is intoxicated› *Bacchanalian* (HS); kwęhs –ek^ʔ –: kwęhs ahrawé·k^ʔęk ‹no unknown-he-be intoxicated› *he is tem-*

perate (HS).

-ek⁷ - Bacchanalian. *dv.n.s.* ha⁷ rawé·k⁷ę ‹the he-is intoxicated› *Bacchanalian* (HS).

-en - be different, be separate. *v.r.-s.i.* stat: -⁷ ~ -ę, prog: -, prp: -, dst: -, caus: -, rvs: -, dat: -, inc.-φ-pat. kawì·re⁷n ‹it-infant-is separate› *its children* (RC 32:12).

-enę - go, travel. *v.r.-a.i.* hab: -hs, pnt: -, stat: -·, prog: -, prp: -, dst: -, caus: -hsT- ~ -⁷T-, rvs: -, dat: -, n-inc. yę̀·nęhs *one goes or travels* (H 447); **-enęhsT -**: yęnę́hstha⁷ ‹one-travel-causes› *a path or road* (H 447); **-enę⁷T -**: è·nę⁷t ‹travel-cause› *a way, passage, road to* (H 447); **-t -**. **-enę⁷T -**: nyawené⁷nę ‹hither-it-travel-caused› *it came from* (RC 12:29), thrawené⁷nę ‹hither-he-travel-caused› *he came from* (RC 12:18); **tha+ne -**. **-enę - -ręhyayęt = ⁷a -**: tha⁷neyawé·nę yuręhyayę́·t⁷ę ‹unusual-apart-it-traveled it-sky-is even with› *horizontal* (HS).

-enęhsT - path, road. *dv.n.s.* yęnę́hstha⁷ ‹one-travel-causes› *a path or road* (H 447).

-enę⁷T - passage, road, way. *dv.n.s.* è·nę⁷t ‹travel-cause› *a way, passage, road to* (H 447).

-er - believe, imagine, presume, suppose, think, want, wish. *v.r.-a.i.* hab: -ha⁷, pnt: -⁷, stat: -ih, prog: -, prp: -ęhe-, dst: -, caus: -, rvs: -, dat: -, n-inc. This verb root is often found in constructions used to introduce direct quotations of an individual's inner, un-verbalized thoughts. sè·rih *you think, you believe* (RC 3:42), rè·rih *he imagines* (HS), sérha⁷ *you are thinking, you are wanting* (R), wáhse⁷r *you thought, you believed* (R), ra⁷na⁷nè·rih *he is presumptuous* (HS), kakawerę́he⁷ *they wanted to* (AW 98); **-erihkaθne -**: rawerihká́θne⁷ ‹he-believe-is strong› *he is insensitive to pain, he is patient, he suffers patiently* (HS); **-yah -**. **-erihθe -**: yękyeríhθek ‹thither-prediction-I-want-be going to› *I will need it* (RC 30:24); **ha⁷ -erih = kaθne -**: ha⁷ rawerihká́θne⁷ ‹the he-believe-is strong› *patience* (HS); **hà·ne⁷ -er -**: hà·ne⁷ rè·rih ‹that is he-wants› *his intention* (HS); yękyeríhθek ‹thither-prediction-I-want-be going to› *I will need it* (RC 30:24); **ha⁷ -erihkaθne -**: ha⁷ rawerihká́θne⁷ ‹the he-believe-is strong› *patience* (HS); **hení·kę· -er- -ętuT -**: hení·kę· wè·rih ęwę́·tu·t ‹that is it-wants prediction-it-rain› *it intends to rain* (R).

-er - intention. *dv.n.s.* hà·ne⁷ rè·rih ‹that is he-wants› *his intention* (HS).

è·re alternatively, away from, elsewhere, opposite, other side (R). *part.* **è·re kę⁷** ‹alternatively where› *away from* (AG); **è·re na⁷ ú⁷ni⁷** ‹alternatively much it-at edge of› *on the other side* (AW 57); **he⁷skę́hę̀·we è·re** ‹somewhere alternatively› *elsewhere* (HS); **è·re -rahkw -**: è·re yuráhkhwa⁷ ‹alternatively it-collects› *it is excluded* (HS).

è·re kę⁷ ‹alternatively where› *away from* (AG). *part.*

è·re –rahkw– be excluded. *v.s.-a.i.* è·re yuráhkhwaʔ ‹alternatively it-collects› *it is excluded* (HS).

–erihkaθne– be patient, suffer patiently. *v.s.-a.i.* rawerihkáθneʔ ‹he-believe-is strong› *he is insensitive to pain, he is patient, he suffers patiently* (HS).

–erihkaθne– patience. *dv.n.s.* haʔ rawerihkáθneʔ ‹the he-believe-is strong› *patience* (HS).

è·rihs runt (HS). *n.*

eríhsęʔ instead (R). *part.* Also: heríhsęʔ.

–erihst– add, add to. *v.r.-t.* hab: -haʔ, pnt: -φ, stat: -, prog: -, prp: -, dst: -, caus: -, rvs: -, dat: -, n-inc. kyeríhsthaʔ *I am adding it* (R); –t–. –erihst–: nakyè·rihst ‹hither-I-add› *I added it* (R).

–eriθk– be distrustful. *v.r.-a.i.* hab: -, pnt: -, stat: -ę, prog: -, prp: -, dst: -, caus: -, rvs: -, dat: -, n-inc. rawerí·θkę *he is distrustful* (HS).

è·riʔ wild cherry (*Prunus virginiana; Prunus serotina*) (H-notebook). *n.* Also: čè·riʔ.

–eryahn– breath. *n.r.* n-poss., inc., n.sfx. -. Found only in compounds. –eryah = nak̯ʷek –: weryáhnakweks ‹it-breath-closes› *asthma* (RC 19:1); ti -. –eryah = natkwarayę –: tyaweryahnatkwarà·yęʔ ‹so-it-breath-is red› *water mocassin (Agkistronden piscivorus), water adder (Natrix* sp.) (R) (also: tyuweryah-natkwarà·yęʔθ).

–eryahnak̯ʷek– asthma. *n.s.* weryáhnakweks ‹it-breath-closes› *asthma* (RC 19:1).

–eryahs– heart. *n.r.* inaln: nweryahsáʔkye *in our hearts* (MP), inc., n.sfx. -eh. aweryáhseh *heart* (R) [Gallatin «auwereahseh» 'Heart'].

–eθ– be long. *v.r.-s.i.* stat: -φ, prog: -, prp: -, dst: -ę-, caus: -T-, rvs: -, dat: -, inc.-φ-pat. Hewitt (2892) notes that, "with the single exception of the pro-

noun characteristic of the singular third person of the inanimate or azoic gender, no pronoun may be prefixed to this root or stem without an intervening pure noun." ì·we·θ *it is long* (H 2892), iwé·θęh *they are long* (H 2892), iweθéheʔ *they were long* (H 2892); –(a)haheθ–: waháhe·θ ‹it-path-is long› *it is a long road, path or row or line of inanimate things* (H 2484); –(a)haheθę–: wahahé·θę ‹it-path-is long-many› *the paths or roads are long* (H 2484); –(a)hęʔneθ–: wahęʔne·θ ‹it-clearing-is long› *the meadow is long* (H 2484); –činęʔthereθ–: kačinęʔthere·θ ‹it-curl-is long› *the curl is long; it is a long curl* (H 2484), yečinęʔthere·θ ‹one-curl-is long› *her curls are long; she has long curls; she has a long curl* (H 2484); –čiʔehneθ–: kačiʔéhne·θ ‹it-claw-is long› *its claw is long; it is a long claw* (H 2484); –(ę)traʔneθę–: wętraʔné·θę ‹it-horn-is long-much› *ox* (R); –(ę)ʔtikęhreθ–: raʔtikęhre·θ ‹he-mind-is long› *he is patient* (HS); –hečheθ–: kahéčhe·θ ‹it-buttocks-is long› *wasp* (R); –hsuʔ = kweθę –: kahsuʔkwé·θę ‹it-finger-is long-much› *butternut (Juglans cinerea)* (RC 11:16); –nęčiʔthereθ–: kanęčíʔthere·θ ‹it-curl of hair-is long› *it is a long curl, the curl is long* (H 2484); –nęheθ–: kanéhe·θ ‹it-corn-is long› *the corn grain is long* (H 2484); –nęhseθ–: kanéhse·θ ‹it-house-is long› *longhouse* (R); –nęhseθkye: kanęhsé·θkye ‹it-house-is long-at› *at longhouse* (RC 26:8); –nęhseθękye: kanęhseθę́·kye ‹it-house-is long-many-at› *at longhouses* (RC 3:4); –nęhsneθ–: kanęhsne·θ ‹it-seed-is long› *the grain is long* (H 2484); –nęʔareθ–.#úʔy: Kanęʔareθ-ʔúʔy ‹it-climbing vine-is long-great› *Long-Vine* (R) [Colonial Records

⟨Coneughauritzhugh⟩ 'Chief's name']; -rę̆weθ -: krę̆·we·θ ⟨I-stature-is long⟩ *I am tall* (AG); -θri'kweθ -: kaθrí'kwe·θ ⟨it-limp thing-is long⟩ *Small (sand or land) Turtle Clan* (R) -ta'=čheθ -: yutá'čhe·θ ⟨it-lower half of body-is long⟩ *corn roaster* (HS); -ta'=reθ -: katá're·θ ⟨it-head-is long⟩ *lettuce* (R); -wiseθ -: yuwí·se·θ ⟨it-ice-is long⟩ *icy* (HS); -'ęyeθ -: yu'ę̆·ye·θ ⟨it-price-is long⟩ *it is expensive, it is dear* (HS); -'ęyeθa'θ -: ęyeθá'θeh ⟨price-be long-is of a size⟩ *appreciate* (HS); -'θę'kareθ -.#ú'y: yu'θę'kare·θ'ú'y ⟨it-brink-is long-great⟩ *it is steep* (HS); -či -. -(a)hyeθ: θhúhye·θ ⟨again-it-fruit-is long⟩ *haw, mulberry* (H-notebook); -či -. -(a)hyeθa'ke: čuhyeθá'kye ⟨again-it-fruit-is long-at⟩ *February* (AG), *April* (R) (HS: June 15-July 15); -či -. -hne'reθ: čuhné'·re·θ ⟨again-it-root-is long⟩ *spikenard (Aralia racemosa)* (L 3); -či -. -hne'reθ -.#áh: čuhne'·re·θ'áh ⟨again-it-root-is long-little⟩ *sarsaparilla* (HS); -či -. -hne'reθ -.#ú'y: čuhne'·re·θ'ú'y ⟨again-it-root-is long-great⟩ *wild sarsaparilla (Aralia nudicaulis)* (HS); -ne+či -. -hsweθ -.#áh: neθkahswe·θ'áh ⟨apart-again-it-back-is long-little⟩ *sparrow hawk* (R); -t -. -'ęyeθ -: nyu'ęyé·θę ⟨hither-it-price-was long⟩ *high prices* (R); ti -. -eθ -: tì·we·θ ⟨so-it-is long⟩ *quality* (HS); ti -. -eθ -.#ú'y: tiwe·θ'ú'y ⟨so-it-is long-great⟩ *it is long* (R); ti -. -eθ -.#áh: tiwe·θ'áh ⟨so-it-is long-little⟩ *it is short* (R); ti -. -(a)haheθ -.#ú'y: tiwa-hahe·θ'ú'y ⟨so-it-path-is long-great⟩ *a long (or big) road* (L 18); ti -. -a'newyeθ -: tihsa'né·wye·θ ⟨so-you-yourself-armspan-is long⟩ *as long as both your arms extended* (RC 30:60); ti -. -čihskę̆hkareθę -.#ú'y: tikačihskę̆hkare-θę̆hú'y ⟨so-it-claw-is long-much-great⟩ *great, long, claws* (RC 28:1); ti -. -eyeθ -: tiwę̆·ye·θ ⟨so-it-hang down-is long⟩ *it is deep* (R); ti -. -ke'weθ -: tikakyé'we·θ ⟨so-it-hair-is long⟩ *long hair* (RC 28:1); ti -. -nęhsneθ -: tikanę̆hsne·θ ⟨so-it-seed-is long⟩ *the grain is long* (H 2484); ti -. -nęhsneθ -.#áh: tikanęhsne·θ'áh ⟨so-it-seed-is long-little⟩ *the grain is short, is not long* (H 2484); ti -. -rihweθ: thwa'karíhwe·θ ⟨so-fact-it-matter-was long⟩ *it was a long time* (RC 15:6); ti -. -rę̆weθ -: tyeré·we·θ ⟨so-one-stature-is long⟩ *one is so tall* (RC 10:15); ti -. -rę̆'eθ -: tikaré'e·θ ⟨so-it-tree-is long⟩ *tall tree* (RC 4:1); ti -. -takareθ -.#ú'y: tikataka-re·θ'ú'y ⟨so-it-point-is long-great⟩ *great long beak, proboscis* (RC 9:11); ti -. -rihweθ -: thwa'karíhwe·θ ⟨so-fact-it-matter-been long⟩ *long time* (RC 15:6); -eθnahkw -: weθnáhkę ⟨it-be long-causes-instrument⟩ *lengthwise* (HS); -eθT -: ré·θtha' ⟨he-be long-causes⟩ *he lengthens it, he prolongs it* (HS), wáhre·θt ⟨he-be long-caused⟩ *he lengthened it* (RC 26:6); -'ęyeθT -: ra'ęyé·θtha' ⟨he-price-be long-causes⟩ *he raises the price* (HS); te' ti -. -eθ -: te' tì·we·θ ⟨what so-it-is long⟩ *how long is it?* (HS), *tapeworm* (R).

-eθnahkw – lengthwise. *dv.n.s.* weθnáhkę ‹it-be long-cause-instrument› *lengthwise* (HS).

-eθT – lengthen, prolong. *v.s.-t.* ré·θtha⁹ ‹he-be long-causes› *he lengthens it, he prolongs it* (HS), wáhre·θt ‹he-be long-caused› *he lengthened it* (RC 26:6).

#eθu⁹ several large (augmentative distributive). *enc.* A relatively rare enclitic that combines the meanings of the augmentative enclitic and the distributive suffix, e.g., **kęhrekshę** –. **#eθu⁹**: kęhrekshęhé·θu⁹ ‹mountain lion-many-several large› *great mountain lions*; **kuhserhę.#eθu⁹**: kuhserhęhé·θu⁹ ‹winter-many great› *December*.

-eshu – pound corn to flour. *v.r.-a.i.* hab: -, pnt: -⁹, stat: -ę, prog: -, prp: -, dst: -, caus: -, rvs: -, dat: -, n-inc. kyéshwę *I pound corn to flour* (R), wa⁹kyéshu⁹ *I pounded corn to flour* (R).

-etayę – prophet. *dv.n.r.* retà·yę⁹ *prophet* (R).

-etihst – consume. *v.r.-t.* hab: -, pnt: -, stat: -ę, prog: -, prp: -, dst: -, caus: -, rvs: -, dat: -, inc.-ɸ-pat. Found only in the construction given below. **-ę⁹re = tihst** –: kakawę⁹retíhstę ‹they-nut-consumed› *they lived on nuts* (RC 10:1).

-eti(y) – make, produce. *v.r.-t.* hab: -( )ahs, pnt: -⁹, stat: -( )ę, prog: -, prp: -, dst: -, caus: -a⁹T-, rvs: -, dat: -, n-inc. rawetì·yę *he made it* (HS), retì·yahs *he makes it* (HS), ęhretiyáhshek *he will make it* (HS), yawetì·yę *it produced it* (HS), wetì·yahs *it produces it* (HS), ęwé·ti⁹ *it will produce it* (HS); **-etyahčihw** –: retyahčíwha⁹ ‹he-produce-very-causes› *he arranges it, he prepares it* (HS), wahratyáhčiw ‹he-produce-very-caused› *he arranged it* (R); **-etya⁹T** –: yakyetyá⁹tha⁹ ‹one-produce-causes› *material, matter* (HS); **-či** –. **-eti(y)** –: θhretì·yahs ‹again-it-makes› *he redresses, he remakes, he revests* (HS); **-a'neti(y)** –: wa⁹ę⁹né·ti⁹ ‹fact-one-oneself-produced› *one got dressed* (R); **-a'netyahčihę** –: ru⁹netyahčíhę· ‹he-himself-produced-very-much› *he is ready, he is fully dressed* (R), yu⁹netyahčíhę· ‹it-itself-produced-very-much› *all ready* (R), ęθa⁹netyahčíhę·k ‹prediction-you-yourself-produce-very-much› *you will get ready* (RC 32:17); **-a'netyahčr** –: u⁹nyetyá⁹čreh ‹self-produce-'ness› *raiment, clothes* (HS); **-a'netyahst** –: u⁹nyetyáhsteh ‹self-produce-'ness› *raiment, clothes* (HS); **-či** –. **-a'neti(y)** –: θaθa⁹né·ti ‹again-you!-yourself-produce› *put your clothes back on!* (RC 3:58), čę⁹né·ti⁹ ‹again-fact-one-oneself-produced› *one put one's clothes back on* (RC 3:59); **-či** –. **-a'netyahstihs⁹a** –: čę⁹netyahstíhs⁹a·⁹ ‹again-one-oneself-produce-'ness-finished› *one finished dressing* (RC 3:59); **ti** –. **-etyahčihwahnę** –: thwa⁹kayętyahčihwáhnę⁹ ‹so-fact-they-produce-very-caused-many› *they got things ready* (R); **-ne+t** –. **-a'netyahčihę** –: ne⁹nyu⁹netyahčíhę⁹ ‹apart-hither-it-itself-produce-very-much› *it was ready there* (RC 25:12); **ha⁹ -eti(y)** –: ha⁹ wetì·yę ‹the it-produced› *artificial* (HS); **kahęwè·ya⁹ -etya⁹T** –: kahęwè·ya⁹ wetyá⁹nę ‹black ash it-produce-caused› *ashen* (HS); **kwęhs -eti(y)** –: kwęhs arwetiyáhshek ‹no unknown-it-produce› *unproductive* (HS).

-eti(y) – artificial. *dv.n.s.* ha⁹ wetì·yę ‹the it-produced› *artificial* (HS).

-etyahčihw – arrange, prepare. *v.s.-t.* retyahčíwha⁹ ‹he-make-very-causes› *he arranges it, he prepares it* (HS), wahratyáhčiw ‹he-produce-very-caused› *he arranged it* (R).

-etya⁹T – material, matter. *dv.n.s.* ya-

kyetyá⁷tha⁷ ‹one-make-causes› *material, matter* (HS).
e⁷ uh (sound of hesitation in conversation) (R). *part.*
e·⁷ yuk (said of something that tastes
awful) (R). *part.*
-e⁷ simple noun suffix. *n.r.sfx.*
-e⁷ stative aspect. *v.r.sfx.*
-e⁷nahkw– insinuate. *v.r.-a.i.* hab: -ha⁷,
pnt: -, stat: -ę̊, prog: -, prp: -, dst: -,
caus: -, rvs: -, dat: -, n-inc. re⁷-
náhkhwa⁷ *he insinuates* (HS); -t-.
-e⁷nahkw–: thrawe⁷náhkę ‹hither-he-
insinuated› *he is fervent, he is unswerving, he has faith* (HS); kwęhs
-t-. -e⁷nahkw–: kwęhs ę⁷nahraweh-
náhkęk ‹no unknown-hither-he-insin-
uate› *he is unfaithful* (HS).
-e⁷r– animal hair, fur. *n.r.* aln: akyé⁷-
rawęh *my fur* (R), inc., n.sfx. -eh (archaic: -ę⁷). Hewitt (notebook) states
that awé⁷rę⁷ is a collective plural
meaning *fur, hair* and awé⁷reh means
a (single) hair. This distinction has not
been noted among modern speakers,
who do not use the form awé⁷rę⁷.
awé⁷reh *animal hair, fur* (R), awé⁷rę⁷
fur (H-notebook) [Lawson «Oowaara»
'Hair']; -e⁷r-.#hči: awe⁷rę́⁷či ‹fur-
very› *furry, hairy: crinosity* (HS);
-e⁷raks–: we⁷rá·ksę· ‹it-fur-is bad›
lamb, mutton, sheep (R); -e⁷rakʷahT–:
na⁷ne⁷rakwáhta⁷ ‹one=another-fur-
cuts› *one crops another's hair* (HS);
-e⁷ra'ne–: aryawe⁷rá·⁷nek ‹unknown-
it-hair-be present› *that hair be present*
(R); -e⁷ra⁷r–: yawé⁷ra⁷r ‹it-fur-is

much› *much fur* (RC 6:11); -či-.
-e⁷rę–: θawé⁷rę⁷ ‹again-fact-it-fur-
dropped› *hair fell back off* (RC 11:
28); -či-. -e⁷ręhT–: ęθwé⁷ręht ‹pre-
diction-again-it-fur-drop-cause› *hair
will fall back off* (RC 11:23); ti-.
-e⁷reθ-.#áh: tiwe⁷re·θ⁷áh ‹so-it-fur-is
long-little› *short fur* (R).
-e⁷r-.#hči furry, hairy; crinosity. *part.*
awe⁷rę́⁷či ‹fur-very› *furry, hairy: curiosity* (HS).
-e⁷raks– lamb, mutton, sheep. *dv.n.s.*
we⁷rá·ksę· ‹it-fur-is bad› *lamb, mutton, sheep* (R).
-e⁷rakʷahT– crop hair. *v.s.-t.* na⁷ne⁷-
rakwáhta⁷ ‹one=another-fur-cuts› *one
crops another's hair* (HS).
-e⁷θ– be in a location, step. *v.r.-a.i.* hab:
-ha⁷, pnt: -φ, stat: -, prog: -, prp: -,
dst: -, caus: -, rvs: -, dat: III (-ati-/-ę-),
n-inc. yé⁷θhahk *one had been here*
(RC 35: 21), ré⁷θhahk *he had been
here* (RC 35: 22), wé⁷θhahk *it was
here* (RC 30:1), *it had stepped* (R), *it
lived (on earth)* (AW 53); -e⁷θ–
{dative III}: θé⁷θę ‹you!-are in a
location-for› *take steps!* (L 51); -či-.
-e⁷θ–: ęθawé⁷θhek ‹un-known-again-
it-be in a location› *that it be walking
around* (RC 7:9); ti-. -e⁷θe⁷–: tyé⁷-
θhe⁷θ ‹so-one-be in a location-begins›
one's step (RC 7:10); -e⁷θayę(T)–
{dative II}: re⁷θayę́·⁷nahθ ‹he-be in a
location-lays-for› *he settles* (HS);
íhskah -e⁷θ–: íhskah arwé⁷θhek ‹no
unknown-it-be in a location› *no more
does it roam* (AW 54).

-eʔθ-{dative III} take steps. *v.s.-a.i.*
θéʔθę ‹you!-are in a location-for› *take
steps!* (L 51).

-eʔθa̱yę(T)-{dative II} settle. *v.s.-a.i.*
reʔθayę́·ʔnahθ ‹he-be in a location-
lays-for› *he settles* (HS).

-eʔwihs- saddle. *n.r.* n-poss., inc., n.sfx.
-eh. aweʔwíhseh *saddle* (HS); -eʔ=
wihsher-: reʔwíhsher ‹he-saddle-
hangs› *he puts saddle upon it* (HS);
áha·θ -eʔwíhsher-: áha·θ reʔwíhsher
‹horse he-saddle-hangs› *he saddles a
horse* (HS); -a'nahsawiʔnahkw- -eʔ=
wihsę́ʔke: yęʔnahsawiʔnáhkhwaʔ a-
weʔwihsę́ʔkye ‹one-oneself-foot-give-
causes-instrument saddle-at› *stirrup*
(HS).

-eʔwihsher- put saddle on. *v.s.-t.*
reʔwíhsher ‹he-saddle-hangs› *he puts
saddle upon it* (HS).

Ę̧

ę- prediction (future mode). *v.pfx.* The
future mode is used to mark the fact
that the speaker is predicting that the
activity or state referred to by the
verb will occur or will have occurred
by some point in time. Therefore, it is
glossed ‹prediction› in this dictionary.

-ę- dative. *v.r.sfx.* Form of dative III
that occurs in the imperative and
when a mode marker is present.

-ę stative aspect. *v.r.sfx.*

-ę̊ stative aspect. *v.r.sfx.*

-ę- fall. *v.r.-a.i.* hab: -h, pnt: -ʔ, stat: -ʔ,
prog: -, prp: -, dst: -, caus: -hT-, rvs:
-, dat: -, inc.-aʔθ-pat. With the
causative suffix this root takes on the
meaning *drop*. It requires an incorporated noun expressing the patient
unless the patient is specified by an

immediately preceding noun or particle. In the absence of an overt patient,
the empty noun root -aʔθ- occurs.
-aʔθęhT-: waʔkáʔθęht ‹fact-I-X-fall-
caused› *I dropped it* (R), raʔθę́hthaʔ
‹he-X-fall-causes› *he knocks off, he
removes it* (HS); -aʔθęʔ-: yuʔθę́ʔę ‹it-
X-fall-began› *it begins to fall* (RC
7:1); -čanęhT-: račanę́htha ‹it-bright-
ness-fall-causes› *he polishes it* (HS);
-čtęhręhT-: naʔnečtęhrę́hthaʔ ‹one=
another-stone-fall-causes› *one throws
another down headlong* (HS); -(ę)ʔ=
tahsę-: yawęʔtáhsęʔ ‹it-tongue-fell›
bee swarm (R); -(ę)terę-: yetè·ręh
‹one-conception-falls› *she is pregnant*
(HS); -(ę)ʔtikęhręʔ-: ruʔtikęhrę́ʔę ‹he-
mind-fall-began› *he is dejected* (HS);
-hraʔnę-: rahráʔnęh ‹he-feather-falls›
he puts feathers on (arrows) (HS);
-hska̱węhT-: yuhskawę́hnę ‹it-raft-fall-
caused› *wreckage* (HS); -hta̱węʔ-:
yuhtawę́ʔę ‹it-stream of water-fall-
began› *waterfall* (R); -kwęhnęhT-:
rakwęhnę́hthaʔ ‹he-rust-fall-causes› *he
knocks off rust* (HS); -nęhsnęhT-:
kanęhsnę́hthaʔ ‹it-seed-fall-causes› *it
causes the grain to fall, it shakes the
grain down* (H 2484); -nęhsnęʔ-: ka-
nę́hsnęʔθ ‹it-seed-fall-begins› *the
grain falls, drops: the grain shells,
said of overripe cereals* (H 2484);
-rętuʔčręhnawę-: yurętuʔčręhnà·węʔ
‹it-coffin-fall-caused-many› *cabinet*
(HS); -rihęhT-: naʔrihę́htha ‹one=an-
other-matter-fall-causes› *one commis-
sions another, one deputizes another*
(HS); -tehwę-: rutéhwęh ‹he-hide-
falls› *he got pale* (RC 30:56); *leech*
(AG), *bloodsucker* (R); -tiʔθrę-: yutíʔθręʔ ‹it-shelf-falls› *it shades* (HS),
ęθwatíʔθręʔ ‹prediction-you-shelf-fall›
you will suspend shelf (RC 3:22);
-tiʔθręhst-: utiʔθrę́hsteh ‹shelf-fall-

'ness› *shade, shadow* (HS); -ti?θrę̨hT -: rati'?θrę̨htha'? ‹he-shelf-fall-causes› *he shades it* (HS); -tkwę? -: rutkwę́'?ę ‹he-stomach-fall-begins› *he has pleurisy* (HS); -wiθrę? -: yuwiθrę́'?ę ‹it-snow-fall-began› *frost* (H 3518); -wyah = sę̨hT -: na'?newyahsę́htha'? ‹one=another- cross-fall-causes› *one crucifies another* (HS); -yenę? -: yuyenę́'?ę ‹it-dead tree-fall-began› *partly fallen down dead tree* (RC 26:16), *fallen tree* (RC 34:2); -ačhukarę̨hnahkw -: yę̨čhuharę̨hnáhkhwa'? ‹one-oneself-beard-fall-cause-instrument› *razor* (HS); -a = čnyu?θę̨hT -: wačnyu'?θrę́htha'? ‹it-it-self-scruf skin-fall-causes› *it (animal, reptile) molts* (HS); -či -. -a?nwirę̨hT -: θwa'?nwirę́hnę ‹again-it-itself-infant-fall-caused› *abortion (by choice)* (HS); -či -. -e?rę -: θawé'?rę'? ‹again-fact-it-hair-fell› *hair fell back off* (RC 11: 28); -či -. -e?rę̨hT -: ę̨θwé'?rę̨ht ‹prediction-again-it-hair-fall-cause› *hair will fall back off* (RC 11:23); -či -. -wirę? -: θkawirę́'?ę ‹again-it-infant-fall-began› *abortion (by accident), miscarriage, premature birth* (HS), čewì·rę'?θ ‹again-one-infant-fall-begins› *one miscarries* (HS); -ne -. -(a)hkarę̨hnahnę -: neyuhkarę̨hnáhnę· ‹apart-it-bark-fall-caused-much› *it is square* (HS); -t -. -či?rę -: nakačí'?rę'? ‹hither-fact-it-ember-fell› *fire fell down* (R); -t -. -hta = wę? -: nyuhtawę́'?ę ‹hither-it-stream of water-fall-began› *at the waterfall* (R), Nyuhtawę́'?ę ‹hither-it-stream of water-fall-began› *Niagara Falls, New York*

(R); -t -. -kθę -: nakákθę̨'? ‹hither-fact-it-dish-fell› *dish fell* (R); -t -. -kerhę -: nahrakyérhę̨'? ‹hither-fact-he-body-fell› *he fell* (R); ti -. -hwe?nę̨hT -: thwa'?kahwé'?nę̨ht ‹so-fact-it-??-fall-caused› *in a trice, suddenly* (HS); -yah -. -a?θę̨hT -: yę̨yę́'?θę̨ht ‹thither-prediction-one-X-fall-cause› *one will drop it there* (RC 12:2); -yah -. -kerhę -: yahwahrakyérhę̨'? ‹thither-fact-he-body-fell› *he fell there* (RC 26:28); -yah -. -trahsę̨hT -: yahwahratráhsę̨ht ‹thither-fact-he-fungus-fall-caused› *he dropped fungus there* (RC 32:10); -ne+t -. -atkerhę̨hT -: nę̨'?nahratkyérhę̨ht ‹apart-fact-thither-he-himself-body-fall-caused› *he cast himself down there* (RC 26:31); tha+ne -. -(a)hkarę̨hT -: tha'?newáhkarę̨ht ‹unusual-apart-it-bark-fall-caused› *it is an unusual kind of square* (RC 23:2); ti+ne -. -(a)hkarę̨hnahnę -: thwa'?thrahkarę̨hnáhnę·'? ‹so-fact-apart-he-bark-fall-caused-much› *he made them square* (RC 12:2); ú·?y ti -. -ę? -: ú·'?y tì·wę'?θ ‹other so-it-fall-begins› *one is pregnant* (HS).

-ę - give. *v.r.-t.* See: -aw -.

-ę - say. *v.r.-t.* See: -a'nę -/ -ę -/ -ihrę -.

ę̨či - future mode+repetitive. *v.pfx.* The form ę̨či - occurs before the consonants θ or t, or the clusters '?n or '?t. The form ę̨č - occurs before the consonant y and the y is dropped. The form ę̨θ - occurs elsewhere.

ę́·či one (RC 24:1) [Lawson «Unche» 'one']. *part.* ti?ę́·či ‹so-one› *another* (RC 12:2); ę̨čihá·?nye? ‹one-going

Tuscarora Pronunciation Key:
/a/ law; /e/ hat; /i/ pizza; /u/ tune; /ę/ hint; /č/ cheese; /h/ hoe; /m/ mother; /s/ same; /t/ do (before a vowel y, or w), too (elsewhere); /k/ gale (before a vowel y or w), kale (elsewhere); /n/ inhale (before a consonant or word-final), note (elsewhere), /r/ hiss (before a consonant or word-final), run (trilled as in Italian, elsewhere); /w/ cuff (before a consonant other than y or word-final), way (elsewhere); /y/ fish (before a consonant or word-final), you (elsewhere), /θ/ thing; /?/ (the sound between the vowels in unh-unh); /·/ long vowel, /'/ high pitch; /`/ low pitch.

along› *one-by-one* (RC 15:2); ę́·či
-a'nę-: ę́·či wá·'ʔnę' ‹one it-becomes›
it coalesces (HS); ę́·či -či-.-(i)har-:
ę́·či θkáheʔr ‹one again-it-hung› *elev-
en* (R) [Lawson «Unche scauwhau»
'eleven']; ę́·či mí·ryę ‹one billion› *one
billion* (HS); ę́·či haʔ hę́ʔtahk tha+
ne-.-yaʔk-: ę́·či haʔ hę́ʔtahk thaʔneka-
yáʔkhęh ‹one the four unusual-apart-
it-breaks-much› *a quarter* (HS); ę́·či
naʔ -yahst- ti-.-yahsti-: ę́·či naʔ uyáhsteh tikayáhstih ‹one much individual
so-it-individual-is a group› *million*
(HS); ę́·či ti-.-(ę)hawi-: ę́·či tikahà·wiʔ
‹one so-it-carried› *one time, once
upon a time* (AW 45).
ę́·či -a'nę- coalesce. *v.s.* ę́·či wá·'ʔnę'
‹one it-becomes› *it coalesces* (HS).
ę́·či -či-.-(i)har- eleven. *dv.n.s.* ę́·či
θkáheʔr ‹one again-it-hung› *eleven*
(R) [Lawson «Unche scauwhau» 'elev-
en'].
ę́·či haʔ hę́ʔtahk tha+ne-.-yaʔk- a quarter. *dv.n.s.* ę́·či haʔ hę́ʔtahk thaʔneka-
yáʔkhęh ‹one the four unusual-apart-
it-breaks-much› *a quarter* (HS).
ę́·či mí·ryę ‹one billion› one billion (HS).
n.s.
ę́·či naʔ -yahst- ti-.-yahsti- million.
dv.n.s. ę́·či naʔ uyáhsteh tikayáhstih
‹one much individual so-it-individual-
is a group› *million* (HS).
ę́·či ti-.-(ę)hawi- one time, once upon a
time. *dv.n.s.* ę́·či tikahà·wiʔ ‹one so-it-
carried-X› *one time, once upon a time*
(AW 45).
ęčihá·ʔnyeʔ ‹one-going along› one-by-
one (RC 15:2). *part.*
-ę̊čiʔwahT- destroy, exterminate, oblit-
erate, stop. *v.r.-t.* hab: -, pnt: -ʔ, stat: -
, prog: -, prp: -, dst: -, caus: -, rvs: -,
dat: -, n-inc. waʔkayakęčíʔwaht *they
destroyed it, they exterminated it, they
obliterated it, they stopped it* (RC

12:11).
ęh uh! (said when lifting something
heavy) (R). *part.*
-ęh- dust, fine grain meal; gunpowder.
n.r. n-poss., inc., n.sfx. -ęʔ. awę́hęʔ
dust, fine grain meal: gunpowder
(HS); -ęhakaʔnę-: rawęhakáʔnęʔ ‹he-
gunpowder-is much› *he had plenty of
gunpowder* (HS); -ęharahkw-: ręharáhkhwaʔ ‹he-gunpowder-gathers› *he
loads gunpowder in it* (HS); -ne-.
-ęhuri-: newęhú·ryeh ‹apart-it-fine
grain meal-stir› *porridge* (HS).
-ęharahkw- load gunpowder. *v.s.-a.i.*
ręharáhkhwaʔ ‹he-gunpowder-gathers›
he loads gunpowder in it (HS).
-(ę)haw-/-haʔw- bear, bring, carry, take.
v.r.-t. hab: -s ~ -ęhs, pnt: -ʔ, stat: -ʔ,
prog: -, prp: -, dst: -ihθę-, caus: -, rvs:
-, dat: -, inc.-ɸ-ag./pat. The basic
meaning is *transport something by
hand.* The form -ęhaw- occurs following certain incorporated noun roots;
the form -haʔw- occurs in the imperative; the form -haw- occurs elsewhere. The morphological signifi-
cance of the final -i- of the stem
-hawi- is uncertain. In the past it has
been taken to be part of the stative
aspect suffix. However, since it also
occurs with the future and factual
modes without the expected final -k it
seems unlikely that it could be part of
an aspect suffix. In word-final position there is apparent free variation in
the pronunciation of the vowel *a* of
this stem between [æ], a principal
allophone of the phoneme *e*, and [*a*],
a principal allophone of the phoneme
a. Here, the stem is written «-hew-»
where the [æ] allophone has been
heard. íkhaʔw *I am holding it* (R),
wá·khaʔw *I take it* (R), wáʔkhaʔw *I
took it* (R), rahà·węhs *he takes it*

(HS), waʔkáheʔw *it brought it* (RC 3:37), θháʔw *take it!* (R); −(ẹ)hawi −: ẹhrahà·wiʔ ‹prediction-he-bring-X› *he will take it* (HS), khà·wiʔ ‹I-bring-X› *I bring it* (R), wakhà·wiʔ ‹I-brought-X› *I am taking it* (R); −či −. −(ẹ)hawi −: čehà·wiʔ ‹again-one-brings-X› *one brings back* (RC 3:28), θhrahà·wiʔ ‹again-he-brings-X› *he carries back* (R); −t −. −(ẹ)haw −: nákhaʔw ‹hither-fact-I-brought› *I brought it back* (R), náhshaʔw ‹hither-fact-you-brought› *you brought it back* (RC 3:29); −t −. −haʔw −: káθhaʔw ‹hither-you-bring› *bring it!* (R); ti −. −(ẹ)hawi −: tikahà·wiʔ ‹so-it-brings-X› *time, at that time* (HS); ti+yah −. −(ẹ)haw −: thwehráhews ‹so-thither-he-brings› *he guesses, he reckons* (HS); ti+yah+či −. −(ẹ)haw −: thwečé·haws ‹so-thither-again-one-brings› *birthday* (HS); −(a)hahẹhawi −: rahahẹhà·wiʔ ‹he-path-brought-X› *guide* (HS); −čihkwẹhawihθẹ −: waʔka-yečihkwẹhawíhθẹʔ ‹fact-they-club-brought-X-many› *they carried clubs* (RC 24:6); −čiʔrẹhawi −: račiʔrẹhà·wiʔ ‹he-ember-brought-X› *Lucifer* (HS); −(ẹ)ʔteyẹhawihT −: kaʔteyẹhawíhthaʔ ‹it-crowd-bring-causes› *bus* (R); −ker = hẹhawihT −: yekyerhẹhawíhthaʔ ‹one-body-bring-causes› *litter, stretcher* (HS); −rihwẹhaw −: rarihwẹhaʔw ‹he-matter-brought› *he held it to be thus* (RC 12:6); −wyahsẹhawi −: rawyah-sẹhà·wiʔ ‹he-cross-brings-X› *he carries the cross* (HS); −yaʔθẹhawiʔ −: rayaʔθẹhà·wiʔθ ‹he-track-bring-X-be-

gins› *he trails* (HS); −'nẹwẹhaw −: waʔkayeʔnẹwẹhaʔw ‹fact-they-kettle-brought› *they carried kettle* (RC 24:6); −či −. −ʔteyhaw −: θkaʔtéyhews ‹again-it-crowd-brings› *it brings crowd repeatedly* (RC 30:29), *bus* (R); ti −. −aʔ = tẹhawi −: tihraʔtẹhà·wiʔ ‹so-he-projectile-brings-X› *he carried so many projectiles* (RC 24:2); −yah −. −(ẹ)ʔti = kẹhrhaw −: wehrẹʔtikẹrhews ‹thither-he-mind-brings› *he apprehends it, he solves it* (HS); −ne+či −. −čheʔwẹhaw −: nẹθahračheʔwẹhaʔw ‹apart-fact-again-he-squash-brought› *he took back two squash* (RC 7:6); −atkẹheyẹʔnẹhawih = nahkw −: yẹtkẹheyẹʔnẹhawihnáhkhwaʔ ‹one-oneself-die-cause-bring-causes-instrument› *litter, stretcher* (HS); eh-náhkye −(ẹ)hawihT −: ehnáhkye raha-wíhthaʔ ‹below he-bring-X-causes› *he abases* (HS); kwẹhs −yah −. −(ẹ)haw − ti −. −nurẹ −: kwẹhs yaryéhaʔw tikanú·rẹ· ‹no thither-unknown-one-bring so-it-is precious› *it is inestimable* (HS).

−(ẹ)hawi − bring, take. *v.s.-t.* ẹhrahà·wiʔ ‹prediction-he-bring-X› *he will take it* (HS), khà·wiʔ ‹I-bring-X› *I bring it* (R), wakhà·wiʔ ‹I-brought-X› *I am taking it* (R).

−ẹhew − hoe. *v.r.-a.i.* hab: -ahs, pnt: -ʔ, stat: -, prog: -, prp: -, dst: -, caus: -, rvs: -, dat: -, n-inc. This root is possibly in Lawson's «Wauche-woc-noc» 'Hoe' if this is a copyists error for *«Wanghe-wocnoc», representing *wẹhewáʔnaʔ, a hypothetical nominal-ization formed with the causative

-ʔT-. ręhè·wahs *he hoes* (R), wah-
ręhe'w *he hoed* (R), waʔnyakęhe'w
the two of them hoed (RC 5:18).

-ęhey- die. *v.s.-a.i.* See: **-ihey-**.

ę̀·hę· yea, yes (RC 3:17) [Gallatin «eahuh» 'Yes']. *part.* Also: **ę̀·hęh**.

ę̀·hęh yea, yes (R) [Gallatin «eahuh»
'Yes']. *part.* Also: **ę̀·hę·**.

-ęhkęrahT- filter, strain. *v.r.-t.* hab: -ha',
pnt: -, stat: -, prog: -, prp: -, dst: -,
caus: -, rvs: -, dat: -, n- inc. ręh-
kęráhtha' *he filters it, he strains it*
(HS).

-ęhkwar-/-ęhkwaruʔčr- bridle. *n.r.* aln:
akęhkwarúʔčrawęh *my bridle* (R),
inc., n.sfx. -eh. The first form occurs
when the root is incorporated, the second when it is unincorporated. awęh-
kwarúʔčreh *bridle* (HS); **-ęhkwaru'nar** =
hu-: ręhkwaruʔnárhuhs ‹he-bridle-
hooks› *he bridles* (HS); **-a'nęhkwaru** =
'narihsi-: raʔnęhkwaruʔnaríhsyęhs ‹he-
himself-bridle-fasten-undoes› *he unbridles it* (HS).

-ęhkwaru'narhu- bridle. *v.s.-a.i.* ręhkwaruʔnárhuhs ‹he-bridle-hooks› *he bridles* (HS).

-ęhkwath- be thick with. *v.r.-s.i.* stat: -ę,
prog: -, prp: -, dst: -, caus: -, rvs: -,
dat: -, n-inc. yawęhkwá·thę *it is thick
with, it is close (as of trees), it is full
of* (RC 32:7); **-ęhkwathaʔT-**: ręhkwa-
tháʔtha' ‹he-be thick with-causes› *he
thickens it* (HS).

-ęhkwathaʔT- thicken. *v.s.-t.* ręhkwa-
tháʔtha' ‹he-be thick with-causes› *he
thickens it* (HS).

-ęhnahkw- expressive. *dv.n.s.* węhnáh-
khwa' ‹it-means-instrument› *expressive* (HS).

-ęhnahkw- indicate, mean. *v.s.-a.i.* ręhnáhkhwa' ‹he-means-instrument› *he
indicates, he means* (HS).

-(ę)hnęθhar- clasp, embrace. *v.r.-t.* stat:
-ɸ, hab: -ɸ, pnt: -ę', prog: -, prp: -,
dst: -, caus: -, rvs: -, dat: -, n-inc.
ręhnę́θhar *he clasps it, he embraces it*
(HS), rawęhnę́θhar *he embraced it*
(HS), ęhręhnę́θharę' *he will embrace
it* (HS): **-(ę)hnęθhar-**: uhnę́θhareh
‹embrace› *armful, embrace* (HS); **-či-**.
-(ę)hnęθhar-: θhręhnę́θhar ‹again-he-
embraces› *he reembraces* (HS); **-či-**.
-(ę)hnęθharaT-: θwęhnę́θhara·t ‹again-
it-embrace-stands› *armful* (HS).

-(ę)hnęθhar- armful, embrace. *n.s.* uh-
nę́θhareh ‹embrace› *armful, embrace*
(HS).

-ęhr- amount, kind, sort. *n.r.* n-poss.,
inc., n.sfx. -. Found only incorporated.
-ęhriyu-: yawęhrí·yu· ‹it-kind-is great›
there are many (RC 3:76), kakawęh-
rí·yu· ‹they-kind-are great› *they are
many* (RC 10:3); **-ęhriyuha'nyeʔ-**:
węhriyuhá·ʔnye' ‹it-kind-is great-going along› *a sequence of many* (RC
24:4); **-ęhrukʷanyę-**: naʔnęhrukwá·-
nyęh ‹one=another-kind-spread out-
much› *one treats another* (HS); **ti-**.
-ęhrake-: tyawęhrá·kye· ‹so-it-kind-is
in number› *it is so many* (RC 6:7),
nęyawęhrá·kye·k ‹so-prediction-it-
kind-be in number› *it will be so many
kinds* (RC 9:5); **ti-**. **-ęhraʔθ-**: tikaka-
wę́hraʔθ ‹so-they-kind-are of a size›
they are larger in number (R); **ti-**.
-ęhriyuha'nyeʔ: nękakawęhriyuhá·ʔ-
nye' ‹so-prediction-they-kind-be great-
going along› *they will be a great
many* (RC 33:8); **-yah+ne-**. **-a'nęh** =
ra'nęʔ-: yaʔnęθwaʔnéhraʔnę' ‹thither-
apart-prediction-you-yourself-kind-be-
come› *you will have your fight* (R).

-ę°hr- dirt, soil. *n.r.* n-poss., inc., n.sfx.
-eh. This root occurs without a pronominal prefix when the external locative is present. It is probably to be
seen in Gallatin's «wunraukwah» 'Val-

ley', from *węhrá·kwę *it picked up dirt.* awę́hreh *dirt, soil* (R); -ę°h=rahęsči: węhrahę́sči ‹it-dirt-is black› *black earth, muck* (R); -ę°hrak‴ahT -: yakęhrakwáhtha' ‹one-dirt-cuts up› *pick ax* (HS); -ę°hrarę -: yawęhrà·rę' ‹it-dirt-added› *aground* (HS); -ę°h=ratkęh -: yawęhrá·tkęh ‹it-dirt-is rotten› *fallow* (HS); -ę°hrayęthu -: yawęhrayę́·thwę ‹it-dirt-planted› *alluvium* (HS); -ę°hrayę'k‴ -: rę́hrayę'kws ‹he-dirt-shoots› *he throws it on the ground* (HS); -ę°hra'k -: ręhrá'kha' ‹he-dirt-digs› *he burrows, he roots* (HS); -ę°hra'ke -: ęhrá'kye ‹dirt-at› *on dirt* (RC 3:41); -ę°hra'rhę -: yawęhrá'rhę· ‹it-dirt-grab-bed-much› *it touches ground, touching ground* (HS); -ę°h=ra'ne -: aryawę́hra'nek ‹unknown-it-dirt-be present› *that there be dirt* (RC 21:2); -ę°hra'neti(y) -: ręhra'netì·yęhs ‹he-dirt-self-produces› *he tills* (H-notebook); -ę°hra'θk‴ahT -: yakęhra'-θkwáhtha' ‹one-dirt-carry away-causes› *rubbish-cart* (HS); -ę°hrihstkę'T -: ręhrihstkę́'tha' ‹he-dirt-jilt-causes› *he enriches land* (HS); -a'nęhrar -: u'nę́hrareh ‹self-dirt-be in› *dirt, filth* (R), yu'nę́hra'r ‹it-itself-dirt-is in› *it is dirty* (R); -a'nęhrar -.#hči: u'nęhraréhči ‹self-dirt-be in-very› *dirty* (HS); -a'nęhrarawęri -: ra'nęhrarawę̀·rih ‹he-himself-dirt-be in-stirs› *he dirties it, he soils it* (HS); -tahskwa'nęhrar -: yutahskwa'nę́hra'r ‹it-domestic animal-dirt-is in› *animals are dirty* (R); -nęhsa'nęhrar -: unęhsa'nę́hrareh ‹house-dirt-be in› *dirty house* (R); -ne -. -ę°hra'netyę -: nehręhra'né·tyęhs ‹apart-he-dirt-is present-much› *he cultivates, he farms* (HS); -ne -. -ę°hrurę -: nehręhrù·ręhs ‹apart-he-dirt-splits› *he plows* (HS); -ne -. -ę°hrurę- -tuhn -: neyakęhrurę́hstha' utúh-neh ‹apart-one-dirt-splits paddle› *plowshare* (HS); -ne -. -a'nęhraT -: nehra'nę́hra'nę ‹apart-he-himself-dirt-was present› *he barricades with earth* (HS); kę' -ne -. -ę°hruręha'nye' -: kę' neyawęhrurę́há·'nye' ‹where apart-it-dirt-split-going along› *furrow* (HS).

-ęhra· - fry. v.r.-t. hab: -, pnt: -, stat: -, prog: -, prp: -he-, dst: -, caus: -hw-, rvs: -, dat: -, inc.-ɸ-pat. węhrá·he' *it is frying* (HS); -ęhrahw -: rę́hraws ‹he-fry-causes› *he fries* (HS); -ta'na=ręhra·he -: kata'naręhrá·heh ‹it-bread-fry-is going to› *fried bread* (R); -'nhęhsęhra·he -: ka'nhęhsęhrá·he' ‹it-egg-fry-is going to› *fried eggs* (R); -'wahręhrahwst -: ye'wahręhráwstha' ‹one-meat-fry-causes› *frying pan* (HS).

-ę°hrahęsči - black earth, muck. *dv.n.s.* węhrahę́sči ‹it-dirt-is black› *black earth, muck* (R).

-ęhrahw - fry. v.s.-t. rę́hraws ‹he-fry-causes› *he fries it* (HS).

-ę°hrak‴ahT - pick ax. *dv.n.s.* yakęhrakáhtha' ‹one-dirt-cuts up› *pick ax* (HS).

-ę°hrayęthu - alluvium. *dv.n.s.* yawęhrayę́·thwę ‹it-dirt-planted› *alluvium* (HS).

-ę°hratkęh - fallow. *dv.n.s.* yawęhrá·tkęh ‹it-dirt-is rotten› *fallow* (HS).

Tuscarora Pronunciation Key:
/a/ law; /e/ hat; /i/ pizza; /u/ tune; /ę/ hint; /č/ cheese; /h/ hoe; /m/ mother; /s/ same; /t/ do (before a vowel y, or w), too (elsewhere); /k/ gale (before a vowel y or w), kale (elsewhere); /n/ inhale (before a consonant or word-final), note (elsewhere), /r/ hiss (before a consonant or word-final), run (trilled as in Italian, elsewhere); /w/ cuff (before a consonant other than y or word-final), way (elsewhere); /y/ fish (before a consonant or word-final), you (elsewhere), /θ/ thing; /'/ (the sound between the vowels in unh-unh); /·/ long vowel, /´/ high pitch; /`/ low pitch.

-ehrayę?kʷ – throw on the ground. *v.s.-t.* ręhrayę'?kws ‹he-dirt-shoots› *he throws it on the ground* (HS).

-ę°hra?k – burrow, root. *v.s.-a.i.* ręhrá'?-kha? ‹he-dirt-digs› *he burrows, he roots* (HS).

-ę°hra?neti(y) – till. *v.s.-a.i.* ręhra?ne-tì·yęhs ‹he-dirt-self-produces› *he tills* (HS).

-ę°hra?θkʷahT – rubbish cart. *dv.n.s.* ya-kęhra'?θkwáhtha? ‹one-dirt-carry away-causes› *rubbish-cart* (HS).

-ęhreθrę? – be apprehensive, be fearful, be in fear. *v.r.-a.i.* hab: -θ, pnt: -ɸ, stat: -ɸ, prog: -, prp: -, dst: -, caus: -T-, rvs: -, dat: -, n-inc. ręhré·θrę'?θ *he is apprehensive, he is fearful, he is in fear, he is alarmed* (HS), ęhręhré·θrę'? *he will be fearful* (HS), wahręh-ré·θrę'? *he was afraid* (RC 34:5); **-ęhreθrę?T** –: awęhreθrę'?neh ‹be fear-ful-cause› *fear* (HS).

-ęhreθrę?T – fear. *dv.n.s.* awęhreθrę'?neh ‹be fearful-cause› *fear* (HS).

-ę°hretihs – hunger, have hunger. *v.r.-s.i.* stat: -ɸ, prog: -, prp: -, dst: -, caus: -, rvs: -, dat: III (-ati-/-ę-), n-inc. This root is unusual in that the bare stem occurs as an independent noun. In addition, the stem requires the connective **-n**– before derivational suffixes such as the dative. ęhré·tihs *hunger* (HS), rawęhré·tihs *he is hungry* (HS); **-ę°hretihsn** –{dative III}: na'?nęh-retihsná·tih ‹one-another-has hunger-for› *one starves another* (HS); **-t** –. **-ę°hretihs** –: nwakęhré·tihs ‹hither-I-have hunger› *I am hungry* (RC 30:38).

-ę°hretihsn –{dative III} starve. *v.s.-t.* na'?-nęhretihsná·tih ‹one=another-has hunger-for› *one starves another* (HS).

-ę°hrihstkę?T – enrich land. *v.s.-a.i.* ręh-rihstké'?tha? ‹he-dirt-jilt-causes› *he enriches land* (HS).

-ęhriyu – be many. *v.s.-s.i.* yawęhrí·yu· ‹it-kind-is great› *there are many* (RC 3:76), kakwęhrí·yu· ‹they-kind-are great› *they are many* (RC 10:3).

-ęhriyuha'nye? – a sequence of many. *dv.n.s.* węhriyuhá·'?nye? ‹it-kind-is great-going along› *a sequence of many* (RC 24:4).

-ęhrukʷanyę – treat. *v.s.-t.* na'?nęhrukwá·-nyęh ‹one=another-kind-spreads out-much› *one treats another* (HS).

-ęhs habitual aspect. *v.r.sfx.*

-ęhsę – bake, broil, parch, roast, toast. *v.r.-t.* hab: -h, pnt: -'?, stat: -·, prog: -, prp: -, dst: -, caus: -, rvs: -, dat: -, inc.-ɸ-/-a'?θk-pat. ręhsęh *he bakes it, he parches it, he roasts it* (HS), ra-węhsę· *he is roasting* (HS); **-a?=θkęhsę** –: aryę'?θkęhsę'? ‹unknown-one-X-parch› *that one parch it* (RC 21:2); **-či?ręhsę** –: ruči'?ręhsę· ‹he-ember-parched› *he bickers* (HS); **-nęhęhsę** –: kanęhęhsęh ‹it-corn-parches› *it parches corn* (RC 28:11), *corn roaster* (R), kanęhęhsęhk ‹it-corn-parched› *parched corn* (RC 15:10); **-nęθęhsę** –: ranęθęhsęh ‹he-potato-parches› *he roasts, bakes potatoes, tubers* (H 2484); **-ta?naręhsęhkw** –: yeta'?naręh-sęhkhwa? ‹one-bread-bake-instrument› *oven* (R); **-a'nę?węhsę** –: wahra'?nę'?-węhsę'? ‹fact-he-himself-back-parched› *he parched his back* (RC 26: 26).

-ęhshek habitual aspect. *v.r.sfx.*

-ę°hskwi(k) – squeeze, wrap up. *v.r.-t.* hab: -hs, pnt: ()-ɸ, stat: -·, prog: -, prp: -, dst: -, caus: -'?T-, rvs: -, dat: -, n-inc. węhskwi· *it is wrapped up* (RC 35:23), wa'?akęhskwik *one wrapped it up* (RC 27:6), ęyakęhskwik *one will squeeze it* (RC 20:1); **-či** –. **-ęhskwi** –: θhręhskwihs ‹again-he-wraps up› *he wraps it up again* (HS); **-ęhskwi?T** –: awęhskwí'?neh ‹wrap up-cause› *pac-*

kage (R); **–ęnhę̄hskwi(k)**–: ręnhę́h-skwihs ‹he-be alive-wraps up› *he swallows* (HS), rawęnhę́hskwi· ‹he-be alive-wrapped up› *he swallowed* (HS), wa'awęnhę́hskwik ‹fact-it-be alive-wrapped up› *it was swallowed up* (RC 7:2); **–ęhskwi'nakęw**: rawęhskwí'na-kęw ‹he-wrap up-cause-in› *in his belongings* (RC 8:27); **–ęhskwi'nihr**–{dative III}: wa'akęhskwi'níhrę' ‹fact-one-wrap-stood up-for› *one had wrapped it up* (RC 27:6).

–ęhskwi'T–package. *n.s.* awęhskwí'neh ‹wrap up-cause› *package* (R).

–ęhT–field. *n.r.* n-poss., inc., n.sfx. -. Found only incorporated in the following form. **–ne**–. **–ęhthyak**–: nehrę́hthya'ks ‹apart-he-field-crosses over› *he crosses a country* (HS).

–ęhta'θrę–shirt, underwear. *dv.n.r.* węhtá'θrę· *shirt, underwear* (RC 34:22).

–ęhuhskwar–mouthful. *n.r.* n-poss., n-inc., n.sfx. -eh. awęhúhskwareh *mouthful* (R); **–či**–. **–ęhuhskwaraT**–: θwęhúhskwara·t ‹again-it-mouthful-stands› *one draught, one mouthful* (HS).

–ę°hwa'nę' be nephew, be niece. *v.r.-k.* kęyęhwá'nę' *my nephew* (RC 25:8), rawęhwá'nę' *his nephew, his niece* (HS); **–ę°hwa'nę'čr**–: awęhwa'né'čreh ‹be nephew-'ness› *nephew(hood)* (R), yakęhwa'né'čreh ‹one-is niece-'ness› *niece(hood)* (R); **–ę°hwa'nę'čhę(T)**–: rawęhwa'né'čhę' ‹he-be nephew-'ness-lay› *his nephew* (RC 11:26).

–ękhe–exist. *v.r.-a.i.* hab: -, pnt: -, stat: -

·, prog: -, prp: -, dst: -tyę-, caus: -, rvs: -, dat: -, n-inc. **–ękhetyę**–: wękhé·-tyęh ‹it-exists-many› *they are alive* (RC 12:5).

–ękhwi–tell legends, be a poet. *v.r.-t.* hab: -h, pnt: -, stat: -, prog: -, prp: -, dst: -, caus: -ahT-, rvs: -, dat: -, n-inc. rę́khwih *he tells legends; poet* (HS); **–ękhwyahT**–: ękhwyaht ‹tell a fable-cause› *myth, story, tale, tradition* (HS), awę́khwyaht ‹tell a fable-cause› *legend, myth* (R); **–ne**–. **–ękhwyurę**–: neyawękhwyú·rę· ‹apart-it-tell a fable-splits› *fabulous* (HS).

–ękhwyahT–legend, myth, story, tale, tradition. *n.s.* ę́khwyaht ‹tell a fable-cause› *myth, story, tale, tradition* (HS), awę́khwyaht ‹tell a fable-cause› *legend, myth* (R).

–ęku–reversive. *v.r.sfx.* The main use of the reversive is to indicate that the action of the verb is undone or reversed (e.g., **wahrę̨hrawihsę́·ku'** ‹fact-he-soil-give-undid-undid› *he took off topsoil*).

–ę°kuh–go through. *v.r.-a.i.* hab: -θ, pnt: -φ, stat: -φ, prog: -, prp: -, dst: -, caus: -T-, rvs: -, dat: -, inc.-φ-pat. When present with this root, an incorporated noun root expresses the medium through which someone/something goes. **–ę°kuhsT**–: kękúhstha' ‹one-goes through-causes› *sifter* (R); **–ę°kuhT**–: rękúhtha' ‹he-go through-causes› *he sifts it* (HS); **–ę°kuhnahkw**–: yakękuh-náhkhwa' ‹one-go through-causes-instrument› *colander, sieve* (HS); **–ne**–.

-ę°kuh -: newę́·kuhθ ‹apart-it-goes through› *diarrhea* (RC 22:1); -ne -. -ę°kuhT -: neyawękúhnę ‹apart-it-go through-caused› *laxative* (RC 18:4); *purgative; it purges* (HS), newękúh- tha⁷ ‹apart-it-go through-causes› *it pierces it, it pervades it* (HS); -a'nę= kuhT -: wa⁷kayę⁷nę́·kuht ‹fact-they- themselves-go through-caused› *they passed through* (RC 26:15), wa⁷nę- kúhtha⁷ ‹it-itself-go through-caused› *it is transient* (HS), ra⁷nękúhtha⁷ ‹he- himself-go through-causes› *he passes by, he surpasses it* (HS), ęka⁷nę́·kuht ‹prediction-I-myself-go through-cause› *I will pass through* (RC 11:23), ę- wa⁷nę́·kuht ‹prediction-it-itself-go through-cause› *it will pass through* (RC 15:4), yu⁷nękúhnę ‹it-itself-go through-caused› *bygone* (HS); -a'nę= kuhnahkw -: yę⁷nękuhnáhkhwa⁷ ‹one- oneself-go through-causes-instrument› *passage* (HS); -a'nękuhnahnę -: ru⁷nę- kuhnáhnę· ‹he-himself-go through- caused-much› *he traversed* (HS), wa⁷- kayę⁷nękuhnáhnę⁷ ‹fact-they-them- selves-go through-caused-much› *they escaped* (AW 102); -ne -. -a'nękuhT -: nehra⁷nękúhtha⁷ ‹apart-he-himself-go through-causes› *he survives* (HS); -yah -. -a'nękuhT -: weyu⁷nękúhnę ‹thither-it-itself-go through-caused› *it passes through there* (RC 3:56); -a'ne= wrękuhT -: yu⁷newrękúhnę ‹it-itself- air-went through› *draft of air* (AG); -t -. -čhe⁷wękuh -: nayučhe⁷wę́·kuh ‹hither-fact-it-gourd-goes through› *it goes through a gourd* (RC 15:4); -ne+t -. -ekękuh -: ne⁷nyawekę́·kuh ‹a- part-hither-it-liquid-goes through› *it goes through liquid* (RC 6:9); ti -. -a'nękuhnahnę -: nę⁷nękuhnáhnę⁷ ‹so- fact-it-itself-go through-caused-many› *it passed through there a number of*

times (RC 17:1); -ne -. -athukstę= kuhT -: newathukstękúhtha⁷ ‹apart-it- itself-light up-'ness-go through-causes› *translucent* (HS); ha⁷ -a'nękuhT -: ha⁷ yu⁷nękúhnę ‹the it-itself-go through- caused› *the past* (HS); kwęhs -yah+ ne -. -ę'nękuhT -: kwęhs ya⁷narę⁷nę- kúhthek ‹no thither-apart-it-day-go through-cause› *it is impenetrable* (HS); thu⁷níhska⁷ -ne -. -ę°kuhT -: thu⁷níhska⁷ nehrękúhtha⁷ ‹here-and- there apart-he-go through-causes› *he bastes it* (HS).

-ę°kuhnahkw - colander, sieve. *dv.n.s.* yakękuhnáhkhwa⁷ ‹one-go through- causes-instrument› *colander, sieve* (HS).

-ę°kuhsT - sifter. *dv.n.s.* From *yakę- kúhstha⁷ *one sifts*, with exceptional loss of the initial syllable. kękúhstha⁷ ‹one-goes through-causes› *sifter* (R).

-ę°kuhT - sift. *v.s.-t.* rękúhtha⁷ ‹he-go through-causes› *he sifts it* (HS).

-ę°kʷe - human being, man, person, woman. *n.r.* n-poss., inc., n.sfx. -h; be human being. *v.r.-a.i.* stat: -, hab: -, pnt: -, prog: -, prp: -, dst: -, caus: -⁷T- , rvs: -, dat: -, n-inc. Possession is expressed by a dative construction. This root requires the increment -hst - when incorporated. ę́·kweh *human being* (RC 1:1), *female human* (R) [Lawson «Unqua» 'Indians'], rę́·kweh *man, male human* (RC 12:1); -ę°kʷe -. #áh: ękweháh ‹human-little› *manne- quin* (R); -ę°kʷe -.#ęwe: ękwehę̀·we ‹hu-man-genuine› *Indian* (R), *Tusca- rora* (RC 30:1) [Lawson «Occoahawa» 'Old Man']; -ę°kʷehčayę -.#áh: ękweh- čayęháh ‹human-be of no account› *person of no account* (RC 28:1); -ę°kʷehke: ękwéhkye ‹human-at› *a- mong the people* (R); -ę°kʷehsayę -: ękwéhsayę⁷ ‹human-vulgar› *dwarf:*

Little People (mythic) (R), *Little Folk*
(AW 45); -(ę°)kʷehst -: ukwéhstch
‹human-'ness› *animal, being, boy,
entity, girl, living (animate) person*
(HS), awękwéhstreh ‹human-'ness›
person (PC); -ę°kʷehstakęre -: wękweh-
stakę̀·reʔ ‹it-human-'ness-is scarce›
persons, men, are scarce (H 2892);
-ę°kʷehstaks -: sękwehstá·ksę· ‹you-
human-'ness-is bad› *you are a bad
person* (R); -ę°kʷehstaks -.#haʔnę?: kayakękwehstaksęháʔnęʔ ‹they-human-
'ness-is bad-many› *bad humans* (RC
27:31); -ę°kʷehstaksę? -: rękwehstá·-
ksęʔθ ‹he-human-'ness-be bad-begins›
he deteriorates (HS); -ę°kʷehsta =
kwahsT -: kękwehstákwahst ‹I-human-
'ness-is good› *I am good, I am a good
person* (R); -ę°kʷehstanęha·ʔ -: awę-
kwehstranęha·ʔ ‹human-'ness-be old›
old person (PC); -ę°kʷehstanehra =
kwahsT -: rawękwehstanehrá·kwahst
‹he-human-'ness-surprise-causes› *he is
majestic, magnificent* (HS); -ę°kʷehsta =
nuręhkwahT -:   rawękwehstanurę́h-
kwaht ‹he-human-'ness-appeal to-
causes› *he is an affable person* (HS);
-ę°kʷehstaθahraʔT -: rawękwehstaθáʔnę
‹he-human-'ness-be soft› *he is agreeable* (HS); -ę°kʷehstaθe·ʔ: awękweh-
stá·θe·ʔ ‹human-'ness-new› *youth*
(HS); -ę°kʷehstaʔęyeθ -{dative I}: naʔ-
nękwehstaʔęyeθáʔθeh ‹one=another-
human-'ness-cost-is long-for› *he has
high regard for another* (HS); -ę°kʷeh =
stęte: rękwehstę́·te ‹he-human-'ness-
certain one› *a particular male human*

(RC 2:1); -ę°kʷehstuʔkręʔT -: rawę-
kwehstuʔkrę́ʔthaʔ ‹he-human-'ness-
float-causes› *he unmans* (HS);
-ę°kʷeʔ -: rawękwéʔę ‹he-be human-
began› *he is subject, he is vanquished*
(HS), kakawękwéʔę ‹they-be human-
began› *they are conquered* (HS),
kayakę́·kweʔθ ‹they-human-begin›
their people (R), rę́·kweʔθ ‹he-human-
begins› *he becomes tame, he succumbs* (HS); -ę°kʷeʔT -: rękwéʔthaʔ
‹he-be human-causes› *he subdues, he
vanquishes* (HS); -t -.-ę°kʷehstayeri -:
thrękwehstayè·riʔ ‹hither-he-human-
'ness-is correct› *he is perfect* (HS);
ti -.-ę°kʷehstuʔnę -: tihrękwehstúʔnę·
‹so-he-human-'ness-is a kind of› *he is
that kind of human* (RC 14:1); -a'nę =
kʷehstawęniyu -: raʔnękwehstawęnì·-
yuʔ ‹he-himself-human-'ness-is God›
he is theandric, he is a man-god (HS);
-a'nękʷehstihsʔa -: raʔnękwehstíhsʔahs
‹he-himself-human-'ness-finishes› *he
matures* (HS), ruʔnękwehstíhsʔę ‹he-
himself-human-'ness-finished› *he is in
the prime of life* (HS); čwe -.-a'nę°kʷe -.
#ęwe.#kęhaʔnę?: čwekaʔnękwehęwe-
kę́haʔnęʔ ‹all kinds of-it-itself-human-
genuine-many› *various Indians* (AW
101); -ę°kʷe - -ʔwahrak -: ę́·kweh raʔ-
wáhraks ‹human he-meat-eats› *cannibal* (R); sè·nę? -a'nękweʔT -: sè·nęʔ
ahruʔnękwéʔnęk ‹never unknown-he-
himself-human-cause› *he is invincible*
(HS).

-ę°kʷe - -ʔwahrak - cannibal. *dv.n.s.*
ę́·kweh raʔwáhraks ‹human he-meat-

eats› *cannibal* (R).

-ę°kʷe -.#áh mannequin. *n.s.* ękwcháh ‹human-little› *mannequin* (R).

-ę°kʷe -.#ęwe Indian; Tuscarora. *n.s.* ękwehę·we ‹human-genuine› *Indian* (R); *Tuscarora* (RC 30:1) [Lawson «Occoahawa» 'Old Man'].

-ę°kʷehčayę -.#áh person of no account. *n.s.* ękwehčayęháh ‹human-be of no account› *person of no account* (RC 28:1).

-ę°kʷehsayę – dwarf; Little People (mythic). *n.s.* ękwéhsayę' ‹human-vulgar› *dwarf: Little People (mythic)* (R). *Little Folk* (AW 45).

-(ę°)kʷehst – animal, being, boy, entity, girl, living (animate) person. *n.s.* ukwéhsteh ‹human-'ness› *animal, being, boy, entity, girl, living (animate) person* (HS). awękwéhstreh ‹human-'ness› *person* (PC).

-ę°kʷehstaksę' – deteriorate. *v.s.-a.i.* rękwehstá·ksę'θ ‹he-human-'ness-be bad-begins› *he deteriorates* (HS).

-ę°kʷehstanehrakwahsT – be majestic, be magnificent. *v.s.-s.i.* rawękwehstanehrá·kwahst ‹he-human-'ness-surprise-causes› *he is majestic, magnificent* (HS).

-ę°kʷehstanuręhkwahT – be affable. *v.s.-s.i.* rawękwehstanurę́hkwaht ‹he-human-'ness-appeal to-causes› *he is an affable person* (HS).

-ę°kʷehstaθahra'T – be agreeable. *v.s.-s.i.* rawękwehstaθá'nę ‹he-human-'ness-be soft› *he is agreeable* (HS).

-ę°kʷehstaθe·' youth. *n.s.* awękwehstá·θe·' ‹human-'ness-new› *youth* (HS).

-ę°kʷehsta'ęyeθ -{dative I} hold another in high regard. *v.s.-t.* na'nękwehsta'ęyeθá'θeh ‹one=another-human-'ness-cost-is long-for› *he has high regard for another* (HS).

-ę°kʷehstukrę'T – unman. *v.s.-a.i.* rawę-kwehstukrę́'tha' ‹he-human-'ness-be loose-causes› *he unmans* (HS).

-ę°kʷe'- be conquered, be subject, be vanquished, become tame, succumb. *v.s.-a.i.* rawękwé'ę ‹he-be human-began› *he is subject, he is vanquished* (HS). kakawękwé'ę ‹they-be human-began› *they are conquered* (HS). kayaké·kwe'θ ‹they-human-begin› *their people* (R), rę́·kwe'θ ‹he-human-begins› *he becomes tame, he succumbs* (HS).

-ę°kʷe'T – subdue, vanquish. *v.s.-t.* rękwé'tha' ‹he-be human-causes› *he subdues, he vanquishes* (HS).

ę́·kye indoors, inside (RC 35:40). *part.* ękye.#ah: ękyeháh ‹in-doors-little› *sedentary* (HS); ę́·kye -ačnahkw-: ę́·kye yęčnáhkhwa' ‹indoors one-oneself-uses-instrument› *furniture* (HS).

ękye.#ah: ękyeháh ‹indoors-little› *sedentary* (HS). *part.*

ę́·kye -ačnahkw – furniture. *dv.n.s.* ę́·kye yęčnáhkhwa' ‹indoors one-oneself-uses-instrument› *furniture* (HS).

-(ę)na·hyę – ally, associate. *v.r.-t.* hab: -, pnt: -, stat: -·, prog: -, prp: -, dst: -tyę-, caus: -hsT-, rvs: -, dat: -, n-inc. -(ę)na·hyęhčr-: unahyę́hčreh ‹ally-'ness› *alliance, association, companionship* (HS); -(ę)na·hyęhsT-: ranahyę́hstha' ‹he-ally-causes› *he allies* (HS); -a'nęna·hyęhsT -: ra'nęnahyę́hstha' ‹he-himself-ally-causes› *he allies himself, he associates himself* (HS); -ne-. -a'nęna·hyęhsT -:nehra'nęná·hyęhst ‹apart-he-himself-ally-caused› *he becomes friends with* (RC 35:41), wa'čha'nęná·hyęhst ‹fact-apart-you-yourself-ally-caused› *you became friends with someone* (RC 30:39); ha' -(ę)na·hyę -: ha' rawęná·hyę· ‹the he-allied› *ally, associate* (HS).

-(ę)na·hyę- ally, associate. *dv.n.s.* ha'' rawęná·hyę· ‹the he-allied› *ally, associate* (HS).

-(ę)na·hyęhčr- alliance, association, companionship. *n.s.* unahyę́hčreh ‹ally-'ness› *alliance, association, companionship* (HS).

-(ę)na·hyęhsT- ally. *v.s.-a.i.* ranahyę́h-stha'' ‹he-ally-causes› *he allies* (HS).

-ęnehkwr- surge, undulate, wave. *v.r.-s.i.* stat: -ę, prog: -, prp: -, dst: -, caus: -, rvs: -, dat: -, n-inc. węnéhkwręh *it undulates, it waves (as water), it surges* (HS); -ęnehkwręti(y)-: węneh-kwręti·yę ‹it-surge-produced› *waves* (SH 375).

-ęnęhyečkT- turn a somersault. *v.r.-a.i.* hab: -ęhs, pnt: -, stat: -, prog: -, prp: -, dst: -, caus: -, rvs: -, dat: -, n-inc. ręnęhyéčknęhs *he turns a somersault* (HS).

-ę°nę- construct. *v.r.-t.* hab: -, pnt: -, stat: -'', prog: -, prp: -, dst: -tyę-, caus: -, rvs: -, dat: -, n-inc. yakę̀·nę'' *building* (RC 1:2) [Gallatin «yaukuhnugh» 'House, Hut'], yakęnę́·tyę'' ‹one-constructed-many› *buildings* (R); tahuré·-tik -ę°nę-: tahuré·tik yawę̀·nę'' ‹chicken it-constructed› *poultry house* (HS), *chicken coop* (R).

-ę°nę- building. *dv.n.s.* yakę̀·nę'' *building* (RC 1:2) [Gallatin «yaukuhnugh» 'House, Hut'], yakęnę́·tyę'' ‹one-constructed-many› *buildings* (R).

-ęnęča'nę''N(e)- poke along. *v.r.-a.i.* hab: -()h, pnt: -()'', stat: -ɸ, prog: -, prp: -, dst: -, caus: -, rvs: -, dat: -, n-inc. ręnęča'nę́''teh *he pokes along* (HS), ręnęčá·''nę''n *he poked along* (HS), ęhręnęča'nę́''tc'' *he will poke along* (HS).

ęnę́hkwa''t drug, medicine (RC 9:1). *n.* See also: -nęhkwa''T-.

-ęnęhkwa''T- cure, remedy. *v.r.-t.* hab: -ha'' ~ ɸ, pnt: -ɸ, stat: -, prog: -, prp: -, dst: -, caus: -, rvs: -, dat: -, n-inc. ręnęhkwá''tha'' *he remedies it* (HS); -či-, -ęnęhkwa''T-: ęθkakawęnę́h-kwa''t ‹prediction-again-they-remedy› *it will cure them* (AW 51); -ęnęh=kwa''T- -hču·''- awę́·te: ręnę́hkwa''t ráhču·'' awę́·te ‹he-remedies he-carves thing› *surgeon* (HS).

-ęnęhkwa''T- -hču·''- awę́·te surgeon. *dv.n.s.* ręnę́hkwa''t ráhču·'' awę́·te ‹he-remedies he-carves thing› *surgeon* (HS).

-(ę)nęhr- scalp, hair with skin attached. *n.r.* inaln: ranęhré''kye *his scalp* (R), inc., n.sfx. -eh. unę́hreh *scalp* (RC 12:29), *hair with skin, especially in forehead* (AG); -(ę)nęhrahstęni-: kaye-nęhrahstè·nih ‹they-scalp-adorn› *they march, they parade* (HS); -(ę)nęhrakT: ranę́hrakwt ‹he-scalp-next to› *next to his scalp* (RC 3:70); -(ę)nęhran=hę''na'nye'': yunęhranhę''ná·''nye'' ‹it-scalp-put in mouth-going along› *it went along with scalp in its mouth* (RC 12:26); -(ę)nęhrayęhnę-: Kunęh-rayę́hnęh ‹o!-scalp-lays-much› *Flying Head (mythic creature)* (RC 28:title), Kwęnęhrayę́hnęh ‹o!-scalp-lays-much› *Flying Head* (AG), Unęhrayę́hnęh ‹scalp-lay-much› *Flying Head (jumped on two legs like grasshopper, 4 foot tall)* (AG); -(ę)nęhra'nihr -: węnęhrá''nihč ‹it-scalp-stands up› *it bunts* (HS), ręnęhrá''nihč ‹he-scalp-stands up› *he bumps* (HS); -(ę)nęhriN -: yenęhrì·ne'' ‹one-scalp-proceeds› *one amasses scalps* (RC 12:9); -(ę)nęhru -: runę́hru·'' ‹he-scalp-is in water› *tulip tree (Liriodendron tulipifera), lignum vitae, whitewood* (RC 9:2); -(ę)nęh= ruhar -: yunęhrúha''r ‹it-scalp-tips› *scalp hangs from tip of pole* (RC 12:24); *lacrosse* (R); -(ę)nęhruhči -: wa'kayę''na''nęhrúhči'' ‹fact-they= another-scalp-removed› *they scalped another* (RC 12:8), ręnęhrúhčęhs ‹he-scalp-removes› *he takes off headdress* (HS); -(ę)nęhruhčr -: unęhrúhčreh ‹scalp-cover-'ness› *hat* (R); -(ę)nęh= ruhčrahrahT -: unęhruhčráhraht ‹scalp-cover-'ness-put up-cause› *terrifying hat* (RC 30:59); -(ę)nęhruhčręti -: ranęhruhčrę́·tih ‹he-scalp-cover-'ness-makes› *hatter* (HS); -(ę)nęhrur -: ranęhrù·rę ‹he-scalp-covered› *he shears* (HS), ęhranęhru''r ‹prediction-he-scalp-cover› *he will shear* (HS); -rir - -(ę)nęhrahstęni'nye' -: urì·reh kayenęhrahstęní·''nye'' ‹row they-scalp-adorn-going along› *parade, procession* (HS); -ne -. -(ę)nęhrya'k- -ah= waryakę -: newęnę́hrya''ks uhwaryá·kę'' ‹two-it-scalp-breaks white› *Canada violet* (HS).

-(ę)nęhrahstęni - march, parade. *v.s.-a.i.* kayenęhrahstè·nih ‹they-scalp-adorn› *they march, they parade* (HS).

-ęnęhrayę - conceal, hide. *v.r.-t.* hab: -, pnt: -'', stat: -, prog: -, prp: -, dst: -, caus: -, rvs: -, dat: I (-''θe-/-''θ-), n-inc. Occurs only in inherently middle voice constructions. -ęnęhrayę -{dative I}: ęθwęnęhrà·yę''θ ‹prediction-youconceal-for› *you will hide* (RC 33:5); -ne+či -.-ęnęhrayę -: neθwęnęhrà·yę'' ‹two-again-it-con-cealed› *it is hidden in two places* (RC 33:9).

-(ę)nęhrayę́hnę - Flying Head. *dv.n.s.* The first two words begin with the rare (in modern Tuscarora) first person singular vocative prefix. Kunęhrayę́hnęh ‹o!-scalp-lays-much› *Flying Head (mythic creature)* (RC 28:title), Kwęnęhrayę́hnęh ‹o!-scalp-lays-much› *Flying Head* (AG), Unęhrayę́hnęh ‹scalp-lay-much› *Flying Head (jumped on two legs like grasshopper, 4 foot tall)* (AG).

-(ę)nęhra'nihr - bump, bunt. *v.s.-a.i.* węnęhrá''nihč ‹it-scalp-stands up› *it bunts* (HS), ręnęhrá''nihč ‹he-scalp-stands up› *he bumps* (HS).

-(ę)nęhru - tulip tree, lignum vitae, whitewood. *dv.n.s.* runę́hru·'' ‹he-scalp-is in water› *tulip tree (Liriodendron tulipifera), lignum vitae, white-wood* (RC 9:2).

-(ę)nęhruhar - lacrosse. *dv.n.s.* yunęhrúha''r ‹it-scalp-tipped› *lacrosse* (R).

-(ę)nęhruhči - scalp; take off headdress. *v.s.-a.i.* wa'kayę''na''nęhrúhči'' ‹fact-they=another-scalp-removed› *they scalped another* (RC 12:8), ręnęhrúhčęhs ‹he-scalp-removes› *he takes off headdress* (HS).

-(ę)nęhruhčr - hat. *n.s.* unęhrúhčreh ‹scalp-cover-'ness› *hat* (R).

-(ę)nęhruhčręti - hatter. *dv.n.s.* ranęhruhčrę́·tih ‹he-scalp-cover-'ness-makes› *hatter* (HS).

-(ę)nęhrur - shear. *v.s.-t.* ranęhrù·rę ‹he-scalp-covered› *he shears it* (HS), ęhranęhru''r ‹prediction-he-scalp-cover› *he will shear it* (HS).

-ęnęhwahs - spend the night, stay over-night. *v.r.-a.i.* See: -ęnęhwači -.

-ęnęhweči -/ -ęnęhwahs - spend the night,

stay overnight. *v.r.-a.i.* hab: -ęhs, pnt: -ʔ, stat: -ę, prog: -, prp: -ęhte-, dst: -, caus: -, rvs: -, dat: -, n-inc. The form **–ęnęhwahs** – occurs before the purposive. The form **–ęnęhweči** – occurs elsewhere. ręnęhwé·čęhs *he stays overnight* (RC 3:5); ti –. **–ęnęhweči** –: thwaʔnyęnęhwé·čiʔ ‹so-fact-two-one-spent the night› *the two of them spent so many nights* (RC 30:3), tihręnęhwé·čęhs ‹so-he-spent the night› *times he stays overnight so many times* (RC 12:2), tiwęnęhwé·čę ‹so-it-spent the night› *it spent so many nights* (RC 3:50), nęhsęnęhwé·čiʔ ‹so-prediction-you-spend the night› *you will spend so many nights* (RC 3:38); ti+ne –. **–ęnęhweči** –: nęʔnęnęhwé·čiʔ ‹so-apart-fact-it-spent the night› *it spent so many nights* (RC 30:18); –či –. **–ęnęhwahshęhte** –: čakęnęhwahshęhteʔ ‹again-one-spend the night-going to› *one was going to spend the night* (RC 3:68).

–ęnęhweT – roost, spend the night, stay overnight, submit to. *v.r.-a.i.* hab: -haʔ, pnt: -ɸ, stat: -, prog: -, prp: -, dst: -, caus: -, rvs: -, dat: -, n-inc. ęhsęnęhwe·t *you will spend the night* (RC 3:51), ręnęhwé·thaʔ *he roosts: he submits to it* (HS); **–ęnęhweʔnahkw** –: kayęnęhweʔnáhkhwaʔ ‹they-spend the night-instrument› *they stayed overnight* (RC 3:5), ręnęhweʔnáhkhwaʔ ‹he-spends the night-instrument› *his roost* (HS).

–ęnęhweʔnahkw – roost. *dv.n.s.* ręnęhweʔnáhkhwaʔ ‹he-spends the night-instrument› *his roost* (HS).

–(ę)nękwir – property, prosperity, riches, thrift, wampum, wealth. *n.r.* n-poss., inc., n.sfx.: -eh. unękwì·reh *property, prosperity, riches, thrift, wampum, wealth* (HS) [Lawson «Nauh-houreot» 'Ronoak']. **–(ę)nękwirawyęhw** –: ręnękwirawyę́hę ‹he-wealth-know how-caused› *he is provident* (HS).

–(ę)nękwirawyęhw – be provident. *v.s.-s.i.* ręnękwirawyę́hę ‹he-wealth-know how-caused› *he is provident* (HS).

–ęnęnhyar – study, watch. *v.r.-t.* hab: -ɸ, pnt: -ęʔ, stat: -ɸ, prog: -, prp: -, dst: -, caus: -, rvs: -, dat: -, n-inc. rawęnę́nhyar *he watches it* (HS), kayęʔnaʔnęnę́nhyar *they guard him* (R), waʔkayęʔnaʔnęnęnhyà·ręʔ *they studied one another* (RC 3:33), ęhsęnęnhyà·ręʔ *you will watch* (R), ęθwęnęnhyà·ręʔ *you will study* (RC 33:5), ęwęnęnhyá·ra·k *it will have watched* (RC 15:10); kwęhs **–ęnęnhyar** –: kwęhs ahrawęnęnhyá·ra·k ‹no unknown-he-watch› *he is inadvertent* (HS); kwęhs **–aˈnęnęnhyar** –: kwęhs ahrawęnęnhyá·ra·k ‹no unknown-he-himself-watch› *he is unguarded* (HS).

ę́·nęʔ *my mother* (RC 3:17). *n.* See: –ʔę –.

–(ę)nęʔyečkw – nest. *n.r.* n-poss., inc., n.sfx. -eh. unęʔyéčkweh *nest* (R); **–(ę)nęʔyečkwhar** –: kanęʔyéčkhwar ‹it-nest-hangs› *it builds nest* (HS); **–(ę)nęʔyečkwatekar** –: wahranęʔyečkwaté·kaʔr ‹fact-he-nest-took from› *he*

took from nest (RC 8:17); -(ę)nę**ʔyeč**=
kwaʔnihr -: yunęʔyečkwaʔníhrę ‹it-
nest-stands up› *nest stands* (RC 17:2);
-(ę)nę**ʔyečkwęy** -: yunęʔyéčkwęy ‹it-
nest-hangs down› *nest is* (RC 26:6);
-(ę)nę**ʔyečkwrahkw** -: węnęʔyečkwráh-
khwaʔ ‹it-nest-gathers› *aerie* (HS).
-(ę)nę**ʔyečkwhar** - build nest. *v..s.-a.i.* kanęʔyéčkhwar ‹it-nest-hangs› *it builds
nest* (HS).
-(ę)nę**ʔyečkwrahkw** - aerie. *dv.n.s.* wę-
nęʔyečkwráhkhwaʔ ‹it-nest-gathers›
aerie (HS).
-ę°**nh(e)** - be alive. *v.r.-a.i.* hab: -hs, pnt:
-, stat: -ʔ, prog: -, prp: -, dst: -, caus:
-aʔT-, rvs: -, dat: -, inc.-ɸ-ag./pat.
rę́nheʔ *he is alive* (RC 25:3), nę́nheʔ
you and I are alive (RC 25:6); -ę°**n**=
he -: awę́nheʔ ‹be alive› *character,
health, life* (HS); -ę°**nhehkT** -: ręnhéh-
kthaʔ ‹he-be alive-instrument-causes›
he enlivens it, he animates it (HS),
naʔnęnhéhkthaʔ   ‹one=another-be
alive-instrument-causes› *one maintains
(enlivens) another* (HS); -ę°**nhehkw** -:
kayakęnhéhkę ‹they-were alive-instrument› *they used it to live on* (RC
10:1); -ę°**nheʔčr** -: awęnhéʔčreh ‹be
alive-'ness› *core, heart* (R); -ę°**nheʔ**=
nehT -: rawę́nheʔneht ‹he-be alive-be
present-causes› *he is gluttonous, he is
a glutton: he is greedy* (H-notebook),
rawęnheʔnehnę́heʔ ‹he-be alive-be
present-caused-remote› *he had been
gluttonous, he had been a glutton, he
had been greedy* (H-notebook), ęhra-
węnheʔnéhnęk ‹prediction-he-be alive-
be present-cause› *he will be gluttonous, he will be a glutton: he will be
greedy* (H-notebook); -či -.-ę°**nhehkw** -:
čawęnhéhkę ‹again-it-is alive-instrument› *liveforever (Sedum triphylum,
S. purpureum)* (H-notebook); -či -.
-ę°**nhehkT** -: čaʔnaʔnęnhéhkthaʔ ‹a-

gain-one=another-bealive-instrument-
complete› *one brings back to life, one
raises the dead, one revivifies another*
(HS); -**nęhsęnhe** -: Kanęhsę́nheʔ ‹it-
house-is alive› *Live-House (male
proper name)* (H 2484); -**wętęn**=
hekari -{dative II}: rawętęnheká·ryęh
‹he-word-be alive-devours-for› *he
suffers* (HS); ti -.-ę°**nhạwę** -{dative II}:
tihrawę́nhawęhθ ‹so-he-be alive-pos-
sess-for› *the way he was feeling* (RC
3:83); ti -.-ę°**nhuhskwarihę** -: tiwęn-
huhskwaríhęh ‹so-it-be alive-is feeble-
much› *breath quivered* (RC 21:8);
ti -.-ę°**nhuʔnę** -: tihręnhúʔnę· ‹so-he-be
alive-is a kind of› *trait* (HS); **ti+či** -.
-ę°**nhe** -.**#áh**: tiθkęnhehsʔáh ‹so-again-
I-am living-little› *my life is coming to
an end/is short* (L 4); **ti+yah** -.-ę°**nhe** -:
thwewę́nheʔ ‹so-thither-it-is alive› *it is
still alive* (RC 33:11); -**yah+či** -.
-ę°**nhayeri** -: wečakęnhayè·riʔ ‹thither-
again-one-be alive-is correct› *one is in
good health again* (RC 18:4); -a**'nęn**=
ha'nę -{dative I}: ęθaʔnęnhá·ʔnęʔθ
‹prediction-you-yourself-be alive-be-
come-for› *you will mourn, it will
deaden your life (said when one
wantonly kills a bird, snake, brute or
insect)* (H-notebook); -a**'nęnhehkčr** -:
uʔnęnhéhkčreh ‹self-be alive-instru-
ment-'ness› *life* (HS); -a**'nęnheh**=
kčrukę ʔ: uʔnęnhehkčrú·kęʔ ‹self-be
alive-instrument-'ness-less› *lifeless*
(HS), ruʔnęnhehkčrú·kęʔ ‹he-himself-
be alive-instrument-'ness-less› *he is
inanimate* (HS); -a**'nęnhehkT** -: uʔ-
nęnhehkt ‹self-be alive-instrument-
cause› *life* (HS), akwaʔnęnhehkt ‹I-
myself-be alive-instrument-causes› *my
life substance* (RC 3:19); -a**'nęn**=
hehkT -.**#keha·**ʔ: uʔnęnhehktkyéha·ʔ
‹self-be alive-in-strument-cause-cus-
tomarily› *spiritual* (HS); -a**'nęnhęT** -:

ra'nęnhę·tha' ‹he-himself-be alive-concludes› *he beseeches, he complains, he invokes* (HS); -a'nęnhih=sakT-: yę'nęnhihsáktha' ‹one-oneself-be alive-seek-causes› *occupation, a trade* (HS); -či-. -a'nęnhehkT-: θahra'nęnhehkt ‹again-fact-he-be alive-instrument-caused› *he came back to life* (RC 12:30); kę' -ę°nhe-: kę' kénhe' ‹where I-am alive› *my heart* (PC); kwęhs -rihwęnhe-: kwęhs akarihwénhek ‹no unknown-it-matter-be alive› *it is invalid* (HS); kwęhs -a='nęnhe'nahkw-: kwęhs ahra'nęnhe'nahkwáhshek ‹no unknown-he-himself-be alive-cause-instrument› *he is impenitent* (HS).

-ę°nhe- character, health, life. *n.s.* awęnhe' ‹be alive› *character, health, life* (HS).

-ę°nhehkT- animate, enliven. *v.s.-t.* ręnhéhktha' ‹he-be alive-instrument-causes› *he enlivens it, he animates it* (HS), na'nęnhéhktha' ‹one=another-be alive-instrument-causes› *one maintains (enlivens) another* (HS).

-ę°nhehkw- use to live on. *v.s.-t.* kayakęnhéhkę ‹they-were alive-instrument› *they used it to live on* (RC 10:1).

-ę°nhe'čr- core, heart. *n.s.* awęnhé'čreh ‹be alive-'ness› *core, heart* (R).

-ę°nhe'nehT- be gluttonous, be a glutton; be greedy. *v.s.-a.i.* rawęnhe'neht ‹he-be alive-be present-causes› *he is gluttonous, he is a glutton: he is greedy* (H-notebook), rawęnhe'nehnéhe' ‹he-be alive-be present-caused-remote› *he had been gluttonous, he had been a glutton, he had been greedy* (H-notebook), çhrawęnhe'néhnęk ‹prediction-he-be alive-be present-cause› *he will be gluttonous, he will be a glutton: he will be greedy* (H-notebook).

-ęnhę?- groan. *v.r.-a.i.* hab: -θ, pnt: -ɸ, stat: -, prog: -, prp: -, dst: -, caus: -, rvs: -, dat: -, n-inc. ręnhę'θ *he groans* (H-notebook), çhrę́nhę' *he will groan* (HS).

-ę°nhi- ignore. *v.r.-t.* hab: -θ, pnt: -, stat: -, prog: -, prp: -, dst: -, caus: -hT-, rvs: -, dat: -, inc.-ɸ-ag. -rihwęnhi?-: rarihwę́nhi'θ ‹he-matter-ignore-begins› *heathen* (HS); -ęnhihT-: na'nęnhíhtha' ‹one=another-ignore-causes› *one disowns another* (HS); -a'nęn=hihT-: ra'nęnhíhtha' ‹he-himself-ignore-causes› *he abjures, he evades it, he renounces it, he reprobates it* (HS); -a'nęnhi?T-{dative III}: ra'nęnihná·ti· ‹he-himself-ignore-causes-for› *he is embarrassed* (HS).

-ęnhihT- disown *v.s.-t.* na'nęnhíhtha' ‹one=another-ignore-causes› *one disowns another* (HS).

-(ę)ni- reflexive. *v.r.pfx.* Lexically determined, rare form.

-(ę)nitęhT- humble. *v.s.-a.i.* wakęnitę́hnę ‹I-myself-am poor› *I humble (myself)* (HS), runitę́hnę ‹he-himself-is poor› *he humbles (himself)* (HS).

-ęr- leave behind. *v.r.-a.i.* hab: -ih, pnt: -', stat: -ę, prog: -, prp: -, dst: -, caus: -, rvs: -, dat: -, inc.-ɸ-pat. -a'nęr-: ra'nę̆·rih ‹he-himself-leaves behind› *he is slight* (HS); -a'nekęr -: uʔnckę·reh ‹self-liquid-leave behind› *dregs, residue* (HS); -a'na'nęr -: yuʔnaʔnę̀·rę ‹it-itself-left behind› *extra one, leftover, left(side)* (R); -či -. -a'na'nęr -: θahraʔná·ʔnęʔr ‹again-fact-he-another-left behind› *he was the exception* (RC 13:3); ti+ či -. -ęr -.#áh: tiθhrawęręháh ‹so-again-he-leave behind-little› *he falters* (RC 36:2); haʔ -a'na'nęr -: haʔ yuʔnaʔnę̀·rę ‹the it-itself-left behind› *leavings, remainder, remains* (HS).

-ęrahθr - moss, algae, scum on stagnant water. *n.r.* n-poss., inc., n.sfx. -eh. awęráhθreh *moss, algae, scum on stagnant water* (R) [Lawson «Auoona hau» 'Moss']; -ęrahθrurę -: yawęrahθrù·rę ‹it-moss-covered› *it is mossy* (R).

-ęrahθrurę - be mossy. *dv.n.s.* yawęrahθrù·rę ‹it-moss-covered› *it is mossy* (R).

ę̀·reʔw locust (R). *n.*

-ę̊ri - breathe. *v.r.-a.i.* hab: -ęhs, pnt: -ʔ, stat: -ę, prog: -, prp: -, dst: -, caus: -, rvs: -, dat: -, n-inc. -ę̊rihshęʔ -: rawęríhshęʔθ ‹he-breathe-'ness-lay-begins› *he is tired, he pants* (HS); -ę̊rihshę='naku -: naʔnęrihshęʔná·kwahs ‹one=another-breathe-'ness-lay-undoes› *one relieves another* (HS); -ę̊rihshukęʔ: rawęrihshú·kęʔ ‹he-breathe-'ness-less› *he is breathless* (HS); -ę̊rihst -: awęríhsteh ‹breathe-'ness› *breath* (HS); -ę̊rihst -.#aka·ʔ: awęrihstʔá·ka·ʔ ‹breathe-'ness-characterized by› *breath* (R); -ę̊ryęhkʷek -: yawęryę́hkwekt ‹it-breathe-X-close-caused› *suffocating* (HS); -ę̊ryę'naʔ -: ręryę́·ʔnaʔθ ‹he-breathe-concludes-begins› *he gets over an attack of sickness, of a spasm, or gets rested* (H-notebook); -a'nęri -: kaʔnę́·ryęhs ‹I-myself-breathe› *I breathe* (RC 3:20), nęyę́ʔnę́·ryę ‹two-one-themselves-breathed› *the two of them breathed* (RC 3:14), waʔkaʔnę̀·riʔ ‹fact-I-myself-breathed› *I breathed* (R); -a'nęri -.#úʔy: raʔnęryęhsʔúʔy ‹he-himself-breathes-great› *he sighs* (HS), ęhraʔnęriʔúʔy ‹prediction-he-himself-breathe-great› *he will sigh* (HS); -a'nęrihshę(T) -: raʔnęríhshęh ‹he-himself-breathe-'ness-lays› *he is resting* (L 22), ruʔnęrihshę́·ʔnahk ‹he-himself-breathe-'ness-laid-had› *he has rested* (L 22), ruʔnęríhshę· ‹he-himself-breathe-'ness-laid› *he has (gone to) rest* (L 22), wahraʔnęríhshę·ʔ ‹fact-he-himself-breathe-'ness-laid› *he rested* (L 22); -a'nęrih=shę'nahkw -: yęʔnęrihshęʔnáhkhwaʔ ‹one-oneself-breathe-'ness-lays-instrument› *resting place* (HS); -a'nęrihsti=yaʔk -: raʔnęrihstì·yaʔks ‹he-himself-breathe-'ness-breaks› *he expires* (H-notebook); -a'nęrihstuhar -: yuʔnęrihstúhar ‹it-itself-breathe-'ness-washes› *din* (HS); -a'nęryehT -: waʔnęryéhthaʔ ‹it-itself-breathe-causes› *gills (of fish)* (SH 375); -či -. -a'nęri -: θhraʔné·ryęhs ‹again-he-himself-breathes› *he breathes again* (R), θahraʔnę̀·riʔ ‹again-fact-he-breathed› *again he breathed* (RC 12:30); -t -. -a'nęrihstaʔ=nihęthu -: thraʔnęrihstaʔnihę́·thuhs ‹hither-he-himself-breathe-'ness-draws in› *he draws a breath* (HS).

-ę̊rihshęʔ - be tired, pant. *v.s.-a.i.* rawęríhshęʔθ ‹he-breathe-'ness-lay-begins› *he is tired, he pants* (HS).

-ę̊rihshę'naku - relieve. *v.s.-t.* naʔnęrihshęʔná·kwahs ‹one=another-breathe-'ness-lay-undoes› *one relieves another* (HS).

-ę̊rihshukęʔ breathless. *dv.n.s.* rawęrihshú·kęʔ ‹he-breathe-'ness-less› *he is breathless* (HS).

-ę̊rihst - breath. *n.s.* awęríhsteh *breath*

‹breathe-'ness› (HS).

-ę̊rihst-.#aka·ʔ breath. *n.s.* awęrihst-ʔá·ka·ʔ ‹breathe-'ness-characterized by› *breath* (R).

ę̀·ru no, not (HS). *part.*

-ęruh- self. *n.r.* aln: rawę̀·ruh *himself* (RC 1:2), n-inc., n.sfx. -φ. ę̀·ruh *herself, oneself* (RC 5:16), awę̀·ruh *itself* (RC 30·27); tha-.-ęruh-: thaʔawę̀·ruh ‹unusual-it-self› *very, most* (RC 24:9); -ęruh-.#áh: θnęruháh ‹you two-self-little› *the two of them by themselves alone* (R), rawęruháh ‹he-self-little› *he is alone* (HS); -ęruha'nyeʔ-: awęruhá·ʔnyeʔ ‹self-going along› *separately* (HS); tha-.-ęruh--akwahsT-: thaʔawę̀·ruh wákwahst ‹unusual-it-self it-is good› *best* (HS).

-ęruh-.#áh self alone. *n.s.* θnęruháh ‹you two-self-little› *the two of them by themselves alone* (R), rawęruháh ‹he-self-little› *he is alone* (HS).

-ęruha'nyeʔ- separately. *n.s.* awęruhá·ʔnyeʔ ‹self-going along› *separately* (HS).

-ę̊ryęhkʷek- suffocate. *v.s.-t.* yawęryę́hkwekt ‹it-breathe-X-close-causes› *suffocating* (HS).

-ę̊ryę'naʔ- get over an attack of sickness, get over a spasm; get rested. *v.s.-a.i.* ręryę́·ʔnaʔθ ‹he-breathe-conclude-begins› *he gets over an attack of sickness, of a spasm, or gets rested* (H-notebook).

ęθa- optative mode+repetitive. *v.r.pfx.*

-ę̊θ(e)r- be so big. *v.r.-a.i.* hab: -φ, pnt: -aʔ, stat: -ʔ, prog: -, prp: -, dst: -aʔθrę̊-, caus: -, rvs: -, dat: -, n-inc. The form -ę̊θr- occurs wherever the root is followed by a stem or suffix beginning with a vowel; the form -ę̊θer- occurs elsewhere. The root requires the partitive unless compounded with another verb. ti-. -ę̊θ(e)r-: tiwę́·θeʔr ‹so-it-is so big› *it is so big* (RC 8:3), nęhrę́·θraʔ ‹so-prediction-he-be so big› *he will be so big* (RC 35:40); ti-.-ę̊θ(e)r-.#áh: tikę·θeʔrʔáh ‹so-I-am so big-little› *I am little* (R); ti-.-ę̊θ(e)r-.#úʔy: tyakę·θeʔrʔúʔy ‹so-one-is so big-great› *big one* (RC 29:9); ti-.-ę̊θraʔθrę-.#úʔy: tiwęθraʔθrę́ʔúʔy ‹so-one-is so big-much-great› *it is gigantic* (RC 3:56); tha+ne-.-ę̊θ(e)r-: thaʔneyakę́·θer ‹unusual-two-one-are so big› *they are of equal size (referring to persons)* (HS); -ę̊θręti-: waʔawęθrę́·tiʔ ‹fact-it-be so big-made› *it made it bigger* (RC 8:6), węθrętíhaʔ ‹it-be so big-makes› *it becomes so big* (RC 35:26), rawę́θrę́·ti· ‹he-be so big-made› *he liked to* (AW 45); -ę̊θrętyaʔT-: naʔnęθrętyáʔthaʔ ‹one=another-be so big-make-causes› *one caresses it* (R); -ę̊θriyu-: sęθrí·yu· ‹you-be so big-are great› *you are big* (R); -a'nęθriyuʔT-: ruʔnęθriyúʔnę ‹he-himself-be so big-be great-caused› *he was contumacious* (HS), raʔnęθriyúʔthaʔ ‹he-himself-be so big-be great-causes› *he is contumacious* (HS); ti-.-ę̊θriyu-: tiwęθrí·yu· ‹so-it-be so big-is great› *it is so big* (RC 6:9); -a'nęθrętyaʔT-: raʔnę-

---

Tuscarora Pronunciation Key:
/a/ l<u>a</u>w; /e/ h<u>a</u>t; /i/ p<u>i</u>zza; /u/ t<u>u</u>ne; /ę/ h<u>in</u>t; /č/ <u>ch</u>eese; /h/ <u>h</u>oe; /m/ <u>m</u>other; /s/ <u>s</u>ame; /t/ <u>d</u>o (before a vowel y, or w), <u>t</u>oo (elsewhere); /k/ <u>g</u>ale (before a vowel y or w), <u>k</u>ale (elsewhere); /n/ i<u>nh</u>ale (before a consonant or word-final), <u>n</u>ote (elsewhere), /r/ hi<u>ss</u> (before a consonant or word-final), <u>r</u>un (trilled as in Italian, elsewhere); /w/ <u>c</u>uff (before a consonant other than y or word-final), <u>w</u>ay (elsewhere); /y/ fi<u>sh</u> (before a consonant or word-final), <u>y</u>ou (elsewhere), /θ/ <u>th</u>ing; /ʔ/ (the sound between the vowels in unh-unh); /·/ long vowel, /ˊ/ high pitch; /ˋ/ low pitch.

θrętyá'²tha'² ‹he-himself-be so big-make-causes› *he fondles* (HS).

-ęθkar- lay in a certain way. *v.r.-a.i.* See: -iθkar-.

-ęθkęri- groan. *v.r.-a.i.* hab: -, pnt: -e'², stat: -, prog: -, prp: -, dst: -, caus: -, rvs: -, dat: -, n-inc. Found only in the following construction with the cislocative and repetitive. -t+či-. -ęθkęri-: nę'²nwęθkę́·rye'² ‹hither-fact-again-it-groaned› *it groaned* (RC 27:26).

-ęθr- relish, taste. *n.r.* n-poss., inc., n.sfx. -eh. awę́·θreh *relish, taste* (HS); -ęθrak'²u'²θrę-: ręθrak'²ú'²θrę· ‹he-taste-releases-much› *he relishes it* (HS); -ęθra'²r-: yawę́·θra'²r ‹it-taste-is much› *tasteful* (HS); -ęθritkę'²-: yawęθritkę́'²ę ‹it-taste-issue-began› *flat taste, insipid* (HS); -ęθrukę'²: awęθrú·kę'² ‹tasteless› *tasteless* (HS); -a'nę=θra'²tyę'²nę-: ra'²nęθra'²tyę́'²nęh ‹he-himself-taste-measures› *he tastes it* (HS); pì·ye'² -ęθrak'²u-{dative I}: pì·ye'² rawęθrak'²ú'²θe· ‹beer he-taste-released-for› *he likes the taste of beer* (HS).

-ęθrak'²u'²θrę- relish. *v.s.-t.* ręθrak'²ú'²θrę· ‹he-taste-releases-much› *he relishes it* (HS).

-ęθra'²r- tasteful. *dv.n.s.* yawę́·θra'²r ‹it-taste-is much› *tasteful* (HS).

-ę°θręti- like to; make bigger. *v.s.-a.i.* wa'²awęθrę́·ti'² ‹fact-it-be so big-made› *it made it bigger* (RC 8:6), węθrętíha'² ‹it-be so big-makes› *it becomes so big* (RC 35:26), rawęθrę́·ti· ‹he-be so big-made› *he liked to* (AW 45).

-ę°θrętya'²T- caress. *v.s.-t.* na'²nęθrętyá'²-tha'² ‹one=another-be so big-make-causes› *one caresses it* (HS).

-ę°θriyu- be big. *v.s.-s.i.* sęθrí·yu· ‹you-be so big-are great› *you are big* (R).

-ęθritkę'²- flat taste, insipid. *dv.n.s.* yawęθritkę́'²ę ‹it-taste-issue-began› *flat taste, insipid* (HS).

-ęθruhnę-/-iθruhnę- flood, gush forth, inundate. *v.r.-a.i.* hab: -h, pnt: -, stat: -'², prog: -, prp: -, dst: -, caus: -, rvs: -, dat: -, n-inc. The form -iθruhnę- appears in the second verb form and in the derived nominalization. The form -ęθruhnę- appears in the first verb form and in the deverbal noun. węθrúhnęh *it gushes forth, it floods* (HS), kęθrúhnęh *it floods, it inundates* (HS), yawęθrúhnę'² *flood* (HS); -iθruhnęhst-: uθruhnę́hsteh ‹flood-'ness› *flood* (HS).

-ęθrukę'² tasteless. *n.s.* awęθrú·kę'² ‹taste-less› *tasteless* (HS).

ęT- future mode+cislocative. *v.r.pfx.* The form ęt- occurs before pronominal prefixes that begin with the consonants *k* or *h*; the final *t* of this prefix coalesces with the cluster *hs* to yield ęčh-. The form ę'n- occurs before pronominal prefixes that begin with the consonants *w* or *y*. The form ę'ni- occurs before pronominal prefixes that begin with the consonants *č* or *θ*, or the clusters '²t or '²n.

-ęT- close, conclude. *v.r.-a.i.* hab: -s, pnt: -a'², stat: -, prog: -, prp: -he-, dst: -, caus: -hu-, rvs: -, dat: II (-ahθ-/-ę-), inc.-?-ag./pat. Found only with incorporated noun roots. -hnęwęthu-: ruhnęwę́·thuhs ‹he-lake bottom-conclude-causes› *it sinks him* (HS); -nęhsęT-: kanęhsę́·the'² ‹it-house-close-is going to› *House Destroyer* (RC 14:title); -rihwęT-: wa'²karihwę́·'²na'² ‹fact-it-matter-closed› *it surceased* (HS), wa'²-karihwę́·'²nahst ‹fact-it-matter-close-caused› *it became silent* (HS); -wi=ręT-: kawí·rę·č ‹it-infant-closes› *it is barren* (HS); -ekęT-{dative II}: wekę́·'²nahθ ‹it-liquid-closes-for› *water subsides* (HS); -khwęT-{dative II}:

rakhwę́·ʼnahθ ‹he-food-closes-for› *he finished eating* (HS); –(ę)ʼtikęhręT– {dative III}: waʼkaʼtikęhrę́·ʼnęʼ ‹fact-it-mind-close-for› *it forgot* (RC 35: 43); –(ę)ʼtikęhręthuhT–: aryęʼnaʼtikęhrę́·thuht ‹unknown-one=another-mind-close-cause-cause› *that one remember another, that one comfort another* (RC 35:19); –či–. –ekęT– {dative II}: θwekę́·ʼnahθ ‹again-it-liquid-close-for› *water settles down again* (HS); tha–. –ęT–.#ęwe: thahrawęʼnehę̀·we ‹unusual-he-conclude-genuine› *he is stupid* (HS); tha–. –(ę)ʼtikęhręT–: thaʼθaʼtikęhrę́·ʼna·k ‹unusual-you!-mind-close› *be calm!* (R); –aʼnewyę=nęT–: wahraʼnewyęnę́·ʼnaʼ ‹fact-he-himself-preparation-closed› *he finished his preparations* (RC 12:3); –aʼrihę='na'nye–: ruʼrihęʼná·ʼnyeʼ ‹he-himself-matter-concluded-going along› *he delegates* (HS); haʼ –ę'nęti–: haʼ yawęʼné·ti· ‹the it-close-made› *misery* (HS).

–ęT– day, daytime. *n.r.* n-poss., inc., n.sfx. -eh. awę·ʼneh *day, daytime* (R) [Gallatin «auwehneh» 'Day']; –ęthar=hu–{dative I}: rawętharhúʼθeh ‹he-day-mix in-for› *he has the ague, he has intercalcated days* (HS); –ę'nah=raT–: wę́·ʼnahra·č ‹it-day-counts› *almanac* (HS); –ę'nakęheyaʼT–: węʼnakęheyáʼthaʼ ‹it-day-die-causes› *blast* (HS); –ę'naks–: węʼná·ksę· ‹it-day-is bad› *stormy* (HS); –ę'naksaʼT–: węʼnaksáʼthaʼ ‹it-day-be bad-causes› *storm* (HS); –ę'nakT–: awę́·ʼnakwt ‹day-next to› *Saturday* (R); –ę'nar–:

rę́·ʼnar ‹he-day-is in› *he dates it (marks the day)* (HS); –ę'natukęhT–: yawęʼnatukę́hthaʼ ‹it-day-is holy› *Sabbath* (HS); –ę'nęhnaʼęha'nyeʼ–: yawęʼnęhnaʼęhá·ʼnyeʼ ‹it-day-drop-cause-began-going along› *decline of day* (HS); –ę'nęte: awęʼnę́·te ‹day-certain› *a certain day* (RC 3:10); –ę'nęti–: yawęʼnę́·ti· ‹it-day-made› *it is disagreeable, it is gloomy, it is terrible, it is too bad, it is unpleasant* (HS); –ę'nę-ti–{dative I}: rawęʼnętyáʼθe· ‹he-day-made-for› *he is gloomy, he is uncomfortable* (HS); –ę'niyu–.#keha·ʼ: awęʼniyuʼkyéha·ʼ ‹day-great-customarily› *diurnal, occurring during the day* (RC 3:2); –či–. –ę'naT–: θwę́·ʼna·t ‹again-it-day-stands› *one day* (RC 21:8); –t–. –ęT–: nyawę́·ʼneh ‹hither-it-day› *o'clock* (R); –t–. –ę'nahręhw–: nawęʼnahrę́hwę ‹hither-it-day-put up-caused› *dawn* (HS), ęʼnayawęʼnahrę́hwak ‹prediction-hither-it-day-put up-cause› *dawn* (RC 15: 3); –t–. –ę'nayęT–: waʼnwęʼnayę́·ʼnaʼ ‹fact-hither-it-day-laid› *the full day* (HS); –t–. –ę'nęte–: nyawęʼné·tehk ‹hither-it-day-was a certain› *time* (R); –t–. –ę'nut: nyawę́·ʼnu·t ‹hither-it-day-stands› *dawn* (HS); ti–. –ę'nake–: nęwęʼná·kye·k ‹so-prediction-it-day-be in number› *it will be so many days* (RC 15:3); ti–. –ę'nęte: tiwęʼné·te ‹so-it-day-certain› *o'clock* (R); ti–. –ę'nyer–: tiwę́·ʼnyer ‹so-it-day-does› *weather* (R); tha+ne–. –ę'nihę: thaʼnyawęʼníhę ‹unusual-apart-it-day-middle of› *noon*

(R); -a'nę'nu'kT-{dative I}: wa''aku'-nę'nú'kthahθ ‹fact-one-oneself-day-ended-for› *one's time came to an end* (RC 3:39); ti+t-. -a'nę'nar-: nę'nyu'-nę́·'nara' ‹so-prediction-hither-it-it-self-day-be in› *week* (G); ha' -ę'nęti-: ha' yawę'nę́·ti· ‹the it-day-made› *grief, what is sad or doleful* (HS); ha' tha+ne-. -a'nę'nare-: ha'' tha'neyu'-nę́·'nare' ‹the unusual-apart-it-itself-day-is distant› *week* (HS); né·kti· ha' tha+ne-. -a'nę'nare-: né·kti· ha' tha'-neyu'nę́·'nare' ‹two the unusual-a-part-it-itself-day-is distant› *biweekly* (HS); kwęhs -ę'nar-: kwęhs aryuwę́·'narak ‹no unknown-it-day-be in› *it is undated* (HS); kwęhs -ę'nehsT-: kwęhs aryawę'néhsnęk ‹no unknown-it-day-strike-cause› *imperceptibly* (HS).

-ę°T- put in fire. *v.r.-t.* hab: -, pnt: -, stat: -. prog: -, prp: -, dst: -, caus: -hu-, rvs: -aku-, dat: -, inc-ɸ-pat. -ę'naku-: yakę'ná·kwahs ‹one-put in fire-undoes› *one took it out of fire* (RC 28: 11); -nęhęthu-: ranęhę́·thuhs ‹he-corn-put in fire-causes› *he puts the corn in the fire* (H 2484).

-ę°T- possess. *v.r.-s.i.* stat: -·, prog: -, prp: -, dst: -, caus: -, rvs: -, dat: -, inc.-ɸ-pat. Requires an incorporated noun root. Hewitt (H 2892) describes the meaning of this verb as follows: "to have, as parts of the body, or the parts of a machine or structure, the limbs or roots, leaves & blossoms of a tree, etc." He also notes that, "the hair of the body is not used with this verb, but may be used of a single hair or tuft of hair." -(ę)takaręT-: yutá·karę·t ‹it-point-possesses› *pointed* (HS); -(ę)ta'ręT-: ratá'rę·t ‹he-head-possesses› *he has a head, as a part of his body, not one that is found or picked up* (H 2892), rata'rę́·'nahk ‹he-head-possessed› *he had a head* (H 2892), ęhrata'rę́·'na·k ‹prediction-he-head-possess› *he will have a head* (H 2892), ęhrata'rę́·'nahk ‹prediction-he-head-possessed› *he will have had a head* (H 2892); -(ę)tu'θęT-: katú'θę·t ‹it-tooth-possesses› *domestic goose: a flageolet* (HS) [Gallatin «kahtosant» 'Goose']; -(ę)tu'θęT-.#ú'y: katu'θę·t-'ú'y ‹it-tooth-possesses-great› *swan* (R); -hne'ręT-: yuhné'rę·t ‹it-root-possesses› *it has a root* (H 2892); -hsukaręT-: rahsú·karę·t ‹he-beard-possesses› *he is bearded* (HS); -i=?nhahnęT-: yu'nháhnę·t ‹it-limb-possesses› *it has a limb or branch* (H 2892); -nęčhęT-: ranę́čhę·t ‹he-arm-possesses› *he has an arm, that is, as part of his body, only* (H 2892); -nęhsęT-: yunę́hsę·t ‹it-house-posses-ses› *there is a room or house to it, said of a room or house that has a connecting room, or of a building that has an outhouse attached to it* (H 2484); -nękwaru'nęT-: yunękwarú'-nę·t ‹it-pin-possesses› *pin* (HS); -ta=kwnęT-: yutákwnę·t ‹it-room-pos-sesses› *story (of a building)* (HS); -yęhwiθnęT-: yuyęhwí·θnę·t ‹it-wing-possesses› *winged* (HS); -'ehnęT-: ra'éhnę·t ‹he-hand-possesses› *he has a hand, as a part of his body* (H 2892); -'tiθkraręT-: yu'tiθkrá·rę·t ‹it-tickle-possesses› *tickling* (HS); -a'rihęT-: ru'ríhę·t ‹he-himself-matter-possesses› *he has it as his business* (RC 26:35); *officer* (HS); -ne-. -ahsęT-: neyúhsę·t ‹two-it-foot-possesses› *biped* (HS); -ne-. -hseyęT-: neyuhsé·yę·t ‹two-it-ear of corn-possesses› *it has two ears of corn* (RC 7:5); ti-. -čhe'węT-: tyučhé'wę·t ‹so-it-gourd-posses-ses› *it has squash* (RC 7:5); ha' -takwnęT-:

ha⁷ yutákwnę·t ‹the it-room-possesses› *cell* (HS); –(ę)tu⁷θęT – –⁷niha –: katú⁷θę·t ka⁷níha· ‹it-tooth-possesses it-is male› *gander* (HS); áhsę ti –. –⁷ęhręT –: áhsę tyu⁷ęhrę·t ‹three so-it-leaf-possesses› *clover* (HS); –⁷nihsęr – –ręryuhkwęT –: u⁷nihsę·reh yuręryúhkwę·t ‹star it-ray-possesses› *comet* (HS); –⁷tihsn – –⁷aręT –: u⁷tíhsneh yu⁷á·rę·t ‹cup it-lower lip-possesses› *pitcher* (HS).

–ętahkera⁷T – betoken. *v.r.-a.i.* hab: -ha⁷, pnt: -, stat: -ę, prog: -, prp: -, dst: -, caus: -, rvs: -, dat: -, n-inc. rętahkyerá⁷tha⁷ *he betokens* (HS); –ne –. –ętahkera⁷T –: neyawętahkyerá⁷nę ‹a-part-it-betokened› *emblem* (HS).

–(ę)tahsn – bat (unhewn), club, pole, rod (of 16½ feet), stick, yoke, wand. *n.r.* aln: aktáhsnawęh *my bat* (R), inc., n.sfx. -eh. utáhsneh *bat (unhewn), club, pole, rod (of 16 ½ feet), stick, yoke, wand* (HS) [Lawson «Ootosne» 'Fishgig']; –(ę)tahsnaku⁷čęri –: wa⁷katahsnaku⁷čę·ri⁷ ‹fact-it-pole-found› *it found pole* (RC 12:26); –(ę)tahsna= nę'nakT –: rętahsnanę⁷náktha⁷ ‹he-pole-affix-causes› *he rams a gun, he packs a gun* (HS); –(ę)tahsna'nek –: yutáhsna⁷neks ‹it-stick-burns› *burning stick* (AW 56); –(ę)tahsnę⁷ke: utahsnę́⁷kye ‹pole-on› *on pole* (RC 12:9); –(ę)tahsniyu –: katahsní·yu· ‹it-pole-is great› *a large stick* (L 78); –(ę)tah= snyeriha –: kakutahsnyeríhę ‹they-pole-straightened› *they spread sticks* (RC 24:9); ti –. –a'nętahsnarę –: tyu⁷nętáh-

snarę⁷ ‹so-it-itself-pole-is in-many› *sticks are in* (RC 6:12).

–(ę)tahsnanę'nakT – pack a gun, ram a gun. *v.s.-a.i.* rętahsnanę⁷náktha⁷ ‹he-pole-affix-causes› *he rams a gun, he packs a gun* (HS).

–(ę)takar – edge, point, steeple. *n.r.* n-poss., inc., n.sfx. -eh. utá·kareh *edge, point, steeple* (HS); –(ę)takaręt: yutá·karę·t ‹it-point-possesses› *pointed* (HS); –(ę)takaręti –: ratakaré·tih ‹he-point-makes› *he sharpens it* (HS); ti –. –(ę)takareθ –.#ú⁷y: tikatakare·θ⁷ú⁷y ‹so-it-point-is long-great› *great long beak, proboscis* (RC 2:3); –ne –. –(ę)takariθ –: newętakarí·θę ‹two-it-point-joined› *framed (e.g., house)* (H 2892); ha⁷ –(ę)takar –.#ha⁷nę⁷: ha⁷ yawętakarhá⁷nę⁷ ‹the it-point-many› *aridity, the drought (the upturned earth, from the fissures in it)* (HS); kę⁷ –ne –. –(ę)takariθ –: kę⁷ neyawętakarí·θę ‹where two-it-point-met› *ridge of house* (HS).

–(ę)takar –.#ha⁷nę⁷ aridity, drought. *n.s.* ha⁷ yawętakarhá⁷nę⁷ ‹the it-point-many› *aridity, the drought (the upturned earth, from the fissures in it)* (HS).

–(ę)takaręt pointed. *dv.n.s.* yutá·karę·t ‹it-point-possesses› *pointed* (HS).

–(ę)takaręti – sharpen. *v.s.-t.* ratakaré·tih ‹he-point-makes› *he sharpens it* (HS).

–ętathrewa⁷T – repent. *v.s.-a.i.* rętathrewá⁷tha⁷ ‹he-??-punishes› *he repents* (HS).

–ętathrewa⁷T – apology. *dv.n.s.* ha⁷ rawętathrewá́'nę ‹the he-??-punished› *his apology* (HS).

–ętatukęht‑ Sunday. *dv.n.s.* yawętatukę́htę ‹it-??-is holy› *Sunday* (HS).

–ętaw‑ filth. *n.r.* n-poss., inc.. n.sfx. ‑eh. awę́·taweh *filth* (HS); –ętawanęhkwi‑: rętawanę́hkwih ‹he-filth-combs› *he sweeps* (HS), wętawanę́hkwih ‹it-filth-combs› *sweepings* (HS); kwęhs –ęta=wanęhkwi‑: kwęhs arwętawanę́hkwik ‹no unknown-it-filth-comb› *unswept* (HS).

–ętawanęhkwi‑ sweep. *v.s.-a.i.* rętawanę́hkwih ‹he-filth-combs› *he sweeps* (HS).

–ętawanęhkwi‑ sweepings. *dv.n.s.* wętawanę́hkwih ‹it-filth-combs› *sweepings* (HS).

–(ę)ta'ker‑ follow (an example). imitate. *v.r.-t.* hab: -ahs, pnt: -', stat: -ę, prog: -, prp: -. dst: -, caus: -ahT-, rvs: -, dat: -, n-inc. ruta'kyè·rę *he followed an example, he imitated it* (HS), rata'kyè·rahs *he follows an example, he imitates it* (HS), ęhratá'kye'r *he will follow an example, he will imitate it* (HS); –ne‑.‑(ę)ta'kerahT‑: wa'tkheyęta'kyè·raht ‹fact-apart-I=another-imitate-caused› *I imitate him/her* (AG).

–(ę)ta'r‑ head; cabbage. *n.r.* aln: ktá'reh *my head* (R), inc., n.sfx. ‑eh. The form –ęta'r‑ occurs following the neuter singular agent pronominal prefix and third person patient pronominal prefixes when the root is incorporated into non-stative verbs; the form –ta'r‑ occurs elsewhere. utá'reh *head* (R) [Lawson «Oo-taure» 'A Head'] [Gallatin «uhtahreh» 'Head']; *cabbage* (HS); –(ę)ta'r‑.#keha·': uta'rę'kyéha·' ‹head-customarily› *cephalic* (HS); –(ę)ta'rahtir‑: ruta'rahtì·ręh ‹he-head-is hard› *he is obstinate* (HS); –(ę)ta'=ranęhwakčr‑: uta'ranęhwákčreh ‹head-

ache-'ness› *cephalalgy* (HS); –(ę)ta'=ranęhwak(T)‑: ruta'ranę́hwaks ‹he-head-aches› *he has a headache* (HS); –(ę)ta'rawerhahsi‑: ręta'rawerháhsyęhs ‹he-head-cover-undoes› *he uncovers head* (R); –(ę)ta'raweθhętyę –: akęta'raweθhę́·tyę' ‹unknown-I=you-head-chop-much› *that I smash up your head* (RC 31:6); –(ę)ta'rawi'T –: ruta'rawí'nę ‹he-head-give to-caused› *it penetrated his head* (RC 30:2); –(ę)=ta'ra'kwar‑.#ú'y: yawęta'ra'kwa'rhú'y ‹it-head-is covered over-great› *its great head is covered over* (RC 28:2); –(ę)ta'ra'ne –: rata'rá·'ne' ‹he-head-is present› *his head sticks out* (H 2892); –(ę)ta'reθ –: katá're·θ ‹it-head-is long› *lettuce* (R); –(ę)ta'ręT –: ratá'rę·t ‹he-head-possesses› *he has a head, as a part of his body, not one that is found or picked up* (H 2892), rata'rę́·'nahk ‹he-head-possessed› *he had a head* (H 2892), ęhrata'rę́·'na·k ‹prediction-he-head-possess› *he will have a head* (H 2892), ęhrata'rę́·'nahk ‹prediction-he-head-possessed› *he will have had a head* (H 2892); –(ę)ta'rhra' –: ratá'rhra'θ ‹he-head-put up-begins› *he knocks his head against something* (HS); –(ę)ta'ruhskę‑: ruta'rúhskę' ‹he-head-bared› *he is bareheaded* (HS); –ne‑.–(ę)ta'rya'k‑: newętá'rya'ks ‹apart-it-head-breaks› *violet (Viola sp.)* (R); –a'ta'rahtręhst‑: yę'ta'rahtrę́hstha' ‹one-oneself-head-tie-causes› *wreath* (HS); –a'ta'rahwan=hahst‑: yę'ta'rahwanháhstha' ‹one-oneself-head-wind-causes› *wreath* (HS).

–(ę)ta'r‑.#keha·' cephalic. *n.s.* uta'rę'kyéha·' ‹head-customarily› *cephalic* (HS).

–(ę)ta'rahtir‑ obstinate. *v.s.-a.i.* ruta'rahtì·ręh ‹he-head-is hard› *he is obstinate*

(HS).

-(ę)taˀranęhwakčr – cephalalgy. *n.s.* utaˀ-ranęhwákčrch ‹head-ache-'ness› *cephalalgy* (HS).

-(ę)taˀranęhwak(T) – have a headache. *v.s.-s.i.* rutaˀranęhwaks ‹he-head-aches› *he has a headache* (HS).

-(ę)taˀreθ – lettuce. *n.s.* katáˀre·θ ‹it-head-is long› *lettuce* (R).

-(ę)taˀruhskę – be bareheaded. *v.s.-s.i.* rutaˀrúhskęˀ ‹he-head-bared› *he is bareheaded* (HS).

-ę̈°te – be a certain one. *v.r.-s.i.* stat: -ˀ, prog: -, prp: -, dst: -, caus: -, rvs: -, dat: -, n-inc. Found only in the constructions cited below. **ti –. -ę̈°te –:** tikayaké·teˀ ‹so-they-are certain ones› *they are certain ones* (R); **-a'nęte –:** waˀné·teˀ ‹it-itself-is a certain one› *it is a certain one* (RC 9:5); **-t –. -ę̈'nęte –:** nyawęˀné·tehk ‹hither-it-day-was a certain one› *time* (R); **ti –. -ę̈'nęte –:** tiwęˀné·teˀ ‹so-it-day-is a certain one› *o'clock* (R).

-ę̈°te certain one (particularizer). *n.r.sfx.* This suffix is typically used to indicate that reference is to a specific member of the class of objects named by the attached root. The specific member may be known (definite) or unknown (indefinite), as suggested by Hewitt's parenthetical comment following the gloss for the first example: **-hehnęte:** uhehné·te ‹field-certain one› *it is this or that kind of field (the definitive this or that is understood here and is expressed outside of the*

sentence) (H 2484), **-hnyęte:** uhnyé·te ‹news-certain one› *a certain story* (AW 54). The suffix may also occur in constructions which have become idiomatic, as in **háhteh –θręwęte:** háhteh uθręwé·te ‹pine resin-certain one› *pitch* (HS).

-ętehst – cellar; dirt floor, hard-packed soil, solid ground. *n.r.* n-poss., inc., n.sfx. -eh. awętéhsteh *dirt floor, hard-packed soil, solid ground* (R); **-ęteh = stakęw:** awętéhstakęw ‹solid ground-in› *in the cellar* (H-notebook); **-ęteh = stahrar –:** yawętehstáhrarę· ‹it-solid ground-is a hole› *it is a hole in the ground* (RC 3:73), *cave* (HS).

-ętehstahrar – cave. *dv.n.s.* yawętehstáhrarę· ‹it-solid ground-is a hole› *cave* (HS).

-ętekęraˀnęti – muddle, roil. *v.r.-t.* hab: -h, pnt: -, stat: -, prog: -, prp: -, dst: -, caus: -, rvs: -, dat: -, n-inc. rętekęraˀné·tih *he muddles it, he roils it* (HS).

-(ę)ter – conception, embryo, fetus, foal, roe. *n.r.* n-poss., inc., n.sfx. -eh. utè·reh *conception, embryo, fetus, foal, roe* (HS); **-(ę)terawak –:** węterà·waks ‹it-conception-shakes› *it spawns* (HS); **-(ę)tera'nę –:** ruterá·ˀnęˀ ‹he-conception-becomes› *he is subject* (HS); **-(ę)terę –:** yetè·ręh ‹one-conception-falls› *she is pregnant* (HS); **-(ę)teri –:** katè·rih ‹it-embryo-is a group› *it is expectant, it is pregnant* (HS); **-(ę)teru –:** ruté·ru·ˀ ‹he-conception-is in water› *perch (Perca sp.)* (H

3518).

-(ę)terawak - spawn. *v.s.-a.i.* węterà·waks ‹it-conception-shakes› *it spawns* (HS).

-(ę)tera'nę - be subject. *v.s.-s.i.* ruterá·ʔ-nęʔ ‹he-conception-becomes› *he is subject* (HS).

-(ę)terę - be pregnant. *v.s.-a.i.* yetè·ręh ‹one-conception-falls› *she is pregnant* (HS).

-(ę)teri - be expectant, be pregnant. *v.s.-a.i.* katè·rih ‹it-embryo-is a group› *it is expectant, it is pregnant* (HS).

-(ę)teru - perch. *dv.n.s.* ruté·ru·ʔ ‹he-conception-is in water› *perch (Perca sp.)* (H 3518).

-ętęʔnyuT - invite to a feast. *v.r.-t.* See: -(i)tęʔnyuT -.

-ęti - nominal plural. *n.r.pfx.* Occurs only with the root -kaθʔah *be a child*.

-(ę)ti - reflexive. *v.r.pfx.* Occurs preceding certain stems that begin with the consonants and clusters *čh, t, n, ʔn, ʔt* or *ʔ*.

-ę°ti -/-eti - make. *v.r.-t.* hab: -h, pnt: -ʔ, stat: -·, prog: -ha'nyeʔ-, prp: -ęhte-, dst: -, caus: -hT-/-aʔT-, rvs: -, dat: III (-ati-/-ę-), inc.-ɸ-pat. The form -eti - occurs following pronominal prefixes that end in *k*, specifically the first person singular agent and patient pronominal prefixes, the third person indefinite agent pronominal prefix, and the third person plural agent pronominal prefix; the form -ę°ti - occurs elsewhere. The fact that the indefinite singular agent pronominal prefix has the form -yak - and the third plural agent pronominal prefix has the form -kayak -, forms normally seen only before the vowels *ę°* and *u*, indicates that the initial vowel of this root was originally *ę°* everywhere, with a subsequent shift of *ę°* to *e* after *k*. ęhrę́·ti·ʔ *he will make it* (R), ękyé·ti·ʔ *I will*

make it (R); -ętihT -: rętíhthaʔ ‹he-make-causes› *he dissects it* (HS), waʔ-kyé·tiht ‹fact-I-make-caused› *I cut it into pieces* (R), wahrę́·tiht ‹fact-he-make-caused› *he cut it into pieces* (RC 12:2); -ętyaʔT -: yakyetyáʔthaʔ ‹one-make-causes› *matter, material* (HS); -ętyaʔnahkw -: yakyetyaʔnáh-khwaʔ ‹one-make-cause-instrument› *mold* (HS); -(a)hahęti -: rahahę́·tih ‹he-path-makes› *he makes, is making a road or path* (HS); -(a)hę'nęti -: ruhęʔ-nę́·ti· ‹he-clearing-made› *he made a clearing* (RC 25:1); -(a)hkaręti -: rahkarę́·tih ‹he-bark-makes› *he chips it, he makes chips* (HS); -(a)hkarętihT -: rahkarętíhthaʔ ‹he-bark-make-causes› *he cuts slices* (HS); -(a)hyęti -: wahyę́·tih ‹he-fruit-makes› *it bears fruit, it fructifies* (HS); -(a)hyętyahnę -: yuhyętyáhnęʔ ‹he-fruit-made-much› *it is fruitful* (HS); -aʔtętyahnę -: wahraʔ-tętyáhnę·ʔ ‹fact-he-projectile-made-many› *he made some projectiles* (RC 6:5); -čanęti -: račanę́·tih ‹he-brightness-makes› *he polishes it, he scours it, he smoothes it* (HS); -čaʔkręti -: račaʔkrę́·tih ‹he-wetness-makes› *he wets it* (HS); -čhaʔręti -: račhaʔrę́·tih ‹he-anger-makes› *he offends it* (HS), naʔčhaʔrę́·tih ‹he-anger-makes› *one angers another* (R); -čhaʔrętyaʔT -: yučhaʔrę́·tyaʔt ‹it-anger-make-caused› *offensive* (HS); -čihkwęti -: θčihkwę́·ti ‹you-mush-make› *make mush!* (RC 3:52); -čihkwętyahnę -: račihkwętyáh-nęh ‹he-fist-makes-many› *he makes fists* (HS); -činęʔthęręti -: račinęʔ-therę́·tih ‹he-curl-makes› *he makes himself curly-headed; lit. he makes himself a curl (i.e., he causes himself to become a curl or curly-headed person)* (H 2484); -čisnęti -: kaku-čisnę́·ti· ‹they-ember-make› *they coun-*

sel, they deliberate (RC 12:26); -či²čęti -: rači²čę·tih ‹he-ruffle-makes› *he plaits, he makes a ruffle* (HS); -ekęti -: aryakyekę·ti² ‹unknown-one-liquid-make› *that one steep it* (RC 23:7), wekę·tih ‹it-liquid-makes› *infusion, wine* (HS); -(ę)tra²nęti -: wętra²nę·tih ‹it-horn-makes› *it is cornific* (HS); -ę'nęti -: yawę²nę·ti· ‹it-day-made› *it is disagreeable, it is gloomy, it is terrible, it is too bad, it is unpleasant* (HS); -(ę)²tikęhręti -: ru²tikęhrę·ti· ‹he-mind-made› *he made up his mind* (HS); rę²tikęhrę·tih ‹he-mind-makes› *he premeditates* (HS); -hseyęti -: kahseyę·tih ‹it-cone-makes› *conifer* (HS); -hskęnę²čręti -: rahskęnę²črę·tih ‹he-peace-'ness-makes› *he is peaceful* (HS); -hwenęti -: kahwenę·tih ‹it-island-makes› *congress, legislature* (HS); -hwenęti -.#ú²y: rahwenętihú²y ‹he-island-makes-great› *senator* (HS); -hwenętihst -: uhwenętíhsteh ‹island-make-'ness› *congress, continent, council, legislature, realm, reign, seat of government, the area of governmental representation* (HS); -hyęhęti -: kahyęhę·tih ‹it-river-makes› *ditch* (HS); -kerhęti -: kakyerhę·tih ‹it-body-makes› *puppet* (HS); -kerhuhčręti -: rakyerhuhčrę·tih ‹he-body-cover-'ness-makes› *tailor* (HS); -ke²čęti -: ęyekye²čę·ti² ‹prediction-one-dough-make› *one will make a bundle* (RC 20:1), *one will make a wad* (RC 23:4); -khęhstęti -: wa²kyekhęhstę·ti² ‹fact-I-soup-made› *I made soup* (R); -khwęti -: wa²kyekhwę·ti² ‹fact-I-food-made› *I cooked a meal* (R); -khwę=tya²T -: yekhwętyá²tha² ‹one-food-make-causes› *kitchen* (HS); -kθęti -: rakθę·tih ‹he-dish-makes› *potter* (HS); -nęhęti -: kanęhę·tih ‹it-corn-makes› *it makes corn, said of growing corn when it is changing from the milk, or when the ears begin to show the grain buds* (H 2484); -nęhkwa²čręti -{dative III}: ęhskwanęhkwa²črę·tyę² ‹prediction-you=me-medicine-'ness-make-for› *you must make medicine for me* (RC 6:4); -nęhsęti -: ranęhsę·tih ‹he-house-makes› *architect* (HS); *he makes a house; he makes a house as a profession, hence, a carpenter* (H 2484); -nęhsnęti -: kanęhsnę·tih ‹it-seed-makes› *it produces grain, seed: is producing grain or seed* (H 2484); -nhu=ręti -: kanhurę·tih ‹it-disease-makes› *unhealthy* (HS); -nhurętya²T -: yunhurętyá²-ne² ‹it-disease-make-caused› *unhealthy* (HS); -nurętyahnę -: wa²kanurętyáhnę² ‹fact-it-braided string of corn-made-many› *it made braided strings of corn* (RC 5:31); -rętu²čręti -: ęθwarętu²črę·ti² ‹prediction-you-coffin-make› *you will make a coffin* (RC 3:22); -rharahčręti -: rarharahčrę·tih ‹he-be confident-'ness-makes› *he gives hope* (HS); -rihstęti -{dative III}: wa²na²rihstę·tyę² ‹fact-one=another-leggings-made-for› *one made leggings for another* (RC 30:59); -rihęti -: rarihę·tih ‹he-matter-makes› *tutor* (HS), yerihę·tih ‹one-matter-makes› *teacher*

Tuscarora Pronunciation Key:
/a/ l̲aw; /e/ h̲at; /i/ p̲izza; /u/ tu̲ne; /ę/ hi̲n̲t; /č/ c̲h̲eese; /h/ h̲oe; /m/ m̲other; /s/ s̲ame; /t/ d̲o (before a vowel y, or w), t̲oo (elsewhere); /k/ g̲ale (before a vowel y or w), k̲ale (elsewhere); /n/ in̲h̲ale (before a consonant or word-final), n̲ote (elsewhere), /r/ hi̲s̲s̲ (before a consonant or word-final), ru̲n (trilled as in Italian, elsewhere); /w/ cuf̲f̲ (before a consonant other than y or word-final), w̲ay (elsewhere); /y/ fi̲s̲h̲ (before a consonant or word-final), y̲ou (elsewhere), /θ/ th̲ing; /²/ (the sound between the vowels in unh̲-unh); /·/ long vowel, /´/ high pitch; /`/ low pitch.

(L 60); –rihęti –{dative III}: wa'urihę́·tyę' ‹fact-it-matter-made-for› *it learned* (RC 8:36), yę'na'rihętyá·tih ‹one=another-matter-makes-for› *school* (R), ra'rihętyá·tih ‹he-himself-matter-makes-for› *he reads* (HS); –rihęti –{dative III} –'T –: ru'rihętyatí'ne' ‹he-himself-matter-makes-for-while moving› *he is studious* (HS); –rihętya'T –: yerihętyá'tha' ‹one-matter-make-causes› *school* (R), wa'rihętyá'tha' ‹it-itself-matter-make-causes› *origin* (HS); –rihętya'T –.#ú'y: yerihętya'thú'y ‹one-matter-make-causes-great› *academy* (R); –ri'węti –: rari'wę́·tih ‹he-blanket-makes› *he quilts* (HS); –θrahkwęti –: kaθrahkwę́·tih ‹it-coagulation-makes› *it coagulates (forms a thick mass)* (HS); –θręwętyahnę –: kaθręwętyáhnęh ‹it-jelly-makes-much› *sweetmeat* (HS); –tahskęti –: wa'etahskę́·ti' ‹fact-one-slave-made› *one picked on* (RC 35:7); –tahθęti –: ratahθę́·tih ‹he-braid-makes› *he braids* (HS); –takaręti –: ratakaрę́·tih ‹he-edge-makes› *he sharpens it* (HS); –(ta)' = čuhkwęti –: rata'čuhkwę́·tih ‹he-heap-makes› *he stacks* (HS); –terhya'čręti –: raterhya'črę́·tih ‹he-be ludicrous-'ness-makes› *he jests, he ridicules* (HS); –tu'karętyahnę –: ratu'karętyáhnęh ‹he-scallop-makes-much› *he scallops* (HS); –tya'kręti –: wa'katya'krę́·ti' ‹fact-it-wetness-made› *it got wet* (L 79), ęktya'krę́·ti' ‹fact-I-wetness-made› *I got wet, it got me wet* (L 79); –węniyuhčręti –: kawęniyuhčrę́·tih ‹it-be God-'ness-makes› *idol* (HS); –wih = ręti –: rawihrę́·tih ‹he-marsh-makes› *he makes dam* (HS); –wiręti –: kawirę́·tih ‹it-infant-makes› *doll* (HS), yewirę́·tih ‹one-infant-makes› *she is prolific* (HS); –yahčęti –: rayahčę́·tih ‹he-be curious-makes› *he is a specific person*

(RC 12:1), kayahčę́·tih ‹it-be curious-makes› *it is certain, it has to be* (RC 3:10); –yęhwanęti –: kayęhwanę́·tih ‹it-leafless tree-makes› *it decays* (HS); –yanręhstęti –: rayanręhstę́·tih ‹he-rule-'ness-makes› *legislator* (HS); –yaręti –: kayarę́·tih ‹it-bag-makes› *wicker* (HS); –yeręti –: kayerę́·tih ‹it-flesh-makes› *it is evident, it is legible, it is obvious, it is perceptible, it is plain, it is visible* (HS); *it shows* (RC 2:12); *indication, vestige* (HS); –yerętihT –: rayerętíhtha' ‹he-flesh-make-causes› *he marks it, he prints, he symbolizes it* (HS); –yeręti' –: rayerę́·ti'θ ‹he-flesh-make-begins› *he appears* (HS); –'na = ręwęti –: yu'naręwę́·ti' ‹it-mud-makes› *mud puddle* (RC 24:7); –'θkęwęti –: ra'θkęwę́·tih ‹he-roast-makes› *he broils it* (HS); –ne –.–ęti –: naryakyé·ti' ‹two-unknown-one-make› *that one make them into two* (RC 3:2); –t –.–ęti –: nahrę́·ti' ‹hither-fact-he-made› *there, he made it* (RC 3:73); –či –.–ekęti –: čawekę́·tye' ‹again-it-liquid-made› *wild honeysuckle (Lonicera* sp.) (H-notebook); –či –.–yeręti –: θkayerę́·tih ‹again-it-flesh-makes› *vestige* (HS); ti –.–nęhsęti –.#ú'y: tihrunęhsętihú'y ‹so-he-house-made-great› *he built a large house* (RC 24:7); ti –.–rhęti –: tikayerhętyéhte' ‹so-they-X-make-are going to› *they are going to make an offering* (RC 11:14); ti –.–yeręti –: thwa'kayerę́·ti' ‹so-fact-it-flesh-made› *it became visible* (RC 9:7); ti+yah –.–(i)'θhęti –: thwehra'θhę́·tih ‹so-thither-he-power-makes› *he conjectures, he guesses* (HS); –a'nęti –: ra'nę́·tih ‹he-himself-makes› *he is born* (HS), wahra'nę́·ti' ‹fact-he-himself-made› *he was born* (HS); –atkwe'nęti –: ratkwe'nę́·tyę ‹he-himself-movement-made› *he moved* (RC

24:10): –atkeʔθręti –: ratkyeʔʔθrę́·tih ‹he-himself-frown-makes› *he scowls* (HS); –aˈnaˈnętihaˈnyeʔ –: yuʔnaʔnęti-háˑʔnyeʔ ‹it-another-make-is going a-long› *it is making itself into* (RC 9:6); –aˈnerʔęhsęti –: čhiyaʔnerʔęhsę́·ti ‹you all!-yourselves-clan-make› *propagate!* (AG), waʔkaʔnerʔęhsę́·tiʔ ‹fact-I-my-self-clan-made› *I flourish, I propagate* (AG); –aˈnęθrętyaʔT –: raʔnęθrętyáʔ-thaʔ ‹he-himself-be so big-make-causes› *he fondles* (HS); –aˈnętuʔθęti –: raʔnętuʔθę́·tih ‹he-himself-tooth-makes› *he teethes* (HS); –aˈnwiręti –: raʔnwirę́·tih ‹he-himself-infant-makes› *he procreates* (HS); –aˈnyerętihnahkw –: yuʔnyerętihnáhkę ‹it-itself-flesh-make-caused-instrument› *sign, symbol* (HS); –aˈnyerętihnęhaˈnyeʔ –: yuʔnyerętihnę-háˑʔnyeʔ ‹it-itself-flesh-made-going along› *apparently* (HS); –aʔręnęti –: ruʔręnę́·tiˑ ‹he-himself-magic-made› *wizard, magician* (RC 14:2), waʔęʔ-ręnę́·tiʔ ‹fact-one-oneself-magic-made› *one made magic* (RC 3:41), waʔka-yęʔręnę́·tiʔ ‹fact-they-themselves-ma-gic-made› *they put it in a state of enchantment* (RC 35:11); –aʔrihęti –{dative III}: raʔrihętyá·tih ‹he-himself-matter-makes› *he reads* (HS); –aʔ= rihęti –{dative III} –ʔT –: ruʔrihętyatíʔ-neʔ ‹he-himself-matter-made-moving› *he is studious* (HS); –aʔrihętyaʔT –: waʔrihętyáʔthaʔ ‹it-itself-matter-make-causes› *origin* (HS); –(ę)tičhaʔręti –: rętičhaʔrę́·tih ‹he-himself-anger-makes› *he is furious* (HS); –(ę)tiʔ=

nyuhkwęti –: rętiʔnyuhkwę́·tih ‹he-himself-group-makes› *he makes an al-liance, he mutinies* (HS), wętiʔnyuh-kwę́·tih ‹it-itself-group-makes› *cluster, league* (HS); –ne –. –atkwaʔnęti –: nehru-tkwaʔnę́·tih ‹two-he-himself-arc-makes› *he is round* (HS); **haʔ** –ęˈnęti –: haʔ yawęʔnę́·tiˑ ‹the it-day-made› *grief, what is sad or doleful* (HS); **haʔ** –taʔnaręti –: haʔ rataʔnarę́·tih ‹the he-bread-makes› *baker* (HS); **haʔ** –aʔ= rihęti –{dative III}: haʔ raʔrihętyá·tih ‹the he-himself-matter-makes› *pupil, student* (HS); **kęʔ** ti –. –aˈnęti –: kęʔ tihraʔnę́·tih ‹where so-he-himself-makes› *Nativity* (HS); **ehnáhkye** –ęˈti –: ehnáhkye rę́·tih ‹low he-makes› *he abases* (HS); **nékw** –ęˈti –: nékw rę́·tih ‹tight he-makes› *he fastens it, he tightens it* (HS); **pámp** –ęˈti –: pámp rę́·tih ‹pump he-makes› *he pumps* (HS).

–ętičhaʔrakʷek – be in a frenzy, be fur-ious. *v.s.-a.i.* rętičháʔrakweks ‹he-himself-anger-closes› *he is in a fren-zy, he is furious* (HS).

–ętičhaʔręti – be furious. *v.s.-a.i.* rętičhaʔ-rę́·tih ‹he-himself-anger-makes› *he is furious* (HS).

#ętíh several little (diminutive distrib-utive). *enc.* The diminutive distribu-tive combines the various meanings of the diminutive (see #áh) with the meaning of the various distributive markers (for example, #haʔnęʔ and #kęhaʔnęʔ). It is fairly infrequent in actual discourse, appearing principally to indicate the diminutive size of a number of objects dispersed spatially (e.g., –**hehn** –.#**ętíh**: uhehnehętíh ‹field-many little› *the fields are small, diminutive* (H 2484)), to constrain the meaning of attributive verbs (e.g., **ti** –. –(a)**haheθ** –.#**ętíh**: tiwahaheθ⁷ętíh ‹so-it-path-is long-many little› *the rows are short* (H 2484)), and to form nouns that are to a greater or lesser extent opaque in meaning (e.g., –**hsęwa⁷r** –.#**ętíh**: uhsęwa⁷rehętíh ‹nail-many little› *tacks* (HS), –**hsir** –.#**ętíh**: uhsirehętíh ‹thread-many little› *cotton, linen* (AG)).

Ętíhę Muncytown, Ontario (90 miles northwest of Brantford) (AG). *n.*

–(**ę**)**tihkw** – down, fur, muff, wool. *n.r.* n-poss., inc., n.sfx. -eh. utíhkweh *down, fur, muff, wool* (HS); –(**ę**)**tihkwi⁷**=θ(e)r –: wętihkwí⁷θręhs ‹it-down-drags› *mud sleigh* (SH 375).

–(**ę**)**tihkwi⁷θ(e)r** – mud sleigh. *dv.n.s.* wętihkwí⁷θręhs ‹it-down-drags› *mud sleigh* (SH 375).

–**ętihręčhę'ni** – back up. *v.r.-a.i.* hab: -ęhs, pnt: -⁷, stat: -, prog: -, prp: -, dst: -, caus: -, rvs: -, dat: -, n-inc. wahrę·tihręčhę́·⁷ni⁷ *he backed into it* (RC 8:4), rętihręčhę́·⁷nyęhs *he backs up* (HS); –**či** –. –**ętihręčhę'ni** –: θhrętihręčhę́·⁷nyęhs ‹again-he-backs up› *he retreats* (HS).

–**ętihse⁷y** – maggot. *n.r.* n-poss., inc., n.sfx. -eh. awętihsé⁷yeh *maggot* (R); –**ne** –. –**ętihse⁷yahkwahnę** –: newętihse⁷yahkwáhnęh ‹apart-it-maggot-picks up-much› *maggots danced around* (RC 26:33).

–**ętihskę⁷nar** – outer bark. *n.r.* n-poss., inc., n.sfx. -eh. awętihskę⁷nà·reh *outer bark* (R); –**a'nętihskę⁷naruhči** –: yu⁷nętihskę⁷narúhčę ‹it-itself-outer bark-removed› *it has removed its outer bark*

(RC 32:9).

–**ę°tihT** – cut into pieces, dissect. *v.s.-t.* rętíhtha⁷ ‹he-make-causes› *he dissects it* (HS), wa⁷kyé·tiht ‹fact-I-make-caused› *I cut it into pieces* (R), wahrę́·tiht ‹fact-he-make-caused› *he cut it into pieces* (RC 12:2).

–(**ę**)**tihtawęhsT** – liniment. *dv.n.s.* yętihtawę́hstha⁷ ‹one-oneself-rub-causes› *liniment* (HS).

–**ęti⁷nęw** – deny. *v.r.-a.i.* hab: -ahs, pnt: -, stat: -, prog: -, prp: -, dst: -, caus: -, rvs: -, dat: -, n-inc. ręti⁷nę̀·wahs *he denies (what he said or did)* (HS).

–(**ę**)**ti⁷nyuhkwęti** – make an alliance, mutiny. *v.s.-a.i.* ręti⁷nyuhkwę́·tih ‹he-himself-group-makes› *he makes an alliance, he mutinies* (HS).

–(**ę**)**ti⁷nyuhkwęti** – cluster, league. *dv.n.s.* węti⁷nyuhkwę́·tih ‹it-itself-group-makes› *cluster, league* (HS).

–(**ę**)**ti⁷rhwęθawihT** – be sheepish. *v.s.-a.i.* ręti⁷rhwęθawíhtha⁷ ‹he-himself-tail-give-causes› *he is sheepish* (HS).

–(**ę**)**ti⁷rhwęθawihT** – sycophant. *dv.n.s.* ręti⁷rhwęθawíhtha⁷ ‹he-himself-tail-give-causes› *sycophant* (HS).

–(**ę**)**ti⁷rhwęθu'narhuhsT** – crupper. *dv.n.s.* węti⁷rhwęθu⁷narhúhstha⁷ ‹it-itself-tail-hook-causes› *crupper* (HS).

–(**ę**)**ti⁷θhahkw** – step. *v.s.-a.i.* ręti⁷θháhkhwa⁷ ‹he-himself-power-picks up› *he steps* (HS).

–**ęti⁷θhar** – leap. *v.r.-a.i.* hab: -ϕ, pnt: -ę⁷, stat: -, prog: -, prp: -, dst: -, caus: -, rvs: -, dat: -, n-inc. rętí⁷θhar *he leaps* (HS), ęhręti⁷θhà·rę⁷ *he will leap* (HS).

–(**ę**)**ti⁷tyę⁷θ(e)r** – blow nose, wipe nose. *v.r.-a.i.* hab: -ęhs, pnt: ()-⁷, stat: -, prog: -, prp: -, dst: -, caus: -, rvs: -, dat: -, n-inc. Almost certainly an old, no longer transparent compound of –(**ę**)**ti** – "reflexive" + –⁷**tyę(hs)** – *nose* + –(i)⁷**θ(e)r** – *drag*. ręti⁷tyę́⁷θręhs *he* *blows his nose, he wipes his nose* (HS), ęhręti⁷tyę́⁷θre⁷r *he will blow his nose, he will wipe his nose* (HS).

–ętkweθ – knee. *n.r.* inaln: kętkweθę́⁷kye *my knee* (R), inc., n.sfx. –eh. awętkwé·θeh *knee* (R).

–ętrahr – limb (of a body), shoulder blade. *n.r.* inaln: kętráhreh *my shoulder blade* (R), inc., n.sfx. –eh. awętráhreh *limb (of a body), shoulder blade* (HS).

–(ę)tra⁷n – horn. *n.r.* n-poss., inc., n.sfx. –eh. awętrá⁷neh *horn* (R), utrá⁷neh *horn* (PC); –(ę)tra⁷neθ –: wętra⁷né·θę ‹it-horn-is long-much› *ox* (R); –(ę)= tra⁷nęti –: wętra⁷-né·tih ‹it-horn-makes› *it is cornific* (HS); –(ę)tra⁷nya⁷k –: rętrá⁷nya⁷ks ‹he-horn-breaks› *he breaks horns* (HS).

–(ę)tra⁷neθ – ox. *dv.n.s.* wętra⁷né·θę ‹it-horn-is long-much› *ox* (R).

–ętręnayę – pray. *v.s.-a.i.* See: –atręna= yę –.

–ętuček – rainy. *dv.n.s.* yawętúčkę ‹it-rains-easily› *rainy* (HS).

–ętuT – rain. *v.r.-a.i.* hab: -s, pnt: -φ, stat: -ę, prog: -, prp: -he⁷, dst: -, caus: -, rvs: -, dat: -, n-inc. Takes an irregular form of the neuter singular agent pronoun, –h –, following the factual mode. wę́·tu·č *it rains: rain* (R) [Lawson «Untuch» 'Rain'] [Gallatin «wuntootch» 'Rain'], wahę́·tu·t *it rained* (RC 3:65), ęwę́·tu·t *it will rain* (R); –ętuT –: awętú·⁷nę ‹rain› *rainwater* (HS); –ętuček –: yawętúčkę ‹it-rains-easily› *rainy* (HS); –t –. –ętuthe⁷ –: nyuwętú·

the⁷› ‹hither-it-rain-going to› *moon dog* (R).

–ętuT – rainwater. *dv.n.s.* awętú·⁷nę ‹rain› *rainwater* (HS).

–(ę)tu⁷θ – tooth. *n.r.* aln: ktú⁷θeh *my tooth* (R), inc., n.sfx. –eh. utú⁷θeh *tooth* (R) [Gallatin «otoatseh, otohseh» 'Tooth']; –(ę)tu⁷θanęhwak(T) –: waktu⁷θanę́hwaks ‹I-tooth-aches› *I have a toothache* (R); –(ę)tu⁷θarik –: rutú⁷θariks ‹he-tooth-bites› *he has a toothache* (HS); –(ę)tu⁷θawihsi –: ratu⁷θawíhsyęhs ‹he-tooth-give to-undoes› *he pulls out teeth, he extracts teeth, he draws teeth* (HS); –(ę)tu⁷= θawihsya⁷T –: yętu⁷θawihsyá⁷tha⁷ ‹one-tooth-give to-undo-causes› *forceps* (HS); –(ę)tu⁷θa'ne –: katu⁷θá·⁷ne⁷ ‹it-tooth-is present› *a tooth sticks out* (H 2892); –(ę)tu⁷θęT –: katú⁷θę·t ‹it-tooth-possesses› *domestic goose* (R); *a flageolet* (HS); *yellow pike* (H 35 18) [Jefferson «kah-toh-sunt» 'goose'] [Gallatin «kahtosant» 'Goose']; –(ę)= tu⁷θęT –.#ú⁷y: katu⁷θę·t⁷ú⁷y ‹it-tooth-possesses-great› *swan* (R); –(ę)tu⁷= θęti –: rętu⁷θę́·tih ‹he-tooth-makes› *he teethes* (HS); –a'nętu⁷θęti –: ra⁷nętu⁷θę́·tih ‹he-himself-tooth-makes› *he teethes* (HS); –ne –. –(ę)tu⁷ča⁷k –: nehrętú⁷ča⁷ks ‹apart-he-tooth-breaks› *he breaks his tooth* (HS); –(ę)tu⁷θęT – –⁷niha –: katú⁷θę·t ka⁷níha· ‹it-tooth-possesses it-is male› *gander* (HS).

–(ę)tu⁷θanęhwak(T) – have a toothache. *v.s.-a.i.* waktu⁷θanę́hwaks ‹I-tooth-aches› *I have a toothache* (R).

-(ę)tuʔθa̱rik – have a toothache. *v.s.-a.i.* rutúʔθariks ‹he-tooth-bites› *he has a toothache* (HS).

-(ę)tuʔθawihsi – pull out teeth, extract teeth, draw teeth. *v.s.-a.i.* ratuʔθawíhsyęhs ‹he-tooth-give to-undoes› *he pulls out teeth, he extracts teeth, he draws teeth* (HS).

-(ę)tuʔθawihsyaʔT – forceps. *dv.n.s.* yetuʔθawihsyáʔthaʔ ‹one-tooth-give to-undo-causes› *forceps* (HS).

-(ę)tuʔθęT – domestic goose; flageolet; yellow pike. *n.s.* katúʔθę·t ‹it-tooth-possesses› *domestic goose; a flageolet* (HS); *yellow pike* (H 3518) [Jefferson «kah-toh-sunt» 'goose'] [Gallatin «kahtosant» 'Goose'].

-(ę)tuʔθęT – -ʔniha – gander. *n.s.* katúʔθę·t kaʔníha· ‹it-tooth-possesses it-is male› *gander* (HS).

-(ę)tuʔθęT -.#uʔy swan. *n.s.* katuʔθę·t-ʔúʔy ‹it-tooth-possesses-great› *swan* (R).

-(ę)tuʔθęti – teethe. *v.s.-a.i.* rętuʔθę́·tih ‹he-tooth-makes› *he teethes* (HS).

-(ę)tuʔT – tooth's edge. *n.r.* poss. ?, inc., n.sfx. -. Found only in the following constructions. -(ę)tuʔthęʔ –: rutúʔthęʔθ ‹he-tooth's edge-?ʔ› *he sets on edge* (HS); -ne -. -ętuʔna̱rik –: nehrętúʔnariks ‹two-he-tooth's edge-bites› *he gnashes teeth, he grits teeth, he shows teeth* (HS).

-(ę)tuʔthęʔ – set on edge. *v.s.-a.i.* rutúʔthęʔθ ‹he-tooth's edge-?ʔ› *he sets on edge* (HS).

-(ę)twahT – miss, overlook. *v.r.-t.* hab: -, pnt:-ɸ, stat: -ɸ, prog: -, prp: -, dst: -, caus: -, rvs: -, dat: -, inc.-ʔʔ-pat. Found only with incorporated noun roots. -nęhętwaht –: kanęhę́·twaht ‹it-corn-overlooks› *the Twelve Mystical Bugs* (RC 15:title); -či -. -(ę)taʔra̱= twahT –: ęθkayęʔnaʔtrá·twaht ‹pre-

diction-again-they=another-head-overlook› *they will miss his head again* (RC 24:8); tha-. -aʔrihwa̱twahT –: thahsaʔrihwá·twaht ‹unusual-fact-you-matter-overlooked› *you did wrong* (AG), thaʔkaʔrihwá·twaht ‹unusual-fact-I-matter-overlooked› *I did wrong* (AG).

-(ę)tyahskariʔčr – bracelet, broach, buckle. *n.r.* n-poss., inc., n.sfx. -eh. utyahskaríʔčreh *bracelet, broach, buckle* (RC 26:9); -(ę)tyahskariʔčru= 'narhu –: rętyahskariʔčruʔnárhuhs ‹he-buckle-hook-causes› *he buckles* (HS); -(ę)tyahskariʔčru'narihsi –: ratyahskariʔčruʔnaríhsyęhs ‹he-buckle-hook-undoes› *he unbuckles* (HS).

-(ę)tyahskariʔčru'narhu – buckle. *v.s.-a.i.* rętyahskariʔčruʔnárhuhs ‹he-buckle-hook-causes› *he buckles* (HS).

-(ę)tyahskariʔčru'narihsi – unbuckle. *v.s.-a.i.* ratyahskariʔčruʔnaríhsyęhs ‹he-buckle-hook-undoes› *he unbuckles* (HS).

-ętyękwęhnę – sniff. *v.r.-a.i.* hab: -h, pnt: -ʔ, stat: -, prog: -, prp: -, dst: -, caus: -, rvs: -, dat: -, n-inc. rętyękwę́hnęh *he sniffs* (HS), ęhrętyękwę́hnęʔ *he will sniff* (HS).

#ęwe genuine (authenticative). *enc.* The authenticative is used on nouns to signal that the entity refered to is the ideal or prototypical case of the noun as in čarhuʔ.#ęwe: čarhuʔę̀·we ‹tobacco-genuine› *ritual tobacco (Nicotiana rustica)* (R); -čheʔw -.#ęwe: učheʔwehę̀·we ‹gourd-genuine› *true gourd (as opposed to, for example, a melon or cucumber which could also be referred to as a type of učhéʔweh)* (R); -ękʷe -.#ęwe: ękwehę̀·we ‹human-genuine› *Indian* (R), *Tuscarora* (RC 30:1); -(ę)ʔtikęhr -.#ęwe: naʔtikęhrehę̀·we ‹one=another-mind-genuine› *volun-*

tarily (HS); **háhteh.#ęwe**: hahtchę·we ‹pine tree-genuine› *Norway spruce (Picea abies)* (H-notebook); **-her-.#ęwe**: uherehę·we ‹green-genuine› *Timothy (grass) (Phleum pratense)* (H-notebook). It is used with verbs to indicate the ideal or ultimate realization of an action or state as in **-aθnerhu-.#ęwe**: raθnerhuhs'ʔę̀·we ‹he-finishes-genuine› *he perfects it* (HS); **-htinę-.#ęwe**: rahtinęhę̀·we ‹he-begs for-genuine› *he implores* (HS). It is also used with particles for emphasis as in **kewę.#ęwe**: kyewęhę̀·we ‹now-genuine› *lately, soon* (R). The boundary # automatically becomes *h* following a vowel-final word, ʔ following a consonant-final word, and φ following a word ending in a laryngeal.

ę̀·we where (R). *part.* See: **hę̀·we**.

ęwéhruʔ at most (RC 3:55). *part.* Also: **ęwè·ruʔ** (R).

ęwè·ruʔ at most (R). *part.* Also: **ęwéhruʔ** (RC 3:55).

-ę°y- cavern, cavity, depression, depths, hole, pit. *n.r.* n-poss., inc., n.sfx. -eh. awę̀·yeh *cavity, hole, pit* (HS); **-ę= yatkahT-**: ahręyátkaht ‹unknown-he-cavern-chase› *that he chase into the cavern* (RC 11:2); **-ęyakuʔčęri-**: waʔnyakęyakuʔčę̀·riʔ ‹fact-two-one-cavern-found› *the two of them found a cavern* (RC 11:1); **-ęyęti-**: ręyę́·tih ‹he-cavern-makes› *he makes a grave* (HS); ti-. **-ęyeθ-**: tiwę̀·ye·θ ‹so-it-cavern-is long› *it is deep* (R); ti-.

-ęyeθ-.#úʔy: tiwęye·θʔúʔy ‹so-it-cavern-is long-great› *it is very deep* (RC 3:73).

-ę°y- be a depression, be at a depth, hang down. *v.r.-a.i.* hab: -, pnt: -eʔ, stat: -φ, prog: -, prp: -, dst: -, caus: -, rvs: -, dat: -, inc.-ʔʔ-pat. Found only with incorporated noun roots. In the Western dialect the final *y* of the root is lost in word-final position, e.g., yúhyę *hanging fruit* (PC). **-(a)hyęy-**: yúhyęy ‹it-fruit-hangs down› *hanging fruit* (R); **-hθęy-**: yúhθęy ‹it-width of cloth-hangs down› *pendant, it hangs* (HS); **-nęʔyęčkwęy-**: yunęʔyę́čkwęy ‹it-nest-hangs down› *nest is* (RC 26:6); **-θkręy-**: yúθkręy ‹it-spittle-hangs down› *drivel* (HS); **-tyaʔnęy-**: yutyáʔnęy ‹it-hornet's nest-hangs down› *hornet's nest* (RC 26:5); **-wisęy-**: yuwí·sęy ‹it-ice-hangs down› *icicle* (HS); ti-. **-kerhęy-**: thwaʔukyerhę̀·yeʔ ‹so-fact-it-body-hung down› *body hung over it* (RC 17:2); ha? **-hθęyehę-**: haʔ yuhθęyéhęh ‹the it-width of cloth-hangs down-many› *hangings* (HS).

-ęʔ simple noun suffix. *n.r.sfx.* Rare, with an archaic flavor.

-ęʔ- empty noun root. *inc.*

-ęʔkʷek- smother. *v.s.-t.* ręʔkweks ‹he-X-closes› *he smothers it* (HS).

-ęʔke simple noun suffix+external locative. *n.r.sfx.* From the examples given by Hewitt (H 2484) it appears that this combination of suffixes had the consistent meaning of "on the surface of, against, attached to" in his time, as opposed to combinations of the external locative with other forms of the simple noun suffix, which meant "on top of" and "at the place of". See: -aʔke and -ehke. -(a)hęʔnęʔke: uhęʔnéʔkye ‹clearing-at› *on or in the meadow as a part of its surface* (H 2484); -aʹnahθehnęʔke: uʔnahθehnéʔkye ‹self-hide-at› *in concealment, in secret, stealthily, stealth, secretly, underhanded* (HS); -aʹnahsawiʔnahkw--eʔwihsęʔke: yęʔnahsawiʔnáhkhwaʔ aweʔwihséʔkye‹one-oneself-foot-give-causes-instrument saddle-at› *stirrup* (HS); -činęʔtheręʔke: učinęʔtheréʔkye ‹curl-at› *on (as a part of) the curl* (H 2484); -čiʔehnęʔke: učiʔehnéʔkye ‹claw-at› *on (as a fixture of) the claw* (H 2484); číˑʔnęʔ -hwihsnęʔkye: číˑʔnęʔ kahwihsnéʔkye ‹bird it-wing-at› *bird's wing* (PC); -čunęʔke: učunéʔkye ‹naked body-at› *on its naked body* (RC 30:44), sčunéʔkye ‹you-naked body-at› *on your naked body* (RC 3:54); -hehnęʔke: uhehnéʔkye ‹field-at› *on the field, or in the field, as a fixture of it* (H 2484); -kahręʔke: ekahręʔkye ‹one-eye-at› *(on) one's eye* (RC 26:10); -ne-.-ahsęʔke: neyęhséʔkye ‹two-one-foot-at› *(on) the two of them's feet* (RC 25:13); -nęčiʔ= theręʔke: unęčiʔtheréʔkye ‹curl of hair-at› *on, on the surface of the curl of hair* (H 2484); -nęhahręʔke: kanęharéʔkye ‹it-corn-puts up-at› *at corn-planting (a subaudition of the word for time), this is the name of the month of April(?)* (H 2484); *March* (R); -nęhęʔke: unęhéʔkye ‹corn-at› *on or against the corn (as a part of it, or a fixture of it)* (H 2484); -nęhsęʔke: unęhséʔkye ‹house-at› *against, or on the side of (as a part of) the house or umbrella* (H 2484); -nęhsnęʔke: unęh-snęʔkye ‹seed-at› *on, against (fastened to) the grain* (H 2484); -ręhsęʔke: uręhséʔkye ‹leg-at› *on its leg* (RC 30:45); -rhahstęʔke: urhahstéʔkye ‹cradle board-at› *in its cradle board* (RC 30:2); -tkwęʔke: utkwéʔkye ‹stomach-at› *on stomach* (RC 26:31), kyetkwéʔkye ‹I-stomach-at› *(on) my stomach* (R); -w(e)ręʔke: uwréʔkye ‹air-at› *on the wind* (R); -wiθręʔke: uwiθréʔkye ‹snow-at› *on snow* (RC 2:12).

ęʹna- optative mode+cislocative. *v.pfx.*

-ęʹnahraT- almanac. *dv.n.s.* węʔnáhraˑč ‹it-day-counts› *almanac* (HS).

-ęʹnakahrę- be intelligent. *v.r.-s.i.* stat: -ˑ, prog: -, prp: -, dst: -, caus: -, rvs: -, dat: -, n-inc. ręʔnakáhręˑ *he is intelligent* (HS).

-ęʹnakęheyaʔT- blast. *dv.n.s.* węʔnakęheyáʔthaʔ ‹it-day-die-causes› *blast* (HS).

-ęʹnaks- stormy. *dv.n.s.* węʔnáˑksęˑ ‹it-day-is bad› *stormy* (HS).

-ęʹnaksaʔT- storm. *dv.n.s.* węʔnaksáʔthaʔ ‹it-day-be bad-causes› *storm* (HS).

-ęʹnakT- Saturday. *n.s.* awéˑʔnakwt ‹day-next to› *Saturday* (R).

-ęʹnaku- take out of fire. *v.s.-t.* yakęʔnáˑkwahs ‹one-put in fire-undoes› *one took it out of fire* (RC 28:11).

-ęʹnar- date. *v.s.-t.* réˑʔnar ‹he-day-is in› *he dates it (marks the day)* (HS).

-ęʹnatukęhT- Sabbath. *dv.n.s.* yawęʔnatukéhthaʔ ‹it-day-is holy› *Sabbath* (HS).

-ęʹnaʹnehsT-/-awęʹnaʹnehsT- make pleasant. *v.r.-t.* hab: -haʔ, pnt: -φ, stat: -φ ~ -ę, prog: -, prp: -, dst: -, caus: -, rvs: -, dat: -, inc.-φ-pat. The form -awęʹnaʹnehsT- occurs with incorporated noun roots; the form -ęʹna= ʹnehsT- occurs elsewhere. ręʔnaʔnéhsthaʔ *he beautifies it, he makes it pleasant* (HS), yawęˑʔnaʔnehst *it feels good* (RC 26:26), rawę́·ʼnaʼnehst *he is agreeable* (HS), waʼawę́·ʼnaʼnehst *it was pleasant* (RC 27:14), yawęʼnaʼ-nehsnę́heʼ *it was very pleasant* (L 32); ti –. **–ę'na̲'nehsT** –: tyawę́·ʼnaʼnehst ‹so-it-made pleasant› *it feels so pleasant* (RC 5:38); **–(a)hę'nawę'na̲'nehsT** –: yuhęʼnawę́·ʼnaʼnehst ‹it-clearing-made pleasant› *it is a pleasant meadow* (H 2484); **–a'nę'na̲'nehsT** –: raʼnęʼnaʼ-néhsthaʼ ‹he-himself-makes pleasant› *he enjoys himself* (HS); **haʔ –ę'na̲ = 'nehsT** –: haʼ yawę́·ʼnaʼnehst ‹the it-made pleasant› *joy* (HS); **kwęhs –ę'na̲'nehsT** –: kwęhs ahrawęʼnaʼnéh-snęk ‹no unknown-he-make pleasant› *he is unhappy* (HS).

–ęʔnewaht – onion. *n.r.* n-poss., n-inc., n.sfx. –ɸ. awęʼnè·waht *onion (Allium cepa)* (R).

–ę'nęti – be disagreeable, be gloomy, be terrible, be too bad, be unpleasant. *v.s.-s.i.* yawęʼné·ti· ‹it-day-made› *it is disagreeable, it is gloomy, it is terrible, it is too bad, it is unpleasant* (HS).

–ę'nęti – {dative I} be gloomy, be uncomfortable. *v.s.-s.i.* rawęʼnętyá·ʼθe· ‹he-day-made-for› *he is gloomy, he is uncomfortable* (HS).

–ęʔnhekʷ – play a game. *v.r.-a.i.* hab: -s, pnt: -t, stat: -ę, prog: -, prp: -, dst: -θę-, caus: -T- ~ -sT-, rvs: -, dat: -, n-inc. θę́ʼnhekw *play!* (R), wakęʼn-hé·kwę *I am playing* (R), ka-yę́ʼnhekws *they play* (RC 11:16), ęθwę́ʼnhekwt *you will play* (RC 27:12); **–ęʔnhekʷ** –: awęʼnhé·kwęʼ ‹play› *game, play* (HS); **–ęʔnhekʷčr** –: awęʼn-hékwčreh ‹play-'ness› *amusement, game, play, toy* (R); **–ęʔnhekʷčrayę** –. **#ke**: kayęʼnhekwčrayę́ʼkye ‹they-play-'ness-lay-at› *gymnasium* (R); **–ęʔn = hekʷsk** –: rawęʼnhékwskę ‹he-played-easily› *he is playful, he is frolicsome* (HS); **–ęʔnhekʷsnahnęhkw** –: yęʼn-hekwsnahnę́hkhwaʼ ‹one-play-causes-much-instrument› *playthings* (H-note-book); **–ęʔnhekʷsT** –: yęʼnhékwsthaʼ ‹one-play-causes› *plaything* (H-note-book); **–ęʔnhekʷθę** –: węʼnhékwθęh ‹it-plays-many› *some are going to play* (RC 27:10), kayęʼnhekwθę́hteʼ ‹they-play-many-are going to› *they are going to play* (RC 11:17); **–ęʔnhekʷT** –: kayęʼnhékwthaʼ ‹they-play-causes› *they play with* (L 33); **–kaθʔah –ęʔn = hekʷT** –: eká·θʼʼah yęʼnhékwthaʼ ‹one-is a child one-play-causes› *child's play* (HS).

–ęʔnhekʷ – game, play. *n.s.* awęʼnhé·kwęʼ ‹play› *game, play* (HS).

–ęʔnhekʷčr – amusement, game, play, toy. *n.s.* awęʼnhékwčreh ‹play-'ness› *amusement, game, play, toy* (R).

–ęʔnhekʷčrayę –.**#ke** gymnasium. *dv.n.s.* kayęʼnhekwčrayę́ʼkye ‹they-play-'ness-lay-at› *gymnasium* (R).

–ęʔnhekʷsk – be frolicsome, be playful. *v.s.-a.i.* rawęʼnhékwskę ‹he-played-easily› *he is playful, he is frolicsome* (HS).

–ęʔnhekʷsnahnęhkw – playthings. *dv.n.s.* yęʼnhekwsnahnę́hkhwaʼ ‹one-play-

Tuscarora Pronunciation Key:
/a/ law; /e/ hat; /i/ pizza; /u/ tune; /ę/ hint; /č/ cheese; /h/ hoe; /m/ mother; /s/ same; /t/ do (before a vowel y, or w), too (elsewhere); /k/ gale (before a vowel y or w), kale (elsewhere); /n/ inhale (before a consonant or word-final), note (elsewhere), /r/ hiss (before a consonant or word-final), run (trilled as in Italian, elsewhere); /w/ cuff (before a consonant other than y or word-final), way (elsewhere); /y/ fish (before a consonant or word-final), you (elsewhere), /θ/ thing; /ʼ/ (the sound between the vowels in unh-unh); /·/ long vowel, /́/ high pitch; /̀/ low pitch.

causes-much-instrument› *playthings* (H-notebook).

-ę^ʔnhek^wsT – plaything. *dv.n.s.* yę^ʔnhékwstha^ʔ ‹one-play-causes› *plaything* (H-notebook).

-(ę)^ʔnhuhskwar– lower part of face, mouthful. *n.r.* n-poss., inc., n.sfx. -eh. u^ʔnhúhskwareh *lower part of face (from nose to chin), mouthful (as of a chipmunk with a mouth full of nuts)* (R); -či-. -(ę)^ʔnhuhskwaraT –: θwę^ʔn-húhskwara·t ‹again-it-mouthful-stands› *one mouthful* (HS).

-ę'ni– throw. *v.r.-t.* See: -a'ni–.

-(ę)^ʔnikęhkari– be uncomfortable. *v.s.-s.i.* ru^ʔnikęhká·ryę ‹he-mind-devoured› *he is uncomfortable* (HS).

-ę^ʔnikęhkarya^ʔn–{dative III} macerate, torture. *v.s.-a.i.* rę^ʔnikęhkarya^ʔná·tih ‹he-mind-devour-causes-for› *he macerates, he tortures it* (HS).

-(ę)^ʔnikęhkarya^ʔt– agony. *dv.n.s.* n-poss., n-inc., n.sfx. -. u^ʔnikęhká·rya^ʔt ‹mind-devour-cause› *agony* (HS).

-(ę)^ʔnikęh(r)– mind. *n.r.* n-poss., inc., n.sfx. -. Occurs only incorporated in verb stems borrowed from other Northern Iroquoian languages. See: -(ę)^ʔ=tikęh(r)–.

-(ę)^ʔnikęhrya^ʔk– despair. *v.s.-a.i.* rę^ʔnikęhrya^ʔks ‹he-mind-breaks› *he despairs* (HS).

-ę^ʔnireT– stay all day. *v.r.-a.i.* hab: -ha^ʔ, pnt: -ɸ, stat: -, prog: -, prp: -, dst: -ahnę-, caus: -, rvs: -, dat: -, n-inc. rę^ʔniré·tha^ʔ *he stays all day* (HS), wa^ʔkayakę^ʔní·re·t *they spent the whole day* (RC 12:14); -ę'nire'nahnę–: rę^ʔnire^ʔnáhnęh ‹he-stays all day-much› *he stays all the day* (HS).

-ę'niyu–.#keha·^ʔ diurnal. *n.s.* awę^ʔniyu^ʔkyéha·^ʔ ‹day-great-customarily› *diurnal, occurring during the day* (RC 3:2).

ę^ʔnyéhči meridian (HS), noon (RC 30:33). *part.* ę^ʔnyéhči na^ʔ-.-a'ni: ę^ʔnyéhči na^ʔú·^ʔni ‹noon some it-at edge of› *meridional (noon-side)* (HS).

ę^ʔnyéhči na^ʔ-.-a'ni meridional. *n.s.* ę^ʔnyéhči na^ʔú·^ʔni ‹noon some it-at edge of› *meridional (noon-side)* (HS).

-ę^{°ʔ}r– nut. *n.r.* n-poss., inc., n.sfx. -eh. awę^ʔreh *nut* (RC 10:1); -ę^{°ʔ}rahwa=ra'nehT–: yawę^ʔrahwà·ra^ʔneht ‹it-nut-is whitish› *almond* (HS); -ę^{°ʔ}retihst–: kakawę^ʔretíhstę ‹they-nut-consumed› *they lived on nuts* (RC 10:1); -ę^{°ʔ}ru–: wa^ʔkayakę^ʔru·^ʔ ‹fact-they-nut-been in water› *they put nuts in water* (RC 10:1); čwe-. -ę^{°ʔ}rake–: čwewę^ʔrá·kye· ‹all kinds of-it-nut-is in number› *all kinds of nuts* (RC 11:6); -ne-. -ę^{°ʔ}rahrih=nahkw–: neyakę^ʔrahrihnáhkhwa^ʔ ‹apart-one-nut-spill-causes-instrument› *nutcracker* (HS).

-ę^{°ʔ}rahwara'nehT– almond. *dv.n.s.* yawę^ʔrahwà·ra^ʔneht ‹it-nut-is whitish› *almond* (HS).

-ę^ʔtahkr– flame. *n.r.* n-poss., inc., n.sfx. -eh. awę^ʔtáhkreh *flame* (R); -ę^ʔtah=kra^ʔnihθk–: yawę^ʔtahkra^ʔníhθkę· ‹it-flame-stood up-easily› *inflammable* (HS); -ne-. -ę^ʔtahkrahkw–: newę^ʔtahkráhkhwa^ʔ ‹apart-it-flame-picks up› *it shoots up flames* (RC 13:9); -ne-. -ę^ʔtahkritkę^ʔnahnę–: newę^ʔtahkritkę^ʔnáhnęh ‹apart-it-flame-issue forth-causes-much› *flames are shooting out* (RC 28:8); -a'nę^ʔtahkra^ʔnihr–: yu^ʔnę^ʔtahkra^ʔníhrę ‹it-itself-flame-stood up› *it blazes, it flames* (HS).

-ę^ʔtahkra^ʔnihθk– inflammable. *dv.n.s.* yawę^ʔtahkra^ʔníhθkę· ‹it-flame-stood up-easily› *inflammable* (HS).

-(ę)^ʔtahs– tongue. *n.r.* inaln: ktáhseh *my tongue* (R), inc., n.sfx. -eh (*West.* -ę^ʔ). awę^ʔtáhseh *tongue* (R), awę^ʔtáhsę^ʔ (PC) [Gallatin «auwuntaway»

'Tongue']; -(ę)ʔtahsę -: yawę'ʔtáhsę'ʔ ‹it-tongue-fell› *bee swarm* (R); -(ę)ʔ = tahsarahkw -: yę'ʔtahsaráhkhwa'ʔ ‹one-tongue-collects› *one is gossiping, one is joking* (R); -ne -. -(ę)ʔtahsęt: neh-rę'ʔtáhsę·t ‹two-he-tongue-possesses› *he is two-tongued* (HS); -t -. -(ę)ʔtah = sitkę'ʔ -: nwę'ʔtahsí·tkę'ʔθ ‹hither-it-tongue-issue forth-begins› *it lolls* (HS).

-(ę)ʔtahsę - bee swarm. *dv.n.s.* yawę'ʔ-táhsę'ʔ ‹it-tongue-fell› *bee swarm* (R).

-(ę)ʔtahsarahkw - gossip, joke. *v.s.-a.i.* yę'ʔtahsaráhkhwa'ʔ ‹one-tongue-collects› *one is gossiping, one is joking* (R).

-(ę)ʔtey - crowd, drove, herd, team; sweet cicely. *n.r.* n-poss., inc., n.sfx. -eh (*crowd*)/ -a'ʔ (*sweet cicely*). u'ʔtè·-yeh *crowd, drove, herd, team* (R), u'ʔtè·ya'ʔ *sweet cicely* (*Osmorhiza* sp.) (H-notebook); -(ę)ʔteyakęw: u'ʔtè·ya-kęw ‹crowd-in› *in the crowd* (RC 26: 10); -(ę)ʔteyanę -.#aka·'ʔ: ra'ʔteyanę'ʔ-á·ka·'ʔ ‹he-crowd-guard-characterized by› *shepherd* (HS); -(ę)ʔteyaruhčrę -: wę'ʔteyarúhčręh ‹it-crowd-gathers› *they are assembled* (HS), kayę'ʔte-yarúhčręh ‹they-crowd-gather› *they congregate* (HS), wahra'ʔteyarúhčrę'ʔ ‹fact-he-crowd-gathered› *he gathered crowd together* (RC 7:7), ęhsteya-rúhčrę'ʔ ‹prediction-you-crowd-gather› *you will gather group together* (MP); -(ę)ʔteyaruhčrę -.#ú'ʔy: wę'ʔteyaruh-črę'ʔú'ʔy ‹it-crowd-gathers-great› *great crowd gathers* (RC 26:8); -(ę)ʔteyę -:

ka'ʔté·yę·k ‹it-crowd-fell› *yeast bread* (R); -(ę)ʔteyęhawihT -: ka'ʔteyęha-wíhtha'ʔ ‹it-crowd-carry-causes› *bus* (R); -(ę)ʔteyęhkw -: u'ʔteyę́hkweh ‹crowd-fall-instrument› *rack, frame* (HS); -(ę)ʔteyhę: u'ʔtéyhę ‹crowd-middle of› *publicly* (HS); -(ę)ʔteyityę -: yu'ʔteyí·tyę· ‹it-crowd-arrived› *a herd got in a field* (H-notebook); -(ę)ʔ = teyu -: ru'ʔté·yu·'ʔ ‹he-crowd-is in water› *mosquito* (RC 2:14); -(ę)ʔte = yuręhT -: ru'ʔteyurę́htha'ʔ ‹he-crowd-split-causes› *he announces (something), he denounces (someone)* (HS); -(ę)ʔteyuʔawi -: yu'ʔteyu'ʔà·wi'ʔ ‹it-crowd-floats› *crowd, moving flock, swarm* (HS); -t -. -(ę)ʔteyitkęhnahkw -: tka'ʔteyitkęhnáhkhwa'ʔ ‹hither-it-crowd-issue-causes-instrument› *exit* (RC 26:6); -ne+či -. -(ę)ʔteyahri -: nę-θakaye'ʔtè·yahri'ʔ ‹apart-fact-again-it-crowd-spill› *again crowd dispersed* (RC 12:29); -či -. -a'nę'ʔteyat'ʔa -: θę'ʔ-nęteyá·t'ʔa·'ʔ ‹again-fact-it-itself-crowd-got in› *crowd got back in* (RC 27:14); ha'ʔ -ne -. -(ę)'ʔteyahrihT -: ha'ʔ wa'ʔ-thra'ʔteyáhriht ‹the fact-apart-he-crowd-spill-caused› *Benediction* (HS); -kθ - -ę'ʔteyęhkw -: úkθeh ye'ʔteyę́h-khwa'ʔ ‹dish one-crowd-fall-instrument› *dripping pan* (HS).

-(ę)ʔteyanę -.#aka·'ʔ shepherd. *dv.n.s.* ra'ʔ-teyanę'ʔá·ka·'ʔ ‹he-crowd-guard-characterized by› *shepherd* (HS).

-(ę)ʔteyaruhčrę - assemble, congregate. *v.s.-a.i.* wę'ʔteyarúhčręh ‹it-crowd-gathers› *they are assembled* (HS),

Tuscarora Pronunciation Key:
/a/ l**a**w; /e/ h**a**t; /i/ p**i**zza; /u/ t**u**ne; /ę/ h**i**nt; /č/ **ch**eese; /h/ **h**oe; /m/ **m**other; /s/ **s**ame; /t/ **d**o (before a vowel y, or w), **t**oo (elsewhere); /k/ **g**ale (before a vowel y or w), **k**ale (elsewhere); /n/ i**nh**ale (before a consonant or word-final), **n**ote (elsewhere), /r/ hi**ss** (before a consonant or word-final), r**u**n (trilled as in Italian, elsewhere); /w/ c**u**ff (before a consonant other than y or word-final), **w**ay (elsewhere); /y/ fi**sh** (before a consonant or word-final), **y**ou (elsewhere), /θ/ **th**ing; /'ʔ/ (the sound between the vowels in u**nh-u**nh); /·/ long vowel, /'/ high pitch; /`/ low pitch.

kayę'teyarúhčręh ‹they-crowd-gather›
they congregate (HS).

–(ę)'teyę – yeast bread. *dv.n.s.* ka'té·yę·k
‹it-crowd-fell› *yeast bread* (R).

–(ę)'teyęhawihT – bus. *dv.n.s.* ka'teyęha-
wíhtha' ‹it-crowd-carry-causes› *bus*
(R).

–(ę)'teyęhkw – frame, rack. *n.s.* u'te-
yęhkweh ‹crowd-fall-instrument› *rack,
frame* (HS).

–(ę)'teyhę publicly. *n.s.* u'téyhę ‹crowd-
middle of› *publicly* (HS).

–(ę)'teyu – mosquito. *dv.n.s.* ru'té·yu·'
‹he-crowd-is in water› *mosquito* (RC
2:14).

–(ę)'teyu'awi – crowd, flock, swarm.
dv.n.s. yu'teyu'à·wi' ‹it-crowd-floats›
crowd, moving flock, swarm (HS).

–(ę)'teyuręhT – announce (something),
denounce (someone). *v.s.-t.* ru'teyu-
réhtha' ‹he-crowd-split-causes› *he announces (something), he denounces
(someone)* (HS).

–(ę)'tikęhn –/–(ę)'tikęh(r) – mind, reason,
temper. *n.r.* aln: aktikęhrà·węh *my
mind* (R), inc., n.sfx. –eh. This root
belongs to a handful that are productively incorporated to create new, idiomatic verb stems. It is used typically
when a new verb expressing a mental
state is required. The form –(ę)'tikęh–
occurs immediately preceding verb
roots beginning with *k* and in a few
archaic constructions; the form –(ę)'=
tikęhn – also occurs only in archaic
constructions; the form –(ę)'tikęhr –
occurs everywhere else. Forms beginning with the vowel ę may occur
following third person agent and
patient pronominal prefixes and following the reflexive and semireflexive
morphemes, although forms beginning
with the consonant ' may also occur
in these positions. u'tikéhreh *mind,*

reason, temper (R); –(ę)'tikęhaw –:
wa'kayę'na'tikéhę·' ‹fact-they=anoth-
er-mind-gave› *they inquired of another*
(R); –(ę)'tikęhkaręhrę –: na'tikęhka-
réhręh ‹one=another-mind-went a-
round-much› *one agitates another*
(HS); –(ę)'tikęhkaręhrahT –: u'tikęh-
karéhraht ‹mind-go around-much-
cause› *commotion* (HS); –(ę)'tikęh =
kaθne –: u'tikęhkáθne' ‹mind-be
strong› *patience* (HS), ru'tikęhkáθne'
‹he-mind-is strong› *he is indefatigable,
he is stout-minded, he is long-suffering* (HS); –(ę)'tikęhkęnyęhčr –: u'-
tikęhkęnyéhčreh ‹mind-excel-'ness›
cheating (HS); –(ę)'tikęhkeya'T –: ru'-
tikęhkyeyá'tha' ‹he-mind-agitates› *he
is oppressed* (HS), ra'tikęhkyeyá'tha'
‹he-mind-agitates› *he is solicitous*
(HS), yu'tikęhkyè·ya't ‹it-mind-agitated› *uncertainty* (HS), wahru'tikęh-
kyè·ya't ‹fact-he-mind-aggitated› *he
concluded* (RC 27:8), na'tikęhkę-
heyá'tha' ‹one=another-mind-agitates›
one discourages another (HS), wa'-
kaku'tikęhkyè·ya't ‹fact-they-mind-
agitated› *they arrived at a conclusion*
(RC 3:72); –(ę)'tikęhtahT –: u'tikéhtaht ‹mind-stand-cause› *danger, dangerous, peril* (HS), yu'tikéhtaht ‹it-
mind-stand-causes› *dangerous, hazardous, perilous* (HS); –(ę)'tikęhthę –:
wa'ka'tikéhthę' ‹fact-it-mind-stood-
much› *it had an idea* (RC 3:40); –ne –.
–(ę)'tikęhkarę'r –: nęθa'tikęhkaré'rę'
‹apart-prediction-you-mind-besloped›
you will be bothered by (HS); –ne –.
–(ę)'tikęhkęni –: nehru'tikęhké·nyę
‹apart-he-mind-excelled› *he is a cheat,
he is a hypocrite, he is dishonest, he
is mistaken, he outwits* (HS), nehra'tikęhké·nyęhs ‹apart-he-mind-excels› *he cheats, he outwits* (HS); –ne –.
–(ę)'tikęhke –: nehru'tikéhkye· ‹two-

he-mind-is in number› *he is dubious, he wavers* (HS), neyuʔtikęhkye· ‹two-it-mind-is in number› *uncertain* (HS); ti -. -(ę)ʔtikęhkaręhrę -: nęθaʔtikęhkaŕęhręʔ ‹so-prediction-you-mind-rock back and forth› *they will bother you* (R); -aʔnęʔtikęhkęni -: yuʔnęʔtikęhkę́·nya·t ‹it-itself-mind-excelled-complete› *it is illusory* (HS); -ne -. -aʔnęʔtikęh = kęy -: nehruʔnęʔtikęhkę̀·yę ‹apart-he-himself-mind-is emptied› *he is a cheat* (HS); -ne -. -aʔnęʔtikęhkęni -: nehruʔnęʔtikęhkę́·nyę ‹apart-he-himself-mind-excelled at› *he is a cheater, he is corrupt, dishonest, he is a hypocrite* (HS); -ne -. -rihwaʔtikęhkęni -: neyurihwaʔtikęhkę́·nyę ‹apart-it-matter-mind-excels› *subterfuge* (HS); haʔ -(ę)ʔtikęhkaθne -: haʔ raʔtikęhkáθneʔ ‹the he-mind-is strong› *his patience* (HS); -(ę)ʔtikęhnę -: ręʔtikę́hnęh ‹he-mind-falls› *he calculates, he intends, he imagines* (HS), waʔę́ʔtikę́hnęʔ ‹fact-one-mind-fell› *one thought* (RC 3:41), ahręʔtikęhnę́hek ‹unknown-he-mind-fall› *that his state of mind be* (RC 2:4); -(ę)ʔtikęhnęhčr -: uʔtikęhnę́hčreh ‹mind-fall-'ness› *behavior, imagination, meditation, thinking, thought* (HS); -(ę)ʔtikęhnęhčrukę?: ruʔtikęhnęhčrú·kęʔ ‹he-mind-fall-'ness-less› *he is thoughtless* (HS); -(ę)ʔti = kęhnęhkw -{dative III}: waʔuʔtikęhnę́hkwęʔ ‹fact-it-mind-fall-picked up-for› *it was baffled, it was stumped* (RC 30:10); -(ę)ʔtikęhnętyę -: ręʔtikęhnę́·tyęh ‹he-mind-falls-much› *he*

thinks, he projects, he meditates (HS), waʔę́ʔtikęhnę́·tyęʔ ‹fact-one-mind-fell-much› *one thought through* (RC 30:6); -t -. -(ę)ʔtikęhnę -: thręʔtikę́hnęh ‹hither-he-mind-falls› *he governs* (H-notebook), thrawęʔtikę́hnęʔ ‹hither-he-mind-fell› *he controls, he sways the rule: forethought* (HS), ętkęʔtikę́hnę·ʔ ‹prediction-hither-I=you-mind-fall› *I will decide for you* (RC 3:36); -t -. -(ę)ʔtikęhnę -{dative I}: thrawęʔtikęhnę́ʔθe· ‹hither-he-mind-fell-for› *he goes involuntarily* (HS); ti -. -(ę)ʔti = kęhnęhčruʔnę -: tiwęʔtikęhnęhčrúʔnę· ‹so-it-mind-fall-'ness-is a kind of› *design, mode of thought* (HS); -yah -. -(ę)ʔtikęhnę -: yęyęʔtikęhnę·ʔ ‹thither-prediction-one-mind-fall› *one will have such thoughts* (RC 3:40); -(ę)ʔ = tikęhr -.#ęwe: naʔtikęhrehę̀·we ‹one=another-mind-genuine› *voluntarily* (HS); -(ę)ʔtikęhr -.#keha·ʔ: uʔtikęhręʔkyéha·ʔ ‹mind-customarily› *spiritual* (HS); -(ę)ʔtikęhrahnę -: raʔtikęhráhnęh ‹he-mind-disappears› *he is lethargic* (HS), wahraʔtikęhráhnęʔ ‹fact-he-mind-disappeared› *he fainted, he lost consciousness* (RC 24:9); -(ę)ʔtikęh = rahnęʔT -: naʔtikęhrahnę́ʔthaʔ ‹one=another-mind-disappear-causes› *one stuns another* (HS), raʔtikęhrahnę́ʔthaʔ ‹he-mind-disappear-causes› *he stupefies it* (HS); -(ę)ʔtikęhrahręhw -: ruʔtikęhráhręw ‹he-mind-put up-caused› *he anticipates* (R); -(ę)ʔtikęhrahruʔT -: ruʔtikęhrahrúʔnę ‹he-mind-is mellow› *he is affable* (HS); -(ę)ʔtikęhrahti =

Tuscarora Pronunciation Key:

/a/ law; /e/ hat; /i/ pizza; /u/ tune; /ę/ hint; /č/ cheese; /h/ hoe; /m/ mother; /s/ same; /t/ do (before a vowel y, or w), too (elsewhere); /k/ gale (before a vowel y or w), kale (elsewhere); /n/ inhale (before a consonant or word-final), note (elsewhere), /r/ hiss (before a consonant or word-final), run (trilled as in Italian, elsewhere); /w/ cuff (before a consonant other than y or word-final), way (elsewhere); /y/ fish (before a consonant or word-final), you (elsewhere), /θ/ thing; /ʔ/ (the sound between the vowels in unh-unh); /·/ long vowel, /ˊ/ high pitch; /ˋ/ low pitch.

ra̲hT –: uʼtikęhrahtiráhtaʼ ‹mind-be hard-cause› *confirmation* (HS); –(ę)ʼ = **tikęhraks** –: Kaʼtikęhrá·ksę· ‹it-mind-is bad› *Bad Mind (one of the primordial twins): evil spirit* (HS); –(ę)ʼtikęhraks – {dative II}: waktikęhrá·ksęhθ ‹I-mind-is bad-for› *I am unhappy* (R); –(ę)ʼ = **tikęhraksaʼT** –: naʼtikęhraksáʼthaʼ ‹one=another-mind-be bad-causes› *one vexes another* (HS), yuʼtikęhrá·ksaʼt ‹it-mind-be bad-caused› *lamentable, saddening* (HS); –(ę)ʼtikęhrakwahsT –: Kaʼtikęhrákwahst ‹it-mind-is good› *Good Mind (one of the primordial twins): good spirit: benevolence* (HS); –(ę)ʼtikęhra̲kweni –: naʼtikęhrakwé·nyęhs ‹one=another-mind-is able› *one influences another* (HS), raʼtikęhrakwé·nyęhs ‹he-mind-is able› *he persuades* (HS); –(ę)ʼtikęhranę̲'nahsi –: naʼtikęhranęʼnáhsyęhs ‹one=another-mind-attach-undoes› *one dissuades another* (HS); –(ę)ʼtikęhra̲nurę –: kaʼ-tikęhranù·ręʼ ‹it-mind-is precious› *drug-free* (R); –(ę)ʼtikęhra̲r –: raʼtikęhrar ‹he-mind-is in› *he is careful, he is cautious, he is mindful* (HS), uʼtikę́hrarę· ‹mind-is in› *caution* (HS); –(ę)ʼtikęhra̲ręhyakę –: ruʼtikęhraręhyá·kę· ‹he-mind-suffered› *he is anxious* (HS); –(ę)ʼtikęhra̲ręhyakęʼT –: ruʼtikęhraręhyaké́ʼthaʼ ‹he-mind-suffer-causes› *he is anxious* (HS); –(ę)ʼ = **tikęhrarhaʼ** –: naʼtikęhrárhaʼθ ‹one=another-mind-ʼʼ› *one distrusts another* (HS); –(ę)ʼtikęhrarheryeti –: raʼtikęhrarheryé·tih ‹he-mind-ʼʼ› *he is candid* (HS); –(ę)ʼtikęhraT –: yuʼtikę́hra·t ‹it-mind-stands› *animal (as opposed to vegetable)* (R), ruʼtikę́hra·t ‹he-mind-stands› *he has discretion* (HS); –(ę)ʼ = **tikęhratukęht** –: uʼtikęhratukę́hti ‹mind-be holy› *Great Spirit: Holy Spirit* (R); –(ę)ʼtikęhratʼa –: ruʼtikęhrá·tʼę ‹he-

mind-put in› *he advises* (HS), naʼ-tikęhrá·tʼahs ‹one=another-mind-puts in› *one advised another* (HS); –(ę)ʼ = **tikęhrawehθa̲yę(T)** –: ruʼtikęhrawéh-θayęʼ ‹he-mind-dark-ness-lay› *he is dark-minded* (HS); –(ę)ʼtikęhrawęri –: naʼtikęhrawę̀·rih ‹one=another-mind-stirs› *one bewilders another* (HS); –(ę)ʼtikęhrayaʼnerę –: naʼtikęhrayaʼ-nè·ręh ‹one=another-mind-wounds› *one chides another* (HS); –(ę)ʼti = **kęhrayerik** –: naʼtikęhrayè·riks ‹one=another-mind-is filled› *one satisfies another* (HS); –(ę)ʼtikęhra̲yę(T) –: naʼ-tikę́hrayęhs ‹one=another-mind-lays› *one comforts another* (R), raʼtikęh-rayęʼ ‹he-mind-lays› *he has confidence* (HS); –(ę)ʼtikęhrayę(T) –{dative II}: ruʼtikęhrayę́·ʼnahθ ‹he-mind-laid-for› *he discerns* (R); –(ę)ʼtikęh = **raʼnihr** –: ruʼtikęhraʼníhrę ‹he-mind-stood up› *his sympathy* (HS), ruʼti-kęhráʼnihč ‹he-mind-stands up› *it interests him* (HS); –(ę)ʼtikęhraʼtyęʼ = **nę** –: raʼtikęhraʼtyéʼnęh ‹he-mind-measures› *he tempts* (HS); –(ę)ʼtikęh = **reθ** –: raʼtikę́hre·θ ‹he-mind-is long› *he is patient* (HS); –(ę)ʼtikęhręT –{dative II}: ruʼtikęhré·ʼnęhθ ‹he-mind-con-cluded-for› *he forgets* (R), waʼkaʼ-tikęhré·ʼnęʼ ‹fact-it-mind-concluded-for› *it forgot* (RC 35:43); –(ę)ʼtikęh = **ręthuhT** –: aryęʼnaʼtikęhrę́·thuht ‹un-known-one=another-mind-close-cause-caused› *that one remember another, that one comfort another* (RC 35:16), naʼtikęhręthúhthaʼ ‹one=another-mind-close-cause-causes› *one soothes another* (HS); –(ę)ʼtikęhręti –: ruʼti-kęhrę́·tih ‹he-mind-makes› *he made up his mind* (HS), ręʼtikęhrę́·tih ‹he-mind-makes› *he premeditates* (HS); –(ę)ʼtikęhręʼ –: ruʼtikęhrę́ʼę ‹he-mind-fall-began› *he is dejected* (HS), waʼ-

kaku'tikęhrę́'ę ⟨fact-they-mind-fall-begaṇ⟩ *they had a thought* (RC 3:72); -(ę)'tikęhrhęreT -: ra'tikęrhęré·tha'' ⟨he-mind-carries away⟩ *he is alluring* (HS); -(ę)'tikęhrihs'a -: rę'tikęhríhs-'ahs ⟨he-mind-finishes⟩ *he resolves* (HS); -(ę)'tikęhriyu -{dative I}: ru'-tikęhriyú'θeh ⟨he-mind-be great-for⟩ *it pleases him* (HS); -(ę)'tikęhriyuhT -: ru'tikęhriyúhtha' ⟨he-mind-be great-causes⟩ *he amuses* (R); -(ę)'ti = kęhrukę'': ru'tikęhrú·kę' ⟨he-mind-less⟩ *he is boisterous, he is impudent, he is mindless, he is rash, he is thoughtless* (HS); -(ę)'tikęhrut -: rę'-tikęhrú·tha' ⟨he-mind-stands⟩ *he invents* (HS); -(ę)'tikęhruryahT -: u'ti-kęhrú·ryaht ⟨mind-stir-cause⟩ *amusement* (R); -(ę)'tikęhru'kręhT -: na'-tikęhru'kréhtha' ⟨one=another-mind-float-causes⟩ *one debauches* (HS); -(ę)'tikęhru'naku -: ra'tikęhru'ná·kwahs ⟨he-mind-send-undoes⟩ *he allures, he beguiles: allurer, tempter* (HS), ęktikęhru'nakwáhshek ⟨prediction-I-mind-send-undo⟩ *I will be at peace* (R); -(ę)'tikęhru'nak"ahT -: yu'-tikęhru'ná·kwaht ⟨it-mind-send-undo-causes⟩ *charm, charming* (HS); -(ę)' = tikęhru'nę -: yękwa'tikęhrú'nę· ⟨we-mind-is a kind of⟩ *(our) philosophy* (R); -(ę)'tikęhrya'khę -: ra'tikęhryá'-khęh ⟨he-mind-breaks-much⟩ *he bothers it* (HS), na'tikęhryá'khęh ⟨one=another-mind-breaks-much⟩ *one disconcerts another* (HS); -(ę)'tikęhryenę -: ra'tikęhryenę́hrę' ⟨he-mind-grabs-

much⟩ *he escorts it* (HS), na'tikęh-ryè·nęh ⟨one=another-mind-grabs⟩ *one accompanies another* (HS); -či -. -(ę)' = tikęhraT-{dative III}: čęktikęhrá·'nę' ⟨again-one=me-mind-is present⟩ *one has given me an idea* (RC 6:18); -či -. -(ę)'tikęhritkę' -: θhra'tikęhrí·tkę'θ ⟨again-he-mind-issue-begins⟩ *he comes to, he revives* (HS); -ne -. -(ę)' = tikęhrayenę -: neyę'nę'tikęhrayé·nę· ⟨apart-one=another-mind-grabs⟩ *one comforts another* (RC 29:1); -t -. -(ę)' = tikęhrayeri -: thra'tikęhrayè·ri' ⟨hither-he-mind-is correct⟩ *he is right-minded* (HS); -t -. -(ę)'tikęhra'nę -: nyaku'ti-kęhrá·'nę' ⟨hither-one-mind-is present⟩ *one has decided* (RC 6:16); -t -. -(ę)'tikęhriyuhT -: nyu'tikęhrì·yuht ⟨hither-it-mind-be great-caused⟩ *satisfaction* (HS); -t -. -(ę)'tikęhriyu -{dative I}: tka'tikęhriyú'θeh ⟨hither-it-mind-is great-for⟩ *it is pleased by* (HS); ti -. -(ę)'tikęhrakhahsyęku -: nęyękwa'ti-kęhrakhahsyé·ku' ⟨so-prediction-we-mind-join-undo-undo⟩ *we will not a-gree* (R); -yah -. -(ę)'tikęhrayeri -: we-ka'tikęhrayè·ri' ⟨thither-it-mind-is correct⟩ *it is sane* (HS); -yah -. -(ę)'ti = kęhrhaw -: wehrę'tikérhews ⟨thither-he-mind-carries⟩ *he apprehends it, he solves it* (HS); -a'nę'tikęhrahręhw -: ru'nę'tikęhráhręw ⟨he-himself-mind-put up-causes⟩ *he anticipates it* (HS); -a'nę'tikęhrar -: ra'nę'tikę́hrar ⟨he-himself-mind-is in⟩ *he is prudent* (HS); -a'nę'tikęhrar -{dative III}: θa'-nę'tikę́hrarę ⟨you-yourself-mind-is in-for› *beware!* (HS); **–a'nę?tikęhrihsak–**: ra?nę?tikęhríhsa·ks ‹he-himself-mind-searches› *he searches his mind* (HS); **–a'nę?tikęhrurihT–**: yę?nę?tikęhruríhtha? ‹one-oneself-mind-stir-causes› *one amuses oneself* (RC 31:4); **–ne–**. **–a'nę?tikęhrahręhw–**: nehru?nę?tikęhráhręw ‹apart-he-himself-mind-put up-causes› *he anticipates* (HS); **–t–**. **–a'nę?tikęhrihs?a–**: thru?tikęhríhs?ę ‹hither-he-himself-mind-finished› *he is prejudice, his mind is made up* (HS); **ha? –(ę)?tikęhraksa?T–**: ha? yu?tikęhrá·ksa?t ‹the it-mind-be bad-caused› *grief* (H-notebook); **ha? –(ę)?tikęh=raręhyakę?T–**: ha? u?tikęhraręhyá·kę?t ‹the mind-suffer-cause› *anxiety* (HS); **ha? –(ę)?tikęhru?nakʷahT–**: ha? yu?tikęhru?ná·kwaht ‹the it-mind-send-undo-causes› *temptation* (HS); **ha? –ne–. –(ę)?tikęhrahręhw–**: ha? nehrawę?tikęhráhręw ‹the apart-he-mind-put up-causes› *his anticipation* (HS); **ha? ti–. –(ę)?tikęhru?nę–**: ha? tihru?tikęhrú?nę· ‹the so-he-mind-is a kind of› *his opinion* (HS); **kwęhs –(ę)?tikęh=ranę–**: kwęhs ahra?tikęhranę·k ‹no unknown-he-mind-guard› *he is unfeeling* (HS); **kwęhs –(ę)?tikęhraye=rik–**: kwęhs ahra?tikęhrayè·rik ‹no unknown-he-mind-be filled› *he is an imbecile* (HS); **kwęhs –(ę)?tikęhr=hawsT–**: kwęhs aryu?tikęrháwsnęk ‹no unknown-it-mind-bring-cause› *it is unknowable* (HS); **kwęhs –(ę)?tikęhriyu–{dative I}**: kwęhs ahru?tikęhriyu?θéhek ‹no unknown-he-mind-be great-for› *he is discontented* (HS); **kwęhs –(ę)?tikęhriyu?T–**: kwęhs aryu?tikęhriyú?nęk ‹no unknown-it-mind-be great-cause› *unsatisfactory* (HS).

–(ę)?tikęhaw– inquire. *v.s.-t.* wa?kayę?na?tikę́hę·? ‹fact-they=another-mind-gave› *they inquired of another* (R).

–(ę)?tikęhkaręhrę– agitate. *v.s.-t.* na?tikęhkarę́?rę ‹one=another-mind-went around-much› *one agitates another* (HS).

–(ę)?tikęhkarę?rahT– commotion. *n.s.* u?tikęhkarę́?raht ‹mind-be sloped-cause› *commotion* (HS).

–(ę)?tikęhkaθne– patience. *n.s.* u?tikęhká·θne? ‹mind-be strong› *patience* (HS), ru?tikęhká·θne? ‹he-mind-is strong› *he is stout-minded, he is long-suffering* (HS).

–(ę)?tikęhkaθne– patience. *dv.n.s.* ha? ra?tikęhká·θne? ‹the he-mind-is strong› *his patience* (HS).

–(ę)?tikęhkęnyęhčr– cheating. *n.s.* u?tikęhkęnyę́hčreh ‹mind-excel-'ness› *cheating* (HS).

–(ę)?tikęhkeya?T– arrive at a conclusion, be solicitous, be oppressed. *v.s.-a.i.* ru?tikęhkyeyá?tha? ‹he-mind-agitates› *he is oppressed* (HS), ra?tikęhkyeyá?tha? ‹he-mind-agitates› *he is solicitous* (HS), wahru?tikęhkyè·ya?t ‹fact-he-mind-agitated› *he concluded* (RC 27:8), na?tikęhkęheyá?tha? ‹one=another-mind-agitates› *one discourages another* (HS), wa?kaku?tikęhkyè·ya?t ‹fact-they-mind-agitated› *they arrived at a conclusion* (RC 3:72).

–(ę)?tikęhkeya?T– uncertainty. *dv.n.s.* yu?tikęhkyè·ya?t ‹it-mind-agitated› *uncertainty* (HS).

–(ę)?tikęhnę– be state of mind, calculate, imagine, intend. *v.s.-a.i.* rę?tikę́hnęh ‹he-mind-falls› *he calculates, he imagines, he intends* (HS), ahrę?tikęhnę́hek ‹unknown-he-mind-fall› *that his state of mind be* (RC 2:4).

–(ę)?tikęhnęhčr– behavior, meditation, thinking. *n.s.* u?tikęhnę́hčreh ‹mind-fall-'ness› *behavior, meditation, thinking* (HS).

–(ę)?tikęhnęhčrukę? be thoughtless. *v.s.-*

s.i. ruˀtikęhnęhčrú·kęˀ ‹he-mind-fall-'ness-less› *he is thoughtless* (HS).

-(ę)ˀtikęhnęhkw -{dative III} be baffled, be stumped. *v. s.-a.i.* waˀuˀtikęhnę́hkwęˀ ‹fact-it-mind-fall-picked up-for› *it was baffled, it was stumped* (RC 30:10).

-(ę)ˀtikęhnętyę - meditate, project, think, think through. *v.s.-a.i.* ręˀtikęhnę́·tyęh ‹he-mind-falls-much› *he thinks, he projects, he meditates* (HS), waˀęˀtikęhnę́·tyę·ˀ ‹fact-one-mind-fell-much› *one thought through* (RC 30: 6).

-(ę)ˀtikęhr -.#ęwe voluntarily. *n.s.* naˀtikęhrehę̀·we ‹one=another-mind-genuine› *voluntarily* (HS).

-(ę)ˀtikęhr -.#keha·ˀ spiritual. *n.s.* uˀtikęhręˀkyéha·ˀ ‹mind-customarily› *spiritual* (HS).

-(ę)ˀtikęhrahnę - be lethargic, faint, lose consciousness. *v.s.-a.i.* raˀtikęhráhnęh ‹he-mind-disappears› *he is lethargic* (HS), wahraˀtikęhráhnęˀ ‹fact-he-mind-disappeared› *he fainted, he lost consciousness* (RC 24:9).

-(ę)ˀtikęhrahnęˀT - stun, stupefy. *v.s.-t.* naˀtikęhrahnę́ˀthaˀ ‹one=another-mind-disappear-causes› *one stuns another* (HS), raˀtikęhrahnę́ˀthaˀ ‹he-mind-disappear-causes› *he stupefies it* (HS).

-(ę)ˀtikęhrahręhw - anticipate. *v.s.-a.i.* ruˀtikęhráhręw ‹he-mind-put up-caused› *he anticipates* (R).

-(ę)ˀtikęhrahruˀT - be affable. *v.s.-s.i.* ruˀtikęhrahrúˀnę ‹he-mind-is mellow›

he is affable (HS).

-(ę)ˀtikęhrahtirahT - confirmation. *dv.n.s.* uˀtikęhrahtiráhthaˀ ‹mind-be hard-cause› *confirmation* (HS).

-(ę)ˀtikęhraks - Bad Mind (one of the primordial twins); evil spirit. *dv.n.s.* Kaˀtikęhrá·ksę· ‹it-mind-is bad› *Bad Mind (one of the primordial twins): evil spirit* (HS).

-(ę)ˀtikęhraks -{dative II} be unhappy. *v.s.-a.i.* waktikęhrá·ksęhθ ‹I-mind-is bad-for› *I am unhappy* (R).

-(ę)ˀtikęhraksaˀT - sadden, vex. *v.s.-t.* naˀtikęhraksáˀthaˀ ‹one=another-mind-be bad-causes› *one vexes another* (HS), yuˀtikęhrá·ksaˀt ‹it-mind-be bad-caused› *saddening* (HS).

-(ę)ˀtikęhraksaˀT - grief. *dv.n.s.* haˀ yuˀtikęhrá·ksaˀt ‹the it-mind-be bad-caused› *grief* (H-notebook).

-(ę)ˀtikęhrakwahsT - Good Mind; good spirit; bene-volence. *dv.n.s.* Kaˀtikęhrákwahst ‹it-mind-is good› *Good Mind (one of the primordial twins): good spirit; benevolence* (HS).

-(ę)ˀtikęhrakweni - influence. *v.s.-t.* naˀtikęhrakwé·nyęhs ‹one=another-mind-is able› *one influences another* (HS).

-(ę)ˀtikęhranurę - drug-free. *n.s.* kaˀtikęhranù·ręˀ ‹it-mind-is precious› *drug-free* (R).

-(ę)ˀtikęhranęˀnahsi - dissuade. *v.s.-t.* naˀtikęhranę́ˀnáhsyęhs ‹one=another-mind-attach-undoes› *one dissuades another* (HS).

-(ę)ˀtikęhrar - be careful, be mindful. *v.s.-a.i.* raˀtikę́hrar ‹he-mind-is in› *he*

---

is careful, he is mindful (HS).

-(ę)ʔtikę̄hrarę̄hyakę - be anxious. *v.s.-a.i.* ruʔtikę̄hrarę̄h-yáˑkę· ‹he-mind-suffered› *he is anxious* (HS).

-(ę)ʔtikę̄hrarę̄hyakęʔT - be anxious. *v.s.-s.i.* ruʔtikę̄hrarę̄hyakę́ʔthaʔ ‹he-mind-suffer-causes› *he is anxious* (HS).

-(ę)ʔtikę̄hrarę̄hyakęʔT - anxiety. *n.s.* haʔuʔtikę̄hrarę̄hyáˑkęʔt ‹the mind-suffer-cause› *anxiety* (HS).

-(ę)ʔtikę̄hrarhaʔ - distrust. *v.s.-t.* naʔtikę̄hrárhaʔθ ‹one=another-mind-ʔʔ› *one distrusts another* (HS).

-(ę)ʔtikę̄hrarheryeti - be candid. *v.s.-a.i.* raʔtikę̄hrarheryéˑtih ‹he-mind-ʔʔ› *he is candid* (HS).

-(ę)ʔtikę̄hraT - animal. *dv.n.s.* yuʔtikę́hraˑt ‹it-mind-stands› *animal (as opposed to vegetable)* (R).

-(ę)ʔtikę̄hraT - have discretion. *v.s.-a.i.* ruʔtikę́hraˑt ‹he-mind-stands› *he has discretion* (HS).

-(ę)ʔtikę̄hratukę̄ht - Great Spirit; Holy Spirit. *dv.n.s.* Uʔtikę̄hratukę́hti ‹mind-be holy› *Great Spirit; Holy Spirit* (R).

-(ę)ʔtikę̄hratʔa - advise. *v.s.-t.* ruʔtikę̄hráˑtʔę ‹he-mind-put in› *he advises* (HS), naʔtikę̄hráˑtʔahs ‹one=another-mind-puts in› *one advised another* (HS).

-(ę)ʔtikę̄hrawehθayę(T) - be darkminded. *v.s.-s.i.* ruʔtikę̄hrawéhθayęʔ ‹he-mind-darkness-lay› *he is dark-minded* (HS).

-(ę)ʔtikę̄hrawę̄ri - bewilder. *v.s.-t.* naʔtikę̄hrawę̀ˑrih ‹one=another-mind-stirs› *one bewilders another* (HS).

-(ę)ʔtikę̄hrayaʔnerę - chide. *v.s.-t.* naʔtikę̄hrayaʔnèˑręh ‹one=another-mind-wounds› *one chides another* (HS).

-(ę)ʔtikę̄hrayerik - satisfy. *v.s.-t.* naʔtikę̄hrayèˑriks ‹one=another-mind-fills up› *one satisfies another* (HS).

-(ę)ʔtikę̄hrayę(T) - comfort. *v.s.-t.* naʔtikę̄hrayę̄hs ‹one=another-mind-lays›

one comforts another (R).

-(ę)ʔtikę̄hrayę(T) - {dative II} discern. *v.s.-t.* ruʔtikę̄hrayę́·ʔnahθ ‹he-mind-laid-for› *he discerns* (HS).

-(ę)ʔtikę̄hraʔnihr - sympathy. *dv.n.s.* ruʔtikę̄hraʔníhrę ‹he-mind-stood up› *his sympathy* (HS).

-(ę)ʔtikę̄hraʔtyęʔnę - tempt. *v.s.-t.* raʔtikę̄hraʔtyę́ʔnęh ‹he-mind-measures› *he tempts* (HS).

-(ę)ʔtikę̄hreθ - be patient. *v.s.-a.i.* raʔtikę́hreˑθ ‹he-mind-is long› *he is patient* (HS).

-(ę)ʔtikę̄hrę - have a thought. *v.s.-a.i.* waʔkakuʔtikę́hręʔ ‹fact-they-mind-fell› *they had an thought* (RC 3:72).

-(ę)ʔtikę̄hręT - {dative II} forget. *v.s.-a.i.* ruʔtikę̄hrę́·ʔnęhθ ‹he-mind-concluded-for› *he forgets* (R), waʔkaʔtikę̄hrę́·ʔnęʔ ‹fact-it-mind-concluded-for› *it forgot* (RC 35: 43).

-(ę)ʔtikę̄hręthuhT - comfort, remember. *v.s.-t.* aryęʔnaʔtikę̄hrę́·thuht ‹unknown-one=another-mind-close-cause-caused› *that one remember another, that one comfort another* (RC 35:16).

-(ę)ʔtikę̄hręti - make up mind, premeditate. *v.s.-a.i.* ruʔtikę̄hrę́ˑtih ‹he-mind-makes› *he made up his mind* (HS), ręʔtikę̄hrę́ˑtih ‹he-mind-makes› *he premeditates* (HS).

-(ę)ʔtikę̄hręʔ - be dejected. *v.s.-a.i.* ruʔtikę̄hrę́ʔę ‹he-mind-fall-began› *he is dejected* (HS).

-(ę)ʔtikę̄hrhę̄reT - be alluring. *v.s.-a.i.* raʔtikę̄rhę̄réˑthaʔ ‹he-mind-carries away› *he is alluring* (HS).

-(ę)ʔtikę̄hrihsʔa - resolve. *v.s.-a.i.* rę̄ʔtikę̄hríhsʔahs ‹he-mind-finishes› *he resolves* (HS).

-(ę)ʔtikę̄hriyu - {dative III} please. *v.s.-t.* ruʔtikę̄hriyú·ʔθeh ‹he-mind-be great-for› *it pleases him* (HS).

-(ę)ʔtikę̄hriyuhT - amuse. *v.s.-t.* ruʔtikę̄hriyúhtha⁷ ‹he-mind-be great-causes› *he amuses* (R).

-(ę)⁷tikęhrukę⁷ be boisterous, be mindless, be rash, be thoughtless. *n.s.* ru⁷-tikęhrú·kę⁷ ‹he-mind-less› *he is boisterous, he is mindless, he is rash, he is thoughtless* (HS).

-(ę)⁷tikęhrut – invent. *v.s.-a.i.* rę⁷tikęhrú·tha⁷ ‹he-mind-stands› *he invents* (HS).

-(ę)⁷tikęhruryahT – amusement. *n.s.* u⁷-tikęhrú·ryaht ‹mind-stir-cause› *amusement* (R).

-(ę)⁷tikęhru⁷kręhT – debauch. *v.s.-t.* na⁷-tikęhru⁷krę́htha⁷ ‹one=another-mind-float-causes› *one debauches* (HS).

-(ę)⁷tikęhru⁷naku – allure, beguile, tempt. *v.s.-a.i.* ra⁷tikęhru⁷ná·kwahs ‹he-mind-send-undoes› *he allures, he beguiles* (HS), ęktikęhru⁷nakwáhshek ‹prediction-I-mind-send-undo› *I will be at peace* (R).

-(ę)⁷tikęhru⁷naku – allurer, tempter. *v.s.-a.i.* ra⁷tikęhru⁷ná·kwahs ‹he-mind-send-undoes› *allurer, tempter* (HS).

-(ę)⁷tikęhru⁷nakʷahT – charm, charming. *dv.n.s.* yu⁷tikęhru⁷ná·kwaht ‹it-mind-send-undo-causes› *charm, charming* (HS).

-(ę)⁷tikęhru⁷nakʷahT – temptation. *dv.n.s.* ha⁷ yu⁷tikęhru⁷ná·kwaht ‹the it-mind-send-undo-causes› *temptation* (HS).

-(ę)⁷tikęhru⁷nę – philosophy. *dv.n.s.* yękwa⁷tikęhrú⁷nę· ‹we-mind-is a kind of› *(our) philosophy* (R).

-(ę)⁷tikęhrya⁷khę – bother, disconcert. *v.s.-t.* ra⁷tikęhryá⁷khęh ‹he-mind-breaks-much› *he bothers it* (HS), na⁷-tikęhryá⁷khę ‹one=another-mind-breaks-much› *one disconcerts another* (HS).

-(ę)⁷tikęhryenę – accompany, escort. *v.s.-t.* ra⁷tikęhryenę́hreh ‹he-mind-grabs-much› *he escorts it* (HS), na⁷tikęhryè·nęh ‹one=another-mind-grabs› *one accompanies another* (HS).

-(ę)⁷tikęhtahT – danger, dangerous, peril. *n.s.* u⁷tikę́htaht ‹mind-stand-cause› *peril* (HS).

-(ę)⁷tikęhtahT – dangerous, hazardous, perilous. *dv.n.s.* yu⁷tikę́htaht ‹it-mind-stand-causes› *perilous* (HS).

-(ę)⁷tikęhthę – have an idea. *v.s.-a.i.* wa⁷ka⁷tikę́hthę⁷ ‹fact-it-mind-stood-caused-much› *it had an idea* (RC 3: 40).

-ę⁷tiθręθę – creep. *v.r.-a.i.* hab: -, pnt: -⁷, stat: -, prog: -, prp: -, dst: -, caus: -, rvs: -, dat: -, n-inc. ęhrę⁷tiθrę́·θę⁷ *he will creep* (RC 35:39).

-ę⁷tuherhu – assail, attack. *v.r.-t.* hab: -hs, pnt: -⁷, stat: -ę, prog: -, prp: -, dst: -, caus: -, rvs: -, dat: -, n-inc. rawę⁷-tuhérhę *he assailed it, he attacked it* (HS), rę⁷tuhérhuhs *he assails it, he attacks it* (HS), ęhrę⁷tuhérhu⁷ *he will assail it, he will attack it* (HS).

-(ę)⁷ty – bay. *n.r.* n-poss., inc., n.sfx. -. Found only incorporated. -(ę)⁷tya = yę(T) –: wę́⁷tyayę⁷ ‹it-bay-lays› *a bay* (HS); -t -. -(ę)⁷tya⁷ke: nyu⁷tyá⁷kye ‹hither-it-bay-at› *France* (R).

-ę⁷w -/-a⁷w – back. *n.r.* inaln: kę⁷wę́⁷kye *on my back* (R), inc., n.sfx. -ę⁷. The form –aʔw– occurs following the reflexive morpheme; the form –ęʔw– occurs elsewhere. awęʔweh *back* (R); –ęʔwa̲keʔy–: rawęʔwakyéʔyeʔ ‹he-himself-back-is humped› *he is humpbacked, he is hunch-backed* (HS); –ęʔ = wa̲nęhwak(T)–: wakęʔwanęhwaks ‹I-back-ache› *my back aches* (R); –ęʔwa = 'nęhT–: rawęʔwá·ʔneht ‹he-back-be present-caused› *he is active* (HS); –a'naʔwyaʔk–: raʔnáʔwyaʔks ‹he-himself-back-breaks› *he limps* (HS); –a = 'naʔwyaʔk–.#úʔy: raʔnaʔwyaʔkhéʔuʔy ‹he-himself-back-break-is going to-great› *he, the big one, is going limping* (RC 25:13); –ęʔw– –hsnahręw–: awęʔweh yuhsnahrę́·wa·t ‹back it-pith-stands› *spine* (HS); haʔ –ęʔwa̲rik–: haʔ ŕęʔwari·ks ‹the he-back-bites› *backbiter* (HS).·

–ęʔw– –hsnahręw– spine. *n.s.* awęʔweh yuhsnahrę́·wa·t ‹back it-pith-stands› *spine* (HS).

–ęʔwa̲keʔy– be hump-backed, be hunch-backed. *v.s.-s.i.* rawęʔwakyéʔyeʔ ‹he-himself-back-is humped› *he is humpbacked, he is hunch-backed* (HS).

–ęʔwa̲nęhwak(T)– have a backache. *v.s.-a.i.* wakęʔwanęhwaks ‹I-back-ache› *my back aches, I have a backache* (R).

–ęʔwa'nęhT– be active. *v.s.-s.i.* rawęʔwá·ʔneht ‹he-back-be present-caused› *he is active* (HS).

–ęʔwa̲rik– backbiter. *dv.n.s.* haʔ ŕęʔwari·ks ‹the he-back-bites› *backbiter* (HS).

–ęʔyT– bob, shake. *v.s.-t.* wę́ʔythaʔ ‹it-hang down-causes› *it shakes* (R), ŕęʔythaʔ ‹he-hang down-causes› *he shakes it* (R); –atʔęhręʔyT–: watʔęhŕęʔythaʔ ‹it-itself-leaf-hang down-causes› *quaking aspen, poplar* (*Populus* sp.) (R).

H

–h habitual aspect. *v.r.sfx.*

hačhíharahst pennyroyal (*Hedoma pulegioides*) (H-notebook). *n.* Archaic: ačhíharahk (HS).

haháh alas! (HS). *part.*

há·hah ha! ha! (laugh of derision) (RC 25:14). *part.*

–hahk habitual aspect. *v.r.sfx.*

–hahkwar– uvula, throat. *n.r.* inaln: khahkwarę́ʔkye *my uvula, my throat* (R), n-inc., n.sfx. –eh. uháhkwareh *uvula, throat* (HS).

–hahst– rail, shingle, sliver, stave, strip of wood. *n.r.* aln: akháhstawęh *my rail, etc.* (R), inc., n.sfx. –eh. uháhsteh *rail, shingle, sliver, stave, strip of wood* (HS); –hahsta̲nę'nakT–: rahahstanęʔnáktha ʔ ‹he-strip of wood-affix-causes› *he splints it* (HS); –hahsti̲har–: rahahstíher ‹he-shingle-puts up› *he shingles it* (HS); –hahsti̲hrahkw–: yehahstihráhkhwaʔ ‹one-shingle-puts up-instrument› *shingle* (HS); –hahstiN–: Kahahstì·nęhs ‹it-strip of wood-proceeds› *Fire Dragon of the White Body* (H-notebook), *dragon fly* (HS); –hah = st– –'nahkwętyaʔT–: uháhsteh yeʔnahkwętyáʔthaʔ ‹stave one-barrel-make-causes› *barrel staves* (HS).

–hahst– –'nahkwętyaʔT– barrel staves. *dv.n.s.* uháhsteh yeʔnahkwętyáʔthaʔ ‹stave one-barrel-make-causes› *barrel staves* (HS).

–hahsta̲nę'nakT– splint. *v.s.-t.* rahahstanęʔnáktha ʔ ‹he-strip of wood-affix-causes› *he splints it* (HS).

–hahsti̲har– shingle. *v.s.-t.* rahahstíher ‹he-shingle-puts up› *he shingles it* (HS).

–hahsti̲hrahkw– shingle. *dv.n.s.* yehahstihráhkhwaʔ ‹one-shingle-puts up-instrument› *shingle* (HS).

-hahstiN- Fire Dragon of the White Body; dragon fly. *dv.n.s.* Kahahstì·nęhs ‹it-strip of wood-proceeds› *Fire Dragon of the White Body* (H-notebook), *dragon fly* (HS).

háhteh pine tree (*Pinus* sp.) (R) [Lawson «Heigta» 'A Pine-Tree']. *n.* **háhteh -θręwęte:** háhteh uθręwę́·te ‹pine resin-certain one› *pitch* (HS); **hahteh.#ęwe:** hahtehę̀·we ‹pine tree-genuine› *Norway spruce (Picea abies)* (H-notebook).

háhteh -θręwęte pitch. *n.s.* háhteh uθręwę́·te ‹pine resin-certain one› *pitch* (HS).

hahteh.#ęwe Norway spruce. hahtehę̀·we ‹pine tree-genuine› *Norway spruce (Picea abies)* (H-notebook). *n.*

hakę́hsu·ˀθ soft maple (M 84). *n.* See: **akę́·suˀr.**

-hakʷ- bowlegged. *n.r.* poss. ?, inc., n.sfx. -. Found only in the cited construction. **-ne-. -hakʷayę(T)-:** nehrahá·kwayęˀ ‹apart-he-bowlegged-lay› *he is bowlegged* (HS).

hà·neˀ that is (RC 12:1). *part.* **hà·neˀ hésnę·** ‹that is then› *so for this reason* (R); **hà·neˀ hésnę· ę·či** ‹that is then one› *at this time* (M 87); **hà·neˀ í·kę·** ‹that is it is› *such* (R); **hà·neˀ nya=wè·rih** ‹that is because› *for the sake of* (AG); **kaˀnę́ hà·neˀ** ‹just! that is› *exactly that, precisely* (R).

hà·neˀ hésnę· ‹that is then› so for this reason (R). *part.*

hà·neˀ hésnę· ę·či ‹that is then one› at this time (M 87). *part.*

hà·neˀ í·kę· ‹that is it is› such (R). *part.*

hà·neˀ nyawè·rih ‹that is because› for the sake of (AG).

-har- hang. *v.r.-t.* See: **-(i)har-.**

-haθa̱r- ham (inside of thigh). *n.r.* inaln: khaθarę́ˀkye *my ham* (R), n-inc., n. sfx. -eh. uhá·θareh *ham (inside of thigh)* (HS).

háuˀ be it so, o.k. (RC 26:20). *part.*

-haw- bear, bring, carry. *v.r.-t.* See: **-(ę)=haw-.**

-hawruhsT- squall. *dv.n.s.* The constituent roots of this stem are uncertain. kahawrúhsthaˀ ‹it-??› *squall* (H-notebook).

háy Thank God!, Hallelujah (RC 26:2). *part.*

-haˀ habitual aspect. *v.r.sfx.*

haˀ the, that (backgrounds or subordinates whatever follows to other information in the phrase or sentence) (R). *part.* **haˀ karáhkęˀ ęhraˀná·ˀnyeˀ** ‹the always sort-stand-going along› *perpetuity* (HS); **haˀ karáhkęˀ kwę́ tì·yuht** ‹the always like it-stands› *ordinarily* (HS); **haˀ karáhkęˀ tì·yuht** ‹the always it-stands› *ordinary* (HS); **haˀ kę́hčih** ‹the maybe› *especially, main* (AW 47), *by rights* (L 58), *really* (L 41); **haˀ kwęhs tikawęnì·yuˀ** ‹the no any position› *not just anyone* (AW 45); **haˀ theˀ** ‹the not› *unless* (R); **haˀ ù·nę** ‹the now› *as soon as* (AW 49), *when* (R).

#ha·ˀ customary. *enc.* Rare form. See: **#kyeha·ˀ. -rha'na̱kęw.#ha·ˀ:** rurhaˀna-

Tuscarora Pronunciation Key:
/a/ l<u>a</u>w; /e/ h<u>a</u>t; /i/ p<u>i</u>zza; /u/ t<u>u</u>ne; /ę/ h<u>in</u>t; /č/ <u>ch</u>eese; /h/ <u>h</u>oe; /m/ <u>m</u>other; /s/ <u>s</u>ame; /t/ <u>d</u>o (before a vowel y, or w), <u>t</u>oo (elsewhere); /k/ <u>g</u>ale (before a vowel y or w), <u>k</u>ale (elsewhere); /n/ i<u>nh</u>ale (before a consonant or word-final), <u>n</u>ote (elsewhere), /r/ hi<u>ss</u> (before a consonant or word-final), r<u>u</u>n (trilled as in Italian, elsewhere); /w/ cu<u>ff</u> (before a consonant other than y or word-final), <u>w</u>ay (elsewhere); /y/ fi<u>sh</u> (before a consonant or word-final), <u>y</u>ou (elsewhere), /θ/ <u>th</u>ing; /ˀ/ (the sound between the vowels in unh-unh); /·/ long vowel, /´/ high pitch; /`/ low pitch.

kę́wha·ʾ ‹he-woods-in-customary› *he is usually in the woods* (H 2892); –nętherhę –.#ha·ʾ: ranętherhę́ha·ʾ ‹he-Turtle Clan-customary› *he is a member of the Turtle Clan* (H 2892).

haʾ karáhkę̄ʾ ęhraʾná·ʾnyeʾ ‹the always sort-stand-going along› perpetuity (HS). *part.*

haʾ karáhkę̄ʾ kwę̄ tì·yuht ‹the always like it-stands› ordinarily (HS). *part.*

haʾ karáhkę̄ʾ tì·yuht ‹the always it-stands› ordinary (HS). *part.*

haʾ kę́hčih ‹the maybe› especially, main (AW 47), by rights (L 58), really (L 41).

haʾ kwę̄hs tikawęnì·yuʾ ‹the no any position› not just anyone (AW 45). *part.*

haʾ theʾ ‹the not› unless (R). *part.*

haʾ ù·nę ‹the now› as soon as (AW 49), when (R). *part.*

–haʾ(č) – collar, neck. *n.r.* inaln: khaʾ-θę́ʾkye *my neck* (R), inc., n.sfx. –eh. Historically, the final segment of this root underwent the shift from *č* to *θ* when followed by a morpheme beginning with any segment other than *i* or *y*. In modern Tuscarora, the form with *θ* has been generalized and may be found before morphemes beginning with *i* (but not *y*) as well. The root occurs without the final consonant *č* when incorporated into the verb root –kʷahT – *cut off.* uháʾθeh *collar, neck* (R); –haʾkʷahT –: rahaʾkwáhtaʾ ‹he-neck-cuts off› *he cuts throat* (HS); –haʾčirwę –: waʾkęhaʾčí·rwęʾ ‹fact-I=you-neck-squeezed› *I strangled you* (R); –haʾčiyu –: kahaʾčí·yu· ‹it-neck-is great› *beautiful neck, great neck* (H-notebook); –haʾθahtrę –: waʾkayehaʾ-θáhtrę·ʾ ‹fact-they-neck-tied› *they tied neck* (RC 6:12); –haʾθiyu –: kahaʾ-θí·yu· ‹it-neck-is great› *beautiful neck,*

great neck (H-notebook).

–haʾčirwę – strangle. *v.s.-t.* waʾkęhaʾčí·-rwęʾ ‹fact-I=you-neck-squeezed› *I strangled you* (R).

–haʾkʷahT – cut throat. *v.s.-a.i.* rahaʾ-kwáhtaʾ ‹he-neck-cuts off› *he cuts throat* (HS).

#haʾnęʾ many, much (distributive). *enc.* This form of the distributive enclitic occurs principally with verb forms comprised of an attributive verb with an incorporated noun. It functions to indicate that a number of instances of the noun with the named attribute are spatially dispersed as in –(a)hahaks –. #haʾnęʾ: wahahaksęháʾnęʾ ‹it-path-is bad-many› *the roads are bad, poor; they are bad, poor roads* (H 2484), and –nęhsahsthu –.#háʾnęʾ: kanęhsah-sthęháʾnęʾ ‹it-house-is small-many› *small houses* (HS). The boundary # is automatically realized as *h* following a vowel, ʾ following a consonant other than *h* or ʾ, and φ following *h* or ʾ. (See also #kęhaʾnęʾ.)

#haʾnęʾt -th (ordinal suffix). *enc.* See: –aˈnęʾT –. –ahθhę –.#haʾnęʾt: wah-θhęháʾnęʾt ‹it-is ten-'th› *tenth* (RC 12: 10).

–(h)(a)ˈnyeʾ – going along (progressive). *r.sfx.* hab: -θ, pnt: -φ, stat: -φ. The form -ˈnyeʾ – occurs after certain roots and stems that end in a vowel; the form –aˈnyeʾ – occurs after certain roots and stems that end in a consonant; the form –haˈnyeʾ – is the most frequent form and occurs after some roots and stems that end in a consonant and some that end in a vowel. While the progressive is typically associated with verb roots and stems, it may also occur with locative nouns to indicate motion in the vicinity of a particular object (e.g., ucę̄hakwthá·ʾ-

nye⁷θ ‹fire-next-going along› *going along next to fire* (RC 12:25).

há⁷θru⁷ ~ hą́⁷θru⁷ thorn apple (*Crataegus punctata*) (R). *n.* Archaic: á⁷θru⁷ (H-notebook). The nasalization of the initial vowel is irregular for the language.

–ha⁷y – appetite. *n.r.* poss. ⁷, inc., n.sfx. –eh. uhá⁷yeh *appetite* (HS); –ha⁷ya̱ = ryu⁷T –: yuha⁷yá·ryu⁷t ‹it-appetite-kill-causes› *unpalatable* (HS); –ha⁷ye̱ = tyahT –: yuha⁷yé̱·tyaht ‹it-appetite-make-caused› *appetizing* (HS).

–ha⁷yaryu⁷T – unpalatable. *dv.n.s.* yuha⁷yá·ryu⁷t ‹it-appetite-kill-causes› *unpalatable* (HS).

–ha⁷ye̱tyahT – appetizing. *dv.n.s.* yuha⁷yé̱·tyaht ‹it-appetite-make-caused› *appetizing* (HS).

–hč – a width of any flexible or flat material. *n.r.* poss. ⁷, inc., n.sfx. –eh. úhθeh *a width of any flexible or flat material* (HS); –hθe̱y –: yúhθe̱y ‹it-width of flexible material-hangs› *pendant, it hangs* (HS); –či –.–hθaT –: θkáhθa·t ‹again-it-width of flexible material-stands› *one pace (of 3 feet), yard* (AG); –ne –.–hčiyu –: neyuhčí·yu· ‹apart-it-width of flexible material-is great› *it is wide* (HS).

#hči very (intensive). *enc.* The principal function of the intensive is to indicate an intensification of an action or an attribute as in á.#hči: áhči ‹stop it-very› *stop it now!* (HS) and –re̱ = 'nakri –.#hči: ure̱⁷nakrí⁷či ‹tree-liquid-very› *much sweetness, it is very sweet* (RC 2:15). It is also frequently used to form adjectives from nouns and noun phrases as in awe̱⁷.#hči: awé̱⁷či ‹water-very› *watery (of food)* (HS) and à·we̱⁷ čikhe⁷.#hči: à·we̱⁷ čikhé⁷či ‹water salt-very› *briny* (HS). The initial *h* of the enclitic is dropped following words that end in a consonant. When this enclitic is added to punctual verbs, it may optionally occur preceding the punctual suffix. The combination of the internal locative with the intensive has a distinct form (see: –a̱ke̱w⁷ahči).

–hči⁷ older sister; older maternal female cousin. *n.r.* aln: ákči⁷ *my older sister: my older maternal female cousin* (R), n-inc., n.sfx. –. ákči⁷ *my older sister: my older maternal female cousin* (R); –hči⁷.#áh: akči⁷áh ‹I-older sister-little› *my older step-sister* (R); –hči⁷čr –: uhčí⁷čreh ‹older sister-'ness› *sisterhood* (HS).

–hči⁷.#áh older step-sister. *n.s.* akči⁷áh ‹I-older sister-little› *my older step-sister* (R).

–hči⁷čr – sisterhood. *dv.n.s.* uhčí⁷čreh ‹older sister-'ness› *sisterhood* (HS).

–hčihre̱ – bear; pear. *n.r.* n-poss., n-inc., n.sfx. –⁷. uhčíhre̱⁷ *bear (Ursus arctos)* (RC 15:6) [Lawson «Oo-chehara» 'Bear-skin']; *pear* (R), rahčíhre̱⁷ *he is a bear* (H 2892).

–hčuhkw – flesh, naked body, raw skin; boy. *n.r.* n-poss., inc., n.sfx. –eh. This root is probably derived from the verb root –hču⁷ – *carve meat* plus the in-

---

Tuscarora Pronunciation Key:
/a/ law; /e/ hat; /i/ pizza; /u/ tune; /e̱/ hint; /č/ cheese; /h/ hoe; /m/ mother; /s/ same; /t/ do (before a vowel y, or w), too (elsewhere); /k/ gale (before a vowel y or w), kale (elsewhere); /n/ inhale (before a consonant or word-final), note (elsewhere), /r/ hiss (before a consonant or word-final), run (trilled as in Italian, elsewhere); /w/ cuff (before a consonant other than y or word-final), way (elsewhere); /y/ fish (before a consonant or word-final), you (elsewhere), /θ/ thing; /⁷/ (the sound between the vowels in unh-unh); /·/ long vowel, /́/ high pitch; /̀/ low pitch.

strumental suffix **-hkw-**. However, the existence of another, probably secondary instrumental construction from this root, uhčú?kweh *dressed meat*, complicates this derivation. uhčúhkweh *flesh, naked body, raw skin; boy* (RC 32:17); **-ačhuhkwhar-**: ručhúhkhwer ‹he-himself-flesh-hung› *male adolescent* (RC 35:43), *boy (10-15 years old)* (AG), kakučhuhkhrá·wę· ‹they-themselves-flesh-hang-many› *boys* (AG); **-ačhuhkwętihT-**: yęčhuhkwę́·tiht ‹one-oneself-raw skin-cuts in pieces› *one will shave it* (R), wa?kayęčhuhkwę́·tiht ‹fact-they-themselves-raw skin-cut in pieces› *they shaved it* (R).

-hčuhkwhar- be adolescent. *v.s.-s.i.* ručúhkhwe?r ‹he-flesh-hung› *male adolescent* (RC 35:43).

-hču?- carve meat, dress meat; carve, cut up. *v.r.-a.i.* hab: -ɸ, pnt: -ɸ, stat: -, prog: -, prp: -, dst: -, caus: -, rvs: -, dat: -, n-inc. ráhču·? *he carves (meat), he cuts it up* (R), wahráhču·? *he dressed meat* (RC 12:2); **-hču?kw-**: uhčú?kweh ‹carve meat-instrument› *chunk of meat, dressed meat, hunk of meat, piece of meat, portion of meat* (R); **-hču?kwahrawę-{dative I}**: wahrahču?kwahrà·wę?θ ‹fact-he-carve meat-instrument-put up-much-for› *he placed portions of meat* (RC 12:2).

-hču?kw- chunk of meat, dressed meat, hunk of meat, piece of meat, portion of meat. *n.s.* uhčú?kweh ‹carve meat-instrument› *chunk of meat, dressed meat, hunk of meat, piece of meat, portion of meat* (R).

-he?- going to (purposive). *v.r.sfx.* hab: -θ, pnt: -ɸ, stat: -ɸ, prog: -, prp: -, dst: -, caus: -, rvs: -, dat: -. The purposive is used to indicate that the speaker is expressing a logical assumption based on available evidence but has not witnessed the event first hand (e.g., **wahraturá·the?** ‹fact-he-hunted-going to› *he was going hunting*).

-he- put on. *v.r.-t.* See: **-(i)he-**.

hé that! (exclamation) (RC 14:6). *part.* **hé hà·ne?** ‹that! that is› *that's that, how awful, how terrible, that's how it is* (R); **hé hà·ne? hę** ‹that! that is ?› *is that so?* (R).

hé hà·ne? ‹that! that is› that's that, how awful, how terrible, that's how it is (R).

hé hà·ne? hę ‹that! that is ?› is that so? (R).

-hečh- buttocks; rear end of a male. *n.r.* inaln: khečhę́?kye *my buttocks* (R), inc., n.sfx. -eh. uhécheh *buttocks; rear end of a male* (R); **-hečheθ-**: kahéče·θ ‹it-buttocks-is long› *wasp* (R); ti-. **-hečhathe-**: tyuhečhá·the? ‹so-it-buttocks-stands-going to› *exposed buttocks* (H-notebook); **-athečhrahkw-**: uthečhráhkweh ‹self-buttocks-collect› *chair, seat, stool* (R), yęthečráhkhwa? ‹one-oneself-buttocks-gathers-instrument› *one uses it to support his buttocks* (Hewitt 1893); **-athečhrahkw-i?rę-**: uthečhráhkweh ré?ę? ‹self-buttocks-collect he-settles› *chairman* (HS).

-hečheθ- wasp. *dv.n.s.* kahéche·θ ‹it-buttocks-is long› *wasp* (R).

hehčę́ atchoo! (sound of a sneeze) (HS). *part.* **hehčę́ -ę°ti-**: hehčę́ rawę́·ti· ‹atchoo he-made› *he sneezes* (HS).

hehčę́ -ę°ti- sneeze. *v.s.-a.i.* hehčę́ rawę́·ti· ‹atchoo he-made› *he sneezes* (HS).

Héhe? Ha-ha (female nickname) (AW 98). *n.*

-hehn- field, garden, lot. *n.r.* n-poss., inc., n.sfx. -eh. In the words recorded by Hewitt (2484) the root is written «-heq-'n-» indicating a phonemicization -heh²n -. The retention of a cluster medial ² before *n* occurs in modern Tuscarora only sporadically following *s*, but never *h*. uhéhneh *field, garden, lot, soil of a field (rare), growing crop of a field or garden (rare)* (H 2484); -hehn -.#áh: uhehneháh ‹field-little› *the field is small, it is a small field, a little field* (H 2484); -hehn -.#ętíh: uhehnehętíh ‹field-many little› *the fields are small, diminutive* (H 2484); -hehn -.#keha·²: uhehna²-kyéha·² ‹field-customarily› *agriculture* (HS), ruhehna²kyéha·² ‹he-field-customarily› *agriculturalist, peasant* (HS); -hehnačhakwahsT -: rahehnačhakwáhstha² ‹he-field-self-X-is good› *he causes the field to look well, puts the field in order and trim* (H 2484); -hehnahrahT -: uhehnáhraht ‹field-put up-cause› *it is an awful field, a field to be feared, on any account whatsoever* (H 2484); -hehnahrehw -: kahehnáhręw ‹it-field-put up-causes› *the field is awry, or of an awkward shape* (H 2484); -hehnahsęht -: rahehnahsęhti ‹he-field-disdains› *he has contempt for the field, he rejects it with disgust* (H 2484); -hehnahwačiyu -: kahehnahwačí·yu· ‹it-field-width-is great› *the field is broad, wide* (H 2484); -hehnah = waθahsthu -: kahehnahwaθáhsthę ‹it-field-width-is small› *it is a narrow field: the field is narrow, not wide* (H 2484); -hehnakehrę -: kahehnakyéhrę² ‹it-field-put up› *the fields are lying together or adjoining* (H 2484); -heh =

nakęri -: rahehnakę·rih ‹apart-he-field-²²› *he is worrying the field (said of one who takes unnecessary time in doing the work on a field)* (H 2484); -hehnaks -: kahehná·ksę· ‹it-field-is bad› *the field is poor, unproductive: the field or garden is bad in shape, is ill-formed, is difficult to till* (H 2484); -hehnakT: uhéhnakwt ‹field-next to› *beside, alongside of the field, garden or lot* (H 2484); -hehnakwahsT -: kahehnákwahst ‹it-field-is good› *the field, soil or crop is good, looks well, is productive or easy to till* (H 2484); -hehnanurę -: kahehnanú·rę² ‹it-field-is precious› *it is a dear, precious field: the field is dear, precious, costly; this is a descriptive sentence which has been applied to the Garden of Eden* (H 2484); -hehnara² -: rahehnà·ra²θ ‹he-field-be in-begins› *he reaches the field, arrives at the field* (H 2484); -hehnaT -: kahéhna·t ‹it-field-stands› *the field is contained (in it) (said of a field, lot or crop surrounded by a wood or other field or crop)* (H 2484); -hehnatihsthu -: kahehnatíhsthę ‹it-field-are small› *the fields are small* (H 2484); -hehnatkwerih -: rahehnatkwè·rihθ ‹he-field-desires› *he longs for the field, desires fondly to own the field* (H 2484); -hehnawerhu -: kahehnawér-huhs ‹it-field-covers› *it covers, over-spreads the field* (H 2484); -hehna = węhte -: kahehnawęhte² ‹it-field-is between› *a field is between (two others)* (H 2484); -hehnayači -: uhehnayá·či

---

Tuscarora Pronunciation Key:
/a/ law; /e/ hat; /i/ pizza; /u/ tune; /ę/ hint; /č/ cheese; /h/ hoe; /m/ mother; /s/ same; /t/ do (before a vowel y, or w), too (elsewhere); /k/ gale (before a vowel y or w), kale (elsewhere); /n/ inhale (before a consonant or word-final), note (elsewhere), /r/ hiss (before a consonant or word-final), run (trilled as in Italian, elsewhere); /w/ cuff (before a consonant other than y or word-final), way (elsewhere); /y/ fish (before a consonant or word-final), you (elsewhere), /θ/ thing; /²/ (the sound between the vowels in unh-unh); /·/ long vowel, /´/ high pitch; /`/ low pitch.

‹field-?'?› *it is a peculiar field: the field has strange, unique or strange qualities* (H 2484); –**hehnayę(T)** –: rahéhnayęhs ‹he-field-lays› *he is laying out a field, he is acquiring a field* (H 2484), kahéhnayę' ‹it-field-lay› *the field lies, is lying* (H 2484), ruhéhnayę' ‹he-field-lays› *he has a field, he owns a field or lot* (H 2484); –**heh**=**nayęhnę** –: kahehnayę·'nęh ‹it-field-lay-many› *the fields lie in groups* (H 2484); –**hehnayęθ(e)r** –: rahehnayę·θręhs ‹he-field-flays› *he is skinning the field (said of one who is taking all the substance from the field without giving back to it any return in the shape of manure)* (H 2484); –**heh**=**na'ke**: uhehná'kye ‹field-at› *on the field (that is, on its surface)* (H 2484); –**hehna'θ** –: kahéhna'θ ‹it-field-is of a size› *the fields are large* (H 2484); –**hehnehke**: uhehnéhkye ‹field-at› *at the field* (H 2484); –**hehneθ** –: kahéhne·θ ‹it-field-is long› *it is a long field, the field is long* (H 2484); –**hehnęr** –: kahehnę·rih ‹it-field-leaves behind› *the field is weak or poor* (H 2484); –**hehnęte**: uhehnę·te ‹field-certain one› *it is this or that kind of field (the definitive this or that is understood here and is expressed outside of the sentence)* (H 2484); –**hehnęti** –: kahehnę·ti· ‹it-field-made› *the field is cleared, one has made it a field, it is cleared ground* (H 2484), rahehnę·tih ‹he-field-makes› *he is making a field, he is clearing land* (H 2484); –**heh**=**nę'ke**: uhehnę'kye ‹field-at› *on the field, or in the field, as a fixture of it* (H 2484); –**hehni** –: kahéhnih ‹it-field-is a group› *the field is full, as of cattle or men* (H 2484); –**hehnihę**: uhehníhę ‹field-in middle of› *in the middle of the field, one half of the*

field or plot (H 2484); –**hehnihs'a** –: rahehníhs'ahs ‹he-field-finishes› *he finishes the field (clearing it), he completes work on the field, as in completing the plowing, curing a crop on the field, or any other labor on it* (H 2484); –**hehnihya'k** –: rahehníhya'ks ‹he-field-crosses over› *he crosses the field or plot of ground* (H 2484); –**hehniyu** –: kahehní·yu· ‹it-field-is great› *it is a large field, a great field* (H 2484); –**hehniyuha'nę'** –: kahehniyúha'nę' ‹it-field-is great-many› *the fields are large, they are large fields* (H 2484); –**hehnuči** –: kahehnú·či' ‹it-field-is a wedge› *the field is cuneiform, wedge-shaped* (H 2484); –**heh**=**nuharaku** –: rahehnuhará·kwahs ‹he-field-tip-undoes› *he takes or cuts off an end of the field* (H 2484); –**heh**=**nur** –: ruhehnù·re' ‹he-field-covers› *he is covering the field (by his operations or labors)* (H 2484); –**hehnut**: yuhéhnu·t ‹it-field-stood› *it shows a part of the field, i.e., it leaves a part of the field, there is part of the field left* (H 2484); –**hehnu'** –: kahéhnu'θ ‹it-field-be in water-begins› *the field is inundated customarily* (H 2484); –**hehnu**='narhu –: kahehnu'nárhuhs ‹it-field-hooks› *it fastens upon, crosses, a part of the field* (H 2484); –**hehnya'k** –: rahéhnya'ks ‹he-field-breaks› *he cuts, divides the field in two, he cuts off a portion of the field* (H 2484); –**heh**=**nyęti** –: kahehnyę·ti' ‹it-field-extended› *the field, plot, lot lies extending away lengthwise* (H 2484); –**ne** –. –**hehnawę**=**ręhT** –: nehrahehnawęręhtha' ‹apart-he-field-diminish-causes› *he takes up unnecessarily needed space or ground, he is an unnecessary person* (H 2484); –**ne** –. –**hehnękuh** –: nehruhehnę·kuhθ ‹apart-he-field-goes through› *he is* *coming out of, is passing through the field* (H 2484); -athehnuri -: ratheh-nù·rih ‹he-himself-field-stirs› *he is driving obnoxious vermin and beasts from the field, he is a scarecrow* (H 2484); -ne -. -athehnakwa?nęti -: neyu-thehnakwa?nę́·ti· ‹two-it-itself-field-arc-made› *the field is round, it is a round field, the field has a round space* (H 2484); ti -. -hehnake -: tika-hehná·kye· ‹so-it-field-is in number› *the fields number as many as* (H 24 84); ti -. -hehna?θ -.#áh: tikahehna?θ?áh ‹so-it-field-is of a size-little› *the field is small, diminutive* (H 2484); ti -. -hehna?θ -.#ú?y: tikahehna?θ?ú?y ‹so-it-field-is of a size-big› *the field is very large* (H 2484); ti+či -. -heh = nęr -.#áh: tiθhruhehnęręháh ‹so-again-he-field-left behind-little› *he has left a small part of the field, as in plowing, or cutting a crop on it* (H 2484); hà·-ne? ti -. -hehnu?nę -: hà·ne? tikaheh-nú?nę· ‹that is so-it-field-is a kind of› *the field is of that shape* (H 2484).

-hehn -.#keha·? agriculture; agricultur-alist, peasant. *n.s.* uhehna?kyéha·? ‹field-customarily› *agriculture* (HS), ruhehna?kyéha·? ‹he-field-customarily› *agriculturalist, peasant* (HS).

-hehst - frame. *n.r.* aln: akhéhstawęh *my frame* (R), inc., n.sfx. -eh. uhéhsteh *frame* (R); -hehstęti -{dative III}: wah-rathehstę́·tyę? ‹fact-he-himself-frame-made-for› *he made frame for it* (RC 5:32).

hè·nę? this (RC 26:13), then (RC 3:56),

at that time (HS). *part.* henę́?kye ‹then-at› *then* (HS); hè·nę? í·kę· ‹then it is› *such* (R).

hè·nę? í·kę· ‹then it is› such (R). *part.*

henę́?kye ‹then-at› then (HS). *part.*

hení·kę· that is, this is, such (R). *part.* Contraction of hè·nę? í·kę·.

her also, so that, in order that (archaic) (R). *part.* her sè·nę? ‹also never› *as never* (AW 103); kwęhs her ‹no so that› *lest* (HS).

her sè·nę? ‹also never› as never (AW 103). *part.*

-her - green; grass. *n.r.* n-poss., inc., n.sfx. -eh. uhè·reh *green* (R), *grass* (PC); -her -.#ęwe: uherehę̀·we ‹green-genuine› *Timothy (grass) (Phleum pratense)* (HS); -herahręhwaku -: rahe-rahręhwá·kwahs ‹he-green-put up-cause-picks up› *he turns over hay* (HS); -herara'ne -: yuherará·?ne? ‹it-green-be in-is present› *nettle* (HS); -hераruhčrę -: raherarúhčręh ‹he-green-gathers› *he rakes* (HS); -heręti -: yu-herę́·tih ‹it-green-makes› *grass is growing* (PC); -heruhkuriθa?T -: yehe-ruhkuriθá?tha? ‹one-green-cover-in-strument-??-causes› *hayfork, pitch-fork* (HS); -heruhkw -: uherúhkweh ‹green-cover-instrument› *grass, ground cover, hay, reed, rush, straw, weed* (RC 11:12); -heruhkw -.#kęha?nę?: ye-heruhkwehkę́ha?nę? ‹one-green-cover-instrument-much› *herbage* (HS); -he = ruhkwayę'nahkw -: yeheruhkwayę?náh-khwa? ‹one-green-cover-instrument-lays-instrument› *hayloft* (HS); -heruh =

kwehsT –: yeheruhkwéhstha'' ‹one-green-cover-instrument-uses› *one uses it for fodder* (HS); –heruhskw –: raherúhskwahs ‹he-green-clears› *he weeds* (HS); –herya'k–: rahé·rya'ks ‹he-green-breaks› *he mows, he reaps* (HS); –herya'kT –: yeheryá'ktha' ‹one-green-break-causes› *grasscutter, lawnmower, scythe, sickle* (HS); –her= 'e(k) –: rahér'ehs ‹he-green-strikes› *he threshes* (HS); –ne –. –herukę –: Neyuherú·kę' ‹apart-it-green-is forked› *a fortified Tuscarora town in colonial North Carolina, "Broken-pasture"* (R) [Colonial Records «Fort Neoheroka», «Fort Noo-he-roo-ka»]; –ne –. –herukę – kì·nę': Neyuherú·kę' kì·nę' ‹apart-it-green-is forked   creek› *Neuse River* (AG); –atherahwanhahsT –: yętherahwanháhstha' ‹one-oneself-green-wind-causes› *bracelet (originally one made of braided grass)* (HS); kę' čhę' –herya'k –: kę' čhę' kaheryá'kę ‹where just it-green-cut› *stubble* (HS); kwęhs –heruhsku –: kwęhs ahruherúhskwę·k ‹no unknown-he-green-clear› *he has not cut the weeds* (HS).

–her–.#ęwe Timothy (grass). *n.s.* uherehę̀·we ‹green-genuine› *Timothy (grass) (Phleum pratense)* (HS).

–herara'ne – nettle. *dv.n.s.* yuherará·'ne' ‹it-green-be in-is present› *nettle* (HS).

–heraruhčrę – rake. *v.s.-a.i.* raherarúhčręh ‹he-green-gathers› *he rakes* (HS).

heríhsę' instead (RC 3:77). *part.* Also: eríhsę'.

–heruhkuriθa'T – hayfork, pitchfork. *dv. n.s.* yeheruhkuriθá'tha' ‹one-green-cover-instrument-'?'-causes› *hayfork, pitchfork* (HS).

–heruhkw – grass, ground cover, hay, reed, rush, straw, weed. *n.s.* uherúhkweh ‹green-cover-instrument› *grass, ground cover, hay, reed, rush, weed*

(RC 11:12).

–heruhkwayę'nahkw – hayloft. *dv.n.s.* yeheruhkwayę·'náh-khwa' ‹one-green-cover-instrument-lays-instrument› *hayloft* (HS).

–heruhkwehsT – use for fodder. *v.s.-a.i.* yeheruhkwéhstha' ‹one-green-cover-instrument-uses› *one uses it for fodder* (HS).

–heruhskw – weed. *v.s.-a.i.* raherúhskwahs ‹he-green-clears› *he weeds* (HS).

–herya'k – mow, reap. *v.s.-a.i.* rahé·rya'ks ‹he-green-breaks› *he mows, he reaps* (HS).

–herya'kT – grasscutter, lawnmower, scythe, sickle. *dv.n.s.* yeheryá'ktha' ‹one-green-break-causes› *grasscutter, lawnmower, scythe, sickle* (HS).

–her'e(k) – thresh. *v.s.-a.i.* rahér'ehs ‹he-green-strikes› *he threshes* (HS).

–heskw – edge. *n.r. poss.* ?, inc., *n.sfx.* –. Found only in the construction cited below. ti –. –athehskwahnę –: tyutheskwáhnę· ‹so-it-itself-edge-disappears› *its edge disappears* (RC 8:10).

hésnę· then (RC 2:4). *part.* hésnę· ì·nę ‹then far› *farther* (R); tyuh hésnę· ‹hence then› *hence, so then* (HS).

hésnę· ì·nę ‹then far› *farther* (R). *part.*

hè·wi enough (RC 25:10). *part.* –he= wihsT –: rahewíhstha' ‹he-enough-causes› *he satisfies it* (HS), ruhewíhstha' ‹he-enough-causes› *he becomes satisfied* (HS), ruhewíhsnę ‹he-enough-caused› *he became satisfied* (HS), wahruhè·wihst ‹fact-he-enough-enough-caused› *he had enough of it* (R).

–hey – die. *v.r.-a.i.* See: –ihey –/–(i)hey –.

–he' remote. *v.r.sfx.* The function of the remote suffix is to mark past anterior or distant past tense (e.g., –t –. –yęthwę-he': tkaycyęthwę́he' ‹hither-they-planted-remote› *they had planted here (e.g., long ago, before others planted in the same place).* It immediately follows the stative aspect suffix.

hé?i·θ you!, you two!, all of you! (second person emphatic pronoun) (RC 30:9). *part.*

hé?i·? I!, we two!, all of us! (first person emphatic pronoun) (RC 30:9). *part.*

hé?kye that one (RC 27:22) [Gallatin «hehkay» 'He']. *part.*

hé?nę? over there, further (RC 26:24). *part.*

-he?nę?nęti- embarrass. *v.r.-t.* hab: -h, pnt: -, stat: -, prog: -, prp: -, dst: -, caus: -, rvs: -, dat: -, n-inc. nathe?-nę?nę́·tih *one embarrasses another* (H-notebook).

he?skęhę̀·we somewhere (RC 30:8). *part.* **he?skęhę̀·we è·re** ‹somewhere opposite› *elsewhere* (HS).

he?skęhę̀·we è·re ‹somewhere opposite› elsewhere (HS). *part.*

hé?thu there (RC 3:8), enough (L 17). *part.* **hé?thu ha? ti-. -hT-:** hé?thu ha? tì·yuht ‹there the so-it-stands› *passable* (HS); **hé?thu -i-:** hé?thu ará·kę·k ‹there unknown-it-is a group› *it is insufficient* (HS).

hé?thu -i- be insufficient. *v.s.-s.i.* hé?thu ará·kę·k ‹there unknown-it-is a group› *it is insufficient* (HS).

hé?thu ha? ti-. -hT- passable. *part.* hé?thu ha? tì·yuht ‹there the so-it-stands› *passable* (HS).

he?thúhči ‹there-very› as a result, fit, just right, proper, right, so that (RC 3:24). *part.* **kwę̨hs he?thúhči -i-:** kwę̨hs

he?thúhči ará·kę·k ‹no fit unknown-it-is a group› *it is unfit* (HS).

he?thúhkye ‹there-at› at that time (RC 3:72). *part.*

hé?tkę̨h high (RC 12:10), on top, publicly (HS). *part.*

hę "?" (yes/no question marker) (R). *part.* Also: **hęh.** See: Lawson «Unta hah» 'Will you go along with me' = ę́?te? hę ? *Will you and I go together?*.

-hę̨či?naw- singe. *v.s.-t.* rahę̨čí?naws ‹he-X-burns› *he singes it* (HS).

-hę̨či?r- black magic; type of magic. *n.r.* n-poss., n-inc., n.sfx. -eh. uhę̨čí?reh *black magic; type of magic* (RC 14:2).

-hę̨hkw- glottis, throat. *n.r.* inaln: khę̨h-kwę́?kye *my glottis* (R), n.sfx. -eh. uhę́hkweh *glottis, throat* (HS).

-hę̨hnarik- have an earache. *v.s.-a.i.* wakhę́hnari·ks ‹I-ear-bite› *I have an earache* (R).

-hę̨hneθę- áha·θ mule. *dv.n.s.* kahę̨h-né·θęh áha·θ ‹it-ear-is long-much horse› *mule* (HS).

-hę̨hθ- throat. *n.r.* inaln: khę̨hθę́?kye *my throat* (R), n-inc., n.sfx. -eh. uhę́hθeh *throat* (HS); **-hę̨hθ?e(k)-:** ruhę́hθ?ehs ‹he-throat-strikes› *he hiccoughed* (HS).

-hę̨hθ?e(k)- hiccough. *v.s.-a.i.* ruhę́hθ-?ehs ‹he-throat-strikes› *he hiccoughed* (HS).

-hę̨hs-/-hę̨hT- ear. *n.r.* inaln: khę́hneh *my ear* (R), inc., n.sfx. -eh. The form -hę̨hs- occurs only incorporated; the form -hę̨hT- occurs both incorporated and unincorporated. uhę́hneh *ear* (R) [Lawson «Ooeth-nat» 'Ears'][Gallatin «ohhuhneh» 'Ear']; **–hęhnạrik –**: wakhę́hnari·ks ‹I-ear-bite› *I have an earache* (R); **–hęhsuri –**: rahęhsù·rih ‹he-ear-stirs› *a bully* (HS); **–hęhsyę –**: ękahę́hsyę⁷ ‹prediction-it-ear-go into› *one will hear it* (RC 17:3), wa⁷kakuhę́hsyę⁷ ‹fact-they-ear-gone into› *they heard* (RC 10:4); **–hęhsyęhT –**: wa⁷kayę⁷nathę́hsyęht ‹fact-they-another-ear-go into-caused› *one caused it to enter their ears* (RC 12:5), nathęhsyę́htha⁷ ‹one-another-ear-go into-causes› *one notifies another* (HS), yuhę́hsyęht ‹it-ear-go into-caused› *audible* (HS); **–ne –**. **–hęhnạkʷek –**: nehrahęhnakwé·kę ‹two-he-ear-closed› *he is deaf* (HS), nęyehęhnakwé·kęk ‹two-prediction-one-ear-close› *one will be deaf* (RC 17:3); **–athęhnačk –**: ruthęhnáčkę· ‹he-himself-ear-stand-easily› *he is docile* (HS); **–athęhnaT –**: rathę́hna·č ‹he-himself-ear-stands› *he listens* (R), wakathęhná·⁷ne⁷ ‹I-myself-ear-stood› *I am listening* (R); **–athęhsuri –**: rathęhsù·rih ‹he-himself-ear-stirs› *he disquiets himself so as not to hear something disagreeable, he is disturbed* (HS); **ti –**. **–athęhnahkwrę –**: tihrathęhnáhkwręh ‹so-he-himself-ear-is in a vertical position› *he pricks up his ears* (R); áha·θ **–hęhneθę –**: áha·θ kahęhné·θęh ‹horse it-ear-is long-much› *ass* (HS); **–hęh= neθę –** áha·θ: kahęhné·θęh áha·θ ‹it-ear-is long-much horse› *mule* (HS); ha⁷ **–athęhnačT –**: ha⁷ kakuthęhnáčtha⁷ ‹the they-themselves-ear-stand-cause› *audience* (HS); kwęhs **–hęhsyę –**: kwęhs ahruhęhsyę́hek ‹no unknown-he-ear-go into› *it is intractable* (HS); **–hęhsyę –** hę skarù·rę⁷: θahę́hsyę⁷ hę skarù·rę⁷ ? ‹you-hear ? Tuscarora› *do you understand Tuscarora?* (R).

–hęhskạw – begrimed face, dirty face. *n.r.* poss. ?, n-inc., n.sfx. –eh. uhę́hskaweh *dirty, begrimed face* (HS).

–hęhsuri – bully. *n.s.* rahęhsù·rih ‹he-ear-stirs› *a bully* (HS).

–hęhsyę – hear; understand a language. *v.s.-t.* ękahę́hsyę⁷ ‹prediction-it-ear-go into› *one will hear it* (RC 17:3), wa⁷kakuhę́hsyę⁷ ‹fact-they-ear-gone into› *they heard* (RC 10:4); **–hęhsyę –** hę skarù·rę⁷: θahę́hsyę⁷ hę skarù·rę⁷ ? ‹you-hear ? Tuscarora› *do you understand Tuscarora?* (R).

–hęhsyęhT – notify. *v.s.-t.* wa⁷kayę⁷nathę́hsyęht ‹fact-they-another-ear-go into-caused› *he caused it to enter their ears* (RC 12:5), nathęhsyę́htha⁷ ‹one-another-ear-go into-causes› *one notifies another* (HS).

–hęhsyęhT – audible. *dv.n.s.* yuhę́hsyęht ‹it-ear-go into-caused› *audible* (HS).

–hęhtkwi⁷r – armpit. *n.r.* inaln: khęhtkwí⁷reh *my armpit* (R), inc., n.sfx. –eh. uhęhtkwí⁷reh *armpit* (R).

–hękạr – delegate, volunteer. *n.r.* n-poss., inc., n.sfx. –eh. uhę́·kareh *delegate, volunteer* (HS); **–hękạrya⁷k –**: rahęká·rya⁷ks ‹he-volunteer-breaks› *he hires, he orders it* (HS), wa⁷kayekhęká·rya⁷k ‹fact-they=me-volunteer-broke› *they chose me as their representative* (RC 12:4); **–athękarya⁷k –**: ruthękaryá⁷kę ‹he-himself-volunteer-broke› *he volunteered* (HS), rathęká·rya⁷ks ‹he-himself-volunteer-breaks› *he volunteers* (HS); *volunteer* (R), ęhruthęká·rya⁷k ‹prediction-he-himself-volunteer-break› *he will volunteer* (HS).

–hękạrya⁷k – hire, order. *v.r.-t.* rahęká·rya⁷ks ‹he-volunteer-breaks› *he hires, he orders it* (HS), wa⁷kayekhęká·rya⁷k ‹fact-they=me-volunteer-broke› *they chose me as their representative* (RC 12:4).

-hẹrehθ – call, holler, shout; cackle, neigh, roar. *v.r.-t.* hab: -φ, pnt: -ę̀ʔ, stat: -ę·, prog: -, prp: -, dst: -, caus: -, rvs: -, dat: -, n-inc. rahę̀·rehθ *he shouts, he is shouting* (L 43), kahę̀·rehθ *it cackles, it gives its note, it neighs, it roars, it shouts (of animals)* (HS), θhẹréhθę· *shout!* (L 43), kayę̀ʔnathẹréhθę· *they hollered at another* (R), ruhẹrehθę́·ʔnahk *he has shouted* (L 43), wahrahẹréhθę̀ʔ *he called* (RC 12:3), waʔehẹréhθę̀ʔ *one hollered* (RC 11:9); –yah+či –. –hẹrehθ –: weθhrahę̀·rehθ ‹thither-again-he-calls› *he recalls* (HS); haʔ –hẹrehθ –: haʔ rahę̀·rehθ ‹the he-calls› *auctioneer* (HS).

-hẹrehθ – auctioneer. *dv.n.s.* haʔ rahę̀·rehθ ‹the he-calls› *auctioneer* (HS).

-hẹreT – carry away, carry off. *v.r.-a.i.* See: -(i)hẹreT –.

-hẹθ – son-in-law. *n.r.* poss. ʔ, n-inc., n. sfx. -eh. uhę́·θeh *son-in-law* (HS).

-hẹθę – mother-in-law, father-in-law. *n.r.* poss. ʔ, n-inc., n.sfx. -eh. uhę́·θę *mother-in-law, father-in-law* (R).

-hẹθę be mother-in-law to, be father-in-law to. *v.r.-k.* yaktihę́·θę *my son-in-law (i.e., my daughter's husband/my sister's daughter's husband)* (RC 30: 14), tihę́·θę *my son-in-law* (RC 30: 20), neyehę́·θę *one's son-in-law: one's father-in-law* (R).

-hẹθhu – have as mother-in-law, have as father-in-law. *v.r.-k.* yaktihę́·θhuʔ *my mother-in-law: my father-in-law* (R).

-hẹsči – be black. *v.r.-s.i.* stat: -φ, prog: -, prp: -, dst: -, caus: -, rvs: -, dat: -,

inc.-φ-ag. kahę́sči *it is black* (RC 12:25) [Lawson «Caw-hunshe» 'Black or Blue, Idem'] [Gallatin «kauhuhstchee» 'Black], Rahę́sči *the black one* (RC 12:21), rahęsčíheʔ *he was black* (H 2892), ęhrahę́sčik *he will be black* (RC 12:20); –hẹsčihT –: rahęsčíhthaʔ ‹he-be black-causes› *he blackens it* (HS); –hẹsčiʔ –: rahę́sčiʔθ ‹he-be black-begins› *he becomes black* (H 2892); –hẹsčiʔr –: uhęsčíʔreh ‹be black-??› *blackness* (HS); –ahθuhkwahęsči –: wahθuhkwahę́sci ‹it-color-instrument-is black› *brown* (HS); –ęhrahęsči –: węhrahę́sči ‹it-dirt-is black› *black earth, muck* (R); –ičahęsči: kęčahę́sči ‹it-fish-is black› *black bass* (H 3518); –nęhsnahęsči –: kanęhsnahę́sči ‹it-seed-is black› *cockle (i.e., any of various weeds that grow in grain fields)* (HS), *the grain is black* (H 2484).

-hẹsčihT – blacken. *v.s.-t.* rahęsčíhthaʔ ‹he-be black-causes› *he blackens it* (HS).

-hẹsčiʔ – become black. *v.s.-a.i.* rahę́sčiʔθ ‹he-be black-begins› *he becomes black* (H 2892).

-hẹsčiʔr – blackness. *n.s.* uhęsčíʔreh ‹be black-??› *blackness* (HS).

-hẹw – boat, canoe, ship, trough. *n.r.* aln: akhę̀·wawęh *my boat* (R), inc., n.sfx. -eh (*West.*: -aʔ). uhę́·weh *boat, canoe, ship, trough* (R), uhę̀·waʔ *boat* (PC); –hẹw –.#keha·ʔ: ruhęwaʔkyéha·ʔ ‹he-boat-customarily› *boatman, sailor, seaman* (HS); –hẹw –.#úʔy: uhęwehúʔy ‹boat-great› *steam boat* (AG), *ship*

(HS), uhęwehúy^ʔ ‹boat-great› *big boat* (PC); **-hęwahtrę** -: rahęwáhtręhs ‹he-boat-ties› *he moors boat* (HS); **-hęwa**= **kęw**: uhę·wakęw ‹boat-in› *in the boat, under the boat* (AG); **-hęwakT**: uhę·wakwt ‹boat-next to› *near the boat, aside of the boat* (AG); **-hęwak**= **tha'nye**ʔ: uhęwakwthá·ʔnye^ʔ ‹boat-next to-going along› *along the boat* (AG); **-hęwak**ʷ**aʔT** -: Yehęwakwáʔthaʔ ‹one-boat-pick up-causes› *Niagara Landing, New York* (former name of Lewiston, New York, "where they take out their canoe or canoes") (AG); **-hęwanę'nahsi** -: rahęwanęʔnáhsyęhs ‹he-boat-affix-undoes› *he disembarks* (HS); **-hęwaʔkye**: uhęwáʔkye ‹boat-at› *upon the boat, on the top of the boat* (AG); **-hęwiN** -: rahęwí·teʔ ‹he-boat-proceeds› *he rows, he goes by boat* (HS); **-hęwuha** -: rahęwúhahs ‹he-boat-puts in water› *he sinks boats* (RC 26:35); **-athęwanę'nakT** -: waʔakyathęwanę·ʔnakt ‹fact-another and I-boat-attach-caused› *we landed* (AG); **-athę**= **wa'nehT** -: wathęwaʔnéhthaʔ ‹it-itself-boat-be present-causes› *dock, quay, pier, port* (HS); **-athęwuha** -: rathęwúhahs ‹he-himself-boat-puts in water› *he goes by boat, he goes by water* (HS); **-ne** -. **-hęwahθhę** -: Nekahęwáhθhę· ‹two-it-boat-is ten› *Twenty-Canoes (Chief of the Beaver Clan)* (H-Handbook); **-ne** -. **-hęwayę'nahkw** -: neyuhęwayęʔnáhkę ‹apart-it-boat-lay-instrument› *concave* (HS); **-yah** -. **-hę**= **wa'ne** -: wekahę·waʔneʔ ‹thither-it-boat-is present› *at the end of the boat, in front of or behind the boat* (AG); **-hęw** -.**#úʔy** **-hsęryuhkw** - **-arekwahT** -: uhęwehúʔy uhsęryúhkweh warekwáhthaʔ ‹boat-great steam-cover-instrument it-go and return-causes› *steam boat* (HS).

-hęw -.**#keha·ʔ** boatman, sailor, seaman. *n.s.* ruhęwaʔkyéha·ʔ ‹he-boat-customarily› *boatman, sailor, seaman* (HS).

-hęw -.**#úʔy** steam boat, ship. *n.s.* uhęwehúʔy ‹boat-great› *steam boat* (AG), *ship* (HS).

-hęw -.**#úʔy** **-hsęryuhkw** - **-arekwahT** - steam boat. *dv.n.s.* uhęwéhuʔy uhsęryúhkweh warekwáhthaʔ ‹boat-great steam-cover-instrument it-go and return-causes› *steam boat* (HS).

-hęwahtrę - moor boat. *v.s.-a.i.* rahęwáhtręhs ‹he-boat-ties› *he moors boat* (HS).

-hęwakʷ**aʔT** - Niagara Landing, New York. *dv.n.s.* Yehęwakwáʔthaʔ ‹one-boat-pick up-causes› *Niagara Landing, New York* (former name of Lewiston, New York, "where they take out their canoe or canoes") (AG).

-hęwanę'nahsi - disembark. *v.s.-a.i.* rahęwanęʔnáhsyęhs ‹he-boat-affix-undoes› *he disembarks* (HS).

-hęwar - flute, pipe, roll, tube, band instrument. *n.r.* aln: akhęwarà·węh *my flute* (R), inc., n.sfx. -eh. This root is pronounced as if it were **-huwar** - by some speakers of modern Tuscarora. uhę·wareh *flute, pipe, roll, tube* (HS), *band instrument* (PC); **-hęwarahT** -. **#áh**: yehęwarahthaʔáh ‹one-tube-cause-little› *fife* (HS); **-hęwaręti** -: kahęwarę·tih ‹it-tube-makes› *making a pipe or tube-like shape around head with a shawl* (L 82).

-hęwarahT -.**#áh** fife. *dv.n.s.* yehęwarahthaʔáh ‹one-tube-cause-little› *fife* (HS).

hę·we where (RC 3:29). *part.* See: ę·we. nęh! séʔči hę·we ‹very because where› *oh, isn't that too bad* (TW).

hęwetéʔ everywhere, where not (HS). *part.*

-hęwiN - go by boat, row. *v.s.-a.i.* rahęwí·te⁷ ‹he-boat-proceeds› *he rows, he goes by boat* (HS).

−hęwuha − sink boat. *v.s.-a.i.* rahęwúhahs ‹he-boat-puts in water› *he sinks boats* (RC 26:35).

hę́⁷ę behold!, look!, see! (H-notebook). *v.*

−hę⁷θahkę − be prompt, be quick. *v.r.-a.i.* hab: -h, pnt: -, stat: -, prog: -, prp: -, dst: -, caus: -, rvs: -, dat: -, n-inc. rahę⁷θáhkęh *he is prompt, he is quick* (HS).

hę́⁷tahk four (RC 3:22) [Lawson «Untoc» 'Four']. *part.* hę́⁷tahk −či −. −(i)har −: hę́⁷tahk θkáhe⁷r ‹four again-it-hangs› *fourteen* (R); hę́⁷tahk ti −. −ahθhę −: hę́⁷tahk tiwáhθhę· ‹four so-it-is ten› *forty* (R); hę́⁷tahk ti+či −. −hterhę −: hę́⁷tahk tičuhtérhę ‹four so-again-it-X-is day› *Thursday* (R).

hę́⁷tahk −či −. −(i)har − fourteen. *dv.n.s.* hę́⁷tahk θkáhe⁷r ‹four again-it-hangs› *fourteen* (R).

hę́⁷tahk ti −. −ahθhę − forty. *dv.n.s.* hę́⁷tahk tiwáhθhę· ‹four so-it-is ten› *forty* (R).

hę́⁷tahk ti+či −. −hterhę − Thursday. *dv.n.s.* hę́⁷tahk tičuhtérhę ‹four so-again-it-X-is day› *Thursday* (R).

hę́⁷te⁷ evident (AW 56). *part.*

híhte⁷ sun (RC 4:4) [Lawson «Heita» 'Sun or Moon'] [Gallatin «heetay, (ahtsuhnyyaihau)» 'Moon', «(ourhukayhaw,) heetay» 'Sun']. *n.* −hihte⁷čr −: uhihté⁷čreh ‹sun-'ness› *month, moon* (HS); −hihte⁷čr −.#kęha⁷nę⁷: uhihte⁷črehkęha⁷nę⁷ ‹sun-'ness-many› *celestial bodies* (RC 3:2); −hihte⁷črahurę⁷ −:

yuhihte⁷črahù·rę⁷θ ‹it-sun-'ness-grow old-begins› *crescent* (HS); −hihte⁷čra= θe·⁷ −: yuhihte⁷črá·θe·⁷ ‹it-sun-'ness-new› *new moon* (R); −hihte⁷čri −: kahihté⁷črih ‹it-sun-'ness-is a group› *second half of moon* (SH 375); −či −. −hihte⁷čraT −: θkahihté⁷čra·t ‹again-it-sun-'ness-stands› *one month* (R); tha −. −hihte⁷črihę: tha⁷uhihte⁷číhę ‹unusual-it-sun-'ness-middle of› *second quarter of moon* (SH 375).

−hihte⁷čr − month, moon. *n.s.* uhihté⁷čreh ‹sun-'ness› *month, moon* (HS).

−hihte⁷čr −.#kęha⁷nę⁷ celestial bodies. *n.s.* uhihte⁷črehkęha⁷nę⁷ ‹sun-'ness-many› *celestial bodies* (RC 3:2).

−hihte⁷črahurę⁷ − crescent. *dv.n.s.* yuhihte⁷črahù·rę⁷θ ‹it-sun-'ness-grow old-begins› *crescent* (HS).

−hihte⁷čraθe·⁷ − new moon. *n.* yuhihte⁷črá·θe·⁷ ‹it-sun-'ness-new› *new moon* (R).

−hihte⁷čri − second half of moon. *dv.n.s.* kahihté⁷črih ‹it-sun-'ness-is a group› *second half of moon* (SH 375).

−hiθ − spread out. *v.r.-a.i.* hab: -, pnt: -, stat: -, prog: -, prp: -, dst: -, caus: -, rvs: -, dat: -, inc.-??-pat. Found only in the construction given below. −ne −. −(ę)⁷teyhi-θahT −: wa⁷tka⁷teyhí·θaht ‹fact-apart-it-crowd-spread out-caused› *it scattered crowd* (RC 5:41).

−hiyu − Allegany Seneca Reservation. *n.r.* poss. ?, n-inc., n.sfx. −⁷. uhì·yu⁷ *Allegany Seneca Reservation* (HS); −hi= yu −.#aka·⁷: uhiyu⁷á·ka·⁷ ‹Allegany Reservation-characterized by› *Resi-*

dent of the *Allegany Seneca Reservation* (HS).

-hiyu-.**#aka·ʔ** Resident of the Allegany Seneca Reservation. *n.s.* uhiyuʔá·ka·ʔ ‹Allegany Reservation-characterized by› *Alleganean* (HS).

híʔnęʔ thunder; the Thunders (legendary embodiments of thunder) (RC 36:title) [Gallatin «heynuh» 'Thunder']. *n.* híʔnęʔ **-weh**-: híʔnęʔ kà·weh ‹thunder it-speaks› *it thunders* (PC).

híʔnęʔ **-weh**- thunder. *v.s.-a.i.* híʔnęʔ kà·weh ‹thunder it-speaks› *it thunders* (HS).

-hk habitual aspect. *v.r.sfx.*

-hkwačh- be unrobed, be unmantled. *v.s.-s.i.* ruhkwáčhę· ‹he-wrap-undid› *he is unrobed, he is unmantled* (HS).

-hkwačr- shroud, wrap. *n.s.* uhkwáčreh ‹wrap-'ness› *shroud, wrap* (HS).

-hkwaθ- wrap. *v.r.-s.i.* stat: -ę, prog: -, prp: -, dst: -, caus: -, rvs: -hsi-, dat: -, n-inc. yuhkwá·θę *it is wrapped* (RC 28:1); **-hkwačh**-: ruhkwáčhę· ‹he-wrap-undid› *he is unrobed, he is unmantled* (HS); **-hkwačr**-: uhkwáčreh ‹wrap-'ness› *shroud, wrap* (HS).

-hkwaʔke plain, high hill. *n.r.* n-poss., n-inc., n.sfx. -. kahkwáʔkye *place where people can see far & wide, either a plain or high hill* (AG).

-hk̈aʔT- pick up. *v.r.-t.* See: **-(i)h=k̈aʔT**-.

-hkwehę- deride, run down. *v.r.-t.* hab: -h, pnt: -, stat: -, prog: -, prp: -, dst: -, caus: -, rvs: -, dat: -, n-inc. rahkwéhęh *he derides it, he runs it down* (HS).

-hkwęni- apparel, raiment. *n.r.* poss. ?, inc. ?, n.sfx. -eh. uhkwę́·nyeh *apparel, raiment* (HS).

-hkwęʔna(w)- assassinate, murder. *v.r.-t.* hab: ()-s, pnt: ()-ɸ, stat: -·, prog: -, prp: -, dst: -, caus: -, rvs: -, dat: -, n-inc. rahkwę́ʔnaws *he assassinates, he murders (never applied to anything except persons)* (H-notebook), ęhrahkwę́ʔnaw *he will murder* (HS): **haʔ-hkwęʔna(w)**-: haʔ ruhkwę́ʔna· ‹the he-assassinated› *assassination* (HS).

-hkwęʔna(w)- assassination. *dv.n.s.* haʔ ruhkwę́ʔna· ‹the he-assassinated› *assassination* (HS).

-hkwi- undo (reversive). *v.r.sfx.* Rare, lexically determined form.

-hkwiʔst- beaded belt, belt, sash. *n.r.* poss. ?, inc. ?, n.sfx. -eh. uhkwíʔsteh *beaded belt, belt, sash* (HS).

-hkwiʔT- move away, remove. *v.r.-a.i.* hab: -haʔ, pnt: -ɸ, stat: -ę, prog: -, prp: -, dst: -, caus: -, rvs: -, dat: -, inc.-ɸ-pat. This root may be the source of Lawson's «Utquichra» 'A Cable', from *utkwíʔčreh, lit. 'itself-move away-'ness'. rahkwíʔthaʔ *he removes it* (HS), ęyéhkwiʔt *one will move away* (RC 23:4); **-atkwiʔT**-: ęwátkwiʔt ‹prediction-it-itself-move away› *it will move away* (RC 23:4); **-(a)hahahkwiʔT**-: rahahahkwíʔthaʔ ‹he-path-moves away› *he switches the road (railroad)* (H 2484); **-(ę)taʔrah=kwiʔT**-: wahrętaʔráhkwiʔt ‹fact-he-head-moved away› *he moved his head away* (RC 24: 9); **-ne+t**-.**-atkwiʔT**-: nethratkwíʔthaʔ ‹apart-hither-he-himself-moves away› *he approaches* (HS); **kwęhs** **-atkwiʔT**-: kwęhs arętkwíʔthek ‹no unknown-it-itself-move away› *it is immovable, it is immutable* (HS).

-hkyerhuhT- hoist. *v.r.-a.i.* hab: -haʔ, pnt: -, stat: -, prog: -, prp: -, dst: -, caus: -, rvs: -, dat: -, n-inc. rahkyerhúhthaʔ *he hoists* (H-notebook).

-hkyuhs- elbow. *n.r.* inaln: rahkyuhséʔkye *on his elbow* (R), inc., n.sfx. -eh. uhkyúhseh *elbow* (R); **-hkyuh=sihar**-: rahkyúhsiher ‹he-elbow-hangs›

he leans upon his elbows (HS);
-**hkyuhsku** -: rahkyúhskwahs ‹he-elbow-picks up› *he elbows it* (HS).
-**hkyuhsihar** - lean on elbows. *v.s.-a.i.* rahkyúhsiher ‹he-elbow-hangs› *he leans upon his elbows* (HS).
-**hkyuhsku** - elbow. *v.s.-t.* rahkyúhskwahs ‹he-elbow-picks up› *he elbows it* (HS).
-**hna** - empty noun root. *v.inc.* See: -**ta** = **wę** - *warm*.
-**hnar** - flint. *n.* n-poss., n-inc., n.sfx. -eh. úhnareh *flint* (AG).
-**hnatawę** - warm. *v.s.-s.i.* yuhnatá·wę·t ‹it-X-warmed› *it is warm* (R).
-**hnatawęhsT** - warm. *v.s.-t.* rahnatawę́hstha› ‹it-X-warm-causes› *he warms it* (R).
-**hnatawę›** - become warm. *v.s.-a.i.* ruhnatà·wę›θ ‹it-X-warms-begins› *he becomes warm* (R).
-**hnaw** - current of water; morass, swamp. *n.r.* n-poss., inc., n.sfx. -eh. When incorporated, the meaning *current of water* predominates. This root refers to the type of watery swamp, verging on a small lake, which is called a fly or vly in some parts of the U.S. Northeast, and which is often created when a stream or river is blocked by a beaver dam. uhnà·weh *morass, swamp* (HS) [Lawson «Oohunawa» 'A Rundlet']; -**hnawahrahT** -: wahrahnawahráhnahk ‹fact-he-current-put up-caused› *he went against the current* (RC 12:29); -**hnawakęw**: uhnà·wakęw ‹current of water-in› *swamp* (R);

-**hnawakęwha'nye›** -: uhnawakęwhá·›nye› ‹current of water-in-going along› *going along in the swamp* (RC 33:8); -**hnawayę(T)** -: yuhnà·wayę› ‹it-current of water-lays› *there is a swamp* (RC 2:13); -**hnawa›ke**: Kahnawá›kye ‹it-current of water-at› *St. Lawrence River* (AG); *Sault St. Louis* (HS); *Kahnawake (Mohawk) Reserve* (R); -**hna** = **wa'nehT** -: yuhnà·wa›neht ‹it-current of water-be present-caused› *it is a sharp current* (RC 12:29).
-**hnawahrahT** - go against the current. *v.s.-a.i.* wahrahnawahráhnahk ‹fact-he-current-put up-caused› *he went against the current* (RC 12:29).
-**hnawakęw** swamp. *n.s.* uhnà·wakęw ‹current of water-in› *swamp* (R).
-**hnawayę(T)** - be a swamp. *v.s.-s.i.* yuhnà·wayę› ‹it-current of water-lays› *there is a swamp* (RC 2:13).
-**hnawa›ke** St. Lawrence River, Sault St. Louis, Kahnawake (Mohawk) Reserve. *n.s.* Kahnawá›kye ‹it-current of water-at› *Sault St. Louis* (HS); *Kahnawake (Mohawk) Reserve* (R).
-**hnek** - alcohol, liquor; juice, sap, water. *n.r.* n-poss., inc., n.sfx. -eh. According to Hewitt & Smith the original meaning of this root was *maple tree sap*. uhné·kyeh *alcohol, liquor; juice, sap, water* (R) [Lawson «Oonaquod» 'Rum']; -**hnekaT** -: kahné·ka·t ‹it-liquid-stands› *there is sap in it, it contains sap* (H 2892); -**hnekayę(T)** - {dative I}: kahné·kayę›θ ‹it-water-lays-for› *a body of water (laying*

there) (H-notebook); **–hnekuhθrahw –**: rahnekúhθraws ‹he-water-strip off-causes› *he sprinkles it* (HS), nathnekuhθráwstha⁹ ‹he-water-strip off-cause-causes› *one baptizes another* (HS); **–athnekạhninę –**: yęthnekahnì·nęh ‹one-oneself-liquor-buys› *inn* (HS).

–hnekuhθrahw – sprinkle. *v.s.-t.* rahnekúhθraws ‹he-water-strip off-causes› *he sprinkles it* (HS).

–hnekuhθrahwsT – baptize. *v.s.-t.* nathnekuhθráwstha⁹ ‹he-water-strip off-causes-causes› *one baptizes another* (HS).

–hnekạyę(T) – {dative I} a body of water (laying there). *dv.n.s.* kahné·kayę⁹θ ‹it-water-lays-for› *a body of water (laying there)* (H-notebook).

–hne⁹r – root, turnip, vegetable. *n.r.* n-poss., inc., n.sfx. -eh. uhné⁹reh *root* (RC 12:18), *turnip, vegetable* (L 70); **–hne⁹rạkahrę(w) –**: yuhne⁹rakáhrę⁹ ‹it-root-is an opening› *there is an opening in the root* (RC 25:2); **–hne⁹= rạkęw**: uhné⁹rakęw ‹root-in› *in root* (RC 15:2); **–hne⁹rạtyenę –**: wahrahne⁹ratyè·nę⁹ ‹fact-he-root-obtained› *he found root* (L 3); **–hne⁹rawihsi –**: rahne⁹rawíhsyęhs ‹he-root-give-undoes› *he uproots it* (HS); **–hne⁹ręt**: yuhné⁹rę·t ‹it-root-possesses› *it has a root* (H 2892); **–hne⁹ręti –**: kahne⁹rę́·tih ‹it-root-makes› *it takes root* (HS); **–hne⁹= ru –**: wa⁹ehné⁹ru·⁹ ‹fact-one-root-put in water› *one put root in water* (RC 22: 1); **–či –**. **–hne⁹reθ –**: čuhné⁹re·θ ‹again-it-root-is long› *spikenard (Aralia racemosa)* (L 3); **–či –**. **–hne⁹reθ –.#áh**: čuhne⁹re·θ⁹áh ‹again-it-root-is long-little› *sarsaparilla (Smilax* sp.) (HS); **–či –**. **–hne⁹reθ –.#ú⁹y**: čuhne⁹re·θ⁹ú⁹y ‹again-it-root-is long-great› *wild sarsaparilla (Aralia nudicaulis)* (H-notebook); **ti –**. **–hne⁹rạtkwạrạyę(T) –**: tikahne⁹ratkwarà·yę⁹ ‹so-it-root-is red›

beet (R).

–hne⁹rawihsi – uproot. *v.s.-a.i.* rahne⁹rawíhsyęhs ‹he-root-give-undoes› *he uproots it* (HS).

–hne⁹ręti – take root. *v.s.-a.i.* kahne⁹rę́·tih ‹it-root-makes› *it takes root* (HS).

–hnęhst – armful. *n.r.* poss. ?, inc. ?, n. sfx. -eh. uhnę́hsteh *armful* (HS).

–hnęhtihčr – (walking) cane, messenger cane, scepter. *n.r.* n-poss., n-inc., n. sfx. -eh. uhnęhtíhčreh *(walking) cane, messenger cane, scepter* (HS).

–hnęhu – upper shoulder. *n.r.* inaln: rahnęhwę́⁹kye *on his upper shoulder* (RC 35:14), inc., n.sfx. -eh. uhnę́hweh *upper shoulder* (R); **–hnęhwakęhčrę –**: wa⁹nathnęhwakę́hčrę⁹ ‹fact-one= another-upper shoulder-whipped› *one slapped another's upper shoulder* (RC 25:10); **–athnęhu'narhuhst –**: rathnęhu⁹narhúhstha⁹ ‹he-himself-upper shoulder-hook-cause-causes› *(his) suspenders* (HS); **–athnęhwạ⁹niha –**: rathnęhwa⁹níhahs ‹he-himself-upper shoulder-sprains› *he sprains his shoulder* (HS), wathnęhwa⁹níhahs ‹it-itself-upper shoulder-sprains› *sparrow hawk* (R).

–hnęhwečh – nape of neck. *n.r.* inaln: rahnęhwečhę́⁹kye *the nape of his neck* (RC 26:21), inc., n.sfx. -eh. uhnęhwéčheh *nape of neck* (R); **–hnęh= wečhara –**: wa⁹nathnęhwécha·⁹ ‹fact-one=another-nape of neck-grabbed› *one grabbed another by the nape of the neck* (RC 3:73); **–hnęhwe= čhạrhenathę –**: ruhnęhwečharhená·thę· ‹he-nape of neck-is rigid› *he has a stiff neck* (H-notebook).

–hnęhwečhạrhenathę – have a stiff neck. *v.s.-a.i.* ruhnęhwečharhená·thę· ‹he-nape of neck-is rigid› *he has a stiff neck* (H-notebook).

–hnęn – butt; trunk. *n.r.* poss. ?, inc. ?, n.sfx. -eh. uhnę̀·neh *butt (of a person),* *trunk (of a tree)* (HS).

-hnęθhar – clasp, embrace. *v.r.-a.i.* See: -(ę)hnęθhar –.

-hnęθhar – armful, embrace. *dv.n.s.* See: -(ę)hnęθhar –.

-hnęw – wife, woman of the house; wife's relatives; mother's relatives. *n.r.* inaln: ráhnęw *his wife's relations* (HS), n-inc., n.sfx. –. yéhnęw *wife, woman of the house* (RC 3:52), ráhnęw *his wife's relations* (HS); -hnęw –.#aka·?: rahnęw?á·ka·? ‹he-mother's relatives-characterized by› *people of his mother's relations, his mother's family, his mother's clan, his mother's tribe* (HS).

-hnęw – bottom of lake, lake bed. *n.r.* n-poss., inc., n.sfx. -eh. uhnę̀·weh *bottom of lake, lake bed* (R); -hnęwa=kęw: uhnę̀·wakęw ‹lake bed-in› *in the lake bed* (RC 3:76); -hnęwyę –: yuhnę́·wyę· ‹it-lake bed-went into› *it is sunken* (HS); -yah –.-hnęwyęhsT –: wekahnęwyę́hstha? ‹thither-it-lake bed-go into-causes› *it sinks in, it is absorbed* (HS); ti+yah –.-hnęwyę –: thwehrahnę́·wyę· ‹so-thither-he-lake bed-went into› *he sinks* (HS); ti+yah –.-(ę)ta?= rahnęwyę –: tyahwa?kata?rahné·wyę? ‹so-thither-fact-it-head-lake bed-went into› *its head disappeared from sight into the mud* (RC 31:7).

-hnęw – course, line, mark. *n.r.* n-poss., inc., n.sfx. -eh. uhnę̀·weh *course, line, mark* (R); -hnęwai?a(k) –: rahnęwaí?ahs ‹he-mark-shoots› *he hits the mark* (HS); -hnęwayę?T –: kahnę̀·wayę?t ‹it-mark-lay-causes› *commerce*

(HS); -hnęwi?θ(e)r –: rahnęwí?θręhs ‹he-mark-drags› *he draws a mark, he traces* (HS); -hnęwyęti?T –: rahnęwyętí?tha? ‹he-mark-extend-causes› *it streaks it* (HS); -ne –.-hnęwayę?T –: nekahnę̀·wayę?t ‹apart-it-mark-lay-causes› *trade, exchange* (HS); kwęhs -hnęwi?θ(e)r –: kwęhs ahruhnęwí?θrę·k ‹no unknown-he-mark-drag› *he has not marked it* (HS); ha? -ne –.-hnęwa=yę?T –: ha? nekahnęwayé?nę ‹the a-part-it-mark-lay-caused› *bargain* (HS).

-hnęw –.#aka·? mother's family, mother's clan, mother's tribe. *n.s.* rahnęw?á·ka·? ‹he-mother's relatives-characterized by› *people of his mother's relations, his mother's family, his mother's clan, his mother's tribe* (HS).

-hnęwai?a(k) – hit the mark. *v.s.-a.i.* rahnęwaí?ahs ‹he-mark-shoots› *he hits the mark* (HS).

-hnęwayę?T – commerce. *dv.n.s.* kahnę̀·wayę?t ‹it-mark-lay-causes› *commerce* (HS).

-hnęwi?θ(e)r – draw a mark, trace. *v.s.-a.i.* rahnęwí?θręhs ‹he-mark-drags› *he draws a mark, he traces* (HS).

-hnęwyę – sink. *v.s.-s.i.* yuhnę́·wyę· ‹it-lake bed-went in-to› *it is sunken* (HS).

-hnęwyęti?T – streak. *v.s.-t.* rahnęwyętí?tha? ‹he-mark-extend-causes› *it streaks it* (HS).

-hnęyahčr – apron. *n.r.* poss. ?, inc. ?, n.sfx. -eh. uhnęyáhčreh *apron* (HS); -hnęyahčr –.#áh: uhnęyahčreháh ‹apron-little› *bib* (HS).

-hnęyahčr –.#áh bib. *n.s.* uhnęyahčreháh

‹apron-little› *bib* (HS).

-hnihsak – go looking for news. *v.s.-a.i.* wahrahnihsá·khe⁷ ‹fact-he-news-seek-was going to› *he went looking for news* (L 12).

-hninę – buy. *v.r.-t.* hab: -h ~ -hs, pnt: -, stat: -, prog: -, prp: -, dst: -, caus: -⁷T-, rvs: -, dat: -, inc.-ɸ-pat. Requires that an incorporated noun be present. –(a)hę'na̱hninę –: rahę⁷nahnì·nęh ‹he-clearing-buys› *he buys the field* (H 24 84); –(a)hę'na̱hninę⁷T –: rahę⁷nahninę⁷-tha⁷ ‹he-clearing-buy-causes› *he buys the field with it* (H 2484); –nęhsna̱h = ninę –: ranęhsnahnì·nęh ‹he-seed-buys› *he buys grain* (H 2484); –nęθa̱hninę –: ranęθahnì·nęh ‹he-potato-buys› *he buys potatoes* (H 2484); –athne = ka̱hninę –: yęthnekahnì·nęh ‹one-one-self-liquor-buys› *inn* (HS); –a'nyah = kwa̱hninę –: ra⁷nyahkwahnì·nęhs ‹he-himself-girth-buys› *he sells fish* (W 74).

-hni⁷ru – sod. *n.r.* poss. ?, inc., n.sfx. -⁷. uhní⁷ru⁷ *sod* (HS); –hni⁷ruken –: kahni⁷rukyè·nę ‹it-sod-divided› *it is underneath the sod* (RC 5:15).

-hnukęw – notice, perceive. *v.r.-a.i.* hab: -, pnt: -, stat: -⁷, prog: -, prp: -, dst: -, caus: -, rvs: -, dat: -, n-inc. rahnú·kę⁷w *he noticed, he perceived* (RC 31:8).

-hny – barb, chisel, spear. *n.r.* poss. ?, n-inc., n.sfx. -eh. úhnyeh *barb, chisel, spear* (HS).

-hny – news, rumor, tale. *n.r.* poss. ?, inc., n.sfx. -eh. úhnyeh *news, rumor, tale* (L 12); –hnihsak –: wahrahnihsá·khe⁷ ‹fact-he-news-seek-was going to› *he went looking for news* (L 12); –hnyahrahT –: uhnyáhraht ‹news-put up-cause› *awful news, awful story* (L 13); –hnyaθe⁷ –: uhnyá·θe⁷ ‹news-be new› *new news* (L 12); –hnya̱wihę –:

rahnyawíhęh ‹he-news-knows-much› *bluffer (best talker)* (L 41); –hnyę̇te: uhnyę́·te ‹news-a certain› *a certain story* (AW 54); –či –. –hnyę̇hawi –: θhrahnyęhà·wi⁷ ‹again-he-news-brings› *he reports* (HS); –ne –. –hnya̱ = karati –: nehrahnyakará·tih ‹apart-he-news-rubs› *he tattles* (HS), nehruhnyakará·tye⁷ ‹apart-he-news-rubbed› *he tattled* (HS); –ne –. –hnyę̇hawihT –: nehrahnyęhawíhtha⁷ ‹apart-he-news-bring-causes› *sycophant, tale-bearer* (HS); –ti –. –hnu⁷nę –: tikahnyú⁷nę· ‹so-it-news-is a kind of› *this story* (AW 53); ha⁷ –hnya̱wę –: ha⁷ ráhnyawęh ‹the he-news-possesses› *his aspersion* (HS).

-hnya – wear, wear around neck. *v.r.-t.* See: –(i)hnya –.

-hnya̱wę – aspersion. *dv.n.s.* ha⁷ ráhnyawęh ‹the he-news-possesses› *his aspersion* (HS).

-hnya̱wihę – bluffer. *dv.n.s.* rahnyawíhęh ‹he-news-knows-much› *bluffer (best talker)* (L 41).

-hra̱ – empty noun root. *v.inc.* See: –tuhsT – *freeze*.

-hra – he (third person singular masculine agent). *v.r.pfx.* The form –hra – occurs before roots and stems that begin with a consonant or the vowel *i*; when the root or stem begins with *i* the final *a* of the prefix coalesces with it to yield the form –hrę –. The form –hr – occurs before roots or stems that begin with a vowel other than *i*. The initial *h* of the prefix is dropped when word-initial.

-hrak –/–hrak** – he...me (third person singular masculine agent=first person singular patient). *v.r.pfx.* The form –hrak** – occurs before roots or stems that begin with the vowel *a*. The form –hrak – occurs elsewhere, with "epenthetic" e inserted between the prefix and roots or stems beginning with certain consonant clusters. The initial *h* is dropped when word-initial.

-hraT – count. *v.r.-a.i.* hab: -s, pnt: -ɸ, stat: -ę, prog: -, prp: -he-, dst: -, caus: -, rvs: -, dat: -, inc.-ɸ-pat. θhrá·t *count!* (R) (variant: í·θhra·t (L 43)), wá·ʔkhra·t *I counted* (R), ruhrá·ʔnę *he has counted* (L 43), ráhra·č *he counts* (L 43), ęyehráčhehk *one will count* (RC 15:3), ęhrahrá·theʔ *he is going to count* (RC 15:5); –či –. **-hraT** –: θhráhra·č ‹again-he-counts› *he renumerates* (HS); ** haʔ** **-hraT** –: haʔ káhra·č ‹the it-counts› *mathematics* (HS); –ę'nahraT –: wę·ʔnahra·č ‹it-day-counts› *almanac* (HS); **-nęhsnahraT** –: ranęhsnáhra·č ‹he-seed-counts› *he counts the grains* (H 2484); **haʔ** **-rihwahraT** –: haʔ yurihwahrá·ʔnę ‹the it-matter-counted› *chapter* (HS); **kwęhs** **-athraT** –: kwęhs aryuthrá·ʔnęk ‹no unknown-it-itself-count› *it is innumerable, it is unnumbered* (HS).

-hraT – mathematics. *dv.n.s.* haʔ káhra·č ‹the it-counts› *mathematics* (HS).

-hratuhsT – freeze. *v.r.-t.* See: **-tuhsT** –.

-hraw –/ **-hru** – he, him (third person singular masculine patient). *v.r.pfx.* The form **-hraw** – occurs before roots or stems that begin with a vowel other than *a*. The form **-hru** – occurs elsewhere with loss of an initial *a* of a root or stem. The initial *h* of the prefix is dropped when word-initial.

-hrawhę – be distraught. *v.s.-a.i.* wah-ruhráwhęʔ ‹fact-he-fear-much› *he was distraught* (RC 1:3).

-hrawʔ – fear. *v.r.-a.i.* hab: -θ, pnt: -, stat: -, prog: -, prp: -, dst: -hę-, caus: -ahT-, rvs: -, dat: -, n-inc. ráhrawʔθ *he fears* (HS); **-hrawhę** –: wahruhráwhęʔ ‹fact-he-fear-much› *he was distraught* (RC 1:3); **-hrawʔahT** –: uhráwʔaht ‹fear-cause› *doleful, lonesome, lonely* (HS).

-hrawʔahT – doleful, lonesome, lonely. *n.s.* uhráwʔaht ‹fear-cause› *doleful, lonesome, lonely* (HS).

-hraʔkw – quill. *n.r.* poss. ?, inc., n.sfx. -eh. uhráʔkweh *quill* (HS); **-hraʔ**= kwaʔr –: yuhráʔkwaʔr ‹it-quill-is much› *tail feather* (RC 12:5).

-hraʔkwaʔr – tail feather. *dv.n.s.* yuhráʔkwaʔr ‹it-quill-is much› *tail feather* (RC 12:5).

-hraʔn – feather. *n.r.* poss. ?, inc., n.sfx. -eh. uhráʔneh *feather* (RC 11:22); **-hraʔnę** –: rahráʔnęh ‹he-feather-falls› *he puts feathers on (arrows)* (HS); **-hraʔnęti** –: kahraʔnę́tih ‹it-feather-makes› *it makes feathers (said of a birdling just starting to grow feathers)* (RC 8:34); **-athraʔnęhT** –: wathraʔnę́htha ʔ ‹it-itself-feather-fall-causes› *it (bird) molts* (HS).

-hraʔn – pestle. *n.r.* n-poss. ?, n-inc., n.sfx. -eh. uhráʔneh *pestle* (RC 5:36).

-hraʔnę – put feathers on. *v.s.-a.i.* rahráʔnęh ‹he-feather-falls› *he puts feathers on (arrows)* (HS).

-hraʔnęti – make feathers. *v.s.-a.i.* kahraʔ-nę́tih ‹it-feather-makes› *it makes*

*feathers (said of a birdling just star-
ting to grow feathers)* (RC 8:34).

–hra?T– bury. *v.r.-t.* See: **–(i)hra?T–**.

–hrek– send. *v.r.-a.i.* hab: -, pnt: -ɸ, stat:
-, prog: -, prp: -, dst: -, caus: -, rvs: -.
dat: -, n-inc. -t-. **–hrek–**: nakayę́?ná-
thre·k ‹hither-fact-they=another-sent›
they sent someone (RC 12:4).

–hren– cut. *v.r.-t.* hab: -ahs, pnt: -?, stat:
-ę, prog: -, prp: -, dst: -, caus: -ahT-,
rvs: -, dat: -, inc.-ɸ-pat. θhré·n *cut it!*
(R), rahrè·nahs *surgeon: he cuts it* (R),
nathrè·nahs *one castrates another* (R),
wá?khre?n *I cut it* (R); **ti-.–hre=
nahthę–**: tyuhrenáhthę· ‹so-it-cut-
caused-much› *it is cut up a lot* (RC
30:46); **–a'nahsahren–**: ru?nahsahrè·nę
‹he-himself-foot-cut› *his foot is cut*
(RC 36:2).

–hren– surgeon. *dv.n.s.* rahrè·nahs ‹he-
cuts› *surgeon* (R).

–hrenathę– be cut up a lot *v.s.-s.i.* ti-.
–hrenathę–: tyuhrenáthę· ‹so-it-cut-
caused-much› *it is cut up a lot* (RC
30:46).

–hrenhętyę– whittle. *v.r.-a.i.* hab: -h, pnt:
-, stat: -, prog: -, prp: -, dst: -, caus: -,
rvs: -, dat: -, n-inc. This root is possible derived historically from the root
–hren– *cut* plus a rare sequence of two
distributive markers, **–hę–** and **–tyę–**.
rahrenhę́·tyęh *he is whittling* (HS).

–hrewa?nęhčr– condemnation, cursing,
punishment. *n.s.* kahrewa?nę́hčra? ‹it-
punish-'ness› *condemnation, cursing,
punishment* (HS).

–hrewa?T– damn, punish. *v.r.-t.* hab: -
ha?, pnt: -ɸ, stat: -ę, prog: -, prp: -,
dst: -, caus: -, rvs: -, dat: -, n-inc.
yuhrewá?nę *penal: it is punishable*
(HS), kahrewá?nę *one is accursed,
one is damned, one is punished* (HS),
nathrewá?tha? *one punishes another*
(HS), ra?nathrewá?tha? *he confesses*

(HS), çyękhihrè·wa?t *one will punish
us* (MP); **–hrewa?nęhčr–**: kahrewa?-
nę́hčra? ‹it-punish-'ness› *condemnation, cursing, punishment* (HS); ti-.
–hrewa?T–: tikayę?nathrewá?tha? ‹so-
they=another-punish› *they are punished* (MP); **–yah+či-.–hrewa?T–**:
yęθakayę?nathrè·wa?t ‹thither-predic-
tion-again-they=another-punish› *they
will repent* (MP); **–ętathrewa?T–**: ręta-
threwá?tha? ‹he-??-punishes› *he repents* (HS); ha? **–ętathrewa?T–**: ha?
rawętathrewá?nę ‹the he-??-punished›
his apology (HS); kwęhs **–ętathre=
wa?T–**: kwęhs ahrętathrewá?thek ‹no
unknown-he-??-punish› *he is unrepenting* (HS).

–hre?– blame, censure. *v.r.-t.* hab: -ahs,
pnt: -, stat: -ę, prog: -, prp: -, dst: -,
caus: -, rvs: -, dat: -, n-inc. yuhré?ę *it
is censured, it is forbidden, it is taboo*
(R), rahré?ahs *he blames it, he censures it* (HS), ruhré?ę *he censured it*
(HS); **–athre?–**: ruthré?ahs ‹he-himself-
censures› *he is blamable* (HS); **–a=
thre?ahsT–**: yuthré?ahst ‹it-itself-cen-
sure-caused› *censure* (HS); **–nh–
–hre?–**: kánhę rahré?ahs ‹it-is full he-
censures› *blameful* (HS).

–hrę– many, much (distributive). *v.r.sfx.*
hab: -h, pnt: -?, stat: -·, prog: -, prp: -,
caus: -, rvs: -, dat: -. The distributive
is used to indicate either that the action of the verb is spread over time or
that the object of the verb is distributed over an area (e.g., **wahratiyę́?-
khrę·?** ‹fact-he-shot-many› *he shot
several (arrows)*.

–hrę– put up, set. *v.r.-t.* hab: -, pnt: -?,
stat: -, prog: -, prp: -, dst: -, caus:
-hw-, rvs: -, dat: -, inc.-ɸ-pat. θhrę́ *set
it down!* (R), ęθwáhrę? *you will put
up* (RC 3:22); **–hręhw–**: wa?khréhwa?
‹fact-I-put up-caused› *I waited* (R),

ęθwahrę́hwaʼ ‹prediction-you-put up-cause› *you will be perfectly still* (RC 33:5). káhręw ‹it-put up-causes› *it leans, it is oblique, it is out of plumb: tendency* (HS); –hrę̨hw –{dative I}: kęhrę̨hwá'ʼθeh ‹I=you-put up-cause-for› *I am waiting for you* (R); –hrę̨h= wahkw –: kahrę̨hwáhkę ‹it-put up-caused-instrument› *it leans toward* (HS); –hrę̨hwaʼθrę –: rahrę̨hwá'ʼθręh ‹he-put up-causes-much› *he sways* (HS); –hrę̨hwhę –: ha'ʼ yuhrę́whę· ‹the it-put up-caused-much› *cessation* (R); –hrę̨hwsT –: rahrę́wstha'ʼ ‹he-put up-causes› *he stops it* (HS); –yah –. –hrę –: yahwahráhrę'ʼ ‹thither-fact-he-put up› *he put it up there* (RC 3:60); –t –. –hrę̨hw –: nayúhręw ‹hither-fact-it-put up-caused› *it is quiet there* (RC 10:4); ti –. –hrę̨hw –: tihruhrę́hę ‹so-he-put up-caused› *he is still* (RC 26: 33), *he is silent, he is taciturn* (HS); tha –. –hrę̨hwaʼke: tha'ʼθahrę̨hwá'ʼkye ‹unusual-you-put up-cause-at› *at your leisure* (R); –či'ʼčihrę̨hw –: rači'ʼčihrę́wha'ʼ ‹he-fringe-put causes› *he puts on fringe* (HS); –(ę)taʼrhrę –.#ú'ʼy: wahrę̨taʼrhrę'ʼú'ʼy ‹fact-he-head-put up-great› *he, the big one, put his head up* (RC 25:17); –(ę)'ʼtikęhrahrę̨hw –: ru'ʼtikęhráhręw ‹he-mind-put up-caused› *he anticipates* (R); –herahrę̨hwaku –: raherahrę̨hwá·kwahs ‹he-green-put up-cause-picks up› *he turns over hay* (HS); –hseʼyuhrę –: ruhse'ʼyúhrę· ‹he-cork-put up› *he plugged it* (RC 11:4); –nę̨hahrę –: ranę̨háhręh ‹he-corn-puts up› *he sets, places corn grains (in the ground); hence, he plants corn* (H 2484); –nę̨hahrę̨ʼkye: kanę̨hahrę́'ʼkye ‹it-corn-puts up-at› *at corn planting (a subaudition of the word for time); this is the name of the month of April (?)* (H 2484); –nę̨hsnahrę̨hw –: runę̨hsnáhręw ‹he-seed-put up-causes› *he has the grain across, has the grain on his shoulder* (H 2484): –ne –. –kahrah= rę̨hw –: nekakahráhręw ‹apart-it-eye-put up-causes› *crooked eyes* (RC 13: 8); –t –. –atrahrę̨hwatyę –: tkakutrahrę̨hwá·tyęh ‹hither-they-pole-put up-cause-much› *they put fence around* (RC 18:13); –t –. –rę̨ʼahrę̨hw –: nakarę'ʼáhręw ‹hither-fact-it-tree-put up-caused› *tree lies down there* (RC 26: 19); –athrę̨hwaku –: wahrathrę̨hwá·ku'ʼ ‹fact-he-himself-put up-cause-picked up› *he turned around* (L 79); rathrę̨hwá·kwahs ‹he-himself-put up-cause-picks up› *he turns about* (R); –athrę̨h= wakuhę –: wathrę̨hwakúhęh ‹it-itself-put up-cause-picks up-much› *it revolves* (HS); –ne –. –athrę̨hw –: nehrathrę́wha'ʼ ‹apart-he-himself-put up-causes› *he opposes it* (HS), nę̨hrathrę́hwe'ʼ ‹apart-prediction-he-himself-put up-cause› *he will oppose it* (HS), neyúthręw ‹apart-it-itself-put up-causes› *crosswise, horizontal, traverse* (HS); –athwaritahrę̨hwa'nye –: ruthwaritahrę̨hwá·'ʼnye'ʼ ‹he-himself-burden-put up-cause-going along› *he carried his backpack along* (RC 26:21); –(ę)= ti'ʼčharihrę –: wahrę̨ti'ʼčharíhrę'ʼ ‹fact-he-himself-branch-put up⟩ *he lifted twig* (RC 26:8); **–ne –**. **–at⁷ehthrę –**: nęhsat⁷éhthrę⁷ ⟨two-prediction-you-yourself-hand-put up⟩ *you will put both your hands up on* (RC 3: 20); **ti+yah –**. **–athwaritạhręw –**: thwewathwarí·tahręw ⟨so-thither-it-itself-burden-put up-causes⟩ *backpack remains there* (RC 26:21); **kę⁷ –ne –**. **–hręhthę –**: kę⁷ neyuhré̜hthę· ⟨where apart-it-put up-caused-much⟩ *base* (HS).

–hrę̜hčihsT – be squeamish. *v.r.-s.i.* stat: –ϕ. prog: –, prp: –, dst: –, caus: –, rvs: –, dat: –, n-inc. ruhré̜hčihst *he is squeamish* (HS).

–hrę̜hkạr – span. *n.r.* n-poss., n-inc., n.sfx. –eh. uhré̜hkareh *span* (HS).

–hrę̜hw – be perfectly still, wait. *v.s.-a.i.* wa⁷khré̜hwa⁷ ⟨fact-I-put up-caused⟩ *I waited* (R), ę̜θwahré̜hwa⁷ ⟨prediction-you-put up-cause⟩ *you will be perfectly still* (RC 33:5).

–hrę̜hw – lean, be oblique, be out of plumb. *v.s.-s.i.* káhręw ⟨it-put up-causes⟩ *it leans, it is oblique, it is out of plumb* (HS).

–hrę̜hw – tendency. *dv.n.s.* káhręw ⟨it-put up-causes⟩ *tendency* (HS).

–hrę̜hw –{dative I} wait for. *v.s.-t.* kę̜hrę̜hwá⁷θeh ⟨I=you-put up-cause-for⟩ *I am waiting for you* (R).

–hrę̜hwahkw – lean toward. *v.s.-a.i.* kahrę̜hwáhkę ⟨it-put up-caused-instrument⟩ *it leans toward* (HS).

–hrę̜hwa⁷θrę – sway. *v.s.-a.i.* rahrę̜hwá⁷θrę̜h ⟨he-put up-causes-much⟩ *he sways* (HS).

–hrę̜hwhę – cessation. *dv.n.s.* ha⁷ yuhré̜whę· ⟨the it-put up-caused-much⟩ *cessation* (HS).

–hrę̜hwsT – stop. *v.s.-t.* rahré̜wstha⁷ ⟨he-puts up-causes⟩ *he stops it* (HS).

–hrę⁷n – grind stone, honing stone, pebble, stone. *n.r.* poss. ⁷, inc., n.sfx. –eh.

uhrę́⁷neh *grind stone, honing stone, pebble, stone* (HS) [Jefferson «o-rehneh» 'stone'] [Gallatin «owrunuay» 'Stone, Rock']: **–hrę⁷naạyę⁷kw –**: rahrę́⁷naye⁷kws ⟨he-stone-shoots⟩ *he stones it* (HS).

–hrę⁷nayę⁷kw – stone. *v.s.-t.* rahré⁷nayę⁷kws ⟨he-stone-shoots⟩ *he stones it* (HS).

–hri – spill. *v.r.-a.i.* hab: –, pnt: –⁷, stat: –, prog: –, prp: –, dst: –⁷θrę-, caus: –hT-, rvs: –, dat: –, inc.-ϕ-/-hwa-ag./pat. In combination with the empty noun root **–hwa –** and the dualic or translocative prefix the root takes on the meaning *break*. wa⁷káhri⁷ *it spilled* (RC 3:65); **–hrihT –**: ruhríhtha⁷ ⟨he-spill-causes⟩ *he demolishes it, he pulls it down, he razes it, he takes it down* (HS); **–hri⁷=θrę –**: kahrí⁷θrę̜h ⟨it-spills-much⟩ *it splatters* (RC 3:55), ękahrí⁷θrę⁷ ⟨prediction-it-spill-much⟩ *it will spill over* (RC 3:54); **–(ę)ta⁷rahrihT –**: wa⁷kayę⁷na⁷ta⁷ráhriht ⟨fact-they=another-head-spill-caused⟩ *they smashed his head* (RC 24:10); **–(i)⁷nyuhkwahrihT –**: rę⁷nyuhkwahríhtha⁷ ⟨he-group-spill-causes⟩ *he disorganizes the group* (HS); **–kę̜hkwạhrihT –**: rakę̜hkwáhrihč ⟨he-??-spill-causes⟩ *he strikes the fire* (HS); **–nę̜hsnạhrihT –**: ranę̜hsnahríhtha⁷ ⟨he-seed-spill-causes⟩ *he breaks, bruises the grain (singular or collective)* (H 2484); **–rihwạhrihT –**: rarihwahríhtha⁷ ⟨he-matter-spill-causes⟩ *he annuls* (HS); **–⁷tehahri⁷ –**: ka⁷teháhri⁷θ ⟨it-sand-spill-begins⟩ *it hails* (H-notebook); **–athriya⁷k –**: yuthriyá⁷kę ⟨it-itself-spill-broke⟩ *precipice* (RC 8:10); **–athriya⁷k –.#ú⁷y**: yuthriya⁷kę̜hú⁷y ⟨it-itself-spill-broke-great⟩ *abyss* (HS); **–ne –**. **–ę̜⁷rạhrihnahkw –**: neyakę⁷rahrihnáhkhwa⁷ ⟨apart-one-nut-spill-causes-instrument⟩ *nutcracker* (HS); **–ne –**.

-hwahrihT -: neθhwáhriht ‹apart-you-X-spill-cause› *break it!* (R), wa'-nyehwáhriht ‹fact-apart-one-X-spill-caused› *one broke it* (RC 15:8), nekahwáhriht ‹apart-it-X-spill-caused› *it burst* (HS), nekhwahríhtha' ‹apart-I-X-spill-cause› *I break things* (L 27); **-ne -. -hwahri' -:** neyuhwahrí'ę ‹apart-it-X-spill-began› *it is broken* (R); **-ne -. -nęhsnahrihT -:** nekanęhsnahríhtha' ‹apart-it-seed-spill-causes› *it grinds, crushes the corn* (H 2484); **-ne -. -nęθahrihT -:** neyenęθahríhtha' ‹apart-one-potato-spill-causes› *one mashes potatoes* (H 2484); **-ne -. -rih = wahrihT -:** nehrarihwahríhtha' ‹apart-he-matter-spill-causes› *he transgresses* (HS); **-ne -. -θuwahri' -:** nekaθuwahrí'ę ‹two-it-animal's-back-spill-began› *bittersweet (Celastrus scandens)* (R) **-ne -. -'wahrahrihT -:** neka'wahrahríhnę ‹apart-it-meat-spill-caused› *hamburger* (R); **-yah -. -hwarihT -:** wekáhrihč ‹thither-it-spill-causes› *it is broken up* (RC 10:2); **-ne+či -. -(ę)'teyahri -:** nęθakaye'tè·yahri' ‹apart-fact-again-they-crowd-spilled› *again crowd dispersed* (RC 12:31); **ha' -ne -. -(ę)' = teyahrihT -:** ha' wa'thra'teyáhriht ‹the fact-apart-he-crowd-spill-caused› *Benediction* (HS); **ha' -athriya'k -:** ha' yuthriyá'kę ‹the it-itself-spill-broke› *extremity* (HS).

-hrihT - demolish, pull down, raze, take down. *v.s.-a.i.* ruhríhtha' ‹he-spill-causes› *he demolishes it, he pulls it down, he razes it, he takes it down*

(HS).

-hri'ę father. *n.r.* aln: akhrí'ę *my father* (R), inc., n.sfx. -. Requires the increment -hst- when incorporated. akuhrí'ę *one's father* (RC 3:25), akhrí'ę *my father* (R); **-hri'ę.#áh:** akhri'ęháh ‹I-father-little› *my paternal uncle* (R); **-hri'ęhst -:** uhri'ęhsteh ‹father-'ness› *fatherhood* (HS); **-hri'ęhstakęheya' = θre -:** ruhri'ęhstakęheyá'θrch ‹he-father-'ness-die-is going to› *he is losing his father, his father is about to die* (HS); **kwęhs -ne -. -hri'ęhsturę -:** kwęhs naryuhri'ęhstú·rę·k ‹no apart-unknown-it-father-'ness-split› *it is unfatherly* (HS).

-hri'ę.#áh paternal uncle. *n.s.* akhri'ęháh ‹I-father-little› *my paternal uncle* (R).

-hri'ęhst - fatherhood. *n.s.* uhri'ęhsteh ‹father-'ness› *fatherhood* (HS).

-hri'θrę - spill over, splatter. *v.s.-a.i.* kahrí'θręh ‹it-spills-much› *it splatters* (RC 3:55), ękahrí'θrę' ‹prediction-it-spill-much› *it will spill over* (RC 3: 54).

#hrunę' people of (populative). *enc.* Occurs only on a few loan words form other Northern Iroquoian languages. In indigenous Tuscarora constructions the same meaning is carried by the characterizer enclitic, **#aka·'.** Examples include: **-ręhy-.-ke.#hrunę':** kayeręhya'kyehrù·nę' ‹they-sky-at-people› *angels* (R) and **Thwahrù·nę'** *Oneida* (RC 21:7).

-hrut be on opposite sides. *v.r.-a.i.* hab: -, pnt: -, stat: -φ, prog: -, prp: -, dst: -, caus: -, rvs: -, dat: -, inc.-ɸ-pat. **-nęh=sahrut**: nekanęhsáhrut ‹two-it-house-are on opposite sides› *the two of them are on opposite sides of the house: the two of them occupy opposite sides of the same fire in a house* (H-notebook).

-hru⁷nęha'nye⁷ - softly. *dv.n.s.* yuhru⁷nęhá·⁷nye⁷ ‹it-is flexible-going along› *softly* (HS).

-hru⁷nęhsT - soften. *v.s.-t.* rahru⁷nę́hstha⁷ ‹he-be flexible-causes› *he softens it* (HS).

-hru⁷T - be flexible, be mellow, be mild, be soft to the touch. *v.r.-s.i.* stat: -ę, prog: -, prp: -, dst: -, caus: -, rvs: -, dat: -, inc.-ɸ-ag. yuhrú⁷nę *it is flexible, it is soft to the touch* (HS), ruhrú⁷nę *he is mild, he is soft* (HS); **-hru⁷nęha'nye** -: yuhru⁷nęhá·⁷nye⁷ ‹it-is flexible-going along› *softly* (HS); **-hru⁷nęhsT** -: rahru⁷nę́hstha⁷ ‹he-be flexible-causes› *he softens it* (HS); **-(ę)⁷tikęhrahru⁷T** -: ru⁷tikęhrahrú⁷nę ‹he-mind-is mellow› *he is affable* (HS); **-yękwirahru⁷T** -: yuyękwirahrú⁷nę ‹it-wood-is soft› *softwood* (PC).

-hryahči⁷ older brother, older maternal male cousin. *n.r.* aln: akhryáhči⁷ *my older brother, my older maternal male cousin* (R), inc., n.sfx. -. akhryáhči⁷ *my older brother, my older maternal male cousin* (R) [Lawson «Wariaugh» 'A Boy']; **-hryahči⁷.#áh**: akhryahči⁷áh ‹I- older brother-little› *my older step-brother* (R).

-hryahči⁷.#áh older step-brother. *n.s.* akhryahči⁷áh ‹I-older brother-little› *my older step-brother* (R).

-hryahsut grandfather, great grandfather (older usage), male ancestor, male relative two or more generations older. *n.r.* aln: akhryáhsu·t *my grandfather, my great grandfather, my (male) ancestor* (R), inc., n.sfx. -. akhryáhsu·t

my grandfather, my great grandfather (older usage), my (male) ancestor (R); **-hryahsut.#kęhe⁷**: ruhryahsutkę́he⁷ ‹he-grandfather-deceased› *forefathers* (R); **-hryahsut.#ú⁷y**: akhryahsu·t⁷ú⁷y ‹I-grandfather-big› *my great grandfather (contemporary usage)* (R).

-hryahsut.#kęhe⁷ forefathers. *n.s.* ruhryahsutkę́he⁷ ‹he-grandfather-deceased› *forefathers* (R).

-hryahsut.#ú⁷y great grandfather (contemporary usage). *n.s.* akhryahsu·t⁷ú⁷y ‹I-grandfather-great› *my great grandfather (contemporary usage)* (R).

-hryatu⁷ maternal uncle. *n.r.* aln: akhryá·tu·⁷ *my maternal uncle* (RC 25:8), inc., n.sfx. -. akhryá·tu·⁷ *my maternal uncle* (RC 25:8), ruhryá·tu·⁷ *his maternal uncle* (RC 11:2); **-hrya=tu⁷čr** -: uhryatú⁷čreh ‹maternal uncle-'ness› *uncle(ness)* (HS).

-hryatu⁷čr - uncle(ness). *n.s.* uhryatú⁷čreh ‹maternal uncle-'ness› *uncle(ness)* (HS).

-hryenę⁷ - break down, topple over; be insolvent. *v.r.-a.i.* hab: -θ, pnt: -, stat: -ę, prog: -, prp: -, dst: -, caus: -, rvs: -, dat: -, n-inc. ráhryenę⁷θ *he breaks down, he topples over* (HS), rahryenę́⁷ę *he has toppled over, he is insolvent* (HS).

-hryuhkw - black muck, marsh, tamarack swamp. *n.r.* n-poss., inc., n.sfx. -eh. uhryúhkweh *black muck, marsh, tamarack swamp* (R); **-hryuhkwakęw**: uhryúhkwakęw ‹marsh-in› *in the tamarack swamp (black muck)* (H 3518); **-hryuhkwa⁷ke**: uhryuhkwá⁷kye ‹marsh-at› *on the border of the marsh* (H 3518); **-hryuhkwyę** -: wa⁷kayehryúhkwyę⁷ ‹fact-they-marsh-entered› *they entered the marsh* (H 3518).

-hθ - empty noun root. *v.inc.* See: **-uke=**

ne̜ -.

-hθ - a width of any flexible or flat material. *n.r.* See: -hč -.

-hθaˀke̜hst - quilt, sheet, width of cloth. *n.r.* poss. ?, n-inc., n.sfx. -eh. uhθaˀ-ke̜hsteh *quilt, sheet, width of cloth* (R).

-hθer - trap. *n.r.* n-poss., inc., n.sfx.: -. Found only in the following construction. -hθerhar -: ruhθérhar ⟨he-trap-hung⟩ *he hung a trap, he sprang a trap* (HS).

-hθerhar - trap. *v.s.-a.i.* ruhθérhar ⟨he-trap-hung⟩ *he hung a trap, he sprang a trap* (HS).

-hθe̜y - pendant. *dv.n.s.* yúhθey ⟨it-width of flexible material-hangs⟩ *pendant* (HS).

-hθe̜ˀka̲r - banks of river, brink, edge, shore. *n.r.* n-poss., inc., n.sfx. -eh. uh-θé̜ˀkareh *banks of river* (AG), *brink, edge, shore* (HS); -hθe̜ˀka̲ra̲ˀke: uh-θe̜ˀkaráˀkye ⟨brink-at⟩ *on the banks of the river* (AG); -hθe̜ˀka̲ra̲'nehT -: yuh-θe̜ˀkará·ˀneht ⟨it-brink-be present-caused⟩ *it is steep* (HS); -hθe̜ˀka̲reθ -. #úˀy: yuhθe̜ˀkare·θˀúˀy ⟨it-brink-is long-great⟩ *it is steep* (HS).

-hθe̜ˀka̲ra̲'nehT - be steep. *v.s.-s.i.* yuh-θe̜ˀkará·ˀneht ⟨it-brink-be present-caused⟩ *it is steep* (HS).

-hθe̜ˀka̲reθ -.#úˀy be steep. *v.s.-s.i.* yuh-θe̜ˀkare·θˀúˀy ⟨it-brink-is long-great⟩ *it is steep* (HS).

-hθraˀr - palm of hand. *n.r.* poss. ?, inc., n.sfx. -eh. uhθráˀreh *palm of hand* (HS); -ne -. -hθraˀrˀe(k) -: nehrahθráˀr-

ˀehs ⟨two-he-palm of hand-strikes⟩ *he claps his hands* (HS).

-hs - empty noun root. *v.inc.* See: -iθ -.

-hs - thou, you alone (second person singular agent). *v.r.pfx.* Before roots and stems beginning with certain consonant clusters an "epenthetic" *e* occurs between this prefix and the root or stem. The initial *h* is dropped when word-initial.

-hsakʷar - clamor, screech, yelling. *n.r.* poss. ?, inc., n. sfx. -eh. uhsá·kwarch *clamor, screech, yelling* (HS); -ačha=kʷa̲raˀnihr -: ručhakwaraˀníhre̜ ⟨he-himself-clamor-stood⟩ *he bawls* (HS); -ačhakʷa̲raˀnihT -: račhakwaraˀníhthaˀ ⟨he-himself-clamor-stand-causes⟩ *he clamors* (HS).

-hsawa̲r - earlobe. *n.r.* poss. ?, inc. ?, n. sfx. -eh. uhsà·wareh *earlobe* (SH 375).

-hsa̲ˀk - be useful. *v.r.-a.i.* hab: -ɸ, pnt: -, stat: -e̜, prog: -, prp: -, dst: -, caus: -, rvs: -, dat: -, n-inc. ráhsaˀk *he is useful* (HS), e̜hráhsaˀke̜k *he would have been useful* (HS), akáhsaˀke̜k *useless (lit., that it might have been useful)* (HS); -hsaˀk - -a'ne̜ -: ráhsaˀk e̜wá·ˀne̜ˀ ⟨he-is useful prediction-it-become⟩ *he will be useful* (HS); -hsaˀk -.#ke̜he?: ráhsaˀk ke̜heˀ ⟨he-is useful-deceased⟩ *he was useful* (HS).

-hsaˀke̜'n - dagger, knife, razor. *n.r.* poss. ?, inc., n.sfx. -eh. uhsáˀke̜ˀneh *dagger, knife, razor* (HS) [Lawson «Oo-socke nauh» 'Knife']; -hsaˀke̜ˀn -.#áh: uhsaˀke̜ˀneháh ⟨knife-little⟩ *penknife* (HS); -ačhaˀke̜ˀnatetˀ -: ručhaˀke̜ˀná·te'̓t ‹he-himself-knife-lined› *he has a knife about him (somewhere on or near him)* (H-notebook).

–hsaʔkę'n –.#áh penknife. *n.s.* uhsa'̓kę'̓ncháh ‹knife-little› *penknife* (HS).

–hsaʔnę – bury, cover with something, cover with earth, hide. *v.r.-t.* See: –(i)hsaʔnę –.

–hsaʔrę –{dative III} get mad, take offense. *v.r.-a.i.* hab: -, pnt: -, stat: -, prog: -, prp: -, dst: -, caus: -, rvs: -, dat: III (-ti-/-ę-), n-inc. ruhsa'̓rę́·ti· ‹he-takes offense-for› *he hates, he takes offense at* (HS). wahruhsá'̓rę'̓θ ‹fact-he-took offense-for› *he got mad* (RC 5:39); –hsaʔrę –{dative III} –ahT –: ruhsa'̓rę́·tyaht ‹he-takes offense-for-caused› *he is hateful* (HS).

–hsaʔrę –{dative III} –ahT – be hateful. *v.s.-s.i.* ruhsa'̓rę́·-tyaht ‹he-takes offense-for-caused› *he is hateful* (HS).

–hsehači – ashes. *n.r.* poss. ?, inc. ?, n. sfx. –·. uhséhači· *ashes* (L 72); –hse = hačihst –: uhsehačíhsteh ‹ashes-'ness› *lividity* (HS).

–hsehačihst – lividity. *n.s.* uhsehačíhsteh ‹ashes-'ness› *lividity* (HS).

–hsehar – ash, lye. *n.r.* poss. ?, inc., n.sfx. –eh. uhséhareh *ash, lye* (R); –hseha = rakęw: uhsehà·rakęw ‹lye-in› *in lye* (RC 10:1); –hseharakri –: uhsehará·kri'̓ ‹lye-liquid› *lye* (HS); –hseharu –: wa'̓ehséharu·'̓ ‹fact-one-lye-was in water› *one put lye in water* (RC 3:53); –či –. –hseharawihsi –: ęθkahseharawíhsi'̓ ‹prediction-again-it-lye-give to-undo› *it will extract lye* (RC 10:1).

–hsekʷar – bayonet, halberd, javelin, lance, spear. *n.r.* poss. ?, inc., n.sfx. –eh. uhsé·kwarch *bayonet, halberd, javelin, lance, spear* (HS); –hsekʷa = riʔθ(e)r –: Sekwarí'̓θre· ‹spear-drag› *Spear-carrier (Turtle Clan chief's name)* (R) [Colonial Records «Sa-

carusa», «Sequareesa»]; –hsekʷaruhar –: uhsekwarúhar ‹spear-tip› *javelin* (HS).

–hsekʷariʔθ(e)r – Spear-carrier. *n.s.* Sekwarí'̓θre· ‹spear-drag› *Spear-carrier (Turtle Clan chief's name)* (R) [Colonial Records «Sacarusa», «Sequareesa»].

–hsekʷaruhar – javelin. *n.s.* uhsekwarúhar ‹spear-tip› *javelin* (HS).

–hser – bark covering, bark roof. *n.r.* poss. ?, inc., n.sfx. –eh. uhsè·reh *bark covering, bark roof* (R); –hserhrawę –: kahserhrà·węh ‹it-bark covering-put up-much› *bark covering is put around* (RC 3:61).

–hsey – cone of a tree, ear of corn. *n.r.* n-poss., inc., n.sfx. –eh. uhsè·yeh *cone of a tree* (HS), *ear of corn* (R); –hse = yęti –: kahseyę́·tih ‹it-cone of tree-makes› *conifer* (HS); –hseyu –: kahsè·yuhk ‹it-ear of corn-had put in water› *boiled ear of corn* (R); –hse = yur –: uhsè·yur ‹ear of corn-cover› *ear of corn* (R); –ne –. –hseyęt: neyuhsé·yę·t ‹two-it-ear of corn-possesses› *it has two ears of corn* (RC 7:5); –ne –. –hseyęhT –: wa'̓thrahsè·yęht ‹fact-two-he-ear of corn-fall-caused› *he dropped two ears of corn* (RC 7:6).

–hseyęti – conifer. *dv.n.s.* kahseyę́·tih ‹it-cone of tree-makes› *conifer* (HS).

–hseyu – boiled ear of corn. *dv.n.s.* kahsè·yuhk ‹it-ear of corn-had put in water› *boiled ear of corn* (R).

–hseyur – ear of corn. *dv.n.s.* uhsè·yur ‹ear of corn-cover› *ear of corn* (R).

–hseʔw – pox, skin lesion, smallpox. *n.r.* n-poss., inc., n.sfx. –eh. uhsé'̓weh *pox, skin lesion, smallpox* (RC 16:1); –hseʔwayę(T) –: kahsé'̓wayę'̓ ‹it-pox-lays› *there is smallpox* (RC 16:1).

–hseʔyu –/–hseʔyuhčr – cork, stopper. *n.r.* poss. ?, inc., n.sfx. –eh. The form –hseʔyuhčr – occurs when the root is not incorporated and with a few verbs when incorporated. The form –hse?yu – is the usual form when incorporated. uhse?yúhčreh *cork, stopper* (R); –hse?yuhčrahT –: yehse?yuhčráhtha? ‹one-cork-grab-causes› *corkscrew* (HS); –hse?yuhčrak –: çkahse?yúhčra·k ‹prediction-it-cork-eat› *it will eat stopper* (RC 15:10); –hse?yuhčraθe·? : uhse?yuhčrá·θe·? ‹cork-is new› *new stopper* (RC 15:8); –hse?yuhčrete: uhse?yuhčré·te ‹cork-certain one› *a certain stopper* (RC 15:3); –hse?yuhrę –: ruhse?yúhrę· ‹he-cork-put up› *he plugged it* (RC 11:4); –hse?yuθnahnęhkw –: yehse?yuθnahnéhkhwa? ‹one-cork-??-disappears-instrument› *shutters* (HS); –či –. –hse?yuhruk –: čehse?yúhruk ‹again-one-cork-struck› *again one struck stopper* (RC 15:8).

–hse?yuhčrahT – corkscrew. *dv.n.s.* yehse?yuhčráhtha? ‹one-cork-grab-causes› *corkscrew* (HS).

–hse?yuθnahnęhkw – shutters. *dv.n.s.* yehse?yuθnahnéhkhwa? ‹one-cork-??-disappears-instrument› *shutters* (HS).

–hsę – be homely, be ugly. *v.r.-s.i.* See: –(i)hsę –.

–hsęhti – disdain, refuse. *v.r.-t.* hab: -h, pnt: -, stat: -, prog: -, prp: -, dst: -, caus: -, rvs: -, dat: -, inc-φ-pat. rahséhtih *he disdains it, he refuses it* (HS); –nęhahsęhti –: ranęhahséhtih ‹he-corn-refuses› *he spurns, refuses (as unworthy) the corn* (H 2484); ha? –hsęhti? –: ha? yuhsęhtí?ę ‹the it-refuse-began› *refuse* (HS).

–hsęhti? – refuse. *dv.n.s.* ha? yuhsęhtí?ę ‹the it-refuse-began› *refuse* (HS).

–hsęn – name. *n.r.* aln: rahsę·nawęh *his name* (R). inc., n.sfx. -ch. uhsę·neh *name* (R); –hsęnahsthu –: rahsęnáhsthę ‹he-name-is small› *he is inferior in rank* (HS); –hsęnakareti –: rahsęnaka-ré·tih ‹he-name-is loud› *he has influence* (HS); –hsęnaksa?T –: načhęnaksá?tha? ‹one=another-name-be bad-causes› *one discredits another* (HS); –hsęnarawę –: kayehsęnarà·węh ‹they-name-are in-many› *list* (HS); –hsęna = tukęht –: θahsęnatukéhti ‹you-name-is holy› *hallowed be Thy name* (G); –hsęnaw –: rahsę·naws ‹he-name-gives to› *he titles it* (HS); –hsęnayeθa?T –: načhęnayeθá?tha? ‹one=another-name-curses› *one denounces another* (HS); –hsęnęnhehkT –.#ęwe: načhęnęnhehktha?ę̀·we ‹one=another-name-be a-live-instrument-causes-genuine› *one immortalizes another* (HS); –hsęnu = wan –: rahsęnuwà·nę ‹he-name-is chief› *colonel, officer, sachem* (HS); –hsę = nyę –{dative I}: rahsęnyę́?θeh ‹he-name-goes into-for› *he despises it: he subscribes to it* (HS); ti –. –hsęnu?nę –: tihrahsęnú?nę· ‹so-he-name-is a kind of› *such is his name* (RC 3: 68); tha+ ne –. –hsęna?θ –: tha?nekahsę·na?θ ‹unusual-two-it-name-is of a size› *coordinate, equal in rank* (HS); –ačhęnar –: račhę·nar ‹he-himself-name-is in› *he signs it, he subscribes to it* (HS); –ačhęnuhar –: račhęnúhar ‹he-himself-name-washes› *he absolves* (HS); –či –.

-ačhẹna'nak?u –: θhračhẹna'ʼná·k'ʼuhs ‹again-he-himself-name-self-releases› *he abdicates* (HS); ha? –hsẹnar –: ha'ʼ kahsẹ̀·nar ‹the it-name-is in› *signature* (HS).

-hsẹnahsthu – be inferior in rank. *v.s.-a.i.* rahsẹnáhsthẹ ‹he-name-is small› *he is inferior in rank* (HS).

-hsẹnakareti – have influence. *v.s.-a.i.* rahsẹnakaré·tih ‹he-name-is loud› *he has influence* (HS).

-hsẹnaksa?T – discredit. *v.s.-t.* načhẹnaksá'ʼtha'ʼ ‹one=another-name-be bad-causes› *one discredits another* (HS).

-hsẹnar – signature. *dv.n.s.* ha'ʼ kahsẹ̀·nar ‹the it-name-is in› *signature* (HS).

-hsẹnarawẹ – list. *dv.n.s.* kayehsẹnarà·wẹh ‹they-name-are in-many› *list* (HS).

-hsẹnaw – title. *v.s.-t.* rahsẹ̀·naws ‹he-name-gives to› *he titles it* (HS).

-hsẹnayeθa?T – denounce. *v.s.-t.* načhẹnayeθá'ʼtha'ʼ ‹one=another-name-curses› *one denounces another* (HS).

-hsẹnẹnhehkT –.#ẹwe immortalize. *v.s.-t.* načhẹnẹnhehktha'ʼẹ̀·we ‹one=another-name-be alive-instrument-causes-genuine› *one immortalizes another* (HS).

-hsẹnuwan – colonel, officer, sachem. *dv.n.s.* rahsẹnuwà·nẹ ‹he-name-is chief› *colonel, officer, sachem* (HS).

-hsẹnyẹ –{dative I} despise, subscribe. *v.s.* rahsẹnyé'ʼθeh ‹he-name-goes into-for› *he despises it, he subscribes to it* (HS).

-hsẹri – savor. *v.r.-t.* hab: -, pnt: -'ʼ, stat: -, prog: -, prp: -, dst: -, caus: -, rvs: -, dat: -, n-inc. –hsẹri –: uhsẹ̀·reh ‹savor› *fetid odor, savor, smell, stench* (HS); –hsẹritkẹ? –: ruhsẹritké'ʼẹ ‹he-steam-issue-began› *he has become tired, he has become still by loss of steam or wind* (HS); –hsẹryuhkw –: uhsẹryúhkweh ‹savor-cover-instrument› *odor,*

savor, steam (HS); –?wahrahsẹri –: aryẹkwa'ʼwahrahsẹ̀·ri'ʼ ‹unknown-we-meat-savor› *that we enjoy meat* (RC 32:4); –hẹw –.#ú?y –hsẹryuhkw – –are= kwahT –: uhẹwéhu'ʼy uhsẹryúhkweh warekwáhtha'ʼ ‹boat-great steam-cover-instrument it-go and return-causes› *steam boat* (HS).

-hsẹri – fetid odor, savor, smell, stench. *n.s.* uhsẹ̀·reh ‹savor› *fetid odor, savor, smell, stench* (HS).

-hsẹritkẹ? – become tired. *v.s.-s.i.* ruhsẹritké'ʼẹ ‹he-steam-issue-began› *he has become tired, he has become still by loss of steam or wind* (HS).

-hsẹryuhkw – odor, savor, steam. *n.s.* uhsẹryúhkweh ‹savor-cover-instrument› *odor, savor, steam* (HS).

-hsẹT – be piquant. *v.r.-s.i.* stat: -ɸ, prog: -, prp: -, dst: -, caus: -, rvs: -, dat: -, n-inc. yúhsẹt *it is piquant* (HS).

-hsẹtathu – sprout. *v.r.-s.i.* hab: -hs, pnt: -, stat: -ẹ°, prog: -, prp: -, dst: -hθẹ-, caus: -, rvs: -, dat: -, n-inc. yuhsẹtá·thẹ *it sprouts (a branch)* (R); –hsẹta= thu –: kahsẹtá·thuhs ‹it-sprouts› *sprout, stool* (HS); –hsẹtathuhθẹ –: yuhsẹtathúhθẹ· ‹it-sprouts-many› *shaggy, dried, pealing outer bark* (RC 30:45).

-hsẹtathu – sprout, stool. *dv.n.s.* kahsẹtá·thuhs ‹it-sprouts› *sprout, stool* (HS).

-hsẹtathuhθẹ – shaggy, dried, peeling outer bark. *dv.n.s.* yuhsẹtathúhθẹ· ‹it-sprouts-many› *shaggy, dried, peel-ing outer bark* (RC 30:45).

-hsẹte be niece, be nephew, be younger brother, be younger sister, be daughter, be son; be any individual in one's clan who is younger. *v.r.-k.* khehsẹ̀·te *my nephew, my niece, my brother, my sister, my daughter, my son (any individual in my clan who is younger than I am)* (R).

-hsẹwati – plane, smooth. *v.r.-a.i.* hab: -h,

pnt: -, stat: -, prog: -, prp: -, dst: -, caus: -hT-, rvs: -, dat: -, n-inc. rahsęwá·tih *he planes it, he smoothes it* (HS); -hsęwa-tihT -: yehsęwatíhtha⁾ ‹one-smooth-causes› *plane (tool for smoothing)* (HS); -(a)hahahsęwati -: kahahahsęwá·tih ‹it-path-smoothes› *it smoothes the road (this is the name for a road scraper)* (H 2484); -ačhę = wati -: yučhęwá·tye⁾ ‹it-itself-smoothed› *it is smooth* (R); -a⁾rę⁾a = čhęwati -: wa⁾rę⁾ačhęwá·tih ‹it-itself-tree-self-smoothes› *sycamore or bottonwood tree* (AG); kwęhs -ačhęwati -: kwęhs aryučhęwá·tyek ‹no unknown-it-itself-smooth› *it is uneven* (HS).

-hsęwatihT - plane. *dv.n.s.* yehsęwatíhtha⁾ ‹one-smooth-causes› *plane (tool for smoothing)* (HS).

-hsęwa⁾r - auger, bolt, fork, key, nail, needle, pitchfork; dwarf pike. *n.r.* aln: aksęwá⁾rawęh *my fork* (R), inc., n. sfx. -eh. uhsęwá⁾reh *auger, bolt, fork, key, nail, needle, pitchfork* (R); *dwarf pike* (H 3518); -hsęwa⁾r -.#ętíh: uhsęwa⁾rehętíh ‹nail-many little› *tacks* (HS); -hsęwa⁾rakęhruk -: ękhehsęwa⁾rakéhruk ‹prediction-I=one-nail-strike› *I will telephone someone* (R); -hsę = wa⁾ra⁾nihr -: rahsęwa⁾rá⁾nihč ‹he-nail-stands up› *he hammers, he rivets* (HS); -hsęwa⁾ra⁾nihθhęku -: rahsęwa⁾ra⁾nihθhę́·kwahs ‹he-nail-stand up-??-undoes› *he unnails, he pulls out nails* (HS).

-hsęwa⁾r -.#ętíh tacks. *n.s.* uhsęwa⁾rehętíh ‹nail-many little› *tacks* (HS).

-hsęwa⁾rakęhruk - telephone. *v.s.-t.* ękhehsęwa⁾rakéhruk ‹prediction-I=one-auger-strike› *I will telephone someone* (R).

-hsęwa⁾ra⁾nihr - hammer, rivet. *v.s.-a.i.* rahsęwa⁾rá⁾nihč ‹he-nail-stands up› *he hammers, he rivets* (HS).

-hsęwireT - degrade. *v.r.-t.* hab: -ha⁾, pnt: -, stat: -ę ~ -ɸ, prog: -, prp: -, dst: -, caus: -, rvs: -, dat: -, n-inc. rahsęwiré·tha⁾ *he degrades it* (HS); -ne -. -hsęwireT -: nehruhsęwiré·⁾nę ‹apart-he-degraded› *he is abused by word* (HS), nehrahsęwiré·tha⁾ ‹apart-he-degrades› *he abuses it, he belittles it, he slanders it* (HS); -ne -. -ačhę = wireT -: neyučhęwí·rę·t ‹apart-it-itself-degrades› *it is humiliating* (HS).

-hsha - fall on back. *v.r.-a.i.* hab: -, pnt: -·⁾, stat: -, prog: -, prp: -, dst: -, caus: -⁾T-, rvs: -, dat: -, n-inc. wa⁾káhsha·⁾ *it fell on its back* (RC 7:4); -hshaT: ráhsha·t ‹he-fall on his back-complete› *he lies on his back, he is supine* (HS); -hsha⁾na⁾ -: ráhsha⁾na⁾θ ‹he-fall on his back-cause-begins› *he falls backward* (HS); -hsharuhkwęt -: yuhsharúhkwę·t ‹it-fall on its back-??› *it alighted* (HS).

-hsharuhkwęt alight. *v.s.-a.i.* yuhsharúhkwę·t ‹it-fall on its back-??› *it alighted* (HS).

-hshaT be supine, lie on back. *v.s.-a.i.* ráhsha·t ‹he-fall on his back-complete› *he lies on his back, he is supine* (HS).

-hshay - be slow. *v.r.-s.i.* stat: -ę, prog: -, prp: -, dst: -, caus: -⁾T-, rvs: -, dat: -,

n-inc. ruhshà·yę *he is slow: dawdler*
(HS); **–hshaya?T** –: rahshayá·'tha·' ‹he-
be slow-causes› *he makes it slow*
(HS); **–ačhaya?T** –: račhayá·'tha·' ‹he-
himself-be slow-causes› *he delays*
(HS).

–hshay – dawdler. *dv.n.s.* ruhshà·yę ‹he-is
slow› *dawdler* (HS).

–hshaya?T – make slow, slow. *v.s.-a.i.*
rahshayá·'tha·' ‹he-be slow-causes› *he
makes it slow, he slows it* (HS).

–hsha̱?na? – fall backward. *v.s.-a.i.* ráh-
sha·'na·'θ ‹he-fall on his back-cause-
begins› *he falls backward* (HS).

–hshe(y) – thou...her, him, one (second
person singular agent=third person
singular patient). *v.r.pfx.* The form
–hshe – occurs before roots and stems
that begin with a consonant. The form
–hshey – occurs before roots and stems
that begin with a vowel. The initial *h*
is dropped when word-initial.

–hshek habitual aspect. *v.r.sfx.*

–hshę – none, scarce. *n.r.* n-poss., n-inc.,
n.sfx. –eh. úhshęh *none, scarce* (HS).

–hshęw – boot; depth, hollow. *n.r.* n-
poss., inc., n.sfx. –eh. uhshę̀·weh *boot;
depth, hollow* (HS) [Lawson «Oosh
unnawa» 'A Canoe']; **–hshęwa̱kęw**: uh-
shę̀·wa-kęw ‹depth-in› *in depths, in
hollow* (RC 11:5); **–ne** –. **–hshęwara** –:
wa·'tkahshę́·wa·' ‹fact-apart-it-depth-
grabbed› *it grabbed hollow* (RC 8:5);
–ne –. **–hshęwirehT** –: nehrahshęwiréh-
tha·' ‹apart-he-depth-wander-causes›
he reproaches (HS); **ti** –. **–hshęwa̱** =
yę(T) –: tihrahshę̀·wayę·' ‹so-he-depth-
lays› *he is light* (HS); **ti** –. **–hshęwa̱** =
yę?T –: tihrahshęwayę́·'tha·' ‹so-he-
depth-lay-causes› *he lightens it* (HS).

–hsir – cord, rope, string, thread, wick,
wire. *n.r.* n-poss., inc., n.sfx. –eh. uh-
sì·reh *cord, rope, string, thread, wick,
wire* (R) [Lawson «Utsera» 'A Rope'];
–hsir –. #ętíh: uhsirehętíh ‹thread-many
little› *cotton, linen* (AG); **–hsirakęθT** –:
kahsirakę́·θnę ‹it-wire-is struck by›
beeline (HS); **–hsirahwanha?θe** –: rah-
sirahwanhá·'θehs ‹he-wire-winds-going
to› *he twines, he winds up spring*
(HS); **–hsiręti** –: rahsirę́·tih ‹he-cord-
makes› *he spins (thread), he makes
rope* (HS), kahsirę́·tih ‹it-cord-makes›
spindle (HS), wa·'nyehsirętyáhnę·'
‹fact-two-one-cord-made-many› *the
two of them made strings* (RC 30:65);
–hsiriyu –: kahsirí·yu· ‹it-cord-is great›
large rope (HS); **–hsiruhar** –: rahsirúhar
‹he-cord-tips› *he threads a needle*
(HS); **–ti** –. **–hsiraT** –.#áh: thwahrahsi-
ra·t'áh ‹so-fact-he-cord-stood-little› *he
made a short string* (RC 8:3).

–hsir –.#ętíh cotton, linen. *n.s.* uhsirehętíh
‹thread-many little› *cotton, linen*
(AG).

–hsirakęθT – beeline. *dv.n.s.* kahsirakę́·-
θnę ‹it-wire-is struck by› *beeline*
(HS).

–hsirahwanha?θe – twine, wind up spring.
v.s.-a.i. rahsirahwanhá·'θehs ‹he-wire-
winds-going to› *he twines, he winds
up spring* (HS).

–hsiręti – make strings, spin (thread). *v.s.-
a.i.* rahsirę́·tih ‹he-cord-makes› *he
spins (thread), he makes rope* (HS),
wa·'nyehsirętyáhnę·' ‹fact-two-one-
cord-made-many› *the two of them
made strings* (RC 30:65).

–hsiręti – spindle. *dv.n.s.* kahsirę́·tih ‹it-
cord-makes› *spindle* (HS).

–hsiruhar – thread. *v.s.-a.i.* rahsirúhar ‹he-
cord-tips› *he threads a needle* (HS).

–hsi?thęhčr – chill, numbness. *n.r.* n-poss.,
inc., n.sfx. –eh. uhsi?thę́hčreh *chill,
numbness* (HS); **–hsi?thęhčręti** –: rah-
si?thęhčrę́·tih ‹he-chill-makes› *he
chills it, he benumbs it* (HS).

–hsi?thęhčreti – benumb, chill. *v.s.-t.* rahsiʔthęhčrę·tih ‹he-chill-makes› *he chills it, he benumbs it* (HS).

-hsk – easily (facilatative). *v.r.sfx.* stat: -ę·. The principal function of this suffix is to indicate that the action of the verb is accomplished with significantly less than usual effort (e.g., **yuʔnékskę·** ‹it-burned-easily› *it is inflammable*). Following the final consonant of a root or stem, the initial *h* is dropped. The *s* of the suffix coalesces with a preceding *t* to yield -čk-. Following *ʔ* or *h*, the *s* of the suffix becomes θ.

-hsk –/**-hskʷ** – thou...me (second person singular agent=first person singular patient). *v.r.pfx.* The form **-hskʷ** – occurs before roots and stems that begin with the vowel *a*. The form **-hsk** – occurs elsewhere, with insertion of "epenthetic" e before roots and stems that begin with certain consonant clusters.

-hska – approach. *v.r.-a.i.* hab: -, pnt: -, stat: -, prog: -, prp: -, dst: -hę-, caus: -hT-, rvs: -, dat: -, n-inc. **-hskahT** –: kayéhskaht ‹they-approach-cause› *they approached* (RC 11:22); -t-. **-hskahęh** = te –: nakahskahęhteʔ ‹hither-fact-it-approached-many-going to› *many were going approaching there* (RC 11:22).

-hskahręw – mouth. *n.r.* See: -(i)hskah = ręw -.

-hskahT – approach. *v.s.-a.i.* kayéhskaht ‹they-approach-cause› *they approached* (RC 11:22).

-hskanen – complexion, countenance. *n.r.*

n-poss., inc., n.sfx. -. Borrowed from another Northern Iroquoian language, see: -hskatet –; found only in the cited construction. **-hskanenahrahT** –: uhskanenáhraht ‹countenance-put up-cause› *awfulness* (RC 28:9), *ferocious* (HS), *how terrible, how awful* (R).

-hskanenahrahT – awfulness, ferocious, how awful, how terrible. *n.s.* uhskanenáhraht ‹countenance-put up-cause› *awfulness* (RC 28:9), *ferocious* (HS), *how terrible, how awful* (R).

-hskar – be jealous. *v.r.-s.i.* stat: -ę, prog: -, prp: -, dst: -, caus: -, rvs: -, dat: -, n-inc. ruhskà·rę *he is jealous* (RC 1:4), wakskà·rę *I am jealous* (R).

-hskar – cloth, linen, shirt. *n.r.* n-poss., inc., n.sfx. -eh. This root is probably at the heart of the Tuscarora self-designation, Skarù·ręʔ, which may have literally meant *flax or hemp-gatherers*, just as the word krirù·ręʔ *whiteman* probably derives from the root seen in ukrì·reh *cotton* and meant *cotton-gatherers*. úhskareh *cloth, linen, shirt* (R); **-hskar** –.#áh: uhskareháh ‹cloth-little› *handkerchief* (HS); **-hskara** = kʷaraθ –: yehskará·kwara·č ‹one-linen-bruise› *flax (Linum usitatissimum)* (H-notebook); **-hskarakʷaraθ**ʔ –: yehskarakwará·θʔę ‹one-linen-bruises-began› *flax (Linum usitatissimum)* (R); **-hskaręyaʔT** –: yuhskaręyáʔthaʔ ‹it-cloth-hang-causes› *curtain* (HS).

-hskar –.#áh handkerchief. *n.s.* uhskareháh ‹cloth-little› *handkerchief* (HS).

-hskarakʷaraθ – flax. *dv.n.s.* yehskará·

kwara·č ‹one-linen-bruises› *flax (Linum usitatissimum)* (H-notebook).

–hskarak^waraθ? – flax. *dv.n.s.* yehskara-kwará·θ'ę ‹one-linen-bruise-began› *flax (Linum usitatissimum)* (R).

–hskaręya?T – curtain. *dv.n.s.* yuhskarę-yá'tha' ‹it-cloth-hang-causes› *curtain* (HS).

–hskari?čr – broach. *n.r.* n-poss., n-inc., n.sfx. -eh. uhskarí'čreh *broach* (HS).

–hskatahT – be exquisite. *v.r.-s.i.* stat: -φ, prog: -, prp: -, dst: -, caus: -, rvs: -, dat: -. n-inc. yúhskataht *it is exquisite* (HS).

–hskatet – complexion, countenance. *n.r.* n-poss., inc., n.sfx. -eh. uhskaté·teh *complexion, countenance* (HS); –hska = tetaks –: rahskatetá·ksę· ‹he-complex-ion-is bad› *he is pallid* (HS).

–hskatetaks – be pallid. *v.s.-s.i.* rahska-tetá·ksę· ‹he-complexion-is bad› *he is pallid* (HS).

–hskaw – bramble, rush; raft. *n.r.* n-poss., inc., n.sfx. -eh. See also: **ú·tkaweh** *raft.* úhskaweh *bramble, rush; raft* (HS); –hskawęhT –: rahskawę́htha' ‹he-raft-fall-causes› *he ruins it* (HS), yuhskawę́hnę ‹it-raft-fall-caused› *wreckage* (HS).

–hskawęhT – ruin. *v.s.-t.* rahskawę́htha' ‹he-raft-fall-causes› *he ruins it* (HS).

–hskawęhT – wreckage. *dv.n.s.* yuhska-wę́hnę ‹it-raft-fall-caused› *wreckage* (HS).

–hska?y – big mouth, jowls. *n.r.* inaln: kská'yeh *my jowls* (R), inc., n.sfx. -eh. uhská'yeh *big mouth, jowls* (R); –hska?yahręhw –: kahska'yáhręw ‹it-jowls-put up-causes› *amiss, oblique* (HS); –ne –. –hska?yak^wahT –: newak-ska'yakwáhtha' ‹two-I-jowls-cut up› *I am yawning* (HS).

–hska?yahręhw – amiss, oblique. *dv.n.s.* kahska'yáhręw ‹it-jowls-put up-

causes› *amiss, oblique* (HS).

–hskeT – wild hemp. *n.r.* n-poss., n-inc., n.sfx. -ę. Requires the masculine prefix; this fact, plus the fact that the suffix -ę resembles more a stative aspect marker than a simple noun suffix suggest that this root is de-verbal in origin. ruhskyé·'nę *wild hemp* (RC 18:1).

–hskękwar – fingernail. *n.r.* inaln: rah-skękwà·reh *his fingernail* (R), inc., n.sfx. -eh. uhskękwà·reh *fingernail* (R).

–hskęn – ghost, phantom. *n.r.* poss. ?, inc., n.sfx. -eh. Perhaps to be seen in some, as yet undeciphered metaphoric use in Lawson's «Oos-skinna» 'A Fish-Hook'. uhskę̀·neh *ghost, phantom* (HS), rahskę̀·neh *he is a ghost* (H 2892); –hskęnakę –: rahskę̀·nakęh ‹he-ghost-sees› *he sees ghost* (HS); –hskę = nakraθ –: yehskęná·kra·θ ‹one-ghost-smells› *one smells of death* (R); –hskęn – –nęh –: uhskę̀·neh unę́heh ‹ghost corn› *ghost corn (planted by the transmigrated spirits of decrepit, old, infants or small children who could not make the journey to Sky-land)* (HS).

–hskęn – –nęh – ghost corn. *n.s.* uhskę̀·neh unę́heh ‹ghost corn› *ghost corn (planted by the transmigrated spirits of decrepit, old, infants or small children who could not make the journey to Skyland)* (HS).

–hskęnakraθ – smell of death. *v.s.-a.i.* yehskęná·kraθ ‹one-ghost-smells› *one smells of death* (R).

–hskęnę? – be at peace. *v.r.-s.i.* stat: -φ, prog: -, prp: -, dst: -, caus: -, rvs: -, dat: -, n-inc. Requires either the nominalizer -čr - or the increment -n - when compounded with another verb root. kayehskę̀·nę' *they are at peace*

(R): –hskęnę⁷–: ahskę̀·nę⁷ ‹unknown-be at peace› *peace, slowly, tranquil, well* (RC 1:4); –hskęnę⁷–.#hči: ahskęnę́⁷či ‹unknown-be at peace-very› *gently, patiently, with security* (HS); –hskęnę⁷naýę(T)–: rahskęnę́⁷nayęhs ‹he-be at peace-lays› *he is peaceful* (HS); –hskęnę⁷čr–: uhskęnę́⁷čreh ‹be at peace-'ness› *peace* (R); –hskęnę⁷=črakęw–: uhskęnę́⁷črakęw ‹be at peace-in› *amicably, in peace, peaceably* (R); –hskęnę⁷čręti–: rahskęnę⁷črę́·tih ‹he-be at peace-'ness-makes› *he is peaceful* (HS); –ne–. –hskęnę⁷naýę(T)–: nehrahskęnę́⁷nayęhs ‹apart-he-be at peace-lays› *he arbitrates* (HS); –ne+či–. –hskęnę⁷na=ýę(T)–: neθhrahskęnę́⁷nayęhs ‹apart-again-he-be at peace-lays› *he reconciles* (HS); –hskęnę⁷– kę́hči: ahskę̀·nę⁷ kę́hči ‹unknown-be at peace perhaps› *slowly* (HS); –hskęnę⁷– tha–. –i⁷rę–: ahskę̀·nę⁷ tha⁷neyé⁷rę⁷ ‹peace unusual-two-one-set› *the two of them live in peace, in union* (H-notebook); kwenikwę́ –hskęnę⁷–: kwenikwę́ θahskè·nę⁷ ‹like you-are at peace› *it seems as though you are well* (TW); čwé·⁷n –hskęnę⁷– hę: čwé·⁷n ahskè·nę⁷ hę ‹again unknown-be at peace ?› *hello* (R); kwęhs –hskęnę⁷– –(ę)⁷=tikęhręT–: kwęhs ahskè·nę⁷ ahrę⁷tikęhrę⁷nę́hek ‹no unknown-be at peace unknown-he-mind-conclude-going to› *he is unpacified* (HS).

–hskęnę⁷– peace, slowly, tranquil, well. *n.s.* ahskè·nę⁷ ‹unknown-be at peace› *peace, slowly, tranquil, well* (RC 1:4).

–hskęnę⁷– kę́hči slowly. *n.s.* ahskè·nę⁷ kę́hči ‹unknown-be at peace perhaps› *slowly* (HS).

–hskęnę⁷– tha–. –i⁷rę– live in peace. *v.s.-a.i.* ahskè·nę⁷ tha⁷neyé⁷rę⁷ ‹peace unusual-two-one-set› *the two of them live in peace, in union* (H-notebook).

–hskęnę⁷–.#hči gently, patiently, with security. *n.s.* ahskęnę́⁷či ‹unknown-be at peace-very› *gently, patiently, with security* (HS).

–hskęnę⁷naýę(T)– be peaceful. *v.s.-a.i.* rahskęnę́⁷nayęhs ‹he-be at peace-lays› *he is peaceful* (HS).

–hskęnę⁷čr– peace. *n.s.* uhskęnę́⁷čreh ‹be at peace-'ness› *peace* (R).

–hskęnę⁷črakęw– amicably, in peace, peaceably. *n.s.* uhskęnę́⁷črakęw ‹be at peace-in› *amicably, in peace, peaceably* (R).

–hskęnę⁷čręti– be peaceful. *v.s.-a.i.* rahskęnę⁷črę́·tih ‹he-be at peace-'ness-makes› *he is peaceful* (HS).

–hskę⁷nar– tree bark. *n.r.* n-poss., n-inc., n.sfx. –eh. uhskę́⁷nareh *tree bark* (R) [Gallatin «oskuhnaureh» 'Bark']; –hskę⁷nara⁷θ–.#u⁷y: kahskę⁷nara⁷θ⁷ú⁷y ‹it-tree bark-is of a size-great› *cottonwood tree (Populus deltoides)* (AG).

–hskę⁷nara⁷θ–.#u⁷y cottonwood tree. *n.s.* kahskę⁷nara⁷θ⁷ú⁷y ‹it-tree bark-is of a size-great› *cottonwood tree (Populus deltoides)* (AG).

–hskę⁷r– bone, skeleton. *n.r.* n-poss., inc., n.sfx. –eh. uhskę́⁷reh *bone, skel-*

Tuscarora Pronunciation Key:
/a/ law; /e/ hat; /i/ pizza; /u/ tune; /ę/ hint; /č/ cheese; /h/ hoe; /m/ mother; /s/ same; /t/ do (before a vowel y, or w), too (elsewhere); /k/ gale (before a vowel y or w), kale (elsewhere); /n/ inhale (before a consonant or word-final), note (elsewhere), /r/ hiss (before a consonant or word-final), run (trilled as in Italian, elsewhere); /w/ cuff (before a consonant other than y or word-final), way (elsewhere); /y/ fish (before a consonant or word-final), you (elsewhere), /θ/ thing; /⁷/ (the sound between the vowels in unh-unh); /·/ long vowel, /́/ high pitch; /̀/ low pitch.

eton (RC 25:10) [Gallatin «oh-skreh» 'Bone']; **–hskę?r –.#hči**: uhskę?réhči ‹bone-very› *bony* (HS); **–hskę?ra̲ = kehT –**: ruhskę?rakyéhne? ‹he-bone-carried on back› *warrior* (R), kakuhskę?rakyéhtha? ‹they-bone-carry on back› *warriors* (RC 24:10); **–hskę? = ra̲kę θhę –**: rahskę?raké θhęh ‹he-bone-gnaws› *he gnaws bone* (HS); **–hskę? = ra̲kę?nahkw –**: uhskę?rakę?náhkhwa? ‹bone-strike-instrument› *white boneset (Eupatorium perfoliatum)* (R); **–hskę? = ra̲rih –**: uhskę́?rarih ‹bone-boil› *ghost-skeleton (departed spirit)* (L 83 — uhskɔ̄?rá·ri·?); **–hskę?ratkęh –**: yuhskę?-rá·tkęhθ ‹it-bone-is rotten› *carries, tooth decay* (HS); **–hskę?ra?θ –**: kahskę́?ra?θ ‹it-bone-is of a size› *they are large bones* (HS); **–hskę?ręti –**: kahskę?rę́·tih ‹it-bone-makes› *it ossifies* (HS); **–hskę?riyu –**: kahskę?rí·yu· ‹it-bone-is great› *it is a large bone* (H-notebook), yuhskę?rí·yu· ‹it-bone-is great› *it has many bones* (H-notebook); **–ačkę?r –**: učkę́?reh ‹self-bone› *bones, skeleton* (R); **–ne –.–ačkę? = rukar –**: neyučkę?rukà·rę ‹apart-it-itself-bone-is broken› *broken bones* (RC 7:10); **ti+yah –.–ačkę?ra̲yę(T) –**: thweyęčkę́?rayęhs ‹so-thither-one-oneself-bone-lays› *consumption, tuberculosis* (RC 23:5); **ti+yah –.–ačkę?ra̲yę(T) – –thwę –**: thweyęčkę́?rayęhs yú·thwę· ‹so-thither-one-oneself-bone-lays it-is good for› *boneset (Eupatorium perfoliatum)* (H-notebook).

–hskę?r –.#hči bony. *n.s.* uhskę?réhči ‹bone-very› *bony* (HS).

–hskę?ra̲kehT – warrior. *dv.n.s.* ruhskę?-rakyéhne? ‹he-bone-carried on back› *warrior* (R), kakuhskę?rakyéhtha? ‹they-bone-carry on back› *warriors* (RC 24:10).

–hskę?ra̲kę θhę – gnaw bones. *v.s.-a.i.*

rahskę?raké θhęh ‹he-bone-gnaws› *he gnaws bone* (HS).

–hskę?ra̲kę?nahkw – white boneset. *n.s.* uhskę?rakę?náhkhwa? ‹bone-strike-instrument› *white boneset (Eupatorium perfoliatum)* (R).

–hskę?ra̲rih – ghost-skeleton. *n.s.* uhskę́?-rarih ‹bone-boil› *ghost-skeleton (departed spirit)* (L 83 — uhskɔ̄?rá·ri·?).

–hskę?ratkęh – carries, tooth decay. *dv. n.s.* yuhskę?rá·tkęhθ ‹it-bone-is rotten› *carries, tooth decay* (HS).

–hskę?ra?θ – be large bones. *v.s.-s.i.* kahskę́?ra?θ ‹it-bone-is of a size› *they are large bones* (HS).

–hskę?ręti – ossify. *v.s.-a.i.* kahskę?rę́·tih ‹it-bone-makes› *it ossifies* (HS).

–hskę?riyu – be a large bone, be many bones. *v.s.-s.i.* kahskę?rí·yu· ‹it-bone-is great› *it is a large bone* (HS), yuhskę?rí·yu· ‹it-bone-is great› *it has many bones* (HS).

–hskhahęnę – gambol. *v.r.-a.i.* hab: -hs, pnt: -, stat: -, prog: -, prp: -, dst: -, caus: -, rvs: -, dat: -, n-inc. kahskhahè·nęhs *they gambol* (HS).

–hskra θ – cough. *v.r.-a.i.* hab: -, pnt: -a?, stat: -, prog: -, prp: -, dst: -, caus: -, rvs: -, dat: -, n-inc. wahrahskrá·θa? *he coughed* (RC 21:6).

–hskruri – grumble. *v.r.-a.i.* hab: -, pnt: -, stat: -·, prog: -, prp: -, dst: -, caus: -, rvs: -, dat: -, n-inc. ruhskrú·ri· *he grumbles* (R).

–hskT(i) – the two of you...me; the two of you...the two of us; thou...the two of us (second person dual agent=first person singular patient; second person dual agent=first person dual patient; second person agent=first person dual patient). *v.r.pfx.* The form **–hskn –** occurs before roots and stems that begin with the vowel ę or the morphophoneme {"u}. The form **–hskt –** occurs before roots and stems that begin with the vowels *i, e,* or *u* (not from {"u}). The form **-hsky** - occurs before roots and stems that begin with the vowel *a.* The form **-hskti** - occurs before roots and stems that begin with a consonant. The initial *h* of the prefix is dropped in word-initial position.

-hskut - south. *n.r.* n-poss., n-inc., n.sfx. -ɸ. **-hskut** -.#áh: uhsku·t'ʔáh ‹south-little› *southward* (HS); **-hskut** -.#ke: uhskú·tkye ‹south-at› *south* (R).

-hskut -.#áh southward. *n.s.* uhsku·t'ʔáh ‹south-little› *southward* (HS).

-hskut -.#ke south. *n.s.* uhskú·tkye ‹south-at› *south* (R).

-hsku'ʔkwar - knob. *n.r.* poss. ?, inc. ?, n. sfx. -eh. uhskú'ʔkwareh *knob* (HS).

-hskwari - be feeble, be old. *v.s.-a.i.* See: **-(i)hskwari** -.

-hskwatkę - become aware of, feel, notice, perceive, realize, suspect. *v.r.-t.* hab: -'ʔθ, pnt: -·ʔ, stat: -, prog: -, prp: -, dst: -, caus: -, rvs: -, dat: -, n-inc. wahrahskwá·tkę·ʔ *he noticed* (RC 3: 69), rahskwá·tkę'ʔθ *he feels it, he perceives it, he realizes it* (HS); **-hskwatkę'ʔčr** -: uhskwatkę́'ʔčreh ‹become aware of-'ness› *curiosity, suspicion* (HS); **-hskwatkę'ʔčręti** -: wahrahskwatkę'ʔčrę́·ti'ʔ ‹fact-he-become aware of-'ness-made› *he took notice of* (RC 27:9), rahskwatkę'ʔčrę́·tih ‹he-become aware of-'ness-makes› *he is apprehensive* (HS).

-hskwatkę'ʔčr - curiosity, suspicion. *n.s.* uhskwatkę́'ʔčreh ‹become aware of-

'ness› *curiosity, suspicion* (HS).

-hskwatkę'ʔčręti - be apprehensive, take notice of. *v.s.-t.* wahrahskwatkę'ʔčrę́·ti'ʔ ‹fact-he-become aware of-'ness-made› *he took notice of* (RC 27:9), rahskwatkę'ʔčrę́·tih ‹he-become aware of-'ness-makes› *he is apprehensive* (HS).

-hskʷa'n - snake. *n.r.* n-poss., n-inc., n.sfx. -eh. rúhskwa'ʔneh *snake* (RC 7:3), úhskwa'ʔneh *snake* (R), ráhskwa'ʔneh *he is a snake* (H 2892) [Lawson «Us-quauh-ne» 'Snake'] [Jefferson «ose-quaw-net» 'snake'] [Gallatin «osequawneh» 'Snake'] (also, probably after the shape and/or decorative motif, Lawson «Oosquaa-na» 'A Tobacco-pipe'); **-ačkʷa'nętyęku** -: račkwa'ʔnę-tyę́·kwahs ‹he-himself-snake-many-picks up› *he squirms* (HS); **-hskʷa'n** - -**(a)hyak** -: úhskwa'ʔneh wáhya·ks ‹snake it-fruit-eats› *partridge vine, partridge berry (Mitchella repens)* (HS).

-hskwa'ʔn - stink. *n.r.* n-poss., n-inc., n.sfx. -eh. uhskwá'ʔneh *stink* (R).

-hskʷa'n - -**(a)hyak** - partridge vine, partridge berry. *dv.n.s.* úhskwa'ʔneh wáhya·ks ‹snake it-fruit-eats› *partridge vine, partridge berry (Mitchella repens)* (HS).

-hskweht - tree stump. *n.r.* n-poss., inc., n.sfx. -eh. uhskwéhteh *tree stump* (R) (also: uhskwíhteh); **-hskwehta'ʔnihr** -: yuhskwehta'ʔníhrę ‹it-tree stump-stood up› *standing tree stump* (RC 26:1); **-hskwehtakę** -: wahrahskwéhtakę'ʔ ‹fact-he-tree stump-saw› *he saw tree*

---

stump (RC 26:3).

–hskweyahčr – square. *n.r.* n-poss., n-inc., n.sfx. –eh. uhskwcyáhčreh *square* (HS): **–hskweyahčri̱hrahkw** –: ychskwc-yahčrihráhkhwa' ‹one-squarc-puts up-instrument› *level (instrument)* (HS).

–hskweyahčri̱hrahkw – level (instrument). *dv.n.s.* ychskwcyahčrihráhkhwa' ‹one-squarc-puts up-instrument› *level (instrument)* (HS).

–hskwe'n – upper lip. *n.r.* inaln: ch-skwe'né'kyc *(on) one's upper lip* (RC 26:10), inc., n.sfx. –eh. uhskwé'neh *upper lip* (R).

–hskwiht – tree stump. *n.r.* n-poss., n-inc., n.sfx. –eh. uhskwíhteh *tree stump* (R) (also: uhskwéhteh).

–hsn – empty noun root. *v.inc.* See: **–ath** – *be dry*.

–hsnahręw – glue, marrow, pith; any sticky substance. *n.r.* n-poss., inc., n.sfx. –eh. Hewitt & Smith cite the form uhs'nahrę·weh, showing the expected (but rare in modern Tuscarora) glottal stop from the shift of Proto-Northern Iroquoian *t* to '*n* after *s*. uhsnahrę·weh *glue, marrow, pith: any sticky substance* (R) (also: uθnahrę·weh); **–hsnahręwawihsi** –: wahrahsnahręwa-wíhsi' ‹fact-he-marrow-give to-un-done› *he extracted marrow* (RC 8:25).

–hsnath – be dry. *v.s.-s.i.* yuhsná·thę ‹it-X-is dry› *it is dry* (R), aryahsná·thęk ‹unknown-it-X-be dry› *that it have been dry* (RC 7:1).

–hsnath –{dative I} be arid. *v.s.-s.i.* yuh-snathá'θe· ‹it-X-is dry-for› *it is arid* (HS).

–hsnathę – aridity. *dv.n.s.* ha' yuhsná·thę· ‹the it-X-is dry-much› *aridity* (HS).

–hsnatha'T – dry. *v.s.-t.* kahsnathá'nę ‹it-X-be dry-caused› *they were dried* (RC 3:61).

–hsna'ku – give up, quit. *v.r.-a.i.* hab: -,

pnt: -', stat: -ę̌, prog: -, prp: -, dst: -, caus: -, rvs: -, dat: -, n-inc. ahruh-sná'ku' *that he quit* (RC 30:19); ti+yah –. **–hsna'ku** –: tyahwahruhsná'ku' ‹so-thither-fact-he-given up› *he got tired and gave up* (RC 8:6); **kwęhs –hsna'ku** –: kwęhs akahsná'kęk ‹no unknown-it-give up› *it is inefficacious* (HS).

–hsna'T – strike. *v.r.-t.* hab: -, pnt: -φ, stat: -, prog: -, prp: -, dst: -, caus: -, rvs: -, dat: -, n-inc. wahrúhsna'*t it struck him* (MG 106:37).

–hsnehw – pony-tail. *n.r.* n-poss., n-inc., n.sfx. –eh. uhsnéhweh *pony-tail* (R).

–hsneręwe – be slender, be tall and thin. *v.r.-a.i.* hab: -h, pnt: -, stat: -, prog: -, prp: -, dst: -, caus: -, rvs: -, dat: -, n-inc. rahsnerę̀·weh *he is slender, he is tall and thin* (HS).

–hsneyę – be lean. *v.r.-a.i.* hab: -, pnt: -', stat: -·, prog: -, prp: -, dst: -, caus: -, rvs: -, dat: II (-ti-/-θ-), n-inc. rahsné·-yę· *he is lean* (RC 21:9); **–hsneyę** –{dative II}: rahsneyę́·tih ‹he-is lean-for› *he emaciates it* (HS); **–hsneyę'** –: yuhsnè·yę'θ ‹it-be lean-begins› *kin-dling* (R), ruhsnè·yę'θ ‹he-be lean-begins› *blue beech (Fagus* sp.*)* (R); **–ne** –. **–hsneyę** –: nęθahsnè·yę' ‹apart-prediction-you-be lean› *you will be lean* (RC 25:11).

–hsneyę –{dative II} emaciate. *v.s.-t.* rahsneyę́·tih ‹he-is lean-for› *he emac-iates it* (HS).

–hsneyę' – blue beech. *dv.n.s.* ruhsnè·-yę'θ ‹he-be lean-begins› *blue beech (Fagus* sp.*)* (R).

–hsneyę' – kindling. *dv.n.s.* yuhsnè·yę'θ ‹it-be lean-begins› *kindling* (R).

–hsne'θar – thistle, thorn. *n.r.* n-poss., n-inc., n.sfx. –eh. uhsné'θareh *thistle, thorn* (R).

–hsnęw – brook, runlet, stream. *n.r.* n-poss., inc., n.sfx. -eh. Hewitt & Smith cite the form uhs'nę·weh, showing the expected (but rare in modern Tuscarora) glottal stop from the shift of Proto-Northern Iroquoian *t to 'n after *s. uhsnę·weh *brook, runlet, stream* (R); –hsnęw–.#áh: uhsnęweháh ‹stream-little› *brooklet, rill* (HS); –hsnęwak̲ęw: uhsnę·wak̲ęw ‹stream-in› *in the stream* (RC 10:1); –hsnęwyę = tihę –: kahsnęwyętí·hę' ‹it-stream-extended-much› *creeks* (AG); –ne –. –hsnęwihya'k –: wa'thrahsnęwíhya'k ‹fact-apart-he-stream-crossed over› *he crossed the stream* (L 26).

–hsnęw –.#áh brooklet, rill. *n.s.* uhsnęweháh ‹stream-little› *brooklet, rill* (HS).

–hsniy – gnaw. *v.r.-t.* hab: -, pnt: -, stat: -, prog: -, prp: -, dst: -ahnę-, caus: -, rvs: -, dat: -, n-inc. –hsniyahnę –: rahsniyáhnęh ‹he-gnaws-much› *he gnaws it clean, he gnaws it to the bone* (HS).

–hsni' – choke. *v.r.-a.i.* hab: -θ, pnt: -φ, stat: -, prog: -, prp: -, dst: , caus: -, rvs: -, dat: -, n-inc. rúhsni'θ *he chokes* (H 2484), ęhrúhsni' *he will choke* (HS); –nehahsni' –: runęháhsni'θ ‹he-corn-chokes› *he chokes on a grain of corn* (H 2484).

–hsnuka'T – be radiant, coruscate, glimmer, scintillate, sparkle, shine, twinkle. *v.s.-a.i.* kahsnuká'tha' ‹it-X-blister-causes› *it is radiant, it coruscates, it shines, it sparkles* (HS), rahsnuká'tha' ‹he-X-blister-causes› *he glimmers, he scintillates, he sparkles, he twinkles* (HS), kahsnuka'náhnęh ‹it-X-blister-causes-much› *dazzling* (AW 50).

–hsnuka'T – firefly. *n.s.* uhsnuká'nęh ‹X-blister-cause› *firefly* (R).

–hsnu'kr – feather. *n.r.* n-poss., n-inc., n.sfx. -eh. *East.* Hewitt & Smith cite the form uhs'nú'kreh, showing the expected (but rare in modern Tuscarora) glottal stop from the shift of Proto-Northern Iroquoian *t to 'n after *s. The Western dialect has the form uhsnú'sreh (PC). uhsnú'kreh *feather* (R) [Lawson «Oosnoo-qua» 'Feather'].

–hsnu'sr – feather. *n.r.* n-poss., n.inc., n.sfx. -eh. *West.* uhsnú'sreh *feather* (PC).

–hsnwe'r – bristle. *n.r.* poss. ?, inc. ?, n.sfx. -eh. uhsnwé'reh *bristle* (HS).

–hsnyar – cheer, excite, exhort, inspire, urge. *v.r.-t.* hab: -, pnt: -', stat: -ę, prog: -, prp: -, dst: -, caus: -, rvs: -, dat: -, n-inc. rahsnyà·rę *he cheers, he excites it, he exhorts it, he inspires it, he urges it* (HS), ęhráhsnya'r *he will cheer* (HS).

–hsnye – attend to. *v.r.-t.* See: –(i)hsnye –.

–hsnyęhθr – spine. *n.r.* poss. ?, inc. ?, n.sfx. -eh. uhsnyęhθreh *spine* (SH 375).

–hsnyu'θr – scruff. *n.r.* poss. ?, inc., n.sfx. -. Found only in the construction cited below. –ačnyu'θręhT –: wačnyu'θréhtha' ‹it-itself-scruff-fall-causes› *it (animal, reptile) molts* (H-notebook).

–hsT – employ (something), use. *v.s.-t.*

See: -(i)hsT-.

-hstač- starch. *n.r.* n-poss., inc., n.sfx. -ɸ. Takes no simple noun prefix in its elicitation form. stá·č *starch* (HS): **-hstačrawę**-: rahstáčrawęh ‹he-starch-'ness-put up-much› *he puts on starch* (HS).

-hstęni- adorn, ornament. *v.r.-t.* hab: -h, pnt: -', stat: -ę, prog: -'nye'-, prp: -, dst: -hę-, caus: -'T-, rvs: -, dat: -, inc.-??-ag./pat. Occurs only with an incorporated noun root. **-(ę)nęhrah** = **stęni**-: kayenęhrahstę̀·nih ‹they-scalp-adorn› *they march, they parade* (HS); **-rihwahstęni**-: rarihwahstę̀·nih ‹he-matter-adorns› *he smoothes away a difficulty* (HS), *mediator (he settles the matter)* (L 60), wa'kayerihwahstę̀·ni' ‹fact-they-matter-adorned› *they make peace* (R); **-rihwahstęnya'T**-: urihwahstę́·nya't ‹matter-adorn-cause› *arbitration* (HS); **-a'nya'tahstęnya'T**-: yę'nya'tahstęnyá'tha' ‹one-body-adorn-causes› *ornament* (HS); **-a'rih** = **wahstęni**-: ra'rihwahstę̀·nih ‹he-him-self-matter-adorns› *he amends it* (HS); **-rir**- **-(ę)nęhrahstęni'nye'**-: urì·reh kayenęhrahstęní·'nye' ‹row they-scalp-adorn-going along› *parade, procession* (HS).

-hsti- inner bark. *n.r.* n-poss., inc., n.sfx. -eh. úhsteh *inner bark* (R); **-hstih** = **rawęku**-: wa'kayehstihrawę́·ku' ‹fact-they-inner bark-undo-much-pick up› *they took down bark* (RC 3:63).

-hstkę'- jilt, reject. *v.s.-t.* See: -(i)h = **stkę'**-.

-hstr- length of back, stature. *n.r.* See: -(i)**hstr**-.

-hstra'nihr- sit up. *v.s.-a.i.* kahstra'níhrę ‹it-stature-stands up› *it is sitting up* (RC 5:37).

-hstra'nihr- **-rę'a'ke** perch. *dv.n.s.* kahstrá'nihč urę'a'kye ‹it-stature-stands

up tree-on› *perch* (HS).

-hstra'nihθne- seat. *v.s.-t.* na'nihstra'-níhθneh ‹one=another-stature-stands up-going to› *one seats another* (HS).

-hstrenę'- be lovesick, pine. *v.r.-a.i.* hab: -θ, pnt: -, stat: -, prog: -, prp: -, dst: -, caus: -, rvs: -, dat: -, n-inc. This is probably derived from the root seen in Lawson's (1709) «Cosserunte» 'Mad' (= *kahsrę́·the' *it is mad or crazy*), literally "begin to be mad or crazy". rahstrè·nę'θ *he is lovesick, he pines* (HS).

-hstruri- mythic prophetic bird; kangaroo, ostrich. *n.r.* n-poss., n-inc., n. sfx. -'. uhstrù·ri' *mythic prophetic bird* (RC 22:title); *kangaroo, ostrich* (HS).

-hstur- be fast. *v.r.-a.i.* hab: -, pnt: -e', stat: -e', prog: -, prp: -, dst: -, caus: -a'T-, rvs: -, dat: -, n-inc. yuhstù·re' *it is fast* (R), ęyuhstù·re' *early* (R); **-hstura'T**-: rahstù·ra'č ‹he-be fast-causes› *he hurries it, he quickens it* (HS); ti-. **-hstur**-: tyuhstù·re' ‹so-it-is fast› *it is so fast* (RC 3:41); **-ačtur**-: ručtù·re' ‹he-himself-is fast› *he hurries* (RC 36:1); ha' **-hstur**-: ha' yuhstù·re' ‹the it-is fast› *celerity* (HS).

-hstur- celerity. *dv.n.s.* ha' yuhstù·re' ‹the it-is fast› *celerity* (HS).

-hstura'T- hurry, quicken. *v.s.-t.* rahstù·ra'č ‹he-be fast-causes› *he hurries it, he quickens it* (HS).

-hstwahr- bird down, fuzz, light fur. *n.r.* n-poss., inc., n.sfx. -eh. uhstwáhreh *bird down, fuzz, light fur* (R); **-hstwahrar**-: uhstwáhrarę ‹light fur-be a hole› *caterpillar* (said to mean "hole with hair around it"; if so, then the word shows haplology from *uhstwahráhrarę) (H-notebook); **-hstwah** = **ręte**: uhstwahrę́·te ‹light fur-certain one› *a particular fine hair* (RC 30:59).

-hstwahrar – caterpillar. *n.s.* uhstwáhrarę ‹light fur-be a hole› *caterpillar* (said to mean "hole with hair around it"; if so, then the word shows haplology from *uhstwahráhrarę) (H-notebook).

-hsučrayę(T) – have forefathers. *v.s.-k.* ruhsučrayę́·ʔnęhk ‹he-ancestor-'ness-lay-had› *his forefathers* (RC 12: 6).

-hsuhkw – lip. *n.r.* inaln: ksuhkwę́ʔkye *(on) my lip* (R), n-inc., n.sfx. -eh. uhsúhkweh *lip* (R).

-hsuhsn – bark from a large tree. *n.* n-poss., n-inc., n.sfx. -eh. uhsúhsneh *elm or other bark from large trees* (H 3518).

-hsukar – beard, facial hair. *n.r.* inaln: ksú·kareh *my beard* (R), inc., n.sfx. -eh. uhsú·kareh *beard, facial hair* (R) [Gallatin «osuhkareh» 'Beard']; -hsu = karęt: rahsú·karę·t ‹he-beard-possesses› *he is bearded* (HS); -ačhuka = ręhT –: račukaré̜hthaʔ ‹he-himself-beard-fall-causes› *he shaves* (HS), waʔkačhú·karęht‹fact-I-myself-beard-fall-caused› *I shaved* (R); -ačhukaręh = nahkw –: yę́čhukaręhnáhkhwaʔ ‹one-oneself-beard-fall-causes-instrument› *razor* (HS).

-hsukaręt be bearded. *v.s.-a.i.* rahsú·karę·t ‹he-beard-possesses› *he is bearded* (HS).

-hsur – sear. *v.r.-t.* hab: -, pnt: -, stat: -ę, prog: -, prp: -, dst: -, caus: -, rvs: -, dat: -, n-inc. ruhsù·rę *he sears it* (HS).

-hsure – be of such a height. *v.r.-s.i.* stat: -ʔ, prog: -, prp: -, dst: -, caus: -, rvs: -, dat: -, inc.-ɸ-pat. ti -. -hsure –: tyuh-sù·reʔ ‹so-it-is of such a height› *its height: altitude* (HS); ti -. -(taʔ)čuh = kwahsure –.#úʔy: thwaʔutaʔčuhkwah-sureʔúʔy ‹so-fact-it-pile-is of such a height-great› *there was a big high pile formed* (RC 30:31).

-hsuryęthu – shatter. *v.r.-t.* hab: -hs, pnt: -, stat: -, prog: -, prp: -, dst: -, caus: -, rvs: -, dat: -, inc.-ɸ-pat. rahsuryę́·thuhs *he shatters it* (HS); -nęh = sahsuryęthu –: ranęhsahsuryę́·thuhs ‹he-house-shatters› *he ruins, destroys the building (by crushing or pulling it to pieces)* (H-notebook).

-hsut grandmother, great grandmother (older usage), ancestor, relative two or more generations older. *n.r.* aln: áksu·t *my grandmother, my great grandmother, my ancestor* (R), inc., n.sfx. -. áksu·t *my grandmother, my great grandmother (older usage), my ancestor* (R); -hsut.#kęhaʔnę́ʔ: yękhihsutkę́haʔnęhk ‹one=us-ancestor-many-had› *our ancestors* (RC 4:1); -hsu = črayę(T) –: ruhsučrayę́·ʔnęhk ‹he-ancestor-'ness-lay-had› *his forefathers had* (RC 12:6); -hsutaʔke: Rahsutáʔkye ‹he-ancestor-at› *King Blunt's Town (a village on the Tuscarora Reservation of 1717 in North Carolina)* [Colonial Records «Ressootska», «Rasewtokee», «Rehorsesky»]; -hsutaʔ = shę̜ʔnę –: yękwahsutaʔshę́ʔnęhk ‹we-ancestor-"plural"-had› *our ancestors* (RC 3:1).

-hsut.#kęhaʔnę́ʔ ancestors. *n.s.* yękhih-sutkę́haʔnęhk ‹one=us-ancestor-many-

Tuscarora Pronunciation Key:
/a/ law; /e/ hat; /i/ pizza; /u/ tune; /ę/ hint; /č/ cheese; /h/ hoe; /m/ mother; /s/ same; /t/ do (before a vowel y, or w), too (elsewhere); /k/ gale (before a vowel y or w), kale (elsewhere); /n/ inhale (before a consonant or word-final), note (elsewhere), /r/ hiss (before a consonant or word-final), run (trilled as in Italian, elsewhere); /w/ cuff (before a consonant other than y or word-final), way (elsewhere); /y/ fish (before a consonant or word-final), you (elsewhere), /θ/ thing; /ʔ/ (the sound between the vowels in unh-unh); /·/ long vowel, /´/ high pitch; /`/ low pitch.

had› *our ancestors* (RC 4:1).

-hsuta?ke King Blunt's Town. *n.s.* Rahsutá?kye ‹he-ancestor-at› *King Blunt's Town (a village on the Tuscarora Reservation of 1717 in North Carolina)* [Colonial Records «Ressootska», «Rasewtokee», «Rehorsesky»].

-hsuta?shę?nę - ancestors. *n.s.* The "plural" suffix here is foreign to Tuscarora and marks this word as borrowed from another Northern Iroquoian language. yękwahsuta?shę́?nęhk ‹we-ancestor-"plural"-had› *our ancestors* (RC 3:1).

-hsu?ku - digit, finger, toe; rake; thimble; herring tooth. *n.r.* inaln: ksu?kwę́?kye *my finger, my toe* (R); aln: aksú?kwawęh *my thimble* (R), inc., n.sfx. -eh. Several of the stems listed below are borrowed from other Northern Iroquoian languages (e.g., Mohawk) that have a noun root **-hso?kw** - 'nut'. Since that root does not occur in Tuscarora, the borrowed stems must be reanalyzed as containing **-hsu?ku** - 'finger'. uhsú?kweh *digit, finger, toe* (RC 30:29); *rake; thimble* (HS); *herring tooth* (PC); **-hsu?kwakanęt** -: su?kwaká·nę·t ‹finger-licked› *red squirrel (Tamiasciurus hudsonicus)* (R); **-hsu?kwaw** -: ękęhsú?kwę? ‹prediction-I=you-finger-give› *I will give you finger* (RC 30:28); **-hsu?kwehčr** -: uhsu?kwéhčreh ‹finger-'ness› *ring* (R); **-hsu?kweθę** -: kahsu?kwé·θę ‹it-finger-is long-many› *butternut (Juglans cinerea)* (RC 11:16); **-či** -. **-hsu?kwakanęt** -: čuhsu?kwaká·nę·t ‹again-it-finger-licked› *red squirrel (Tamiasciurus hudsonicus)* (AG); **-či** -. **-hsu?kwihę**: θkahsu?kwíhę ‹again-it-finger-middle of› *middle of finger* (RC 30:44); **tha+ne** -. **-hsu?=kuken** -.**#kęha?nę?**: tha?nehrahsu?kukyenękę́ha?nę? ‹unusual-two-he-finger-put down-many› *to the tips of each one of his fingers* (RC 14:5); **ti** -. **-hsu?kwake** -: tikahsu?kwá·kye· ‹so-it-finger-is in number› *so many fingers* (RC 17:2); **-hsu?ku** - **-iyu** -: uhsú?kweh wì·yuh ‹finger it-is great› *thumb* (SH 375).

-hsu?ku - **-iyu** - thumb. *n.s.* uhsú?kweh wì·yuh ‹finger it-is great› *thumb* (SH 375).

-hsu?kwakanęt - red squirrel. *dv.n.s.* su?kwaká·nę·t ‹finger-licked› *red squirrel (Tamiasciurus hudsonicus)* (R).

-hsu?kwehčr - ring. *n.s.* uhsu?kwéhčreh ‹finger-'ness› *ring* (R).

-hsu?kweθę - butternut. *dv.n.s.* kahsu?kwé·θę ‹it-finger-is long-many› *butternut (Juglans cinerea)* (RC 11:16).

-hsu?n - nipple. *n.r.* poss. ?, inc. ?, n.sfx. -eh. uhsú?neh *nipple* (HS).

-hsu?ranę - be mellow. *v.r.-s.i.* stat: -·, prog: -, prp: -, dst: -, caus: -hT-, rvs: -, dat: -, n-inc. yuhsu?rá·nę· *mellowness* (HS); **-hsu?ranęhT** -: rahsu?ranę́htha? ‹he-be mellow-causes› *he loosens it, he mollifies it, he softens it* (HS).

-hsu?ranęhT - loosen, mollify, soften. *v.s.-t.* rahsu?ranę́htha? ‹he-be mellow-causes› *he loosens it, he mollifies it, he softens it* (HS).

-hsu?θhę - be in a corner. *v.r.-s.i.* stat: -?, prog: -, prp: -, dst: -, caus: -, rvs: -, dat: -, inc.-ϕ-pat. **-nęhsahsu?θhę** -: yunęhsahsú?θhę? ‹it-house-is in a corner› *in corner of house* (RC 34:5); **-t** -. **-hsu?θhę** -: nyuhsú?θhę? ‹hither-it-is in a corner› *into a corner* (RC 11:16).

-hsu?θr - cone (shape), point, tapered thing, tower. *n.r.* poss. ?, inc., n.sfx. -eh. uhsú?θreh *cone (shape), point, tapered thing, tower* (HS); **-hsu?=θrukę?**: uhsu?θrú·kę? ‹point-less› *pointless* (HS); **-ne** -. **-hsu?θrya?k** -:

nehrahsú'²θrya'²ks ‹apart-he-point-breaks› *he breaks the point off* (HS).

-hsu²θrukę² pointless. *n.s.* uhsu'²θrú·kę² ‹point-less› *pointless* (HS).

-hsu²ye – be a libertine, be licentious, be profligate. *v.r.-s.i.* stat: -², prog: -, prp: -, dst: -, caus: -, rvs: -, dat: -, n-inc. ruhsú'²ye² *he is a libertine, he is licentious, he is profligate* (HS); **-hsu²ye²** –: uhsu'²yé'²ę ‹be licentious-begin› *lust* (HS).

-hsu²ye² – lust. *n.s.* uhsu'²yé'²ę ‹be licentious-begin› *lust* (HS).

-hsw – back, bust, lower back, vest, waist. *n.r.* inaln: rahswę́'²kye *on his back* (RC 3:35), inc., n.sfx. -eh. úhsweh *back, bust, lower back, waist* (HS), *vest* (SH 375); **-hsw**-.**#keha·²**: uhswę'²kyéha·² ‹back-customary› *dorsal* (HS); **-hswai²a(k)** –: kayehswaí'²aks ‹they-back-shoot› *longball (game)* (R); **-hswakwęrihT** –: rahswakwęríhtha² ‹he-back-appear-causes› *he revealed* (HS); **-hswakwęri²** –: rahswakwę̀·ri'²θ ‹he-back-appear-begins› *he is found out* (H-notebook); **-hswakwę²n** –: rahswakwę́'²na·t ‹he-back-turned down› *he is lying face down* (R), uhswakwę́'²neh ‹back-turn down› *something or someone lying face down on the ground* (R); **-hswakwę²nar** –: rahswakwę́'²na'²r ‹he-back-turn down-was in› *he lies prone with the back upward* (HS), kahswakwę́'²nar ‹it-back-turn down-is in› *it is upside down, turned upside down* (HS); **-hswayę(T)** –: ráhswayę² ‹he-back-lays› *he sits (or lies)*

bent low forward (H-notebook); **-hsweni²e(k)** –: načwení'²ehs ‹one=another-back-strikes› *one fells another, one slays another* (HS), rahswení'²ehs ‹he-back-strikes› *he hits it in the back* (HS); **-ne** –. **-hswate'nahkw** –: nekahswate'²náhkwę ‹apart-it-back-was in a line-instrument› *duplicate, what is copied* (HS); **-ne+či** –. **-hswatet²** –: neθhrahswaté·t'²ahs ‹apart-again-he-back-is in a line› *he redoubles it* (HS); **-ne** –. **-hswate²narhy** –: nehrahswate'²nárhyę ‹apart-he-back-was in a line-??› *he multiplies* (H-notebook); **-ne+či** –. **-hsweθ** –.**#áh**: neθkahswe·θ'²áh ‹apart-again-it-back-is long-little› *sparrow hawk* (R); **-yah+či** –. **-hswakwę²** = **narhu** –: yęčęktihswakwę'²nárhu² ‹thither-prediction-again-we-back-turn down-be in-cause› *we will make a dark secret of it by covering it up* (RC 30:18).

-hsw –.**#keha·²** dorsal. *n.s.* uhswę'²kyéha·² ‹back-custom-ary› *dorsal* (HS).

-hswai²a(k) – longball (game). *dv.n.s.* kayehswaí'²aks ‹they-back-shoot› *longball (game)* (R).

-hswakwęrihT – reveal. *v.s.-t.* rahswakwęríhtha² ‹he-back-appear-causes› *he revealed* (HS).

-hswakwęri² – be found out. *v.s.-a.i.* rahswakwę̀·ri'²θ ‹he-back-appear-begins› *he is found out* (H-notebook).

-hswakwę²n – be lying face down. *v.s.-a.i.* rahswakwę́'²na·t ‹he-back-turned down› *he is lying face down* (R), uhswakwę́'²neh ‹back-turn down› *some-*

thing or someone lying face down on the ground (R).

-hswakwę?n – lying face down. *n.s.* uhswakę́?neh ‹back-turn down› *something or someone lying face down on the ground* (R).

-hswakwę?nar – be upside down, lie prone with the back upward, turn upside down. *v.s.-a.i.* rahswakwę́?na?r ‹he-back-turned down› *he lies prone with the back upward* (HS), kahswakwę́?nar ‹it-back-turns down› *it is upside down, turned upside down* (HS).

-hswayę(T) – sit (or lie) bent forward. *v.s.-a.i.* ráhswayę? ‹he-back-lays› *he sits (or lies) bent low forward* (H-notebook).

-hsweni?e(k) – fell, hit in the back, slay. *v.s.-t.* načwení?ehs ‹one=another-back-strikes› *one fells another, one slays another* (HS), rahswení?ehs ‹he-back-strikes› *he hits it in the back* (HS).

-hswę?n – dry-rot, rotted out log, rotted out fallen tree. *n.r.* poss. ?, inc., n.sfx. -eh. uhswę́?neh *dry-rot, rotted out log, rotted out fallen tree* (HS); **-hswę?na = węhsthę** –: wa?ehswę?nawę́hsthę? ‹fact-one-rotted out log-possess-caused-much› *one had rotten wood* (RC 11:23); **-hswę?na?ke** –: uhswe?ná?kye ‹rotted out log-at› *at hollow (log)* (RC 30:9).

-hsy – empty noun root. *v.inc.* See: **-aks** – *be bad*, **-akwahsT** – *be good*.

-hsy – palm of the hand. *n.r.* inaln: ksyę́?kye *my palm* (R), inc., n.sfx. -eh. úhsyeh *palm of the hand* (HS); **-hsyawęri** –: rahsyawę̀·rih ‹he-palm of the hand-stirs› *he handles it* (HS); **-hsyur** –: úhsyu? ‹palm-cover› *grip* (HS); **-hsyuhčrę** –: rahsyúhčręh ‹he-palm of the hand-cover-'ness-falls› *he pampers it* (HS); **-hsyu?kaθne** –: rah-

syu?ká·θne? ‹he-palm-cover-is strong› *his grip is strong* (HS).

-hsyakęw in the body. *n.r.* n-poss., n-inc., n.sfx. -ɸ. uhsyá·kęw *in the body* (H-notebook); **-hsyakęw.#áh**: uhsyakę́w?ah ‹in the body-little› *of in the body (applied generally to fat, etc. of a dressed hog, etc.)* (H-notebook).

-hsyakęw.#áh of in the body. *dv.n.s.* uhsyakę́w?ah ‹in the body-little› *of in the body (applied generally to fat, etc. of a dressed hog, etc.)* (H-notebook).

-hsyaks – be mean, be unkind. *v.s.-s.i.* kahsyá·ksę· ‹it-X-is bad› *it is mean* (RC 24:2), rahsyá·ksę· ‹he-X-is bad› *he is unkind* (HS), rahsyaksę́·?nye? ‹he-X-is bad-going along› *he is unkindly* (HS).

-hsyakwahsT – have good taste. *v.s.-a.i.* rahsyákwahst ‹he-X-is good› *he has good taste* (HS); **weyúhre -hsya = kwahsT** –: weyúhre rahsyákwahst ‹very he-X-is good› *he is scrupulous* (HS).

-hsyawęri – handle. *v.s.-t.* rahsyawę̀·rih ‹he-palm of the hand-stirs› *he handles it* (HS).

-hsyuhčrę – pamper. *v.s.-t.* rahsyúhčręh ‹he-palm of the hand-cover-'ness-falls› *he pampers it* (HS).

-hsyur – grip. *n.s.* úhsyu? ‹palm-cover› *grip* (HS).

-hs?a – exhaust, finish. *v.s.-a.i.* See: **-(i)hs?a** –.

-hs?ahT – go rapidly, flee. *v.s.-a.i.* See: **-(i)hs?ahT** –.

-hT – stand. *v.r.-a.i.* hab: -, pnt: -ɸ, stat: -ɸ, prog: -, prp: -, dst: -, caus: -, rvs: -, dat: -, inc.-ɸ-ag. Although the basic meaning of this root is *stand*, the root is generally used in constructions in which a more abstract sense of *exist* dominates. **-t** –. **-hT** –: ná?uht ‹hither-fact-it-stood› *it was* (L 38); **ti** –. **-hT** –: tì·yuht ‹so-it-stood› *so it stands, so it* *is, thus it is* (RC 10:5); ti –. –rihwahT –: thwa'karíhwaht ‹so-fact-it-matter-stood› *it did that* (RC 30:27); –ne+t –. –hT –: ne̜·'nyuht ‹apart-fact-again-it-stood› *incessantly* (HS), ná·'nyuht ‹apart-again-it-stood› *constantly* (HS), e̜·'ne̜·'nyuht‹prediction-apart-again-it-stand› *over and over* (HS); tha+ne –. –hT –: tha'ne̜·yuht ‹unusual-two-it-stood› *same, similar, they two are alike* (HS), tha'neyuhné̜he' ‹unusual-two-it-stand-remote› *they were similar* (HS); tha+t –. –hT –: thá'nyuht ‹unusual-hither-it-stood› *of equal age (things)* (HS), tha'nyá·kuht ‹unusual-hither-one-stood› *of equal age (persons)* (HS); kwe̜hs –ne –. –ya'tahT –: kwe̜hs naryuyá'taht ‹no apart-unknown-it-body-stand› *it is unfit* (HS).

–ht̲aw – current of water, stream of water; rain shower. *n.r.* n-poss., inc., n.sfx. –eh. When incorporated, the meaning *stream of water* predominates. úhtaweh˙ *current of water, stream of water; rain shower* (HS); –ht̲awaka= reru –: yuhtawakaré·ru· ‹it-stream of water-is rolling› *shoal* (AG); –ht̲a= wakareru?T –: yuhtawakarerú'ne̜ ‹it-stream of water-be rolling-causes› *rapids* (HS); –ht̲awa'nehT –: yuhtawá·'neht ‹it-stream of water-be present-caused› *sharp current* (RC 35:31); –ht̲awe̜? –: yuhtawé̜'e̜ ‹it-stream of water-fall-began› *waterfall* (R); –ht̲awiyu –.#ke: Uhtawiyú'kye ‹stream of water-be great-at› *Mississippi River* (HS); –ht̲awT –: rahtáwtha' ‹he-stream of

water-causes› *he sops* (HS); –ht̲awye̜ = ti –: yuhtawyé̜·ti' ‹it-stream of water-extends› *there is a current* (AG); –či –. –ht̲awah(e)r –: θakahtáwhra' ‹again-fact-it-stream of water-put up› *stream of water again gushed up* (RC 6:9); –ne –. –ht̲awakwa?nahT –: nekahtawakwá'nahč ‹apart-it-stream of water-arc-causes› *it is eddying; eddy, whirlpool* (AG); –t –. –ht̲awah(e)r –: nakahtawáhra' ‹hither-fact-it-stream of water-put up› *stream of water gushed up* (RC 6:9); –t –. –ht̲awe̜? –: nyuhtawé̜'e̜ ‹hither-it-stream of water-fall-began› *at the waterfall* (R), Nyuhtawé̜'e̜ ‹hither-it-fall-began› *Niagara Falls, New York* (R); –a'ne̜htawhar – –čte̜h= ra?ke: yu'ne̜htáwher učte̜hrá'kye ‹it-itself-stream of water-hung rock-at› *a sheet of water over a rock* (AG).

–ht̲awakareru – shoal. *dv.n.s.* yuhtawakaré·ru· ‹it-stream of water-is rolling› *shoal* (AG).

–ht̲awakareru?T – rapids. *dv.n.s.* yuhtawakarerú'ne̜ ‹it-stream of water-be rolling-causes› *rapids* (HS).

–ht̲awa'neht – sharp current. *dv.n.s.* yuhtawá·'neht ‹it-stream of water-be present-caused› *sharp current* (RC 35:31).

–ht̲awe̜ – rub. *v.r.-t.* See: –(i)htawe̜ –.

–ht̲awe̜? – waterfall. *dv.n.s.* yuhtawé̜'e̜ ‹it-stream of water-fall-began› *waterfall* (R).

–ht̲awiyu –.#ke Mississippi River. *n.s.* Uhtawiyú'kye ‹stream of water-be great-at› *Mississippi River* (HS).

–ht̲awT – sop. *v.s.-a.i.* rahtáwtha' ‹he-stream of water-causes> *he sops* (HS).

-htehn - loblolly pine. *n.r.* n-poss., inc., n.sfx. -eh. uhtéhneh *loblolly pine (Pinus tardea)* (RC 34:2); **-htehnakęw**: uhtéhakęw <loblolly pine-in> *in the pine bush* (R); **-htehnu** -: Kahtéhnu·ʔ <loblolly pine-is in water> *name of a Tuscarora village in colonial North Carolina, occupied up to the eighteenth century* (R) [Lawson «Cauteghna»], *Neuse River* (AG); **-htehnu** -.**#aka·ʔ**: kahtehnuʔá·ka·ʔ <loblolly pine-is in water-characterized by> *Tuscarora residents of the village of Kahtéhnu·ʔ* (Hewitt 1910).

-htehnu - name of a Tuscarora village in colonial North Carolina, Neuse River. *dv.n.s.* Kahtéhnu·ʔ <loblolly pine-is in water> *name of a Tuscarora village in colonial North Carolina, occupied up to the eighteenth century* (R) [Lawson «Cauteghna»], *Neuse River* (AG).

-htehnu -.**#aka·ʔ** Tuscarora residents of the village of Kahtéhnu·ʔ. *dv.n.s.* kahtehnuʔá·ka·ʔ <loblolly pine-is in water-characterized by> *Tuscarora residents of the village of Kahtéhnu·ʔ* (Hewitt 1910).

-hthar - converse, talk. *v.r.-a.i.* hab: -, pnt: -ʔ, stat: -ę, prog: -, prp: -, dst: -ętyę-, caus: -, rvs: -, dat: -, n-inc. ráhtharę *he conversed, he talked* (HS), neyéhtharę *the two of them conversed* (HS), nękáhthaʔr *the two of them will converse* (R); **-htharętyę** -: rahtharę́·tyęh <he-converses-much> *he parleys* (HS).

-htharętyę - parley. *v.s.-a.i.* rahtharę́·tyęh <he-converses-much> *he parleys* (HS).

-htič̌h - hip, knee. *n.r.* inaln: ktič̌hę́ʔkye *my hip, my knee* (R), n-inc., n.sfx. -eh. uhtíč̌heh *hip, knee* (HS).

-htikariʔn - hoe. *n.r.* n-poss., n-inc., n.sfx. -eh. uhtikaríʔneh *hoe* (R).

-htinę - beg for, borrow, plead, request. *v.r.-t.* hab: -h, pnt: -ʔ, stat: -· ~ -ʔ, prog: -, prp: -, dst: -, caus: -, rvs: -, dat: III. inc.-φ-ag. rahtì·nęh *he begs for it, he borrows it* (HS), ruhtí·nę· *he has borrowed it* (L 25), ruhtì·nęʔ *he has borrowed it* (L 25), wahrahtì·nęʔ *he borrowed it* (L 61); **-htinę** -.**#ęwe**: rahtinęhę̀·we <he-begs for-genuine> *he implores* (HS), wahrahtinęʔę̀·we <fact-he-begged for-genuine> *he implored* (HS); **-htinęT** -: ruhtinę́·ʔneh <he-begs for-moving> *he is importunate* (HS); **-rihwahtinę** -: rarihwahtì·nęh <he-matter-begs for> *he asks leave* (HS); **-rihwahtinę** -{dative I}: ękayęʔnaʔ-rihwahtì·nęʔθ <prediction-they=another-matter-beg for-for> *they will order another* (RC 12:20), waʔeθarihwahtì·nęʔθ <fact-one=you-matter-begged for-for> *one ordered you* (RC 23:3), ękęrihwahtì·nęʔθ <prediction-I=you-matter-beg> *I will beg of you* (MP); **haʔ** **-htinę** -: haʔ rahtì·nęh <the he-begs> *beggar* (HS).

-htinę - beggar. *dv.n.s.* haʔ rahtì·nęh <the he-begs> *beggar* (HS).

-htinę -.**#ęwe** implore. *v.s.-a.i.* rahtinęhę̀·we <he-begs for-genuine> *he implores* (HS), wahrahtinęʔę̀·we <fact-he-begged for-genuine> *he implored* (HS).

-htinęT - be importunate. *v.s.-s.i.* ruhtinę́·ʔneh <he-begs for-moving> *he is importunate* (HS).

-htir - be durable, be hard, be solid. *v.r.-a.i.* hab: -, pnt: -ʔ, stat: -ę, prog: -ęhaʔnyeʔ-, prp: -, dst: -, caus: -ahT- ~ -aʔT-, rvs: -, dat: III, inc.-φ-ag./pat. yuhtì·rę *it is hard, it is durable, it is solid* (HS), waʔnyúhtiʔr *the two of them were matched in strength, the two of them are even* (RC 30:40), *it is even* (MG 106:34); **-htirahT** -: rahtì·-

rahč ‹he-be hard-causes› *he hardens it, he solidifies it* (HS), ęhstì·raht ‹prediction-you-be hard-cause› *you will reinforce it* (RC 35:40); –htirahT –{dative II}: naktiráhthahθ ‹you!=me-be hard-cause-for› *strengthen me!* (R); –(a)hahahtir –: yuhahahtì·rę ‹it-path-is hard› *the road is hard, firm* (H 2484); –(a)hahahtí'r –: yuhahahtí·'rę ‹it-path-be hard-began› *the road has become hard* (H 2484); –(ę)'tikęhrahtirahT –: wa'ktikęhrahtì·raht ‹fact-I-mind-be hard-caused› *I agreed to it* (R); –ker = hahtiręha'nye' –: kakukyerhahtirę·há·'nye' ‹they-body-be hard-going along› *they are all strong bodied* (RC 3:85); –nęhsahtirahT –: ranęhsahtì·rahč ‹he-house-be hard-causes› *he strengthens the house* (HS); –rihwahtirahT –: wa'krihwahtì·raht ‹fact-I-matter-be hard-caused› *I accepted it* (R), rarihwahtì·rahč ‹he-matter-be hard-causes› *he ratifies it* (HS); –yękwirahtir –: yuyękwirahtì·rę ‹it-wood-be hard› *hardwood* (PC); –a'nęhtir –{dative III}: ę'·nęhtì·rę' ‹fact-it-itself-been hard-for› *it was hardy* (RC 26:34); tha –.–htir –: tha'stì·rę ‹unusual-you-are hard› *stop messing around (said by a mother to misbehaving children)* (R); –a'nęhti = ra'T: ra'nęhtirá'tha' ‹he-himself-be hard-causes› *he dares, he hazards (e.g., a guess)* (H-notebook), ra'nęhtì·ra'č ‹he-himself-be hard-causes› *he dares, he hazards (e.g., a guess)* (H-notebook), ra'nęhtirá'nę ‹he-himself-be hard-caused› *he dared* (H-note-

book); **ha'** –htir –: ha' uhtì·rę ‹the be hard› *hardness, rigidity* (HS).

–htir – hardness, rigidity. *n.s.* ha' uhtì·rę ‹the be hard› *hardness, rigidity* (HS).

–htirahT – harden, reinforce, solidify. *v.s.-t.* rahtì·rahč ‹he-be hard-causes› *he hardens it, he solidifies it* (HS), ęhstì·raht ‹prediction-you-be hard-cause› *you will reinforce it* (RC 35:40).

–htirahT –{dative II} strengthen. *v.s.-t.* naktiráhthahθ ‹you!=me-be hard-cause-for› *strengthen me!* (R).

–htiθT – support. *v.r.-t.* hab: -ha', pnt: -ɸ, stat: -ę, prog: -, prp: -, dst: -, caus: -, rvs: -, dat: -, n-inc. Probably an archaic causative in –hT – of the root –htir – *be hard* with the expected change of *rhT* to *θT*. rahtíθtha' *he supports it* (HS), ruhtíθnę *he has supported it* (HS), ęhráhtiθt *he supported it* (R).

–htite – remove shell, shell. *v.r.-a.i.* hab: -, pnt: -', stat: -, prog: -, prp: -, dst: -, caus: -, rvs: -, dat: -, n-inc. wahrahtí·te' *he shelled it* (RC 12:29).

–htkwir – spoon. *n.r.* aln: aktkwì·reh *my spoon* (R), inc., n.sfx. -eh. uhtkwì·reh *spoon* (R); –či –.–htkwiraT –: θkahtkwí·ra·t ‹again-it-spoon-stand› *spoonful* (HS).

–htr – penis. *n.r.* poss. ?, inc., n.sfx. -eh. úhtreh *penis* (R); –htra'nihr –: wahstrá'nihr ‹fact-you-penis-stand up› *you stick your dick in* (PC).

–htrę – bind, tie. *v.s.-t.* See: –(i)htrę –.

–htwęh – plant, sprout. *n.r.* n-poss., n-inc., n.sfx. -eh. uhtwę́heh *a plant or the*

Tuscarora Pronunciation Key:
/a/ law; /e/ hat; /i/ pizza; /u/ tune; /ę/ hint; /č/ cheese; /h/ hoe; /m/ mother; /s/ same; /t/ do (before a vowel y, or w), too (elsewhere); /k/ gale (before a vowel y or w), kale (elsewhere); /n/ inhale (before a consonant or word-final), note (elsewhere), /r/ hiss (before a consonant or word-final), run (trilled as in Italian, elsewhere); /w/ cuff (before a consonant other than y or word-final), way (elsewhere); /y/ fish (before a consonant or word-final), you (elsewhere), /θ/ thing; /'/ (the sound between the vowels in unh-unh); /·/ long vowel. /´/ high pitch; /`/ low pitch.

plants of any cultivated crop, as corn, wheat, oats, etc.; sprout (HS).

-htyakayę – be backward, be slow. *v.r.-a.i.* hab: -h, pnt: -, stat: -·, prog: -, prp: -, dst: -, caus: -, rvs: -, dat: -, n-inc. rahtyakà·yęh *he is backward, he is slow* (HS), ruhtyaká·yę· *he is backward, he is slow* (HS).

-htyanę – bark, bay. *v.r.-a.i.* hab: -h, pnt: -·ʔ, stat: -ʔ, prog: -, prp: -, dst: -, caus: -, rvs: -, dat: -, n-inc. kahtyà·nęh *it barks* (R), rahtyà·nęh *he bays, he barks* (HS), ruhtyà·nęʔ *he had bayed, he barked* (HS), ęhrahtyá·nę·ʔ *he will bay, he bark* (HS); **-htyanę'ne** –: yuhtanę·ʔne·ʔ ‹it-bark-moving› *it barks at every little thing* (W 74).

-htyarh – caterpillar, worm. *n.r.* n-poss., n-inc., n.sfx. -eh/-ʔ. uhtyárheh *caterpillar, worm* (R), rúhtyaʔr *worm* (L 80).

-htyaw – hip. *n.r.* poss. ?, inc. ?, n.sfx. -eh. uhtyà·weh *hip* (AG).

-htyehs – soot. *n.r.* n-poss., n-inc., n.sfx. -ɸ/-eh. úhtyehs *soot* (HS), uhtyéhseh *soot* (HS), **-htyehs** –.#hči: uhtyehséhči ‹soot-very› *sooty* (HS).

-htyehs –.#hči sooty. *n.s.* uhtyehséhči ‹soot-very› *sooty* (HS).

-htyer – corn shuck. *n.r.* n-poss., inc., n.sfx. -eh. uhtyè·reh *corn shuck* (R); **-či** –.**-htyera'n** –: ęθakahtyè·raʔnak ‹unknown-again-it-corn shuck-stood› *that corn shucks have remained* (RC 10:2).

-htyękʷ – mischief, teasing. *n.s.* uhtyę́·kweh ‹be mischievous› *mischief, teasing* (R).

-htyękʷ – be mischievous. *v.r.-s.i.* stat: -ę·, prog: -, prp: -, dst: -, caus: -, rvs: -, dat: -, n-inc. ruhtyę́·kwę· *he is mischievous* (HS); **-htyękʷ** –: uhtyę́·kweh ‹be mischievous› *mischief, teasing* (R); **-htyękʷęhsthę** – rahtyękwę́hsthęh ‹he-mischief-possess-causes-much› *he torments it* (HS).

-htyękʷęhsthę – torment. *v.s.-t.* rahtyękwę́hsthęh ‹he-mischief-possess-causes-much› *he torments it* (HS).

-htyuhar – haft, handle. *n.r.* n-poss., n-inc., n.sfx. -eh. uhtyúhareh *haft, handle* (HS).

-htyuhkw – shuck. *n.r.* n-poss., n-inc., n.sfx. -eh. uhtyúhkweh *shuck (of nuts)* (HS).

-htyuT – sprout. *v.r.-a.i.* hab: -haʔ, pnt: -ʔ, stat: -·, prog: -, prp: -, dst: -, caus: -, rvs: -, dat: III (-ati-/-ę-), n-inc. kahtyú·thaʔ *it is sprouting* (L 23), rahtyú·thaʔ *he is sprouting it (grain, corn, etc.)* (L 23), yúhtyu·t *it has sprouted* (L 24), waʔkáhtyuʔt *it sprouted, it came out of the seed* (L 24); **-htyuT** –{dative III}: waʔkahtyú·ʔnęʔ ‹fact-it-sprouted-for› *it will sprout there for* (RC 21:2); **-či** –. **-htyuT** –: θkahtyú·thaʔ ‹again-it-sprouts› *it springs up again* (HS); **-t** –. **-htyuT** –{dative III}: ęʔnakahtyú·ʔnęʔ ‹unknown-hither-it-sprout› *that it sprout there for* (RC 21:2).

-htyuT –{dative III} sprout for. *v.s.-a.i.* waʔkahtyú·ʔnęʔ ‹fact-it-sprouted-for› *it sprouted there for* (RC 21:2).

-htyuw – rump. *n.r.* poss. ?, inc. ?, n.sfx. -eh. uhtyù·weh *rump* (SH 375).

hú hey!. *part.* hú *hey!*.

-hu – causative. *v.r.sfx.* hab. -s, pnt: -ʔ, stat. -ę°, prp: -, dst: -, dat: -. This form of the causative appears principally in more or less idiomatic constructions. The final *u* of the prefix becomes *w* before the habitual aspect suffix and is elided before the stative aspect suffix.

-huhst – basswood. *n.r.* n-poss., n-inc., n.sfx. -eh. uhúhsteh *basswood (Tilia americana)* (RC 30:34).

-huk- light up, shine. *v.r.-a.i.* hab: -s,
pnt: -ɸ, stat: -, prog: -, prp: -, dst: -,
caus: -, rvs: -, dat: I (-θe-/-θ-), inc.-ɸ-
ag. yú·huks *it lights up, it shines: light*
(R), wa'ú·huk *it became light: daybreak* (HS); -hukčr-: uhúkčreh ‹light
up-'ness› *brightness, light, radiance*
(HS); -rȩhyahuk-: yurȩhyáhuks ‹it-
sky-lights up› *Aurora Borealis* (HS):
Milky Way: rainbow (R); -rihwahu=
ka'T-: rarihwahuká'tha' ‹he-matter-
light up-causes› *he defines it, he dis-
cusses it, he demonstrates it, he en-
lightens it, he explains it, he sheds
light on it* (HS); -'ȩhrahuk-: yu'ȩ́h-
rahuks ‹it-leaf-lights up› *brilliant, gorgeous (leaves are lighted—in primitive times a fire that would light up
the leaves to any considerable distance about was considered extraordinary & only on great occasions was
it seen)* (HS); -ne-.-huka'T-{dative
II}: neyuhuka'ná·ti· ‹apart-it-light up-
caused-for› *it lit up for* (RC 3:38),
wa'nyuhuká'thahθ ‹fact-apart-it-light
up-caused-for› *it started to shine* (RC
3:75); -ne-.-athukstȩkuhT-: newathuk-
stȩkúhtha' ‹apart-it-itself-light up-
'ness-passes through› *translucent* (HS);
-ne-.-ȩ'nahuka'T-{dative II}: nȩkaka-
wȩ'nahuká'thahθ ‹apart-prediction-
they-daylight up-cause-for› *day will
be lit up for them* (RC 4:5); -t-.
-huk-{dative I}: nayuhúkθe· ‹hither-it-
light up-for› *aurora* (HS); ti+yah-.
-huk-: thweyú·huks ‹so-thither-it-lights
up› *clear, transparent* (HS).

-hukčr- brightness, light, radiance. *n.s.*
uhúkčreh ‹light up-'ness› *brightness,
light, radiance* (HS).
-hur- grow, grow old. *v.r.-a.i.* hab: -ɸ,
pnt: -', stat: -ȩ, prog: -, prp: -, dst: -,
caus: -ahT-, rvs: -, dat: III (-ati-/-ȩ-),
inc.-ɸ-pat. rúhur *old man* (RC 1:4),
káhur *dirty old man, licentious old
man* (R); -hur-.#kȩha'nȩ': kaku'-
nihurkȩ́ha'nȩ' ‹they-plural-grow old-
many› *old men* (R); -hurȩ'-: yuhù·-
rȩ'θ ‹it-grow old-begins› *it grows old*
(RC 6:14), ruhurȩ́'ȩ ‹he-grow old-
began› *he is an adult* (HS); -hurȩ'=
ȩha'nye'-: kahurȩ'ȩhá·'nye' ‹it-grow
old-began-going along› *it is growing
older* (RC 3:25), yuhurȩ'ȩhá·'nye' ‹it-
grow old-began-going along› *it is
growing* (HS); -yah-.-hur-: weθahù·rȩ
‹thither-you-grew old› *you are growing old* (R), yahwahráhu'r ‹thither-
fact-he-grew old› *he grew old* (R);
-hihte'črahurȩ'-: yuhihte'črahù·rȩ'θ
‹it-sun-'ness-grow old-begins› *crescent
(moon)* (HS); -tkwahur-{dative III}:
wahrutkwahù·rȩ' ‹fact-he-stomach-
grew old-for› *his stomach began to
swell* (R); -athurahT-: rathuráhtha'
‹he-himself-grow old-causes› *oldest
male* (RC 13:3), *senior* (HS), yȩthu-
ráhtha' ‹one-oneself-grow old-causes›
eldest (RC 29:2).
-hur- old man; licentious old man. *dv.
n.s.* rúhur ‹he-grows old› *old man* (RC
1:4), káhur ‹it-grows old› *dirty old
man, licentious old man* (R).
-hurȩ'- grow old. *v.s.-a.i.* yuhù·rȩ'θ ‹it-

grow old-begins⟩ *it grows old* (RC 6: 14), ruhurę́ʼę ⟨he-grow old-began⟩ *he is an adult* (HS).

–hurę̨ʼęha'nyeʼ – grow older. *v.s.-a.i.* kahurę̨ʼęhá·ʼnyeʼ ⟨it-grow old-began-going along⟩ *it is growing older* (RC 3: 25), yuhurę̨ʼęhá·ʼnyeʼ ⟨it-grow old-began-going along⟩ *it is growing* (HS).

Hutyuhkwawáʼkę He-Holds-The-Multitude (Chief of the Turtle Clan) (H-Handbook). *n.*

–huʼkr – mucilage, phlegm, slime. *n.r.* n-poss., n-inc., n.sfx. -eh. uhúʼkreh *mucilage, phlegm, slime* (HS).

húʼks slippery elm (*Ulmus fulva*) (R). *n.*

–huʼs – cold (disease). *n.r.* n-poss., inc., n.sfx. -ɸ/-eh. húʼs *cold (disease)* (R), uhúʼseh *cold (disease)* (R); –athuʼ = seryę(T) –{dative I}: rathuʼseryę́ʼθe· ⟨he-himself-cold-X-lays-for⟩ *he has a cold* (HS); –huʼs – -(ę)-taʼrakęw –ye = nę̨ –: húʼs ratáʼrakęw ruyé·nę̨·t ⟨cold he-head-in he-grabbed⟩ *he has a head cold* (HS).

–huʼs – -(ę)taʼrakęw –yenę̨ – have a head cold. *v.s.* húʼs ratáʼrakęw ruyé·nę̨·t ⟨cold he-head-in he-grabbed⟩ *he has a head cold* (HS).

–hwa – empty noun root. *v.inc.* See: –hri – *spill.*

–hwač – breadth, flatness. *n.r.* n-poss., inc., n.sfx. -eh. uhwá·θeh *breadth, flatness* (HS), yuhwá·θeh *flat* (HS); –hwačeriha –.#úʼy: yuhwačerihęhúʼy ⟨it-breadth-straightened-great⟩ *it is scattered around a lot* (RC 2:10); –hwačiyu –: kahwačí·yu· ⟨it-breadth-is great⟩ *broad* (H-notebook), *wide* (L 75); –hwačiyuhT –: rahwačiyúhthaʼ ⟨he-breadth-be great-causes⟩ *he widens it* (HS); –hwačiʼe(k) –: rahwačíʼehs ⟨he-breadth-strikes⟩ *he crushes it, he jams it* (L 75); –hwaθiyu –: kahwaθí·yu· ⟨it-breadth-is great⟩ *broad* (H-

notebook); –nę̨hsahwačiyu –: kanę̨hsahwačí·yu· ⟨it-house-breadth-is great⟩ *it is a wide house* (HS); –nę̨hsahwa = θahsthu –: kanę̨hsahwaθáhsthę ⟨it-house-breadth-is small⟩ *it is a narrow house or room, the house or room is narrow* (H 2484); –nę̨hsnahwačiyu –: kanę̨hsnahwačí·yu· ⟨it-seed-breadth-is great⟩ *the grain is wide, it is the nature of the grain to be wide* (H 2484); ti –. –hwaθaʼθ –.#áh: tikahwaθaʼθʼáh ⟨so-it-breadth-is of a size-little⟩ *it is so narrow* (L 75); ti –. –hwa = θaʼθ –.#úʼy: tikahwaθaʼθʼúʼy ⟨so-it-breadth-is of a size-great⟩ *it is so wide* (R); ti –. –kerhahwaθaʼθa'nyeʼ –: tikakyerhahwaθaʼθá·ʼnyeʼ ⟨so-it-body-breadth-is of a size-going along⟩ *of body width* (RC 15:2); –ne –. –athwa = čiʼθ(e)r –: newathwačíʼθręhs ⟨apart-it-itself-flatness-drags⟩ *sleigh* (H 3518).

–hwačeriha –.#úʼy scatter. *v.s.-t.* yuhwačerihęhúʼy ⟨it-breadth-straightened-great⟩ *it is scattered around a lot* (RC 2:10).

–hwačir – clan segment, extended family. *n.r.* n-poss., inc., n.sfx. -eh. uhwačì·reh *clan segment, extended family* (R); –hwačirakweʼniyu –: rahwačirakweʼnì·yuʼ ⟨he-extended family-is principal⟩ *he is head of the family* (RC 27:2).

–hwačirakweʼniyu – be head of family. *v.s.-s.i.* rahwačirakweʼnì·yuʼ ⟨he-extended family-is principal⟩ *he is head of family* (RC 27:2).

–hwačiyu – be broad, be wide. *v.s.-s.i.* kahwačí·yu· ⟨it-breadth-is great⟩ *broad* (H-notebook), *wide* (L 75) (also: kahwaθí·yu·).

–hwačiyuhT – widen. *v.s.-t.* rahwačiyúhthaʼ ⟨he-breadth-be great-causes⟩ *he widens it* (HS).

–hwačiʼe(k) – crush, jam. *v.s.-t.* rahwačí'ehs ‹he-breadth-strikes› *he crushes it, he jams it* (L 75).

-hwahst – effervescence, froth, scum, thin foam. *n.r.* n-poss., inc., n.sfx. -eh. uhwáhsteh *effervescence, froth, scum, thin foam* (HS); -athwahsthar -.#ú'y: yuthwahsther'ú'y ‹it-itself-scum-hangs-great› *there is much scum* (RC 30:54).

-hwanh – wind, wrap. *v.r.-t.* hab: -ahs, pnt: -a', stat: -ę, prog: -, prp: -a'θe-, dst: -, caus: -, rvs: -ahsi-, dat: -, inc.-ɸ-pat. rahwánhahs *he winds it, wraps it up* (HS); -hwanhahsi -: rahwanháhsyęhs ‹he-wind-undoes› *he unravels, he unwinds* (HS); -hwan= hahsT -: yehwanháhstha' ‹one-wind-causes› *wrapper* (HS); -hwanha'θe -: rahwanhá'θehs ‹he-winds-going to› *he winds it, he twists it, he wraps it up* (HS); -hsirahwanha'θe -: rahsirahwanhá'θehs ‹he-wire-wind-is going to› *he twines, he winds up spring* (HS); -atherahwanhahsT -: yętherahwanháhstha' ‹one-oneself-green-wind-causes› *bracelet (originally one made from braided grass)* (R); -a'ta'rah= wanhahsT -: yę'ta'rahwanháhstha' ‹one-oneself-head-wind-causes› *wreath* (HS); -ne -. -hwanhatihsi -: nehrahwanhatíhsyęhs ‹apart-he-wind-for-undoes› *he untwists it, he unwinds it* (HS); -ne -. -athwanha'θehę -: neyuthwanha'θéhę· ‹apart-it-itself-wound-going to-much› *spiral* (HS).

-hwanhahsi – unravel, unwind. *v.s.-t.* rahwanháhsyęhs ‹he-wind-undoes› *he un-*

ravels, he unwinds (HS).

-hwanhahsT – wrapper. *dv.n.s.* yehwanháhstha' ‹one-wind-causes› *wrapper* (HS).

-hwanha'θe – twist, wind, wrap up. *v.s.-t.* rahwanhá'θehs ‹he-winds-going to› *he winds it, he twists it, he wraps it up* (HS).

-hwarit – backpack, belongings; body (as a physical container for the non-corporal spirit). *n.r.* n-poss., inc., n. sfx. -eh. uhwarí·teh *backpack, belongings; body (as a physical container for the non-corporal spirit)* (R); -hwa= ritę'ni -: wa'uhwaritę·'ni' ‹fact-it-backpack-thrown› *it left behind backpack* (RC 11:24); -athwarit -: uthwarí·teh ‹self-backpack› *backpack, belongings; body* (HS); -athwaritę'ni -: ęwakathwaritę·'ni' ‹prediction-I-myself-backpack-throw› *my spirit will leave my body in death* (R); ti -. -athwa= rita'θ -.#áh: tiwathwaritá'θ'ah ‹so-it-itself-backpack-is of a size-little› *small backpack* (RC 26:17); ti+yah -. -athwaritahręhw -: thwewathwarí·tahręw ‹so-thither-it-itself-backpack-put up-caused› *backpack remains there* (RC 26:21).

-hwari'n – load, lump, mass. *n.r.* n-poss., inc., n.sfx. -eh. uhwarí·'neh *load, lump, mass* (R); -athwari'neti -: rathwari'né·tih ‹he-himself-load-makes› *he packs up* (HS).

-hwaθiyu – be broad, be wide. *v.s.-s.i.* kahwaθí·yu· ‹it-breadth-is great› *broad* (H-notebook) (also: kahwačí·yu·).

-**hwaθr** – strip clothes from. *v.r.-t.* hab: -çhs, pnt: -, stat: -, prog: -, prp: -, dst: -, caus: -, rvs: -, dat: -, n-inc. nathwá·θręhs *one strips another's clothes off* (HS).

-**hwaʔn** – whiteness. *n.r.* n-poss., n-inc., n.sfx. -eh. uhwáʔneh *whiteness* (HS).

-**hwaʔr** – thick foam. *n.r.* n-poss., n-inc., n.sfx. -eh. uhwáʔreh *thick foam* (HS).

-**hwekst** – asthma. *n.s.* uhwéksteh ‹close-'ness› *asthma* (HS).

-**hwen** – scar. *n.r.* inaln: rahwè·neh *his scar, he is scarred* (HS), inc., n.sfx. -eh. uhwè·neh *scar* (HS); -**hwenar** –: rahwè·nar ‹he-scar-is in› *he scars it* (HS), ruhwè·naʔr ‹he-scar-was in› *he is scarred* (HS).

-**hwen** – island; continent, country. *n.r.* n-poss., inc., n.sfx. -. Found only incorporated. The basic meaning of the root is *island*. The meaning *country, continent* is secondary and derives from the Tuscarora mythic tradition that the earth is an island created on the back of a turtle in the primordial sea. (See Rudes & Crouse 1987, legend 3.) -**hwen** –.#ke.#hrunę**ʔ**: uhwenaʔkyehrù·nęʔ ‹island-at-people› *islander* (HS); -**hwenęti** –: kahwenę́·tih ‹it-island-makes› *congress, legislature* (HS); -**hwenęti** –.#úʔy: rahwenętihúʔy ‹he-island-makes-big› *Senator* (HS); -**hwenętihst** –: uhwenętíhsteh ‹island-make-'ness› *congress, continent, council, legislature, realm, reign, seat of government, the area of governmental representation* (HS); -**hwenętihsta** = **kari** –: rahwenętihstaká·ryahs ‹he-island-'ness-devours› *he devastates a continent/country* (HS); -**hwenu** –: yuhwè·nuʔ ‹it-island-is in water› *island* [Gallatin «youwaynote» 'Island']; kę̀·neʔ –**hwen** –.#ke.#aka·ʔ: kę̀·neʔ kahwenaʔkyehá·ka·ʔ ‹here it-island-at-

characterized by› *Americans* (HS); ha**ʔ** kę̀·ne**ʔ** -**hwenu** –: haʔ kę̀·neʔ yuhwè·nu·ʔ ‹the here it-island-is in water› *America* (HS).

-**hwen** –.#ke.#hrunę**ʔ** islander. *n.s.* uhwenaʔkyehrù·nęʔ ‹is-land-at-people› *islander* (HS).

-**hwenar** – scar. *v.s.-t.* rahwè·nar ‹he-scar-is in› *he scars it* (HS), ruhwè·naʔr ‹he-scar-was in› *he is scarred* (HS).

-**hwenęti** – congress, legislature. *dv.n.s.* kahwenę́·tih ‹it-island-makes› *congress, legislature* (HS).

-**hwenęti** –.#ú**ʔ**y Senator. *dv.n.s.* rahwenętihúʔy ‹he-is-land-makes-big› *Senator* (HS).

-**hwenętihst** – congress, continent, council, legislature, realm, reign, seat of government, the area of governmental representation. *n.s.* uhwenętíhsteh ‹island-make-'ness› *congress, continent, council, legislature, realm, reign, seat of government, the area of governmental representation* (HS).

-**hwenętihstakari** – devastate a continent/a country. *v.s.-a.i.* rahwenętihstaká·ryahs ‹he-island-'ness-devours› *he devastates a continent or a country* (HS).

-**hwenu** – island. *dv.n.s.* yuhwè·nuʔ ‹it-island-is in water› *island* (R) [Gallatin «youwaynote» 'Island'].

-**hweθn** – belly, underbelly, underside. *n.r.* poss. ?, inc., n.sfx. -eh. uhwé·θneh *belly, underbelly, underside* (R); ti –.-**hweθnaʔθ** –.#ú**ʔ**y: tikahweθnaʔθʔúʔy ‹so-it-belly-is of a size-big› *it has a big belly* (RC 2:4).

-**hweʔn** – furrow. *n.r.* n-poss., inc., n.sfx. -eh. uhwéʔneh *furrow* (HS); -**hweʔ** = **nar** –: uhwéʔnareh ‹furrow-be in› *raised flat land between two furrows in a plowed field* (R); ti –.-**hweʔnęhT** –: thwaʔkahwéʔnęht ‹so-fact-it-fur-row-fall-caused› *abruptly, quickly, precip-*

itously (HS); ti –. **–hwe?na̱ra?** –: tikah-
we'nará'ę ‹so-it-furrow-be in-began›
land begins to be cultivated (RC 30:
1); **–athwe?nęti** –: ęthwe'nę́·ti'' ‹fact-
it-itself-furrow-made› *it (animal)
charged* (AW 57); **–athwe?nętyęha =
'nye?** –: ruthwe''nętyęhá·'nye'' ‹he-himself-furrow-makes-going along› *he
pushes forward*; **–t** –. **–athwe?nęti** –: nakayęthwe'nę́·ti'' ‹hither-fact-they-
themselves-furrow-made› *they made a
challenge* (RC 24:10); **–yah** –. **–athwe? =
nę** –: yęθwathwé'nę'' ‹thither-prediction-you-yourselves-furrow-fall› *you
will rush forward* (RC 33:5); **–yah** –.
–athwe?nęti –: wewathwe''nę́·tyęhs
‹thither-it-itself-furrow-makes› *it darts
forth* (HS).

–hwe?na̱r – raised flat land between two
furrows in a plowed field. *n.s.* uh-
wé''nareh ‹furrow-be in› *raised flat
land between two furrows in a plowed
field* (R).

–hwe'nu – be round. *v.r.-a.i.* stat: –, hab: –,
pnt: –'', prog: –, prp: –, dst: –, caus: –,
rvs: –, dat: –, n-inc. ęyehwé·''nu'' *one
will be round* (RC 23:4).

–hweθtkę – disgusting substance, gangrene. *dv.n.r.* The verb root from
which this is derived is unknown.
yuhwéθtkę· *disgusting substance, gangrene* (RC 21:6).

–hwęr – win from. *v.r.-a.i.* stat: –, hab: –,
pnt: –'', prog: –, prp: –, dst: –, caus: –,
rvs: –, dat: –, n-inc. wáhskhwę''r *you
won from me* (RC 25:15).

–hwę?khar – board, plank, timber, wood.

n.r. n-poss., inc., n.sfx. –eh. uh-
wę''khareh *board, plank, timber, wood*
(HS); **–hwę?khara̱kʷahnahkw** –: yeh-
wę''narakwahnáhkhwa'' ‹one-board-
cuts off-instrument› *saw* (HS); **–hwę? =
kha̱ręθkar** –: kahwę''kharéθka''r ‹it-
board-lay down› *floor* (RC 8:9);
–ne –. **–hwę?kha̱rurę** –: nekahwę''kharu-
rę́hshahk ‹apart-it-board-splits› *sawmill* (HS).

–hwę?khara̱kʷahnahkw – saw. *dv.n.s.* yeh-
wę''kharakwahnáhkhwa'' ‹one-board-
cuts off-instrument› *saw* (HS).

–hwę?kha̱ręθkar – floor. *dv.n.s.* kahwę''-
kharéθka''r ‹it-board-lay down› *floor*
(RC 8:9).

–hwę̱?n – distended stomach. *n.r.* n-poss.,
inc., n.sfx. –eh. uhwę́''neh *distended
stomach* (HS); **–athwę?nak?u** –: ra-
thwę''ná·k''uhs ‹he-himself-distended
stomach-releases› *he bloats* (HS).

–hwihsn – wing. *n.r.* poss. ?, inc., n.sfx.
–eh. *West.* uhwíhsneh *wing* (PC); čí·''-
nę'' **–hwihsnę?kye**: čí·''nę'' kahwih-
snę́''kye ‹bird it-wing-at› *bird's wing*
(PC).

–hwihst – cash, metal, money. *n.r.* n-
poss., inc., n.sfx. –eh (archaic –a''.).
uhwíhsteh *cash, metal, money* (R),
uhwíhsta'' *cash, money* (HS); **–hwih =
stakęre** –: kahwihstakę̀·re'' ‹it-money-is
scarce› *money is scarce* (H 2892);
–hwihstanę –: rahwíhstanęh ‹he-money-
guards› *cashier, treasurer* (HS);
–hwihsta̱nurę –: kahwihstanù·rę'' ‹it-
metal-is precious› *silver* (RC 21:1);
–hwihsta̱rahkw –: yehwihstaráhkhwa''

‹one-money-collects› *purse* (HS);
-hwihstaθerhu -{dative I}: rahwihsta-
θerhú⁊θeh ‹he-money-covers-for› *he
guilds* (HS); -hwihstatak(e)r -: ękah-
wihstatá·krę⁊ ‹prediction-it-metal-be
plentiful› *money will become plenteous, abundant, plenty* (H 2892);
-hwihstaw -: ękayę⁊nathwíhstę⁊ ‹pre-
diction-they=another-money-give to›
they will give money (to another) (L
35); -hwihsta?k -: rahwihstá⁊kha⁊ ‹he-
metal-digs› *he mines gold* (HS);
-hwihstiyu -: kahwihstí·yu· ‹it-money-
is great› *much money* (AW 98);
-hwihstur -: yuhwíhstu⁊ ‹it-money-cov-
ers› *lucrative* (HS), *metal is imbedded
(now, most commonly used of gold,
silver, copper, etc.)* (H 2892); -hwih=
stukę?: ruhwihstú·kę⁊ ‹he-metal-less›
he is impotent, he is insolvent (HS);
-athwihstarahkw -:   rathwihstaráh-
khwa⁊ ‹he-himself-money-collects› *he
ravishes* (HS), wa⁊kayęthwíhstrarahk
‹fact-they-themselves-money-collected› *they violated (females)* (AG); -a=
thwihstarahkw -{dative III}: wa⁊khe-
yathwihstraráh-kę⁊   ‹fact-I=another-
myself-money-collected-for› *I violated her* (AG), kęyathwihstrarahkwá·tih
‹I=you-myself-money-collect-for› *I am
violating (you)* (AG); -athwihstę=
tyahT -: yuthwihstę́·tyaht ‹it-itself-
money-make-causes› *money-making,
profitable* (HS); -či -. -hwihstaT -:
θkahwíhsta·t ‹again-it-money-stands›
one dollar (HS); -hwihstanurę - -ah=
waryakę -: kahwihstanù·rę⁊ uhwa-
ryá·kę⁊ ‹it-metal-is precious it-is
white› *silver* (HS); -hwihstanurę -
-a'nya⁊tahstęnya?T -: kahwihstanù·rę⁊
yę⁊nya⁊tahstęnyá⁊tha⁊ ‹it-metal-is precious one-oneself-body-adorn-causes›
jewelry (HS).
-hwihstanę - cashier, treasurer. *dv.n.s.*

rahwíhstançh ‹he-money-guards› *cashier, treasurer* (HS).
-hwihstanurę - silver. *dv.n.s.* kahwih-
stanù·rę⁊ ‹it-metal-is precious› *silver*
(RC 21:1).
-hwihstanurę - -ahwaryakę - silver. *dv.n.s.*
kahwihstanù·rę⁊ uhwaryá·kę⁊ ‹it-metal-is precious it-is white› *silver* (HS).
-hwihstanurę - -a'nya⁊tahstęnya?T - jewelry. *dv.n.s.* kahwihstanù·rę⁊ yę⁊nya⁊-
tahstęnyá⁊tha⁊ ‹it-metal-is precious
one-oneself-body-adorn-causes› *jewelry* (HS).
-hwihstarahkw - purse. *dv.n.s.* yehwihsta-
ráhkhwa⁊ ‹one-money-collects› *purse*
(HS).
-hwihstaθerhu -{dative I} guild. *v.s.-t.*
rahwihstaθerhú⁊-θeh ‹he-money-covers-for› *he guilds* (HS).
-hwihsta?k - mine gold. *v.s.-a.i.* rahwih-
stá⁊kha⁊ ‹he-metal-digs› *he mines
gold* (HS).
-hwihstur - be lucrative, be imbedded (of
metals). *v.s.-s.i.* yuhwíhstu⁊ ‹it-mon-
ey-covers› *it is lucrative* (HS), *metal
is imbedded (now, most commonly
used of gold, silver, copper, etc.)* (H
2892).
-hwihstukę? be impotent, be insolvent.
v.s.-s.i. ruhwihstú·kę⁊ ‹it-metal-less›
he is impotent, he is insolvent (HS).
-hyatęhst - book, card, newspaper, paper.
n.r. n-poss., inc., n.sfx. -eh. uhyatę́h-
steh *book, card, newspaper, paper* (R);
-hyatęhst -.#kęha?nę?: uhyatęhsta⁊kę́-
ha⁊nę⁊ ‹paper-much› *stationary* (HS);
-hyatęhstanę'nak -: yuhyatęhstanę⁊ná·-
kę ‹one-paper-affixed› *notice, posted
notice, poster* (HS); -hyatęhstatukęht -:
uhyatęhstatukę́hti ‹book-be holy› *Bible*
(HS); -hyatęhstayę'nahkw -: yehyatęh-
stayę⁊náhkwa⁊ ‹one-book-lays-instrument› *library* (HS); -hyatęhstayę'ner -:
rahyatęhstayę⁊nè·rih ‹he-book-knew›

he learned; scholar (HS); -athyatęh=
statęhninę -: rathyatęhstatęhnì·nęh ‹he-
him-self-paper-sells› *stationer* (HS);
-ne -. -hyatęhstayę'nahkw -: neyehyatęhstayę'náhkhwa' ‹apart-one-paper-
lays-instrument› *playing cards* (HS);
kę? -hyatęhstayę'nahkw -: kę'' yehyatęhstayę'náhkhwa' ‹where one-paper-
lays-instrument› *bookcase, desk* (HS).
-hyatęhst -.#kęha?nę? stationary. *n.s.* uh-
   yatęhsta'kęha'nę' ‹paper-much› *stationary* (HS).
-hyatęhstanę'nak - notice, posted notice,
   poster. *dv.n.s.* yuhyatęhstanę'ná·kę
   ‹one-paper-affixed› *notice, posted notice, poster* (HS).
-hyatęhstatukęhT - Bible. *n.s.* uhyatęh-
   statukęhti ‹book-be holy› *Bible* (HS).
-hyatęhstayę'nahkw - library. *dv.n.s.* yehyatęhstayę'náhkhwa' ‹one-book-lays-
   instrument› *library* (HS).
-hyatęhstayę'ner - learn. *v.s.-a.i.* rahyatęh-
   stayę'nè·rih   ‹he-book-knew›   *he
   learned* (HS).
-hyatęhstayę'ner - scholar. *dv.n.s.* rahya-
   tęhstayę'nè·rih ‹he-book-knew› *scholar* (HS).
-hya?k - cross over. *v.r.-a.i.* See: -(i)h=
   ya?k -.
-hyęh - river. *n.r.* See: -(i)yh(ęh) -.

I

í - prothetic vowel. *v.pfx.* Occurs on
verbs that would not otherwise have

an accentable penultimate or antepenultimate vowel. It adds no meaning
to the word.
-i stative aspect. *v.r.sfx.*
-i -/-ę° - be, be a group, be all, be the
only one, exist. *v.r.-a.i.* hab: -h, pnt: -
', stat: -·, prog: -ha'nye'-, prp: -, dst:
-, caus: -, rvs: -, dat: -, inc.-ɸ-ag. The
form -ę° - occurs following the third
person feminine/indefinite pronouns
and the third person plural pronoun.
The form -i - occurs elsewhere. The
number of members of the "group" is
determined by the pronominal prefix
unless the partitive prefix is present,
which occurs only when the pronominal prefix is singular. When the partitive prefix is present, the group consists of a number of members determined by reference to information
outside the immediate domain of the
particular verb form. Otherwise, if the
pronominal prefix is plural, the group
has more than two members; if the
pronominal prefix is dual, the group
has two members; if the pronominal
prefix is singular, the group has one
member. í·kę· *it is* (RC 30:40), íhrę·
he is (R), yá·kę· *one is* (R), ará·kę·k
that it be (RC 31:4), ę́·kę·k *it will be;
completely, totally* (RC 3:54); -i -.
#hči: ikę́hči ‹it-is a group-very› *first,
in the first place* (HS); -či -. -i -:
ęθá·kę·k ‹again-it-is a group› *that it
again be* (R), nečá·kę· ‹two-again-one-
is a group› *there are two* (RC 32:5);
-ne -. -i -: nę́·kę·k ‹two-prediction-it-be

a group› *it will be two* (R). né·kę· ‹two-it-is a group› *two things: they are two; pair (non-human)* (HS). neyá·kę· ‹they two-are a group› *two persons; pair (human)* (HS); ti -. -i -: tí·kę· ‹so-it-is a group› *it is so many* (R). tikayá·kę· ‹so-they-are a group› *there are so many* (R). thwá·ʔkęʔ ‹so-fact-it-was a group› *it was a group* (R). thwáhę· ‹so-fact-it-was a group› *occasion* (RC 32:1); -nęhsi -: kanęhsih ‹it-house-is a group› *the house is full (of people)* (HS); -yahsti -: rayáhstih ‹he-individual-is a group› *male individual* (R), kayáhsti· ‹it-individual-is a group› *one hundred* (R) [Lawson «Ki you se» 'Thousand']; -a'natʔah = θrihkT -: ęhsaʔnatʔáhθrihkt ‹prediction-you-yourself-basket-be a group-instrument-cause› *you will fill your basket* (RC 3:37); -či -. -yahsti -: θkayáhsti· ‹again-it-individual-is a group› *one hundred* (L 13); -ne -. -yahsti -: nekayáhsti· ‹two-it-individual-is a group› *two hundred* (L 13); tha+ne -. -yaʔtihaʹnye -: thaʔneyeyaʔtihá·ʔnyeʔ ‹unusual-apart-one-body-is a group-going a-long› *every-one-alone (each one)* (RC 12:18); ù·nę -khwiʔ -: ù·nę wakyekhwíʔę ‹now I-meal-be a group-began› *I have finished eating* (L 56), ù·nę rukhwíʔę ‹now he-meal-be a group-began› *he finished eating* (L 55); nyà·wę -khwiʔ -: nyà·wę ękyékhwiʔ ‹thanks fact-I-meal-be a group-began› *thanks, I am through eating* (L 56); kwęhs héʔthu -i -: kwęhs héʔthu ará·kę·k ‹no there unknown-it-be a group› *it is insufficient* (HS); kwęhs heʔthúhči -i -: kwęhs heʔthúhči ará··kę·k ‹no just right unknown-it-be a group› *it is unfit* (HS); kwęhs -kęʔT -i -: kwęhs ú·kęʔt ará·kę·k ‹no see-cause unknown-it-be a group› *it is in-*

visible (HS); kwęhs wehreʔę̀·we -i -: kwęhs wehreʔę̀·we ará·kę·k ‹no truly unknown-it-be a group› *unreal* (HS).

-i -.#hči first, in the first place. *n.s.* ikę́hči ‹it-is a group-very› *first, in the first place* (HS).

-ič - fish. *n.r.* n-poss., inc., n.sfx. -ęh. kę́·čęh *fish* (R) [Lawson «Cunshe» 'Fish'] [Jefferson «kun-junh» 'fish'] [Gallatin «kuhtchyuh» 'Fish']; -ič -.#ętíh: kęčęhętíh ‹it-fish-many little› *little fishes* (AW 48); -ič -.#hči: kęčę́hči ‹it-fish-very› *fishy* (HS); -iča̱ = hęsči: kęčahę́sči ‹it-fish-is black› *black bass (Micropterus* sp.*)* (H 3518); -ičahwaryakę -: kęčahwaryá·kęʔ ‹it-fish-white› *white fish* (H 3518); -iča = yaʔnerę -: waʔkičayaʔnè·ręʔ ‹fact-I-fish-harmed› *I wounded fish* (R); -ičihsak -: ęhsičíhsa·k ‹prediction-you-fish-seek› *you will go (spear)fishing* (R); -či -. -iča̱nę -: θkę́·čanęh ‹again-it-fish-guards› *dog-fish* (H 3518); -nęʔr -ičihsakT -: unę́ʔreh yečihsákthaʔ ‹net one-fish-seek-causes› *fish net* (SH 375).

-ič -.#ętíh little fishes. *n.s.* kęčęhętíh ‹it-fish-many little› *little fishes* (AW 48).

-ič -.#hči fishy. *n.s.* kęčę́hči ‹it-fish-very› *fishy* (HS).

-iča̱hęsči black bass. *dv.n.s.* kęčahę́sči ‹it-fish-is black› *black bass (Micropterus* sp.*)* (H 3518).

-ičahwaryakę - white fish. *n.s.* kęčahwaryá·kęʔ ‹it-fish-white› *white fish* (H 3518).

-ičihsak - go (spear)fishing. *v.s.-a.i.* ęhsičíhsa·k ‹prediction-you-fish-seek› *you will go (spear)fishing* (R).

-ih stative aspect. *v.r.sfx.*

-(i)har - hang. *v.r.-a.i.* hab: -ɸ, pnt: -ʔ, stat: -ʔ, prog: -aʹnyeʔ-, prp: -, dst: -awę-, caus: -ahT-, rvs: -aku-, dat: III (-ati-/-ę-/-ę-), inc.-ɸ-pat. The form -i =

har- occurs following noun roots ending in *č θ n h*; the form **-har**- occurs elsewhere. This root is one of a half dozen that have a special form for noting plural patients, **-atihar**-. This form of the root is both archaic (it is found principally in the material recorded by J.N.B. Hewitt) and optional. Furthermore, its use does not preclude the presence of the distributive suffix to further mark the plurality of the patient. In word-final position there is apparent free variation in the pronunciation of the vowel of this stem between [æ], usually indicating the vowel *e*, and [a], usually indicating the vowel *a*. Here, the stem is regularly written «-her-» where [æ] has been heard. The dative suffix is irregular with this root in that, rather than the expected alternation between a form **-ati**- with the habitual and stative aspects and a form **-ę**- with the imperative and punctual, the form **-ę**- occurs in all aspects. **-(i)har**-: ráha'r ‹he-hung› *he belongs to or has membership in (it), he is present at a meeting or assembly, he is one of a party* (H 2892), *he is a member* (M 87), *he is interested* (HS); **-(i)har**-{dative III}: rahà·ręh ‹he-hangs-for› *executioner, hangman* (HS), ęyehà·rę' ‹prediction-one-hang-for› *one will hang for* (RC 21:1), wa'khehà·rę' ‹fact-I=another-hung-for› *I enrolled someone (on the tribal rolls)* (R); **-(i)harahkw**-: yeharáhkhwa'

‹one-hangs-instrument› *hanger* (R); **-(i)haraku**-: rahará·kwahs ‹he-hang-undoes› *he takes it down* (HS); **-(i)=hara'nye'**-: rahará·'nye'θ ‹he-hangs-going along› *he is going toward* (RC 35:44); **-(i)harawę'nye'**-: kaharawę·'-nye' ‹it-hangs-much-going along› *it is in the midst* (RC 27:2); **-t**-. **-(i)har**-: thráher ‹hither-he-hangs› *he increases* (HS), tkáher ‹hither-it-hangs› *it increases* (RC 3:34); **ti+yah**-. **-(i)ha=ra'nye'**-: tyękahará·'nye' ‹so-there-prediction-it-hang-going along› *it will be going along with it* (RC 16:1); **ti+yah+či**-. **-(i)har**-: thweθkáhe'r ‹so-there-again-it-hung› *anniversary* (HS); **-(a)čęhihar**-: neyečęhíha'r ‹two-one-fire-hung› *the two of them formed a family* (RC 35:1); **-(a)hahihar**-: waha-híhe'r ‹it-path-hangs› *(it is) a road upon something (as on a ledge or hill)* (H 2484); **-a'θriharhuhsT**-: yę'θrihar-húhstha' ‹one-aim-hang-cause-uses› *tomahawk* (HS); **-čaratiharahkw**-: yu-čaratiharáhkę ‹it-door-several-hung-instrument› *hinge* (HS); **-čihskw=harahT**-: kačihskhwà·rahč ‹it-mush-hang-causes› *it mires, it sticks in mud* (HS); **-e'wihshar**-: re'wíhsher ‹he-saddle-hangs› *he puts saddle upon it* (HS); **-ha'čihar**-: kaha'číhe'r ‹it-neck-hung› *collar* (R); **-hčuhkwhar**-: ruh-čúhkhwe'r ‹he-flesh-hung› *male adolescent* (RC 35:43); **-hkyuhsihar**-: rahkyúhsiher ‹he-elbow-hangs› *he leans upon his elbows* (HS); **-hseya=tiharawę**-: yuhseyatihará·wę ‹it-ear of

---

corn-several-hang-many⟩ *ears of corn
are hanging around* (RC 2:6); **–kahr** =
har -{dative III}: wahrakarhà·rę⁷ ⟨fact-
he-eye-hung-for⟩ *he laid down a snare*
(R); **–kerhihar** –: kakyerhíhe⁷r ⟨it-body-
hung⟩ *body hangs* (RC 6:14) **–kerhi** =
har -{dative III}: wahrakyerhihà·rę⁷
⟨fact-he-body-hung-for⟩ *he hung body*
(RC 27:17); **–nęhsatihar** –: kanęhsatíhar
⟨he-house-several-hangs⟩ *he makes an
addition to the house* (H 2484); **–nę⁷** =
yečkhwar –: kanę⁷yéčkhwar ⟨it-nest-
hangs⟩ *it builds nest* (HS); **–nuri** =
harawę –: wahranurihará·wę·⁷ ⟨fact-he-
string of corn-hung-many⟩ *he hung
strings of corn* (RC 5:32); **–rętu⁷** =
črihar –: karętu⁷čríhe⁷r ⟨it-coffin-
hangs⟩ *coffin hangs* (RC 3:25); **–rihw** =
haraku –: rariwhará·kwahs ⟨he-matter-
hang-undoes⟩ *he allows, he permits*
(HS), na⁷riwhará·kwahs ⟨one=another-
matter-hang-undoes⟩ *one gives another
sanction* (HS) **–tya⁷thar** –: katyá⁷thar
⟨it-puffed-up bag-hangs⟩ *hornet's nest*
(RC 26:5); **–wiθerhar** –: yuwiθérha⁷r
⟨it-snow-hangs⟩ *snow held up by
reeds, etc.* (H 3518); **–⁷nęwahar** –
{dative III}: ęye⁷nęwahà·rę⁷ ⟨predic-
tion-one-kettle-hang-for⟩ *one will hang
kettle for* (RC 15:6); **–ne** –. **–tehwhar** –:
nehrutéwhe⁷r ⟨apart-he-skin-hangs⟩ *he
has a fur-cap* (AG); **–a'natihar** –: ra⁷na-
tíhar ⟨he-himself-several-hangs⟩ *he
fastens (them) to it* (HS); **–ne** –. **–a'ni** =
har –: nehra⁷níhar ⟨apart-he-himself-
hangs⟩ *he skips, he transgresses* (HS),
he goes over or beyond it (H-notebook); **–a⁷či⁷erhar** –: ra⁷či⁷érhar ⟨he-
himself-scarlet-hangs⟩ *he blushes*
(HS); **–a'nętakwthar** –: wa⁷nętákwthe⁷r
⟨it-itself-bed-hung⟩ *it hung its bed
there* (RC 3:8); **–a'nyahkwhar** –: ra⁷-
nyáhkhwar ⟨he-himself-girth-hangs⟩ *he
swings* (HS), yu⁷nyáhkhwar ⟨it-itself-

girth-hangs⟩ *it oscillates, it swings*
(HS); **–a⁷rihwharhu** –: yu⁷riwhárhę ⟨it-
itself-matter-hang-caused⟩ *it is a difficulty* (HS), wa⁷riwhárhuhs ⟨it-itself-
matter-hang-causes⟩ *difficulty (abstract)* (HS); **ha⁷** **–rihwharaku** –: ha⁷
ruriwhará·kwę ⟨the he-matter-hang-un-
did⟩ *his allowance* (HS); **kę⁷** **–(i)har** –:
kę⁷ káher ⟨where it-hangs⟩ *foundation*
(HS); **áhsę** **–či** –. **–(i)har** –: áhsę θkáhe⁷r
⟨three again-it-hung⟩ *thirteen* (R);
čá·⁷nahk **–či** –. **–(i)har** –: čá·⁷nahk θkáhe⁷r ⟨seven again-it-hung⟩ *seventeen*
(R); **ę́·či** **–či** –. **–(i)har** –: ę́·či θkáhe⁷r
⟨one again-it-hung⟩ *eleven* (R); **hę́⁷-
tahk** **–či** –. **–(i)har** –: hę́⁷tahk θkáhe⁷r
⟨four again-it-hung⟩ *fourteen* (R);
né·krę·⁷ **–či** –. **–(i)har** –: né·krę·⁷ θkáhe⁷r
⟨eight again-it-hung⟩ *eighteen* (R);
né·kti· **–či** –. **–(i)har** –: né·kti· θkáhe⁷r
⟨two again-it-hung⟩ *twelve* (R); **níhręh**
–či –. **–(i)har** –: níhręh θkáhe⁷r ⟨nine
again-it-hung⟩ *nineteen* (R); **úhya⁷k**
–či –. **–(i)har** –: úhya⁷k θkáhe⁷r ⟨six
again-it-hung⟩ *sixteen* (R); **wísk** **–či** –.
–(i)har –: wísk θkáhe⁷r ⟨five again-it-
hung⟩ *fifteen* (R); **ę́·či** **ti+yah+
či** –. **–(i)har** –: ę́·či thweθkáhe⁷r ⟨one so-
there-again-it-hung⟩ *1:30 (thirty minutes past one o'clock)* (R); **kwęhs**
–a⁷rihwharaku –: kwęhs aryu⁷riwha-
rá·kwęk ⟨no unknown-it-itself-matter-
hang-undo⟩ *it is illicit* (HS).

–(i)har – be a member, be interested. *v.s.-
a.i.* ráha⁷r ⟨he-hung⟩ *he belongs to or
has membership in (it), he is present
at a meeting or assembly, he is one of
a party* (H 2892), *he is a member* (M
87), *he is interested* (HS).

–(i)har -{dative III} enroll (on the tribal
rolls). *v.s.-t.* wa⁷khehà·rę⁷ ⟨fact-I=
another-hung-for⟩ *I enrolled someone
(on the tribal rolls)* (R).

–(i)har -{dative III} executioner, hangman. *dv.n.s.* rahà·ręh ‹he-hangs-for› *executioner, hangman* (HS).

-(i)harahkw - hanger. *dv.n.s.* yeharáhkhwa⁷ ‹one-hangs-instrument› *hanger* (R).

-(i)haraku - take down. *v.s.-t.* rahará·kwahs ‹he-hang-undoes› *he takes it down* (HS).

-(i)hara'nye⁷ - go toward. *v.s.-a.i.* rahará·⁷nye⁷θ ‹he-hangs-going along› *he is going toward* (RC 35:44).

-(i)harawę'nye⁷ - be in the midst. *v.s.-a.i.* kaharawę́·⁷nye⁷ ‹it-hangs-much-going along› *it is in the midst* (RC 27:2).

-ihaw - bring. *v.r.-t.* See: **-(ę)haw -.** Occurs when the repetitive prefix is present.

-iha⁷T - be in a line, be in a row. *v.r.-a.i.* hab: -, pnt: -ɸ, stat: -ę, prog: -ę'nye⁷-, prp: -, dst: -, caus: -, rvs: -, dat: -, inc.-ɸ-pat. Related to the enclitic **#ha⁷nę⁷t. -ne -. -iha⁷nę'nye⁷ -:** nekęha⁷né·⁷nye⁷ ‹two-it-is in a line-going along› *lining up in twos* (R); **-tkwari = ha⁷T -:** wahratkwaríha⁷t ‹fact-he-blood-was in a line› *he drained blood* (RC 8:11).

-(i)he - put on. *v.r.-a.i.* hab: -h, pnt: -, stat: -·, prog: -, prp: -, dst: -, caus: -, rvs: -, dat: -, inc.-ɸ-pat. rúhe· *he put on* (RC 8:34); **-kerhihe -:** yukyerhíhe· ‹it-body-put on› *bodies were put on* (RC 8:12); **-nę⁷yeckwihe -:** kanę⁷yeckwíheh ‹it-nest-puts on› *it perches* (RC 7:10); **-yah -. -(ę)ta⁷rihe -:** wekata⁷ríheh ‹thither-it-head-puts on› *it puts head back on* (RC 34:14); **kwęhs**

-(i)he -: kwęhs aryúhek ‹no unknown-it-put on› *untimely* (HS); **kwęhs -yah -. -(i)he -:** kwęhs yaryúhek ‹no thither-unknown-it-put on› *undue* (HS); **kwęhs -yah+ne -. -(i)he -:** kwęhs ya⁷naryúhek ‹no thither-apart-unknown-it-put on› *it is incomprehensible* (HS).

-ihey -/ -(i)hey -/ -ęhey -/ -kęhey - die. *v. r.-a.i.* hab: -ęhs, pnt: -⁷, stat: -ę, prog: -, prp: -ęhθre- ~ -ęhθe-, dst: -, caus: -ahT-, rvs: -, dat: -, inc.-ɸ-pat. The form **-kęhey -** occurs following the reflexive and semireflexive morphemes, with incorporated noun roots and in compound verb stems. The form **-ęhey -** occurs following third person patient prefixes. The form **-(i) = hey -** occurs with the habitual aspect when no modal affixes or derivational suffixes are present. The form **-ihey -** occurs elsewhere. rawęhè·yę *he is dead: corpse* (RC 26:33) [Lawson «Whaharia» 'Dead'], kęhè·yę *death, mortality* (HS) [Gallatin «kuhhayyuh» 'Dead, Death'], rahè·yęhs *he is dying* (R), wa⁷kęhe⁷y *it died* (RC 15:7), ękíhe⁷y *I will die* (RC 3:18), kiheyęhθre⁷ *I am going to die* (RC 3:17), akayaiheyęhθek *that they be going to die* (RC 3:21); **-iheyahT -:** yękwęhè·yaht ‹we-die-caused› *our mortality* (HS), ręheyáhtha⁷ ‹he-die-causes› *it deadens him* (HS); **-kęhe = yę -:** natkęhè·yę ‹one=another-died› *one debilitates another* (HS); **-iheyę⁷ -:** kęhè·yę⁷θ ‹it-die-begins› *it is dying*

(HS): **ti** –. –**ęhey** –: tiwęhè·yę ‹so-it-died› *so it died* (RC 8:48); –**kęheyę?na** = **yę(T)** –: rakęheyę́?nayę? ‹he-die-caused-lay› *he is lying there dying* (R); –**(a)hk̲a̲ra̲kęhey** –: yuhkarakęhà·yę ‹it-bark-died› *bark has been dead* (RC 26:3); –**ę'nakęheya?T** –: węʔnakęheyá?thaʔ ‹it-day-die-causes› *blast* (HS); –**rihwa̲kęhey** –: waʔkarihwakę́heʔy ‹fact-it-matter-died› *thing died* (RC 26:9); –**?wahkęheyę?** –: kaʔwahkęhè·yęʔθ ‹it-meat-die-begins› *it mortifies* (HS); –**atkęheyę?nayę'nahkw** –: yętkęheyę́ʔnayę́ʔnáhkhwaʔ ‹one-oneself-die-cause-lay-in-strument› *hospital, infirmary* (HS); –**atkęheyę?nęhawi?** = **nahkw** –: yętkęheyę́ʔnęhawiʔnáhkhwaʔ ‹one-oneself-die-cause-carries-instrument› *litter, stretcher* (HS); –**ne** –. –**ę** = **heyęhsturę** –: neyawęheyęhstù·rę· ‹two-it-die-'ness-split› *cadaverous* (HS); **á·** **tha** –. –**ihey** –: á· thahsíheʔy ‹aw unusual-unknown-you-die› *aw, you might as well die* (L 53); **kwęhs** –**iheyęhθe** –: kwęhs akęheyę́hθek ‹no unknown-it-die-going to› *it is undying* (HS), kwęhs ahręheyę́hθek ‹no unknown-he-die-going to› *he is immortal* (HS).

–**iheyàhT** – mortality. *dv.n.s.* yękwęhè·yaht ‹we-die-caused› *our mortality* (HS).

–**iheyę?** – be dying. *v.s.-a.i.* kęhè·yęʔθ ‹it-die-begins› *it is dying* (HS).

–**(i)hę** medial locative. *n.r.sfx.* The form –ihę occurs after roots and stems that end in a single laryngeal or certain consonant clusters. The form –hę occurs elsewhere. –**(a)hahihę**: uhahíhę ‹path-in middle of› *in the middle of the road, path or way* (H 2484); –**(a)** = **hę?nihę**: uhęʔníhę ‹clearing-in middle of› *in the middle of the meadow, in the very center of the meadow* (H 2484); –**(a)hę?thę** –: wahę́ʔthę ‹it-front-in middle of› *in the middle of* (RC 25:12); –**a?wna?wthęha?**: uʔwnaʔwthę́haʔ ‹earth-earth-in middle of-customarily› *of the wilds, from the wilderness* (RC 18:1); –**a?wthę**: á·ʔwthę ‹earth-in middle of› *waste, a wild* (HS); –**či** –. –**hsu?kwihę**: θkahsuʔkwíhę ‹again-it-finger-middle of› *middle of finger* (RC 30:44); –**(ę)?teyhę**: uʔtéyhę ‹crowd-middle of› *publicly* (HS); –**hehnihę**: uhehníhę ‹field-in middle of› *in the middle of the field, one half of the field or plot* (H 2484); –**(i)y** = **hęhihę**: uyhęhíhę ‹river-in the middle of› *in the middle of river* (RC 26:20); –**nęčihę**: unęčíhę ‹potato-in the middle of› *in the middle of the potato or tuber, one half of the potato or tuber* (H 2484); –**nęhshę**: kanę́hshę ‹it-house-in the middle of› *in the middle of the house* (modern) (R), unę́hshę ‹house-in the middle of› *in the middle of the house, in the middle of the floor* (H 2484); –**nęhskhę**: kanę́hskhę ‹it-house-in the middle of› *in the middle of the house* (archaic) (H 2484); –**nęhsnihę**: unęhsníhę ‹seed-in the middle of› *in the middle of the grain or seed* (H 2484); –**nęθihę**: unęθíhę ‹potato-in the middle of› *in the middle of the potato or tuber, one half of the potato or tuber* (H 2484); –**nęthę**: unę́·thę ‹hill-in the middle of› *halfway* (R); –**ręthę**: urę́·thę ‹tree-in the middle of› *middle of tree* (RC 10:5); **tahuré·tik a?wthęha·?** ‹chicken earth-in middle of-characterized by› *pheasant* (L 35); **tha+ne** –. –**kčihę**: thaʔnyukčíhę ‹unusual-apart-it-dish-in middle of› *half a dish* (RC 18:3), thaʔnyukθíhę ‹unusual-apart-it-dish-in middle of› *middle of dish* (RC 20:1); **tha+ne** –. –**wenęthę** –: thaʔnyuwenę́·thę ‹unusual-apart-it-measure of liquid-middle of› *pint* (HS).

-(i)hereT – carry away, carry off. *v.r.-a.i.* hab: -ha', pnt: -ɸ, stat: -ę, prog: -, prp: -, dst: -, caus: -, rvs: -, dat: -, inc.-ɸ-ag. rahęré·tha' *he carries off, it bears away* (HS). wa'kayę'nathę́·re·t *they took another away* (HS). wahrahę́·re·t *he carried away* (RC 25:13); -t -. -hęreT -: nakahę́·re·t ‹hither-it-carried away› *May* (R); ti -. -hęreT -: tihruhęré·'nę ‹so-he-carried away› *he had been taken from* (RC 8:45); -(ę)'tikęhrhęreT -: ra'tikęrhęré·tha' ‹he-mind-carries away› *he is alluring* (HS); -nęhsnihęreT -: ranęhsnihęré·tha' ‹he-seed-carries away› *he carries away the grain* (H 2484).

-(i)hkʷa'T – pick up. *v.r.-t.* hab: -ha', pnt: -ɸ, stat: -ę, prog: -, prp: -, dst: -, caus: -, rvs: -, dat: -, n-inc. The root occurs optionally with and without the dualic prefix, with no apparent difference in meaning. wa'kíhkwa't *I picked it up* (L 18), wahsíhkwa't *you picked it up* (L 18); -ne -. -(i)hkʷa'T -: nehrúhkwa'nę ‹apart-he-picked up› *he lifts it, he upholds it* (HS), wa'thráhkwa't ‹fact-apart-he-picked up› *he picked it up* (L 18), wa'chíhkwa't ‹fact-apart-you-picked up› *you picked it up* (L 18), wa'tkíhkwa't ‹fact-apart-I-picked up› *I picked it up* (L 18), nękíhkwa't ‹apart-prediction-I-pick up› *I will pick it up* (L 18); -t -. -(i)hkʷa'T -: načíhkwa't ‹hither-you-pick up› *pick it up!* (L 18); -yah -. -(i)hkʷa'T -: wehráhkwa'nę ‹thither-he-picked up› *he*

yearns for it (RC 34:3).

-ihn – cloth, parchment, patch, piece, shred; buckskin, skin. *n.r.* n-poss., inc., n.sfx. -eh/-ę'. The meaning *skin* occurs only when this root is incorporated. úhneh *parchment, patch, piece (of cloth or leather), shred* (HS), *cloth* (AW 50), kę́hnę' *buckskin* (HS); -ihnar -: ręhnar ‹he-patch-is in› *he patches, he pieces it together* (HS), úhnareh ‹skin-be in› *pieces of leather, scraps of leather* (RC 8:3); -ihna = tyenę -: akęhnatyè·nę' ‹unknown-it-hide-obtain› *that it get into skin* (RC 32:12), ręhnatyè·nęh ‹he-hide-obtains› *he penetrates the skin* (HS); -ihna = węhte -: yuhnawę́htę' ‹it-cloth-is between two things› *a piece of cloth (skin) is between (two others)* (H 2892); -či -. -ihnakwahsT -: θkęhnakwáhsna' ‹again-it-skin-is good› *skin was good and strong again* (RC 11:28); -ne -. -ihnęhya'k -: nehruhnęhyá'kę ‹apart-he-piece of leather-crossed over› *(he has a leather) scarf (over left shoulder)* (AG); -ne -. -ih = nuhrarak -: nehręhnúhraraks ‹two-he-skin-presses› *he pinches* (HS); -ti -. -ihnakarahrę -: tyehnakaráhrę· ‹so-one-skin-is thin› *one's skin is so delicate* (RC 3:57); -ihn - -ahčakewa'T -: úhneh yęhčakyewá'tha' ‹cloth one-fist-wipe-causes› *napkin* (HS); kę' -ihnę = ti -: kę' yehnę́·tih ‹where one-skin-makes› *tannery* (HS).

-ihn - -ahčakewa'T – napkin. *dv.n.s.* úhneh yęhčakyewá'tha' ‹cloth one-fist-wipe-causes› *napkin* (HS).

-**ihnar**- patch, piece together. *v.s.-t.* rǫ́hnar ‹he-patch-is in› *he patches, pieces it together* (HS).

-**ihnar**- pieces of leather, scraps of leather. *n.s.* úhnareh ‹skin-be in› *pieces of leather, scraps of leather* (RC 8:3).

-(i)**hnęk**- send for, summon. *v.r.-t.* hab: -s, pnt: -, stat: -, prog: -, prp: -, dst: -, caus: -, rvs: -, dat: -, n-inc. ráhnęks *he summons, he sends for it* (R); -**yah**-. -**ihnęk**-: weyę'na'níhnęks ‹thither-one=another-sends for› *one sends for another* (HS).

-(i)**hnya**- wear; wear around neck. *v.r.-a.i.* hab: -, pnt: -', stat: -ę, prog: -ęha'nye'-, prp: -, dst: -, caus: -, rvs: -, dat: -, n-inc. rúhnyę *he wore* (RC 35:14), ęhráhnya' *he will wear* (R); -(i)**hnyahθ**-: uhnyáhθeh ‹wear around one's neck-?'› *cape, mantle* (HS); -(i)**hnyahčiyu**-: kahnyahčí·yu· ‹it-wear around one's neck-?'-is great› *large cape* (H-notebook) (alternative: kahnyahθí·yu· (H-notebook)); -(i)**h**= **nyahst**-: uhnyáhsteh ‹wear around one's neck-'ness› *necklace* (RC 3:30); -a'**nihnyahsT**-: yę'nihnyáhstha' ‹one-oneself-wears around neck-cause› *stole* (HS); -**či**-. -(ę)**tihnyęha'nye'**-: θwętihnyęhá·'nye' ‹again-it-itself-wore-going along› *she is wearing* (RC 3:30).

-(i)**hnyahθ**- cape, mantle. *n.s.* uhnyáhθeh ‹wear around neck-?'› *cape, mantle* (HS).

-(i)**hnyahst**- necklace. *n.s.* uhnyáhsteh ‹wear around neck-'ness› *necklace* (RC 3:30).

-**ihr**- drink. *v.r.-t.* hab: -ha', pnt: -φ, stat: -ę, prog: -, prp: -, dst: -, caus: -a'T-, rvs: -, dat: -, n-inc. The form -**ehr**- occurs following the masculine singular and neuter singular agent pronominal prefixes. The form -**ihr**- occurs elsewhere. čír *drink!* (R), kírha' *I drink* (R), rérha' *he drinks* (RC 21:8), ęyáir *one will drink* (RC 22:2), wá'kir *I drank* (R), wáhrer *he drank* (RC 6:9); -**ïhra?T**-: rehrá'tha' ‹he-drink-causes› *he waters (the animals)* (HS), wa'na'níhra't ‹fact-one=another-drink-caused› *one made another drink* (RC 30:55); -**ïhra?nahnę**-: wa'-kayę'na'nihra'náhnę' ‹fact-they=another-drink-caused-much› *they gave another much to drink* (RC 21:4); -**akwahst?**-**ha?** -**ihr**-: yukwáhst'ę ha' yaírha' ‹it-be good-began the one-drinks› *drinkable* (HS); **pì·ye?** -**ihr**-: pì·ye' wakíhrę ‹beer I-drank› *I drank beer* (HS).

-**ïhra?T**- water. *v.s.-t.* rehrá'tha' ‹he-drink-causes› *he waters (the animals)* (HS).

-(i)**hra?T**- bury. *v.r.-t.* hab: -e', pnt: -φ, stat: -, prog: -, prp: -, dst: -ę-, caus: -, rvs: -, dat: -, inc.-φ-pat. wa'na'níhra't *one buried another* (R), wahrahrá'nek *he had buried it* (R); **yah+ne**-. -**a?nehra?nę**-: ya'nęθwa'nehrá'nę·' ‹thither-apart-prediction-you-yourselves-bury-much› *you will conceal yourselves there* (RC 33:8); -**hnawah**= **ra?T**-: wahrahnawahrá'nahk ‹fact-he-current of water-buried› *he went against the current* (RC 12:29).

-**ihreks** mountain lion. *n.r.* n-poss., n-inc., n.sfx. -φ. kę́hreks *mountain lion* (AW 97); -**ihreks** -**čisnuhkw**-: kę́hreks učísnuhkweh ‹it-mountain lion spot› *leopard* (HS).

-**ihreks** -**čisnuhkw**- leopard. *n.s.* kę́hreks učísnuhkweh ‹it-mountain lion spot› *leopard* (HS).

-**ihrę**- say. *v.r.-t.* See: -a'nę-.

-**ihsak**- look for, search, seek. *v.r.-t.* hab:

-s, pnt: -ɸ, stat: -ę, prog: -ęha'nye'-, prp: -he-, dst: -hę-, caus: -T-, rvs: -, dat: -, inc.-ɸ-pat. The form -ehsak- occurs following third person singular pronominals, the imperative plural pronominal, transitive pronominals ending in y, the third person masculine singular agent pronominal, and the first and second person plural marker. The form -ihsak- occurs elsewhere. réhsaks *he searches for it* (HS), wahréhsa·k *he sought* (RC 13:5), ę'nwéhsa·k *you and I will seek* (RC 3:79), rawehsakęhá·'nye' *he is going seeking* (RC 12:24), kayę'na'níhsaks *they seek another* (RC 26:14), čhiyéhsa·k *you all go seek!* (RC 29:10); –čihkwnihsak –: nakčihkwníhsa·k ‹you=me-louse-seek› *seek my lice!* (RC 27:4), wa'na'čihkwníhsa·k ‹fact-one=another-louse-sought› *one sought another's lice* (RC 27:4); –či= nę'therihsak –: račinę'theríhsaks ‹he-curl-seeks› *he is looking for a curl: he is looking for a curly-haired person* (H 2484); –ęnęhkwa'črihsakhę –: węnęhkwa'črihsá·khęh ‹it-medicine-'ness-seeks-many› *she went looking for medicines* (AW 97); –hnihsakhe –: wahrahnihsá·khe' ‹fact-he-news-sought-going to› *he went looking for news* (L 12); –ičihsak –: ęhsičíhsa·k ‹prediction-you-fish-seek› *you will go (spear)fishing* (R); –kčihsak –: rakčíhsaks ‹he-dish-seeks› *he seeks dish* (H-notebook); –nęhkwa'črihsakhe –: wahranęhkwa'črihsá·khe' ‹fact-he-med-icine-'ness-sought-going to› *he went looking for medicine* (L 3); –nęčih= sakhę –: kanęčihsá·khęh ‹it-potato-seeks-many› *it seeks some potatoes* (RC 27:16); –yękwirihsak –: wa'kaye-yękwiríhsa·k ‹fact-they-wood-sought› *they look for wood* (AW 55); –yę'= kwarihsakhe –: wahrayę'kwarihsá·khe' ‹fact-he-smoke-sought-going to› *he went looking for smoke* (RC 12: 22); –'čkawihsakhe –: θwa'čkawihsá·kheh ‹you-branch-seek-going to› *you all go looking for branches* (RC 29:7); –a'nekhwihsakT –: wa'nekhwihsáktha' ‹it-itself-meal-seek-causes› *pasturage* (HS); –a'nęnhihsakT –: yę'nęnhihsáktha' ‹one-oneself-be alive-seek-causes› *occupation, a trade* (HS); –a'nę'tikęhrihsak –: ra'nę'tikęhríhsaks ‹he-himself-mind-seeks› *he searches his mind* (HS); –nę'r – –ičihsakT –: unę'reh yečihsáktha' ‹net one-fish-seek-causes› *fish net* (SH 375).

-(i)hsa̲'nę – bury, cover with something, cover with earth, hide. *v.r.-t.* hab: -, pnt: -·', stat: -', prog: -, prp: -, dst: -, caus: -hT-, rvs: -, dat: -, inc.-ɸ-pat. wahráhsa'nę·' *he buried it* (RC 34:5), ęhsihsá'nę·' *you will hide it* (MG 106:41); –či -. –(i)hsa̲'nęhnaku –: čehsa'nęhná·ku' ‹again-fact-one-bury-cause-undid› *one unburied it* (RC 34: 10); –(ę)ta'ra̲hsa̲'nę –: ruta'rahsá'nęhk ‹he-head-buried› *he buried his head* (RC 34:10); –nęha̲hsa'nę –: kanęháhsa'nę' ‹it-corn-buried› *one has buried corn: it is buried corn* (H 2484); –rih=

Tuscarora Pronunciation Key:
/a/ law; /e/ hat; /i/ pizza; /u/ tune; /ę/ hint; /č/ cheese; /h/ hoe; /m/ mother; /s/ same; /t/ do (before a vowel y, or w), too (elsewhere); /k/ gale (before a vowel y or w), kale (elsewhere); /n/ inhale (before a consonant or word-final), note (elsewhere), /r/ hiss (before a consonant or word-final), run (trilled as in Italian, elsewhere); /w/ cuff (before a consonant other than y or word-final), way (elsewhere); /y/ fish (before a consonant or word-final), you (elsewhere), /θ/ thing; /'/ (the sound between the vowels in unh-unh); /·/ long vowel, /́/ high pitch; /̀/ low pitch.

wihsa?nę -:   wa'?kayerihwihsá'?nę·'?
‹fact-they-matter-buried› *they made a
pledge* (AW 101): -a?nwętahsa?nę -:
ru'?nwętahsá'?nę'? ‹he-himself-word-
buried› *he is monotonous* (HS); ti-.
-(i)hsa?nęhkwakęhyaT -: tikahsa'?nęh-
kwakęhya·t ‹so-it-bury-instrument-is at
the edge of› *as far as the graves lay*
(RC 3:74).
-ihsa?nę? -[1]/-ihse? -[2] be carried on shoulders, ride bareback. *v.r.-t.* hab: [1]-θ,
pnt: [1]-φ, stat: [2]-φ, prog: -, prp: -, dst:
-, caus: -, rvs: -, dat: -, n-inc. The
form -ihse? - occurs with the stative
aspect. The form -ihsa?nę? - occurs
elsewhere. Hewitt & Smith, however,
cite one anomalous form: ęhrúhse'? *he
will ride*, with -ihse? - in a punctual
aspect construction. rúhse'? *he rides a
horse* (HS), akęhsá'?nę'? *that it ride
bareback* (RC 26:19), wa'?na'?nihsá'?-
nę'? *one rode another bareback* (RC
26:21); -ihsa?nę'nye? -: yakuhse'?nę́·'?-
nye'? ‹one-is carried on shoulders-go-
ing along› *calvary* (HS); ti-.-ihse? -:
tyę'?na'?níhse'? ‹so-one=another-was
carried on shoulders› *one had ridden
another bareback* (RC 26:21); -a=
čhe?T -: račhé'?tha'? ‹he-himself-be carried on shoulders-causes› *he causes
himself to be mounted* (H-notebook);
-ačhe?naku -: račhe'?ná·kwahs ‹he-himself-be carried on shoulders-cause-undoes› *he dismounts* (H-notebook).
-ihsa?nę'nye? - calvary. *dv.n.s.* yakuhsa'?-
nę́·'?nye'? ‹one-is carried on shoulders-
going along› *calvary* (HS).
-(i)hsę - be homely, be ugly. *v.r.-a.i.* hab:
-, pnt: -, stat: -h, prog: -, prp: -, dst: -,
caus: -hT-, rvs: -, dat: I (-'?θc-/-'?θ-),
n-inc. kíhsęh *I am homely, I am ugly*
(R), síhsęh *you are homely, you are
ugly* (R), ráhsęh *he is homely, he is
ugly* (R); -(i)hsę -{dative I}: ruhsę́'?θc'?

‹he-was ugly-for› *he takes offense*
(HS), načhę́'?θeh ‹one=another-is ugly-
for› *one hates another* (HS); -ačhę -
{dative I}: neyęčhę́'?θeh ‹two-one-
themselves-are ugly-for› *the two of
them are enemies, the two of them
hate each other* (HS); -a'nwętahsęhT -:
ra'?nwętahsę́htha'? ‹he-himself-word-be
ugly-causes› *he boasts, he mocks*
(HS).
-(i)hsę -{dative I} take offense. *v.s.-a.i.*
ruhsę́'?θe'? ‹he-was ugly-for› *he takes
offense* (HS), načhę́'?θeh ‹one=an-
other-is ugly-for› *one hates another*
(HS).
íhskah not (RC 30:62). *part.* (also: ih-
skáh (R)).
íhskah -a?čtehrihsT - ignore, leave alone.
v.s.-t. íhskah wa'?kačtéhriht ‹not fact-I-
become involved with› *I ignored it*
(R), íhskah wa'?kheyačtéhriht ‹not
fact-I=another-become involved with›
*I left another alone, I did not bother
another* (R).
ihskáhkye rarely, seldom (HS); occasionally, someday (RC 35:18). *part.*
-(i)hskahręw - mouth. *n.r.* inaln: kih-
skahrę̀·weh *my mouth* (R), inc., n.sfx.
-eh. Some speakers of modern Tuscarora use a variant of this root that
lacks the final *w*, e.g., uhskáhrę'?
mouth, kihskáhrę'? *my mouth*. The
form -ihskahręw - occurs only following the first and second person singular pronominal prefixes. The form
-hskahręw - occurs elsewhere. Historically, this noun root is a compound
of PNI * -hs - *mouth* plus the verb root
-kahręw - *be an opening*. Although
this compound is treated as an indivisible whole in Tuscarora, its historical origin as a noun-verb compound explains the lack of an overt
verb root in the stem meaning *gape*.

uhskahrę·weh *mouth* (R) [Gallatin «oskawruh-weigh» 'Mouth']; **–ne –**. **–(i)hskahręwahT –**:nehruhskahręwáh-tha⁹ ‹apart-he-mouth-causes› *he gapes, he yawns* (HS); **–ne –**. **–(i)hskahrę = wahT –**. **–hsk –**: nehruhskahręwahthá⁹-θkę· ‹apart-he-mouth-causes-easily› *yawner* (HS); **–ačkahręwuhar –**: ručkah-ręwúhar ‹he-himself-mouth-washes› *he gargles* (HS).

–(i)hskwari – be feeble, be old (female). *v.r.-a.i.* hab: -h, pnt: -, stat: -⁹, prog: -, prp: -, dst: -, caus: -, rvs: -, dat: -, inc.-ɸ-pat. The form **–ihskwari –** occurs following the first and second person singular agent pronominal prefixes. The initial vowel behaves like an "epenthetic" vowel as shown by the fact that the accent unexpectedly falls on root-medial *a* in the penultimate syllable of the first word cited below. It is perhaps the case that all instances of root-initial (i) have the same origin as other "epenthetic" vowels. The form **–hskwari –** occurs elsewhere. kih-skwà·rih *I am feeble, I am old (female)* (R); **–(i)hskwari –**: káhskwari⁹ ‹it-is feeble› *old woman* (idiolectally also: káhskwarih) (R) [Lawson «Cusquerre» 'Old Woman']; **–(i)hskwa = ri –.#áh**: kahskwari⁹áh ‹it-is feeble-little› *little old woman* (RC 26:17); **–(i)hskwari –.#ú⁹y**: kahskwari⁹ú⁹y ‹it-is feeble-big› *very old woman* (RC 6: 18); **–nęhahskwari –**: unęháhskwari⁹ ‹corn-be feeble› *the mother-corn, that is, the corn from which a certain kind*

may have been derived: corn of an older growth (H 2484); ti –. **–ęnhuh = skwarihę –**: tiwęnhuhskwaríhę· ‹so-it-be alive-cover-is feeble-much› *breath quivered* (RC 21:8).

–(i)hskwari – old woman. *dv.n.s* káh-skwari⁹ ‹it-is feeble› *old woman* (R) (idiolectally also: káhskwarih (R)) [Lawson «Cusquerre» 'Old Woman'].

–(i)hskwari –.#áh little old woman. *dv.n.s* kahskwari⁹áh ‹it-is old woman-little› *little old woman* (RC 26:17).

–(i)hskwari –.#ú⁹y very old woman. *dv. n.s* kahskwari⁹ú⁹y ‹it-is feeble-big› *very old woman* (RC 6:18).

–(i)hsnahnęhkw – materials. *dv.n.s* yeh-snahnę́hkhwa⁹ ‹one-use-cause-instrument› *materials* (HS).

–(i)hsT – employ (something), use. *v.r.-t.* hab: -ha⁹, pnt: -ɸ, stat: -, prog: -, prp: -ha'nye⁹-, dst: -ha⁹nę-, caus: -ahT-, rvs: -, dat: -, inc.-ɸ-pat. The form **–ihsT –** occurs following the first and second person singular agent pronominal prefixes. The form **–hsT –** occurs elsewhere. ráhstha⁹ *he employs it, he uses it* (R), wá⁹kihst *I used it* (R), ęhsihst *you will use it* (RC 30:28), wa⁹kayehsthá⁹nę⁹ *they served (e.g. food)* (R), wa⁹kayehsthá·⁹nye⁹ *they are using it* (R); **–(i)hsnahnęhkw –**: yehsnahnę́hkhwa⁹ ‹one-use-cause-instrument› *materials* (HS); **–ačT –**: ę̀·yęčt ‹prediction-one-oneself-use› *one will use it* (RC 15:9), yę́čtha⁹ ‹one-oneself-uses› *weapon* (HS), wáčtha⁹ ‹it-itself-uses› *it uses it* (RC 12:15);

Tuscarora Pronunciation Key:
/a/ law; /e/ hat; /i/ pizza; /u/ tune; /ę/ hint; /č/ cheese; /h/ hoe; /m/ mother; /s/ same; /t/ do (before a vowel y, or w), too (elsewhere); /k/ gale (before a vowel y or w), kale (elsewhere); /n/ inhale (before a consonant or word-final), note (elsewhere), /r/ hiss (before a consonant or word-final), run (trilled as in Italian, elsewhere); /w/ cuff (before a consonant other than y or word-final), way (elsewhere); /y/ fish (before a consonant or word-final), you (elsewhere), /θ/ thing; /⁹/ (the sound between the vowels in unh-unh); /·/ long vowel, /´/ high pitch; /`/ low pitch.

-**ačnahkw** -: ęyęčnáhkhwek ‹prediction-one-oneself-use-instrument› *one
will use it for* (RC 6:15); -**aʔθrihar**=
huhsT -: yę·ʔθriharhúhstha·ʔ ‹one-aim-
hang-cause-uses› *tomahawk* (HS);
-**nęhkwaʔčrawęhsT** -: ękayenęhkwa·ʔ-
črà·węhst ‹prediction-they-medicine-
'ness-possess-use› *they will use their
medicine* (RC 10:7); **theʔ t** -. -**(i)h**=
snahkw -: theʔ nakahsnáhkęk ‹not
hither-unknown-it-use-instrument› *it is
worn out, it is worthless* (R).

-**(i)hstkę?** - jilt, reject. *v.r.-t.* hab: -θ, pnt:
-, stat: -ę, prog: -, prp: -, dst: -, caus:
-, rvs: -, dat: -, inc.-ɸ-pat. ráhstkę·ʔθ
he rejects it (HS), na·ʔníhstkę·ʔθ *one
jilts another* (H-notebook); -**ęhrih**=
stkęʔT -: ręhrihstkę·ʔtha·ʔ ‹he-soil-jilt-
causes› *he enriches land* (H-notebook); -**rihwahstkę?** -: rarihwáhstkę·ʔθ
‹he-matter-jilts› *he jilts the matter* (H-
notebook), urihwahstkę·ʔę ‹matter-
jilted› *a jilted matter, or one not fav-
orably received, or one that has not
been received but discarded, and dis-
owned* (H-notebook).

-**(i)hstkukr** - be a filthy lout, be profligate. *v.r.-s.i.* stat: -e·ʔ, prog: -, prp: -,
dst: -, caus: -, rvs: -, dat: -, n-inc.
kihstkú·kre·ʔ *I am a filthy lout* (SH
375); rahstkú·kreh *he is profligate*
(HS).

-**(i)hstr** - stature. *n.r.* n-poss., inc., n.sfx.
-eh. úhstreh *stature* (HS); -**(i)hstraʔ**=
nihr -: wa·ʔkihstrá·ʔnir ‹fact-I-stature-
stood up› *I sat down* (PC) (*East:* wa·ʔ-
kstrá·ʔnir *I was seated* (R)); -**(i)h**=
straʔnihr -: na·ʔnihstrá·ʔnihč ‹one=an-
other-stature-stands up› *one inducts
another* (HS).

-**(i)hstraʔnihr** - be seated, be sitting. *v.s.-
a.i. West.* wa·ʔkihstrá·ʔnir ‹fact-I-X-
stood up› *I sat down* (PC) (*East.:* wa·ʔ-
kstrá·ʔnir *I was seated* (R)).

-**(i)hstraʔnihr** - induct. *v.s.-t.* na·ʔnih-
strá·ʔnihč ‹one=another-X-stands up›
one inducts another (HS).

-**(i)hsuʔku** - finger. *n.r.* inaln: kihsu·ʔ-
kwę·ʔkye *my finger* (PC), inc., n.sfx.
-ch. *West.* kihsu·ʔkwę·ʔkye *my finger*
(PC) (*East.:* ksu·ʔkwę·ʔkye (R)), sih-
su·ʔkwę·ʔkye *your finger* (PC) (*East.:*
sehsu·ʔkwę·ʔkye (R)).

-**(i)hsw** - back. *n.r.* inaln: kihswę·ʔkye *my
back* (PC), inc., n.sfx. -eh. *West.*
kihswę·ʔkye *my back* (PC) (*East.:*
kswę·ʔkye (R)).

-**(i)hsʔa** - exhaust, finish, use up. *v.r.-t.*
hab: -hs, pnt: -·ʔ, stat: -ę, prog: -, prp:
-, dst: -, caus: -hT-, rvs: -, dat: III (-ti-
/-ę-), inc.-ɸ-ag./pat. Hewitt gives two
alternative forms for the first person
singular habitual of this root. číhsʔa·
finish it (food)! (L 56), íksʔahs *I eat
up* (H-notebook), kíhsʔahs *I eat up*
(H-notebook), ráhsʔahs *he exhausts it*
(HS), *he finishes eating (as in he usually finishes eating by 2 o'clock)* (L
55), wa·ʔkíhsʔa·ʔ *I finished* (R), wa·ʔ-
káhsʔa·ʔ *it finished* (RC 10:5); -**(i)hs**=
ʔahT -: yuhsʔáhnę ‹it-exhaust-caused›
bulk, totality (HS); -**(a)hę'nihsʔa** -: ra-
hę·ʔníhsʔahs ‹he-clearing-finishes› *he
completes, he finishes the meadow
(i.e., the work he has to do on it, as
gathering the hay, plowing or harrowing it, etc.)* (H 2484); -**ahskwihsʔa** -:
wahrahskwíhsʔa·ʔ ‹fact-he-hard
ground-finished› *he finished (preparing) field* (RC 5:21); -**atheʔčrihsʔa** -:
wa·ʔęthe·ʔčríhsʔa·ʔ ‹fact-one-pound-
'ness-finished› *one finished powder*
(RC 3:54); -**nęhsihsʔa** -: ranęhsíhsʔahs
‹he-house-exhausts› *he finishes the
house* (H-notebook); -**rihwihsʔa** -: yu-
rihwíhsʔę ‹it-matter-exhausted› *decree*
(HS), rarihwíhsʔahs ‹he-matter-ex-
hausts› *he makes a compact* (H-note-

book), *he agrees, he researches, he orders to charge* (HS); **-rihwihs?a-** {dative III}: na?rihwihs?á·tih ‹one=another-matter-exhausts-for› *one enjoins another* (HS); **-ta?nihs?a-**: wa?nyeta?níhs?a·? ‹fact-two-one-village-exhausted› *the two of them finished camp* (RC 30:28); **-?wahrihs?a-**: yu?wahríhs?ę ‹it-meat-exhausted› *meat is eaten up* (RC 17:4); **-athwaritihs?a-**: ęhsathwaritíhs?a·? ‹prediction-you-yourself-backpack-exhaust› *you will finish backpack* (RC 3:38); **-atkerhihs=?a-**: wa?ętkyerhíhs?a·? ‹fact-one-oneself-body-finish-ed› *one grew to adulthood* (RC 3:37); **-a'naθnęhkwihs?a-**: wa?ę?naθnęhkwíhs?a·? ‹fact-one-oneself-burden-finished› *one finished packing* (RC 3:39); **-a'netyahstihs?a-**: čę?netyahstíhs?a·? ‹again-fact-one-oneself-produce-'ness-finished› *one finished redressing* (RC 3:59); **-a'nę=kʷehstihs?a-**: ra?nękwehstíhs?ahs ‹he-himself-human-'ness-exhausts› *he matures* (HS), ru?nękwehstíhs?ę ‹he-himself-human-'ness-exhausted› *he is in the prime of life* (HS); **-a?rihwihs=?a-**: kaku?rihwíhs?ę ‹they-themselves-matter-exhausted› *they plotted, they promised* (RC 26:8), ra?rihwíhs?ahs ‹he-himself-matter-exhausts› *he bargains, he contrasts, he stipulates* (HS), yu?rihwíhs?ę ‹it-itself-matter-exhausted› *behest* (HS); **-a?rihwihs?a-** {dative III}: ra?rihwihs?á·tih ‹he-himself-matter-exhausts-for› *he makes a resolution* (HS); **-t-.-(i)hs?a-**: nakahs?áh-

nahk ‹hither-fact-it-finish-caused› *it used up* (RC 2:4); **-t-.-(i)hs?ahT-**: nahráhs?aht ‹hither-fact-he-exhaust-caused› *he went rapidly* (RC 6:9), nakayéhs?aht ‹hither-fact-they-exhaust-caused› *they fled* (RC 24:9); **-yah-.-ač?ahT-**: yahwa?kayéč?aht ‹thither-fact-they-themselves-exhaust-caused› *they hurried themselves away* (RC 3:9), *they went forth* (RC 32:5), weyuč?áhnę ‹thither-it-itself-exhaust-caused› *it is all gone* (R); **ti-.-a?rih=wihs?a-**: tiyakya?rihwíhs?ahs ‹so-we two-ourselves-matter-exhaust› *we two promised one another* (RC 30:23); **ha?-ač?a-**: ha? kakúč?ę ‹the they-themselves-exhausted› *the dead* (R); **kwęhs-ač?ahT-**: kwęhs aręč?áhthek ‹no unknown-it-itself-exhaust-cause› *it is inexhaustable* (HS); **kwęhs-a'nuh=stihs?a-**: kwęhs ahru?nuhstíhs?ęk ‹no unknown-he-himself-year-exhaust› *a minor* (HS).

-(i)hs?ahT- bulk, totality. *dv.n.s* yuhs-?áhnę ‹it-exhaust-caused› *bulk, totality* (HS).

íhs?ę beyond, more (RC 30:62). *part.* **íhs?ę ti+yah-.-?ęyuhar-** {dative I}: íhs?ę thweyę?nat?ęyúharθeh ‹more so-thither-one=another-cost-washes-for› *one overpays* (HS); **íhs?ę -yah+či-.-rhę?-**: íhs?ę yęčúrhę? ‹more thither-prediction-again-it-be day-begin› *day after tomorrow* (HS).

íhs?ę ti+yah-.-?ęyuhar- {dative I} overpay. *v.s.-a.i.* íhs?ę thweyę?nat?ęyú-harθeh ‹more so-thither-one=another-

---

cost-tips-for> *one overpays* (HS).

íhs⁷ę -yah+či -. -rhę⁷ - day after tomorrow. *dv.n.s.* íhs⁷ę yęčúrhę⁷ ‹more thither-prediction-again-it-be day-begin› *day after tomorrow* (HS).

ihs⁷ęhah the more (RC 2:11). *part.*

-(i)htawę - rub. *v.r.-t.* hab: -, pnt: -⁷, stat: -, prog: -, prp: -, dst: -, caus: -, rvs: -, dat: -, n-inc. The initial vowel behaves like an "epenthetic" vowel as shown by the fact that the accent unexpectedly falls on root medial *a* in the penultimate syllable of the first word cited below. It is perhaps the case that all instances of root initial (i) have the same origin as other "epenthetic" vowels. ęyehtà·wę⁷ *one will rub* (RC 11:23), wa⁷na⁷níhtawę⁷ *one rubbed another* (RC 11:28).

-ihteθ - signify, tell. *v.r.-t.* hab: -, pnt: -ɸ, stat: -, prog: -, prp: -, dst: -, caus: -, rvs: -, dat: -, n-inc. wahréhte·θ *he told* (RC 2:4), ęyaíhte·θ *one will tell* (RC 30:7), wa⁷kayę⁷na⁷níhte·θ *one told them* (RC 6:2), ęhréhte·θ *he will signify* (HS).

-ihte⁷-/-ęhte⁷-/-ęhn - mean. *v.r.-a.i.* hab: -ɸ, pnt: -, stat: -ɸ, prog: -, prp: -, dst: -, caus: -, rvs: -, dat: I (-θe-/-θ-), n-inc. The form -ęhte⁷ - occurs following the third person neuter singular agent and third person patient pronominal prefixes. The unusual form -ęhn - occurs before the instrumental suffix. The form -ihte⁷ - occurs elsewhere. kíhte⁷ *I mean* (R), síhte⁷ *you mean* (RC 3:18), réhte⁷ *he means* (R), węhte⁷ *it means* (RC 3:19), rawęhte⁷ *he meant* (HS); -ęhnahkw -: ręhnáhkhwa⁷ ‹he-means-instrument› *he indicates, he means* (HS), węhnáhkhwa⁷ ‹it-means-instrument› *expressive* (HS).

-(i)htrę - tie. *v.r.-t.* hab: -h ~ -hs, pnt: -·⁷ ~ -·t, stat: -, prog: -ha⁷nye⁷-, prp: -,

dst: -, caus: -, rvs: -hsi-, dat: -, inc.-ɸ-pat. This root is probably to be seen in Lawson's «Ough-tre's» 'Shirt' from *uhtréhsteh "something that is tied". káhtręh *it ties* (RC 23:4), na⁷níhtręhs *one dresses another's wound* (HS), ęhsíhtrę·⁷ *you will tie* (RC 32:17), wahráhtrę·⁷ *he tied it* (R), wa⁷kayę⁷na⁷níhtrę·t *they tied him up* (M 87); -(i)htręhsi -: rahtréhsyęhs ‹he-tie-undoes› *he loosens it, he unlaces it, he unties it* (HS), wahrahtréhsi⁷ ‹fact-he-tie-undid› *he untied it* (R); -(i)h = tręhsi -{dative III}: wahrakihtréhsyę⁷ ‹fact-he=me-tie-undone-for› *he untied it for me* (R); -ne -. -(i)htręhsthę -: nehrahtréhsthęh ‹apart-he-tie-cause-much› *he binds it up, he enchains it* (HS), wa⁷nyehtréhsthę·⁷ ‹fact-apart-one-tie-cause-much› *one bound it* (RC 17:1); -(a)hkarahtręha'nye⁷ -: ruhkarahtręhá·⁷nye⁷ ‹he-bark-tied-going along› *bark is tied to him* (RC 32:10); -ha⁷ = θahtrę -: wa⁷kayeha⁷θáhtrę⁷ ‹fact-they-neck-tied› *they tied neck* (RC 6:12); -hęwahtrę -: rahęwáhtręhs ‹he-boat-ties› *he moors boat* (HS); -a = tkahrahtrę -: ratkahráhtręhs ‹he-himself-eye-ties› *he is blindfolded* (HS); -a'netkwahtręhsT -: wa⁷netkwahtréhstha⁷ ‹it-itself-stomach-tie-causes› *belt* (HS); -a'nihtręhsT -: yę⁷nihtréhstha⁷ ‹one-oneself-tie-causes› *poultice* (HS); -a⁷ta⁷ahtręhsT -: yę⁷ta⁷rahtréhstha⁷ ‹one-oneself-head-tie-causes› *wreath* (HS); -ne -. -at⁷ahstrę -: wa⁷thrat⁷áhstrę·⁷ ‹fact-apart-he-himself-breast-tied› *he tied it on breast* (RC 30:58); -čhiku⁷r - -(i)htręhsT -: učhikú⁷reh yehtréhstha⁷ ‹manufactured shoe one-tie-causes› *shoelace* (HS).

-(i)htręhsi - loosen, unlace, untie. *v.s.-t.* rahtréhsyęhs ‹he-tie-undoes› *he loosens it, he unlaces it, he unties it* (HS), wahrahtréhsi ‹fact-he-tie-undid› *he untied it* (R).

-(i)hya?k – cross over. *v.r.-t.* hab: -s, pnt: -ɸ, stat: -ę, prog: -, prp: -, dst: -, caus: -T-, rvs: -, dat: -, inc.-ɸ-pat. aryéhyak *that one cross over it* (RC 26: 19), wahréhyak *he crossed over it* (RC 26:23), waéhyak *one crossed* (RC 3:47); **-(i)hya?k-**: úhyak ‹cross over› *six* (RC 30:62) [Lawson «Houe-yoc» 'Six']; **-(i)hya?kT-**: yehyáktha ‹one-cross over-causes› *ford* (HS); **-yah+či-. -(i)hya?k-.#hči. -hę-**: weθ-hruhyakę-číhę· ‹thither-again-he-crossed over-very-much› *he had already crossed back over there* (RC 31:9); **-ne-. -hsnęwihya?k-**: wathrahsnęwíhyak ‹fact-apart-he-stream-crossed over› *he crossed the stream* (L 26); **-ne-. -ihnęhya?k-**: nehruhnęhyákę ‹apart-he-piece of leather-crossed over› *(he has a leather) scarf (over left shoulder* (AG); **-ne-. -nę'nihya?khę-**: watkayenęnihyakhę ‹fact-apart-they-hill-crossed over-many› *they crossed over mountains* (AG); **-t-. -iyhęhya?k-**: načiyhéhyak ‹hither-you!-river-cross over› *come back across river!* (RC 31:6); **ti-. -uhstih=ya?k-**: tyawuhstihyákę ‹so-it-year-crossed over› *it is that many years old* (L 38); thwaakuhstíhyak ‹so-fact-one-year-crossed over› *one is so many years old* (RC 3:25); **-a'nęrihstihya?k-**: ranęrihstíhyaks‹he-himself-breathe-'ness-crosses over› *he expires* (H-notebook); **-ne-. -a'nihya?kT-**: wanwa-níhyakt ‹fact-apart-it-it-self-cross over-caused› *it took steps* (RC 9:4), watkaníhyakt ‹fact-apart-I-myself-cross over-caused› *I stepped somewhere else* (RC 31:8); **-ne-. -ęh=thya?k-**: nehréhthyaks ‹apart-he-field-crosses over› *he crosses a country* (HS); **-(i)hya?k-. -či-. -(i)har-**: úhyak θkáhar ‹cross over again-it-hung› *sixteen* (R); **-(i)hya?k-ti-. -ahθhę-**: úhyak tiwáhθhę· ‹cross over so-it-is ten› *sixty* (R).

-(i)hya?k- – six. *n.s.* úhyak ‹cross over› *six* (RC 30:62) [Lawson «Houeyoc» 'Six'].

-(i)hya?k-. -či-. -(i)har- – sixteen. *n.s.* úhyak θkáhar ‹cross over again-it-hung› *sixteen* (R).

-(i)hya?k-ti-. -ahθhę- – sixty. *n.s.* úhyak tiwáhθhę· ‹cross over so-it-is ten› *sixty* (R).

-(i)hya?kT- – ford. *dv.n.s* yehyáktha ‹one-cross over-causes› *ford* (HS).

-(i)hyęhah(e)r- – river. *dv.n.s* kahyęháhrę ‹it-river-put up› *river* (R).

-(i)hyęhęti- – ditch. *dv.n.s* kahyęhę́·tih ‹it-river-makes› *ditch* (HS).

-iN- – go, lead, proceed. *v.r.-a.i.* hab: -ęhs, pnt: -, stat: -e, prog: -, prp: -, dst: -, caus: -T-, rvs: -, dat: -, inc.-ɸ-pat. Encountered only with incorporated noun roots. The form of the root with the stative aspect (-in-(e?)) in the second example is irregular; -it-(e?)- would be expected as in the first example. **-hęwiN-**: rahęwí·te ‹he-boat-led› *he rows, he goes by boat*

(HS); **-nęhriN -**: yenęhrì·ne[?] ⟨one-scalp-led⟩ *they advanced as a war party* (RC 12:9); **-ręhyiN -**: wahrarę́hyi[?]n ⟨fact-he-sky-led⟩ *he "climbed the sky"* (*said of the sun as it rises and crosses the sky*) (RC 4:6); **-či -.-nęčhiN -**: θahranę́čhi[?]n ⟨again-fact-he-arm-led⟩ *he led back someone by the arm* (R); **-athahiN -**: rathahì·nęhs ⟨he-himself-path-leads⟩ *he travels* (HS), rathahí·tc[?] ⟨he-himself-path-led⟩ *he is traveling* (H 2484); **-a'nyahkwiN -**: ra[?]nyahkwì·nęhs ⟨he-himself-girth-proceeds⟩ *he peddles goods* (HS).

-inę - turkey. *n.r.* n-poss., n-inc., n.sfx. -[?]. kę̀·nę[?] *turkey (Meleagris gallopavo)* (R) [Lawson «Coona» 'Turkey'] [Jefferson «ken-nengh» 'turkey'] [Gallatin «kennengh» 'turkey'].

ì·nę far (RC 12:12). *part.* **inę.#ah**: inę́hah ⟨far-little⟩ *a little ways* (RC 6:13); *aloof* (HS); **ì·nę -(i)[?]rę -**: ì·nę yú[?]rę[?] ⟨far it-is settled⟩ *infrequent, rare* (HS).

ì·nę -(i)[?]rę - infrequent, rare. *dv.n.s* ì·nę yú[?]rę[?] ⟨far it-is settled⟩ *infrequent, rare* (HS).

inę.#ah a little ways; aloof. *part.* inę́hah ⟨far-little⟩ *a little ways* (RC 6:13); *aloof* (HS).

-inęht - February; late April through early May. *n.r.* n-poss., n-inc., n.sfx. -i (archaic: -eh). kęnę́hteh *April 15-May 15* (HS), kęnę́hti *February* (R).

-inęr - August. *n.r.* n-poss., n-inc., n.sfx. -[?]. kę̀·nę[?]r *August;* **-inęr -.#ke**: kęnę́[?]rkye ⟨August-at⟩ *June 15-July 15* (HS).

-inęr -.#ke late June through early July. *n.s.* kęnę́[?]rkye ⟨August-at⟩ *June 15-July 15* (HS).

-inę[?]kyęhst - bow, nod. *v.r.-a.i.* hab: -ha[?], pnt: -, stat: -, prog: -, prp: -, dst: -, caus: -, rvs: -, dat: -, n-inc. ręnę[?]kyęhstha[?] *he bows, he nods* (HS).

-ir - bit, grain, particle, soil, small piece.
n.r. n-poss., inc., n.sfx. -[?]. à·wi[?]r *soil* (RC 5:1); **-ir -.#ke**: awí[?]rkye ⟨grain-at⟩ *on soil* (RC 5:7); **-ir -.#keha·[?]**: awi[?]rkyéha·[?] ⟨grain-customarily⟩ *of the soil* (RC 15:1); **-irya[?]k -.#áh**: kęrya[?]k[?]áh ⟨it-grain-break-little⟩ *it broke in small pieces* (RC 12:29); **awę́·te -ira'ne -**: awę́·te kęrá·[?]ne[?] ⟨thing it-grain-is present⟩ *muddy, soiled, turbid* (HS).

-ir - move across, move through, roam, rove. *v.r.-a.i.* hab: -ęhs, pnt: -[?], stat: -ę, prog: -, prp: -, dst: -, caus: -ehT-, rvs: -, dat: -, inc.-φ-pat. rì·ręhs *he roams through* (HS), ę́hri[?]r *he will roam* (HS); **-ahčir -{dative I} -hrę -**: na[?]nahčira[?]θéhręh ⟨one=another-fist-moves through-for-much⟩ *one insults another* (HS); **-nęhsirehT -**: Kanęhsiréhtha[?] ⟨it-house-move through-causes⟩ *Move-Through-House (female proper name)* (H 2484); **-nyatarir -**: ranyatarì·rę ⟨he-lake-moved through⟩ *he wades in lake* (RC 26:35); **-[?]a=wyir -**: ra[?]awyì·ręhs ⟨he-dew-moves through⟩ *he rambles about or through the dew* (H-notebook); **-ne -.-hshę =wirehT -**: nehrahshęwiréhtha[?] ⟨apart-he-hollow-move through-causes⟩ *he reproaches* (HS).

-irya[?]k -.#áh break in small pieces. *v.s.-a.i.* kęrya[?]k[?]áh ⟨it-grain-break-little⟩ *it broke in small pieces* (RC 12: 29).

-(i)r[?]ęhs - clan, blood, descent, dynasty, family line, lineage, race. *n.r.* aln: akir[?]ęhsę́·te *my clan* (R), inc., n.sfx. -eh. The initial cluster of this root is pronounced ['r[?]] due to the historic spread of glottalization backward across resonants in the language. ur[?]ę́hseh *clan, blood, descent, dynasty, family line, lineage, race* (HS); **-(i)r=[?]ęhsęte**: ur[?]ęhsę́·te ⟨clan-certain one⟩ *species* (HS), akir[?]ęhsę́·te ⟨I-clan-a certain one⟩ *my clan* (R), sir[?]ęhsę́·te

‹you-clan-a certain one› *your clan* (R);
-(i)r²ęhsa²na'nye² -: kar²ęhsa²ná·²nye²
‹it-clan-cause-going along› *posterity*
(HS); -a'ner²ęhsęti -: čhiya²ner²ęhsé·ti
‹you all!-yourselves-clan-make› *propagate!* (AG), wa²ka²ner²ęhsé·ti² ‹fact-I-myself-clan-made› *I flourish, I propagate* (AG).

-(i)r²ęhsa²na'nye² - posterity. *dv.n.s.* kar-²ęhsa²ná·²nye² ‹it-clan-cause-going along› *posterity* (HS).

-(i)r²ęhsęte clan, species. *n.s.* ur²ęhsé·te ‹clan-certain one› *species* (HS), akir-²ęhsé·te ‹I-clan-a certain one› *my clan* (R), sir²ęhsé·te ‹you-clan-a certain one› *your clan* (R).

í·θ second person; you, the two of you, you all (R) [Lawson «Eets» 'Thou'] [Gallatin «eets» 'You']. *part.*

-iθkar -/-ęθkar - lay something down, spread something out. *v.r.-t.* hab: -φ ~ -ęh ~ -ęhs pnt: -ę·t, stat: -ę², prog: -, prp: -, dst: -, caus: -, rvs: -, dat: -, inc.-φ-pat. This root is unusual in that three different forms of the habitual aspect marker are attested, two in the writings of Hewitt and another in the modern language. The form in the modern language suggest this root may have been restructured to -iθ = karę -. The form -ęθkar - occurs when an incorporated noun is present. kíθkar *I spread out on the ground or floor* (H-notebook), ręθkà·ręhs *he spreads it* (HS), kiθkà·ręh *I am laying it down* (R), wakiθkà·rę² *I lay it down* (R), wa²kiθká·rę·t *I laid it down* (R);

-iθkar -: úθkareh ‹spread something out› *carpet, sheet, spread* (HS); -iθ = karęhkw -: yęθkaréhkhwa² ‹one-spreads something out-instrument› *cloth, rug, sheet* (R); -čtęhręθkar -: račtęhrę́θkar ‹he-stone-spreads out› *he paves* (HS), kačtęhrę́θkar ‹it-stone-spreads out› *pavement* (HS); -²ęhręθ = karahkw -: ka²ęhręθkaráhkhwa² ‹it-leaf-spreads out› *Virginia water plant* (R); kwęhs -iθkar -: kwęhs aké²θkaręk ‹no unknown-it-spread something out› *it is unspread (used only of spreads, cloths, etc.)* (HS).

-iθkar - sheet, spread. *n.s.* úθkareh ‹spread something out› *sheet, spread* (HS).

-iθkaręhkw - cloth, rug, sheet. *dv.n.s* yęθkaréhkhwa² ‹one-spreads something out-instrument› *cloth, rug, sheet* (R).

-iθn - scab, scale (of a fish), scar. *n.r.* n-poss., inc., n.sfx. -eh. úθneh *scab, scale (of a fish), scar* (R); -iθn -: ré²θne² ‹he-scabs› *he is all scabs* (HS); -iθn -.#hči: uθnéhči ‹scale-very› *scaly* (HS); -iθnahwaryakę -: uθnahwaryá·kę² ‹scale-white› *shad (Alosa sp.)* (HS); -iθnakęrat: kęθnakę̀·rat ‹it-scale-is white› *white bass (Roccus chrysops)* (H 3518); -iθnayę(T) -: ré²θnayę² ‹he-scab-lays› *he is all scabs* (HS); -iθnęhT -: ręθnéhtha² ‹he-scale-fall-causes› *he scales it (e.g., the fish)* (HS); ti -. -iθna² -: ‹so-it-scale-is of a size› tiké²θna²θ *size of scale* (RC 35: 23).

–iθn – be all scabs. *v.s.-a.i.* ręθneˀ ‹he-
scabs› *he is all scabs* (HS).

–iθn–.#hči scaly. *n.s.* uθnéhči ‹scale-
very› *scaly* (HS).

–iθnahwaryakę – shad (*Alosa* sp.). *n.s.*
uθnahwaryá·kęˀ ‹scale-white› *shad
(Alosa* sp.*)* (HS).

–iθnakęrat white bass. *dv.n.s.* kęθnakę̀·rat
‹it-scale-is white› *white bass (Roccus
chrysops)* (H 3518).

–iθnayę(T) – be all scabs. *v.s.-a.i.* ręθ-
nayęˀ ‹he-scab-lays› *he is all scabs*
(HS).

–iθnęhT – scale. *v.s.-t.* ręθnéhthaˀ ‹he-
scale-fall-causes› *he scales it (e.g., the
fish)* (HS).

–iθruhnę – flood, gush forth, inundate.
v.r.-a.i. See: –ęθruhnę–.

–(i)tęhT –/ –ętęhT – be poor. *v.r.-a.i.* hab: -
ɸ, pnt: -, stat: -ę , prog: -, prp: -he-,
dst: -, caus: -, rvs: -, dat: -, inc.-ɸ-pat.
This root inexplicably fails to show
the shift of root-final *t* to *n* before the
inchoative suffix, although it does
show the change before the stative
suffix. The form –ętęhT– occurs with
incorporated noun roots. wakí·tęht *I
am poor* (R), rú·tęht *he is indigent*
(HS), ęhrutę́hnęk *he will be poor*
(HS); –(i)tęhtaˀ–: rutęhtáˀ̨ę ‹he-be
poor-began› *he got poor* (L 55), wak-
tęhtáˀ̨ę ‹I-be poor-began› *I got poor*
(R), wahrutę́htaˀ ‹fact-he-be poor-begun› *he has gotten poor* (L 55),
utęhtáˀ̨ę ‹be poor-begun› *indigence,
poverty* (HS); –(i)tęhtheˀčręti –: ratęh-
theˀčrę́·tih ‹he-be poor-going to-'ness-
makes› *he beggars it* (HS), naˀ-
tęhtheˀčrę́·tih ‹one=another-be poor-
going to-'ness-makes› *one impov-
erishes another* (HS); –nęhętęhT–: yu-
nęhę́·tęht ‹it-corn-is poor› *the corn is
poor (referring to corn that is growing)* (H 2484); –nęhsętęhT–: yunęh-

sę́·tęht ‹it-house-is poor› *it is a poorly
furnished house, a house bespeaking
poverty* (H 2484); –(ę)nitęhT–: wakę-
tę́hnę ‹I-myself-am poor› *I humble
(myself)* (HS), runitę́hnę ‹he-himself-
is poor› *he humbles (himself)* (HS);
–a'nęnitęhT–: raˀnęnitę́hthaˀ ‹he-him-
self-himself-is poor› *he humbles himself* (HS); –(i)tęhT– –asθhar–: yakú·
tęht wásθhar ‹one-is poor it-cares for›
*alms house, poor house, homeless
shelter* (HS).

–(i)tęhT– –asθhar – alms house, poor
house, homeless shelter. *dv.n.s* ya-
kú·tęht wásθhar ‹one-is poor it-cares
for› *alms house, poor house, homeless
shelter* (HS).

–(i)tęhtaˀ – become poor. *v.s.-a.i.* rutęh-
táˀ̨ę *he got poor* (L 55) ‹he-be poor-
began›, waktęhtáˀ̨ę ‹I-be poor-began›
I got poor (R), wahrutę́htaˀ ‹fact-he-
be poor-begun› *he has gotten poor* (L
55).

–(i)tęhtaˀ – indigence, poverty. *n.s.* utęh-
táˀ̨ę ‹be poor-begun› *indigence, poverty* (HS).

–(i)tęhtheˀčręti – beggar, impoverish. *v.s.-
t.* ratęhtheˀčrę́·tih ‹he-be poor-going
to-'ness-makes› *he beggars it* (HS),
naˀtęhtheˀčrę́·tih ‹one=another-be
poor-going to-'ness-makes› *one im-
poverishes another* (HS).

–itkęˀ – appear, come forth, issue. *v.r.-a.i.*
hab: -θ, pnt: -ɸ, stat: -ɸ, prog: -, prp:
-he-, dst: -θrę- ~ -hę-, caus: -hw-, rvs:
-, dat: -, inc.-ˀˀ-pat. Occurs only with
an incorporated noun present. –čaˀtuh=
stitkęˀθrę –: yučaˀtuhstitkę́ˀθrę· ‹it-be
cool-'ness-came forth-many› *springs
of water* (RC 12:29); –čaˀtuhstitkęhę –:
yučaˀtuhstitkę́hę· ‹it-be cool-'ness-
came forth-much› *running spring of
water* (RC 12:29); –ekitkęhw –: wekí·
tkęws ‹it-liquid-come forth-causes›

press (e.g., for wine, cider) (HS), ęyakyekí·tkęw ‹prediction-one-liquid-come forth-cause› *one will draw liquid out* (RC 19:2); ‑ekitkę⁊‑: wekí·tkę⁊θ ‹it-liquid-comes forth› *it distills* (HS), yawekitké⁊ę ‹it-liquid-came forth› *juice* (HS); ‑ęθritkę⁊‑: yawęθritké⁊ę ‹it-taste-came forth› *flat taste, insipid* (HS); ‑(ę)ta⁊ritkę⁊‑: wa⁊nyeta⁊rí·tkę⁊ ‹fact-two-one-head-came forth› *their two heads came forth* (RC 27:25); ‑(ę)⁊teyitkę⁊‑: wa⁊ka⁊teyí·tkę⁊ ‹fact-it-crowd-came forth› *crowd came forth* (RC 11:24); ‑kahritkę⁊‑: yukahrí·tkę⁊ ‹it-eye-came forth› *protruding eyes* (AW 57); ‑rihwitkęhw‑: rarihwí·tkęws ‹he-matter-come forth-causes› *he divulges; informer* (HS); ‑θręwitkę⁊‑: kaθręwí·tkę⁊θ ‹it-syrup-comes forth› *it extrudes syrup* (RC 2:15); ‑tehwitkę⁊‑: ratehwí·tkę⁊θ ‹he-skin-comes forth› *he grows pale* (HS), yutehwitké⁊ę ‹it-skin-came forth› *it is pale* (HS); ‑thekʷitkę⁊‑: rathekwí·tkę⁊θ ‹he-sweat-comes forth› *he sweats* (HS); ‑tkwaritkę⁊‑: ratkwarí·tkę⁊θ ‹he-blood-comes forth› *he bleeds* (HS); ‑tya⁊nitkę⁊θręhte‑: katya⁊nitkę⁊θréhteh ‹it-sprout-come forth-many-going to› *plants are sprouting up* (RC 31:7); ‑wętitkę⁊‑: rawętí·tkę⁊θ ‹he-word-comes forth› *he speaks* (HS); ‑či‑. ‑(ę)⁊tikęhritkę⁊‑: θahra⁊tikęhrí·tkę⁊ ‹again-fact-he-mind-came forth› *he regained consciousness* (RC 36:4), *he revived* (HS); ‑ne‑. ‑(ę)⁊tahkritkę⁊nah=nę‑: newę⁊tahkritkę⁊náhnęh ‹apart-it-flame-comes forth-much› *flames are shooting out* (R); ‑ne‑. ‑wętitkę⁊‑: nehrawętí·tkę⁊ ‹apart-he-word-came forth› *he spoke out* (RC 3:56); ‑t‑. ‑(ę)⁊tahsitkę⁊‑: nwę⁊tahsí·tkę⁊θ ‹hither-it-tongue-comes forth› *it lolls* (HS); ‑t‑. ‑(ę)⁊teyitkę⁊nahkw‑: tka⁊teyitkę⁊náhkhwa⁊ ‹hither-it-crowd-come forth-causes-instrument› *exit* (RC 26:6); ‑t‑. ‑wętitkę⁊‑: nyewętí·tkę⁊ ‹hither-one-word-came forth› *one stated* (RC 30:11); ‑t‑. ‑⁊ehnitkę⁊‑: naka⁊ehní·tkę⁊ ‹hither-fact-hand-came forth› *hand came forth there* (RC 10:5).

í·tyate⁊ yellow dock (*Rumex crispus*) (RC 21:11). *n.*

‑ityę‑ arrive at, go to. *v.r.-t.* hab: -h, pnt: -⁊, stat: -·, prog: -, prp: -, dst: -, caus: -⁊T-, rvs: -, dat: -, inc.-φ-ag./pat. ‑yah‑. ‑ityę‑: yęyawí·tyę·k ‹thither-prediction-it-have gone to› *it will have arrived there* (RC 15:4); ‑(ę)⁊teyityę‑: yu⁊teyí·tyę· ‹it-crowd-went to› *a herd got in a field* (H-notebook); ‑htawi=tyę‑: kahtawí·tyęh ‹it-stream of water-goes to› *it gushes in* (H-notebook); ‑nehsnityę⁊T‑: ranęhsnityé⁊tha⁊ ‹he-seed-go to-causes› *he carries grain to cover, brings grain into the barn, etc.* (H 2484); ‑nurityę⁊T‑: wa⁊nyenurí·tyę⁊t ‹fact-two-one-string of corn-go to-caused› *the two of them took strings of corn into* (RC 5:33), kanurityé⁊nę ‹it-string of corn-go to caused› *it took string of corn into* (RC 5:23); ‑rihwityę⁊T‑: wa⁊krihwí·tyę⁊t ‹fact-I-matter-went to› *I enter com-*

plaint (AG), wa'kayę'na'rihwí·tyę't ‹fact-they=another-matter-went to› *they made their complaints* (AG); -'ęyityę -: ru'ęyí·tyęh ‹he-debt-goes to› *he is in debt, he is indebted to, he owes* (H-notebook); -at'ęyityę'T -: rat-'ęyityę'tha' ‹he-himself-debt-go to-causes› *he runs into debt* (H-notebook).

-(i)t'uh - sleep. *v.r.-a.i.* hab: -s, pnt: -ɸ, stat: -ɸ, prog: -, prp: -he-, dst: -hę-, caus: -T-, rvs: -, dat: -, inc.-ɸ-pat. wakí·t'uhs *I am sleeping* (R), wakit-'úhshek *I was sleeping* (R), ęwakí·t-'uh *I will go to sleep* (R), ękí·t'uh *I will sleep* (R); -(i)t'uhe -: ęwakit'úhe' ‹prediction-I-sleep-going to› *I will go to bed* (R); -(i)t'uhT -: yakut'úhtha' ‹one-sleep-causes› *laudanum, opium* (HS), yut'úhne' ‹it-sleep-caused› *opiate, somnific* (HS), rut'úhne' ‹he-sleep-caused› *sleeper* (HS); -(i)t'uhT -{dative II}: wa'kayę'na'nit'úhthahθ ‹fact-they=another-sleep-caused-for› *one put them to sleep* (R), ęhrat'úhthahθ ‹prediction-he-sleep-cause-for› *he will put it to sleep* (HS), rat'uhná·tih ‹he-sleep-causes-for› *he puts it to sleep* (HS); ti -. -(i)t'uhęhte -: tikęt-'uhęhteh ‹so-it-sleep-many-is going to› *everyone is sleeping* (RC 35:7).

-(i)t'uhe - go to bed. *v.s.-a.i.* ęwakit'úhe' ‹prediction-I-sleep-going to› *I will go to bed* (R).

-(i)t'uhT - laudanum, opiate, opium, sleeper, somnific. *n.s.* yakut'úhtha' ‹one-sleep-causes› *laudanum, opium* (HS), yut'úhne' ‹it-sleep-caused› *opiate, somnific* (HS), rut'úhne' ‹he-sleep-caused› *sleeper* (HS).

-(i)t'uhT -{dative II} put to sleep. *v.s.-t.* wa'kayę'na'nit'úhthahθ ‹fact-they=another-sleep-caused-for› *one put them to sleep* (R), ęhrat'úhthahθ ‹pre-

diction-he-sleep-cause-for› *he will put it to sleep* (HS), rat'uhná·tih ‹he-sleep-causes-for› *he puts it to sleep* (HS).

ì·ya·k it is said (RC 1:1). *part.*

-iye - grease, oil. *n.r.* n-poss., n-inc., n. sfx. -'. kę·ye' *grease, oil* (R); -iye -. #hči: kęyé'či ‹oil-very› *oily* (HS); či'ení·či' -iye -: či'ení·či' kę·ye' ‹??› oil› *castor oil* (HS); -sherę·t -iye -: ushè·rę·t kę·ye' ‹cow grease› *tallow* (HS).

-iye -.#hči oily. *n.s.* kęyé'či ‹oil-very› *oily* (HS).

-(i)yh(ęh) -/-(i)hyęh - river. *n.r.* n-poss., inc., n.sfx. -eh. The form -(i)yh - is found only preceding the verb root -akT - *be next to* and the verb root -nu - of uncertain meaning. The form -(i)hyęh - is the product of a metathesis of the initial consonant cluster and is found only in a few common constructions. Elsewhere, the form -(i)yhęh - occurs. Although the older pronunciation of the initial cluster of this root shows the expected voiceless resonant (i.e., [yh]), many speakers pronounce it with an alveopalatal fricative (i.e., [ʰš]). This latter pronunciation may be old, as suggested by words cited in the colonial records of the Carolinas. uyhęheh *river* (AG); -(i)yhęhaka'ne -: yuyhęhaká'ne' ‹it-river-is abundant› *many rivers* (AG); -(i)yhakT -: akęyha·kwt ‹unknown-it-river-be next to› *that it be next to river* (RC 26:19); -(i)yhęha'ne'nye' -: kayhęha'né·'nye' ‹it-river-is present-going along› *river goes along* (RC 3:38); -(i)hyęhah(e)r -: kahyęháhrę ‹it-river-put up› *river* (R); -(i)yhęhakęw: uyhęhakęw ‹river-in› *in river* (R); -(i)yhęha'ni: uyhęha'ni ‹river-at edge of› *at edge of river* (RC 31:10);

–(i)hyẹhẹti –: kahyẹhẹ́·tih ‹it-river-makes› *ditch* (HS); –(i)yhẹhihẹ: uyhẹhíhẹ ‹river-in the middle of› *in the middle of river* (RC 26:20); –(i)yhẹ = hakT: Uyhẹha·kwt ‹river-next to› *next to river: Lewiston, New York* (RC 9:4); –(i)yhẹhar –: wa'eyhẹhara' ‹fact-one-river-was in› *one was in river* (RC 3:40); –(i)yhẹhsT –: úyhẹhst ‹river-cause› *salmon* (H 3518); –(i)yhnu –: kẹ́yhnu·' ‹it-river-??› *river* (R) [Colonial Records «Cashie» 'River'] [Gallatin «keynugh» 'river']; –ne –. –a'niy = hakT –: neyu'niyhá·knẹ ‹apart-it-itself-river-is next to› *it lies across river* (RC 26:16); –t –. –(i)yhẹhya'k –: načiyhẹ́hya'k ‹hither-you!-river-cross over› *come back across river!* (RC 31:6); kẹ' –(i)hyẹhẹti –: kẹ' kahyẹhẹ́·tih ‹where it-river-makes› *channel* (HS).

–(i)yhẹhakT Lewiston, New York. *n.s.* Uyhẹha·kwt ‹river-next to› *Lewiston, New York* (RC 9:4).

–(i)yhẹhsT – salmon. *n.s.* úyhẹhst ‹river-cause› *salmon* (H 3518).

–(i)yhnu – river. *dv.n.s.* kẹ́yhnu·' ‹it-river-??› *river* (R) [Colonial Records «Cashie» 'River'] [Gallatin «key-nugh» 'river'].

–iyu – be beautiful, be great. *v.r.-a.i.* hab: –, pnt: –', stat: –·, prog: –, prp: –, dst: –, caus: –hT–, rvs: –, dat: I (–'θe-/–'θ-), inc.-ɸ-pat. wí·yu· *it is beautiful, it is great* (R) [Gallatin «weeyou» 'Great, Big'], wì·yuhk *it was beautiful* (HS), ẹwì·yu' *it will be beautiful* (HS); –iyuhe': wiyúhe' ‹it-was great-remote› *it was beautiful* (HS); –iyuhT –: rẹyúhtha' ‹he-be great-causes› *he amplifies it* (R); –či –. –iyuhT –: θhriyúhtha' ‹again-he-be great-causes› *he enlarges it* (HS); –(a)hahiyu –: wahahí·yu· ‹it-path-is great› *great path* (RC 26:3); –(a)hahiyuhT –: rahahiyúhtha' ‹it-path-be great-causes› *he enlarges, is enlarging, widens the road* (H 2484); –(a)hẹ'niyu –: wahẹ'ní·yu· ‹it-clearing-is great› *the meadow is large* (H 2484); –(a)hkariyu –: yuhkarí·yu· ‹it-bark-is great› *it is pliant (limber)* (HS), ruhkarí·yu· ‹he-bark-is great› *he is agile, he is limber, he is spry, he is supple (limber)* (HS), *he is nimble* (H-notebook); –atra'θwiyu –: θatra'θwí·yu· ‹you-luck-is great› *you have good luck* (R); –činẹ'theriyu –: yečinẹ'therí·yu· ‹one-curl-is great› *she has a large head of curly hair; her hair is abundant, luxuriant* (H 2484); –či'eh = niyu –: kači'ehní·yu· ‹it-claw-is great› *the claw is large, its claw is large* (H 2484); –čtẹhriyu –: kačtẹhrí·yu· ‹it-stone-is great› *a large stone* (AW 45); –ẹhriyu –: yawẹhrí·yu· ‹it-sort-is great› *there are many* (RC 3:76), kakawẹhrí·yu· ‹they-sort-is great› *they are many* (RC 10:3); –ẹhriyuha'nye' –: wẹhriyuhá·'nye' ‹it-sort-be great-going along› *a sequence of many* (RC 24:4); –ẹθriyu –: sẹθrí·yu· ‹you-be so big-are great› *you are big* (R); –(ẹ) = tahsniyu –: katahsní·yu· ‹it-stick-is great› *a large stick* (L 78); –ẹ'niyu –. #keha·': awẹ'niyu'kyéha·' ‹day-be great-customarily> *diurnal, occurring during the day* (RC 3:2); -(ę)ʔtikęh = riyu -{dative I}: ruʔtikęhriyúʔθeh <he-mind-is great-for> *it pleases him* (HS); -(ę)ʔtikęhriyuhT -: ruʔtikęhriyúhtha? <he-mind-be great-causes> *he amuses* (HS); -haʔčiyu -: kahaʔčí·yu· <it-neck-is great> *large collar or neck* (H-notebook); -haʔθiyu -: kahaʔθí·yu· <it-neck-is great> *large collar or neck* (H-notebook); -hskęʔriyu -: kahskęʔrí·yu· <it-bone-is great> *it is a large bone* (H-notebook), yuhskęʔrí·yu· <it-bone-is great> *it has many bones* (H-notebook); -htawiyu -.#ke: Uhtawiyúʔkye <it-current of water-is great> *Mississippi River* (R), -hwačiyu -: kahwačí·yu· <it-breadth-is great> *broad* (H-notebook), *wide* (L 75); -hwačiyuhT -: rahwačiyúhtha? <it-breadth-be great-causes> *he widens it* (HS); -hwaθi = yu -: kahwaθí·yu· <it-breadth-is great> *broad* (H-notebook); -hwihstiyu -: kahwihstí·yu· <it-money-is great> *much money* (AW 98); -(i)hnyahčiyu -: kahnyahčí·yu· <it-cape-is great> *large cape* (H-notebook); -(i)hnyahθiyu -: kahnyahθí·yu· <it-cape-is great> *large cape* (H-notebook); -iʔnyuhkwiyu -: kęʔnyuhkwí·yu· <it-group-is great> *big group, congregation* (HS); -kahriyu -: kakahrí·yu· <it-eye-is great> *large eyes* (AW 45); -kčiyu -: kakčí·yu· <it-dish-is great> *large dish* (H-notebook); -kęh = siyu -: kakęhsí·yu· <it-face-is great> *a very large face* (AW 45); -khwiyu -: rakhwí·yu· <he-meal-is great> *he is a great eater* (HS); -kθiyu -: kakθí·yu· <it-dish-is great> *large dish* (H-notebook); -nęhiyu -: kanęhí·yu· <it-corn-is great> *the corn grain is large* (H 24 84); -nęhsiyuhT -: ęʔtinęhsì·yuht <prediction-we two-house-be great-cause> *you and I will enlarge house, you and*

I will build an addition (RC 30:24); -ręʔiyu -: karęʔí·yu· <it-tree-is great> *beautiful, great, large tree* (AW 56); -ręʔiyuhT -: karęʔiyúhtha? <it-tree-be great-causes> *it makes a great tree* (RC 6:15); -rihwiyu -: urihwí·yu· <matter-be great> *it is sure* (HS); -rihwi = yuhsT -: rurihwiyúhsnę <he-matter-be great-caused> *he is religious* (HS), karihwiyúhsnahk <it-matter-be great-caused> *Christianity* (HS); -rihwiyuh = snęhčr -: urihwiyuhsnęhčreh <matter-be great-cause-'ness> *Christianity* (HS); -taʔniyu -.#áh: kataʔniyuháh <it-village-is great-little> *it is quite a city* (H-notebook); -tkwiyu -: waʔetkwì·yuʔ <fact-one-stomach-was great> *one's stomach grew* (RC 35:25); -wętiyu -: kawętí·yu· <it-word-is great> *bass (versus treble), it is sonorous* (HS); -ʔęyi = yu -: kaʔęyí·yu· <it-enclosure-is great> *large fort* (H-notebook); -ʔnehsi = yuhsT -: kaʔnehsiyúhstha? <it-band-be great-causes> *announcement is made* (RC 34:18); -ʔnęwiyu -: kaʔnęwí·yu· <it-kettle-is great> *great kettle* (RC 3:54); -ʔtuθhaʔniyu -: ruʔtuθhaʔní·yu· <he-jealousy-is great> *he is envious* (H-notebook); -či -. -nyatariyu -: Θkanyatarí·yu· <again-it-lake-is great> *Handsome Lake* (R); -ne -. -hčiyu -: neyuhčí·yu· <apart-it-width of cloth-is great> *it is wide* (HS); -t -. -(ę)ʔtikęh = riyuhT -: nyuʔtikęhrì·yuht <hither-it-mind-be great-caused> *satisfaction* (HS); ti -. -ęθriyu -: tiwęθrí·yu· <so-it-be so big-is great> *it is so big* (RC 6:9); ti -. -taʔčuhkwiyu -: tikataʔčuhkwí·yu· <so-it-pile-is great> *large pile* (AW 53); -aʔrihwiyuhsT -: raʔrihwiyúhstha? <he-himself-matter-be great-causes> *he pretends to be religious* (HS); -t -. -(ę)ʔtikęhriyu -{dative I}: tkaʔtikęhriyúʔθeh <hither-it-mind-is

great-for› *it is pleased by* (RC 35:12); -rihwiyuhsT- -ęheya?nahkw-: karihwiyúhsnak rawęheya?náhkę ‹it-matter-be great-caused he-die-caused-instrument› *martyr* (HS); kwęhs -rih=wiyuhsT-: kwęhs ahrurihwiyúhsnęk ‹no unknown-he-matter-be great-cause› *he is unchristian* (HS); kwęhs -t-. -(ę)?tikęhriyuhT-: kwęhs a?nayu?-tikęhriyúhnęk ‹no unknown-hither-it-mind-be great-cause› *unsatisfactory* (HS).

-iyuhT- amplify. *v.s.-t.* ręyúhtha? ‹he-be great-causes› *he amplifies it* (R).

í·? first person; I, we [Lawson «Ee» 'I'] [Gallatin «ie», «hei» 'I']. *part.* Also: í·?i·. -at?ihsT-: rat?íhstha? ‹he-himself-I-causes› *he arrogates, he egotizes* (HS), rut?íhsnę ‹he-himself-I-caused› *he egotized* (HS); ha? -at?ihsT-: ha? rat?íhstha? ‹the he-himself-I-causes› *his egoism* (HS).

-i?a(k)-¹/-yę?kw-² shoot. *v.r.-t.* hab: ¹-ahs ~ ²-s, pnt: ²-?, stat: ¹-(), prog: -, prp: -, dst: -hrę-, caus: -, rvs: -, dat: -, inc.-ti-ag./pat. This is one of only two suppletive verbs in Tuscarora. Note, however, the two forms of the habitual indicating either that the suppletion of these roots is recent and not yet complete or that the suppletion is being eliminated by the development of full inflection for both roots. The data do not permit a determination of which of these scenarios is the correct one. This root is also unusual, or rather the form -i?a(k)- is unusual in

that it conditions the presence of the "stem-joiner" vowel *a*, thus producing one of the rare cases of contiguous vowels in the language. However, like other sequences of *ai* the cluster is broken up phonetically by a brief *r*-like sound, i.e., rarihwaí?ahs is pronounced [ra.rih.wa.ˈí?.ahs]. waktí?ak *I shot it* (R), ratì·yę?kws *he shoots* (RC 30:29); -yę?khrę-: wahratiyę́?khrę? ‹fact-he-X-shot-many› *he shot some* (R); -hnęwai?a(k)-: rahnęwaí?ahs ‹he-mark-shoots› *he hits the mark* (HS); -hswai?a(k)-: kayehswaí?ahs ‹they-back-shoot› *longball (game)*; -rę?ati=yę?khrę-.#ú?y: wa?karę?atiyę?khrę?-ú?y ‹fact-it-tree-X-shot-many-great› *it shot many trees* (RC 5:41); -rihwai?=a(k)-/-rihwayę?kw-: rarihwaí?ahs ‹he-matter-shoots› *he is opposed* (HS), raríhwayę?kws ‹he-matter-shoots› *he disapproves, he objects* (HS).

-(i)?čkaw- branch, fagot, kindling, twig. *n.r.* n-poss., inc., n.sfx. -eh. ú?čkaweh *branch, fagot, kindling, twig* (RC 30:27); -(i)?čkawę?ke: u?čkawę́?kye ‹branch-on› *on twig* (RC 17:1); -yah-. -(i)?čkawa?nihr-: yahwa?e?čkawá?nir ‹thither-fact-one-branch-stood up› *one stood up twig there* (RC 17:2); -(ę)=ti?čkawya?khe-.#ú?y: węti?čkawya?-khe?ú?y ‹it-itself-branch-break-going to-great› *branches are breaking* (RC 30:19); ti-. -(ę)ti?čkawya?khęhte-. #ú?y: nęti?čkawya?khęhte?ú?y ‹so-fact-it-itself-branch-break-many-going to-great› *a great many branches were being broken* (RC 9:4).

-(i)²e(k) - strike. *v.r.-t.* hab: -hs, pnt: -( ),
stat: -·, prog: -, prp: -, dst: -, caus: -,
rvs: -, dat: -, inc.-ɸ-ag./pat. rá²ehs *he
strikes* (HS), rú²e· *he has struck* (HS),
ehrá²ek *he will strike* (HS); -her =
²e(k) -: rahér²ehs ‹he-green-strikes› *he
threshes* (HS); -hehθ²e(k) -: rahéhθ-
²ehs ‹he-throat-strikes› *he hiccoughed*
(HS); -hsweni²e(k) -: rahswení²ehs
‹he-back-X-strikes› *he hits it in the
back* (HS), načwení²ehs ‹one=another-
back-X-strikes› *one slays another*
(HS); -ht²e(k) -: rúht²ehs ‹he-X-
strikes› *he stumbles, he trips* (HS);
-hwači²e(k) -: rahwačí²ehs ‹he-
breadth-strikes› *he crushes, he jams*
(HS); -kahθ²e(k) -: yukáhθ²e· ‹it-tear-
struck› *it is hollow-eyed* (HS); -nęhs =
²e(k) -: runęhs²ę· ‹he-house-struck› *he
struck house* (HS); -nęhwar²ehsT -:
yenęhwar²éhstha² ‹one-brain-strike-
causes› *war club* (SH 375); -ręhya² =
ehsT -: yuręhya²éhsnę ‹it-sky-strike-
caused› *it gathers the sky together*
(RC 4:1); -θkwar²e(k) -: raθkwár²ehs
‹he-lip-strikes› *he shouts, he whoops*
(HS); -wenęt²e(k) -: kawenę·t²ehs ‹it-
iron-strikes› *clock* (HS); -wenęt =
²ehst -: yewenę·t²éhstha² ‹one-iron-
strikes-'ness› *bell* (HS); -²ęhr²e(k) -:
ra²ęr²ehs ‹he-leaf-strikes› *he strikes
leaf (archaic mode of signalling one's
lover in the woods by cupping leaf
and striking it like a drum)* (HS);
-ne -, -hθra²r²e(k) -: nehrahθrá²r²ehs
‹two-he-palm of hand-strikes› *he claps
his hands* (HS); ę·či -wenęt²e(k) -: ę·či
kawenę·t²ehs ‹one it-iron-strikes› *hour*
(R); -(ę)tahsn - -her²ehst -: utáhsneh
yeher²éhstha² ‹stick one-green-strike-
causes› *flail: one uses it to thresh*
(HS); -²θkwehs - -ht²ehst -: u²θkwéh-
seh yakuht²éhstha² ‹cutting block

one-X-strike-causes› *stumbling block*
(HS).

í·²i· first person; I, we. *part.* Also: í·².
-i²khar - breechcloth, frock, petticoat,
skirt; clothes. *n.r.* n-poss., inc., n.sfx.
-eh. u²khà·reh *breechcloth, frock,
petticoat, skirt; clothes* (HS) [Lawson
«Oukaure» 'A Flap']; -i²kharęti -
{dative III}: wa²na²ni²kharę·tyę²
‹fact-one=another-skirt-made-for› *one
made skirt for another* (RC 30:52).
-i²khaw - frock, skirt; clothes. *n.r.* n-
poss., inc., n.sfx. -eh. u²khà·weh
frock, skirt; clothes (HS).
-i'n - eel. *n.r.* n-poss., n-inc., n.sfx. -eh.
kę·²neh *eel* (R) [Lawson «Cuhn-na»
'Eel'].
-i²naw - burn. *v.r.-t.* hab: -s, pnt: -², stat:
-, prog: -, prp: -, dst: -, caus: -, rvs: -,
dat: -, inc.-ɸ-pat. rę²naws *he burns it*
(HS); -hę²či²naw -: rahę²čí²naws ‹he-
??-burns› *he singes* (HS); -i²θkeri² =
naw -: ęhsi²θkyerí²na²w ‹prediction-
you-??-burn› *you will singe the fur off
by throwing it on the coals* (R).
-i²ner - feel, have a presentiment. *v.r.-a.i.*
hab: -h, pnt: -, stat: -, prog: -, prp: -,
dst: -, caus: -, rvs: -, dat: -, n-inc.
rę²ner *he feels: his presentiment* (HS);
-i²nersT -: rę²nérstha² ‹he-feel-causes›
his nerve(s) (HS).
-i²nersT - have nerve. *dv.n.s.* rę²nérstha²
‹he-feel-causes› *his nerve(s)* (HS).
-i'nęr - have compassion for, pity. *v.r.-t.*
hab: -ɸ, pnt: -, stat: -ę, prog: -, prp: -,
dst: -, caus: -ahT-, rvs: -, dat: -, n-inc.
kę²nę̀·rę *compassion, pity* (R), rę·²nęr
he pities (HS); -i'nęrahT -: yu²nę̀·raht
‹it-pity-caused› *it is pitiable* (HS);
-a'ni'nęr -: ru²ni²nę̀·rę ‹he-himself-
pitied› *he is compassionate, he is
gracious, he is pitiful* (HS); -a'ni'nę =
rahsk -: ru²ni²nęráhskę ‹he-himself-pit-
ies-easily› *he is merciful, he is prone*

to pity (HS); -a'ni'n<u>e</u>rahT -: yu'ni'n<u>e</u>·raht ‹it-itself-pity-caused› *it is pitiable* (HS); -a'ni'n<u>e</u>r<u>e</u>hĕr -: u'ni'n<u>e</u>r<u>e</u>hĕrch ‹self-pity-'ness› *charity, mercy, pity* (HS); -a'ni'n<u>e</u>r<u>e</u>hĕruk<u>e</u>?: ru'ni'n<u>e</u>r<u>e</u>h-ĕrú·k<u>e</u>' ‹he-himself-pity-'ness-less› *he is implacable, pitiless, remorseless* (HS); kw<u>e</u>hs -a'ni'n<u>e</u>rahsk -: kw<u>e</u>hs ahru'ni'n<u>e</u>ráhsk<u>e</u>k ‹no unknown-he-himself-pity-easily› *he is inhospitable* (HS).

-i'n<u>e</u>rahT - be pitiable. *v.s.-s.i.* yu'n<u>e</u>·raht ‹it-pity-caused› *it is pitiable* (HS).

-(i)'nhahT - large branch, tree limb. *n.r.* n-poss., inc., n.sfx. -eh (archaic -φ). u'nháhneh *large branch, tree limb* (R), ú'nhaht *tree limb* (HS); -(i)'nhahna' = nihrh<u>e</u> -: yu'nhahna'nírh<u>e</u>· ‹it-large branch-stands up-many› *limbs were* (RC 4:2); -(i)'nhahn<u>e</u>te: u'nhahn<u>é</u>·te ‹large branch-a certain-one› *a certain limb* (RC 4:2); -(i)'nhahnu -: Ka'n-háhnu·' ‹it-large branch-is in water› *Kanhato, New York (an old Tuscarora village in south central New York)* (R); -(i)'nhahnut.#áh: yu'nhahnu·t'áh ‹it-large branch-stood-little› *shoot (of a plant)* (HS); -(i)'nhahnu'θk<u>a</u>rh -: ra'nhahnú'θkarhahs ‹he-large branch-chips› *he lops it off* (HS); -ne -. -(i)'n = hahnya'k -: wa'tki'nháhnya'k ‹fact-two-I-large branch-broke› *I split branch in two* (R); ti -. -(i)'nhahneθ<u>e</u> -: tika'nhahn<u>é</u>·θ<u>e</u>· ‹so-it-large branch-is long-many› *so its limbs are long* (RC 4:1); ti -. -(i)'nhahnuk<u>e</u> -: tyu'nhahnú·k<u>e</u>· ‹so-it-large branch-is forked›

forked branch (RC 4:1).

-(i)'nhahnu - Kanhato, New York. *n.s.* Ka'nháhnu·' ‹it-large branch-is in water› *Kanhato, New York (an old Tuscarora village in south central New York)* (R).

-(i)'nhahnut.#áh shoot (of a plant). *dv. n.s.* yu'nhahnu·t'áh ‹it-large branch-stood-little› *shoot (of a plant)* (HS).

-(i)'nhahnu'θk<u>a</u>rh - lop off. *v.s.-t.* ra'n-hahnú'θkarhahs ‹he-large branch-chips› *he lops it off* (HS).

-(i)'nh<u>e</u>hθ - rawhide strip, rein, strap. *n.r.* n-poss., inc., n.sfx. -eh. u'nh<u>é</u>hθeh *rawhide strip, rein, strap* (R); -(i)'n = h<u>e</u>hθaw<u>e</u> -: ra'nh<u>é</u>hθaw<u>e</u>hs ‹he-raw-hide strip-possesses› *he strops it* (HS); -(i)'nh<u>e</u>hθ<u>e</u>ti -{dative III}: wa'na'-ni'nh<u>e</u>hθ<u>é</u>·ty<u>e</u>' ‹fact-one=another-raw-hide strip-made-for› *one made strips of rawhide for another* (RC 30:60); -(i)'nh<u>e</u>hθu'narhuhst -: ye'nh<u>e</u>hθu'nar-húhstha' ‹one-rawhide strip-hook-cause-causes› *belt* (HS).

-(i)'nh<u>e</u>hθ<u>a</u>w<u>e</u> - strop. *v.s.-t.* ra'nh<u>é</u>h-θaw<u>e</u>hs ‹he-rawhide strip-possesses› *he strops it* (HS).

-(i)'nh<u>e</u>hθu'narhuhst - belt. *dv.n.s.* ye'n-h<u>e</u>hθu'narhúhstha' ‹one-rawhide strip-hook-cause-causes› *belt* (HS).

-i'nyuhkw - army, body, company, class, group, league, organization, troop. *n.r.* aln: θw<u>e</u>'nyúhkway<u>e</u>' *your group* (RC 13:5), inc., n.sfx. -eh. u'nyúhkweh *army, body, company, class, group, league, organization, troop* (R); -i' = nyuhkwahrahT -: u'nyuhkwáhraht

‹group-put up-cause› *multitude* (HS);
-i'nyuhkwahrihT -: rę'nyuhkwahríhtha' ‹he-group-spill-causes› *he disor-*
ganizes the group (HS); -i'nyuh=
kwayę(T) -: yakwę'nyúhkwayę' ‹we-
group-lay› *our organization: Temper-*
ance Society (i.e., 6-Nations Temper-
ance Soc(iety) over 100 yrs. old–Sen-
eca, Onondaga and Tuscarora) (L
37–[yakwa'nyúhkwayə̃']); -i'nyuh=
kwęti -: rę'nyuhkwę́·tih ‹he-group-
makes› *he classifies* (HS); -i'nyuh=
kwiyu -: kę'nyuhkwí·yu· ‹it-group-is
great› *big group, congregation* (HS);
tha+t -. -i'nyuhkwuken -: tha'nyu'-
nyuhkwukyé·nę· ‹unusual-hither-it-
group-divided› *to both ends of group*
(RC 33:8); -(ę)ti'nyuhkwęti -: węti'-
nyuhkwę́·tih ‹it-itself-group-makes›
cluster, league (HS); **-ne** -. -(ę)ti'nyuh=
kwakenę -: nęθwę'nyuhkwukyè·nę'
‹two-prediction-you-yourself-group-put
down› *you will divide your group in*
two (RC 33:8).
-**i'nyuhkwahrahT** - multitude. *n.s.* u'-
nyuhkwáhraht ‹group-put up-cause›
multitude (HS).
-**i'nyuhkwahrihT** - disorganize the group.
v.s.-a.i. rę'nyuhkwahríhtha' ‹he-
group-spill-causes› *he disorganizes the*
group (HS).
-**i'nyuhkwayę(T)** - Temperance Society.
dv.n.s. yakwę'nyúhkwayę' ‹we-group-
lay› *Temperance Society (i.e., 6-Na-*
tions Temperance Soc(iety) over 100
yrs. old–Seneca, Onondaga and Tus-
carora) (L 37–[yakwa'nyúhkwayə̃']).
-**i'nyuhkwęti** - classify. *v.s.-t.* rę'nyuh-
kwę́·tih ‹he-group-makes› *he classifies*
(HS).
-**i'nyuhkwiyu** - congregation. *dv.n.s.* kę'-
nyuhkwí·yu· ‹it-group-is great› *big*
group, congregation (HS).
-**i'rę** - abide, be placed, be seated, re-

main, set, settle, stay. *v.r.-a.i.* hab: -
hs, pnt: -', stat: -', prog: -, prp: -htc'-
, dst: -, caus: -'T-, rvs: -, dat: -, inc.-
ɸ-pat. Hewitt & Smith also record an
exceptional imperative form, θá'rę *be*
still!, as if the root were *-a'rę-. In
the same place, they record an equally
exceptional second person dual imperative form, θtí'rę *you two be still!*
Tuscarora otherwise has special forms
only for singular and non-singular
[dual/plural] imperatives. Other exceptional forms are found occasionally in
different sources. For example, yah-
wahré'rę' *he placed it there* (MG 88)
rather than expected *yahwahrę́'rę'
suggest that the root was originally
-(i)'rę- and has been restructured
to -i'rę-. čí'rę *set it down!* (R), kí'rę'
I am at home (R), yé'rę' *one lives*
(RC 35:37), rę́'rę' *he abides, he is*
placed, he is seated, he remains (HS),
yaktí'rę' *you and I stay together:*
husband and wife (HS); -**i'rę'T** -:
ękí'rę́'nak ‹prediction-I-set-cause› *I*
will be staying (R), akí'rę́'nak ‹unknown-I-set-cause› *that I be settled*
(RC 30:69), kę'rę́'nahk ‹it-set-caused-
had› *it is situated* (RC 33:2); -**či** -.
-**i'rę** -: θhrę́'ęhs ‹again-he-sets› *he*
readjusts it, he resets it (HS), θah-
rú'rę' ‹again-fact-he-set› *it took him*
back (RC 8:45); -**či** -. -**i'ręhte'** -: ęθ-
kę'ręhte' ‹prediction-again-I=you-set-
going to› *I will take you back* (RC 8:
41); -**yah** -. -**i'rę** -: yahwa'kayę'na'-
ní'rę' ‹thither-fact-they=another-set›
they left (abandoned) him (M 87);
-**ne+či** -. -**i'rę'na'** -: neθkę'rę́'na'θ ‹a-
part-again-it-set-cause-begins› *it steps*
(RC 28:6), nęθakę'rę́'na' ‹apart-
again-fact-it-set-cause-begun› *it step-*
ped (RC 28:6); -**kerhi'rę** -: ękayekyer-
hí'rę' ‹prediction-they-body-set› *they*

will set body (RC 6:13); -a'ni?rę -: yu'ní'rę' ‹it-itself-set› *it is fixed in place* (HS); ì·nę -i?rę -: ì·nę yú'rę' ‹far it-sets› *infrequent, rare* (HS); -hskęnę - tha -. -i?rę -: ahskè·nę tha'neyé'rę' ‹peace unusual-two-one-set› *the two of them live in peace, in union* (H-notebook); kwęhs -i?rę - -a? = tak(e)r -: kwęhs aré'rę' aryę'takyé·ra·t ‹no unknown-it-set unknown-one-one-self-dwell-complete› *it is uninhabited* (HS).

-i?rę?T - be settled, be situated, be staying. *v.s.-a.i.* ęki'rę'nak ‹prediction-I-set-cause› *I will be staying* (R), aki'rę'nak ‹unknown-I-set-cause› *that I be settled* (RC 30:69), kę'rę'nahk ‹it-set-caused-had› *it is situated* (RC 33:2).

-(i)?rhwęθ - tail. *n.r.* inaln: ki'rhwę́·θeh *my tail* (M 87), inc., n.sfx. -eh. u'rhwę́·θeh *tail* (R); -(i)?rhwęθ -.#ke: u'rhwęθę́'kye ‹tail-on› *on its tail* (RC 12:5); -(i)?rhwęθ -.#keha·?: u'rhwęθę'kyéha·' ‹tail-customarily› *caudal* (HS); -(i)?rhwęθukę?: u'rhwęθú·kę' ‹tail-less› *tailless* (HS); ti -. -(i)?rhwęθu?nę -: tika'rhwęθú'nę· ‹so-it-tail-is a kind of› *so its kind of tail is* (RC 12:5); -(ę)ti?rhwęθawihT -: ręti'rhwęθawíhtha' ‹he-himself-tail-give-causes› *he is sheepish; sycophant* (HS); -(ę)ti?rhwęθu'narhuhsT -: węti'rhwęθu'narhúhstha' ‹it-itself-tail-hook-cause-causes› *crupper (of a horse)* (HS).

-(i)?rhwęθ -.#keha·? caudal. *n.s.* u'rhwęθę'kyéha·' ‹tail-customarily› *caudal*

(HS).

-(i)?rhwęθukę? tailless. *n.s.* u'rhwęθú·kę' ‹tail-less› *tailless* (HS).

-(i)?θ(e)r - drag. *v.r.-t.* hab: -ęhs, pnt: ()-', stat: -ę, prog: -, prp: -, dst: -ehθę-, caus: -ehT-, rvs: -, dat: -, inc.-φ-pat. This root is perhaps to be seen in Lawson's «Utsera» root, from *ú'θreh "thing dragged", unless Lawson's form represents a divergent recording of uhsì·reh *string, thread*. rú'θrę *he has dragged it* (HS), rá'θręhs *he drags it* (HS), wahrá'θe'r *he dragged it* (R); -či?ri?θrehT -: yeči'ri'θréhtha' ‹one-spark-drag-causes› *lantern* (HS); -hnę = wi?θ(e)r -: rahnęwí'θręhs ‹he-mark-drags› *he draws a mark, he traces* (HS); -hsekwari?θ(e)r -: Sekwarí'θre·' ‹spear-drag› *Spear-carrier (Turtle Clan chief's name)* (R) [Colonial Records «Sacarusa», «Sequaressa»]; -kerhi? = θ(e)r -: wa'kayekyerhí'θe'r ‹fact-they-body-dragged› *they dragged body* (RC 6:12), wahrakyerhi'θréhθę·' ‹fact-he-body-dragged-many› *he dragged bodies* (RC 30:62); -te?kwi?θrehT -: yete'kwi'θréhtha' ‹one-bag-drag-causes› *portmanteau* (HS); -?ahθri?θ(e)r -: wahra'ahθrí'θe'r ‹fact-he-basket-dragged› *he dragged basket* (RC 27:14); -či -. -a'nwiri?θ(e)r -: nęčę'nwirí'θe'r ‹two-prediction-again-one-oneself-infant-drag› *the two of them will take the infant home* (RC 11:15); -ne -. -athwači?θ(e)r -: newathwačí'θręhs ‹a-part-it-itself-flatness-drags› *sleigh* (H 3518).

–(i)ʔθ(e)r – ride. *v.r.-a.i.* hab: -ęhs, pnt: ()-ʔ ~ -eʔ, stat: -e·ʔ, prog: -, prp: -, dst: -ehθę-, caus: -hT-, rvs: -, dat: -, n-inc. This root is derived from –(i)ʔθ(e)r – *drag*. The fact that it requires patient forms of the pronominal prefixes suggests that the original meaning was *X is dragged by Y*. However, the distinctive form of the stative aspect that now occurs with this root indicates that it has become a separate morpheme in the language. Lounsbury also gives a remodeled factual mode form with the punctual aspect suffix -eʔ and states "< [comes form] *it is dragging him (this may be a "going" form)," presumably a reference to a form with the purposive suffix. However, this seems unlikely since nowhere else does the purposive suffix have the form -e- and analogical remodeling is a preferable explanation. rúʔθre·ʔ *he rode* (HS), wakíʔθre·ʔ *I am riding* (R), θáʔθre·ʔ *you are riding* (R), arękíʔ-θeʔr *that I ride* (R), wahrúʔθeʔr *he rode* (HS), wahrúʔθreʔ *he's riding (in something) off* (L 52); –(i)ʔθręheʔ: ruʔθręheʔ ‹he-rode-remote› *he has ridden* (L 52); –(i)ʔθrehT–: ruʔθréhnę ‹he-ride-caused› *he has ridden (off)* (L 52); –(i)ʔθrehθę–: wahruʔθréhθę·ʔ ‹fact-he-rode-much› *he rode around* (L 52); –(i)ʔθrehčr–: uʔθréhčreh ‹ride-'ness› *automobile, car, vehicle* (R); –(i)ʔθrehčr–.#áh: uʔθrehčreháh ‹ride-'ness-little› *buggy* (HS); –(i)ʔθrehčra=węhsT–: yeʔθrehčrawęhshthaʔ ‹one-ride-'ness-possess-causes› *tar* (HS); –(i)ʔθrehčr– –ne–.–ahčarahkw–: uʔθréhčreh neyęhčaráhkhwaʔ ‹ride-'ness a-part-one-fist-is in-instrument› *wheelbarrow* (HS); čwe–.–ę'nake– –(i)ʔ=θ(e)r–: čwewę·ʔná·kye· rúʔθręhs ‹all-

day-is in number he-rides› *every day he rides* (L 52).

–(i)ʔθh – cogency, force, power; pace, step, stride. *n.r.* n-poss., inc., n.sfx. -eh. úʔθheh *cogency, force, power; pace, step, stride* (HS); –(i)ʔθhah=rahT–: ruʔθháhraht ‹he-power-put up-caused› *his manner of doing is violent, he is violent* (HS); –(i)ʔθha=nęhT–: raʔθhanęhthaʔ ‹he-power-guard-causes› *he alleviates, he assuages, he deadens force, he moderates* (HS); –(i)ʔθhaθn–: uʔθhá·θneh ‹power-be strong› *authority, power, strength* (R), yuʔθhá·θneh ‹it-power-is strong› *acrid, cogent, strength* (HS), weʔθhá·θneʔ ‹it-power-is strong› *it is enduring, it lasts* (HS), kaʔθhá·θneʔ ‹it-power-is strong› *it is potent* (HS), *it is powerful* (RC 28:7), reʔθhá·θneʔ ‹he-power-is strong› *he is enduring* (HS); –(i)ʔθhaθnęhčr–: uʔθhaθnęhčreh ‹power-be strong-'ness› *authority, power, strength* (R); –(i)ʔθhaθnęh=črayę(T)–: wakyeʔθhaθnęhčrayęʔ ‹I-power-be strong-'ness-lay› *I am strong* (R); –(i)ʔθhaθnęhst–: uʔθhaθnęhsteh ‹power-be strong-'ness› *prerogative, right* (R); –(i)ʔθhaθnęhstakʷek–: raʔθhaθnęhstakwé·kę ‹he-power-be strong-'ness-is whole› *he is almighty* (HS), ęhsiʔθhaθnęhstakwé·kęk ‹prediction-you-power-be strong-'ness-be whole› *you will have the authority* (RC 23:3); –(i)ʔθhaθnęhstaw–: raʔθhaθnęhstaws ‹he-power-be strong-'ness-gives› *he authorizes it* (HS); –(i)ʔθhęti–: waʔkaʔθhę́·tiʔ ‹fact-it-power-made› *it judged* (RC 30:32); ti+yah–.–(i)ʔθhęti–: thwehraʔθhę́·tih ‹so-thither-he-power-makes› *he conjectures, he guesses* (HS); –t–.–(i)ʔ=θhanę–: nyúʔθhanęhs ‹hither-it-power-guards› *it abates* (HS); –a'niʔθhah=

nę**ʔT** –: raʔniʔθhahnę́ʔthaʔ ⟨he-himself-power-disappear-causes⟩ *he relents* (HS); **–(ę)ti ʔθhahkw** –: rętiʔθháhkhwaʔ ⟨he-himself-power-picks up⟩ *he steps* (HS).

–(i)ʔθhahrahT – be violent. *v.s.-a.i.* ruʔθháhraht ⟨he-power-put up-caused⟩ *his manner of doing is violent, he is violent* (HS).

–(i)ʔθhanęhT – alleviate, assuage, deaden force, moderate. *v.s.-t.* raʔθhanę́hthaʔ ⟨he-power-guard-causes⟩ *he alleviates, he assuages, he deadens force, he moderates* (HS).

–(i)ʔθhaθn – authority, power, strength. *n.s.* uʔθhá·θneh ⟨power-be strong⟩ *authority, power, strength* (R).

–(i)ʔθhaθn – acrid, cogent, strength. *dv.n.s.* yuʔθhá·θneh ⟨it-power-is strong⟩ *acrid, cogent, strength* (HS).

–(i)ʔθhaθn – be enduring, be potent, be powerful, last. *v.s.-a.i.* weʔθhá·θneʔ ⟨it-power-is strong⟩ *it is enduring, it lasts* (HS), kaʔθhá·θneʔ ⟨it-power-is strong⟩ *it is potent* (HS), *it is powerful* (RC 28:7), reʔθhá·θneʔ ⟨he-power-is strong⟩ *he is enduring* (HS).

–(i)ʔθhaθnęhčr – authority, power, strength. *n.s.* uʔθhaθnę́hčreh ⟨power-be strong-'ness⟩ *authority, power, strength* (R).

–(i)ʔθhaθnęhčrayę(T) – be strong. *v.s.-s.i.* wakyeʔθhaθnę́hčrayęʔ ⟨I-power-be strong-'ness-lay⟩ *I am strong* (R).

–(i)ʔθhaθnęhst – prerogative, right. *n.s.* uʔθhaθnę́hsteh ⟨power-be strong-'ness⟩ *prerogative, right* (R).

–(i)ʔθhaθnęhstakʷ**ek** – be almighty, have the authority. *v.s.-a.i.* raʔθhaθnęhstakwé·kę ⟨he-power-be strong-'ness-is whole⟩ *he is almighty* (HS), ęhsiʔθhaθnęhstakwé·kek ⟨prediction-you-power-be strong-'ness-be whole⟩ *you will have the authority* (RC 23:3).

–(i)ʔθhaθnęhstaw – authorize. *v.s.-t.* raʔθhaθnę́hstaws ⟨he-power-be strong-'ness-gives⟩ *he authorizes it* (HS).

–(i)ʔθhęni – conquer, defeat, master, overpower. *v.r.-t.* hab: -ęhs, pnt: -ʔ, stat: -ę, prog: -, prp: -, dst: -, caus: -, rvs: -, dat: -, n-inc. waʔkheʔθhę̀·niʔ *I conquer him, her, one* (AG), *I defeated another* (R), waʔkakheʔθhę̀·niʔ *I conquer them* (AG); **–rihwaʔθhęni** –: rurihwaʔθhę́·nyęhs ⟨he-matter-defeats⟩ *he backslides* (HS); **–a'niʔθhęni** –: raʔniʔθhę́·nyęhs ⟨he-himself-defeats⟩ *he masters it, he overpowers it* (HS), ęyakwaʔniʔθhę̀·niʔ ⟨prediction-we-ourselves-defeat⟩ *we will defeat another* (RC 33:8); **–či** –. **–a'niʔθhęni** –: θhraʔniʔθhę́·nyęhs ⟨again-he-himself-defeats⟩ *he reconquers* (HS); **kwęhs –(i)ʔθhę=nyęʔT** –: kwęhs ahruʔθhęnyę́ʔthek ⟨no unknown-he-defeat-cause⟩ *he is unrelenting* (HS).

–(i)ʔθhęti – judge. *v.s.-t.* waʔkaʔθhę́·tiʔ ⟨fact-it-power-made⟩ *it judged* (RC 30:32).

–(i)ʔθk – empty noun root. *v.inc.* See: **–u** – *be in liquid,* **–uha** – *put in liquid,* **–u=har** – *wash,* **–uʔk(e)r** – *float on water.*

–(i)ʔθkuʔ – drown. *v.s.-a.i.* waʔkayéʔθkuʔ ⟨fact-they-X-be in water-began⟩ *they*

Tuscarora Pronunciation Key:
/a/ law; /e/ hat; /i/ pizza; /u/ tune; /ę/ hint; /č/ cheese; /h/ hoe; /m/ mother; /s/ same; /t/ do (before a vowel y, or w), too (elsewhere); /k/ gale (before a vowel y or w), kale (elsewhere); /n/ inhale (before a consonant or word-final), note (elsewhere), /r/ hiss (before a consonant or word-final), run (trilled as in Italian, elsewhere); /w/ cuff (before a consonant other than y or word-final), way (elsewhere); /y/ fish (before a consonant or word-final), you (elsewhere), /θ/ thing; /ʔ/ (the sound between the vowels in unh-unh); /·/ long vowel, /́/ high pitch; /̀/ low pitch.

drowned (R), rá'²θku'²θ ‹hc-X-bc in water-begins› *he drowns* (HS), ru'²-θkú'²ç ‹he-X-bc in water-began› *he drowned* (HS).

–(i)²θkuha – baptize, immerse. *v.s.-t.* na'²-ni'²θkúhahs ‹one=another-X-put in water› *one baptizes another, one immerses another* (HS).

–(i)²θkuha – baptism. *dv.n.s.* ha'² na'²-ni'²θkúhahs ‹the one=another-X-put in water› *baptism* (HS).

–(i)²θkurę'nye² – whirlwind. *dv.n.s.* yu'²-θkurę·'²nye'² ‹it-X-split-going along› *whirlwind* (HS).

–i²θkeri²naw – singe the fur off. *v.s.-a.i.* ęhsi'²θkyerí'²na'²w ‹prediction-you-'²?²-burn› *you will singe the fur off by throwing it on the coals* (R).

–(i)²θrehčr – automobile, car, vehicle. *n.s.* u'²θréhčreh ‹ride-'ness› *automobile, car, vehicle* (R).

–(i)²θrehčr –.#áh buggy. *n.s.* u'²θrehčre-háh ‹ride-'ness-little› *buggy* (HS).

–(i)²θrehčr – –ne –. –ahčarahkw – wheelbarrow. *n.s.* u'²θréhčreh neyęhčaráh-khwa'² ‹ride-'ness apart-one-fist-is in-instrument› *wheelbarrow* (HS).

–(i)²θrehčrawęhsT – tar. *dv.n.s.* ye'²θreh-črawę́hshtha'² ‹one-ride-'ness-possess-causes› *tar* (HS).

–(i)²θwa²nihu – be left-handed; be left side. *v.r.-s.i.* stat: -ę, prog: -, prp: -, dst: -, caus: -, rvs: -, dat: -, n-inc. ki'²θwa'²níhę *I am left-handed* (R); *my left side* (L 81) (*West.:* ki'²swa'²ni-hę́'²kye (PC)), ra'²θwa'²níhę *he is left-handed* (R); *his left side* (L 81), ye'²-θwa'²níhę *her left side* (L 81).

–i²ta²nath – thirst. *v.r.-s.i.* stat: -ę, prog: -, prp: -, dst: -, caus: -a'²T-, rvs: -, dat: -, n-inc. –i²ta²natha²T –: yaku'²ta'²nathá'²-tha'² ‹one-thirst-causes› *thirst* (HS); –i²ta²nathę² –: ki'²ta'²ná·thę'²θ ‹I-thirst-begin› *I am thirsty* (R), waki'²ta'²ná·-

thę'²θ ‹I-thirst-begin› *I got thirsty* (R). u'²ta'²nathę́'²ç ‹thirst-began› *thirst* (HS).

–i²ta²natha²T – thirst. *dv.n.s.* yaku'²ta'²-nathá'²tha'² ‹one-thirst-causes› *thirst* (HS).

–i²ta²nathę² – be thirsty. *v.s.-a.i.* ki'²ta'²-ná·thę'²θ ‹I-thirst-begin› *I am thirsty* (R), waki'²ta'²ná·thę'²θ ‹I-thirst-begin› *I got thirsty* (R).

–i²ta²nathę² – thirst. *n.s.* u'²ta'²nathę́'²ç ‹thirst-began› *thirst* (HS).

–(i)²tyęhs – nose. *n.r. West.* inaln: ki'²-tyę́hseh *my nose* (PC), inc., n.sfx. -eh. Western dialect form of the root –(ę)²tyęhs –. ki'²tyę́hseh *my nose* (PC), si'²tyę́hseh *your nose* (PC).

–i²yęT – regain strength, revitalize. *v.r.-s.i.* stat: -a'², prog: -, prp: -, dst: -, caus: -a'²T-, rvs: -, dat: -, n-inc. waki'²yę́·'²na'² *I have regained my strength* (RC 3:74).

K

k – my (first person singular inalienable). *n.r.pfx.* When followed by a noun root or stem beginning with certain consonant clusters, an "epenthetic" e intervenes between the prefix and the root or stem.

–k – I (first person singular agent). *v.r. pfx.* When followed by a verb root or stem beginning with certain consonant clusters, an "epenthetic" e intervenes between the prefix and the root or stem.

–k – empty noun root. *v.inc.* See: –uwan – *be chief.*

–k habitual aspect. *v.r.sfx.* Occurs following certain roots and stems that end in a short vowel when a modal prefix is also present.

-k stative aspect. *v.r.sfx.* Occurs following certain roots and stems that end in a short vowel when either the future or optative modal prefixes are present.

-k- eat. *v.r.-t.* hab: -s, pnt: -ɸ, stat: -ę, prog: -, prp: -he-, dst: -, caus: -, rvs: -, dat: -, inc.-ʔʔ-pat. Requires an incorporated noun specifying what is eaten. Perhaps seen in Lawson's «Utta-ana-wox» 'Have you got anything to eat,' from *-taʔnara·ks *...bread-eat-habitual.* -(a)hy**ak**he-: waʔkayehyá··kheʔ ‹fact-they-fruit-ate-going to› *they were going to eat fruit* (RC 11:17); -atkęhθr**ak**-: ętkęhθra·k ‹fact-it-pus-ate› *it ate pus* (RC 21:10); -či**h**= kwn**ak**-: kačíhkwna·ks *monkey* (R) ‹it-louse-eats›; -čihkwn**ak**-.#úʔy: kačih-kwnaksʔúʔy ‹it-louse-eats-great› *ape* (R); -či ʔr**ak**-: yučíʔra·ks ‹it-ember-eats› *one eats embers* (RC 28:12); -nęh**ak**- ranęhaks ‹he-corn-eats› *he eats corn* (H 2484); -nęhsn**ak**-: kanęhsna·ks ‹it-seed-eats› *it eats grain* (H 2484); -nęθ**ak**-: θnę·θa·k ‹you!-potato-eat› *eat your potato(es)!* (L 25), runęθá·kę ‹he-potato-ate› *he has eaten potatoes* (L 5); -taʔnar**ak**-: ktáʔnara·ks ‹I-bread-eat› *I am eating bread* (R); -tkuriʔn**ak**-: ęhratkuriʔnákshek ‹prediction-he-corn whey-eat› *he will be eating corn whey* (RC 24:8); -ʔwah= r**ak**-: kaʔwáhra·ks ‹it-meat-eats› *cannibal, carnivore* (RC 10:5), yuʔwáhra·ks ‹it-meat-eats› *cancer* (R), wak-ʔwáhra·ks ‹I-meat-eat› *it is eating me* (R); -či-.-a'nwęt**ak**-: θhraʔnwę·ta·ks ‹again-he-himself-word-eats› *he retracts it* (HS); -či-. -(i)hn**aks**- -(a)h= y**ak**-: θkęhná·ksęʔ wáhya·ks ‹wolf it-fruit-eats› *false Solomon's seal (Smilacina sp.)* (H-notebook); čír -(a)h= y**ak**-: čír wáhya·ks ‹dog it-fruit-eats› *nightshade (Solanum sp.)* (H-notebook); -hskwa'n- -(a)hy**ak**-: úhskwaʔ-neh wáhya·ks ‹snake it-fruit-eats› *partridge vine, partridge berry (Mitchella repens)* (H-notebook).

ka- hither, here (cislocative). *v.pfx.* Occurs in the imperative. (See: -t-.)

ka- its (third person singular neuter inalienable). *n.r.pfx.* Occurs preceding roots and stems that begin with a consonant or the vowel *i*, with which vowel it coalesces to yield -kę-. (See: **w-**.)

-ka- it (third person singular neuter agent). *v.r.pfx.* Occurs preceding roots and stems that begin with a consonant or the vowel *i*, with which vowel it coalesces to yield -kę-. (See: **w-**.)

ká·či come! (L 14). *v.*

-kahčęʔr-/-kahčiʔr- blink. *n.r.* poss. ?, inc., n.sfx. -eh. The form -kahčiʔr- occurs when incorporated. The form -kahčęʔr- occurs elsewhere. ukah-čęʔreh *a blink* (H-notebook); -atkah= čiʔraʔniha-: ratkahčiʔraʔníhahs ‹he-himself-blink-sprains› *he squints* (HS); -ne-. -atkahčiʔraʔniha-: nehratkahčiʔ-raʔníhahs ‹two-he-himself-blink-sprains› *he winks* (HS).

-kahčuʔn- eyelash. *n.r.* inaln: kkahčúʔ-neh *my eyelash* (R), n-inc., n.sfx. -eh.

ukahčú·'neh *eyelash* (R).

kahęwè·ya' black ash (*Fraxinus* sp.) (H-notebook). *n.* **kahęwè·ya'** **-etya'T -:** kahęwè·ya' wetyá·'nę ‹black ash it-produce-caused› *ashen* (HS).

kahęwè·ya' -etya'T - ashen. *dv.n.s.* kahęwè·ya' wetyá·'nę ‹black ash it-produce-caused› *ashen* (HS).

ká·hka·h raven (*Corvus corax*) (R) [Jefferson «cau-cau» 'raven']. *n.*

-kahkarihn - loop. *n.r.* poss. '?, inc. '?, n. sfx. -eh. ukahkaríhneh *loop* (HS).

-kahkaθn - have good vision. *v.s.-a.i.* rakahká·θne' ‹he-eye-is strong› *he has good vision* (R).

-kahkawę'n - bleary-eyed. *n.r.* poss. '?, inc. '?, n.sfx. -eh. ukahkawę́·'neh *bleary-eyed* (HS).

-kahkę - catch sight of. *v.s.-t.* wa'akukáhkę·' ‹fact-one-eye-saw› *it caught sight of one* (RC 28:11).

-kahkęhey - have haggard eyes. *v.s.-a.i.* rukahkęhè·yę ‹he-eye-died› *he has haggard eyes* (HS).

-kahkęni - discover. *v.s.-t.* rukahkę́·nyę ‹he-eye-excelled at› *he has discovered* (HS), rakahkę́·nyęhs ‹he-eye-excels at› *he discovers* (HS), wahrakahkę̀·ni' ‹fact-he-eye-excelled at› *he discovered* (RC 24:3).

Káhkwahs Erie (AG). *n.*

-kahkwahsT - be sharp-sighted. *v.s.-a.i.* rakáhkwahst ‹he-eye-is good› *he is sharp-sighted* (HS).

-kahkʷeksi - alarm. *v.s.-t.* natkahkwé·ksyęhs ‹one=another-ear-close-undoes› *one alarms another* (HS).

-kahkwe'r - eye-circles. *n.r.* poss. '?, inc. '?, n.sfx. -. Found only incorporated in the cited construction. **-kahkwe'ran =ha -:** kakahkwe'ránhę ‹it-eye-circles-is full› *it is full of eye-circles (said of a place, thicket, or other thing full of game that are at bay and looking out)*

(HS).

-kahkwiruh - give a black eye to. *v.r.-t.* hab: -ahs, pnt: -, stat: -, prog: -, prp: -, dst: -, caus: -, rvs: -, dat: -, n-inc. natkahkwirúhahs *one gives another a black eye* (HS).

-kahke'n - loop. *n.r.* poss. '?, inc. '?, n.sfx. -eh. ukahkyé·'neh *loop* (HS).

káhne·' someone, who, whoever (L 38). *part.* kwęhs káhne·' ‹no who› *no one* (AW 101).

-kahnę - boil, cook. *v.r.-t.* hab: -, pnt: -'', stat: -·, prog: -, prp: -hte''-, dst: -tyę-, caus: -, rvs: -ku-, dat: II (-ti-/-hθ-), inc.-ɸ-pat. Theoretically, it should not be possible to combine the reversive suffix with this root since one cannot "unboil" or "uncook" something. Nevertheless, the reversive does occur, adding an interruptive or completive sense. wakkáhnę· *I boil it* (R), ękayekáhnę·' *they will boil (stew) it* (L 35), wa'ekáhnę·' *one cooked it* (RC 29:9); **-kahnę -{dative II}:** wa'natkáhnęhθ ‹fact-one=another-boiled-for› *one cooked for another* (R); **-kahnęhte'-:** yekahnę́hte' ‹one-boil-going to› *stew* (SH 375); **-kahnęku -:** wa'ekahnę́·ku' ‹fact-one-boil-undid› *one took it off the fire* (RC 29:11); **-atkahnęhkw -:** yętkahnę́hkhwa' ‹one-oneself-boils-instrument› *things for starting a fire (e.g., flints)* (RC 8:13); **-atkahnętyę -:** wa'ętkahnę́·tyę' ‹fact-one-oneself-boiled-much› *one built a fire* (RC 3:39).

-kahnę -{dative II} cook for. *v.s.-t.* wa'natkáhnęhθ ‹fact-one=another-boiled-for› *one cooked for another* (R).

-kahnęhte - stew. *dv.n.s.* yekahnę́hte' ‹one-boil-going to› *stew* (SH 375).

-kahnęku - take off the fire. *v.s.-t.* wa'ekahnę́·ku' ‹fact-one-boil-undid› *one took it off the fire* (RC 29:11).

kahnę́ʔkye when (R). *part.*

-kahnę́ʔnaku- be out of sight. *v.r.-a.i.*
hab: -, pnt: -ʔ, stat: -, prog: -, prp: -,
dst: -, caus: -, rvs: -, dat: -, n-inc.
waʔekahnę́ʔnakuʔ *one is out of sight*
(RC 29: 12).

-kah(r)- eye; glasses, spectacles. *n.r.* inaln: kkáhreh *my eye* (R), aln: akkáh-
rawęh *my glasses, spectacles* (R).
n.sfx. -eh. The form -kah- occurs
when the root is incorporated before
stems beginning with the consonant *k.*
The form -kahr- occurs elsewhere.
ukáhreh *eye* (R); *glasses, spectacles*
(HS) [Gallatin «ookawreh»]; -kah=
kaθn-: rakahkáθneʔ ‹he-eye-is strong›
he has good vision (R); -kahkę-: waʔ-
akukáhkęʔ ‹fact-one-eye-saw› *it
caught sight of one* (RC 28:11); -kah=
kęhey-: rukahkęhè·yę ‹he-eye-died› *he
has haggard eyes* (HS); -kahkęni-:
rukahkę́·nyę ‹he-eye-excelled at› *he
has discovered* (HS), rakahkę́·nyęhs
‹he-eye-excels at› *he discovers* (HS),
wahrakahkę̀·niʔ ‹fact-he-eye-excelled
at› *he discovered* (RC 24:13); -kah=
kwahsT-: rakáhkwahst ‹he-eye-is
good› *he is sharp sighted* (HS); -kah=
kʷeksi-: natkahkwé·ksyęhs ‹one=an-
other-ear-close-undoes› *one alarms another* (HS); -kahranęhsku-: wahrakahranęhskuʔ ‹fact-he-eye-stole› *he
peaked at it* (RC 7:8); -kahrat-.#hči:
nakwakahratáhči ‹you!=us-eye-stand-
very› *share our vision* (R); -kahra=
yę(T)-{dative I}: ęhskáhrayęʔθ ‹pre-
diction-you-eye-lay-for› *you must*

*leave a trap (leave something (as bait)
to catch the eye)* (R); -kahręʔke: e-
kahrę́ʔkye ‹one-eye-at› *(on) one's eye*
(RC 26:10); -kahrę́ʔkeha·ʔ: ukahrę́ʔ-
kyéha·ʔ ‹eye-customarily› *ocular* (HS);
-kahrhar-{dative III}: wahrakarhà·ręʔ
‹fact-he-eye-hung-for› *he laid down a
snare* (R); -kahritkę-: yukahrí·tkęʔ ‹it-
eye-comes forth› *protruding eyes* (AW
57); -kahriyu-: kakahrí·yu· ‹it-eye-is
great› *large eyes* (AW 45); -či-.
-kahraks-: θkakahrá·ksęʔ ‹again-it-
eye-is bad› *pickerel* (H 3518); -ne-.
-kahkʷek-: nehrakahkwé·kę ‹two-he-
eye-closed› *he is blind* (R); -ne-.
-kahrahręhw-: nekakahráhręw ‹two-it-
eye-put up-causes› *crooked eyes* (RC
13:8); -ne-. -kahrare-: nehrakáhrareʔ
‹two-he-eye-is distant› *he looks upward* (RC 3:77); ti-. -kahraʔθrę-.#úʔy:
tikakahraʔθręʔúʔy ‹so-it-eye-is so big-
great› *huge eyes* (RC 28:9); -atkah=
keθku-: waʔkayętkahkyé·θkuʔ ‹fact-
they-themselves-eye-raised› *they
raised their eyes* (RC 3:77); -atkah=
rahtrę-: ratkahráhtręhs ‹he-himself-
eye-ties› *he is blindfolded* (HS); -a=
tkahratʔahst-: yętkahratʔáhstha ‹one-
oneself-eye-put in-causes› *telescope*
(HS); -ne-. -atkahkʷek-: nęwakatkah-
kwé·kęk ‹two-prediction-I-myself-eye-
close› *my eyes will be closed* (RC 3:
20), neyutkahkwé·kę ‹two-it-itself-eye-
closed› *its eyes are closed* (RC 7:12);
-ne-. -atkahraʔnihr-: waʔnwatkahráʔnir
‹fact-two-it-itself-eye-stood up› *it opened its eyes* (RC 8:22); -t-. -atkahr=

ʔu -: nahratkárʔuʔ ⟨hither-fact-he-him-self-eye-showed⟩ *he blinked, he winked* (RC 26:28); -yah -. -atkahrawiʔT -: weyutkahrawíʔnę ⟨thither-it-itself-eye-give to-caused⟩ *it was peaking* (RC 8:35); -čisnuhku - -kahrakęw: yučisnúhkuʔ ukáhrakęw ⟨it-spot-covered eye-in⟩ *pupil (of the eye)* (HS).

-kahranęhsku - peak at. *v.s.-t.* wahrakahranęhskuʔ ⟨fact-he-eye-stole⟩ *he peaked at it* (RC 7:8).

-kahrat -.#hči share a vision. *v.s.-t.* nakwakahratáhči ⟨you!=us-eye-stand-very⟩ *share our vision* (R).

-kahrayę(T) -{dative I} leave a trap. *v.s.-a.i.* çhskáhrayęʔθ ⟨prediction-you-eye-lay-for⟩ *you must leave a trap (leave something to catch the eye)* (R).

-kahreʔn - brow, eyebrow. *n.r.* poss. ʔ, inc. ʔ, n.sfx. -eh. ukahréʔneh *brow, eyebrow* (HS).

-kahreʔwar - eye-like spots over the eyes. *n.r.* poss. ʔ, inc., n.sfx. -. Found only in the cited construction. -kahreʔwa=rawę -: yukahreʔwà·rawęʔ ⟨it-eye-like spots over the eyes-possesses⟩ *it has eye-like spots over its eyes (the presence of such spots on dogs is believed to mean that these dogs are more "witchy")* (HS).

-kahrę(w) - be an opening. *v.r.-s.i.* stat: -·ʔ, prog: -, prp: -, dst: -, caus: -, rvs: -, dat: -, inc.-ɸ-pat. The form -kah=ręw - occurs whenever a vowel-initial suffix follows. It may also occur in other positions for a few speakers. For most, however, the form -kahrę - occurs elsewhere. See: -(i)hskahręw - *mouth.* -kahręw -: ukahrè·weh ⟨be an opening⟩ *breach, fissure, hole, opening* (HS); -hneʔrakahrę(w) -: yuhneʔrakáhrę·ʔ ⟨it-root-is an opening⟩ *there is an opening in the root* (RC 25:2); -ʔęya=kahrę(w) -: yuʔęyakáhrę·ʔ ⟨it-enclos-

ure-is an opening⟩ *lane* (HS); -nęh=sakahrę(w) -: yunęhsakáhrę·ʔ ⟨it-house-is an opening⟩ *the house has an opening, an aperture* (H 2484); -ta'na=kahrę(w) -: yuta'nakáhrę·ʔ ⟨it-settle-ment-is an opening⟩ *street* (HS); -ʔnyehrakahrę(w) -: yuʔnyehrakáhrę·ʔ ⟨it-chimney-is an opening⟩ *chimney hole* (RC 27:17); -ne -. -a'naʔwnakah=ręwa'ne -: nęwa'na'wnakahrè·wa'neʔ ⟨apart-prediction-it-itself-land-be an opening-be present⟩ *it will create an opening in the land* (RC 3:70); wa'-nwa'na'wnakahrè·wa'neʔ ⟨fact-apart-it-itself-land-be an opening-was present⟩ *it created an opening in the land* (RC 3:73); kwęhs -rihwakahręʔT -: kwęhs aryurihwakahrę́'nak ⟨no un-known-it-matter-be an opening-cause⟩ *unreasonable* (HS).

-kahręw - breach, fissure, hole, opening. *n.s.* ukahrè·weh ⟨be an opening⟩ *breach, fissure, hole, opening* (HS).

-kahręʔkeha·ʔ ocular. *n.s.* ukahręʔkyé-ha·ʔ ⟨eye-customarily⟩ *ocular* (HS).

-kahrhar -{dative III} lay down a snare. *v.s.-a.i.* wahrakarhà·ręʔ ⟨fact-he-eye-hung-for⟩ *he laid down a snare* (R).

-kahθ - tear. *n.r.* n-poss., inc., n.sfx. -. Found only incorporated in the cited construction. -kahθʔe(k) -: yukáhθʔe· ⟨it-tear-struck⟩ *it is hollow-eyed* (H-notebook).

-kahθariʔn - tattered. *n.r.* n-poss., n-inc., n.sfx. -eh. ukahθaríʔneh *tattered* (H-notebook).

-kahθr - tear. *n.r.* inaln: kkáhθreh *my tear* (R), inc., n.sfx. -eh (archaic: -iʔ). ukáhθreh *tear* (R), ukáhθriʔ *tear* (HS); -kahθrakęw: rakáhθrakęw ⟨he-tear-in⟩ *he is in tears* (HS); -ne -. -kahθraruh=θrę -: nehrakahθrarúhθręh ⟨apart-he-tear-ʔʔ⟩ *he sheds tears* (HS).

-kahθʔe(k) - be hollow eyed. *v.s.-s.i.* yukáhθ'e· ‹it-tear-struck› *it is hollow eyed* (H-notebook).

-kahshe(y) - all of you...all of them; all of you...him, her; you alone...all of them (second person non-singular agent=third person singular patient; second person non-singular agent= third person non-singular patient; second person singular agent=third person non-singular patient). *v.r.pfx.* The form -kahshey - occurs before roots and stems that begin with a vowel. The form -kahshe - occurs before roots and stems that begin with a consonant.

-kahT - catch sight of. *v.r.-t.* hab: -ha', pnt: -ɸ, stat: -, prog: -, prp: -, dst: -, caus: -, rvs: -, dat: -, inc.-ɸ-pat. wá'kkaht *I caught sight of it* (R); čwe -. -kahT -: čweyú·kaht ‹all kinds of-it-caught sight of› *commonality* (HS); -yah -. -a'nwętakahT -: weyę'-nwętakáhtha' ‹thither-one-oneself-word-catches sight of› *one overhears* (RC 4:3).

káhwih coffee (R). *n.*

ka·kakáh cluck (sound of a chicken) (R). *part.*

kakaw -/kaku - their (third person plural alienable). *n.r. pfx.* The form kakaw - occurs before roots and stems that begin with a vowel other than *a*. The form kaku - occurs before roots and stems that begin with a consonant or the vowel *a*, which vowel drops.

-kakaw -/-kaku - they, them (third person plural patient). *v.r.pfx.* The form

-kakaw - occurs before roots and stems that begin with a vowel other than *a*. The form -kaku - occurs before roots and stems that begin with a consonant or the vowel *a*, which vowel drops.

-kakhe(y) - I...them (first person singular agent=third person plural patient). *v.r. pfx.* The form -kakhey - occurs before roots and stems that begin with a vowel. The form -kakhe - occurs before roots and stems that begin with a consonant.

kà·nar colonel (HS). *n.*

-kanęT - lick. *v.r.-t.* hab: -, pnt: -ɸ, stat: -, prog: -, prp: -, dst: -hę-, caus: -, rvs: -, dat: -, inc.-ɸ-pat. čhiká·nę·t *lick it, you all!* (RC 3:58), wa'nyakuká·nę·t *the two of them licked it* (RC 3:57); -kanęthę -: nekakané·thęh ‹two-it-lick-much› *the two of them lick a lot* (RC 3: 58); -hsu'kwakanęt -: su'kwaká·nę·t ‹finger-licked› *red squirrel (Tamiasciurus hudsonicus)* (R); -či -. -hsu' = kwakanęt -: čuhsu'kwaká·nę·t ‹again-it-finger-licked› *red squirrel (Tamiasciurus hudsonicus)* (AG).

Kanętakaryáhskye Washington, District of Columbia (AG). *n.*

Kanętayę́'ku Philadelphia, Pennsylvania (AG). *n.*

kanyú' as soon as, provided that (HS). *part.*

-kar - cost, debt, expense, price. *n.r.* n-poss., inc., n.sfx. -eh. ú·kareh *cost, debt, expense, price* (HS); -karanę -: natkarà·nęh ‹one=another-debt-guards›

Tuscarora Pronunciation Key:
/a/ law; /e/ hat; /i/ pizza; /u/ tune; /ę/ hint; /č/ cheese; /h/ hoe; /m/ mother; /s/ same; /t/ do (before a vowel y, or w), too (elsewhere); /k/ gale (before a vowel y or w), kale (elsewhere); /n/ inhale (before a consonant or word-final), note (elsewhere), /r/ hiss (before a consonant or word-final), run (trilled as in Italian, elsewhere); /w/ cuff (before a consonant other than y or word-final), way (elsewhere); /y/ fish (before a consonant or word-final), you (elsewhere), /θ/ thing; /'/ (the sound between the vowels in unh-unh); /·/ long vowel, /´/ high pitch; /`/ low pitch.

surety (lit., one guards another's debt)
(HS); -k**a**ra**ʔ**tyenę -: rakara**ʔ**tyè·nęh
‹he-debt-measures› *he values* (HS);
-k**a**ruhar -: rakarúhar ‹he-debt-washes›
he indemnifies (HS); -k**a**rya**ʔ**k -: na-
tká·rya**ʔ**ks ‹one=another-debt-breaks›
one credits another (HS); -k**a**rya**ʔ**kčr -:
ukaryá**ʔ**kčreh ‹debt-break-'ness› *hireage, salary, wages* (HS); -atk**a**rayę =
'n**a**hkw -: ratkarayę**ʔ**náhkhwa**ʔ** ‹he-himself-debt-lays-instrument› *he pledges*
(HS); -atk**a**ruharT -: yutkaruhárnę ‹it-
itself-debt-wash-caused› *indemnity*
(HS); -atk**a**rut -: yękyátkaru·t ‹we two-
debt-stand› *I owe another or you, another or you owe me* (SH 375); -atk**a** =
rya**ʔ**k -: rutkaryá**ʔ**ki ‹he-himself-debt-
broke› *his pension* (HS).
-kar - clank, make a noise. *v.r.-s.i.* stat:
-ɸ, prog: -, prp: -, dst: -, caus: -, rvs:
-, dat: -, inc.-ɸ-pat. yú·kar *it clanks, it
makes a noise* (HS); kwè·ni**ʔ** -θa**ʔ** =
r**a**kar -: kwè·ni**ʔ** yuθá**ʔ**rakar ‹like it-
bacon-makes a noise› *you can even
hear the fat rattle (said when a very
fat woman sings)* (R); -ne -. -aθnar =
čr**a**kar -: newaθnárčrakar ‹apart-it-cry-
'ness-makes a noise› *it sobs* (HS);
-ne -. -**ʔ**tyęhkr**a**kar -: nehra**ʔ**tyęhkrakar
‹apart-he-snot-makes a noise› *he snivels* (HS).
ká·ra· dandelion (*Taraxacum officinale*)
(H-notebook). *n.*
karáhkę**ʔ** always (RC 25:9). *part.* karahkę**ʔ**.#eθu**ʔ**: karahkę**ʔ**é·θu**ʔ** ‹always-
great · many› *perpetually* (HS); ha**ʔ**
karáhkę**ʔ** -ęhra**ʔ**na'nye**ʔ** -: ha**ʔ** karáhkę**ʔ**
ęhra**ʔ**ná·**ʔ**nye**ʔ** ‹the always sort-stand-
going along› *perpetuity* (HS); ha**ʔ**
karáhkę**ʔ** kwę -ti -. -hT -: ha**ʔ** karáhkę**ʔ**
kwę tì·yuht ‹the always like so-it-
stands› *ordinarily* (HS); ha**ʔ** karáhkę**ʔ**
-ti -. -hT -: ha**ʔ** karáhkę**ʔ** tì·yuht ‹the
always so-it-stands› *ordinary* (HS).

karahkę**ʔ**.#eθu**ʔ** perpetually. *part.* karahkę**ʔ**é·θu**ʔ** ‹always-great many› perpetually (HS).
-karahrę - be thin. *v.r.-s.i.* stat: -·, prog: -,
prp: -, dst: -hę-, caus: -, rvs: -, dat: -,
inc.-ɸ-pat. Found only with incorporated noun roots. -nęhs**a**karahrę -: ka-
nęhsakaráhrę· ‹it-house-is thin› *the
(sides of the) house are thin* (H-notebook); ti -. -(i)hn**a**karahrę -: tyehnaka-
ráhrę· ‹so-one-skin-is thin› *one's skin
is so delicate* (RC 3:57).
-k**a**ranę - surety. *dv.n.s.* natkarà·nęh
‹one=another-debt-guards› *surety (lit.,
one guards another's debt)* (HS).
kà·rarih cholera (HS). *n.*
-karati - rub against. *v.r.-t.* hab: -h, pnt: -,
stat: -e**ʔ**, prog: -, prp: -, dst: -hę-,
caus: -hT-, rvs: -, dat: -, inc.-ɸ-pat.
rakará·tih *he rubs it against it* (HS);
-čikęw**a**karati -: račikęwakará·tih ‹he-
fiddle-rubs› *he is playing the fiddle*
(R); -ręhsk**a**ratihT -: yeręhskaratíhtha**ʔ**
‹one-leg-rub against-causes› *violin*
(HS); -rihst**a**karati -: rarihstakará·tih
‹he-iron-rubs› *he files* (HS); -ne -.
-hny**a**karati -: nehruhnyakará·tye**ʔ** ‹a-
part-he-news-rubbed› *he tattled* (HS),
nehrahnyakará·tih ‹apart-he-news-rubs›
he tattles (HS).
karátkwar red oak (*Quercus rubens*), elm
(*Ulmus* sp.); any reddish colored tree
(H-notebook) [Jefferson «kau-raunt-
qual» 'oaks']. *n.*
kà·ra**ʔ** sturgeon (R) *n.* Lounsbury, p. 78,
gives the form [gá·rah].
-k**a**ra**ʔ**tyenę - value. *v.s.-t.* rakara**ʔ**tyè·nęh
‹he-debt-measures› *he values (i.e., as-
signs a value to) it* (HS).
-kareru - roll. *v.r.-a.i.* stat: -·, prog: -,
prp: -, dst: -, caus: -**ʔ**T-, rvs: -, dat: -
, inc.-ɸ-ag./pat. Found only with an
incorporated noun root. -ht**a**wakareru -:
yuhtawakaré·ru· ‹it-stream of water-

rolls *shoal* (AG); -ht̲awakareru?T -: yuhtawakarerú'̓nę ‹it-stream of water-roll-causes› *rapids* (HS); -atkerh̲a̲ka = reru?nahnę -: watkyerhakareru'̓náhnęh ‹it-itself-body-roll-causes-much› *some roll themselves* (RC 27: 10).

-kare(ti) - be loud. *v.r.-a.i.* stat: -·, prog: -, prp: -, dst: -, caus: -, rvs: -, dat: -, inc.-ɸ-pat. The form -kare- occurs before the inchoative. The form -kare = ti - occurs elsewhere. -hsęn̲akareti -: ruhsęnakaré·tih ‹he-name-is loud› *he has influence* (HS); -θręhn̲akareti -: ruθręhnakaré·tih ‹he-dream-is loud› *he snores* (HS); -węt̲akareti -: ruwętakaré·ti· ‹he-voice-is loud› *his voice is loud* (RC 12:3); -yaθęhst̲akareti -: ruyaθęh-stakaré·ti· ‹he-be called-'ness-is loud› *he is famous* (HS); kwęhs -rih = w̲akare? -: kwęhs aryurihwakaré'̓ęk ‹no unknown-it-matter-be loud-begin› *it is unheard (of)* (HS).

-karę(hw) - bypass, go around. *v.r.-t.* hab: ()-s, pnt: ()-?, stat: ()-ę°, prog: -, prp: -, dst: ()-θę- ~ -hrę-, caus: -hT-, rvs: -, dat: -, inc.-ɸ-ag./pat. No generalization about the occurrence of the form -karęhw- versus the occurrence of -karę- can be made on the basis of the available data. Historically, the form -karęhw- may be derived from the form -karę- through the addition of the causative -hw-, but the meaning difference has been lost and the two forms function as alternants of a single root. ę'̓nwakà·ręw *we will go around* (AW 55); -ne -. -karehrę -: neh-rakaréhrçh ‹apart-he-goes around-much› *he agitates it* (HS), nakaka-réhrę'̓ ‹apart-unknown-it-go around-much› *that it disturb its position* (RC 3:22); -(a)hah̲akarę(hw) -: rahahakà·ręws ‹he-path-goes around› *he turns back, retraces his way; he puts a turn in the road* (H 2484); -a?wn̲akaręhrę -: wa'̓wnakahréhrę'̓ ‹it-earth-goes a-round-much› *earthquake* (R); -rihw̲a = karę(hw) -: rarihwakà·ręws ‹he-matter-goes around› *he stirs up strife* (HS); -atkarę(hw) -: ratkà·ręws ‹he-himself-goes around› *he turns (out or away)* (HS), yutkaréhę ‹it-itself-went around› *it has turned; turn* (HS); -arahska = rę(hw) -: warahskà·ręws ‹it-itself-foot-goes around› *it paws* (HS); -yah -. -atkaręhwθę -: yahwa'̓kayętkaréwθę·'̓ ‹thither-fact-they-themselves-went a-round-much› *they traveled greatly* (RC 29:11); tha+ne -. -atkaręhT -: tha'̓-newatkaréhnę ‹unusual-apart-it-itself-go around-caused› *it rocks back and forth* (RC 3:2); ti+yah -. -atkarę(hw) -: thwewatkà·ręws ‹so-thither-it-itself-goes around› *it travels back and forth* (RC 8:38); -či -. -athah̲akarę(hw) -: θakayęthahakà·ręw ‹again-fact-they-themselves-path-went around› *they returned* (RC 12:11); -atkaręhrę - -?θkwehs -: ęhsatkaréhrę'̓ u'̓θkwéhseh ‹prediction-you-yourself-go around-much chair› *rocking chair* (R).

-karęni - damage, injure. *v.r.-t.* hab: -h, pnt: -, stat: -, prog: -, prp: -, dst: -, caus: -, rvs: -, dat: -, n-inc. rakarę·nih

Tuscarora Pronunciation Key:
/a/ l̲aw; /e/ h̲at; /i/ p̲izza; /u/ t̲une; /ę/ h̲int; /č/ c̲heese; /h/ h̲oe; /m/ m̲other; /s/ s̲ame; /t/ do (before a vowel y, or w), too (elsewhere); /k/ gale (before a vowel y or w), k̲ale (elsewhere); /n/ in̲hale (before a consonant or word-final), n̲ote (elsewhere). /r/ his̲s̲ (before a consonant or word-final), run (trilled as in Italian, elsewhere); /w/ cuff (before a consonant other than y or word-final), w̲ay (elsewhere); /y/ fish (before a consonant or word-final), you (elsewhere). /θ/ thing; /'̓/ (the sound between the vowels in unh-unh); /·/ long vowel, /'/ high pitch; /`/ low pitch.

he damages it, he injures it (HS); **-ka=rẹnyahT** -: ukarẹ·nyaht ‹injury-cause› *harm, injury* (HS); ** haʔ -atkarẹniʔ** -: haʔ kakutkarẹníʔẹ ‹the they-themselves-damage-began› *the damned* (HS).

-karẹnyahT - harm, injury. *n.s.* ukarẹ·nyaht ‹injury-cause› *harm, injury* (HS).

-karhaT - turn upward. *v.r.-t.* hab: -, pnt: -, stat: -, prog: -, prp: -, dst: -ahnẹ-, caus: -hu-, rvs: -, dat: -, inc.-ɸ-pat. **-karhathu** -: rakarhá·thuhs ‹he-turn upward-causes› *he turns it over, he inverts it* (HS); **-tehwakarha'nahnẹ** -: ratehwakarhaʔnáhnẹh ‹he-skin-turns upward-much› *he stretches out skins* (RC 8:21).

-karhathu - invert, turn over. *v.s.-t.* rakarhá·thuhs ‹he-turn upward-causes› *he turns it over, he inverts it* (HS).

-kari - consume, devour. *v.r.-t.* hab: -ahs, pnt: -ʔ, stat: -ẹ, prog: -, prp: -ahθeʔ-, dst: -, caus: -aʔT-, rvs: -, dat: -, inc.-ɸ-pat. raká·ryahs *he devours it* (R), ahskà·riʔ *that you devour it* (RC 11:13), ẹkhekà·riʔ *I will eat someone* (RC 30:39); **-(a)čẹhakari** -: ẹyakučẹhakà·riʔ ‹prediction-one-fire-devour› *one's family will be consumed* (RC 15:10); **-hwenẹtihstakari** -: rahwenẹtihstaká·ryahs ‹he-island-make-'ness-devours› *he devastates a continent or a country* (HS); **-nẹhskari** -: ranẹhská·ryahs ‹he-house-devours› *he robs the house, i.e., he creates a disturbance in the house* (H-notebook), *burglar* (HS), kanẹhská·ryahs ‹it-house-devours› *it devours the house (as a disease when it attacks successively the members of the same family)* (HS); **-ta'nakari** -: rataʔnaká·ryahs ‹he-village-devours› *he is raising a ruckus (lit., eating up the settlement or in the house)* (L 44), *he pillages, he ravages* (HS), rutaʔ-

nakáryẹ ‹he-village-devoured› *he has raised a fuss* (L 44), θtaʔnakà·ri ‹you!-village-devour› *raise a fuss!* (L 44); **-werakari** -: kweraká·ryahs ‹I-air-devour› *I am inhaling* (RC 9:7); **-(ẹ)ʔni=kahkaryaʔT** -{dative III}: rẹʔnikẹhkaryaʔná·tih ‹he-mind-devour-causes-for› *he macerates, he tortures it* (HS); **-yah** -. **-e** - **-ta'naka-ryahθe** -: wáʔθe θtaʔnakaryáhθe ‹thither-you!-go you!-village-devour-going to› *go raise a fuss!* (L 44).

-karuhar - indemnify. *v.s.-t.* rakarúhar ‹he-debt-washes› *he indemnifies* (HS).

kà·ruʔ hither (RC 3:56), less than (AG). *part.* **karúʔ.#kye**: karúʔkye ‹hither-at› *since* (HS).

karúʔ.#kye since. *part.* karúʔkye ‹hither-at› *since* (HS).

-karyaʔk - credit. *v.s.-t.* natká·ryaʔks ‹one=another-debt-breaks› *one credits another* (HS).

-karyaʔkčr - hireage, salary, wages. *n.s.* ukaryáʔkčreh ‹debt-break-'ness› *hireage, salary, wages* (HS).

-kaθn - be heavy (of animates), be strong. *v.r.-s.i.* See: **-aθn** -.

-kaθʔah be a child, be a boy, be a girl. *v.r.-k.* This root is unusual in two ways. First, it shows a unique plural form that is created through infixation, i.e., **kayekẹtí·θʔah** *children*. Second, it may take either the verbal or the nominal form of the third person feminine/indefinite singular agent pronoun. yeká·θʔah *child: girl* (R) (also: eká·θʔah (RC 1:2)), raká·θʔah *boy* (R); **-kaθ=ʔah.#keha·ʔ**: ekaθʔahkyéha·ʔ ‹one-is a child-customarily› *childish* (HS); **-kaθʔah.#kẹheʔ**: kkaθʔahkẹheʔ ‹I-am a child-deceased› *I was young* (R); **-kaθʔah -ẹ°ʔnhekʷT** -: eká·θʔah yẹʔnhékwthaʔ ‹one-is a child one-play a game-causes› *child's play* (HS).

-kaθ⁷ah -ę°⁷nhek^wT - child's play. *dv.n.s.* eká·θ⁷ah yę⁷nhékwtha⁷ ‹one-is a child one-play a game-causes› *child's play* (HS).

-kaθ⁷ah.#keha·⁷ childish. *n.s.* ekaθ⁷ah-kyéha·⁷ ‹one-is a child-customarily› *childish* (HS).

-kaθ⁷ah.#kęhe⁷ be young. *v.s.-a.i.* kkaθ-⁷ahkęhe⁷ ‹I-am a child-deceased› *I was young* (R).

Katarakraθ⁷á·ka·⁷ Cattaraugus Seneca (R). *n.*

katéčra⁷θ pumpkin (H-notebook). *n.*

-kawe - row a boat. *v.r.-a.i.* hab: -, pnt: -·⁷, stat: -, prog: -, prp: -, dst: -, caus: -, rvs: -, dat: -, n-inc. wa⁷kká·we·⁷ *I rowed a boat* (R); -kaweȟčr-: uka-wéhčreh ‹row a boat-'ness› *oar* (HS).

-kaweȟčr - oar. *n.s.* ukawéhčreh ‹row a boat-'ness› *oar* (HS).

-kawehs - corn cob. *n.r.* n-poss., n-inc., n.sfx. -eh. ukawéhseh *corn cob* (HS).

kà·winar governor (HS). *n.*

kaya -/kayak -/kaye - their (third person plural inalienable). *n.r.pfx.* The form kaya - occurs before certain roots and stems that begin with the vowel *i*. The form kayak - occurs before roots and stems that begin with the vowel *u* or the morphophoneme {ę°}. The form kaye - occurs before roots and stems that begin with consonants, the vowels *a* and certain cases of *i*, the vowel *e*, with which the final vowel of the prefix coalesces to yield kayę -, and the vowel *ę* which causes the final *e* of the prefix to be dropped.

-kaya -/-kayak -/-kaye - they (third person plural agent). *v.r.pfx.* The form -kaya - occurs before certain roots and stems that begin with the vowel *i*. The form -kayak - occurs before roots and stems that begin with the vowel *u* or the morphophoneme {ę°}. The form -ka = ye - occurs before roots and stems that begin with consonants, the vowels *a* and certain cases of *i*, the vowel *e*, with which the final vowel of the prefix coalesces to yield -kayę -, and the vowel *ę* which causes the final *e* of the prefix to be dropped.

-kayeθa - they...you alone (third person plural agent=second person singular patient). *v.r.pfx.* The final *a* of the prefix is dropped before roots and stems that begin with a vowel other than *i*. When the initial vowel of the roots or stem is *i*, the final *a* coalesces with it to yield -kayeθę -.

-kayę - be willing to, permit. *v.r.-t.* hab: -, pnt: -·⁷, stat: -, prog: -, prp: -, dst: -, caus: -, rvs: -, dat: -, n-inc. ękà·yę⁷ *it permitted* (RC 35:10), eθakà·yę⁷ *that you permit* (RC 35:5), wahrukà·yę⁷ *he agreed to it* (RC 3:13).

-kayęk -/-kayęk^w - they...me (third person plural agent=first person singular patient). *v.r.pfx.* The form -kayęk^w - occurs before roots and stems that begin with the vowel *a*. The form -kayęk - occurs elsewhere with insertion of "epenthetic" e before roots and stems that begin with certain consonant clusters.

kayę'naT(ę) - he, she...them; the two of them...them; they...him, her; they...the two of them; they...them (third person (singular, dual, plural) agent=third person plural patient; third person plural agent=third person (singular, dual, plural) patient). *v.r.pfx.* The form **kayę'na'nę** - occurs before certain roots and stems that begin with the consonant *n* or the consonant clusters *hn* or *ht*. The form **kayę'nat-** occurs before roots and stems that begin with the consonants *k, ', * or *h*; when the root or stem begins with the cluster *hs*, this cluster coalesces with the final *t* of the prefix to yield **kayę'načh-**. The form **kayę'na'n** - occurs before roots and stems that begin with a vowel. The form **kayę'na'** - occurs before roots and stems that begin with the consonants *t, č, r* or, sometimes, *n*. The form **kayę'na'ne** - occurs before roots and stems that begin with clusters that condition the appearance of "epenthetic" e.

kayhá·ya· no wonder (R). *part.*

-ka'n - circle, hoop, ring, round, wheel. *n.r.* n-poss., inc., n.sfx. -eh. uká'neh *circle, hoop, ring, round, wheel* (HS); **-ka'n-.#áh:** uka'neháh ‹ring-little› *ringlet* (HS); **-ka'na'ni:** uká'na'ni ‹ring-at edge of› *at edge of circle* (RC 31:3); **-ka'nayę(T)** -: wahraká'nayę' ‹fact-he-ring-laid› *he went in a circle* (RC 31:3); **-ka'nęte:** uka'nę́·te ‹ring-certain one› *wheel* (AG); **-ne-.-ka'=nuhrarak** -: nehraka'núhraraks ‹two-he-wheel-presses› *brakeman* (HS).

-ka'n-.#áh ringlet. *n.s.* uka'neháh ‹ring-little› *ringlet* (HS).

-ka'nayę(T) - go in a circle. *v.s.-a.i.* wahraká'nayę' ‹fact-he-ring-laid› *he went in circle* (RC 31:3).

-ka'ne - have many, have much. *v.r.-s.i.* stat: -', prog: -, prp: -, dst: -, caus: -, rvs: -, dat: -, inc.-φ-pat. This root may also appear as **-ka'nę** -, i.e., with a final nasal rather than oral vowel. wakká'ne' *I have an abundance, I have much* (HS). ruká'ne' *he has many or much* (H-notebook); **-ahθuh=kwaka'ne** -: yuhθuhkwaká'ne' ‹it-paint-instrument-has much› *having many colors* (HS); **-ęhaka'ne** -: rawę́haká'ne' ‹he-gun-powder-has much› *he had plenty of gunpowder* (HS); **-nęhsnaka'ne** -: runęhsnaká'ne' ‹he-seed-has much› *he has abundance of grain, much grain* (H 2484); **-węta=ka'ne** -: yuwętaká'ne' ‹it-word-has many› *wordy* (HS); **-'ęhraka'ne** -: yu'ęhraká'ne' ‹it-leaf-has many› *lettuce* (HS).

ka'nehnę́ although, even though (H 34 83). *part.*

ka'nę́ just! (RC 2:11), very (L 29). *part.* **ka'nę́ hà·ne'** ‹just! that is› *exactly that, precisely* (HS); **ka'nę́ kyè·nę·** ‹just this is› *exactly that, precisely* (HS); **ha' ka'nę́** ‹the just!› *definitely* (AW 45); **ha' ka'nę́ -tukę'** -: ha' ka'nę́ utukę́'ę ‹the just ??-began› *for sure* (AW 98); **ka'nę́ -tukę'** -: ka'nę́ utukę́'ę ‹just ??-began› *for sure* (AW 50).

ka'nę́ hà·ne' ‹just! that is› exactly that, precisely (HS). *part.*

ka'nę́ kyè·nę· ‹just this is› exactly that, precisely (HS). *part.*

ka'nę́ -tukę' - for sure. *dv.n.s.* ka'nę́ utukę́'ę ‹just ??-began› *for sure* (AW 50).

-ka'nęte wheel. *n.s.* uka'nę́·te ‹ring-certain one› *wheel* (AG).

ka'nęwehę̀·we actually (H-notebook). *part.*

Ka'tárhwaht Spirit of the North Wind (SH 375), The Pythoness (RC 5:title),

mythic reptile, dinosaur (RC 6:title).
n.

ka²ti²í²i· crow (morning call of a rooster) (R). *part.*

-kč- cup, dish, plate; cymbal. *n.r.* aln:
akyékθawẹh *my dish* (R), inc., n.sfx.
-eh. úkθeh *cup, dish, plate* (R);
cymbal (HS); -kčihsak-: rakčíhsa·ks
‹he-dish-seeks› *he looks for dish* (H-
notebook); -kčiyu-: kakčí·yu· ‹it-dish-
is great› *large dish* (H-notebook);
-kθakewa²T-: yekθakyewá²tha² ‹one-
dish-wipe-causes› *washcloth* (HS);
-kθẹti-: rakθẹ́·tih ‹he-dish-makes› *potter* (HS); -kθhar-{dative II}-.#ú²y:
wa²na²nekθherhahθ²²ú²y ‹fact-one=
another-dish-hung-for-big› *one put a
big dish before another* (RC 30:49);
-kθhraku-: θekθrá·ku ‹you!-dish-put
up-undo› *take the dishes off* (L 54);
-kθhrawẹ-: ẹhsekθrà·wẹ² ‹prediction-
you-dish-put up-several› *you will set
the table, you will put dishes around*
(R); -kθhrawẹhte-: θekθrawẹ́hte
‹you!-dish-put up-many-going to› *set
the dishes (on the table)* (L 54);
-kθiyu-: kakθí·yu· ‹it-dish-is great›
large dish (H-notebook); -kθuharT-:
kakθuhárnẹ ‹it-dish-wash-caused›
dishwater (H-notebook); -či-.-kθaT-:
θkákθa·t ‹again-it-dish-stands› *one
dish, panful* (HS); -ne-.-kθahkw-:
wa²thrákθahkw ‹fact-apart-he-dish-
pick up› *he picked up dish* (RC 6:9);
-t-.-kθẹ-: nakákθẹ² ‹hither-fact-it-
dish-fell› *dish fell* (R); -yah-.-kθẹ²ni-:
yahwa²kakθẹ́·²ni² ‹thither-fact-it-dish-

threw› *it threw dish there* (RC 11:22);
tha+ne-.-kčihẹ: tha²nyukčíhẹ ‹unusual-apart-it-dish-in middle of› *half a
dish* (RC 18:3), tha²nyukθíhẹ ‹unusual-apart-it-dish-in middle of› *middle of dish* (RC 20:1); -kč- -ya²=
tarahsT-: úkθeh yeya²taráhstha² ‹dish
one-body-be in-causes› *chalice* (HS);
-kθanurẹ- -ẹtya²T-: kakθanú·rẹ· ya-
kyetyá²tha² ‹it-dish-is precious one-
make-causes› *porcelain* (HS).

-kč- -ya²tarahst- chalice. *n.s.* úkθeh
yeya²taráhstha² ‹dish one-body-be in-
causes› *chalice* (HS). -

#ke at (external locative). *enc.* See also:
-a²ke, -ehke, and -ẹ²ke. athu².#ke:
athú²kye ‹cold-at› *north* (R) [Lawson
«Hothooka» 'Northwest wind']; awẹ².
#ke: awẹ́²kye ‹water-at› *watery (of
roads)* (HS); -a'nu²knahkw.#ke: u²-
nu²knahkẹ́·kye ‹self-end-instrument-at›
ultimate (HS); -a²ruhčrẹhkw-.#ke:
yẹ²ruhčrẹhkhwá²-kye ‹one-oneself-
gathers-instrument-at› *(at) church*
(HS); -a²wnanẹha·².#ke: u²wnanẹ-
há·²kye ‹land-be old-at› *in the old
country* (L 61); -či-.-hterhẹ.#ke: θuh-
terhẹ́·kye ‹again '?-it ?-X-is day-at›
forenoon (HS), *in the morning* (H
447); -či-.-w(e)r-.#ke: θkawé²rkye ‹a-
gain-it-air-at› *January* (R) (HS:
February 15-March 15); čikhe².#ke:
čikhé²kye ‹salt-at› *ocean* (HS); -ẹ²kʷe-
.#ke: ẹkwéhkye ‹human-at› *among the
people* (R); henẹ².#ke: henẹ́²kye
‹then-at› *then* (HS); he²thu.#ke: he²-
thúhkye ‹there-at› *at that time* (RC

3:72); -**hskut**.#**ke**: uhskú·tkyc ‹south-at› *south* (R); -**inẹr**.#**ke**: kẹnẹ́ʔrkyc ‹August-at› *June 15-July 15* (HS); -**ir**-.#**ke**: awíʔrkyc ‹grain-at› *on soil* (RC 5:7); -**nẹhseθ**-.#**ke**: kanẹhsé·θkye ‹it-house-is long-at› *at longhouse* (RC 26:8); -**nẹhseθẹ**-.#**ke**: kanẹhseθẹ́·kye ‹it-house-is long-many-at› *at longhouses* (RC 3:4); -**rẹhy**-.#**ke**.#**hrunẹ**ʔ: kayerẹhyaʔkyehrù·nẹʔ ‹they-sky-at-pcople› *angels* (R); -**taˈnaθe**-ʔ.#**ke**: Utaʔnaθéʔkyc ‹settlement-new-at› *Geneva, New York* (R) [Morgan, League «O-tä-nä-sä´-ga»]; -**taˈn**-.#**ke**.-**hrẹ**-: kataʔnaʔkyéhrẹʔ ‹it-settlement-at-many› *towns* (R); **ti**-.-**re**-.#**ke**-: tyuréʔkye ‹so-it-is distant-at› *anterior, previously* (HS); **tuʔaka·**ʔ.#**ke**: tuʔaká·ʔkye ‹Seneca-at› *to the Senecas* (AW 102); **uhtaʔkẹ́ʔkye** ‹before-at› *following* (RC 3:24).

#**keha·**ʔ customary. *enc.* The primary function of the customary enclitic is to indicate a behavior or condition that is typically associated with the preceding noun, e.g., **akʷ**-.#**keha·**ʔ: akwehkyéha·ʔ ‹deer-customarily› *cervine* (HS), **awẹ**ʔ.#**keha·**ʔ: awẹʔkyéha·ʔ ‹water-customarily› *aquatic, of the water* (RC 3:76), *fond of water* (H-notebook), **čir**.#**kéha·**ʔ čirkyéha·ʔ ‹dog-customarily› *canine* (HS), -**ẹˈni**=**yu**-.#**keha·**ʔ: awẹʔniyuʔkyéha·ʔ ‹day-great-customarily› *diurnal, occurring during the day* (RC 3:2), -(**ẹ**)**taʔr**-.#**keha·**ʔ: utaʔrẹʔkyéha·ʔ ‹head-customarily› *cephalic* (HS), and -(**ẹ**)ʔ=**tikẹhr**-.#**keha·**ʔ: uʔtikẹhrẹʔkyéha·ʔ ‹mind-customarily› *spiritual* (HS). As indicated by the preceding examples, the resulting constructions are typically glossed as adjectives in English. However, the customary may also be used to form words that are translated into English as nouns, e.g., -**hehn**-.#**keha·**ʔ: uhchnaʔkyéha·ʔ ‹field-customarily› *agriculture* (HS), ruhehnaʔkyéha·ʔ ‹he-field-customarily› *agriculturalist, peasant* (HS).

-**kehn**- headstrap, belt used to fasten loads. *n.s.* ukyéhneh ‹carry on back› *headstrap, belt used to fasten loads* (HS).

-**kehnahsi**- unburden. *v.s.-t.* natkyehnáhsyẹhs ‹one=another-carry on back-undoes› *he unburdens* (HS).

-**kehr**- distribute, heap, pile up, put around, put up. *v.r.-t.* hab: -ẹhs, pnt: -ẹ´ʔ, stat: -ẹ´ʔ, prog: -, prp: -, dst: -, caus: -, rvs: -, dat: -, inc.-ɸ-pat. yukyéhrẹʔ *it is placed* (RC 3:75), rakyéhrẹhs *he heaps it, he piles it* (HS), wahrakyéhrẹʔ *he put around* (RC 7:7); -**kehrẹhst**-: ukyehrẹ́hsteh ‹pile-'ness› *pile* (HS); -**či**-.-**kehr**-: čukyéhrẹʔ ‹again-it-piled› *it is a pile* (R); -**hskẹ́ʔrạkehr**-: kahskẹ́ʔrakyéhrẹʔ ‹it-bone-piled› *pile of bones* (RC 8:12); -**kθạkehr**-: waʔkayekθakyéhrẹʔ ‹fact-they-dish-piled› *they put up dishes* (RC 6:7); -**kerhạkehr**-: kakyerhakyéhrẹʔ ‹it-body-piled› *pile of bodies* (RC 8:12); -**atkehr**-: yutkyéhrẹʔ ‹it-itself-piled› *they are heaped, they are piled, they are stacked (applicable to a collection of inanimate objects)* (H 2892), utkyéhreh ‹self-pile› *lump, tumor* (HS).

-**kehrẹhst**- pile. *n.s.* ukyehrẹ́hsteh ‹pile-'ness› *pile* (HS).

-**kehsT**- dangle. *v.r.-t.* hab: -haʔ, pnt: -, stat: -, prog: -, prp: -, dst: -, caus: -, rvs: -, dat: -, inc.-ɸ-pat. Found only in the cited construction. -**aʔnahskehsT**-: kayẹʔnahskyéhsthaʔ ‹they-themselves-foot-dangle› *they dangled their feet* (RC 12:13).

-**kehT(aT)**- carry on one's back (tra-

ditionally, fastened by a headstrap).
v.r.-t. hab: -ha' ~ ()-s, pnt: -ɸ ~ ()-ɸ,
stat: -c' ~ ()-ɸ, prog: -, prp: -, dst: -,
caus: -, rvs: -ahsi-, dat: -, inc.-ɸ-pat.
The form –**kehnaT** – occurs in the presence of the semireflexive when no
other suffix (e.g., the reversive) is
present. The form –**kehT** – occurs elsewhere. natkyéhna·č *one burdens another* (HS); –**kehn** –: ukyéhneh ‹carry
on back› *headstrap, belt used to fasten
loads* (HS); –**kehnahsi** –: natkyehnáh-
syęhs ‹one=another-carry on back-undoes› *he unburdens* (HS); –**hskę'ra** =
kehT –: kakuhskę'rakyéhtha' ‹they-
bone-carry on back› *warriors* (RC 24:
10), ruhskę'rakyéhne' ‹he-bone-carried on back› *warrior* (R); –**atkehnaT** –:
yętkyéhna·č ‹one-oneself-carries on
back› *one carries a burden* (R); –**a** =
tkehnahsi –: wa'ętkyehnáhsi' ‹fact-
one-oneself-carry on back-undid› *one
unfastened it and took it off one's
back* (RC 3:41); –**a'na'wnakehnaT** –:
ęhra'na'wnakyéhna·t ‹prediction-he-
himself-earth-carry on back› *he will
bear the earth on his back* (RC 3:79);
–**či** –. –**atkehnaT** –: čętkyéhna·t ‹again-
fact-one-oneself-carried on back› *a-
gain one carried on one's back* (RC
3:46).

–**kehu** – be starlit, be unclouded (night
sky). *v.r.-s.i.* stat: -ę, prog: -, prp: -,
dst: -, caus: -, rvs: -, dat: -, n-inc.
yukyéhę *it is starlight, it is starlit, it is
unclouded* (HS).

–**kekT(i)** –/–**keky** – the two of us...you a-
lone; the two of us...the two of you;
the two of us...all of you; I...the two
of you (first person dual exclusive
agent=second person (singular, dual,
plural) patient; first person singular
agent=second person dual patient). *v.
r.pfx.* The form –**kekn** – occurs before
roots and stems that begin with the
vowel ę or the morphophoneme {"u}.
The form –**kekt** – occurs before roots
and stems that begin with the vowels
e, i, or u not from {"u}. The form
–**keky** – occurs before roots and stems
that begin with the vowel a. The form
–**kekti** – occurs before roots and stems
that begin with a consonant.

–**kekwa** – all of us...you alone; all of
us...the two of you; all of us...all of
you; I...all of you (first person plural
exclusive agent=second person (singular, dual, plural) patient; first person
singular agent=second person plural
patient). *v.r.pfx.* The final *a* of the
prefix combines with an initial *i* of a
root or stem to yield –**kekwę** –. Before
other root or stem-initial vowels, the
final *a* of the prefix is dropped.

–**kenę** – put down. *v.r.-t.* hab: -, pnt: -,
stat: -·, prog: -, prp: -, dst: -, caus: -,
rvs: -, dat: -, n-inc. yukyé·nę· *it put
down* (RC 3:60).

–**kenha** – strive. *v.r.-t.* hab: -hs, pnt: -',
stat: -ę, prog: -, prp: -, dst: -, caus:
-a'T-, rvs: -, dat: I (-'θe-/-'θ-), inc.-ɸ
~-ahθ-ag./pat. –**atkenha** –: wahsatkyén-
ha' ‹fact-you-yourself-strove› *you got
up (out of bed)* (R); –**ahθkenha** –: rah-

θkyénhahs ‹he-X-strives› *he is fighting for it, he is competing for it* (R);
–ahθkenha? –: uhθkyenhá''ę ‹X-strive-
begin› *avarice, avidity, covetousness,
greediness* (HS); –ahθkenha –{dative
I}: ruhθkyenhá''θc· ‹he-X-strove-for›
he is greedy (HS); –a'nahθkenha –: ra''-
nahθkyénhę ‹he-himself-X-strove› *he
bustles, he defends, he hurries, he
hastens, he strives for* (HS), wahra''-
nahθkyénha'' ‹fact-he-himself-X-
strove› *he pushed himself harder, he
struggled to help* (RC 36:2); –kerha =
kenha –: ękękyerhakyénha'' ‹prediction-
I=you-body-strive› *I will help you*
(RC 11:7), ęhskwakyerhakyénha''
‹prediction-you=I-body-strive› *you all
will help me* (RC 6:2), rakyerha-
kyénhahs ‹he-body-strives› *he is helping* (HS); –kerhakenha?T –: ukyerhakyénha''t ‹body-strive-cause› *aid, assistance, favor* (HS); –rihwakenha –
{dative I}: na''rihwakyenhá''θeh ‹one=
another-matter-strives-for› *one intercedes for another* (HS); –ne –, –rihwa =
kenha –: nęyerihwakyénha'' ‹apart-prediction-one-matter-strive› *the two of
them will argue* (L 41), nehrarihwakyénhahs ‹apart-he-matter-strives› *advocate, lawyer: he argues* (HS), nehrurihwakyénhę ‹apart-he-matter-strove›
he debates (HS), neyurihwakyénhę ‹a-
part-it-matter-strove› *discussion* (HS);
–a'natkerhakenha –: ękayę''natkyerha-
kyénha'' ‹prediction-they-themselves-
body-strive› *they will help themselves*
(R); ha? –ahθkenha –: ha'' rahθkyénhahs ‹the he-X-strives› *competitor*
(HS); ha? –a'nahθkenha –: ha'' ru''nahθkyénhę ‹the he-himself-X-strove› *his
ardor* (HS).

–kerh – body; letter (of the alphabet), *n.r.*
inaln: kkyerhę́''kyę *(on) my body* (R),
inc., n.sfx. –eh. ukyérheh *body* (RC

28:1); *letter (of the alphabet)* (HS);
–kerhačiwak –: yukyerhači·wakę ‹it-
body-is bitter› *bitter hickory* (H-notebook); –kerhahtir –: rukyerhahtì·rę ‹he-
body-is durable› *he is able-bodied*
(HS); –kerhahtir –.#ha?nę?: kakukyer-
hahtiręhá''nę'' ‹they-body-is durable-
many› *they are strong people* (RC 24:
6); –kerhakehrę –: kakyerhakyéhrę'' ‹it-
body-put up› *piles of bodies* (RC 8:
12); –kerhakenha –: ękękyerhakyénha''
‹prediction-I=you-body-strive› *I will
help you* (RC 6:2), ęhskwakyerhakyénha'' ‹prediction-you=me-body-
strive› *you all will help me* (R); –ker =
hakenha?T –: ukyerhakyénha''t ‹body-
strive-cause› *aid, assistance, favor*
(HS); –kerhakęhey –: rukyerhakęhè·yę
‹he-body-died› *he is enfeebled* (HS);
–kerhakęw: rakyérhakęw ‹he-body-in›
in his body (RC 21:3); –kerhakraθ –:
kakyerhá·kra·θ ‹it-body-smells› *goat*
(R), skyerhá·kra·θ ‹you-body-smell›
you have body odor (R); –kerhaks –:
skyerhá·kse· ‹you-body-is bad› *you
have body odor* (R); –kerhakT: ukyér-
hakwt ‹body-next to› *side of body*
(RC 12:28); –kerhaku?čęri –: wahra-
kyerhaku''čę·ri'' ‹fact-he-body-found›
he found bodies (RC 12:15); –ker =
hakʷek –: kayekyerhakwé·kę ‹they-
body-closed› *they have entire body*
(RC 6:11); –kerhar –: yukyérhar ‹body-
is in› *engraving, portrait* (HS), natkyérhar ‹one=another-body-is in› *one
takes another's picture, one paints
another's picture* (HS); –kerhar –{dative
III}: wa''kkyerhà·rę'' ‹fact-I-body-was
in-for› *I drew it* (R), wa''khekyer-
hà·rę'' ‹fact-I=another-body-was in-
for› *I drew someone, I photographed
someone* (R), wa''katkyerhà·rę'' ‹fact-
I-myself-body-was in-for› *I drew myself* (R); –kerhat?a –: ęhskwakyerhá·t-

ʼaˑʼ ‹prediction-you=me-body-put in›
all of you will put me in it (RC 3:22);
–kerhawyesT –: rukyerhawyésnę ‹he-
body-is seemly› *he has grace of body*
(HS); –kerhayenę –: rukyerhayèˑnęhs
‹he-body-grabs› *he has spasms* (HS);
–kerhayę(T) –: kakyérhayęʼ ‹it-body-
lays› *there is body* (RC 8:32); –ker=
hęhawihT –: yekyerhęhawíhthaʼ ‹one-
body-carry-causes› *litter, stretcher*
(HS); –kerhęT –: rakyerhęˑʼneʼ ‹he-
body-concludes› *he commends* (HS);
–kerhęti –: kakyerhęˑtih ‹it-body-makes›
puppet (HS); –kerhihar –: kakyerhíheʼr
‹it-body-hung› *body hangs* (RC 6:14);
–kerhihe –: yukyerhíheʼ ‹it-body-put
on› *bodies were put on* (RC 8:12);
–kerhiʼrę –: ękayekyerhíʼręʼ ‹prediction-they-body-set› *they will set body*
(RC 6:13); –kerhiʼθ(e)r –: waʼkaye-
kyerhíʼθeʼr ‹fact-they-body-dragged›
they dragged body (RC 6:12); –ker=
huhar –: natkyerhúhar ‹one=another-
body-tips› *one affixes ones body to
the end of a pole or other pole-like instrument or thing* (H-notebook); –ker=
huhar –: natkyerhúhar ‹one=another-
body-washes› *one exculpates, one
washes one's body* (H-notebook);
–kerhuhčr –: ukyerhúhčreh ‹body-cov-
er-'ness› *clothes, coat, dress* (R); –ker=
huhčręti –: rakyerhuhčręˑtih ‹he-body-
cover-'ness-makes› *he makes clothing:
tailor* (HS); –kerhuhsku –: rukyerhúhskę ‹he-body-bared› *he is alone, he is
single* (HS); –kerhukęʼ: yukyerhúˑkęʼ
‹it-body-less› *incorporeal* (HS); –ker=

hur –: natkyérhuč ‹one=another-body-is
in› *one dresses another* (HS); –ker=
huʼawi –: yukyerhuʼàˑwiʼ ‹it-body-
floated› *body floated along* (RC 3:75);
–kerhuʼkT –{dative III}: waʼnyaku-
kyerhúʼknęʼ ‹fact-two-one-body-en-
ded-for› *the two of them came to end
of its body* (RC 3:58); –kerhuˈnarhu –:
nakkyerhuʼnárhęhk ‹you!=me-body-
hook-cause› *defend me from it!* (RC
3:57); –ne –. –kerhaʼθku –: nekakyerháʼ-
θkwahs ‹apart-it-body-take along› *it
brings bodies* (RC 32:14); –t –. –kerhę –:
nahrakyérhęʼ ‹hither-fact-he-body-fell›
he fell (R); ti –. –kerhahwaθaʼθra=
ˈnyeʼ –: tikakyerhahwaθaʼθráˑʼnyeʼ
‹so-it-body-width-is so big-going a-
long› *body width* (RC 15:2); ti –.
–kerhaʼθ –: tikayekyérhaʼθ ‹so-they-
body-are of a size› *size of their bodies*
(RC 6:11); ti –. –kerhęy –: thwaʼukyer-
hęˑyeʼ ‹so-fact-it-body-hang down›
body hung over it (RC 17:2); –yah –.
–kerhę –: yahwahrakyérhęʼ ‹thither-
fact-he-body-fell› *he fell there* (RC
26:28); –ne+t –. –kerhuʼkrahteʼ –: nęʼna-
yakukyerhuʼkráhteʼ ‹apart-fact-hither-
one-body-floated on top-going to›
one's body was floating (RC 3:77);
–atkerhanę –: aryętkyérhanęˑt ‹un-
known-one-oneself-body-guard› *that
one protect oneself* (RC 17:2); –a=
tkerharaku –: ętkyerharáˑkuʼ ‹fact-it-it-
self-body-collected› *it took itself away*
(RC 2:8); –atkerhaʼneʼku –: ęhsatkyer-
haʼnéʼkuʼ ‹prediction-you-yourself-
body-flee› *you will pull back, you*

---

will withdraw (RC 3:54); **–atkerhihs** =
ʔa –: waʔǫtkyerhíhsʔa·ʔ ‹fact-one-oneself-body-finished› *one grew to adulthood* (RC 3:37); **–atkerhur** –: rutkyer-
hù·rę ‹he-himself-body-cover-was in›
he has coat on (RC 2:1); **–či** –. **–ker** =
hakuhe –: θahrakyerhakúheʔ ‹again-
fact-he-body-pick up-going to› *he was
going picking bodies back up* (RC
11:25); **–či** –. **–kerhęhawi** –: θkakyerhę-
hà·wiʔ ‹again-it-body-carried› *it brings
back bodies* (RC 8:20); **–či** –. **–atker** =
hęti –: čutkyerhę́·tih ‹again-it-itself-
body-makes› *it remakes its body* (RC
15:10); **–či** –. **–atkerhuʔkrahT** –: θahra-
tkyerhúʔkraht ‹again-fact-he-himself-
body-floated on top› *he came floating
back up* (RC 3:90); **–ne+t** –. **–atker** =
hęhT –: nęʔnahratkyérhęht ‹apart-fact-
hither-he-himself-body-fall-caused› *he
cast himself down there* (RC 26:31);
tha+ne –. **–atkerhayaʔθ(e)r** –: thaʔneyutkyerhayáʔθer ‹unusual-apart-it-itself-
body-crosses› *body is crisscrossed*
(RC 30:31); **haʔ** **–kerhęti** –: haʔ ka-
kyerhę́·tih ‹the it-body-makes› *statue*
(HS); **–kerhakęw kęʔnáʔkę**: ukyérhakęw kęʔnáʔkę ‹body-in side› *inward*
(HS); **–kerhętyahnę** – **–weniyuhčręti** –:
kakyerhętyáhnęh rawęniyuhčrę́·tih ‹it-
body-makes-much he-be God-'ness-
makes› *idolater* (HS).

–**kerhačiwak** – bitter hickory. *n.s.* yukyer-
hačì·wakę ‹it-body-is bitter› *bitter hickory (Carya sp.)* (R).

–**kerhahtir** – be able-bodied. *v.s.-s.i.* ru-
kyerhahtì·rę ‹he-body-is durable› *he is
able-bodied* (HS), kakukyerhahtirę̨háʔ-
nęʔ ‹they-body-is durable-many› *they
are strong people* (RC 24:6).

–**kerhakenha** – help. *v.s.-t.* ękękyerha-
kyénhaʔ ‹prediction-I=you-body-
strive› *I will help you* (RC 6:2), ęh-
skwakyerhakyénhaʔ ‹prediction-you=

me-body-strive› *you all will help me*
(R).

–**kerhakenhaʔT** – aid, assistance, favor.
n.s. ukyerhakyénhaʔt ‹body-strive-
cause› *aid, assistance, favor* (HS).

–**kerhakęhey** – be enfeebled. *v.s.-s.i.* ru-
kyerhakęhè·yę ‹he-body-died› *he is
enfeebled* (HS).

–**kerhakęw kęʔnáʔkę** inward. *n.s.* ukyérhakęw kęʔnáʔkę ‹body-in side› *inward*
(HS).

–**kerhakraθ** – goat. *n.s.* kakyerhá·kra·θ ‹it-
body-smells of› *goat (Capra sp.)* (R).

–**kerhakraθ** – have body odor. *v.s-s.i.*
skyerhá·kra·θ ‹you-body-smell› *you
have body odor* (R).

–**kerhaks** – have body odor. *v.s-s.i.* skyer-
há·ksę ‹you-body-is bad› *you have
body odor* (R).

–**kerhar** – engraving, portrait. *dv.n.s.* yukyérhar ‹body-is in› *engraving, portrait* (HS).

–**kerhar** – paint a picture of, take a picture. *v.s.-t.* natkyérhar ‹one=another-
body-is in› *one takes another's picture,
one paints a picture of someone* (HS).

–**kerhar** –**{dative III}** draw, photograph.
v.s.-t. waʔkkyerhà·ręʔ ‹fact-I-body-
was in-for› *I drew it* (R), waʔkhe-
kyerhà·ręʔ ‹fact-I=another-body-was
in-for› *I drew someone, I photographed someone* (R), waʔkatkyer-
hà·ręʔ ‹fact-I-myself-body-was in-for›
I drew myself (R).

–**kerhatʔa** – put in. *v.s.-t.* ęhskwakyer-
há·tʔa·ʔ ‹prediction-you=me-body-put
in› *all of you will put me in it* (RC 3:
22).

–**kerhayenę** – have spasms. *v.s.-a.i.* ru-
kyerhayè·nęhs ‹he-body-grabs› *he has
spasms* (HS).

–**kerhęhawihT** – litter, stretcher. *dv.n.s.*
yekyerhęhawíhthaʔ ‹one-body-carry-
causes› *litter, stretcher* (HS).

-**kerhęT** – commend. *v..s.-t.* rakyerhę̨·'ne'⁾ ‹he-body-concludes› *he commends* (HS).

-**kerhęti** – puppet. *dv.n.s.* kakyerhę́·tih ‹it-body-makes› *puppet* (HS).

-**kerhęti** – statue. *dv.n.s.* ha'⁾ kakyerhę́·tih ‹the it-body-makes› *puppet* (HS).

-**kerhętyahnę** – -**weniyuhčręti** – idolater. *dv.n.s.* kakyerhętyáhnęh rawęniyuhčrę́·tih ‹it-body-makes-much he-be God-'ness-makes› *idolater* (HS).

-**kerhuhar** – exculpate, wash body. *v..s.-t.* natkyerhúhar ‹one=another-body-washes› *one exculpates another, one washes one's body* (H-notebook).

-**kerhuha̲r** – affix to the end of a pole. *v.s.-t.* natkyerhúhar ‹one=another-body-tips› *one affixes one's body to the end of a pole or other pole-like instrument or thing* (H-notebook).

-**kerhuhčr** – clothes, coat, dress. *n.s.* ukyerhúhčreh ‹body-cover-'ness› *clothes, coat, dress* (R).

-**kerhuhčręti** – tailor. *dv.n.s.* rakyerhuhčrę́·tih ‹he-body-cover-'ness-makes› *tailor* (HS).

-**kerhuhsku** – be alone, be single. *v.s.-s.i.* rukyerhúhskę ‹he-body-bared› *he is alone, he is single* (HS).

-**kerhukę'** incorporeal. *dv.n.s.* yukyerhú·kę'⁾ ‹it-body-less› *incorporeal* (HS).

-**kerhur** – dress. *v.s.-t.* natkyérhuč ‹one=another-body-is in› *one dresses another* (HS).

-**kerhu'narhu** – defend someone from. *v.s.-t.* nakkyerhu'nárhęhk ‹you=me-body-hook-cause› *defend me from it!*

(RC 3:57).

-**kerwę'** – be in motion. *v.r.-a.i.* hab: -θ, pnt: -, stat: -, prog: -, prp: -, dst: -, caus: -, rvs: -, dat: -, n-inc. yukyérwę'θ *it is in motion* (H-notebook).

-**keθku** – lift, raise. *v.r.-t.* hab: -ahs, pnt: -', stat: -ę, prog: -, prp: -, dst: -, caus: -, rvs: -, dat: -, inc.-ɸ-pat. wa'⁾-kkyé·θku'⁾ *I raised it up (said of a chief at a Condolence Ceremony or of an inanimate object)* (R), natkyé·-θkwahs *one elects another* (HS); -či -. -**keθku** -: θhrakyé·θkwahs ‹again-he-raises› *he reestablishes it, he reordains it* (HS); -**atkeθku** -: rutkyé·θkwę ‹he-himself-raised› *he has raised himself* (HS), wahratkyé·θku'⁾ ‹fact-he-himself-raised› *he raised himself* (R); -či -. -**atkeθku** -: θhratkyé·θkwahs ‹again-he-himself-raises› *he recovers* (HS); -**nęhsakeθku** -: ranęhsakyé·θkwahs ‹he-house-raises› *he erects a house, he is rearing a house* (HS); -**atkahkeθku** -: wa'⁾kayętkahkyé·θku'⁾ ‹fact-they-themselves-eye-raised› *they raised their eyes* (RC 3:77); -**a'nwętakeθku** -: ra'⁾-nwętakyé·θkwahs ‹he-himself-voice-raises› *he raises his voice* (HS).

-**keT** – scrape. *v.r.-t.* hab: -, pnt: -ɸ, stat: -, prog: -, prp: -, dst: -hę-, caus: -, rvs: -, dat: -, inc.-ɸ-pat. wá'⁾kkye·t *I scraped it* (PC); -**kethę** -: wa'⁾kkyé·-thę·'⁾ ‹fact-I-scraped-much› *I scratched it, I sawed it* (R), wa'⁾kakyé·thę·'⁾ ‹fact-it-scraped-much› *it (a nail) scratched it* (HS), ęhskyé·thę·'⁾ ‹prediction-you-scrape-much› *you will*

---

scratch (as for an itch) (HS); **-ke=
thᶒhkw** -:   yekyethᶒhkhwa⁷   ‹one-
scrapes-much-instrument›   *scraper*
(HS);   **-či⁷rurakethᶒ** -:   ᶒyeči⁷rura-
kyé·thᶒ·⁷   ‹prediction-one-medicine
stick-scrape-much›   *one   will   scrape
(bark) from medicine stick* (RC 19:2).
-kethᶒ - saw, scrape, scratch. *v.s.-t.* wa⁷-
kkyé·thᶒ·⁷   ‹fact-I-scraped-much›   *I
scratched it, I sawed it* (R), wa⁷-
kakyé·thᶒ·⁷ ‹fact-it-scraped-much› *it (a
nail) scratched it* (HS), ᶒhskyé·thᶒ·⁷
‹prediction-you-scrape-much› *you will
scratch (as for an itch)* (HS).
-kethᶒhkw - scraper. *dv.n.s.* yekyethᶒhkhwa⁷ ‹one-scrapes-much-instrument›
scraper (HS).
-keya⁷T - ??. *v.r.-a.i.* hab: -ha⁷, pnt: -ɸ,
stat: -, prog: -, prp: -, dst: -, caus: -,
rvs: -, dat: -, inc.-ɸ-ag. Found only in
composition with the incorporated
noun root **-(ᶒ)⁷tikᶒh(r)** -. **-(ᶒ)⁷tikᶒh =
keya⁷T** -: na⁷tikᶒhkyeyá⁷tha⁷ ‹one=
another-mind-??› *one is solicitous of
another/one discourages another* (HS),
wahru⁷tikᶒhkyè·ya⁷t ‹fact-he-mind-??›
he concluded (RC 27:8), ru⁷tikᶒhke-
yá⁷tha⁷ ‹he-mind-??› *he is oppressed*
(HS), ra⁷tikᶒhkeyá⁷tha⁷ ‹he-mind-??›
he is solicitous (HS), wa⁷kaku⁷tikᶒh-
kyè·ya⁷t ‹fact-they-mind-??› *they arrived at a conclusion* (RC 3:72).
-ke⁷č - bundle, burden, dough, lump,
mass, ointment. *n.r.* n-poss., inc., n.
sfx. -eh. ukyé⁷čeh *bundle, burden,
dough, lump, mass, ointment* (HS);
-ke⁷č -: yukyé⁷čeh ‹it-dough› *doughy,
soggy* (HS); **-ke⁷č** -.**#hči**: ukye⁷čéhči
‹dough-very› *doughy* (HS); **-ke⁷ča̲ =
čirwᶒ** -: rakye⁷čačí·rwᶒhs ‹he-dough-
strangles› *he kneads* (HS); **-ke⁷ča̲ =
tkᶒhnahkw** -: yekye⁷čatkᶒhnáhkhwa⁷
‹one-dough-be rotten-causes-instru-
ment› *one leavens it* (HS); **-ke⁷čᶒti** -:

ᶒyekye⁷čᶒ́·ti⁷ ‹prediction-one-dough-
make› *one will make a bundle* (RC
20:1), *one will make a wad* (RC 23:
4), *one will knead* (HS); **-ne** -.
-atke⁷čahkw -: nehratkye⁷čáhkhwa⁷
‹apart-he-himself-dough-picks up› *he
hops, he jumps* (HS); **-ne** -. **-atke⁷ =
čahkwahte** -.**#ú⁷y**:   newatkye⁷čah-
kwahte⁷ú⁷y ‹apart-it-itself-dough-pick
up-going to-great› *big thing is jumping around a lot* (R); **ti+ne** -.
-atke⁷čahkw -: thwa⁷nwatkyé⁷čahkw
‹so-fact-apart-it-itself-dough-picked
up› *it jumped together* (RC 9:4);
kwᶒhs -ke⁷čatkᶒh -: kwᶒhs aryukye⁷-
čatkᶒ́hᶒk ‹no unknown-it-dough-be
rotten-begin› *it is unleavened* (HS).
-ke⁷č - doughy, soggy. *n.s.* yukyé⁷čeh
‹it-dough› *doughy, soggy* (HS).
-ke⁷č -.**#hči** doughy. *n.s.* ukye⁷čéhči
‹dough-very› *doughy* (HS).
-ke⁷ča̲čirwᶒ - knead. *v.s.-a.i.* rakye⁷ča-
čí·rwᶒhs ‹he-dough-strangles›   *he
kneads* (HS).
-ke⁷čatkᶒhnahkw - leaven. *v.s.-t.* yekye⁷-
čatkᶒhnáhkhwa⁷ ‹one-dough-be rotten-
causes-instrument›   *one   leavens it*
(HS).
-ke⁷čᶒti - knead. *v.s.-a.i.* ᶒyekye⁷čᶒ́·ti⁷
‹prediction-one-dough-make› *one will
knead* (HS).
-ke⁷nuθerhu - squirt. *v.r.-a.i.* hab: -hs,
pnt: -, stat: -, prog: -, prp: -, dst: -,
caus: -, rvs: -, dat: -, n-inc. rakye⁷nu-
θérhuhs *he squirts* (HS).
-ke⁷θr - frown, scowl, wrinkling of skin
between eyes in grimacing, cock's
comb. *n.r.* inaln: rakyé⁷θreh *he is
august, scowling* (HS), inc., n.sfx. -eh.
ukyé⁷θreh *frown, scowl, wrinkling of
skin between one's eyes in grimacing,
cock's comb* (R); **-ne** -. **-ke⁷θrur** -: nehrukyé⁷θru⁷ ‹apart-he-frown-cover› *he
is grave* (H-notebook); **-atke⁷θra̲rurᶒ** -:

ratkye⁷θrarù·ręh ‹he-himself-frown-donates› *he scowls* (HS); –atke⁷θręti –:
ratkye⁷θrę́·tih ‹he-himself-frown-
makes› *he scowls* (HS).
–ke⁷w – broom; hair. *n.r.* inaln: kkye⁷-
wę́⁷kye *my hair* (R), aln: akkyé⁷-
wawęh *my broom* (R), inc., n.sfx. –eh.
ukyé⁷weh *broom: hair* (R); –ke⁷w –.
#hči: ukye⁷wéhči ‹hair-very› *crinosity,
hairy* (HS); –ke⁷w –.#ú⁷y: ukye⁷wehú⁷y ‹hair-great› *shaggy* (HS); –ke⁷ =
ware –: skyé⁷ware⁷ ‹you-hair-is distant› *your disheveled hair* (RC 3:11);
–ke⁷wuhθręku –:wa⁷natkye⁷wuhθrę́·-
ku⁷ ‹fact-one=another-hair-peel-undid›
one rubbed another's hair (RC 3:13);
ti –. –ke⁷we –: tikakyé⁷we·θ ‹so-it-hair-is
long› *long hair* (RC 28:1); –atke⁷w =
rahkw –: yętkye⁷wráhkhwa⁷ ‹one-oneself-hair-collects› *wig* (HS); –ke⁷w –
–htyuharęte: ukyé⁷weh uhtyuharę́·te
‹hair handle-certain one› *broomstick*
(HS).
–ke⁷w – –htyuharęte broomstick. *n.s.*
ukyé⁷weh uhtyu-harę́·te ‹hair handle-
certain one› *broomstick* (HS).
–ke⁷w –.#hči crinosity, hairy. *n.s.* u-
kye⁷wéhči ‹hair-very› *crinosity, hairy*
(HS).
–ke⁷w –.#ú⁷y shaggy. *n.s.* ukye⁷wehú⁷y
‹hair-great› *shaggy* (HS).
–ke⁷ware – have disheveled hair. *v.s.-s.i.*
skyé⁷ware⁷ ‹you-hair-is distant› *your
disheveled hair* (RC 3:11).
–ke⁷y – be humped. *v.r.-s.i.* stat: -e⁷,
prog: -, prp: -, dst: -, caus: -, rvs: -,
dat: -, inc.-φ-pat. –ke⁷yęhst –: ukye⁷-
yęhsteh ‹be humped-'ness› *hump*
(HS); –ę⁷wake⁷y –: rawę⁷wakyé⁷ye⁷
‹he-himself-back-is humped› *he is
hump-backed, he is hunch-backed*
(HS).
–ke⁷yęhst – hump. *n.s.* ukye⁷yęhsteh ‹be
humped-'ness› *hump* (HS).
kę directly, right (R) [Lawson «Ka»
'There'; «Kakoo» 'A little while ago'
from kę kyè·wę *just today*]. *part.*
–kę – see. *v.r.-t.* hab: -h, pnt: -⁷, stat: -·,
prog: -, prp: -⁷θe-, dst: -, caus: -hsT-
~-⁷T-, rvs: -, dat: -, n-inc. This root is
perhaps to be seen in Lawson's «Oo-
nu-tsauka» 'I remember it' from ù·nę
θá·kę· *now, you have seen it* . í·kkęh *I
see it* (R), rú·kę· *he has seen it* (R),
wa⁷kayé·kę⁷ *they saw it* (RC 10:5);
–kęhsT –: rakę́hstha⁷ ‹he-see-causes›
his sight (HS); –kę⁷T –: yú·kę⁷t ‹it-see-
causes› *it is visible* (HS); –hskweh =
takę –: wahrahskwehtá·kę⁷ ‹fact-he-tree
stump-saw› *he saw a tree stump* (RC
26:3); –rihwakę⁷θe –:na⁷rihwaké⁷θeh
‹one=another-matter-sees-going   to›
one criticizes another (HS); –atkę⁷θe –:
kayętkę́⁷θeh ‹they-themselves-see-going to› *they are watching* (R), ra-
tkę́⁷θeh ‹he-himself-sees-going to› *he
examines, he investigates, he views*
(HS); –atkę⁷θehstaw –: kayętkę⁷θéhstaws ‹they-themselves-see-going to-
'ness-come› *they come to look at* (RC
5:37); –ne –. –kę⁷θahnę –:neθkę⁷θáhnę
‹apart-you!-see-going to-much› *examine it!* (AW 51), nehrakę⁷θáhnęh
‹apart-he-sees-going to-much› *he ex-*

amines it (H-notebook); **tha+ne** –. **–kę?** = **θahnę** –: tha?neθkę?θáhnę ‹unusual-apart-you!-see-going to-much› *examine it more closely!* (AW 50); **–ne** –. **–rihwakę?θahnę** –: nehrarihwakę?θáhnęh ‹apart-he-matter-sees-going to-much› *he researches* (HS); **–ne** –. **–rihwakę?θahnę** –.**#hči**: nehrarihwakę?θahnéhči ‹apart-he-matter-sees-going to-much-very› *he examines the matter closely, he analyzes* (HS); **–yah** –. **–kę** –: wehrá·kęh ‹thither-he-sees› *he foresees* (HS); **–yah** –. **–atkę?θahnę** –: yahwa?nyekę?θáhnę·? ‹thither-fact-two-one-saw-going to-much› *the two of them look over the place* (R); **–yah** –. **–atkę?θehrę** –: weyętkę?θéhręhs ‹thither-one-oneself-sees-going to-much› *one went to look at it* (RC 3:27); **–ne+či** –. **–rihwakę?θahnę** –: neθhrarihwakę?θáhnęh ‹apart-again-he-matter-sees-going to› *he reconsiders* (HS); **ha?** **–atkę?θe** –: ha? ratké?θeh ‹the he-himself-sees-going to› *spectator* (HS); **kwęhs** **–kę?T** –: kwęhs aryuké?nęk ‹no unknown-it-see-cause› *it is invisible* (HS); **kwęhs** **–kę?T** – **–i** –: kwęhs ú·kę?t ará·kęk ‹no see-cause unknown-it-be a group› *it is invisible* (HS).

–kęh – hem, seam; mane. *n.r.* n-poss., n-inc., n.sfx. -eh. ukéheh *hem, seam: mane* (HS); **–kęhuhčr** –: ukęhúhčreh ‹hem-cover-'ness› *ribbon: silk* (HS); **–kęhur** –: yekéhuč ‹one-hem-covers› *one covers, one hems, one ribbons* (HS).

–kęha – erect, raise. *v.r.-t.* hab: -hs, pnt: -?, stat: -ę, prog: -, prp: -?θe-, dst: -, caus: -, rvs: -, dat: -, inc.-ɸ-pat. rakéhahs *he erects it, he raises it* (HS); **–yanręhstakęha** –: rayanręhstakéhahs ‹he-rule-'ness-raises› *policeman* (HS); **–atkęha** –: θatkęha ‹you!-yourself-raise›

get up!, get out of bed! (R), ratkéhahs ‹he-himself-raises› *he rises, he gets up* (HS), wahratkéha? ‹fact-he-himself-raised› *he arose* (RC 5:19); **–či** –. **–atkęha** –: θhrutkéhę ‹again-he-himself-raised› *he got back out of bed* (RC 26:30), θhratkéhahs ‹again-he-himself-raises› *he rises again* (HS); **–ne+t** –. **–atkęha** –: nę?nyętkéha? ‹apart-fact-hither-one-oneself-raised› *one got back out, one arose again* (RC 30:42); **–t** –. **–atkęha?T** –: thrutkęhá?nę ‹hither-he-himself-raised-caused› *as soon as he got up, right from his bed* (R); **–ačhu?kuwahčratkęha** –: ručhu?kuwahčratkéhę ‹he-be rich-'ness-self-raised› *he is magnificent* (HS); **ha?** **–či** –. **–atkęha?θe** –: ha? ęčętkęhá?θe? ‹the unknown-again-one-oneself-raise-going to› *resurrection* (HS); **–či** –. **–a** = **tkęha** – **–(i)hey** –: čę?natkéhahs węhè·yę ‹again-one=another-raises it-died› *one raises the dead* (HS).

#kęha?nę? several, various (distributive). *enc.* This form of the distributve occurs following nouns, attributive verbs with incorporated noun roots, and kinship terms. It functions to indicate that there are a number of the named entity or object distributed spatially, as in ak^w –.**#kęha?nę?**: akwakéha?nę? ‹deer-many› *deer* (RC 12:4), **–a'nę** = **ru?**.**#kęha?nę?**: ra?nęru?kéha?nę? ‹he-is close friends-many› *his close friends* (RC 14:6), and **čwe** –. **–a'nęk^we** –. **#ęwe**.**#kęha?nę?**: čweka?nękwehęwekéha?nę? ‹all kinds of-it-itself-human-genuine-many› *various Indians* (AW 101). Hewitt (2892) suggests that this enclitic is the plural form of í·kę· *it is* (see: **–i** –/**–ę°** –). (See also **#ha?nę?**.)

kéhčih maybe, perhaps (R) *part.* ha? kéhčih ‹the maybe› *especially, main* (AW 47), *by rights* (L 58), *really* (L

41).

-kęhčrę – mistreat. *v.r.-t.* hab: -h, pnt: -ʔ, stat: -·, prog: -, prp: -, dst: -, caus: -, rvs: -, dat: -, inc.-ɸ-pat. rukę́hčręh *he is mistreated* (RC 11:18), ahrukęhčrę́hek *that he be mistreated* (RC 11:19); **-hnęhwakęhčrę** –: nathnęhwakę́hčrę· ‹one=another-upper shoulder-mistreated› *one slapped another's upper shoulder* (RC 25:11); **-aʔčarakęh = črę** –: waʔkayęʔčarakę́hčręʔ ‹fact-they-themselves-door-mistreated› *they pounded on door* (R).

-kęhey – die. *v.r.-a.i.* See: **-(i)hey** –.

#kęheʔ ex-, deceased, former (decessive). *enc.* When present with words denoting living entities (nouns, attributive verbs containing incorporated nouns, and kinship verbs) the decessive functions to indicate that the entity no longer exists in the named state, as in **-kuwan** –.**#kęheʔ**: rakuwanękę́heʔ ‹he-is chief-deceased› *the ex-chief, the former chief* (R), **-tyak** –. **#kęheʔ**: waktyakękę́heʔ ‹I-married-deceased› *my ex-wife, my deceased wife* (R), and **-hryahsut.#kęheʔ**: ruhryahsutkę́heʔ ‹he-has as grandfather-deceased› *forefathers (lit. "former grandfathers")* (R). Note that in these cases the only word-accent is on the decessive. When present with stative verbs, it denotes past tense as in **-(a)hwihsT** – **#kęheʔ**: kahwíhsneʔ kę́heʔ ‹it-is strong deceased› *it was strong or powerful* (H 2892) and **-hsaʔk** – **#kęheʔ**: ráhsaʔk kę́heʔ ‹he-is

useful-deceased› *he was useful* (HS). Note that both the decessive and the stative verb are typically accented in such constructions.

-kęhkwahrihr – strike the fire. *v.r.-a.i.* hab: -s, pnt: -, stat: -, prog: -, prp: -, dst: -, caus: -, rvs: -, dat: -, n-inc. This "root" is almost certainly an old compound of the verb **-ahrihr** – *scatter* plus a noun root **-kęhkw** –, the meaning of which is not decipherable today but probably meant something like *ashes*. rakęhkwáhrihč *he strikes the fire* (HS).

-kęhr – contempt, disdain. *n.r.* n-poss., inc., n.sfx. -. Found only incorporated. **-kęhraT** –: ukęhrá·ʔnę ‹contempt-stands› *derision, humility* (HS); **-kęh = raT** –**{dative II}**: rukęhraʔná·tih ‹he-contempt-stands-for› *he disdains it, he holds it common* (HS); **-kęhręti** –: rakęhrę́·tih ‹he-contempt-makes› *he depreciates it, he humiliates it, he pokes fun at it, he ridicules it* (HS); **-kęh = rętyahnę** –: natkęhrętyáhnęh ‹one=another-contempt-makes-much› *one scoffs at another* (HS); **-kęhrętyahT** –: yukęhrę́·tyaht ‹it-contempt-make-causes› *it is contemptible* (HS).

-kęhraT – derision, humility. *n.s.* ukęhrá·ʔnę ‹contempt-stands› *derision, humility* (HS).

-kęhraT –**{dative II}** disdain, hold common. *v.s.-t.* rukęhraʔná·tih ‹he-contempt-stands-for› *he disdains it, he holds it common* (HS).

-kęhręti – depreciate, humiliate, poke fun

at, ridicule. *v.s.-t.* rakęhrę́·tih ‹he-contempt-makes› *he depreciates it, he
humiliates it, he pokes fun at it, he
ridicules it* (HS).
–**kęhrętyahnę** – scoff at. *v.s.-t.* natkęhrętyáhnęh ‹one=another-contempt-
makes-much› *one scoffs at another*
(HS).
–**kęhretyahT** – be contemptible. *v.s.-t.* yu-
kęhrę́·tyaht ‹he-contempt-mak̆e-causes›
it is contemptible (HS).
–**kęhre?w** – kind of elm tree. *n.r.* n-poss.,
n-inc., n.sfx. -a?. ukęhré?wa? *a kind
of elm* (H-notebook).
–**kęhruk** – punch, strike. *v.r.-t.* hab: -, pnt:
-ɸ, stat: -ɸ, prog: -, prp: -, dst: -, caus:
-, rvs: -, dat: -, inc.-ɸ-pat. ęhrakę́hruk
he will strike (HS), ęhshekę́hruk *you
will strike another* (RC 30:35), wa?-
natkę́hruk *one punched another* (R);
–**yah** –. –**kęhruk** –: weθkę́hruk ‹thither-
you!-strike› *strike it!* (R); –**(ę)ta?ra** =
kęhruk –: wa?na?ta?rakę́hruk ‹fact-
one=another-head-struck› *one struck
another's head* (RC 25:9); –**hsęwa?** =
rakęhruk –: ękhehsęwa?rakę́hruk ‹pre-
diction-I=another-needle-strike› *I will
telephone someone* (R); –**nęhsakęh** =
ruk –: wa?kanęhsakę́hruk ‹fact-it-
house-struck› *it struck house* (RC 5:
41); **ti** –. –**hrę?kęhruk** –·: thwahrahrę?-
kę́hruk ‹so-fact-he-??-struck› *he killed
so much* (RC 30:29).
–**kęhs** – face. *n.r.* inaln: kkę́hseh *my face*
(R) (also: kkęhsę́?kye (R)), inc., n.sfx.
-eh (older -a?). ukę́hseh *face* (R), ka-
kę́hsa? *face* (W 74); –**kęhsahtir** –: ru-
kęhsahtí·rę· ‹he-face-is hard› *he is serious* (HS); –**kęhsakę?T** –: natkę́hsakę?č
‹one=another-face-strikes› *one slaps
another's face* (HS); –**kęhsawęręhT** –
{**dative II**}: ahrukęhsawęrę́hthahθ ‹unknown-he-face-diminish-for› *that he
have bad luck* (RC 12:2); –**kęhsiyu** –:

kakęhsí·yu· ‹it-face-is great› *a very
large face* (AW 45); –**kęhsya?k** –: ę?-
nwakę́hsya?k ‹prediction-we-face-
break› *we'll eat* (R); –**atkęhsahθuh** –:
ratkęhsahθúhahs ‹he-himself-face-
paints› *he paints his face* (HS); –**a** =
tkęhsayata?T –: ratkęhsayatá?tha? ‹he-
himself-face-pouts› *he makes grimaces* (H-notebook); –**atkęhsayata?nah** =
nę –: ratkęhsayata?náhnęh ‹he-himself-
face-pouts-much› *he makes grimaces*
(H-notebook), *he grimaces* (HS); –**a** =
tkęhsa'nę?θahnę –: watkęhsa?nę?θáh-
nęh ‹it-itself-face-writes-much› *tattoo
marks* (SH 375); –**atkęhsuhči** –: ratkęhsúhčęhs ‹he-himself-fact-removes› *he
unmasks himself* (HS); –**atkęhsuh** =
θręku –: wahratkęhsuhθrę́·ku? ‹fact-he-
himself-face-strip-undid› *he stripped
off his face* (RC 26:13); –**atkęhsur** –:
utkęhsù·rę ‹self-face-covered› *False
Face, mask* (HS), yutkęhsù·rę ‹it-itself-face-covered› *mask* (AW 46); –**a** =
tkęhsu'narhuhsT –: watkęhsu?narhúh-
stha? ‹it-itself-face-hook-causes› *halter*
(HS); –**ne** –. –**atkęhsatihar** –: nehratkęhsatíhar ‹apart-he-himself-face-runs a-
way› *he faces it* (HS); –**ne** –. –**atkęhsiθ** –:
wa?thratkęhsi·θ ‹fact-two-he-himself-
face-joined› *he hit face* (AW 46);
–**ne** –. –**atkęhsurę** –: nehrutkęhsú·rę· ‹a-
part-he-himself-face-split› *he is scarred on his face* (H-notebook); **ú·?y**
–**kęhsęT** –: ú·?y rakęhsé·tha? ‹other he-
face-possesses› *he disguises it* (H-
notebook); –**wenęt?e(k)** – –**kęhsawę** –:
kawenę́·t?ehs ukę́hsawęh ‹it-iron-
strikes face-possess› *dial (of a clock)*
(HS).
–**kęhsahtir** – be serious. *v.s.-s.i.* rukęhsah-
tí·rę· ‹he-face-is hard› *he is serious*
(HS).
–**kęhsakę?T** – slap face. *v.s.-t.* natkę́h-
sakę?č ‹one=another-face-strikes› *one*

slaps another's face (HS).

-kę̆hsawę̆rę̆hT -{dative II} have bad luck. *v.s.-a.i.* ahrukę̆hsawę̆rę̆hthahθ ‹unknown-he-face-diminish-for› *that he have bad luck* (RC 12:2).

-kę̆hskwar- big face, jowls. *n.r.* inaln: kkę̆hskwareh *my big face, my jowls* (R), n-inc., n.sfx. -eh. ukę̆hskwareh *big face, jowls* (R).

-kę̆hsT- sight. *dv.n.s.* rakę̆hstha⁷ ‹he-see-causes› *his sight* (HS).

-kę̆huhčr- ribbon, silk. *n.s.* ukę̆húhčreh ‹hem-cover-'ness› *ribbon, silk* (HS).

-kę̆huhs- gills. *n.r.* poss. ?, inc. ?, n.sfx. -eh. ukę̆húhseh *gills* (AG).

-kę̆hur- cover, hem, ribbon. *v.s.-t.* yekę̆huč ‹one-hem-covers› *one covers, one hems, one ribbons* (HS).

-kę̆hya⁷k- trouble mind. *v.r.-t.* hab: -s, pnt: -, stat: -, prog: -, prp: -, dst: -hę̆-, caus: -, rvs: -, dat: -, n-inc. natkę̆hya⁷ks *one troubles another's mind* (RC 9:title), wa⁷kayę̆⁷natkę̆hyá⁷khę̆·⁷ *they were distressed* (RC 9:2).

kę̆·nę̆⁷ here (RC 3:2). *part.* kę̆·ne⁷ -hwen-.#ke.#aka·⁷: kę̆·ne⁷ kahwena⁷kyehá·ka·⁷ ‹here it-island-at-characterized by› *Americans* (HS); ha⁷ kę̆·ne⁷ -hwenu-: ha⁷ kę̆·ne⁷ yuhwè·nu⁷ ‹the here it-island-is in water› *America* (HS).

kę̆·ne⁷ -hwenu- America. *n.s.* ha⁷ kę̆·ne⁷ yuhwè·nu⁷ ‹the here it-island-is in water› *America* (HS).

kę̆·ne⁷ -hwen-.#ke.#aka·⁷ Americans. *n.-s.* kę̆·ne⁷ kahwena⁷kyehá·ka·⁷ ‹here it-island-at-characterized by› *Americans*

-kę̆nh- season. *n.r.* n-poss., n-inc., n.sfx. -eh. ukę̆nheh *season* (HS); -kę̆nha=tukę̆ht-: ukę̆nhatukę̆hti ‹season-be holy› *holiday season* (R); -kę̆nha⁷ke: kę̆nhá⁷kye ‹season-at› *(in the) summer* (HS).

-kę̆nhatukę̆ht- holiday season. *n.s.* ukę̆nhatukę̆hti ‹season-be hold› *holiday season* (R).

-kę̆nha⁷ke summer, in the summer. *n.s.* kę̆nhá⁷kye ‹season-at› *(in the) summer* (HS).

kę̆nhyeháh June (HS July 15 - August 15). *n.*

kę̆nhyehé·θu⁷ July (HS August 15 - September 15). *n.*

-kę̆ni- excel. *v.r.-a.i.* See: -ne-. -kę̆ni-.

-kę̆rat be white. *v.r.-s.i.* stat: -ɸ, prog: -, prp: -, dst: -, caus: -, rvs: -, dat: -, inc.-??-pat. Found only with incorporated noun roots in words that appear to be loanwords from other Northern Iroquoian languages. -iθnakę̆=rat: kę̆θnakę̆·rat ‹it-scale-is white› *white bass (Roccus chrysops)* (H 35 18); -nę̆hakę̆rat: kanę̆hakę̆·rat ‹it-corn-is white› *white corn* (RC 5:18), *flour corn* (H 2484); -rihstakę̆rat-.#áh: karihstakę̆rat⁷áh ‹it-metal-is white-little› *basin (lit., little tin thing)* (HS).

-kę̆raT -{dative I} appear to, have visions. *v.r.-a.i.* hab: -h, pnt: -ɸ, stat: -, prog: -, prp: -, dst: -, caus: -, rvs: -, dat: I (-a⁷θe-/-a⁷θ), n-inc. rukę̆ra⁷ná⁷θeh *he has visions, it appears to him* (HS), wa⁷ukę̆rá·⁷na⁷θ *it had vis-*

ions, it appeared to it (RC 33:7).

kęrhaˀnę̀·we it has a mind of its own (said when an inanimate object refuses to stay put, such as a broom that falls over each time it is stood in a corner) (R). *part.*

–kęryaˀk – cut a crease around, cross with gray streaks. *v.r.-t.* hab: -s, pnt: -, stat: -, prog: -, prp: -, dst: -hę- , caus: -, rvs: -, dat: -, n-inc. rakę́·ryaˀks *he cuts a crease around it, he crosses it with gray streaks* (H-notebook); **–atkę = ryaˀkhę –**: yutkęryáˀkhę· ‹it-itself-cut a crease around-much› *grizzly bear* (HS); **–ne –. –atkęryaˀkhę –**: neyutkęryáˀkhęh ‹apart-it-itself-cuts a crease around-much› *it is brindled* (H-notebook).

kę·θ as a rule, customarily (L 28). *part.*

–kęθhę – gnaw at. *v.r.-t.* hab: -h, pnt: -, stat: -, prog: -, prp: -, dst: -, caus: -, rvs: -, dat: -, inc.-ϕ-ag./pat. rakę́θhęh *he gnaws at it* (HS); **–hskęˀrakęθhę –**: rahskęˀrakę́θhęh ‹he-bone-gnaws at› *he gnaws bone* (HS); **–rihwakęθhę –**: naˀrihwakę́θhęh ‹one=another-matter-gnaws at› *one criticizes another* (HS).

–kęθręhn – burly, corpulence; a coarse, rough or fat person. *n.r.* n-poss., n-inc., n.sfx. -eh. ukęθrę́hneh *burly, corpulence: a coarse, rough or fat person* (HS).

–kętiθˀah be children. *v.r.-k.* The irregular plural of **–kaθˀah**. kayekętí·θˀah *group of young children* (RC 29:6).

–kęty – hump. *n.r.* poss. ?, inc., n.sfx. -. Found only in the cited constructions. **–či –. –kętyanę'nakT –**: θayukętyanę́·ˀnakt ‹again-fact-it-hump-attached› *again its body was hunched up* (RC 26:31); **–atkętyęyaˀT –**: rutkętyęyáˀnę ‹he-himself-hump-hang down-caused› *he clung* (HS).

–kę(y) – I...you alone (first person sin-gular agent=second person singular patient). *v.r.pfx.* The form **–kęy –** occurs before roots and stems that begin with a vowel. The form **–kę –** occurs before roots and stems that begin with a consonant.

–kęyaw – empty. *v.r.-t.* hab: -s, pnt: -, stat: -, prog: -, prp: -, dst: -, caus: -, rvs: -, dat: -, n-inc. rakę̀·yaws *he empties it* (HS).

kęˀ where (RC 2:2). *part.* kęˀ sáˀ ‹where look!› *look here!* (H-notebook).

kęˀ –athaharuhčrę – crossroads, four-corners. *n.s.* kęˀ yuthaharúhčręˀ ‹where it-itself-path-gathered› *where the roads are collected (this is another name for the four-corners or crossroads of high-ways)* (H 2484).

kęˀ –athahayahθ(e)r – four-corners, intersection. *n.s.* kęˀ yuthahayáhθeˀr ‹where it-itself-path-crossed› *where the roads are folded one on the other, or are tiered (this is the term applied to the four corners at the juncture of roads or where one crosses the other)* (H 2484).

kęˀ čhęˀ –heryaˀk – stubble. *n.s.* kęˀ čhęˀ kaheryáˀkę ‹where just it-green-cut› *stubble* (HS).

kęˀ –ę̇nhe – heart. *n.s. West.* kę kęnheˀ ‹where I-am alive› *my heart* (PC).

kęˀ –hyatęhstayę'nahkw – bookcase, desk. *n.s.* kęˀ yehyatęhstayęˀnáhkhwaˀ ‹where one-paper-lays-instrument› *bookcase, desk* (HS).

kęˀ –(i)har – foundation. *n.s.* kęˀ káher ‹where it-hangs› *foundation* (HS).

kęˀ –ihnęti – tannery. *n.s.* kęˀ yehnę́·tih ‹where one-skin-makes› *tannery* (HS).

kęˀ –(i)hyęhęti – channel. *n.s.* kęˀ kahyęhę́·tih ‹where it-river-makes› *channel* (HS).

kęˀ kwę́ –yah –. –ręhyaˀniha – horizon. *dv. n.s.* kęˀ kwę́ weyuręhyaˀníhę ‹where like thither-it-sky-sprains⟩ *horizon* (HS).

kę⁷ -ne -. -ę°hruręha'nye⁷ - furrow. *n.s.* kę⁷ neyawęhruręhá·⁷nye⁷ ⟨where a-part-it-dirt-split-going along⟩ *furrow* (HS).

kę⁷ -ne -. -(ę)takariθ - ridge of house. *n.s.* kę⁷ neyawętakarí·θę ⟨where two-it-point-met⟩ *ridge of house* (HS).

kę⁷ -ne -. -hręhthę - base. *n.s.* kę⁷ ne-yuhręhthę· ⟨where apart-it-put up-caused-much⟩ *base* (HS).

kę⁷ -rihuwana⁷nahkw - pulpit. *dv.n.s.* ha⁷ kę⁷ yerihuwana⁷náhkhwa⁷ ⟨the where one-matter-be chief-causes-instrument⟩ *pulpit* (HS).

kę⁷ sá⁷ look here! (H-notebook). *part.*

kę⁷ -t -. -wenę'na⁷tawę⁷T - foundry. *dv.n. s.* kę⁷ nyewenę⁷na⁷tawę́⁷tha⁷ ⟨where hither-one-iron-warm-causes⟩ *foundry* (HS).

kę⁷ -takwthrahkw - bed chamber. *dv.n.s.* kę⁷ yetakwthráhkhwa⁷ ⟨where one-bed-puts up-instrument⟩ *bed chamber* (HS).

kę⁷ -tak(e)r - country. *dv.n.s.* kę⁷ ratá·-kre⁷ ⟨where he-dwells⟩ *his country* (HS).

kę⁷ ti -. -akęhya'na'nye⁷ - the coast, the edge. *n.s.* kę⁷ tiwakęhya⁷ná·⁷nye⁷ ⟨where so-it-extend from-going along⟩ *the coast, the edge* (HS).

kę⁷ ti -. -a'nęti - Nativity. *n.s.* Kę⁷ Tih-ra⁷ńę́·tih ⟨where so-he-himself-makes⟩ *Nativity* (HS).

kę⁷ -yah -. -a'nu⁷kT - extreme, extremity. *dv.n.s.* kę⁷ weyú·⁷nu⁷kt ⟨where thith-er-it-itself-ended⟩ *extreme, extremity* (HS).

kę⁷ -yu⁷nęhT - laboratory. *dv.n.s.* kę⁷ kayu⁷nę́htha⁷ ⟨where it-work-causes⟩ *laboratory* (HS).

kę⁷ -'nęhT - grave, tomb. *dv.n.s.* ha⁷ kę⁷ rá·⁷nęht ⟨the where he-buries⟩ *grave, tomb* (HS).

-kę⁷črę - hammer. *v.s.-t.* rakę́⁷čręh ⟨he-strike-'ness-falls⟩ *he hammers* (HS).

kę́⁷kahwa⁷ mud hen (RC 3:77). *n.*

-kę⁷n - brow, forehead. *n.r.* poss. ?, n-inc., n.sfx. -eh. ukę́⁷neh *brow, fore-head* (HS).

#kę⁷na⁷kę side. *enc.* kę⁷ná⁷kę *side* (R); -kerhakęw kę⁷ná⁷kę: ukyérhakęw kę⁷-ná⁷kę ⟨body-in side⟩ *inward* (HS); -akT -.#kę⁷na⁷kę: ukwtkę⁷ná⁷kę ⟨be next to-side⟩ *lateral* (HS).

-kę⁷θr - pillow, support. *n.r.* poss. ?, inc., n.sfx. -eh. ukę́⁷θreh *pillow, support* (HS); -kę⁷θrahkw -: kkę⁷θráhkhwa⁷ ⟨I-support-pick up⟩ *I support it* (HS), rakę⁷θráhkhwa⁷ ⟨he-support-picks up⟩ *he underlays it* (HS); -kę⁷θruhčr -: u-kę⁷θrúhčreh ⟨pillow-cover-'ness⟩ *pillow case* (HS); -atkę⁷θrahkw -: yu-tkę⁷θráhkę ⟨it-it-self-supported-instru-ment⟩ *it is supported by*; *foundation* (HS); -atkę⁷θrur -: watkę́⁷θruh ⟨it-it-self-support-covers⟩ *it forms matter, it suppurates* (HS); ha⁷ -a'nęhskę⁷ = θrahkw -: ha⁷ yu⁷nęhskę⁷θráhkę ⟨the it-itself-house-supported-instrument⟩ *basis* (HS).

-kę⁷θrahkw - support. *v.s.-t.* kkę⁷θráh-khwa⁷ ⟨I-support-instrument⟩ *I support it* (HS).

-kę?θruhčr – pillow case. *n.s.* ukę?θrúh-čreh ‹pillow-cover-'ness› *pillow case* (HS).

-kę?T – be visible. *v.s.-s.i.* yú·kę?t ‹it-see-causes› *it is visible* (HS).

-kę?T – hammer, rap, strike. *v.r.-t.* hab: -s, pnt: -ɸ, stat: -, prog: -, prp: -, dst: -, caus: -, rvs: -, dat: -, inc.-ɸ-ag./pat. rá·kę?č *he hammers it, he raps it, he strikes it* (RC 30:42); **-kę?črę** –: raké?čręh ‹he-strike-'ness-falls› *he hammers* (HS); **-kęhsakę?T** –: natkęhsakę?č ‹one=another-face-strikes› *one slaps another's face* (HS); **-hskę?rakę?** = **nahkw** –: uhskę?rakę?náhkhwa? ‹bone-strike-instrument› *white boneset (Eupatorium perfoliatum)* (R); **-rihwa** = **kę?T** –: raríhwakę?č ‹he-matter-strikes› *he condemns* (HS); **-wirakę?T** –: wa?-ewi·rakę?t ‹fact-one-infant-struck› *one stole a child* (RC 35:title); **-w(e)ra** = **kę?T** –: ká·wrakę?č ‹it-air-strikes› *squall of wind* (AG).

-khahsyęku – disunite, parcel out. *v.r.-t.* rakhahsyę́·kwahs ‹he-divide-undo-un-does› *he disunites, he parcels it out* (HS).

-khe(y) – I...him, her (first person singular agent=third person singular patient). *v.r.pfx.* The form **-khey** – occurs before roots and stems that begin with a vowel. The form **-khe** – occurs before roots and stems that begin with a consonant.

-khę – soup. *n.r.* aln: akyekhę́hstawęh *my soup* (R), inc., n.sfx. -h. Requires the increment **-hst** – when incorporated. ú-khęh *soup* (R) [Lawson «Ook-hoo» 'Broath']; **-khęhstęti** –: wa?kyekhęh-stę́·ti? ‹fact-I-soup-made› *I made soup* (R).

-khręw – evergreen. *n.r.* n-poss., n-inc., n.sfx. -eh. ukhrę̀·weh *evergreen* (RC 20:1); **-khręw** – **-trahn** –: ukhrę̀·weh utráhneh ‹evergreen plant› *common yarrow (Achillea millefolium)* (RC 20:1).

-khręw – **-trahn** – common yarrow. *n.s.* ukhrę̀·weh utráhneh ‹evergreen plant› *common yarrow (Achillea millefolium)* (RC 20:1).

-khw – food, meal. *n.r.* aln: akyékhwawęh *my food, my meal* (R), inc., n. sfx. -eh. úkhweh *food, meal* (R); **-khwah(e)r** –: yakwakhwáher ‹we-food-put up› *we make a feast* (L 34); **-khwaruhčrę** –: ęyakwakhwarúhčrę·? ‹fact-I-food-made› *we gather food* (L 34); **-khwa?nehT** –: rúkhwa?neht ‹he-food-be present-caused› *he is hungry* (HS); **-khwanęT** –{dative III}: wa?nya-kukhwané·?nę? ‹fact-two-one-food-fed-for› *it was the two of them's meal* (RC 3:55); **-khwęT** –{dative II}: rakhwę́·?nahθ ‹he-food-concludes-for› *he finishes eating* (HS); **-khwęti** –: wa?kyekhwę́·ti? ‹fact-I-food-made› *I cook a meal* (R); **-khwętya?T** –: yekhwętyá?tha? ‹one-food-make-causes› *kitchen* (HS); **-khwiyu** –: rakhwí·yu· ‹he-food-is great› *he is a great eater* (HS); **-a'nekhwah(e)r** –: ra?nekhwáher ‹he-himself-food-puts up› *he takes his meal* (HS), ęhra?nekhwáhrę? ‹prediction-he-himself-food-put up› *he will take his meal* (HS); **-a'nekhwahrahčr** –: u?nekhwahráhčreh ‹self-food-put up-'ness› *table* (RC 17:5); **-a'nekhwah** = **ruhT** –: yę?nekhwahrúhtha? ‹one-oneself-food-put up-cover-causes› *tablecloth* (HS); **-a'nekhwayę(T)** –: wa?né-khwayę? ‹it-itself-food-lays› *there is food* (RC 17:5); **-a'nekhwihsakT** –: wa?nekhwihsáktha? ‹it-itself-food-seek-causes› *pasturage* (HS); **nyà·wę** **-khwi?** –: nyà·wę ękyékhwi? ‹thanks fact-I-food-be a group-began› *thanks,*

I'm full (L 56); **ù·nę -khwi?-**: ù·nę rukhwí'ę ‹now he-food-be a group-began› *he finished eating* (L 55), ù·nę wakyekhwí'ę ‹now I-food-be a group-began› *I have finished eating* (L 55), ù·nę ękyékhwi' ‹now fact-I-food-be a group-began› *I am through eating* (L 56); **θuhtérhę -a'nekhwah(e)r-**: θuhtérhę yę'nekhwáher ‹morning one-one-self-food-puts up› *breakfast* (HS).

-khwah(e)r- make a feast. *v.s.-a.i.* yakwakhwáher ‹we-food-put up› *we make a feast* (L 34).

-khwa?nehT- be hungry. *v.s.-s.i.* rúkhwa'neht ‹he-food-be present-caused› *he is hungry* (HS).

-khwęti- cook a meal. *v.s.-a.i.* wa'kyekhwę́·ti' ‹fact-I-food-made› *I cook a meal* (R).

-khwętya?T- kitchen. *dv.n.s.* yekhwętyá'tha' ‹one-food-make-causes› *kitchen* (HS).

-khwiyu- be a great eater. *v.s.-a.i.* rakhwí·yu· ‹he-food-is great› *he is a great eater* (HS).

-khwi?- finish eating. *v.s.-a.i.* nyà·wę ękyékhwi' ‹thanks fact-I-food-be a group-began› *thanks, I'm full* (L 56). ù·nę rukhwí'ę ‹now he-food-be a group-began› *he finished eating* (L 55), ù·nę wakyekhwí'ę ‹now I-food-be a group-began› *I have finished eating* (L 55), ù·nę ękyékhwi' ‹now fact-I-food-be a group-began› *I am through eating* (L 56).

kì·nę? creek (RC 3:43) [Lawson «Wackena» 'A Creek']. *n.* This word is un-usual in that it appears with a verbal prefix (the cislocative) to indicate what with other nouns would be indicated with the external locative. **tkì·=nę?** ‹hither-creek› *at creek* (RC 31:4); **kì·nę?.#ha?nę?**: kinęhá'nę? ‹creek-many› *rivers* (AG); **-ne-.-herukę-kì·nę?**: Neyuherú·kę? Kì·nę? ‹apart-it-green-is forked creek› *Neuse River* (AG); **kì·nę?.#aka·?**: rakinęhá·ka·' ‹he-creek-characterized by› *he is of the Beaver Clan* (H 2892).

kì·nę?.#aka·? Beaver Clan. *n.s.* rakinęhá·ka·' ‹he-creek-characterized by› *he is of the Beaver Clan* (H 2892).

kí?ah listen! (R). *v.*

krá·kra· bat (mammal) (R). *n.*

-krar- persist in doing good. *v.r.-a.i.* hab: -ɸ, pnt: -, stat: -, prog: -, prp: -, dst: -, caus: -, rvs: -, dat: -, n-inc. rú·krar *he is persistent in a good cause* (HS).

-krehw- clevis. *n.r.* n-poss., n-inc., n.sfx. -eh. ukréhweh *clevis* (HS).

krę́·r weeping willow *(Salix babylonica)*, willow *(Salix* sp.) (H-notebook). *n.* Also: krę̀·yu (HS), krę́rhyu (H-notebook).

krę́rhyu weeping willow *(Salix babylonica)*, willow *(Salix* sp.) (H-notebook). *n.* Also: krę̀·yu (HS), krę́·r (H-notebook).

krę̀·yu weeping willow *(Salix babylonica)*, willow *(Salix* sp.) (HS). *n.* Also: krę́·r (H-notebook), krę́rhyu (H-notebook).

-krir- cotton, wool. *n.r.* n-poss., inc., n.sfx. -eh. This root appears to be at the heart of the Tuscarora name for whitemen, krirù·rę^ʔ, which may literally have meant *cotton or wool-gatherers* just as the Tuscarora self-designation, Skarù·rę^ʔ, may derive from the root seen in uhskà·reh and have literally meant *hemp-gatherers*. ukrì·reh *cotton, wool* (RC 34:22); **-kri,rurę -**: krirù·rę^ʔ ‹cotton-split› *whiteman* (RC 30:1) [Lawson «Nickreruroh» 'Englishman']; **-aˈnekrirurę -** θáhe^ʔ: yu^ʔnekrirù·rę^ʔ θáhe^ʔ ‹it-itself-cotton-split bean› *peas* (HS); **θáhe^ʔ -aˈnekrirurę -**: θáhe^ʔ u^ʔnekrirù·rę^ʔ ‹bean self-cotton-split› *peas* (HS).

krirù·rę^ʔ ‹cotton-split› whiteman (RC 30:1) [Lawson «Nickreruroh» 'Englishman']. *n.*

-kri^ʔr - rags, tatters. *n.r.* n-poss., n-inc., n.sfx. -eh. This was the name of Dorothy Crouse's dog, a small, blond shiatsu. ukrí^ʔreh *rags, tatters* (HS).

krú·si^ʔ grocery store (R). *n.*

-kru^ʔr - corn silk. *n.r.* n-poss., n-inc., n.sfx. -eh. ukrú^ʔreh *corn silk* (HS).

-kθakewaʔT - washcloth. *dv.n.s.* yekθakyewá^ʔtha^ʔ ‹one-dish-wipe-causes› *washcloth* (HS).

-kθanurę - -ętyaʔT - porcelain. *dv.n.s.* kakθanú·rę· yakyetyá^ʔtha^ʔ ‹it-dish-is precious one-make-causes› *porcelain* (HS).

-kθęti - potter. *dv.n.s.* rakθę́·tih ‹he-dish-makes› *potter* (HS).

-kθhrawę - set the table. *v.s.-a.i.* ęhsekθrà·wę^ʔ ‹prediction-you-dish-put up-many› *you will set the table, you will put dishes around* (R).

-kθuharT - dishwater. *dv.n.s.* kakθuhárnę ‹it-dish-wash-caused› *dishwater* (H-notebook).

kú aw, now-now (expression of sympathy) (R). *part.*

ku- O my (first person singular vocative agent). *v.r.pfx.* Occurs only on kinship verb roots. Before roots beginning with a vowel, the final *u* automatically becomes *w*. kúrhak *my paternal aunt (vocative, i.e, used in addressing one's aunt)* (R), kwá^ʔreh *my grandchild, my grandniece, my grandnephew, my great grandchild (vocative)* (RC 26:31).

-ku - get, pick up, take. *v.r.-a.i.* hab: -ahs, pnt: -^ʔ, stat: -ę, prog: -, prp: -he-, dst: -hę-, caus: -ahT-, rvs: -hsi-, dat: -, inc.-ɸ-pat. Lounsbury lists two unusual forms for this verb, an imperative with an atypical prothetic í- and a first person singular habitual that is atypically absent a prothetic í-. The explanation for the unusual distribution of prothesis on this verb in Lounsbury's data is uncertain. θkú *get it!* (L 46), í·θku *get it!* (L 46), wá·kkwę *I have picked it up, I have gotten it* (R), kkwáhs *I do get it* (L 46), í·kkwahs *I do get it* (L 46), rá·kwahs *he accepts it, he takes it* (HS), wá^ʔkku^ʔ *I picked it up, I got it* (R), ę́·kku^ʔ *I will pick it up, I will get it* (R); **-kuhe -**: θkúhe ‹you!-get-going to› *go get it!* (L 46), ękkúhe^ʔ ‹prediction-I-get-going to› *I will go after it* (R); **-yah -. -kuhe -**: wa^ʔθkúhe ‹thither-you!-get-going to› *go get it over there!* (L 46); **-athnęhstakuhe -**: wahrathnęhstakúhe^ʔ ‹fact-he-play a game-'ness-got-going to› *he was going picking up game ball* (RC 25:6); **-hkyuhsku -**: rahkyúhskwahs ‹he-elbow-gets› *he elbows it* (HS); **-nęha= kwaʔnahkw -**: yenęhakwa^ʔnáhkhwa^ʔ ‹one-corn-pick up-causes-instrument› *corn-planter, sickle* (HS); **-nęhsku -**: ranę́hskwahs ‹he-house-picks up› *he steals, is stealing (literally, he takes the house, but use has made it mean* *to steal)* (H 2484), ǫhranę́hsku·ˀ ‹prediction-he-house-pick up› *he will steal* (HS); –rihwaku –: raríhwakwahs ‹he-matter-gets› *he accedes, he accepts, he approves* (HS); –atku –: rá·tkwahs ‹he-himself-gets› *he takes away, he usurps* (HS), rú·tkwę ‹he-himself-got› *he usurped* (HS), ęhrá·tkwaˀ ‹prediction-he-himself-get› *he will usurp* (HS); –či –. –ˀahθrakuhe –: θakayeˀahθrakúheˀ ‹again-fact-they-basket-got-going to› *they were picking basket back up* (RC 10:2); –ne –. –aˀčihskukuhę –: nęwaˀčihskukúhęˀ ‹apart-prediction-it-itself-mush-get-much› *mush will splatter* (RC 3:54); –yah –. –athahakuhsi –: waˀθathahakúhsi ‹thither-you!-yourself-path-get-undo› *straighten out your path there!* (RC 3:44); **ha·ˀ –atku –:** ha·ˀ rú·tkwę ‹the he-himself-got› *his conquest of, his usurpation* (HS); **čhęˀ ti –. –ku –:** čhęˀ thwáˀkkuˀ ‹just so-fact-I-got› *I just now got it* (L 46).

kúhkwih quail (R). *n.*

kuhsérhę winter (R) [Gallatin «kooseh-ha» 'Winter']. *n.* **kuhserhęháh** ‹winter-little› *November* (R) (HS: November 15-December 15); **kuhserhęhé·θuˀ** ‹winter-many great› *December* (R) (HS: December 15-January 15).

kuhserhęháh ‹winter-little› November (R) (HS: November 15-December 15). *n.*

kuhserhęhé·θuˀ ‹winter-many great› December (R) (HS: December 15-January 15). *n.*

Kuhyá·kę Ottawa, Ontario (R). *n.*

kunikwę́ as, like (RC 28:1). *part.* Contraction of kù·niˀ kwę.

kù·niˀ as, like (R). *part.* Also: kwù·niˀ (R).

kunúhθraks minnow (H 3518). *n.*

kù·rah Indian agent (HS). *n.*

Kuráhku· British (M 87). *n.* **kuráhku·-aˈnyęˈnahkw –:** kuráhku· yęˀnyęˀnáhkhwaˀ ‹British one-oneself-lays-instrument› *throne* (HS).

kuráhku· -aˈnyęˈnahkw – throne. *n.s.* kuráhku· yęˀnyęˀnáhkhwaˀ ‹British one-oneself-lays-instrument› *throne* (HS).

Kurahkuháh English; prince, princess (HS). *n.*

kuráhkuwaˀ governor, king (RC 21:1). *n.*

kù·reh acorn, black oak (RC 10:1); beech (RC 11:16); red oak (H-notebook) [Lawson «Kooawa» 'Acorns']. *n.*

kúskus pig (R). *n.* Variant of kwískwis (R).

kutí·kęˀ blackhaw (*Vibernum* sp.) (RC 6:14). *n.*

kutíˀ perhaps (RC 1:4). *part.* Also: kuˀtíˀ (RC 1:4), kwetíˀ (R), kwutíˀ (R), kwuˀtíˀ (R).

kù·wahk pike (fish) (R). *n.*

–kuwan – be chief. *v.s.-s.i.* See: –uwan – be chief.

–kuwanaˀT – exalt. *v.s.-t.* rakuwanáˀthaˀ ‹he-X-be a chief-causes› *he exalts it* (HS).

–kuwanaˀT – clan mother, mock chief, little old man. *n.s.* ukuwanáˀthaˀ ‹X-be a chief-cause› *clan mother* (RC 7: 7), *a mock chief, a little old man* (HS).

–kuwanęhčr – chiefship. *n.s.* ukuwanę́hčreh ‹X-be a chief-'ness› *chiefship* (HS).

-kuʔč - cock's comb. *n.r.* n-poss., n-inc., n.sfx. -eh. ukúʔčeh *cock's comb* (R).

-kuʔčęri - find. *v.r.-t.* hab: -ęhs, pnt: -ʔ, stat: -ę, prog: -, prp: -, dst: -, caus: -, rvs: -, dat: -, inc.-φ-pat. wahrakuʔčę·riʔ *he found it* (RC 3:89); -či-. **-kuʔčęri** -: θhrakuʔčę́·ryęhs ‹again-he-finds› *he recovers* (HS); **-(ę)tah= snaku ʔčęri** -: waʔkatahsnakuʔčę̀·riʔ ‹fact-it-pole-found› *it found pole* (RC 12:26); **-ęyakuʔčęri** -: waʔnyakęyakuʔčę̀·riʔ ‹fact-two-one-cavern-found› *the two of them found a cavern* (RC 11:1); **-kerhakuʔčęri** -: wahrakyerhakuʔčę̀·riʔ ‹fact-he-body-found› *he found body* (RC 12:15); **-yęʔkwa= kuʔčęri** -: ruyęʔkwakuʔčę́·ryę ‹he-smoke-found› *he found smoke* (RC 12:23); -či-. **-rihwakuʔčęri** -: θkarihwakuʔčę́·ryę *it discovered a way again* (RC 21:2) ‹again-it-matter-found›; **-a= tkuʔčęri** -: watkuʔčę́·ryęhs ‹it-itself-finds› *it finds itself* (RC 12:18); **kwęhs -atkuʔčęri** -: kwęhs aryutkuʔčę́·ryę·k ‹no unknown-it-itself-find› *it is unfound* (HS); **kwęhs -či-. -atkuʔ= čęri** -: kwęhs ęθętkuʔčęryę́hshek ‹no unknown-again-it-itself-find› *it is incomparable* (HS).

kúʔr gulp (sound of liquid being swallowed) (R). *n.*

kuʔteʔtù·ręʔ dewberry (*Rubus* sp.) (RC 22:title). *n.*

kuʔtíʔ perhaps (RC 1:4). *part.* Also: kutíʔ (R), kwetíʔ (R), kwutíʔ (R), kwuʔtíʔ (R).

-kw - empty noun root. *v.inc.* See: -a= 'naθ(e) - *go around.*

kwačì·rah wood sorrel (*Oxalis montana*) (H-notebook). *n.* **kwačirahúʔy** ‹wood sorrel-big› *red sorrel (Oxalis acetosella)* (H-notebook).

kwačirahúʔy ‹wood sorrel-big› red sorrel (*Oxalis acetosella*) (H-notebook). *n.*

kwáhrak peach (R). *n.* Also: kwáhraʔk (H-notebook).

kwáhraʔk peach (H-notebook). *n.* Also: kwáhrak (R).

-kwahs - like. *v.r.-t. West.* hab: -, pnt: -, stat: -ę·, prog: -, prp: -, dst: -, caus: -, rvs: -, dat: -, n-inc. Found only in the Western dialect. wakkwáhsę· *I like it* (PC), sakwáhsę· *you like it* (PC).

kwáhst cheap (AG). *part.* See: -a= **kwahsT** - *be good.*

-kʷahT - cut off. *v.r.-t.* hab: -haʔ, pnt: -φ, stat: -ę, prog: -, prp: -, dst: -ahnę-, caus: -ahT-, rvs: -aku-, dat: -, inc.-φ-pat. θkwáht *cut it off!* (R), íθkwaht *cut it off!* (L 44), rakwáhthaʔ *he cuts it* (L 44), rukwáhnę *he has cut it off* (L 44), *he is anxious* (HS); **-kʷahnah= nęhteʔ** -: wahrakwahnahnę́hteʔ ‹fact-he-cut off-caused-going to› *he is going to cut it* (L 26); **-čiʔehnakʷahT** -: račiʔehnakwáhthaʔ ‹he-claw-cuts off› *he cuts off claw (or claws)* (H 2484); **-čiʔrakʷahT** -: račiʔrakwáhthaʔ ‹he-ember-cuts off› *he snuffs a candle out* (HS); **-čiʔrakʷahnahkw** -: yečiʔrakwahnáhkhwaʔ ‹one-ember-cuts off-instrument› *candle snuffer* (HS); **-eʔra= kʷahT** -: naʔneʔrakwáhthaʔ ‹one=another-hair-cuts off› *one crops another's hair* (HS); **-ę°hrakʷahT** -: yakęhrakwáhthaʔ ‹one-dirt-cuts off› *pick ax* (HS); **-(ę)tahsnakʷahT** -: waʔktáhsnakwaht ‹fact-I-stick-cut off› *I cut off a stick* (R); **-(ę)tahsnakʷahnahnę** -: waʔkayetahsnakwahnáhnę·ʔ ‹fact-they-stick-cut off-many› *they cut off some sticks* (R); **-haʔkʷahT** -: rahaʔkwáhthaʔ ‹he-neck-cuts off› *he cuts throat* (HS); **-hwęʔnarakʷahnahkw** -: yehwęʔnarakwahnáhkhwaʔ ‹one-board-cuts off-instrument› *saw* (HS); **-nęhakʷahnaʔ** =

nahkw –: yenęhakwahna⁷⁷náhkhwa⁷⁷ ‹one-corn-cut off-causes-instrument› *cornplanter, sickle* (HS); –ręhsak̮ʷah = nahnę –: ękręhsakwahnáhnę·⁷ ‹prediction-I-leg-cut off-many› *I will cut its legs off* (AW 58); –ne –. –hska⁷ya = k̮ʷahT –: newakska⁷yakwáhtha⁷ ‹apart-I-jowls-cut off› *I am yawning* (R); –atk̮ʷahT –: ęwátkwaht ‹prediction-it-itself-cut off› *it will stop itself* (RC 3:20), watkwáhtha⁷ ‹it-itself-cuts off› *it is brittle* (HS); –atk̮ʷahnahkw –: yutkwahnáhkę ‹it-itself-cut off-instrument› *it is abrupt* (HS); –atk̮ʷahnaku –: ratkwahná·kwahs ‹he-himself-cut off-undoes› *he has success* (HS); –t –. –atk̮ʷahT –: nyutkwáhnę ‹hither-it-itself-cut off› *fourth quarter of moon* (SH 375); ča⁷úhshę⁷ –t –. –atk̮ʷahT –: ča⁷úhshę⁷ nyutkwáhnę ‹almost hither-it-itself-cut off› *third quarter of moon* (SH 375).

–kwahy – be cute, be handsome. *v.r.-s.i.* stat: -ę, prog: -, prp: -, dst: -, caus: -, rvs: -, dat: -, n-inc. yekwáhyę *she (young girl) is cute* (R), rakwáhyę *he is handsome* (R); –kwahyęhčr –: u-kwahyęhčreh ‹be handsome-'ness› *beauty* (HS); ti –. –kwahy –: tihrakwáhyę ‹so-he-is handsome› *he is so handsome* (RC 35:11); –kwahyęhčręti –: rakwahyęhčrę́·tih ‹he-be handsome-'ness-makes› *he beautifies it* (HS).

–kwahyęhčr – beauty. *n.s.* ukwahyęhčreh ‹be handsome-'ness› *beauty* (HS).

–kwahyęhčręti – beautify. *v.s.-t.* rakwahyęhčrę́·tih ‹he-be handsome-'ness-makes› *he beautifies it* (HS).

–kwanaku – overcome a difficulty. *v.r.-a.i.* hab: -ahs, pnt: -, stat: -, prog: -, prp: -, dst: -, caus: -, rvs: -, dat: -, n-inc. rakwaná·kwahs *he overcomes a difficulty* (HS).

kwà·nę a lot, great, many, much (RC 11:3). *part.* sé⁷či kwà·nę ‹since much› *it's too much* (R).

–kwanihst – be handsome, be pretty. *v.r.-s.i.* stat: -ɸ, prog: -, prp: -, dst: -, caus: -, rvs: -, dat: -, n-inc. rakwà·nihst *he is handsome* (R), kakwà·nihst *it is pretty* (HS).

kwanya⁷tarahkwáhnęh choke cherries *(Prunus virginiana)* (H-notebook). *n.*

–k̮ʷara·θ – batter, bruise. *v.r.-t.* hab: -s, pnt: -ɸ, stat: -ę, prog: -, prp: -, dst: -ahnę-, caus: -, rvs: -, dat: -, n-inc. rukwará·θę *he has battered it* (HS), rá·kwara·č *he batters it* (HS), ęyé·kwara·θ *one will bruise it* (RC 20:1).

kwà·rerar zzzzz (sound of snoring) (R). *part.*

kwà·rę⁷r northern tree frog (RC 17:1). *n.*

–kwarih – hasten. *v.r.-t.* hab: -, pnt: -, stat: -ę, prog: -, prp: -, dst: -, caus: -a⁷T-, rvs: -, dat: -, n-inc. The bare root has not been encountered. It is found only with the causative or the inchoative suffix. –kwariha⁷T –: θkwaríha⁷t ‹you!-haste-cause› *hurry up!* (R), khekwarihá⁷tha⁷ ‹I=another-haste-cause› *I hasten another* (HS), kwaríha⁷t ‹haste-cause› *fast, quick* (R); –kwarihę⁷ –: rukwaríhę⁷θ ‹he-hasten-begins› *he is in haste* (HS); –kwa =

---

rihęˀčr –: ukwarihę́ˀčreh ‹hasten-begin-'ness› *impatiently* (HS); –kwarihęˀT –: ukwarihę́ˀneh ‹hasten-begin-cause› *haste* (HS); –atkwarihaˀT –: rutkwariháˀnę ‹he-himself-haste-caused› *he is hurrying* (HS); –ne –. –kwarihęˀ –: neyukwaríhęˀθ ‹apart-it-has-ten-begins› *it quakes* (HS); –ne –. –aˀwnakwarihęˀ –: waˀnyuˀwnakwaríhęˀ ‹fact-apart-it-earth-hasten-began› *land trembled, earthquake* (RC 28:6); –ne –. –ręˀakwa = rihęˀ –: nęyuręˀakwaríhęˀ ‹apart-prediction-it-tree-hasten-begin› *tree will be shaken* (RC 27:27).

–kwarihaˀT – hasten, hurry. *v.s.-t.* θkwaríhaˀt ‹you!-hasten-cause› *hurry up!* (R), khekwariháˀthaˀ ‹I=another-hasten-cause› *I hasten another* (HS).

kwaríhaˀt ‹haste-cause› fast, quick (R). *part.*

–kwarihęˀ – be in haste. *v.s.-a.i.* rukwaríhęˀθ ‹he-hasten-begins› *he is in haste* (HS).

–kwarihęˀčr – impatiently. *n.s.* ukwarihę́ˀčreh ‹hasten-begin-'ness› *impatiently* (HS).

–kwarihęˀT – haste. *n.s.* ukwarihę́ˀneh ‹hasten-begin-cause› *haste* (HS).

–kwarit – dower, love present. *n.r.* n-poss., n-inc., n.sfx. –eh. ukwarí·teh *a dower, love present, a gift given before betrothal, any gift of affection or regard* (H-notebook).

–kwari(y) – be inseparable. *v.r.-s.i.* stat: -eˀ, prog: -, prp: -, dst: -, caus: -, rvs: -, dat: II (-ati-/-hθ-), n-inc. kayekwarì·yeˀ *they travel together, they are inseparable* (R); –kwari(y) –{dative II}: natkwà·rihθ ‹one=another-is inseparable-for› *one is another's lover* (RC 17:4).

–kwari(y) –{dative II} be someone's lover. *v.s.-t.* natkwà·rihθ ‹one=another-is inseparable-for› *one is another's lover*

(RC 17:4).

kwarù·wak screech owl *(Otus asio)* (R). *n.* Also: kwaruwaˀáh (R) and kwarù·waˀ (HS).

kwarù·waˀ screech owl *(Otus asio)* (HS). *n.* Also: kwaruwaˀáh (R) and kwarù·wak (R).

kwaruwaˀáh screech owl *(Otus asio)* (R). *n.* Also: kwarù·wak (R) and kwarù·waˀ (HS).

–kwati – be young male. *v.r.-a.i.* hab: -hs, pnt: -, stat: -, prog: -, prp: -, dst: -, caus: -, rvs: -, dat: -, n-inc. rakwá·tihs *young man* (RC 27:2) [Lawson «Quottis» 'Young Man']; –kwatih = čayę –: rakwatíhčayęˀ ‹he-be young male-is cowardly› *he is bold* (HS); –kwatihčayęhčr –: ukwatihčayę́hčreh ‹be young male-be cowardly-'ness› *audacity, bravery* (HS); –kwati – -ę° = kʷehstahtir –: rakwá·tihs rękwehstahtì·rę ‹he-is young male he-human-'ness-is durable› *he is athletic* (HS); –kwati – -kwatihčrahtir –: rakwá·tihs rukwatihčrahtì·rę ‹he-is young male he-be young male-'ness-is durable› *he is athletic* (HS).

–kwati – -ę°kʷehstahtir – be athletic. *v.s.-a.i.* rakwá·tihs rękwehstahtì·rę ‹he-is young male he-human-'ness-is durable› *he is athletic* (HS).

–kwati – -kwatihčrahtir – be athletic. *v.s.-a.i.* rakwá·tihs rukwatihčrahtì·rę ‹he-is young male he-be young male-'ness-is durable› *he is athletic* (HS).

–kwatihčayę – be bold. *v.s.-s.i.* rukwatíhčayęˀ ‹he-be young male-is cowardly› *he is bold* (HS).

–kwatihčayęhčr – audacity, bravery. *n.s.* ukwatihčayę́hčreh ‹be young male-be cowardly-'ness› *audacity, bravery* (HS).

kwa·ˀáh arrgh (wail of mourning said when a chief dies) (TW). *part.*

kwá?ks pow! (sound of hitting someone in the head) (R). *part.*

kwa?kúrhyeh whippoorwill (*Caprimulgus vociferus*) (R). *n.*

-kwa?n - arc, curve. *n.r.* n-poss., inc., n.sfx. -eh. ukwá'neh *arc, curve* (R); -ne -. -atkwa?neti -: nehratkwa'né·tih ‹two-he-himself-arc-makes› *he rounds it* (HS), nehrutkwa'né·tih ‹two-he-himself-arc-makes› *he is round* (HS); -ne -. -htawakwa?nahT -: nekahtawakwá'nahč ‹apart-it-stream of water-arc-causes› *it is eddying: eddy, whirlpool* (AG); -ne -. -a'nẹnẹhsnakwa? = nẹti -: neyu'nẹnẹhsnakwa'né·ti· ‹apart-it-itself-seed-arc-made› *the grain is round, it is a round grain* (H 2484).

-kwehčrẹ - pucker. *v.r.-a.i.* hab: -h, pnt: -·', stat: -', prog: -, prp: -, dst: -, caus: -, rvs: -, dat: -, n-inc. rukwéhčrẹ' *he puckered* (HS), rakwéhčrẹh *he puckers* (HS), ẹhrakwéhčrẹ·' *he will pucker* (HS).

-kʷek - close, make whole. *v.r.-t.* hab: -s, pnt: -ɸ, stat: -ẹ, prog: -ẹha'nye'-, prp: -, dst: -, caus: -T-, rvs: -si-, dat: I (-θe-/-θ-), inc.-ɸ-pat. kayekwé·kẹ *they closed it* (RC 12:7); -kʷekT -: kakwéktha' ‹it-close-causes› *it takes all: inclusively* (HS); -akʷek -: wakwé·kẹ ‹it-closed› *it is whole, total* (HS); tha+t -. -kʷekT -: thẹ'naká·kwekt ‹unusual-unknown-hither-it-close-cause› *that it come to pass* (RC 3:80); -(a)haha = kʷek -: raháhakweks ‹he-path-closes› *he obstructs a road* (HS), kaháhakweks ‹it-path-closes› *it closes the*

road (as a fallen tree or drifted-snow in winter) (H 2484); -eryahnakʷek -: weryahnákweks ‹it-breathe-cause-closes› *asthma* (RC 19:1); -ẹryẹhkʷekT -: yawẹryẹhkwekt ‹it-breathe-X-close-caused› *suffocating* (HS); -ẹ?kʷek -: rẹ'?kweks ‹he-X-closes› *he smothers it* (HS); -(i)?θhaθnẹhstakʷek -: ẹhsi'?θha-θnẹhstakwé·kẹk ‹prediction-you-power-be heavy-'ness-close› *you will have authority* (RC 25:3), ra'?θhaθnẹhstakwé·kẹ ‹he-power-be heavy-'ness-closed› *he is almighty* (HS); -kah = kʷeksi -: natkahkwéksyẹhs ‹one=another-ear-close-undoes› *one alarms another* (HS); -kerhakʷek -: kayekyerhakwé·kẹ ‹they-body-closed› *they have the entire body* (RC 6:11); -nẹh = sakʷek -: kanẹhsakwé·kẹ ‹it-house-closed› *the whole house, i.e., the entire audience in a building* (H-notebook); -wiskʷek -: wa'?kawískwe·k ‹fact-it-ice-closed› *the water freezes* (AG); -?ẹhrakʷek -: ẹka'?ẹhrakwek ‹prediction-it-leaf-close› *its leaves will be intact* (RC 22:3); -(ẹ)ti?čha? = rakʷek -: rẹti'?čhá'rakweks ‹he-himself-anger-closes› *he is in a frenzy* (HS); -?nhẹhakʷek -: ru'?nhẹhakweks ‹he-urine-closes› *he has the strangury (lit., "it closes or shuts up his urine")* (H 2484); -ne -. -ahčakʷekẹha'nye? -: nehruhčakwekẹhá·'nye' ‹two-he-fist-closed-going along› *he was carrying it in his clenched fists* (RC 3:90); -ne -. -(a)čẹhakʷekT -: nekakučẹhakwé·kẹ ‹two-they-fire-closed› *whole family*

(RC 13:10); **-ne -**. **-hęhnak̲ʷek -**: nehra-
hęhnakwé·kę ‹two-he-ear-closed› *he is
deaf* (HS), nęyehęhnakwé·kęk ‹two-
prediction-one-ear-close› *one will be
deaf* (RC 17:3); **-ne -**. **-kahk̲ʷek -**: nehra-
kahkwé·kę ‹two-he-eye-closed› *he is
blind* (R); **-aʔnęʔk̲ʷek -**: yuʔnęʔkwé·kę
‹it-itself-X-closed› *it smolders* (HS);
-ne -. **-atkahk̲ʷek -**: nęwakatkahkwé·kęk
‹two-prediction-I-myself-eye-closed›
my eyes will be closed (RC 3:20), ne-
yutkahkwé·kę ‹two-it-itself-eye-closed›
its eyes are closed (RC 7:12); **ti -**.
-aʔrih-wa̲k̲ʷek -{dative I}: thwahruʔ-
ríhwakwekθ ‹so-fact-he-himself-matter-closed-for› *he becomes puzzled*
(SH 375).
-k̲ʷekT - inconclusively. *dv.n.s.* kakwék-
thaʔ ‹it-close-causes› *inclusively* (HS).
-kwen - blunt, dull. *n.r.* n-poss., n-inc.,
n.sfx. **-eh** (older: **-ęʔ**). ukwè·neh
blunt, dull (M 87), ukwè·nęʔ *dull (as
of a knife)* (L 72).
-kweni - be able. *v.r.-a.i.* hab: -ęhs, pnt: -
ʔ, stat: -ę, prog: -, prp: -, dst: -, caus:
-aʔT-, rvs: -, dat: -, inc.-ɸ-ag. yu-
kwé·nyę *it is able, it is possible* (RC
15:1), ękakwè·niʔ *it will be able* (RC
15:1), akakwè·niʔ *that it be possible*
(RC 24:7); **-kweni -**: natkwé·nyęhs
‹one=another-enables› *one induces another* (HS); **-kwenyaʔT -**: yukwé·nyaʔt
‹it-be able-causes› *feasible* (HS);
-kwenyęhčr -: ukwenyę́hčreh ‹be able-
'ness› *ability, might* (R); **-kwenyęh =
črayę(T) -**: rukwenyę́hčrayęʔ ‹be able-
'ness› *he has ability* (HS); **-(ę)ʔti =
kęhra̲kweni -**: raʔtikęhrakwé·nyęhs ‹he-
mind-is able› *he persuades* (HS), naʔ-
tikęhrakwé·nyęhs ‹one=another-mind-
is able› *one influences another* (HS);
-atkweni -: rutkwé·nyę ‹he-himself-was
able› *he has won* (L 40), ratkwé·-
nyęhs ‹he-himself-is able› *he wins*

(HS), waʔkayętkwè·niʔ ‹fact-they-
themselves-were able› *they won* (R);
-a'natkweni -: ruʔnatkwé·nyę ‹he-himself-was able› *he is independent*
(HS); **haʔ ti -**. **-kweni -**: haʔ tihra-
kwé·nyęhs ‹the so-he-is able› *his
capacity* (HS); **kwęhs -kweni -**: kwęhs
ahrakwè·niʔ ‹no unknown-he-be able›
he is incompetent (HS), kwęhs ahra-
kwenyę́hshek ‹no unknown-he-be
able› *he is incapable* (HS); **kwęhs
-kwenyaʔT -**: kwęhs aryukwenyáʔnęk
‹no unknown-it-be able-cause› *it is
impossible* (HS); **kwęhs -kwenyaʔT -
-atkwiʔT -**: kwęhs aryukwenyáʔnęk
arętkwiʔt ‹no unknown-it-be able-
cause unknown-it-itself-move› *it is irremovable* (HS).
-kweni - induce. *v..s.-t.* natkwé·nyęhs
‹one=another-enables› *one induces another* (HS).
kwè·nihs cents, pennies (L 73), copper
(or, by custom, a kettle) (H-notebook).
n. A loan word from English pennies.
kwè·niʔ copper, penny, kettle (HS). *n.* A
loan word from English penny. **-kwe =
niʔt -**: ukweníʔteh ‹penny› *one penny*
(L 73); **-kweniʔtahsthu -**: kakweniʔ-
táhsthę ‹it-penny-is small› *a few pennies* (L 73).
kwè·niʔ commonly, just, simply; gratis,
free (R); near (RC 3:57). *part.* kwè·niʔ
ę́·kweh ‹commonly human› *common
man, layman* (HS); kweníʔsayę
‹commonly-vulgar› *vaguely* (HS);
kwęhs kwè·niʔ ‹no commonly› *impunity, for nothing* (HS).
kwè·niʔ ę́·kweh ‹commonly human›
common man, layman (HS). *part.*
kweníʔsayę ‹commonly-vulgar› vaguely
(HS). *part.*
-kweniʔt - one penny. *n.s.* ukweníʔteh
‹penny› *one penney* (L 73).
-kweniʔtahsthu - a few pennies. *dv.n.s.*

kakweni''táhsthę ‹it-penny-is small› *a few pennies* (L 73).

-kwenya'T - feasible. *dv.n.s.* yukwé·-nya''t ‹it-be able-causes› *feasible* (HS).

-kwenyęhčr - ability, might. *n.s.* ukwe-nyéhčreh ‹be able-'ness› *ability, might* (R).

-kwer - ankle. *n.r.* inaln: rakwerę''kye *(at) his ankle* (RC 6:9), inc., n.sfx. -eh. ukwè·reh *ankle* (R); -kwera'niha -: wahrukwera'níhak ‹fact-he-ankle-sprained› *he twisted his ankle* (RC 25:13); ti -. -kwera'Θrę -.#ú'y: tihrakwera''Θrę'ú'y ‹so-he-ankle-is so big-great› *his ankles are large* (RC 25:13).

kwè·ru' rabbit *(Sylvilagus floridanus)* (R). *n.*

kwe'kú·rye' u'náhkweh yellow lady's slipper (H-notebook). *n.*

kwé'kwek duck (R). *n.*

kwé'kwe' female green lizard (R). *n.*

-kwe'n - movement. *n.r.* n-poss., inc., n.sfx. -eh. ukwé'neh *movement* (R); -atkwe'nęti -: ratkwe'né·tyę ‹he-him-self-movement-made› *he moved* (RC 24:10); -ne -. -atkwe'nęti -.#ú'y: neyutkwe'nętíhu'y ‹apart-it-itself-move-ment-makes-great› *it makes a move* (RC 25:12); ti -. -atkwe'nęti -: tiwatkwe'né·tyę ‹so-it-itself-movement-made› *it has moved* (RC 15:7).

-kwe'niyu - be the main one, be the principal one. *v.r.-s.i.* hab: -, pnt: -, stat: -', prog: -, prp: -, dst: -, caus: -, rvs: -, dat: -, inc.-φ-pat. -(a)hahakwe'niyu -: wahahakwe'nì·yu' ‹it-path-is the main one› *principal path* (RC 13:5), *main,*

principal road; it is the highway, public way (H 2484); -čisnakwe'niyu -: Kayečisnakwe'nì·yu' ‹they-ember-are the main ones› *Onondaga sachems ("Keepers-of-the-Fire")* (R); -hwači= rakwe'niyu -: rahwačirakwe'nì·yu' ‹he-nuclear family-is the main one› *he is head of the family* (RC 27:2); -nęhsakwe'niyu -: ranęhsakwe'nì·yu' ‹he-house-is the main one› *proprietor* (HS); -rihwakwe'niyu -: rarihwakwe'nì·yu' ‹he-matter-is the main one› *master: the one in charge* (RC 13:5); -ta'nakwe'niyu -: kata'nakwe'-nì·yu' ‹it-settlement-is the main one› *capitol city* (HS); -ya'takwe'niyu -: kaya'takwe'nì·yu' ‹it-body-is the main one› *principal* (HS); -a'nya'ta= kwe'niyuhsT -: ra'nya'takwe'niyúh-stha' ‹he-himself-body-be the main one-causes› *he monopolizes* (HS); ha' -ta'nakwe'niyu -: ha' rata'nakwe'-nì·yu' ‹the he-village-is the main one› *mayor* (HS).

kwe'tí' perhaps (RC 1:4). *part.* Also: kutí' (R), ku'tí' (R), kwutí' (R), kwu'tí' (R).

kwé'yę·' barely, middling, moderate, temperate (HS). *part.* kwe'yę. -ha= 'nye': kwe'yęhá·'nye' ‹barely-going along› *moderately* (HS); kwé'yę·' ti -. -a'narih -: kwé'yę·' tyu'naríhę· ‹barely so-it-is hot› *tepid* (HS).

kwe'yę. -ha'nye' moderately. *part.* kwe'-yęhá·'nye' ‹barely-going along› *moderately* (HS).

kwé'yę·' ti -. -a'narih - tepid. *n.s.* kwé'-

yę·ʼ tyuʼnaríhę· ‹barely so-it-is hot›
tepid (HS).

kwę́ as, like (RC 11:16). *part.*

-kwęhčr – ocher, red paint, vermillion.
n.r. n-poss., inc., n.sfx. -eh. ukwę́h-
čreh *ocher, red paint, vermillion* (R);
  -kwęhčrarhu –: rakwęhčrárhuhs ‹he-
vermillion-mixes in› *he reddens it*
(HS); **-kwęhčręθhaʔk** –: rakwęhčrę́-
θhaʔk ‹he-vermillion-??› *he has scarlet fever* (HS).

-kwęhčrarhu – redden. *v.s.-t.* rakwęhčrárhuhs ‹he-vermillion-mixes in› *he reddens it* (HS).

-kwęhčręθhaʔk – have scarlet fever. *v.s.-
a.i.* rakwęhčrę́θhaʔk ‹he-vermillion-??›
he has scarlet fever (HS).

kwę́hkwęh raven (HS). *n.*

-kwęhnakew – wipe off rust. *v.s.-a.i.* ra-
kwęhnakyè·wahs ‹he-rust-wipes› *he
wipes off rust* (HS).

-kwęhnar – throw down. *v.r.-t.* hab: -ɸ,
pnt: -ʼ, stat: -ę, prog: -, prp: -, dst: -,
caus: -hu-, rvs: -, dat: -, inc.-ɸ-pat.
  -kwęhnarhu –: rakwęhnárhuhs ‹he-
throw down-causes› *he strikes it down
flat, he causes it to lie flat* (H-notebook); **-θwạkwęhnar** –: raθwakwę́hnar
‹he-short cloak-throws down› *he
prostrates* (HS); **-tehạkwęhnarhu** –: katehakwęhnárhuhs ‹it-sand-throw down-
causes› *it hails* (HS); **-tehạkwęh=
narhu** –: yutehakwęhnárhę ‹it-sand-
throw down-caused› *sandy country,
plains (a desert would be called so)*
(AG); **-tehạkwęhnarhu –.#úʔy**: yuteha-
kwęhnarhęhúʔy ‹it-sand-throw down-
caused-great› *desert* (HS); **-atʼehnạ=
kwęhnar** –: rutʼehnakwęhnà·rę ‹he-him-
self-hand-threw down› *he slapped*
(HS), ratʼehnakwę́hnar ‹he-himself-
hand-throws down› *he slaps* (HS), ęh-
ratʼehnakwę́hnaʼr ‹prediction-he-himself-hand-turn down› *he will slap*

(HS).

-kwęhnaraʔ – get rusty. *v.s.-a.i.* kakwę́h-
naraʔθ ‹it-rust-be in-begins› *it gets
rusty* (HS).

-kwęhnarhu – cause to lie flat, strike
down flat. *v.s.-t.* rakwęhnárhuhs ‹he-
throw down-causes› *he strikes it down
flat, he causes it to lie flat* (H-notebook).

-kwęhnęhT – knock off rust. *v.s.-a.i.* ra-
kwęhnę́hthaʔ ‹he-rust-fall-causes› *he
knocks off rust* (HS).

kwęhs no, not (RC 2:13); un-, in-, a- (R)
[Gallatin «kwuhss» 'No']. *part.* This
particle is used to denote lexical ne-
gation and is, thus, equivalent to the
English prefixes un- (unimportant), in-
(independent), and a- (amoral). The
negated lexical item immediately follows the particle and, if a verbal construction, is marked for the optative
mode.

kwęhs **-ačhęwati** – be uneven. *v.s.-s.i.*
kwęhs aryučhęwá·tyek ‹no unknown-
it-itself-smooth› *it is uneven* (HS).

kwęhs **-ačʔahT** – be inexhaustible. *v.s.-
a.i.* kwęhs aręčʔáhthek ‹no unknown-
it-itself-exhaust-cause› *it is inexhaustible* (HS).

kwęhs **-(a)hyęti** – be unfruitful. *v.s.-a.i.*
kwęhs aręhyętíhek ‹no unknown-it-
fruit-make› *it is unfruitful* (HS).

kwęhs **-ạkęwaT** – be unique. *v.s.-s.i.*
kwęhs aryukęwá·ʔnęk ‹no unknown-it-
lie within-stand› *it is unique* (HS).

kwęhs **-akwahsT** – be impracticable. *v.s.-
a.i.* kwęhs arę́kwahst ‹no unknown-it-
be good› *it is impracticable* (HS).

kwęhs **-(a)nha** – be unfilled. *v.s.-s.i.*
kwęhs akánhęk ‹no unknown-it-fill› *it
is unfilled* (HS).

kwęhs **-athraT** – be innumerable, be unnumbered. *v.s.-s.i.* kwęhs aryuthrá·ʔ-
nęk ‹no unknown-it-itself-count› *it is*

innumerable, it is unnumbered (HS).

kwęhs –athwęr – be undeserving. *v.s.-s.i.* kwęhs ahruthwę·ręk ‹no unknown-he-deserve› *he is undeserving* (HS).

kwęhs –atkahrye?T – be inexpressible. *v. s.-s.i.* kwęhs aryutkahryé?nek ‹no un-known-it-tell-cause› *it is inexpressible* (HS).

kwęhs –atku?čęri – be unfound. *v.s.-s.i.* kwęhs aryutku?čę·ryę·k ‹no unknown-it-itself-find› *it is unfound* (HS).

kwęhs –atkwęnyęhsT – be indecent. *v.s.-s.i.* kwęhs aryutkwęnyéhsnęk ‹no un-known-it-itself-treat with respect› *it is indecent* (HS).

kwęhs –atkwi?T – be immovable, be im-mutable. *v.s.-s.i.* kwęhs arętkwí?thek ‹no unknown-it-itself-move away› *it is immovable, it is immutable* (HS).

kwęhs –at?wahT – be infallible. *v.s.-s.i.* kwęhs ahrat?wáhthek ‹no unknown-he-escape-cause› *he is infallible* (HS).

kwęhs –a?čtehrihsT – be inadvertent. *v.s.-a.i.* kwęhs wahračtéhrihst ‹no fact-he-become involved with› *he was in-advertent* (HS).

kwęhs –a'nahča'nahkw – be unspoiled. *v. s.-a.i.* kwęhs aryu?nahča?náhkęk ‹no unknown-it-itself-spoil› *unspoiled* (HS).

kwęhs –a'nahθkw – be unfaded, be unfa-ding. *v.s.-a.i.* kwęhs aryu?náhθkwęk ‹no unknown-it-itself-fade› *it is un-faded* (HS), kwęhs aryu?nahθkwáh-shek ‹no unknown-it-itself-fade› *it is unfading* (HS).

kwęhs –a'nęhwatyę?T – be unsearchable. *v.s.-s.i.* kwęhs aryu?nęhwatyę́?nek ‹no unknown-it-cheat-cause› *it is unsear-chable* (HS).

kwęhs –a'nękwehstakwęnyęhsT – be im-polite. *v.s.-a.i.* kwęhs ahru?nękweh-stakwęnyéhsnęk ‹no unknown-he-him-self-human-'ness-treat with respect› *he is impolite* (HS).

kwęhs –a'nęnęhwih – be unrelated. *v.s.-t.* kwęhs ahra?nęnęhwíhek ‹no un-known-he-himself-be related to› *he is unrelated* (HS).

kwęhs –a'nęnęnhyar – be unguarded. *v.s.-s.i.* kwęhs ahrawęnęnhyá·ra·k ‹no un-known-he-himself-watch› *he is un-guarded* (HS).

kwęhs –a'nęnhe?nahkw – be impenitent. *v.s.-a.i.* kwęhs ahra?nęnhe?nahkwáh-shek ‹no unknown-he-himself-be a-live-cause-instrument› *he is impenitent* (HS).

kwęhs –a?nęrhw – be unclouded. *v.s.-s.i.* kwęhs aryu?nęrhwek ‹no unknown-it-cloud› *it is unclouded* (HS).

kwęhs –a?nihθkwa?T – be impregnable, be invulnerable. *v.s.-s.i.* kwęhs aryu?-nihθkwá?nęk ‹no unknown-it-pick off-cause› *it is impregnable, it is in-vulnerable* (HS).

kwęhs –a'ni'nęrahsk – be inhospitable. *v. s.-a.i.* kwęhs ahru?ni?nęráhskęk ‹no unknown-he-himself-pity-easily› *he is inhospitable* (HS).

kwęhs –a'nuhstihs?a – a minor. *dv.n.s.* kwęhs ahru?nuhstíhs?ęk ‹no unknown-he-himself-year-exhaust› *a minor* (HS).

kwęhs -a'nuryahnę- be immovable, be inactive. *v.s.-a.i.* kwęhs ahra'nuryahnę́hek ‹no unknown-he-himself-stir-much› *he is inactive* (HS), kwęhs arę'nuryahnę́hek ‹no unknown-it-itself-stir-much› *it is immovable* (HS).

kwęhs -a'nu?kT - be infinite, be unlimited. *v.s.-s.i.* kwęhs aryu'nú'knak ‹no unknown-it-itself-end› *it is infinite, it is unlimited* (HS).

kwęhs -a'nwętanh - be irresponsible. *v.s.-a.i.* kwęhs ahru'nwę́·tanhęk ‹no unknown-he-himself-word-fill› *he is irresponsible* (HS).

kwęhs -a'nwętarahkw - be insubordinate, disobey. *v.s.-a.i.* kwęhs ahru'nwętaráhkęk ‹no unknown-he-himself-word-collect› *he is insubordinate, he disobeys, he is disobedient* (HS).

kwęhs -a?rakew - be ineffaceable. *v.s.-a.i.* kwęhs arę'rakyewáhshek ‹no unknown-it-itself-X-wipe› *it is ineffaceable* (HS).

kwęhs -a?rihwahnę?T - be inexcusable. *v.s.-a.i.* kwęhs arę'rihwahnę́'thek ‹no unknown-it-itself-matter-disappear-cause› *it is inexcusable* (HS).

kwęhs -a?rihwara? - ta?awę́·te be innocent. *v.s.-a.i.* kwęhs ahru'rihwará'ęk ta'awę́·te ‹no unknown-he-himself-matter-be in-begin something› *he is innocent* (HS).

kwęhs -a?rihwharaku - be illicit. *v.s.-s.i.* kwęhs aryu'riwhará·kwęk ‹no unknown-it-itself-matter-hang-undo› *it is illicit* (HS).

kwęhs -a?θwahT - be unquenchable. *v.s.-s.i.* kwęhs aryu'θwáhnęk ‹no unknown-it-extinguish-cause› *it is unquenchable* (HS).

kwęhs -čha?nahkw - be incorruptible. *v.s.-a.i.* kwęhs arę'na'čha'náhkhwek ‹no unknown-it=another-gall-pick up› *it is incorruptible* (HS).

kwęhs -či-.-ačhakwahsT - be irreparable, be incorrigible. *v.s.-s.i.* kwęhs ęθayuchakwáhsnęk ‹no unknown-again-it-X-be good› *it is irreparable, it is incorrigible* (HS).

kwęhs -či-.-atku?čęri - be incomparable. *v.s.-a.i.* kwęhs ęθętku'čęryę́hshek ‹no unknown-again-it-itself-find› *it is incomparable* (HS).

kwęhs -či-.-a?rihwahnę?T - be inexplicable, be irremissible. *v.s.-a.i.* kwęhs ęθę'rihwahnę́'thek ‹no unknown-again-it-itself-matter-disappear-cause› *it is inexplicable, it is irremissible* (HS).

kwęhs -či-.-nęhkwa'nę? - be irremediable. *v.s.-s.i.* kwęhs ęθayunęhkwá·'nę'k ‹no unknown-again-it-medicine-become› *it is irremediable* (HS).

kwęhs -ek? - be intemperate. *v.s.-a.i.* kwęhs ahrawé·k'ęk ‹no unknown-he-be intoxicated› *he is temperate* (HS).

kwęhs -eti(y) - be unproductive. *v.s.-a.i.* kwęhs arwetiyáhshek ‹no unknown-it-produce› *unproductive* (HS).

kwęhs -ęnęnhyar - be inadvertent. *v.s.-s.i.* kwęhs ahrawęnęnhyá·ra·k ‹no unknown-he-watch› *he is inadvertent* (HS).

kwęhs -ętathrewa?T - be unrepenting. *v.s.-a.i.* kwęhs ahrętathrewá'thek ‹no unknown-he-?'?-punish› *he is unrepenting* (HS).

kwęhs -ętawanęhkwi - be unswept. *v.s.-a.i.* kwęhs arwętawanę́hkwik ‹no unknown-it-filth-comb› *unswept* (HS).

kwęhs -ę'na'nehsT - be unhappy. *v.s.-s.i.* kwęhs ahrawę'na'néhsnęk ‹no unknown-he-make pleasant› *he is unhappy* (HS).

kwęhs -ę'nar - be undated. *v.s.-s.i.* kwęhs aryawę́·'narak ‹no unknown-it-day-be in› *it is undated* (HS).

kwęhs -ę'nehsT - be imperceptible. *v.s.-

s.i. kwęhs aryawę·'néhsnęk ‹no unknown-it-day-use› *imperceptibly* (H-notebook).

kwęhs **-(ę)'tikęhranę** - be unfeeling. *v.s.-a.i.* kwęhs ahra'tikęhranę·k ‹no unknown-he-mind-guard› *he is unfeeling* (HS).

kwęhs **-(ę)'tikęhrayerik** - imbecile. *dv.n. s.* kwęhs ahra'tikęhrayè·rik ‹no unknown-he-mind-be filled› *imbecile* (HS).

kwęhs **-(ę)'tikęhrayę'nahsT** - inexplicable. *n.s.* kwęhs u'tikęhrayę́·'nahst ‹no mind-lay-cause› *inexplicable* (HS).

kwęhs **-(ę)'tikęhrhawsT** - be unknowable. *v.s.-s.i.* kwęhs aryu'tikęrháwsnęk ‹no unknown-it-mind-bring-cause› *it is unknowable* (HS).

kwęhs **-(ę)'tikęhriyu** -{dative I} be discontented. *v.s.-a.i.* kwęhs ahru'tikęhriyu'θéhek ‹no unknown-he-mind-be great-for› *he is discontented* (HS).

kwęhs **-(ę)'tikęhriyu'T** - be unsatisfactory. *v.s.-s.i.* kwęhs aryu'tikęhriyú'nęk ‹no unknown-it-mind-be great-cause› *unsatisfactory* (HS).

kwęhs her ‹no so that› lest (HS). *part.*

kwęhs hè·wi **-i'rę** - **-a'tak(e)r** - be uninhabitable. *v.s.-a.i.* kwęhs hè·wi aŕę́'-rę' aryę'takyé·ra·t ‹no enough unknown-it-settle unknown-one-oneself-dwell› *it is uninhabitable* (HS).

kwęhs **-hewihsT** - be insatiable. *v.s.-a.i.* kwęhs ahruhewíhsthek ‹no unknown-he-enough-cause› *he is insatiable* (HS).

kwęhs hé'thu **-i** - be insufficient. *v.s.-s.i.* kwęhs hé'thu ará·kę·k ‹no there unknown-it-be a group› *it is insufficient* (HS).

kwęhs he'thúhči **-i** - be unfit. *v.s.-s.i.* kwęhs he'thúhči ará·kę·k ‹no just right unknown-it-be a group› *it is unfit* (HS).

kwęhs **-hęhsyę** - be intractable. *v.s.-a.i.* kwęhs ahruhęhsyéhek ‹no unknown-he-ear-go into› *it is intractable* (HS).

kwęhs **-hskęnę'** - **-(ę)'tikęhręT** - be unpacified. *v.s.-a.i.* kwęhs ahskè·nę' ahrę'tikęhrę'néhek ‹no unknown-be at peace unknown-he-mind-conclude-going to› *he is unpacified* (HS).

kwęhs **-hsna'ku** - be inefficacious. *v.s.-s.i.* kwęhs akahsná'kęk ‹no unknown-it-give up› *it is inefficacious* (HS).

kwęhs **-(i)he** - be untimely. *v.s.-s.i.* kwęhs aryúhek ‹no unknown-it-put on› *untimely* (HS).

kwęhs **-iheyęhθe** - be immortal, be undying. *v.s.-s.i.* kwęhs akęheyéhθek ‹no unknown-it-die-going to› *it is undying* (HS), kwęhs ahręheyéhθek ‹no unknown-he-die-going to› *he is immortal* (HS).

kwęhs **-i'rę** - **-a'tak(e)r** - be uninhabited. *v.s.-a.i.* kwęhs aŕę́'rę' aryę'takyé·ra·t ‹no unknown-it-set unknown-one-oneself-dwell-complete› *it is uninhabited* (HS).

kwęhs **-(i)'θhęnyę'T** - be unrelenting. *v.s.-a.i.* kwęhs ahru'θhęnyę́'thek ‹no unknown-he-defeat-cause› *he is unrelenting* (HS).

Tuscarora Pronunciation Key:
/a/ l<u>a</u>w; /e/ h<u>a</u>t; /i/ p<u>i</u>zza; /u/ t<u>u</u>ne; /ę/ h<u>i</u>nt; /č/ <u>ch</u>eese; /h/ <u>h</u>oe; /m/ <u>m</u>other; /s/ <u>s</u>ame; /t/ <u>d</u>o (before a vowel y, or w), <u>t</u>oo (elsewhere); /k/ <u>g</u>ale (before a vowel y or w), <u>k</u>ale (elsewhere); /n/ i<u>nh</u>ale (before a consonant or word-final), <u>n</u>ote (elsewhere), /r/ hi<u>ss</u> (before a consonant or word-final), <u>r</u>un (trilled as in Italian, elsewhere); /w/ c<u>uff</u> (before a consonant other than y or word-final), <u>w</u>ay (elsewhere); /y/ fi<u>sh</u> (before a consonant or word-final), <u>y</u>ou (elsewhere), /θ/ <u>th</u>ing; /'/ (the sound between the vowels in unh-unh); /·/ long vowel, /´/ high pitch; /`/ low pitch.

kwẹhs káhne·ˀ ‹no who› no one (AW
101). *part.*

kwẹhs –keˀčatkẹh– be unleavened. *v.s.-
s.i.* kwẹhs aryukycˀčatkẹ́hẹk ‹no unknown-it-dough-be rotten-begin› *it is
unleavened* (HS).

ķwẹhs –kẹˀT– be invisible. *v.s.-s.i.*
kwẹhs aryukẹ́ˀnẹk ‹no unknown-it-
see-cause› *it is invisible* (HS).

kwẹhs –kẹˀT– –i– be invisible. *v.s.-s.i.*
kwẹhs ú·kẹˀt ará·kẹk ‹no see-cause
unknown-it-be a group› *it is invisible*
(HS).

kwẹhs kwè·niˀ ‹no commonly› impunity,
for nothing (HS). *part.*

kwẹhs –kweni– be incapable, be incompetent. *v.s.-a.i.* kwẹhs ahrakwè·niˀ ‹no
unknown-he-be able› *he is incompetent* (HS). kwẹhs ahrakwenyẹ́hshek
‹no unknown-he-be able› *he is incapable* (HS).

kwẹhs –kwenyaˀT– be impossible. *v.s.-
s.i.* kwẹhs aryukwenyá́ˀnẹk ‹no unknown-it-be able-cause› *it is impossible* (HS).

kwẹhs –kwenyaˀT– –atkwiˀT– be irremovable. *v.s.-a.i.* kwẹhs aryukwe-
nyáˀnẹk arẹ́tkwiˀt ‹no unknown-it-be
able-cause unknown-it-itself-move› *it
is irremovable* (HS).

kwẹhs –ne–. –atkẹˀneti– be invariable.
v.s.-a.i. kwẹhs narẹtkẹ́ˀné·tiˀ ‹no a-
part-unknown-it-itself-change› *it is invariable* (HS).

kwẹhs –ne–. –atkẹˀneti–{dative III} be
unalterable. *v.s.-a.i.* kwẹhs narẹtkẹ́ˀ-
netyẹ́hshek ‹no apart-unknown-it-it-
self-change-for› *it is unalterable* (HS).

kwẹhs –ne–. –atkẹˀnetyaˀT– be unalterable. *v.s.-a.i.* kwẹhs naryutkẹ́ˀnetyáˀ-
nẹk ‹no apart-unknown-it-itself-
change-cause› *it is unalterable* (HS).

kwẹhs –ne–. –aˈnekhahsi– be indivisible.
v.s.-a.i. kwẹhs narẹˀnekhahsyẹ́hshek

‹notwo-unknown-it-itself-divide-undo›
it is indivisible (HS).

kwẹhs –ne–. –aˈnekhahsyaˀT– be inseparable. *v.s.-a.i.* kwẹhs narẹˀnekhah-
syáˀnẹk ‹no two-unknown-it-itself-di-
vide-undo-cause› *it is inseparable*
(HS).

kwẹhs –ne–. –aˈnewyẹhw– be inconsistent,
be incompatible, be incongruous. *v.s.-
a.i.* kwẹhs narẹˀné·wyẹw ‹no two-it-
itself-know how-cause› *the two of
them are inconsistent, the two of them
are incongruous, the two of them are
incompatible* (HS).

kwẹhs –ne–. –aˀrihuhθ(e)r– be undecided.
v.s.-s.i. kwẹhs naryuˀrihúhθrẹk ‹no
apart-unknown-it-itself-matter-strip
off› *it is undecided* (HS).

kwẹhs –ne–. –aˀrihukaˀT– be inexplicable.
v.s.-a.i. kwẹhs narẹˀrihukáˀthek ‹no
apart-unknown-it-itself-matter-blister-
cause› *it is inexplicable* (HS).

kwẹhs –ne–. –hriˀẹhsturẹ– be unfatherly.
v.s.-s.i. kwẹhs naryuhriˀẹhstú·rẹ·k ‹no
apart-unknown-it-be father to-ˈness-
split› *it is unfatherly* (HS).

kwẹhs –ne–. –kwaˀnẹti– be unrounded. *v.
s.-s.i.* kwẹhs nahrukwaˀnẹ́·tik ‹no a-
part-unknown-he-arc-makes› *he is unrounded* (HS).

kwẹhs –ne–. –tkwarihT–{dative III} have
indigestion. *v.s.-a.i.* kwẹhs nahrutkwarihnatíhek ‹no apart-unknown-he-
stomach-be ripe-cause-for› *he has indigestion* (HS).

kwẹhs –ne–. –wẹtakẹˀneti– be untranslated. *v.s.-s.i.* kwẹhs nakawẹtakẹ́ˀ-
né·tyẹk ‹no apart-unknown-it-word-
change› *it is untranslated* (HS).

kwẹhs –ne–. –yaˀtahT– be unfit. *v.s.-s.i.*
kwẹhs naryuyáˀtaht ‹no apart-unknown-it-body-stand› *it is unfit* (HS).

kwẹhs –nẹheratẹhT– be ungrateful. *v.s.-
s.i.* kwẹhs ahrunẹheratẹ́hnek ‹no un-

known-he-thank-cause› *he is ungrateful* (HS).

kwęhs –rę'nha? – be unaccustomed to.
v.s.-t. kwęhs ahrurę'nhá'ęk ‹no unknown-he-frequent-begin› *he is unaccustomed to it* (HS).

kwęhs –rharahT – be unexpected, be unhoped for, be unpromising. *v.s.-s.i.*
kwęhs aryurharáhnęk ‹no unknown-it-
be confident-cause› *it is unexpected, it
is unhoped for, it is unpromising*
(HS).

kwęhs –rihwakahrę?T – be absurd, be unreasonable. *v.s.-s.i.* kwęhs aryurih-
wakahrę'nak ‹no unknown-it-matter-
be an opening-cause› *it is absurd, (it
is) unreasonable* (HS).

kwęhs –rihwakare? – be unheard of. *v.s.-
s.i.* kwęhs aryurihwakaré'ęk ‹no un-
known-it-matter-be loud-begin› *it is
unheard (of)* (HS).

kwęhs –rihwar – be unapproachable, be
unsocial. *v.s.-s.i.* kwęhs ahruríhwarak
‹no unknown-he-matter-be in› *he is
unapproachable, he is unsocial* (HS).

kwęhs –rihwarhu – fail to heed. *v.s.-a.i.*
kwęhs ahrarihwárhęk ‹no unknown-
he-matter-mix› *he does not heed it*
(HS).

kwęhs –rihwater?(ak) – be infallible. *v.s.-
a.i.* kwęhs ahrarihwater'áhshek ‹no
unknown-he-matter-make a mistake›
he is infallible (HS).

kwęhs –rihwęnhe – be invalid. *v.s.-a.i.*
kwęhs akarihwęnhek ‹no unknown-it-
matter-be alive› *it is invalid* (HS).

kwęhs –rihwiyuhsT – be unchristian. *v.s.-
s.i.* kwęhs ahrurihwiyúhsnęk ‹no unknown-he-matter-be great-cause› *he is
unchristian* (HS).

kwęhs sawę́·te –wyęhw – be incompetent.
v.s.-s.i. kwęhs sawę́·te ahrawyę́hęk
‹no nothing unknown-he-know how-
cause› *he is incompetent* (HS).

kwęhs –t–. –ehnahkw – be unfaithful. *v.s.-
a.i.* kwęhs ę'nahrawehnáhkęk ‹no un-
known-hither-he-go-causes-instrument›
he is unfaithful (HS).

kwęhs –t–. –(ę)?tikęhriyuhT – be unsatisfactory. *v.s.-s.i.* kwęhs ę'nayu'tikęhriyúhnęk ‹no unknown-hither-it-
mind-be great-cause› *unsatisfactory*
(HS).

kwęhs –t–. –rihwarahkw – be neutral. *v.s.-
s.i.* kwęhs ę'nahrurihwaráhkęk ‹no
unknown-hither-he-matter-collect› *he
is neutral* (HS).

kwęhs –t–. –rihwayerik – be unjust. *v.s.-a.i.*
kwęhs ę'nakarihwayè·rik ‹no unknown-hither-it-matter-fill up› *it is unjust* (HS), kwęhs ę'nahrarihwayè·rik
‹no unknown-hither-he-matter-fill up›
he is unjust (HS).

kwęhs –tak(e)r – be uninhabited. *v.s.-s.i.*
kwęhs aryetá·krek ‹no unknown-one-
dwell› *it is uninhabited* (HS).

kwęhs –ta'nakęw.#áh rustic. *n.s.* kwęhs
uta'nakęw'áh ‹no settlement-in-little›
rustic (HS).

kwęhs tha –. –a'na?wnyeriha – be uneven.
v.s.-s.i. kwęhs tharyu'na'wnyeríhęk
‹no unusual-unknown-it-itself-earth-
straighten› *it is uneven (earth)* (HS).

kwęhs tha –. –a'nya?čerih – be indirect. *v.*

s.-s.i. kwęhs tharyu'³nya'³čeríhçhs ‹no unusual-unknown-it-itself-track-straighten› *it is indirect* (HS).

kwęhs tha –. **-ehsT** – be indifferent. *v.s.-a.i.* kwęhs thahréhsthek ‹no unusual-unknown-he-go-causes› *he is indifferent* (HS).

kwęhs -tuwęhT – be credible. *v.s.-s.i.* kwęhs aryutuwę́hnęk ‹no unknown-it-tell a lie-cause› *it is credible, it is incontestible* (HS).

kwęhs -tyak – bachelor. *dv.n.s.* kwęhs ahrutyákshek ‹no unknown-he-marry› *bachelor* (HS).

kwęhs wehre'³ę̀·we –i– be unreal. *v.s.-s.i.* kwęhs wehre'³ę̀·we ará·kę·k ‹no truly unknown-it-be a group› *unreal* (HS).

kwęhs -wyesT – be indecorous, be unbecoming. *v.s.-s.i.* kwęhs aryuwyésnęk ‹no unknown-it-is seemly› *it is indecorous, it is unbecoming* (HS).

kwęhs -yah –. –(ę)haw – ti –. **-nurę** – be inestimable. *v.s.-s.i.* kwęhs yaryéha'³w tikanú·rę· ‹no thither-unknown-one-bring so-it-is precious› *it is inestimable* (HS).

kwęhs -yah –. –(i)he – be undue. *v.s.-s.i.* kwęhs yaryúhek ‹no thither-unknown-it-put on› *undue* (HS).

kwęhs -yah+ne –. **-ę'nękuhT** – be impenetrable. *v.s.-a.i.* kwęhs ya'³narę'³nękúhthek ‹no thither-apart-it-day-go through-cause› *it is impenetrable* (HS).

kwęhs -yah+ne –. –(i)he – be incomprehensible. *v.s.-s.i.* kwęhs ya'³naryúhek ‹no thither-apart-unknown-it-put on› *it is incomprehensible* (HS).

kwęhs -yan(e)(r) – –i– innocently. *dv.n.s.* kwęhs yuya-né·rę·t ará·kę·k ‹no it-rule-possesses unknown-it-is a group› *innocently* (HS).

kwęhs -yanręhsta'³ke –i– unlawful. *n.s.* kwęhs uyanręhstá'³kye ará·kę·k ‹no rule-'ness-at unknown-it-is a group› *it is unlawful* (HS).

kwęhs -ya'³tawyesT – be unseemly. *v.s.-s.i.* kwęhs aryuya'³tawyésnęk ‹no unknown-it-body-is seemly› *unseemly* (HS).

kwęhs -ya'³ta'nę – be unbecoming. *v.s.-s.i.* kwęhs ahruya'³tá·'³nęk ‹no unknown-he-body-become› *he is unbecoming* (HS).

kwęhs -ya'³tatukęhT – –i– be unholy. *v.s.-s.i.* kwęhs ruya'³tatukę́hti ará·kę·k ‹no he-body-is holy unknown-it-is a group› *he is unholy* (HS).

kwęhs -ya'³tatukęhtiha'nye'³ – be unholy. *v.s.-s.i.* kwęhs aryuya'³tatukęhtihá·'³nye'³ ‹no unknown-it-body-be holy-going along› *it is unholy* (HS).

kwęhs -ya'³čęti – be indefinite. *v.s.-s.i.* kwęhs akaya'³čę́·tik ‹no unknown-it-track-extend› *it is indefinite* (HS).

kwęhs -yęwahT – be unblessed. *v.s.-s.i.* kwęhs ahruyęwáhnęk ‹no unknown-he-bless› *he is unblessed* (HS).

kwęhs -yę'nerT – be unknown. *v.s.-s.i.* kwęhs aryuyę'³nérnęk ‹no unknown-it-know-cause› *it is unknown* (HS).

kwęhs -'nek – be incombustible. *v.s.-a.i.* kwęhs aryu'³nékshek ‹no unknown-it-burn› *it is incombustible* (HS).

kwęhs -'neksk – be incombustible. *v.s.-s.i.* kwęhs aryu'³nékskę·k ‹no unknown-it-burn-easily› *it is incombustible* (HS).

kwęhs -'³nihahstayę'ner – chaste woman, maidenhood. *dv.n.s.* kwęhs arye'³nihahstayę'³nè·rihk ‹no unknown-one-be young male-'ness-know› *chaste woman, maidenhood* (HS).

-kwęhT – rust; face paint, vermillion. *n.r. n-poss., inc., n.sfx.* **-eh.** ukwę́hneh *rust* (HS), kwę́ht *face paint, vermillion* (HS) [Lawson «Quaunt» 'Paint']; **-kwęhčr** –: ukwę́hčreh ‹vermillion-'ness› *ocher, red paint, vermillion* (R);

-kwęhčrarhu –: rakwęhčrárhuhs ‹he-vermillion-'ness-mixes in› *he reddens it* (HS); -kwęhčręθha?k –: rakwęhčrę́θha?k ‹he-vermillion-'ness-?'?› *he has scarlet fever* (HS); -kwęhnakew –: rakwęhnakyè·-wahs ‹he-rust-wipes› *he wipes off rust* (HS); -kwęhnara? –: kakwę́hnara?θ ‹it-rust-be in-begins› *it gets rusty* (HS); -kwęhnęhT –: rakwęhnę́htha? ‹he-rust-fall-causes› *he knocks off rust* (HS).

kwęnę?ará·yę·θ grape, grapevine (HS). *n.*

-kwęnyęhsT – treat with respect. *v.r.-t.* hab: -ha?, pnt: -, stat: -ɸ, prog: -ęha-'nye?-, prp: -, dst: -, caus: -, rvs: -, dat: -, n-inc. rakwęnyę́hstha? *he treats it with respect, he esteems it, he honors it, he respects it, he solemnizes it* (HS), natkwęnyę́hstha? *one receives another, one treats another well* (HS); -atkwęnyęhsT –: yutkwę́·nyęhst ‹it-itself-treats with respect› *civility, decency, politeness* (HS); -a= tkwęnyęhsnęha'nye? –: yutkwęnyęhsnęhá·?nye? ‹it-itself-treated with respect-going along› *decently* (HS); -a= 'natkwęnyęhsT –: ra?natkwęnyę́hstha? ‹he-himself-self-treats with respect› *he respects himself* (HS); ha? -atkwę= nyęhsT –: ha? yutkwę́·nyęhst ‹the it-itself-treated with respect› *respectability* (HS); kwęhs -atkwęnyęhsT –: kwęhs aryutkwęnyę́hsnęk ‹no unknown-he-himself-treat with respect› *it is indecent* (HS); kwęhs -a?nę= kwehstakwęnyęhsT –: kwęhs ahru?nękwehstakwęnyę́hsnęk ‹no unknown-

he-himself-human-'ness-treat with respect› *he is impolite* (HS).

-kwęri – appear, turn up. *v.r.-a.i.* hab: -ehs, pnt: -?, stat: -, prog: -, prp: -, dst: -, caus: -hT-, rvs: -, dat: -, inc.-ɸ-pat. rakwę́·ryehs *he appears, he turns up* (H-notebook); -yah –. -kwęri –: yęhrakwę̀·ri? ‹thither-prediction-he-appear› *he will appear there* (RC 12:4); -hswakwęrihT –: rahswakwęríhtha? ‹he-back-appear-causes› *he revealed* (HS); -hswakwęri? –: rahswakwę̀·ri?θ ‹he-back-appear-begins› *he is found out* (H-notebook).

kwęθnè·reh buzzard (RC 12:18). *n.* kwę= θnereháh ‹buzzard-little› *kind of buzzard* (RC 12:29).

kwęθnereháh ‹buzzard-little› kind of buzzard (RC 12: 29). *n.*

Kwęyukuhá·ka·? Cayuga (AG). *n.* Also: Kwęyukwęhá·ka·?.

Kwęyukwęhá·ka·? Cayuga (R). *n.* Also: Kwęyukuhá·ka·?.

-kwę?rar – be spotted. *v.s.-s.i.* stat: -ɸ, prog: -, prog: -, prp: -, dst: -, caus: -, rvs: -, dat: -, inc.-?'?-pat. Found in the cited construction. -yęhwiθkwę?rar –: uyęhwiθkwę́?ra?r ‹wing-be spotted› *spotted wing* (H-notebook).

kwę?ráhsi? crab apple (*Malus* sp.) (R). *n.*

-kwihsT – be heavy. *v.r.-t.* hab: -, pnt: -e?, stat: -, prog: -, prp: -, dst: -, caus: -, rvs: -, dat: -, n-inc. wahrukwíhsne? *it hit him badly* (RC 3:16).

kwíhstet run fast! (R). *v.*

kwí·ks squeek (R). *part.*

Tuscarora Pronunciation Key:
/a/ l<u>a</u>w; /e/ h<u>a</u>t; /i/ p<u>i</u>zza; /u/ t<u>u</u>ne; /ę/ h<u>i</u>nt; /č/ <u>ch</u>eese; /h/ <u>h</u>oe; /m/ <u>m</u>other; /s/ <u>s</u>ame; /t/ <u>d</u>o (before a vowel y, or w), <u>t</u>oo (elsewhere); /k/ <u>g</u>ale (before a vowel y or w), <u>k</u>ale (elsewhere); /n/ i<u>nh</u>ale (before a consonant or word-final), <u>n</u>ote (elsewhere), /r/ hi<u>ss</u> (before a consonant or word-

final), <u>r</u>un (trilled as in Italian, elsewhere); /w/ c<u>u</u>ff (before a consonant other than y or word-final), <u>w</u>ay (elsewhere); /y/ fi<u>sh</u> (before a consonant or word-final), <u>y</u>ou (elsewhere), /θ/ <u>th</u>ing; /?/ (the sound between the vowels in unh-unh); /·/ long vowel, /´/ high pitch; /`/ low pitch.

-**kwir**- brush, shrub, tree, twig. *n.r.* n-poss., n-inc., n.sfx. -eh. ukwì·reh *brush, shrub, twig* (HS), *a tree (applied to standing ones)* (H-notebook); -**kwirak**-: kakwí·ra·ks ‹it-tree-eats› *it browses* (HS); -**kwiraʔr**-: yukwì·raʔr ‹it-tree-is much› *there are some trees standing* (H-notebook); -**kwiruhsku**-: kakwirúhskwahs ‹it-tree-picks off› *it browses* (HS).

-**kwirak**- browse. *v.s.-a.i.* kakwí·ra·ks ‹it-tree-eats› *it browses* (HS).

-**kwiruhsku**- browse. *v.s.-a.i.* kakwirúh-skwahs ‹it-tree-picks off› *it browses* (HS).

kwískwis pig. *n.* Also: kúskus. **kwískwis néʔči** ‹pig like› *hoggish* (HS); **kwískwis** -**areʔnęwθę**-: kwískwis waręʔ-nę́wθęh ‹pig it-snorts-much› *pig is grunting* (AG); **kwískwis** -**khwawę**-: kwískwis úkhwawęh ‹pig food-possess› *swill* (HS); **kwískwis** -**ʔniha**-: kwískwis kaʔníha· ‹pig it-is male› *boar* (HS).

kwískwis -**khwawę**- swill. *n.s.* kwískwis úkhwawęh ‹pig food-possess› *swill* (HS).

kwískwis néʔči ‹pig like› hoggish (HS). *n.s.*

kwískwis -**ʔniha**- boar. *n.s.* kwískwis kaʔníha· ‹pig it-is male› *boar* (HS).

kwù·niʔ as, like (R). *part.* Also: kù·niʔ (R).

kwutíʔ perhaps (R). *part.* Also: kutíʔ (RC 1:4), kuʔtíʔ (R), kwetíʔ (R), kwuʔtíʔ (R).

kwuʔtíʔ perhaps (R). *part.* Also: kutíʔ (RC 1:4), kuʔtíʔ (R), kwetíʔ (R), kwu-tíʔ (R).

-**kyaʔw**- quiver. *v.r.-s.i.* stat: -i, prog: -, prp: -, dst: -, caus: -, rvs: -, dat: III, inc.-ɸ-pat. ę́·či -**kyaʔw**-: ę́·či waʔu-kyáʔwik ‹one fact-it-quivered› *a jolt* (HS); -**kerhakyaʔwihsthę**-: ęθakyerha-

kyaʔwíhsthęʔ ‹unknown-you-body-quiver-causes-much› *that your body quiver* (RC 3:54).

kyé·nę· this (RC 3:21). *part.* **kaʔnę́ kyé·-nę·** ‹just! this is› *precisely, exactly that* (HS).

kyení·kę· this is (RC 3:21). *part.* Contraction of kyé·nę· í·kę· *this it is.*

kyérhiʔ standing tree, the tree (RC 3:38) *n.* Occurs with the cislocative, the dualic, and the partitive, prefixes that normally are found only on verbs. **kyerhíʔnęʔ** ‹standing tree-many› *trees* (R); **nekyérhiʔ** ‹two-standing tree› *two standing trees* (RC 25:2); **tikyérhiʔ** ‹so-standing tree› *standing tree* (RC 2:15); **tkyérhiʔ** ‹hither-standing tree› *at standing tree* (RC 2:15).

kyè·wę now, today (RC 30:33). *part.* **kyewę.#ęwe:** kyewęhę̀·we ‹now-genuine› *lately, soon* (R); **kyè·wę** -**rhęʔ**-: kyè·wę yurhę́ʔę ‹now it-became day› *today* (HS); **haʔ kyè·wę ti**-. -**rhęʔθrę**-: haʔ kyè·wę tyurhę́ʔ-θręʔ ‹the now so-it-became day-much› *now-a-days* (HS).

kyè·wę -**rhęʔ**- today. *part.* kyè·wę yur-hę́ʔę ‹now it-became day› *today* (HS).

kyè·wę ti-. -**rhęʔθrę**- now-a-days. *part.* haʔ kyè·wę tyurhę́ʔθręʔ ‹the now so-it-became day-much› *now-a-days* (HS).

kyewę.#ęwe lately, soon. *part.* kyewę-hę̀·we ‹now-genuine› *lately, soon* (R).

kyeʔ aforesaid (RC 26:4). *part.* **teʔ kyeʔ** ‹what afore-said› *whatever* (MG 88).

kyé·ʔnyęʔ nearby (RC 7:6). *part.*

-**kyęr**- be smoky. *v.r.-s.i.* stat: -ɸ, prog: -, prp: -, dst: -, caus: -, rvs: -, dat: -, n-inc. yú·kyęr *it is smoky* (HS).

-**kʔęyę**- perceive. *v.r.-t.* hab: -, pnt: -, stat: -ʔ, prog: -, prp: -, dst: -, caus: -, rvs: -, dat: -, n-inc. wakyekʔę̀·yęʔ *I am perceived* (RC 30:69).

L

lè·mun lemon (HS). *n.* lè·mun -ek̨eti-:
lè·mun wek̨é·tih ‹lemon it-liquid-
makes› *lemonade* (HS).

lè·mun -ek̨eti- lemonade. *dv.n.s.* lè·mun
wek̨é·tih ‹lemon it-liquid-makes› *lemonade* (HS).

lí·li· lily (HS). *n.*

M

má'ma' moccasin (R). *n.* Pronounced
mé'me' by some speakers. -ma'ma'=
ęhT-: wa'kma'má'ęht ‹I-moccasin-
fell-caused› *I dropped a moccasin* (R).

mę̀·nit minute (R). *n.*

mę́·teh Monday (R). *n.*

mí·ryę billion (HS). *n.* ę́·či mí·ryę ‹one
billion› *one billion* (HS); na' mí·ryę
‹much billion› *one billion* (HS).

N

-nač- rice. *n.r.* n-poss., n-inc., n.sfx. -a'.
uná·ča' *rice* (R); -nač- -tkuri'nęte: u-
ná·ča' utkuri'ńę́·te ‹rice hominy-certain one› *rice pudding* (HS).

-nač- -tkuri'nęte rice pudding. *n.s.* u-
ná·ča' utkuri'ńę́·te ‹rice porridge-cer-
tain one› *rice pudding* (HS).

-nač̌r- bow (weapon). *n.r.* n-poss., n-inc.,

n.sfx. -eh. unáč̌reh *bow (weapon)* (R).

-nahe'r- species of wild boar; bear fat;
peanut (?). *n.r.* n-poss., n-inc., n.sfx.
-eh. In a list of plant names Hewitt
indicates that this root may also mean
peanut. unahé'reh *species of wild
boar; bear fat* (R); *peanut* (?) (H-
notebook).

náhst quiet! (R). *part.*

náhwęr yes, I have (R). *part.*

-na·hyę- ally, associate. *v.r.-a.i.* See:
-(ę)na·hyę-.

-na·hyęhč̌r- alliance, association, companionship. *n.s.* See: -(ę)na·hyęhč̌r-.

-na·hyęhsT- ally. *dv.n.s.* See: -(ę)na·h=
yęhsT-.

-nak- birch. *n.r.* n-poss., n-inc., n.sfx.
-eh. uná·kyeh *birch (Betula sp.)* (R).

nak-/nakᵂ- you alone!...me (second person singular imperative=first person
singular patient). *v.r.pfx.* The form
nakᵂ- occurs before roots and stems
that begin with the vowel *a.* The form
nak- occurs elsewhere with insertion
of "epenthetic" e between the prefix
and roots and stems that begin with
certain consonant clusters.

nakT(i)-/naky- you alone!...the two of us
(second person singular imperative=
first person dual patient). *v.r.pfx.* The
form naky- occurs before roots and
stems that begin with the vowel *a.*
The form nakn- occurs before roots
and stems that begin with the vowel ę
or the morphophoneme {ᵘu}. The
form nakt- occurs before other roots
and stems that begin with the vowels

Tuscarora Pronunciation Key:
/a/ l<u>a</u>w; /e/ h<u>a</u>t; /i/ p<u>i</u>zza; /u/ t<u>u</u>ne; /ę/ h<u>i</u>nt; /č/
<u>ch</u>eese; /h/ <u>h</u>oe; /m/ <u>m</u>other; /s/ <u>s</u>ame; /t/ <u>d</u>o
(before a vowel y, or w), <u>t</u>oo (elsewhere); /k/ <u>g</u>ale
(before a vowel y or w), <u>k</u>ale (elsewhere); /n/
i<u>n</u>hale (before a consonant or word-final), <u>n</u>ote
(elsewhere), /r/ hi<u>ss</u> (before a consonant or word-

final), <u>r</u>un (trilled as in Italian, elsewhere); /w/ cu<u>ff</u>
(before a consonant other than y or word-final),
<u>w</u>ay (elsewhere); /y/ fi<u>sh</u> (before a consonant or
word-final), <u>y</u>ou (elsewhere), /θ/ <u>th</u>ing; /'/ (the
sound between the vowels in unh-<u>u</u>nh); /·/ long
vowel, /´/ high pitch; /`/ low pitch.

e, i, or *u* not from {"u}. The form **nakti-** occurs before roots and stems that begin with a consonant.

nakwa- you alone!...all of us (second person singular imperative=first person plural patient). *v.r.pfx.* Before roots and stems that begin with the vowel *i,* the final *a* of the prefixes coalesces with the *i* to yield **nakwę-**. Before other vowels the final *a* of the prefix is dropped.

nakwę́čha⁷ mythic diminutive deer (RC 8:32), antelope (AG). *n.* Gatschet adds the comment "to be fortunate" with a footnote stating that "to kill an antelope and prepare it in a certain way is a sign of everlasting luck."

na(r)(a)- dualic+optative. *v.pfx.* The form **nara-** occurs when the word accent falls on this prefix. The form **nar-** occurs before the glides *w* or *y.* When the prefix is follow by a *w* followed by the vowel *a* the sequence coalesces to yield **nę-**. The form **na-** occurs elsewhere.

nará·kwi⁷ sumac *(Rhus* sp.) (R). *n.*

nà·ra⁷r red headed woodpecker (R). *n.*

narà·we⁷st a few, a little (L 73), shortly (L 4). *part.*

naré⁷re rock bass *(Ambloplites rupestris)* (H 3518), sunfish (HS). *n.*

nà·re⁷θ not too much (R). *part.*

narú⁷naru⁷ coo-coo (R). *n.*

-nawa⁷čt- lead, pewter. *n.r.* n-poss., inc., n.sfx. -eh. unawá⁷čteh *lead, pewter* (HS); **-nawa⁷čtarhu-**: ranawa⁷čtár-huhs ‹he-lead-mixes in› *he leads it, he plumbs it, he solders it* (HS).

-nawa⁷čtarhu- lead, plumb, solder. *v.s.-t.* ranawa⁷čtárhuhs ‹he-lead-mixes› *he leads it, he plumbs it, he solders it* (HS).

nà·werk flea (R) [Lawson «Nauocq» 'A Flea']. *n.* **-nawerkčrar-**: yunawérkčrar ‹it-flea-'ness-is in› *it is afflicted with fleas* (HS).

-nawerkčrar- be afflicted with fleas. *v.s.-a.i.* yunawérkčrar ‹it-flea-'ness-is in› *it is afflicted with fleas* (HS).

-nawęhkr- oats. *n.r.* n-poss., n-inc., n.sfx. -i⁷. unawę́hkri⁷ *oats* (HS).

náwnę⁷ swift (bird) (HS). *n.*

-naye⁷- be proud. *v.r.-s.i.* stat: -ɸ, prog: -, prp: -, dst: -, caus: -sT-, rvs: -, dat: -, n-inc. ranà·ye⁷ *he is proud* (HS); **-naye⁷-**: unayé⁷ę ‹be proud› *pride, vanity* (HS); **-naye⁷čr-**: unayé⁷čreh ‹be proud-'ness› *pride, vanity* (HS); **-a'nęnaye⁷sT-**: ra⁷nęnayé⁷stha⁷ ‹he-himself-be proud-causes› *he makes himself proud* (HS).

-naye⁷- pride, vanity. *n.s.* unayé⁷ę ‹be proud› *pride, vanity* (HS).

-naye⁷čr- pride, vanity. *n.s.* unayé⁷čreh ‹be proud-'ness› *pride, vanity* (HS).

Nayuhkawé⁷ah Chief of the Wolf Clan (literal meaning uncertain) (H-Handbook). *n.*

na⁷ already, more, much (RC 3:10). *part.* è·re na⁷ ú⁷ni⁷ ‹alternatively much it-at edge of› *on the other side* (AW 57); na⁷ -rihwa⁷ke: na⁷ urihwá⁷kye ‹much matter-at› *concerning* (HS); ę́·či na⁷ -yahst-ti-. -yahsti-: ę́·či na⁷ uyáhsteh tikayáhstih ‹one much individual so-it-individual-is a group› *million* (HS); ę⁷nyéhči na⁷ -a'ni: ę⁷nyéhči na⁷ ú·⁷ni ‹noon some it-at edge of› *meridional (noon-side)* (HS), -⁷tehsnakT na⁷ -(a)'ni: u⁷téhsnakwt na⁷ ú·⁷ni ‹back much-it-at the edge of› *backward, reverse* (HS).

na⁷ -rihwa⁷ke concerning. *n.s.* na⁷ urihwá⁷kye ‹much matter-at› *concerning* (HS).

na⁷ ti-. -(a)hahu⁷nę- course. *dv.n.s.* na⁷ tyuhahú⁷nę· ‹much so-it-path-is a kind of› *course* (HS).

-na'č - pail. *n.r.* n-poss., n-inc., n.sfx. -a'. uná'ča' *pail* (R), kaná'ča' *pail* (R)).

-na'čuhkw - cowl, helmet, hood. *n.r.* n-poss., n-inc., n.sfx. -eh. una'čúhkweh *cowl, helmet, hood* (HS).

ná'ku' boil (anatomical) (R); jack-in-the-pulpit *(Arisaema atrorubens)* (H-notebook); devil's darning needle (causing a sore similar to a boil) (H 3518). *n.* na'ku'.#ú'y: na'ku'ú'y ‹boil-great› *carbuncle* (HS).

na'ku'.#ú'y carbuncle. *n.* na'ku'ú'y ‹boil-great› *carbuncle* (HS).

-na'θrar - bail (of a pail). *n.r.* n-poss., n-inc., n.sfx. -eh. uná'θrareh *bail (of a pail)* (HS).

-na'kwey - cattail. *n.r.* n-poss., n-inc., n. sfx. -a'. una'kwè·ya' *cattail (Typha latifolia)* (H-notebook).

ná'wak already (R). *part.*

ná'wnę' assaparic, eft, newt (HS). *n.*

ne - dualic. *v.pfx.* Occurs in word-initial position in the absence of modal markers.

-ne - two, apart (dualic). *v.pfx.* The dualic serves three basic functions in Tuscarora: an attributive function, as a replacement for né·kti· *two*; an inflectional function, as the marker of dual number for third person pronouns; and, a derivational function, indicating that the verb refers to a change in location or state. Although the dualic serves three functions, no word may contain more than one dualic prefix. This results in some cases of polysemy such as neyętkhwa' *one dances/the two of them dance*. The meanings of the dualic in its attributive and inflectional functions is usually transparent and, thus, such forms are not normally listed as separate entries in this work. (A few exceptions exist; specifically, forms with the dualic in its attributive function that have been lexicalized with idiomatic meanings.) However, in its derivational function, the meaning of the dualic is more opaque. Such cases are listed here.

-ne -. -(a)čęhahkw - jack o' lantern. *dv.n.s.* nekačęháhkhwa' ‹apart-it-fire-picks up› *jack o' lantern* (AG).

-ne -. -(a)čęhuhkwahkw - jack o' lantern. *dv.n.s.* nekačęhuhkwáhkhwa' ‹apart-it-fire-cover-instrument-picks up› *jack o' lantern* (AG).

-ne -. -(a)čęhak"ekT - whole family. *dv. n.s.* nekakučęhakwé·kę ‹two-they-fire-closed› *whole family* (RC 13:10).

-ne -. -(a)čęhatekę - neighbor. *dv.n.s.* neyękyačęhaté·kę· ‹two-we two-fire-join› *my neighbor* (R).

-ne -. -ačhęwireT - be humiliating. *v.s.-s.i.* neyuchęwí·rę·t ‹apart-it-itself-degrades› *it is humiliating* (HS).

-ne -. -ačhiθ - meet. *v.s.-a.i.* nehruchí·θę ‹two-he-himself-X-met› *he met* (HS), nehrachí·θahs ‹two-he-himself-X-meets› *he meets* (HS), wa'nyęčhi·θ ‹fact-two-one-one-self-X-met› *the two of them met* (RC 34:22).

-ne -. -ačkanekęT - juggle. *v.s.-a.i.* nehrač-

Tuscarora Pronunciation Key:
/a/ law; /e/ hat; /i/ pizza; /u/ tune; /ę/ hint; /č/ cheese; /h/ hoe; /m/ mother; /s/ same; /t/ do (before a vowel y, or w), too (elsewhere); /k/ gale (before a vowel y or w), kale (elsewhere); /n/ inhale (before a consonant or word-final), note (elsewhere), /r/ hiss (before a consonant or word-final), run (trilled as in Italian, elsewhere); /w/ cuff (before a consonant other than y or word-final), way (elsewhere); /y/ fish (before a consonant or word-final), you (elsewhere), /θ/ thing; /'/ (the sound between the vowels in unh-unh); /·/ long vowel, /´/ high pitch; /`/ low pitch.

kanekę́·tha⁷ ‹apart-he-himself-is strange› *he juggles* (HS).

–ne –. –(a)hahahkw – walk on a path. *v.s.-a.i.* wa⁷tkayeháhahkw ‹fact-they-path-picked up› *they walked on a path* (RC 32:2).

–ne –. –(a)hahiθ – meet. *v.s.-t.* nehrahahí·θahs ‹apart-he-path-meets› *he meets it* (H 2484), nehrahahí·θhe⁷ ‹apart-he-path-meet-is going to› *he is about to meet it* (H 2484).

–ne –. –ahča⁷nihrhę – pot. *dv.n.s.* neyuhča⁷nírhę· ‹apart-it- fist-stood-much› *pot* (HS).

–ne –. –(a)hkarayę'nahkw – draughthead. *dv.n.s.* neyęhkarayę⁷náhkhwa⁷ ‹apart-one-bark-lays-instrument› *draughthead* (HS).

–ne –. –(a)hkaręhnahnę – be square. *v.s.-s.i.* neyuhkaręhnáhnę· ‹apart-it-bark-fall-cause-much› *it is square* (HS).

–ne –. –(a)hkarstraku – unyoke. *v.s.-t.* nehrahkarstrá·kwahs ‹apart-he-bark-'ness-collects› *he unyokes* (HS), nehruhkarstrá·kwę ‹apart-he-bark-'ness-collected› *he unyoked* (HS).

–ne –. –(a)hkaruθT – wild geranium. *dv.n.s.* neyuhkarúθ⁷ne⁷ ‹apart-it-bark-cover-causes› *wild geranium (Geranium maculatum)* (H-notebook).

–ne –. –ahk(e)T – fold. *v.s.-t.* nehrúhknęhs ‹apart-he-goes back and forth› *he folds it* (HS), nęhrúhkye·t ‹apart-prediction-he-go back and forth› *he will fold it* (HS).

–ne –. –ahna – approach. *v.r.-a.i.* hab: -, pnt: -⁷, stat: -·, prog: -, prp: -, dst: -, caus: -, rvs: -, dat: -, n-inc. nętkayę́hnahk ‹apart-prediction-hither-they-approach› *they will be approaching there* (RC 33:8).

–ne –. –ahθęhT –{dative I} faint. *v.s.-s.i.* wa⁷nwakahθę́hnę⁷θ ‹fact-apart-I-hid-for› *I fainted* (AG), nęwakahθę́hnę⁷θ ‹prediction-I-hide-for› *I will faint* (AG).

–ne –. –(a)hθę⁷n(e)r – fasten end-to-end, graft, join, lengthen, splice. *v.s.-a.i.* neyúhθę⁷r ‹apart-it-hung down› *it is spliced, it is grafted* (R), nehrahθę́⁷ner ‹apart-he-hangs down› *he grafts it, he joins it, he splices it, he lengthens it* (R), nęhrahθę́⁷re⁷ ‹apart-prediction-he-hang down› *he will fasten it end-to-end, he will splint it* (R).

–ne –. –(a)hθę⁷n(e)r – joint (of bones). *dv. n.s.* neyuhθę́⁷ner ‹apart-it-hangs down› *joint (of bones)* (SH 375).

–ne –. –ahsęt biped. *dv.n.s.* neyúhsę·t ‹two-it-foot- possesses› *biped* (HS).

–ne –. –ahsukę – be an ungulate. *v.s.-s.i.* neyuhsú·kę⁷ ‹two-it-foot-is forked› *it is ungulate* (HS).

–ne –. –(a)hwihshęhey – be fatigued, be tired. *v.s.-s.i.* nehruhwihshęhé·yę· ‹a-part-he-be strong-died› *he is tired, he is fatigued* (R).

–ne –. –(a)hwihshęheyahT – fatigue. *v.s.-t.* neyuhwihshęhè·yaht ‹apart-it-be strong-die-causes› *it is fatiguing* (HS).

–ne –. –arahsiθa⁷T – applaud. *v.s.-a.i.* nehrarahsiθá⁷tha⁷ ‹two-he-himself-foot-join-causes› *he applauds* (HS).

–ne –. –arahstahkw – stamp (feet). *v.s.-a.i.* nehrarahstáhkhwa⁷ ‹apart-he-himself-foot-collects› *he stamps (with his feet)* (HS).

–ne –. –areti – radiate. *v.r.-a.i.* hab: -ęhs, pnt: -, stat: -, prog: -, prp: -, dst: -, caus: -a⁷T-, rvs: -, dat: -, n-inc. newaré·tyęhs *it radiates* (HS); –ne –. –aretya⁷T –: nehraretyá⁷tha⁷ ‹apart-he-radiate-causes› *he disperses it, he scatters it, he strews it* (HS), wa⁷tkaré·tya⁷t ‹fact-apart-I-radiate-caused› *I spread* (AG), newakaretyá⁷nę ‹apart-I-radiate-caused› *I have spread it long ago, or I had spread* (AG); –ne –.

-athnyaretyaʔT -: waʔthrathnyaré·tyaʔt ⟨fact-apart-he-himself-news-radiate-caused⟩ *he reported news* (RC 24:4); -ne -. -aʔrihwaretyaʔT -: waʔthraʔrihwaré·tyaʔt ⟨fact-apart-he-himself-matter-radiate-caused⟩ *he spread the news* (RC 12:15).

-ne -. -aretyaʔT - disperse, scatter, spread, strew. *v.s.-t.* nehraretyáʔthaʔ ⟨apart-he-radiate-causes⟩ *he disperses it, he scatters it, he strews it* (HS), waʔtkaré·tyaʔt ⟨fact-apart-I-radiate-caused⟩ *I spread* (AG), newakaretyáʔnę ⟨apart-I-radiate-caused⟩ *I have spread it long ago, or I had spread* (AG).

-ne -. -aθkwaraw - open mouth. *v.s.-a.i.* nehráθkwaraws ⟨apart-he-lips-gives⟩ *he opens his mouth* (H-notebook).

-ne -. -aθkwaru'narhę - embroider. *v.s.-a.i.* nehraθkwaruʔnárhęh ⟨apart-he-lip-hooks-much⟩ *he embroiders* (HS).

-ne -. -aθnarčrakar - sob. *v.s.-a.i.* newaθnárčrakar ⟨apart-it-cry-'ness-makes a noise⟩ *it sobs* (HS).

-ne -. -asθr - foam over, swell up. *v.r.-a.i.* hab: -ęhs, pnt: -, stat: -ę, prog: -, prp: -, dst: -, caus: -, rvs: -, dat: -, n-inc. newásθręhs ⟨apart-it-swells up⟩ *it foams over, it swells (as of something boiling)* (HS).

-ne -. -athahahkw - walk. *v.s.-a.i.* nehruthaháhkę ⟨aoart-he-himself-path-picks up⟩ *he is walking* (L 13), nehruthahahkęhá·ʔnyeʔ ⟨apart-he-himself-path-picked up-going along⟩ *he is walking along* (L 13).

-ne -. -athahahkwaʔT - ground, baked, white corn. *dv.n.s.* neyuthahahkwáʔthaʔ ⟨apart-it-itself-path-pick up-causes⟩ *ground, baked, white corn (a provision traditionally taken along on a trip)* (R).

-ne -. -athahskwahnę - be slippery. *v.s.-s.i.* neyuthahskwáhnę ⟨apart-it-itself-slip-much⟩ *it is slippery* (HS).

-ne -. -atharuʔčinet - slide. *v.r.-a.i.* hab: -haʔ, pnt: -, stat: -, prog: -, prp: -, dst: -, caus: -, rvs: -, dat: -, n-inc. nehratharuʔčiné·thaʔ *he slides* (H-notebook).

-ne -. -athnę - play ball. *v.s.-a.i.* nehráthnę· *he plays ball* (RC 25:title), nehrathnęhsthaʔ *he plays ball* (RC 25:3), waʔthráthnęʔ *he played ball* (R).

-ne -. -athnyaretyaʔT - report news. *v.s.-a.i.* waʔthrathnyaré·tyaʔt ⟨fact-apart-he-himself-news-radiate-caused⟩ *he reported news* (RC 24:4).

-ne -. -athręhw - oppose. *v.s.-t.* nęhrathréhweʔ ⟨apart-prediction-he-himself-put up-cause⟩ *he will oppose it* (HS).

-ne -. -athręhw - crosswise, horizontal, traverse. *dv.n.s.* neyúthręw ⟨apart-it-itself-put up-causes⟩ *crosswise, horizontal, traverse* (HS).

-ne -. -athukstękuhT - translucent. *dv.n.s.* newathukstękúhthaʔ ⟨apart-it-itself-light up-'ness-passes through⟩ *translucent* (HS).

-ne -. -athwači ʔθ(e)r - sleigh. *dv.n.s.* newathwačíʔθ ręhs ⟨apart-it-itself-flatness-drags⟩ *sleigh* (H 3518).

-ne -. -athwaʔnaθehę - spiral. *dv.n.s.* neyęthwaʔnaθéhęh ⟨apart-one-oneself-X-encircles-much⟩ *spiral* (HS).

-ne -. -atkahčira̱ʔniha - wink. *v.s.-a.i.* nehratkahčiraʔníhahs ⟨apart-he-himself-blink-sprains⟩ *he winks* (HS).

-ne -. -atkahkʷek - close eyes. *v.s.-a.i.* nęwakatkahkwé·kęk ⟨two-prediction-I-myself-eye-closed⟩ *my eyes will be closed* (RC 3:20); neyutkahkwé·kę ⟨two-it-itself-eye-closed⟩ *its eyes are closed* (RC 7:12).

-ne -. -atkahraʔnihr - open eyes. *v.s.-a.i.* waʔnwatkahráʔnir ⟨fact-two-it-itself-eye-stood up⟩ *it opened its eyes* (RC 8:22).

-ne -. -atkahrehna̱rik - lightning. *v.s.-a.i.* newatkahréhnari·ks ⟨apart-it-itself-eye-??-bites⟩ *lightning* (HS—with secondary gloss "it naps its eye, shuts its eye quickly"), nęhratkahréhnari·k ⟨apart-prediction-he-himself-eye-??-bite⟩ *he will make lightning* (RC 35:39).

-ne -. -atkęhsurę - have a scar on face. *v.s.-s.i.* nehrutkęhsú·rę· ⟨apart-he-himself-face-split⟩ *he is scarred on his face* (H-notebook).

-ne -. -atkęni - fair, market. *dv.n.s.* neyętkę́·nyęhs ⟨apart-one-oneself-excels at⟩ *fair, market* (HS).

-ne -. -atkęni - compete for, emulate. *v.s.-t.* nehrutkę́·nyę ⟨apart-he-himself-excelled at⟩ *he emulates* (HS), nehratkę́·nyęhs ⟨apart-he-himself-excels at⟩ *he competes for it* (HS), waʔtkatkę̀·niʔ ⟨fact-apart-I-myself-excelled⟩ *I competed for it* (R).

-ne -. -atkęryaʔkhę - be brindled. *v.s.-s.i.* neyutkęryáʔkhęh ⟨apart-it-itself-cuts a crease around-much⟩ *it is brindled* (H-notebook).

-ne -. -atkęʔnetyęku - transform into. *v.s.-t.* waʔnwatkęʔnetyé·kuʔ ⟨fact-apart-it-itself-change-undid⟩ *it transformed into* (RC 15:1).

-ne -. -atkw - dance. *v.s.-a.i.* nehrátkhwaʔ ⟨apart-he-himself picks up⟩ *he dances* (R), wáʔthratkw ⟨fact-apart-he-himself-picked up⟩ *he danced* (R).

-ne -. -atkweʔnęti -.#úʔy make a move. *v.s.-a.i.* neyutkweʔnętihúʔy ⟨apart-it-itself-movement-makes-great⟩ *it makes a move* (RC 25:12).

-ne -. -atkeʔčahkw - hop, jump. *v.s.-a.i.* nehratkyeʔčáhkhwaʔ ⟨apart-he-himself-dough-picks up⟩ *he hops, he jumps* (HS).

-ne -. -atreʔrukęhsthę - be V-shaped. *v.s.-s.i.* neyutreʔrukę́hsthęʔ ⟨apart-it-pole-be forked-caused-much⟩ *it is V-shaped* (RC 6:11).

-ne -. -atʔniha - change, differ, vary. *v.s.-a.i.* newatʔníhahs ⟨two-it-itself-sprains⟩ *it changes, it varies* (HS), nęwatʔníhaʔ ⟨two-prediction-it-itself-sprains⟩ *it will change, it will vary* (HS), neyutʔníhę ⟨two-it-itself-sprained⟩ *dissimilar, the two of them differ* (HS).

-ne -. -aw - barter, reciprocate. *v.s.-a.i.* nehrá·ʔnaʔnaws ⟨apart-he=another-gives to⟩ *he barters, he reciprocates* (HS).

-ne -. -awęręh - diminish. *v.r.-a.i.* hab: -θ, pnt: -, stat: -, prog: -, prp: -, dst: -, caus: -T-, rvs: -, dat: II (-ati-/-ahθ-), inc.-ɸ-pat. Requires the dualic unless the dative is present. -kęhsawęręhT - {dative II}: ahrukęhsawęré̜hthahθ ⟨unknown-him-face-diminish-for⟩ *that he have bad luck* (RC 12:2); -ne -. -(a)ha=hawęręh -: neyuhahawę̀·ręhθ ⟨apart-it-path-diminishes⟩ *the road cramps it, is too narrow for it* (H 2484); -ne -. -(a)hahawęręhT -: newahahawęré̜hthaʔ ⟨apart-it-path-diminish-causes⟩ *it takes up a part of the road (said of an obstruction on a road, lit; it encroaches upon the road, it makes the road too small, is a free rendering of this)* (H 2484); -ne -. -hehnawęręhT -: nehrahehnawẹrẹ́htha⁷ ‹apart-he-field-diminish-causes› *he takes up unnecessarily needed space or ground, he is an unnecessary person* (H 2484); –ne–. –nẹhsawẹrẹhT –: nekanẹhsawẹrẹ́htha⁷ ‹apart-it-house-diminish-causes› *it takes up the room in the house uselessly, it is in the way in the house, it unnecessarily takes up room in the house* (H 2484).

–ne–. –a⁷čihskẹhka̲ra⁷nihr – pinch. *v.s.-t.* wa⁷tka⁷na⁷čihskẹhkará⁷nir ‹fact-apart-I-myself-self-fingernail-stood up› *I pinched myself* (AG), wa⁷nyakya⁷-čihskẹhkará⁷nir ‹fact-apart-the two of us-ourselves-fingernail-stood up› *we pinched each other* (AG), wa⁷tkheya⁷-čihskẹhkará⁷nir ‹fact-apart-I=another-self-fingernail-stood up› *I pinched him/her* (AG).

–ne–. –a'nahθẹ⁷raku – follow, succeed. *v.s.-t.* nehra⁷nahθẹ⁷rá·kwahs ‹apart-he-himself-hang down-undoes› *he succeeds another, he follows another* (HS).

–ne–. –a'nahθẹ⁷raku – luxate. *v.s.-a.i.* newa⁷nahθẹ⁷rá·kwahs ‹apart-it-itself-hang down-undoes› *it luxates* (HS).

–ne–. –a'naT – compare. *v.r.-t.* hab: -s, pnt: -, stat: -, prog: -, prp: -, dst: -, caus: -, rvs: -, dat: -, n-inc. nehrá·⁷na·č *he compares* (HS).

–ne–. –a'na⁷nihr – strive. *v.s.-a.i.* nehru⁷-na⁷níhrẹ ‹apart-he-himself-stood up› *he strives* (HS).

–ne–. –a'na⁷nihrhẹ – rival. *dv.n.s.* nehru⁷na⁷nírhẹh ‹apart-he-himself-stands up-much› *rival* (HS).

–ne–. –a'nekha̲ – be separate. *v.s.-s.i.* neyu⁷né·khẹ ‹apart-it-itself-divided› *separate: they are separate* (HS).

–ne–. –a'nekhahsi – schism. *dv.n.s.* ha⁷ neyu⁷nekháhsyẹ ‹the two-it-itself-divide-undid› *schism* (HS).

–ne–. –a'netyak – husband and wife. *dv.n.s.* newa⁷netyá·kẹ ‹two-it-themselves-were married› *husband and wife* (HS).

–ne–. –a'ne'nihẹthu – elastic. *dv.n.s.* newa⁷ne⁷nihẹ́·thuhs ‹apart-it-itself-pulls› *elastic* (AG).

–ne–. –a'nẹkuhT – survive. *v.s.-a.i.* nehra⁷-nẹkúhtha⁷ ‹apart-he-himself-go through-causes› *he survives* (HS).

–ne–. –a'nẹna·hyẹhsT – become friends with. *v.s.-t.* nehra⁷nẹná·hyẹhst ‹apart-he-himself-is a gang-for› *he becomes friends with* (RC 35:41), wa⁷čha⁷nẹná·hyẹhst ‹fact-apart-you-yourself-were a gang-for› *you became friends with someone* (RC 30:39).

–ne–. –a'nẹnẹheratẹ – be thankful. *v.s.-a.i.* neka⁷nẹnẹherá·tẹh ‹apart-I-myself-thank› *I am thankful* (AG).

–ne–. –a'nẹnẹheratẹnyẹ – give thanks. *v.s.-a.i.* wa⁷tkayẹ⁷nẹnẹheratẹ́·nyẹ⁷ ‹fact-apart-they-themselves-thanked-much› *they gave thanks* (RC 12:12).

–ne–. –a⁷nẹniharhu – interfere. *v.s.-a.i.* nehru⁷nẹnihárhẹ ‹apart-he-intermeddled› *he interferes* (HS).

–ne–. –a'nẹt – entertain. *v.s.-a.i.* wa⁷tkayẹ́·⁷nẹ·t ‹fact-apart-they-took along food› *they entertained* (RC 36:title).

-ne -. -a'nętahθęT - join together. *v.s.-a.i.* neyuʔnętahθę́·ʔnę ‹two-it-itself-braid-concluded› *it's joined together* (L 24), neyuʔnętahθę·t ‹two-it-itself-braid-con-cludes› *it's joined together* (L 24).

-ne -. -a'nętak - open. *v.s.-a.i.* newaʔnętá·kę ‹two-it-itself-opened›· *it opens (itself)* (HS), neyuʔnętá·kę ‹two-it-itself-opened› *it is open* (HS).

-ne -. -a'nęʔtikęhkęni - be dishonest, be a hypocrite. *v.s.-s.i.* nehruʔnęʔtikęhkę́·nyę ‹apart-he-himself-mind-excelled at› *he is dishonest, he is a hypocrite* (HS).

-ne -. -a'nęʔtikęhkęy - be a cheat. *v.s.-s.i.* nehruʔnęʔtikęhkę̀·yę ‹apart-he-himself-mind-is emptied› *he is a cheat* (HS).

-ne -. -a'nęʔtikęhrahręhw - anticipate. *v.s.-a.i.* nehruʔnęʔtikęhráhręw ‹apart-he-himself-mind-put up-causes› *he anticipates* (HS).

-ne -. -a'nihar - go beyond, go over, omit, skip, transgress. *v.r.-t.* hab: -ɸ, pnt: -, stat: -, prog: -, prp: -, dst: -, caus: -, rvs: -, dat: -, n-inc. nehraʔníhar *he discriminates (makes unequal), he goes over it, he omits it, he skips it, he transgresses* (HS); *he goes over or beyond it* (H-notebook).

-ne -. -a'nihθkawęhsT - commixture. *dv.n.s.* haʔ neyuʔnihθkawę́hsnę ‹the two-it-commixed› *commixture* (HS).

-ne -. -a'nihyaʔkT - step, take steps. *v.s.-a.i.* waʔnwaʔníhyaʔkt ‹fact-apart-it-itself-cross over-caused› *it took steps* (RC 9:4), waʔtkaʔníhyaʔkt ‹fact-apart-I-myself-cross-over-caused› *I stepped somewhere else* (RC 31:8).

-ne -. -a'nuk"ahT - disarrange, scatter. *v.s.-t.* nehraʔnukwáhthaʔ ‹apart-he-himself-be spread out-causes› *he disarranges it, he scatters it* (HS).

-ne -. -a'nuk"ahnahnę - splatter. *v.s.-a.i.* newaʔnukwahnáhnęh ‹apart-it-itself-be spread out-causes-much› *it splatters* (RC 3:55).

-ne -. -a'nurę - be split. *v.s.-s.i.* neyuʔnú·rę· ‹apart-it-itself-split› *it is split* (HS).

-ne -. -a'nurę - crack, crevice. *dv.n.s.* neyuʔnú·rę· ‹apart-it-itself-split› *crack, crevice* (HS).

-ne -. -a'nuʔkT - be bent, be crooked, be curved. *v.s.-s.i.* neyuʔnúʔknę ‹apart-it-itself-ended› *it is bent, it is crooked, it is curved* (HS).

-ne -. -a'nuʔknęku - be crooked, be winding, be zigzag. *v.s.-s.i.* neyuʔnuʔknę́·kwę ‹apart-it-itself-end-undid› *it is crooked, it is winding, it is zigzag* (HS).

-ne -. -a'nwiryaʔk - pup. *v.s.-a.i.* newaʔnwì·ryaʔks ‹two-it-itself-offspring-breaks› *it pups* (HS).

-ne -. -a'nyaʔk - break in two. *v.s.-a.i.* nęwáʔnyaʔk ‹two-prediction-it-itself-break› *I will break it in two* (RC 24:8).

-ne -. -a'nyaʔkhę - break in two. *v.s.-a.i.* newaʔnyáʔkhę· ‹two-it-itself-broke-much› *it broke in two* (RC 30:42).

-ne -. -a'nyehrakθę - mixture. *dv.n.s.* neyuʔnyehrákθęʔ ‹two-it-itself-mixed in-much› *mixture* (HS).

-ne -. -a'nyehsakęʔneti - change appearance, metamorphose. *v.s.-a.i.* newaʔnyehsakęʔné·tyęhs ‹apart-it-itself-appearance-changes› *it metamorphoses* (HS), waʔthraʔnyehsakęʔné·tiʔ ‹fact-apart-he-himself-appearance-changed› *he changed his appearance* (RC 26:13).

-ne -. -a'nyenę - wrestle. *v.s.-a.i.* nehraʔnyè·nęhs ‹apart-he-himself-grabs› *he wrestles* (HS).

-ne -. -a'nyeręhnahkw - firstly. *dv.n.s.* nyuʔnyeręhnáhkę ‹apart-it-have an unexpected experience-caused-instrument› *firstly* (R).

-ne -. -a'nyerẹhnyẹ - be haunting. *v.s.-a.i.* newa?nyeréhnyẹ? ‹apart-it-have an unexpected experience-cause-went into› *it is haunting; spirit is going around, mysterious movements* (L 83), wa?nwakyeréhnyẹ? ‹fact-apart-I-have an unexpected experience-cause-went into› *it disturbs me* (RC 32:11).

-ne -. -a'nyerẹhnyẹ - be a prodigy, be deformed. *v.s.-s.i.* nehru?nyeréhnyẹ? ‹apart-he-have an unexpected experience-cause-went into› *he is a prodigy, he is deformed* (HS).

-ne -. -a'nyerẹhnyẹ -{dative I} foretell a bad experience. *v.s.-a.i.* wa?thru?nyeréhnyẹ?θ ‹apart-he-have a bad experience-cause-went into-for› *he foretold a bad experience* (RC 26:22).

-ne -. -a'nyerẹnyẹ - monster; monstrous. *dv.n.s.* neyu?nyeré·nyẹ· ‹apart-it-had an unexpected experience-much› *monster (it is deformed), monstrous* (HS).

-ne -. -a'nyerẹ'nye? - act. *v.s.-a.i.* nehra?nyeré·?nye? ‹apart-he-has an unexpected experience-going along› *he is acting* (R).

-ne -. -a?ra'nyehnẹ - be infamous. *v.s.-a.i.* nehru?ra?nyéhnẹ· ‹apart-he-himself-is in-going along-much› *he is infamous* (HS).

-ne -. -a?rẹhyayerẹ'nye - Aurora Borealis, Northern Lights. *dv.n.s.* newa?rẹhyayeré·?nye? ‹apart-it-itself-sky-has an unexpected experience-going along› *Aurora Borealis, Northern Lights* (R).

-ne -. -a?rihstuhrarak - printing. *dv.n.s.* neyu?rihstuhrará·kẹ ‹two-it-itself-met-

al-pressed› *printing* (HS).

-ne -. -a?rihukwa?T - announce. *v.s.-a.i.* nehra?rihukwáhtha? ‹apart-he-himself-matter-be spread out-causes› *he announces* (HS).

-ne -. -a?rihukwa?T - proclamation. *dv.n.s.* neyu?rihukwá?tha? ‹apart-it-itself-matter-spread out-causes› *proclamation* (HS).

-ne -. -a?rihuk"ahT - announcement, declaration. *dv.n.s.* ha? nehru?rihukwáhnẹ· ‹the apart-he-himself-matter-be spread out-caused› *his announcement of* (HS), ha? neyu?rihukwáhnẹ· ‹the apart-it-itself-matter-be spread out-causes› *declaration* (HS).

-ne -. -a?rihwahkw - sing. *v.s.-a.i.* wa?thra?ríhwahkw ‹fact-apart-he-himself-matter-picked up› *he sang* (R).

-ne -. -a?rihwahkw -{dative I} sing about. *v.s.-t.* wa?nyẹ?na?rihwáhkẹ?θ ‹fact-apart-one=another-matter-picked up-for› *one sang about another* (R).

-ne -. -a?rihwahkwahT - hymnal, song book. *dv.n.s.* neyẹ?rihwahkwáhtha? ‹apart-one-oneself-matter-pick up-causes› *hymnal, song book* (HS).

-ne -. -a?rihwaretya?T - spread the news. *v.s.-a.i.* wa?thra?rihwaré·tya?t ‹fact-apart-he-himself-matter-radiate-caused› *he spread the news* (RC 12:15).

-ne -. -a?rihwiθ - alliance. *dv.n.s.* nehru?rihwí·θẹ ‹two-he-himself-matter-joined› *his alliance* (HS).

-ne -. -a?rihwaya?θraku - retort. *v.s.-a.i.* nehra?rihwaya?θrá·kwahs ‹two-he-himself-matter-fold-undoes› *he retorts*

(HS).

–ne –. –aˀθku – carry away. *v.r.-t.* hab: - ahs, pnt: -ˀ, stat: -, prog: -, prp: -, dst: -, caus: -ahT-, rvs: -, dat: -, inc.-ˀˀ- pat. Requires the dualic unless the causative is present; encountered only with an incorporated noun present. **–ęʰhraˀθkʷahT –:** yakęhraˀθkwáhtha[?] ‹one-dirt-carry away-causes› *rubbish-cart* (HS); **–ne –. –kerhaˀθku –:** neka-kyerháˀθkwahs ‹apart-it-body-carries away› *it brings bodies* (RC 32:14); **–ne –. –nęhaˀθku –:** nehranęháˀθkwahs ‹apart-he-corn-carries away› *he is drawing, carrying corn (from one place to another)* (H 2484); **–ne –. –ręˀaˀθku –:** waˀtkaręˀáˀθkuˀ ‹fact-apart-it-tree-carried away› *it carried away tree* (RC 30:26); **–ne –. –wętaˀ = θku –:** nekawętáˀθkwahs ‹apart-it-word-carries away› *it carries away language* (RC 4:3).

–ne –. –aˀtęhękari – suffer. *v.s.-t.* newakaˀ-tęhęká·ryę ‹apart-I-myself-suffered› *I suffer* (AG).

–ne –. –aˀtęhękaryaˀT –{dative II} commit cruelty. *v.s.-t.* waˀtkayęˀnaˀnaˀtęhę-karyáˀthahθ ‹fact-apart-they=another-themselves-suffer-caused-for› *they committed cruelty* (AG), nekheyęˀtę-hękaryaˀná·tih ‹apart-I=another-my-self-suffer-cause-for› *I am committing cruel acts* (AG).

–ne –. –aˀwnakwarihę[?] – earthquake. *dv.n.s.* waˀnyuˀwnakwaríhęˀ ‹fact-apart-it-earth-hasten-began› *earthquake* (RC 28:6).

–ne –. –aˀwnihyaˀkθę – traverse. *v.s.-a.i.* nehruˀwnihyáˀkθę· ‹apart-he-earth-cross over-much› *he traverses* (HS).

–ne –. –čha'nayę(T) – be foggy. *v.s.-s.i.* ne-yučhá·ˀnayęˀ ‹apart-it-fog-lays› *it is foggy, it is misty* (R).

–ne –. –čhaˀnuhT – exhale, sweat. *v.s.-a.i.*

nekačhaˀnúhtha[?] ‹apart-it-be difficult-causes› *it exhales, it sweats* (H-note-book).

–ne –. –čhaˀrhu – be sullen. *v.s.-s.i.* neh-ručháˀrhu[?] ‹apart-he-anger-caused› *he is sullen* (HS).

–ne –. –čisnahkwa'nę – falling star. *n.s.* ne-kačisnahkwáˀnęˀ ‹apart-it-spark-in-strument-fly› *falling star* (PC).

–ne –. –ekahkwaˀnahT – eddy. *v.s.-a.i.* ne-wekáhkwaˀnahč ‹apart-it-liquid-wrap up-causes› *it eddies* (HS).

–ne –. –ekanę – casement of a window. *dv. n.s.* newé·kanęh ‹apart-it-liquid-guards› *casement of a window* (R).

–ne –. –ęheyęhsturę – cadaverous. *dv.n.s.* neyawęheyęhstú·rę· ‹two-it-die-'ness-split› *cadaverous* (HS).

–ne –. –ęhra'netyę – cultivate, farm. *v.s.-a.i.* nehręhraˀné·tyęhs ‹apart-he-dirt-is present-much› *he cultivates, he farms* (HS).

–ne –. –ęhrurę – plow. *v.s.-a.i.* nehręhrù·-ręhs ‹apart-he-dirt-splits› *he plows* (HS).

–ne –. –ęhrurę – –tuhn – plowshare. *dv.n.s.* neyakęhruréhstha[?] utúhneh ‹apart-one-dirt-splits paddle› *plowshare* (HS).

–ne –. –ęhthyaˀk – go across country. *v.s.-a.i.* nehréhthyaˀks ‹apart-he-field-cros-ses over› *he crosses a country* (HS).

–ne –. –ęhuri – porridge. *dv.n.s.* newęhú·-ryeh ‹apart-it-fine grain meal-stirs› *porridge* (HS).

–ne –. –ęhyaˀnahčręti – drive crazy. *v.r.-t.* hab: -h, pnt: -, stat: -·, prog: -, prp: -, dst: -, caus: -, rvs: -, dat: -, n-inc. This root is clearly a stem in origin, composed of the verb **–ęˀti –** *make* with an incorporated noun **–ęhyaˀnahčr –**, it-self a noun stem composed of the nominalizer **–hčr –** plus a root **–ęhyaˀn –** which, however, is of unknown mean-ing since it does not occur independently. For this reason, the construction must be considered a root rather than a stem. nehręhya'nahčrę·tih *he drives another crazy* (HS).

-ne -. -ękhwyurę - fabulous. *dv.n.s.* neyawękhwyú·rę· ‹apart-it-tell a fable-split› *fabulous* (HS).

-ne -. -ę°kuh - diarrhea. *dv.n.s.* newę·kuhθ ‹apart-it-goes through› *diarrhea* (RC 22:1).

-ne -. -ę°kuhT - laxative, purgative. *dv.n.s.* neyawękúhnę ‹apart-it-go through-caused› *laxative* (RC 18:4), *purgative* (HS).

-ne -. -ę°kuhT - pervade, pierce, purge. *v.s.-t.* neyawękúhnę ‹apart-it-go through-caused› *it purges* (HS), newękúhtha' ‹apart-it-go through-causes› *it pierces it, it pervades it* (HS).

-ne -. -(ę)nęhrya'k - -ahwaryakę - Canada violet (HS). *n.s.* newęnęhrya'ks uhwaryá·kę' ‹two-it-scalp-breaks white› *Canada violet (Viola* sp.*)* (HS).

-ne -. -ęnękT - bow. *v.r.-a.i.* hab: -ęhs, pnt: -, stat: -, prog: -, prp: -, dst: -, caus: -, rvs: -, dat: -, n-inc. nehrę-nę́·knęhs *he bows* (HS).

(-ne -.) -ęnu'kęhw - grin. *v.r.-a.i.* hab: -s, pnt: -, stat: -, prog: -, prp: -, dst: -, caus: -, rvs: -, dat: -, n-inc. ręnú'-kęws *he grins* (H-notebook); nehrę-nú'kęws *he grins* (HS).

-ne -. -ętahkruT - float to the top. *v.r.-a.i.* hab: -s, pnt: -, stat: -, prog: -, prp: -, dst: -, caus: -, rvs: -, dat: -, n-inc. newętáhkruč ‹apart-it-floats to the top› *it floats to the top* (RC 8:26).

-ne -. -ętahkera'T - emblem. *dv.n.s.* neyawętahkyerá'nę ‹apart-it-betokened› *emblem* (HS).

-ne -. -(ę)ta'rya'k - violet. *dv.n.s.* newętá'rya'ks ‹apart-it-head-breaks› *violet (Viola* sp.*)* (H-notebook).

-ne -. -ętkʷ - pulsate, pulse. *v.r.-a.i.* hab: -ha', pnt: -, stat: -, prog: -, prp: -, dst: -, caus: -, rvs: -, dat: -, n-inc. newę́·-tkhwa' *it pulsates, it pulses* (HS).

-ne -. -(ę)tu'ča'k - break tooth. *v.s.-a.i.* nehrętú'ča'ks ‹apart-he-tooth-breaks› *he breaks his tooth* (HS).

-ne -. -ę°'rahrihnahkw - nutcracker. *dv.n.s.* neyakę'rahrihnáhkhwa' ‹apart-one-nut-spill-causes-instrument› *nutcracker* (HS).

-ne -. -(ę)'tahsęt be two-tongued. *v.s.-s.i.* nehrę'táhsę·t ‹two-he-tongue-possesses› *he is two-tongued* (HS).

-ne -. -(ę)'tikęhkarę'r - bother. *v.s.-t.* nę-θa'tikęhkarę́'rę' ‹apart-prediction-you-mind-be sloped› *you will be bothered by* (HS).

-ne -. -(ę)'tikęhkęni - cheat, outwit. *v.s.-a.i.* nehru'tikęh-kę́·nyę ‹apart-he-mind-excelled› *he is a cheat, he is corrupt, he is a hypocrite, he is dishonest, he is mistaken* (HS), nehra'tikęhkę́·nyęhs ‹apart-he-mind-excels› *he cheats, he outwits* (HS).

-ne -. -(ę)'tikęhke - be dubious, be uncertain, waver. *v.s.-a.i.* nehru'tikę́hkye· ‹two-he-mind-is in number› *he is dubious, wavers* (HS), neyu'tikę́hkye· ‹two-it-mind-is in number› *uncertain* (HS).

Tuscarora Pronunciation Key:
/a/ law; /e/ hat; /i/ pizza; /u/ tune; /ę/ hint; /č/ cheese; /h/ hoe; /m/ mother; /s/ same; /t/ do (before a vowel y, or w), too (elsewhere); /k/ gale (before a vowel y or w), kale (elsewhere); /n/ inhale (before a consonant or word-final), note (elsewhere), /r/ hiss (before a consonant or word-final), run (trilled as in Italian, elsewhere); /w/ cuff (before a consonant other than y or word-final), way (elsewhere); /y/ fish (before a consonant or word-final), you (elsewhere), /θ/ thing; /'/ (the sound between the vowels in unh-unh); /·/ long vowel, /´/ high pitch; /`/ low pitch.

-**ne**-.-(ę)ʔ**tikęhrayenę**-comfort. *v.s.-t.* neyęʔnęʔtikęhrayé·nę· ‹apart-one=another-mind-grasps› *one comforts another* (RC 29:1).

-**ne**-.-**hahskw**- slip. *v.r.-a.i.* hab: -ahs, pnt: -, stat: -, prog: -, prp: -, dst: -ahnę-, caus: -, rvs: -, dat: -, n-inc. nehruháhskwahs *he slips* (HS); -**ne**-.-**athahskwahnę**-: neyuthahskwáhnęʔ ‹apart-it-itself-slip-much› *it is slippery* (HS).

-**ne**-.-**hčiyu**- be wide. *v.s.-s.i.* neyuhčí·yu· ‹apart-it-width of flexible material-is great› *it is wide* (HS).

-**ne**-.-**hehnawęręhT**- take up space, be unnecessary. *v.s.-a.i.* nehrahehnawęréhthaʔ ‹apart-he-field-diminish-causes› *he takes up unnecessarily needed space or ground, he is an unnecessary person* (H 2484).

-**ne**-.-**herukę**- Fort Neoheroka. *dv.n.s.* Neyuherú·kęʔ ‹apart-it-green-is forked› *a fortified Tuscarora town in colonial North Carolina, "Broken-pasture"* (AG) [Colonial Records «Fort Neoheroka», «Fort Noo-he-roo-ka»].

-**ne**-.-**herukę**- **kì·nęʔ** Neuse River. *dv.n.s.* Neyuherú·kęʔ Kì·nęʔ ‹apart-it-green-is forked creek› *Neuse River* (AG).

-**ne**-.-**hęhnak"ek**- be deaf. *v.s.-a.i.* nehrahęhnakwé·kę ‹two-he-ear-closed› *he is deaf* (HS), nęyehęhnakwé·kęk ‹two-prediction-one-ear-close› *one will be deaf* (RC 17:3).

-**ne**-.-**hęwahθhę**- Twenty-Canoes (Chief of the Beaver Clan). *dv.n.s.* Nekahęwáhθhę· ‹two-it-boat-is ten› *Twenty-Canoes (Chief of the Beaver Clan)* (H-Handbook).

-**ne**-.-**hęwayę'nahkw**- concave. *dv.n.s.* neyuhęwayęʔnáhkę ‹apart-it-boat-lay-instrument› *concave* (HS).

-**ne**-.-**hkętihsT**- be ambient, be visible, surround. *v.r.-s.i.* stat: -ę, prog: -, prp: -, dst: -ę·-, caus: -, rvs: -, dat: -, n-inc. neyuhkętíhsnę *it can be seen* (RC 13: 8), *it is ambient, it surrounds* (HS).

-**ne**-.-**hkw**- lift, pick up, raise. *v.r.-t.* hab: -haʔ, pnt: -ɸ, stat: -ę, prog: -, prp: -hte-, dst: -ahnę-, caus: -aʔT-, rvs: -, dat: -, inc.-ɸ-ag. nehráhkhwaʔ *he raises, lifts it* (HS), *he <u>does</u> pick it up* (L 43), wáʔthrahkw *he picked it up* (L 18), wáʔnyehkw *they two picked it up* (RC 6:15), nekęhkwę *I lift you up* (RC 26:18); -**ne**-.-**hkwaʔT**-: nehrahkwáʔthaʔ ‹apart-he-pick up-causes› *he makes it higher, lifts it* (HS), waʔthráhkwaʔt ‹fact-apart-he-pick up-caused› *he picked <u>it</u> up* (L 43), načíhkwaʔt ‹apart-you-pick up-cause› *pick it up!* (L 18); -**ne**-.-**ahθhahkw**-: waʔthráhθhahkw ‹fact-apart-he-handful-picked up› *he picked up handful* (RC 14:3); -**ne**-.-**čiʔrahkw**-.#úʔy: waʔtkačiʔrahkwʔúʔy ‹fact-apart-it-spark-picked up-great› *a big flash of light appeared* (RC 9:9); -**ne**-.-(ę)**tih**=**seʔyahkwahnę**-: newętihseʔyahkwáhnę· ‹apart-it-maggot-picked up-many› *maggots dance around* (RC 26:33); -**ne**-.-**kerhahkw**-: nehrakyerháhkhwaʔ ‹apart-he-body-picks up› *adulterer* (HS); -**tehwahkwaʔT**-: yutehwáhkwaʔt ‹it-hide-pick up-caused› *startling* (HS); -**tehwahkw**-: naʔtehwáhkhwaʔ ‹one=another-hide-picks up› *one affrights another, one scares another* (HS); -**tehwahkwaʔT**-: yutehwáhkwaʔt ‹it-hide-pick up-caused› *startling* (HS); -**ne**-.-**uhstahkw**-: nęwúhstahkw ‹apart-prediction-it-year-pick up› *spring (time)* (R); -**atkwahčr**-: utkwáhčreh ‹self-pick up-'ness› *dance* (HS); -**ne**-.-**atkw**-: nehrátkhwaʔ ‹apart-he-himself picks up› *he dances* (R), wáʔthratkw ‹fact-apart-he-himself-picked up› *he danced* (R), wáʔnyetkw ‹fact-two-one-

oneself-picked up› *the two off them danced* (R); -yah+ne -. -a'nehkw -: wewa'néhkwę ‹thither-it-itself-picked up› *it comes to an end there* (RC 25:2); -ne -. -atke'čahkwahte -.#ú'y: newatkye'čahkwahte'ú'y ‹apart-it-itself-burden-pick up-is going to-much› *big thing is going jumping up and down* (RC 28:5); -ne -. -athahahkw -: nehruthaháhkę ‹he-himself-path- picks up› *he is walking* (L 13), nehruthahahkęhá·'nye' ‹he-himself-path-picked up-going along› *he is walking along* (L 13); -ne -. -athahahkwa'T -: neyuthahahkwá'tha' ‹apart-it-itself-path-pick up-causes› *ground, baked, white corn (a provision traditionally taken along on a trip)* (R); -ne -. -a'rihwahkw -: wa'thra'ríhwahkw ‹fact-apart-he-himself-matter-picked up› *he sang* (R); -ne -. -a'rihwahkw -{dative I}: wa'-nyę'na'rihwáhkę'θ ‹fact-apart-one=another-matter-picked up-for› *one sang about another* (R); -ne -. -a'rih= wahkwahT -: neyę'rihwahkwáhtha' ‹apart-one-oneself-matter-pick up-causes› *hymnal, song book* (R); tha+ne -. -atke'čahkw -: thwa'nwatkyé'čahkw ‹unusual-fact-apart-it-itself-dough-picked up› *it jumped together* (RC 9: 4).

-ne -. -hkwa'T - lift, make higher, pick up. *v.s.-t.* nehrahkwá'tha' ‹apart-he-pick up-causes› *he makes it higher, lifts it* (HS), wa'thráhkwa't ‹fact-a-part-he-pick up-caused› *he picked it up* (L 43), načíhkwa't ‹apart-you-pick up-cause› *pick it up!* (L 18).

-ne -. -hnyakarati - tattle. *v.s.-a.i.* nehrahnyakará·tih ‹apart-he-news-rubs› *he tattles* (HS), nehruhnyakará·tye' ‹apart-he-news-rubbed› *he tattled* (HS).

-ne -. -hnyęhawihT - sycophant. *dv.n.s.* nehrahnyęhawíhtha' ‹apart-he-news-bring-causes› *sycophant* (HS).

-ne -. -hra - the two male's (third person dual masculine inalienable). *n.r.pfx.* With roots and stems that begin with the vowel *i* the final *a* of the prefix coalesces with the initial *i* to yield -ne -. -hrę -. Before other intial vowels of roots and stems, the final a of the prefix is dropped.

-ne -. -hra - the two of them (males) (third person dual masculine agent). *v.r.pfx.* With roots and stems that begin with the vowel *i* the final *a* of the prefix coalesces with the initial *i* to yield -ne -. -hrę -. Before other initial vowels of roots and stems, the final a of the prefix is dropped.

-ne -. -hraw -/-ne -. -hru - the two male's (third person dual masculine alienable). *n.r.pfx.* The form -ne -. -hraw - occurs before roots and stems that begin with a vowel other than the vowel *a*. The form -ne -. -hru - occurs elsewhere.

-ne -. -hraw -/-ne -. -hru - the two of them (males) (third person dual masculine patient). *n.r.pfx.* The form -ne -. -hraw - occurs before roots and stems that begin with a vowel other than the vowel *a*. The form -ne -. -hru - occurs elsewhere.

−**ne** −. −**hθrarʔe(k)** – clap. *v.s.-a.i.* nehrahθrárʔehs ‹two-he-palm of hand-strikes› *he claps his hands* (HS).

−**ne** −. −**hsęwireT** – abase, abuse by word, belittle, reproach, slander. *v.s.-t.* nehruhsęwiré·ʔnę ‹apart-he-degraded› *he is abused by word* (HS), nehrahsęwiré·thaʔ ‹apart-he-degrades› *he abases, he belittles, he reproaches it, he slanders it* (HS).

−**ne** −. −**hshe(y)** – the two of you…him, her; you alone…the two of them (second person dual agent=third person singular patient, second person singular agent=third person dual patient). *n. r.pfx.* The form −**ne** −. −**hshey** – occurs before roots and stems that begin with a vowel. The form −**ne** −. −**hshe** – occurs before roots and stems that begin with a consonant.

−**ne** −. −**hsiharʔ** – swarm. *v.r.-a.i.* hab: -, pnt: -, stat: -ę, prog: -, prp: -, dst: -, caus: -, rvs: -, dat: -, inc.-ɸ-ag. neyuʔteyahsihárʔę *crowd swarms* (RC 26:10).

−**ne** −. −**hsiθ** – attach, put together, join. *v. s.-t.* nehrahsí·θahs ‹apart-he-X-meets› *he joins two things* (HS), nęhráhsi·θ ‹apart-prediction-he-X-meet› *he will join two things* (HS).

−**ne** −. −**hsiθhę** – attach, put together. *v.s.-t.* waʔthrahsí·θhęʔ ‹fact-apart-he-X-metmuch› *he attached it, he put it together* (R).

−**ne** −. −**hskanekęT** – be odd, be peculiar, be queer, be strange. *v.r.-s.i.* stat: -ɸ, prog: -, prp: -, dst: -hę-, caus: -hT-, rvs: -, dat: -, inc.-ɸ-pat. neyuhskané·kę·t *it is peculiar* (AW 50), *it is queer* (AW 45), *it is strange* (R); −**ne** −. −**nęθahskanekęT** –: neyunęθahskané·kę·t ‹apart-it-potato-is odd› *it is a curious, strange potato* (H 2484);

−**ne** −. −**rihwahskanekęT** –: neyurihwahskané·kę·t ‹apart-it-matter-is odd› *curiosity* (HS); −**ne** −. −**wętahskanekęT** –: (ne)yuwętahskané·kę·t ‹apart-it-word-is odd› *ambiguous* (HS); −**ne** −. −**ačkane**=**kęT** –: nehračkanekę́·thaʔ ‹apart-hehimself-is odd› *he juggles* (HS); **tha+ne** −. −**hskanekęT** –: thaʔneyuhskané·kę·t ‹unusual-apart-it-is odd› *it surprises* (RC 27:7).

−**ne** −. −**hskaʔyakʷahT** – yawn. *v.s.-a.i.* newakskaʔyakwáhthaʔ ‹apart-I-jowls-cut off› *I am yawning* (R).

−**ne** −. −**hskęnęʔnayę(T)** – arbitrate. *v.s.-a.i.* nehrahskęnę́ʔnayęhs ‹apart-he-be at peace-lays› *he arbitrates* (HS).

−**ne** −. −**hsneyę** – be lean. *v.s.-a.i.* nęθahsnè·yęʔ ‹apart-prediction-you-be lean› *you will be lean* (RC 25:11).

−**ne** −. −**hswaʔteˈnahkw** – duplicate. *dv.n.s.* nekahswaʔteʔnáhkwę ‹apart-it-backwas in a line-instrument› *duplicate, what is copied* (HS).

−**ne** −. −**hswaʔteʔnarhy** – multiply. *v.s.-a.i.* nehrahswaʔteʔnárhyę ‹apart-he-backwas in a line-??› *he multiplies* (Hnotebook).

−**ne** −. −**htawakwaʔnahT** – eddy, whirlpool. *dv.n.s.* nekahtawakwáʔnahč ‹apart-itstream of water-arc-causes› *it is eddying; eddy, whirlpool* (AG).

−**ne** −. −**hukaʔT** – {dative II} light up for, start to shine for. *v.s.-t.* neyuhukaʔná·ti· ‹apart-it-light up-caused-for› *it lit up* (RC 3:38), waʔnyuhukáʔthahθ ‹fact-apart-it-light up-caused-for› *it started to shine* (RC 3:75).

−**ne** −. −**hwahrihT** – break. *v.s.-t.* neθhwáhriht ‹apart-you!-X-spill-cause› *break it!* (R), waʔnyehwáhriht ‹fact-apartone-X-spill-caused› *one broke it* (RC 15:8), nekhwahríhtha ʔ ‹apart-I-X-spillcause› *I break things* (L 27).

−**ne** −. −**hwahriʔ** – become broken. *v.s.-a.i.*

neyuhwahrí'ʔę ⟨apart-it-X-spill-began⟩ *it is broken* (R).

—ne —. —hwanhatihsi — untwist, unwind. *v.s.-t.* nehrahwanhatíhsyęhs ⟨apart-he-wind-for-undoes⟩ *he untwists it, unwinds it* (HS).

—ne —. —hwar'e(k) — crush, crush together. *v.s.-t.* wa'thrahwár'ek ⟨fact-apart-he-??-struck⟩ *he crushed it, he crushes it together* (HS).

—ne —. —hwa'ri'ne — be fragile. *v.r.-s.i.* stat: -', prog: -, prp: -, dst: -, caus: -, rvs: -, dat: -, n-inc. neyuhwa'rí'ne' *it is fragile* (HS).

—ne —. —hwek — surround. *v.r.-t.* hab: -s, pnt. -, stat: -, prog: -, prp: -, dst: -, caus: -, rvs: -, dat: -, n-inc. nehráhweks *he surrounds* (HS).

—ne —. —hwek — be choking, have asthma. *v.r.-a.i.* hab: -s, pnt. -, stat: -, prog: -, prp: -, dst: -, caus: -, rvs: -, dat: -, n-inc. nehrúhweks *he has asthma, he is choking* (HS); —ne —. —hweksturę —: neyuhwekstù·rę' ⟨apart-it-have asthma-'ness-split⟩ *asthmatic* (HS).

—ne —. —hweksturę — asthmatic. *dv.n.s.* neyuhwekstù·rę' ⟨apart-it-have asthma-'ness-split⟩ *asthmatic* (HS).

—ne —. —hwę'kharurę — sawmill. *dv.n.s.* nekahwę'kharuréhshahk ⟨apart-it-board-splits⟩ *sawmill* (R).

—ne —. —hyatęhstayę'nahkw — playing cards. *dv.n.s.* neyehyatęhstayę'náhkwa' ⟨apart-one-paper-lays-instrument⟩ *playing cards* (HS).

—ne —. —i — pair. *dv.n.s.* né·kę· ⟨two-it-is a group⟩ *pair (neuter)* (HS), neyá·kę·

⟨they two-are a group⟩ *pair (human)* (HS).

—ne —. —(i)hkw — lift, pick up, raise. *v.s.-t.* nehráhkhwa' ⟨apart-he-picks up⟩ *he raises, lifts it* (HS), *he does pick it up* (L 43), wá'thrahkw ⟨fact-apart-he-picked up⟩ *he picked it up* (L 18), nekéhkwę ⟨apart-I=you-picked up⟩ *I lift you up* (RC 26:18).

—ne —. —(i)hkʷa'T — elevate, lift, pick up, raise, uphold. *v.s.-t.* nehrahkwá'tha' ⟨apart-he-pick up-causes⟩ *he makes it higher, he lifts it* (HS), nehrúhkwa'nę ⟨apart-he-picked up⟩ *he lifts it, he upholds it* (HS), wa'thráhkwa't *he picked it up* (L 18) ⟨fact-apart-he-picked up⟩, wa'čhíhkwa't ⟨fact-apart-you-picked up⟩ *you picked it up* (L 18), wa'tkíhkwa't ⟨fact-apart-I-picked up⟩ *I picked it up* (L 18), nękíhkwa't ⟨apart-prediction-I-pick up⟩ *I will pick it up* (L 18), načíhkwa't ⟨apart-you!-pick up-cause⟩ *pick it up!* (L 18).

—ne —. —ihnuhrarak — pinch. *v.s.-t.* nehręhnúhraraks ⟨two-he-skin-presses⟩ *he pinches* (HS).

—ne —. —(i)hskahręwahT — gape, yawn. *v.s.-a.i.* nehruhskahręwáhtha' ⟨apart-he-mouth-causes⟩ *he gapes, he yawns* (HS).

—ne —. —(i)hskahręwahT —. —hsk — yawner. *dv. n.s.* nehruhskahręwahthá'θkę· ⟨apart-he-mouth-causes-easily⟩ *yawner* (HS).

—ne —. —(i)hsnye — attend to. *v.r.-t.* hab: -, pnt: -', stat: -, prog: -, prp: -, dst: -, caus: -, rvs: -, dat: -, n-inc. wa'thráhsnye' *he attended to it* (RC 36:

---

2).

-ne -. -(i)htręhstę - bind, enchain. *v.s.-t.* nehrahtrę́hstęh ‹apart-he-tie-caused-much› *he binds it up, he enchains it* (HS), wa⁷nyehtrę́hsthę⁷ ‹fact-apart-one-tie-caused-much› *one bound it* (RC 17:1).

-ne -. -iθ - join together. *v.r.-t.* hab: -ahs, pnt: -ɸ, stat: -ę, prog: -, prp: -, dst: -ę·-, caus: -a⁷T-, rvs: -, dat: -, inc.-hs-pat. Requires the dualic unless the causative or dative are present. **-ne -. -hsiθ -:** nehrahsí·θahs ‹two-he-X-joins› *he joins two things together* (HS), nęhráhsi·θ ‹two-he-X-joins› *he will join two things together* (HS); **-ne -. -ačhiθ -:** nehruchí·θę ‹two-he-himself-X-joined› *he met* (HS), nehračhí·θahs ‹two-he-himself-X-joins› *he meets* (HS), wa⁷nyę́chi·θ ‹fact-two-one-oneself-X-joined› *one met* (RC 34:22); **-ne -. -(a)hahiθ -:** wa⁷nyeháhi·θ ‹fact-two-one-path-joined› *the two of them met* (MG 105:21); **-ne -. -anęhtriθ -:** wa⁷nyęnę́htri·θ ‹fact-two-one-top of head-joined› *the two of them butted heads* (RC 30:40); **-ne -. -a⁷rihwiθ -:** nehru⁷rihwí·θę ‹two-he-himself-matter-joined› *alliance* (HS); **-ne -. -(ę)ta = kariθ -:** newętakarí·θę ‹two-it-point-joined› *framed (e.g., house)* (H 2892); **-ne -. -atkęhsiθ -:** wa⁷thratkę́hsi·θ ‹fact-two-he-himself-face-joined› *he hit face* (AW 46); **-wętiθa⁷T -:** ruwętiθá⁷tha⁷ ‹he-word-join-caused› *he alludes to, he mentions, he refers to it* (HS); **-ne -. -arahsiθa⁷T -:** nehrarahsiθá⁷tha⁷ ‹two-he-himself-foot-join-causes› *he applauds* (HS); **-yah+ne -. -(a)hahiθ -:** ya⁷nęθwaháhi·θ ‹thither-two-prediction-you-path-join› *you will wait there* (RC 33:4); **ti+yah+ne -. -(a)hahiθ -:** tyahwa⁷nyeháhi·θ ‹so-thither-fact-two-one-path-join› *one met there* (RC 30:

40); **ti+yah+či -. -(a)hahiθę -:** tyahę́θah-ruhahí·θę⁷ ‹so-thither-again-fact-he-path-met-much› *he returned to his own path* (RC 31:3); **ha⁷ -ne -. -⁷tehiθa⁷T -:** ha⁷ neyu⁷tehiθá⁷nę ‹the apart-it-sand-join-caused› *hail* (HS).

-ne -. -(i)'nę - fly. *v.r.-a.i.* hab: -, pnt: -⁷, stat: -, prog: -, prp: -, dst: -, caus: -. rvs: -, dat: -, n-inc. *West.* wa⁷chí·⁷nę⁷ *you flew* (PC), wa⁷tkí·⁷nę⁷ *I flew* (PC).

-ne -. -ka - the two of them's (two females or a male and a female) (third person dual feminine/zoic inalienable). *n.r. pfx.* Occurs before roots and stems that begin with a consonant or the vowel *i*, with which vowel the final *a* of the prefix coalesces to yield **-ne -. -kę -.**

-ne -. -ka - the two of them (two females or a female and a male) (third person dual feminine/zoic agent). *v.r.pfx.* Occurs before roots and stems that begin with a consonant or the vowel *i*, with which vowel the final *a* of the prefix coalesces to yield **-ne -. -kę -.**

(-ne -.) -kahkʷek - be blind. *v.s.-a.i.* nehrakahkwé·kę ‹two-he-eye-closed› *he is blind* (R), rakahkwé·kę ‹he-eye-closed› *he is blind* (R).

-ne -. -kahkweθrathe - be dazzled. *v.r.-a.i.* hab: -, pnt: -, stat: -⁷, prog: -, prp: -, dst: -, caus: -, rvs: -, dat: -, n-inc. nehrukahkweθrá·the⁷ *it dazzles him, he is dazzled* (H-notebook).

-ne -. -kahrahręhw - crooked eyes. *dv.n.s.* nekakahráhręw ‹apart-it-eye-put up-causes› *crooked eyes* (RC 13:8).

-ne -. -kahθraruhθrę - shed tears. *v.s.-a.i.* nehrakahθrarúhθręh ‹apart-he-tear-?⁷› *he sheds tears* (HS).

-ne -. -karehrę - agitate. *v.s.-t.* nehraka-réhręh ‹apart-he-goes around-much› *he agitates it* (HS).

-ne -. -ka?nuhrarak - brakeman. *dv.n.s.*
nehraka?núhraraks ‹two-he-wheel-
presses› *brakeman* (HS).

-ne -. -kerhahkw - adulterer. *dv.n.s.* nehrakyerháhkhwa? ‹apart-he-body-picks
up› *adulterer* (HS).

-ne -. -ke?θrur - be grave. *v.s.-s.i.* nehrukyé?θru? ‹apart-he-frown-covered›
he is grave (H-notebook).

-ne -. -kęhu - have around mouth. *v.r.-t.*
hab: -, pnt: -, stat: -ę, prog: -, prp: -,
dst: -, caus: -, rvs: -, dat: -, n-inc.
nehrukę́hę *he has it all around his
mouth* (HS).

-ne -. -kęni - excel at, outdo. *v.r.-t.* hab:
-ęhs, pnt: -, stat: -ę, prog: -, prp: -,
dst: -, caus: -, rvs: -, dat: -, inc.-φ-pat.
Requires the dualic unless an incorporated noun is present. nehrakę́·nyęhs
he excels at it, he outdoes (HS); -ne -.
-atkęni -: neyętkę́·nyęhs ‹apart-one-
oneself-excels at› *fair, market* (HS),
nehrutkę́·nyę ‹apart-he-himself-excel-
led at› *he emulates* (HS); nehratkę́·-
nyęhs ‹apart-he-himself-excels at› *he
competes for it* (HS); -kahkęni -: ru-
kahkę́·nyę ‹he-eye-excelled at› *he has
discovered* (HS), rakahkę́·nyęhs ‹he-
eye-excels at› *he discovers* (HS), wah-
rakahkę̀·ni? ‹fact-he-eye-excelled at›
he discovered (RC 24:13); -atkę =
nihs?a -: kakutkęníhs'?ę ‹they-them-
selves-excel at-finished› *they counseled* (RC 12:8); eθwatkęníhs?a·? ‹un-
known-you-yourselves-excel at-finish›
that you hold council (RC 12:8); -a =
tkęnihs?a?T -: yętkęnihs?á?tha? ‹one-
oneself-excel at-finish-causes› *council
house* (R); -atkęnihs?a -.#ú?y: wa?ka-
yętkęnihs?a·?ú?y ‹fact-they-themselves-excel-finished-great› *they had a
great council* (RC 12:16); -a'nę?tikęh =
kęni -: yu?nę?tikęhkę́·nya·t ‹it-itself-
mind-excelled-complete› *it is illusory*
(HS); -(ę)?tikęhkęnyęhčr -: u?tikęhkę-
nyę́hčreh ‹mind-excel-'ness› *cheating*
(HS); -ne -. -(ę)?tikęhkęni -: nehru?ti-
kęhkę́·nyę ‹apart-he-mind-excelled at›
*he is a cheat, he is a hypocrite, he is
dishonest, he is mistaken, he outwits*
(HS), nehra?tikęhkę́·nyęhs ‹apart-he-
mind-excels› *he cheats, he outwits*
(HS); -ne -. -rihwa?tikęhkęni -: neyurihwa?tikęhkę́·nyę ‹apart-it-matter-
mind-excels› *subterfuge* (HS); -ne -.
-a'nę?tikęhkęni -: nehru?nę?tikęhkę́·-
nyę ‹apart-he-himself-mind-excelled
at› *he is dishonest, he is a hypocrite*
(HS).

-ne -. -kę?neti - change, exchange, modify,
replace, substitute. *v.r.-t.* hab: -ęhs,
pnt: -?, stat: -ę, prog: -, prp: -, dst: -,
caus: -a?T-, rvs: -ęku-, dat: III (-ati-/-
ę-), inc.-φ-pat. Usually requires the
dualic. For many speakers of modern
Tuscarora, this root is pronounced as
if it were -ne -. -ku?neti -. nehrukę?-
né·tyę *he substitutes* (HS), nehrakę?-
né·tyęhs *he exchanges it, he modifies
it, he replaces it* (HS); -či -. -rihwa =
kę?neti -: θhrarihwakę?né·tyęhs ‹again-
he-matter-changes› *he alters his resolution* (HS); -ne -. -wętakę?neti -: neh-
rawętakę?né·tyęhs ‹apart-he-word-

changes› *translator* (HS), wa›nyakti-
wętakę›né·ti› ‹fact-apart-we-word-
changed› *the two of us translated* (RC
i); **-ne -. -yehsakę›neti -**: rayehsakę›né·-
tyęhs ‹he-appearance-changes› *he disguises it* (HS); **-yah -. -takwnakę›neti -**:
wehratakwnakę›né·tyęhs ‹thither-he-
place-changes› *he transposes it* (HS);
-atkę›netya›T -: yutkę›netyá›nę ‹it-
itself-change-caused› *it is changeable,
it is mutable* (HS); **-ne -. -atkę›netyę =
ku -**: wa›nwatkę›netyę́·ku› ‹fact-apart-
it-itself-change-undid› *it transformed
into* (RC 15:1); **-ne -. -a'nyehsakę› =
neti -**: newa›nyehsakę›né·tyęhs ‹a-part-
it-itself-appearance-changes› *it metamorphoses* (HS), wa›thra›nyehsakę›-
né·ti› ‹fact-apart-he-himself-appearance-changed› *he changed his appearance* (RC 26:13); **kwęhs -ne -.
-wętakę›neti -**: kwęhs nakawętakę›-
né·tyęk ‹no apart-unknown-it-word-
change› *it is untranslated* (HS); **kwęhs
-ne -. -atkę›neti -**: kwęhs narętkę›né·ti›
‹no apart-unknown-it-itself-change› *it
is invariable* (HS); **kwęhs -ne -.
-atkę›neti -{dative III}**: kwęhs narętkę›netyę́hshek ‹no apart-unknown-it-
itself-change-for› *it is unalterable*
(HS); **kwęhs -ne -. -atkę›netya›T -**:
kwęhs naryutkę›netyá›nęk ‹no apart-
unknown-it-itself-change-cause› *it is
unalterable* (HS).

-ne -. -kę›θahnę - examine. *v.s.-t.* neθkę›-
θáhnę· ‹apart-you!-see-going to-much›
examine it! (AW 51), nehrakę›θáh-
nęh ‹apart-he-sees-going to-much› *he
examines it* (H-notebook).

-ne -. -kha - divide; be twins. *v.r.-t.* hab:
-hs, pnt: -, stat: -ę, prog: -, prp: -, dst:
-, caus: -, rvs: -hsi-, dat: -, inc.-ϕ-
ag./pat. neyé·khę *twins* (HS), nehrá·-
khę *he is a twin* (HS), nehrá·khahs *he
divides it* (HS); **-khahsyęku -**: rakhah-

syę́·kwahs ‹he-divide-undo-undoes› *he
apportions, he disunites, he parcels it
out* (HS), rukhahsyę́·kwę ‹he-divide-
undo-undid› *he apportioned* (HS);
-rihwakha -: yurihwá·khę ‹it-matter-divided› *discord* (HS); **-yerakha -**: raye-
rá·khę ‹he-flesh-divided› *he mingles*
(HS); **-ne -. -khahnę -**: nehrakháhnęh
‹two-he-divide-many› *he separates
several things* (HS); **-ne -. -khahsi -**:
nekakukháhsyę ‹two-they-divide-un-
done› *they were separated from* (R),
nehrakháhsyęhs ‹two-he-divide-un-
does› *he disunites* (HS); **-ne -. -(a)ha =
hakhahsi -**: nęyehahakháhsi› ‹two-pre-
diction-one-path-divide-undo› *the two
of them will go separate ways* (RC
35:39); **-ne -. -rihwakha -**: neyakurih-
wá·khahs ‹two-one-matter-divides› *the
two of them disagree* (HS); **-ne -.
-a'nekha -**: neyu›né·khę ‹two-it-itself-
divided› *separate: they are separate*
(HS); **-ne+či -. -kha›nyęku -**: neθhra-
kha›nyę́·kwahs ‹apart-again-he-divide-
throw-undoes› *he divides it* (HS); **ha›
-ne -. -a'nekhahsi -**: ha› neyu›nekháh-
syę ‹the two-it-itself-divide-undid›
schism (HS); **kwęhs -a'nekhahsi -**:
kwęhs narę›nekhahsyę́hshek ‹no two-
unknown-it-itself-divide-undo› *it is indivisible* (HS); **kwęhs -a'nekhah =
sya›T -**: kwęhs narę›nekhahsyá›nęk
‹notwo-unknown-it-itself-divide-undo-
cause› *it is inseparable* (HS).

-ne -. -khahnę - separate several. *v.s.-t.*
nehrakháhnęh ‹apart-he-divide-many›
he separates several things (HS).

-ne -. -khahsi - disunite, separate from. *v.
s.-t.* nekakukháhsyę ‹apart-they-divide-
undone› *they were separated from* (R),
nehrakháhsyęhs ‹apart-he-divide-un-
does› *he disunites* (HS).

-ne -. -khe(y) - the two of us...him, her;
I...the two of them (first person dual

agent=third person singular patient, first person singular agent=third person dual patient). *v.r.pfx.* The form -ne-.-khey- occurs before roots and stems that begin with a vowel. The form -ne-.-khe- occurs before roots and stems that begin with a consonant.

-ne-.-kwarihę?- quake. *v.s.-a.i.* neyukwaríhę?θ ‹apart-it-hasten-begins› *it quakes* (HS).

-ne-.-kwa?nęti- make round, round. *v. s.-t.* nehrakwa?nę́·tih ‹apart-he-arc-makes› *he rounds it* (HS), nehrukwa?nę́·tih ‹apart-he-arc-makes› *he is round* (HS).

-ne-.-ne?kęθnahnę- shake. *v.r.-t.* hab: -h, pnt: -?, stat: -, prog: -, prp: -, dst: -, caus: -, rvs: -, dat: -, n-inc. neθne?kęθnáhnę *shake it!* (R), nehrane?kęθnáhnęh *he shakes it* (HS); ę́·či -ne-.-ne?kęθnahnę-: ę́·či wa?tkane?kęθnáhnę? ‹one fact-apart-it-shakes› *a jolt* (HS).

-ne-.-nęhruhkwanyę- attest. *v.r.-a.i.* hab: -h, pnt: -·?, stat: -?, prog: -, prp: -, dst: -, caus: -, rvs: -, dat: -, n-inc. nehranęhruhkwá·nyęh *he attests* (HS), nehrunęhruhkwá·nyę? *he attested* (HS), nęhranęhruhkwá·nyę·? *he will attest* (HS); ha? -ne-.-nęhruhkwanyę-: ha? nehrunęhruhkwá·nyę? ‹the apart-he-attested› *his attestation, his swearing* (HS).

-ne-.-nęhruhkwanyę- attestation. *dv.n.s.* ha? nehrunęhruhkwá·nyę? ‹the apart-he-attested› *his attestation, his swear-ing* (HS).

-ne-.-nęhsya?khę- partition. *dv.n.s.* nekanęhsyá?khęh ‹two-it-house-breaks-much› *partition: the house is divided (into two rooms)* (H-notebook).

-ne-.-nęθnahkwahshayę- kestrel. *dv.n.s.* The meanings of the constituent roots are uncertain. nekanęθnahkwáhshayę? *kestrel* (HS).

-ne-.-nę?riye- entangle, perplex, tangle. *v.s.-t.* neyunę?rì·ye? ‹apart-it-net-??› *it is intricate, it is tangled* (HS), nehranę?rì·yehs ‹apart-he-net-??› *he is entangled, he is perplexed, he tangles it* (HS).

-ne-.-nę?riyehsi- disentangle. *v.s.-t.* nehranę?riyéhsyęhs ‹apart-he-net-??-undoes› *he disentangles it* (HS).

-ne-.-nę?yar- look at, regard, stare at, study. *v.r.-t.* hab: -φ, pnt: -?, stat: -?, prog: -, prp: -, dst: -, caus: -, rvs: -, dat: -, inc.-φ-pat. nehranę?yar *he regards it, he studies it* (RC 26:11), nehrunę?ya?r *he studied it* (RC 26: 28), nehsknę?yar *you are looking at me, you are staring at me* (R), naryęknę?yà·rahk *that one has studied me* (RC 24:2); -ne-.-nę?yar-.#ú?y: nehranę?yarhú?y ‹apart-he-looks at-great› *he stares* (HS); -nę?yaręhčra?niha-: runę?yaręhčra?níhahs ‹he-look at-'ness-sprains› *he pricks his conscience* (HS); -ne-.-wiranę?yar-: nakawiranę?ya?r ‹apart-fact-it-infant-looked at› *it studied infant* (RC 30:5).

-ne-.-nę?yar-.#ú?y stare at. *v.s.-t.* nehranę?yar?ú?y ‹apart-he-looks at-great›

Tuscarora Pronunciation Key:
/a/ l<u>a</u>w; /e/ h<u>a</u>t; /i/ p<u>i</u>zza; /u/ t<u>u</u>ne; /ę/ h<u>i</u>nt; /č/ <u>ch</u>eese; /h/ <u>h</u>oe; /m/ <u>m</u>other; /s/ <u>s</u>ame; /t/ <u>d</u>o (before a vowel y, or w), <u>t</u>oo (elsewhere); /k/ <u>g</u>ale (before a vowel y or w), <u>k</u>ale (elsewhere); /n/ i<u>nh</u>ale (before a consonant or word-final), <u>n</u>ote (elsewhere), /r/ hi<u>ss</u> (before a consonant or word-final), <u>r</u>un (trilled as in Italian, elsewhere); /w/ cu<u>ff</u> (before a consonant other than y or word-final), <u>w</u>ay (elsewhere); /y/ fi<u>sh</u> (before a consonant or word-final), <u>y</u>ou (elsewhere), /θ/ <u>th</u>ing; /?/ (the sound between the vowels in unh-unh); /·/ long vowel, /´/ high pitch; /`/ low pitch.

he stares (HS).

-ne -. -nhę'nara ⁷θrę – gasp for air, gasp for breath. *v.s.-a.i.* wa⁷thranhę⁷nará⁷θrę⁷ ‹fact-apart-he-have in mouth-was in-much› *he gasped for breath* (RC 3: 22).

-ne -. -niθku⁷ru'narihsi – unbutton. *v.s.-t.* newakniθku⁷ru⁷naríhsyę ‹apart-I-but-ton-hook-undo› *I have unbuttoned it* (R).

-ne -. -ra⁷nyeT – humiliate, insult, traduce. *v.r.-t.* hab: -ha⁷, pnt: -, stat: -, prog: -, prp: -, dst: -, caus: -, rvs: -, dat: -, n-inc. nehrara⁷nyé·tha⁷ *he traduces it* (HS), na⁷ra⁷nyé·tha⁷ *one humiliates another, one insults another* (HS).

-ne -. -ra⁷tekę – be joined in marriage; re-join. *v.s.-a.i.* nehrara⁷té·kęhs ‹two-he-X-joins› *he is joined in marriage: he rejoins* (HS).

-ne -. -ręharayę – hoar-frost. *dv.n.s.* The meanings of constituent roots are uncertain. neyuręharà·yę⁷ *hoar-frost* (HS).

-ne -. -ręhyayę(T) -.#áh watermelon. *dv.n. s.* neyuręhyayę⁷áh ‹apart-it-sky-lay-little› *watermelon (Citrullus vulgaris)* (R).

-ne -. -ręryuhkwitkę⁷ – be resplendent. *v. s.-s.i.* neyuręryuhkwitkę́⁷ę ‹apart-it-ray-come forth-began› *it is resplendent* (HS).

-ne -. -rę⁷aręhwahkw – joist. *dv.n.s.* neye-rę⁷aręhwáhkhwa⁷ ‹apart-one-tree-add-causes-instrument› *joist* (HS).

-ne -. -rę⁷kęni – cast a spell on, foresee the future of; be infatuated with. *v.r.-t.* hab: -ęhs, pnt: -⁷, stat: -ę, prog: -, prp: -, dst: -, caus: -, rvs: -, dat: -, n-inc. nehrurę⁷kę́·nyęhs *it casts a spell on him* (RC 31:2), nehrurę⁷kę́·nyę *he foresaw the future (he is clairvoyant)* (RC 6:1); *he cast a spell on someone* (RC 31:2), nęyerę⁷kę̀·ni⁷ *one will be*

infatuated (RC 17:4); neyurę⁷kę́·nyę *witch-medicine* (AG); **tha+ne -. -rę⁷ = kęni -:** tha⁷neyurę⁷kę́·nyę ‹unusual-apart-it-casts a spell on› *one is infatuated* (RC 17:5).

-ne -. -rę'na'ne – log house. *dv.n.s.* ne-karę́·⁷na⁷ne⁷ ‹apart-it-log-is present› *log house* (R).

-ne -. -rę⁷neti – be dizzy, be giddy. *v.r.-a.i.* hab: -ęhs, pnt: -, stat: -, prog: -, prp: -, dst: -, caus: -, rvs: -, dat: -, n-inc. nehrarę⁷né·tyęhs *he is dizzy, he is giddy* (HS).

-ne -. -rę'nya⁷kT – saw. *dv.n.s.* neyerę⁷-nyá⁷ktha⁷ ‹two-one-log-cut-causes› *saw* (R).

-ne -. -rhęhT – be somewhere all night, stay overnight. *v.s.-a.i.* nehrarhę́htha⁷ ‹apart-he-be day-causes› *he stays overnight* (HS), wa⁷tkayérhęht ‹fact-apart-they-be day-caused› *they were all night* (RC 12:13).

-ne -. -rhu – mix. *v.s.-t.* nehrárhuhs ‹two-he-mixes› *he mixes the two* (HS), nę-yérhu⁷ ‹two-prediction-one-mix› *one will mix it* (RC 17:4).

-ne -. -rhuhθę – season. *v.s.-t.* neyerhúhθęh ‹two-one-mixes-much› *one seasons it* (HS).

-ne -. -rhuhsT – season. *v.s.-t.* neyerhúh-stha⁷ ‹two-one-mix-causes› *one is seasoning it* (HS).

-ne -. -rhuhsT – seasoning. *dv.n.s.* neyer-húhstha⁷ ‹two-one-mix-causes› *seasoning* (HS).

-ne -. -rhuθhwahnęhkw – aromatics, cologne, perfume. *dv.n.s.* neyurhu-θhwahnę́hkhwa⁷ ‹two-it-mix-smell-much-instrument› *aromatics, cologne, perfume* (HS).

-ne -. -rihurę – be guilty. *v.s.-a.i.* nehru-rihù·ręh ‹apart-he-matter-splits› *he is guilty* (HS).

-ne -. -rihwahčar – promote. *v.s.-t.* nehrarihwáhčar ‹apart-he-matter-fist-is in› *he promotes it* (HS).

-ne -. -rihwahkwaʔT - psalms, tune. *dv.n.s.* neyerihwahkwáʔthaʔ ‹apart-one-matter-pick up-causes› *psalms, tune* (HS).

-ne -. -rihwahrihT - transgress. *v.s.-a.i.* nehrarihwahríhthaʔ ‹apart-he-matter-spill-causes› *he transgresses* (HS).

-ne -. -rihwahskanekęT - curiosity. *dv.n.s.* neyurihwahskané·kę·t ‹apart-it-matter-is odd› *curiosity* (HS).

-ne -. -rihwakenha - argue with, debate. *v. s.-t.* nęyerihwakyénhaʔ ‹apart-prediction-one-matter-strive› *the two of them will argue* (L 41), nehrarihwakyénhahs ‹apart-he-matter-strives› *he argues* (HS), nehrurihwakyénhę ‹apart-he-matter-strove› *he debates* (HS).

-ne -. -rihwakenha - advocate, lawyer. *dv. n.s.* nehrarihwakyénhahs ‹apart-he-matter-strives› *advocate, lawyer* (HS).

-ne -. -rihwakenha - discussion. *dv.n.s.* neyurihwakyénhę ‹apart-it-matter-strove› *discussion* (HS).

-ne -. -rihwakęti - banter. *v.s.-a.i.* This stem is clearly a compound of -rihw - *matter* with a verb root; however, the verb root has not otherwise been attested for the language. nehrarihwakę́·tih *he banters* (HS).

-ne -. -rihwakęʔθahnę - research. *v.s.-t.* nehrarihwakęʔθáhnęh ‹apart-he-matter-sees-going to-much› *he researches* (HS).

-ne -. -rihwakęʔθahnę -.#hči analyze, examine closely. *v.s.-t.* nehrarihwakęʔ-

θahnę́hči ‹apart-he-matter-sees-going to-much-very› *he examines the matter closely, he analyzes* (HS).

-ne -. -rihwayaʔθraku - answer. *v.s.-a.i.* nehrarihwayaʔθrá·kwahs ‹two-he-matter-fold-undoes› *he answers* (HS).

-ne -. -rihwayaʔθrakʷahT - answerable. *dv. n.s.* neyurihwayaʔθrá·kwaht ‹two-it-matter-fold-undo-caused› *answerable* (HS).

-ne -. -rihwayęT -{dative I} decide. *v.s.-a.i.* nehrurihwayęʔnáʔθe· ‹apart-he-matter-laid-for› *he decides* (HS).

-ne -. -rihwayę'nahT - be decisive. *v.s.-s.i.* neyurihwayę́·ʔnaht ‹apart-it-matter-lay-caused› *it is decisive* (HS).

-ne -. -rihwaʔtikęhkęni - subterfuge. *dv.n. s.* neyurihwaʔtikęhkę́·nyę ‹apart-it-matter-mind-excels› *subterfuge* (HS).

-ne -. -rihstuhrarak - print. *v.s.-t.* nehrarihstúhraraks ‹two-he-metal-presses› *he prints it (printer, publisher)* (HS).

-ne -. -rihstuhrarak - printing press. *dv.n.s.* nekarihstúhraraks ‹two-it-metal-presses› *printing press* (HS).

-ne -. -θa - the two of them...you alone (third person dual feminine/zoic agent=second person singular patient). *v.r.pfx.* With roots and stems that begin with the vowel *i* the final *a* of the prefix coalesces with the initial *i* to yield -ne -.-θę -. Before roots and stems beginning with other vowels, the final *a* of the prefix is dropped.

-ne -. -θčuhčha - gnash teeth. *v.r.-s.i.* stat: -ʔ, prog: -, prp: -, dst: -, caus: -, rvs: -, dat: -, n-inc. nehraθčúhčhaʔ *he*

---

gnashes his teeth (HS).

-ne –. -θręwya ʔk – break seal. *v.s.-a.i.* nehraθrę·wyaʔks ‹apart-he-wax-breaks› *he breaks the seal* (HS).

-ne –. -θuwa̱hriʔ – bittersweet. *dv.n.s.* nekaθuwahríʔę ‹two-it-animal's backspill-began› *bittersweet (Celastrus scandens)* (R)

-ne –. -tahθęT – annex, join. *v.s.-t.* nehratahθę́·thaʔ ‹two-he-braid-concludes› *he annexes it* (R), waʔthratahθę́·ʔnęʔ ‹fact-two-he-braid-concluded› *he joined it* (L 24–gives [waʼthr³tdaʼθ³·ʼn³ʼ] with an unexpected nasal vowel in the second syllable).

-ne –. -tahwečü –{dative II} need, want. *v.r.-a.i.* hab: -, pnt: -, stat: -, prog: -, prp: -, dst: -, caus: -, rvs: -, dat: II (-ni-/-hθ-), n-inc. The form of the dative with the habitual aspect is irregular in that it shows *n* where *t* is expected. nehrutahwęčü·nih ‹apart-he-needs-for› *he requires it* (RC 1:8), nęhrutahwę́·čuhθ ‹apart-prediction-he-need-for› *it will behoove him* (HS).

-ne –. -tahwęčuhu – be necessary. *v.r.-s.i.* hab: -, pnt: -, stat: -ę°, prog: -, prp: -, dst: -, caus: -, rvs: -, dat: -, n- inc. Clearly related to the preceding root, with absence of the dative and addition of the causative **-hu –.** neyutahwęčúhę ‹apart-it-need-caused› *it is necessary* (HS).

-ne –. -tak – open, remove a covering so as to reveal an opening (as in opening a door). *v.r.-t.* hab: -ęhs, pnt: -, stat: -ę, prog: -, prp: -, dst: -, caus: -, rvs: -, dat: -, n-inc. The dualic is dropped in nominal constructions. **-takęhst –**: utakę́hsteh ‹open-'ness› *doorway, enclosed porch, foyer, portal* (R); **-ta= kęhsta'ni**: utakę́hstaʔni ‹open-'ness-at the edge of› *side of enclosed porch* (RC 3:8); **-ne –. -tak –**: nekatá·kę ‹two-

it-opened› *it is open* (RC 26:10), nehratá·kęhs ‹two-he-opens› *he opens it* (HS); **-ne –. -a'nętak –**: newaʔnętá·kę ‹two-it-itself-opened› *it opens (itself)* (HS), neyuʔnętá·kę ‹two-it-itself-opened› *it is open* (HS).

-ne –. -tak(e)r – one's people. *dv.n.s.* nehratá·kyer ‹apart-he-dwells› *his own people* (RC 12:1).

-ne –. -takeraʔnahkw – parable. *dv.n.s.* neyetakyeraʔnáhkhwaʔ ‹apart-one-dwell-causes-instrument› *parable* (HS).

-ne –. -takręte tribe. *dv.n.s.* nehratakrę́·te ‹apart-he-dwell-certain one› *his tribe* (RC 3:72).

-ne –. -ta'ni – be notorious. *v.s.-a.i.* nehratá·ʔnih ‹apart-he-settlement-is all› *he is notorious* (HS).

-ne –. -taʔwęthu – fight one another. *v.s.-t.* nekayęʔtaʔwę́·thuhs ‹two-they-themselves-slaughter› *they fight each other* (R).

-ne –. -tehwhar – have a fur cap. *v.s.-s.i.* nehrutéwheʔr ‹apart-he-skin-hangs› *he has a fur cap* (AG).

-ne –. -tekar – brace. *v.s.-t.* nehrutekà·rę ‹two-he-took from› *he braced* (HS).

-ne –. -tekar – brace, prop. *dv.n.s.* haʔ neyutekà·rę ‹the two-it-took from› *a prop, a brace* (HS).

-ne –. -tekę – join, put together. *v.r.-t.* hab: -h, pnt: -ʔ, stat: -·, prog: -, prp: -, dst: -hrę-, caus: -, rvs: -, dat: -, inc.-ahθr-pat. **-ne –. -athahatekę –**: neyuthahaté·kę· ‹two-it-itself-path-put together› *the two roads are side by side* (H 2484); **-ne –. -ahθratekę –**: newahθraté·kę· ‹two-it-X-joined› *they two are together* (R); **-ne –. -(a)čę̱hatekę –**: neyęktičęhaté·kęh ‹two-we two-fire-join› *neighbor* (HS); **-ne –. -(a)čę̱hatekę̱hrę –**: nekačęhatekę́hręh ‹two-it-fire-joins-many› *among members of a family* (R), neyękwačęhatekę́hręh ‹two-we-fire-join-many› *neighbors* (HS): –ne–. **–wyatekę** –: wa'-thrawyaté·kę' ⟨fact-two-he-preparation-joined⟩ *he put two preparations together* (RC 14:3); **–'washaratekę** –: Ra'washaraté·kęhs ⟨he-earring-joins⟩ *He-Puts-Earrings-Together (male proper name)* (RC 16:11); **–a'nęnęh = satekę** –: yu'nęnęhsaté·kę· ⟨it-itself-house-joined⟩ *the houses are side by side (this is a singular form, but use has given it a dual sense)* (H 2484).

–ne–. **–tęharę'rę** – appall, awe. *v.r.-t.* hab: -h, pnt: -, stat: -ę, prog: -, prp: -, dst: -, caus: -'T-, rvs: -, dat: -, n-inc. nehrutęharę'ręh *it appalls him, it awes him* (HS); –ne–. **–tęharę'rę'T** –: nehrutęharę'rę't ⟨apart-he-awe-causes⟩ *he is awe-inspiring* (HS); ha' –ne–. **–tęharę' = rę'T** –: ha' neyutęharę'rę't ⟨the apart-it-awe-causes⟩ *awe* (HS).

–ne–. **–tęharę'rę'T** – be awe-inspiring. *v.s.-s.i.* nehrutęharę'rę't ⟨apart-he-awe-causes⟩ *he is awe-inspiring* (HS).

–ne–. **–tęharę'rę'T** – awe. *dv.n.s.* ha' neyutęharę'rę't ⟨the apart-it-awe-causes⟩ *awe* (HS).

–ne–. **–tęnhekari** – be afflicted, be in distress. *v.s.-s.i.* nehrutęnheká·ryę ⟨apart-he-is afflicted⟩ *he is afflicted, he is in distress* (HS).

–ne–. **–thunęhyani'n** – be horrible. *v.r.-s.i.* stat: -ę, prog: -, prp: -, dst: -, caus: -, rvs: -, dat: -, n-inc. neyuthunęhyaní'nę *it is horrible* (HS).

–ne–. **–tihar** – run away. *v.r.-a.i.* hab: -ɸ, pnt: -, stat: -, prog: -, prp: -, dst: -, caus: -hu-, rvs: -, dat: II (-ati-/-ahθ),

inc.-ɸ-ag./pat. Requires the dualic unless the dative is present. nehrutihárhę *he has fled* (RC 26:30); –ne+či –. **–tiharhu** –: nęθahratihárhu' ⟨apart-fact-again-he-run away-caused⟩ *he again fled* (RC 6:10); –ne+t –. **–tiharhu** –: nętktihárhu' ⟨apart-prediction-hither-I-run away-cause⟩ *I will run there* (R); –ne–. **–atkęhsatihar** –: nehratkęhsatíhar ⟨apart-he-himself-face-runs away⟩ *he faces it* (HS).

–ne–. **–tihurę** – have a heart attack, have a stroke. *v.r.-s.i.* hab: -, pnt: -', stat: -, prog: -, prp: -, dst: -, caus: -, rvs: -, dat: -, n-inc. wa'nyakutihù·rę' ⟨fact-apart-one-had a stroke⟩ *one had a heart attack, one had a stroke* (R).

–ne–. **–tkwa'nihθT** – convex-o-convex. *dv.n.s.* neyutkwa'níhθnę ⟨two-it-stomach-stand up-caused⟩ *convex-o-convex (shaped like a lens or a magnifying glass)* (HS).

–ne–. **–uhkwanęT** – stir. *v.r.-t.* hab: -, pnt: -, stat: -ę, prog: -, prp: -, dst: -, caus: -, rvs: -, dat: -, n-inc. nehruhkwanę·'nę *he stirs it* (HS).

–ne–. **–uhrarak** – pinch, press (a thing together). *v.r.-t.* hab: -s, pnt: -, stat: -, prog: -, prp: -, dst: -, caus: -T-, rvs: -, dat: I (-θe-/-θ), inc.-ɸ-pat. The dualic is optionally–but frequently–deleted in the words for *nightmare* and *stake*. nehrúhraraks *he pinches* (HS); –ne–. **–čisnuhrarakT** –: neyečisnuhraráktha' ⟨two-one-ember-press-causes⟩ *tongs* (HS); –ne–. **–ihnuhrarak** –: nehręhnúhraraks ⟨two-he-skin-presses⟩ *he pinch-*

es (HS); **-ne -. -ka'nuhrarak -**: nehraka'núhraraks ‹two-he-wheel-presses› *brakeman* (HS); **-ne -. -ya'tuhrarak -**: (ne)yakuya'túhraraks‹(two)-one-body-presses› *nightmare* (R); **-ne -. -'ę = yuhrarakT -**: (ne)ye'ęyuhraráktha' ‹(two)-one-cost-press-causes› *stake* (HS); **-ne -. -'tuhrarak -**: nehra'túhraraks ‹two-he-X-presses› *he presses (a thing together)* (HS), neka'túhraraks ‹two-it-X-presses› *pincers, it presses together* (HS); **-ne -. -rihstuhrarak -**: nehrarihstúhraraks ‹two-he-metal-presses› *he prints it (printer, publisher)* (HS), nekarihstúhraraks ‹two-it-metal-presses› *printing press* (HS); **-ne+či -. -rihstuhrarak -**: neθhrahrihstúhraraks ‹two-again-he-metal-presses› *he reprints it* (HS); **-ne -. -a'rihstuhrarak -**: neyu'rihstuhrará·kę ‹two-it-itself-metal-pressed› *printing* (HS); **-ne -. -a'ri = huhrarakT -**: neyu'rihúhrarakt ‹two-it-itself-matter-press-caused› *pressing: it is in great strength* (HS); **-ne -. -a'rihu = hrarak -{dative I}**: nęθa'rihúhrarakθ ‹apart-prediction-you-yourself-matter-press-for› *it will disturb you* (RC 25: 16).

-ne -. -uhstahkw - spring, springtime. *dv. n.s.* nęwúhstahkw ‹apart-prediction-it-year-pick up› *spring, springtime* (R).

-ne -. -uhstakeha'nye' - biennial. *dv.n.s.* newuhstakyehá·'nye' ‹two-it-year-is in number-going along› *biennial* (HS).

-ne -. -uhst' - double. *v.r.-t.* hab: -ahs, pnt: -, stat: -ɸ, prog: -, prp: -, dst: -, caus: -, rvs: -, dat: -, n-inc. nehrúhst'ahs *he doubles it* (HS); **-ne -. -a'nuhst' -**: neyú·'nuhst ‹two-it-itself-doubles› *double* (HS).

-ne -. -ukar - be broken up. *v.r.-a.i.* hab: -, pnt: -', stat: -ę·, prog: -, prp: -, dst: -, caus: -, rvs: -, dat: -, inc.-ɸ-pat. Requires the semireflexive or an incor-

porated noun root. **-a'nyękwirukar -**: yu'nyękwiruká·rę· ‹it-it-self-wood-is broken up› *split wood* (HS); **-ne -. -turahčrukar -**: wa'thraturahčrú·ka'r ‹fact-apart-he-rib-broke up› *he broke his rib* (RC 21:3); **-ne -. -a'nukar -**: neyu'nuká·rę ‹apart-it-itself-is broken up› *it is broken up crosswise* (RC 24: 2); **-ne -. -ačkę'rukar -**: neyučkę'ruká·rę· ‹apart-it-itself-bone-is broken up› *broken bones* (RC 7:10).

-ne -. -ukę - be bent, be forked. *v.r.-s.i.* stat: -', prog: -, prp: -, dst: -, caus: -hsT-, rvs: -, dat: -, inc.-ɸ-pat. neyawú·kę' *it is forked* (HS); **-(a)ha = hukęhsT -**: yuhahukęhsthę' ‹it-path-be forked-caused-many› *the road is divided in branches or forks* (H 2484); **-nęhsukęhsthę -**: yunęhsukęhsthę· ‹it-house-be forked-caused-much› *the house has rooms, that is, the house is divided into branches or parts* (H 24 84); **-ne -. -ahsukę -**: neyuhsú·kę' ‹apart-it-foot-is forked› *cloven foot, pronged foot: it is ungulate* (HS); **-ne -. -atre'rukę -**: neyutre'rú·kę·k ‹apart-prediction-it-pole-be forked› *it will be forked pole* (R); **-ne -. -atre' = rukęhsthę -**: neyutre'rukęhsthęh ‹apart-it-pole-be forked-causes-much› *it is V-shaped* (RC 6:11); **-ne -. -herukę -**: Neyuherú·kę' ‹apart-it-green-is forked› *a fortified Tuscarora town in colonial North Carolina, "Broken Pasture"* (AG) [Colonial Records «Fort Neoheroka», «Fort Noo-he-roo-ka»]; **-ne -. -rę'ukę -**: neyurę'ú·kę' ‹apart-it-tree-is forked› *forked tree* (RC 27:6); **tha+ne -. -ręhsukę -**: tha'nehruręhsú·kę' ‹unusual-apart-he-leg-is forked› *his legs gave out from under him* (RC 24:8); **ti -. -(i)'nhahnukę -**: tyu'nhahnú·kę' ‹so-it-limb-is forked› *forked branch* (RC 4:1).

-ne -. -uk̨eni - ??. *v.r.-a.i.* hab: -, pnt: -?,
stat: -, prog: -, prp: -, dst: -, caus: -,
rvs: -, dat: -, inc.-??-pat. Found only
in the following construction. -ne -.
-rętuk̨eni -: wa?nyękrętuk̨ė·ni? ‹fact-
apart-one=me-magic-??› *one cheated
me, one bested me* (RC 28:12).

-ne -. -ⁿurę - split. *v.s.-t.* neθù·rę ‹apart-
you!-split› *split it!* (R), nehrù·ręhs ‹a-
part-he-splits› *he splits* (HS), neθnù··
ręh ‹apart-you two-split› *you two are
splitting it* (R), newakú·rę· ‹apart-I-
split› *I had split it* (R), wa?tkù·rę? *I
split it* (R) ‹fact-apart-I-split›, narya-
wú·rę·k ‹apart-unknown-it-split› *that it
split* (RC 30: 45).

-ne -. -ⁿuręhsthę - split. *v.s.-t.* newakuréhs-
sthę· ‹apart-I-split-much› *I had split it*
(R).

-ne -. -u?k(e)T - hem. *v.r.-t.* hab: -ęhs,
pnt: ()-φ, stat: -ę, prog: -, prp: -, dst:
-, caus: -, rvs: -, dat: -, n-inc. neyakú?knęhs *one hems it* (H-notebook),
newú?knę *one hemmed it* (H-notebook), nęyakú?kye·t *one will hem it*
(H-notebook).

-ne -. -u?kę - hold up, sustain. *v.r.-t.* hab:
-h, pnt: -, stat: -, prog: -, prp: -, dst: -,
caus: -, rvs: -, dat: -, n-inc. nehrú?kęh
he holds it up, he sustains it (HS).

-ne -. -u?knęhsi - unbend. *v.s.-t.* nehru?-
knéhsyęhs ‹apart-he-end-undoes› *he
unbends it* (HS).

-ne -. -u?kT - bend. *v.s.-t.* hab: -ęhs, pnt: -
, stat: -ę. nehrú?knęhs ‹apart-he-ends›
he bends it, he turns it over (HS).

-ne -. -w - the two of them's (two females
or a male and a female) (third person
dual feminine/zoic inalienable). *n.r.
pfx.* Occurs before roots and stems
that begin with a vowel other than *i*.

-ne -. -w - the two of them (two females
or a male and a female) (third person
dual feminine/zoic agent). *v.r.pfx.* Occurs before roots and stems that begin
with a vowel other than *i*.

-ne -. -wak -/-ne -. -wakʷ - the two of
them...me (third person dual femi-
nine/zoic agent=first person singular
patient). *v.r.pfx.* The form -ne -. -wakʷ -
occurs before roots and stems that
begin with the vowel *a*. The form
-ne -. -wak - occurs elsewhere with insertion of "epenthetic" e before roots
and stems that begin with certain consonant clusters.

-ne -. -weh - parley. *v.s.-t.* nehrà·weh ‹a-
part-he-speaks› *he parleys* (HS), neya-
kwà·weh ‹apart-we-speak› *we all talk
together* (R).

(-ne -.) -wętahskanek̨ęT - ambiguous. *dv.n.
s.* (ne)yuwętahskané·k̨ę·t ‹apart-it-
word-is odd› *ambiguous* (HS).

-ne -. -wętak̨ę?neti - translator. *dv.n.s.*
nehrawętak̨ę?né·tyęhs ‹apart-he-word-
changes› *translator* (HS).

-ne -. -wętitk̨ę? - speak out. *v.s.-a.i.* neh-
rawęti·tk̨ę? ‹apart-he-word-came forth›
he spoke out (RC 3:56).

-ne -. -ya -/-ne -. -yak -/-ne -. -ye - the two of
them's (two females or a male and a
female) (third person dual feminine/
indefinite inalienable). *n.r.pfx.* The
form -ne -. -ya - before certain roots

Tuscarora Pronunciation Key:
/a/ law; /e/ hat; /i/ pizza; /u/ tune; /ę/ hint; /č/
cheese; /h/ hoe; /m/ mother; /s/ same; /t/ do
(before a vowel y, or w), too (elsewhere); /k/ gale
(before a vowel y or w), kale (elsewhere); /n/
inhale (before a consonant or word-final), note
(elsewhere), /r/ hiss (before a consonant or word-
final), run (trilled as in Italian, elsewhere); /w/ cuff
(before a consonant other than y or word-final),
way (elsewhere); /y/ fish (before a consonant or
word-final), you (elsewhere), /θ/ thing; /?/ (the
sound between the vowels in unh-unh); /·/ long
vowel, /´/ high pitch; /`/ low pitch.

and stems that begin with the vowel *i*. The form –**ne** –.–**yak**– occurs before roots and stems that begin with the vowel *u* or the morphophoneme {ę°}. The form –**ne** –.–**ye** – occurs elsewhere with coalescence of the final *e* of the prefix with following ę (not from {ę°}) or *e* to yield –**ne** –.–**yę** –.

–**ne** –.–**ya** –/–**ne** –.–**yak** –/–**ne** –.–**ye** – the two of them (two females or a male and a female) (third person dual feminine/indefinite agent). *v.r.pfx.* The form –**ne** –.–**ya** – before certain roots and stems that begin with the vowel *i*. The form –**ne** –.–**yak** – occurs before roots and stems that begin with the vowel *u* or the morpho-phoneme {ę°}. The form –**ne** –.–**ye** – occurs elsewhere with coalescence of the final *e* of the prefix with following ę (not from {ę°}) or *e* to yield –**ne** –.–**yę** –.

–**ne** –.–**yahserhar**ʔ – be busy. *v.r.-s.i.* stat: -ę, prog: -, prp: -, dst: -, caus: -, rvs: -, dat: -, inc.-ϕ-pat. newakyahserhárʔę *I am busy* (R), nehruyahserhárʔę *he is busy* (HS), *he is overcrowded with work or very busy* (H-notebook).

–**ne** –.–**yakaw** –/–**ne** –.–**yaku** – the two of them's (two females or a male and a female) (third person dual feminine/indefinite alienable). *n.r.pfx.* The form –**ne** –.–**yakaw** – occurs before roots and stems that begin with a vowel other than *a*. The form –**ne** –.–**yaku** – occurs before roots and stems that begin with a consonant or the vowel *a*, which vowel is dropped.

–**ne** –.–**yakaw** –/–**ne** –.–**yaku** – the two of them (two females or a male and a female) (third person dual feminine/indefinite patient. *v.r.pfx.* The form –**ne** –.–**yakaw** – occurs before roots and stems that begin with a vowel other than *a*. The form –**ne** –.–**yaku** – occurs

before roots and stems that begin with a consonant or the vowel *a*, which vowel is dropped.

–**ne** –.–**ya**ʔ**ta'nę**ʔ – be seemly. *v.s.-s.i.* neyuyaʔtá·ʔnęʔ ‹apart-it-body-becomes› *it is seemly* (HS).

(–**ne** –.)–**ya**ʔ**tuhra̱rak** – nightmare. *dv.n.s.* (ne)yakuyaʔtúhraraks‹(two)-one-body-presses› *nightmare* (R).

–**ne** –.–**yehrak** – alloy, intermingle, mix in, mix together. *v.s.-t.* nęyakwayéhrak ‹apart-prediction-we-bring together› *we will mix it in* (R), waʔthrayéhrak ‹fact-apart-he-brought together› *he mixed together* (RC 30:53), nehrayéhraks ‹apart-he-brings together› *he alloys, he mixes two things* (HS).

–**ne** –.–**yehrak** –{dative III} Feast of the Dead. *dv.n.s.* Waʔnyęʔnyehrá·kęʔ ‹fact-apart-one-brought together-for› *Feast of the Dead* (AG).

–**ne** –.–**yehraksT** – ingredient. *dv.n.s.* neyeyehrákstha›‹apart-one-bring together-causes› *ingredient* (HS).

–**ne** –.–**ye**θ**a** – the two of them...you alone (third person dual feminine/indefinite agent=second person singular patient). *v.r.pfx.* With roots and stems that begin with the vowel *i* the final *a* of the prefix coalesces with the initial *i* to yield –**ne** –.–**ye**θ**ę** –. Before roots and stems that begin with other vowels, the final *a* of the prefix is dropped.

–**ne** –.–**yęk** –/–**ne** –.–**yęk**ʷ – the two of them...me (third person dual feminine/zoic agent=first person non-singular patient). *v.r.pfx.* The form –**ne** –.–**yęk**ʷ – occurs before roots and stems that begin with the vowel *a*. The form –**ne** –.–**yęk** – occurs elsewhere with insertion of "epenthetic" e before roots and stems that begin with certain consonant clusters.

–**ne** –.–**yę'naT(e)** – the two of them...him,

her; she, one...the two of them (third person dual feminine/indefinite agent= third person feminine/indefinite patient, third person singular feminine/ indefinite agent=third person dual feminine/indefinite patient). *v.r.pfx.* The form **-ne-.-yę'nat-** occurs before roots and stems that begin with the consonants *k*, *ʔ*, or *h*; when the roots or stem begins with the cluster *hs*, this cluster coalesces with the final *t* of the prefix to yield **-ne-.-yę'nač-**. The form **-ne-.-yę'na'n-** occurs before roots and stems that begin with a vowel. The form **-ne-. -yę'naʔ-** occurs before roots and stems that begin with the consonants *t*, *č*, *r* or, sometimes, *n*. The form **-ne-.-yę'na'nę-** occurs before certain roots and stems that begin with the consonant *n* or the consonant clusters *hn* or *ht*. The form **-ne-. -yę'na'ne-** occurs before roots and stems that begin with clusters that condition the appearance of "epenthetic" e.

-ne-.-ʔčisne- be acid, be sour. *v.r.-s.i.* stat: -ʔ, prog: -, prp: -, dst: -, caus: -, rvs: -, dat: -, n-inc. neyuʔčísneʔ *it is acid, it is sour* (HS).

(-ne-.)-ʔęyuhrarakT- stake. *dv.n.s.* (ne)-yeʔęyuhrarákthaʔ ‹(two)-one-cost-press-causes› *stake* (HS).

-ne-.-'nę- fly. *v.r.-a.i.* hab: -, pnt: -ʔ, stat: -ʔ, prog: -, prp: -, dst: -tyę-, caus: -, rvs: -, dat: -, n-inc. nekáʔnęʔ *it flies* (R), waʔthráʔnęʔ *he flew* (RC 12:22), wáʔtknęʔ *I flew* (R); **-ne-.**

-'nętyę-: neθwaʔnę·tyçʔ ‹apart-you-fly-much› *you all are flying* (RC 12: 3); **-ne+či-.-'nę-**: nęθakáʔnęʔ ‹apart-fact-again-it-flew› *again it flew* (RC 12:26).

-ne-.-'nęʔθ- engrave, write. *v.r.-t.* hab: -haʔ, pnt: -φ, stat: -ę, prog: -, prp: -, dst: -ahnę-, caus: -, rvs: -, dat: -, inc.-φ-pat. The dualic is absent with the characterizer enclitic and when an incorporated noun is present. né·θnęʔθ *write it!* (R), nehruʔnęʔθę *he has written* (L 23), nekaʔnęʔθę *manuscript* (HS), nehraʔnęʔθhaʔ *he writes* (R), *he engraves* (HS), waʔtká·ʔnęʔθ *it wrote* (R), waʔčhá·ʔnęʔθ *you wrote* (R); **-'nęʔθ-.#aka·ʔ**: raʔnęʔθhaʔáka·ʔ ‹he-writes-characterized by› *writer* (L 23—[raʔnꝍʔθaháka·ʔ]); **-'nęʔθęhst-**: uʔnęʔθęhsteh ‹write-'ness› *writing* (HS); **-ne-.-'nęʔθahkw-**: neyeʔnęʔθáhkhwaʔ ‹apart-one-writes-instrument› *pencil, pen* (R); **-ne-.-a'nę= 'nęʔθ-**: neyuʔnęʔnęʔθę ‹apart-it-itself-wrote› *inscription, manuscript* (HS); **-atkęhsa'nęʔθahnę-**: watkęhsaʔnęʔθáhnęh ‹it-itself-face-writes-much› *tattoo marks* (SH 375); ha? **-ne-. -'nęʔθ-**: haʔ nehruʔnęʔθę ‹the apart-he-wrote› *author* (HS).

-ne-.-'nęʔθ- author. *dv.n.s.* haʔ nehruʔnęʔθę ‹the apart-he-wrote› *author* (HS).

-ne-.-'nęʔθahkw- pencil, pen. *dv.n.s.* neyeʔnęʔθáhkhwaʔ ‹apart-one-writes-instrument› *pencil, pen* (R).

-ne-.-ʔθkwehsukwahT- {dative III} cyl-

inder. *n.s.* neyu'ʔθkwehsukwahná·ti·
‹apart-it-round block of wood-spread
out-caused-for› *cylinder* (AG).

-ne -. -ʔtiθkrarę - tickle. *v.r.-t.* hab: -h,
pnt: -, stat: -, prog: -, prp: -, dst: -,
caus: -, rvs: -, dat: -, n-inc. nehra'ʔtiθ-
krà·ręh *he tickles it* (HS); -ʔtiθkraręt:
yu'ʔtiθkrá·rę·t ‹it-tickle-possesses› *tickling* (HS), yu'ʔtiθkrarę·'ʔnę ‹it-tickle-
possessed› *ticklish* (HS).

-ne -. -ʔtuhrarak - press. *v.s.-t.* nehra'ʔtúh-
rara·ks ‹two-he-'?ʔ-presses› *he presses
(a thing together)* (HS), neka'ʔtúh-
rara·ks ‹two-it-'?ʔ-presses› *it presses
together* (HS).

-ne -. -ʔtuhrarak - pincers. *dv.n.s.* neka'ʔ-
túhrara·ks ‹two-it-'?ʔ-presses› *pincers*
(HS).

-ne -. -ʔtyęhk - have a nose bleed. *v.r.-a.i.*
hab: -ɸ, pnt: -, stat: -, prog: -, prp: -,
dst: -, caus: -, rvs: -, dat: -, n-inc.
Possibley an old compound of -(ę)ʔ =
tyęh(s) - *nose* and -k - *eat.* newáktyęhk
‹apart-I-have a nose bleed› *I have a
nose bleed* (R).

-ne -. -ʔtyęhkrakar - snivel. *v.s.-a.i.* nehra'ʔtyęhkrakar ‹apart-he-snot-makes a
noise› *he snivels* (HS).

-ne -. -ʔtyę'nęhsT - measure by. *v.s.-a.i.*
nehru'ʔtyę'ʔnęhsnę ‹apart-he-measure-
caused› *he measured by* (RC 12:2).

-ne -. -ʔtyę'nęhsT - model, pattern. *dv.n.s.*
neye'ʔtyę'ʔnęhstha' ‹apart-one-measure-causes› *model, pattern* (HS).

-ne -. -ʔwahrahrihT - hamburger. *dv.n.s.*
neka'ʔwahrahríhnę ‹apart-it-meat-spill-
caused› *hamburger* (R).

-ne -. -ʔwaʔT - play hoop & javelin game.
v.r.-a.i. hab: -ha', pnt: -, stat: -, prog:
-, prp: -, dst: -, caus: -, rvs: -, dat: -,
n-inc. Hewitt (notebook) describes the
hoop & javelin game as follows:
"stand at a distance while one rolls a
hoop, wooden or metal about 15 feet,

before them & they try to throw their
(javelin) so that they may fasten it to
the ground." nehra'ʔwá'ʔtha' *he plays
hoop & javelin game* (H-notebook);
-ʔwaʔčr -: u'ʔwá'ʔčreh ‹play hoop &
javelin game› *hoop & javelin game*
(H-notebook).

-ne+či -. -a'ʔnahwyar - recoil. *v.r.-a.i.* hab:
-ɸ, pnt: -ę', stat: -', prog: -, prp: -,
dst: -, caus: -, rvs: -, dat: -, n-inc. ne-
ču'ʔnáhwya'ʔr *it recoiled* (HS), ne-
θwa'ʔnáhwyar *it recoils* (HS), nęθwa'ʔnahwyà·rę' *it will recoil* (HS).

-nehraku(h) - amaze, astonish, surprise.
v.r.-t. hab: -ahs, pnt: ()-ɸ, stat: -, prog:
-ęha'nye'-, prp: -, dst: -, caus: -ahT-,
rvs: -, dat: -, n-inc. runehrá·kwahs *he
is astonished* (HS), wa'ʔunehrá·kuh *it
was surprised* (RC 30:10), wa'ʔkaku-
nehrá·kuh *they were surprised* (RC
3:73), ęknehrá·kuh *I was amazed, I
was surprised* (R); **-nehrakwahnę =
ha'nye' -:** yunehrakwahnęhá·'ʔnye' ‹it-
surprise-caused-going along› *wonderfully* (HS), runehrakwahnęhá·'ʔnye'
‹he-surprise-caused-going along› *he
grew great* (HS); **-nehrakwahT -:** yu-
nehrá·kwaht ‹it-surprise-causes› *a-
stonishing, extraordinary* (HS), runeh-
rá·kwaht ‹he-surprise-causes› *he is illustrious* (HS); **ha' -nehrakwahT -:** ha'
yunehrá·kwaht ‹the it-surprise-causes›
a wonder (HS).

-nehrakwahnęha'nye' - wonderfully. *dv.n.
s.* yunehrakwahnęhá·'ʔnye' ‹it-surprise-
caused-going along› *wonderfully*
(HS).

-nehrakwahnęha'nye' - grow great. *v.s.-
a.i.* runehrakwahnęhá·'ʔnye' ‹he-surprise-caused-going along› *he grew
great* (HS).

-nehrakwahT - be illustrious. *v.s.-s.i.* ru-
nehrá·kwaht ‹he-surprise-causes› *he is
illustrious* (HS).

-nehrakwahT – a wonder; astonishing, extraordinary. *dv.n.s.* yunehrá·kwaht ‹it-surprise-causes› *astonishing, extraordinary* (HS), ha'² yunehrá·kwaht ‹the it-surprise-causes› *a wonder* (HS).

-nehs – film. *n.r.* n-poss., inc., n.sfx. -eh. unéhseh *film (for a camera)* (HS); -nehsur –: runéhsuh ‹he-film-covers› *he has film, he films* (HS).

-nehsur – film. *v.s.-a.i.* runéhsuh ‹he-film-covers› *he films* (HS).

-nehuhčr – sheath. *n.r.* n-poss., n-inc., n. sfx. -eh. unehúhčreh *sheath* (R); -ne = huhčrakęw: unehúhčrakęw ‹sheath-in› *in sheath* (RC 8:3).

-nehuθer – Atlantides. *n.r.* n-poss., n-inc., n.sfx. -ɸ. unehú·θer *Atlantides* (HS).

Nekayę́·tę² Chief of the Bear Clan (literal meaning uncertain) (H-Handbook). *n.*

nekčihę́hrę·t cricket *(Gryllus domesticus)* (R). *n.*

nekčirè·re chickadee (R); an early riser (H-notebook). *n.*

né·kre· early spring frog (H 3518). *n.*

né·krę² eight (R) [Lawson «Nec-kara» 'Eight']. *part.* né·krę² -či -. -(i)har -: né·krę² θkáhe'²r ‹eight again-it-hangs› *eighteen* (R); né·krę² ti -. -ahθhę -: né·krę² tiwáhθhę· ‹eight so-it-is ten› *eighty* (R).

né·krę² -či -. -(i)har – eighteen. *part.* né·krę² θkáhe'²r ‹eight again-it-hangs› *eighteen* (R).

né·krę² ti -. -ahθhę – eighty. *part.* né·krę² tiwáhθhę· ‹eight so-it-is ten› *eighty* (R).

né·kti· two (R) [Lawson «Necte» 'Two']. *part.* né·kti· -či -. -(i)har -: né·kti· θkáhe'²r ‹two again-it-hangs› *twelve* (R) [Lawson «Nectec scaukhau» 'Twelve']; né·kti· ti+či -. -hterhę -: né·kti· tičuhtérhę ‹two so-again-it-X-is day› *Tuesday* (R); né·kti· ha² tha+ne -. -a'nę'nare -: né·kti· ha² tha'²neyu'²nę́·'²nare² ‹two the unusual-apart-it-itself-day-is distant› *biweekly* (HS).

né·kti· -či -. -(i)har – twelve. *part.* né·kti· θkáhe'²r ‹two again-it-hangs› *twelve* (R) [Lawson «Nectec scau-khau» 'Twelve'].

né·kti· ti+či -. -hterhę – Tuesday. *dv.n.s.* né·kti· tičuhtérhę ‹two so-again-it-X-is day› *Tuesday* (R).

né·kw tightness (R). *n.* né·kw -a'nę -: né·kw yú'²nę· ‹tightness it-became› *it is fastened up* (H-notebook); né·kw -ę°ti -: né·kw rę́·tih ‹tightness he-makes› *he fastens it, he tightens it* (HS).

né·kw -a'nę – fasten. *v.s.-a.i.* né·kw yú'²nę· ‹tightness it-became› *it is fastened up* (H-notebook).

né·kw -ę°ti – fasten, tighten. *v.s.-t.* né·kw rę́·tih ‹tightness he-makes› *he fastens it, he tightens it* (HS).

nér²ę skunk *(Mephitis mephitis)* (R). *n.*

-neθtwa²r – pubic hair. *n.r.* aln: akunéθtwa'²reh *one's pubic hair* (RC 6:6), n-inc., n.sfx. -eh. unéθtwa'²reh *pubic hair* (R).

-neshę – Hell. *n.r.* n-poss., n-inc., n.sfx. -'². unéshę² *Hell* (HS) (also: uné'²sę² (HS), unę́'²sę·'² (HS)).

Tuscarora Pronunciation Key:
/a/ l<u>a</u>w; /e/ h<u>a</u>t; /i/ p<u>i</u>zza; /u/ t<u>u</u>ne; /ę/ h<u>i</u>nt; /č/ <u>c</u>heese; /h/ <u>h</u>oe; /m/ <u>m</u>other; /s/ <u>s</u>ame; /t/ <u>d</u>o (before a vowel y, or w), <u>t</u>oo (elsewhere); /k/ <u>g</u>ale (before a vowel y or w), <u>k</u>ale (elsewhere); /n/ i<u>nh</u>ale (before a consonant or word-final), <u>n</u>ote (elsewhere), /r/ hi<u>ss</u> (before a consonant or word-final), <u>r</u>un (trilled as in Italian, elsewhere); /w/ <u>c</u>uff (before a consonant other than y or word-final), <u>w</u>ay (elsewhere); /y/ fi<u>sh</u> (before a consonant or word-final), <u>y</u>ou (elsewhere), /θ/ <u>th</u>ing; /'²/ (the sound between the vowels in unh-unh); /·/ long vowel, /'/ high pitch; /`/ low pitch.

-neshęhrunę? devil. *n.r.* n-poss.. n-inc..
n.sfx. -. uneshęhrù·nę? *devil* (HS) (also: unishehrù·nę? (L 7), unęshęhrù·-
nę? (HS). une?sęhrù·nę? (HS)).

netyá?kiw   just as soon as (RC 8:41).
part.

newęta?ę́·nya?ks spicebush *(Lindera ben-
zoin)* (H-notebook). *n.*

newętikhwáhkęh   bastard (HS). *n.*

newętikwęhčha?ks?ú?y bloodroot *(San-
guinaria canadensis)* (RC 23:2). *n.*

Neyuchá?ktę It-Is-Bent (Chief of the
Wolf Clan) (H-Handbook). *n.*

neyukuyaná·tręhs ground hemlock *(Ly-
copodium* sp.*)* (H-notebook). *n.*

neyuna?kwéyher fawn (R). *n.*

neyurę?nę́?ę mist (R). *n.*

ne? if, when; o that (RC 30:18). *part.*
   ne? the? ‹if not› *unless, if not* (HS).

ne? the? ‹if not› unless, if not (HS). *part.*

né?či as, as if, for instance, just like,
like, very like (RC 25:4). *part.*

-ne?sę- Hell. *n.r.* n-poss., n-inc., n.sfx.
   -?. uné?sę? *Hell* (HS) (also: unéshę?
   (HS), uné?sę·? (HS)).

-ne?sęhrunę? devil. *n.r.* n-poss., n-inc.,
   n.sfx. -. une?sęhrù·nę? *devil* (HS) (also: unishehrù·nę? (L 7), unęshęhrù·-
   nę? (HS), uneshęhrù·nę? (HS)).

nę – dualic+future. *v.pfx.* Occurs in word-
initial position.

nę – partitive+future. *v.pfx.* Occurs in
word-initial position.

nę – dualic+optative. *v.pfx.* A portmanteau in word-initial position of the dualic, the optative, and a pronominal
prefix beginning with the sequence
wa, which is lost.

nę – dualic+optative+third person singular
agent. *v.pfx.* A portmanteau in word-
initial position of the dualic, the optative, and the third person neuter
singular -w – before a stem beginning
with the vowel *a.*

nę if (subjunctive marker) (RC 26:4).
part.

-nę – guard, tend. *v.r.-t.* hab: -h ~ -ha?.
pnt: -, stat: -, prog: -, prp: -, dst: -,
caus: -, rvs: -, dat: -, inc.-ɸ-pat. The
completive suffix -·t occurs where the
punctual aspect marker would be expected. rà·nęh *he tends it: occupant
(of a house)* (HS), yè·nęh *wife* (R);
ranę́ha? *he guards it* (R), ná?nęh *one
guards another* (HS); -nęhsanę -: ka-
nę́hsanęh ‹it-house-guards› *a cricket
(its literal meaning being it watches
the house, so called from a habit of
the cricket: when it gains entrance
into the house, it remains quiet so
long as it hears someone moving
about)* (H 2484); -rę?anę -: karę́?anęh
‹it-tree-guards› *it guards tree* (RC 4:
2), *liverwort* (H-notebook); -rihwanę -:
uríhwanęh ‹matter-guard› *because of*
(R); -ta?nanę -: neyetá?nanęh ‹two-
one-village-guard› *the two of them
guard camp* (RC 32:5); -atkerhanę -:
aryętkyérhanę·t ‹unknown-one-oneself-
body-guard-complete› *that one protect
oneself* (RC 16:2); -a'nwiranę -: ra?-
nwì·ranęh   ‹he-himself-offspring-
guards› *he nurses* (HS).

-nę – occupant (of a house). *dv.n.s.* rà·-
nęh ‹he-guards› *occupant (of a house)*
(HS).

-nę – wife. *dv.n.s.* yè·nęh ‹one-guards›
wife (R).

-nę – be soft. *v.s.-a.i.* See: -(a)nę -.

-nęč – bulb, potato, tuber. *n.r.* n-poss.,
inc., n.sfx. -eh. As with other roots
and stems ending in *č*, the final *č*
shifts to θ everywhere except before *i,*
where it appears optionally as θ in
some constructions. unę́·θeh *bulb, potato, tuber* (R), kanę́·θeh *bulb; tuber,
tuberous or bulbous* (H 2484); -nęč -.
#áh: unęθeháh ‹potato-little› *it is*

small potatoes, the potato is small (H 2484); **-nęčihę:** unęčíhę ‹potato-in the middle of› *in the middle of the potato or tuber, one half of the potato or tuber* (H 2484); **-nęčihsak -:** kanęčihsá··khę· ‹it-potato-sought-many› *it seeks some potatoes* (RC 27:16), ranęčíhsa·ks ‹he-potato-seeks› *he is hunting for potatoes* (H 2484); **-nęčityę?T -:** ranęčityę?tha? ‹he-potato-arrive at-causes› *he is bringing in the potatoes* (H 2484); **-nęčiyu -:** kanęčí·yu· ‹it-potato-is great› *large potato* (H 2484); **-nęθača?kr -:** unęθačá?kreh ‹potato-wet› *the potatoes are, the potato is wet or soggy* (H 2484); **-nęθahča? = nahkw -:** ranęθahča?náhkhwa? ‹he-potato-spoils› *he is wasting potatoes, he is destroying potatoes* (H 2484); **-nęθah(e)r -:** ranę·θar ‹he-potato-puts up› *he drops potato, he sets potato, as one does when planting* (H 2484); **-nęθahęsči -:** kanęθahęsči ‹it-potato-black› *it is a black potato, the potato is black* (H 2484); **-nęθahninę -:** ranęθahnì·nęh ‹he-potato-buys› *he is buying potato* (H 2484); **-nęθahsa = 'nęhkw -:** yenęθahsa?nęhkhwa? ‹one-potato-buried-instrument› *cache for potatoes* (H 2484); **-nęθahs?a -:** ranęθáhs?ahs ‹he-potato-finishes› *he eats up potatoes* (H 2484); **-nęθahsthu -:** kanęθáhsthę ‹it-potato-is small› *small potato* (H 2484); **-nęθakari -:** ranęθaká·ryahs ‹he-potato-devours› *he devours the potato or tuber* (H 2484); **-nęθakęre -:** kanęθakę̀·re? ‹it-potato-is scarce› *potatoes are scarce* (H 2892); **-nęθaks -:** kanęθá·ksę· ‹it-potato-is bad› *the potato is bad, unfit for use, ill-favored* (H 2484); **-nęθakuhę -:** ranęθakúhęhs ‹he-potato-picks up-many› *he goes after potatoes, goes to bring potatoes* (H 2484); **-nęθakwahsT -:** kanęθákwahst ‹it-potato-is good› *good potato* (H 2484); **-nęθanha -:** kanęθánhę ‹it-potato-filled› *full of potatoes* (H 2484); **-nęθahrihnęhe? -:** kanęθahrihnę́he? ‹it-potato-spill-caused-going to› *mashed potatoes* (R); **-nęθaθe·?:** unęθá·θe·? ‹potato-new› *new potato, new potatoes* (H 2484); **-nęθaθray -:** unęθaθrà·yeh ‹potato-fresh› *the potato is raw, uncooked, not done* (H 2484); **-nęθathę? -:** kanęθá·thę?θ ‹it-potato-be dry-begins› *potato is (or are) drying, potato is (or are) becoming dry* (H 2484); **-nęθatya?T -:** ranęθatyá?tha? ‹he-potato-buys› *he buys potatoes* (H 2484); **-nęθawerhu -:** ranęθawérhuhs ‹he-potato-covers› *he covers potato, he is covering potato* (H 2484); **-nęθawih = si -:** ranęθawíhsyęhs ‹he-potato-give-undoes› *he pulls out potatoes, as from a cache or pit* (H 2484); **-nęθawi?T -:** ranęθawí?tha? ‹he-potato-give-causes› *he inserts potatoes, he sets potatoes* (H 2484); **-nęθa?k -:** ranęθá?kha? ‹he-potato-digs› *he digs (is digging) potatoes or tubers* (H 2484); **-nęθa?ke:** unęθá?kye ‹potato-at› *on (on the top of) the potato, or tuber* (H 2484); **-nę = θa?θ -:** kanę·θa?θ ‹it-potato-is of a size› *large potatoes* (H 2484); **-nęθeh =**

Tuscarora Pronunciation Key:
/a/ l<u>a</u>w; /e/ h<u>a</u>t; /i/ p<u>i</u>zza; /u/ t<u>u</u>ne; /ę/ h<u>in</u>t; /č/ <u>ch</u>eese; /h/ <u>h</u>oe; /m/ <u>m</u>other; /s/ <u>s</u>ame; /t/ <u>d</u>o (before a vowel y, or w), <u>t</u>oo (elsewhere); /k/ <u>g</u>ale (before a vowel y or w), <u>k</u>ale (elsewhere); /n/ i<u>nh</u>ale (before a consonant or word-final), <u>n</u>ote (elsewhere), /r/ hi<u>ss</u> (before a consonant or word-final), <u>r</u>un (trilled as in Italian, elsewhere); /w/ cuff (before a consonant other than y or word-final), <u>w</u>ay (elsewhere); /y/ fi<u>sh</u> (before a consonant or word-final), <u>y</u>ou (elsewhere), /θ/ <u>th</u>ing; /?/ (the sound between the vowels in unh-unh); /·/ long vowel, /́/ high pitch; /̀/ low pitch.

ke: unǫθéhkye ‹potato-at› *at the potato, at the place of the potato, at the
potato field* (H 2484); -nǫθehčrukri?:
unǫθehčrú·kri? ‹potato-'ness-rubbish›
*rejected or castaway potatoes, pieces
of decayed or old potatoes* (H 2484);
-nǫθehshayǫ?: unǫθéhshayǫ? ‹potato-
ill-favored› *an ill-favored, mean potato* (H 2484); -nǫθǫhrahw -: yenǫθǫ́h-
raws ‹one-potato-fry-causes› *she fries
potatoes* (H 2484); -nǫθǫhsǫ -: ranǫ-
θǫ́hsǫh ‹he-potato-parches› *he roasts
potato or tuber, he bakes potato or
tuber* (H 2484), kanǫθǫ́hsǫhk ‹it-po-
tato-was parched› *baked potato* (R);
-nǫθǫtihT -: yenǫθǫtíhtha? ‹one-potato-
make-causes› *she is cutting up the
potato or potatoes* (H 2484); -nǫ=
θǫ?ke: unǫθǫ́?kye ‹potato-at› *on, a-
gainst (as part of) the potato* (H 24
84); -nǫθihǫ: unǫθíhǫ ‹potato-in the
middle of› *in the middle of the potato
or tuber, one half of the potato or tuber* (H 2484); -nǫθu -: ranǫ́·θuh ‹he-
potato-is in water› *he boils potatoes*
(H 2484); -nǫθuha -: ranǫθúhahs ‹he-
potato-puts in water› *he puts potato or
tuber in liquid; hence, he boils potatoes* (H 2484); -nǫθuhča?T -: yenǫθuh-
čá?tha? ‹one-potato-remove-causes›
knife or other tool for paring potatoes
(H 2484); -nǫθuhči -: ranǫθúhčǫhs ‹he-
potato-removes› *he peals potatoes, he
pares potatoes* (H 2484); -nǫθuhkw -:
yenǫθúhkhwa? ‹one-potato-is in water-instrument› *pot or kettle for boiling
potatoes* (H 2484); -nǫθukri?: unǫθú·-
kri? ‹potato-rubbish› *rejected or castaway potatoes, pieces of decayed or
old potatoes* (H 2484); -nǫθuku -: ra-
nǫθú·kwahs ‹he-potato-be in water-undoes› *he takes potatoes out of the pot
or out of any liquid* (H 2484); -nǫ=
θu? -: kanǫ́·θu?θ ‹it-potato-be in wat-

er-begins› *potato(es) is (or are) becoming flooded over* (H 2484); ti -.
-nǫθa?θ -.#ú?y: tikanǫθa?θ?ú?y ‹so-it-
potato-is of a size-great› *potato is
very large* (H 2484); ti -. -nǫθa?θrǫ -.
#ú?y: tikanǫθa?θrǫ?ú?y ‹so-it-potato-is
so big-great› *potatoes are very large*
(H 2484); tha -. -nǫθane -: thyunǫθá·?-
ne? ‹unusual-it-potato-is present› *potatoes lie scattered about, lie about or
around* (H 2484).

-nǫčh - arm, sleeve. *n.r.* inaln: yenǫ́čheh
one's arm (RC 26:21), inc., n.sfx. -eh.
unǫ́čheh *arm* (R), *sleeve* (HS) [Gal-
latin «onuntcheh» 'Arm']; -nǫčhahra =
rak -: na?nǫčháhrara·ks ‹one=another-
arm-be a hole-eats› *one inoculates another* (HS); -nǫčhahwihsT -: ranǫčhah-
wíhs-ne? ‹he-arm-is strong› *his arm is
strong* (RC 24:9); -nǫčha?nihθku -:
wa?na?nǫčha?níhθku? ‹fact-one=an-
other-arm-picked off› *she picked the
arms out* (AG); -nǫčhǫt: ranǫ́čhǫ·t ‹he-
arm-possesses› *he has an arm, that is,
as part of his body, only* (H 2892);
-nǫčhukǫ?: unǫčhú·kǫ? ‹arm-less›
sleeveless (HS); tha -. -nǫčha?nihrhǫ -:
thayunǫčha?nírhǫk ‹unusual-it-arm-
stood up-much› *he had arms on* (AG).
-nǫčhahrarak - inoculate. *v.s.-t.* na?nǫ-
čháhrara·ks ‹one=another-arm-be a
hole-eats› *one inoculates another*
(HS).
-nǫčhukǫ? sleeveless. *n.s.* unǫčhú·kǫ?
‹arm-less› *sleeveless* (HS).
nǫči - dualic+future+repetitive. *v.pfx.* The
form nǫč - occurs before pronominal
prefixes that begin with the consonant
y, which consonant is dropped. The
form nǫθ - occurs before pronominal
prefixes that begin with the consonants *k* or *h*; with pronominal prefixes
that begin with *hs*, the final θ of the
prefix coalesces with the cluster to

yield **nęčh –**. The form **nęči –** occurs elsewhere.

–nęči ʔther – curl of hair. *n.r.* inaln: ranęčí ʔthereh *he is curly-headed, has curly hair* (H 2484), inc.. n.sfx. –eh. See also: **–či ʔther –**. unęčí ʔthereh *a curl of hair* (H 2484); **–nęči ʔtherakęw**: unęči ʔtherá·kęw ‹curl of hair-in› *in or under curls or a curled hair* (H 2484); **–nęči ʔtheraks –**: kanęči ʔtherá·ksę· ‹itcurl of hair-is bad› *the curl of hair is of poor quality, is ill-looking: the curl looks frowsy* (H 2484); **–nęči ʔ = therakT –**: unęčí ʔtherakwt ‹curl of hair-next to› *beside the curl, or curl of hair* (H 2484); **–nęči ʔtherakwahsT –**: kanęči ʔtherákwahst ‹it-curl of hair-is good› *the curl of hair is of good quality, looks well, is fine-looking* (H 2484), yenęči ʔtherákwahst ‹one-curl of hair-is good› *her curls are fine-looking, she has a fine head of curly hair, her curly locks are beautiful* (H 2484); **–nęči ʔ = therakweʔnh(e)r –**: kanęči ʔtherakwéʔnheʔr ‹it-curl of hair-is too short› *the curl of hair is short, the curl does not reach* (H 2484); **–nęči ʔtherara –**: ranęčí ʔtherahs ‹he-curl of hair-grabs› *he seizes the curl of hair, the head of curly hair, the person having the head of curly hair* (H 2484); **–nęči ʔthe = ra ʔke**: unęči ʔtherá ʔkye ‹curl of hair-at› *on, on the top of the curl of hair* (H 2484); **–nęči ʔtherehke**: unęči ʔtheréhkye ‹curl of hair-at› *at, in the curl or curls of hair* (H 2484); **–nęči ʔthereθ –**: kanęčí ʔthere·θ ‹it-curl of hair-is long›

it is a long curl, the curl is long (H 2484); **–nęči ʔtherę ʔ –**: kanęčí ʔtherę ʔθ ‹it-curl of hair-fall-begins› *the curl of hair falls, is falling* (H 2484); **–nęči ʔ = therę ʔke:** unęči ʔtherę ʔkye ‹curl of hair-at› *on, on the surface of the curl of hair* (H 2484); **–nęči ʔtheriyu –**: yenęči ʔtherí·yu· ‹one-curl of hair-is great› *her curls are large or fluffy, being abundant and long* (H 2484); **–nęči ʔtheru ʔthiy –**: ranęči ʔtheruthì·yę ‹he-curl of hair-sharpen› *he is handling, passing his hands over or through the curl or curls of hair* (H 2484).

nę́h very (emphatic) (RC 26:26). *part.* nę́h ì·nę ‹very far› *so far* (H-notebook); nę́h séʔči hę̀·we ‹very because where› *really, that's too bad* (R); **–yehnę – nę́h**: čéhnę nę́h ‹you!-allow very› *well, let's see now* (R); nę́h **–akwahsT –**: nę́h wákwahst ‹very it-is good› *very good* (HS).

–nęh – corn. *n.r.* n-poss., inc., n.sfx. –eh. unę́heh *corn (Zea mays)* (RC 3:65) [Lawson «Oonaha» 'Corn']; **–nęhači –**: kanęhači ʔ ‹it-corn-??› *the corn is black, it is black corn* (Hewitt considers this a shortened form of expected *kanęhahę́sči*, but this is unlikely on phonetic grounds) (H 2484); **–nę = hah(e)r –**: ranęháhrę ‹he-corn-puts up› *he sets, places corn grains (in the ground), hence, he plants corn* (H 2484); **–nęhahrę ʔke:** kanęharę́ ʔkye ‹itcorn-puts up-at› *at corn-planting (a subaudition of the word for time), this*

Tuscarora Pronunciation Key:
/a/ l**a**w; /e/ h**a**t; /i/ p**i**zza; /u/ t**u**ne; /ę/ h**i**nt; /č/ **ch**eese; /h/ **h**oe; /m/ **m**other; /s/ **s**ame; /t/ **d**o (before a vowel y, or w), **t**oo (elsewhere); /k/ **g**ale (before a vowel y or w), **k**ale (elsewhere); /n/ in**h**ale (before a consonant or word-final), **n**ote (elsewhere), /r/ hi**ss** (before a consonant or wordfinal), **r**un (trilled as in Italian, elsewhere); /w/ c**uff** (before a consonant other than y or word-final), **w**ay (elsewhere); /y/ fi**sh** (before a consonant or word-final), **y**ou (elsewhere), /θ/ **th**ing; /ʔ/ (the sound between the vowels in unh-unh); /·/ long vowel, /´/ high pitch; /`/ low pitch.

is the name of the month of April(?)
(H 2484); *March* (R); –nęhahsa'nę –:
kanęháhsa'nę' ‹it-corn-buries› *one has
buried corn, it is buried corn, one has
buried the corn (in a cache)* (H 2484);
–nęhahsęhti –: ranęhahsę́htih ‹he-corn-
refuses› *he spurns, refuses (as unworthy) the corn* (H 2484); –nęhahskwa =
ri –: unęháhskwari' ‹corn-be feeble›
*the mother-corn, that is, the corn from
which a certain kind may have been
derived: corn of an older growth (than
some other)* (H 2484); –nęhahsthu –:
kanęháhsthę ‹it-corn-is small› *the corn
grain is small* (H 2484); –nęhahwa =
ryakę –: unęhahwaryá·kę' ‹corn-white›
*white corn, the corn is white, it is
white corn* (H 2484); –nęhak– ranę́-
haks ‹he-corn-eats› *he eats corn* (H
2484); –nęhakaθne –: kanęhaká́θne' ‹it-
corn-is hard› *flint corn* (HS); –nęha =
kęrat: kanęhakę̀·rat ‹it-corn-is white›
white corn (RC 5:18), *flour corn* (H
2484); –nęhakęw: unę́hakęw ‹corn-in›
*in the corn, that is, in the grain or in
the growing corn* (H 2484); –nęha =
kęw.#hči: unęhakęw'áhči ‹corn-in-
very› *far into the corn heap or corn
field* (H 2484); –nęhakhwi' –: runęhá-
khwi'θ ‹he-corn-food-be the only one-
begins› *he is finishing a meal of corn*
(H 2484); –nęhaks –: kanęhá·ksę· ‹it-
corn-is bad› *the corn is bad (as to
quality)* (H 2484); –nęhakwahsT –: kanęhákwahst ‹it-corn-is good› *the corn
is good, it is good corn* (H 2484);
–nęhakwa'nahkw –: yenęhakwa'náhkhwa' ‹one-corn-pick up-causes-instrument› *corn-planter, sickle* (HS);
–nęhanęhwak(T) –: ranęhanę́hwaks ‹he-
corn-aches› *he longs for, desires corn*
(H 2484); –nęhanęT –: wa'na'nę́hanę·t
‹fact-one=another-corn-fed› *one gave
another corn to eat* (R); –nęhar –: ra-

nę́har ‹he-corn-is in› *he sets, places
corn grains (in the ground), hence, he
plants corn* (H 2484); –nęharihT –: ra-
nęharíhtha' ‹he-corn-be ripe-causes›
he cooks, is cooking the corn (H
2484), kanęharíhtha' ‹it-corn-be ripe-
causes› *a locust, its name means literally, it ripens corn (as a habit), perhaps, because it sings when the
weather is hottest* (H 2484); –nęhar =
kęhw –: runęharkę́hę ‹he-corn-has plenty› *he has an abundance of corn* (H
2484); –nęhaθri'r –: unęhaθrí'reh
‹corn-wrinkle› *corn that is shrunken,
a name of a certain kind of corn (this
is the common sweet corn)* (H 2484);
–nęhaT –: unę́ha·t ‹corn-stand› *pip*
(HS); –nęhath –: yunęhá·thę ‹it-corn-is
dry› *the corn is dry or seasoned* (H
2484); –nęhatha'T –: ranęhathá'tha'
‹he-corn-be dry-causes› *he is drying,
seasoning the corn* (H 2484); –nęha =
tihsthu –: kanęhatíhsthę ‹it-corn-are
small› *the corn grains are small* (H
2484); –nęhatkwerih –: ranęhatkwè·-
rihθ ‹he-corn-de-sires› *he fondly
wants the corn, desires the corn with
longing* (H 2484); –nęhaturę –: ranę-
hatù·ręh ‹he-corn-stores› *he puts corn,
the corn, away* (H 2484), runęhatù·ręh
‹he-corn-stores› *he fails to do with the
corn (as he would)* (H 2484); –nęha =
tyuθer –: unęhatyú·θer ‹corn-scrape
corn› *the corn is green, is yet in the
milk* (H 2484); –nęhayęthu –: wahranę-
hayę́·thu' ‹fact-he-corn-planted› *he
planted corn* (R); –nęha'ke: unęhá'kye
‹corn-at› *on, on the top of the corn,
either a single grain or on a heap of
ears or grains* (H 2484); –nęha'nihr –:
kanęhá'nihč ‹it-corn-stands up› *it sets
corn (grains), said of corn ears when
the grain buds begin to appear* (H
2484); –nęha'θ –: kanęha'θ ‹it-corn-is

of a size› *the corn grains are large (no singular form)* (H 2484); –nęha⁷θręn –: yunęhá⁷θrę· ‹it-corn-is clean› *the corn is clean, free from dirt* (H 2484); –nę = hehke: unęhéhkye ‹corn-at› *at the corn, at the place of corn* (H 2484); –nęheθ –: kanęhe·θ ‹it-corn-is long› *the corn grain is long* (H 2484); –nęhęh = sę –: kanęhéhsęhk ‹it-corn-parched› *parched corn* (RC 15:8); *canaille (canail or canell), a kind of coarse flour, it is between bran and the flour* (H 2484), ranęhéhsęh ‹he-corn-parches› *he roasts, parches corn* (H 2484); –nę = hętęhT –: yunęhé·tęht ‹it-corn-is poor› *the corn is poor (referring to corn that is growing)* (H 2484); –nęhethu –: ranęhé·thuhs ‹he-corn-put in fire-causes› *he puts the corn in the fire* (H 2484); –nęhęti –: kanęhé·tih ‹it-corn-makes› *it makes corn, said of growing corn when it is changing from the milk, or when the ears begin to show the grain buds* (H 2484); –nęhętwahT –: Kanęhé·twaht ‹it-corn-overlooks› *a certain fabulous insect, of which there were supposed to be only twelve in existence, for a part of the year only. In the fall, all the insects of creation collected themselves into twelve individuals, and these bore the name cited. Of course they were esteemed greatly by the sorcerers* (H 2484); –nęhę⁷ke: unęhę⁷kye ‹corn-at› *on or against the corn (as a part of it, or a fixture of it)* (H 2484); –nęhiyu –: kanęhí·yu· ‹it-corn-is great› *the corn grain is large*

(H 2484); –nęhu –: ranęhuh ‹he-corn-is in water› *he puts corn to soak, he puts corn in liquid (to soak or to cook)* (H 2484), ranęhu⁷ ‹he-corn-was in water› *he has corn cooking (in liquid)* (H 2484); –nęhučhę(T) –: kanęhúchę⁷ ‹it-corn-be in water-'ness-lays› *corn bread* (R); –nęhuhar –: ranęhúhar ‹he-corn-washes› *he washes, is washing the corn* (H 2484), wa⁷enęhuhà·re⁷ ‹fact-one-corn-washed› *one washed corn* (RC 3:53); –nęhuhare⁷T –: yenęhuharé⁷tha⁷ ‹one-corn-wash-causes› *a basket for washing corn, lit., one uses it to wash corn* (H 2484); –nęhukę⁷: runęhú·kę⁷ ‹he-corn-less› *he is cornless, without corn, has no corn* (H 2484); –nęhukey –: ranęhukę·yahs ‹he-corn-shells› *he shells, is shelling the corn* (H 2484); –nęhuku –: ranęhú·kwahs ‹he-corn-be in water-undoes› *he takes the corn from the kettle, he takes the corn from the water, as corn bread, etc.* (H 2484); –nęhuku –{dative III}.#ha·⁷: Akunęhukwatíha·⁷ ‹one-corn-put in water-undoes-for-characterized by› *Eel Clan* (AG); –nęhu = rahsT –: ranęhuráhstha⁷ ‹he-corn-??› *he soaks, wets or dampens the corn* (H 2484); –nęhu⁷kręr –: ranęhu⁷krę·rahs ‹he-corn-floats› *he is taking out the floating corn* (H 2484); –ne –. –nęhah = rihT –: nekanęhahríhtha⁷ ‹apart-it-corn-spill-causes› *it grinds, crushes the corn* (H 2484); –ne –. –nęha⁷θku –: nehranęhá⁷θkwahs ‹apart-he-corn-carries away› *he is drawing, carrying corn*

Tuscarora Pronunciation Key:
/a/ law; /e/ hat; /i/ pizza; /u/ tune; /ę/ hint; /č/ cheese; /h/ hoe; /m/ mother; /s/ same; /t/ do (before a vowel y, or w), too (elsewhere); /k/ gale (before a vowel y or w), kale (elsewhere); /n/ inhale (before a consonant or word-final), note (elsewhere), /r/ hiss (before a consonant or word-final), run (trilled as in Italian, elsewhere); /w/ cuff (before a consonant other than y or word-final), way (elsewhere); /y/ fish (before a consonant or word-final), you (elsewhere), /θ/ thing; /⁷/ (the sound between the vowels in unh-unh); /·/ long vowel, /´/ high pitch; /`/ low pitch.

(from one place to another) (H 2484);
ti -.-**nęhači**ʔ**tkwahnayę(T)** -: tikanęha-
čiʔtkwáhnayęʔ ‹so-it-corn-yellow-lays›
it is yellow corn (H 2484); **ti** -.-**nę** =
haʔθ -.**#ú**ʔ**y**: tikanęhaʔθʔúʔy ‹so-it-
corn-is of a size-great› *the corn grain
is very large* (H 2484); **te**ʔ -**nęhęte**:
teʔ unęhę́·te ‹what corn-certain one›
What kind (species) of corn is it? (H
2484); **te**ʔ **ti** -.-**nęhu**ʔ**nę** -: teʔ tikanę-
húʔnę· ‹what so-it-corn-is a kind of›
What kind (shape) of corn is it? (H
2484); **ù·nę** -**weh**- **ha**ʔ -**nęharihT** -:
ù·nę kà·weh haʔ kanęharíhthaʔ ‹now
it-speaks the it-corn-boil-causes› *now
speaks the corn-ripener (said when
you can hear the locusts buzzing —the
hotter the day, the more they will
buzz)* (L 49).

nę́h -**akwahsT** - very good. *part.* nę́h
wákwahst ‹very it-is good› *very good*
(HS).

nę́h ì·nę ‹very far› *so far* (H-notebook).
part.

nę́h séʔ**či hę̀·we** ‹very because where›
really, that's too bad (R). *part.*

-**nęhači** - black corn. *dv.n.s.* A loanword
from another Northern Iroquoian language. kanę́hačiʔ ‹it-corn-??› *the corn
is black, it is black corn* (Hewitt considers this a shortened form of expected *kanęhahę́sči*, but this is unlikely
on phonetic grounds) (H 2484).

-**nęhah(e)r** - plant corn. *v.s.-a.i.* ranęháhrę
‹he-corn-puts up› *he sets, places corn
grains (in the ground), hence, he
plants corn* (H 2484).

-**nęhahrę**ʔ**ke** corn-planting time; March;
April. *n.s.* kanęharę́ʔkye ‹it-corn-puts
up-at› *at corn-planting (a subaudition
of the word for time), this is the name
of the month of April(?)* (H 2484);
March (R).

-**nęhahskwari** - mother-corn. *n.s.* unęháhskwariʔ ‹corn-be feeble› *the mother-
corn, that is, the corn from which a
certain kind may have been derived:
corn of an older growth (than some
other)* (H 2484).

-**nęhahwaryakę** - white corn. *n.s.* unęhah-
waryá·kęʔ ‹corn-white› *white corn, the
corn is white, it is white corn* (H 24
84).

-**nęhaka**θ**ne** - flint corn. *dv.n.s.* kanęhakáθneʔ ‹it-corn-is hard› *flint corn*
(HS).

-**nęhakęrat** - white corn, flour corn. *dv.
n.s.* A loanword from another Northern Iroquoian language. kanęhakę̀·-
rat ‹it-corn-is white› *white corn* (RC
5:18), *flour corn* (H 2484).

-**nęhakwa**ʔ**nahkw** - corn-planter, sickle.
dv.n.s. yenęhakwaʔnáhkhwaʔ ‹one-
corn-pick up-causes-instrument› *corn-
planter, sickle* (HS).

-**nęhar** - plant corn. *v.s.-a.i.* ranę́har ‹he-
corn-is in› *he sets, places corn grains
(in the ground), hence, he plants corn*
(H 2484).

-**nęharihT** - locust. *dv.n.s.* kanęharíhthaʔ
‹it-corn-be ripe-causes› *a locust, its
name means literally, it ripens corn
(as a habit), perhaps, because it sings
when the weather is hottest* (H 2484).

-**nęha**θ**ri**ʔ**r** - sweet corn. *n.s.* unęhaθríʔreh
‹corn-wrinkle› *corn that is shrunken,
a name of a certain kind of corn (this
is the common sweet corn)* (H 2484).

-**nęhaT** - pip. *n.s.* unę́ha·t ‹corn-stand›
pip (HS).

-**nęhatyu**θ**er** - green corn. *n.s.* unęha-
tyú·θer ‹corn-scrape corn› *the corn is
green, is yet in the milk* (H 2484).

-**nęha·**ʔ - be old. *v.r.-s.i.* stat: -ɸ, prog: -,
prp: -, dst: -, caus: -, rvs: -, dat: -,
inc.-ɸ-ag./pat. yunęha·ʔ *it is old* (R);
-**nęha·**ʔ -: unęha·ʔ ‹be old› *long ago*
(MP); -**nęha·**ʔ**.#áh**: unęha·ʔáh ‹be old-

little⟩ *old, oldness: long ago, once u-pon a time* (R); **-nẹha·ʔ.#áh.#kẹheʔ:** kakunẹhaʔahkẹheʔ ⟨they-are old-little-deceased⟩ *ancients, old ones* (R); **-nẹ=ha·ʔ.#kẹhaʔnẹʔ:** kakunẹhaʔkẹhaʔnẹʔ ⟨they-are old-many⟩ *old-timers* (AW 55), *old-fashioned people* (AW 98); **-aʔwnanẹha·ʔke:** uʔwnanẹhá·ʔkye ⟨land-be old-at⟩ *in the old country* (L 61); **-nẹhsanẹha·ʔ-:** unẹhsanẹha·ʔ ⟨house-be old⟩ *old house* (PC); **-rih=wanẹha·ʔ-:** urihwanẹha·ʔ ⟨matter-be old⟩ *old songs* (R); **-nẹha·ʔ.#áh -aʔnẹ-:** unẹha·ʔáh wá·ʔnẹʔ ⟨be old-little it becomes⟩ *it becomes inveterate* (HS); **haʔ -nẹha·ʔ.#áh.#kẹheʔ:** haʔ kakunẹhaʔahkẹheʔ ⟨the they-are old-little-deceased⟩ *the old ones* (HS).

-nẹha·ʔ- long ago. *n.s.* unẹha·ʔ ⟨be old⟩ *long ago* (MP).

-nẹha·ʔ.#áh old, oldness; long ago, once upon a time. *n.s.* unẹha·ʔáh ⟨be old-little⟩ *old, oldness; long ago, once u-pon a time* (R).

-nẹha·ʔ.#áh -aʔnẹ- become inveterate. *v.s-a.i.* unẹha·ʔáh wá·ʔnẹʔ ⟨be old-lit-tle it becomes⟩ *it becomes inveterate* (HS).

-nẹha·ʔ.#áh.#kẹheʔ ancients, old ones. *n.s.* kakunẹhaʔahkẹheʔ ⟨they-are old-little-deceased⟩ *ancients, old ones* (R); haʔ kakunẹhaʔahkẹheʔ ⟨the they-are old-little-deceased⟩ *the old ones* (HS).

-nẹha·ʔ.#kẹhaʔnẹʔ old-timers, old-fash-ioned people. *n.s.* kakunẹhaʔkẹhaʔnẹʔ ⟨they-are old-many⟩ *old-timers* (AW 55), *old-fashioned people* (AW 98).

-nẹheratẹ- thank. *v.r.-t.* hab: -hs ~ -h, pnt: -, stat: -, prog: -, prp: -, dst: -Nyẹ-, caus: -hT-, rvs: -, dat: -, n-inc. naʔnẹherá·tẹhs *one thanks another* (HS); **-aʔnẹnẹheratẹhT-:** yuʔnẹnẹhe-rá·tẹht ⟨it-itself-thank-causes⟩ *meritor-ious* (HS); **-ne-.-aʔnẹnẹheratẹ-:** nekaʔ-nẹnẹherá·tẹh ⟨apart-I-myself-thank⟩ *I am thankful* (AG); **-ne-.-aʔnẹnẹhe=ratẹnyẹ-:** waʔtkayẹʔnẹnẹheratẹ·nyẹʔ ⟨fact-apart-they-themselves-thanked-much⟩ *they gave thanks* (RC 12:12); **haʔ -nẹheratehT-:** haʔ kanẹherá·tẹht ⟨the it-thank-causes⟩ *welcome* (HS); **kwẹhs -nẹheratẹhT-:** kwẹhs ahrunẹhe-ratẹ́hnek ⟨no unknown-he-thank-cause⟩ *he is ungrateful* (HS).

-nẹheratehT- welcome. *dv.n.s.* haʔ ka-nẹherá·tẹht ⟨the it-thank-causes⟩ *wel-come* (HS).

-nẹhẹhsẹ- canaille, coarse corn flour, parched corn. *dv.n.s.* kanẹhẹ́hsẹhk ⟨it-corn-parched⟩ *parched corn* (RC 15:8); *canaille (canail or canell), a kind of coarse flour, it is between bran and the flour* (H 2484).

-nẹhẹtwahT- Twelve Mystical Bugs. *dv.n.s.* Kanẹhẹ́·twaht ⟨it-corn-over-looks⟩ *a certain fabulous insect, of which there were supposed to be only twelve in existence, for a part of the year only. In the fall, all the insects of creation collected themselves into twelve individuals, and these bore the name cited. Of course they were es-teemed greatly by the sorcerers* (H 24 84).

-**nęhka̲r** – cut hair. *v.r.-a.i.* hab: -çhs, pnt: -, stat: -ę·, prog: -, prp: -, dst: -, caus: -, rvs: -, dat: -, n-inc. ranę́hkaręhs *he cuts hair* (HS); -**nęhka̲rahčr** –: yunęhkaráhčreh ‹it-cuts hair-'ness› *scissors* (HS); -**a'nęnęhka̲r** –: yu'nęnę́hkarę· ‹it-itself-cut hair› *it is shorn* (HS).

-**nęhka̲rahčr** – scissors. *dv.n.s.* yunęhkaráhčreh ‹it-cuts hair-'ness› *scissors* (HS).

-**nęhkʷahT** – behead, cut off head. *v.s.-a.i.* ranęhkwáhtha' ‹he-X-cuts off› *he beheads, he cuts off its head* (HS).

-**nęhkwa'čra̲yę'ner** – healer, medicine man, medical practitioner. *dv.n.s.* ranęhkwa'črayę'nè·rih ‹he-medicine-'ness-knows› *medicine man, medical practitioner, healer* (HS).

-**nęhkwa'T** – anodyne, antidote, drug, medicine. *n.r.* aln: runęhkwá'čhę' *he has medicine* (R), inc., n.sfx. -eh. Requires the addition of the nominalizer when incorporated. See also **ęnę́hkwa'T.** yunę́hkwa't *anodyne, antidote, drug, medicine* (RC 6:7); -**nęhkwa'T** –. **#ęwe:** unęhkwa'tʔę̀·we ‹medicine-genuine› *brandy* (HS); -**nęhkwa'čra̲raku** –: ęknęhkwa'črará·ku' ‹prediction-I-medicine-'ness-choose› *I will choose a medicine* (RC 15:3), wa'kayenęhkwa'črarakúhę' ‹fact-they-medicine-'ness-chose-much› *they chose medicine for themselves* (RC 10:7); -**nęh=kwa'čra̲tya'T** –: ękayenęhkwá'čratya't ‹prediction-they-medicine-'ness-buy› *they will buy medicine* (AW 98); -**nęhkwa'čra̲yę'ner** –: ranęhkwa'črayę'nè·rih ‹he-medicine-'ness-knows› *medicine man, medical practitioner, healer* (HS); -**nęhkwa'črę̲te:** unęhkwa'črę́·te ‹medicine-'ness-certain one› *a certain medicine* (R); **kwęhs –či** -. -**nęhkwa̲'nę'** –: kwęhs ęθayunęhkwá·'nę'k ‹no unknown-again-it-medicine-become› *it is irremediable* (HS).

-**nęhkwa'T** –.**#ęwe** brandy. *n.s.* unęhkwa'tʔę̀·we ‹medicine-genuine› *brandy* (HS).

-**nęhkʷekT** – close-minded person, ninny. *n.s.* unę́hkwekt ‹X-close-cause› *close-minded person, ninny* (HS).

-**nęhkwihskri** – spruce *(Picea* sp.). *n.r.* n-poss., n-inc., n.sfx. -'. unęhkwíhskri' *spruce (Picea* sp.) (H-notebook).

-**nęhkwihst** – pod. *n.r.* n-poss., n-inc., n.sfx. -eh. unęhkwíhsteh *pod* (R).

-**nęhnur** – swamp oak. *n.r.* n-poss., n-inc., n.sfx. -ę'. unęhnù·rę' *swamp oak* (H-notebook).

-**nęhnyeyę** – desire. *v.r.-t.* hab: -, pnt: -', stat: -, prog: -, prp: -, dst: -, caus: -, rvs: -, dat: -, n-inc. wa'enęhnyè·yę' *one desired* (RC 29:4).

-**nęhr** – scalp. *n.r.* See: -**(ę)nęhr** -.

-**nęhra̲yehnę** – Flying Head. *n.s.* See: -**(ę)nęhra̲yehnę** -.

-**nęhra'nihr** – bump, bunt. *v.s.-t.* See: -**(ę)nęhra'nihr** -.

-**nęhra's** – milk; pap, udder. *n.r.* n-poss., inc., n.sfx. -eh. unęhrá'seh *milk* (R); *pap, udder* (HS); -**nęhra'sahkw** –: na'nęhra'sáhkwahs ‹one=another-milk-takes› *one weans, one takes milk from another* (HS); -**nęhra'saku** –: kanęhra'sá·ku' ‹it-milk-picks up› *cow* (R); -**nęhra'sarhu** –: yenęhra'sárhuhs ‹one-milk-mixes› *one churns* (HS); -**nęh=ra'sarhuhsT** –: yenęhra'sarhúhstha' ‹one-milk-mix-causes› *one churns* (HS); -**nęhra'saT** –: yunęhrá'sa·t ‹it-udder-stands› *it has milk in it; cow* (HS); -**nęhra'sa'nahkw** –: ranęhra'sa'náhkhwa' ‹he-milk-causes-instrument› *he milks it* (HS).

-**nęhra'sahkw** – wean. *v.s.-t.* na'nęhra'sáhkwahs ‹one=another-milk-takes› *one weans, one takes milk from another* (HS).

-nęhra²saku - cow. *dv.n.s.* kanęhra²sá·-ku² ‹it-milk-picks up› *cow* (R).

-nęhra²sarhu - churn. *v.s.-a.i.* yenęhra²sárhuhs ‹one-milk-mixes› *one churns* (HS).

-nęhra²sarhuhsT - churn. *v.s.-a.i.* yenęhra²sarhúhstha² ‹one-milk-mix-causes› *one churns* (HS).

-nęhra²saT - cow. *dv.n.s.* yunęhrá²sa·t ‹it-udder-stands› *cow* (HS).

-nęhra²sa²nahkw - milk. *v.s.-t.* ranęhra²sa²náhkhwa² ‹he-milk-causes-instrument› *he milks it* (HS).

-nęhru - tulip tree, lignum vitae, whitewood. *n.s.* See: -(ę)nęhru -.

-nęhruhar - lacrosse. *n.s.* See: -(ę)=nęhruhar -.

-nęhruhči - scalp; take of headdress. *v.s.-a.i.* See: -(ę)-nęhruhči -.

-nęhruhčr - hat. *n.s.* See: -(ę)nęhruhčr -.

-nęhruhčręti - hatter. *dv.n.s.* See: -(ę)=nęhruhčręti -.

-nęhrur - shear. *v.s.-t.* See: -(ę)nęhruhčr -.

-nęhs - cage, cottage, house, hut; umbrella; hut or lodge of an animal such as a beaver or muskrat. *n.r.* aln: aknéhsawęh *my house* (R), inc., n.sfx. -eh. unéhseh *cage, cottage, house, hut, umbrella; hut or lodge of an animal such as a beaver or muskrat* (HS) [Lawson «Oinouse» 'House']; -nęhs -. #áh: unęhseháh ‹house-little› *a small house or umbrella, houseling* (H 248 4); -nęhs -.#ęwe: unęhsehę·we ‹house-genuine› *the genuine house, the natural or original house; this is the modern name of the ancient bark-*

house (H 2484); -nęhs -.#ú²y: unęhsehú²y ‹house-great› *a great or large house or umbrella* (H 2484); -nęh=sača²tuh -: yunęhsačá²tuh ‹it-house-is cool› *the house is cool, chilly; the house is cold; said of a house that is so poorly built that it is difficult to keep it warm in winter or cold weather* (H 2484); -nęhsačhu²kuw -: unęhsačhú²ku· ‹house-be rich› *(it is) a richly furnished house* (H 2484); -nęhsah=rahT -: unęhsáhraht ‹house-put up-cause› *it is a great, massive house; it is an awful house* (H 2484); -nęh=sahrar -: yunęhsáhrarę ‹it-house-is a hole› *window* (R); -nęhsah0uh -: ranęhsah0úhahs ‹he-house-paints› *he paints the house, he paints houses, he is painting the house* (H 2484); -nęh=sahsthu -: kanęhsáhsthę ‹it-house-is small› *it is a small house or umbrella* (H 2484); -nęhsahtirahT -: ranęhsahtì·rahč ‹he-house-be durable-causes› *he strengthens the house* (H 2484); -nęhsahwačiyu -: kanęhsahwačí·yu· ‹it-house-breadth-is great› *the house or room is wide, it is a wide house* (H 2484); -nęhsahwaryakę -: unęhsahwaryá·kę² ‹house-white› *white house* (PC); -nęhsahwa0ahsthu -: kanęhsahwa0áhsthę ‹it-house-breadth-is small› *it is a narrow house or room, the house or room is narrow* (H 2484); -nęhsakahrę(w) -: yunęhsakáhrę·² ‹it-house-is an opening› *the house has an opening, an aperture* (H 2484); -nęh=sakarahrę -: kanęhsakaráhrę· ‹it-house-*

---

is thin› *the house is thin, that is, its sides are thin* (H 2484); **-nęhsakęw**: unę́hsakęw ‹house-in› *in a house* (RC 11:16); *in the house, under the house* (H 2484); **-nęhsakęw.#hči**: unęhsakęwʔáhči ‹house-in-very› *far into or under the house* (H 2484); **-nęhsakT**: unę́hsakwt ‹house-next to› *beside, near the house* (H 2484); **-nęhsa = kwahsT –**: kanę́hsákwahst ‹it-house-is good› *it is a good house or room (in the latter sense, it means the parlor of modern houses)* (H 2484); **-nęhsa = kʷek –**: kanę́hsakwé·kę ‹it-house-is closed› *the whole house, meaning the entire audience in a building* (H 2484); **-nęhsakweʔniyu –**: ranę́hsakweʔnì·yuʔ ‹he-house-is the principal one› *proprietor* (HS); **-nęhsakeθku –**: ranę́hsakyé·θkwahs ‹he-house-raises› *he erects a house, is rearing a house* (H 2484); **-nęhsanę –**: kanę́hsanęh ‹it-house-guards› *a cricket (its literal meaning being it watches the house, so called from a habit of the cricket: when it gains an entrance into the house, it remains quiet so long as it hears someone moving about)* (H 2484), ranę́hsanęh ‹he-house-guards› *he watches the house, is watching the house* (H 2484); **-nęhsanęha·ʔ –**: unę́hsanęha·ʔ ‹house-be old› *old house* (PC); **-nęhsanurę –**: kanę́hsanú·rę· ‹it-house-is precious› *palace, parlor* (HS); **-nęhsaθtkaʔT –**: unęhsáθtkaʔt ‹house-vomit-cause› *it is a filthy house* (H 2484); **-nęhsatarinę –**: kanę́hsatarí·nę·ʔ ‹it-house-??› *death, disease, pestilence, or misfortune that brings death* (H 2484); **-nęhsatawę –**: yunęhsatá·wę· ‹it-house-is warm› *it is a warm house, or the house is warm: it is a warm house, meaning hereby that it is so built that it is an easy matter to keep

it warm in cold weather (H 2484); **-nęhsataʔkwar –**: yunęhsatáʔkwaʔr ‹it-house-pressed close to› *house hugged it* (RC 34:10); **-nęhsatekar –**: runęhsatekà·rę ‹he-house-took from› *he despoils house* (HS); **-nęhsatetʔ –**: ranęhsaté·tʔahs ‹he-house-lines› *he lathes* (HS), ęhranęhsaté·tʔaʔ ‹prediction-he-house-line› *he will lathe* (HS); **-nęh = satetʔahsT –**: yenęhsatetʔáhsthaʔ ‹one-house-line-causes› *lathe* (HS); **-nęh = sathęʔ –**: kanęhsá·thęʔθ ‹it-house-be dry-begins› *the house is drying, is becoming dry* (H 2484); **-nęhsathuʔ**: yunęhsá·thuʔ ‹it-house-cold› *the house is cold, is subject to cold, it not built warm: it is a cold house* (H 2484); **-nęhsatihar –**: ranęhsatíhar ‹he-house-hang› *he makes an addition to the house* (H 2484); **-nęhsatihsthu –**: kanęhsatíhsthę ‹it-house-are small› *the houses are small, diminutive* (H 24 84); **-nęhsatukęht –**: unęhsatukę́hti ‹house-holy› *sanctuary* (HS); **-nęhsa = tyaʔT –**: ranęhsatyáʔthaʔ ‹he-house-buys› *he buys, is buying the house* (H 2484); **-nęhsawęhte –**: yunęhsawę́hteʔ ‹it-house-is between two things› *it is a house between (two others)* (H 28 92), Kanęhsawę́hteʔ ‹it-house-is between two things› *House-In-Between (male proper name)* (H 2484); **-nęh = sawyęhw –**: ranęhsawyę́hę ‹he-house-know how-caused› *he knows how to build a house: this is another name of a carpenter* (H 2484); **-nęhsayę(T) –**: kanę́hsayęʔ ‹it-house-lays› *the house lies, is established, stands* (H 2484); **-nęhsaʔke**: unęhsáʔkye ‹house-at› *on, on the top of the house or umbrella* (H 2484); *roof* (HS); **-nęhsa'nek –**: yunę́hsaʔneks ‹it-house-burns› *burning house* (PC), waʔunę́hsaʔnek ‹fact-it-house-burned› *house burned* (PC);

-nẹhsa̱ʔnẹθ -: kanę́hsaʔnẹ·θ ‹it-house-is thick› *the house is thick, that is, its sides are: the sides of the house are thick* (H 2484); -nẹhsa'ne -: kanęhsá·ʔneʔ ‹it-house-is present› *house protrudes, house stands out* (H 2892); -nẹhsa'nẹhra̱r -: unẹhsaʔnę́hrareh ‹house-self-dirt-be in› *it is a dirty house* (H 2484); -nẹhsaʔnihθT -: yenẹhsaʔníhθthaʔ ‹one-house-stand up-causes› *the house one erects: this is the descriptive name of an umbrella* (H 2484); -nẹhsaʔθ -: kanęhsaʔθ ‹it-house-is of a size› *the houses are large* (H 2484); -nẹhsaʔθrẹn -: yunęhsá·ʔθrẹ·n ‹it-house-is clean› *the house is clean* (H 2484); -nẹhsehke: unęhséhkye ‹house-at› *at the house or at the place of the house* (H 2484); -nẹhseθ -: kanęhse·θ ‹it-house-is long› *the house is long, it is a long house* (H 2484); *longhouse* (R); -nẹhseθ -.#áh: kanęhse·θʔáh ‹it-house-is long-little› *the house is quite long, is rather long* (H 2484); -nẹhseθ.#ke: kanęhsé·θkye ‹it-house-is long-at› *at longhouse* (RC 26:8); -nẹhseθẹ.#ke: kanęhseθẹ́·kye ‹it-house-is long-many-at› *at longhouses* (RC 3:4); -nẹhsẹt: yunę́hsẹ·t ‹it-house-possesses› *there is a room or house to it, said of a room or house that has a connecting room, or of a building that has an outhouse attached to it* (H 2484); -nẹhsẹnhe -: Kanęhsę́nheʔ ‹it-house-is alive› *Live-House (male proper name)* (H 2484); -nẹhsẹtẹhT -: yunęhsę́·tẹht ‹it-house-is

poor› *it is a poorly furnished house, a house bespeaking poverty* (H 2484); -nẹhsẹti -: ranęhsę́·tih ‹he-house-makes› *architect* (HS); *he makes a house: he makes a house as a profession, hence, a carpenter* (H 2484); -nẹhsẹʔke: unęhsę́ʔkye ‹house-at› *against, or on the side of (as a part of) the house or umbrella* (H 2484); -nẹh=sẹ'ni -: ranęhsę́·ʔnyẹhs ‹he-house-throws› *he leaves the house (habitually) (said of one who leaves his house daily or periodically)* (H 2484); -nẹhshẹ: kanę́hshẹ ‹it-house-in the middle of› *in the middle of the house (modern)* (R), unę́hahẹ ‹house-in the middle of› *in the middle of the house, in the middle of the floor* (H 2484); -nẹhi -: kahnę́hsih ‹it-house-is a group› *the house is full (said of a house full of people)* (H 2484); -nẹhsirehT -: Kahnęhsiréhthaʔ ‹it-house-move through-causes› *Move-Through-House (female proper name)* (H 2484); -nẹh=siyu -: kahnęhsí·yu· ‹it-house-is great› *it is a large, spacious house* (H 2484); -nẹhskarẹʔre -: kanęhskarę́ʔreʔ ‹it-house-is sloped› *the house is inclined, is out of plumb* (H 2484); -nẹhskari -: ranęhská·ryahs ‹he-house-devours› *he creates a disturbance in the house, he robs the house by breaking into the house* (H 2484); *burglar* (HS), kanęhská·ryahs ‹it-house-devours› *it devours the house (as a disease when it attacks successively the members of the same family), it disorders, commits outrages in the house* (H 2484); **-nęhskęhyaT** -: kanęhskę́hya·t ‹it-house-extends from› *the bounds of the house; hence, at the very side of the house* (H 2484); **-nęhskhę**: kanę́hskhę ‹it-house-in the middle of› *in the middle of the house* (archaic) (H 2484); **-nęhsku** -: ranę́hskwahs ‹he-house-picks up› *he steals, is stealing (literally, he takes the house, but use has made it mean to steal)* (H 2484), ęhranę́hskuʔ ‹prediction-he-house-pick up› *he will steal* (HS); **-nęhskuʔye** -: runęhskúʔye· ‹he-house-bends› *thief*; **-nęhskuʔyehčr** -: unęhskuʔyéhčreh ‹house-bends-'ness› *theft* (HS); **-nęhsuhar** -: unęhsúhareh ‹house-tip› *the roof or top-surface of the house* (H 2484); **-nęhsuhar** -: ranęhsúhar ‹he-house-washes› *he dedicates* (H 2484); **-nęhsuharaʔke**: unęhsuharáʔkye ‹house-tip-at› *on the top of the house, on the summit of the house* (H 2484); **-nęhsuhriʔ** -: kanęhsúhriʔθ ‹it-house-ruin-begins› *the house is falling to pieces, is tottering to its fall or ruin* (H 2484); **-nęh=sukęhsthę** -: yunęhsukę́hsthęʔ ‹it-house-be forked-caused-many› *the house has rooms, that is, the house is divided into branches or parts* (H 24 84); **-nęhsuryęthu** -: ranęhsuryę́·thuhs ‹he-house-??› *he ruins, destroys the house (by crushing or pulling it to pieces)* (H 2484); **-nęhsut**: kanę́hsu·t ‹it-house-stands› *the house stands* (H 2484), yunę́hsu·t ‹it-house-stands› *its house stands, there is room in the house to spare* (H 2484); **-nęhsuʔ=k(e)r** -: yunęhsúʔkyer ‹it-house-floats› *the house floats, is floating (the liquid is understood)* (H 2484); **-nęhsuʔ=krahteʔ** -: yunęhsuʔkráhteʔ ‹it-house-floats-going to› *the house goes floating* (H 2484); **-nęhsyęti** -: kanęhsyę́·tiʔ

‹it-house-extends out› *it is an extended house, one lengthened by making an addition to its end* (H 2484), ranęhsyę́·tiʔ ‹he-house-extends out› *he extends house, he builds an addition* (HS), *he extends the house (lengthwise)* (H 2484); **-nęhsyętiʔT** -: ękęnęhsyę́·tiʔt ‹prediction-I=you-house-extend-cause› *I will confederate you* (AG), kakhenęhsyętíʔthaʔ ‹I=them-house-extend-cause› *I am confederating them* (AG), kakhenęhsyętíʔnę ‹I=them-house-extend-caused› *I have confederated them* (AG); **-či** -. **-nęh=seθ** -: θhrunę́hse·θ ‹again-he-house-is long› *His-House-Is-Very-Long (name of a male person)* (H 2484); **-ne** -. **-nęhsahruT** -: nekanęhsáhrut ‹two-it-house-??› *they two are on opposite sides of the house, they two occupy opposite sides of the same fire in a house* (H 2484); **-ne** -. **-nęhsake** -: nekanęhsá·kye· ‹two-it-house-is in number› *there are two houses (modern)* (H 2484); **-ne** -. **-nęhsawęręhT** -: nekanęhsawęrę́hthaʔ ‹a-part-it-house-diminish-causes› *it takes up room in the house uselessly, it is in the way in the house, it unnecessarily takes up room in the house* (H 2484); **-ne** -. **-nęhske** -: nekanę́hskye· ‹two-it-house-is in number› *there are two houses (archaic)* (H 2484); **-ne** -. **-nęhsyaʔk** -: nekanęhsyáʔkę ‹two-it-house-broke› *the house is divided (into two rooms) (said of a partition)* (H 2484); ti -. **-nęhsaʔθ** -. **#úʔy**: tikanęhsaʔθʔúʔy ‹so-it-house-is of a size-great› *it is a great large house* (H 2484); ti -. **-nęhseθ** -. **#áh**: tikanęhse·θʔáh ‹so-it-house-is long-little› *it is a short house* (H 2484); ti -. **-nęhsęti** -. **#úʔy**: tihrunęhsęti·ʔúʔy ‹so-he-house-made-great› *he built a large house* (RC 24:7); **-aʔnęhstahkw** -: yuʔ-

nẹhstáhkẹ ‹it-itself-house-gathered› *foundation* (HS); –a'nẹnẹhsatekẹ –: yu'ẹnẹnẹhsaté·kẹ· ‹it-itself-house-joined› *the houses are side by side (this is a singular form, but use has given it a dual sense)* (H 2484); –a'nẹnẹhsẹ' = neT –: ra'nẹnẹhsẹ'né·tha' ‹he-himself-house-hides behind› *he goes alongside of the house, he hides behind the house* (H 2484); –a'nẹnẹhskwahčra = kẹw: u'nẹnẹhskwáhčrakẹw ‹self-house-pick up-'ness-in› *stealthily* (HS); –a'nẹnẹhskwahT –: u'nẹnẹ́hskwaht ‹self-house-pick up-cause› *stealth* (HS), ra'nẹnẹhskwáhtha' ‹he-himself-house-pick up-causes› *he goes stealthily* (HS); –nẹhs –.#áh –ahtki' = ẹhkw –: unẹhseháh yẹhtki'ẹ́hkhwa' ‹house-little one-excretes-instrument› *outhouse, privy* (HS); –nẹhsakT –ter = 'ahθẹti –: unẹhsakwt kater'ahθẹ́·tih ‹house-next to it-sod-makes› *grass* (HS); ha' –nẹhsku –: ha' yenẹ́hskwahs ‹the one-house-picks up› *theft* (HS); ha' –a'nẹhskẹ'θrahkw –: ha' yu'nẹhskẹ'θráhkẹ ‹the it-itself-house-supported-instrument› *basis* (HS); ì·nẹ –a'nẹnẹhsarẹ –: ì·nẹ yu'nẹnẹ́hsarẹ' ‹far it-itself-house-added› *the houses are, set far apart* (H 2484); núhskẹ –a = 'nẹnẹhsarẹ –: núhskẹ yu'nẹnẹ́hsarẹ' ‹near it-itself-house-??› *the houses are close together* (H 2484).

–nẹhs –.#áh –ahtki'ẹhkw – outhouse, privy. *n.s.* unẹhseháh yẹhtki'ẹ́hkhwa' ‹house-little one-excretes-instrument› *outhouse, privy* (HS).

–nẹhs –.#ẹwe ancient bark-house. *n.s.* unẹhsehẹ̀·we ‹house-genuine› *the genuine house, the natural or original house: this is the modern name of the ancient bark-house* (H 2484).

–nẹhsahrar – window. *dv.n.s.* yunẹhsáhrarẹ ‹it-house-is a hole› *window* (R).

–nẹhsakT –ter'ahθẹti – grass. *n.s.* unẹ́hsakwt kater'ahθẹ́·tih ‹house-next to it-sod-makes› *grass* (HS).

–nẹhsakwahsT – parlor. *dv.n.s.* kanẹhsákwahst ‹it-house-is good› *it is a good house or room (in the latter sense, it means the parlor of modern houses)* (H 2484).

–nẹhsak"ek – the house (audience). *dv.n.s.* kanẹhsakwé·kẹ ‹it-house-is closed› *the whole house, meaning the entire audience in a building* (H 2484).

–nẹhsakwe'niyu – proprietor. *dv.n.s.* ranẹhsakwe'nì·yu' ‹he-house-is the principal one› *proprietor* (HS).

–nẹhsakeθku – erect a house, rear a house. *v.s.-a.i.* ranẹhsakyé·θkwahs ‹he-house-raises› *he erects a house, he is rearing a house* (H 2484).

–nẹhsanẹ – cricket. *dv.n.s.* kanẹ́hsanẹh ‹it-house-guards› *a cricket (its literal meaning being it watches the house, so called from a habit of the cricket; when it gains an entrance into the house, it remains quiet so long as it hears someone moving about)* (H 24 84).

–nẹhsanurẹ – parlor. *dv.n.s.* kanẹhsanú·rẹ· ‹it-house-is precious› *parlor* (HS).

–nẹhsatarinẹ – death, disease, misfortune,

pestilence. *dv. n.s.* kanęhsatarí·nę·ˀ ‹it-house-??› *death, disease, pestilence, or misfortune that brings death* (H 2484).

-nęhsatihar – build an addition. *v.s.-a.i.* ranęhsatíhar ‹he-house-hang› *he makes an addition to the house* (H 24 84).

-nęhsatukęhT – sanctuary. *n.s.* unęhsatukęhti ‹house-holy› *sanctuary* (HS).

-nęhsawęhte – House-In-Between. *dv.n.s.* Kanęhsawęhteˀ ‹it-house-is between two things› *House-In-Between (male proper name)* (H 2484).

-nęhsawyęhw – carpenter. *dv.n.s.* ranęhsawyęhę ‹he-house-know-caused› *he knows how to build a house: this is another name of a carpenter* (H 2484).

-nęhsaˀke roof. *n.s.* unęhsáˀkye ‹house-at› *roof* (HS).

-nęhsaˀnihθT – umbrella. *dv.n.s.* yenęhsaˀníhθthaˀ ‹one-house-stand up-causes› *the house one erects: this is the descriptive name of an umbrella* (H 2484).

-nęhsęnhe – Live-House. *dv.n.s.* Kanęhsęnheˀ ‹it-house-is alive› *Live-House (male proper name)* (H 2484).

-nęhsęti – architect, carpenter. *dv.n.s.* ranęhsę́·tih ‹he-house-makes› *architect* (HS); *he makes a house: he makes a house as a profession, hence, a carpenter* (H 2484).

-nęhsirehT – Move-Through-House. *dv.n.s.* Kanęhsiréhthaˀ ‹it-house-move through-causes› *Move-Through-House (female proper name)* (H 2484).

-nęhskari – burglar. *dv.n.s.* ranęhská·ryahs ‹he-house-devours› *he creates a disturbance in the house, he robs the house by breaking into the house* (H 2484); *burglar* (HS).

-nęhsku – steal. *v.s.-a.i.* ranę́hskwahs ‹he-house-picks up› *he steals, is stealing (literally, he takes the house, but use*

has made it mean to steal) (H 2484); ęhranę́hskuˀ ‹prediction-he-house-pick up› *he will steal* (HS).

-nęhsku – theft. *dv.n.s.* haˀ yenę́hskwahs ‹the one-house-picks up› *theft* (HS).

-nęhskuˀye – thief. *dv.n.s.* runęhskúˀye· ‹he-house-bends› *thief* (R).

-nęhskuˀyehčr – theft. *n.s.* unęhskuˀyéhčreh ‹house-bend-'ness› *theft* (HS).

-nęhsn – grain, pit, stone, seed. *n.r.* aln: aknę́hsnawęh *my seed* (R), inc., n.sfx. -eh. Hewitt (2484) occasionally writes this root **-nĕⁿs-ˀn-** indicating the presence of a glottal stop between *s* and *n*. This glottal stop is not present in the speech of living speakers, but is the expected result of the shift of **t* to *ˀn*. unę́hsneh *a grain of wheat, corn, etc., a seed, pit or stone of fruit, the seed of a plant* (H 2484); **-nęhsn-.#áh:** unęhsneháh ‹seed-little› *a small grain, it is a small grain* (H 2484); **-nęhsna=čhakwahsT-:** ranęhsnačhakwáhsthaˀ ‹he-seed-self-X-is good› *he cares for the grain, is getting it ready to house or to put into the barn, as cutting it and binding it, etc:* (H 2484); **-nęh=snačiwak-:** yunęhsnačì·wakę ‹it-seed-is bitter› *black pepper (Piper nigrum)* (R); **-nęhsnahęsči-:** kanęhsnahę́sči ‹it-seed-is black› *cockle (i.e., any of various weeds that grow in grain fields)* (HS), *the grain is black* (H 2484); **-nęhsnahninę-:** ranęhsnahnì·nęh ‹he-seed-buys› *he buys the grain* (H 24 84); **-nęhsnahraT-:** ranęhsnáhra·č ‹he-seed-counts› *he counts the grains* (H 2484); **-nęhsnahręhw-:** runęhsnáhręw ‹he-seed-put up-causes› *he has the grain across, has the grain on his shoulder* (H 2484); **-nęhsnahrihr-:** ranęhsnáhrihč ‹he-seed-scatters› *he sows the grain, spills the grain* (H 2484); **-nęhsnahrihT-:** ranęhsnahríhthaˀ ‹he-seed-scatters⟩ *he sows the grain, spills the grain* (H 2484); −nȩhsnahrihT −: ranȩhsnahríhtha⟩ ⟨he-seed-spill-causes⟩ *he breaks, bruises the grain (singular or collective)* (H 2484); −nȩhsnah = wačiyu −: kanȩhsnahwačí·yu· ⟨it-seed-breadth-is great⟩ *the grain is wide, it is the nature of the grain to be wide* (H 2484); −nȩhsnahwaryakȩ −: unȩhsnahwaryá·kȩ⟩ ⟨seed-white⟩ *the grain is white* (H 2484); −nȩhsnak −: kanȩ́hsna·ks ⟨it-seed-eats⟩ *it eats grain* (H 2484); −nȩhsnaka⟩ne −: runȩhsnaká⟩ne⟩ ⟨he-seed-is much⟩ *he has abundance of grain, has much grain* (H 2484); −nȩhsnakȩre −: kanȩhsnakȩ̀·re⟩ ⟨it-seed-is scarce⟩ *the grain is scarce, not plentiful* (H 2484); −nȩhsnaks −: kanȩhsná·ksȩ· ⟨it-seed-is bad⟩ *it is bad, poor grain, it is a bad or poor grain* (H 2484); −nȩhsnakwahsT −: kanȩhsnákwahst ⟨it-seed-is good⟩ *it is good grain: the grain is good, fine* (H 24 84); −nȩhsnanȩhsku −: ranȩhsnanȩ́hskwahs ⟨he-seed-house-picks up⟩ *he steals the grain (customarily) or is stealing the grain* (H 2484); −nȩhsna = nȩsne −: runȩhsnanȩ́sne⟩ ⟨he-seed-holds dear⟩ *he cherishes fondly the grain, is not willing to part with the grain* (H 2484); −nȩhsnanha −: kanȩhsnánhȩ ⟨it-seed-is full⟩ *it is full of grain (said of a barn or bin, or bag; it is applied in this sense to grain yet in the straw)* (H 2484); −nȩhsnarik −: ranȩ́hsnariks ⟨he-seed-bites⟩ *he bites the grain (singly or collectively)* (H 2484); −nȩhsnaruh = črȩ −: kanȩhsnarúhčrȩh ⟨it-seed-gathers⟩ *it gathers grain: places the grain in a heap, in one spot* (H 2484); −nȩh = snaθhu −: yunȩhsnáθhwahs ⟨it-seed-smell⟩ *it smells the grain* (H 2484); −nȩhsnaθri⟩r −: unȩhsnaθrí⟩reh ⟨seed-wrinkle⟩ *shriveled or wrinkled grain* (H 2484); −nȩhsnatawȩ −: yunȩhsnatá·wȩ· ⟨it-seed-warmed⟩ *the grain is warm, the grain is damp* (H 2484); −nȩhsnath −: yunȩhsnáthȩ ⟨it-seed-is dry⟩ *the grain is dry or seasoned* (H 2484); −nȩhsnaturȩ −: ranȩhsnatù·rȩh ⟨he-seed-stores⟩ *he puts away, stores grain* (H 24 84); −nȩhsnatya⟩T −: ranȩhsnatyá⟩tha⟩ ⟨he-seed-buys⟩ *he buys grain, is buying; is a grain merchant* (H 2484); −nȩhsnawihsi −: ranȩhsnawíhsyȩhs ⟨he-seed-give-undoes⟩ *he pulls out a grain, or grain* (H 2484); −nȩhsnayači −: unȩhsnayá·či⟩ ⟨seed-be singular⟩ *it is a peculiar, strange grain; a singular grain* (H 2484); −nȩh = snayȩ(T) −: ranȩhsnayȩ⟩ ⟨he-seed-lays⟩ *he lays grain down* (H 2484); −nȩh = snayȩhnȩ −: ranȩhsnayȩ́hnȩhs ⟨he-seed-lays-much⟩ *he goes habitually to leave grain (said of a person taking grain to market or other depot)* (H 2484); −nȩhsna⟩ke: unȩhsná⟩kye ⟨seed-at⟩ *on, on the top of the grain or seed; literally, on grain, meaning that the ground or floor is covered with grain* (H 2484); −nȩhsna⟩ke.#ú⟩y: unȩhsna⟩kyehú⟩y ⟨seed-at-great⟩ *on much grain; that is, much grain lies on the ground or floor* (H 2484); −nȩhsnayȩ =

Tuscarora Pronunciation Key:
/a/ law; /e/ hat; /i/ pizza; /u/ tune; /ȩ/ hint; /č/ cheese; /h/ hoe; /m/ mother; /s/ same; /t/ do (before a vowel y, or w), too (elsewhere); /k/ gale (before a vowel y or w), kale (elsewhere); /n/ inhale (before a consonant or word-final), note (elsewhere), /r/ hiss (before a consonant or word-final), run (trilled as in Italian, elsewhere); /w/ cuff (before a consonant other than y or word-final), way (elsewhere); /y/ fish (before a consonant or word-final), you (elsewhere), /θ/ thing; /⟩/ (the sound between the vowels in unh-unh); /·/ long vowel, /́/ high pitch; /̀/ low pitch.

'**nahkw** –: yenǫhsnayę'ʼnáhkhwa'ʼ ‹onc-see-lays-instrument› *granary* (HS); –**nǫhsna'ʼθ** –: kanǫ́hsna'ʼθ ‹it-seed-is of a size› *the grains are large* (H 2484); –**nǫhsnatawę** –: yunǫhsnatá·wę· ‹it-seed-is warm› *the grain is warm, the grain is damp* (H 2484); –**nǫhsnehke**: unǫh-snéhkye ‹seed-at› *at the seed or pit, at the place of the seed or pit* (H 2484); –**nǫhsneθ** –: kanǫ́hsne·θ ‹it-seed-is long› *the grain is long* (H 2484); –**nǫhsnǫhT** –: kanǫhsnǫ́htha'ʼ ‹it-seed-fall-causes› *it causes the grain to fall, it shakes the grain down* (H 2484); –**nǫhsnęti** –: kanǫhsnę́·tih ‹it-seed-makes› *it produces grain, seed; is producing grain or seed* (H 2484); –**nǫhsnę'ʼ** –: kanǫ́hsnę'ʼθ ‹it-seed-fall-begins› *the grain falls, drops: the grain shells, said of overripe seeds* (H 2484); –**nǫhsnę'ʼke**: unǫhsnę́'ʼkye ‹seed-at› *on, against (fastened to) the grain* (H 2484); –**nǫhsnihę**: unǫhsníhę ‹seed-in the middle of› *in the middle of the grain or seed* (H 2484); –**nǫh= snihęreT** –: ranǫhsnihęré·tha'ʼ ‹he-seed-carries away› *he carries away the grain* (H 2484); –**nǫhsnityę'ʼT** –: ranǫh-snityę́'ʼtha'ʼ ‹he-seed-go to-causes› *he carries grain to cover, brings grain into the barn, etc*: (H 2484); –**nǫh= snuhsku** –: unǫhsúhskę ‹seed-be bare› *the grain is unmingled, the grain is clear* (H 2484); –**nǫhsnuhkw** –: unǫh-snúhkweh ‹seed-cover-instrument› *samp* (H 2484); –**nǫhsnuhkwętya'ʼT** –: yenǫhsnuhkwętyá'ʼtha'ʼ ‹one-seed-cov-er-instrument-make-causes› *one uses it to make samp* (H 2484); –**nǫhsnu= kę'ʼ**: runǫhsnú·kę'ʼ ‹he-seed-less› *he is grainless, he is without grain* (H 2484); –**nǫhsnukęy** –: kanǫhsnukę̀·yahs ‹it-seed-shells› *it shells the grain, from ears of corn or wheat heads* (H 2484);

–**nǫhsnu'ʼ** –: kanǫ́hsnu'ʼθ ‹it-seed-be in water-begins› *the grain is customarily flooded, is subject to floods* (H 2484); –**či** –. –**nǫhsnaT** –: θkanǫ́hsna·t ‹again-it-seed-stands› *one seed* (RC 23:6); –**ne** –. –**a'nęnǫhsnakwa'ʼnęti** –: neyu'ʼnęnǫh-snakwa'ʼ-nę́·ti· ‹apart-it-itself-seed-arc-made› *the grain is round, it is a round grain* (H 2484); **ti** –. –**nǫhsnači'ʼtkwah = nayę(T)** –: tikanǫhsnači'ʼtkwáhnayę'ʼ ‹so-it-seed-yellow-lays› *the grain is yellow* (H 2484); **ti** –. –**nǫhsna'ʼθ** –. **#ú'ʼy**: tikanǫhsna'ʼθ'ʼú'ʼy ‹so-it-seed-is of a size-great› *the grain is very large* (H 2484); **ti** –. –**nǫhsneθ** –.**#áh**: tikanǫh-sne·θ'ʼáh ‹so-it-seed-is long-little› *the grain is short, is not long* (H 2484); **kwà·nę** –**nǫhsnitkę'ʼ** –: kwà·nę kanǫh-sní·-tkę'ʼθ ‹much it-seed-come forth-begins› *it produces, yields much grain (said of wheat, oats, and other grain producing plants)* (H 2484); –**nǫhsn** – –**nęhaT** –: unǫ́hsneh yunǫ́ha·t ‹seed it-corn-stands› *grain, it has seed in it (this is the name of any grain used or intended to be used for planting)* (H 2484).

–**nǫhsnačiwak** – black pepper. *dv.n.s.* yu-nǫhsnači·wakę ‹it-seed-is bitter› *black pepper (Piper nigrum)* (R).

–**nǫhsnahęsči** – cockle. *dv.n.s.* kanǫhsna-hę́sči ‹it-seed-is black› *cockle (i.e., any of various weeds that grow in grain fields)* (HS), *the grain is black* (H 2484).

–**nǫhsnayę'nahkw** – granary. *dv.n.s.* ye-nǫhsnayę'ʼnáhkhwa'ʼ ‹one-see-lays-in-strument› *granary* (HS).

–**nǫhsnuhkw** – samp. *n.s.* unǫhsnúhkweh ‹seed-cover-in-strument› *samp* (H 2484).

–**nǫhsuhar** – roof. *n.s.* unǫhsúhareh ‹house-tip› *the roof or top-surface of the house* (H 2484).

-**nęhsuhar** - dedicate. *v.s.-t.* ranęhsúhar ‹he-house-washes› *he dedicates it* (HS).

-**nęhsyęti** - build an addition, extend house. *v.s.-a.i.* kanęhsyę́·ti'' ‹it-house-extends out› *it is an extended house, one lengthened by making an addition to its end* (H 2484), ranęhsyę́·ti'' ‹he-house-extends out› *he extends house, he builds an addition* (HS), *he extends the house (lengthwise)* (H 2484).

-**nęhsyęti'T** - confederate. *v.s.-t.* ękęnęhsyę́·ti''t ‹prediction-I=you-house-extend-cause› *I will confederate you* (AG), kakhenęhsyętí''tha'' ‹I=them-house-extend-cause› *I am confederating them* (AG), kakhenęhsyętí''nę ‹I=them-house-extend-caused› *I have confederated them* (AG).

-**nęhučhę(T)** - corn bread. *dv.n.s.* kanęhúchę'' ‹it-corn-be in water-'ness-lays› *corn bread* (R).

-**nęhuhare'T** - basket for washing corn. *dv.n.s.* yenęhuharé''tha'' ‹one-corn-wash-causes› *a basket for washing corn, lit., one uses it to wash corn* (H 2484).

-**nęhuku** -{dative III}.#ha·'' Eel Clan. *dv. n.s.* Akunęhukwatíha·'' ‹one-corn-put in water-undoes-for-characterized by› *Eel Clan* (AG).

-**nęhwakčr** - illness, sickness. *n.s.* unęhwákčreh ‹be ill-'ness› *illness, sickness* (R).

-**nęhwakčrawę** - menstruation. *dv.n.s.* kakunęhwakčrà·węh ‹they-be ill-'ness-possess› *menstruation* (R).

-**nęhwaknęčr** - illness. *n.s.* unęhwaknę́hčreh ‹be ill-'ness› *illness* (RC 23:2).

-**nęhwakskhę** - be sickly. *v.s.-s.i.* runęhwákskhę· ‹he-is ill-easily-much› *he is sickly* (HS).

-**nęhwak(T)** - ail, ache, be hurt, be ill, be sick, be sore. *v.r.-a.i.* hab: -s, pnt: -ɸ, stat: ()-e'', prog: -, prp: -, dst: -, caus: -, rvs: -, dat: -, inc.-ɸ-ag./pat. yunęhwá·kne'' *it is painful* (R), runę́hwaks *he is ill* (RC 3:70) [Lawson «Connauwox» 'I am sick'], wa''unę́hwa·k *it got sick* (RC 33:11), wahrunę́hwa·k *he was ill* (RC 3:16); -**nęhwakčr** -: unęhwákčreh ‹be ill-'ness› *illness, sickness* (R); -**nęhwakčrawę** -: kakunęhwakčrà·węh ‹they-be ill-'ness-possess› *menstruation, they are menstruating* (R); -**nęhwaknęčr** -: unęhwaknę́hčreh ‹be ill-'ness› *illness* (RC 23:2); -**nęh**=**wakskhę** -: runęhwákskhę· ‹he-is ill-easily-much› *he is sickly* (HS); ti -. -**nęhwak(T)** -: tihrunę́hwaks ‹so-he-is ill› *he is indisposed, he is a little sick* (HS); -**a'nęnęhwak(T)** -: ru''nęnęhwá·knę ‹he-himself-was ill› *he pretends to be sick* (HS); -**nęhanęh**=**wak(T)** -: ranęhanę́hwaks ‹he-corn-is ill› *he longs for, desires corn* (H 2484); -**rihwanęhwak(T)** -: wahrarihwanę́hwa·k ‹fact he-matter-was ill› *he challenged* (HS), na''rihwanę́hwaks ‹one=another-matter-is ill› *one challenges another, one menaces another* (HS); -**tahkwanęhwak(T)** -: ratahkwanę́hwaks ‹he-marriage-is ill› *he is amorous, he wants the other sex* (HS);

-tkwan̨ęhwak(T) -: katkwanę́hwaks ‹it-stomach-is ill› *belly-ache, upset stomach* (RC 19:11); -r̨ę'nakri- -n̨ęh=wak(T)-: ur̨ę'ná·kri' kakunę́hwaks ‹tree-liquid they-are ill› *diabetes: diabetics* (R).

-n̨ęhwar̨- brain. *n.r.* poss. ?, inc., n.sfx. -eh. unę́hwareh *brain* (R); -n̨ęhwar̨-. #keha·?: unęhwar̨ę'kyéha·' ‹brain-customarily› *cephalic* (HS); -n̨ęhwar̨u=ri-: runęhwarù·rih ‹he-brain-stirs› *he bellows, he roars* (HS); -n̨ęhwar̨u?=yehčr-: unęhwaru'yéhčreh ‹brain-bend-'ness› *adultery* (HS); -n̨ęhwar̨='ehsT-: yenęhwar'éhstha' ‹one-brain-strike-causes› *war club* (SH 375); -či-. -n̨ęhwar̨iyu-: čunęhwarí·yu· ‹again-it-brain-is great› *catfish* (AG), *sucker (fish)* (H 3518); -a'n̨ęn̨ęhwar̨u?=yehsT-: ra'nęnęhwaru'yéhstha' ‹he-himself-brain-bend-causes› *he fornicates, he is licentious* (HS).

-n̨ęhwar̨-.#keha·? cephalic. *n.s.* unęhwar̨ę'kyéha·' ‹brain-customarily› *cephalic* (HS).

-n̨ęhwar̨uri - bellow, roar. *v.s.-a.i.* runęhwarù·rih ‹he-brain-stirs› *he bellows, he roar* (HS).

-n̨ęhwar̨u?yehčr - adultery. *n.s.* unęhwaru'yéhčreh ‹brain-bend-'ness› *adultery* (HS).

-n̨ęhwar̨?ehsT - war club. *dv.n.s.* yenęhwar'éhstha' ‹one-brain-strike-causes› *war club* (SH 375).

-n̨ęhwih be related to. *v.r.-k.* Anthony F.C. Wallace records an irregular form of the stem -a'nęhwih- in ka'nę́hwih *my relatives* (AW 98) from Dan Smith. ranę́hwih *his relative* (HS); -n̨ęhwihčr-: unęhwíhčreh ‹be related to-'ness› *affinity, kindred, relation, relationship* (HS); -a'nęn̨ęh=wih-: yę'nęnę́hwih ‹one-oneself-is related to› *her relatives* (AW 99); kwę̨hs

-a'n̨ęn̨ęhwih -: kwę̨hs ahra'nęnęhwíhck ‹no unknown-he-himself-be related to› *he is unrelated* (HS).

-n̨ęhwihčr- affinity, kindred, relation, relationship. *n.s.* unęhwíhčreh ‹be related to-'ness› *affinity, kindred, relation, relationship* (HS).

-n̨ęhyaθ- sinew, vein; plantain *(Plantago* sp.). *n.r.* n-poss., inc., n.sfx. -eh. unęhyá·θeh *sinew, vein* (RC 15:4); *(road) plantain (Plantago* sp.*)* (H-notebook); -n̨ęhyaθ-.#kęha?nę̨?: unęhyaθe'kę́ha'nę' ‹sinew-many› *muscles* (R); -t-. -n̨ęhyaθak-: ętkanęhyá·θa·k ‹prediction-hither-it-sinew-eat› *it will eat sinew there* (RC 15:5).

-n̨ęhyaθ-.#kęha?nę̨? muscles. *n.s.* unęhyaθe'kę́ha'nę' ‹sinew-many› *muscles* (R).

-n̨ęhyuT- sinew. *n.r.* poss. ?, inc., n.sfx. -. Found only in the following construction. -n̨ęhyu'narik-: wa'kayenęhyu'ná·ri·k ‹fact-they-sinew-bit› *they spell-bound it (literally, they bit its sinews)* (RC 35:10), snęhyu'ná·ri·ks ‹you-sinew-bite› *you are witchy* (R).

-n̨ęhyu'narik- spell-bind. *v.s.-t.* wa'kayenęhyu'ná·ri·k ‹fact-they-sinew-bit› *they spell-bound it (literally, they bit its sinews)* (RC 35:10), snęhyu'ná·ri·ks ‹you-sinew-bite› *you are witchy* (R).

nę́knę but otherwise (RC 21:11). *part.*

nę́·ku? hornbeam *(Carpinus caroliniana)* (H-notebook). *n.*

-nękwaru?n- pin. *n.r.* n-poss., inc., n.sfx. -. Found only in the following constructions. -nękwaru?nęt: yunękwarú'nę·t ‹it-pin-possesses› *pin* (HS); -nękwaru?na?nihr-: ranękwaru'ná'nihč ‹he-pin-stands up› *he sets a pin, he strikes a pin* (HS).

-nękwaru?nęt pin. *dv.n.s.* yunękwarú'nę·t ‹it-pin-possesses› *pin* (HS).

-nękwaruʔnaʔnihr – set a pin, strike a pin. *v.s.-a.i.* ranękwaruʔnáʔnihč ‹he-pin-stands up› *he sets a pin, he strikes a pin* (HS).

nę́·kwer also (RC 11:13). *part.* kwęhs nę́·kwer ‹no also› *not also* (HS).

-nęnhur – food, forage. *n.r.* n-poss., n-inc., n.sfx. -eh. unęnhù·reh *food, forage* (HS).

-nęnyuhr – clod, lump of earth. *n.r.* n-poss., n-inc., n.sfx. -eh. unęnyúhreh *a clod, lump of earth* (HS).

nęθa(r)(a) – dualic+repetitive+optative. *v. pfx.* The form **nęθara** – occurs whenever the prefix receives word accent; if this form is followed by a pronominal prefix that begins with the sequence *wa*, the final vowel contracts with the sequence to give **nęθarę** –. The form **nęθar** – occurs when the prefix is unaccented before pronominal prefixes that begin with the glides *w* or *y*. The form **nęθa** – occurs elsewhere.

-nęθehwit – black-eyed Susan. *n.r.* n-poss., n-inc., n.sfx. -eh. unęθéhwi·t *black-eyed Susan (Rudbeckia sp.)* (R).

-nęθhuʔ – be disappointed. *v.r.-s.i.* stat: -ę, prog: -, prp: -, dst: -, caus: -, rvs: -, dat: -, n-inc. runęθhúʔę *he is disappointed* (H-notebook).

-nęθkar – pimple. *n.r.* n-poss., n-inc., n.sfx. -eh. unę́·θkareh *pimple* (HS).

-nęθkwaruri – portulaca. *n.r.* n-poss., n-inc., n.sfx. -h. unęθkwarù·rih *portulaca (Portulaca grandiflora)* (HS).

-nęθnar – put a stop to. *v.r.-t.* hab: -, pnt: -, stat: -, prog: -aʔnyeʔ-, prp: -, dst: -, caus: -, rvs: -, dat: -, n-inc. Encountered only in the construction cited below. -nęθnaraʔnyeʔ-.#áh: knęθnaraʔnyeʔáh ‹I-put a stop to-going along-little› *I am stopping it* (RC 30:9).

-nęshę – Hell. *n.r.* n-poss., n-inc., n.sfx. -·ʔ. unéshę·ʔ *Hell* (HS) (also: unéshęʔ (R), uné·ʔsęʔ (R)).

-nęshęhrunęʔ devil. *n.r.* n-poss., n-inc., n.sfx. -. unęshęhrù·nęʔ *devil* (HS) (also: unishehrù·nęʔ (L 7), uneshęhrù·nęʔ (R), uneʔsęhrù·nęʔ (R)).

-nęsnaT – deny, forbid, prohibit. *v.r.-t.* hab: -s, pnt: -ęʔ, stat: -, prog: -aʔnyeʔ-, prp: -, dst: -, caus: -, rvs: -, dat: -, n-inc. ranę́snač *he denies it, he prohibits it* (HS), waʔkhenę́snaʔnęʔ *I forbid (another)* (AG), waʔkayęʔnaʔnę́snaʔnęʔ *he forbid them (lit. one forbade them)* (AG).

-nęsne – hold dear, love. *v.r.-t.* hab: -, pnt: -, stat: -ʔ, prog: -, prp: -, dst: -, caus: -, rvs: -, dat: -, inc.-ɸ-pat. runę́sneʔ *it loves him* (RC 8:23), kayęʔnaʔnę́sneʔ *they love another* (RC 3:72); -nęhsnanęsne –: runęhsnanę́sneʔ ‹he-seed-holds dear› *he cherishes fondly the grain, is not willing to part with the grain* (H 2484); -aʔnęnęsne –: raʔnęnę́sneʔ ‹he-himself-holds dear› *he loves himself* (R).

nęt – dualic+future+cislocative. *v.pfx.* The form **nęt** – occurs before pronominal prefixes that begin with the consonants *k* or *h*; when the prefix precedes the cluster *hs*, the cluster coalesces with the preceding final *t* of the prefix to yield **nęčh**-. The form **nę'n**- occurs before pronominal prefixes that begin with the consonants *w* or *y*. The form **nę'ni**- occurs elsewhere.

-**nęT**- hill, mountain; billow. *n.r.* n-poss., inc., n.sfx. -eh. unę́·ʔneh *hill, mountain* (R); *billow* (HS) [Gallatin «yooneneuntee» 'Mountain']; -**nęT**-.#hči: unęʔnéhči ‹hill-very› *billowy* (HS); -**nęth(e)r**-: yunę́·ther ‹it-hill-puts up› *peak* (HS), *hill* (PC) [Gallatin «younunthehr» 'Hill']; -**nęth(e)r**-.#ha·ʔ: A-kunętheríha·ʔ ‹one-hill-puts up-characterized by› *Turtle Clan* (AG), ranęthere̜ha·ʔ ‹he-hill-puts up-characterized by› *he is of the Turtle Clan* (H 2892); -**nęth(e)r**-.#ke: unęthráʔkye ‹hill-puts up-at› *top of mountain* (AG); -**nęth(e)r**-.#úʔy: yunętherʔúyʔ ‹it-hill-puts up-great› *mountain* (PC); -**nęthę**: unę́·thę ‹hill-in the middle of› *halfway* (R); -**nę-thrawę**-.#úʔy: yunęthrawęʔúʔy ‹it-hill-put up-much-great› *mountainous* (HS); -**nę'nahrar**-: yunęʔnáharę ‹it-hill-is a hole› *cave, cavern* (AG); -**nę'nahrarahsthę**-: yunęʔnaharáhsthę· ‹it-hill-be a hole-causes-many› *caves, caverns* (AG); -**nę'naʔ**=kehę: yunęʔnaʔkyéhę ‹it-hill-at-middle of› *slope of a mountain* (AG); -**nę'na**=kęw: unę́·ʔnakęw ‹hill-in› *in, below hill* (RC 11:1); -**nę'nakęwha'nye?**-: unęʔnakęwhá·ʔnyeʔ ‹hill-in-going along› *going along in hill* (RC 33:3); -**nę'nareθ**-: Yunę́·ʔnare·θ ‹it-hill-be in-is long› *Utica, New York* (R) [Morgan League «Ya-nun-nä´-rats» 'Utica']; -**nę'naʔke**: unęʔnáʔkye ‹hill-at› *on, at hill* (R); -**nęʔnaʔnaθ**-: Yenęʔná·ʔnač ‹one-hill-encircles› *Mohawk Valley* (AG); -**nę'nu**-: Kanę́·ʔnu·ʔ ‹it-hill-is in water› *New York City* (AG); -**nę'nu**-.

#aka·ʔ: Kanęʔnu·ʔá·ka·ʔ ‹it-hill-is in water-characterized by› *New Yorkers* (AG); -**nę'nuharaʔkeha'nye?**-: unęʔnuharaʔkyehá·ʔnyeʔ ‹hill-tip-at-going along› *going along at the summit of hill* (RC 33:5); -**nę'nyęti**-: yunęʔnyę́·tiʔ ‹it-hill-extends› *ridge* (HS); -**a'nęnę'na'ne?T**-: yuʔnęnęʔnaʔnéʔnę ‹it-it-self-hill-be present-caused› *cliff* (HS); -**ne**-.-**nę'nihyaʔkhę**-: waʔtkayenęʔnihyáʔkhęʔ ‹fact-apart-they-hill-crossed over-many› *they crossed over mountains* (AG).

-**nęT**- feed, give food to, nourish. *v.r.-t.* hab: -s, pnt: -φ, stat: -ę, prog: -, prp: -, dst: -, caus: -, rvs: -, dat: III (-ati-/-ę-), inc.-φ-ag./pat. θnę́·t *feed it!* (R), naʔné·ʔnę *one maintains (feeds) another* (HS), rá·nę·č *he feeds it, he nourishes it* (HS), wahrá·nę·t *he fed it* (RC 8:14), waʔkhé·nę·t *I fed it to him* (R); -**khwanęT**-{dative III}: waʔnyakukhwanę́·ʔnęʔ ‹fact-two-one-food-fed-for› *it was the two of them's meal* (RC 3:55); -**nęhanęT**-: waʔnaʔnę́hanę·t ‹fact-one=another-corn-fed› *one gave another corn to eat* (R); -**nę'nah**=staw-: ranęʔnáhstaws ‹he-feed-'ness-comes› *he gives it to eat* (RC 18:23); -**ʔwahranęT**-: wahraʔwáhranę·t ‹fact-he-meat-fed› *he fed it meat* (RC 30:32); -**či**-.-**(ę)ʔtikęhranęT**-: čękti-kęhranę́·ʔnę ‹again-we two-mind-fed› *one gives me an idea* (RC 6:18).

-**nęT**-.#hči billowy. *n.s.* unęʔnéhči ‹hill-very› *billowy* (HS).

-**nętakaryahs** President. *dv.n.r.* n-poss., n-inc., n.sfx. -. A partially nativized loan word from Seneca. Kanętaká·ryahs *The President of the U.S.* (AG); haʔ Ranętaká·ryahs *President* (HS).

-**nętawętyanę** tobacco pipe. *n.r.* n-poss., n-inc., n.sfx. -φ. kanętawętyà·nę *tobacco pipe* (M 87).

-nẹth(e)r – peak, hill. *dv.n.s.* yuné·ther ‹it-hill-puts up› *peak* (HS), *hill* (PC) [Gallatin «younunthehr» 'Hill'].

-nẹth(e)r –.#ha·ʔ Turtle Clan. *n.s.* A-kunẹtheríha·ʔ ‹one-hill-puts up-characterized by› *Turtle Clan* (AG), ranẹthéṛha·ʔ ‹he-hill-puts up-characterized by› *he is of the Turtle Clan* (H 2892).

-nẹth(e)r –.#úʔy mountain. *dv.n.s.* yunẹther'úyʔ ‹it-hill-puts up-great› *mountain* (PC).

-nẹthẹ halfway. *n.s.* uné·thẹ ‹hill-in the middle of› *halfway* (R).

-nẹthrawẹ –.#úʔy mountainous. *dv.n.s.* yunẹthrawẹʔúʔy ‹it-hill-put up-much-great› *mountainous* (HS).

nẹ·tu·ʔ wild potato; water hemlock *(Cicuta maculata)*; tuber; any plant with a tuberous root that grows near springs of water (RC 27:16). *n.*

-nẹwẹ – female. *n.r.* n-poss., n-inc., n.sfx. –ʔ. kanẹ̀·wẹʔ *female human* (RC 10:5) [Lawson «Con-noowa» 'Woman'], u-nẹ̀·wẹʔ *female non-human* (RC 30: 43); -nẹwẹ –.#áh: kanẹwẹʔáh ‹female-little› *little female* (RC 27:1); Twaʔ-á·ka·ʔ -nẹwẹ –: Twaʔá·ka·ʔ kanẹ̀·wẹʔ ‹Seneca it-is female› *a Seneca female* (AG).

-nẹwẹthu – sink. *v.r.-t.* hab: -hs, pnt: -, stat: -, prog: -, prp: -, dst: -, caus: -hT-, rvs: -, dat: -, n-inc. runẹwé·-thuhs *it sinks him* (HS); -nẹwẹthuhT –: ranẹwẹthúhtha'ʔ ‹he-sink-causes› *he drowns it* (RC 26: 35), *he submerges it* (HS), wahrunẹwé·thuht ‹fact-he-sink-caused› *it drowned him* (RC 3:

82), ahrunẹwé·thuht ‹unknown-he-sink-cause› *that it drown him* (RC 3: 85).

-nẹwẹthuhT – drown, submerge. *v.s.-t.* ranẹwẹthúhtha'ʔ ‹he-sink-causes› *he drowns it* (RC 26:35), *he submerges it* (HS), wahrunẹwé·thuht ‹fact-he-sink-caused› *it drowned him* (RC 3:82), ahrunẹwé·thuht ‹unknown-he-sink-cause› *that it drown him* (RC 3:85).

-nẹy – brick. *n.r.* n-poss., n-inc., n.sfx. -eh. unẹ̀·yeh *brick* (R).

-nẹyẹhθ – have ringworm. *v.r.-s.i.* stat: -φ, prog: -, prp: -, dst: -, caus: -, rvs: -, dat: -, n-inc. runẹ̀·yẹhθ *he has ringworm* (H-notebook).

nẹʔ also (RC 28:13) *part.*

-nẹʔahčir – burdock. *n.r.* n-poss., n-inc., n.sfx. -eh. unẹʔahčì·reh *burdock (Arctium sp.)* (H-notebook).

-nẹʔar – briar; climbing vine; prickly pear. *n.r.* n-poss., inc., n.sfx. -eh. Possibly to be seen in Colonial Records «Coneughauritzhugh», name of a Tuscarora chief in 1727, a leader of a "renegade" group (= (?) kanẹʔ-are·θʔúʔy *Great Long Vine*). unẹʔ-à·reh *briar; climbing vine; prickly pear* (RC 16:1); -nẹʔarara'ʔ –: yakunẹʔà·ra-raʔθ ‹one-climbing vine-be in-begins› *ivy (Hedera helix)* (HS); -nẹʔara = yẹ(T) –: unẹʔà·rayẹʔ ‹climbing vine-lays› *wild grape (Vitis sp.)* (R); -nẹʔ = araʔnihr –: yunẹʔaraʔníhrẹ ‹it-climbing vine-stood up› *climbing vine stands* (RC 7:5); -nẹʔaruha –: ẹyenẹʔarúha'ʔ ‹prediction-one-climbing vine-put in

Tuscarora Pronunciation Key:
/a/ law; /e/ hat; /i/ pizza; /u/ tune; /ẹ/ hint; /č/ cheese; /h/ hoe; /m/ mother; /s/ same; /t/ do (before a vowel y, or w), too (elsewhere); /k/ gale (before a vowel y or w), kale (elsewhere); /n/ inhale (before a consonant or word-final), note (elsewhere), /r/ hiss (before a consonant or word-final), run (trilled as in Italian, elsewhere); /w/ cuff (before a consonant other than y or word-final), way (elsewhere); /y/ fish (before a consonant or word-final), you (elsewhere), /θ/ thing; /ʔ/ (the sound between the vowels in unh-unh); /·/ long vowel, /ʹ/ high pitch; /ˋ/ low pitch.

water› *one will put climbing vine in
water* (RC 16:1); ‑**ne** ‑. ‑**a'nęnę²a** =
rya²k ‑: wa²nwa²nęnę²á·rya²k ‹fact-
apart-it-itself-climbing vine-broke› *the
vine broke* (AG).

-**nę²arara²** ‑ ivy. *dv.n.s.* yakunę²à·rara²θ
‹one-climbing vine-be in-begins› *ivy
(Hedera helix)* (HS).

-**nę²arayę(T)** ‑ wild grape. *n.s.* unę²-
à·rayę² ‹climbing vine-lays› *wild
grape (Vitis sp.)* (R).

-**nę²ker** ‑ suck. *v.r.-a.i.* hab: -ha², pnt: -²,
stat: -ę, prog: -, prp: -, dst: -, caus:
-a²T-, rvs: -, dat: -, n-inc. runę²kyè·rę
he nursed (HS), kanę²kyérha² *it sucks*
(L 78), ękanę́²kye²r *it will suck* (R),
wa²knę́²kye²r *I sucked* (R); -**nę²ke** =
ra²T ‑: yenę²kyerá²tha² ‹one-suck-
causes› *one nurses it* (RC 30:2), *one
suckles it* (HS); -t-. -**nę²kera²T** ‑: ę²-
naknę²kyerá²thahk ‹unknown-hither-I-
suck-cause› *that I have nursed here*
(RC 27:30).

-**nę²kera²T** ‑ nurse, suckle. *v.s.-t.* yenę²-
kyerá²tha² ‹one-suck-causes› *one nurses it* (RC 30:2), *one suckles it* (HS).

-**nę²kw** ‑ bunch, heap, pile. *n.r.* n-poss.,
n-inc., n.sfx. -eh. unę́²kweh *bunch,
heap, pile* (HS).

-**nę'nahrar** ‑ cave, cavern. *dv.n.s.* yunę²-
náharę ‹it-hill-is a hole› *cave, cavern*
(AG).

nę'na(r)(a) ‑ dualic+cislocative+optative.
v.pfx. The form **nę'nara** ‑ occurs whenever the prefix receives word accent;
if this form is followed by a pronominal prefix that begins with the sequence *wa*, the final vowel contracts
with the sequence to give **nę'narę** ‑.
The form **nę'nar** ‑ occurs when the prefix is unaccented before pronominal
prefixes that begin with the glides *w*
or *y*. The form **nę'na** ‑ occurs elsewhere.

-**nę'na(k)** ‑ affix, attach, fasten. *v.r.-t.*
hab: -, pnt: ()-², stat: ()-ę, prog: -, prp:
-, dst: -, caus: ()-T-, rvs: -hsi-, dat: -,
inc.-ra²-pat. -**hyatęhstanę'nakT** ‑: rah-
yatęhstanę²náktha² ‹he-paper-attach-
causes› *he posts papers* (HS); -**nę²** =
θkwanę'na(k) ‑: yunę²θkwanę²ná·kę
‹it-burden-attached› *burden is fastened*
(RC 26:27), wa²unę²θkwanę́·²nak
‹fact-it-burden-attached› *burden was
fastened* (RC 26:27); -**ra²nę'nahsi** ‑: ra-
ra²nę²náhsyęhs ‹he-X-attach-undoes›
he detaches it (HS); -**ra²nę'nakT** ‑: ę-
yera²nę́·nakt ‹prediction-one-X-attach-
cause› *one will stick close to it* (RC
23:3); -**θręwanę'nakT** ‑: raθręwanę²-
náktha² ‹he-wax-attach-causes› *he
seals it* (HS); -**²tuhsanę'nahsi** ‑: wah-
ra²tuhsanę²náhsi² ‹fact-he-clam-at-
tach-undid› *he unfastened clam(shell)*
(RC 35:16); -**²tuhsanę'nakT** ‑: ra²tuh-
sanę²náktha² ‹fact-he-clam-attach-
causes› *he packs* (HS); -**či** ‑. -**kętyanę** =
'nakT ‑: θayukętyanę́·²nakt ‹again-fact-
it-hump-attach-caused› *again its body
was hunched up* (RC 26:31); -**či** ‑.
-**nę'nakarath** ‑: θahranę²nakará·thę²
‹again-fact-he-attach-climbed› *he
climbed back up the precipice* (RC 6:
31); -**athęwanę'nakT** ‑: wa²akyathęwa-
nę́·²nakt ‹fact-another and I-boat-attach-caused› *we landed* (AG); -**a²ra²** =
nę'nahsi ‑: ę²ra²nę²náhsi² ‹fact-it-it-
self-X-attach-undid› *it came off* (RC
26:27).

-**nę'nahstaw** ‑ give to eat. *v.s.-t.* ranę²-
náhstaws ‹he-feed-'ness-gives› *he
gives it to eat* (RC 18:23).

-**nę'nareθ** ‑ Utica, New York. *dv.n.s.* Yu-
nę́·²nare·θ ‹it-hill-be in-is long› *Utica,
New York* (R) [Morgan League «Ya-
nun-nä´-rats» 'Utica'].

-**nę'na²kehę** slope of a mountain. *dv.n.s.*
yunę²nakyéhę ‹it-hill-at-middle of›

slope of a mountain (AG).

–nę꞉ʔnaʔna·θ–. Mohawk Valley. *n.s.* Ye-
nęʔná·ʔna·č ‹one-hill-encircles› *Mohawk Valley* (AG).

–nę'nu– New York City. *n.s.* Kanę́·ʔnu·ʔ
‹it-hill-is in water› *New York City*
(AG).

–nę'nu–.#aka·ʔ New Yorkers. *n.s.* Kanęʔ-
nu·ʔá·ka·ʔ ‹it-hill-is in water-characterized by› *New Yorkers* (AG).

–nę'nyęti– ridge. *dv.n.s.* yunęʔnyę́·tiʔ ‹it-
hill-extends› *ridge* (HS).

nę́·ʔnyuht ‹apart-hither-it-stands› over
and over again (RC 3:71). *part.*

–nęʔr– cobweb, net, lace, sieve, veil. *n.r.*
n-poss., inc., n.sfx. -eh. unę́ʔreh *cobweb, net, lace, sieve, veil* (HS); –nęʔ=
raʔr–: yunę́ʔraʔr ‹it-net-is much› *web*
(AG); –ne–. –nęʔriye–: neyunęʔrì·yeʔ
‹apart-it-net-??› *it is intricate, it is tangled* (HS), nehranęʔrì·yehs ‹apart-he-
net-??› *he is entangled, he is perplexed, he tangles it* (HS); –ne–.
–nęʔriyehsi–: nehranęʔriyéhsyęhs ‹a-
part-he-net-??-undoes› *he disentangles
it* (HS); rukiʔyáhskę –nęʔr–: rukiʔ-
yáhskę unę́ʔreh ‹spider net› *spider
web* (HS); –nęʔr– –ičihsakT–: unę́ʔreh
yečihsáktaʔ ‹net one-fish-seek-causes› *fish net* (SH 375).

–nęʔr– –ičihsakT– fish net. *dv.n.s.* unę́ʔ-
reh yečihsáktaʔ ‹net one-fish-seek-
causes› *fish net* (SH 375).

–nęʔrar– pollution. *n.r.* n-poss., inc., n.
sfx. -eh. Encountered only in the constructions cited below. –nęʔraratyaʔ=
kʷahT–: unęʔraratyáʔkwaht ‹pollution-

be nauseous-cause› *pollution* (HS);
–nęʔrarawęri–: ranęʔrarawę̀·rih ‹he-
pollution-stirs› *he pollutes it* (HS).

–nęʔraratyaʔkʷahT– pollution. *n.s.* unę́ʔ-
raratyáʔkwaht ‹pollution-be nauseous-
cause› *pollution* (HS).

–nęʔrarawęri– pollute. *v.s.-t.* ranęʔrara-
wę̀·rih ‹he-pollution-stirs› *he pollutes
it* (HS).

–nęʔraʔr– web. *dv.n.s.* yunęʔraʔr ‹it-net-
is much› *web* (AG).

–nęʔθkw– burden. *n.r.* n-poss., inc., n.
sfx. -. Found only incorporated. –nęʔ=
θkwanę'na(k)–: yunęʔθkwanęʔná·kę
‹it-burden-attached› *burden is fastened*
(RC 26:27), waʔunęʔθkwanę·ʔnak
‹fact-it-burden-at-tached› *burden was
fastened* (RC 26: 27).

–nęʔs– bottom. *n.r.* n-poss., n-inc., n.sfx.
-. unęʔsę́ʔkye *at the bottom* (AG).

–nęʔt– hemlock; larch. *n.r.* n-poss., n-
inc., n.sfx. -eh. unę́ʔteh *hemlock
(Tsuga canadensis)* (H-notebook);
larch (Larix sp.) (H-notebook); –nęʔ=
takęw.#áh: unęʔtakęwʔáh ‹hemlock-in-
little› *second Wolf Clan ("under-the-
pine")* (L 47).

–nęʔtakęw.#áh Little Wolf Clan, second
Wolf Clan. *n.s.* unęʔtakęwʔáh ‹hemlock-in-little› *Little Wolf Clan* (L 5),
second Wolf Clan ("under-the-pine")
(L 47).

–nęʔtakwęte juniper *(Juniperus sp.)*. *n.r.*
n-poss., n-inc., n.sfx. -. unęʔtakwę́·te
juniper (Juniperus sp.) (H-notebook).

–nęʔtęhs tamarack. *n.r.* n-poss., n-inc.,
n.sfx. -ɸ. kanęʔtęhs *tamarack (Larix*

laricina, Larix sp.*)* (R) (also: kanę́ʔ-tę́ʔθ (H-notebook)).

-nę́ʔtę́ʔθ tamarack. *n.r.* n-poss., n-inc., n.sfx. -ϕ. kanę́ʔtę́ʔθ *tamarack (Larix laricina, Larix* sp.*)* (H-notebook) (also: kanę́ʔtęhs (R)).

-nę́ʔy - intoxicate. *v.r.-t.* hab: -ahs, pnt: -, stat: -, prog: -, prp: -, dst: -, caus: -ahsT-, rvs: -, dat: -, n-inc. Possibly to be seen in Lawson's «Connaugh jost twane» 'All the <u>Indians</u> are drunk', representing *kanę́ʔyahs thwé·ʔn it is drunk all*. runę́ʔyahs *he is drunk* (HS), naʔnę́ʔyahs *one intoxicates another* (HS), kakunę́ʔyahs *alcoholics* (R); **-nę́ʔy** -: unę́ʔyeh ‹intoxicate› *liquor* (L 37); *drunkenness* (HS); **-nę́ʔyahsT** -: yakunę́ʔyáhstha? ‹one-intoxicate-causes› *alcohol* (R); **-a'nęnę́ʔyahsT** -: raʔ-nęnę́ʔyáhstha? ‹he-himself-intoxicate-causes› *he makes merry* (HS).

-nę́ʔy - alcoholic. *dv.n.s.* kakunę́ʔyahs ‹they-intoxicate› *alcoholics* (R).

-nę́ʔy - liquor; drunkenness. *n.s.* unę́ʔyeh ‹intoxicate› *liquor* (L 37); *drunkenness* (HS).

-nę́ʔyahsT - alcohol. *dv.n.s.* yakunę́ʔyáhstha? ‹one-intoxicate-causes› *alcohol* (R).

-nę́ʔyaręhčraʔniha - prick conscience. *v.s.-a.i.* runę́ʔyaręhčraʔníhahs ‹he-look at-'ness-sprains› *he pricks his conscience* (HS).

-nę́ʔyečkwhar - build nest. *v.s.-a.i.* See: **-(ę)nę́ʔyečkwhar** -.

-nę́ʔyečkw - nest. *n.r.* See: **-(ę)nę́ʔ=yečkw** -.

-nę́ʔyečkwrahkw - aerie. *n.s.* See: **-(ę)=nę́ʔyečkwrahkw** -.

-nę́ʔyuhčr - comb. *n.r.* n-poss., n-inc., n.sfx. -eh. unę́ʔyúhčreh *comb* (HS).

-nhaʔ - employ, hire. *v.r.-t.* hab: -θ, pnt: -ϕ, stat: -, prog: -, prp: -, dst: -, caus: -, rvs: -, dat: -, n-inc. waʔkhénhaʔ *I*

hired him (R), ęyénhaʔ *one will be employed* (RC 15:9); **-nhaʔčr** -: unháʔ-čreh ‹employ-'ness› *a hand, emissary, hackman, orderly, servant* (HS); **-a='nenhaʔ** -: raʔnénhaʔθ ‹he-himself-employs› *he hires out, he serves* (HS), waʔę́ʔnénhaʔ ‹fact-one-oneself-employed› *one served* (RC 27:31).

-nhaʔčr - emissary, hackman, hired hand, orderly, servant. *n.s.* unháʔčreh ‹employ-'ness› *a hand, emissary, hackman, orderly, servant* (HS).

-nhaʔnę - deplore, mourn for, mourn the loss of, regret. *v.r.-t.* hab: -h, pnt: -, stat: -, prog: -, prp: -, dst: -, caus: -ʔT-, rvs: -, dat: -, n-inc. ranháʔnę *he deplores, he mourns for, he mourns the loss of, he regrets* (HS); **-nhaʔ=nęʔT** -: yunháʔnęʔt ‹it-regret-caused› *it is pitiful, it is to be regretted* (HS).

-nhaʔnęʔT - be pitiful, be to be regretted. *v.s.-s.i.* yunháʔnęʔt ‹it-regret-caused› *it is pitiful, it is to be regretted* (HS).

-nhęT - have in the mouth. *v.r.-t.* hab: -, pnt: -ęʔ, stat: -, prog: -a'nyeʔ-, prp: -, dst: -, caus: -hu-, rvs: -aku-, dat: -, inc.-ϕ-pat. **-nhęthu** -: naʔnenhę́·thuhs ‹one=another-have in the mouth-causes› *one puts in another's mouth* (HS); **-nhę'naku** -: ranhęʔná·kwahs ‹he-have in mouth-undoes› *he unclogs it* (HS); **-nęhranhę'na'nyeʔ** -: yunęhranhęʔná·ʔ-nyeʔ ‹it-scalp-has in mouth-going a-long› *it went along with scalp in mouth* (RC 12:26); **-tihsanhęthu** -: ra-tihsanhę́·thuhs ‹he-poison-have in mouth-causes› *he poisons it, he gives it poison* (HS); **-a'nenhęT** -: ęyęʔnen-hę́·ʔnęʔ ‹prediction-one-oneself-have in the mouth› *one will have it in one's mouth* (RC 23:6); **-ne** -. **-nhę'nara?θrę** -: waʔthranhęʔnáráʔθręʔ ‹fact-apart-he-have in mouth-was in-much› *he gasped for breath* (RC 3:22).

-**nhęthu** – put in someone's mouth. *v.s.-t.* na'nenhę́·thuhs ‹one=another-have in the mouth-causes› *one puts in another's mouth* (HS).

-**nhę'naku** – unclog. *v.s.-t.* ranhę'nákwahs ‹he-have in mouth-undoes› *he unclogs it* (HS).

-**nhihT** – be awkward, be embarrassing, be inconvenient, be unhandy. *v.r.-s.i.* stat: -ɸ, prog: -, prp: -, dst: -, caus: -, rvs: -hrę-, dat: III (-ati-/-ę-), inc.-ɸ- pat. rúnhiht *he is awkward* (HS), yúnhiht *it is awkward, it is embarrassing, it is inconvenient, it is unhandy* (HS); -**nhihT** –: únhiht ‹be awkward› *awkward* (HS); -**nhihthrę** –: runhíhthręh ‹he-is awkward-much› *he bungles, he makes mistakes* (R) (Hewitt & Smith give «ru-nhi´'-çrěⁿ»); -**takwnan** = **hihT** –: yutakwnánhiht ‹it-space-is awkward› *it is embarrassing (position)* (HS); -**a'nenhihT** –{dative III}: ru'nenhihná·ti· ‹he-himself-is awkward-for› *he is embarrassed* (HS).

-**nhihT** – awkward. *n.s.* únhiht ‹be awkward› *awkward* (HS).

-**nhihthrę** – bungle, make mistakes. *v.s.-a.i.* runhíhthręh ‹he-is awkward-much› *he bungles, he makes mistakes* (R) (Hewitt & Smith give «ru-nhi´'-çrěⁿ»).

-**nhučę** – be an angle, be a corner, be narrow. *v.r.-s.i.* stat: -', prog: -, prp: -, dst: -, caus: -'T-, rvs: -, dat: -, n-inc. yunhú·čę' *it is an angle, it is a corner, it is narrow; cape, cave, nook* (HS); -**nhučę'nawę** –: yunhučę'nà·wę' ‹it-be a corner-causes-many› *corners* (RC 27:17); -**nhučę'T** –: yunhučę'tha' ‹it-be a corner-causes› *it results* (HS); -**nhučę'T** –{dative I}: wahranhučę'-thahθ ‹fact-he-be a corner-caused-for› *he cornered it* (R).

-**nhučę** – cape, cave, nook. *dv.n.s.* yunhú·čę' ‹it-is a corner› *cape, cave, nook* (HS).

-**nhučę'T** – result. *v.s.-a.i.* yunhučę'tha' ‹it-be a corner-causes› *it results* (HS).

-**nhučę'T** –{dative I} corner. *v.s.-t.* wahranhučę'thahθ ‹fact-he-be a corner-caused-for› *he cornered it* (R).

-**nhur** – disease (with visible symptoms). *n.r.* n-poss., inc., n.sfx. -eh. unhù·reh *disease (with visible symptoms)* (R); -**nhurahrahT** –: unhù·rahraht ‹disease-put up-cause› *it is a tough or serious disease* (RC 16:3); -**nhura'na'r** –: kanhurá'na'r ‹it-disease-cause-is much› *epidemic* (HS); -**nhuręti** –: kanhurę́·tih ‹it-disease-makes› *unhealthy* (HS); -**nhurętya'T** –: yunhurętyá'ne' ‹it-disease-make-caused› *unhealthy* (HS).

-**nhura'na'r** – epidemic. *dv.n.s.* kanhurá'-na'r ‹it-disease-is much› *epidemic* (HS).

-**nhuręti** – unhealthy. *dv.n.s.* kanhurę́·tih ‹it-disease-makes› *unhealthy* (HS).

-**nhurętya'T** – unhealthy. *dv.n.s.* yunhurętyá'ne' ‹it-disease-make-caused› *unhealthy* (HS).

-**nhu'w** – areola of nipple; cheek. *n.r.* inaln: yenhú'weh *one's areola; one's cheek* (R), inc., n.sfx. -eh. unhú'weh *areola of nipple; cheek* (HS); **ti** –.

-nhu?wa?θ-: tyenhú'?wa'?θ ‹so-one-
areola-is of a size› *size of areola of
one's nipple* (RC 35:23).

Nihawęná?ah His-Voice-Is-Small (Chief
of the Turtle Clan) (H-Handbook). *n.*

-nihkehw- thistle. *n.r.* n-poss., n-inc.,
n.sfx. -eh. unihkyéhweh *thistle* (HS).

Nihnuhkà·we? He-Anoints-The-Hide
(Chief of the Beaver Clan) (H-Handbook). *n.*

níhrę? nine (R). *part.* **níhrę?** -či-. -(i)har-:
níhrę'? θkáhe'?r ‹nine again-it-hangs›
nineteen (R); **níhrę?** ti-. **-ahθhę**-: níhrę'? tiwáhθhę· ‹nine so-it-is ten› *ninety*
(R).

níhrę? -či-. -(i)har- nineteen. *part.* níhrę'?
θkáhe'?r ‹nine again-it-hangs› *nineteen*
(R).

níhrę? ti-. **-ahθhę**- ninety. *part.* níhrę'?
tiwáhθhę· ‹nine so-it-is ten› *ninety*
(R).

-nikyehw- Canada thistle. *n.r.* n-poss., n-
inc., n.sfx. -eh. unikyéhweh *long, high
thistle, Canada thistle (Cirsium ar-
vense)* (AG).

-niθku?r- button. *n.r.* n-poss., inc., n.sfx.
-eh. uniθkú'?reh *button* (HS); **-niθku?** =
ru'narhu-: raniθku'?ru'?nárhuhs ‹he-
button-hook-causes› *he buttons it*
(HS); **-ne**-. **-niθku?ru'narihsi**-: newakniθku'?ru'?naríhsyę ‹apart-I-button-
hook-undo› *I have unbuttoned it* (R).

-niθku?ru'narhu- button. *v.s.-t.* raniθku'?-
ru'?nárhuhs ‹he-button-hook-causes› *he
buttons it* (HS).

-nishęhrunę? devil. *n.r.* n-poss., n-inc.,
n.sfx. -. unishęhrù·nę'? devil (HS) (also: unęshęhrù·nę'? (L 7), unęshęh-
rù·nę'? (R), une'?sęhrù·nę'? (R)).

-nitęhT- humble. *v.s.-t.* See: **-(ę)nitęhT**-.

-ni?ke.#aka·? Mohawks. *n.r.* n-poss., n-
inc., n.sfx. -ɸ. Kani'?kyehá·ka·'? *Mohawks* (R) (also: Kanyę'?kyehá·ka·'?).

ní?ni? jay (R). *n.*

ní?sni?s speckled woodpecker (AG). *n.*

-nręh- have worms. *v.r.-a.i.* hab: -ahs,
pnt: -, stat: -, prog: -, prp: -, dst: -,
caus: -, rvs: -, dat: -, n-inc. runrę́hahs
he has worms (HS).

núhi? white-flowering dogwood *(Cornus
florida)* (RC 6:14). *n.*

núhskę almost, near (RC 29:1). *part.*
núhskę -(i)?rę-: núhskę yú'?rę'? ‹near
it-is settled› *nearness, propinquity*
(HS).

núhskę -(i)?rę- nearness, propinquity.
dv.n.s. núhskę yú'?rę'? ‹near it-is
settled› *nearness, propinquity* (HS).

-nuhskwi?θr- muscle of upper arm. *n.r.,*
poss. ?, inc. ?, n.sfx. -eh. unuhskwí'?-
θreh *muscle of upper arm* (AG).

nú·kwer also (RC 12:5). *part.*

nú·k?ah few, sparse (RC 2:15). *part.*
nú·k?ah kwę́ ‹few like› *sparse* (HS).

nú·k?ah kwę́ ‹few like› sparse (HS). *part.*

-nur- braided string of corn. *n.r.* n-poss.,
inc., n.sfx. -eh. unù·reh *braided string
of corn* (RC 5:31); **-nurętyahnę**-: wa'?-
kanurętyáhnę'? ‹fact-it-braided string
of corn-made-many› *it made braided
strings of corn* (RC 5: 30).

-nurę- be expensive, be precious. *v.r.-s.i.*
stat: -'?, prog: -, prp: -, dst: -, caus: -,
rvs: -, dat: I (-'?θe-/-'?θ-), inc.-ɸ-ag./
pat. kanù·rę'? *it is expensive* (R); **-nu** =
rę -{dative I}: runurę́'?θeh ‹he-is precious-for› *he appreciates it* (HS); **-nu** =
ręhkw-: knurę́hkwa'? ‹I-am precious-
instrument› *I love it* (R) [Gallatin
«yainoruhkwhau» 'To Love'], ranurę́h-
khwa'? ‹he-is precious-instrument› *it is
precious to him, he loves it* (R), a-
ryęknurę́hkhwek ‹unknown-one=me-
be precious-instrument› *that one love
me* (RC 3:54), kayeknurę́hkhwa'?
‹they=me-are precious-instrument›
they love me (RC 24:6), kayę'?-
na'?nurę́hkhwa'? ‹they=another-are

precious-instrument› *they love him* (RC 12:1), ra'na'nɛnurɛ́hkhwa' ‹he-himself-is precious-instrument› *he thinks highly of himself* (R); **-nurɛh= kwahčr -**: unurɛhkwáhčreh ‹be precious-instrument-'ness› *love* (HS); **-(ɛ)'= tikɛhranurɛ -**: ka'tikɛhranù·rɛ' ‹it-mind-is precious› *drug-free* (R); **-nɛh= sanurɛ -**: kanɛhsanù·rɛ' ‹it-house-is precious› *palace, parlor* (HS); **-rih= wanurɛ -**: karihwanù·rɛ' ‹it-matter-is precious› *precious matter, precious subject* (R); **-ya'tanurɛhsT -**: raya'ta-nurɛ́hstha' ‹he-body-be precious-causes› *he ennobles it* (HS); **-yɛra= nurɛ -**: kayɛranù·rɛ' ‹it-odor-is precious› *perfume* (HS); **-kθanurɛ - -ɛ= tya'T -**: kakθanú·rɛ· yakyetyá'tha' ‹it-dish-is precious one-make-causes› *porcelain* (HS).

-nurɛ -{dative I} appreciate. *v.s.-t.* ru-nurɛ́'θeh ‹he-is precious-for› *he appreciates it* (HS).

-nurɛhkw - be precious to, love, think highly of. *v.s.-t.* knurɛ́hkhwa' ‹I-am precious-instrument› *I love it* (R) [Gallatin «yainoruhkwhau» 'To Love'], ranurɛ́hkhwa' ‹he-is precious-instru-ment› *it is precious to him, he loves it* (R), aryɛknurɛ́hkhwek ‹unknown-one=me-be precious-instrument› *that one love me* (RC 3:54), kayeknurɛ́hkhwa' ‹they=me-are precious-instrument› *they love me* (RC 24:6), kayɛ'na'nu-rɛ́hkhwa' ‹they=another-are precious-instrument› *they love him* (RC 12:1), ra'na'nɛnurɛ́hkhwa' ‹he-himself-is

precious-in-strument› *he thinks highly of himself* (R).

-nurɛhkwahčr - love. *n.s.* unurɛhkwáh-čreh ‹be precious-instrument-'ness› *love* (HS).

nú·θri' magnolia *(Magnolia* sp.) (H-notebook); spotted alder *(Alnus* sp.) (R). *n.*

-nuta - white corn; up-so-quick-none-so-pretty. *n.r.* n-poss., n-inc., n.sfx. -·'. kanú·ta·' *white corn* (RC 7:5); *up-so-quick-none-so-pretty* (H-notebook).

-nu'čit calico corn. *n.r.* n-poss., n-inc., n.sfx. -ɸ. kanú'či·t *calico corn* (R).

nwa - our (yours, mine and others') (first person inclusive plural inalienable). *n.r.pfx.* The final *a* of the prefix co-alesces with a following *i* to yield **nwɛ -**. Before other vowels, the final *a* of the prefix is dropped.

Nwá'kan barbarian, enemy; Penobscot; any Algonquian (RC 33:2), Ojibwe, Mississaugas (AG). *n.*

nwí'nwi' chicken hawk, hen harrier *(Circus* sp.) (R). *n.*

ny - first person inclusive dual in-alienable. *n.r.pfx.* Occurs in word-ini-tial position before roots or stems that begin with the vowel *a*.

-nyarutarhu - steer (a vessel). *v.r.-a.i.* hab: -, pnt: -, stat: -ɛ, prog: -, prp: -, dst: -, caus: -, rvs: -, dat: -, n-inc. ru-nyarutárhɛ *he steered (a vessel)* (HS).

-nyatanawɛ - be melted, be thawed (of snow). *v.r.-s.i.* stat: -·, prog: -, prp: -, dst: -, caus: -, rvs: -, dat: -, inc.-ɸ-pat. yunyataná·wɛ· *it (snow) is thawed, it* *is melted: slush* (HS).

-nyatanawę – slush. *dv.n.s.* yunyataná·wę· *slush* (HS).

-nyatar – lake, sea. *n.r.* n-poss., inc., n. sfx. -eh. unyá·tareh *lake, sea* (R) (also: kanyá·tareh) [Gallatin «kaunyautauray» 'Lake']; **-nyatar**-.#keha·ʔ: u-nyataraʔkyé-ha·ʔ ‹lake-customarily› *maritime* (HS); **-nyatar**-.#úʔy: kanya-tarehúʔy ‹it-lake-great› *sea* (HS) [Gallatin «kaunyautaurayohe» 'Sea']; **-nya=tarakęwha'nyeʔ** –: unyatarakęwhá·ʔnyeʔ ‹lake-in-going along› *going into lake* (RC 26:34); **-nyatarar** –: wahranyata-rà·raʔ ‹fact-he-lake-was in› *he was in lake* (RC 26:34); -či-.**-nyatariyu** –: Θkanyatarí·yu· ‹again-it-lake-is great› *Handsome-Lake (male proper name)* (R); -či-.**-nyatarati**.#aka·ʔ: Θkanyatara-tihá·ka·ʔ ‹again-it-lake-ʔʔ-character-ized by› *Nanticokes* (probably, "near the ocean") (AG); -či-.**-nyatara=tiʔku**-.#aka·ʔ: Θkanyataratiʔkuʔá·ka·ʔ ‹again-it-lake-ʔʔ-characterized by› *Europeans* (HS).

-nyatar-.#keha·ʔ maritime. *n.s.* unyata-raʔkyéha·ʔ ‹lake-customarily› *mari-time* (HS).

-nyatar-.#úʔy sea. *n.s.* kanyatarehúʔy ‹it-lake-great› *sea* (HS) [Gallatin «kau-nyautaurayohe» 'Sea'].

nyawè·rih because (RC 35:24). *part.* hà·neʔ nyawè·rih ‹that is because› for the sake of (AG).

nyà·wę please, thank you, you're welcome (general acknowledgment of exchange) (RC 30:12). *part.* nyá·wę ù·nę –čarhu –: nyá·wę! ù·nę ęʔnwačarhuʔ ‹thank you now prediction-we-smoke› *thank you! now, let all of us smoke together (invocation spoken while sprinkling tobacco over a medicine that one is about to gather)* (TW); nyá·wę.#úʔy: nyawęhúʔy ‹thank you-great› *thank you very much* (TW).

nyá·wę.#úʔy thank you very much. *part.* nyawęhúʔy ‹thank you-great› *thank you very much* (TW).

nyę – partitive+translocative+future. *v. pfx.*

nyę́·nyę hen hawk (AG). *n.*

Nyę́·tkye Brotherton, New York (eighteenth century community of New England Algonquian refugees on Oneida territory) (AG). *n.*

nyęʔę̀·we papaw *(Aimina triloba)* (H-notebook). *n.*

-nyęʔke.#aka·ʔ Mohawk. *n.r.* inaln: ra-nyęʔkyehá·ka·ʔ *he is Mohawk* (H 28 92), n-inc. Kanyęʔkyehá·ka·ʔ *Mohawk* (R) (also: Kaniʔkyehá·ka·ʔ).

Nyučirhéʔę Tuscarora Reservation in New York (archaic) (RC 21:7). *n.*

Nyuθrù·ręʔ Buffalo, New York (R) [Morgan League «Ne-o-thro´-ra» 'Buffalo']. *n.*

Nyú·ya· New Year's Day (L 34). *n.* nyú·ya·.#áh: nyuyaʔáh! ‹New Year's Day-little› *Happy New Year! (cry yelled out when arriving at someone's house on New Year's Day)* (TW).

nyú·ya·.#áh Happy New Year. *part.* nyuyaʔáh! ‹New Year's Day-little› *Happy New Year's! (cry yelled out when arriving at someone's house on New Year's Day)* (TW).

P

pámp pump (HS). *n.*

pà·rih barley *(Hordeum* sp.) (HS). *n.*

píhskit biscuit, roll (R). *n.* The final *t* is dropped in composition. **-pihski=tyaʔT** –: waʔkpíhskityaʔt ‹fact-I-biscuit-bought› *I bought biscuits* (R).

pí·kak peacock *(Pavo cristatus)* (HS). *n.*

pì·yeʔ beer (HS). *n*. pì·yeʔ –ęθrakʔu –
{dative I}: pì·yeʔ rawęθrakʔúʔθc·
‹beer he-taste-released-for› *he likes
the taste of beer* (HS); pì·yeʔ –ïhr –:
pì·yeʔ wakíhrę ‹beer I-drank› *I drank
beer* (HS).

plúks plop (sound of something mushy,
like mashed potatoes, hitting the floor)
(R). *part*.

pó·ks thwuck (sound of an arrow hitting
a deer or other animal in a fleshy
part) (R). *part*.

pú·ks phlat (sound of a noisy fart) (R).
part.

R

–r– empty noun root. *v.inc*. See: –akew–
wipe, –atʔa– *put in*.

–r– be in. *v.r.-a.i*. stat: -ʔ, hab: -ɸ, pnt:
-aʔ, prog: -, prp: -aʔθre-, dst: -aʔθrę-
~ -awę-, caus: -ahsT- ~ -ʔT-, rvs: -,
dat: III (-ati-/-ę-), inc.-ɸ-ag./pat.
–raʔ –: yù·raʔθ ‹it-be in-begins› *it gets
into things* (R), rù·raʔθ ‹he-be in-begins› *it infects him* (HS); waʔù·raʔ
‹fact-it-be in-began› *it touched upon it*
(RC 30:42); *it got into it* (L 53), rà·-
raʔθ ‹he-be in-begins› *he responds*
(HS), ruráʔę ‹he-be in-began› *he
responded* (HS), ęhrà·raʔ ‹fact-it-be
in-began› *he will respond* (HS); –raʔ =
θreʔ –: ráraʔθreʔθ ‹he-be in-going to-
begins› *he goes about joining it, he*

goes about reaching it (HS); –t –. –raʔ –:
nahrà·raʔ ‹hither-fact-he-was in› *he
replies* (RC 26:29); –(a)haharaku –:
rahahará·kwahs ‹he-path-be in-undoes›
he averts it (HS), *he turns it off the
road or track, as a train or cart, or
other things* (H 2484); –(a)hahara ʔ –:
raháharaʔθ ‹he-path-be in-begins› *he
reaches, gets on the road* (H 2484);
–(a)hęʔnaraʔ –: rahęʔʔnaraʔθ ‹he-clearing-be in-begins› *he reaches, arrives at
the meadow* (H 2484), waʔehęʔʔnaraʔ
‹fact-one-clearing-be in-began› *one
was in a clearing* (RC 25:5); –aʔwna =
rawę –: yuʔwnarà·węʔ ‹it-earth-is in-
much› *atlas* (HS); –kerhar –: yukyérhar ‹it-body-is in› *picture* (R); –ker =
har –{dative III}: waʔkkyerhà·rę ‹fact-
I-body-was in-for› *I drew it* (R), waʔ-
khekyerhà·rę ‹fact-I=another-body-
was in-for› *I drew someone, I photographed someone* (R); –kwęhnaraʔ –:
kakwęhnaraʔθ ‹it-rust-be in-begins› *it
gets rusty* (H 2484); –nawerkčrar –: yunawérkčrar ‹it-flea-'ness-is in› *it is
afflicted with fleas* (HS); –nęhar –: ra-
nęhar ‹he-corn-is in› *he sets, places
corn grains (in the ground), hence, he
plants corn* (H 24 84); –nęθar –: ra-
nę́·θar ‹he-potato-is in› *he drops potatoes (as in planting)* (HS); –nęʔara =
raʔ –: yakunęʔà·raraʔθ ‹one-climbing
vine-be in-begins› *ivy (Hedera helix)*
(HS); –nę'nareθ –: Yunęʔʔnare·θ ‹it-hill-
be in-was long› *Utica, New York* (R)
[Morgan, League «Ya-nun-nä´-rats»];
–nyatarar –: wahranyatarà·raʔ ‹fact-

he-lake-was in› *he was in lake* (RC 26:34); –re̦war –: rare̦·war ‹he-length of body-is in› *he frames a picture* (HS); –rihwar –: yuríhwar ‹it-matter-is in› *circumstantial* (HS); –rihwarahsT –: rarihwaráh-stha᾿ ‹he-matter-be in-causes› *he tamed it* (HS); –rihwara᾿ –: wahruríhwara᾿ ‹fact-he-matter-was in› *he got blamed for it* (RC 30:72); –rihwa= ra᾿θk –: yurihwará᾿θke̦· ‹it-matter-be in-began-easily› *it is tamable* (HS); –θre̦hnara᾿ –: ruθre̦hnara᾿θ ‹he-sleep-be in-begins› *he is sleepy* (HS); –θre̦= wara᾿ –: yuθre̦·wara᾿θ ‹it-wax-be in-begins› *it sticks* (HS); –θri᾿rar –: θrí᾿rar ‹wrinkle-be in› *alligator (Alligator* sp.*)* (R) [Lawson «Utsererauh»]; –tah= skwar –: ratáhskwar ‹he-slave-is in› *he annoys, he enslaves* (R), rutáhskwar ‹he-slave-is in› *he tantalizes it: he is harassed, he is teased* (HS), kakutáhskwar ‹they-slave-is in› *it plagues them* (RC 2:2); –tuhnar –: yutúhnar ‹it-fin-is in› *it has fins* (HS); –tukarar –: yutú·karar ‹it-point-is in› *it is indented* (HS); –ya᾿θar –: uyá᾿θareh ‹track-be in› *tracks, footprints* (R), kayá᾿θar ‹it-track-is in› *print* (HS); –ya᾿θarawe̦ –: kaya᾿θarà·we̦h ‹it-track-be in-posses-ses› *its tracks* (RC 2:11); –yerara᾿T –: ruye̦·rara᾿t ‹he-flesh-be in-caused› *he is incarnate* (HS); –᾿nihse̦rarawe̦ –: u᾿nihse̦rarà·we̦᾿ ‹star-be in-much› *it is starred* (HS); –᾿rhuhkwar –: u᾿rhúhkwareh ‹cultiver-be in› *plot of land* (HS); –᾿tye̦hkrar –: ru᾿tye̦hkrar ‹he-snot-is in› *he is soiled by snot* (HS); –athahar –: rutháha᾿r ‹he-himself-path-was in› *he lays in wait* (R); –athahar – {dative III}: akatháhre̦᾿ ‹unknown-I-myself-path-be in-for› *that I join* (RC 13:6); –atkerhar –{dative III}: wa᾿katkye̦rhà·re̦᾿ ‹fact-I-myself-body-was in-for› *I drew myself* (R); –a᾿rakare=

rahsT –: ye̦᾿rakareráhstha᾿ ‹one-one-self-sound-be in-causes› *noisemaker, rattle* (HS); –ne –. –nhe̦᾿nara᾿θre̦ –: wa᾿-thranhe̦᾿nará᾿θre̦᾿ ‹fact-apart-he-be in mouth-cause-was in-much› *he gasped for breath* (RC 3:22); tha –. –atke̦hθrar –: thahe̦tke̦hθrarahk ‹unusual-fact-it-pus-was in› *pus was in it* (RC 21:6); ha᾿ –t –. –᾿nare̦war –: ha᾿ nyu᾿nare̦·war ‹the hither-it-mud-was in› *ceiling* (HS); kwe̦hs –rihwar –: kwe̦hs ahruríhwarak ‹no unknown-he-matter-be in› *he is unapproachable, he is unsocial* (HS); kwe̦hs –a᾿rihwara᾿ – ta᾿awe̦·te: kwe̦hs ahru᾿rihwará᾿e̦k ta᾿awe̦·te ‹no un-known-he-himself-matter-be in-begin anything› *he is innocent* (HS); –re̦hya= rawe̦ – –hyate̦hst –: yure̦hyarà·we̦᾿ uhyate̦hsteh ‹it-sky-is in-many book› *astronomy* (HS).

–r – be moon; be present in the sky above the horizon. *v.r.-s.i.* stat: -᾿, prog: -, prp: -, dst: -, caus: -, rvs: -, dat: -, n-inc. Hewitt (2892) describes the meaning of this root as follows: "to be present at, to appear at. A demonstrative prefix usually completes the predicate. This verb is used only to mark or predicate the point where the sun, moon or any one of the solar bodies is. The circumstances of time & place being expressed by suitable inflections." í·ka᾿r *moon* (R) [Jefferson «e-gaur» 'moon'], *it is present, that the sun, moon, or planet is above the horizon, is present in the firmament* (H 2892), ikà·rahk *it was present, etc. etc.* (H 2892), e̦ká·ra·k *it will be present, etc. etc.* (H 2892); ti –. –r –.#ú᾿y: tika᾿rhú᾿y ‹so-it-is moon-great› *great moon* (RC 8:3).

ra – his (third person singular masculine inalienable). *n.r.pfx.* The form ra – occurs before roots and stems that begin with a consonant or the vowel *i*; when the root or stem begins with *i* the final *a* of the prefixes coalesces with it to yield the form re̜-. The form r- occurs before roots and stems that begin with a vowel other than *i*.

-ra- empty noun root. *v.inc.* See: -tawe̜- *warn.*

-rače̜- rend, rip, tear. *v.r.-t.* stat: -ʔ, hab: -hs, pnt: -, prog: -, prp: -, dst: -, caus: -ku-, rvs: -, dat: -, n-inc. Rather than denoting an activity opposite from that of the root alone, the combination of the root plus the reversive suffix produces negligible change in meaning. If anything, the reversive serves to slightly emphasize the force of the activity. rará·če̜hs *he rips it, he tears it* (HS); **-rače̜ku-**: raráče̜·kwahs ⟨he-tear-undoes⟩ *he rends it, he tears it* (HS), kračé̜·kwahs ⟨I-tear-undo⟩ *I tear it* (AG); **-aʔrače̜-**: yuʔrá·če̜ʔ ⟨it-itself-tore⟩ *it is torn* (HS); **-aʔrače̜ku-**: waʔ-račé̜·kwahs ⟨it-itself-tear-undoes⟩ *the tearing (ripping noise of thunder)* (AG); **haʔ -aʔrače̜-**: haʔ yuʔrá·če̜ʔ ⟨the it-itself-tore⟩ *rent, tear: it is torn* (HS).

-rače̜ku- rend, tear. *v.s.-t.* raráče̜·kwahs ⟨he-tear-undoes⟩ *he rends it, he tears it* (HS), kračé̜·kwahs ⟨I-tear-undo⟩ *I tear* (AG).

-rahkw- collect, load, ship. *v.r.-t.* stat: -e̜°, hab: -haʔ, pnt: -φ, prog: -, prp: -, dst: -, caus: -ahT-, rvs: -, dat: III (-ati-/-e̜-), inc.-φ-pat. The shift of initial *r* to *t* in this root when immediately preceded by *s* is historically predic-

table, although such sequences are rare. raráhkhwaʔ *he loads it, he ships it* (HS), akà·rahkw *that it collect it* (RC 21:11); **-atke̜hθrarahkw-**: yutke̜h-θraráhke̜ ⟨it-pus-collected⟩ *it collects pus* (RC 21:10); **-(e̜)ʔtahsarahkw-**: ye̜ʔtahsaráhkhwaʔ ⟨one-tongue-col-lects⟩ *one is gossiping, one is joking* (R); **-θkrarahkwahT-**: yeθkrarahkwáh-thaʔ ⟨one-spit-collect-causes⟩ *spittoon* (HS); **-taˈnarahkw-**: Utaʔnaráhkhwaʔ ⟨settlement-col-lects⟩ *Canandaigua, New York* (R) [Morgan, League «Cä́-tä-na-rä́-qua»]; **-tkwararahkw-**: yu-tkwararáhke̜ ⟨it-blood-collected⟩ *hemorrhage* (RC 7:7); **-we̜tarahkw-**: waʔ-kayewé·tarahkw ⟨fact-they-word-col-lected⟩ *they followed word, they obeyed* (RC 33:10); **-či-, -rahkw-**: θhraráhkhwaʔ ⟨again-he-collects⟩ *he loads again* (HS); **-aʔrahkw-**: é̜ʔrahkw ⟨fact-it-itself-collected⟩ *it is collected* (RC 27:18); **-athaharahkw-**: yuthaha-ráhkwe̜ ⟨it-itself-path-collected⟩ *it is out of the way* (H 2484), rathaharáh-kwahs ⟨he-himself-path-collects⟩ *he deviates, he turns aside* (HS); **-a=thwihstarahkw-**: rathwihstaráhkhwaʔ ⟨he-himself-money-collects⟩ *he rav-ishes* (HS), waʔkaye̜thwíhstrarahk ⟨fact-they-themselves-money-collec-ted⟩ *they violated (females)* (AG); **-athwihstarahkw-{dative III}**: waʔkhe-yathwihstraráhke̜ʔ ⟨fact-I=another-my-self-money-collected-for⟩ *I violated* (AG), ke̜yathwihstrarahkwá·tih ⟨I=you-myself-money-collect-for⟩ *I am*

Tuscarora Pronunciation Key:
/a/ law; /e/ hat; /i/ pizza; /u/ tune; /e̜/ hint; /č/ cheese; /h/ hoe; /m/ mother; /s/ same; /t/ do (before a vowel y, or w), too (elsewhere); /k/ gale (before a vowel y or w), kale (elsewhere); /n/ inhale (before a consonant or word-final), note (elsewhere). /r/ hiss (before a consonant or word-final), run (trilled as in Italian, elsewhere); /w/ cuff (before a consonant other than y or word-final), way (elsewhere); /y/ fish (before a consonant or word-final), you (elsewhere), /θ/ thing; /ʔ/ (the sound between the vowels in unh-unh); /·/ long vowel, /´/ high pitch; /`/ low pitch.

violating (you) (AG); -atke?wrahkw -: yętkye'wráhkhwa' ‹one-oneself-hair-collects› *wig* (HS); -a'nwętarahkw -: na'na'nwętaráhkhwa' ‹one=another-self-word-collects› *one follows another's command, one obeys* (R); -ne -. -arahstahkw -: nehrarahstáhkhwa' ‹apart-he-himself-foot-collects› *he stamps (with his feet)* (HS); è·re -rah = kw -: è·re yuráhkhwa' ‹opposite it-collects› *it is excluded* (HS); kwęhs -t -. -rihwarahkw -: kwęhs ę'nahrurihwaráhkęk ‹no unknown-hither-he-matter-collect› *he is neutral* (HS).

-rahr - be thin. *v.r.-s.i.* stat: -ę·, prog: -, prp: -, dst: -, caus: -a'T-, rvs: -, dat: -, n-inc. karáhrę· *it is thin (not thick)* (HS); -rahra?T -: rarahrá'tha' ‹he-be thin-causes› *he thins it* (HS).

-rahra?T - thin. *v.s.-t.* rarahrá'tha' ‹he-be thin-causes› *he thins it* (HS).

rahθé?kye autumn, fall (RC 12:2); goldenrod (*Solidago* sp.) (R). *n.* rahθe? = kyeháh ‹autumn-little› *August* (R); *September* (HS: *September 15-October 15*); rahθe?kyehé·θu? ‹autumn-many great› *October* (R) (HS: *October 15-November 15*).

rahθe?kyeháh ‹autumn-little› August (R); September (HS: September 15-October 15). *n.*

rahθe?kyehé·θu? ‹autumn-many great› October (R) (HS: October 15-November 15). *n.*

-rahu?t - sweetflag. *n.r.* n-poss., n-inc., n.sfx. -a'. urahú'ta' *sweetflag (Acorus calamus)* (H-notebook).

-rakar(e) - sound. *v.r.-a.i.* stat: -ɸ, hab: -, pnt: ()-'. prog: -, prp: -, dst: -, caus: -, rvs: -, dat: II (-ti-/-hθ), n-inc. yurá·kar *it sounds* (HS), *the noise, sound* (AG), ęyurakà·re' *it will sound* (HS); -ra = kar(e)-{dative II}: yurakaré·ti· ‹it-sounds-for› *low, sharp noise* (AG). *it*

is loud; aloud (HS); -rakarerahsthę -: yurakareráhsthę· ‹it-sound-be in-causes-much› *noises* (AG); -rakarere -: yurakarè·re' ‹it-sound-is distant› *it rumbles* (HS); -či -. -rakar(e) -: čurá·kar ‹again-it-sounds› *it resounds* (HS); -t -. -rakar -: nyurá·kar ‹hither-it-sounds› *a noise* (AW 57); -a?rakarerahsT -: yę'rakareráhstha' ‹one-oneself-sound-be in-causes› *noisemaker, rattle* (HS); kwęhs -rakar(e)-{dative II}: kwęhs aryurakaré·ti' ‹no unknown-it-sound-be in-for› *a low, mild noise* (AG).

-rakar(e)-{dative II} be loud. *v.s.-s.i.* yurakaré·ti· ‹it-sounds-for› *it is loud* (HS).

-rakarere - rumble. *v.s.-s.i.* yurakarè·re' ‹it-sound-is distant› *it rumbles* (HS).

-raku - choose, prefer, select, take from, unload. *v.r.-t.* stat: -ę, hab: -ahs, pnt: -', prog: -, prp: -he-, dst: -, caus: -, rvs: -, dat: III (-ati-/-ę-), inc.-ɸ-ag./pat. rará·kwahs *he chooses, he prefers, he unloads* (HS), rurá·kwę *he has unloaded* (HS), ęhrará·ku' *he will unload* (HS), wa'krá·ku' *I chose it, I selected it,* wahsrá·ku' *you chose it, you selected it;* -raku -: yurá·kwę ‹it-chose› *deduction* (HS); -t -. -raku -: thrará·kwahs ‹hither-he-chooses› *he deducts* (HS), nyerá·ku' ‹hither-one-chose› *she took out* (AW 50); -ahθharaku -: rahθhará·kwahs ‹he-handful-chooses› *he snatches it* (HS); -rihwaraku -: nakrihwará·ku ‹you!=me-matter-choose› *permit me!* (RC 3:11), aryękhirihwará·ku' ‹unknown-one=us-matter-choose› *that one permit us* (MP); -rihwaraku -{dative III}: na'rihwarakwá·tih ‹one=another-matter-chooses-for› *one trusts another* (HS); -wętaraku -: rawętará·kwahs ‹he-word-chooses› *he extracts from a book* (HS); -wira = rakuhe -: wa'ewirarakúhe' ‹fact-one-infant-chose⟩ *one selected infant* (RC 9:2); **-atkerharaku -**: ękycrhará·ku⟩ ⟨fact-it-itself-body-chose⟩ *it took itself away* (RC 2:8); **-a'nwiraraku -**: wa⟩-ka⟩nwirará·ku⟩ ⟨fact-I-myself-infant-chose⟩ *I adopted child* (R); **-a'nwi = rarakwa⟩ -**: yakwa⟩nwirará·kwa⟩θ ⟨we-ourselves-infant-choose-begin⟩ *Adoption Ceremony* (R); **áhsę ę·či -raku -**: áhsę ę·či ękará·ku⟩ ⟨three one prediction-it-choose⟩ *one third* (AG).

-raku - deduction. *dv.n.s.* yurá·kwę ⟨it-chose⟩ *deduction* (HS).

-rakwn - deep detritus on the forest floor. *n.r.* n-poss., n-inc., n.sfx. -eh. urá·kw-neh *dead leaves, etc., thick and deep on the forest floor in dense woods and forests* (H-notebook).

-ran - corn soup. *n.r.* n-poss., n-inc., n. sfx. -eh. urà·neh *corn soup* (R).

-rakew - wipe. *v.r.-t.* See: **-akew -**.

rà·ruh black oak (RC 11:16). *n.*

-raθkęws blueweed. *n.r.* n-poss., n-inc., n.sfx. -. kará·θkęws *blueweed (Echium vulgate)* (H-notebook).

-rat - lie down. *v.r.-a.i.* stat: -, hab: -φ, pnt: -φ, prog: -, prp: -, dst: -, caus: -, rvs: -, dat: -, n-inc. í·kra·t *I lie down* (RC 3:22), wahrá·ra·t *he lay down* (RC 26:27), θá·ra·t *lie down!*; **-rat -**: rá·ra·t ⟨he-lies down⟩ *occupant (of a conveyance)* (HS); **-a⟩rat -**: yú⟩ra·t ⟨it-itself-lies down⟩ *it is formidable* (HS).

-rat - occupant (of a conveyance). *dv.n.s.* rá·ra·t ⟨he-lies down⟩ *occupant (of a conveyance)* (HS).

-ratawę - be a warmed tree (i.e., fit to give sap, ready for peeling bark off). *v.s.-s.i.* yuratá·wę· ⟨it-X-warmed⟩ *it is a warmed tree (i.e., it is fit to give sap or in a condition for peeling its bark off)* (H-notebook).

-rath - climb. *v.r.-a.i.* stat: -ę, hab: -ęhs, pnt: -φ ~ -ę⟩, prog: -, prp: -, dst: -ehrę-, caus: -ahsT- ~ -⟩T-, rvs: -, dat: -, inc.-φ-pat. By regular rule, word-final clusters of an obstruent plus a laryngeal metathesize. Thus, the final *th* of this root becomes *ht* when the punctual marker -φ is used. wa⟩kará·thę⟩ *it climbed* (RC 15:2); **-rath -**: rurá·thę ⟨he-climbed⟩ *blacksnake (Elaphe obsoleta)* (R); **-rathehrę -**: wa⟩ka-yerathéhrę⟩ ⟨fact-they-climbed-much⟩ *they climbed up* (RC 3:85); **-t -. -rath -**: ę⟩nyè·raht ⟨prediction-hither-one-climb⟩ *one will climb there* (RC 15:2); **-yah -. -rath -**: wekará·thę ⟨thither-it-climbed⟩ *it climbed up there* (RC 3:33), weyerá·thęhs ⟨thither-one-climbs⟩ *one climbs there* (RC 3:27); **-rathah = snahkw -**: yerathahsnáhkhwa⟩ ⟨one-climb-causes-instrument⟩ *staircase* (HS); **-či -. -nę'nakarathę -**: θahranę⟩nakará·thę⟩ ⟨again-fact-he-attach-climbed⟩ *he climbed back up the precipice* (RC 26:31); **-a⟩rathę⟩T -**: ru⟩rathę́⟩nę ⟨he-himself-climb-caused⟩ *he ascended* (HS).

-rath - blacksnake. *dv.n.s.* rurá·thę ⟨he-climbed⟩ *blacksnake (Elaphe obsoleta)* (R).

-rathahsnahkw - staircase. *dv.n.s.* yerathahsnáhkhwa⟩ ⟨one-climb-causes-instrument⟩ *staircase* (HS).

–rati – grind, rub. *v.r.-t.* stat: –, hab: -h,
pnt: -e·', prog: –, prp: –, dst: -chę-,
caus: –, rvs: –, dat: –, inc.-ɸ-pat.
rará·tih *he grinds it, he rubs it* (HS);
–ratyehę –: wa·'kratyéhę·' ⟨fact-I-rub-
bed-much⟩ *I rubbed it (as after hurting
an arm or rubbed clothes: e.g., If one
says* wa·'ktuharéhę·' *'I washed (clothes)'–and she asks "how", then answer
"I rubbed them (by hand)"* (L 75);
–ne –. **–ahθharati** –: wa·'thrahθhará·tye'
⟨fact-two-he-handful-rubbed⟩ *he rubbed two handfuls together* (RC 14:3).

raw –/**ru** – third person singular masculine
alienable. *n.r.pfx.* The form **raw** –
occurs before roots and stems that
begin with a vowel other than *a*. The
form **ru** – occurs elsewhere with loss
of an root or stem-initial *a*.

–ra? – empty noun root. *v.inc.* See: **–nę** =
'na(k)** – *affix, attach.*

–ra? – get in, get into, infect, touch upon.
v.s.-a.i. yù·ra·'θ ⟨it-be in-begins⟩ *it
gets into things,* rù·ra·'θ ⟨he-be in-be-
gins⟩ *it infects him* (HS), yurá·'ę ⟨it-be
in-began⟩ *it's gotten into it* (into anything) (L 53), wa·'ù·ra·' ⟨fact-it-be in-
began⟩ *it touched upon it* (RC 30:42);
it got into it (L 53).

–ra? – respond. *v.s.-a.i.* rà·ra·'θ ⟨he-be in-
begins⟩ *he responds* (HS), rurá·'ę ⟨he-
be in-began⟩ *he responded* (HS), ęh-
rà·ra·' ⟨prediction-it-be in-began⟩ *he
will respond* (HS).

–ra?kar – pluck. *v.r.-a.i.* stat: –, hab: -ęhs,
pnt: -·', prog: –, prp: –, dst: –, caus: –,
rvs: –, dat: –, n-inc. rará·'karęhs *he
plucks* (HS), wa·'kará·'ka·'r *I plucked
(feathers)* (R).

–ra?karhu – accompany, come along with.
v.r.-t. stat: –, hab: –, pnt: -·', prog: –,
prp: –, dst: –, caus: –, rvs: –, dat: –, n-
inc. ękakura·'kárhu·' *they will come*

along as well (RC 33:3); **–ra?kar** =
hu?ęha'nye? –: rura·'karhu·'ęhá··'nye'
⟨he-accompany-began-going along⟩ *he
is approaching* (H-notebook).

rá?kwihs turtle (RC 3:85), Turtle Clan
(R). *n.*

–ra?nahkw – be along, be exempt. *v.r.-a.i.*
stat: –, hab: -ahs, pnt: –, prog: -ę·ha-
'nye'-, prp: -he-, dst: –, caus: –, rvs: –,
dat: II (-θe-/-θ-), n-inc. rura·'náhkwahs
he is exempt (HS), rura·'nahkęhá··'-
nye' *he's along* (L 58); **–ra?nahkhe** –:
rara·'náhkhe' ⟨he-is along-going to⟩
he's along (as: with them in the car)
(L 58); **–ra?nahkw** –{dative I}: rara·'-
nahkθéhahk ⟨he-was along-for⟩ *he
used to be along* (L 58).

–ra?nar – hollow interior of an old, rotten
or dead tree. *n.r.* n-poss., n-inc., n.sfx.
-eh. ura·'nà·reh *hollow interior of an
old, rotten or dead tree* (R); -t-. **–ra?** =
naryę –: tkara·'ná·ryę' ⟨hither-it-hollow
tree-goes into⟩ *in the hollow tree* (RC
10:19).

–ra'nę – tree. *v.r.-t.* stat: –, hab: -h, pnt: –,
prog: –, prp: –, dst: –, caus: –, rvs: –,
dat: –, n-inc. rará··'nęh *he trees it*
(HS).

rá?θ moth (HS). *n.*

–ra?θ – cloud. *n.r.* n-poss., n-inc., n.sfx.
-ɸ ~ -eh. See also: **–ra?θr** –. ù·ra·'θ
cloud (RC 8:6), urá·'θeh *cloud* (R).

–ra?θr – cloud; spleen. *n.r.* inaln: kra·'-
θré·'kye *my spleen* (R), inc., n.sfx.
-eh. See also: **–ra?θ** –. urá·'θreh *cloud*
(HS), *spleen* (SH 375); **–ra?θr** –.
#kęha?nę?: ura·'θrehkę·'ha·'nę' ⟨cloud-
many⟩ *clouds* (HS); **–ra?θrutyę** –: yu-
ra·'θrú·tyę' ⟨it-cloud-covers-many⟩ *it
is clouded (dotted with clouds)* (HS).

–ra?θre? – go about joining, go about
reaching. *v.s.-t.* rará·'θre·'θ ⟨it-be in-
going to-begins⟩ *he goes about joining
it, he goes about reaching it* (HS).

-ra[?]θrutyę̧ – be clouded. *v.s.-s.i.* yura[?]-θrú·tyę̧[?] ‹it-cloud-covers-many› *it is clouded (dotted with clouds)* (HS).

réhse·n raisin (HS). *n.*

-rehsT – stretch. *v.r.-t.* stat: -φ, hab: -ha[?], pnt: -, prog: -, prp: -, dst: -, caus: -, rvs: -, dat: -, inc.-φ-ag. raréhstha[?] *he stretches it*; -a[?]θrarehsT –: ru[?]θraréhstha[?] ‹he-aim-stretches› *he is excessive, he is outrageous, he overdoes it* (HS), yú[?]θrarehst ‹it-aim-stretched› *excessively, extravagant, outrageous* (HS); -rihwarehsT –: rarihwaréhstha[?] ‹he-matter-stretches› *he amplifies it* (HS); -yah –. -rihwarehsT –: wehrarihwaréhstha[?] ‹thither-he-matter-stretches› *he exaggerates it* (HS).

ré·ti·θ radish *(Raphanus sativus)* (R). *n.*

-rę – empty noun root. *v.inc.* See: -aθhu – *smell.*

-rę – add, pick, put among, put in, set out, set on, take. *v.r.-t.* stat: -·, hab: -h, pnt: -[?], prog: -, prp: -, dst: -, caus: -hw-, rvs: -ku-, dat: -, inc.-φ-pat. rà·rę̧h *he adds, he picks, he puts among others, he puts in, he sets out, he sets on, he takes* (HS), rú·rę· *he added, etc.,* ę̧hrà·rę[?] *he will add, etc;* -rę̧ku –: raré·kwahs ‹he-add-undoes› *he culls, he picks out, he prunes, he sorts* (HS), ę̧hsré·ku[?] ‹prediction-you-add-undo› *you will sort* (L 75); -rę̧hsarę̧ku –: rarę̧hsaré·kwahs *he abases, he defames* (HS) ‹he-leg-add-undoes›, na[?]rę̧hsaré·kwahs ‹one=another-leg-add-undoes› *one dishonors another* (HS); -teh=warę̧ –: rutéhwarę̧hs ‹he-hide-adds› *he is skittish, he is timid* (HS); -teh=warę̧hsk –: rutehwarȩ́hskę̧· ‹he-hide-added-easily› *he is apt to frighten, he is timid* (HS); -ne –. -rę̧[?]arę̧hwahkw –: neyerę̧[?]arę̧hwáhkhwa[?] ‹apart-one-tree-add-causes-instrument› *joist* (HS); -t –. -ę'narę̧hw –: ę̧[?]nayawę̧[?]narę̧hwak ‹unknown-hither-it-day-add-cause› *it is dawn* (RC 14:3); -a[?]rę̧[?]arę̧ –: θa[?]rȩ́[?]arę̧h ‹you!-yourself-tree-add› *go behind tree!* (M 87); ì·nę̧ -a'nę̧nę̧hsarę̧ –: ì·nę̧ yu[?]nę̧nȩ́hsarę̧[?] ‹far it-itself-house-added› *the houses are, set far apart* (H 2484).

-rę̧ha[?] – be dexterous, be skillful. *v.r.-s.i.* stat: -ę̧, prog: -, prp: -, dst: -, caus: -, rvs: -, dat: -, n-inc. rurę̧há[?]ę̧ *he is dexterous, he is skillful* (HS).

-rę̧hkuhę̧hte – stagger, tipple. *v.r.-a.i.* stat: -, hab: -h, pnt: -[?], prog: -, prp: -, dst: -, caus: -, rvs: -, dat: -, n-inc. rurę̧hkuhę̧hteh *he staggers, he tipples* (HS).

-rę̧hkw – feel itchy. *v.r.-a.i.* stat: -·, hab: -ha[?], pnt: -, prog: -, prp: -, dst: -ahnę̧-, caus: -, rvs: -, dat: -, n-inc. rarȩ́hkhwa[?] *he feels itchy* (HS); -rę̧hkwah=nę̧ –: yurę̧hkwáhnę̧· ‹it-felt itchy-much› *it itches* (HS).

-rę̧hkwahnę̧ – itch. *v.s.-s.i.* yurę̧hkwáhnę̧· ‹it-felt itchy-much› *it itches* (HS).

-rę̧hθ – leg. *n.r.* n-poss., inc., n.sfx. -. See: -rę̧hs –. -rę̧hθa[?]nihr –: yurę̧hθa[?]níhrę̧ ‹it-leg-stood up› *its leg* (RC 24:8); -rę̧hθu'narhu –: ę̧krę̧hθu[?]nárhu[?] ‹prediction-I-leg-hook› *I will hook my leg* (RC 24:8).

-rę̧hs – leg. *n.r.* aln: akrȩ́hseh *my leg,*

inc., n.sfx. -eh. See: -rẹhθ -. urẹ́hsch *leg* (RC 28:1); -rẹhsaks -: rarẹhsá·ksẹ· ‹he-leg-is bad› *his leg is bad* (H 24 84); -rẹhsak"ahnahnẹ -: ẹkrẹhsakwah-náhnẹ·ʔ ‹prediction-I-leg-cut off-much› *I will cut its legs off* (AW 58); -rẹhsarẹku -: rarẹhsarẹ́·kwahs ‹he-leg-add-undoes› *he abases, he defames* (HS), naʔrẹhsarẹ́·kwahs ‹one=another-leg-add-undoes› *one dishonors another* (HS); -rẹhsẹʔke: urẹhsẹ́ʔkye ‹leg-at› *on its leg* (RC 30:45); -rẹhskaratihT -: yerẹhskaratíhthaʔ ‹one-leg-rub against-causes› *violin* (HS); -rẹhsuhskẹ -: rurẹhsúhskẹʔ ‹he-leg-is bare› *he is bare-legged* (HS); ti -. -rẹhsaʔθ -: tyerẹ́hsaʔθ ‹so-one-leg-is of a size› *size of one's leg* (RC 30:34); tha+ne -. -rẹhsukẹ -: thaʔnehrurẹhsú·kẹ· ‹unusual-apart-he-leg-is forked› *his leg gave out from under him* (RC 24:8).

-rẹhsarẹku - abase, defame, dishonor. *v.s.-t.* rarẹhsarẹ́·kwahs ‹he-leg-add-un-does› *he abases, he defames* (HS), naʔrẹhsarẹ́·kwahs ‹one=another-leg-add-undoes› *one dishonors another* (HS).

-rẹhskaratihT - violin. *dv.n.s.* yerẹhskara-tíhthaʔ ‹one-leg-rub against-causes› *violin* (HS).

-rẹhy - sky, blue. *n.r.* n-poss., inc., n.sfx. -eh. The meaning *blue* is present only in the Western dialect. urẹ́hyeh *sky* (RC 12:5), *blue* (PC) [Gallatin «ough-ruhyai» 'Sky, Heaven']; -rẹhyah(e)r -: wahrarẹhyáhraʔ ‹fact-he-sky-put up› *he "climbed the sky" (i.e., traveled from horizon to zenith)* (RC 12:19); -rẹhyahuk -: yurẹ́hyahuks ‹it-sky-lights up› *Aurora Borealis* (HS); *Milky Way; rainbow* (R); -rẹhyakẹw: urẹ́h-yakẹw ‹sky-in› *in sky* (R), *Heaven* (modern) (R), *Sky Land* (archaic) (RC 3:3); -rẹhyakẹw.#áh: urẹhyakẹwʔáh

‹sky-in-little› *celestial* (HS); -rẹhyaʔ = kehrunẹʔ: kayerẹhyaʔkyehrù·nẹʔ ‹they-sky-at-people› *angels* (R); -ne -. -rẹhyayẹ(T) -.#áh: neyurẹhyayẹʔáh ‹a-part-it-sky-lay-little› *watermelon (Citrullus vulgaris)* (R); tha -. -rẹhya = waʔk -: Tharẹhyawáʔkẹ ‹unusual-sky-held› *Creator, He-Holds-the-Heavens* (RC 1:1); tha -. -rẹhyurẹʔT -: thahra-rẹhyù·rẹʔt ‹unusual-fact-he-sky-split› *he splits the sky* (RC 14:5); -yah -. -rẹhyaʔniha -: weyurẹhyaʔníhẹ ‹thith-er-it-sky-sprains› *horizon* (HS); -rẹh = yarawẹ - -hyatẹhst -: yurẹhyarà·wẹʔ uh-yatẹ́hsteh ‹it-sky-is in-many book› *astronomy* (HS); -ne -. -aʔrẹhyayerẹ = ʔnye -: newaʔrẹhyayerẹ́·ʔnyeʔ ‹apart-it-itself-sky-does-going along› *Aurora Borealis, Northern Lights* (R); -rẹhy -ti -. -ahθuhkuʔnẹ -: urẹ́hyeh tiwahθuh-kúʔnẹ· ‹sky so-it-color-instrument-is a kind of› *azure* (HS); kẹʔ kwẹ́ -yah -. -rẹhyaʔniha -: kẹʔ kwẹ́ weyurẹhyaʔ-níhẹ ‹where like thither-it-sky-sprains› *horizon* (HS).

-rẹhy - ti -. -ahθuhkuʔnẹ - azure. *n.s.* urẹ́hyeh tiwahθuhkúʔnẹ· ‹sky so-it-color-instrument-is a kind of› *azure* (HS).

-rẹhyah(e)r - climb the sky. *v.s.-a.i.* wah-rarẹhyáhraʔ ‹fact-he-sky-put up› *he "climbed the sky" (i.e., traveled from horizon to zenith)* (RC 12:19).

-rẹhyahuk - Aurora Borealis; Milky Way; rainbow. *dv.n.s.* yurẹ́hyahuks ‹it-sky-lights up› *Aurora Borealis; Milky Way; rainbow* (R).

-rẹhyakẹ - suffer. *v.r.-a.i.* stat: -, hab: -, pnt: -ʔ, prog: -, prp: -, dst: -, caus: -ʔT-, rvs: -, dat: -, n-inc. waʔerẹ́h-yakẹʔ *one suffered* (RC 35:35); -rẹh = yakẹʔčr -: urẹhyakẹ́ʔčreh ‹it-suffer-'ness› *suffering* (HS); -rẹhyakẹʔT -: yurẹ́hyakẹʔt ‹it-suffer-caused› *it is fa-*

tiguing (HS), urę́hyakę́'t ‹suffer-cause› *suffering* (HS); **-a'rę̧hyakę?T -:** ra'rę̧hyakę́'tha' ‹he-himself-suffer-causes› *he toils* (HS), ru'rę̧hyakę́'nę ‹he-himself-suffer-caused› *he is toiling* (HS).

-rę̧hyakę̧w Heaven, Sky Land. *n.s.* urę́hyakęw ‹sky-in› *Heaven (modern), Sky Land (archaic)* (RC 3:3).

-rę̧hyakę̧w.#áh celestial. *n.s.* urę̧hyakęw-'áh ‹sky-in-little› *celestial* (HS).

-rę̧hyakę?čr - suffering. *n.s.* urę̧hyakę́'-čreh ‹it-suffer-'ness› *suffering* (HS).

-rę̧hyakę?T - be fatiguing. *v.s.-a.i.* yurę́hyakę't ‹it-suffer-caused› *it is fatiguing* (HS).

-rę̧hyakę?T - suffering. *n.s.* urę́hyakę't ‹suffer-cause› *suffering* (HS).

-rę̧hyarawę̧ - -hyatę̧hst - astronomy. *n.s.* yurę̧hyarà·wę' uhyatę́hsteh ‹it-sky-is in-many book› *astronomy* (HS).

-rę̧hya?kehrunę̧' angels. *n.s.* kayerę̧h-ya'kyehrù·nę' ‹they-sky-at-people› *angels* (R).

-rę̧hya?nahčr - craziness, frenzy *n.s.* urę̧h-ya'náhčreh ‹be crazy-'ness› *craziness, frenzy* (HS).

-rę̧hya?T - be crazy. *v.r.-a.i.* stat: -, hab: -ahs, pnt: -, prog: -, prp: -, dst: -, caus: -, rvs: -, dat: -, n-inc. rurę̧h-yá'nahs *he is crazy; lunatic* (HS); **-rę̧hya?nahčr -:** urę̧hya'náhčreh ‹be crazy-'ness› *craziness, frenzy* (HS).

-rę̧hya?T - lunatic. *dv.n.s.* rurę̧hyá'nahs *lunatic* (HS).

-rę̧kru?riθ - succumb. *v.r.-a.i.* hab: -, pnt: -, stat: -φ, prog: -, prp: -, dst: -, caus: -, rvs: -, dat: -, n-inc. rarę̧krú'ri·θ *he succumbs* (HS).

-rę̧ku - cull, pick out, prune, sort. *v.s.-t.* rarę́·kwahs ‹he-add-undoes› *he culls, he picks out, he prunes, he sorts* (HS). ę̧hsrę́·ku' ‹prediction-you-add-undo› *you will sort* (L 75).

-rę̧N - magic, witchcraft. *n.r.* n-poss., inc., n.sfx. -eh. urę́·teh *magic, witchcraft* (RC 27:27); **-rę̧ta?r -:** rurę́·ta'r ‹he-magic-is much› *soothsayer* (RC 6:1); **-rę̧tukę?:** karę̧tú·kę' ‹it-magic-less› *ginseng (Palax quinquefolius)* (HS); **-ne -. -rę̧tukę̧ni -:** wa'nyękrę̧tu-kę̧·ni' ‹fact-apart-one=me-magic-?'?› *one has bested me* (RC 28:12); **-a'rę̧ = nę̧ti -:** ru'rę̧nę́·ti· ‹he-himself-magic-makes› *magician, wizard* (RC 14:2), wa'ę́'rę̧nę́·ti' ‹fact-one-oneself-magic-made› *one made magic* (RC 3:41), wa'kayę̧'rę̧nę́·ti' ‹fact-they-themselves-magic-made› *they put it in a state of enchantment* (RC 35:11).

-rę̧r - dry, withered leaves. *n.r.* n-poss., inc., n.sfx. -eh. urę̧·reh *dry, withered leaves* (HS).

-rę̧ryuhkw - flame, halo, ray. *n.r.* n-poss., inc., n.sfx. -eh. urę̧ryúhkweh *flame, halo, ray* (HS); **-rę̧ryuhkwa?r -:** yurę̧-ryúhkwa'r ‹it-ray-is much› *it has a halo* (HS); **-ne -. -rę̧ryuhkwitkę? -:** ne-yurę̧ryuhkwitkę́'ę ‹apart-it-ray-come forth-began› *it is resplendent* (HS).

-rę̧ryuhkwa?r - have a halo. *v.s.-s.i.* yurę̧-ryúhkwa'r ‹it-ray-is much› *it has a halo* (HS).

-rę̧θ - bowstring; trigger. *n.r.* n-poss., n-inc., n.sfx. -eh. uŗé·θeh *bowstring: trigger* (HS) [Lawson «Ooratsa» 'Jew's-Harp'].

-ŗeθhu– smell. *v.s.-t.* See: -aθhu–. ękŗéθhu^ʔ ‹fact-I-X-smelled› *I smelled it* (R), weθaŗéθhu^ʔ ‹fact-you-X-smelled› *you smelled it* (R).

-ŗeθhwahT– smell. *v.s.-a.i.* raŗeθhwáhtha^ʔ ‹he-X-smell-causes› *he smells* (HS).

-ŗet– tree. *n.r.* n-poss., inc., n.sfx. -. Suppletive with -ŗe^ʔ–, found incorporated in a few constructions that have the appearance of loans from other Northern Iroquoian languages. -ŗetah= steni–: raŗetahstè·nih ‹he-tree-adorns› *he hews trees, he squares trees* (HS); -ŗetahstenya^ʔT–: yeŗetahstenyá^ʔtha^ʔ ‹one-tree-adorn-causes› *adz, broad-ax* (HS); -ŗetahstenihsi–: raŗetahsteníhsyęhs ‹he-tree-adorn-undoes› *he rough-hews, he hews miserably* (HS); -ŗetawa^ʔk–: Kaŗetawá^ʔkę ‹it-tree-held› *One-Is-Holding-the-Tree (Chief of the Snipe Clan)* (H-Handbook); -ŗetu^ʔčr–: uŗetú^ʔčreh ‹tree-cover-'ness› *coffin, receptacle, trunk* (RC 3:22); -ŗetu^ʔ= čŗehnawę–: yuŗetu^ʔčŗehnà·wę^ʔ ‹it-tree-cover-'ness-fall-caused-much› *cabinet* (HS); -ŗetu^ʔčŗeti–: ęθwaŗetu^ʔčŗé·ti^ʔ ‹prediction-you-tree-cover-'ness-make› *you will make a coffin* (RC 3:22); -ŗetu^ʔčrurukT–: yeŗetu^ʔčrurúktha^ʔ ‹one-tree-cover-'ness-cover-causes› *pall* (HS).

-ŗeT– ax; log, tree. *n.r.* n-poss., inc., n.sfx. -eh. uŗé·^ʔneh *ax; log* (R) [Gallatin «orenneh, orenhna» 'Wood']; -ŗe= thę: uŗé·thę ‹tree-in the middle of› *middle of tree* (RC 10:5); -ŗe'nahrar–: uŗe^ʔnáhrareh ‹log-is a hole› *ladder* (HS); -ŗe'nahrar–.#kęhe^ʔ: kaŗe^ʔnahraŗekéhe^ʔ ‹it-tree-is a hole-deceased› *maple sap* (R); -ŗe'nakri–: uŗe^ʔná·kri^ʔ ‹tree-liquid› *sugar* (R); -ŗe'nakri–.#hči: uŗe^ʔnakrí^ʔči ‹tree-liquid-very› *much sweetness, it is very sweet* (RC 2:15); -ŗe'nakri^ʔčrarhu–{dative I}: kaŗe^ʔnakri^ʔčrarhú^ʔθeh ‹it-tree-liquid-'ness-mixes in-for› *sweetmeat* (HS); -ŗe'na= kri^ʔčra^ʔr–: yuŗe^ʔnakrí^ʔčra·^ʔr ‹it-tree-liquid-'ness-is much› *cake* (R); -ŗe= 'nya^ʔk–: raŗé·^ʔnya^ʔks ‹he-log-cuts› *he saws* (R); -ne–. -ŗe'na̱ne–: nekaŗé·^ʔna^ʔne^ʔ ‹apart-it-log-is present› *log house* (R); -ne–. -ŗe'nya^ʔkT–: neyeŗe^ʔnyá^ʔktha^ʔ ‹two-one-log-cut-causes› *saw* (R); -ŗe'nakri– -nęhwak(T)–: uŗe^ʔná·kri^ʔ kakunéhwaks ‹tree-liquid they-are ill› *diabetes; diabetic* (R); -ŗe'nakri– -θŗęw–: uŗe^ʔná·kri^ʔ uθŗè·weh ‹tree-liquid syrup› *osier* (HS), *syrup* (R); -ŗe'nakri–.#hči -ta'nar–: uŗe^ʔnakrí^ʔči utá·^ʔnareh ‹tree-liquid-very bread› *cake* (R).

-ŗetahsteni– hew trees, square trees. *v.s.-a.i.* raŗetahstè·nih ‹he-tree-adorns› *he hews trees, he squares trees* (HS).

-ŗetahstenya^ʔT– adz, broad-ax. *dv.n.s.* yeŗetahstenyá^ʔtha^ʔ ‹one-tree-adorn-causes› *adz, broad-ax* (HS).

-ŗetahstenihsi– rough-hew, hew miserably. *v.s.-a.i.* raŗetahsteníhsyęhs ‹he-tree-adorn-undoes› *he rough-hews, he hews miserably* (HS).

-ŗetawa^ʔk– One-Is-Holding-the-Tree. *dv. n.s.* Kaŗetawá^ʔkę ‹it-tree-held› *One-Is-Holding-the-Tree (Chief of the Snipe Clan)* (H-Handbook).

-ŗeta^ʔr– soothsayer. *dv.n.s.* ruŗé·ta^ʔr ‹he-magic-is much› *soothsayer* (RC 6:1).

ŗéthę buck (male deer). *n.* Possibly from the same root as Lawson's «Ottea» 'Fawn-skin' (= (?) uthę^ʔáh).

-ŗeti– pick away, pick out. *v.s.-t.* stat: -, hab: -, pnt: -, prog: -, prp: -, dst: -ahnę-, caus: -, rvs: -ęku-, dat: -, inc.-ɸ-pat. Found only in the constructions cited below. **ti+či –. –rętyahnę –**: tiθkayerętyáhnę· ‹so-again-they-picked out-much› *they picked it out* (RC 29:21); **–ahθharętyęku –**: rahθharętyę́·kwahs ‹he-handful-pick out-undoes› *he claws, he scratches* (HS); **–ʔwahra = rętyęku –**: yuʔwahrarętyę́·kwę ‹it-meat-pick out-undid› *it picked away meat* (RC 17:3).

–rętukęʔ ginseng. *dv.n.s.* karętú·kęʔ ‹it-magic-less› *ginseng (Palax quinquefolius)* (R).

–rętuʔčr – coffin, receptacle, trunk. *n.s.* urętúʔčreh ‹tree-cover-'ness› *coffin, receptacle, trunk* (RC 3:22).

–rętuʔčręhnawę – cabinet. *dv.n.s.* yurętuʔčręhnà·węʔ‹it-tree-cover-'ness-fall-caused-much› *cabinet* (HS).

–rętuʔčrurukT – pall. *dv.n.s.* yerętuʔčrurúkthaʔ ‹one-tree-cover-'ness-cover-causes› *pall* (HS).

–ręw – length of body, stature. *n.r.* n-poss., inc., n.sfx. –eh. urę·weh *length of body, stature* (R); **–ręwar –**: rarę̀·war ‹he-length of body-is in› *he frames a picture* (HS); **–ręweθ –**: krę́·we·θ ‹I-length of body-is long› *I am tall* (AG); **ti –. –ręweθ –**: tiyerę́·we·θ ‹so-one-length of body-is long› *so one is tall* (RC 10:15); **ti –. –ręweθ –.#áh**: tikręwe·θʔáh ‹so-it-length of body-is long-little› *I am short* (R); **ti –. –rę = weθ –.#úʔy**: tikaręwe·θʔúʔy ‹so-it-length of body-is long-great› *it is so tall* (RC 30:21); **–aʔręwaʔnihr –**: yuʔręwaʔníhrę ‹it-itself-length of body-stood up› *it stands on end* (HS), waʔ

ręwáʔnihč ‹it-itself-length of body-stands up› *it rears (e.g., a horse)* (HS).

–ręwar – frame a picture. *v.s.-a.i.* rarę̀·war ‹he-length of body-is in› *he frames a picture* (HS).

–ręweθ – be tall. *v.s.-a.i.* krę́·we·θ ‹I-length of body-is long› *I am tall* (AG).

–ręʔ – tree; shaft of a cart. *n.r.* n-poss., inc., n.sfx. –eh. urę́ʔeh *tree; shaft of a cart* (HS) [Gallatin «ough-ruhch» 'Tree']; **–ręʔahrar –**: neyuręʔáhrarę ‹two-it-tree-is a hole› *two trees with holes in them* (RC 25:2); **–ręʔahrarak –**: raręʔáhrara·ks ‹he-tree-be a hole-eats› *he mortises* (HS); **–ręʔahrarakT –**: yęręʔahrarákthaʔ ‹one-tree-be a hole-eat-causes› *carpenter's (large) bore* (HS); **–ręʔanę –**: karęʔanęh ‹it-tree-guards› *it guards tree* (HS); *liverwort* (R); **–ręʔ = aʔnihθku –**: ękayeręʔaʔníhθkuʔ ‹prediction-they-tree-pick off› *they will uproot tree* (RC 3:70); **–ręʔiyu –**: karęʔí·yu· ‹it-tree-is great› *great, beautiful tree* (R); **–ne –. –ręʔakwarihęʔ –**: nęyuręʔakwaríhęʔ‹apart-prediction-it-tree-hasten-began› *tree will be shaken* (RC 27:27); **–ne –. –ręʔaręhwahkw –**: neyeręʔaręhwáhkhwaʔ ‹apart-one-tree-add-causes-instrument› *joist* (HS); **–ne –. –ręʔaʔθku –**: nękręʔáʔθkuʔ ‹apart-prediction-I-tree-carry away› *I will carry away tree* (RC 30:25), waʔtkaręʔáʔθkuʔ ‹fact-apart-it-tree-carried away› *it carried away tree* (RC 30:26); **–ne –. –ręʔukę –**: neyuręʔú·kęʔ ‹two-it-tree-is bent› *fork of trees* (RC 27:6);

(RC 27:6); ti -. -rẹʔaʔθrẹ -: nẹkarẹʔáʔ-
θrẹ·k ‹so-prediction-it-tree-be so big›
tree will be so big (RC 30:25); -aʔ=
rẹʔačhẹwati -: waʔrẹʔačhẹwá·tih ‹it-
itself-tree-self-smoothes› *sycamore or
bottonwood tree* (AG).

-rẹʔahrarak - mortise. *v.s.-a.i.* rarẹʔáh-
rara·ks ‹he-tree-be a hole-eats› *he
mortises* (HS).

-rẹʔahrarakT - carpenter's bore. *dv.n.s.*
yẹrẹʔahrarákthaʔ ‹one-tree-be a
hole-eat-causes› *carpenter's (large)
bore* (HS).

-rẹʔanẹ - liverwort. *dv.n.s.* karẹʔanẹh ‹it-
tree-guards› *liverwort* (R).

-rẹʔeʔčr - thigh. *n.r.* n-poss., n-inc., n.sfx.
-eh. urẹʔéʔčreh *thigh* (HS).

-rẹʔkar - finger span. *n.* poss. ?, inc.,
n.sfx. -. Found only incorporated.
-rẹʔkarah(e)r -: waʔkarẹʔkaráhrẹʔ
‹fact-it-finger span-put up› *to reach,
span the fingers, extend, etc.* (AG);
-či -. -rẹʔkarat: čurẹʔkara·t ‹again-it-
finger span-is one› *one stretch/reach
of fingers* (AG); -aʔrẹʔkaraʔr -: waʔ-
rẹ́ʔkaraʔr ‹it-itself-finger span-is
much› *geometrical caterpillar* (AG).

-rẹʔkẹʔr - massacre, slaughter, strike
down. *v.r.-t.* stat: -, hab: -s, pnt: -,
prog: -, prp: -, dst: -, caus: -hu-, rvs:
-, dat: -, n-inc. rarẹ́ʔkẹʔč *he massacres, he slaughters, he strikes down*
(HS); -rẹʔkẹʔrhu -: ẹhrarẹʔkẹ́ʔrhuk
‹prediction-he-slaughter-cause› *he will
slaughter* (HS).

-rẹʔkẹʔrhu - slaughter. *v.s.-t.* ẹhrarẹʔkẹ́ʔ-
rhuk ‹prediction-he-slaughter-cause›
he will slaughter (HS).

-rẹʔkruʔriʔ - swag, sway. *v.r.-a.i.* stat: -ẹ,
hab: -θ, pnt: -ɸ, prog: -, prp: -, dst: -,
caus: -, rvs: -, dat: -, n-inc. ra-
rẹʔkrúʔriʔθ *he swags, he sways* (HS),
rurẹʔkruʔríʔẹ *he swagged, he swayed*
(HS), ẹhrarẹʔkrúʔriʔ *he will swag, he*

will swayed (HS).

-rẹʔkuhw - swag, sway. *v.r.-a.i.* stat: -ẹ°,
hab: -, pnt: -, prog: -, prp: -, dst: -,
caus: -, rvs: -, dat: -, n-inc. rarẹʔkúhẹ
he swags, he sways (HS).

-rẹ'nahrar - ladder. *n.s.* urẹʔnáhrareh ‹log-
be a hole› *ladder* (HS).

-rẹ'nahrar -.#kẹheʔ maple sap. *n.s.* ka-
rẹʔnahrarẹkẹ́heʔ ‹it-tree-is a hole-deceased› *maple sap* (R).

-rẹ'nakri - sugar. *n.s.* urẹʔná·kriʔ ‹tree-liquid› *sugar* (R).

-rẹ'nakri - -nẹhwak(T) - *dv.n.s.* urẹʔná·
kriʔ kakunẹ́hwaks ‹tree-liquid they-
are ill› *diabetes; diabetics* (R).

-rẹ'nakri - -θrẹw - osier; syrup. *n.s.*
urẹʔná·kriʔ uθrẹ̀·weh ‹tree-liquid syrup› *osier; syrup* (HS).

-rẹ'nakri -.#hči -ta'nar - cake. *n.s.* u-
rẹʔnakríʔči utáʔnareh ‹tree-liquid-very
bread› *cake* (R).

-rẹ'nakriʔčrarhu -{dative I} sweetmeat.
dv.n.s. karẹʔnakriʔčrarhúʔθeh ‹it-tree-
liquid-'ness-mixes in-for› *sweetmeat*
(HS).

-rẹ'nakriʔčraʔr - cake. *dv.n.s.* yurẹʔna-
kríʔčra·ʔr ‹it-tree-liquid-'ness-is much›
cake (R).

-rẹʔnh - frequent. *v.r.-a.i.* stat: -ẹ, hab:
-ẹhs, pnt: -, prog: -, prp: -, dst: -,
caus: -ahsT-, rvs: -, dat: -, n-inc.
rarẹ́ʔnhẹhs *he frequents* (HS);
-rẹʔnhahsT -: rurẹʔnháhsthaʔ ‹he-frequent-causes› *it inures him* (HS);
-rẹʔnhaʔ -: naʔrẹʔnháʔẹ ‹one=another-
frequent-began› *one is familiar with
another* (HS), rarẹ́ʔnhaʔθ ‹he-frequent-begins› *he becomes familiar
with it, he gets used to it* (HS),
rurẹʔnháʔẹ ‹he-frequent-began› *he
knows how* (L 50), wahrarẹ́ʔnhaʔ
‹fact-he-frequent-began› *he got used
to it* (L 50), *he learned* (L 49), ah-
rurẹʔnháʔẹk ‹unknown-he-frequent-be-

gin› *that he become accustomed to it* (R); -rę?nha?T -: khe?rę?nhá?tha? ‹I=another-frequent-begin-cause› *I accustom another. I familiarize another* (HS); **tha -. -yę - -rę?nha? -:** thikà·yę? ahrarę?nha? ‹unusual-it-goes into unknown-he-frequent-begin› *easily he learns* (L 49); **ti -. -a?rę?nh -:** tyu?rę?nhę ‹so-it-itself-frequented› *at intervals, occasionally* (HS); **kwęhs -rę?nha? -:** kwęhs ahrurę?nháhęk ‹no unknown-he-frequent-begin› *he is unaccustomed to it* (HS).

-rę?nhahsT - inure. *v.s.-t.* rurę?nháhstha? ‹he-frequent-causes› *it inures him* (HS).

-rę?nha? - become accustomed, learn. *v.s.-a.i.* na?rę?nhá?ę ‹one=another-frequent-began› *one is familiar with another* (HS), rarę?nha?θ ‹he-frequent-begins› *he becomes familiar with it, he gets used to it* (HS), rurę?nhá?ę ‹he-frequent-began› *he knows how* (L 50), wahrarę?nha? ‹fact-he-frequent-began› *he got used to it* (L 50), *he learned* (L 49), ahrurę?nhá?ęk ‹unknown-he-frequent-begin› *that he become accustomed to it* (R).

-rę?nha?T - accustom, familiarize. *v.s.-t.* khe?rę?nhá?tha? ‹I=another-frequent-begin-cause› *I accustom another, I familiarize another* (HS).

-rę'nya?k - saw. *v.s.-a.i.* rarę·?nya?ks ‹he-log-cuts› *he saws* (R).

-rhahkw - reed (plant). *n.r.* n-poss., n-inc., n.sfx. -eh. urháhkweh *reed* (HS).

-rhahst - cradle board; jack-in-the-pulpit. *n.r.* n-poss., inc. (with the meaning 'cradle board'), n.sfx. -eh. urháhsteh *cradle board: jack-in-the-pulpit (Arisaema atrorubens)* (H-notebook); **-rhahstę?ke:** urhahstę?kye ‹cradle board-at› *in its cradle board* (RC 30:2); **-rhahsta?nihr -:** wa?erhahstá?nir ‹fact-one-cradle board-stood up› *one stood up cradle board* (RC 30:4).

-rhar - be confident, be willing. *v.r.-s.i.* stat: -e?, prog: -a'nye?-, prp: -, dst: -, caus: -ahT-, rvs: -, dat: -, n-inc. rurhà·re? *he is confident, he is willing* (HS), rurhará·?nye? *he goes confidently* (HS); **-rharahčr -:** urharáhčreh ‹be confident-'ness› *confidence, hope, zeal* (HS); **-rharahčrayę(T) -:** rurharáhčrayę? ‹he-be confident-'ness-lays› *he has hope* (HS); **-rharahčręti -:** rarharahčrę·tih ‹he-be confident-'ness-makes› *he gives hope* (HS); **-rha=rahT -:** rarhà·rahč ‹he-be confident-causes› *he promises* (HS), ęhrarhà·raht ‹prediction-he-be confident-causes› *he will promise* (HS); **kwęhs -rharahT -:** kwęhs aryurharáhnęk ‹no unknown-it-be confident-cause› *it is unexpected, it is unhoped for, it is unpromising* (HS).

-rharahčr - confidence, hope, zeal. *n.s.* urharáhčreh ‹be confident-'ness› *confidence, hope, zeal* (HS).

-rharahčrayę(T) - have hope. *v.s.-a.i.* rurharáhčrayę? ‹he-be confident-'ness-lays› *he has hope* (HS).

-rharahčręti - give hope. *v.s.-t.* rarharahčrę·tih ‹he-be confident-'ness-makes› *he gives hope* (HS).

−**rharahT** − promise. *v.s.-a.i.* rarhà·rahč ‹he-be confident-causes› *he promises* (HS), ęhrarhà·raht ‹prediction-he-be confident-causes› *he will promise* (HS).

−**rha̱'n** −/ −**rha'n** − forest, woods. *n.r.* n-poss., inc., n.sfx. −eh. The form −**rha̱'n** − appears only in the citation from of the root. Elsewhere, the root has the form −**rha'n** −. úrha'neh *forest, woods* (HS); −**rha'na̱kęw**: urhá·'nakęw ‹forest-in› *in the forest* (RC 24:2); −**rha** = **'na̱kęw.#ha·'**: rurha'nakęwha·' ‹he-woods-in-customary› *he is usually in the woods* (H 2892); −**rha'na̱kęw.#ú'y**: urha'nakęw'ú'y ‹forest-in-great› *desert* (HS); −**rha'nęti** −: karha'nę́·tih ‹it-forest-makes› *orchard* (HS); −**rha'nyę** −: wahrarhá·'nyę' ‹fact-he-forest-went into› *he went into the forest* (RC 26:15).

−**rha'n** − catch, trap. *v.r.-t.* stat: -e', hab: -, pnt: -, prog: -, prp: -, dst: -, caus: -, rvs: -, dat: -, n-inc. yurhá'ne' *adhesive: it is catching* (HS); −**rha'ę'** = **nuhsk** −: yurha'nę'núhskę· ‹it-catch-cause-covered-easily› *it adheres, it sticks to* (HS).

−**rha'n** − adhesive. *dv.n.s.* yurhá'ne' ‹it-caught› *adhesive* (HS).

−**rha'na̱kęw.#ú'y** desert. *n.s.* urha'na̱kęw'ú'y ‹forest-in-great› *desert* (HS).

−**rha'nęti** − orchard. *dv.n.s.* karha'nę́·tih ‹it-forest-makes› *orchard* (HS).

−**rha'ę'nuhsk** − adhere, stick to. *v.s.-a.i.* yurha'nę'núhskę·‹it-catch-cause-covered-easily› *it adheres, it sticks to* (HS).

−**rhenath** − be stiff. *v.r.-s.i.* stat: -ę, prog: -, prp: -, dst: -, caus: -a'T-, rvs: -, dat: -, n-inc. ti −. −**rhenath** −: tyurhená·thę ‹so-it-is stiff› *it is stiff* (HS); −**rhena** = **tha'T** −: rarhenathá'tha' ‹he-be stiff-causes› *he stiffens it* (HS).

−**rhenatha'T** − stiffen. *v.s.-t.* rarhenathá'-tha' ‹he-be stiff-causes› *he stiffens it* (HS).

−**rhew** − sift. *v.r.-t.* stat: -, hab: -ahs, pnt: -, prog: -, prp: -, dst: -, caus: -ahT-, rvs: -, dat: -, n-inc. −**rhewahčr** −: urhewáhčreh ‹sift-'ness› *fanning-mill* (HS); −**rhewahT** −: yerhewáhtha' ‹one-sift-causes› *one fans with it: fanning-mill* (HS); −**a'rhew** −: ka'rhè·wahs ‹I-myself-sift› *I fan it, I sift it* (H-notebook); −**či** −. −**rhew** −: θhrarhè·wahs ‹again-he-sifts› *he resifts* (HS).

−**rhewahčr** − fanning-mill. *n.s.* urhewáhčreh ‹fan with-'ness› *fanning-mill* (HS).

−**rhewahT** − fan with. *v.r.-t.* stat: -, hab: -ha', pnt: -, prog: -, prp: -, dst: -, caus: -, rvs: -, dat: -, n-inc. yerhewáhtha' *one fans with it* (HS).

−**rhę** − be day. *v.r.-s.i.* stat: -ϕ, prog: -, prp: -, dst: -, caus: -hT-, rvs: -, dat: -, n-inc. This root is irregular in two respects. First, it is the only vowel-final root that takes the −ϕ stative suffix. Second, while it is clearly a part of the words meaning *morning* and *day of the week*, these words are otherwise partially or completely morphologically opaque. The question marks in the angle-bracketed (‹›) portion are there to indicate that, from the combination of the repetitive and the neuter third singular objective pronoun, one would expect ***ču** − and not θu −. −**rhę'** −: wa'úrhę' ‹fact-it-be day-began› *it became day(time), daylight* (RC 27:2), *daily* (HS), ęyúrhę' ‹prediction-it-be day-begin› *tomorrow* (RC 30:14) [Lawson «Jureha» 'To morrow']; −**rhę'** −.#**keha·'**: urhę'ękyéha·' ‹be day-begin-customarily› *daily, diurnal, pertaining to day* (HS); −**rhę'** =

θrę –: yurhę́ʼθrę· ‹it-be day-began-many› *days* (RC 3:14); –či –. –hterhę –: θuhtérhę ‹again ʼ-it ʼ-X-is day› *morning* (RC 4:7); –či –. –hterhę.#áh: θuhterhę́ʼáh ‹again ʼ-it ʼ-X-is day-little› *morning* (HS); –či –. –hterhę.#ke: θuhterhę́·kye ‹again ʼ-it ʼ-X-is day-at› *forenoon* (HS); –ne –. –rhęhT –: nehrarhę́htha⁹ ‹apart-he-be day-causes› *he stays overnight* (HS), waʼtkayérhęht ‹fact-apart-they-be day-caused› *they were all night* (RC 12:13); –ne –. –rhęhnahnę –: nehrarhęhnáhnęh ‹apart-he-be day-causes-many› *he stays over nights* (HS), nękarhęhnáhnę·⁹ ‹apart-prediction-it-be day-cause-many› *it will be so many days* (RC 30:18); –t –. –rhę⁹ –: nayúrhę⁹ ‹hither-it-be day-began› *daybreak, very early dawn* (HS); –t –. –rhę⁹ –.#aka·⁹: nyurhęʼθʼáka·⁹ ‹hither-it-be day-begins-characterized by› *English* (HS); –t –. –rhę⁹ –. #ú⁹y: nayurhęʼúʼy ‹hither-it-be day-began-great› *day-break, just after midnight, very early dawn* (HS); ti+ či –. –rhę⁹ –: tičurhę́ʼę ‹so-again-it-be day-began› *days* (RC 4:8), *everyday* (RC 27:2), *daily* (HS); áhsę ti+ či –. –hterhę –: áhsę tičuhtérhę ‹three so-again-it-X-is day› *Wednesday* (R); hę́ʼtahk ti+či –. –hterhę –: hę́ʼtahk tičuhtérhę ‹four so-again-it-X-is day› *Thursday* (R); né·kti· ti+či –. –hterhę –: né·kti· tičuhtérhę ‹two so-again-it-X-is day› *Tuesday* (R); wísk ti+či –. –hterhę –: wísk tičuhtérhę ‹five so-again-it-X-is day› *Friday* (R); íhsʼę

–yah+či –. –rhę⁹ –: íhsʼę yęčúrhę⁹ ‹more thither-prediction-again-it-be day-begin› *day after tomorrow* (HS); kyè·wę –rhę⁹ –: kyè·wę yurhę́ʼę ‹now it-be day-began› *today* (HS); ha⁹ kyè·wę ti –. –rhę⁹ –: ha⁹ kyè·wę tyurhę́ʼθrę· ‹the now so-it-be day-began-many› *now-a-days* (HS).

–rhęhskri – artichoke. *n.r.* n-poss., n-inc., n.sfx. –⁹. urhę́hskri⁹ *artichoke (Cynara scolymus)* (H-notebook).

–rhęrhu – howl. *v.r.-a.i.* stat: -, hab: -h, pnt: -, prog: -, prp: -, dst: -, caus: -, rvs: -, dat: -, n-inc. rarhę́rhuh *he howls, he ululates* (HS).

–rhę⁹ – daily, daylight. *dv.n.s.* waʼúrhę⁹ ‹fact-it-be day-began› *daylight* (RC 27:2), *daily* (HS).

–rhę⁹ – tomorrow. *dv.n.s.* ęyúrhę⁹ ‹prediction-it-be day-begin› *tomorrow* (RC 30:14) [Lawson «Jureha» 'To morrow'].

–rhę⁹ –.#keha·⁹ daily, diurnal. *n.s.* urhęʼękyéha·⁹ ‹be day-begin-customarily› *daily, diurnal, pertaining to day* (HS).

–rhę⁹θrę – days. *dv.n.s.* yurhę́ʼθrę· ‹it-be day-began-many› *days* (RC 3:14).

–rhu – apply, mix, put on. *v.r.-t.* stat: -, hab: -hs, pnt: -⁹, prog: -, prp: -, ´dst: -hθę-, caus: -hsT-, rvs: -, dat: -, inc.-ɸ-ag./pat. rárhuhs *he applies it, he mixes it, he puts it on* (HS); –ne –. –rhu –: nehrárhuhs ‹two-he-mixes› *he mixes the two* (HS), nęyérhu⁹ ‹two-prediction-one-mix› *one will mix it* (RC 17:4); –ne –. –rhuhθę –: neyerhúhθ ̨ęh ‹two-one-mixes-much› *one sea-sons it* (HS); **-ne -**. **-rhuhsT -**: neyer-húhstha⁷ ‹two-one-mix-causes› *one is seasoning it: seasoning* (HS); **-ne -**. **-rhuθhwahn ̨ęhkw -**:neyurhuθhwahn ̨ęh-khwa⁷‹two-it-mix-smell-much-instrument› *aromatics, cologne, perfume* (HS); **-nawa⁷čt ̲arhu -**: ranawa⁷čtárhuhs ‹he-lead-mixes› *he leads it, he plumbs it, he solders it* (HS); **-n ̨ęhra⁷s ̲arhu -**: yen ̨ęhra⁷sárhuhs ‹one-milk-mixes› *one churns* (HS); **-n ̨ęhra⁷s ̲arhuhsT -**: yen ̨ęhra⁷sarhúhstha⁷ ‹one-milk-mix-causes› *one churns* (HS); **-r ̨ę'nakri⁷ = črarhu -{dative I}**: kar ̨ę⁷nakri⁷črar-hú⁷θeh ‹it-tree-liquid-'ness-mixes in-for› *sweetmeat* (HS); **-rihw ̲arhu -**: wa⁷-na⁷rihwárhu⁷ ‹fact-one=another-matter-mixed› *one blamed another* (R), na⁷ríhwarhuhs ‹one=another-matter-mixes› *one accuses another* (HS); **-ye = t ̲arhu -**: rayétarhuhs ‹he-fat-mixes› *he lards it* (HS).

-rhuhčraw ̨ę - make sick by witchcraft. *v. s.-t.* wa⁷na⁷nerhuhčrà·w ̨ę⁷ ‹fact-one=another-charm-'ness-possessed› *one made someone else sick by witchcraft* (R).

-rhuh ̲t - lady slipper; charm, love potion. *n.r.* n-poss., inc., n.sfx. **-φ**. úrhuht *lady slipper (Cypripedium* sp.*)* (H-notebook); *charm* (HS), *love potion* (RC 17:title); **-rhuhčraw ̨ę -**: wa⁷na⁷nerhuh-črà·w ̨ę⁷ ‹fact-one=another-charm-'ness-possessed› *one made someone else sick by witchcraft* (R).

-rhw ̲ar - swan. *n.r.* n-poss., n-inc., n.sfx. **-eh**. This root may be related to, but shows different morphology from the word for swan given in Lawson (1709), «Oorhast». úrhwareh *swan (Cygnus* sp.*)* (RC 8:34).

-rhweht - plague, witch-induced illness. *n.r.* n-poss., n-inc., n.sfx. **-φ**. Hewitt &

Smith's transcription suggest únr-hweht. If correct, the initial *n* of the root has been lost in modern Tuscarora. úrhweht *plague* (HS), *witch-induced illness* (R).

-rih - boil, cook, ripen. *v.r.-a.i.* hab: -θ, pnt: -φ, stat: -ę ~ -φ, prog: -, prp: -, dst: -ę-, caus: -a⁷T- ~ -T-, rvs: -, dat: I (-θe-/-θ-), inc.-φ-pat. kà·rihθ *it ripens* (HS), yù·rih *it is ripe, it is mellow* (HS), wa⁷kà·rih *it boiled* (RC 3:56), aryù·rihk *that it be cooked* (RC 30:48); **-rih -{dative I}**: wa⁷kakù·rihθ ‹fact-they-boiled-for› *it was done (cooked) for them* (RC 12:14); **-ri = ha⁷T -**: rarihá⁷tha⁷ ‹he-boil-causes› *he seethes* (HS); **-rih ̨ę -**: ̨ęyuríh ̨ę⁷ ‹prediction-it-boil-much› *it will boil* (RC 15:6), wa⁷uríh ̨ę⁷ ‹fact-it-boiled-much› *it was cooked* (RC 3:54); **-rih ̨ę⁷ -**: yu-ríh ̨ę⁷θ ‹it-boil-begins› *it boils, it bubbles* (HS); **-rihθkahn ̨ę -**: karihθkáhn ̨ęh ‹it-boil-easily-much› *it is precocious* (HS); **-rihT -**: θríht ‹you!-boil-cause› *cook!, boil it!* (R), karíhn ̨ę ‹it-boil-caused› *it cooked* (RC 30:68), raríh-tha⁷ ‹it-boil-causes› *he cooks* (HS), karíhtha⁷ ‹it-boil-causes› *it ripens* (HS); **-(a)hy ̲arih -**: yúhyarih ‹it-fruit-boiled› *mellowness, ripe fruit* (HS); **-a⁷k ̨ęhr ̲arihT -**: wa⁷k ̨ęhraríhn ̨ę ‹it-ash-boil-caused› *cement, lime* (HS); **-a⁷ = θk ̲arihT -**: ra⁷θkaríhtha⁷ ‹he-X-boil-causes› *he scalds it* (HS); **-čihskw ̲a = rih ̨ę⁷ -**: yučihskwaríh ̨ę⁷θ ‹it-mush-boil-begins› *it cooks mush* (RC 3:55); **-hsk ̨ę⁷r ̲arih -**: uhsk ̨ę́⁷rarih ‹bone-boil› *skeleton* (HS); **-n ̨ęharihT -**: ran ̨ęharíh-tha⁷ ‹he-corn-boil-causes› *he cooks, is cooking the corn* (H 2484); **-tku = ri⁷n ̲arih ̨ę⁷ -**: yutkuri⁷naríh ̨ę⁷θ ‹it-hominy-boil-begins› *it sputters* (HS); **-ye = t ̲arih ̨ę⁷ -**: yuyetaríh ̨ę⁷θ ‹it-great-boil-begins› *grease has been boiling* (RC

15:10); **kwęhs** –ne –. –tkwa̱rihT –{dative III}: kwęhs nahrutkwarihnatíhek ‹no apart-unknown-he-stomach-be ripe-causes-for› *he has indigestion* (HS); **ù·nę** –weh – ha? –nęha̱rihT –: ù·nę kà·weh ha? kanęharíhtha? ‹now it-speaks the it-corn-boil-causes› *now speaks the corn-ripener (said when you can hear the locusts buzzing—the hotter the day, the more they will buzz)* (L 49).

–**riha?T** – seethe. *v.s.-a.i.* rarihá?tha? ‹he-boil-causes› *he seethes* (HS).

–**rihęt** – be in the business of, be in charge of. *v.s.-s.i.* raríhę·t ‹he-matter-possesses› *he is in business, he is in charge of* (HS).

–**rihęt** – circumstance. *dv.n.s.* yuríhę·t ‹it-matter-possesses› *circumstance* (HS).

–**rihęti** – teach. *v.s.-a.i.* rarihę́·tih ‹he-matter-makes› *he teaches* (HS), yerihę́·tih ‹one-matter-makes› *she teaches* (HS).

–**rihęti** – teacher, tutor. *dv.n.s.* rarihę́·tih ‹he-matter-makes› *tutor* (HS), yerihę́·tih ‹one-matter-makes› *teacher* (HS).

–**rihęti** – It-Goes-Along-Teaching (Chief of the Beaver Clan). *dv.n.s.* Karihę́·tye? ‹it-matter-makes› *It-Goes-Along-Teaching* (Chief of the Beaver Clan) (HS).

–**rihęti** –{dative III} learn; teach, train. *v.s.-t.* na?rihę́·tyę? ‹one=another-matter-made-for› *one taught another, one trained another* (RC 30:20), wa?urihę́·tyę? ‹fact-it-matter-made-for› *it learned* (RC 8:36).

–**rihęti** –{dative III} school. *dv.n.s.* yę?na?rihętyá·tih ‹one=another-matter-makes-for› *school* (R).

–**rihętya?T** – school. *dv.n.s.* yerihętyá?tha? ‹one-matter-make-causes› *school* (R).

–**rihę?** – boil, bubble. *v.s.-a.i.* yuríhę?θ ‹it-boil-begins› *it boils, it bubbles* (HS).

–**rihθkahnę** – be precocious. *v.s.-a.i.* karihθkáhnęh ‹it-boil-easily-much› *it is precocious* (HS).

–**rihst** – leggings. *n.r.* n-poss., inc., n.sfx. -eh. uríhsteh *leggings* [Lawson «Owissera» 'Stockings']; –rihstęti –{dative III}: wa?na?rihstę́·tyę? ‹fact-one=another-leggings-made-for› *one made leggings for someone else* (RC 30:59).

–**rihst** – metal. *n.r.* n-poss., inc., n.sfx. -. Found only incorporated in constructions that appear to be loans from other Northern Iroquoian languages. –rihstakęrat –.#áh: karihstakęrat?áh ‹it-metal-is white-little› *basin (lit. little tin thing)* (HS); –rihstarh –: rarihstárhahs ‹he-metal-??› *he gilds it* (HS); –rihsti?θ(e)r –: rarihstí?θręhs ‹he-metal-drags› *he surveys* (HS); –rihstuh =θerhę –: yurihstuhθérhę· ‹he-metal-stripped-much› *immaculate* (AG); –ne+či –. –rihstuhra̱rak –: neθhrarihstúhraraks ‹apart-again-he-metal-presses› *he reprints it* (HS).

–**rihstarh** – gild. *v.s.-t.* rarihstárhahs ‹he-metal-??› *he gilds it* (HS).

–**rihsti?θ(e)r** – survey. *v.s.-a.i.* rarihstí?θręhs ‹he-metal-drags› *he surveys* (HS).

–**rihstuhθerhę** – be immaculate. *v.s.-s.i.* yurihstuhθérhę· ‹he-metal-stripped-much› *immaculate* (AG).

–rihT – boil, cook, ripen. *v.s.-t.* θríht ‹you!-boil-cause› *cook!, boil it!* (R), karíhnẹ ‹it-boil-caused› *it cooked* (RC 30:68), raríhtha᾿ *he cooks* (HS) ‹he-boil-causes›, karíhtha᾿ ‹it-boil-causes› *it ripens* (HS).

–rihuwan –{dative III} disclaim. *v.s.-t.* na᾿rihuwaná·tih ‹one=another-matter-is chief-for› *one disclaims another* (HS).

–rihuwana᾿T – announce, preach. *v.s.-a.i.* rarihuwaná᾿tha᾿ ‹he-matter-be chief-causes› *he preaches* (HS), θrihù·-wana᾿t ‹you!-matter-be chief-cause› *announce it!, preach!* (MP).

–rihuwana᾿T –{dative III} declaim, sermonize against. *v.s.-t.* na᾿rihuwana᾿-ná·tih ‹one=another-matter-be chief-causes-for› *one declaims another, one sermonizes against another* (HS).

–rihu᾿kT – finish speaking. *v.s.-a.i.* wa᾿-erihú᾿knẹ᾿ ‹fact-one-matter-ended› *she had finished speaking* (AG).

–rihw – affair, business, event, habit, matter, news, song, theme, thing, tune. *n.r.* n-poss., inc., n.sfx. –eh. This root is one of a handful that are productively incorporated to create new, idiomatic verb stems. It appears, generally, when a new verb expressing an abstract concept other than a mental state is required. uríhweh *affair, business, event, habit, matter, news, song, theme, thing, tune* (HS); **–rihẹt –**: raríhẹ·t ‹he-matter-possesses› *he is in business, he is in charge of* (HS), yuríhẹ·t ‹it-matter-possesses› *circumstance* (HS); **–rihẹti –**: rarihẹ́·tih ‹he-matter-makes› *tutor* (HS), yerihẹ́·tih ‹one-matter-makes› *she teaches: teacher* (HS); Karihẹ́·tye᾿ ‹it-matter-makes› *It-Goes-Along-Teaching* (Chief of the Beaver Clan) (HS); **–rihẹti –{dative**

III}: na᾿rihẹ́·tyẹ᾿ ‹one=another-matter-made-for› *one taught another, one trained another* (RC 30:20), wa᾿uri-hẹ́·tyẹ᾿ ‹fact-it-matter-made-for› *it learned* (RC 8:36), yẹ᾿na᾿rihẹtyá·tih ‹one=another-matter-makes-for› *school* (R); **–rihẹtya᾿T –**: yerihẹtyá᾿tha᾿ ‹one-matter-make-causes› *school* (R); **–ri = huwan –{dative III}**: na᾿rihuwaná·tih ‹one=another-matter-is chief-for› *one disclaims another* (HS); **–rihuwana᾿T –**: rarihuwaná᾿tha᾿ ‹he-matter-be chief-causes› *he preaches* (HS), θrihù·wa-na᾿t ‹you!-matter-be chief-cause› *announce it!, preach!* (MP); **–rihu = wana᾿T –{dative III}**: na᾿rihuwana᾿-ná·tih ‹one=another-matter-be chief-causes-for› *one declaims another, one sermonizes against another* (HS); **–ri = hu᾿kT –**: wa᾿erihú᾿knẹ᾿ ‹fact-one-matter-ended› *she had finished speaking* (AG); **–rihw –.#ẹwe**: urihwehẹ̀·we ‹matter-genuine› *authentic* (HS); **–rih = wahčrukr –**: urihwahčrú·kri᾿ ‹matter-'ness-rubbish› *trifles* (HS); **–rihwah = nẹ᾿T –**: rarihwahnẹ́᾿tha᾿ ‹he-matter-disappear-causes› *he pardons* (HS), yẹkwarihwahnẹ́᾿tha᾿ ‹we-matter-disappear-cause› *we forgive* (G); **–rih = wahrahT –**: urihwáhraht ‹matter-put up-cause› *crime, terrible thing* (MP); **–rihwahrihT –**: rarihwahríhtha᾿ ‹he-matter-spill-causes› *he annuls* (HS), yẹkwarihwahríhnẹ ‹we-matter-spill-cause› *we owe (e.g., a debt)* (G); **–rih = wahθehT –**: na᾿rihwahθéhtha᾿ ‹one=another-matter-hides› *one entrusts another with a secret* (HS), rurihwahθéh-nẹ ‹he-matter-hid› *he doesn't tell* (HS), rarihwahθéhtha᾿ ‹he-matter-hides› *he keeps it secret* (HS), yurihwahθéhnẹ ‹it-matter-hid› *it is a mystery, it is a secret* (HS); **–rihwahstẹni –**: rarihwah-stẹ̀·nih ‹he-matter-adorns› *he smoothes* *away a difficulty* (HS), *mediator (he settles the matter)* (L 60), waʔkayerihwahstę̇·niʔ ‹fact-they-matter-a-dorned› *they make peace* (R); −rih = **wahstęnyaʔT** −: urihwahstę́·nyaʔt ‹matter-adorn-cause› *arbitration* (HS); −rih = **wahsthu** −: yurihwáhsthę ‹it-matter-is small› *frivolous* (HS); −**rihwahtinę** −: rarihwahtì·nęh ‹he-matter-begs› *petitioner* (HS); −**rihwahtinę** −{dative I}: ękayę̇ʔnaʔrihwahtì·nę̇ʔθ ‹prediction-they=another-matter-beg for-for› *they will order another* (RC 12:20), waʔ-eθarihwahtì·nę̇ʔθ ‹fact-one=you-matter-begged for-for› *one ordered you* (RC 23:3), ękęrihwahtì·nę̇ʔθ ‹prediction-I=you-matter-beg› *I will beg of you* (MP); −**rihwahtirahT** −: rarihwahtì·rahč ‹he-matter-be durable-causes› *he approves* (HS); −**rihwakarę(hw)** −: rarihwakà·ręws ‹he-matter-goes a-round› *he stirs up strife* (HS); −rih = **wakayę** −: urihwakà·yęʔ ‹matter-be old› *olden times* (RC 9:1), *culture, old ways, tradition* (R); −**rihwakenha** −: nęyerihwakyénhaʔ ‹two-prediction-one-matter-strive› *the two of them will argue* (L 41); −**rihwakenha** −{dative I}: naʔrihwakyenháʔθeh ‹one=another-matter-strives-for› *one intercedes for another* (HS); −**rihwakayęʔčrakęw**: urihwakayę́ʔčrakęw ‹matter-be old-'ness-in› *in antiquity* (RC 3:1); −rih = **wakę̇θhe** −: naʔrihwakę́θheh ‹one=another-matter-gnaws at› *one criticizes another* (HS); −**rihwakęʔT** −: raríhwakę̇ʔč ‹he-matter-strikes› *he con-*

demns (HS); −**rihwakha** −: yurihwákhę ‹it-matter-divided› *discord* (HS), neyakurihwá·-khahs ‹two-one-matter-divides› *the two of them disagree* (HS); −**rihwaksaʔT** −: rarihwaksáʔthaʔ ‹he-matter-be bad-causes› *he profanes, he swears* (HS); −**rihwaksaʔT** −{dative III}: naʔrihwaksaʔná·tih ‹one=another-matter-be bad-causes-for› *one damns another, one vilifies another* (HS); −**rihwaku** −: raríhwakwahs ‹he-matter-picks up› *he accedes, he accepts, he approves* (HS); −**rihwa** = **kwahsT** −: rurihwákwahst ‹he-matter-is good› *he is beneficent* (HS); −rih = **wakwahsT** −{dative III}: waʔkakurihwakwáhsnęʔ ‹fact-they-matter-was good-for› *they believed it to be true* (RC 26:9); −**rihwakweʔniyu** −: rarihwakweʔnì·yuʔ ‹he-matter-is principal one› *master: the one in charge* (RC 13:5); −**rihwakʔuhsi** −: karihwakʔúhsyęhs ‹it-matter-release-undoes› *decisive* (HS), rarihwakʔúhsyęhs ‹he-matter-release-undoes› *he authenticates, he justifies* (HS); −**rihwanę** −: uríhwanęh ‹matter-guard› *because of* (MP); −**rihwanęha ʔ** −: urihwanę́haʔ ‹matter-old› *old songs* (R); −**rihwar** −: yuríhwar ‹it-matter-is in› *circumstantial* (HS); −**rihwarahsT** −: rarihwaráhstha ʔ ‹he-matter-be in-causes› *he tamed it* (HS); −**rihwaraʔ** −: wahruríhwaraʔ ‹fact-he-matter-be in-began› *he got blamed for it* (RC 30:72); −**rihwaraʔθk** −: yurihwaráʔθkę· ‹it-matter-be in-began-easily› *it is tamable* (HS); −**rihwarekwaʔT** −:

rurihwarekwá'nę ‹he-matter-go and return-caused› *he officiates* (HS); –rih= waretya?T –: rarihwaretyá'tha' ‹he-matter-spread-causes› *herald* (HS): –rihwarhu –: wa'na'rihwárhu' ‹fact-one=another-matter-mixed› *one blamed another* (R), nä'ríhwarhuhs ‹one=another-matter-mixes› *one accuses another* (HS); –rihwarikhę –: rarihwaríkhęh ‹he-matter-bites› *he mutters* (HS); –rihwaruhčrę –: rarihwarúhčręh ‹he-matter-gather› *he sums up* (HS); –rihwaθe·?: urihwá·θe·' ‹matter-new› *new fashioned, modern* (RC 21: 2), *innovation, novelty* (HS); –rihwa?= θhęni –: rurihwa'θhę́·nyęhs ‹he-matter-defeats› *he backslides* (HS); –rihwa= ter?(ak) –: urihwatér'ę ‹matter-make a mistake› *sinfulness, wickedness* (MP), kakurihwatér'ę ‹they-matter-made a mistake› *they are wicked: sinners* (MP), rurihwatér'ahs ‹he-matter-makes a mistake› *he sins* (HS), wa'-kayerihwatér'ak ‹fact-they-matter-made a mistake› *they sinned, they were wicked* (MP); –rihwater?akčra?= nyeręhT –: yurihwater'akčra'nyeréhnę ‹it-matter-make a mistake-'ness-have an unusual experience-caused› *original sin* (HS); –rihwater?ęhčrawę –: kakurihwater'ęhčrawęh ‹they-matter-mistake-'ness-possess› *their sins* (MP); –rihwatkę –: urihwátkę' ‹matter-inherent power› *medicine story* (AW 47); –rihwatukęhT –: rarihwatukę́htha' ‹he-matter-??-causes› *he specifies* (HS); –rihwatukęht –: rurihwatukę́hti ‹he-matter-is holy› *he is holy* (MP); –rihwatukęht –.#keha·?: urihwatukęhtikyéha·' ‹matter-be holy-customarily› *ecclesiastic* (HS); –rihwatukę? –: urihwatukę́'ę ‹matter-??-began› *it is improbable* (HS); –rihwaw –: na'ríhwaws ‹one=another-matter-gives› *one im-*

putes (HS); –rihwawehθayę –: yurihwawéhθayę' ‹it-matter-be dark› *abstruse, enigma* (HS); –rihwawę –: uríhwawęh ‹matter-possess› *cause, occasion, purpose, reason* (HS), *because* (MP); –rihwawihw –: rarihwawíhę ‹he-matter-know how-causes› *he palliates* (HS); –rihwawsT –: rarihwáwstha' ‹he-matter-give-causes› *his pretext* (HS); –rihwayę –: ękarihwà·yę' ‹prediction-it-matter-go into› *it will result* (RC 3: 20), rarihwà·yęhs ‹he-matter-goes into› *agent: he causes* (HS), karihwà·yęhs ‹it-matter-goes into› *causal* (HS); –rihwayęti –: rarihwayę́·tih ‹he-matter-extends› *he idolizes it, he worships it* (HS); –rihwayę?kw –: raríhwayę?kws ‹he-matter-shoots› *he protests* (HS); –rihwayu?n(ę) –: rurihwayú'ne' ‹he-matter-works› *he plots* (HS); –rih= wa?ke: urihwá'kye ‹matter-at› *in regard to: official* (HS); –rihwa?narih –: rarihwa'naríhę ‹he-matter-is hot› *he is ardent* (HS); –rihwa'naT –: raríhwa'na·č ‹he-matter-goes around› *he proposed* (HS); –rihwa?tyęT –.{dative III}: kayę'na'rihwa'tyę'ná·ti· ‹they=another-matter-measured-for› *they complained* (AG); –rihwa?tyę'nęhku –: rarihwa'tyę'nę́hkwahs ‹he-matter-measure-undoes› *he philosophizes* (HS); –rihwehsayę –: yurihwéhsayę' ‹it-matter-vulgar› *frivolous* (HS); –rih= węhsT –: rarihwę́hstha' ‹he-matter-give-causes› *he inculcates* (HS); –rihwharaku –: rariwhará·kwahs ‹he-matter-hang-undoes› *he allows, he permits* (HS), na'riwhará·kwahs ‹one=another-matter-hang-undoes› *one gives another sanction* (HS); –rihwihs?a –: yurihwíhs'ę ‹it-matter-exhausted› *decree* (HS); rarihwíhs'ahs ‹he-matter-finishes› *he makes a compact* (H-notebook), *he agrees, he researches,*

he orders to charge (HS); –rihwih =
s?a –{dative III}: na?rihwihs?á·tih
‹one=another-matter-finishes-for› *one
enjoins another* (HS); –rihwihs?ahnę –:
wa?kayerihwihs?áhnę? ‹fact-they-matter-finished-much› *they made a pledge*
(AW 101); –rihwitkęhw –: rarihwí·-
tkęws ‹he-matter-come forth-causes›
he divulges (HS); –rihwityę?T –: wa?-
krihwí·tyę?t ‹fact-I-matter-went to› *I
enter complaint* (AG), wa?kayę?na?-
rihwí·tyę?t ‹fact-they=another-matter-
went to› *they made their complaints*
(AG); –rihwiyu –: urihwí·yu ‹matter-be
great› *it is sure* (HS); –rihwiyuhčr –:
urihwiyúhčreh ‹matter-be great-'ness›
Christianity, religion (HS); –rihwi =
yuhsT –: karihwiyúhsnahk ‹it-matter-be
great-caused› *Christianity, religion*
(HS), rarihwiyúhsnę ‹he-matter-be
great-caused› *he is religious* (HS);
–rihwiyuhsnęhčr –: urihwiyuhsnęhčreh
‹matter-be great-cause-'ness› *Christianity* (HS); –rihwya?k –{dative I}:
na?rihwyá?kθeh ‹one=another-matter-
break-for› *one interrupts another* (HS);
–či –. –rihwahtinę –: θahrarihwahtì·nę?
‹again-fact-he-matter-begged› *he begged* (AW 56); –či –. –rihwakę'neti –:
θhrarihwakę?né·tyęhs ‹again-he-mat-
ter-changes› *he alters his resolution*
(HS); –či –. –rihwaku?čęri –: θkarihwa-
ku?čę́·ryę ‹again-it-matter-found› *it re-
discovered a way* (RC 21:2); –ne –.
–rihurę –: nehrurihù·ręh ‹apart-he-matter-splits› *he is guilty* (HS); –ne –.
–rihwahčar –: nehrarihwáhčar ‹apart-he-

matter-fist-is in› *he promotes it* (HS);
–ne –. –rihwahkwa?T –: neyerihwah-
kwá?tha? ‹apart-one-matter-pick up-
causes› *psalms, tune* (HS); –ne –.
–rihwahrihT –: nehrarihwahríhtha? ‹a-
part-he-matter-spill-causes› *he transgresses* (HS); –ne –. –rihwahskane =
kęhT –: neyurihwahskané·kęht ‹apart-it-
matter-is strange› *curiosity* (HS); –ne –.
–rihwakę?θahnę –: nehrarihwakę?θáh-
nęh ‹apart-he-matter-sees-going to-
much› *he researches, he examines the
matter closely* (HS); –ne –. –rihwakę? =
θahnę –.#hči: nehrarihwakę?θahnę́hči
‹apart-he-matter-sees-going to-much-
very› *he analyzes* (HS); –ne –. –rih =
wakenha –: nehrarihwakyénhahs ‹apart-
he-matter-strives› *advocate, lawyer; he
argues, he disputes it, he pleads* (HS),
nehrurihwakyénhę ‹apart-he-matter-
strove› *his discussion; he debates*
(HS); –ne –. –rihwaya?θraku –: nehrarih-
waya?θrá·kwahs ‹two-he-matter-fold-
undoes› *he answers* (HS); –ne –. –rih =
waya?θrakʷahT –: neyurihwaya?θrá·-
kwaht ‹two-it-matter-fold-undo-caused› *answerable* (HS); –ne –. –rihwayęT –
{dative I}: nehrurihwayę?ná?θe· ‹a-
part-he-matter-laid-for› *he decides*
(HS); –ne –. –rihwayę'nahT –: neyurih-
wayę́·?naht ‹apart-it-matter-lay-caused›
it is decisive (HS); –ne –. –rihwa?ti =
kęhkęni –: neyurihwa?tikęhkę́·nyę ‹a-
part-it-matter-mind-excels› *subterfuge*
(HS); –t –. –rihu?kT –{dative III}: nyę?-
na?rihu?kná·tih ‹hither-one=another-
matter-puts an end to-for› *one crit-*

Tuscarora Pronunciation Key:
/a/ law; /e/ hat; /i/ pizza; /u/ tune; /ę/ hint; /č/
cheese; /h/ hoe; /m/ mother; /s/ same; /t/ do
(before a vowel y, or w), too (elsewhere); /k/ gale
(before a vowel y or w), kale (elsewhere); /n/
inhale (before a consonant or word-final), note
(elsewhere), /r/ hiss (before a consonant or word-
final), run (trilled as in Italian, elsewhere); /w/ cuff
(before a consonant other than y or word-final),
way (elsewhere); /y/ fish (before a consonant or
word-final), you (elsewhere), /θ/ thing; /?/ (the
sound between the vowels in unh-unh); /·/ long
vowel, /´/ high pitch; /`/ low pitch.

icizes another (HS); -t -. -**rihwara** -: tkaríhwahs ‹hither-it-matter-grabs› *echo* (HS); -t -. -**rihware** -: thruríhware'' ‹hither-he-matter-is distant› *he maintains* (HS); -t -. -**rihwature** -: nahskrihwatú·re· ‹hither-you=me-matter-store› *you save me* (MP); -t -. -**rihwaya'** = **θraku** -: tkarihwaya''θrá·kwahs ‹hither-it matter-fold-undoes› *echo* (HS); -t -. -**rihwayeri** -: tkarihwayè·ri'' ‹hither-it-matter-is straight› *correct, right* (HS); -t -. -**rihwayerik** -: tkarihwayè·rik ‹hither-it-matter-filled up› *it is trustable* (R); -t -. -**rihwaye** -: tkarihwà·ye'' ‹hither-it-matter-went into› *it is difficult* (RC 25:7); -t -. -**rihwa'nihθT** -: nyurihwa''níhθne ‹hither-it-matter-stand up-caused› *principal* (HS); -t -. -**rihwa're** -: thrarihwá''rehs ‹hither-he-matter-??› *he insists* (HS); **tha** -. -**rihwa'netye** -: thyurihwa''né·tye'' ‹un-usual-it-matter-is present-much› *other things* (AG); **ti** -. -**rihuhθ(e)r** -: nehsrihúhθe''r ‹so-you-matter-strip off› *you will carry the matter through to its legitimate conclusion* (R); **ti** -. -**rihu'ne** -: tikarihú''ne· ‹so-it-matter-is a kind of› *it was that kind of event* (RC 3:10), tiwakrihú''ne· ‹so-I-matter-is a kind of› *I have a habit* (RC 25:9), tyurihú''ne· ‹so-it-matter-is a kind of› *it is a custom* (RC 25:16); **ti** -. -**rih** = **weθ** -: thwa''karíhwe·θ ‹so-fact-it-matter-was long› *long time* (RC 15:6); -**ne+či** -. -**rihwake'θahne** -: neθhrarihwake''θáhneh ‹apart-again-he-matter-sees-going to-much› *he reconsiders* (HS); **ti+yah** -. -**rihwakeθnahne** -: thwekarihwakeθnáhneh ‹so-thither-it-matter-gnaws at-much› *it reverberates* (HS); -**a'rihet**: ru''ríhe·t ‹he-himself-matter-possesses› *he has as his business* (RC 26:35); *officer* (HS); -**a'ri** = **heti** -{dative III}: ra''rihetyá·tih ‹he-himself-matter-makes-for› *he reads* (HS); -**a'riheti** -{dative III} -'T -: ru''rihetyatí·''ne'' ‹he-himself-matter-made-for-moving› *he is studious* (HS); -**a'rihetya'T** -: wa''rihetyá''tha'' ‹it-it-self-matter-make-causes› *origin* (HS); -**a'rihe'na'nye** -: ru''rihe''ná·''nye'' ‹he-himself-matter-concluded-going along› *he delegates* (HS); -**a'rihuk''ahT** -: ru''rihú·kwaht ‹he-himself-matter-spread out-caused› *he is haughty, he is insolent, he is overbearing* (HS), ru''rihukwáhne ‹he-himself-matter-spread out-caused› *he is audacious, he is boastful* (HS); -**a'rihurya'T** -: are''rihú·rya''t ‹unknown-it-itself-matter-stir-cause› *that it bother it, that it spoil it, that it make it nasty* (RC 3:22), ra''rihuryá''tha'' ‹he-himself-matter-stir-causes› *he abuses, he stultifies, he trifles with* (HS), neye''na''na''rihú·rya''t ‹two-prediction-one=another-self-matter-stir-cause› *one will mistreat another two* (RC 27:31), na''na''rihuryá''tha'' ‹one=another-matter-stir-causes› *one is teasing another* (R); -**a'rihwahne'T** -: yu''rihwáhne''t ‹it-itself-matter-disappear-cause› *(it is) pardonable* (HS); -**a'rihwahsteni** -: ra''rihwahstè·nih ‹he-himself-matter-adorns› *he amends it* (HS); -**a'rih** = **wakse'na'T** -: ru''rihwakse''ná''ne'' ‹he-himself-matter-bebad-begin-caused-moving› *he is quarrelsome* (HS); -**a'rihwakse'T** -: ra''rihwaksé''tha'' ‹he-himself-matter-be bad-begin-causes› *he quarrels* (HS); -**a'rihwak'uhsi** -: ra''rihwak''úhsye ‹he-himself-matter-release-undid› *upright (sober) man* (RC 12:31), *(he is) pious* (HS); -**a'** = **rihwanet(a')** -: yekwa''rihwané·ta'' ‹we-ourselves-matter-suffer› *we forgive* (MP); -**a'rihwanet(a')** -{dative I}: nakwa''rihwané·ta''θ ‹you!=us-yourself-

matter-suffer-for⟩ *forgive us!* (MP);
-aʔrihw**a**ruręk**ʷ**ahT -: yuʔrihwarurę́·kwaht ⟨it-itself-matter-contribute-undo-caused⟩ *revocable* (HS); -aʔrihw**a**tetʔ -: raʔrihwaté·tʔahs ⟨he-himself-matter-lines⟩ *notary* (HS); -aʔrihw**a**tiheθ -{dative III}: waʔkaʔrihwatihé·θę́ʔ ⟨fact-I-myself-matter-was dependent-for⟩ *I am trusting* (AG); -aʔrih= w**a**tukęhT -: raʔrihwatukę́htha⟨he-himself-matter-ʔʔ-causes⟩ *he recapitulates* (HS); -aʔrihw**a**yaʔθrak**ʷ**ahT -: yuʔrihwayaʔθrá·kwaht ⟨it-itself-matter-fold-undo-caused⟩ *expiatory* (HS); -aʔrihwa'ne -: yuʔrihwá·ʔneʔ ⟨it-itself-matter-is present⟩ *account* (HS); -aʔ= rihwa'neku -: raʔrihwaʔné·kwahs ⟨he-himself-matter-be present-undoes⟩ *he dissembles* (HS); -aʔrihw**a**ʔtikęh= ryaʔkhę -: raʔrihwaʔtikęhryáʔkhęh ⟨he-himself-matter-mind-breaks-much⟩ *he inconveniences* (HS); -aʔrihwharhu -: yuʔriwhárhę· ⟨it-itself-matter-hung-caused⟩ *it is a difficulty* (R), waʔriwhárhuhs ⟨it-itself-matter-hang-causes⟩ *difficulty (abstract)* (HS); -aʔ= rihwihsʔa -: yuʔrihwíhsʔę ⟨it-itself-matter-finished⟩ *behest* (HS), raʔrihwíhsʔahs ⟨he-himself-matter-finishes⟩ *he bargains, he contracts, he stipulates* (HS), kakuʔrihwíhsʔę ⟨they-themselves-matter-finished⟩ *they plotted, they promised* (RC 24:8); -aʔ= rihwihsʔa -{dative III}: raʔrihwihsʔá·tih ⟨he-himself-matter-finishes-for⟩ *he makes a resolution* (HS); -aʔrih= wiyuhsT -: raʔrihwiyúhsthaʔ ⟨he-him-

self-matter-be great-causes⟩ *he pretends to be religious* (HS); -ne -. -aʔrihuhr**a**rak -{dative II}: neθaʔrihúhrarakθ ⟨apart-prediction-you-matter-press⟩ *it troubles you* (RC 25:16); -ne -. -aʔrihukwaʔT -: neyuʔrihwukwáʔtha⟨apart-it-itself-matter-spread out-causes⟩ *proclamation* (HS); -ne -. -aʔrihurę -: nehruʔrihù·ręʔ ⟨apart-he-himself-matter-split⟩ *he is guilty of a crime* (H-notebook); -ne -. -aʔrih= w**a**hkw -: waʔthraʔríhwahkw ⟨fact-apart-he-himself-matter-picked up⟩ *he sang* (R); -ne -. -aʔrihw**a**hkw -{dative I}: waʔnyęʔnaʔrihwáhkęʔθ ⟨fact-apart-one=another-matter-pickedup-for⟩ *one sang about another* (R); -ne -. -aʔrihwahkwahT -: neyęʔrihwahkwáhthaʔ ⟨apart-one-oneself-matter-pick up-causes⟩ *hymnal, song book* (HS); -ne -. -aʔrihwaretyaʔT -: waʔthraʔrihwaré·tyaʔt ⟨fact-apart-he-himself-matter-radiate-caused⟩ *he spread the news* (RC 12:15); -ne -. -aʔrihwiθ -: nehruʔrihwí·θę ⟨two-he-himself-matter-joined⟩ *his alliance* (HS); -ne -. -aʔrih= waya?θraku -: nehraʔrihwayaʔθrá·kwahs ⟨two-he-himself-matter-fold-undoes⟩ *he retorts* (HS); -t -. -aʔrihęti -: nwaʔrihę́·tih ⟨hither-it-itself-matter-makes⟩ *incipient* (HS); tha -. -aʔrih= w**a**twahT -: thahsaʔrihwá·twaht ⟨unusual-fact-you-matter-overlooked⟩ *you did wrong* (AG), thaʔkaʔrihwá·twaht ⟨unusual-fact-I-matter-overlooked⟩ *I did wrong* (AG); haʔ -rihuwanaʔT -: haʔ rarihuwanáʔthaʔ ⟨the he-matter-be

---

Tuscarora Pronunciation Key:
/a/ l**a**w; /e/ h**a**t; /i/ p**i**zza; /u/ t**u**ne; /ę/ h**i**nt; /č/ **ch**eese; /h/ **h**oe; /m/ **m**other; /s/ **s**ame; /t/ do (before a vowel y, or w), too (elsewhere); /k/ g**a**le (before a vowel y or w), **k**ale (elsewhere); /n/ i**nh**ale (before a consonant or word-final), **n**ote (elsewhere), /r/ hi**ss** (before a consonant or word-final), run (trilled as in Italian, elsewhere); /w/ cu**ff** (before a consonant other than y or word-final), **w**ay (elsewhere); /y/ fi**sh** (before a consonant or word-final), **y**ou (elsewhere), /θ/ **th**ing; /ʔ/ (the sound between the vowels in unh-unh); /·/ long vowel, /ˊ/ high pitch; /ˋ/ low pitch.

chief-causes⟩ *preacher* (HS); **ha? -rih=waye -**: ha? karihwà·yęhs ⟨the it-matter-goes into⟩ *agency* (HS); **ha? -rih=wayęti -**: ha? rarihwayę́·tih ⟨the he-matter-extends⟩ *his adoration* (HS); **ha? -rihwa'ne -**: ha? yuríhwa?ne? ⟨the it-matter-is present⟩ *an unfinished matter, a matter to attend to, a chore* (HS); **ha? -rihwharaku -**: ha? ruriwhará·kwę ⟨the he-matter-hang-undid⟩ *his allowance* (HS); **ha? -rihwihs?a -**: ha? rurihwíhs?ę ⟨the he-matter-finished⟩ *his promise* (HS); **ha? -ne -. -rihu?kT -**: ha? nyuríhu?kt ⟨the apart-it-matter-comes to an end⟩ *defect* (HS); **ha? -ne -. -rihwaya?θrakʷahT -**: ha? neyurihwaya?θrá·kwaht ⟨the two-it-matter-fold-undo-caused⟩ *answer* (HS); **ha? -t -. -rihuka?T -**: ha? thrurihuká?nę ⟨the hither-he-matter-blister-caused⟩ *author* (HS); **ha? ti -. -rihu?nę -**: ha? tyurihú?nę· ⟨the so-it-matter-is a kind of⟩ *usually* (HS), ha? tihrurihú?nę· ⟨the so-he-matter-is a kind of⟩ *his policy* (HS); **ha? -a?rihęti -{dative III}**: ha? ra?rihętyá·tih ⟨the he-him-self-matter-makes-for⟩ *pupil, student* (HS); **ha? -a?rihwaksę? -**: ha? ra?rihwaksę́?ę ⟨the he-himself-matter-be bad-began⟩ *his quarrel* (HS); **ha? -ne -. -a?rihukʷa?T -**: ha? nehra?rihukwá?tha? ⟨the apart-he-himself-matter-spread out-causes⟩ *he announces* (HS); ha? nehru?rihukwá?nę ⟨the apart-he-himself-matter-spread out-caused⟩ *his announcement of* (HS), ha? neyu?rihwukwá?nę ⟨the apart-it-itself-matter-spread out-caused⟩ *declaration* (HS); **ha? -ne -. -a?rihwater?aksturę -**: ha? neyu?rihwater?akstú·rę· ⟨the two-it-itself-matter-mistake-'ness-split⟩ *turpitude* (HS); **hà·ne? (na?) -rihwa?ke**: hà·ne? urihwá?kye ⟨that is matter-at⟩ *regarding* (HS), hà·ne? na? urihwá?-

kye ⟨that is   much   matter-at⟩ *regarding* (HS); **kę? -rihuwana?nahkw -**: kę? yerihuwana?náhkhwa? ⟨where one-matter-be chief-causes-instrument⟩ *pulpit* (HS); **kwęhs -rihwakahrę?T -**: kwęhs aryurihwakahrę́?nak ⟨no un-known-it-matter-be an opening-caus-ed⟩ *it is absurd, it is unreasonable* (HS); **kwęhs -rihwakare? -**: kwęhs aryurihwakaré?ęk ⟨no unknown-it-mat-ter-be loud-begin⟩ *it is unheard (of)* (HS); **kwęhs -rihwar -**: kwęhs ahruríh-warak ⟨no unknown-he matter-be in⟩ *he is unapproachable, he is unsocial* (HS); **kwęhs -rihwater?(ak) -**: kwęhs ahrarihwater?áhshek ⟨no unknown-he-matter-make a mistake⟩ *he is infallible* (HS); **kwęhs -rihwiyuhsT -**: kwęhs ah-rurihwiyúhsnęk ⟨no unknown-he-mat-ter-be great-cause⟩ *he is unchristian* (HS); **kwęhs -t -. -rihwarahkw -**: kwęhs ę?nahrurihwaráhkęk ⟨no unknown-hither-he-matter-choose⟩ *he is neutral* (HS); **kwęhs -t -. -rihwayerik -**: kwęhs ę?nakarihwayè·rik ⟨no unknown-hith-er-it-matter-fill up⟩ *it is unjust* (HS), kwęhs ę?nahrarihwayè·rik ⟨no un-known-hither-he-matter-fill up⟩ *he is unjust* (HS); **kwęhs -a?rihwharaku -**: kwęhs aryu?riwhará·kwęk ⟨no un-known-it-itself-matter-hang-undo⟩ *it is illicit* (HS); **kwęhs -ne -. -a?rihuhθ(e)r -**: kwęhs naryu?rihúhθręk ⟨no apart-unknown-it-itself-matter-strip off⟩ *it is undecided* (HS); **na? -rihwa?ke**: na? urihwá?kye ⟨much matter-at⟩ *con-cerning* (HS); **-rihwiyuhsT - -ęheya? =nahkw -**: karihwiyúhsnahk rawęheya?-náhkę ⟨it-matter-be great-caused he-die-caused-instrument⟩ *martyr* (HS).

-rihw -.#ęwe authentic. *n.s.* urihwehę̀·we ⟨matter-genuine⟩ *authentic* (HS).

-rihwahčrukr - trifles. *n.s.* urihwahčrú·kri? ⟨matter-'ness-rubbish⟩ *trifles* (HS).

–rihwahnę^ʔT – forgive, pardon. *v.s.-t.* ra-rihwahnę́^ʔtha^ʔ ‹he-matter-disappear-causes› *he pardons* (HS), yękwarih-wahnę́^ʔtha^ʔ ‹we-matter-disappear-causes› *we forgive* (G).

–rihwahrahT – crime. *n.s.* urihwáhraht ‹matter-put up-cause› *crime* (HS).

–rihwahrihT – annul. *v.s.-t.* rarihwahríh-tha^ʔ ‹he-matter-spill-causes› *he annuls* (HS).

–rihwahrihT – owe. *v.s.-t.* yękwarihwah-ríhnę ‹we-matter-spill-cause› *we owe (e.g., a debt)* (G).

–rihwahθehT – entrust with a secret, keep a secret. *v.s.-t.* na^ʔrihwahθéhtha^ʔ ‹one=another-matter-hides› *one entrusts another with a secret* (HS), ru-rihwahθéhnę ‹he-matter-hid› *he doesn't tell* (HS), rarihwahθéhtha^ʔ ‹he-matter-hides› *he keeps it secret* (HS).

–rihwahθehT – be a mystery, be a secret. *v.s.-s.i.* yurihwahθéhnę ‹it-matter-hid› *it is a mystery, it is a secret* (HS).

–rihwahstęni – make peace, smooth away a difficulty. *v.s.-a.i.* rarihwahstę̀·nih ‹he-matter-adorns› *he smoothes away a difficulty* (HS), wa^ʔkayerihwahstę̀·ni^ʔ ‹fact-they-matter-adorned› *they make peace* (R).

–rihwahstęni – mediator. *dv.n.s.* rarihwah-stę̀·nih ‹he-matter-adorns› *mediator* (L 60).

–rihwahstęnya^ʔT – arbitration. *n.s.* urih-wahstę́·nya^ʔt ‹matter-adorn-cause› *arbitration* (HS).

–rihwahsthu – frivolous. *dv.n.s.* yurih-wáhsthę ‹it-matter-is small› *frivolous*

(HS).

–rihwahtinę – petitioner. *dv.n.s.* rarihwah-tì·nęh ‹he-matter-begs› *petitioner* (HS).

–rihwahtinę –{dative I} beg of, order. *v.s.-t.* ękayę^ʔna^ʔrihwahtì·nę^ʔθ ‹prediction-they=another-matter-beg for-for› *they will order another* (RC 12:20), wa^ʔeθarihwahtì·nę^ʔθ ‹fact-one=you-matter-begged for-for› *one ordered you* (RC 23:3), ękęrihwahtì·nę^ʔθ ‹prediction-I=you-matter-beg-for› *I will beg of you* (HS).

–rihwahtirahT – approve. *v.s.-a.i.* rarih-wahtì·rahč ‹he-matter-be durable-causes› *he approves* (HS).

–rihwakaręhw – stir up strife. *v.s.-a.i.* ra-rihwakà·ręws ‹he-matter-goes around› *he stirs up strife* (HS).

–rihwakayę – olden times, culture, old ways, traditions. *n.s.* urihwakà·yę^ʔ ‹matter-be old› *olden times* (RC 9:1), *culture, old ways, traditions* (R).

–rihwakayę^ʔčrakęw in antiquity. *n.s.* u-rihwakayę́^ʔčrakęw ‹matter-be old-'ness-in› *in antiquity* (RC 3:1).

–rihwakenha – argue. *v.s.-a.i.* nęyerih-wakyénha^ʔ ‹two-prediction-one-matter-strive› *the two of them will argue* (L 41).

–rihwakenha –{dative I} intercede for. *v.s.-t.* na^ʔrihwakyenhá^ʔθeh ‹one=another-matter-strives-for› *one intercedes for another* (HS).

–rihwakęθhe – criticize. *v.s.-t.* na^ʔrihwa-kę́θheh ‹one=another-matter-gnaws at› *one criticizes another* (HS).

-rihwakę?T - condemn. *v.s.-t.* raríhwakę'č ‹he-matter-strikes› *he condemns*
(HS).

-rihwakha - disagree. *v.s.-t.* neyakurihwákhahs ‹two-one-matter-divides› the
two of them disagree (HS).

-rihwakha - discord. *dv.n.s.* yurihwákhę
‹it-matter-divided› *discord* (HS).

-rihwaksa?T - profane, swear. *v.s.-a.i.*
rarihwaksá'tha' ‹he-matter-be bad-
causes› *he profanes, he swears* (HS).

-rihwaksa?T -{dative III} damn, vilify.
v.s.-t. na'rihwaksa'á·tih ‹one=another-
matter-be bad-causes-for› *one damns
another, one vilifies another* (HS).

-rihwaku - accede, accept, approve. *v.s.-
a.i.* raríhwakwahs ‹he-matter-picks up›
he accedes, he accepts, he approves
(HS).

-rihwakwahsT - be beneficent. *v.s.-s.i.* rurihwákwahst ‹he-matter-is good› *he is
beneficent* (HS).

-rihwakwahsT -{dative III} believe to be
true. *v.s.-a.i.* wa'kakurihwakwáhsnę'
‹fact-they-matter-was good› *they believed it to be true* (RC 26:9).

-rihwakwe?niyu - master. *dv.n.s.* rarihwakwe'nì·yu' ‹he-matter-is principal
one› *master* (R).

-rihwak?uhsi - authenticate, justify. *v.s.-
a.i.* rarihwak'úhsyęhs ‹he-matter-release-undoes› *he authenticates, he justifies* (HS).

-rihwak?uhsi - decisive. *dv.n.s.* karihwak-
'úhsyęhs ‹it-matter-release-undoes›
decisive (HS).

-rihwanę - because of. *n.s.* uríhwanęh
‹matter-guard› *because of* (MP).

-rihwanęha·? - old songs. *n.s.* urihwa-
nęha·' ‹matter-old› *old songs* (R).

-rihwar - circumstantial. *dv.n.s.* yuríhwar
‹it-matter-is in› *circumstantial* (HS).

-rihwarahsT - tame. *v.s.-t.* rarihwaráhstha' ‹he-matter-be in-causes› *he

tamed it* (HS).

-rihwara? - blame. *v.s.-t.* wahruríhwara'
‹fact-he-matter-be in-began› *he got
blamed for it* (RC 30:72).

-rihwara?θk - be tamable. *v.s.-s.i.* yurih-
wará'θkę· ‹it-matter-be in-began-easily› *it is tamable* (HS).

-rihwarekwa?T - officiate. *v.s.-a.i.* rurihwarekwá'nę ‹he-matter-go and return-
caused› *he officiates* (HS).

-rihwaretya?T - herald. *dv.n.s.* rarihwaretyá'tha' ‹he-matter-spread-causes›
herald (HS).

-rihwarhu - accuse, blame. *v.s.-t.* wa'-
na'rihwárhu' ‹fact-one=another-mat-
ter-mixed› *one blamed another* (R),
na'ríhwarhuhs ‹one=another-matter-
mixes› *one accuses another* (HS).

-rihwarikhę - mutter. *v.s.-a.i.* rarihwaríkhęh ‹he-matter-bites› *he mutters*
(HS).

-rihwaruhčrę - sum up. *v.s.-a.i.* rarihwarúhčręh ‹he-matter-gather› *he sums
up* (HS).

-rihwaθe·? new fashioned, innovation,
modern, novelty. *n.s.* urihwá·θe·'
‹matter-new› *modern, new fashioned*
(RC 21:2), *innovation, novelty* (HS).

-rihwaθhęni - backslide. *v.s.-a.i.* rurihwa-
θhę·nyęhs ‹he-matter-??› *he backslides*
(HS).

-rihwater?(ak) - sin, be wicked. *v.s.-a.i.*
urihwatér'ę ‹matter-make a mistake›
sinfulness, wickedness (MP), kakurihwatér'ę ‹they-matter-made a mistake› *they are wicked: sinners* (MP),
rurihwatér'ahs ‹he-matter-makes a
mistake› *he sins* (HS), wa'kayerihwa-
tér'ak ‹fact-they-matter-made a mistake› *they sinned, they were wicked*
(MP).

-rihwater?akčra?nyeręhT - original sin.
dv.n.s. yurihwater'akčra'nyeręhnę ‹it-
matter-make a mistake-'ness-have an

unusual experience-caused⟩ *original sin* (HS).

–rihwater?ẹhčrawẹ – sin. *dv.n.s.* kakurihwater'ẹhčrawẹh ⟨they-matter-mistake-'ness-possess⟩ *their sins* (MP).

–rihwatkẹ – medicine story. *n.s.* urihwátkẹ' ⟨matter-inherent power⟩ *medicine story* (AW 47).

–rihwatukẹhT – specify. *v.s.-a.i.* rarihwatukẹ́htha' ⟨he-matter-??-causes⟩ *he specifies* (HS).

–rihwatukẹht – be holy. *v.s.-s.i.* rurihwatukẹ́hti ⟨he-matter-is holy⟩ *he is holy* (MP).

–rihwatukẹht-.#keha·? ecclesiastic. *n.s.* urihwatukẹhtikyéha·' ⟨matter-be holy-customarily⟩ *ecclesiastic* (HS).

–rihwatukẹ? – be improbable. *dv.n.s.* urihwatukẹ́'ẹ ⟨matter-??-began⟩ *it is improbable* (HS).

–rihwaw – impute. *v.s.-t.* na'ríhwaws ⟨one=another-matter-gives⟩ *one imputes* (HS).

–rihwawehθayẹ – abstruse, enigma. *dv. n.s.* yurihwawéhθayẹ' ⟨it-matter-be dark⟩ *abstruse, enigma* (HS).

–rihwawẹ – because, cause, occasion, purpose, reason. *n.s.* uríhwawẹh ⟨matter-possess⟩ *cause, occasion, purpose, reason* (HS), *because* (MP).

–rihwawihw – palliate. *v.s.-a.i.* rarihwawíhẹ ⟨he-matter-know how-caused⟩ *he palliates* (HS).

–rihwawsT – pretext. *dv.n.s.* rarihwáwstha' ⟨he-matter-give-causes⟩ *his pretext* (HS).

–rihwayẹ – cause, result. *v.s.-a.i.* ẹka-rihwà·yẹ' ⟨prediction-it-matter-go into⟩ *it will result* (RC 3:20), rarihwà·yẹhs ⟨he-matter-goes into⟩ *he causes* (HS).

–rihwayẹ – causal. *dv.n.s.* karihwà·yẹhs ⟨it-matter-goes into⟩ *causal* (HS).

–rihwayẹ – agent. *dv.n.s.* rarihwà·yẹhs ⟨he-matter-goes into⟩ *agent* (HS).

–rihwayẹ – agency. *dv.n.s.* ha' karihwà·yẹhs ⟨the it-matter-goes into⟩ *agency* (HS).

–rihwayẹti – idolize, worship. *v.s.-t.* rarihwayẹ́·tih ⟨he-matter-extends⟩ *he idolizes it, he worships it* (HS).

–rihwayẹti – adoration. *dv.n.s.* ha' rarihwayẹ́·tih ⟨the he-matter-extends⟩ *his adoration* (HS).

–rihwayẹ?kw – protest. *v.s.-a.i.* raríhwayẹ?kws ⟨he-matter-shoots⟩ *he protests* (HS).

–rihwayu?n(ẹ) – plot. *v.s.-a.i.* rurihwayú'ne' ⟨he-matter-works⟩ *he plots* (HS).

–rihwa?ke in regard to; official. *n.s.* urihwá'kye ⟨matter-at⟩ *in regard to; official* (HS).

–rihwa?narih – be ardent. *v.s.-s.i.* rarihwa'naríhẹ· ⟨he-matter-is hot⟩ *he is ardent* (HS).

–rihwa'naT – propose. *v.s.-a.i.* raríhwa'na·č ⟨he-matter-goes around⟩ *he proposed* (HS).

–rihwa'ne – unfinished matter, matter to attend to, chore. *dv.n.s.* ha' yuríhwa'ne' ⟨the it-matter-is present⟩ *an unfinished matter, a matter to attend to, a chore* (HS).

–rihwa̱ʔtyę̄T –.{dative III}: complain. *v.s.-t*. kayę̄ʔnaʔrihwaʔtyęʔná·ti· ‹they=another-matter-measured-for› *they complained* (AG).

–rihwa̱ʔtyę'nę̄hku – philosophize. *v.s.-a.i.* rarihwaʔtyęʔnę́hkwahs ‹he-matter-measure-undoes› *he philosophizes* (HS).

–rihwehsa̱yę – frivolous. *dv.n.s.* yurihwéhsayęʔ ‹it-matter-vulgar› *frivolous* (HS).

–rihwę̱hsT – inculcate. *v.s.-t.* rarihwę́hstha ʔ ‹he-matter-give-causes› *he inculcates* (HS).

–rihwharaku – allow, permit, sanction. *v.s.-a.i.* rariwhará·kwahs ‹he-matter-hang-undoes› *he allows, he permits* (HS), naʔriwhará·kwahs ‹one=another-matter-hang-undoes› *one gives another sanction* (HS).

–rihwharaku – allowance. *dv.n.s.* ha ʔ ruriwhará·kwę ‹the he-matter-hang-undid› *his allowance* (HS).

–rihwihsʔa – make a compact, order to charge, research. *v.s.-a.i.* rarihwíhs-ʔahs ‹he-matter-finishes› *he makes a compact, he researches, he orders to charge* (HS).

–rihwihsʔa – promise. *dv.n.s.* ha ʔ rurihwíhsʔę ‹the he-matter-finished› *his promise* (HS).

–rihwihsʔa –{dative III} enjoin. *v.s.-t.* naʔrihwihsʔá·tih ‹one=another-matter-finishes-for› *one enjoins another* (HS).

–rihwihsʔahnę – make a pledge. *v.s.-a.i.* waʔkayerihwihsʔáhnę ʔ ‹fact-they-matter-finished-much› *they made a pledge* (AW 101).

–rihwitkę̱hw – divulge. *v.s.-a.i.* rarihwí·tkęws ‹he-matter-come forth-causes› *he divulges* (HS).

–rihwityęʔT – enter complaint. *v.s.-t.* waʔkrihwí·tyęʔt ‹fact-I-matter-went to› *I enter complaint* (AG), waʔkayę̄ʔnaʔ-

rihwí·tyęʔt ‹fact-they=another-matter-went to› *they made their complaints* (AG).

–rihwiyu – sure. *n.s.* urihwí·yu· ‹matter-be great› *it is sure* (i.e., *O yeh, that's right!*) (HS).

–rihwiyuhčr – Christianity, religion. *n.s.* urihwiyúhčreh ‹matter-be great-'ness› *Christianity, religion* (HS).

–rihwiyuhsnę̱hčr – Christianity. *n.s.* urihwiyuhsnę́hčreh ‹matter-be great-cause-'ness› *Christianity* (HS).

–rihwiyuhsT – Christianity, religion. *dv. n.s.* karihwiyúhsnahk ‹it-matter-be great-caused› *Christianity, religion* (HS).

–rihwiyuhsT – be Christian, be religious. *v.s.-s.i.* rurihwiyúhsnę ‹he-matter-be great-caused› *he is Christian, he is religious* (HS).

–rihwiyuhsT – –ę̱heyaʔnahkw – martyr. *dv. n.s.* karihwiyúhsnahk rawę̱heyaʔnáhkę ‹it-matter-be great-caused he-die-caused-instrument› *martyr* (HS).

–rihwyaʔk –{dative I} interrupt. *v.s.-t.* naʔrihwyáʔkθeh ‹one=another-matter-break-for› *one interrupts another* (HS).

–rik – bite. *v.r.-t.* hab: -s, pnt: -ɸ, stat: -ę, prog: -, prp: -, dst: -hę-, caus: -, rvs: -, dat: -, inc.-ɸ-pat. rurí·kę *he has bit it* (L 44), rá·ri·ks *he bites it* (R), wáʔkri·k *I bit it* (R), θrí·k *bite it!* (R); –rikhę –: ęyurí·khę ʔ ‹prediction-it-bite-much› *it will be bitten all over* (RC 17:3), rarí·khęh ‹he-bites-much› *he chomps* (HS); –t –. –rik –: ná·θri·k ‹hither-you-bite› *bite it!* (L 44–gives [ná·θri·k], but the medial glottal stop represented by the ['] must be an error]; –hę̱hna̱rik –: wakhę́hnari·ks ‹I-ear-bite› *I have an earache* (R); –nę̱h=sna̱rik –: ranę́hsnariks ‹he-seed-bites› *he bites the grain (singly or collectively)* (H 2484); –nę̱hyuʔna̱rik –: waʔ-

kayenęhyú'′nari·k ‹fact-they-sinew-bit› *they cast a spell* (RC 33:12); –rih = **warikhę** –: rarihwarí·khęh ‹he-matter-bites-much› *he mutters* (HS); –θrę = **warikhę** –: kaθręwarí·khęh ‹it-gum-bites-much› *it ruminates* (HS); –ne –. –**atkahrehnarik** –: newatkahréhnari·ks ‹apart-it-itself-eye-'?'-bites› *lightning* (HS–with secondary gloss "it naps its eye, shuts its eye quickly"), nęhratkahréhnari·k ‹apart-prediction-he-himself-eye-'?'-bite› *he will make lightning* (RC 35:39).

–**rikhę** – bite all over, chomp. *v.s.-t.* ęyurí·khę' ‹prediction-it-bite-much› *it will be bitten all over* (RC 17:3), rarí·khęh ‹he-bites-much› *he chomps* (HS).

–**rir** – chain, row. *n.r.* n-poss., n-inc., n.sfx. –eh. urì·reh *chain, row* (HS); –**rir** – –**nęhrahstęni'nye'** –: urì·reh kakunęhrahstęní·'nye' ‹row they-scalp-adorned-going along› *procession* (HS).

–**rir** – –**nęhrahstęni'nye'** – procession. *n.s.* urì·reh kakunęhrahstęní·'nye' ‹row they-scalp-adorned-going along› *procession* (HS).

–**riraw** – rebuke, scolds. *v.r.-t.* hab: -s, pnt: -, stat: -, prog: -, prp: -, dst: -, caus: -, rvs: -, dat: -, n-inc. rarì·raws *he rebukes it, he scolds it* (HS).

–**r(i)yu** – butcher, kill. *v.r.-t.* hab: -hs, pnt: -', stat: -·', prog: -, prp: -, dst: -, caus: -'T-, rvs: -, dat: -, inc.-φ-pat. The form –**riyu** – occurs following any morpheme ending in a consonant. The form –**ryu** – occurs elsewhere. rá·ryuhs

he butchers (HS), yakú·ryuhs *it kills someone* (RC 24:2), wahrú·ryu' *he had been killed* (RC 24:2), wa'khé·ryu' *I killed someone* (RC 24:2), wa'na'rì·yu' *one killed another* (RC 29:14); –**r(i)yu** –: ká·ryu·' ‹it-killed› *beast, prey, wild animal* (HS); –**r(i)** = **yu** –.#**kęha'nę'**: karyu'kęha'nę' ‹it-killed-many› *wild animals* (MP); –**r(i)** = **yu'T** –: uryú'neh ‹kill-cause› *beast* (HS); –**r(i)yu'T** –.#**ú'y**: uryu'nehú'y ‹kill-cause-great› *big or large creature* (AW 57); –**r(i)yu'nahrahT** –.#**kęha'nę'**: uryu'nahrahtkęha'nę' ‹kill-cause-put up-cause-many› *large awful beasts* (AW 47); –**r(i)yu'nakwahsT** –: karyu'nákwahst ‹it-kill-is good› *gracious person* (AW 50); –'**wahraryu** –: ra'wahrá·ryuhs ‹he-meat-kills› *butcher* (HS); –**a'riyu** –: wa'ka'rì·yu' ‹fact-I-myself-killed› *I fought* (R); –**a'ri** = **yu'T** –: wa'ka'riyú'ne' ‹fact-I-myself-kill-caused› *I am a fighter* (R); –**a'** = **riyu'čr** –: u'riyú'čreh ‹self-kill-'ness› *war* (HS); –**a'riyu'črarę'nha'** –: ra'riyu'črarę'nha'θ ‹self-kill-'ness› *he wars* (HS); á·**thu'** –**r(i)yu** –: á·thu' wakrì·yuhs ‹cold I-kill› *I am cold* (R); –**thekw** –**r(i)yu** –: ú·thekw yú·ryuhs ‹sweat it-kills› *one perspires* (HS), ú·thekw rú·ryuhs ‹sweat he-kills› *he sweats* (HS).

–**r(i)yu** – beast, prey, wild animal. *dv.n.s.* ká·ryu·' ‹it-killed› *beast, prey, wild animal* (HS).

–**r(i)yu'nakwahsT** – gracious person. *dv. n.s.* karyu'nákwahst ‹it-kill-is good› *gracious person* (AW 50).

-r(i)yu?T – beast. *n.s.* uryú'?neh ‹kill-cause› *beast* (HS).

-ri'n – dove, pigeon. *n.r.* n-poss., n-inc., n.sfx. -eh. urí·'?neh *dove, pigeon* (R) [Gallatin «oreneh» 'Pigeon'].

-ri?r – bran, chaff, epidermis, peel, rind, shuck, siftings, skin; sheet of paper; divorce. *n.r.* n-poss., inc., n.sfx. -eh. urí'?reh *bran, chaff, epidermis, peel, rind, shuck, siftings, skin; sheet of paper; divorce* (HS); -ri?ruhči -: rari'?rúhčęhs ‹he-peel-removes› *he peels it* (HS); -a?ri?ruhči -: ęwa'?ri'?rúhči'? ‹prediction-it-itself-peel-remove› *it will peel off* (R).

-ri?ruhči – peel. *v.s.-t.* rari'?rúhčęhs ‹he-peel-removes› *he peels it* (HS).

-ri?w – bedding, blanket, covering, quilt; flag; mullein. *n.r.* n-poss., inc., n.sfx. -eh. urí'?weh *bedding, blanket, covering, quilt; flag; mullein (Verbascum sp.)* (HS) [Lawson «Oorewa» 'Blankets']; -ri?w-.#ęwe: uri'?wehę̀·we ‹bedding-genuine› *sheet* (HS); *Indian blanket; bedding* (RC 34:22); -ri?wak?uh = si -: rari'?wak'?úhsyęhs ‹he-flag-release-undoes› *he unfurls it* (HS); -ri?wa? = nihr -: rari'?wá'?nihč ‹one-flag-stands up› *he hoists sail* (HS); -ri?wa?nihr = hę -: rari'?wa'?nírhęh ‹one-flag-stands up› *he sails* (HS); -ri?wa?nihθT -: yeri'?wa'?íhθtha'? ‹one-flag-stand up-causes› *she raises a flag* (HS); -ri?węti -: rari'?wę́·tih ‹he-bedding-makes› *he quilts* (HS).

-ri?w-.#ęwe – sheet; Indian blanket; bedding. *n.s.* uri'?wehę̀·we ‹bedding-genuine› *sheet* (HS); *Indian blanket; bedding* (RC 34:22).

-ri?wak?uhsi – unfurl. *v.s.-t.* rari'?wak'?úhsyęhs ‹he-flag-release-undoes› *he unfurls it* (HS).

-ri?wa?nihr – hoist sail. *v.s.-a.i.* rari'?wá'?-nihč ‹one-flag-stands up› *he hoists sail* (HS).

-ri?wa?nihrhę – sail. *v.s.-a.i.* rari'?wa'?nírhęh ‹one-flag-stands up› *he sails* (HS).

-ri?wa?nihθT – raise a flag. *v.s.-a.i.* yeri'?wa'?níhθtha'? ‹one-flag-stand up-causes› *she raises a flag* (HS).

-ri?węti – quilt. *v.s.-a.i.* rari'?wę́·tih ‹he-bedding-makes› *he quilts* (HS).

-rkęhw – have plenty. *v.r.-a.i.* hab: -, pnt: -, stat: -ę̊, prog: -, prp: -, dst: -, caus: -, rvs: -, dat: -, inc.-ɸ-pat. wakrkę́hę *I have plenty* (R); -nęharkęhw -: runęharkę́hę ‹he-corn-has plenty› *he has an abundance of corn* (H 2484); -a = 'nerkęhw -: yu'?nerkę́hę ‹it-itself-have plenty› *it is abundant* (HS).

ruči·nękw – ant (AG). *n.*

ruhákwaręt – white crane, whooping crane *(Grus americana)* (SH 375). *n.*

-ruhčrę – accumulate, bring together, collect, gather, rally. *v.r.-t.* hab: -h, pnt: -'?, stat: -·, prog: -, prp: -, dst: -, caus: -hT-, rvs: -, dat: -, inc.-ɸ-ag./pat. rarúhčręh *he accumulates, he collects, he gathers, he rallies* (HS), wahrarúhčrę'? *he gathered*; -(ę)?teyaruhčrę -: wę'?teyarúhčręh ‹it-crowd-gathers› *they are assembled* (HS), kayę'?teyarúhčręh ‹they-crowd-gather› *they congregate* (HS); wahra'?teyarúhčrę'? ‹fact-he-crowd-gathered› *he gathered crowd together* (RC 7:7), ęhsteyarúhčrę'? ‹prediction-you-crowd-gather› *you will gather group together* (MP); -(ę)?teya = ruhčrę-.#ú?y: wę'?teyaruhčrę'?ú'?y ‹it-crowd-gathers-great› *great crowd gathers* (RC 26:8); -nęhsnaruhčrę -: kanęhsnarúhčręh ‹it-seed-gather› *it gathers grain; places the grain in a heap, in one spot* (H 2484); -rihwaruhčrę -: rarihwarúhčręh ‹he-matter-gather› *he sums up* (HS); -a?ruhčrę -: wa'?rúhčręh ‹it-itself-gathers› *assembly* (HS);

-athaharuhčrę -: yuthaharúhčrch ‹it-itself-path-gathers› *crossroads* (HS);
-a?ruhčręhkw-.#ke: yę?ruhčręhkhwá?-
kye ‹one-oneself-gathers-instrument-
at› *(at) church* (HS); -a?ruhčręhT -:
ru?ruhčrę́hnę· ‹he-himself-gather-caused› *he's gone to church* (L 25), ru?-
ruhčrę́hnęhs ‹he-himself-gather-causes›
he goes to church (L 25); -a?ruh=
čręhthe -: wahra?ruhčrę́hthe? ‹fact-he-
himself-gather-caused-go-ing to› *he's
going to church* (L 25), θa?ruhčrę́hthe
‹you!-yourself-gather-cause-going to›
go to church! (L 25).

ruhnyárhar Baltimore oriole *(Icterus gal-
bula)* (R). *n.*

ruhsá·tu·? raccoon *(Procyon lotor)* (R)
[Lawson «Roo-sotto» 'Raccoon-skin'].
n.

ruhséhkwrę water lily *(Nymphaeacea
sp.)* (H-notebook). *n.*

ruhsè·nu? crab (H-notebook). *n.*

ruhskwé·?nę? rat *(Rattus sp.)* (R) [Law-
son «Rusquiane» 'A Rat']. *n.*

ruhsné·kri? horned owl (R) [probabaly
Jefferson «roh suck-ra» 'owl']. *n.*

ruhsnyáhrę gnat (H-notebook). *n.*

ruhsù·warę mandragora, mandrake, may
apple *(Podophyllum pelatum)* (H-notebook). *n.*

ruhtkę̀·ye·? millipede (H-notebook). *n.*

ruhtyéhrawik chokeberry *(Aronia sp.)*
(H-notebook). *n.*

rukayę́heh minnow (AG). *n.*

ruki?yáhskę spider (RC 25:9). *n.* ruki?-
yáhskę -nę?r -: ruki?yáhskę unę́?reh
‹spider net› *spider web* (HS).

ruki?yáhskę -nę?r - spider web. *n.s.* ruki?yáhskę unę́?reh ‹spider net› *spider
web* (HS).

rukwéhu newt (R); mythic lizard (RC
10:19). *n.* Also: arekwéhu?y *lizard*
(AW 58), rukwéhu?y *lizard* (AW 58).

rukwéhu?y lizard (AW 58). *n.* Also:
arekwéhu?y *lizard* (AW 58), rukwéhu
newt (R), *mythic lizard* (RC 10:19).

rukwé?kwe? common lizard (R). *n.*

rukyé·kę? smartweed (H-notebook). *n.*

rukyé?nę·t catfish (H 3518). *n.*

runáwher high bush blueberry *(Vaccinium sp.)* (R). *n.*

runá?kę·t woodchuck, ground hog *(Mar-
mota monax)*; Irish (HS). *n.* According to Hewitt & Smith, the Irish
were named "woodchuck" from that
nation first being seen digging canals.

runehúhu turtledove *(Streptopelia sp.)*
(H-notebook). *n.*

runęhkwrę̀·rę wood betony *(Pedicularis
canadensis)* (H-notebook). *n.*

runęhnù·rę? white oak *(Quercus alba)*
(H-notebook). *n.*

runę́hθkwarę? toad; wart (MG 84). *n.*

runęká?nęt dogwood *(Cornus sp.)* (H-
notebook). *n.*

runyá?rha?r golden robin (AG).

rurakwnyę́hre? red-spotted lizard (H-
notebook). *n.*

-rur - wean. *v.r.-t.* hab: -ahs, pnt: -, stat:
-, prog: -, prp: -, dst: -, caus: -, rvs: -,
dat: -, n-inc. na?rù·rahs *one weans
another* (HS); -rurahshę(T) -: raruráhshęh ‹he-wean-'ness-lays› *he weans
himself from, he fasts* (HS).

-rurahshę(T) – fast, wean from. *v.s.-a.i.*
raruráhshęh ‹he-wean-'ness-lays› *he
weans himself from, he fasts* (HS).
-rurę – contribute to, donate to, share
with, tithe. *v.r.-t.* hab: -h, pnt: -ʾ, stat:
-, prog: -, prp: -, dst: -, caus: -, rvs:
-ku-, dat: II (-ti-/-θ), n-inc. rarù·ręh *he
contributes to it, he donates to it, he
tithes* (HS), wa'ʾkayerù·rę' *they do-
nated to it* (RC 26:9); –rurę –{dative
II}: na'ʾrurę·tih ‹one=another-contrib-
utes to-for› *alms: one shares with another* (HS); –ruręku –: rarurę·kwahs
‹he-contribute to-undoes› *he disorganizes it, he pulls it in pieces* (HS); –či –.
–ruręku –: ęθkrurę·ku' ‹prediction-a-
gain-I-contribute to-undo› *I will again
tear it down* (HS); –a'ʾruręku –: wa'ʾru-
rę·kwahs ‹it-itself-contribute to-undoes› *it (un)ravels* (HS); –ačri'ʾrarurę –:
wačri'ʾrarù·ręh ‹it-itself-wrinkle-contributes to› *it shrivels up, it wrinkles*
(HS); –a'ʾrihwạrurękʷahT –: yu'ʾrihwa-
rurę·kwaht ‹it-itself-matter-contribute
to-undo-caused› *revocable* (HS); té·ks
–rurę –: té·ks rarù·ręh ‹tax he-tithes› *he
collects taxes* (HS).
-rurę –{dative II} share with. *v.s.-t.* na'ʾ-
rurę·tih ‹one=another-contributes to-
for› *one shares with another* (HS).
-rurę –{dative II} alms. *dv.n.s.* na'ʾrurę·tih
‹one=another-contributes to-for› *alms*
(HS).
-ruręku – disorganize, pull in pieces. *v.s.-
t.* rarurę·kwahs ‹he-contribute to-undoes› *he disorganizes it, he pulls it in
pieces* (HS).
rurę̀·narę mallard duck (*Anas platyrhyn-
chos*) (H-notebook). *n.*
rurę́·w'ʾeh mythic occult monster (RC
10:title). *n.*
ruθè·rę sheep-tick, wood-tick (AG). *n.*
ruté·krar green frog (H 3518). *n.*
rutihkę·t'ʾú'ʾy woodcock (*Philhela minor*)

(HS). *n.*
rutkwe'ʾnúhę' copperhead snake (*Agkis-
trodon contortrix*) (H-notebook). *n.*
rutyá·ktę' speckled trout (H 3518). *n.*
ru'ʾkę̀·rarahs gnat (H-notebook). *n.*
rú'ʾki' agreed? (R). *part.* The meaning of
this particle is roughly equivalent to
French *n'est pas?*.
ru'ʾné·tuk red oak (*Quercus velutina, Q.
borealis*) (RC 26:5). *n.* ru'ʾné·tuk –ę' =
ręte: ru'ʾné·tuk awę'ʾrę́·te ‹red oak nut-
certain one› *acorn* (R).
ru'ʾné·tuk –ę'ʾręte acorn. *n.s.* ru'ʾné·tuk
awę'ʾrę́·te ‹red oak nut-certain one› *a-
corn* (R).
ru'ʾθé'ʾtę bedbug (*Cimex lectularius*)
(AG), punese (HS). *n.*
ru'ʾtáhkę bee, hornet, wasp (RC 26:5). *n.*
ru'ʾtáhkę –ęnę –: ru'ʾtáhkę yawę̀·nę·
‹bee it-constructed› *beehive* (HS); ru'ʾ-
táhkę –θręw –: ru'ʾtáhkę uθrę̀·weh ‹bee
syrup› *honey* (R); ru'ʾtáhkę –tihu'ʾsT –:
ru'ʾtáhkę yetihú'ʾstha' ‹bee one-arrive-
causes› *beehive* (HS).
ru'ʾtáhkę –ęnę – beehive. *n.s.* ru'ʾtáhkę
yawę̀·nę· ‹bee it-constructed› *beehive*
(HS).
ru'ʾtáhkę –θręw – honey. *n.s.* ru'ʾtáhkę
uθrę̀·weh ‹bee syrup› *honey* (R).
ru'ʾtáhkę –tihu'ʾsT – beehive. *dv.n.s.*
ru'ʾtáhkę yetihú'ʾstha' ‹bee one-arrive-
causes› *beehive* (HS).
rú'ʾta'ʾrw hickory (*Carya* sp.) (R) [Law-
son «Roo tau» 'Hickory Nuts']. *n.* ru'ʾ-
ta'ʾrw'ʾú'ʾy ‹hickory-great› *walnut* (*Juglans* sp.) (R) [Lawson «Roo tau-ooe»
'Walnuts'].
ru'ʾta'ʾrw'ʾú'ʾy ‹hickory-great› walnut (*Juglans* sp.) (R) [Lawson «Roo tau-ooe»
'Walnuts']. *n.*
rú'ʾta'ʾw male milk snake (R). *n.*
ru'ʾterhęruhú'ʾy bumblebee (*Bumbus* sp.)
(R). *n.*
ru'ʾtúhsarę milk snake (*Lampropeltis do-*

liata triangulum) (R). *n.*

ruʔtúrher yellow-spotted lizard (H-notebook). *n.*

-ruʔwẹhs -.#ẹtíh wild sunflower. *n.r.* n-poss., n-inc., n.sfx. -aʔ. uruʔwẹhsaʔ-ẹtíh *wild sunflower (Helianthus* sp.*)* (H-notebook).

-ryaʔnar - be crazy, be delirious from illness. *v.r.-s.i.* pnt: -, stat: -ɸ, prog: -, prp: -, dst: -, caus: -, rvs: -, dat: -, n-inc. θaryáʔnar *you are crazy, you are delirious from illnesses* (TW).

Θ

θ -/č - you alone! (imperative singular). *v.r.pfx.* The form č - occurs before roots and stems that begin with the vowel *i* or the consonant *y*, with loss of the *y*. The form θ - occurs elsewhere with insertion of "epenthetic" e between the prefix and roots or stems beginning with certain consonant clusters.

-θ - put on. *v.r.-t.* hab: -s, pnt: -, stat: -eʔ, prog: -, prp: -, dst: -, caus: -, rvs: -, dat: -, inc.-ɸ-pat. Found only in the constructions cited below in combination with the dualic and the noun root **-arahsu -** *shoe.* **-ne+či -.-arah = suθ -:** neθhrarahsú·θeʔ ‹apart-again-he-shoe-put on› *he shoed it again* (HS), neθhraráhsuč ‹apart-again-he-shoe-puts on› *he shoes it again* (HS); **á·ha·θ -ne -.-arahsuθ -:** á·ha·θ nehrarahsú·θeʔ ‹horse apart-he-shoe-put on› *he shoed a horse* (HS).

θa - yours alone (second person singular alienable). *n.r.pfx.* With roots and stems that begin with the vowel *i* the final *a* of the prefix and the *i* coalesce to yield θẹ -. Before roots and stems beginning with other vowels the final *a* of the prefix is dropped.

-θa - you alone (second person singular patient). *v.r.pfx.* With roots and stems that begin with the vowel *i* the final *a* of the prefix and the *i* coalesce to yield θẹ -. Before roots and stems beginning with other vowels the final *a* of the prefix is dropped.

θa - yours alone (second person singular alienable). *n.r.pfx.* With roots and stems that begin with the vowel *i* the final *a* of the prefix and the *i* coalesce to yield θẹ -. Before roots and stems beginning with other vowels the final *a* of the prefix is dropped.

-θa - you alone (second person singular patient). *v.r.pfx.* With roots and stems that begin with the vowel *i* the final *a* of the prefix and the *i* coalesce to yield θẹ -. Before roots and stems beginning with other vowels the final *a* of the prefix is dropped.

θučá·kʔu kingfisher (SH 375). *n.*

-θaheʔ(r) - bean. *n.r.* n-poss., inc., n.sfx. -ɸ. In modern Tuscarora, the elicitation form of this root occurs without a simple noun prefix or a simple noun suffix and the final *r* appears only in composition. However, Hewitt and

---

Tuscarora Pronunciation Key:

/a/ law; /e/ hat; /i/ pizza; /u/ tune; /ẹ/ hint; /č/ cheese; /h/ hoe; /m/ mother; /s/ same; /t/ do (before a vowel y, or w), too (elsewhere); /k/ gale (before a vowel y or w), kale (elsewhere); /n/ inhale (before a consonant or word-final), note (elsewhere), /r/ hiss (before a consonant or word-final), run (trilled as in Italian, elsewhere); /w/ cuff (before a consonant other than y or word-final), way (elsewhere); /y/ fish (before a consonant or word-final), you (elsewhere), /θ/ thing; /ʔ/ (the sound between the vowels in unh-unh); /·/ long vowel, /ʹ/ high pitch; /ˋ/ low pitch.

Smith also list a form **uθahé'reh** *bean* alongside of **θáhe'**. **θáhe'** *bean* (RC 26:9) [Lawson «Saugh-he» 'Pease']: **θáhe' -a'nekrirurę-**: θáhe' u'nekrirù·rę' ‹bean self-cotton-split› *peas (lit., Whiteman's bean)* (HS); yu'nekrirù·rę' θáhe' ‹it-itself-cotton-split bean› *peas (lit., Whiteman's bean)* (HS); **-θahe'raka'ne-**: Ruθahe'raká'ne' ‹he-bean-is abundant› *He-Has-Plenty-of-Beans* (male proper name in use in the late 1800s near Brantford, Ontario) (AG); **-θahe'rakęre-**: kaθahe'rakę·re' ‹it-bean-is scarce› *beans are scarce* (H 2892), kaθahe'rakę·rehk ‹it-bean-was scarce› *beans were scarce* (H 2892), ękaθahe'rakę·re·k ‹prediction-it-bean-be scarce› *beans will be scarce* (H 2892); **-θahe'ratya'T-**: wa'kθahe'rá·tya'r ‹fact-I-bean-bought› *I bought beans* (R).

θáhe' -a'nekrirurę- peas. *n.s.* θáhe' u'nekrirù·rę' ‹bean self-cotton-split› *peas (lit., Whiteman's bean)* (HS), yu'nekrirù·rę' θáhe' ‹it-itself-cotton-split bean› *peas (lit., Whiteman's bean)* (HS).

-θahe'raka'ne- He-Has-Plenty-of-Beans. *dv.n.s.* Albert S. Gatschet comments that this is the proper name of a very old man near Brantford, whose real name is **Nyukawéhę**, which he compares with the Tutelo name **Nikǫha**. Ruθahe'raká'ne' ‹he-bean-is abundant› *He-Has-Plenty-of-Beans* (male proper name in use in the late 1800s near Brantford, Ontario) (AG).

-θahru'T- be smooth, be soft. *v.r.-s.i.* stat: -ę, prog: -, prp: -, dst: -, caus: -, rvs: -, dat: -, inc.-φ-pat. See also: **-hru'T-**. yuθahrú'nę *it is smooth, it is soft* (R) [Lawson «Utsauwanne» 'Soft']; **-ę'kʷehstaθahru'T-**: rawękwehstaθahrú'nę ‹he-human-'ness-is soft› *he is sociable* (HS); **-wętaθah=ru'T-**: ruwętaθahrú'nę ‹he-word-is soft› *his voice was so soft* (RC 35: 10).

θá·st black squirrel (AG) [Lawson «Sost» 'Squirrel-skin'] [Jefferson «sahst» 'squirrel']. *n.* θá·st ti-. **-a'kęh=rayę(T)-**: θá·st tiwa'kęhrayę' ‹black squirrel so-it-ashes-lays› *gray squirrel (Sciuris carolinensis)* (AG).

θá·st ti-. -a'kęhrayę(T)- gray squirrel. *dv.n.s.* θá·st tiwa'kęhrayę' ‹black squirrel so-it-ashes-lays› *gray squirrel (Sciuris carolinensis)* (AG).

θatiwéhek rabble (HS). *n.*

-θa'r- bacon, fat back, salt pork. *n.r.* n-poss., n-inc., n.sfx. -eh. uθá'reh *bacon, fat back, salt pork* (R) [Lawson «Ootsaure» 'Fat']; **kwè·ni' -θa'rakar-**: kwè·ni' yuθá'rakar ‹like it-bacon-makes a noise› *you can even hear the fat rattle (said when a very fat woman sings)* (R).

-θa'w- be parent-in-law (male speaking). *v.r.-k.* yé·θa'w *my father-in-law, my mother-in-law (male speaking)* (R)

-θa'w- daughter-in-law, granddaughter-in-law; female in-law of a younger generation. *n.r.* aln: á·kθa'w *my daughter-in-law, my niece-in-law, my granddaughter-in-law, my great granddaughter-in-law* (R), n-inc., n.sfx. -φ ~ -eh. uθá'weh *daughter-in-law* (HS).

-θehru'n- field daisy. *n.r.* n-poss., n-inc., n.sfx. -ę'. uθehrú'nę' *field daisy (Chrysanthemum leucanthemum)* (H-notebook).

-θ(e)r- clean, purify. *v.r.-t.* hab: -ęhs, pnt: ()-', stat: -ę, prog: -, prp: -, dst: -, caus: -, rvs: -, dat: -, n-inc. See also: **-a'θręn-**. rá·θręhs *he cleans it, he purifies it* (HS), rú·θrę *he has cleaned it* (HS), ęhrá·θe'r *he will clean it* (HS).

-θer- wrist. *n.r.* inaln: kθeré'kye *my wrist* (R), n-inc., n.sfx. -eh. This root is pronounced with the vowel *a* as in uθà·reh *wrist* (R) by some contemporary speakers of the language. uθè·reh *wrist* (HS); -(ę)tiθerahtręhsT-: yę̨tiθerahtrę́hstha' ‹one-oneself-wrist-tie-causes› *bracelet* (HS).

-θerhu- pour. *v.r.-t.* hab: -, pnt: -', stat: -, prog: -, prp: -, dst: -, caus: -hT-, rvs: -, dat: -, n-inc. ęyeθérhu' *one will pour* (RC 16:1); -yah-. -θerhu-: yahwa'kayeθérhu' ‹thither-fact-they-poured› *they poured there* (RC 12:30); -θerhuhnahkw-: yeθerhuhnáhkhwa' ‹one-pour-causes-instrument› *funnel* (HS).

-θerhuhnahkw- funnel. *dv.n.s.* yeθerhuhnáhkhwa' ‹one-pour-causes-instrument› *funnel* (HS).

θenę́·ku·t mink *(Mustela vison)* (R). *n.*

θę́hru' until (R). *part.* Also: θę́'ru' (RC 6:15), θhę́'ru' (L 6).

-θęnęn- calf of leg. *n.r.*, poss. ?, inc. ?, n.sfx. -eh. uθęnè·neh *muscle and calf of leg* (AG).

-θęr- rattle (of a snake). *n.r.* n-poss., inc., n.sfx. -eh. uθę̀·reh *rattle of a snake* (SH 375); -θęręt: ruθę́·rę·t ‹he-rattle-possesses› *rattlesnake (Sistrurus sp., Crotalus sp.)* (RC 7:1).

-θęręt rattlesnake. *n.s.* ruθę́·rę·t ‹he-rattle-possesses› *rattlesnake (Sistrurus sp., Crotalus sp.)* (RC 7:1).

-θęy- fundament, rump. *n.r.* n-poss., n-inc., n.sfx. -eh. See: -ti'θęy-. uθę̀·yeh *fundament, rump* (HS).

θę́'ru' until (RC 6:15). *part.* Also: θę́hru' (R), θhę́'ru' (L 6).

θharé'ku get that knife! (M 84). *v.* Possibly shortened from *θeθharé'ku ‹you!-knife-take› (containing an archaic word for knife), the expected imperative form.

θhę́'ru' until (L 6). *part.* Also: θę́hru' (R), θę́'ru' (RC 6:15).

Θhuhtyerę́hskę' Mischief-Maker (RC 26: title). *n.* Also: Θhuhtyerúhskę' (R), which also has the meaning *mirthful.*

Θhuhtyerúhskę' Mischief-Maker; mirthful (R). *n.* Also: Θhuhtyerę́hskę' (RC 26:title).

-θhuhwahkw- be an upstart. *v.r.-s.i.* stat: -ę°, prog: -, prp: -, dst: -, caus: -, rvs: -, dat: -, n-inc. raθhuhwáhkę *he is an upstart* (H-notebook).

-θhukwyęhte'- prowl about. *v.r.-a.i.* hab: -θ, pnt: -, stat: -, prog: -, prp: -, dst: -, caus: -, rvs: -, dat: -, n-inc. raθhukwyę́hte'θ *he prowls about* (H-notebook).

θkahę́'θkahę' wild black currant *(Ribes sp.)* (H-notebook). *n.*

Θkahnéhtati Albany, New York (archaic) (R), Schenectady, New York (modern) (R), Hudson River (AG) [Morgan, League «Skaw-na-taw´-te» 'Albany']. *n.*

θkanatanę́hwe' pigweed (H-notebook). *n.*

θkarihstù·wa' mullet *(Moxostoma sp.)* (H-notebook). *n.*

θka'nyę́hsa' reindeer *(Rangifer tarandus)* (HS). *n.*

Tuscarora Pronunciation Key:
/a/ law; /e/ hat; /i/ pizza; /u/ tune; /ę/ hint; /č/ cheese; /h/ hoe; /m/ mother; /s/ same; /t/ do (before a vowel y, or w), too (elsewhere); /k/ gale (before a vowel y or w), kale (elsewhere); /n/ inhale (before a consonant or word-final), note (elsewhere), /r/ hiss (before a consonant or word-final), run (trilled as in Italian, elsewhere); /w/ cuff (before a consonant other than y or word-final), way (elsewhere); /y/ fish (before a consonant or word-final), you (elsewhere), /θ/ thing; /'/ (the sound between the vowels in unh-unh); /·/ long vowel, /´/ high pitch; /`/ low pitch.

θkaʔnyę́hseh moose *(Alces americana)* (R). *n.*

-θkr- spittle. *n.r.* n-poss., inc., n.sfx. -eh. úθkreh *spittle* (HS); **-θkrₐrahkwahT-**: yeθkrarahkwáhtha' ‹one-spittle-collect-causes› *spittoon* (HS); **-θkręy-**: yúθkręy ‹it-spittle-hung down› *drivel* (HS), rúθkręy ‹he-spittle-hung down› *he slobbers* (HS); **-(ę)tiθkrę'ni-**: ręti-θkrę́·'nyęhs ‹he-himself-spittle-throws› *he spits* (HS); **-ne-**. **-θkraw-**: nehrúθ-kraws ‹apart-he-spittle-gives› *he salivates* (HS).

-θkrₐrahkwahT- spittoon. *dv.n.s.* yeθkra-rahkwáhtha' ‹one-spittle-collect-causes› *spittoon* (HS).

-θkręy- slabber. *v.s.-a.i.* rúθkręy ‹he-spittle-hung down› *he slobbers* (HS).

-θkręy- drivel. *dv.n.s.* yúθkręy ‹it-spittle-hung down› *drivel* (HS).

-θkrawęri- mince. *v.r.-t.* hab: -h, pnt: -, stat: -, prog: -, prp: -, dst: -, caus: -, rvs: -, dat: -, n-inc. raθkrawę̀·rih *he minces it* (H-notebook).

θkwarì·nę wolf *(Canis lupus)* (RC 11:13) [Lawson «Squarrena» 'Wolf']; Wolf Clan (R). *n.*

-θkwehthar- scratch. *v.r.-a.i.* hab: -ɸ, pnt: -, stat: -, prog: -, prp: -, dst: -, caus: -, rvs: -aku-, dat: -, n-inc. With this root the reversive suffix, rather than adding the meaning *undo* as usual, merely serves to transitivize the stem. raθkwéhthar *he scratches* (HS); **-θkwehtharaku-**: raθkwehthará·kwahs ‹he-scratch-undoes› *he claws it, he scratches it (with his nails)* (HS), ruθkwehthará·kwę ‹he-scratch-undid› *he clawed it, he scratched it* (HS), ęhraθkwehthará·ku' ‹prediction-he-scratch-undo› *he will claw it, he will scratch it* (HS).

-θkwehtharaku- claw, scratch. *v.s.-t.* raθkwehthará·kwahs ‹he-scratch-undoes› *he claws it, he scratches it (with his nails)* (HS), ruθkwehthará·kwę ‹he-scratch-undid› *he clawed it, he scratched it* (HS), ęhraθkwehthará·ku' ‹prediction-he-scratch-undo› *he will claw it, he will scratch it* (HS).

-θkʷek- be dumb; shut one's lips. *v.s.-a.i.* Possibly a rather radical shortening of a stem *-θ(kwₐra)kʷek- ‹lips-close› (H-notebook). ráθkwe·ks ‹he-X-closes› *he shut his lips* (H-notebook); ti-. **-θkʷek-**: tihruθkwé·kę ‹so-he-shut his lips› *he is dumb* (H-notebook).

-θn- wear (clothes). *v.r.-s.i.* stat: -ę, prog: -, prp: -, dst: -, caus: -, rvs: -, dat: -, n-inc. wákθnę *I'm wearing it* (R), θá·θnę *you're wearing it* (R), rú·θnę *he's wearing it* (R).

-θnahr- human skin. *n.r.* n-poss., n-inc., n.sfx. -eh. uθnáhreh *human skin* (R).

-θnahręw- marrow. *n.r.* n-poss., n-inc., n.sfx. -eh. Also: **-hsnahręw-**. uθnah-rę̀·weh *marrow* (R).

-θnur- feather. *n.r.* n-poss., n-inc., n.sfx. -eh. uθnù·reh *feather* (R).

-θnyarę- be assiduous, be diligent, be industrious, be smart. *v.r.-s.i.* stat: -', prog: -, prp: -, dst: -, caus: -, rvs: -, dat: -, n-inc. Also: **-θteʔnyarę-**. ruθ-nyà·rę' *he is assiduous, he is diligent, he is industrious, he is smart* (HS); **-θnyaręʔčr-**: uθnyarę́'čreh ‹be diligent-'ness› *diligence* (HS).

-θnyaręʔčr- diligence. *n.s.* uθnyarę́'čreh ‹be diligent-'ness› *diligence* (HS).

-θrahrehst- be impetuous. *v.r.-s.i.* stat: -ɸ, prog: -, prp: -, dst: -, caus: -, rvs: -, dat: -, n-inc. ruθráhrehst *he is impetuous* (HS).

-θrahkw- clabber, coagulation, custard, thickening. *n.r.* n-poss., inc., n.sfx. -eh. uθráhkweh *clabber, coagulation, custard, thickening, thickness of any liquid* (HS); **-θrahkwa'nę-**: ęhsθrahkwá·'nę' ⟨prediction-you-coagulation-become⟩ *you will can it, you will preserve it* (R); **-θrahkwęti -**: kaθrahkwę́·tih ⟨it-coagulation-makes⟩ *it coagulates (forms a thick mass)* (HS).

-θrahkwa'nę - can, preserve. *v.,s.-t.* ęhs-θrahkwá·'nę' ⟨prediction-you-coagulation-become⟩ *you will can it, you will preserve it* (R).

-θrahkwęti - coagulate. *v.,s.-a.i.* kaθrahkwę́·tih ⟨it-coagulation-makes⟩ *it coagulates (forms a thick mass)* (HS).

-θrahwi'r - fritter, pancake. *n.r.* n-poss., n-inc., n.sfx. -eh. uθrahwí'reh *fritter, pancake* (R).

-θrar - flutter, palpitate, quiver, shiver, shudder, stir, tremble. *v.r.-a.i.* hab: -ha', pnt: -', stat: -, prog: -, prp: -, dst: -, caus: -ahsT-, rvs: -, dat: -, n-inc. ruθrárha' *he quivers, he shivers, he shudders, he stirs, he trembles* (HS), yuθrárha' *it flutter, it palpitates, it shakes, it trembles* (HS), ęyú·θra'r *it will palpitate* (HS); **-θrarahsT -**: ruθrà·rahst ⟨he-palpitate-caused⟩ *he is severe* (HS); **-t-.-θrar -**: nyuθrárha' ⟨hither-it-palpitates⟩ *quivering* (AW 45).

-θrarahsT - be severe. *v.s.-s.i.* ruθrà·rahst ⟨he-palpitate-caused⟩ *he is severe* (HS).

-θray - fresh; roe. *n.r.* n-poss., n-inc., n.sfx. -eh. uθrà·yeh *fresh* (RC 30:47), *roe* (AG); **-θray -**: eθrà·yeh ⟨one-fresh⟩ *young girl* (RC 35:1), yeθrà·yeh ⟨one-fresh⟩ *young woman: damsel* (HS); **-θray -.#áh**: yeθrayeháh ⟨one-fresh-lit-

tle⟩ *young person* (R); **-ekaθray -**: awekaθrà·yeh ⟨liquid-fresh⟩ *fresh liquid* (RC 19:2); **-nęθaθray -**: unęθa-θrà·yeh ⟨potato-fresh⟩ *the potato is raw, uncooked, not done* (H 2484) **-'ęhraθray -**: u'ęhraθrà·yeh ⟨leaf-fresh⟩ *lettuce (Lactuca sp.)* (R); **-ačraya=yę'θk -**: yęčrayayę́'θkę ⟨one-oneself-fresh-laid-easily⟩ *tuberculosis* (AW 98).

-θray - damsel, young girl, young woman. *n.s.* eθrà·yeh ⟨one-fresh⟩ *young girl* (RC 35:1), yeθrà·yeh ⟨one-fresh⟩ *young woman: damsel* (HS).

-θray -.#áh young person. *n.s.* yeθra-yeháh ⟨one-fresh-little⟩ *young person* (R).

-θra'nę - stretch. *v.r.-t.* hab: -h, pnt: -, stat: -, prog: -, prp: -, dst: -, caus: -, rvs: -, dat: -, n-inc. raθrá'nęh *he stretches it* (HS).

-θręhn - dream, sleep. *n.r.* n-poss., inc., n.sfx. -eh. uθrę́hneh *dream, sleep* (HS); **-θręhnakareti -**: ruθręhnakaré·tih ⟨he-sleep-is loud⟩ *he snores* (HS); **-θręhnaksę' -**: ruθręhnaksę́'ę ⟨he-sleep-be bad-began⟩ *he had a bad dream: his dream* (HS), raθręhná·ksę'θ ⟨he-sleep-be bad-begins⟩ *he dreams* (HS), ękθręhná·ksę' ⟨fact-I-sleep-be bad-began⟩ *I dreamt (had a bad dream)* (AW 50); **-θręhnak'u -**: ruθręhná·k'ę ⟨he-sleep-released⟩ *he likes sleep* (HS); **-θręhnara' -**: ruθręh-nara'θ ⟨he-sleep-be in-begins⟩ *he is sleepy* (HS); **-θręhnukę'**: ruθręhnú·-kę' ⟨he-sleep-less⟩ *he is sleepless*

Tuscarora Pronunciation Key:
/a/ law; /e/ hat; /i/ pizza; /u/ tune; /ę/ hint; /č/ cheese; /h/ hoe; /m/ mother; /s/ same; /t/ do (before a vowel y, or w), too (elsewhere); /k/ gale (before a vowel y or w), kale (elsewhere); /n/ inhale (before a consonant or word-final), note (elsewhere), /r/ hiss (before a consonant or word-final), run (trilled as in Italian, elsewhere); /w/ cuff (before a consonant other than y or word-final), way (elsewhere); /y/ fish (before a consonant or word-final), you (elsewhere), /θ/ thing; /'/ (the sound between the vowels in unh-unh); /·/ long vowel, /´/ high pitch; /`/ low pitch.

(HS); -θrẹhnuri -: wahraθrẹhnù·ri'' ‹fact-he-sleep-stirred› *he awoke* (RC 8:15), načrẹhnù·rih ‹one=another-sleep-stirs› *one awakens another* (HS).

-θrẹhnakareti – snore. *v.s.-a.i.* ruθrẹhna-karé·tih ‹he-sleep-is loud› *he snores* (HS).

-θrẹhnaksẹ' – have a bad dream. *v.s.-a.i.* ruθrẹhnaksẹ·''ẹ ‹he-sleep-be bad-began› *he had a bad dream* (HS), raθrẹhná·ksẹ·''θ ‹he-sleep-be bad-begins› *he dreams* (HS), ẹkθrẹhná·ksẹ·' ‹fact-I-sleep-be bad-began› *I dreamt (had a bad dream)* (AW 50).

-θrẹhnak'u – like sleep. *v.s.-a.i.* ruθrẹhná·k''ẹ ‹he-sleep-released› *he likes sleep* (HS).

-θrẹhnara' – be sleepy. *v.s.-a.i.* ruθrẹhnara''θ ‹he-sleep-be in-begins› *he is sleepy* (HS).

-θrẹhnukẹ' be sleepless. *v.s.-s.i.* ruθrẹhnú·kẹ' ‹he-sleep-less› *he is sleepless* (HS).

-θrẹhnuri – awake. *v.s.-a.i.* wahraθrẹhnù·ri' ‹fact-he-sleep-stirred› *he awoke* (RC 8:15).

-θrẹshay – ill-luck, misfortune. *n.r.* n-poss., inc., n.sfx. -ẹ'. uθréshayẹ' *ill-luck, misfortune* (HS); -θrẹshay -. #ú'y: uθrẹshayẹ''ú'y ‹misfortune-great› *great misfortune* (RC 12:7).

-θrẹw – cement, glue, gum, jam, jelly, molasses, resin, syrup, tar, wax. *n.r.* n-poss., inc., n.sfx. -eh. uθrẹ̀·weh *cement, glue, gum, jam, jelly, molasses, resin, syrup, tar, wax* (R); -θrẹw -. #hči: uθrẹwéhči ‹gum-very› *gummy, resinous* (HS); -θrẹwanẹ'nakT -: raθrẹwanẹ''náktha' ‹he-wax-attach-causes› *he seals it* (HS); -θrẹwara' -: yuθrẹ̀·wara''θ ‹it-gum-be in-begins› *it sticks* (HS); -θrẹwarikhẹ – kaθrẹwarí·khẹh ‹it-gum-bites-much› *it ruminates* (HS); -θrẹwawẹ -: raθrẹ̀·wawẹhs ‹he-gum-

possesses› *he puts gum on it, he seals it, he tars it, he taints it with gum* (HS); -θrẹwawẹhsthẹ -: raθrẹwawẹ́hsthẹh ‹he-gum-possess-causes-much› *he gums them* (HS); -θrẹwẹtyahnẹ -: kaθrẹwẹtyáhnẹh ‹it-syrup-makes-much› *sweetmeat* (HS), yeθrẹwẹtyáhnẹh ‹one-syrup-makes-much› *one preserves, one makes jelly* (HS); -θrẹwi= tkẹ' -: kaθrẹwí·tkẹ''θ ‹it-syrup-issues› *it extrudes syrup* (RC 2:15); -ne -. -θrẹwya'k -: nehraθrẹ́·wya''ks ‹apart-he-wax-breaks› *he breaks the seal* (HS); -θrẹw - -ne -. -(a)hkaruθne -: uθrẹ̀·weh neyuhkarúθneh ‹gum apart-it-bark-?'?› *alum* (HS); háhteh -θrẹ= wẹte: háhteh uθrẹwẹ́·te ‹pine resin-certain one› *pitch* (HS); ru'táhkẹ -θrẹw -: ru''táhkẹ uθrẹ̀·weh ‹bee syrup› *honey* (R).

-θrẹw -.#hči gummy, resinous. *n.s.* uθrẹwéhči ‹gum-very› *gummy, resinous* (HS).

-θrẹwanẹ'nakT – seal. *v.s.-t.* raθrẹwanẹ'náktha' ‹he-wax-attach-causes› *he seals it* (HS).

-θrẹwara' – stick. *v.s.-a.i.* yuθrẹ̀·wara''θ ‹it-gum-be in-begins› *it sticks* (HS).

-θrẹwawẹ – put gum on, seal, tar, taint with gum. *v.s.-a.i.* raθrẹ̀·wawẹhs ‹he-gum-possesses› *he puts gum on it, he seals it, he tars it, he taints it with gum* (HS).

-θrẹwawẹhsthẹ – gum. *v.s.-a.i.* raθrẹwa-wẹ́hsthẹh ‹he-gum-possess-causes-much› *he gums them* (HS).

-θrẹwẹtyahnẹ – sweetmeat. *dv.n.s.* kaθrẹ-wẹtyáhnẹh ‹it-syrup-makes-much› *sweetmeat* (HS).

-θrẹwẹtyahnẹ – make jelly, preserve. *v.s.-a.i.* yeθrẹwẹtyáhnẹh ‹one-syrup-makes-much› *one preserves, one makes jelly* (HS).

θrẹ'kye hardly (HS). *part.*

-θriʔkw - limp thing. *n.r.* n-poss., inc., n.sfx. -eh. uθríʔkweh *limp thing* (R); -θriʔkweθ -: kaθríʔkwe·θ ‹it-limp thing-is long› *land turtle, sand turtle: Small Turtle Clan* (R).

-θriʔkweθ - land turtle, sand turtle; Small Turtle Clan. *dv.n.s.* kaθríʔkwe·θ ‹it-limp thing-is long› *land turtle, sand turtle: Small Turtle Clan* (R).

-θriʔr - wrinkle; snail. *n.r.* n-poss., inc., n.sfx. -eh (in the meaning *wrinkle*) /-aʔ (in the meaning *snail*). uθríʔreh *wrinkle* (RC 26:13), uθríʔraʔ *snail* (HS); -θriʔr -.#úʔy: uθriʔrehúʔy ‹wrinkle-great› *elephant* (R); -θriʔrar -: θríʔ-rar ‹wrinkle-is in› *alligator (Alligator sp.)* (R) [Lawson «Utsererauh» 'Alligator']; -nęhaθriʔr -: unęhaθríʔreh ‹corn-wrinkle› *corn that is shrunken, a name of a certain kind of corn (this is the common sweet corn)* (H 2484); -nęhsnaθriʔr -: unęhsnaθíʔreh ‹seed-wrinkle› *shriveled or wrinkled grain* (H 2484); -ačriʔrarurę -: wačriʔrarù·ręh ‹it-itself-wrinkle-contributes› *it shrivels up, it wrinkles* (HS).

-θriʔr -.#úʔy elephant. *n.s.* uθriʔrehúʔy ‹wrinkle-great› *elephant* (R).

-θriʔrar - alligator. *n.s.* θríʔrar ‹wrinkle-is in› *alligator (Alligator sp.)* (R) [Lawson «Utsererauh» 'Alligator'].

-θruʔT - flood, flow copiously. *v.r.-s.i.* stat: -e·, prog: -, prp: -, dst: -, caus: -, rvs: -, dat: -, n-inc. yuθrúʔnę· *it is flowing copiously, it flows in force, water is flowing* (L 82), *it floods, it flows* (HS); -θruʔT -: uθrúʔnę· ‹flow› *deluge* (HS).

-θruʔT - deluge. *n.s.* uθrúʔnę· ‹flow› *deluge* (HS).

-θteʔnyarę - be assiduous, be industrious, be smart. *v.r.-s.i.* stat: -ʔ, prog: -, prp: -, dst: -, caus: -, rvs: -, dat: -, n-inc. Also: -θnyarę -. ruθteʔnyà·ręʔ *he is assiduous, he is industrious, he is smart* (HS).

θT(i) -/č - the two of yours (second person dual possessor). *n.r.pfx.* The distinction between alienable and inalienable is not marked by distinct pronominal prefixes for the second person dual. The form θn - occurs before roots and stems that begin with the vowel ę or the morphophoneme {ᵘu}. The form θt - occurs before roots and stems that begin with the vowels *i, e,* or *u* (not from {ᵘu}). The form -č - occurs before roots and stems that begin with the vowel *a*. The form θti - occurs before roots and stems that begin with a consonant.

-θT(i) -/-č - the two of you (second person dual actor). *v.r.pfx.* The distinction between agent and patient is not marked by distinct pronominal prefixes for the second person dual. The form -θn - occurs before roots and stems that begin with the vowel ę or the morphophoneme {ᵘu}. The form -θt - occurs before roots and stems that begin with the vowels *i, e,* or *u* (not from {ᵘu}). The form -č - occurs before roots and stems that begin with the vowel *a*. The form

-θti - occurs before roots and stems that begin with a consonant.

-θuhra?t - white cedar. flat-leafed cedar. *n.r.* n-poss., inc., n.sfx. -a?. uθuhrá?ta? *white cedar, flat-leafed cedar* (R); -θuhra?tayẹ(T) -: yuθuhrá?tayẹ? ‹it-flat-leafed cedar-lies› *there is a flat-leafed cedar* (RC 2:13).

θútahs soldier. *n.* Hewitt and Smith give the form θúter *soldier*. -θutahs: raθútahs ‹he-soldier› *he is a soldier* (L 43). kθútahs ‹I-soldier› *I am a soldier* (L 43); θútahs -a?rihẹt: θútahs waka?ríhẹ·t ‹soldier I-myself-matter-possess› *I am a soldier* (L 43).

-θutahs be a soldier. *v.s.-a.i.* raθútahs ‹he-soldier› *he is a soldier* (L 43), kθútahs ‹he-soldier› *I am a soldier* (L 43).

θútahs -a?rihẹt be a soldier. *v.s.-a.i.* θútahs waka?ríhẹ·t ‹soldier I-myself-matter-possess› *I am a soldier* (L 43).

-θuw - animal's back. *n.r.* n-poss., inc., n.sfx. -eh. uθù·weh *animal's back* (R); čwe -. -θuwake -: čwekaθuwá·kye· ‹all kinds of-it-animal's back-is in number› *all different kinds of animals' backs* (RC 3:76); -ne -. -θuwahri? -: nekaθuwahrí?ẹ ‹two-it-animal's back-spill-began› *bittersweet (Celastrus scandens)* (R).

θú·yẹ·t duck (R) [Lawson «Sooeau» 'A Duck']. *n.* Also: θú?yẹ·t (R).

θú?krihst red-winged blackbird *(Agelaius phaeniceus)* (R). *n.*

θú?yẹ·t duck (R) [Lawson «Sooeau» 'A Duck']. *n.* Also: θú·yẹ·t (R).

-θw - short cloak. *n.r.* n-poss., inc., n.sfx. -eh. ú·θweh *short cloak* (HS); -θwa = kwẹhnar -: raθwakwẹ́hnar ‹he-short cloak-throws down› *he prostrates* (HS).

θwa - all of yours (second person plural possessor). *n.r.pfx.* The distinction be-

tween alienable and inalienable is not marked by distinct pronominal prefixes for the second person plural. With roots and stems that begin with the vowel *i* the final *a* of the prefix coalesces with the *i* to yield θwẹ -. Before roots and stems that begin with other vowels the final *a* of the prefix is lost.

-θwa - all of you (second person plural actor). *v.r.pfx.* The distinction between agent and patient is not marked by distinct pronominal prefixes for the second person plural. With roots and stems that begin with the vowel *i* the final *a* of the prefix coalesces with the *i* to yield -θwẹ -. Before roots and stems that begin with other vowels the final *a* of the prefix is lost.

θwahyù·wa? apple *(Malus sp.)* (H-notebook). *n.*

-θwakwẹhnar - prostrate. *v.s.-a.i.* raθwakwẹ́hnar ‹he-short cloak-throws down› *he prostrates* (HS).

θwará·rẹ·k lamprey eel (H 3518). *n.*

-θwẹtahrahT - be rude. *v.s.-s.i.* ruθwẹtáhraht ‹he-??-put up-caused› *he is rude* (HS).

S

s - yours alone (second person singular inalienable). *n.r.pfx.* Before roots and stems that begin with certain consonant clusters "epenthetic" e occurs between the prefix and the root or stem.

sá·iter cider (HS). *n.*

sáw saw (HS). *n.* sáw -ẹ°ti -: sáw rẹ́·tih ‹saw he-makes› *he saws* (HS).

sáw -ẹ°ti - saw. *v.s.-a.i.* sáw rẹ́·tih ‹saw he-makes› *he saws* (HS).

Sawà·nu Shawnee (AG). *n.* Sawanu.#a =

ka·ʔ: Sawanuʔá·ka·ʔ ‹Shawnee-characterized by› *Shawnee* (AG).

Sawanu.#aka·ʔ Shawnee. *n.* Sawanuʔ-á·ka·ʔ ‹Shawnee-characterized by› *Shawnee* (AG).

sawá·thuʔ setting of the sun, setting of a star, star-set, sunset (H-notebook). *n.*

sawę́·te something (RC 24:5); nothing (RC 3:22). *part.*

sawętawę́·te something (HS). *part.* A blend of **sawę́·te** *something* and **awę́·te** *thing*.

sáy shiver (from fear) (HS). *part.* sáy -ę°ti -: sáy wakyé·tih ‹shiver I-make› *it chills me, it is atrocious to me* (HS).

sáy -ę°ti - chill, be atrocious to. *v.s.-t.* sáy wakyé·tih ‹shiver I-make› *it chill me, it is atrocious to me* (HS).

sáʔ look!, see! (HS). *v.* kęʔ sáʔ ‹where look!› *look here!* (H-notebook); sáʔ.#áh: saʔáh ‹look!-little› *look!* (TW).

sáʔ.#áh look!. *v.* This verb differs from **sáʔ** in that the former directs the listener's to look at a spot away from the speaker, whereas **saʔáh** directs the listener to look at something closer. saʔ-áh ‹look!-little› *look!* (TW).

saʔkáhne·ʔ somebody, someone, who (RC 3:79). *part.*

sáʔrkę́ʔ ostensibly, pretence, sham (RC 24:5). *part.*

sáʔthu season of the year (HS), fall (H-notebook). *part.*

séher also, however, nevertheless, yet (RC 3:55). *part.*

sè·nęʔ never (RC 12:2). *part.* her sè·nęʔ ‹also never› *as never* (AW 103); wah

sè·nęʔ ‹o! never› *o come now, that's not true* (R).

séʔči because, since (RC 3:73). *part.* nę́h séʔči hę̀·we ‹very because where› *really, that's too bad* (R); séʔči kwà·nę ‹since much› *it's too much* (R); ù·nę séʔči hę̀·we ‹now since where› *isn't that awful?* (R).

séʔči kwà·nę ‹since much› it's too much (R).

sę́·nyęʔ hate (RC 30:48). *part.*

sę́·r à·rę notwithstanding, still (HS). *part.*

sękwéh nobody (AG). *part.*

sę̀·weʔ all (RC 25:2), both (RC 3:20). *part.*

-sheręt cow. *n.r.* n-poss., n-inc., n.sfx. -φ. ushé·rę·t *cow* (R) [Lawson «Oussarunt» 'A Cow']; -sheręt.#áh: ushe-rę·tʔáh ‹cow-little› *bovine* (HS), *calf* (L 78); -sheręt.#kęʔnaʔnęʔ: usheręt-kę́ʔnaʔnęʔ ‹cow-many› *cattle* (HS); -sheręt.#keha·ʔ: usherętkyéha·ʔ ‹cow-customarily› *bovine* (HS); -sheręt -iye -: ushé·rę·t kę̀·yeʔ ‹cow grease› *tallow* (HS); -sheręt -ʔniha -: ushé·rę·t kaʔníha· ‹cow it-is male› *bull* (HS).

-sheręt -iye - tallow. *n.s.* ushé·rę·t kę̀·yeʔ ‹cow grease› *tallow* (HS).

-sheręt -ʔniha - bull. *n.s.* ushé·rę·t kaʔ-níha· ‹cow it-is male› *bull* (HS).

-sheręt.#áh bovine; calf. *n.s.* ushe·rę·tʔáh ‹cow-little› *bovine* (HS), *calf* (L 78).

-sheręt.#kęʔnaʔnęʔ cattle. *n.s.* usheręt-kę́ʔnaʔnęʔ ‹cow-many› *cattle* (HS).

-sheręt.#keha·ʔ bovine. *n.s.* usherętkyé-ha·ʔ ‹cow-customarily› *bovine* (HS).

-sir - canoe. *n.r.* n-poss., n-inc., n.sfx.

Tuscarora Pronunciation Key:
/a/ law; /e/ hat; /i/ pizza; /u/ tune; /ę/ hint; /č/ cheese; /h/ hoe; /m/ mother; /s/ same; /t/ do (before a vowel y, or w), too (elsewhere); /k/ gale (before a vowel y or w), kale (elsewhere); /n/ inhale (before a consonant or word-final), note (elsewhere), /r/ hiss (before a consonant or word-final), run (trilled as in Italian, elsewhere); /w/ cuff (before a consonant other than y or word-final), way (elsewhere); /y/ fish (before a consonant or word-final), you (elsewhere), /θ/ thing; /ʔ/ (the sound between the vowels in unh-unh); /·/ long vowel, /ʹ/ high pitch; /ʽ/ low pitch.

-ch. usì·rch *canoe* (R).

-**skarurę** - be Tuscarora. *v.r.-s.i.* stat: -ʔ, prog: -, prp: -, dst: -, caus: -, rvs: -, dat: -, n-inc. raskarù·rę^ʔ *he is Tuscarora* (H 2892), yakwaskarù·rę^ʔ *we Tuscarora* (L 34), nwaskarù·rę^ʔ *we Tuscarora* (AW 102); -**skaruręʔ**: Skarù·rę^ʔ ‹be Tuscarora› *Tuscarora* (RC 33:1); -**ačkarurę** -: kayęčkarù·rę^ʔ ‹they-themselves-are Tuscarora› *they are Tuscarora* (HS).

Skarù·ręʔ ‹be Tuscarora› Tuscarora (RC 33:1). *n.*

Skwakíhahs Erie (AG). *n.*

-**skwenę** - mouse. *n.r.* n-poss., n-inc., n.sfx. -ʔ. Like a few other animal names, this root inexplicably takes the masculine singular patient pronominal prefix in its elicitation form. ruskwè·nę^ʔ *mouse (Mus* sp.) (R) [Lawson «Rusquiane» 'A Rat'].

spì·nič spinach *(Spinacia oleracea)* (R). *n.*

stá·kwiʔ aloft (HS), up high (RC 25:2) *part.* **stá·kwiʔ.#áh**: stakwiʔáh ‹up high-little› *eagle* (12:4) [Jefferson «sauh-quih-hau» 'eagle']; **stá·kwiʔ -enęʔT** -: stá·kwi^ʔ è·nę^ʔt ‹up high travel-cause› *highway* (H-notebook), *stairs, stairway* (HS); **haʔ stá·kwiʔ**: ha^ʔ stá·kwi^ʔ ‹the up high› *chamber* (HS); **haʔ stá·kwiʔ naʔ -nęhsa'ni**: ha^ʔ stá·kwi^ʔ na^ʔ unę́hsa^ʔni ‹the up high much house-at edge of› *chamber* (HS).

stá·kwiʔ chamber. *n.s.* ha^ʔ stá·kwi^ʔ ‹the up high› *chamber* (HS).

stá·kwiʔ -enęʔT - highway, stairs, stairway. *n.s.* stá·kwi^ʔ è·nę^ʔt ‹up high travel-cause› *highway* (H-notebook), *stairs, stairway* (HS).

stá·kwiʔ.#áh eagle. *n.s.* Albert S. Gatschet gives **strakwiʔáh** with an *r* not found in other sources. stakwiʔáh ‹up high-little› *eagle* (RC 12:4) [Jefferson

«sauh-quih-hau» 'eagle'].

-**stawęʔčr** - rattle. *n.r.* n-poss., n-inc., n. sfx. -eh. ustawę́^ʔčreh *rattle* (R).

sté·t párkkye at the state park, to the state park (R). *n.*

steʔ some (AW 53), a certain, some specific (L 34). *part.* ste^ʔ ti -. -ake -: ste^ʔ tiwá·kye· ‹some so-it-is in number› *several* (HS).

steʔ ti -. -ake - several. *part.* ste^ʔ tiwá·kye· ‹some so-it-is in number› *several* (HS).

sté?kę·θ afterwards (RC 15:7). *part.*

stí·yu· instead (R). *part.*

stiʔkà·reh anus, disgusting thing (R). *n.*

stúw oven, stove (R). *n.* -**stuhčrayę(T)** -: kakustúhčrayę^ʔ ‹they-stove-'ness-lay› *they have an oven, they have a stove* (R).

súhweʔt witch hazel *(Hamamelis virginiana)* (H-notebook). *n.*

suká·we·θ crocodile *(Crocodylus* sp.) (R). *n.*

Sukuhęté·thaʔ title of the Shawnee chief on the Tuscarora Chiefs Council, responsible for the descendants of adopted Shawnee (AG). *n.*

Swé·kęʔ Canada (R). *n.* **Swekęʔ.#aka·ʔ**: Swekęʔá·ka·^ʔ ‹Canada-characterized by› *Grand River Indians* (AG).

Swekęʔ.#aka·ʔ Grand River Indians. *n.* Swekęʔá·aka·^ʔ ‹Canada-characterized by› Grand River Indians (AG). *n.*

sy·· hush! (HS). *part.*

syah oh nuts! (R). *part.*

syà·wę some (R). *part.*

T

-**t** - empty noun root. *v.inc.* See: -**iʔak** - *shoot,* -**uha** - *put in water,* -**uhar** - *wash.*

-t- hither, here (cislocative). *v.pfx.* The form t- occurs before pronominal prefixes that begin with the consonants *k* or *h*. When followed by the sequence *hs* the prefix coalesces with the sequence to yield -čh-. The form n- occurs before pronominal prefixes that begin with the consonants *w* or *y*. The form ni- occurs before pronominal prefixes that begin with the consonants *č* or *θ*. (See also ka-.) The cislocative in ninety percent of its occurrences carries the meaning "away from speaker, near hearer". Its usual English translation is *there* and its gloss in this dictionary is the more archaic, but more accurate ⟨hither⟩. In meaning, it is opposed to the translocative, which generally carries the meaning "away from the speaker and hearer." With a number of verb roots and stems, however, the meaning of the cislocative is more opaque. With some it adds the meaning of "location at or near", with others it adds a meaning of action or movement "toward both the speaker and hearer", with others it adds the notion of "motion downward." With still others it is impossible to determine precisely what the cislocative adds to the meaning of the whole. Where the meaning of the cislocative is opaque, it is a discontinuous part of the verb stem. In a few cases, the cislocative is obligatory with a particular verb root or stem. In most cases, however, a root or stem

occurs with the cislocative with a particular meaning and with other affixes or unaffixed with other meanings. Below are listed all those cases that have been encountered in the data base from which this dictionary has been constructed where the cislocative is opaque in meaning and forms part of a verb or deverbal noun stem.

-t-. -ačnęhsT-.#hči come down. *v.s.-a.i.* nęčnęhsná'či ⟨hither-fact-it-descended-very⟩ *it came down* (RC 32: 12).

-t-. -ahθę'nayę(T)- get dark. *v.s.-a.i.* wa'-nwahθę'nayę·'na' ⟨fact-hither-it-become dark-laid⟩ *it got dark* (RC 3: 65).

-t-. -ahθę'nar- be dark. *v.s.-a.i.* ę'nyuh-θę·'nara' ⟨prediction-hither-it-darkness-be in⟩ *it will be dark* (RC 8: 13).

-t-. -ahsthu'ęha'nye'- grow to be less. *v.s.-a.i.* ę'nyuhsthu'ęhá·'nye' ⟨prediction-hither-it-be small-begin-going along⟩ *it will grow to be less* (RC 3: 20).

-t-. -(a)karę'r- disturb position. *v.s.-a.i.* nakakarę'rę' ⟨hither-unknown-it-be sloped⟩ *that it disturb its position* (RC 3:22).

-t-. -akT- be near to, replace. *v.s.-t.* na'á·ktakwt ⟨hither-we-be next to⟩ *that the two of us be near one another, that I replace another* (R).

-t-. -ar(e)ku- come from. *v.s.-a.i.* nwaré·kwę· ⟨hither-it-moves on⟩ *it comes from* (RC 34:12).

-t-. -athwe'nęti- make a challenge. *v.s.-a.i.* nakayęthwe'né·ti' ⟨hither-fact-they-themselves-furrow-made› *they made a challenge* (RC 24:10).

-t-. -atkar²u – blink, wink. *v.s.-a.i.* nahratkár²u² ‹hither-he-himself-eye-showed› *he blinked, he winked* (RC 26:28).

-t-. -atkęha²n – get up, get out of bed. *v.s.-a.i.* thrutkęhá²nę ‹hither-he-himself-rose-while moving› *as soon as he got up; right out of his bed* (R).

-t-. -atkwahT – fourth quarter of moon. *dv.n.s.* nyutkwáhnę ‹hither-it-itself-cut off› *fourth quarter of moon* (SH 375).

-t-. -atrahręhwatyę – put fence around. *v.s.-a.i.* tkakutrahręhwá·tyęh ‹hither-they-pole-put up-cause-much› *they put fence around* (RC 18:13).

-t-. -aw – give to. *v.s.-t.* tkę̀·yaws ‹hither-I=you give to› *I give it to you* (R), čkà·wi ‹hither-you=me-gave to› *you handed it to me* (R).

-t-. -a'na²nihr – arise (from a sitting position). *v.s.-a.i.* thra²ná²nihč ‹hither-he-himself-stands up› *he arises (from a sitting position)* (HS).

-t-. -(a)'ne – loom, project, protrude. *v.s.-s.i.* nwá·²ne² ‹hither-it-is present› *it looms, it projects, it protrudes* (HS).

-t-. -a²netkę² – east. *dv.n.s.* nwa²né·tkę²θ ‹hither-it-rises› *east* (RC 4:1).

-t-. -a²nęrhwitkę – clouds come forth. *v.s.-a.i.* nę²nęrhwí·tkę² ‹hither-it-storm cloud-came forth› *clouds came forth there* (RC 36:1).

-t-. -a'nęrihsta²nihęthu – draw a breath. *v.s.-a.i.* thra²nęrihsta²nihę́·thuhs ‹hither-he-himself-breathe-'ness-draws in› *he draws a breath* (HS).

-t-. -a'nę'nu²kT – be abnormal, be mentally deficient, be retarded. *v.s.-a.i.* nyu²nę́·²nu²kt ‹hither-it-itself-day-ended› *it is abnormal, it is mentally deficient, it is retarded* (HS).

-t-. -a'ni – throw to. *v.s.-t.* kaθá·²ni ‹hith-er-you-throw› *throw it to me!* (R).

-t-. -a'nihęthu – withdraw. *v.s.-a.i.* thra²nihę́·thuhs ‹hither-he-pulls› *he withdraws* (R).

-t-. -a'nu²kT – end. *v.s.-a.i.* nę²nú²knę² ‹hither-fact-it-itself-ended› *it ended* (RC 15:6).

-t-. -a'nu²nę'nye² – go along being in such and such a condition. *v.s.-a.i.* nayu²nu²nę́·²nye² ‹hither-it-itself-was a kind of-going along› *it goes along being in such a way* (RC 3:69).

-t-. -a'nwehra²T – above-mentioned. *dv.n.s.* nyu²nwehrá²nę ‹hither-it-itself-speak-caused› *above-mentioned* (HS).

-t-. -a'nwętahT – mock. *v.s.-t.* nwa²nwętáhtha² ‹hither-it-itself-word-stands› *it mocks* (HS).

-t-. -a'nwętahT – echo. *dv.n.s.* nwa²nwętáhtha² ‹hither-it-itself-word-stands› *echo* (HS).

-t-. -a'nyehsayer – conduct oneself. *v.s.-a.i.* naka²nyéhsaye²r ‹apart-fact-I-myself-appearance-did› *I conduct myself* (RC 26:4).

-t-. -a'nyeręhT – make happen. *v.s.-t.* nahra²nyè·ręht ‹hither-he-have an unexpected experience-caused› *he made it happen* (RC 3:84).

-t-. -a'nyeręhT – first time. *dv.n.s.* nę²nyè·ręht ‹hither-fact-it-have an unexpected experience-caused› *first time* (RC 6:6), nę²nyerę́hnahk ‹hither-fact-it-have an unexpected experience-caused› *first time* (RC 6:7).

-t-. -a²rihęti – incipient. *dv.n.s.* nwa²rihę́·tih ‹hither-it-itself-matter-makes› *incipient* (HS).

-t-. -a²rihwahθaw² – rudiments. *dv.n.s.* nyu²rihwáhθa²w ‹hither-it-itself-matter-began› *rudiments* (HS).

-t-. -a²θrenęhT – clean. *v.s.-t.* nayu²θrè·nęht ‹hither-fact-it-be clean-caused› *it cleaned it* (RC 6:10).

-t-. -ča?urya?T - be preoccupied. *v.r.-a.i.* hab: -ha?, pnt: -, stat: -, prog: -, prp: -, dst: -, caus: -, rvs: -, dat: -, n-inc. thruča?uryá?tha? *he is preoccupied* (HS).

-t-. -čęwa?nihrhę - stand up burial poles. *v.s.-a.i.* tkakučęwa?nírhę? ⟨hither-they-burial pole-stand up-many⟩ *they stand up burial poles* (RC 3:13).

-t-. -čhe?wękuh - go through gourd. *v.s.-a.i.* nayučhe?wę·kuh ⟨hither-it-gourd-goes through⟩ *it goes through a gourd* (RC 15:4).

-t-. -či?rę - fire fall down. *v.s.-a.i.* naka-čí?ręh ⟨hither-it-ember-falls⟩ *fire fell down* (RC 10:6).

-t-. -e - come. *v.s.-a.i.* ęčhę? ⟨prediction-hither-you-go⟩ *you will come* (R), ę́-tkye? ⟨prediction-hither-I-go⟩ *I will come* (R), náhre? ⟨hither-he-goes⟩ *he is coming* (R).

-t-. -e - future. *dv.n.s.* ha? nà·we? ⟨the hither-it-goes⟩ *future* (HS).

-t-. -ekę - mouth of river. *dv.n.s.* nyawé·-kę? ⟨hither-it-liquid-fell⟩ *mouth of river* (AG).

-t-. -eku?nętyę - blister. *dv.n.s.* naweku?-nę́·tyę? ⟨hither-it-liquid-was a kind of-much⟩ *blister* (RC 3:57).

-t-. -enę?T - come from. *v.s.-t.* nyawe-nę́?nę ⟨hither-it-travel-caused⟩ *it came from* (RC 12:29), thrawenę́?nę ⟨hither-he-travel-caused⟩ *he came from* (RC 12:18).

-t-. -erihst - add. *v.s.-t.* nakyè·rihst ⟨hither-I-add⟩ *I added it* (R).

-t-. -e?nahkw - be fervent, be unswerving, have faith. *v.s.-s.i.* thrawe?náhkę ⟨hither-he-is faithful⟩ *he is fervent, he is unswerving, he has faith* (HS).

-t-. -ę -/ -t-. -ihrę - reply. *v.s.-a.i.* nahrá·wę· ⟨hither-he-said⟩ *he replied* (R), nahrę́h-rę? ⟨hither-fact-he-said⟩ *he replied* (RC 12:19).

-t-. -(ę)haw - bring back. *v.s.-t.* nákha?w ⟨hither-fact-I-brought⟩ *I brought it back* (R), náhsha?w ⟨hither-fact-you-brought⟩ *you brought it back* (RC 3:29).

-t-. -ęhretihs - be hungry. *v.s.-s.i.* nwakęh-ré·tihs ⟨hither-I-have hunger⟩ *I am hungry* (RC 30:38).

-t-. -ętuthe? - moon dog. *dv.n.s.* nyuwę-tú·the? ⟨hither-it-rain-going to⟩ *moon dog* (R).

-t-. -ę'nahręhw - dawn. *dv.n.s.* nawę?nah-rę́hwę ⟨hither-it-day-put up-caused⟩ *dawn* (HS), ę?nayawę?nahrę́hwak ⟨prediction-hither-it-day-put up-cause⟩ *dawn* (RC 15:3).

-t-. -ę'nęte - time. *dv.n.s.* nyawę?nę́·tehk ⟨hither-it-day-was a certain⟩ *time* (R).

-t-. -ę'nut dawn. *dv.n.s.* nyawę·?nu·t ⟨hither-it-day-stands⟩ *dawn* (HS).

-t-. -(ę)?tahsitkę? - loll. *v.s.-a.i.* nwę?tah-sí·tkę?θ ⟨hither-it-tongue-issue forth-begins⟩ *it lolls* (HS).

-t-. -(ę)?teyitkęhnahkw - exit. *dv.n.s.* tka?-teyitkęhnáhkhwa? ⟨hither-it-crowd-issue-causes-instrument⟩ *exit* (RC 26:6).

-t-. -(ę)?tikęhnę - control, decide for, govern. *v.s.-t.* thrę?tikę́hnęh ⟨hither-he-mind-falls⟩ *he governs* (HS), thrawę?-

tik**ę́**hnę**ˀ** ‹hither-he-mind-fell› *he controls, he sways the rule* (HS), ętkę**ˀ**tikę́hnę**ˀ** ‹prediction-hither-I=you-mind-fall› *I will decide for you* (RC 3:36).

–t–. –(ę)**ˀtikęhnę** – forethought. *dv.n.s.* thrawę**ˀ**tikę́hnę**ˀ** ‹hither-he-mind-fell› *his forethought* (HS).

–t–. –(ę)**ˀtikęhrayeri** – be right-minded. *v.s.-a.i.* thra**ˀ**tikęhrayè·ri**ˀ** ‹hither-he-mind-is correct› *he is right-minded* (HS).

–t–. –(ę)**ˀtikęhraˈnę** – decide. *v.s.-a.i.* nyaku**ˀ**tikęhrá·**ˀ**nę**ˀ** ‹hither-one-mind-is present› *one has decided* (RC 6:16).

–t–. –(ę)**ˀtikęhrihsˀa** – be prejudice, make mind up. *v.s.-a.i.* thru**ˀ**tikęhríhs**ˀ**ę ‹hither-he-himself-mind-finished› *he is prejudice, his mind is made up* (HS).

–t–. –(ę)**ˀtikęhriyu** –{dative I} be pleased by. *v.s.-t.* tka**ˀ**tikęhriyú**ˀ**θeh ‹hither-it-mind-is great-for› *it is pleased by* (HS).

–t–. –(ę)**ˀtikęhriyuhT** – satisfaction. *dv.n.s.* nyu**ˀ**tikęhrì·yuht ‹hither-it-mind-be great-caused› *satisfaction* (HS).

–t–. –(ę)**ˀtyaˀke** France. *dv.n.s.* Nyu**ˀ**tyá**ˀ**kye ‹hither-it-bay-at› *France* (R).

–t–. –**hęreT** – May. *dv.n.s.* nakahę́·re·t ‹hither-fact-it-carried away› *May* (R).

–t–. –**hratuhsT** – freeze. *v.s.-a.i.* nakáhratuhst ‹hither-fact-it-froze› *it froze* (R).

–t–. –**hsuˀθhę** – into a corner. *dv.n.s.* nyuhsú**ˀ**θhę**ˀ** ‹hither-it-is in a corner› *into a corner* (RC 11:16).

–t–. –**ht** – be. *v.s.-s.i.* ná**ˀ**uht ‹hither-fact-it-stood› *it was* (L 38).

–t–. –**htawah(e)r** – stream of water gush up. *v.s.-a.i.* nakahtawáhra**ˀ** ‹hither-fact-it-stream of water-put up› *stream of water gushed up* (RC 6:9).

–t–. –**htawęˀ** – at the waterfall. *dv.n.s.* nyuhtawę́**ˀ**ę ‹hither-it-stream of water-fall-began› *at the waterfall* (R).

–t–. –**htawęˀ** – Niagara Falls, New York.

dv.n.s. Nyuhtawę́**ˀ**ę ‹hither-it-fall-began› *Niagara Falls, New York* (R).

–t–. –**huk** –{dative I} aurora. *dv.n.s.* nayuhúkθe· ‹hither-it-light up-for› *aurora* (HS).

–t–. –(i)**har** – increase. *v.s.-t.* thráher ‹hither-he-hangs› *he increases* (HS), tkáher ‹hither-it-hangs› *it increases* (RC 3:34).

–t–. –(i)**hkᵂaˀT** – pick up. *v.s.-t.* načíhkwa**ˀ**t ‹hither-you-pick up› *pick it up!* (L 18).

–t–. –(i)**hsˀa** – use up. *v.s.-t.* nakahs**ˀ**áhnahk ‹hither-fact-it-exhaust-caused› *it used up* (RC 2:4).

–t–. –(i)**hsˀahT** – flee, go rapidly. *v.s.-a.i.* nahráhs**ˀ**aht ‹hither-fact-he-exhaust-caused› *he went rapidly* (RC 6:9), nakayéhs**ˀ**aht ‹hither-fact-they-exhaust-caused› *they fled* (RC 24:9).

–t–. –(i)**yhęhyaˀk** – come back across river. *v.s.-a.i.* načiyhę́hya**ˀ**k ‹hither-you-river-cross over› *come back across river!* (RC 31:6).

–t–. –(i)**ˀθhanę** – abate. *v.s.-a.i.* nyú**ˀ**θhanęhs ‹hither-it-power-guards› *it abates* (HS).

–t–. –**kurarhu** – be French. *v.r.-s.i.* stat: -ę, prog: -, prp: -, dst: -, caus: -, rvs: -, dat: -, n-inc. Found only in the cited construction. Tkayekurárhę *Kingdom of France* (HS).

–t–. –**rakar** – noise. *dv.n.s.* nyurá·kar ‹hither-it-sounds› *a noise* (AW 57).

–t–. –**raku** – deduct. *v.s.-t.* thrará·kwahs ‹hither-he-chooses› *he deducts* (HS).

–t–. –**raˀ** – reply. *v.s.-a.i.* nahrà·ra**ˀ** ‹hither-fact-he-was in› *he replies* (RC 26:29).

–t–. –**rhęˀ** – daybreak, very early dawn. *dv.n.s.* nayúrhę**ˀ** ‹hither-it-be day-began› *daybreak, very early dawn* (HS).

–t–. –**rhęˀ** –.#**aka·ˀ** English. *dv.n.s.* nyurhę**ˀ**θ**ˀ**á·ka·**ˀ** ‹hither-it-be day-begins-characterized by› *English* (HS).

-t-. -rhę?-.#ú?y daybreak, just after midnight, very early dawn. *dv.n.s.* nayurhę?ú?y ‹hither-it-be day-began-great› *daybreak, just after midnight, very early dawn* (HS).

-t-. -rihu?kT -{dative III} criticize. *v.s.-t.* nyę?na?rihu?kná·tih ‹hither-one=another-matter-puts an end to-for› *one criticizes another* (HS).

-t-. -rihwara - echo. *dv.n.s.* tkaríhwahs ‹hither-it-matter-grabs› *echo* (HS).

-t-. -rihware - maintain. *v.s.-s.i.* thruríhware? ‹hither-he-matter-is distant› *he maintains* (HS).

-t-. -rihwaturę - save. *v.s.-t.* nahskrihwatú·rę· ‹hither-you=me-matter-store› *you save me* (MP).

-t-. -rihwaya?θraku - echo. *dv.n.s.* tkarihwaya?θrá·kwahs ‹hither-it-matter-fold-undoes› *echo* (HS).

-t-. -rihwayeri - be correct, be right. *v.s.-a.i.* tkarihwayè·ri? ‹hither-it-matter-is straight› *it is correct, it is right* (HS).

-t-. -rihwayerik - be trustable. *v.s.-a.i.* tkarihwayè·rik ‹hither-it-matter-filled up› *it is trustable* (HS).

-t-. -rihwayę - be difficult. *v.s.-a.i.* tkarihwà·yę? ‹hither-it-matter-went into› *it is difficult* (RC 25:7).

-t-. -rihwa?nihθT - principle. *dv.n.s.* nyurihwa?níhθnę ‹hither-it-matter-stand up-caused› *principle* (HS).

-t-. -takar - whistle. *v.s.-a.i.* nyetá·kare? ‹hither-one-whistled› *one whistles* (RC 32:15).

-t-. -tehękari - in the place of torment. *dv.n.s.* nyutehęká·rya? ‹hither-it-sand-de-voured› *in the place of torment* (AG).

-t-. -turę - lacking. *dv.n.s.* nyutú·rę· ‹hither-it-store› *lacking* (R).

-t-. -wehr - above-mentioned. *dv.n.s.* ha? nyuwéhrę ‹the hither-it-spoke› *above-mentioned* (HS).

-t-. -wętitkę? - state. *v.s.-a.i.* nyewętí·tkę? ‹hither-one-word-came forth› *one stated* (RC 30:11).

-t-. -yakę? - emanate. *v.s.-a.i.* thrayá·kę?θ ‹hither-he-go out-begins› *he emanates* (HS), thruyakę́?ę ‹hither-he-go out-began› *he has emanated* (HS).

-t-. -yer - be diligent. *v.s.-s.i.* ha? thruyè·rę ‹the hither-he-did› *he is diligent* (HS).

-t-. -yer - Amen. *dv.n.s.* ha? nakà·yer ‹the hither-it-does› *Amen* (HS).

-t-. -yeri - be complete, be fit, be just, be perfect. *v.s.-s.i.* tkayè·ri? ‹hither-it-is correct› *it is complete, it is fit, it is just, it is perfect* (HS).

-t-. -yę - entry(way), ingress; income. *dv.n.s.* ha? tkà·yę? ‹the hither-it-went into› *entry(way), ingress; income* (HS).

-t-. -yęhT - bring in, introduce. *v.s.-t.* thrayę́htha? ‹hither-he-go into-causes› *he brings in, he introduces* (HS).

-t-. -yę?khwar - swarm. *dv.n.s.* nakayę?khwà·ra? ‹hither-fact-it-smoke-hung› *a swarm* (RC 26:10).

-t-. -?ęyeθ - high prices. *dv.n.s.* nyu?ęyé·θę ‹hither-it-price-was long› *high prices* (R).

-t-. -?naręwar - ceiling. *dv.n.s.* ha? nyu?narę̀·war ‹the hither-it-mud-is in› *ceiling* (HS).

−tačit− guide. *n.r.* n-poss., n-inc., n.sfx. -ch. utačí·teh *guide* (HS).

−tahki?w − catch up to, outrun. *v.r.-t.* hab: -ahs, pnt: -ɸ, stat: -ę, prog: -, prp: -, dst: -, caus: -, rvs: -, dat: -, n-inc. rutahkí?wę *he outran it* (HS), ratahkí?-wahs *he outruns it* (HS), wa?nyetáhki?w *the two of them outran it* (RC 30:63), ęhrutáhki?w *it will catch up to him* (R).

−tahkukę?čr − celibacy. *n.s.* utahkukę́?čreh ‹marriage-less-'ness› *celibacy* (HS).

−tahkw − marriage, matrimony; mistress, spouse. *n.r.* n-poss., inc., n.sfx. -eh. utáhkweh *marriage, matrimony* (R); *mistress, spouse* (HS); −tahkukę?čr −: utahkukę́?čreh ‹marriage-less-'ness› *celibacy* (HS); −tahkwahrihT −: ratahkwahríhtha? ‹he-marriage-spill-causes› *he divorces* (HS); −tahkwaks −: katahkwá·ksę· ‹it-marriage-is bad› *mis-marriage* (HS); −tahkwanęhwak(T) −: ratahkwanę́hwaks‹he-marriage-aches› *he is amorous, he wants the other sex* (R); −tahkwatyenę −: waθatahkwatyè·-nę? ‹fact-you-marriage-obtained› *you got a husband/a wife* (R); −tahkwa= yeθa?čr −: utahkwayeθá?čreh ‹marriage-curse-'ness› *cursed marriage, un-chastity* (HS); −tahkwę'ni −: rutahkwę́·?nyęhs ‹he-marriage-throws› *he leaves his spouse* (HS).

−tahkwahrihT − divorce. *v.s.-t.* ratahkwahríhtha? ‹he-marriage-spill-causes› *he divorces* (HS).

−tahkwaks − mis-marriage. *dv.n.s.* katahkwá·ksę· ‹it-marriage-is bad› *mis-marriage* (HS).

−tahkwanęhwak(T) − be amorous. *v.s.-a.i.* ratahkwanę́hwaks‹he-marriage-aches› *he is amorous, he wants the other sex* (R).

−tahkwatyenę −get a husband/a wife. *v.s.-a.i.* waθatahkwatyè·nę? ‹fact-you-mar-

riage-obtained› *you got a husband/a wife* (R).

−tahkwayeθa?čr − cursed marriage, un-chastity. *n.s.* utahkwayeθá?čreh ‹marriage-curse-'ness› *cursed marriage, un-chastity* (HS).

tahkwà·yę? red raspberry *(Rubus stri-gosus)* (H-notebook). *n.* tahkwayę?. #ú?y: tahkwayę?ú?y ‹red raspberry-great› *red-flowering raspberry (Rubus sp.)* (H-notebook).

tahkwayę?.#ú?y red-flowering raspberry. *n.s.* tahkwayę?ú?y ‹red raspberry-great› *red-flowering raspberry (Rubus sp.)* (H-notebook).

−tahkwę'ni − leave spouse. *v.s.-a.i.* rutahkwę́·?nyęhs ‹he-marriage-throws› *he leaves his spouse* (HS).

Tahnawá·teh Tonawanda, New York; Tonawanda Seneca Reservation (R) [Morgan, League ‹Tä´-nä-wä-teh›]. *n.* Tahnawateh.#aka·?:Tahnawatehá·ka·? ‹Tonawanda Reservation-characterized by› *Tonawanda Reservation Senecas* (R).

Tahnawateh.#aka·? Tonawanda Reservation Senecas. *n.s.* Tahnawatehá·ka·? ‹Tonawanda Reservation-characterized by› *Tonawanda Reservation Senecas* (R).

−tahrek − touch. *v.r.-t.* hab: -s, pnt: -ɸ, stat: -, prog: -, prp: -, dst: -, caus: -, rvs: -, dat: -, n-inc. akatáhre·k *that it touch* (AW 53); −či −. −tahrek −: θhratáhreks ‹again-he-touches› *he retouches it* (HS); −yah −. −tahrek −: yahwa?ktáhre·k ‹thither-fact-I-touched› *I touched it* (R), yahwahratáhre·k ‹thither-fact-he-touched› *he touched it* (R), yahwahstáhre·k ‹thither-fact-you-touched› *you touched it* (R).

−tahθ − braid. *n.r.* aln: aktáhθawęh *my braid* (R), inc., n.sfx. -eh. utáhθeh *braid* (HS); −tahθęti −: ratahθę́·tih ‹he-

braid-makes› *he braids it* (R); -ne -.
-tahθęT -: nehratahθę́·tha⁷ ‹two-he-
braid-concludes› *he annexes it* (R),
wa⁷thratahθę́·⁷nę⁷ ‹fact-two-he-braid-
concluded› *he joined it* (L 24–gives
[wa'thrᴈtda'θᴈ·'nᴈ'] with an unexpected nasal vowel in the second syllable); -ne -. -tahθę'nawę -: nehratah-
θę⁷nà·węh ‹two-he-braid-concludes-
many› *he joins them* (L 24–gives
[næhrᴈtda'θᴈ'nà·wᴈ'] with an unexpected nasal vowel in the second syllable); -ne -. -a'nętahθęT -: neyu⁷nętah-
θę́·⁷nę ‹two-it-itself-braid-concluded›
it's joined together (L 24), neyu⁷nę-
táhθę·t ‹two-it-itself-braid-concludes›
it's joined together (L 24).
-tahθęti - braid. *v.s.-t.* ratahθę́·tih ‹he-
braid-makes› *he braids it* (R).
-tahs - assail, assault, invade, menace. *v.
r.-a.i.* hab: -ha⁷, pnt: -ɸ, stat: -ę, prog:
-, prp: -, dst: -ahnę-, caus: -, rvs: -,
dat: -, n-inc. rú·tahsę *he assailed, he
assaulted, he invaded, he menaces*
(HS), ratáhsha⁷ *he assails, he assaults,
he invades, he menaced* (HS), ęh-
rá·tahs *he will assail, he will assault,
he will invade, he will menace* (HS);
-tahsahnę -: ratahsáhnęhs ‹he-assails-
much› *he makes incursions* (HS);
-tahsahstaw -: wa⁷kayetahsáhsta⁷w
‹fact-they-assail-'ness-came› *they attacked, they came looking for a fight*
(RC 33:2), ękayetahsáhsta⁷w ‹predic-
tion-they-assail-'ness-come› *they will
attack, they will come looking for a
fight* (RC 33:3).

-tahsahnę - make incursions. *v.s.-a.i.*
ratahsáhnęhs ‹he-assails-much› *he
makes incursions* (HS).
-tahsahstaw - attack, come looking for a
fight. *v.s.-a.i.* wa⁷kayetahsáhsta⁷w
‹fact-they-assail-'ness-came› *they attacked, they came looking for a fight*
(RC 33:2), ękayetahsáhsta⁷w ‹predic-
tion-they-assail-'ness-come› *they will
attack, they will come looking for a
fight* (RC 33: 3).
táhsę dozen (HS). *n.* áhsę na⁷ táhsę
‹three much dozen› *three dozen* (HS).
-tahskęti - pick on. *v.s.-t.* wa⁷etahskę́·ti⁷
‹fact-one-slave-made› *one picked on*
(RC 35:7).
-tahskęti - prisoner. *dv.n.s.* na⁷tahskę́·tih
‹one=another-slave-makes› *prisoner*
(HS).
-tahskuhar - hitch up. *v.s.-t.* ratahskúhar
‹he-slave-tips› *he hitches up (the
horse)* (HS).
-tahskuhči - acquit, rescue. *v.s.-t.* ratahskúhčęhs ‹he-slave-removes› *he rescues it* (HS), ktahskúhčęhs ‹I-slave-
remove› *I acquit* (HS), khetahskúhčęhs ‹I=another-slave-remove› *I acquit
someone* (HS).
-tahskw - domestic animal, pet, prisoner,
slave; copy, model, pattern, plan, śam-
ple. *n.r.* inaln: ratáhskweh *his prisoner*
(HS), inc., n.sfx. -eh. utáhskweh *domestic animal, pet, prisoner, slave;
copy, model, pattern, plan, sample*
(HS); -tahskęti -: wa⁷etahskę́·ti⁷ ‹fact-
one-slave-made› *one picked on* (RC
35:7), na⁷tahskę́·tih ‹one=another-

slave-makes› *prisoner* (HS); **-tahsku = har –**: ratahskúhar ‹he-slave-tips› *he hitches up (the horse)* (HS); **-tah = skuhči –**: ratahskúhčęhs ‹he-slave-removes› *he rescues it* (HS), ktahskúhčęhs ‹I-slave-remove› *I acquit* (HS), khetahskúhčęhs ‹I=another-slave-remove› *I acquit someone* (HS); **-tah = skwah(e)r –**: ratáhskwar ‹he-slave-puts up› *he annoys, he enslaves* (HS), rutáhskwar ‹he-slave-puts up› *he tantalizes it: he is harassed, he is teased* (HS), kakutáhskwar ‹they-slave-put up› *it plagues them* (RC 2:2); **-tah = skwahrahT –**: utahskwáhraht ‹slave-put up-cause› *annoyance* (HS); **-tahskwa = 'nęhra⁷r –**: yutahskwa⁷nęhra⁷r ‹it-slave-self-dirt-is much› *animals are dirty* (R); **-či –. -tahskwayę(T) –**: θkakutahskwayę́·⁷nak ‹again-they-slave-laid› *they had a pet again* (RC 33:1); **kwęhs –a'nętahskuhči –**: kwęhs ahru⁷nętahskúhčęk ‹no unknown-he-himself-slave-remove› *he is unrescued* (HS).

–tahskwah(e)r – annoy, enslave, harass, plague, tantalize, tease. *v.s.-t.* ratáhskwar ‹he-slave-puts up› *he annoys, he enslaves* (HS), rutáhskwar ‹he-slave-puts up› *he tantalizes it: he is harassed, he is teased* (HS), kakutáhskwar ‹they-slave-put up› *it plagues them* (RC 2:2).

–tahskwahrahT – annoyance. *n.s.* utahskwáhraht ‹slave-put up-cause› *annoyance* (HS).

–tahsn – bat (unhewn), club, pole, rod (of 16½ feet), stick, yoke, wand. *n.r.* See: **-(ę)tahsn –**.

–tahsnanę'nakT – pack a gun, ram a gun. *v.s.-a.i.* See: **-(ę)tahsnanę'nakT –**.

tahuré·tik chicken. *n.* a⁷wthę́ha·⁷ tahuré·tik ‹earth-in middle of-characterized by chicken› *pheasant* (L 35); tahu-

ré·tik a⁷wthę́ha·⁷ ‹chicken earth-in middle of-characterized by› *pheasant* (L 35); **tahuré·tik –⁷niha –**: tahuré·tik ka⁷níha· ‹chicken it-is male› *cock* (HS).

tahuré·tik a⁷wthę́ha·⁷ ‹chicken earth-in middle of-characterized by› pheasant (L 35). *n.s.*

tahuré·tik –⁷niha – cock. *n.s.* tahuré·tik ka⁷níha· ‹chicken it-is male› *cock* (HS).

–tahwęhn – temple. *n.r.* n-poss., n-inc., n.sfx. -eh. utahwę́hneh *temple* (HS).

–takar – whistle. *v.r.-a.i.* hab: -ɸ, pnt: -, stat: -e⁷, prog: -, prp: -, dst: -, caus: -, rvs: -, dat: -, n-inc. ratá·kar *he is whistling*; **-t –. -takar –**: nyetá·kare⁷ ‹hither-one-whistled› *one whistles* (RC 32:15).

–tak(e)r – dwell, inhabit, live, reside; abound, be plentiful. *v.r.-a.i.* hab: ()-ɸ, pnt: -ę⁷, stat: -e⁷, prog: -, prp: -, dst: -, caus: ()-a⁷T-, rvs: -, dat: -, inc.-ɸ pat. With an incorporated noun root this verb has the meaning *abound, be plentiful*. Without an incorporated noun root it means *dwell, inhabit, live, reside.* yetá·kre⁷ *one dwells, one inhabits, one lives, one resides: village* (R), ratá·kre⁷ *inhabitant* (HS), kayetá·kre⁷ *they dwell; villagers, inhabitants* (RC 26:4), *populace* (HS), yetá·krehk *one dwelt* (RC 12:11); **-tak(e)r –**: utá·kre⁷ ‹dwell› *nation* (HS); **-tak(e)r –. #keha·⁷**: utakrę́⁷kyéha·⁷ ‹dwell-customarily› *national* (HS); **-takręte**: kayetakrę́·te ‹they-dwell-certain one› *kinds of inhabitants* (RC 12:7), stakrę́·te ‹you-dwell-certain one› *your tribe* (R); **-ne –. -tak(e)r –**: nehratá·kyer ‹apart-he-dwells› *his own people* (RC 12:1); **-ne –. -takyera⁷nahkw –**: neyetakyera⁷náhkhwa⁷ ‹apart-one-dwell-causes-instrument› *parable* (HS); **-ne –.**

-takrę̨te: nehratakrę́·te ‹apart-he-dwell-certain one› *his tribe* (RC 3:72); -t-. -tak(e)r-: nyetá·kreʔ ‹hither-one-dwelt› *one dwells there* (RC 26:2); -hwih=statak(e)r-: ękahwihstatá·kręʔ ‹prediction-it-metal-be plentiful› *money will become plenteous, abundant, plenty* (H 2892); -yuʔnę̨hčratak(e)r-: ękayuʔnę̨hčratá·kręʔ ‹prediction-it-work-'ness-be plentiful› *work will become abundant* (H 2892), akayuʔnę̨hčratá·krę́ʔ ‹unknown-it-work-'ness-be plentiful› *work would become abundant* (H 2892); haʔ -tak(e)r-: haʔ ratá·kreʔ ‹the he-dwells› *native* (HS), haʔ katá·kreʔ ‹the it-dwells› *fauna* (HS), haʔ yetá·kreʔ ‹the one-dwells› *the public* (HS); kęʔ -tak(e)r-: kęʔ ratá·kreʔ ‹where he-dwells› *his country* (HS); kwę̨hs -tak(e)r-: kwę̨hs aryetá·krek ‹no unknown-one-dwell› *it is uninhabited* (HS).

-tak(e)r- village. *dv.n.s.* yetá·kreʔ ‹one-dwells› *village* (R).

-tak(e)r- inhabitant. *dv.n.s.* ratá·kreʔ ‹he-dwells› *inhabitant* (HS).

-tak(e)r- inhabitants, populace, villagers. *dv.n.s.* kayetá·kreʔ ‹they-dwells› *villagers, inhabitants* (RC 26:4), *populace* (HS).

-tak(e)r- nation. *n.s.* utá·kreʔ ‹dwell› *nation* (HS).

-tak(e)r- native. *dv.n.s.* haʔ ratá·kreʔ ‹the he-dwells› *native* (HS).

-tak(e)r- fauna. *dv.n.s.* haʔ katá·kreʔ ‹the it-dwells› *fauna* (HS).

-tak(e)r- the public. *dv.n.s.* haʔ yetá·kreʔ ‹the one-dwells› *the public* (HS).

-tak(e)r-.#kehaʔ national. *n.s.* utakrę̨ʔkyéha·ʔ ‹dwell-customarily› *national* (HS).

-takę̨hst- doorway, enclosed porch, foyer, portal. *n.s.* utaką́hsteh ‹open-'ness› *doorway, enclosed porch, foyer, portal* (R); -takę̨hsta'ni: utaką́hstaʔni ‹open-'ness-at the edge of› *side of enclosed porch* (RC 3:8).

-takrę̨ʔkehaʔ national. *n.s.* utakrę̨ʔkyéha·ʔ ‹dwell-customarily› *national* (HS).

tá·kteh doctor (R). *n.* Also: tá·ktę̨h (AW 98).

tá·ktę̨h doctor (AW 98). *n.* Also: tá·kteh (R).

tá·ku·θ cat (R). *n.* tá·ku·θ -ʔę̨hrak-: tá·ku·θ kaʔę́hra·ks ‹cat it-leaf-eats› *catnip* (H-notebook).

tá·ku·θ -ʔę̨hrak- catnip. *n.s.* tá·ku·θ kaʔę́hra·ks ‹cat it-leaf-eats› *catnip* (H-notebook).

takwaká·yę· raspberries (L 45). *n.*

-takwnakT bedside. *n.s.* utákwnakwt ‹bed-next to› *bedside* (HS).

-takwnę̨T- story (of a building). *dv.n.s.* yutákwnę̨·t ‹it-stage-possesses› *story (of a building)* (HS).

-takwnę̨T- cell. *dv.n.s.* haʔ yutákwnę̨·t ‹the it-room-possesses› *cell* (HS).

-takwnut interval, vacancy. *dv.n.s.* haʔ yutákwnu·t ‹the it-space-stood› *interval, vacancy* (HS).

-takwT- apartment, bed, position, room, space, stage. *n.r.* aln: aktákwnayęʔ *my apartment* (R), inc., n.sfx. -eh. utákwnch *apartment, bed, position, room, space, stage* (HS); **-takwnakT**: utákwnakwt ‹bed-next to› *bedside* (HS); **-takwnaw -**: wa'²kayę'²na'²tákwnę'² ‹fact-they=another-space-gave› *they gave them a place* (AW 102); **-takw= nayę(T) -**: eθatakwnayę̆·'²nak ‹unknown-you-bed-lay› *that you had a bed* (RC 11:12); **-takwnęT -**: yutákwnę·t ‹it-stage-possesses› *story (of a building)* (HS); **-takwthrawę'nye² -**: katakwthrawę̆·'²-nye'² ‹it-bed-put up-many-going along› *one is setting up beds* (RC 3:5); ti -. **-takwnayer -**: tihrutakwnayè·rę ‹so-he-position-did› *his posture* (HS); ti -. **-takwna²θ -.#áh**: tikatakwna'²θ'²áh ‹so-it-room-is of a size-little› *cell* (HS); **-yah -. -takwnakę'neti -**: wehratakwnakę'²né·tyęhs ‹thither-he-position-changes› *he transposes* (HS); **-a'nętakwnahθehT -**: yu'²nętakwnahθéhnę ‹it-itself-room-hid› *arcanum* (HS); **ha² -takwnęT -**: ha'² yutákwnę·t ‹the it-room-possesses› *cell* (HS); **ha² -takwnut**: ha'² yutákwnu·t ‹the it-space-stood› *interval, vacancy* (HS); **kę² -takwthrahkw -**: kę'² yetakwthráhkhwa'² ‹where one-bed-puts up-instrument› *bed chamber* (HS).

tatíhstatih lizard (R). *n.*

tatukę́hti Sunday (R). *n.*

-tatur - be lazy. *v.r.-s.i.* stat: -, prog: -, prp: -, dst: -, caus: -, rvs: -, dat: -, n-inc. Found only in the two cited constructions. **-tature²w -**: utaturé'²weh ‹be lazy-??› *idleness, laziness* (HS); **ti+yah -. -tatura² -{dative I}**: tyahwahrutatù·ra'²θ ‹so-thither-fact-he-be lazy-became-for› *he got lazy* (R).

-tature²w - idleness, laziness. *n.s.* utaturé'²weh ‹be lazy-??› *idleness, laziness* (HS).

-tawę - heat up, warm. *v.r.-t.* hab: -h, pnt: -, stat: -'², prog: -, prp: -, dst: -,

caus: -hsT- ~ -hT-, rvs: -, dat: II (-ati-/-ahθ-), inc.-hna-/-ta'²-/-ra-pat. With the empty noun root **-hna -**, the stem takes on the inchoative meaning of *become warm, heat up*. In such cases, the stative meaning *be warm* is expressed by the presence of the completive aspect suffix -·t. With the empty noun root **-ta² -**, the stem means *dissolve, melt*. **-a²wnatawęhT -**: ęk[a'²wnatà·węht](#) ‹prediction-I-earth-warm-cause› *I will warm earth* (RC 4:5); **-hnatawę -**: yuhnatá·wę·t ‹it-X-warmed› *it is warm* (R), rahnatawę́hstha'² ‹it-X-warms› *he warms it* (R); **-hnatawę -{dative II}**: ruhnatà·węhθ ‹it-X-warms-for› *he becomes warm* (R); **-nęhruhčratawę -**: yunęhruhčratà·wę'² ‹it-scalp-'ness-is warm› *warm hat* (H-notebook); **-nęhsatawę -**: yunęhsatà·wę'² ‹it-house-warmed› *it is a warm house, or the house is warm, it is a warm house, meaning that it is built so that it is an easy matter to keep it warm in cold weather* (H 24 84); **-nęhsatawęhsT -**: yenęhsatawę́hstha'² ‹one-house-warm-causes› *stove (archaic)* (HS); **-nęhsnatawę -**: yunęhsnatá·wę· ‹it-seed-warmed› *the grain is warm, the grain is damp* (H 2484); **-ratawę -**: yuratá·wę· ‹it-X-warmed› *it is a warmed tree (i.e., it is fit to give sap or in a condition for peeling its bark off)* (H-notebook); **-ta²tawę -**: yuta'²tá·wę· ‹it-X-melted› *humid: it is melted* (R), wa'²kata'²tà·wę'² ‹fact-it-X-melted› *it melted* (R), kata'²tà·węhs ‹it-X-melted› *it thaws* (R), wa'²kta'²tà·wę'² ‹fact-I-X-melted› *I dissolved it* (R), ękata'²tà·wę'² ‹prediction-it-X-melt› *it will be soaked* (R); **-ta² = tawęhT -**: rata'²tawę́htha'² ‹he-X-melt-causes› *he infuses it, he soaks it* (HS); **-ta²tawę² -**: yuta'²tawę́'²ę ‹it-X-melt-began⟩ *it begins to melt* (RC 2:12), kata⁷tà·wę⁷θ ⟨it-X-melt-begins⟩ *it melts, it is soaked* (R); –ta⁷tawę⁷T –: yuta⁷-tawę́⁷ne⁷ ⟨it-X-melted-moving⟩ *dissoluble; it melts easily* (HS); –wenę = 'natawęhT –: rawenę⁷na⁷tawę́htha⁷ ⟨he-iron-warm-causes⟩ *he melts iron* (HS); ti –. –hnatawę –: tyuhnatà·węh ⟨so-it-X-warms⟩ *it got warm* (R); kwęhs –ta⁷ = tawę⁷ –: kwęhs akata⁷tawę́⁷θek ⟨no unknown-it-X-melt-begin⟩ *it is indissoluble, it is infusible* (HS).

tawę́·nya⁷ks touch-me-not (*Impatiens* sp.) (R). *n.*

tawę́·te anything (R). *part.* Contraction of ta⁷awę́·te.

–tawę⁷nę – celebrate, compliment, laud, praise. *v.r.-t.* hab: -h, pnt: -, stat: -, prog: -, prp: -, dst: -, caus: -hT-, rvs: -, dat: -, n-inc. ratawę́⁷nęh *he celebrates it, he lauds it, he praises it* (HS), na⁷tawę́⁷nęh *one compliments another* (HS); **–tawę⁷nęhčr –**: utawę⁷néhčreh ⟨celebrate-'ness⟩ *celebrity* (HS); **–tawę⁷nęhT –**: utawę́⁷nęht ⟨celebrate-cause⟩ *adulation, praise* (HS), yutawę́⁷nęht ⟨it-celebrate-causes⟩ *praiseworthy* (HS).

–tawę⁷nęhčr – celebrity. *n.s.* utawę⁷néhčreh ⟨celebrate-'ness⟩ *celebrity* (HS).

–tawę⁷nęhT – adulation, praise. *n.s.* utawę́⁷nęht ⟨celebrate-cause⟩ *adulation, praise* (HS).

–tawę⁷nęhT – praiseworthy. *dv.n.s.* yutawę́⁷nęht ⟨it-celebrate-causes⟩ *praiseworthy* (HS).

tawístawis snipe, Snipe Clan (R). *n.*

tawistawis⁷ú⁷y ⟨snipe-great⟩ *plover* (HS).

tawistawis⁷ú⁷y ⟨snipe-great⟩ plover (HS). *n.*

–tawn – clay. *n.r.* n-poss., n-inc., n.sfx. -eh. utáwneh *clay* (R).

–ta⁷ – empty noun root. *v.inc.* See: –ta = wę –.

ta⁷awę́·te anything (RC 26:16) *part.*

–ta⁷čh – lower half of human body (from waist to ankles); Half-Body. *n.r.* n-poss., inc., n.sfx. -eh. Utá⁷čheh *Half-Body (a mythic creature that affixes itself to promiscuous persons* (R); **–ta⁷čheθ –**: yutá⁷čhe·θ ⟨it-lower half of body-is long⟩ *corn roaster* (R); **–ta⁷ = čhuhčr –**: uta⁷čhúhčreh ⟨lower half of body-cover-'ness⟩ *breeches, pants* (HS).

–ta⁷čheθ – corn roaster. *dv.n.s.* yutá⁷čhe·θ ⟨it-lower half of body-is long⟩ *corn roaster* (R).

–ta⁷čhuhčr – breeches, pants. *n.s.* uta⁷čhúhčreh ⟨lower half of body-cover-'ness⟩ *breeches, pants* (HS).

–(ta)⁷čuhkw – barrow, heap, pile, stack. *n.r.* n-poss., inc., n.sfx. -eh. Both the forms **–⁷čuhkw –** and **–ta⁷čuhkw –** may occur when the root is unincorporated; however, only the form **–ta⁷čuhkw –** occurs in incorporation. uta⁷čúhkweh *barrow (of earth), heap (of corn, earth, wheat), pile, stack, shock* (HS); **–(ta)⁷ = čuhkw –.#áh**: uta⁷čuhkweháh ⟨heap-little⟩ *jag, little load* (HS); **–(ta)⁷ = čuhkw –.#ętíh**: u⁷čuhkwehętíh ⟨heap-many little⟩ *small bunches* (RC 30:

Tuscarora Pronunciation Key:
/a/ l**a**w; /e/ h**a**t; /i/ p**i**zza; /u/ t**u**ne; /ę/ h**i**nt; /č/ **ch**eese; /h/ **h**oe; /m/ **m**other; /s/ **s**ame; /t/ **d**o (before a vowel y, or w), **t**oo (elsewhere); /k/ **g**ale (before a vowel y or w), **k**ale (elsewhere); /n/ i**nh**ale (before a consonant or word-final), **n**ote (elsewhere), /r/ hi**ss** (before a consonant or word-final), **r**un (trilled as in Italian, elsewhere); /w/ c**uff** (before a consonant other than y or word-final), **w**ay (elsewhere); /y/ fi**sh** (before a consonant or word-final), **y**ou (elsewhere), /θ/ **th**ing; /⁷/ (the sound between the vowels in unh-unh); /·/ long vowel, /´/ high pitch; /`/ low pitch.

66); –(ta)ʔčuhkwęti –: rataʔčuhkwę́·tih ‹he-heap-makes› *he stacks* (HS); –t–. –(ta)ʔčuhkwaʔnihr –: nyutaʔčuhkwaʔ-níhrę ‹hither-it-heap-stood up› *great heap stands* (R); ti–. –(ta)ʔčuhkwah = surę –.#úʔy: thwaʔutaʔčuhkwahsuręʔ-úʔy ‹so-fact-it-heap-was of a height-great› *there was a big high pile formed* (RC 30:31).

–(ta)ʔčuhkw –.#áh jag, little load. *n.s.* utaʔčuhkwehá́h ‹heap-little› *jag, little load* (HS).

–(ta)ʔčuhkwęti – stack. *v.s.-a.i.* rataʔčuhkwę́·tih ‹he-heap-makes› *he stacks* (HS).

–taʔk– dig. *v.s.-t.* See: –aʔk–.

–taʔker – follow (an example), imitate. *v.r.-t.* See: –(ę)taʔker –.

–taʔkęha'nyeʔ – trench. *dv.n.s.* kataʔkęhá·ʔnyeʔ ‹it-X-digs-going along› *trench* (HS).

táʔks pop (R). *part.*

–taʔkwar – hug, press close to. *v.r.-t.* hab: -, pnt: -, stat: -ʔ, prog: -, prp: -, dst: -, caus: -, rvs: -, dat: -, inc.-ɸ-pat. –(ę)taʔrataʔkwar –.#úʔy: yawętaʔrataʔ-kwaʔrʔúʔy ‹it-head-pressed close to-great› *its head was greatly covered* (RC 24:11); –nęhsataʔkwar –: yunęhsatáʔkwaʔr ‹it-house-pressed close to› *house hugged it* (RC 34: 10).

táʔkwnęʔ small gray woodpecker (R). *n.*

–ta'n – camp, city, settlement, village. *n.r.* aln: kakutá·ʔnayęʔ *their village* (RC 9: 1), inc., n.sfx. –eh. utá·ʔneh *camp, city, settlement, village* (R); –ta'nakah = rę(w) –: yutaʔnakáhręʔ ‹it-settlement-is an opening› *street* (HS); –ta'nakari –: rataʔnaká·ryahs ‹he-settlement-devours› *he invades, he pillages, he ravages* (HS); –ta'nakęw.#áh: utaʔnakęw-ʔáh ‹settlement-in-little› *urbane* (HS); –ta'nakweʔniyu –: kataʔnakweʔnì·yuʔ ‹it-settlement-is the main one› *capitol*

city (HS); –ta'narahkw –: Utaʔnaráh-khwaʔ ‹settlement-col-lects› *Canandaigua, New York* (R) [Morgan, League «Cä́-tä-na-rä́-qua»]; –ta'na = θe·ʔke: Utaʔnaθé·ʔkye ‹settlement-new-at› *Geneva, New York* (R) [Morgan, League «O-tä-nä-sä́-ga»]; –ta'na = yęhte –: wahrataʔnayę́hteʔ ‹fact-he-settlement-laid-going to› *he was going to make camp* (RC 8:2); –ta'nayę(T) –.#áh: kataʔnayęʔáh ‹it-settlement-lays-little› *small town, village* (R) [Gallatin «kautaunauyuhah» 'Town, Village']; –ta'naʔkyehrę –: kataʔnaʔkyéhrę́ʔ ‹it-settlement-at-many› *towns* (R); –ta'nu = rihT –: rataʔnuríhthaʔ ‹he-settlement-stir-causes› *he dislodges it* (HS); –ta = 'nyę –: ratá·ʔnyęh ‹he-settlement-goes into› *he visits, he enters the camp* (HS); –ta'nyę –{dative I}: waʔktá·ʔ-nyęʔθ ‹fact-I-settlement-went into-for› *one visited me* (RC 25:9); –ne –.–ta'ni –: nehratá·ʔnih ‹apart-he-settlement-is all› *he is notorious* (HS); ti–. –ta'na = yęʔnahkw –: tihrataʔnayęʔnáhkhwaʔ ‹so-he-settlement-lay-causes-instrument› *he has a campsite* (RC 30:3); haʔ –ta'nakweʔniyu –: haʔ rataʔnakweʔ-nì·yuʔ ‹the he-settlement-is the main one› *mayor* (HS); kwęhs –ta'nakęw. #áh: kwęhs utaʔnakęwʔáh ‹no settlement-in-little› *rustic* (HS).

–taʔn – shank. *n.r.* n-poss., n-inc., n.sfx. –eh. utáʔneh *shank* (HS).

–ta'nakahrę(w) – street. *dv.n.s.* yutaʔnakáhręʔ ‹it-settlement-is an opening› *street* (HS).

–ta'nakari – invade, pillage, ravage. *v.s.-a.i.* rataʔnaká·ryahs ‹he-settlement-devours› *he invades, he pillages, he ravages* (HS).

–ta'nakęw.#áh urbane. *n.s.* utaʔnakęwʔáh ‹settlement-in-little› *urbane* (HS).

–ta'nakweʔniyu – capitol city. *dv.n.s.* kata'ʔnakweʔnì·yuʔ ‹it-settlement-is the main one› *capitol city* (HS).

-ta'nakweʔniyu – mayor. *dv.n.s.* haʔ rataʔnakweʔnì·yuʔ ‹the he-settlement-is the main one› *mayor* (HS).

ta'na(r)(a) – partitive+dualic+optative. *v. pfx.* The form ta'nara – occurs whenever the prefix receives word accent; if this form is followed by a pronominal prefix that begins with the sequence *wa*, the final vowel contracts with the sequence to give ta'narę –. The form ta'nar – occurs when the prefix is unaccented before pronominal prefixes that begin with the glides *w* or *y*. The form ta'na – occurs elsewhere.

-taʔnar – biscuit, bread, cake (e.g., of yeast). *n.r.* aln: akta'ʔnarà·węh *my bread* (R), inc., n.sfx. -eh. utá'ʔnareh *bread* (RC 3:37), *biscuit, cake (e.g., of yeast)* (HS) [Lawson «Ootocnare» 'Bread'] [Gallatin «otau-nareh» 'Bread']; –ta'ʔnaręhra·he –: kata'ʔnaręhrá·heh ‹it-bread-fries-going to› *fried bread* (R).

-ta'narahkw – Canandaigua, New York. *n.s.* Uta'ʔnaráhkhwaʔ ‹settlement-collects› *Canandaigua, New York* (R) [Morgan, League «Cä´-tä-na-rä´-qua»].

-taʔnaręhra·he – fried bread. *dv.n.s.* kata'ʔnaręhrá·heh ‹it-bread-fries-going to› *fried bread* (R).

-ta'naθe·ʔke Geneva, New York. *n.s.* Uta'ʔnaθé·ʔkye ‹settlement-new-at› *Geneva, New York* (R) [Morgan, League «O-tä-nä-sä´-ga»].

-ta'nayęhte – be going to make camp. *v.s.-a.i.* wahrata'ʔnayęhteʔ ‹fact-he-settlement-laid-going to› *he was going to make camp* (RC 8:2).

-ta'nayę(T)–.#áh small town, village. *dv.n.s.* kata'ʔnayęʔáh ‹it-settlement-lays-little› *small town, village* [Gallatin «kautaunauyuhah» 'Town, Village'].

ta'ne – partitive+dualic. *v.pfx.* Occurs in word-initial position when no modal marker is present.

ta'nę – partitive+dualic+future. *v.pfx.* Occurs in word-initial position.

-ta'nurihT – dislodge. *v.s.-t.* rata'ʔnuríhthaʔ ‹he-settlement-stir-causes› *he dislodges it* (HS).

-ta'nyę – enter camp, visit. *v.s.-a.i.* ratá·ʔnyęh ‹he-settlement-goes into› *he visits, he enters the camp* (HS).

-ta'nyę –{dative I} visit. *v.s.-t.* wa'ʔktá·ʔnyęʔθ ‹fact-I-settlement-went into-for› *one visited me* (RC 25:9).

-taʔr – head. *n.r.* See: –(ę)taʔr –.

-taʔr –.#keha·ʔ cephalic. *n.s.* See: –(ę)=taʔr –.#keha·ʔ.

-taʔrahtir – obstinate. *v.s.-a.i.* See: –(ę)=taʔrahtir –.

-taʔranęhwakčr – cephalalgy. *n.* See: –(ę)=taʔranęhwakčr –.

-taʔranęhwak(T) – have a headache. *v.s.* See: –(ę)taʔranęhwak(T) –.

-taʔreθ – lettuce. *n.s.* See: –(ę)taʔreθ –.

-taʔruhskę – be bareheaded. *v.s.-s.i.* See: –(ę)taʔruhskę –.

-taʔθru – young squash. *n.* n-poss., n-inc., n.sfx. -eh. utáʔθruh *young squash* (H

Tuscarora Pronunciation Key:
/a/ law; /e/ hat; /i/ pizza; /u/ tune; /ę/ hint; /č/ cheese; /h/ hoe; /m/ mother; /s/ same; /t/ do (before a vowel y, or w), too (elsewhere); /k/ gale (before a vowel y or w), kale (elsewhere); /n/ inhale (before a consonant or word-final), note (elsewhere), /r/ hiss (before a consonant or word-final), run (trilled as in Italian, elsewhere); /w/ cuff (before a consonant other than y or word-final), way (elsewhere); /y/ fish (before a consonant or word-final), you (elsewhere), /θ/ thing; /ʔ/ (the sound between the vowels in unh-unh); /·/ long vowel, /´/ high pitch; /`/ low pitch.

3518).

-ta?T – lie down. *v.r.-a.i.* hab: -s, pnt: -, stat: -, prog: -, prp: -, dst: -, caus: -, rvs: -, dat: -, n-inc. rá·ta²č *he lies down* (RC 26:33); -t-. **-ta?T** -: thrá·ta²č ‹hither-he-lies down› *he lay there* (RC 3:11); **kwęhs -ta?T** -: kwęhs ahratá²čhek ‹no unknown-he-lies down› *unreclining* (HS).

-ta?tawę – dissolve, melt, thaw. *v.s.-t.* yuta²tá·wę· ‹it-X-warmed› *it is melted* (R), wa²kata²tà·wę² ‹fact-it-X-warmed› *it melted* (R), kata²tà·węhs ‹it-X-warmed› *it thaws* (R), wa²kta²tà·wę² ‹fact-I-X-warmed› *I dissolved it* (R), ękata²tà·wę² ‹prediction-it-X-warm› *it will be soaked* (R).

-ta?tawę – humid. *dv.n.s.* yuta²tá·wę· ‹it-X-warmed› *humid* (R).

-ta?tawęhT – infuse, soak. *v.s.-t.* rata²tawę́htha² ‹he-X-warm-causes› *he infuses it, he soaks it* (HS).

-ta?tawę² – melt, soak. *v.s.-a.i.* yuta²tawę́²ę ‹it-X-warm-began› *it begins to melt* (RC 2:12), kata²tà·wę²θ ‹it-X-warm-begins› *it melts, it is soaked* (R).

-ta?tawę?T – dissoluble. *dv.n.s.* yuta²tawę́²ne² ‹it-X-warmed-moving› *dissoluble* (HS).

ta?ta?tá? knock knock knock (R). *part.*

-ta?węthu – slaughter. *v.r.-t.* hab: -hs, pnt: -², stat: -hstę, prog: -, prp: -hstęhe-, dst: -, caus: -, rvs: -, dat: -, n-inc. wa²kayę²na²ta²wę́·thu² *they slaughtered them* (RC 12:7); **-ne** -. **-ta?wę=thu** -: nekayę²ta²wę́·thuhs ‹two-they-themselves-slaughter› *they fight each other* (R); **ti** -. **-ta?węthu** -: tikakuta²węthuhstę́he² ‹so-they-slaughtered-going to› *they went along exterminating* (RC 12: 12).

-ta?ya?nihr – squat. *v.s.-a.i.* This and the next two entries are clearly related,

this entry composed of the verb root **-a?nihr** – *stand up* plus a noun root **-ta?y** -, and the next entry composed of **-ur** – *cover* and **-hkw** – "instrumental" with, again, the noun root **-ta?y** -. However, the noun root **-ta?y** – has not been encountered outside of these two constructions and, thus, its precise meaning remains uncertain. ruta²ya²níhrę ‹he-??-stood up› *he is squatting* (HS).

-ta?yuhkw – squatting figure. *n.s.* See note at **-ta?ya?nihr** -. uta²yúhkweh ‹??-cover-instrument› *a squatting figure* (H-notebook); **-ta?yuhkwa̲yę(T)** -: rata²yúhkwayę² ‹he-??-cover-instrument-lays› *he is a cripple* (H 3518).

-ta?yuhkwa̲yę(T) – be a cripple. *v.s.-s.i.* See note at **-ta?ya?nihr** -. rata²yúhkwayę² ‹he-??-cover-in-strument-lays› *he is a cripple* (H 3518).

tehčíhę² maybe, supposedly (RC 32:13). *part.*

tehéhsnę· then (W 74). *part.*

téher why (HS). *part.* **téher hę í·θ** ‹why ? you› *and what did you expect* (R); **téher ú?nę²** ‹why alternatively› *and what did you expect, that's what you get* (R).

téher hę í·θ ‹why ? you› *and what did you expect* (R). *part.*

téher ú?nę² ‹why alternatively› *and what did you expect, that's what you get* (R). *part.*

-tehęhčrę – flog, whip. *v.r.-t.* hab: -h, pnt: -·², stat: -, prog: -, prp: -, dst: -, caus: -, rvs: -, dat: -, n-inc. wa²na²tehę́hčrę·² *one whipped another* (RC 11:13), wa²utehę́hčrę·² *it was whipped* (RC 11:18); **ti** -. **-tehęhčrę** -: tyę²na²tehę́hčręh ‹so-one=another-whips› *one whips another* (RC 11:3).

-tehęr(uk) – flog, whip. *v.r.-t.* hab: -s, pnt: ()-ɸ, stat: -, prog: -, prp: -, dst: -, caus: -, rvs: -, dat: -, n-inc. Found only in Hewitt and Smith's manuscript dictionary. The alternation of -teh̨r- in the habitual aspect with -teh̨ruk- in the punctual is unique. ratéheč *he flogs, he whips* (HS), na'téheč *one whips another* (HS), ehrateh̨·ruk *he will flog* (HS), eye'na'teh̨·ruk *one will flog another* (HS).

-tehr- peel off bark. *v.r.-a.i.* hab: -, pnt: -ɸ, stat: -e·, prog: -, prp: -, dst: -, caus: -, rvs: -, dat: -, n-inc. rutéhre· *he had peeled off bark* (RC 12:2), katéhre· *one peels off bark from tree* (R), wahrá·ter *he peeled off bark* (RC 12:2), wa'é·ter *one peeled off bark from tree* (R).

-tehr- pass time. *v.r.-a.i.* hab: -, pnt: -ɸ, stat: -, prog: -, prp: -, dst: -, caus: -, rvs: -, dat: -, n-inc. ti -. -tehr -: neyú·ter ‹so-prediction-it-pass time› *so many days will pass* (RC 13:7).

-tehra'- be afraid of, be scared of. *v.r.-t.* hab: -θ, pnt: -ɸ, stat: -, prog: -, prp: -, dst: -, caus: -T-, rvs: -, dat: -, n-inc. ratéhra'θ *he is afraid* (RC 11:2), kaye'na'téhra'θ *they are afraid of another* (RC 11:16), ehstéhra' *you will be afraid* (RC 3:54); -tehra'T -{dative II}: na'tehra'ná·tih ‹one=another-be afraid of-causes-for› *one intimidates another* (HS).

-tehra'T -{dative II} intimidate. *v.s.-t.* na'tehra'ná·tih ‹one=another-be afraid of-causes-for› *one intimidates another* (HS).

-tehθ- rushtail. *n.r.* n-poss., n-inc., n.sfx.

-eh. utéhθeh *rushtail* (HS).

-tehskr- stink. *v.r.-a.i.* hab: -ahs, pnt: -, stat: -, prog: -, prp: -, dst: -, caus: -, rvs: -, dat: -, n-inc. katéhskrahs *it stinks; goat* (R).

-tehskr- goat. *dv.n.s.* katéhskrahs ‹it-stinks› *goat* (R).

-tehw- hide, pelt, skin. *n.r.* aln: aktéhweh *my hide* (R), inaln: ktéhweh *my skin* (R), inc., n.sfx. -eh. utéhweh *hide, skin* (RC 26:31) [Lawson «Ootahawa» 'Raw skin undrest']; -teh=wahkw -: na'tehwáhkhwa' ‹one=another-hide-picks up› *one affrights another, one scares another* (HS); -teh=wahkwa'T -: yutehwáhkwa't ‹it-hide-pick up-caused› *startling* (HS); -teh=ware -: rutéhwarehs ‹he-hide-adds› *he is skittish, he is timid* (HS); -teh=warehsk -: rutehwaréhske· ‹he-hide-added-easily› *he is apt to frighten, he is timid* (HS); -tehwa'neθ -: rutéhwa'-ne·θ ‹he-hide-is thick› *he has a thick hide* (R); -tehwe -: rutéhweh ‹he-hide-falls› *he got pale* (RC 30: 56); *leech* (AG), *bloodsucker* (R); -tehwitke' -: yutehwitké'e ‹it-hide-came forth› *it is pale* (HS); -tehwitke'e' -: ratehwitké'e'θ ‹he-hide-come forth-begins› *he grows pale* (HS); -ne -. -tehure -: wa'thratehù·re' ‹fact-two-he-hide-split› *he split hide in two* (RC 30: 58); -ne -. -tehwhar -: nehrutéwhe'r ‹apart-he-skin-hangs› *he has a fur-cap* (AG); -a'tehwatehnine'T -: ye'tehwatehniné'tha' ‹one-oneself-hide-sell-causes› *peltry, selling of furs* (HS);

čuhstekyerhyá?kę –**tehwęte:** čuhstekyerhyá'?kę utehwę́·te ‹buffalo hide-a certain one› *buffalo robe* (HS).

–**tehwahkw** – affright, scare. *v.s.-t.* na'?tehwáhkhwa'? ‹one=another-hide-picks up› *one affrights another, one scares another* (HS).

–**tehwahkwahT** – startling. *dv.n.s.* yutehwáhkwaht ‹it-hide-pick up-caused› *startling* (HS).

–**tehwarę** – be skittish, be timid. *v.s.-a.i.* rutéhwaręhs ‹he-hide-adds› *he is skittish, he is timid* (HS).

–**tehwaręhsk** – apt to frighten, be timid. *v.s.-a.i.* rutehwaréhskę· ‹he-hide-added-easily› *he is apt to frighten, he is timid* (HS).

–**tehwę** – get pale. *v.s.-a.i.* rutéhwęh ‹hehide-falls› *he got pale* (RC 30:56).

–**tehwę** – bloodsucker, leech. *dv.n.s.* rutéhwęh ‹he-hide-falls› *leech* (AG), *bloodsucker* (R).

–**tehwitkę?** – be pale. *v.s.-s.i.* yutehwitkę́'?ę ‹it-hide-came forth› *it is pale* (HS).

–**tehwitkę?ę?** – grow pale. *v.s.-a.i.* ratehwitkę́'?ę'?θ ‹he-hide-come forth-begins› *he grows pale* (HS).

–**tekar** – take from. *v.r.-a.i.* hab: -, pnt: -'?, stat: -ę, prog: -, prp: -, dst: -, caus: -, rvs: -, dat: -, inc.-ɸ-pat. –**(ę)nę?yeč=kwatekar** –: wahranę'?yeckwaté·ka'?r ‹fact-he-nest-took from› *he took from nest* (RC 8:17); –**nęhsatekar** –: runęhsatekà·rę ‹he-house-took from› *he despoils house* (HS); –**ne** –.–**tekar** –: nehrutekà·rę ‹two-he-took from› *he braces* (HS); **ha?** –**ne** –.–**tekar** –: ha'? neyutekà·rę ‹the two-it-took from› *a prop, a brace* (HS).

té·ks tacks (R); tax (HS). *n.* **té·ks** –**rurę** –: té·ks rarù·ręh ‹tax he-tithes› *he collects taxes* (HS); **té·ks** –**?ęyuhar** –: té·ks ra'?ęyúhar ‹tax he-cost-washes› *he*

pays taxes (HS).

té·ks –**rurę** – collect taxes. *v.s.-a.i.* té·ks rarù·ręh ‹tax he-tithes› *he collects taxes* (HS).

té·ks –**?ęyuhar** – pay taxes. *v.s.-a.i.* té·ks ra'?ęyúhar ‹tax he-cost-washes› *he pays taxes* (HS).

–**tekwęnarę** – recline. *v.r.-a.i.* hab: -, pnt: -'?, stat: -, prog: -, prp: -, dst: -, caus: -, rvs: -, dat: -, n-inc. Found only in the cited construction. –**yah** –.–**a?te=kwęnarę** –: yahwa'?nyę'?tekwę̀·narę'? ‹thither-fact-two-one-oneself-reclined› *the two of them reclined there together* (RC 3:11).

–**tenę** – be sunny. *v.r.-a.i.* hab: -, pnt: -'?, stat: -, prog: -, prp: -, dst: -, caus: -hsT-, rvs: -, dat: -, n-inc. wa'?utè·nę'? *it got sunny* (R), yutè·nę'? *it is sunny* (R), ayutè·nę'? *that it be sunny* (R); –**tenęhserh** –: utenęhsérhę· ‹be sunny?'?› *lying in sunshine* (RC 35:26); –**te=nęhst** –: utenę́hsteh ‹be sunny-'ness› *sunshine* (R); –**tenęhstr** –: utenę́hstreh ‹be sunny-'ness› *sun* (PC); –**tenęhsta='nehT** –: yutenęhstá·'?neht ‹it-be sunny'ness-be present-causes› *sunny* (HS); –**a'nętenęhsT** –: ru'?nętenę́hsnę ‹he-himself-be sunny-caused› *he basks in the sun* (HS).

–**tenęhserh** – lying in sunshine. *n.s.* utenęhsérhę· ‹be sunny-?'?› *lying in sunshine* (RC 35:26).

–**tenęhsta'nehT** – sunny. *dv.n.s.* yutenęhstá·'?neht ‹it-be sunny-'ness-be presentcauses› *sunny* (HS).

–**tenęhst** – sunshine. *n.s. East.* utenę́hsteh ‹be sunny-'ness› *sunshine* (R).

–**tenęhstr** – sun. *n.s. West.* utenę́hstreh ‹be sunny-'ness› *sun* (PC).

–**ter** – conception, embryo, fetus, foal, roe. *n.r.* See: –**(ę)ter** –.

–**terawak** – spawn. *v.s.-a.i.* See: –**(ę)te=rawak** –.

–tera'nę – be subject. *v.s.-s.i.* See: –(ę)te= ra'nę –.

–terę – be pregnant. *v.s.-a.i.* See: –(ę)= terę –.

–teri – be expectant, be pregnant. *v.s.-a.i.* See: –(ę)teri –.

–teru – perch. *dv.n.s.* See: –(ę)teru –.

–terhu – sink. *v.r.-a.i.* hab: -, pnt: -ʔ, stat: -, prog: -, prp: -, dst: -, caus: -, rvs: -, dat: -, n-inc. waʔkatérhuʔ *it sunk* (RC 31:9).

–terhyaʔčr – shovel, spade. *n.r.* n-poss., inc., n.sfx. -eh. uterhyáʔčreh *shovel, spade* (HS); –terhyaʔčraT –: katerhyáʔčraˑt ‹it-shovel-stands› *there is a spade or shovel in it, it contains a shovel* (H 2892).

–terhyaʔčręti – jest. *v.s.-a.i.* raterhyaʔčrę́ˑtih ‹he-be ludicrous-'ness-makes› *he jests* (HS).

–terhyaʔT – be comic, be ludicrous, be ridiculous, be whimsical. *v.r.-s.i.* stat: -ɸ, prog: -, prp: -, dst: -, caus: -, rvs: -, dat: III (-ati-/-ę-), n-inc. yutérhyaʔt *it is comic, it is ludicrous, it is ridiculous, it is whimsical* (HS); –terhyaʔ= čręti –: raterhyaʔčrę́ˑtih ‹he-be ludicrous-'ness-makes› *he jests* (HS); –ter= hyaʔT –.{dative III}.#úʔy: ruterhyaʔnatihúʔy ‹he-is ridiculous-for-great› *he laughs immoderately* (HS).

–terhyaʔT –.{dative III}.#úʔy laugh immoderately. *v.s.-a.i.* ruterhyaʔnatihúʔy ‹he-is ridiculous-for-great› *he laughs immoderately* (HS).

–terʔ(ak) – choose wrongfully, make a mistake. *v.r.-a.i.* hab: -ahs, pnt: ()-ɸ, stat: -ę, prog: -, prp: -, dst: -, caus: -, rvs: -, dat: -, inc.-ɸ-ag. naryęʔnaʔtér- ʔak *that the two of them mistake one another* (RC 34:22); –rihwaterʔ(ak) –: urihwatérʔę ‹matter-made a mistake› *sinfulness, wickedness* (MP), kakurihwatérʔę ‹they-matter-made a mistake› *they are wicked: sinners* (MP), rurihwatérʔahs ‹he-matter-makes a mistake› *he sins* (HS), waʔkayerihwatérʔak ‹fact-they-matter-made a mistake› *they sinned, they were wicked* (MP); –rihwaterʔakčraʔnyeręhT –: yurihwaterʔakčraʔnyerę́hnę ‹it-matter-make a mistake-'ness-have an unusual experience-caused› *original sin* (HS); kwęhs –rihwaterʔ(ak) –: kwęhs ahrarihwaterʔáhshek ‹no unknown-he-matter-make a mistake› *he is infallible* (HS).

–terʔęhčeriha – spread out sod, turf. *v.s.-a.i.* raterʔęhčeríhahs ‹he-sod-straightens› *he turfs, he spreads out sod* (HS).

–terʔęhθ – sod, turf; bushy head of hair. *n.r.* n-poss., inc., n.sfx. -eh. uterʔęhθeh *sod, turf: bushy head of hair* (HS); –terʔęhčeriha –: raterʔęhčeríhahs ‹he-sod-straigh-tens› *he turfs, he spreads out sod* (HS); –nęhsakT –terʔęhθęti –: unęhsakwt katerʔęhθę́ˑtih ‹house-next to it-sod-makes› *grass* (HS).

–teθkwi(k) - pucker. *v.r.-t.* hab: -hs, pnt: ()-ɸ, stat: -, prog: -, prp: -, dst: -, caus: -, rvs: -, dat: -, n-inc. ratéθkwihs *he puckers it* (H-notebook).

-tet⁷- make a groove in, make an indentation in, make a line in, line. *v.r.-t.* hab: -ahs, pnt: -a⁷, stat: -ɸ, prog: -, prp: -, dst: -, caus: -hsT-, rvs: -, dat: -, inc.-??-ag./pat. Occurs only with an incorporated noun root. **-nęh = sạtet⁷a** -: ranęhsaté·t⁷ahs ‹he-house-lines› *he lathes* (HS), ęhranęhsaté·t⁷a⁷ ‹prediction-he-house-line› *he will lathe* (HS); **-nęhsạtet⁷ahsT** -: yenęhsatet-⁷áhstha⁷ ‹one-house-line-causes› *lathe* (HS); **-⁷nhęhsukrạtet⁷** -: ru⁷nhęhsú·krate⁷t ‹he-egg-juice-lined› *he has beside him a slatternly woman, a woman disgustingly filthy* (H 2484); **-ačha⁷kę⁷natet⁷** -: ručha⁷kę⁷ná·te⁷t ‹he-himself-knife-lined› *he has a knife about him (somewhere on or near him)* (H-notebook); **-a⁷rihwạtet⁷** -: ra⁷-rihwaté·t⁷ahs ‹he-himself-matter-lines› *notary* (HS).

te⁷ what (RC 30:28) *part.* **te⁷** **-ihrę** -: te⁷ číhrę· ‹what you!-say› *I guess so, whatever you say* (R); **te⁷** **ti** -. **-eθ** -: te⁷ tì·we·θ ‹what so-it-is long› *how long is it?* (HS), *tapeworm* (R).

te⁷ **-ihrę** - I guess so, whatever you say. *part.* te⁷ číhrę· ‹what you!-say› *I guess so, whatever you say* (R).

te⁷ **ti** -. **-eθ** - tapeworm. *n.* te⁷ tì·we·θ ‹what so-it-is long› *tapeworm* (R).

-te⁷khwarhu - pocket. *v.s.-t.* rate⁷khwár-huhs ‹he-bag-hang-causes› *he pockets it* (HS).

-te⁷kw - bag, cushion, mattress, pocket, purse. *n.r.* aln: akté⁷kwayę⁷ *my bag* (R), inc., n.sfx. -eh. uté⁷kweh *bag, cushion, mattress, pocket, purse* (HS) [Lawson «Uttaqua» 'A Bag']; **-te⁷ = khwarhu** -: rate⁷khwárhuhs ‹he-bag-hang-causes› *he pockets it* (HS); **-te⁷ = kwa⁷nihr** -: kate⁷kwá⁷nihč ‹it-bag-stands up› *it bags it* (HS), kate⁷kwa⁷-níhrę ‹it-bag-stood up› *circus* (HS);

-te⁷kwi⁷θrehT -: yete⁷kwi⁷θréhtha⁷ ‹one-bag-ride-causes› *portmanteau* (HS); ti -. **-te⁷kwa⁷θrę** -.#ętíh. **-a'nye⁷** -: tikate⁷kwa⁷θrę⁷ętihá·⁷nye⁷ ‹so-it-bag-is so big-many little-going along› *each had a small bag* (RC 32:1); **-⁷nhęh-** **-te⁷kwawę** -: u⁷nhę́heh uté⁷kwareh ‹urine bag-possess› *bladder* (HS).

-te⁷kwa⁷nihr - bag. *v.s.-t.* kate⁷kwá⁷nihč ‹it-bag-stands up› *it bags it* (HS).

-te⁷kwa⁷nihr - circus. *dv.n.s.* kate⁷kwa⁷-níhrę ‹it-bag-stood up› *circus* (HS).

-te⁷kwik - drift (of snow). *v.r.-a.i.* hab: -s, pnt: -ɸ, stat: -, prog: -, prp: -, dst: -, caus: -, rvs: -, dat: -, n-inc. katé⁷kwiks *it (snow) is drifting* (R), ękaté⁷kwik *it will drift* (R).

-te⁷kwi⁷θrehT - portmanteau. *dv.n.s.* yete⁷kwi⁷θréhtha⁷ ‹one-bag-ride-causes› *portmanteau* (HS).

-te⁷naku - hollow out. *v.r.-t.* hab: -ahs, pnt: -, stat: -, prog: -, prp: -, dst: -, caus: -, rvs: -, dat: -, n-inc. kate⁷ná·kwahs *it hollows out* (H-notebook).

-te⁷nyętęhčr - bushel. *n.r.* n-poss., n-inc., n.sfx. -eh. ute⁷nyętę́hčreh *bushel* (HS).

-te⁷θT - build a fire. *v.r.-t.* hab: -ha⁷, pnt: -ę⁷, stat: -, prog: -, prp: -, dst: -, caus: -, rvs: -, dat: -, n-inc. wah-ruté⁷θnę⁷ *he built a fire* (RC 26:26), eθaté⁷θthek *that you build fires* (RC 11:12).

te⁷té⁷ *et alia, et cetera,* and others (RC 26:9) *part.*

-te⁷wahrahT - be frightening. *v.s.-s.i.* yute⁷wáhraht ‹it-??-put up-caused› *it is frightful* (HS), ute⁷wáhraht ‹??-put up-cause› *something terrible* (R).

-te⁷wahrahT -{dative III} frighten. *v.s.-t.* na⁷te⁷wahrahná·tih ‹one=another-??-put up-causes-for› *one frightens another* (HS).

-tęnhekari- be afflicted, be in distress. *v.r.-s.i.* stat: -ę, prog: -, prp: -, dst: -, caus: -, rvs: -, dat: III (-ati-/-ę-), n-inc. Requires the dualic unless the dative is present. -tęnhekari-{dative III}: na'tęnhekaryá·tih ‹one=another-is afflicted-for› *one afflicts another* (HS); -ne-.-tęnhekari-: nehrutęnheká·ryę ‹apart-he-is afflicted› *he is afflicted, he is in distress* (HS).

-tęnhekari-{dative III} afflict. *v.s.-t.* na'tęnhekaryá·tih ‹one=another-is afflicted-for› *one afflicts another* (HS).

tę́hči' mythic little head that eats entire families (R). *n.*

tha- unusual (contrastive). *v.pfx.* The form th- occurs before pronominal prefixes that begin with *w* or *y*. The form thi- occurs elsewhere; however, this form is optionally replaced by the form tha- before pronominal prefixes that begin with the consonant *h* and by the form tha'- before the third person neuter singular patient prefix yaw-/yu- with loss of the initial y of the pronominal prefix. The contrastive, when present, always occurs in absolute word-initial position. It indicates that the action or state signified by the verb root or stem is contrary to what would be expected given the physical laws of the universe or the norms of Tuscarora culture. Since the prefix does not indicate how the activity or state deviates from the norm, but only that it is deviant, the meaning of the word to which it is affixed

is nearly always opaque. Thus, in all its occurrences, the contrastive is considered a discontinuous part of the verb root or stem. Below are listed those verb roots or stems that occur in this dictionary with the contrastive.

tha-.-ahstaw- leave alone. *v.r.-t.* hab: -, pnt: -, stat: -ih, prog: -, prp: -, dst: -, caus: -, rvs: -, dat: -, n-inc. thę-θahstá·wi·k ‹unusual-prediction-you-leave alone› *you will leave it alone* (RC 30:40) [Lawson «Tnotsau-rau-week» 'Let it alone' = *«Tsosserau-week» *θahstrá·wi·k].

tha-.-a'nya'čeriha- be equitable. *v.s.-s.i.* thyu'nya'čeríhę ‹unusual-it-itself-path-straightened› *it is equitable* (H-notebook).

tha-.-a'rihwatwahT- do wrong. *v.s.-a.i.* thahsa'rihwá·twaht‹unusual-fact-you-matter-overlooked› *you did wrong* (AG), tha'ka'rihwá·twaht ‹unusual-fact-I-matter-overlooked› *I did wrong* (AG).

tha-.-ča'narih- continue boiling. *v.s.-t.* thayuča'naríhę ‹unusual-it-X-is hot› *let it boil! (said to someone who wants to remove something from the heat which appears to have already boiled long enough)* (L 50).

tha-.-eh-.#ęwe be a dolt, be a simpleton. *v.s.-s.i.* tha'awehę̀·we ‹unusual-it-little-genuine› *a dolt, a simpleton* (HS), thahrawehę̀·we ‹unusual-he-little-genuine› *he is a simpleton* (HS).

tha-.-ekat-.#áh lobelia, great lobelia (*Lobelia* sp). *dv.n.s.* thyakyekatha'áh

---

Tuscarora Pronunciation Key:
/a/ law; /e/ hat; /i/ pizza; /u/ tune; /ę/ hint; /č/ cheese; /h/ hoe; /m/ mother; /s/ same; /t/ do (before a vowel y, or w), too (elsewhere); /k/ gale (before a vowel y or w), kale (elsewhere); /n/ inhale (before a consonant or word-final), note (elsewhere), /r/ hiss (before a consonant or word-final), run (trilled as in Italian, elsewhere); /w/ cuff (before a consonant other than y or word-final), way (elsewhere); /y/ fish (before a consonant or word-final), you (elsewhere), /θ/ thing; /'/ (the sound between the vowels in unh-unh); /·/ long vowel, /´/ high pitch; /`/ low pitch.

‹unusual-one-liquid-stands-little› *lobelia, great lobelia (Lobelia sp.)* (H-notebook).

tha-. -ęruh - most, very. *n.s.* thaʼawę̀·ruh ‹unusual-it-self› *most, very* (RC 24:9).

tha-. -ęT-.#ęwe be stupid. *v.s.-s.i.* thahrawęʼnehę̀·we ‹unusual-he-conclude-genuine› *he is stupid* (HS).

tha-. -(ę)ʼtikęhręT- be calm. *v.s.-a.i.* thaʼθaʼtikęhrę́·ʼna·k ‹unusual-you!-mind-close› *be calm!* (R).

tha-. -hihteʼčrihę second quarter of moon. *n.s.* thaʼuhihteʼčríhę ‹unusual-it-sun-'ness-middle of› *second quarter of moon* (SH 375).

tha-. -hręhw-.#ke at your leisure. *dv.n.s.* thaʼθahręhwáʼkye ‹unusual-you-put up-cause-at› *at your leisure* (R).

tha-. -htir- stop messing around. *v.s.-a.i.* thaʼshtì·rę ‹unusual-you!-be hard› *stop messing around! (said by a mother to misbehaving children)* (R).

tha-. -ręhyuręʼT- split the sky. *v.s.-a.i.* thahraręhyù·ręʼt ‹unusual-he-sky-split› *he splits the sky (said of the sun as it travels from the east horizon to the west horizon or of a person who travels in a north to south direction)* (RC 14:5).

tha-. -ręhyawaʼk- Creator, He-Holds-The-Heavens. *dv.n.s.* The absence of a pronominal prefix in this name is unusual and may mark the word as a loan word from another Northern Iroquoian language. Tharęhyawáʼkę ‹unusual-sky-grasped› *Creator, He-Holds-The-Heavens* (RC 1:1).

tha-. -yeriha- go straight. *v.s.-a.i.* thahrayeríhaʼ ‹unusual-he-straightened› *he goes straight* (RC 31:2).

tha+ne-. -athwęhnęti- be round. *v.r.-s.i.* stat: -·, prog: -, prp: -, dst: -, caus: -, rvs: -, dat: -, n-inc. thaʼneyuthwęhnę́·ti· ‹unusual-apart-it-is round› *it is*

round (R).

tha+ne-. -atkweʼnęti- hané?či **-athnęhst-** globular. *dv.n.s.* thaʼneyutkweʼnę́·ti·hané?či uthnę́hsteh ‹unusual-apart-it-itself-arc-made that is-very play ball-'ness› *globular (round like a ball)* (AG).

tha+ne-. -ęʼnihę noon. *dv.n.s.* thaʼnyawęʼníhę ‹unusual-apart-it-day-middle of› *noon* (R).

tha+ne-. -yeri-.#haʼnę? be equidistant away from. *v.s.-s.i.* thaʼneyuyerihá?nę? ‹unusual-apart-it-is correct-much› *it is equidistant away from* (RC 31:10), *it is opposite* (HS).

thahęθa- contrastive+repetitive+factual. *v.pfx.* Occurs in word-initial position.

-thahkwęy- goods. *n.r.* n-poss., n-inc., n.sfx. -eh. uthahkwę̀·yeh *goods* (HS).

thakękʼáh that it be a little different (RC 35:15). *part.*

Thanetáhkhwaʼ Chief of the Snipe Clan (literal meaning uncertain) (H-Handbook). *n.*

tha(r)(a)- contrastive+optative. *v.pfx.* The form **thara-** occurs whenever the prefix receives word accent; if this form is followed by a pronominal prefix that begins with the sequence *wa*, the final vowel contracts with the sequence to give **tharę-**. The form **thar-** occurs when the prefix is unaccented before pronominal prefixes that begin with the glides *w* or *y*. The form **tha-** occurs elsewhere.

Tharę́·tu·ʼ Toronto, Ontario (AG). *n.*

thaʼ- contrastive. *v.pfx.* Occurs in word-initial position in the imperative.

thaʼahsę̀·nę half (RC 1:2), halfway (RC 18:2). *part.* See: **ahsę̀·nę**.

thaʼne- contrastive+dualic. *v.pfx.* The final *e* is dropped before pronominal prefixes that begin with *y* in verb forms that are three or more syllables in length.

tha?we – contrastive+translocative. *v.pfx*. Occurs in word-initial position in the imperative.

théhstement testament (HS). *n.*

-thekw – perspiration, sweat. *n.r.* n-poss., inc., n.sfx. -φ. Requires the stem increment -n- with suffixes and when incorporated. ú·thekw *perspiration, sweat* (HS); **-thekwnakęw**: uthékwnakęw ‹sweat-in› *sweaty* (HS); **-thekw = nitkę?** -: rathekwní·tkę?θ ‹he-sweat-comes forth› *he perspires, he sweats* (HS); **-ne-.-thekwnu?na** -: nehrathekwnú?nę ‹apart-he-sweat-receives› *he sweats* (HS); **-thekw** - -r(i)yu -: ú·-thekw rú·ryuhs ‹sweat he-kills› *he sweats* (HS).

-thekw - -r(i)yu – perspire, sweat. *v.s.-a.i.* ú·thekw rú·ryuhs ‹sweat he-kills› *he sweats* (HS).

-thekwnakęw sweaty. *n.s.* uthékwnakęw ‹sweat-in› *sweaty* (HS).

-thekwnitkę? - perspire, sweat. *v.s.-a.i.* rathekwní·tkę?θ ‹he-sweat-comes forth› *he perspires, he sweats* (HS).

the? no, not (RC 11:21). *part.* More emphatic a negative than either **íhskah** or **kwęhs**. à·rę **the?** ‹about not› *if not* (AW 48); áθę **the?** ‹when not› *not yet* (AW 52); ne? **the?** ‹if not› *unless, if not* (HS).

the? t -. -(i)hsnahkw – worn out, be worthless. *v.s.-a.i.* the? nakahsnáhkęk ‹not hither-unknown-it-use-instrument› *it is worn out, it is worthless* (R).

thé·?nę? yesterday (R). *part.*

the?nę·reh afternoon, evening (RC 8:20). *part.*

thę – contrastive+future. *v.pfx*. Occurs in word-initial position.

thęhčí?na· grizzly bear *(Ursus horribilis)* (R). *n.*

thę'na(r)(a) – contrastive+dualic+optative. *v.pfx*. The form **thę'nara** – occurs whenever the prefix receives word accent; if this form is followed by a pronominal prefix that begins with the sequence *wa*, the final vowel contracts with the sequence to give **thę'narę** -. The form **thę'nar** – occurs when the prefix is unaccented before pronominal prefixes that begin with the glides *w* or *y*. The form **thę'na** – occurs elsewhere.

thí· tea (R). *n.*

thikawęnì·yu? anywhere (RC 1:8) *part.*

-thit?ah – be little ones. *v.s.-s.i.* See: -t?ah -.

thúh there (RC 30:8), to, up to ("not used in the same manner as English 'to'") (HS). *part.* The parenthetical addendum in Hewitt & Smith's dictionary is correct in that the Tuscarora particle is very rare in discourse and has either the meaning *there, near the speaker* (in which case it is the lexical counterpart to the cislocative prefix [see: -t-]) or the meaning *close to* (in which case it is the lexical counterpart to the external locative suffix in one of its meanings [see: -ke] and to the lateral locative in one of its meanings [see: -akT]). **thuh hè·wi**: thuh hè·wi ‹there enough› *good enough* (R).

thuh hè·wi ‹there enough› good enough (R). *part.*

thuhkyę́ʔthu on the sly, stealthily, very quietly (RC 23: 4). *part.*

thuhwáʔne·ʔ no matter (L 40). *part.*

thumé·tuhs tomato(es) (R). *n.*

thunęhyárhę́ʔ mythic Stone Giant (RC 30:1). *n.*

thuʔníhskah here and there, rare (HS). *part.*

thuʔù·nę immediately, promptly, right away (RC 3:26). *part.*

Thwahrù·nęʔ Oneida (RC 21:7). *n.*

thwaʔ– contrastive+factual. *v.pfx.* The final ʔ of the prefix is dropped before pronominal prefixes that begin with the consonant *h.*

thwaʔT(i)– contrastive+cislocative+factual. *v.pfx.* The form **thwaʔn–** occurs before pronominal prefixes that begin with the consonants *w* or *y.* The form **thwaʔt–** occurs before pronominal prefixes that begin with the consonants *k* or *h.* The form **thwaʔni–** occurs elsewhere.

thwaʔT(i)– contrastive+dualic+factual. *v. pfx.* The form **thwaʔn–** occurs before pronominal prefixes that begin with the consonants *w* or *y.* The form **thwaʔt–** occurs before pronominal prefixes that begin with the consonants *k* or *h.* The form **thwaʔni–** occurs elsewhere.

thwe– partitive+translocative. *v.pfx.* Occurs in word-initial position when no modal marker is present.

thwé·ʔn all (RC 30:31) [Lawson «(Connaugh jost) twane» 'All (the Indians are drunk)' = *(kanę́ʔyahst) thwé·ʔn "(it is drunk) all"]. *part.*

thweʔnhé·θuʔ besides (RC 25:5). *part.*

–thwę– be good for, cure. *v.r.-s.i.* stat: -·, prog: -, prp: -, dst: -, caus: -, rvs: -, dat: -, n-inc. yú·thwę· *it is good for* (RC 22:1), *it cures* (AW 98); –či–. **–thwęhętyę–:** čuthwęhę́·tyę· ‹again-it-cure-much-much› *(it) had healed* (AW 98); –ʔtuθ(e)r– –thwę–: uʔtú·θer yú·thwę· ‹itch it-is good for› *elecampagne (Inula helenium)* (H-notebook).

thyá·ryęhst it is not known (RC 24:12). *part.*

tí⋯ bzzz (sound of a mosquito) (R). *part.*

T(i)–/ny– ours (yours and mine) (first person inclusive dual inalienable). *n.r. pfx.* The form **n–** occurs before roots and stems that begin with the vowel ę or the morphophoneme {ʰu}. The form **t–** occurs before roots and stems that begin with the vowels *i, e,* or *u* (not from {ʰu}). The form **ny–** occurs before roots and stems that begin with the vowel *a.* The form **ti–** occurs before roots and stems that begin with a consonant.

ti– so (partitive). *v.pfx.* The form **n–** occurs before pronominal prefixes that begin with the sequence *yę.* The form **t–** occurs before pronominal prefixes that begin with *y* followed by the vowels *i, e, a,* or *u* in words that are three or more syllables in length. The form **ti–** occurs elsewhere. The principal use of the partitive is to mark the head noun in an attributive relationship. For this reason, the partitive is obligatory with a number of verb roots and stems that indicate generic notions of quality and incorporate the noun root representing the head noun (e.g., *be so big, be so many in number, be of such a size*). With such predicates, the specific nature of the quality is indicated outside the predicate, either by another word or by an enclitic. The partitive also occurs as a fossilized element of certain attributive predicates (e.g., **tika-tkwarà·yę⁷** *it is red*), a number of deverbal nouns, and certain verb stems. In these cases, the partitive must be considered a discontinuous part of the stem. All such cases encountered in this work are listed below.

-ti- empty noun root. *v.inc.* See: **-yę⁷=kw-** *shoot.*

ti-. -ahereθT-.#áh be dispersed. *v.r.-a.i.* hab: -ha⁷, pnt: -, stat: -, prog: -, prp: -, dst: -, caus: -, rvs: -, dat: -, n-inc. tiwahereθtha⁷áh ‹so-it-is dispersed-little› *it is infrequent, it is rare* (RC 18:1).

ti-. -(a)hk̲a̲r̲a̲či⁷tkwahnayę(T)- yellow oak (*Quercus* sp.). *dv.n.s.* tiwahkarači⁷-tkwáhnayę⁷ ‹so-it-bark-yellow-lays› *yellow oak* (*Quercus* sp.) (H-notebook).

ti-. -ahθę'nę'ni- {dative III} become puzzled. *v.s.-a.i.* thwahrahθę⁷nę·⁷nyę⁷ ‹so-fact-he-become dark-threw-for› *he becomes puzzled* (SH 375).

ti-. -akęhyaT- coast, edge, limit. *dv.n.s.* tiwakęhya·t ‹so-it-extends from› *its edge* (H-notebook), ha⁷ tiwakęhya·t ‹the so-it-extends from› *the coast, the limit* (HS).

ti-. -aθrę- be so big, be so much. *v.r.-s.i.* stat: -⁷, prog: -'nye⁷-, prp: -, dst: -, caus: -, rvs: -, dat: -, inc.-ɸ-ag. tiwá··θręk ‹so-it-is so big› *it will be that much* (RC 20: 1); **ti-. -aθrę-.#áh:** tiwaθrę⁷áh ‹so-it-is so big-little› *shallow* (HS); **ti-. -aθrę-.#ú⁷y:** tiwaθrę⁷ú⁷y ‹so-it-is so big-great› *it will be so big;*

deep (water) (HS); **ti-. -rihwaθrę-.#ętíh:** tyurihwaθrę⁷ętíh ‹so-it-matter-is so big-many little› *trifles* (HS); **ti-. -aθrę'nye⁷-.#áh -atęhninę-:** tiwaθrę⁷nye⁷áh ratęhnì·nęh ‹so-it-is so big-going along-little he-sells› *he sells retail* (HS).

ti-. -aT-. -ahkwrę- be in a vertical position. *v.r.-a.i.* hab: -h, pnt: -⁷, stat: -·, dst: -, caus: -, rvs: -, dat: -, inc.-ɸ-pat. tihru⁷náhkwrę· ‹so-he-himself-is in a vertical position› *he is upright, he is vertical* (HS); **ti-. -a'nahkwrę-.#hči:** tyu⁷nahkwręhči ‹so-it-itself-is in a vertical position-very› *it is perfectly upright, it is plumb* (HS); **ti-. -athęh=nahkwrę-:** tihrathęhnáhkwręh ‹so-he-himself-ear-is in a vertical position› *he pricks up his ears* (HS).

ti-. -athęhnahkwrę- prick up ears. *v.s.-a.i.* tihrathęhnáhkwręh ‹so-he-himself-ear-is in a vertical position› *he pricks up his ears* (HS).

ti-. -a⁷- become of a size. *v.r.-a.i.* hab: -, pnt: -ɸ, stat: -, prog: -, prp: -, dst: -, caus: -, rvs: -, dat: -, n-inc. Hewitt (2892) implies that this root is related to the root **-a⁷θ-** *be of a size*, the latter being the habitual aspect form; however, various morphological features of the latter verb root indicate that this is not the case. **ti-. -a⁷-.#áh:** nęwa⁷áh ‹so-prediction-it-become of a size-little› *there will be not much, it will become or amount to small quantity* (H 2892); **ti-. -a⁷-.#ú⁷y:** nęwa⁷-ú⁷y ‹so-prediction-it-become of a size-

great› *it will become large* (H 2892):
te⁷ ti –. –a⁷–: te⁷ nę̀·wa⁷ ‹what so-prediction-it-become of a size› *how large
will it become* (H 2892).

ti –. –a'nahkwrę –.#hči be perfectly upright,
be plumb. *v.s.-s.i.* tyu⁷nahkwrę́⁷či ‹so-
it-itself-is in a vertical position-very›
it is perfectly upright, it is plumb
(HS).

ti –. –a⁷narih – temperature. *dv.n.s.* ha⁷
tyu⁷naríhę· ‹the so-it-is hot› *the temperature* (HS).

ti –. –(a)'ne – another, some other; besides.
dv.n.s. tihrá·⁷ne⁷ ‹so-he-is present› *he
is another person (not the one meant,
an outsider), he is somebody else (i.e.,
he is an odd one, in the sense of projecting or protruding beyond the complement of persons)* (H 2892), *some
other male* (RC 3:83), tiká·⁷ne⁷ ‹so-it-
is present› *another, a different, besides*
(HS).

ti –. –a⁷neθ –.#áh pistol. *dv.n.s.* tiwa⁷ne·θ-
⁷áh *pistol* ‹so-it-gun-is long-small›
(HS).

ti –. –a'newyaT – armspan (unit of measurement). *dv.n.s.* thwa⁷né·wya·t ‹so-it-
itself-armspan-stands› *measure as long
as the arms extend from tip of one
hand to the other* (AG).

ti –. –a'nwęniyu – be at liberty. *v.s.-a.i.* tih-
ra⁷nwęnì·yu⁷ ‹so-he-himself-is God›
he is at liberty (HS).

ti –. –a'nwęniyuhsT – take liberties. *v.s.-a.i.*
tihra⁷nwęniyúhstha⁷ ‹so-he-himself-be
God-causes› *he takes liberties* (HS).

ti –. –a'nyer – wonder. *v.s.-a.i.* tikayę́·⁷nyer
‹so-they-themselves-do› *they wonder*
(R).

ti –. –a'nyerę –.#hči be surprised. *v.s.-a.i.*
thwahra⁷nyeréhči⁷ ‹so-fact-he-had an
unexpected experience-very› *he was
quite surprised* (R).

ti –. –a'nyeręhθrę – have accidents. *v.s.-a.i.*
thwa⁷kaku⁷nyerę́hθrę⁷ ‹so-fact-they-
had an unexpected experience-many›
accidents happened to them (RC 32:
1).

ti –. –a'nyeriha – be straight. *v.s.-s.i.* tyu⁷-
nyeríhę· ‹so-it-it-self-is straight›
straight (L 82).

ti –. –a⁷rę⁷nh – at intervals, occasionally.
dv.n.s. tyu⁷rę́⁷nhę ‹so-it-itself-frequented› *at intervals, occasionally* (HS).

ti –. –a⁷rihwak̲ʷek –{dative I} become puzzled. *v.s.-s.i.* thwahru⁷ríhwakwekθ
‹so-fact-he-himself-matter-closed-for›
he becomes puzzled (SH 375).

ti –. –a⁷θr – be so big, be so huge, be so
much. *v.r.-s.i.* stat: -ę·, prog: -ę'nye⁷-,
prp: -, dst: -, caus: -, rvs: -, dat: -,
inc.-φ-pat. It is very likely that one
form of the distributive morpheme,
-a⁷θrę -, originally derives from this
verb. tiwá⁷θrę· ‹so-it-is so big› *it is so
big* (RC 35:14); ti –. –a⁷θr –.#ętíh: ti-
wa⁷θrę⁷ętíh ‹so-it-is so big-many little› *small pieces* (RC 10:7); ti –. –a⁷=
θrę'nye⁷ –: tiwa⁷θrę́·⁷nye⁷ ‹so-it-is so
big-going along› *they are so large*
(RC 12:2); ti –. –a⁷θrę'nye⁷ –.#áh: tiwa⁷-
θrę⁷nye⁷áh ‹so-it-is so big-going a-
long-little› *it goes along being small*
(RC 7:9); ti –. –kahra⁷θr –.#ú⁷y: tikakah-
ra⁷θrę⁷ú⁷y ‹so-it-eyes-is so big-great›
huge eyes (RC 28:9); ti –. –kwera⁷θr –.
#ú⁷y: tihrakwera⁷θrę⁷ú⁷y ‹so-he-an-
kle-is so big-great› *his ankles are
large* (RC 25:13); ti –. –nęha⁷θr –.#ú⁷y:
tikanęha⁷θrę⁷ú⁷y ‹so-it-corn-is so big-
great› *the corn grains are very large*
(H 2484); ti –. –rę⁷a⁷θr –: nękarę⁷á⁷-
θrę·k ‹so-prediction-it-tree-be so big›
tree will be so big (RC 30:25); ti –.
–te⁷kwa⁷θr –.#ętíh. –ha'nye⁷ –: tikate⁷-
kwa⁷θrę⁷ętihá·⁷nye⁷ ‹so-it-bag-is so
big-many little-going along› *each had
a small bag* (RC 32:1); te⁷ ti –. –a⁷θr –:

te·ʔ tiwáʔθrahk ‹what so-it-was so big› *how large was it?* (H 2892); hà·neʔ ti –. –aʔθr –: hà·neʔ tiwáʔθrahk ‹that is so-it-was so big› *it was that large* (H 2892).

ti –. –aʔtaʔwęthuhst – exterminate. *v.s.-t.* tikakuʔtaʔwęthuhsthę́he·ʔ ‹so-they-them-selves-combat-cause-much-going to› *they went along exterminating* (RC 12:12).

ti –. –čirwęhsthę – squeeze out. *v.s.-t.* nę-yečirwę́hstę·ʔ ‹so-prediction-one-strangle-cause-for› *one will squeeze it out* (RC 20:1).

ti –. –čiʔruratkwarayę(T) – rose willow. *dv. n.s.* tikačiʔruratkwarà·yę·ʔ ‹so-it-medicine stick-is red› *rose willow (Salix purpurea)* (RC 6:6).

ti –. –čiʔtkwahnayę(T) – gold. *dv.n.s.* tikačiʔtkwáhnayę ‹so-it-yellow-lays› *gold* (R) [Gallatin «ticottcheet kwaunaugeh» 'Yellow'].

ti –. –čiʔtkwahnayę(T) –.#ętíh yellow jackets, hornets. *dv.n.s.* tikačiʔtkwahnayę·ʔętíh ‹so-it-yellow-lays-many little› *yellow jackets, hornets (Vespa maculata)* (R).

ti –. –eryahnatkwarayę(T) – water moccasin, water adder. *dv.n.s.* tyaweryahnatkwarà·yę·ʔ ‹so-it-breath-is red› *water moccasin (Agkistronden piscivorus), water adder (Natrix sp.)* (R) (Also: tyuweryahnatkwarà·yę·ʔθ (R)).

ti –. –(ę)hawi – time, at that time. *dv.n.s.* tikahà·wi·ʔ ‹so-it-brings-X› *time, at that time* (HS).

ti –. –ęhrahsthu – paucity. *dv.n.s.* haʔ tikakawęhráhsthę ‹the so-they-sort-are small› *paucity* (HS).

ti –. –ę'nęte – o' clock. *dv.n.s.* tiwęʔnę́·te·ʔ ‹so-it-day-is a certain› *o' clock* (R).

ti –. –ę'nyer – weather. *dv.n.s.* tiwę́·ʔnyer ‹so-it-day-does› *weather* (R).

ti –. –hehskwahT – –ihrę – be succinct. *v.s.-a.i.* The stem ti –. –hehskwahT – has not been encountered outside the cited construction. thwahrahéhskwaht wahréhrę·ʔ ‹so-fact-he-?? fact-he-said› *he is succinct* (H-notebook).

ti –. –hneʔratkwarayę(T) – beet. *dv.n.s.* tikahneʔratkwarà·yę·ʔ ‹so-it-root-is red› *beet* (R).

ti –. –hweʔnęht – abruptly, in a trice, quickly, precipitously, suddenly. *dv.n.s.* thwaʔkahwéʔnęht ‹so-fact-it-furrow-fall-caused› *abruptly, in a trice, quickly, precipitously, suddenly* (HS).

ti –. –hweʔnęʔn – be perpendicular. *v.r.-s.i.* stat: -ę, prog: -, prp: -, dst: -, caus: -, rvs: -, dat: -, n-inc. tyuhweʔnę́ʔnę ‹so-it-is perpendicular› *it is perpendicular* (HS).

ti –. –i – occasion. *dv.n.s.* thwáhę· ‹so-fact-it-was a group› *occasion* (RC 32:1).

ti –. –re – be distant, be far. *v.r.-s.i.* stat: -ʔ, prog: -, prp: -, dst: -, caus: -, rvs: -, dat: -, inc.-ɸ-pat. tyù·re·ʔ ‹so-it-is distant› *aloof, apart* (HS), *it is distant* (RC 12:2); ti –. –re –.#áh: tyureʔáh ‹so-it-is distant-little› *frequently* (HS); ti –. –reʔke –: tyuréʔkye ‹so-it-is distant-at› *anterior, previously* (HS); tha+ne –. –aʔre –: thaʔneyúʔrehk ‹unusual-apart-it-itself-was distant› *so far apart* (RC

23:2); **- keʔwa̲re** -: skyéʔwareʔ ‹you-hair-is distant› *your disheveled hair* (RC 3:11); **-ne** -. **-kahra̲re** -: nehrakáh-rareʔ ‹apart-he-eye-is distant› *he looked upward* (RC 3:77); **-t** -. **-rih=wa̲re** -: thruríhwareʔ ‹hither-he-matter-is distant› *he maintains* (HS).

ti -. **-re** - aloof, apart. *dv.n.s.* tyù·reʔ ‹so-it-is distant› *aloof, apart* (HS).

ti -. **-re** -.**#áh** frequently. *dv.n.s.* tyureʔáh ‹so-it-is distant-little› *frequently* (HS).

ti -. **-reʔke** - anterior, previously. *dv.n.s.* tyuréʔkye ‹so-it-is distant-at› *anterior, previously* (HS).

ti -. **-takwna̲yer** - posture. *dv.n.s.* tihru-takwnayè·rę ‹so-he-position-did› *his posture* (HS).

ti -. **-ta'na̲yęʼnahkw** - have a campsite. *v.s.-a.i.* tihrataʔnayęʔnáhkhwaʔ ‹so-he-set-tlement-lay-causes-instrument› *he has a campsite* (RC 30:3).

ti -. **-tkwa̲ra̲yę(T)** - be red. *v.s.-s.i.* tika-tkwará·yę·t ‹so-it-blood-lays-complete› *it is red* (M 87).

ti -. **-uhkarahsT** - scratch. *v.r.-s.i.* stat: -ęʔ, prog: -, prp: -, dst: -, caus: -, rvs: -, dat: -, n-inc. tyawuhkaráhsneʔ ‹so-it-scratched› *so it scratches* (RC 3:57).

ti -. **-ukr** - be lax, be limber, be loose, be slack. *v.s.-s.i.* tyawú·krę· ‹so-it-is loose› *it is lax, it is limber, it is loose, it is slack* (HS).

ti -. **-ukrahkw** - loosen. *v.s.-t.* tihrukráh-khwaʔ ‹so-he-is loose-instrument› *he loosens it* (HS).

ti -. **-wętaʔθ** -.**#áh** have a small, thin voice. *v.s.-t.* tihrawętaʔθʔáh ‹so-he-word is of a size-little› *he has a small, thin voice* (AG).

ti -. **-yer** - happen. *v.s.-a.i.* tyuyè·rę ‹so-it-did› *it happened* (RC 30:8), tikà·yer ‹so-it-does› *it happens* (RC 25:9).

ti -. **-yer** -.**#áh** lightly. *dv.n.s.* tyuyeręháh ‹so-it-did-little› *lightly* (HS).

ti -. **-yeraT** - toward. *dv.n.s.* tyuyerá·ʔnę ‹so-it-went in a specific direction› *toward* (HS).

ti -. **-yeraT** - direction. *dv.n.s.* haʔ tyu-yerá·ʔnę ‹the so-it-went in a specific direction› *direction* (HS).

ti -. **-yerę̲ti** -.**#áh** indistinct. *dv.n.s.* tika-yerętiháh ‹so-it-flesh-makes-little› *indistinct* (HS).

ti -. **-yę(T)** - be easy. *v.s.-s.i.* tikà·yęʔ ‹so-it-laid› *it is easy* (R).

ti -. **-ʔtyatih** - during, in the meantime. *dv.n.s.* tyuʔtyá·tihθ ‹so-it-is a long time› *during, as long as it lasts* (HS), tyuʔ-tyatíhę ‹so-it-was a long time› *during, as long as it lasted* (HS), thwaʔuʔ-tyá·tih ‹so-fact-it-was a long time› *in the meantime (present and past)* (RC 3:75), nęyuʔtyá·tih ‹so-prediction-it-be a long time› *in the meantime (future)* (HS).

ti -. **-ʔtyatih** - duration. *dv.n.s.* haʔ tyuʔ-tyá·tihθ ‹the so-it-is a long time› *duration* (HS).

ti -. **-ʔtyeh** - casual, it just happens. *dv.n.s.* tyúʔtyehθ ‹so-it-happens by chance› *casual, it just happens* (R).

ti -. **-ʔtyę'nęhsT** - acquiesce. *v.s.-a.i.* tihraʔtyęʔnę́hsthaʔ ‹so-he-measure-caus-es› *he acquiesces* (HS).

ti -. **-ʔtyę'nęhsT** - acquiescence. *dv.n.s.* tih-ruʔtyęʔnę́hsnę ‹the so-he-measure-caused› *his acquiescence* (HS).

ti+yah -. **-(ę)haw** - guess, reckon. *v.s.-a.i.* thwehráhews ‹so-thither-he-brings› *he guesses, he reckons* (HS).

ti+yah -. **-tatura** ʔ -**{dative I}** become lazy. *v.s.-a.i.* tyahwahrutatù·raʔθ ‹so-thither-fact-he-be lazy-became-for› *he got lazy* (R).

ti+yah+či -. **-(ę)haw** - birthday. *dv.n.s.* thwečé·haws ‹so-thither-again-one-brings› *birthday* (HS).

tiči - partitive+repetitive. *v.pfx.* The form

tiči – occurs before the consonants *θ* or *t*, or the clusters *ʔn* or *ʔt*. The form tič – occurs before the consonant *y* and the *y* is dropped. The form tiθ – occurs elsewhere.

–tičkeʔn – bell. *n.r.* n-poss., n-inc., n.sfx. –eh. utičkyéʔneh *bell* (R).

–tičkẹr – eggshell; scalp. *n.r.* inaln: ktičkẹ·reh *my scalp* (R), inc., n.sfx. –eh. utičkẹ·reh *eggshell; scalp* (R).

tičunuwéhnẹ continuous (RC 21:8) *part.*

–tihahku – kill, massacre. *v.r.-t.* hab: -h, pnt: -aʔ, stat: -, prog: -, prp: -, dst: -, caus: -, rvs: -, dat: -, n-inc. kakutiháhkuh *it massacres them* (R), ahratiháhkwaʔ *that he kill* (AW 58).

tihčaryéhsteh who knows? (R). *part.*

tihčayẹ́hah coward, cowardly, timid (HS). *n.*

–tihčayẹhah – be a coward, be pusillanimous. *v.r.-s.i.* stat: -ɸ, prog: -, prp: -, dst: -, caus: -, rvs: -, dat: -, n-inc. stihčayẹ́hah *you are a coward* (AW 55), ratihčayẹ́hah *he was a coward* (AW 56), *he is pusillanimous* (HS).

–tihe – hover. *v.r.-a.i.* hab: -h, pnt: -, stat: -, prog: -, prp: -, dst: -, caus: -, rvs: -, dat: -, n-inc. rutíheh *he hovers* (HS).

–tiheθ – be dependent. *v.r.-s.i.* stat: -ɸ, prog: -, prp: -, dst: -, caus: -aʔT-, rvs: -, dat: III (-ati-/-ẹ-), inc.-ɸ-ag. rutíhe·θ *he is dependent* (R); –tiheθ –{dative III}: ẹkayetiheθẹ́hek ‹prediction-they-be dependent-for› *they shall trust, they shall confide in* (AG), waʔkẹtihé·θẹʔ ‹fact-I=you-was dependent-for› *I depend on you* (RC 23:27); –tiheθaʔT –:

rutihé·θaʔt ‹he-be dependent-caused› *he is dependable, he is to be depended upon* (RC 9:5); –aʔrihwatiheθ – {dative III}: waʔkaʔrihwatihé·θẹʔ ‹fact-I-myself-matter-was dependent-for› *I am trusting* (AG).

–tiheθ –{dative III} confide in, depend on, trust. *v.s.-t.* ẹkayetiheθẹ́hek ‹prediction-they-be dependent-for› *they shall trust, they shall confide in* (AG), waʔkẹtihé·θẹʔ ‹fact-I=you-was dependent-for› *I depend on you* (RC 23:27).

–tiheθaʔT – be dependable, be to be depended upon. *v.s.-a.i.* rutihé·θaʔt ‹he-be dependent-caused› *he is dependable, he is to be depended upon* (RC 9:5).

–tihẹhy – blue. *n.r.* n-poss., n-inc., n.sfx. –eh. *West.* See: –tihẹry –. utihẹ́·hyeh *blue* (PC).

–tihẹry – blue. *n.r.* n-poss., n-inc., n.sfx. –eh. *East.* See: –tihẹhy –. utihẹ́·ryeh *blue* (RC 12:5) [Gallatin «otee-huh-ryeh» 'Blue']; –tihẹryahẹsči –: katihẹryahẹ́sči ‹it-blue-black› *dark blue, purple* (AW 111); –tihẹryahwaryakẹ –: utihẹryahwaryá·kẹʔ ‹blue-white› *light blue* (AW 111).

–tihẹryahẹsči – dark blue, purple. *dv.n.s.* katihẹryahẹ́sči ‹it-blue-black› *dark blue, purple* (AW 111).

–tihẹryahwaryakẹ – light blue. *n.s.* utihẹryahwaryá·kẹʔ ‹blue-white› *light blue* (AW 111).

–tihkẹhrẹw – anus. *n.r.* n-poss., n-inc., n.sfx. –eh. utihkẹhrẹ̀·weh *anus* (R).

–tihkw – down, fur, muff, wool. *n.r.* See:

Tuscarora Pronunciation Key:
/a/ l<u>a</u>w; /e/ h<u>a</u>t; /i/ p<u>i</u>zza; /u/ t<u>u</u>ne; /ẹ/ h<u>i</u>nt; /č/ <u>ch</u>eese; /h/ <u>h</u>oe; /m/ <u>m</u>other; /s/ <u>s</u>ame; /t/ <u>d</u>o (before a vowel y, or w), <u>t</u>oo (elsewhere); /k/ <u>g</u>ale (before a vowel y or w), <u>k</u>ale (elsewhere); /n/ i<u>nh</u>ale (before a consonant or word-final), <u>n</u>ote (elsewhere), /r/ hi<u>ss</u> (before a consonant or word-final), <u>r</u>un (trilled as in Italian, elsewhere); /w/ cu<u>ff</u> (before a consonant other than y or word-final), <u>w</u>ay (elsewhere); /y/ fi<u>sh</u> (before a consonant or word-final), <u>y</u>ou (elsewhere), /θ/ <u>th</u>ing; /ʔ/ (the sound between the vowels in unh-unh); /·/ long vowel, /́/ high pitch; /̀/ low pitch.

-(ę)tihkw -.

-tihkwi?θ(e)r - mud sleigh. *dv.n.s.* See: -(ę)tihkwi?θ(e)r -.

-tihkwekne - astringent. *dv.n.r.* This root is encountered only in the cited construction. The form of the pronominal prefix shows that it is deverbal in origin. yutihkwékne? *astringent* (HS).

-tihrečha?k - Bear Clan, White Bear Clan. *n.r.* inaln: ratihréčha?k *he is of the Bear Clan* (H 2892), n-inc. tihréčha?ks *White Bear Clan* (L 47), tihréčha?k *Bear Clan* (AG).

-tihθur - reed, rushtail. *n.r.* n-poss., inc., n.sfx. -eh. utihθù·reh *reed* (H-notebook), *rushtail* (HS).

-tihs - poison. *n.r.* n-poss., inc., n.sfx. -eh. utíhseh *poison*; -tihsar -: ratíhsar ‹he-poison-is in› *he envenoms* (HS); -tihsanhęthu -: ratihsanhę́·thuhs ‹he-poison-put in mouth-causes› *he poisons it, he gives it poison* (HS); -tih = sayę'ner -: yetihsayę?nè·rih ‹one-poison-knows› *witch* (RC 9:1); -tihsayę = 'nerihe-.#ú?y: ratihsayę?'nerihe?ú?y ‹he-poison-knows-going to-great› *great wizard, he is practicing much wizardry* (RC 14:1); ha? -tihsayę'ner -: ha? yetihsayę?'nè·rih ‹the one-poison-knows› *witchcraft* (HS).

-tihsar - envenom. *v.s.-a.i.* ratíhsar ‹he-poison-is in› *he envenoms* (HS).

-tihsanhęthu - poison, give poison to. *v. s.-t.* ratihsanhę́·thuhs ‹he-poison-put in mouth-causes› *he poisons it, he gives it poison* (HS).

-tihsayę'ner - witch. *dv.n.s.* yetihsayę?-nè·rih ‹one-poison-knows› *witch* (RC 9:1).

-tihsayę'ner - witchcraft. *dv.n.s.* ha? yetihsayę?'nè·rih ‹the one-poison-knows› *witchcraft* (HS).

-tihse?y - eyelid. *n.r.* n-poss., n-inc., n. sfx. -eh. utihsé?yeh *eyelid* (R).

tíhsnę? and (RC 12:1). *part.* Several early sources, including works by J.N.B. Hewitt and Albert Gatschet, record another form for this particle, specifically, tíhsę?. This pronunciation is unknown in the modern language.

-tihstę - cohabit, be a pair. *v.r.-s.i.* stat: -?, prog: -, prp: -, dst: -, caus: -a?T-, rvs: -, dat: -, n-inc. yutíhstę? *it cohabits: a pair* (HS).

-tihstę?re - be a housefly. *v.r.-s.i.* stat: -?, prog: -, prp: -, dst: -, caus: -a?T-, rvs: -, dat: -, n-inc. rutihstę́?re? *housefly (Musca domestica)* (R), wa?katihstę́?rek *housefly stuck to* (RC 26:28).

-tihtawęhsT - liniment. *dv.n.s.* See: -(ę) = tihtawęhsT -.

-tihtwęy - sore, tumor, ulcer. *n.r.* aln: rutihtwę̀·yayę? *he has an abscess* (HS), inc., n.sfx. -eh. See: -htwęy -. utihtwę̀·yeh *sore, tumor, ulcer* (HS).

-tihtyuhčr - claw, spur of bird's leg. *n.r.* n-poss., n-inc., n.sfx. -eh. utihtyúhčreh *claw, spur of bird's leg* (HS).

-tihu? - arrive, be placed, be at home, be in a customary seat or place of abode. *v.r.-a.i.* hab: -θ, pnt: -ɸ, stat: -ę, prog: -, prp: -, dst: -θrę-, caus: -, rvs: -, dat: -, n-inc. Hewitt (2892) gives the meaning of this root as, "to be in a customary seat or place of abode or habitation; to be at home; to abide; to be in a pasture (of animals)." He also makes the erroneous statement that, "this stem is now used only in the plural...". kakutihú?ę *they have arrived* (RC 33:1), *they are placed (sitting), are at home, are in their pen or house, or are perched* (H-notebook), katíhu?θ *it exists* (RC 35:29), ękayetíhu? *they will arrive* (RC 33:4), kayetihú?θrę? *they remain* (RC 3:4), *they abide in their places in groups* (H 2892); -yah+ či -.-tihu? -: yęčękwatihú?ęk ‹thither-prediction-again-we-arrive⟩ *we will re-turn there* (R).

–t(i)kahT– chase, pursue. *v.r.-t.* hab: -e⟩. pnt: -φ. stat: -, prog: -, prp: -, dst: -, caus: -, rvs: -, dat: -, inc.-φ-pat. The form –tikahT– occurs following the reflexive. The form –tkahT– occurs elsewhere. kyetkáhne⟩ *I chase it* (R), wakyetkáhne⟩ *it chases me* (R), ratkáhne⟩ *he chases it, he pursues it* (HS), rutkáhne⟩ *he is chased* (RC 6: 10), wahrátkaht *he chased it* (RC 2:9), wahrútkaht *it chased him* (R); –ęya= tkahT–: ahręyátkaht ⟨unknown-he-cavern-chase⟩ *that he follow the windings of a cavern* (RC 11:2); –yanręh= statkahT–: rayanręhstatkáhne⟩ ⟨he-rule-'ness-chases⟩ *he observes laws* (HS); –a'nętikahT–: ra'nętikáhne⟩ ⟨he-himself-chases⟩ *he chases* (RC 25:14), *he pursues it closely* (HS), wahra'nę-tí·kaht ⟨fact-he-himself-chased⟩ *he chased* (RC 25:10).

tikawęnì·yu? any position (RC 8:12), as soon as, pell-mell, whenever (HS). *part.*

tí·kę· as many as are (RC 12:4) *part.* See: –i–.

–tikę– blackhaw. *n.r.* n-poss., n-inc., n. sfx. -φ. rutí·kę *blackhaw* (R), kutí·kę *blackhaw* (R).

tikętéh, tikętéh clomp, clomp (sound of a horse running) (R). *part.*

tí·pi· T.B., tuberculosis (AW 51). *n.*

–tirher– be exempted from work, be king, be queen. *v.r.-s.i.* stat: -φ, prog: -, prp: -, dst: -, caus: -, rvs: -, dat: -,

n-inc. This verb was used in traditional narratives to refer to teenagers isolated from infancy to puberty, and to refer to the first human beings. Boyce (1978, p. 283) also notes the use of this verb to refer to village chiefs among the Tuscarora (Lawson «Teeth-ha» 'A King') and the Nottoway (Wood [Rudes 1981] «Tirer» 'A King'). ratírher *he is exempt from labor; king* (RC 3:8), etírher *one is exempt from work; queen* (RC 3:8) (also: yetírher (R)), neyetírher *the two of them are exempt from work* (RC 3:10).

tit– partitive+cislocative. *v.pfx.* The form ti'n– occurs before pronominal prefixes that begin with the consonants *w* or *y*. The form tit– occurs before pronominal prefixes that begin with the consonants *k* or *h*. The form ti'ni– occurs elsewhere.

–tiyę'kw– shoot. *v.r.-t.* See: –i'ak–/ –yę'kw–.

–tiyheh– blot out, float over, cover over, darken out. *v.r.-s.i.* stat: -φ, prog: -, prp: -, dst: -, caus: -a'?T-, rvs: -, dat: -, n-inc. yutíyheh *it blotted out, it floated over, it covered over, it darkened out* (RC 8:3).

tì·yuht so it is, so it stood (RC 11:16). *part.* See: –hT–.

–ti'ak– shoot. *v.r.-t.* See: –i'ak–/–yę'kw–.

tí'er besides (RC 12:5). *part.*

–ti'k– copulate, have sex with spouse. *v.r.-t.* hab: -, pnt: -a·t, stat: -, prog: -, prp: -, dst: -, caus: -a'?T-, rvs: -, dat: -, n-inc. The precise meaning of the root is uncertain. In modern Tuscarora it is clearly used to refer to heterosexual intercourse, in particular between married couples. It is unclear whether it also refers to other forms of intercourse (e.g., homosexual). The completive aspect suffix (-a·t) replaces the punctual with this root. wahratí$^{\gamma}$ka·t *he copulates, he has sex with his spouse* (R).

-ti$^{\gamma}$kar̨ewe – inject. *v.r.-t.* hab: -h, pnt: -, stat: -, prog: -, prp: -, dst: -, caus: -a$^{\gamma}$T-, rvs: -, dat: -, n-inc. **-ti$^{\gamma}$ka = r̨ewe** –: ti$^{\gamma}$kar̨ȩ·weh ‹inject› *hoop snake (mythic, turns into a hoop by biting its sharp-boned tail)* (R); à·w̨ȩ$^{\gamma}$ **-ti$^{\gamma}$= kar̨ewe** –: à·w̨ȩ$^{\gamma}$ na$^{\gamma}$ti$^{\gamma}$kar̨ȩ·weh ‹water one=another-injects› *one injects* (HS).

-ti$^{\gamma}$kar̨ewe – hoop snake (mythic). *dv.n.* ti$^{\gamma}$kar̨ȩ·weh ‹inject› *hoop snake (mythic, turns into a hoop by biting its sharp-boned tail)* (R)

-ti$^{\gamma}$n – fart, fetor, flatulence. *n.r.* n-poss., n-inc., n.sfx. -eh. utí$^{\gamma}$neh *fart, fetor, flatulence* (HS) [Lawson «Ut-tena» 'A F--t']; **-ti$^{\gamma}$n̨ȩ** –: katí$^{\gamma}$n̨ȩh ‹it-fart-falls› *flicker (Colaptes auratus)* (R).

-ti$^{\gamma}$nehθr – Roman wormwood, ragweed. *n.r.* n-poss., n-inc., n.sfx. -eh. uti$^{\gamma}$néhθreh *Roman wormwood, ragweed (Ambrosia sp.)* (H-notebook).

-ti$^{\gamma}$n̨ȩhkw – bowl, crock. *n.r.* n-poss., n-inc., n.sfx. -eh. uti$^{\gamma}$n̨ȩhkweh *bowl, crock* (HS).

-ti$^{\gamma}$n̨ȩw – fundament, rump. *n.r.* n-poss., n-inc., n.sfx. -eh. uti$^{\gamma}$n̨ȩ·weh *fundament, rump* (HS).

-ti$^{\gamma}$nyuhkw̨ȩti – make an alliance, mutiny. *v.s.-a.i.* See: -(ȩ)ti$^{\gamma}$nyuhkw̨ȩti –.

-ti$^{\gamma}$nyuhkw̨ȩti – cluster, league. *dv.n.s.* See: -(ȩ)ti$^{\gamma}$nyuhkw̨ȩti –.

-ti$^{\gamma}$r – provisions, treasure. *n.r.* n-poss., n-inc., n.sfx. -eh. utí$^{\gamma}$reh *provisions, treasure (anything, food or money, put up for future use)* (HS).

-ti$^{\gamma}$reθh(e)r – sword, swordguard. *n.r.* n-poss., n-inc., n.sfx. -ϕ ~ -eh. yuti$^{\gamma}$ré·θher *swordguard* (HS), uti$^{\gamma}$ré·θhreh *sword* (HS).

-ti$^{\gamma}$rhw̨ȩθawihT – be sheepish. *v.s.-a.i.* See: -(ȩ)ti$^{\gamma}$rhw̨ȩθawihT –.

-ti$^{\gamma}$rhw̨ȩθawihT – sycophant. *dv.n.s.* See: -(ȩ)ti$^{\gamma}$rhw̨ȩθawihT –.

-ti$^{\gamma}$rhw̨ȩθu'narhuhsT – crupper. *dv.n.s.* See: -(ȩ)ti$^{\gamma}$rhw̨ȩθu'narhuhsT –.

-ti$^{\gamma}\theta$(e)r – cupboard, overhang, stage, shelf. *n.r.* n-poss., inc., n.sfx. -eh. utí$^{\gamma}\theta$reh *cupboard, overhang, stage, shelf* (HS); **-ti$^{\gamma}\theta$erhar** –: kati$^{\gamma}\theta$érhe$^{\gamma}$r ‹it-overhang-hangs› *shelf hangs, there is a shelf* (RC 3:60); **-ti$^{\gamma}\theta$rat̨ek̨ȩ** –: kakuti$^{\gamma}\theta$raté·k̨ȩ$^{\gamma}$ ‹they-overhang-joined› *they set up an ambuscade* (RC 10:8); **-ti$^{\gamma}\theta$r̨ȩ** –: ȩθwatí$^{\gamma}\theta$r̨ȩ$^{\gamma}$ ‹prediction-you-overhang-fall› *you will suspend shelf* (RC 3:22), yutí$^{\gamma}\theta$r̨ȩ$^{\gamma}$ ‹it-overhang-fell› *it shades* (HS), ȩyuti$^{\gamma}\theta$r̨éhek ‹prediction-it-overhang-fall› *it will shade* (HS); **-ti$^{\gamma}\theta$r̨ȩhst** –: uti$^{\gamma}\theta$r̨éhsteh ‹overhang-fall-'ness› *shade, shadow* (HS); **-ti$^{\gamma}\theta$r̨ȩhsT** –: kati$^{\gamma}\theta$r̨éhstha$^{\gamma}$ ‹it-overhang-fall-causes› *it overshadows* (HS); **-ti$^{\gamma}\theta$r̨ȩhstara$^{\gamma}$** –: yuti$^{\gamma}\theta$r̨éhstara$^{\gamma}\theta$ ‹overhang-fall-'ness-be in-begins› *it overshadows* (HS); **-ti$^{\gamma}\theta$r̨ȩhT** –: rati$^{\gamma}\theta$r̨éhtha$^{\gamma}$ ‹he-overhang-fall-causes› *he shades it* (HS).

-ti$^{\gamma}\theta$ȩy – rump. *n.r.* n-poss., n-inc., n.sfx. -eh. uti$^{\gamma}\theta$ȩ̀·yeh *rump* (HS).

-ti$^{\gamma}\theta$hahkw – step. *v.s.-a.i.* See: -(ȩ)ti$^{\gamma}$= θhahkw –.

-ti$^{\gamma}\theta$rat̨ek̨ȩ – set up an ambuscade. *v.s.-a.i.* kakuti$^{\gamma}\theta$raté·k̨ȩ$^{\gamma}$ ‹they-overhang-joined› *they set up an ambuscade* (RC 10:8).

-ti$^{\gamma}\theta$r̨ȩ – shade. *v.s.-a.i.* yutí$^{\gamma}\theta$r̨ȩ$^{\gamma}$ ‹it-overhang-fell› *it shades* (HS), ȩyuti$^{\gamma}$-

θréhek ‹prediction-it-overhang-fall› *it will shade* (HS).

–ti²θrehst – shade, shadow. *n.s.* uti²θréhsteh ‹overhang-fall-'ness› *shade, shadow* (HS).

–ti²θrehsT – overshadow. *v.s.-a.i.* kati²θréhstha² ‹it-over-hang-fall-causes› *it overshadows* (HS).

–ti²θrehstara² – overshadow. *v.s.-a.i.* yuti²θréhstara²θ ‹overhang-fall-'ness-be in-begins› *it overshadows* (HS).

–ti²θrehT – shade. *v.s.-t.* rati²θréhtha² ‹he-overhang-fall-causes› *he shades it* (HS).

–ti²tyę²θ(e)r – blow nose, wipe nose. *v. r.-a.i.* See: –(ę)ti²tyę²θ(e)r –.

tkaré·nyę·² angelica *(Angelica* sp.) (H-notebook). *n.*

–tkaw – raft. *n.r.* n-poss., n-inc., n.sfx. –eh. ú·tkaweh *raft* (HS) (Also: úhskaweh).

–tka²n – musk, musk bag. *n.r.* n-poss., n-inc., n.sfx. –eh. utká²neh *musk, musk bag* (R).

tka²ne²náhkwahs black raspberry *(Rubus occidentalis)* (H-notebook). *n.*

–tka²T – follow. *v.r.-a.i.* hab: -e², pnt: -ϕ, stat: -ę, prog: -, prp: -, dst: -, caus: -, rvs: -, dat: -, n-inc. yutká²nę *it followed* (HS), katká²ne² *it follows: according to* (HS), yutká²ne² *commonly, off and on, often* (R), ękátka²t *it will follow* (HS).

–tka²T – according to. *d.v.n.s.* katká²ne² *according to* (HS).

–tka²T – commonly, off and on, often. *d.v.n.s.* yutká²ne² *commonly, off and on, often* (R).

–tkę – blood, gore. *n.r.* n-poss., n-inc., n.sfx. –². This root is irregular in that it appears with the pronominal prefix **ka**– rather than **u**– in its elicitation form. This is perhaps to avoid homophony with the noun útkę² *inherent power.* ká·tkę² *blood, gore* (RC 2:4) [Lawson «Cotcoo» 'Drest-skin'] [Gallatin «cotnuh» 'Blood']; –tkę–.#ęwe: katkę²ę̀·we ‹it-blood-genuine› *real blood* (R).

tkęhwè·nuh bobcat *(Lynx rufus)*, mountain lion *(Felis concolor)*, panther, wildcat (R) [Lawson «Cauhau-weana» 'Wildcat-skin']. *n.* tkęhwenuhkę́ha²nę² ‹panther-many› *panthers* (RC 12:4).

–tkęwa²θ – gum (of the mouth). *n.r.* n-poss., n-inc., n.sfx. –eh. utkęwá²θeh *gum (of the mouth)* (HS).

–tkę²r – nutshell. *n.r.* n-poss., n-inc., n.sfx. –eh. utkę́²reh *nutshell* (R).

–tkuhkw – corpulent and pertuberant stomach or belly. *n.s.* utkúhkweh ‹stomach-cover-instrument› *a large, corpulent and pertuberant stomach or belly* (H-notebook).

tkurehčì·yu lark (R). *n.*

–tkuri – corn porridge, corn whey, hominy, rests from boiling corn. *n.r.* n-poss., inc., n.sfx. –². This root is irregular in that it appears with the pronominal prefix **ka**– rather than **u**– in its elicitation form, which suggests that it is deverbal in origin. Cognates in other Northern Iroquoian language mean *stir*; a similar meaning for Tuscarora is suggested by the presence of what appears to be the same root in the word **utkuryá?čreh** *paddle; shoulder blade*. Also, this root requires the increment **-?n-** when incorporated. katkù·ri? *corn porridge, corn whey, hominy, rests from boiling corn* (RC 25:6) [Lawson «Cotquerre» 'Homine']; **-tkuri?nak-**: ęhratkuri?ná·ksek ‹prediction-he-hominy-eat› *he will eat corn porridge* (RC 25:8); **-tkuri?narihę?-**: yutkuri?naríhę?θ ‹it-hominy-boil-begins› *it sputters* (HS); **-nač- -tkuri = 'nęte -**: uná·ča? utkuri?nę́·te ‹rice hominy-certain one› *rice pudding* (HS).

-tkuri?narihę?- sputter. *v.s.-a.i.* yutkuri?naríhę?θ ‹it-hominy-boil-begins› *it sputters* (HS).

-tkurya?čr- paddle, shoulder blade. *n.r.* inaln (in meaning *shoulder blade*): kyetkuryá?čreh *my shoulder blade* (R), aln (in meaning *paddle*): akyetkuryá?črayę? *my paddle* (R), n.sfx. -eh. utkuryá?čreh *paddle, shoulder blade* (R).

-tkuθt- be bashful, be shy. *v.r.-s.i.* stat: -φ, prog: -, prp: -, dst: -, caus: -, rvs: -, dat: -, n-inc. rútkuθt *he is bashful, he is shy* (R).

-tku?θr- baby. *n.r.* n-poss., n-inc., n.sfx. -eh. utkú?θreh *baby* (RC 35:39); **-tku?θr-.#keha·?**: utku?θra?kyéha·? ‹baby-customarily› *babyish* (HS), utku?θrehkyéha·? ‹baby-customarily› *babyish* (HS).

-tku?θr-.#keha·? babyish. *n.s.* utku?θra?kyéha·? ‹baby-customarily› *babyish* (HS), utku?θrehkyéha·? ‹baby-customarily› *babyish* (HS).

-tkw- abdomen, belly, groin, paunch, pleura, stomach. *n.r.* inaln: yétkweh *one's stomach* (RC 26:21), inc., n.sfx. -eh. útkweh *abdomen, belly, groin, paunch, pleura, stomach* (HS) [Gallatin «otqueh» 'Belly']; **-tkuhkw-**: utkúhkweh ‹stomach-cover-instrument› *a large, corpulent and pertuberant stomach or belly* (H-notebook); **-tkw-.#keha·?**: utkwehkyéha·? ‹stomach-customarily› *abdominal, celiac* (HS); **-tkwanęhwak(T)-**: katkwanę́hwaks ‹it-stomach-aches› *bellyache, upset stomach* (RC 19:1); **-tkwat?a-**: katkwá·t?ę ‹it-stomach-put in› *pie, pudding* (R); **-tkwat?a?T-**: ękayetkwat?á?ne·? ‹prediction-they-stomach-put in-moving› *they will make pies* (L 36); **-tkwa?=nihr-**: yutkwa?níhrę ‹it-stomach-stood up› *it bulges, it is convex* (HS); **-tkwę?-**: rutkwę́?ę ‹he-stomach-fall-began› *he has a rupture, he has pleurisy* (HS); **-tkwę?ke**: utkwę́?kye ‹stomach-at› *on stomach* (RC 26:31), kyetkwę́?kye ‹I-stomach-at› *(on) my stomach* (R); **-tkwiyu?-**: wa?etkwì·yu? ‹fact-one-stomach-be great-began› *one's stomach grew* (RC 35:25); **-a='netkwahtręhsT-**: wa?netkwahtrę́hstha? ‹it-itself-stomach-tie-causes› *belt* (HS); **-(a)hy- -tkwat?ahsT-**: úhyeh katkwat?áhsnę ‹fruit it-stomach-put in-caused› *fruit pie* (HS); **kwęhs -ne-. -tkwarihT- {dative III}**: kwęhs nahrutkwarihnatíhek ‹no apart-unknown-he-stomach-be ripe-causes-for› *he has indigestion* (HS).

-tkw-.#keha·? abdominal, celiac. *n.s.* utkwehkyéha·? ‹stomach-customarily› *abdominal, celiac* (HS).

-tkwanak͏ʷę- success, thrift. *n.r.* n-poss., n-inc., n.sfx. -·?. utkwaná·kwę·? *success, thrift* (HS).

-tkwanęhwak(T)- bellyache, upset stomach. *dv.n.s.* katkwanę́hwaks ‹it-stomach-aches› *bellyache, upset stomach* (RC 19:1).

-tkwar-/-tkwar- blood. *n.r.* aln: akyetkwà·reh *my blood* (R), inc., n.sfx. -?.

This root looks almost as if it were a stem derived from –tkw– *stomach* and –r– *be in*. From such a compound one would expect the elicitation form to be **ú·tkwareh**, which is in fact the pronunciation of the word in the Western dialect. The accentuation of the stem meaning *be red*, which clearly contains the root meaning *blood*, also suggests a stem form –tkwar–. However, in the Eastern dialect the accent on the elicitation form (**utkwà·reh**) points to a stem form –tkwar–. (The other words cited below could contain either –a– or –a–.) It is perhaps the case that –tkwar– is the original form of the stem and that the accentuation of the elicitation form has been regularized to the penultimate syllable. u·tkwà·reh *blood* (R), ú·tkwareh *blood* (PC): –tkwararahkw–: yutkwararáhkę ‹it-blood-collected› *hemorrhage* (RC 7:7); –tkwaraθe?.#hči: utkwaraθé?či ‹blood-new-very› *very new blood* (RC 21:11); –tkwarayę(T)–: katkwarà·yę? ‹it-blood-lays› *it is red* (R) [Lawson «Cotcoo-rea» 'Red'] [Gallatin «tucotquaurauyuh» 'Red']; –tkwara?ke: u·tkwará?kye ‹blood-at› *sanguinary* (HS); –tkwaritkę?–: ratkwarí·tkę?θ ‹he-blood-comes forth› *he bleeds* (HS); –tkwariyu–: ratkwarí·yu· ‹he-blood-is great› *he is sanguine* (HS); –či–. –tkwara'nehT–: čutkwará·?neht ‹again-it-blood-be present-caused› *cardinal: any reddish-colored bird* (R); ti–. –tkwarayę(T)–: tikatkwará·yę·t ‹so-it-blood-lays-complete› *it is red* (M 87); ti–. –tkwarayę'na?–: tikatkwarayę́·?na?θ ‹so-it-blood-lay-begins› *it is reddened* (HS).

–tkwararahkw– hemorrhage. *dv.n.s.* yutkwararáhkę ‹it-blood-collected› *hemorrhage* (RC 7:7).

–tkwarayę(T)– be red. *v.s.-s.i.* katkwarà·yę? ‹it-blood-lays› *it is red* (R) [Lawson «Cotcoo-rea» 'Red'] [Gallatin «tucotquaurauyuh» 'Red'].

–tkwara?ke sanguinary. *n.s.* utkwará?kye ‹blood-at› *sanguinary* (HS).

–tkwaritkę?– bleed. *v.s.-a.i.* ratkwarí·tkę?θ ‹he-blood-comes forth› *he bleeds* (HS).

–tkwariyu– be sanguine. *v.s.-s.i.* ratkwarí·yu· ‹he-blood-is great› *he is sanguine* (HS).

–tkwat?a– pie, pudding. *dv.n.s.* katkwá·t-?ę ‹it-stomach-put in› *pie, pudding* (R).

–tkwat?a?T– make pies. *v.s.-a.i.* ękaye-tkwat?á?ne·? ‹prediction-they-stomach-put in-moving› *they will make pies* (L 36).

–tkwa?nihr– bulge, be convex. *v.s.-s.i.* yutkwa?níhrę ‹it-stomach-stood up› *it bulges, it is convex* (HS).

–tkwehr– dung, feces, shit, turd. *n.r.* inaln: etkwéhreh *one's shit* (R), inc., n.sfx. –eh. utkwéhreh *dung, feces, shit, turd* [Lawson «Utquera» 'A T---d']; –tkwehr–.#hči: yetkwehréhči ‹one-shit-very› *one moves one's bowels often* (H-notebook).

–tkwehr–.#hči move bowels often. *v.s.-*

a.i. yetkwehréhči ‹one-shit-very› *one moves one's bowels often* (H-notebook).

–tkwehθętíh little bloodroot. *n.* yutkwehθętíh *little bloodroot* (R).

–tkwehθęthu – staunch the flow of blood. *v.r.-a.i.* hab: -hs, pnt: -, stat: -, prog: -, prp: -, dst: -, caus: -, rvs: -, dat: -, n-inc. ratkwehθę́·thuhs *he staunches blood* (HS).

–tkwęhn – frying pan, spider (footed skillet). *n.r.* n-poss., n-inc., n.sfx. -eh. utkwę́hneh *frying pan, spider (footed skillet)* (HS); **–tkwęhnarahęsči** –: katkwęhnarahę́sči ‹frying pan-be in-black› *maroon, scarlet* (AW 111).

–tkwęnuhθr – gizzard. *n.r.* n-poss., n-inc., n.sfx. -eh. utkwęnúhθreh *gizzard* (HS).

–tkwę? – begin to snow. *v.r.-a.i.* hab: -, pnt: -?, stat: -, prog: -, prp: -, dst: -, caus: -, rvs: -, dat: -, n-inc. wa?ká·tkwę? *it started snowing* (R) [Lawson «Acaun-que» 'Snow'], ęká·tkwę? *it will be snowing* (R).

–tkwę? – have a rupture, have pleurisy. *v.s.-s.i.* rutkwę́?ę ‹he-stomach-fall-began› *he has a rupture, he has pleurisy* (HS).

–tkwęhnarahęsči – maroon, scarlet. *dv.n.s.* Probably originally a reference to the blackish coating that develops with use on an iron skillet. katkwęhnarahę́sči ‹frying pan-be in-black› *maroon, scarlet* (AW 111).

–trahn – plant, sprout; leaf (archaic). *n.r.* n-poss., inc., n.sfx. -eh. utráhneh *plant, sprout: leaf (archaic)* (HS); **ti** –. **–trahna?nihr** –: nęyutrahna?níhręk ‹so-prediction-it-leaf-stand› *so many leaves will be standing* (RC 23:2); **–khręw** – **–trahn** –: ukhrę̇·weh utráhneh ‹evergreen plant› *common yarrow (Achillea millefolium)* (RC 20:1).

–trahθn – plate. *n.r.* n-poss., n-inc., n.sfx. -eh. utráhθneh *plate* (HS).

–trahs – fungus, mushroom. *n.r.* n-poss., inc., n.sfx. -eh. This root is probably the source of Lawson's «Trossa» 'Hat'. utráhseh *fungus, mushroom* (RC 32: 10); **–yah** –. **–trahsęhT** –: yahwahratráhsęht ‹thither-he-fungus-fall-caused› *he dropped fungus there* (RC 32:10).

–trahwęhte – snowsnake. *n.* n-poss., n-inc., n.sfx. -?. utrahwę́hte? *snowsnake* (H 3518).

–tra?n – horn. *n.r.* See: **–(ę)tra?n** –.

–tra?neθ – ox. *dv.n.s.* See: **–(ę)tra?neθ** –.

–trehn – bird tail, fish tail. *n.r.* poss. ?, inc. ?, n.sfx. -eh. utréhneh *bird tail, fish tail* (AG).

–tre?r – small sleigh, trevoy. *n.r.* n-poss., n-inc., n.sfx. -eh. utré?reh *small sleigh, trevoy* (SH 375).

trí?tri? parrot (AG). *n.*

–tuhar – wash. *v.r.-t.* See: **–uhar** –.

–tuharehčrawę – soap. *v.s.-t.* ratuharéhčrawęhs ‹he-X-wash-'ness-possesses› *he soaps it* (HS).

–tuharęhe? – washer. *dv.n.s.* wa?katuharę́he? ‹fact-it-X-wash-was going to› *washer* (R).

–tuha?čr – soap. *n.s.* utuhá?čreh ‹X-put in water-'ness› *soap* (HS).

–tuha?st – soap; red trillium, wake-robin. *n.s.* utuhá?sta? ‹X-put in water-'ness› *soap: red trillium (Trillium erectum), wake-robin* (HS).

túhkwak guinea hen *(Numida meleagris)* (R). *n.*

–tuhn – fin, keel of a ship, paddle, wing-like shelf. *n.r.* n-poss., inc., n.sfx. -eh/-a?. utúhneh *fin, paddle* (HS), utúhna? *fin, keel of a ship, wing-like shelf* (HS); **–tuhnar** –: yutúhnar ‹it-fin-is in› *it has fins* (HS).

–tuhnar – have fins. *v.s.-s.i.* yutúhnar ‹it-fin-is in› *it has fins* (HS).

-tuhrar – detain. *v.r.-t.* hab: -ɸ, pnt: -, stat: -ę, prog: -, prp: -, dst: -, caus: -, rvs: -, dat: -, n-inc. rutuhrà·rę *he detains it* (HS), naʔtúhrar *one detains another* (RC 35:42).

-tuhs wheat. *n.r.* n-poss., n-inc., n.sfx. -ɸ. ú·tuhs *wheat* (RC 23:6).

-tuhsT – freeze. *v.r.-t.* hab: -haʔ, pnt: -ɸ, stat: -ę, prog: -, prp: -he-, dst: -, caus: -, rvs: -, dat: -, inc-hra-pat. –hra= tuhsT –: yuhratúhsnę *it is frozen* (L 74), kahratúhstha* *freezing* (L 73); –t –. –hratuhsT –: nakáhratuhst ‹hither-fact-it-froze› *it froze* (R); –a'nęnha= tuhsT –: ruʔnęnhatúhsnę ‹he-himself-be alive-froze› *he is chilled, he shivers* (HS).

tuhtíʔ in spite of (RC 15:7), nevertheless (HS). *part.*

-tukar – cog, cam; scallop; point. *n.r.* n-poss., inc., n.sfx. -eh. utú·kareh *cog, cam; scallop; point* (HS); –tukarar –: yutú·karar ‹it-point-is in› *it is indented* (HS); –tukaraʔnihr –: waʔktukaráʔnir ‹fact-I-point-stood up› *I sharpened it (e.g., pencil)* (HS); –tukaręT –: yutú·-karę·t ‹it-point-possesses› *it is sharp, it is pointed* (R); –tukaręti–: waʔktuka-rę·tiʔ ‹fact-I-point-made› *I sharpened it (e.g., pencil)* (HS); –tukarętyahnę –: ratukarętyáhnęh ‹he-point-makes-many› *he scallops (the edges)* (HS).

-tukarar – be indented. *v.s.-s.i.* yutú·karar ‹it-point-is in› *it is indented* (HS).

-tukaraʔnihr – sharpen. *v.s.-t.* waʔktuka-ráʔnir ‹fact-I-point-stood up› *I sharpened it (e.g., pencil)* (HS).

-tukaręti – sharpen. *v.s.-t.* waʔktukarę·tiʔ ‹fact-I-point-made› *I sharpened it (e.g., pencil)* (HS).

-tukarętyahnę – scallop. *v.s.-t.* ratukarę-tyáhnęh ‹he-point-makes-many› *he scallops (the edges)* (HS).

-tukę –{dative I} appear to. *v.s.-t.* The root upon which this stem is apparently based does not occur independently. It is found only in this stem and in the stems –tukęhT – *bring to show, indicate* and –tukęʔ – *be definite.* Hewitt's secondary gloss suggests that the bare root originally meant *come to, come ashore.* rutukę́ʔθe· ‹he-??-for› *he trows, it appears to him* ("it comes a-shore to him, i.e., it becomes a matter of knowledge to him") (H-notebook).

-tukęhT – bring to show, indicate. *v.s.-t.* See note at –tukę –{dative I}. ratukę́h-thaʔ ‹he-??-causes› *he brings to show, he indicates* (HS); –rihwatukęhT –: ra-rihwatukę́hthaʔ ‹he-matter-??-causes› *he specifies* (HS); –aʔrihwatukęhT –: raʔrihwatukę́hthaʔ ‹he-himself-matter-??-causes› *he recapitulates* (HS).

-tukęht – be holy, be sacred. *v.r.-s.i.* stat: -i/-ę, prog: -iha'nyeʔ-, prp: -, dst: -hę-, caus: -ihsT-, rvs: -, dat: -, inc.-ɸ-ag./ pat. The word for *Sunday* is clearly a loanword containing the noun root for *day.* The Tuscarora form of this root would give **yawęʔnatukę́htę. It is probable that most all of the words containing the root –tukęht – are loanwords from other Northern Iroquoian languages borrowed with the introduction of Christianity to the Nation in the nineteenth century. **-tukęh= tihsT** -: ratukęhtíhstha⁷ ‹he-be holy-causes› *he sanctifies* (HS); **-ętatu= kęht** -: yawętatukę́htę ‹it-⁷⁷-is holy› *Sunday* (HS); **-(ę)⁷tikęhratukęht** -: u⁷-tikęhratukę́hti ‹mind-be holy› *Great Spirit: Holy Spirit* (R); **-hsęnatukęht** -: θahsęnatukę́hti ‹you-name-is holy› *hallow be Thy name* (G); **-hyatęh= statukęht** -: uhyatęhstatukę́hti ‹book-be holy› *Bible* (R); **-kęnhatukęht** -: ukęnhatukę́hti ‹season-be holy› *holiday season* (R); **-nęhsatukęht** -: unęhsatukę́hti ‹house-be holy› *sanctuary* (HS); **-rihwatukęht** -: rurihwatukę́hti ‹he-matter-is holy› *he is holy* (MP), *reverend* (HS); **-rihwatukęhthę** -: neyękhirihwatukę́hthę· ‹two-one=us-matter-is holy-much› *one makes the two of us holy* (R); **-ya⁷tatukęht** -: ruya⁷tatukę́hti ‹he-body-is holy› *saint* (HS), raya⁷tatukę́hti ‹he-body-is holy› *monk* (HS); **-ya⁷tatukęhtihsT** -: raya⁷tatukęhtíhstha⁷ ‹he-body-be holy-causes› *he consecrates, he sanctifies* (HS); **-yeta= tukęht** -: uyetatukę́hti ‹grease-be holy› *chrism, holy oil* (HS); **-t-. -rihwa= tukęht** -: nayękhirihwatukę́hnę ‹hither-one=us-matter-is holy› *one is holy to us* (MP); **kwęhs -ya⁷tatukęht- -i** -: kwęhs ruya⁷tatukę́hti ará·kę·k ‹no he-body-is holy unknown-it-is a group› *he is unholy* (HS); **kwęhs -ya⁷tatu= kęhtiha'nye⁷** -: kwęhs aryuya⁷tatukęhtihá·⁷nye⁷ ‹no unknown-it-body-be holy-going along› *it is unholy* (HS).

-tukęhtihsT - sanctify. *v.s.-t.* ratukęhtíhstha⁷ ‹he-be holy-causes› *he sanctifies* (HS).

-tukę⁷ - be definite, be sure, be true. *v.s.-s.i.* See note at **-tukę-{dative I}**. yutukę́⁷ę ‹it-⁷⁷-began› *it is sure, it is true* (HS); **-tukę⁷** -: utukę́⁷ę ‹⁷⁷-began› *def-*

initely (RC 14:3), *truly* (RC 3:76); **-tukę⁷-.#hči**: utukę⁷ę́hči ‹⁷⁷-began-very› *in effect, really* (HS); **-rihwa= tukę⁷** -: urihwatukę́⁷ę ‹matter-⁷⁷-began› *it is improbable* (HS); **ha⁷ ka⁷nę́ -tukę⁷** -: ha⁷ ka⁷nę́ utukę́⁷ę ‹the just ⁷⁷-began› *for sure* (AW 98); **ka⁷nę́ -tukę⁷** -: ka⁷nę́ utukę́⁷ę ‹just ⁷⁷-began› *for sure* (AW 50).

-tukę⁷ - definitely, truly. *dv.n.s.* utukę́⁷ę ‹⁷⁷-began› *definitely* (RC 14:3), *truly* (RC 3:76).

-tukę⁷-.#hči in effect, really. *dv.n.s.* utukę⁷ę́hči ‹⁷⁷-began-very› *in effect, really* (HS).

-tur - chaff, cornhusk, husk, stalk. *n.r.* n-poss., inc., n.sfx. -eh. This root is related historically to **-nur** - *braided string of corn*, both of which are from Proto-Northern Iroquoian * **-nor** - *chaff, husk*. The latter root fails to show the regular shift of *n* to Tuscarora *t*. utù·reh *chaff, corn-husk, husk, stalk* (R); **-tura⁷nihr** -: yutura⁷níhrę ‹it-husk-stood up› *it has a husk* (RC 7:5); **-tura⁷nihθku** -: ęyetura⁷níhθku⁷ ‹prediction-one-husk-pick off› *one will pick off stalk* (RC 20:1); **-turuhči** -: akaturúhči⁷ ‹unknown-it-husk-remove› *that husk be removed* (RC 5:30).

-turahčr - rib. *n.r.* inaln: kturáhčreh *my rib* (R), inc., n.sfx. -eh. uturáhčreh *rib* (R); **-ne** -. **-turahčrukar** -: wa⁷thraturahčrú·ka⁷r ‹fact-apart-he-rib-broke up› *he broke his rib* (RC 21:3).

-tura⁷nihr - have a husk. *v.s.-s.i.* yutura⁷níhrę ‹it-husk-stood up› *it has a husk* (RC 7:5).

-turę - preserve, put away, save, store, stow, treasure; fail. *v.r.-t.* hab: -h, pnt: -⁷, stat: -·, prog: -, prp: -, dst: -, caus: -, rvs: -, dat: -, inc.-φ-ag./pat. This root is related historically to **-nurę** - *be precious*, both of which are from Proto-Northern Iroquoian *-norę- *preserve, save, treasure*. The latter root fails to show the regular shift of *n* to Tuscarora *t*. rutú·rę· *he put it away, he stored it* (RC 8:19), ratù·ręh *he preserves it, he puts it away, he stows it, he treasures it; he fails (to do it)* (HS), θtù·rę *put it away!, store it!* (R), wa²kakutù·rę² *they failed, they were unable* (RC 3:25); -t-. -turę-: nyutú·rę· ‹hither-it-store› *lacking* (R); -a²na=turę-: wa²ka²natù·rę² ‹fact-I-gun-stored› *I put away my gun, I stored my gun* (R); -nęhaturę-: ranęhatù·ręh ‹he-corn-stores› *he puts corn, the corn, away* (H 2484); -nęhsnaturę-: ranęhsnatù·ręh ‹he-seed-stores› *he puts away, stores grain* (H 2484); -t-. -rihwaturę-: nahskrihwatú·rę· ‹hither-you=me-matter-store› *you save me* (MP).

-turiyę- press down on, step on. *v.r.-t.* hab: -, pnt: -², stat: -·, prog: -, prp: -, dst: -, caus: -, rvs: -, dat: -, n-inc. na²turí·yę· *one oppressed another* (HS), ęhsturì·yę² *you will press down on* (RC 3:21), wa²kturì·yę² *I stepped on it* (R).

-turuhkw- flag iris. *n.r.* n-poss., n-inc., n.sfx. -eh. uturúhkweh *flag iris* (AG).

-tuwę- fib, lie, prevaricate, tell a lie. *v.r.-a.i.* hab: -h, pnt: -², stat: -·, prog: -, prp: -, dst: -, caus: -hT-, rvs: -, dat: -, n-inc. θatú·wę· *you are a liar* (RC 2:7), kakutú·wę· *liars* (R), katù·węh *it tells a lie* (R), yutù·węh *it is false* (HS), wahrutù·wę² *he lied* (R); -tu=węhnawęri-: ratuwęhnawę̀·rih ‹he-tell a lie-cause-stirs› *he belies* (HS), ęhratuwęhnawę̀·ri² ‹prediction-he-tell a lie-cause-stir› *he will belie* (HS); -tu=węhnęti-: ratuwęhnę́·tih ‹he-tell a lie-cause-makes› *he falsifies it* (HS); -tu=węhnur-: yutuwęhnù·rę ‹it-tell a lie-cause-covered› *doubtful* (HS); -tu=węhT-: utù·węht ‹tell a lie-cause› *doubt, lie, skepticism* (R), utuwę́hneh ‹tell a lie-cause› *falsehood, lie* (HS), yutù·węht ‹it-tell a lie-caused› *incredible, incredulous* (HS), ratuwę́htha² ‹he-tell a lie-causes› *he disbelieves it, he doubts it, he is incredulous* (HS), na²tuwę́htha² ‹one=another-tell a lie-causes› *one mistrusts another* (HS); -a²tuwęhT-: ęka²tù·węht ‹prediction-I-myself-tell a lie-cause› *I will tell a lie* (RC 30:19); kwęhs -tuwęhT-: kwęhs aryutuwę́hnęk ‹no unknown-it-tell a lie-cause› *it is credible, it is incontestible* (HS).

-tuwęhnawęri- belie. *v.s.-a.i.* ratuwęhnawę̀·rih ‹he-tell a lie-cause-stirs› *he belies* (HS), ęhratuwęhnawę̀·ri² ‹prediction-he-tell a lie-cause-stir› *he will belie* (HS).

-tuwęhnęti- falsify. *v.s.-t.* ratuwęhnę́·tih ‹he-tell a lie-cause-makes› *he falsifies it* (HS).

-tuwęhnur- doubtful. *dv.n.s.* yutuwęhnù·rę ‹it-tell a lie-cause-covered› *doubtful* (HS).

-tuwęhT- doubt, falsehood, lie, skepticism. *n.s.* utù·węht ‹tell a lie-cause› *doubt, lie, skepticism* (R), utuwę́hneh

Tuscarora Pronunciation Key:
/a/ law; /e/ hat; /i/ pizza; /u/ tune; /ę/ hint; /č/ cheese; /h/ hoe; /m/ mother; /s/ same; /t/ do (before a vowel y, or w), too (elsewhere); /k/ gale (before a vowel y or w), kale (elsewhere); /n/ inhale (before a consonant or word-final), note (elsewhere), /r/ hiss (before a consonant or word-final), run (trilled as in Italian, elsewhere); /w/ cuff (before a consonant other than y or word-final), way (elsewhere); /y/ fish (before a consonant or word-final), you (elsewhere), /θ/ thing; /²/ (the sound between the vowels in unh-unh); /·/ long vowel, /´/ high pitch; /`/ low pitch.

‹tell a lie-cause› *falsehood, lie* (HS).

-tuwęhT - incredible, incredulous. *dv.n.s.* yutù·węht ‹it-tell a lie-caused› *incredible, incredulous* (HS).

-tuwęhT - disbelieve, doubt, mistrust. *v. s.-t.* ratuwę́htha⁷ ‹he-tell a lie-causes› *he disbelieves it, he doubts it, he is incredulous* (HS), na⁷tuwę́htha⁷ ‹one=another-tell a lie-causes› *one mistrusts another* (HS).

Tu⁷á·ka·⁷ Seneca (R). *n.* See: Twa⁷á·ka·⁷. tu⁷aka·⁷.#kye: tu⁷aká·⁷kye ‹Seneca-at› *to the Senecas* (AW 102).

-tu⁷kr - saliva, spit. *n.r.* n-poss., inc., n.sfx. -eh. utú⁷kreh *saliva, spit* (R); -tu⁷krę'ni -: wa⁷ktu⁷krę́·⁷ni⁷ ‹fact-I-saliva-throw› *I spit* (HS).

-tu⁷krę'ni - spit. *v.s.-a.i.* wa⁷ktu⁷krę́·⁷ni⁷ ‹fact-I-saliva-throw› *I spit* (HS).

tú⁷ks cranberry (R). *n.* Onomatopoeic in origin, imitative of the noise produced by cranberries when they burst during cooking. tú⁷ks -a'nę -: tú⁷ks wá·⁷nęh ‹cranberry it-says› *cranberry* (R).

tú⁷ks -a'nę - cranberry. *dv.n.s.* tú⁷ks wá·⁷nęh ‹cranberry it-says› *cranberry* (R).

-tu⁷θ - tooth. *n.r.* See: -(ę)tu⁷θ -.

-tu⁷θanęhwak(T) - have a toothache. *v.s.-a.i.* See: -(ę)tu⁷θanęhwak(T) -.

-tu⁷θarik - have a toothache. *v.s.-a.i.* See: -(ę)tu⁷θarik -.

-tu⁷θawihsi - pull out teeth, extract teeth, draw teeth. *v.s.-a.i.* See: -(ę)tu⁷θa=wihsi -.

-tu⁷θawihsya⁷T - forceps. *dv.n.s.* See: -(ę)tu⁷θawihsya⁷T -.

tú⁷θeh meadow lily, wood lily *(Lillium* sp.) (H-notebook). *n.*

-tu⁷θęT - domestic goose; flageolet; yellow pike. *n.s.* See: -(ę)tu⁷θęt.

-tu⁷θęT - -⁷niha - gander. *n.s.* See: -(ę)=tu⁷θęt -⁷niha -.

-tu⁷θęT -.#u⁷y swan. *n.s.* See: -(ę)tu⁷θęt.

#u⁷y.

-tu⁷θęti - teethe. *v.s.-a.i.* See: -(ę)tu⁷θę =ti -.

-tu⁷θr - butter. *n.r.* n-poss., n-inc., n.sfx. -eh. utú⁷θreh *butter* (R); -tu⁷θr -.#hči: utu⁷θréhči ‹butter-very› *buttery* (HS); -tu⁷θr - -či⁷ręte: utú⁷θreh uči⁷rę́·te ‹butter ember-certain one› *candle* (R).

-tu⁷θr - -či⁷ręte candle. *n.s.* utú⁷θreh u-či⁷rę́·te ‹butter ember-certain one› *candle* (R).

-tu⁷θr -.#hči buttery. *n.s.* utu⁷θréhči ‹butter-very› *buttery* (HS).

-tu⁷t - wave. *n.r.* n-poss., n-inc., n.sfx. -a⁷. utú⁷ta⁷ *wave (of water)* (R).

-tu⁷T - tooth's edge. *n.r.* See: -(ę)tu⁷T -.

-tu⁷thę⁷ - set on edge. *v.s.-a.i.* See: -(ę)=tu⁷thę⁷ -.

-twahT - miss, overlook. *v.r.-t.* See: -(ę)=twahT -.

Twa⁷á·ka·⁷ Seneca (language or people) (AG). *n.* Albert S. Gatschet states that this word is from a shortened form of an archaic činętwa⁷á·ka·⁷ (see Seneca (o)nǫtawá⁷ka: *Seneca* [Chafe 1967, entry 1274]). Twa⁷á·ka·⁷ -uwan -: Twa⁷á·ka·⁷ rakuwá·nę· ‹Seneca he-X-is chief› *a Seneca chief* (AG); Twa⁷-á·ka·⁷ -nęwę -: Twa⁷á·ka·⁷ kanę̀·wę⁷ ‹Seneca it-is female› *a Seneca female* (AG).

-tyačhayę - girl (10-15 years old). *n.s.* etyáčhayę⁷ *girl (10-15 years old)* (AG).

tyahęθa - partitive+translocative+repetitive+factual. *v.pfx.*

-tyahskari⁷čr - bracelet, brooch, buckle. *n.r.* See: -(ę)tyahskari⁷čr -.

-tyahskari⁷čru'narhu - buckle. *v.s.-a.i.* See: -(ę)tyahskari⁷čru'narhu -.

-tyahskari⁷čru'narihsi - unbuckle. *v.s.-a.i.* See: -(ę)tyahskari⁷čru'narihsi -.

tyahwa⁷ - partitive+translocative+factual. *v.pfx.* The final ⁷ is dropped before a pronominal prefix that begins with *h*. The sequence *wa*ʔ of the prefix coalesces with an initial sequence *wa* of a following pronominal prefix to yield **tyahę̄ -**.

tyahwaʔT(i) - partitive+translocative+cislocative+factual. *v.pfx.* The form **tyahwaʔn -** occurs before pronominal prefixes that begin with the consonants *w* or *y*. The form **tyahwaʔt -** occurs before pronominal prefixes that begin with the consonants *k* or *h*. The form **tyahwaʔni -** occurs elsewhere.

tyahwaʔT(i) - partitive+translocative+dualic+factual. *v.pfx.* The form **tyah = waʔn -** occurs before pronominal prefixes that begin with the consonants *w* or *y*. The form **tyahwaʔt -** occurs before pronominal prefixes that begin with the consonants *k* or *h*. The form **tyahwaʔni -** occurs elsewhere.

-tyak - marry. *v.r.-t.* hab: -, pnt: -φ, stat: -ę, prog: -, prp: -, dst: -θę- ~ -hę-, caus: -, rvs: -, dat: -, n-inc. katyá·kę *husband, spouse, wife* (R) [Lawson «Kateocca» 'Wife'], ęyęktí·tya·k *the two of us will marry one another* (RC 3:50); **-tyakθę -**: neyutyákθę· ‹two-it-married-many› *pairs of spouses* (RC 11:10); **-ne -. -tyakhę -**: nekakutyá·khęh ‹two-they-marry-much› *they intermarry* (HS); **-a'netyak -**: newaʔnetyá·kę ‹two-it-itself-married› *husband and wife* (RC 27:1); **kwęhs -tyak -**: kwęhs ahrutyákshek ‹no unknown-he-marries› *bachelor* (HS).

-tyak - husband, spouse, wife. *dv.n.s.* ka-

tyá·kę *husband, spouse, wife* (R) [Lawson «Kateocca» 'Wife'].

-tyan - pod, shell. *n.r.* n-poss., n-inc., n.sfx. -eh. utyà·neh *pod, shell* (HS).

tya(r)(a) - partitive+translocative+optative. *v.pfx.* The form **tyara -** occurs whenever the prefix receives word accent; if this form is followed by a pronominal prefix that begins with the sequence *wa*, the final vowel contracts with the sequence to give **tyarę -**. The form **tyar -** occurs when the prefix is unaccented before pronominal prefixes that begin with the glides *w* or *y*. The form **tya -** occurs elsewhere. The final *a* of this form coalesces with an initial sequence *wa* of a pronominal prefix to yield **nyę -**.

tyà·reʔ before, first (RC 11:27). *part.*

-tyaʔkr - wetness. *n.r.* n-poss., inc., n.sfx. -eh. utyáʔkreh *wetness, condition of being wet* (R); **-tyaʔkręti -**: waʔkatyaʔkrę́·tiʔ ‹fact-it-wetness-made› *it got wet* (L 79), ęktyaʔkrę́·tiʔ ‹fact-I-wetness-made› *I got wet, it got me wet* (L 79).

-tyaʔkręti - get wet. *v.s.-a.i.* waʔkatyaʔkrę́·tiʔ ‹fact-it-wetness-made› *it got wet* (L 79), ęktyaʔkrę́·tiʔ ‹fact-I-wetness-made› *I got wet, it got me wet* (L 79).

-tyaʔkʷ - be nauseous, gag, retch. *v.r.-a.i.* hab: -, pnt: -, stat: -, prog: -, prp: -, dst: -hrę-, caus: -ahT-, rvs: -, dat: -, inc.-φ-pat. Found only with a derivational suffix—either the causative suffix or the distributive suffix—present.

-tya?kʷahT -: utyá?kwaht ‹be nause-ous-cause› *nastiness* (R), yutyá?kwaht ‹it-be nauseous-caused› *it is obscene* (HS), rutyá?kwaht ‹he-be nauseous-caused› *he is dirty (in speech, con-duct), he is nasty, he is obscene, he is perverted, he is unclean* (HS); -tya? = kʷahT -{dative III}: rutya?kwahná·ti· ‹he-be nauseous-caused-for› *he gags, he is nauseous* (HS); -tya?kʷhrę -: ra-tyá?kwręh ‹he-is nauseous-much› *he retches* (HS), rutyá?kwrę· ‹he-was nauseous-much› *he gags, he is nau-seous* (HS); -ne+t -. -tya?kʷahT - {da-tive III}: nę?nahrutya?kwáhnę·? ‹a-part-fact-hither-he-be nauseous-caus-ed-for› *he again got nauseated* (RC 30:56); -nę?aratya?kʷahT -: unę?ara-tyá?kwaht ‹pollution-be nasty› *pollu-tion* (HS); -?nhęhatya?kʷahT -: ru?nhę-hatyá?kwaht ‹he-urine-is nasty› *his ur-ine is disgusting, nauseating (said of one who is so dirty as to have an of-fensive effluvia from his person)* (H 2484).

-tya?kʷahT - nastiness. *n.s.* utyá?kwaht ‹be nauseous-cause› *nastiness* (R).

-tya?kʷahT - be dirty (in speech, in con-duct), be obscene, be unclean. *v.s.-s.i.* yutyá?kwaht ‹it-be nauseous-caused› *it is obscene* (HS), rutyá?kwaht ‹he-be nauseous-caused› *he is dirty (in speech, in conduct), he is obscene, he is unclean* (HS).

-tya?kʷahT -{dative III} be nauseous, gag. *v.s.-s.i.* rutya?kwahná·ti· ‹he-be nauseous-caused-for› *he gags, he is nauseous* (HS).

-tya?kʷhrę - be nauseous, gag, retch. *v.s.-a.i.* ratyá?kwręh ‹he-is nauseous-much› *he retches* (HS), rutyá?kwrę· ‹he-was nauseous-much› *he gags, he is nauseous* (HS).

-tya?nęy - hornet's nest. *dv.n.s.* yutyá?nęy ‹it-puffed-up bag-hangs down› *hor-net's nest* (RC 26:5).

tya?nuhθrę́hę· weasel *(Mustela frenata)* (RC 27:17). *n.* Hewitt & Smith's com-ment, "prob. from the manner of skin-ning it," suggests that this noun con-tains the root -tya?T - *puffed-up bag* and the root -uhθ(e)r - *strip off*.

-tya?nuka?T- belch. *v.s.-a.i.* rutya?nu-ká?tha? ‹he-puffed-up bag-blister-causes› *he belches* (HS), ęhrutya?-nú·ka?t ‹prediction-he-puffed-up bag-blister-cause› *he will belch* (HS).

-tya?T - coach, puffed-up bag. *n.r.* n-poss., inc., n.sfx. -eh. utyá?neh *coach, puffed-up bag* (HS); -tya?nakęw: u-tyá?nakęw ‹puffed-up bag-in› *in hor-net's nest* (RC 26:6); -tya?nęy -: yu-tyá?nęy ‹it-puffed-up bag-hangs down› *hornet's nest* (RC 26:5); -tya?nuka?T -: rutya?nuká?tha? ‹he-puffed-up bag-blister-causes› *he belches* (HS), ęhru-tya?nú·ka?t ‹prediction-he-puffed-up bag-blister-cause› *he will belch* (HS); -tya?thar -: katyá?thar ‹it-puffed-up bag-hangs› *hornet's nest* (RC 26:5); ti -. -tya?na?θ -.#ú?y: tikatya?na?θ-?ú?y ‹so-it-puffed-up bag-is of a size-great› *large hornet's nest* (RC 26:5).

-tya?T - bribe, buy. *v.r.-t.* hab: -ha?, pnt: -φ, stat: -ę, prog: -, prp: -, dst: -, caus: -, rvs: -, dat: -, inc.-φ-pat. θtyá?t *buy it!* (R), nwá·tya?t *let all of us buy it!* (RC 26:8), kakutyá?nę *they bought it* (RC 26:9), eθá·tya?t *you would buy it* (RC 26:8), na?tyá?tha? *one bribes another* (HS); -nęhkwa?čratya?T -: ę-kanęhkwá?čratya?t ‹prediction-it-med-icine-buy› *they will buy medicine* (AW 98); -nęhsatya?T -: ranęhsa-tyá?tha? ‹he-house-buys› *he buys, is buying the house* (H 2484); -nęh = snatya?T -: ranęhsnatyá?tha? ‹he-seed-buys› *he buys grain, is buying; is a*

grain merchant (H 2484); -n**ęθa**=
tya?T-: ranęθatyá'?tha? ‹he-potato-
buys› *he buys potatoes* (H 2484);
-pihskitya?T-: wa'?kpíhskitya'?t ‹fact-I-
biscuit-bought› *I bought biscuits* (R);
-θahe?r**a**tya?T-: wahsθahé'?ratya'?t
‹fact-you-bean-bought› *you bought
beans* (R).

tya?tarahkwáhnęh choke cherry *(Prunus
virginiana)* (H-notebook). *n.*

-tya?thar- hornet's nest. *dv.n.s.* katyá'?-
thar ‹it-puffed-up bag-hangs› *hornet's
nest* (RC 26:5).

-tyenę- get, get into, obtain, penetrate,
procure. *v.r.-t.* hab: -h, pnt: -'?, stat: -·,
prog: -, prp: -, dst: -, caus: -hsT-, rvs:
-, dat: -, inc.-ɸ-pat. ratyè·nęh *he obtains it, he penetrates it, he procures it*
(HS); -tyenę-: utyé·nę· ‹obtain› *chance*
(HS); -tyenęhsT-: ęktyenęhsthek ‹pre-
diction-I-obtain-cause› *I will be getting it* (R); -hne?r**a**tyenę-: wahrah-
ne'?ratyè·nę'? ‹fact-he-root-obtained› *he
found root* (L 3); -ihn**a**tyenę-: akęhna-
tyè·nę'? ‹unknown-it-hide-obtain› *that
it get into skin* (RC 32:12), ręhnatyè··
nęh ‹he-hide-obtains› *he penetrates the
skin* (HS); -tahkw**a**tyenę-: waθatah-
kwatyè·nę'? ‹fact-you-marriage-obtained› *you got a husband/a wife* (R).

-tyenę- chance. *n.s.* utyé·nę· ‹obtain›
chance (HS).

-tyęw**a**r- pond, puddle. *n.r.* n-poss., n-
inc., n.sfx. -eh. utyę̀·wareh *pond,
puddle* (HS).

-tyę?kwiN- storm. *v.r.-a.i.* hab: -ęhs, pnt:
-'?, stat: -, prog: -, prp: -he-, dst: -,
caus: -, rvs: -, dat: -, n-inc. ratyę'?-
kwì·nęhs *he storms* (HS), katyę'?-
kwì·nęhs *stormy* (HS), ękatyé'?kwi'?n
it will storm (RC 5:40); -tyę?kwiN-:
wa'?katyé'?kwi'?n ‹fact-it-stormed› *hurricane* (AG); -tyę?kwithe-: katyę'?-
kwí·the'? ‹it-storms-going to› *storm*
(HS).

-tyę?kwiN- hurricane. *dv.n.s.* wa'?katyé'?-
kwi'?n ‹fact-it-stormed› *hurricane*
(AG).

-tyę?kwithe- storm. *dv.n.s.* katyę'?kwí·-
the'? ‹it-storms-go-ing to› *storm* (HS).

-tyę?nari- dogtooth violet, yellow adder's
tongue. *n.r.* n-poss., n-inc., n.sfx. -'?.
utyę'?nà·ri'? *dogtooth violet, yellow adder's tongue (Erythronium* sp.) (H-
notebook).

tyuh hence, so, therefore (RC 12:10).
part. tyuh hésnę· ‹hence then› *hence,
so then* (HS).

tyuh hésnę· ‹hence then› hence, so then
(HS). *part.*

-tyur- swim (as a means of locomotion).
v.r.-a.i. hab: -ęhs ~ -e'?, pnt: -'?, stat: -
, prog: -, prp: -, dst: -, caus:-, rvs: -,
dat: -, n-inc. ktyù·ręhs *I swim* (R),
ratyù·re'? *he's swimming (swimming
to get somewhere)* (L 82), wa'?ká·-
tyu'?r *it swam* (RC 15:6); -tyur**a**=
wihw-: ratyurawíhę ‹he-swim-know
how-caused› *he is a good swimmer* (L
82).

-tyur**a**wihw- be a good swimmer. *v.s.-
s.i.* ratyurawíhę ‹he-swim-know how-
caused› *he is a good swimmer* (L 82).

-tyuθ(e)r- scrape corn. *v.r.-a.i.* hab: -,

pnt: ()-ˀ, stat: -, prog: -, prp: -, dst: -, caus: -, rvs: -, dat: -, inc.-ɸ-pat. wahstyú·θeˀr *you scrape corn* (R); –tyu = θ(e)r –: utyú·θer ‹scrape corn› *green corn* (R), utyú·θreh ‹scrape corn› *green corn* (H-notebook); –nęhatyu = θ(e)r –: unęhatyú·θer ‹corn-scrape corn› *the corn is green, is yet in the milk* (H 2484).

–tyuθ(e)r – green corn. *n.s.* utyú·θer ‹scrape corn› *green corn* (R), utyú·θreh ‹scrape corn› *green corn* (H-notebook).

tyúˀrę̌ˀ sometimes (RC 8:26). *part.*

–tˀah – be little one, be infant. *v.r.-s.i.* stat: -ɸ, prog: -, prp: -, dst: -, caus: -, rvs: -, dat: -, n-inc. The plural formation is unique to this root. yú·tˀah *it is little* (HS), yuthí·tˀah *they are little* (HS); –tˀah –: ú·tˀah ‹be little one› *little one* (RC 8:22); –thitˀah –: uthí·tˀah ‹plural-be little one› *young ones of animals* (HS); –tˀah –.#úˀy: ut-ˀahúˀy ‹be little one-great› *big baby* (RC 8:12).

–tˀah – little one. *n.s.* ú·tˀah ‹be little one› *little one* (RC 8:22).

–tˀah –.#úˀy big baby. *n.s.* utˀahúˀy ‹be little one-great› *big baby* (RC 8:12).

U

–u – cover. *v.r.-s.i.* See: –ur –.

–u – be in liquid, be in water, float. *v.r.-a.i.* hab: -h, pnt: -·ˀ, stat: -·ˀ, prog: -, prp: -, dst: -, caus: -, rvs: -ku-, dat: -, inc.-ɸ- ~ -(i)ˀθk-pat. Hewitt (2892) gives the meaning of this root as, "to float or be floating, as a cloud (in the air), or to be immersed as a log, etc., to be imbedded or set, as ore, mineral, waters, coal, etc. and as a stone in the setting of a ring, and as water in a blister, and as cranberry (bushes) in swampy lands." yá·wu·ˀ *it floats* (HS); –(a)hęˀnuˀ –: wahę́ˀnuˀθ ‹it-clearing-be in water-begins› *the meadow is subject to overflow (from some stream of water), the meadow customarily becomes inundated* (H 2484); –ahryu –: ráhryuh ‹he-fishing gear-is in water› *he fishes* (HS); –(a)hyu –: yúhyu·ˀ ‹it-fruit-is in water› *berry or fruit is imbedded, set, or are, in swampy land (said of cranberry patches)* (H 2892); –čikheˀnuku –: račikheˀnú·kwahs ‹he-salt-be in water-undoes› *he freshens it* (HS); –eku –: yawé·ku·ˀ ‹it-liquid-is in water› *a liquid or liquid is imbedded (in it) (said of water in a blister or serum in a sore)* (H 2892); –ę°ˀru –: waˀkayakę́ˀru·ˀ ‹fact-they-nut-was in water› *they put nuts in water* (RC 10:1); –(ę)ˀteyu –: ruˀté·yu·ˀ ‹he-crowd-is in water› *mosquito* (RC 2:14); –heh = nuˀ –: kahéhnuˀθ ‹it-field-be in water-begins› *the field is inundated customarily* (H 2484); –hneˀru –: waˀehnéˀ-ru·ˀ ‹fact-one-root-was in water› *one put root in water* (R); –hseharu –: waˀ-ehséharu·ˀ ‹fact-one-lye-was in water› *one put lye in water* (RC 3:53); –hse = yu –: kahsè·yuhk ‹it-ear of corn-was in water› *boiled ear of corn* (R); –hteh = nu –: Kahtéhnu·ˀ ‹it-pine-is in water› *name of Tuscarora village in colonial North Carolina, occupied up to the 18th century* (R) [Lawson «Cauteghna»]; –htehnu –.#aka·ˀ: Kahtehnuˀá·-ka·ˀ ‹it-pine-is in water-characterized by› *Tuscarora residents of the village of Kahtéhnu·ˀ* (R); –hwihstu –: yuh-wíhstu·ˀ ‹it-metal-is in water› *metal is imbedded, now most commonly used of gold, silver, copper, etc.* (H 2892); –(i)ˀnhahnu –: Kaˀnháhnu·ˀ ‹it-limb-is in water› *Kanhato, New York (an old Tuscarora village in south central New York)* (R); –(i)ʔθkuʔ–: waʔkayéʔθkuʔ ‹fact-they-X-be in water-began› *they drowned* (R), ráʔθkuʔθ ‹he-X-be in water-begins› *he drowns* (HS), ruʔθkúʔę ‹he-X-be in water-began› *he drowned* (HS); –nęhsnuʔ–: kanęhsnuʔθ ‹it-seed-be in water-begins› *the grain is customarily flooded, is subject to floods* (H 2484); –nęhu–: ranęhuh ‹he-corn-is in water› *he puts corn to soak, he puts corn in liquid (to soak or to cook)* (H 2484); –nęhu=čhę(T)–: kanęhúchęʔ ‹it-corn-be in water-'ness-lays› *corn bread* (R); –nę=huku–: ranęhú·kwahs ‹he-corn-be in water-undoes› *he takes the corn from the kettle, he takes the corn from the water, as corn bread, etc.* (H 2484); –nęθu–: ranę́·θuh ‹he-potato-is in water› *he boils potato* (H 2484); –nę=θuhkw–: yenęθúhkhwaʔ ‹one-potato-is in water-instrument-lays› *pot or kettle for boiling potatoes* (H 2484); –nęθu=ku–: ranęθú·kwahs ‹he-potato-be in water-undoes› *he takes potatoes out of the pot or out of any liquid* (H 2484); –nęθuʔ–: kanę́·θuʔθ ‹it-potato-be in water-begins› *potato(es) is (are) becoming flooded over* (H 2484); –raʔ=θru–: yuráʔθru·ʔ ‹it-cloud-is in water› *a cloud floats, is floating* (H 2892).

ú·č oats *(Avena sativa)* (R) *n.*

–uči– be cuneate, taper. *v.r.-s.i.* stat: -ʔ, prog: -, prp: -, dst: -, caus: -, rvs: -, dat: -, inc.-ɸ-pat. wú·čiʔ *it is cuneate,*

it tapers (HS); –(a)hęʔnuči–: kahęʔnú·čiʔ ‹it-meadow-is cuneate› *sharp point of land, land pointing into water* (AG); –hehnuči–: kahehnú·čiʔ ‹it-field-is cuneate› *the field is cuneiform, wedge-shaped* (H 2484).

učʔáhči ‹self-finish-cause-very› the last (RC 28:11). *part.*

učʔahná·te·t ‹self-finish-cause-line› lastly, solely, ultimately (HS). *part.*

účʔaht ‹self-finish-cause› but, except, only (RC 12:5) [Lawson «Ut chat» 'That's all']. *part.*

–uha– put in liquid, put in water. *v.r.-t.* hab: -hs, pnt: -ʔ, stat: -ę, prog: -, prp: -, dst: -, caus: -ʔT-, rvs: -, dat: -, inc.-ɸ-~-(i)ʔθk-pat. ęyakúhaʔ *one will put it in water* (RC 19:2); –yah–. –uha–: waʔθúha ‹thither-you!-X-put in water› *put it in water!* (R); –hęwuha–: rahęwúhahs ‹he-boat-puts in water› *he sinks boats* (RC 26:35); –nęθuha–: ranęθúhahs ‹he-potato-puts in water› *he puts potato or tuber in liquid; hence, he boils potatoes* (H 2484); –nęʔ=aruha–: ęyenęʔarúhaʔ ‹prediction-one-climbing vine-put in water› *one will put vine in water* (RC 16: 1); –θkwa=ruha–: raθkwarúhahs ‹he-lips-puts in water› *he sips* (HS); –wenęʔnuhaʔT–: yewenęʔnuháʔthaʔ ‹one-iron-put in water-causes› *one sets anchor* (HS); –ʔehnuha–: wahraʔehnúhaʔ ‹fact-he-hand-put in water› *he put his hand in water* (RC 12:29); –či–. –(i)ʔθkuha–: čęʔnaʔniʔθkúhaʔ ‹again-one=another-X-put in water› *one rebaptizes another*

(HS); -yah-.-ʔahθruha-: yahwaʔkaycʔ-ahθrúhaʔ ‹thither-fact-they-basket-put in water› *they put basket in water* (RC 10:1); -yah-.-(i)ʔθkuha-: yɛyeʔθkúhaʔ ‹thither-prediction-one-X-put in water› *one will submerge there* (RC 15:6); -athɛwuha-: rathɛwúhahs ‹he-himself-boat-puts in water› *he goes by boat, he goes by water* (HS); -aʼnɛhruha-: raʔnɛhrúhahs ‹he-himself-scalp-puts in water› *diver: he dives in, he plunges* (HS); -aʼnwenɛʼnuha-: yuʔnwenɛʼnúhɛ ‹it-itself-iron-put in water› *it is at anchor* (HS); haʔ -aʼniʔθkuhaʔT-: haʔ yɛʼniʔθkuháʔthaʔ ‹the one-oneself-X-put in water-causes› *bath* (HS).

-uhar- fasten to the end, tip. *v.r.-t.* hab: -ɸ, pnt: -, stat: -ʔ, prog: -, prp: -, dst: -, caus: -, rvs: -aku-, dat: -, inc.-ɸ-pat. rúhar *he fastens to the end, he tips* (HS); -uharaku-: ruhará·kwahs ‹he-tip-undoes› *he cuts off the end, he un-hafts it* (HS); -hehnuharaku-: rahehnuhará·kwahs ‹he-field-tip-undoes› *he takes or cuts off an end of the field* (H 2484); -hsekwaruhar-: uhsekwarúhar ‹speak-tip› *javelin* (HS); -hsi=ruhar-: rahsirúhar ‹he-wire-tips› *he threads a needle* (HS); -kerhuhar-: natkyerhúhar ‹one=another-body-tips› *one affixes one's body to the end of a pole or other pole-like instrument or thing* (H-notebook); -nɛhruhar-: yunɛhrúhaʔr ‹it-scalp-tipped› *scalp hangs from tip of pole* (RC 12:24); -nɛh=suhar-: unɛhsúhareh ‹house-tip› *the roof or top-surface of the house* (H 2484); -nɛhsuharaʔke: unɛhsuharáʔkye ‹house-tip-at› *on the top of the house* (H 2484); -nɛʼnuharaʔkehaʼnyeʔ-: unɛʼnuharaʔkyehá·ʼnyeʔ ‹hill-tip-at-going along› *going around the summit of the hill* (RC 33:5).

-uhar- wash. *v.r.-t.* hab: -ɸ, pnt: -eʔ ~ -

ʔ, stat: -ʔ, prog: -, prp: -, dst: -, caus: -T-, rvs: -, dat: -, inc.-t-~-iʔθk-pat. -čikheʔnuhar-: račikheʔnúhar ‹he-salt-washes› *he freshens* (HS); -čunuhar-: waʔnaʔčunuhà·reʔ ‹fact-one=another-torso-washed› *one washed another* (R); -(i)ʔθrehčruhar-: ruʔθrchčrúhaʔr ‹he-ride-'ness-washed› *he had washed his car* (R), waʔkheʔθrehčrúhaʔr ‹fact-I=one-ride-'ness-washed› *I washed one's car* (R), waʔkθrehčrúhaʔr ‹fact-I-ride-'ness-washed› *I washed car* (R), waʔkθrehčruhà·reʔ ‹fact-I-ride-'ness-washed› *I washed car* (R); -karuhar-: rakarúhar ‹he-debt-washes› *he indemnifies* (HS); -kθuharT-: kakθuhárnɛ ‹it-dish-wash-caused› *dishwater* (H-notebook); -kerhuhar-: natkyerhúhar ‹one=another-body-washes› *one washes one's body* (H-notebook); -nɛhsu=har-: ranɛhsúhar ‹he-house-washes› *he dedicates* (HS); -nɛhuhar-: waʔenɛhuhà·reʔ ‹fact-one-corn-washed› *one washed corn* (RC 3:53), ranɛhúhar ‹he-corn-washes› *he washes, is washing the corn* (H 2484); -nɛhuhareʔT-: yenɛhuharéʔthaʔ ‹one-corn-wash-causes› *a basket for washing corn, lit., one uses it to wash corn* (H 2484); -tu=har-: waʔktuhà·reʔ ‹fact-I-X-washed› *I washed it* (R), ratúhar ‹he-X-washes› *he washes* (HS), waʔkatuharɛ́heʔ ‹fact-it-X-wash-was going to› *washer* (R); -ʔɛyuhar-: raʔɛyúhar ‹he-cost-washes› *he pays* (HS); -či-.-ʔɛyuhar-: θhraʔɛyúhar ‹again-he-cost-washes› *he reimburses, he repays, he revenges* (HS); -ačhɛnuhar-: račhɛnúhar ‹he-himself-name-washes› *he absolves* (HS); -ačkahrɛwuhar-: ručkahrɛwúhar ‹he-himself-mouth-washes› *he gargles* (HS); -atkaruharT-: yutkaruhárnɛ ‹it-itself-debt-wash-caused› *indemnity* (HS); -aʼnɛrihstuhar-: yuʔnɛrihstúhar ‹it-itself-breathe-'ness-washes› *din* (HS); -a'niʔθkuhar -: ra'ni'ʔθkúhar ‹he-himself-X-washes› *he bathes, he is bathing* (R); haʔ -či -. -atʔęyuhar -: ha'ʔ θwat'ʔęyúhar ‹the again-it-itself-cost-washes› *retaliation* (HS); íhsʔę ti+ yah -. -ʔęyuhar -{dative I}: íhs'ʔę thweyę'ʔnat'ʔęyúharθeh ‹more so-thither-one=another-cost-washes-for› *one overpays* (HS); sé'ʔči kwà·nę -ʔęyuhar -: sé'ʔči kwà·nę nat'ʔęyúhar ‹since much one=another-cost-washes› *one overpays* (HS).

-uharaku - cut off end, unhaft. *v.s.-t.* ruhará·kwahs ‹he-tip-undoes› *he cuts off the end, he unhafts it* (HS).

-uhči - peel, remove. *v.r.-t.* hab: -ęhs, pnt: -'ʔ, stat: -ę, prog: -, prp: -ęhe-, dst: -θrę-, caus: -a'ʔT-, rvs: -, dat: -, inc.-ɸ-pat. rúhčęhs *he peels* (HS), ęhrúhči'ʔ *he peeled* (HS); -čaruhči -: račarúhčęhs ‹he-door-removes› *he is taking the door off its hinges, he unhinges door* (HS); -nęhruhči -: wa'ʔ-kayę'ʔna'ʔnęhrúhči'ʔ ‹fact-they=another-scalp-removed› *they scalped another* (RC 12:8); -nęθuhčaʔT -: yenęθuhčá'ʔtha'ʔ ‹one-potato-remove-causes› *knife or other tool for paring potatoes* (H 2484); -nęθuhči -: ranęθúhčęhs ‹he-potato-removes› *he peals potatoes, he pares potatoes* (H 2484); -riʔruhči -: rari'ʔrúhčęhs ‹he-peel-removes› *he peels it* (HS); -tahskuhči -: na'ʔtahskúhčęhs ‹one=another-domestic animal-washes› *he liberates* (HS); -či -. -(ę)taʔruhči -: ęθahrata'ʔrúhči'ʔ ‹un-

known-again-he-head-remove› *that his head be again removed* (RC 7:2); -atkęhsuhči -: ratkęhsúhčęhs ‹he-himself-face-removes› *he unmasks himself* (HS); -a'nahsuhčęhe -: ra'ʔnahsuhčęhe'ʔ ‹he-himself-foot-removes-going to› *he is going kicking it* (RC 25:13); -a'narahsuhči -: ru'ʔnarahsúhčę ‹he-himself-shoe-removed› *he took off his shoes* (R), wahra'ʔnarahsúhči'ʔ ‹fact-he-himself-shoe-removed› *he took off his shoes* (R); -a'nętihskęʔnaruhči -: yu'ʔnętihskę'ʔnarúhčę ‹it-itself-outer bark-removed› *it has removed its outer bark* (RC 32:9); -aʔriʔruhči -: ęwa'ʔ-ri'ʔrúhči'ʔ ‹prediction-it-itself-peel-removes› *it will peel off* (R); -či -. -a'nuhči -: θhra'ʔnúhčęhs ‹again-he-himself-removes› *he pays up, he repays, he retaliates* (HS).

uhęʔręʔ Canadian goose (R), wild goose (AW 85) [Jefferson «oh-henh-ren»]. *n.*

-uhk - of one kind, pure. *n.r. n-poss., n-inc., n.sfx.* -ę'ʔ. awúhkę'ʔ *of one kind, pure* (HS).

-uhriʔ - decay, fall to pieces. *v.r.-t.* hab: -θ, pnt: -, stat: -, prog: -, prp: -, dst: -, caus: -, rvs: -, dat: -, inc.-ɸ-pat. wúhri'ʔθ *it decays, it falls to pieces* (HS); -uhriʔθrę -: yawuhrí'ʔθrę· ‹it-fall to pieces-began-much› *ruins* (HS); -čiʔ = čihstuhriʔ -: yuči'ʔčihstuhrí'ʔę ‹it-flower-ruined› *wilted flower* (R); -nęh = suhriʔ -: kanęhsúhri'ʔθ ‹it-house-falls to pieces› *the house is falling to pieces, i.e., it tottering to its fall or ruin* (H 2484); haʔ -uhriʔ -: ha'ʔ yawuhrí'ʔę ‹the it-fall to pieces-began> *ruin* (HS).

-uhri?- ruin. *dv.n.s.* ha? yawuhrí?ę <the it-fall to pieces-began> *ruin* (HS).

-uhri?θrę- ruins. *dv.n.s.* yawuhrí?θrę· <it-fall to pieces-began-much> *ruins* (HS).

-uhθ(e)r- pull off, skim, strip off, take off, unstring. *v.r.-t.* hab: -ęhs, pnt: ()-?, stat: -ę, prog: -ęha'nye?-, prp: -, dst: -, caus: -ahw-, rvs: -ęku-, dat: I (-θe-/-θ), inc.-φ-pat. rúhθręhs *he pulls off, he skims, he unstrings* (HS); -(a)h=karuhθręha'nye? -: kakuhkaruhθręhá·?-nye? <they-bark-stripped off-going along> *they are stripping bark off* (RC 6:11); -hnekuhθrahw -: rahnekúhθraws <he-liquid-strip off-causes> *(he is) Christian, he sprinkles it* (HS); -hne=kuhθrahwsT -: nathnekuhθráwstha? <one=another-liquid-strip off-cause-causes> *one baptizes another* (HS); -ke?wuhθręku -: wa?'natkye?'wuhθrę́·ku? <fact-one=another-hair-strip off-undid> *one rubbed another's hair* (RC 3:13); -rę?uhθ(e)r -: wa?kayerę?úhθe?r <fact-they-tree-stripped off> *they took bark off trees* (RC 9:7); -rihstuh=θerhę -: yurihstuhθérhę· <it-metal-stripped off-much> *(it is) immaculate* (AG); -yetuhθ(e)r-: rayetúhθręhs <he-grease-strips off> *he skims* (HS); -a=tkęhsuhθręku -: wahratkęhsuhθrę́·ku? <fact-he-himself-face-strip off-undid> *he stripped off his face* (RC 26:13); -(ę)tičha?ruhθ(e)r -: ręticha?rúhθręhs <he-himself-anger-strips off> *(his) passion* (HS); -ne -. -rihuhθ(e)r -: nęhsrihúhθe?r <apart-prediction-you-matter-strip off> *you will carry the matter through to its legitimate conclusion* (R); ha? -ne -. -(ę)tičha?ruhθ(e)r -: ha? nehręticha?rúhθręhs <the apart-he-himself-anger-strips off> *his rage* (HS).

uhsęnę́·thę? just at the right time (R). *part.*

-uhsk- all of a kind, all of a sort; clear, pure. *n.r.* n-poss., n-inc., n.sfx. -ę. awúhskę *all of a sort, all of a kind; clear, pure* (HS).

-uhsku- pick (plural objects). *v.r.-t.* hab: -ahs, pnt: -ę?, stat: -ę, prog: -ęha'nye?-, prp: -, dst: -, caus: -, rvs: -, dat: -, inc.-φ-pat. Hewitt and Smith cite three anomalous forms in their manuscript dictionary that point to a stem of the form -**urku** -: ruhsúrkę *he is barefoot*, ruhsurkęhá·?nye? *he is barefoot*, and ruręhsúrkę *he is bare-legged*. All of these words are pronounced with *hs* rather than *r* in modern Tuscarora (see below). Either there were two roots, -**urku** - and -**uhsku** -, that had partially merged in late 19th century Tuscarora and are fully merged today, or there was only one root and the variation in Hewitt and Smith's dictionary needs to be explained. In the latter case, any explanation must entail the dialectal shift of syllable-final voiceless *r* to *s*. Either the root early underwent this shift and the shifted form was generalized and adopted by speakers who otherwise retain syllable-final voiceless *r* (since these speakers of modern Tuscarora have -**uhsku** - for this verb root) or Hewitt and Smith recorded the cited forms from a speaker whose dialect had undergone the shift of *r* to *s* and mistakenly assumed that where they heard syllable-final [hs] from this speaker it should be written *r*. Related forms in other Northern Iroquoian languages point to the latter explanation as the correct one and to -**uhsku** - as the inherited form of the root. rúhskwahs *he picks (plural objects)* (HS), wa?kúhskę? *I picked it (e.g., flowers)* (R); -**ahsuhsku** -: wakahsúhskę <I-foot-picked off> *I am barefoot* (R), ruhsúhskę ‹he-foot-picked off› *he is barefoot* (HS), ruhsuhskęhá·ʔnyeʔ ‹he-foot-picked off-going along› *he is barefoot* (HS); –čiʔčihstuhsku –: račiʔčihstúhskwahs ‹he-flower-picked off› *he deflowers it* (HS), waʔkčiʔčihstúhskęʔ ‹fact-I-flower-picked off› *I picked flowers* (HS); –(ę)taʔruhsku –: utaʔrúhskę ‹head-picked off› *headless* (RC 28:1), rutaʔrúhskę ‹he-head-picked off› *he is pure-headed, he is bare headed* (HS); –kerhuhsku –: rukyerhúhskę ‹he-body-picked off› *he is a-lone, he is single* (HS); –nęhsnuh = sku –: unęhsnúhskęʔ ‹seed-pick off› *the grain is unmingled, the grain is clear* (H 2484); –ręhsuhsku –: ruręhsúhskę ‹he-leg-picked off› *he is bare-legged* (HS); –ʔcharuhsku –: ruʔcharúhskę ‹he-branch-picked off› *he has lots of humor* (R); –aʔcunuhsku –: θaʔcunúhskę ‹you!-yourself-torso-pick off› *make yourself naked!, take your clothes off!* (RC 3:54); kwęhs –heruhsku –: kwęhs ahruherúhskwęk ‹no unknown-he-green-pick off› *he has not cut the weeds* (HS).

uhskwaríʔnaʔ cat's paw, wild ginger *(Asarum canadense)*. *n.*

–uhsnari – double. *v.r.-t.* hab: -, pnt: -, stat: -ę, prog: -, prp: -, dst: -, caus: -, rvs: -, dat: -, n-inc. ruhsná·ryę *he doubles them* (HS).

uhsné·krik hoot owl (R). *n.*

–uhst – year. *n.r.* n-poss., inc., n.sfx. -eh. awúhsteh *year* (R); –uhstaθe·ʔ: awuhstá·θe·ʔ ‹year-new› *New Year's Day*

(R); –uhstayahčęti –: wuhstayahčę·tiʔ ‹it-year-be curious-made› *a certain year* (RC 12:7); –či –. –uhstathaˈnyeʔ –: θwuhstathá·ʔnyeʔ ‹again-it-year-stands-going along› *yearly* (HS); –ne –. –uhstahkw –: waʔnwúhstahkw ‹fact-apart-it-year-picked up› *summertime* (R), newúhstahkw ‹apart-it-year-picks up› *springtime* (RC 15:1), neyawuhstáhkę ‹apart-it-year-picked up› *spring* (HS); –ne –. –uhstakehaˈnyeʔ –: newuhstakyehá·ʔnyeʔ ‹two-it-year-is in number-going along› *biennial* (HS); –ne+ či –. –uhstahkw –: nęθawúhstahkw ‹apart-again-unknown-it-year-pick up› *next spring* (R); ti –. –uhstihyaʔk –: ti-wuhstihyáʔkę ‹so-it-year-crossed› *it is so many years old* (RC 29:2), tyawuhstihyáʔkę ‹so-it-year-crossed› *it is that many years old* (L 38), thwaʔakuhstíhyaʔk ‹so-fact-one-year-crossed› *one is so many years old* (RC 3:25); ti+či –. –uhstęʔ –: tičawuhstęʔę ‹so-again-it-year-fall-began› *annual, every year* (HS); –aˈnuhstę –: raʔnúhstęh ‹he-himself-year-falls› *he hibernates, he winters* (HS); haʔ –uhstaˈnaˈnyeʔ –: haʔ wuhstaʔná·ʔnyeʔ ‹the it-year-stands-going along› *the current year* (HS); –yahsti – ti –. –uhstake –: kayáhstih ti-wuhstá·kye· ‹it-individual-is a group so-it-year-is in number› *century* (HS); kwęhs –aˈnuhstihsʔa –: kwęhs ahruʔnuhstíhsʔęk ‹no unknown-he-himself-year-finish› *minor* (HS).

–uhstaθe·ʔ New Year's Day. *n.s.* awuhstá·θe·ʔ ‹year-new› *New Year's Day*

(R).

uhsú·kawe·θ whale (HS). *n.*

uhtá?kę before, behind (RC 11:23). *part.* **uhta?kę́?kye** ‹before-at› *following* (RC 3:24).

uhta?kę́?kye ‹before-at› following (RC 3:24), after (AG). *part.*

-uk- blister. *v.r.-a.i.* hab: -s, pnt: -, stat: -, prog: -, prp: -, dst: -, caus: -a?T-, rvs: -, dat: -, inc.-φ-pat. rà·wuks *he is blistered* (HS); **-uk-**: awú·kę? ‹blister› *blister* (HS); **-čatuka?T-**: kačatuká?tha? ‹it-brightness-blister-causes› *it is glossy, it shines* (HS); **-čęhuka?=nahkw-**: wa?kayečęhuká?nahkw ‹fact-they-fire-blister-caused› *they used it to start fire* (RC 6:14); **-čisnuka?T-**: kačisnuká?tha? ‹it-ember-blister-causes› *it sparkles* (HS); **-hsnuka?T-**: kahsnuká?tha? ‹it-??-blister-causes› *it is radiant, it coruscates, it shines, it sparkles* (HS), rahsnuká?tha? ‹he-??-blister-causes› *he glimmers, he scintillates, he sparkles, he twinkles* (HS); **-hsnuka?T-**: uhsnuká?nęh ‹??-blister-cause› *firefly* (R); **-yakę?čruk-**: ruyakę?čruks ‹he-go out-begin-'ness-blisters› *he goes to stool* (HS); **-?nhęhsuk-**: ru?nhęhsuks ‹he-egg-blisters› *he desires to urinate (lit., "his urine chafes or blisters him")* (H 2484); **-a'nuka?T-**: wa?nuká?tha? ‹it-itself-blister-causes› *it inflames, it ulcerates* (HS); **kwęhs -a'nuka?T-**: kwęhs aryu?nú·ka?t ‹no unknown-it-itself-blister-cause› *it is uninflamed* (HS); **kwęhs -ne-.-a?=rihuka?T-**: kwęhs narę?rihuká?thek ‹no apart-unknown-it-itself-matter-blister-cause› *it is inexplicable* (HS).

-uk- blister. *n.s.* awú·kę? ‹blister› *blister* (HS).

-ukaw- smear. *v.r.-t.* hab: -, pnt: -?, stat: -, prog: -, prp: -, dst: -, caus: -, rvs: -, dat: -, n-inc. wa?kayakú·ka?w *they*

smeared it (RC 12:30).

-uka?T- inflame. *v.s.-a.i.* **-čatuka?T-**: kačatuká?tha? ‹it-brightness-blister-causes› *it is glossy, it shines* (HS); **-čęhu=ka?nahkw-**: wa?kayečęhuká?nahkw ‹fact-they-fire-blister-caused› *they used it to start fire* (RC 6:14); **-čisnuka?T-**: kačisnuká?tha? ‹it-ember-blister-causes› *it sparkles* (HS); **-hsnuka?T-**: kahsnuká?tha? ‹it-??-blister-causes› *it is radiant, it coruscates, it shines, it sparkles* (HS), rahsnuká?tha? ‹he-??-blister-causes› *he glimmers, he scintillates, he sparkles, he twinkles* (HS); **-hsnuka?T-**: uhsnuká?nęh ‹??-blister-cause› *firefly* (R); **kwęhs -a'nuka?T-**: kwęhs aryu?nú·ka?t ‹no unknown-it-itself-blister-cause› *it is uninflamed* (HS); **kwęhs -ne-.-a'rihuka?T-**: kwęhs narę?rihuká?thek ‹no apart-unknown-it-itself-matter-blister-cause› *it is inexplicable* (HS).

-ukenę- divide. *v.r.-t.* hab: -h, pnt: -?, stat: -·, prog: -, prp: -, dst: #kęha?nę?, caus: -, rvs: -, dat: -, inc.-hθ-pat. This root is unusual in that it marks the distributive with the nominal enclitic. **-hni?rukenę-**: kahni?rukyè·nęh ‹it-sod-divides› *it is underneath sod* (RC 5:15); **-ne-.-i?nyuhkwukenę-**: nęθwę?nyuhkwukyè·nę? ‹apart-you-group-divide› *you will divide your group in two* (RC 33:8); **tha+ne-.-ukenę-**: tha?nyukyé·nę· ‹unusual-two-it-divide› *between two things, intermediate* (HS); **tha+ne-.-čtęhrukenę-**: tha?nekačtęhrukyé·nę· ‹unusual-apart-it-stone-divided› *between the stones* (AG); **tha+ne-.-hθukenę-**: tha?nyehθukyé·nę· ‹unusual-apart-one-X-divided› *one's crotch* (RC 30:35); **tha+ne-.-hsu?kukenę-. #kęha?nę?**: tha?nehrahsu?kukyenęhkęha?nę? ‹unusual-apart-he-finger-divides-many› *to tips of each one of his fingers* (RC 14:5).

-ukęy - shell. *v.r.-t.* hab: -ahs, pnt: -ɸ, stat: -, prog: -, prp: -, dst: -, caus: -, rvs: -, dat: -, inc.-ɸ-pat. rukę̀·yahs *he shells* (HS), ęhrú·kęy *he will shell* (HS); **-nęhsnukęy -**: kanęhsnukę̀·yahs ‹it-seed-shells› *it shells the grain, from ears of corn or wheat heads* (H 2484); **-nęhukęy -**: ranęhukę̀·yahs ‹he-corn-shells› *he shells, is shelling the corn* (H 2484).

ukę́ʔ or (RC 12:2) *part.*

-ukęʔ -less. *n.b.sfx.* **-a'nwęʔeręʔčrukęʔ**: ra'nwęʔeręʔčrú·kęʔ ‹he-play music-'ness-less› *he is songless, he is tuneless* (HS); **-čikuhsukęʔ**: učikuhsú·kęʔ ‹hoof-less› *hoofless* (HS); **-ęrihshukęʔ**: rawęrihshú·kęʔ ‹he-breathe-'ness-less› *he is breathless* (HS); **-ęθrukęʔ**: awęθrú·kęʔ ‹taste-less› *tasteless* (HS); **-ę='nukęʔ**: rawę'nú·kęʔ ‹he-day-less› *he is distracted* (HS); **-(ę)ʔtikęhnęhčru=kęʔ**: ru'tikęhnęhčrú·kęʔ ‹he-mind-fall-'ness-less› *he is thoughtless* (HS); **-(ę)ʔtikęhrukęʔ**: ru'tikęhrú·kęʔ ‹he-mind-less› *he is boisterous, he is impudent, he is mindless, he is rash, he is thoughtless* (HS); **-hsuʔθrukęʔ**: uhsu'ʔθrú·kęʔ ‹point-less› *pointless* (HS); **-hwihstukęʔ**: rahwihstú·kęʔ ‹he-money-less› *he is impotent, he is insolvent* (HS); **-kerhukęʔ**: yukyerhú·kęʔ ‹it-body-less› *incorporeal* (HS); **-nęh=snukęʔ**: runęhsnú·kęʔ ‹he-seed-less› *he is grainless, he is without grain* (H 2484); **-nęhukęʔ**: runęhú·kęʔ ‹he-corn-less› *he is cornless, without corn, has no corn* (H 2484); **-rętukęʔ**: karętú·kęʔ ‹it-magic-less› *ginseng (Palax quinquefolius)* (H-notebook); **-θręhnukęʔ**: ruθręhnú·kęʔ ‹he-dream-less› *he is sleepless* (HS); **-wętukęʔ**: ruwętú·kęʔ ‹he-word-less› *he is dumb* (HS); **-ʔne=hahčrukęʔ**: ru'nehahčrú·kęʔ ‹he-shame-'ness-less› *he is immodest, he is shameless, he has lost all shame* (HS); **-ʔnhęhsukęʔ**: ru'nhęhsú·kęʔ ‹he-eggs-less› *eunuch* (HS); **-ʔrhwęθukęʔ**: u'rhwęθú·kęʔ ‹tail-less› *tailless* (HS); **-a'nęnhehkčrukęʔ**: ra'nęnhehkčrú·kęʔ ‹he-himself-be alive-instrument-'ness-less› *he is inanimate* (HS), u'nęnhehkčrú·kęʔ ‹self-be alive-instrument-'ness-less› *lifeless* (HS); **-a'niʔnęręh=črukęʔ**: ru'niʔnęręhčrú·kęʔ ‹he-himself-pity-'ness-less› *he is implacable, he is pitiless, he is remorseless* (HS).

ú·kęʔt between (RC 3:69) *part.*

-ukr - be loose, be slack. *v.r.-s.i.* stat: -ę·, prog: -, prp: -, dst: -, caus: -ę'ʔT-, rvs: -, dat: -, inc.-ɸ-pat. **tha -. -ukr -**: thyawú·krę· ‹unusual-it-is loose› *it is loose, it is slack* (HS); thęyawú·krę·k ‹unusual-prediction-it-be loose› *it will be loose, it will be slack* (HS); **-u=kręʔT -**: rukrę́ʔtha' ‹he-be loose-causes› *he defaces it, he impairs it, he perverts it, he spoils it* (HS); **-ę̊kʷeh=stukręʔT -**: rawękwehstukrę́ʔtha' ‹he-human-'ness-be loose-causes› *he unmans* (HS); **-(ę)ʔtikęhrukręʔT -**: na'tikęhrukrę́ʔtha' ‹one=another-mind-be loose-causes› *one debauches* (HS);

-**yehsukrę°T** -: rayehsukrę́°tha° ‹he-ap-pearance-be loose-causes› *he disfig-ures* (HS); **ti** -. -**ukr** -: tyawú·krę· ‹so-it-is loose› *it is lax, it is limber, it is loose, it is slack* (HS); **ti** -. -**ukrahkw** -: tihrukráhkhwa° ‹so-he-is loose-instru-ment› *he loosens it* (HS).

-**ukr** - bits, fragments, rubbish. *n.r.* n-poss., n-inc., n.sfx. -i° ~ -eh. This noun root frequently occurs as the second element of noun stems. awú·-kri° *bits, fragments, rubbish* (HS); -**ehčrukr** -: awehčrú·kri° ‹little-'ness-rubbish› *stuff, trifles* (HS); -**ehukr** -: awehú·kri° ‹little-rubbish› *stuff, trifles* (HS); -**hsyukr** -: rahsyú·kri° ‹he-X-rub-bish› *he is careless, he is improvident, he is prodigal, he is wasteful* (HS); -**nęθukr** -: unęθú·kri° ‹potato-rubbish› *rejected or cast away potatoes, pieces of decayed old potatoes* (H 2484); -**nęθahčrukr** -: unęθahčrú·kri° ‹potato-'ness-rubbish› *rejected or cast away potatoes, pieces of decayed old po-tatoes* (H 2484); -**rihwahčrukr** -: urih-wahčrú·kri° ‹matter-'ness-rubbish› *tri-fles* (HS); -**ta'narukr** -: uta°narú·kri° ‹bread-rubbish› *crumbs of bread* (HS); -**°nhęhsukr** -: u°nhęhsú·kreh ‹egg-rub-bish› *urine (disgusting), foul or dis-gusting urine: a slovenly or slatternly person so filthy as to emit an odor of urine* (H 2484), u°nhęhsú·kri° ‹egg-rubbish› *what is exuded from eggs or testicles* (H 2484); -**°nhęhsukrakęw**: u°nhęhsú·krakęw ‹egg-rubbish-in› *in, amidst urine (that is offensive)* (H 24 84); -**°nhęhsukraθ** -: ka°nhęhsú·kra·θ ‹it-egg-rubbish-smells› *it emits a foul odor of urine (said of an animal)* (H 2484); -**°nhęhsukraθhu** -: ru°nhęhsu-kráθhwahs ‹he-egg-rubbish-smell-causes› *he smells (filthy) urine* (H 24 84); -**°nhęhsukratet°** -: ru°nhęhsú·kra-

te°t ‹he-egg-rubbish-lined› *he has be-side him a slatternly woman, a wo-man disgustingly filthy* (H 2484); -**°nhęhsukrayę(T)** -: ra°nhęhsú·krayę° ‹he-egg-rubbish-lays› *he lies in offen-sive urine; his garments emit the dis-gusting odor of urine* (H 2484); -**°nhęhsukra°ke**: u°nhęhsukrá°kye ‹egg-rubbish-at› *on foul urine* (H 24 84); -**°nhęhsukryęti** -: ka°nhęhsukryę́·-ti° ‹it-egg-rubbish-extends› *he lies ex-tended in (foul) urine, its urine lies spanned out* (H 2484).

-**ukrę°T** - deface, impair, pervert, spoil. *v.s.-t.* rukrę́°tha° ‹he-be loose-causes› *he defaces it, he impairs it, he per-verts it, he spoils it* (HS).

-**uks** mythic crow-like bird. *n.r.* n-poss., n-inc., n.sfx. -. Á·kuks *mythic crow-like bird* (RC 12:5), há°uks *mythic crow-like bird* (RC 12:5).

-**uk** - spread out. *v.r.-s.i.* stat: -ę·, prog: -, prp: -, dst: -atyę-, caus: -ahT- ~ehT-, rvs: -, dat: -, inc.-φ-ag./pat. -u° = čiruk - : ru°čirú·kwahs ‹he-sting-spreads out› *he smarts, it stings him* (HS); -**a'nuk atyę** -: ra°nukwá·tyęh ‹he-himself-spreads out-much› *he hurts himself or causes a relapse of sickness* (H-notebook); -**a°rihuk ahT** -: ra°rihú·kwaht ‹he-himself-matter-spread out-causes› *he is haughty, he is imperti-nent, he is impudent* (HS), ru°rihu-kwáhnę· ‹he-himself-matter-spread out-caused› *he is audacious, he is boastful* (HS); -**ne** -. -**°θkwehsukwehT** - {dative III}: neyu°θkwehsukwehná·ti· ‹apart-it-round block of wood-spread out-caused-for› *cylinder* (AG) -**ne** -. -**at°wahθruk** -: neyut°wahθrú·kwę· ‹a-part-it-itself-drop-is spread out› *drops spread out* (RC 2:14); -**ne** -. -**a'nu** = k ahT - : nehra°nukwáhtha° ‹apart-he-himself-be spread out-causes› *he dis-*

arranges, he scatters (HS); -ne-. -a'nu =
k"ahnahnę -: newa'?nukwahnáhnęh ‹a-
part-it-itself-be   spread   out-causes-
much› *it splatters* (RC 3:55); -ne-. -a'? =
rihuk"ahT -: nehra'?rihukwáhtha'? ‹a-
part-he-himself-matter-be spread out-
causes› *he announces* (HS), neyu'?-
rihukwáhtha'? ‹apart-it-itself-matter-be
spread out-causes› *proclamation* (HS);
ha'? -ne-. -a'?rihuk"ahT -: ha'? nehru'?-
rihukwáhnę· ‹the apart-he-himself-
matter-be spread out-caused› *his announcement of* (HS), ha'? neyu'?rihu-
kwáhnę· ‹the apart-it-itself-matter-be
spread out-causes› *declaration* (HS).

-ukyę'?neT - trickle. *v.r.-a.i.* hab: -ha'?,
pnt: -, stat: -, prog: -, prp: -, dst: -,
caus: -, rvs: -, dat: -, n-inc. wukyę'?-
né·tha'? *it trickles* (HS).

ù·nę at this time, at that time, now, when
(RC 1:8) *part.* ù·nę ha'? ‹now the›
immediately (R); ù·nę hésnę· ‹now
then› *when* (R); ù·nę séher ‹now also›
finally (R); ù·nę sé'?či hę·we ‹now
since where› *isn't that awful?* (R).

ù·nę ha'? ‹now the› immediately (R).
part.

ù·nę hésnę· ‹now then› when (R). *part.*

ù·nę séher ‹now also› finally (R). *part.*

ù·nę sé'?či hę·we ‹now since where› isn't
that awful (R). *part.*

Unęta'?kyehá·ka·'? Onondaga (people)
(AG). *n.*

-unhik - make a mistake. *v.r.-a.i.* hab: -s,
pnt: -ɸ, stat: (Hewitt & Smith give the
anomalous form runhí'?ę *he has made
mistakes*), prog: -, prp: -, dst: -, caus:

-, rvs: -, dat: -, n-inc. rúnhiks *he is
making a mistake* (HS), ęhrúnhik *he
will be making a mistake* (HS).

Unyut'?á·ka·'? Oneida people (archaic)
(AG). *n.*

-ur - coarse; whole. *n.r.* n-poss., n-inc.,
n.sfx. -. à·wur *coarse; whole (of
things)* (HS).

-ur - cover. *v.r.-t.* hab: -s, pnt: -'?, stat: -ę
~ -e'? ~ -'?, prog: -, prp: -, dst: -,
caus: -hT-, rvs: -, dat: -, inc.-ɸ-pat.
The final *r* of the root is typically lost
before suffixes that begin with the
laryngeal consonants *h* and '? (including the punctual aspect suffix and
the rare -'? stative aspect suffix). íhruč
he covers (HS); -(a)hčuhčr -: uhčúhčreh ‹fist-cover-'ness› *gloves, mittens*
(R); -(a)hčuhčrę -: ruhčúhčrę'? ‹he-fist-
cover-'ness-possesses› *he is wearing
gloves* (HS); -(a)hkarur -: ráhkaruč
‹he-bark-covers› *he panels* (HS), ruh-
karù·rę ‹he-bark-covered› *he paneled*
(HS); -atkęhθrur -: ętkę́hθru'? ‹fact-it-
pus-covered› *it got pustular* (R);
-atkęhθrur -.#ú'?y: ętkęhθru'?ú'?y ‹fact-
it-pus-covered-great› *it was covered
greatly with pus* (RC 21:3); -čę =
huhkw -: učę́húhkweh ‹fire-cover-instrument› *type of fire-witch, flickering-light witch* (RC 7:8); -či'?tkwah =
nur -: kači'?tkwáhnuč ‹it-yellow-covers›
it grows yellow (HS); -ęrahθur -: ya-
węrahθù·rę ‹it-moss-covered› *it is
mossy* (HS); -hehnur -: ruhehnù·re'?
‹he-field-covered› *he is covering the
field (by his labors)* (H 2484); -he =

---

ruhkw –: uherúhkweh ‹green-cover-instrument› *grass* (R); **–hseyur** –: uhsè·yur ‹ear of corn-cover› *ear of corn* (R); **–hsęryuhkw** –: uhsęryúhkweh ‹savor-cover-instrument› *odor, savor, steam* (HS); **–hsyuhčr** –: rahsyúhčreh ‹he-palm of hand-cover-'ness› *he pampers it* (HS); **–hwihstur** –: yuhwíhstu' ‹it-money-covered› *lucrative* (HS); **–kerhuhčr** –: ukyerhúhčreh ‹body-cover-'ness› *clothes, coat, dress* (R); **–ker=huhčręti** –: rakyerhuhčrę́·tih ‹he-body-cover-'ness-makes› *tailor; he makes clothes* (HS); **–kerhur** –: natkyérhuč ‹one=another-body-covers› *one dresses another* (HS); **–kęhuhčr** –: ukęhúhčrch ‹hem-cover-'ness› *ribbon, silk* (HS); **–kęhur** –: yekę́huč ‹one-hem-covers› *one covers, one hems, one ribbons* (HS); **–kę'θruhčr** –: ukę'θrúhčreh ‹support-cover-'ness› *pillow case* (HS); **–nehsur** –: runéhsuh ‹he-film-covers› *he has film, he films* (HS); **–nęhruhčr** –: unęhrúhčreh ‹scalp-cover-'ness› *hat* (R); **–nęhrur** –: ranęhrù·rę ‹he-scalp-covered› *he shears* (HS), ęhranę́hru'r ‹prediction-he-scalp-cover› *he will shear* (HS); **–nęhsnuhkw** –: unęhsnúhkweh ‹seed-cover-instrument› *samp* (H 2484); **–nęhsnuhkwętya'T** –: yenęhsnuhkwętyá'tha' ‹one-seed-cover-instrument-make-causes› *one uses it to make samp* (H 2484); **–wisur** –: kawí·suč ‹it-ice-covers› *it covers with ice, it freezes* (HS), yuwisù·rę ‹it-ice-covered› *icy* (HS); **–yuhkuhčr** –: uyuhkúhčreh ‹border-cover-'ness› *lace* (HS); **–yuhkur** –: yeyúhkuč ‹one-border-covers› *one borders it, one makes a border* (HS), rayúhkuč ‹he-border-covers› *he rims it* (HS); **–'ęyuhT** –: ye'ęyúhtha' ‹one-enclosed area-cover-causes› *pasture* (HS); **–ne** –.–(a)h=karuhT** –: neyuhkarúhne' ‹apart-it-

bark-cover-causes› *wild geranium (Geranium maculatum)* (H-notebook); **–ne** –.–ke'θrur** –: nehrukyé'θru' ‹apart-he-frown-covered› *he is grave* (H-notebook); **ti** –.–ę̈nhuhskwarihę** –: ti-węnhuhskwaríhę· ‹so-it-be alive-cover-was feeble-much› *breath quivered* (RC 21:8); **–ačhęryuhkwa'nihr** –: wačhęryuhkwá'nihč ‹it-itself-savor-cover-instrument-stands up› *it exhales* (HS); **–atkęhsur** –: utkęhsù·rę ‹self-face-covered› *False Face, mask* (HS), yutkęhsù·rę ‹it-itself-face-covered› *mask* (AW 46); **–atkę'θrur** –: watkę́'θruh ‹it-itself-support-covers› *it forms matter, it suppurates* (HS); **–atkerhur** –: rutkyerhù·rę ‹he-himself-body-covered› *he has a coat on* (RC 2:1); **–a'neh=karur** –: yu'nehkarù·rę ‹it-itself-bark-covered› *paneling* (HS); **–a'nekhwah=ruhT** –: ye'nekhwahrúhtha' ‹one-oneself-food-put up-cover-causes› *tablecloth* (HS).

–urę – be damp, be moist. *v.r.-s.i.* stat: -', prog: -, prp: -, dst: -, caus: -, rvs: -, dat: -, n-inc. yawù·rę' *it is damp, it is moist* (HS).

–ⁿurę – split. *v.r.-t.* hab: -hs ~ -h, pnt: -·', stat: -', prog: -'nye'-, prp: -, dst: -hsthę-, caus: -'T-, rvs: -, dat: -, inc.-φ ~-(i)'θk-ag./pat. With the exception of the first four examples, this root requires the dualic. **–(ę)'teyurę'T** –: ru'teyurę́'tha' ‹he-crowd-split-causes› *he announces (something), he denounces (someone)* (HS); **–hskarurę** –: Skarù·rę' ‹flax-split› *Tuscarora* (R); **–(i)'θkurę'nye'** –: yu'θkurę́·'nye' ‹it-X-split-going along› *whirlwind* (HS); **–krirurę** –: krirù·rę' ‹cotton-split› *whiteman* (RC 30:1) [Lawson «Nickreruroh» 'English-man']; **–ne** –.–ⁿurę** –: neθù·rę ‹apart-you-split› *split it!* (R), nehrù·ręhs ‹apart-he-splits› *he splits*

(HS), neθnù·rẹh ⟨apart-you two-split⟩ *you two are splitting it* (R), newakú·rẹ· ⟨apart-I-split⟩ *I had split it* (R), wa'tkù·rẹ·' ⟨fact-apart-I-split⟩ *I split it* (R), naryawú·rẹ·k ⟨apart-unknown-it-split⟩ *that it split* (RC 30:45); –ne –. –ⁿurẹhsthẹ –: newakurẹhsthẹ· ⟨apart-I-split-much⟩ *I had split it* (R); –ne –. –ẹhrurẹ –: nehrẹhrù·rẹhs ⟨apart-he-dirt-splits⟩ *he plows* (HS); –ne –. –ẹkhwyu = rẹ –: neyawẹkhwyú·rẹ· ⟨apart-it-tell a fable-split⟩ *fabulous* (HS); –ne –. –hwẹ'khạrurẹ –: nekahwẹ'kharurẹhshahk ⟨apart-it-board-split⟩ *sawmill* (HS); –ne –. –rẹ'urẹhsthẹ –.#ú'y: wa'tkarẹ'urẹhsthẹ'ú'y ⟨fact-apart-it-tree-split-much-great⟩ *it split great tree in two* (RC 30:28); –ne –. –rẹhyurẹ –: nẹhsrẹhyú·rẹ·' ⟨apart-prediction-you-sky-split⟩ *you will go south* (RC 3:38); tha –. –rẹhyurẹ'T –: thahrarẹhyù·rẹ't ⟨unusual-fact-he-sky-split⟩ *he splits the sky* (RC 14:5); –ne –. –'rhuhkwạrurẹ –: nehra'rhuhkwarù·rẹh ⟨apart-he-cultiver-be in-splits⟩ *he harrows it* (HS); –ne+či –. –'rhuhkwạrurẹ –: nẹču'rhuhkwarú·rẹ·' ⟨apart-fact-again-it-cultiver-be in-split⟩ *it stirred land, it divided land, it poked up through land* (HS); –ne –. –a'nurẹ –: neyu'nú·rẹ ⟨apart-it-itself-split⟩ *crack, crevice; it is split* (HS); –ne –. –atkẹhsurẹ –: nehrutkẹhsú·rẹ· ⟨apart-he-himself-face-split⟩ *he is scarred on his face* (H-notebook); –ne –. –a'rihurẹ –: nehru'rihú·rẹ ⟨apart-he-himself-matter-split⟩ *he is guilty of a crime* (H-notebook).

–ⁿuri – stir. *v.r.-t.* hab: -h ~ -ha', pnt: -' ~ -e', stat: -·, prog: -, prp: -, dst: -ahnẹ- ~ -ehẹ-, caus: -(a)'T-, rvs: -, dat: III (-ati-/-ẹ-). inc.-φ-ag./pat. weθnù·ri' *you two mixed it, you two stirred it* (R); –ⁿuryahnẹ –: ẹwuryáhnẹ' ⟨prediction-it-stir-much⟩ *it will shake it up* (R), ruryáhnẹh ⟨he-stirs-much⟩ *he moves it* (HS); –(a)čẹhuryahnẹ –: ẹhsčẹhuryáhnẹ·' ⟨prediction-you-fire-stir-much⟩ *you will poke up the fire* (R); –(a)čẹhuri'thẹ –: račẹhuri'thẹh ⟨he-fire-stir-causes-much⟩ *he pokes the fire, he stirs the fire* (HS); –čha' = ruri –: wakcha'rú·ri· ⟨I-anger-stirred⟩ *I am mad* (R) [Lawson «Cotcheroore» 'Angry'], rucha'rú·ri· ⟨he-anger-stirred⟩ *he raves* (HS), rucha'ruríhahk ⟨he-anger-stirred⟩ *he was angry* (R), wa'ucha'rù·ri' ⟨fact-it-anger-stirred⟩ *it got mad* (RC 31:10); –čha'ruryehẹ –: yucha'ruryéhẹ' ⟨it-bile-stir-much⟩ *it angers them* (RC 26:7); –či'čihstuhri' –: yuči'čihstuhrí'ẹ ⟨it-flower-ruined⟩ *wilted flower* (R); –či'tkwahnuri –{dative III}: wakči'tkwahnuryá·ti·k ⟨I-yellow-stirred-for⟩ *I am feeling bilious* (L 80); –(ẹ)'tikẹhrurya'T –: u'tikẹhrú·rya't ⟨mind-stir-cause⟩ *amusement* (HS); –hẹhsuri –: rahẹhsù·rih ⟨he-ear-stirs⟩ *bully* (HS); –nẹhwạruri –: ranẹhwarù·rih ⟨he-brain-stirs⟩ *he bellows, he roars* (HS); –rihurya'T –: rarihuryá'tha' ⟨he-matter-stir-causes⟩ *he neglects it* (HS); –θrẹhnuri –: wahraθrẹhnù·ri' ⟨fact-he-dream-stirred⟩ *he awoke* (RC 8:15); –wẹturi –: ruwẹtú·ri·

‹he-word-stirred› *he moans, he murmurs, he mutters* (RC 3:71), yuwętú·ri· ‹it-word-stirred› *resonant* (HS); –ʔnhęhsuri –: raʔnhęhsù·rih ‹he-egg-stirs› *intruder* (HS); –či –. –rihuri –: θakayęʔnaʔrihú·ryeʔ ‹again-fact-they=another-matter-stirred› *they made fun of him* (AW 56); –ne –. –ęhuri –: newęhú·ryeh ‹apart-it-fine grain meal-stir› *porridge* (HS); ti –. –aʔwnuri –: tiwaʔwnù·rih ‹so-it-earth-stirs› *it disturbs earth* (RC 12:4); –a'nuri –: waʔkaʔnù·riʔ ‹fact-I-myself-stirred› *I drove* (R), raʔnù·rih ‹he-himself-stirs› *he drives* (HS); –a'nuryahnę –: wahraʔnuryáhnę·ʔ ‹fact-he-himself-stirred-much› *he struggled* (RC 7:2), ruʔnuryáhnę· ‹he-himself-stirred-much› *he made an attempt* (RC 8:21); –athehnuri –: rathehnù·rih ‹he-himself-field-stirs› *he is driving obnoxious vermin and beasts from the field, he is a scarecrow* (H 2484); –athęhsuri –: rathęhsù·rih ‹he-himself-ear-stirs› *he disquiets himself so as not to hear something disagreeable, he is disturbed* (HS); –a'naʔwnuri –: waʔnaʔwnù·rih ‹it-itself-earth-stirs› *it drives earth* (RC 12:15); –a'nęʔtikękhruri –: yęʔnęʔtikęhruríhaʔ ‹one-oneself-mind-stirs› *one amuses oneself* (RC 31:4); –aʔri = huryaʔT –: naʔnaʔrihuryáʔthaʔ ‹one=another-matter-stir-causes› *one is abusing another, one is teasing another* (R), aręʔrihú·ryaʔt ‹unknown-it-itself-matter-stir-cause› *that it bother it, that it make it nasty, that it spoil it* (RC 3:22), raʔrihuryáʔthaʔ ‹he-himself-matter-stir-causes› *he abuses, he stultifies, he trifles with it* (HS), nęyęʔnaʔaʔrihú·ryaʔt ‹two-prediction-one=another-self-matter-stir-cause› *one will mistreat another two* (RC 27:31); kwęhs –a'nuryahnę –: kwęhs ahraʔnuryahnę-

hek ‹no unknown-he-himself-stir-much› *he is inactive* (HS), kwęhs aręʔnuryahnęhek ‹no unknown-it-itself-stir-much› *it is immovable* (HS); –ʔnewak – –a'nuri –: uʔné·wa·k waʔnù·rih ‹ghost it-itself-stirs› *pussytoes (Antennaria* sp.) (R).

–uruk – cover. *v.r.-t.* hab: -s, pnt: -, stat: -, prog: -, prp: -, dst: -, caus: -T-, rvs: -, dat: -, inc.-ɸ-pat. rù·ruks *he covers it* (HS); –rętuʔčrurukT –: yurętuʔčrurúkthaʔ ‹it-tree-cover-'ness-cover-causes› *pall* (HS).

–ⁿuryahnę – move, shake up. *v.s.-t.* ęwuryáhnę·ʔ ‹prediction-it-stir-much› *it will shake it up* (R), ruryáhnęh ‹he-stirs-much› *he moves it* (HS).

–uθkrir – fumble. *v.r.-t.* hab: -ęhs, pnt: -ʔ, stat: -, prog: -, prp: -, dst: -, caus: -, rvs: -, dat: -, n-inc. ruθkrì·ręhs *he fumbles it* (HS), ęhrúθkriʔr *he will fumble it* (HS).

uθę́·theʔ until (RC 30:1). *part.*

–uθʔ – caul, covering. *n.r.* n-poss., n-inc., n.sfx. -eh. awú·θʔeh *caul, covering* (HS).

–ut be in an upright position, stand. *v.r.-s.i.* stat: -ɸ, prog: -, prp: -, dst: -, caus: -, rvs: -, dat: -, inc.-ɸ-pat. Requires an incorporated noun root. **–hehnut:** yuhéhnu·t ‹it-field-stood› *it shows a part of the field, i.e., it leaves a part of the field, there is part of the field left* (H 2484); –(i)ʔnhahnut.#áh: yuʔnhahnu·tʔáh ‹it-branch-stood-little› *shoot (of a plant)* (HS); –nęhsut: kanę́hsu·t ‹it-house-stood› *the house stands* (H 2484), yunę́hsu·t ‹it-house-stood› *its house stands, there is room in the house to spare* (H 2484); –ne –. –čtęhrut: nekačtę́hru·t ‹apart-it-stone-stood› *masonry* (HS); –t –. –ę'nut: nyawę́·ʔnu·t ‹hither-it-day-stood› *dawn* (HS); –atkạrut –: yękyátkạru·t ‹we two-

debt-stand⟩ *I owe another or you, another or you owe me* (SH 375); **-a'nę =
nęhsut:** ru'nęnęhsu·t ⟨he-himself-house-stood⟩ *his house stood* (RC 3: 50).

Utekwahtę'áh The-Bear-Cub (Chief of the Bear Clan) (H-Handbook). *n.*

-uthę - wound. *v.r.-t.* hab: -, pnt: -', stat: -, prog: -, prp: -, dst: -, caus: -, rvs: -, dat: -, n-inc. wahrú·thę' *he wounded* (AW 62).

-uwan -/-uwan - be chief. *v.r.-s.i.* stat: -ę·, prog: -, prp: -, dst: -ha'nę', caus: -a'T-, rvs: -, dat: II (-ati-/-ę-), inc.-k-ag./pat. **-kuwan -:** rakuwà·nę· ⟨he-X-is chief⟩ *(he is a) chief* (RC 3:50) [Gallatin ⟨yaikowaunuh⟩ 'Chief'], wakkuwà·nę· ⟨I-X-am chief⟩ *I am chief* (M 87), kayę'natkuwà·nę· ⟨they=another-X-are chief⟩ *their chief* (RC 12:5); **-kuwan -.#ha'nę':** kayekuwanęhá'nę' ⟨they-X-are chief-many⟩ *they are chiefs* (RC 26:11); **-kuwan -.#kęhe':** rukuwanękę́he' ⟨he-X-is a chief-deceased⟩ *dead chief, former chief* (RC 12:10); **-kuwana'T -:** rakuwaná'tha' ⟨he-be a chief-causes⟩ *he exalts it* (HS), ukuwaná'tha' ⟨be a chief-cause⟩ *clan mother* (RC 7:7); *a mock chief, a little old man* (HS); **-kuwanęhčr -:** u-kuwanęhčreh ⟨X-be a chief-'ness⟩ *chiefship* (HS); **-rihuwan -{dative III}:** na'rihuwaná·tih ⟨one=another-matter-is chief-for⟩ *one disclaims another, one sermonizes another* (HS); **-rihu = wana'T -:** rarihuwaná'tha' ⟨he-matter-be chief-causes⟩ *he preaches* (HS),

θrihù·wana')t ⟨you!-matter-be chief⟩ *announce it!, preach!* (MP); **ha' -rihu = wana'T -:** ha' rarihuwaná'tha' ⟨the he-matter-be chief-causes⟩ *he preaches* (HS); **ha' kę' -rihuwana'nahkw -:** ha' kę' yerihuwana'náhkhwa' ⟨the where one-matter-be chief-causes-instrument⟩ *pulpit* (HS); **Twa'á·ka·' -uwan -:** Twa'á·ka·' rakuwá·nę· ⟨Seneca he-X-is chief⟩ *a Seneca chief* (AG).

ù·wa' owl (RC 27:title). *n.*

ù·wa' thimbleberry *(Rubus occidentalis)* (H-notebook). *n.*

uwá'čeh elsewhere (L 62). *n.*

Uyá·ta' Cherokee (RC 32:1). *n.*

uyá'či it is queer (HS). *part.*

uya'kwáher any large prehistoric beast (e.g., dinosaur, mastodon), behemoth, hyena, mythic bear, tough meat (RC 29:1). *n.*

#úy' augmentative. *enc.* Variant used in the Western dialect and by some speakers of the Eastern dialect.

-u'awi - float (on air). *v.r.-s.i.* stat: -', prog: -, prp: -, dst: -hθę-, caus: -, rvs: -, dat: -, inc.-??-pat. Found only with an incorporated noun root present. **-čunu'awihθę -:** Čunu'awíhθę' ⟨torso-float-many⟩ *Naked-Bodies-Floating (female proper name)* (RC 24:4); **-(ę)'teyu'awi -:** yu'teyu'à·wi' ⟨it-crowd-floats⟩ *crowd, moving flock, swarm* (HS); **-kerhu'awi -:** yukyerhu'-à·wi' ⟨it-body-floats⟩ *body floated along* (RC 3:75); **-rihu'awi -:** Yurihu'-à·wi' ⟨it-matter-floats⟩ *Indian name given to Mrs. Bowman, advertising*

---

manager in charge of Carborundum Band—"a song through the air." from radio broadcasting (L 16).

-uʔčir- suck. *v.r.-a.i.* hab: -haʔ, pnt: -, stat: -, prog: -, prp: -, dst: -ahnę-, caus: -aʔT-, rvs: -, dat: -, inc.-ɸ-pat. ruʔčírhaʔ *he sucks* (HS); **-uʔčiraʔT-**: wuʔčiráʔthaʔ ‹it-suck-causes› *it sucks it* (RC 2:3); **-uʔčirahnę-**: ękuʔčiráhnęʔ ‹prediction-I-suck-many› *I will suck them* (RC 25:10); **-ʔaruʔčir-**: raʔaruʔčírhaʔ ‹he-lower lip-sucks› *he kisses* (HS).

-uʔčiraʔT- suck. *v.s.-t.* wuʔčiráʔthaʔ ‹it-suck-causes› *it sucks it* (RC 2:3).

-uʔk(e)r- float (on water). *v.r.-a.i.* hab: ()-ɸ ~ ()-haʔ, pnt: -ęʔ, stat: -ę, prog: -, prp: -ahte-, dst: -awę-, caus: -, rvs: -aku-, dat: -, inc.-ɸ- ~ -(i)ʔθk-ag./pat. yawúʔkyer *it floats* (HS), yawuʔkyérhaʔ *(it) is floating around in it* (L 53); **-uʔkrahte-**: yawuʔkráhteʔ ‹it-floated-going to› *it floats along, it drifts* (HS), *it is floating* (L 53); **-uʔkrahtehnęheʔ**: yawuʔkrahtehnę́·heʔ ‹it-float-going to-much-remote› *it has floated* (L 53); **-uʔkrahteʔ-**: yawuʔkráhteʔθ ‹it-float-going to-begins› *it drifts (floats)* (HS), *it is floating (has been and still is ?)* (L 53), yawuʔkrahtéʔθhahk ‹it-float-going to-began› *it had floated (but no longer)* (L 53); **tha-.-uʔk(e)r-**: thyawúʔkrę ‹unusual-it-floated› *it is lax, it is loose* (HS); **ti-.-uʔk(e)r-**: thwaʔawúʔkręʔ ‹so-fact-it-floated› *it floated on it* (RC 5:1); **-(i)ʔθkuʔkrawę-**: yuʔθkuʔkrá·wę· ‹it-X-floated-many› *some float on it* (RC 3:76), kakuʔθkuʔkrá·wę· ‹they-X-floated-many› *they were floating around* (RC 3:78); **-nęh=suʔk(e)r-**: yunęhsúʔkyer ‹it-house-floats› *the house floats, is floating (the liquid is understood)* (H 2484); **-nęh=suʔkrahte-**: yunęhsuʔkráhteʔ ‹it-house-

float-going to› *the house goes floating along* (H 2484); **-nęhuʔkręr-**: ranęhuʔkrę̀·rahs ‹he-corn-float-leaves behind› *he is taking out the floating corn* (H 2484); **-ne+t-.-kerhuʔkrahte-**: nęʔna-yakukyerhuʔkráhteʔ ‹apart-fact-hither-one-body-floated-going to› *one's body was floating* (RC 3:77); **-aꞌnuʔ=krahkw-**: raʔnuʔkráhkhwaʔ ‹he-him-self-floats-instrument› *he floats* (HS), yuʔnuʔkráhkę ‹it-itself-floated-instrument› *it is floating* (HS); **-aꞌnuʔ=krakwahte-**: waʔnuʔkrakwáhteh ‹it-itself-float-undoes-going to› *it is floating up* (RC 3:76); **-či-.-atkerhuʔ=k(e)r-**: θahratkyerhúʔkrahk ‹again-fact-he-himself-body-floated› *he came floating back up* (RC 3:90).

-uʔkT- end. *v.r.-a.i.* hab: -haʔ, pnt: -ęʔ, stat: -ɸ, prog: -, prp: -, dst: -, caus: -, rvs: -ęhsi- ~ -ęku-, dat: -, inc.-ɸ-ag./pat. With the dualic, this root takes on the meaning of *bend* and takes a different set of aspect suffixes (hab: -ęhs, pnt: -, stat: -ę). In addition, the stem with the dualic can occur with either of two different reversive suffixes, with different meanings. **-ne-. -uʔkT-**: nehrúʔknęhs ‹apart-he-ends› *he bends it, he turns it over* (HS); **-ne-.-uʔknęhsi-**: nehruʔknę́hsyęhs ‹a-part-he-end-undoes› *he unbends it* (HS); **-ne-.-rihuʔkT-{dative III}**: nyęʔnaʔrihuʔkná·tih ‹apart-one=anoth-er-matter-ends-for› *one criticizes another* (HS); **-aꞌnuʔkT-**: yú·ʔnuʔkt ‹it-itself-ended› *it came to an end; the end* (RC 2:15), waʔnúʔktha ‹it-itself-ends› *it terminates* (HS), waʔkayę́ʔnúʔknęʔ ‹fact-they-themselves-ended› *they ran out of it* (R); **-aꞌnuʔknahkw-. #ke**: uʔnuʔknahkę́·kye ‹self-end-instru-ment-at› *ultimate* (HS); **-ne-.-a='nuʔkT-**: neyuʔnúʔknę ‹apart-it-itself-ended⟩ *it is bent* (HS); **-ne-. -a'nu⟩ = kn̨eku -:** neyu'nu'kn̨ę·kwę ⟨apart-it-itself-end-undid⟩ *it is crooked, it is winding, it is zigzag* (HS); **-t-. -a= 'nu⟩kT -:** nę'nú'kn̨ę⟩ ⟨hither-fact-it-itself-ended⟩ *it ended* (RC 15:6); **-ker= hu⟩kT -:** wa'nyakukyerhú'kn̨ę⟩ ⟨fact-two-one-body-ended⟩ *the two of them came to end of its body* (RC 3:58); **-rihu⟩kT -:** wa'erihú'kn̨ę⟩ ⟨fact-one-matter-ended⟩ *she had finished speaking* (AG); **-yah-. -r̨ehyu⟩kT -:** yahwahrar̨ehyú'kn̨ę⟩ ⟨thither-fact-he-sky-ended⟩ *he came to the end of the sky* (RC 4:6); **-a'n̨enhu⟩kT -{dative II}:** wa'aku'n̨enhú'kthahθ ⟨fact-one-oneself-be alive-ended-for⟩ *one's time came to an end* (R); **-ne-. -a⟩rihu⟩kT -:** neyu'rihú'kn̨ę ⟨apart-it-itself-matter-ended⟩ *droll* (HS); **-t-. -a'n̨e'nu⟩kT -:** nyu'n̨ę·'nu'kt ⟨hither-it-itself-day-ended⟩ *it is abnormal, it is mentally deficient, it is retarded* (HS); **ha⟩ -ne-. -rihu⟩kT -:** ha' nyuríhu'kt ⟨the apart-it-matter-ended⟩ *defect* (HS); **ha⟩ -yah-. -a'nu⟩kT -:** ha' weyú·'nu'kt ⟨the thither-it-itself-ended⟩ *summit* (HS); **kę⟩ -yah-. -a'nu⟩kT -:** kę' weyú·'nu'kt ⟨where thither-it-itself-ended⟩ *extreme, extremity* (HS); **kwęhs -a'nu⟩kT -:** kwęhs aryu'nú'knak ⟨no unknown-it-itself-end⟩ *it is infinite, it is unlimited* (HS).

-u⟩na- receive. *v.r.-t.* hab: -, pnt: -·', stat: -, prog: -, prp: -, dst: -, caus: -, rvs: -ku-, dat: -, inc.-'?'-ag./pat. Requires an incorporated noun root.

-(ę)⟩tik̨ehru⟩naku -: ̨ektik̨ehru'nakwáhshek ⟨prediction-I-mind-receive-undo⟩ *I will be at peace* (R), ra'tik̨ehru'ná·kwahs ⟨he-mind-receive-undoes⟩ *he allures, he beguiles; allurer, tempter* (HS); **-(ę)⟩tik̨ehru⟩nakʷahT -:** yu'tik̨ehru'ná·kwaht ⟨it-mind-receive-undo-causes⟩ *charm, charming* (HS); **-hyat̨ehstu⟩na -:** ahruhyat̨ehstú'na·' ⟨unknown-he-book-received⟩ *that he receive letter* (R); **-w̨etu⟩na -:** wa'ew̨etú'na·' ⟨fact-one-word-received⟩ *one received a message* (R); **ha⟩ -(ę)⟩ti= k̨ehru⟩nakʷahT -:** ha' yu'tik̨ehru'ná·kwaht ⟨the it-mind-receive-undo-causes⟩ *temptation* (HS).

-ⁿu'narhu- hook. *v.r.-t.* hab: -hs, pnt: -', stat: -ę·, prog: -, prp: -, dst: -ę-, caus: -hsT-, rvs: -, dat: -, inc.-ɸ-ag./pat. **-̨ehkwaru'narhu -:** r̨ehkwaru'nárhuhs ⟨he-bridle-hooks⟩ *he bridles* (HS); **-(ę)tyahskari⟩čru'narhu -:** r̨etyahskari'čru'nárhuhs ⟨he-buckle-hooks⟩ *he buckles* (HS); **-hehnu'narhu -:** kahehnu'nárhuhs ⟨it-field-hooks⟩ *it fastens upon, crosses a part of the field* (H 24 84); **-kerhu'narhę -:** nakkyerhu'nárhę·k ⟨you!=me-body-hook-much⟩ *defend me from!* (RC 16:1); **-niθku⟩ru'nar= hu -:** raniθku'ru'nárhuhs ⟨he-button-hooks⟩ *he buttons it* (HS); **-r̨ehθu= 'narhu -:** ̨ekr̨ehθu'nárhu' ⟨prediction-I-leg-hook-cause⟩ *I will hook leg* (RC 24:8); **-⟩nh̨ehθu'narhuhsT -:** ye'nh̨ehθu'narhúhstha' ⟨one-rawhide strip-hook-causes⟩ *belt* (HS); **-ne-. -θkwa= ru'narhę -:** nehraθkwaru'nárhęh ⟨aparthc-lip-hooks-many⟩ *he embroiders* (HS); **-ne** -. **-węnę'nu'narhu** -: nehrawenę'²nu'²nárhuhs ⟨apart-he-iron-hooks⟩ *he locks it* (HS); **-a'nu'narhu** -: ra'²-nu'²nárhę· ⟨he-himself-hooked⟩ *he avoids it* (HS); **-athnęhu'narhuhsT** -: rathnęhu'²narhúhstha'² ⟨he-himself-upper shoulder-hook-causes⟩ *(his) suspenders* (HS); **-atkęhsu'narhuhsT** -: watkęhsu'²narhúhstha'² ⟨it-itself-face-hook-causes⟩ *halter* (HS); **-(ę)ti'² = rhwęθu'narhuhsT** -: węti'²rhwęθu'²narhúhstha'² ⟨it-itself-tail-hook-causes⟩ *crupper (of a horse)* (HS); **-ne** -. **-a'nya'²ka̲ru'narhu** -: nę'²nya'²karu'²nárhu'² ⟨apart-fact-it-itself-upper body-hooked⟩ *it hooked upper part of body* (RC 32:14).

-ⁿu'nari - fasten. *v.r.-t.* hab: -, pnt: -'², stat: -, prog: -, prp: -, dst: -, caus: -, rvs: -hsi-, dat: -, inc.-ɸ-pat. weθnú·'²-nari'² *you two fastened it* (R); **-ⁿu'na = rihsi** -: ru'²naríhsyęhs ⟨he-fasten-undoes⟩ *he unloosens it* (HS), rawu'²naríhsyę ⟨he-fasten-undid⟩ *he has unloosened it* (HS), ęhru'²naríhsi'² ⟨prediction-he-fasten-undo⟩ *he will unloosen it* (HS); **-(ę)tyahskari'²čru = 'narihsi** -: ratyahskari'²čru'²naríhsyęhs ⟨he-buckle-fasten-undoes⟩ *he unbuckles* (HS); **-ne** -. **-niθku'²ru'narihsi** -: newakniθku'²ru'²naríhsyę ⟨apart-I-button-fasten-undid⟩ *I have unbuttoned it* (R); **-a'nu'narihsi** -: ra'²nu'²naríhsyęhs ⟨he-himself-fasten-undoes⟩ *he disengages himself* (HS); **-a'²nęhkwaru'na = rihsi** -: ra'²nęhkwaru'²naríhsyęhs ⟨he-himself-bridle-fasten-undoes⟩ *he unbridles it* (HS).

-ⁿu'narihsi - unloosen. *v.s.-t.* ru'²naríhsyęhs ⟨he-fasten-undoes⟩ *he unloosens it* (HS), rawu'²naríhsyę ⟨he-fasten-undid⟩ *he has unloosened it* (HS), ęhru'²naríhsi'² ⟨prediction-he-fasten-undo⟩ *he will unloosen it* (HS).

-u'na̲T - blow (as of the wind). *v.r.-a.i.* hab: -s, pnt: -ɸ, stat: -ę, prog: -, prp: -, dst: -, caus: -, rvs: -, dat: -, n-inc. yawú·'²na'²nę *aired* (HS), wahú·'²na·t *it blew* (R) [Jefferson «wauh-hoh-naut» 'wind']; **-u'na̲T** -: wú·'²na·č ⟨it-blows⟩ *wind* (R) (Also: ú·'²na·č (R)) [Lawson «Hoonach» 'Wind']; **-u'na̲T -.#ú'²y**: wahu'²na·t'²ú'²y ⟨fact-it-blew-great⟩ *a big wind blew* (L 77).

-u'na̲T - wind. *dv.n.s.* wú·'²na·č ⟨it-blows⟩ *wind* (R) (Also: ú·'²na·č (R)) [Lawson «Hoonach» 'Wind'].

-u'²nę - be a kind of, be like, resemble. *v.r.-t.* hab: -, pnt: -'², stat: -·, prog: -'nye'²-, prp: -, dst: -, caus: -, rvs: -, dat: I (-'²θe-/-θ), inc.-ɸ-pat. **-u'²nę** - {dative I}: wahrú'²nę'²θ ⟨fact-he-was a kind of-for⟩ *he got the idea* (RC 13: 4); **-t** -. **-a'nu'²nę'nye'²** -: nayu'²nu'²nę·'²-nye'² ⟨hither-it-itself-is a kind of-going along⟩ *it goes along being in such a way* (RC 3:69); **tha** -. **-athe'²čru'²nę** -: thahęthe'²črú'²nę'² ⟨unusual-fact-it-pound-'ness-was a kind of⟩ *it was an unusual kind of powder* (RC 15:8); **ti** -. **-u'²nę** -: tiwú'²nę ⟨so-it-is a kind of⟩ *it is like, it resembles* (HS), tihsú'²nę· ⟨so-you-are a kind of⟩ *well, what did you expect, that's what you get (e.g., said to a child who has gotten hurt doing something naughty)* (R); **ti** -. **-ahθuhku'²nę** -: tiwahθuhkú'²nę· ⟨so-it-paint-instrument-is a kind of⟩ *it is such a color* (R); **ti** -. **-atkahrye'² = čru'²nę** -: tiwatkahrye'²črú'²nę· ⟨so-it-tell-'ness-is a kind of⟩ *such is the kind of account or report* (R); **ti** -. **-eh = su'²nę** -: tiwehsú'²nę· ⟨so-it-log-is a kind of⟩ *that kind of log* (RC 3:47); **ti** -. **-eku'²nę** -: tiwekú'²nę· ⟨so-it-liquid-is a kind of⟩ *kind of liquid* (R), thwahekú'²nę'² ⟨so-fact-it-liquid-is a kind

of› *it became such a liquid* (RC 12:
29); ti –. –ẹ°kʷehstuʔnẹ –: tihrẹkweh-
stúʔnẹ· ‹so-he-name-is a kind of› *he is
that kind of human* (RC 14:1); ti –.
–ẹ°nhuʔnẹ –: tihrẹnhúʔnẹ· ‹so-he-be a-
live-is a kind of› *(his) trait* (HS);
ti –. –(ẹ)ʔtikẹhnẹhčruʔnẹ –: tiwẹʔtikẹh-
nẹhčrúʔnẹ· ‹so-it-mind-fall-'ness-is a
kind of› *design, mode of thought*
(HS); ti –. –hnyuʔnẹ –: tikahnyúʔnẹ· ‹so-
it-news-is a kind of› *this story* (AW
53); ti –. –hsẹnuʔnẹ –: tihrahsẹnúʔnẹ·
‹so-he-name-is a kind of› *such is his
name* (RC 3:68); ti –. –rihuʔnẹ –: tiwa-
krihúʔnẹ· ‹so-I-matter-am a kind of› *I
have a habit* (RC 25:9), tikarihúʔnẹ·
‹so-it-matter-is a kind of› *it was that
kind of event* (RC 3:10), tyurihúʔnẹ·
‹so-it-matter-is a kind of› *usually*
(HS), *it is a custom* (RC 25:16); ti –.
–yehsuʔnẹ –: tikayehsúʔnẹ· ‹so-it-appearance-is a kind of› *so its appearance is* (RC 28:9); ti –. –ʔrhwẹθuʔnẹ –:
tikaʔrhwẹθúʔnẹ· ‹so-it-tail-is a kind
of› *so its kind of tail is* (RC 12:5);
tha+či –. –yehsuʔnẹ –: thahẹθahrayeh-
súʔnẹʔ ‹unusual-fact-again-he-appearance-was a kind of› *he transformed
himself again* (RC 26:15); hà·neʔ ti –.
–hehnuʔnẹ –: hà·neʔ tikahehnúʔnẹ· ‹that
is so-it-field-is a kind of› *the field is
of that shape* (H 2484); haʔ ti –. –(ẹ)ʔ =
tikẹhruʔnẹ –: haʔ tihruʔtikẹhrúʔnẹ· ‹the
so-he-mind-is a kind of› *his opinions*
(HS).

–uʔnẹ –{dative I} get the idea. *v.s.-a.i.*
wahrúʔnẹʔθ ‹fact-he-was a kind of-

for› *he got the idea* (RC 13:4).

úʔnẹʔ alternatively, as well, on the other
side (RC 28:3) *part.* **téher úʔnẹʔ** ‹why
alternatively› *and what did you expect, that's what you get* (R).

uʔnhé·taʔ porcupine *(Erethizon dorsatus)*,
porcupine quill (R). *n.*

uʔníhskaʔ everywhere (HS), here and
there (RC 3:55). *part.*

–uʔθkarh – clip. *v.r.-t.* hab: -ẹhs, pnt: -ɸ,
stat: -ẹ·, prog: -, prp: -, dst: -, caus: -,
rvs: -, dat: -, inc.-ɸ-pat. rúʔθkarhẹhs
he clips (HS), rawúʔθkarhẹ· *he clip-
ped* (HS), ẹhrúʔθkar *he will clip* (HS);
–ʔẹhruʔθkarh –: raʔẹhrúʔθkarhẹhs ‹he-
leaf-clips› *he strips off leaves* (HS).

uʔtéhsnakwt behind, rear (HS). *part.*

–uʔthiy – sharpen. *v.r.-t.* hab: -, pnt: -,
stat: -ẹ, prog: -, prp: -, dst: -, caus: -,
rvs: -, dat: -, inc.-ɸ-pat. Found only in
the cited construction. –nẹčiʔtheruʔ =
thiy –: ranẹčiʔtheruthì·yẹ ‹he-curl of
hair-sharpen› *he is handling, passing
his hands over or through the curl or
curls of hair* (H 2484).

#úʔy augmentative. *enc.* Variant used by
most speakers of the Eastern dialect.
See: –úyʔ.

ú·ʔy other (R). *part.* **ú·ʔy.#hči:** ú·ʔyči
‹other-very› *differently* (HS); **héʔu·ʔy**
‹that!-other› *another one* (RC 24:1);
rá·ku·ʔy ‹he-X-other› *stranger* (HS),
another male (RC 24:2); **akuʔykẹ =
haʔnẹʔ** ‹one-other-many› *others* (HS);
ú·ʔy –kẹhsẹT –: ú·ʔy rakẹhsẹ́·thaʔ ‹other he-face-possesses› *he disguises it*
(H-notebook).

ú·ʔy **–kęhsęT–** disguise. *v.s.-t.* ú·ʔy rakęhsę́·tha*ʔ* ‹other he-face-possesses› *he disguises it* (H-notebook).

ú·ʔy.**#hči** differently. *part.* ú·ʔyči ‹other-very› *differently* (HS).

–uʔy(e)– bend. *v.r.-t.* hab: -ęhs, pnt: -, stat: -, prog: -, prp: -, dst: -, caus: ()-hsT- ~ ()-hT-, rvs: -, dat: -, inc.-ɸ pat. **-aʔnuʔy(e)-**: uʔnúʔyeh ‹gun-bend› *ramrod* (HS); **–nęhskuʔye –**: runęhskúʔye· ‹he-house-picks up-bend› *thief* (R); **–nęhskuʔyehčr –**: unęhskuʔyéhčreh ‹house-pick up-bend-'ness› *theft* (HS); **–nęhwaruʔyehčr –**: unęhwaruʔyéhčreh ‹brain-bend-'ness› *adultery* (HS); **–yaʔ= karuʔyehT –**: ęyeyaʔkarúʔyeht ‹prediction-one-upper body-bend-cause› *one will entrap upper body* (RC 24:8); **–a'nęnęhwaruʔyehsT –**: raʔnęnęhwaruʔyéhstha*ʔ* ‹he-himself-brain-bend-causes› *he fornicates, he is licentious* (HS); **–ne –.-atkwiruʔy(e) –**: nehratkwirúʔyęhs ‹apart-he-himself-twig-bends› *he bends the sapling to himself* (HS).

W

w– it (third person singular neuter agent). *v.r.pfx.* Occurs preceding roots and stems that begin with a vowel.

wah oh!. *part.* wah sè·nę*ʔ* ‹oh! never› *oh come now, that's not true* (R).

wah – factual mode+third person singular neuter agent. *v.r.pfx.* Occurs as a redundant marker of factual mode and third person singular neuter agent on verbal constructions in which the basic factual mode marker has coalesced with the basic third person singular neuter agent prefix and the initial vowel *a* of a verb root or stem, e.g., {waʔ–w–ačhuri–ʔ} "factual mode-third singular neuter agent-eat-punctual" → {ęčhù·riʔ} → wahęčhù·ri*ʔ it ate* (R).

wah sè·nę*ʔ* oh come now, that's not true. *part.* wah sè·nę*ʔ* ‹oh! never› *oh come now, that's not true* (R).

wáhiʔr isn't it, it is so, it is true (RC 3:76). *part.*

Wáhstę Boston, Massachusetts (AG). *n.*

Wahstęhá·ka·ʔ American(s) (R) *n.*

wáht white ash *(Fraxinus americana)* (RC 19:title) *n.* Also: wáhtw (R).

–wak –/–wakʷ – I, me (first person singular patient). *v.r.pfx.* The form **–wakʷ –** occurs before roots and stems that begin with the vowel *a*. The form **–wak –** occurs elsewhere with insertion of "epenthetic" e before roots and stems that begin with certain consonant clusters.

warè·reh bull frog *(Rana catesbeiana)* (HS) *n.* warereh.**#ah**: warereháh ‹bull frog-little› *tadpole* (HS).

warereh.#ah tadpole. *n.* warereháh ‹bull frog-little› *tadpole* (HS).

warę́ʔkrę́ʔθ muskmelon *(Cucumis melo)* (R). *n.*

wáthnyu· shucks (R). *part.*

wawahúʔy mythic tree (translated by Hewitt as *Celandine*) that marked the home of Ruʔwnawáʔkę (RC 3:38); touch-me-not, impatiens *(Impatients sp.)* (H-notebook). *n.*

wáyway locust (H 447). *n.*

waʔ – fact (factual mode). *v.pfx.* The final *ʔ* is dropped before pronominal prefixes that begin with the consonant *h*. The prefix coalesces with a following sequence *wa* to yield ę –.

waʔ – thither, there (translocative). *v.pfx.* Occurs in word-initial position in the imperative.

–waʔk – grasp, hold. *v.r.-t.* hab: -s, pnt: -ɸ, stat: -ę, prog: -, prp: -, dst: -, caus: -, rvs: -, dat: -, inc.-ɸ-pat. **-aʔwna=**

wa?k –: Ru·?wnawá?ke̜ ‹he-earth-grasped› *He-Holds-the-Earth* (RC 3:69); –c̆una̱wa?k –: ruc̆unawa?ke̜he? ‹he-torso-grasped-past› *it had held his body* (RC 30:56); –(i)?θhaθne̜hste̜hawa?k –: akaye?θhaθne̜hste̜hà·wa?k ‹unknown-they-power-be strong-'ness-?'?-grasp› *they would hold supreme power* (M 87); –re̜ta̱wa?k –: Kare̜tawá?ke̜ ‹it-tree-grasped› *One-Is-Holding-the-Tree (Chief of the Snipe Clan)* (H-Handbook); –yeta̱wa?k –: ruyetawá?ke̜ ‹he-?'?-grasped› *he holds it* (HS); –ne –. –hswa̱wa?k –: neθahswawá?ke̜ ‹apart-you-back-grasped› *it is holding onto your back* (R); tha –. –re̜hyawa?k –: Thare̜hyawá?ke̜ ‹unusual-sky-grasped› *Creator, He- Holds-the-Heavens* (RC 1:1).

wa?ne – translocative+dualic. *v.pfx.*

wa?newakstaks?ú?y shark (H 3518). *n.*

*wá?re̜? nine (obsolete) [Lawson «Wearah» 'Nine']. *part.* Replaced in Tuscarora by the mid-1800s with níhre̜?. Cognate with Oneida wá·tlu̜?, Onondaga wá?te̜·?, and Laurentian «madellon».

wa?T(i) – factual mode+cislocative. *v.pfx.* The form wa?n – occurs before pronominal prefixes that begin with the consonants *w* or *y*. The form wa?t – occurs before pronominal prefixes that begin with the consonants *k* or *h*. The form wa?ni – occurs elsewhere.

wa?T(i) – factual mode+dualic. *v.pfx.* The form wa?n – occurs before pronominal prefixes that begin with the consonants *w* or *y*. The form wa?t – occurs before pronominal prefixes that begin with the consonants *k* or *h*. The form wa?ni – occurs elsewhere.

–wa?tke̜ – be loquacious, be talkative. *v. r.-s.i.* stat: -·, prog: -, prp: -, dst: -, caus: -hsT-, rvs: -, dat: -, n-inc. ruwá?tke̜· *he is loquacious, is talkative* (HS); –wa?tke̜hc̆r –: uwa?tke̜hc̆reh ‹be loquacious-'ness› *garrulity* (HS).

–wa?tke̜hc̆r – garrulity. *dv.n.s.* uwa?tke̜hc̆reh ‹be loquacious-'ness› *garrulity* (HS).

wa?wa?wa? blah, blah, blah (sound of people talking too much) (R). *part.*

wa̜wa̜wa̜ woof (bark of a dog) (R). *part.*

we – thither, there (translocative). *v.pfx.* Occurs in word-initial position when no modal marker is present.

wec̆i – translocative+repetitive. *v.pfx.* The form wec̆i – occurs before the consonants *θ* or *t*, or the clusters *?n* or *?t*. The form wec̆ – occurs before the consonant *y* and the *y* is dropped. The form weθ – occurs elsewhere.

–weh – speak, talk. *v.r.-a.i.* hab: -φ, pnt: -φ, stat: -φ, prog: -, prp: -, dst: -, caus: -sT-, rvs: -, dat: -, n-inc. θwéh *talk!* (R), kà·weh *it speaks* (RC 12:25), í·kweh *I am speaking* (R), wá?kweh *I talked* (R), rawéhahk *he talked* (L 16), ne̜?tì·weh *let's talk!* (R); –wehsT –: yewéhstha? ‹one-speak-causes› *palate* (HS); –ne –. –weh –: nehrà·weh ‹apart-he-speaks› *he parleys* (HS), neyakwà·weh ‹apart-we-speak› *we all talk together* (R); –yah –. –weh –: wehrà·weh ‹thither-he-speaks› *he talks (as over the phone) in a distant place* (L 16); -a'nwehaks -: ru'nwehá·ksę· ‹he-himself-speak-is bad› *he talks nonsense* (HS); hí'nę' -weh -: hí'nę' kà·weh ‹thunder it-speaks› *it thunders* (PC); ù·nę -weh - ha' -nęharihT -: ù·nę kà·weh ha' kanęharíhtha' ‹now it-speaks the it-corn-boil-causes› *now speaks the corn-ripener (said when you can hear the locusts buzzing—the hotter the day, the more they will buzz)* (L 49); -wyęhw - ha' -weh -: rawyéhę ha' rà·weh ‹he-know how-caused the he-speaks› *he is eloquent* (HS).

-wehr - speak. *v.r.-a.i.* stat: -ę, hab: -, pnt: -, prog: -ęha'nye'-, prp: -, dst: -, caus: -a'T-, rvs: -, dat: II (-ati-/ahθ-), n-inc. ruwéhrę *he spoke* (RC 3:23), *his deposition* (HS), kawehręhá·'nye' *it is speaking along* (RC 6:15); -wehr -{dative II}: ęyewérhahθ ‹prediction-one-speak-for› *one will speak to it* (RC 23:1), na'nwéhratih ‹one=another-speaks-for› *one addresses oneself to another* (HS); -wehra'T -: rawehrá'tha' ‹he-speak-causes› *he speaks (a language); he mentions, speaks of, speaks about* (HS), akwéhra't ‹unknown-I-speak-cause› *that I speak (a language)* (R); -wehręhčr -: uwehréhčreh ‹speak-'ness› *speech* (HS); -či -.-wehręhčaT -: čewehréhčra·t ‹again-one-speak-'ness-is one› *one manner of speech* (RC 1:1); -t -. -a'nwehra'T -: nyu'nwehrá'nę ‹hither-it-itself-speak-caused› *above-mentioned* (HS); ha' -t -.-wehr -: ha' nyuwéhrę ‹the hither-it-spoke› *above-mentioned* (HS).

-wehr -{dative II} address, speak to. *v.s.-t.* ęyewérhahθ ‹prediction-one-speak-for› *one will speak to it* (RC 23:1), na'nwéhratih ‹one=another-speaks-for› *one addresses oneself to another* (HS).

-wehra'T - speak (a language); mention, speak about, speak of. *v.s.-t.* rawehrá'tha' ‹he-speak-causes› *he speaks (a language): he mentions, he speaks of, he speaks about* (HS), akwéhra't ‹unknown-I-speak-cause› *that I speak (a language)* (R).

-wehręhčr - speech. *n.s.* uwehréhčreh ‹speak-'ness› *speech* (HS).

wehrę'ę̀·we indeed (R), in truth (HS), truly (RC 3:50). *part.* Also: wehręhę̀·we (W 74); wehrę'ę̀·we -ę̊ti -: wehrę'ę̀·we ŕę·tih ‹truly he-makes› *he assures it* (HS).

wehrę'ę̀·we -ę̊ti - assure. *v.s.-t.* wehrę'ę̀·we ŕę·tih ‹truly he-makes› *he assures it* (HS).

-wehsT - palate. *dv.n.s.* yewéhstha' ‹one-speak-causes› *palate* (HS).

-wenę - iron, rainbow. *n.r.* n-poss., n-inc., n.sfx. -'. uwè·nę' *iron* (R), yuwè·nę' *rainbow* (L 83); -wenę - -a'načnahnę -: uwè·nę' yu'načnáhnę· ‹iron it=another-used-much› *ironworks* (HS); -we = nę - -a'načT -: uwè·nę' yu'náčnę ‹iron it=another-used› *ironworks* (HS).

-wenę - -a'načnahnę - ironworks. *dv.n.s.* uwè·nę' yu'načnáhnę· ‹iron it=another-used-much› *ironworks* (HS).

-wenę - -a'načT - ironworks. *dv.n.s.* uwè·nę' yu'náčnę ‹iron it=another-used› *ironworks* (HS).

-wenęT - anchor, iron, measure of liquids. *n.r.* n-poss., inc., n.sfx. -eh. This root is undoubtedly derived from -wenę - *iron* with the addition of a root increment -T -. However, since this root has its own elicitation form, it must be treated as a distinct root. When the meaning *measure of liquids* is present, the specific measure of liquid (pint, quart, gallon) is determined contextually, for example, based on the type of liquid being measured and the purpose for which it is being measured. Historically, according to Lawson (1709), the Tuscarora defined the standard measure for liquids such as rum as being the amount that the person in the tribe with the greatest oral capacity could hold in his or her mouth at one time. uwenę·'neh *anchor, iron: measure of liquids* (R) [Lawson «Owa-iana» 'A Kettle']; **-wenęt'ehsT** –: yewenęt'éhstha' ‹one-iron-strike-causes› *bell (one strikes iron with)* (HS); **-wenęt'e(k)** –: kawenę·t'ehs ‹it-iron-strikes› *clock* (HS), rawenę·t'ehs ‹he-iron-strikes› *he rings bell* (HS); **-wenę'nahtir** –: yuwenę'nahtì·rę ‹it-iron-is durable› *steel* (HS); **-wenę'nahtira?T** –: rawenę'nahtì·ra'č ‹he-iron-be durable-causes› *he steels it* (HS); **-wenę'natawęhT** –: rawenę'natawéhtha' ‹he-iron-warm-causes› *he melts iron* (HS); **-wenę='natkęh** –: yuwenę'ná·tkęh ‹it-iron-is rotten› *witch-stone, load-stone* (HS); **-wenę'nayętihsT** –: yewenę'nayętíhstha' ‹one-iron-extend-causes› *trap* (HS); **-wenę'nuha?T** –: yewenę'nuhá'tha' ‹one-iron-put in water-causes› *one sets anchor* (HS); **-či** –. **-wenę'naT** –. **#áh**: θkawenę'na·t'áh ‹again-it-measure of liquid-is one-little› *one quart* (RC 18:2); **-ne** –. **-wenę'nake** –: nekawenę'ná·kye· ‹two-it-measure of liquid-is in number› *two quarts* (RC 16:1); **-ne** –. **-wenę'nu'narhu** –: nehrawenę'nu'nárhuhs ‹apart-he-iron-hooks› *he*

locks it (HS); **-a'nwenę'nanę'na =knahkw** –: yę'nwenę'nanę'naknáhkhwa' ‹one-oneself-iron-attaches-instrument› *ice skates* (HS); **-a'nwenę='nuha** –: yu'nwenę'núhę ‹it-itself-iron-put in water› *it is at anchor* (HS); **tha+ne** –. **-wenęthę** –: tha'nyuwené·thę ‹unusual-apart-it-measure of liquid-middle of› *pint* (HS); **ę·či -wenęt='e(k)** –: ę·či kawenę·t'ek ‹one it-iron-struck› *hour* (HS); **kę? -t** –. **-wenę='na'tawę?T** –: kę' nyewenę'na'tawę'tha' ‹where hither-one-iron-warm-causes› *foundry* (HS); **-wenęt'e(k) --kęhsawę** –: kawenę·t'ehs ukę́hsawęh ‹it-iron-strikes face-possess› *dial (of a clock)* (HS).

-wenęt'ehsT – bell. *dv.n.s.* yewenęt'éhstha' ‹one-iron-strike-causes› *bell (one strikes iron with)* (HS).

-wenęt'e(k) – clock. *dv.n.s.* kawenę·t'ehs ‹it-iron-strikes› *clock* (HS).

-wenęt'e(k) – ring bell. *v.s.-a.i.* rawenę·t'ehs ‹he-iron-strikes› *he rings bell* (HS).

-wenęt'e(k) --kęhsawę – dial (of a clock). *dv.n.s.* kawenę·t'ehs ukę́hsawęh ‹it-iron-strikes face-possess› *dial (of a clock)* (HS).

-wenę'nahtir – steel. *dv.n.s.* yuwenę'nahtì·rę ‹it-iron-is durable› *steel* (HS).

-wenę'nahtira?T – steel. *v.s.-t.* rawenę'nahtì·ra'č ‹he-iron-be durable-causes› *he steels it* (HS).

-wenę'natkęh – load-stone, witch-stone. *dv.n.s.* yuwenę'ná·tkęh ‹it-iron-is rotten› *witch-stone, load-stone* (HS).

Tuscarora Pronunciation Key:
/a/ law; /e/ hat; /i/ pizza; /u/ tune; /ę/ hint; /č/ cheese; /h/ hoe; /m/ mother; /s/ same; /t/ do (before a vowel y, or w), too (elsewhere); /k/ gale (before a vowel y or w), kale (elsewhere); /n/ inhale (before a consonant or word-final), note (elsewhere), /r/ hiss (before a consonant or word-final), run (trilled as in Italian, elsewhere); /w/ cuff (before a consonant other than y or word-final), way (elsewhere); /y/ fish (before a consonant or word-final), you (elsewhere), /θ/ thing; /'/ (the sound between the vowels in unh-unh); /·/ long vowel, /ˊ/ high pitch; /ˋ/ low pitch.

-wenę'nayętihsT - trap. *dv.n.s.* yewenę'-nayętíhstha'' ‹one-iron-extend-causes› *trap* (HS).

-wenę'nuha?T - set anchor. *v.s.-a.i.* yewenę'nuhá'tha'' ‹one-anchor-put in water-causes› *one sets anchor* (HS).

-w(e)r - air, wind. *n.r.* n-poss., inc., n.sfx. -eh. The form -wr- occurs when the word-accent falls after the root, unless an impermissible cluster would result (e.g., word-initial *kwr- in *I am inhaling*, below). The form -wer- occurs elsewhere. In the older records the form -wr- also occurs in the elicitation form where the accent precedes the root. This indicates that there was a late epenthesis of *e* in this root. ú·wreh *air, wind* (HS) [Gallatin «oghre» 'Wind'], ù·wereh *air, wind* (R); -w(e)r-.#keha·?: uwrę'kyéha·' ‹air-customarily› *acrid, aerial, atmospheric* (HS); -w(e)rača?tuh -: yuwračá'tuh ‹it-air-is cool› *cool breeze* (R); -w(e)rahwihsT -: kawrahwíhsne' ‹it-air-is strong› *strong wind* (R); -w(e)=rakari -: kweraká·ryahs ‹I-air-devour› *I am inhaling* (RC 9:7); -w(e)rakęθnę -: yuwrakę́θnę' ‹it-air-gnaws at› *it is bleak* (HS); -w(e)rakę?T -: ká·wrakę'č ‹it-air-strikes› *squall of wind* (AG); -w(e)rę?ke: uwrę́'kye ‹air-at› *on the wind* (R) -či-. -w(e)?rke: θkawé'rkye ‹again-it-air-at› *January* (R) (HS: *February 15-March 15*); -a'newrę=kuhT -: yu'newrękúhnę ‹it-itself-air-went through› *draft of air* (AG).

-w(e)r-.#keha·? acrid, aerial, atmospheric. *n.s.* uwrę'kyéha·' ‹air-customarily› *acrid, aerial, atmospheric* (HS).

-w(e)rača?tuh - cool breeze. *dv.n.s.* yuwračá'tuh ‹it-air-is cool› *cool breeze* (R).

-w(e)rahwihsT - strong wind. *dv.n.s.* ka-

wrahwíhsne' ‹it-air-is strong› *strong wind* (R).

-w(e)rakari - inhale. *v.s.-a.i.* kweraká·ryahs ‹I-air-devour› *I am inhaling* (RC 9:7).

-w(e)rakęθnę - be bleak. *v.s.-s.i.* yuwrakę́θnę' ‹it-air-gnaws at› *it is bleak* (HS).

-w(e)rakę?T - squall of wind. *n.s.* ká·wrakę'č ‹it-itself-air-strikes› *squall of wind* (AG).

wé·tnya? pshaw! (expression of disbelieve) (HS) (R). *part.*

weyúhre· very (RC 12:1). *part.*

we? barf (sound of vomiting) (RC 30:56). *part.*

-we?θra?θe - loathe. *v.r.-a.i.* hab: -h, pnt: -, stat: -, prog: -, prp: -, dst: -, caus: -, rvs: -, dat: -, n-inc. rawe?θrá?θeh *he loathes* (HS).

-wę - belong to. *v.r.-t.* hab: -h, pnt: -, stat: -?, prog: -, prp: -hte?-, dst: -, caus: -, rvs: -, dat: II (-ati-/-ahθ-), inc.-φ-pat. ákwęh *it is my or mine* (H 2892), θà·węh *it is thy or thine* (H 2892), kakù·węh *it is their or theirs* (H 2892); -a'nawę -: ru'nà·węh ‹he-himself-belongs to› *he possesses it* (RC 24:8); -(a)hę?nawę -: ruhę́'nawęh ‹he-field-belongs to› *the meadow belongs to him, it is his meadow* (H 2484); -hnyawę -: ha' ráhnyawęh ‹the he-news-belongs to› *his aspersion* (HS); -khwawę -: yękwákhwawęh ‹we-food-belong to› *our food* (RC 35:34); -nęhkwa?črawęhst: ękayenęhkwá'črawęhst ‹prediction-they-medicine-'ness-belong to-use› *they will have medicine to use* (RC 10:7); -nęhrawę -. #kęhe?: runęhrawęhkęhe' ‹he-scalp-belongs to-deceased› *his scalp was* (RC 12:10); ti-. -ęnhawę -{dative II}: tihrawę́nhawęhθ ‹so-he-be alive-belongs to-for› *such is his life* (RC 3:

72); **ti+yah** -. **-yehsawę** -: thweθaych-
sà·wę᾽ ‹so-thither-you-appearance-be-
longed to› *it has happened to you* (RC
11:5).

-wę - put on dabs, smear. *v.r.-a.i.* hab: -
hs, pnt: -, stat: -, prog: -, prp: -, dst: -,
caus: -, rvs: -, dat: -, n-inc. rà·węhs *he
puts on dabs, he smears* (HS); **-ye =
rawę** -: yeyè·rawęhs ‹one-flesh-smears›
goldplate, silverplate (HS), rayè·ra-
węhs ‹he-flesh-smears› *he soils it, he
taints it* (HS);

-węnar - speak to. *v.r.-t.* hab: -, pnt: -a᾽,
stat: -ę, prog: -, prp: -, dst: -, caus: -,
rvs: -, dat: -, n-inc. aθahshewę̀·nara᾽
that you speak to someone (RC 3:38).

-węna᾽T - surrender. *v.r.-a.i.* hab: -ha᾽,
pnt: -, stat: -, prog: -, prp: -, dst: -,
caus: -, rvs: -, dat: -, n-inc. ruwę-
ná᾽tha᾽ *he surrenders* (HS).

-węniyu - be God *v.r.-s.i.* stat: -᾽, prog: -,
prp: -, dst: -, caus: -, rvs: -, dat: -,
inc.-φ-ag. rawęnì·yu᾽ *God* (R), swę-
nì·yu᾽ *you are God* (R); **-węni =
yuhčręti** -: kawęniyuhčrę́·tih ‹it-be
God-'ness-makes› *idol* (HS); **-a᾽nwę =
niyu** -: ka᾽nwęnì·yu᾽ ‹I-myself-am
God› *I am free* (AG); **-a᾽nwęniyu᾽** -:
ru᾽nwęniyú᾽ę ‹he-himself-be God-
began› *he is freed from slavery* (HS),
ra᾽nwęnì·yu᾽θ ‹he-himself-be God-
begins› *he is freed, he is set free*
(HS); **-a᾽nwęniyuhsT** -: ra᾽nwęniyúh-
stha᾽ ‹he-himself-be God-causes› *rebel* (HS); ti-. **-a᾽nwęniyu** -: tihra᾽nwę-
nì·yu᾽ ‹so-he-himself-is God› *he is at
liberty, he is independent* (HS); ti-.

-a᾽nwęniyuhsT -: tihra᾽nwęniyúhstha᾽
‹so-he-himself-be God-causes› *he
takes liberties* (HS); **-a᾽nękʷehstawę =
niyu** -: ru᾽nękwehstawęnì·yu᾽ ‹he-him-
self-human-'ness-is God› *he is theandric, he is a man-god* (HS); í·θ **-wę =
niyu** -: í·θ swęnì·yu᾽ ‹you you-are
God› *te deum* (HS); **-kerhętyahnę** -
-węniyuhčręti -: kakyerhętyáhnęh ra-
węniyuhčrę́·tih ‹it-body-makes-much
he-be God-'ness-makes› *idolater* (HS).

-węniyuhčręti - idol. *dv.n.s.* kawęniyuh-
črę́·tih ‹it-be God-'ness-makes› *idol*
(HS).

-węt - command, language, letter (postal),
message, music, order, speech, voice,
word. *n.r.* n-poss., inc., n.sfx. -eh. u-
wę́·teh *command, language, letter
(postal), message, music, order,
speech, voice, word* (RC 4:1); **-wę =
tahčr** -: uwętáhčreh ‹word-'ness› *dictionary, lexicon, vocabulary* (R); **-wę =
tahrahT** -: uwętáhraht ‹word-put up-
cause› *terrible noise* (RC 28:7); **-wę =
tahru᾽T** -: rawętahrú᾽nę ‹he-word-is
soft› *he is courteous* (HS); **-wętah =
stur** -: rawętahstù·re᾽ ‹he-word-is fast›
he is a rapid speaker (HS), yuwętah-
stù·re᾽ ‹it-word-is fast› *volubility*
(HS); **-wętakareti** -: ruwętakaré·tih ‹he-
voice-is loud› *his voice is loud* (RC
12:3); **-wętaka᾽ne** -: yuwętaká᾽ne᾽ ‹it-
word-is much› *wordy* (HS); **-węta =
kęhey** -: ękawętakę́he᾽y ‹prediction-it-
music-die› *music will die* (RC 6:9);
-wętaks -: rawętá·ksę· ‹he-word-is bad›
he has coarse speech (HS); **-węta =**

rahkw –: waˀkayewę́·tarahkw ‹fact-they-word-collected› *they followed word* (RC 33:9), ęhskwę́·tarahkw ‹prediction-you=me-word-collect› *you will mind me* (AW 57); **–wętaraku** –: rawętará·kwahs ‹he-word-chooses› *he extracts from a book* (HS); **–wętaT** –: aryuwętá·ˀnahk ‹unknown-it-word-stand› *that its word stand* (RC 33:6); **–wętitkę** –: rawętí·tkęˀθ ‹he-word-come forth-begins› *he speaks* (HS); **–wętiyu** –: kawętì·yuh ‹it-word-is great› *it is sonorous* (HS); **–węturi** –: ruwętù·rih ‹he-voice-stirs› *he bemoans, he hums, he moans, he mutters* (HS), yuwętú·ri· ‹it-word-stirred› *resonant* (HS); –či–. **–wętęhawihT** –: Čewętęhawíhti ‹again-one-word-bring-causes› *Bringer-of-Language (mythic bird, said to have brought language from God to man)* (RC 2); –ne–. **–wętaˀ** = **θku** –: nekawętáˀθkwahs ‹apart-it-word-carries away› *it carries away language* (RC 4:3); ti–. **–wętaˀθ** –: tikawę́·taˀθ ‹so-it-word-is of a size› *size of word* (RC 26:7); ti–. **–wętaˀθ** –. **#áh**: tihrawętaˀθˀáh ‹so-he-word-is of a size-little› *he has a small, thin voice* (AG); **–aˈnwętahęˀT** –: raˀnwętáhęˀč ‹he-himself-word-in front of› *he proposes* (HS); **–aˈnwętahθawˀahsT** –: yuˀ-nwętahθáwˀahst ‹it-itself-word-begin-caused› *it is legible* (HS); **–aˈnwętah** = **saˀnę** –: ruˀnwętáhsaˀnęˀ ‹he-himself-voice-buried› *he is monotonous* (HS); **–aˈnwętahsęhT** –: raˀnwętahsę́hthaˀ ‹he-himself-word-be evil-causes› *he boasts, he mocks* (HS); **–aˈnwętahska** = **nekęT** –: yuˀnwętahskané·kę·t ‹it-itself-word-is strange› *allegory* (HS); **–a** = **ˈnwętakaraˀnaT** –: raˀnwętakaráˀna·č ‹he-himself-word-ˀ?› *he interprets* (HS); **–aˈnwętakeθku** –: raˀnwętakyé·θkwahs ‹he-himself-word-raises› *he*

raises his voice (HS); **–aˈnwętanh** –: wahsaˀnwętánhek ‹fact-you-yourself-word-aided› *you are responsible* (HS); **–aˈnwętarahkw** –: raˀnwętaráhkhwaˀ ‹he-himself-word-collects› *he obeys* (HS), naˀnaˀnwętaráhkhwaˀ ‹one=another-self-word-collects› *one follows another's command, one obeys another* (MP), ruˀnwę́·tarahkw ‹he-himself-word-collected› *he is obedient, he is obliging* (HS); **–aˈnwętayerik** –: raˀnwętayè·riks ‹he-himself-word-fills up› *he fulfills, he realizes* (HS); **–aˈnwęta** = **yęhT** –: raˀnwętayę́hthaˀ ‹he-himself-word-go into-causes› *he speaks ill of it* (HS), uˀnwę́·tayęht ‹self-word-go into-cause› *invective* (HS); **–aˈnwęta** = **ˈnahT** –: raˀnwętáˀnahč ‹he-himself-word-be present-causes› *he intones* (HS); **–aˈnwętaˈnanye** –: yuˀnwętaˀná·ˀnyeˀ ‹it-itself-word-is present-going along› *it goes by humming* (HS); **–aˈnwętaˈne** –: yuˀnwętá·neˀ ‹it-itself-word-is present› *it hums, it intones* (HS); **–aˈnwętaˈnetyę** –: yuˀnwętaˀné·tyęˀ ‹it-itself-word-is present-much› *there is noise* (RC 26:7); **–aˈnwę** = **tuhnę** –: raˀnwętúhnęh ‹he-himself-word-swells› *he is hoarse* (HS); –ne–. **–aˈnwętaˈnaT** –: newaˀnwę́·taˀna·č ‹apart-it-itself-word-is around› *it chimes* (HS); –t–. **–aˀnwętahT** –: nwaˀnwętáhthaˀ ‹hither-it-itself-word-stands› *echo; it mocks* (HS); **haˀ –wętiyu** –: haˀ kawętì·yuh ‹the it-word-is great› *bass (voice)* (HS); **haˀ –aˈnwętanh** –: haˀ ruˀnwętánhę ‹the he-himself-word-aided› *his responsibility* (HS); **kwęhs –a** = **ˈnwętarahkw** –: kwęhs ahruˀnwętaráhkęk ‹no unknown-he-himself-word-collect› *he is insubordinate* (HS); **kwęhs –aˈnwętanh** –: kwęhs ahruˀnwę́·tanhęk ‹no unknown-he-himself-word-aide› *he is irresponsible* (HS).

-**wętahčr** – dictionary, lexicon, vocabulary. *n.s.* uwętáhčreh ‹word-'ness› *dictionary, lexicon, vocabulary* (R).

-**wętahru?T** – be courteous. *v.s.-s.i.* rawętahrú·?nę ‹he-word-is soft› *he is courteous* (HS).

-**wętahstur** – be a rapid speaker, talk fast. *v.s.-a.i.* rawętahstù·re? ‹he-word-is fast› *he is a rapid speaker* (HS).

-**wętahstur** – volubility. *dv.n.s.* yuwętahstù·re? ‹it-word-is fast› *volubility* (HS).

-**wętaka?ne** – wordy. *dv.n.s.* yuwętaká?ne? ‹it-word-is much› *wordy* (HS).

-**wętaks** – have coarse speech. *v.s.-s.i.* rawętá·ksę· ‹he-word-is bad› *he has coarse speech* (HS).

-**wętarahkw** – mind someone, follow another's word. *v.s.-t.* wa?kayewę́·tarahkw ‹fact-they-word-collected› *they followed word* (RC 33:9), ęhskwę́·tarahkw ‹prediction-you=me-word-collect› *you will mind me* (AW 57).

-**wętaraku** – extract from a book. *v.s.-a.i.* rawętará·kwahs ‹he-word-chooses› *he extracts from a book* (HS).

-**wętitkę?** – speak. *v.s.-a.i.* rawętí·tkę?θ ‹he-word-come forth-begins› *he speaks* (HS).

-**wętiyu** – be sonorous. *v.s.-a.i.* kawętì·yuh ‹it-word-is great› *it is sonorous* (HS).

-**wętiyu** – bass. *dv.n.s.* ha? kawętì·yuh ‹the it-word-is great› *bass (voice)* (HS).

-**węturi** – bemoan, hum, moan, mutter. *v.s.-a.i.* ruwętù·rih ‹he-voice-stirs› *he bemoans, he hums, he moans, he mutters* (HS).

-**węturi** – resonant. *dv.n.s.* yuwętú·ri· ‹it-word-stirred› *resonant* (HS).

-**wi** – know. *v.r.-a.i.* hab: -, pnt: -·t, stat: -ę, prog: -, prp: -, dst: -, caus: -hw-, rvs: -, dat: -, inc.-φ-ag./pat. The form -**wi** – occurs before suffixes that begin with a consonant; the form -**wy** – occurs before suffixes that begin with a vowel. ęhskwi·t *you will know me* (R); -**wihw** –: wahrà·wiw ‹fact-he-know how-caused› *he learned* (R), rawíhę ‹he-know how-caused› *he knows how* (L 49); -**wyęhw** –: rá·wyęws ‹he-know how-causes› *he learns* (HS); -**nęhsawyęhw** –: ranęhsawyę́hę ‹he-house-know how-caused› *he knows how to build a house; this is another name of a carpenter* (H 2484); -**rihwawihw** –: rarihwawíhę ‹he-matter-know how-caused› *he palliates* (HS); -**tahskwawihw** –: ratahskwawíhę ‹he-slave-know how-caused› *he annoys* (HS); -**tyurawihw** –: ratyurawíhę ‹he-swim-know how-caused› *he is a good swimmer* (L 82); -**a?newyęhw** –: ra?newyę́hę ‹he-himself-know how-caused› *carpenter* (R); *he is adroit, he is crafty, he is ingenious, he is skillful* (HS); -**a'newyęhsT** –: ra?newyę́hstha? ‹he-himself-know how-causes› *he retains (knowledge)* (HS); -**atkwahčra** = **wihw** –: ratkwahčrawíhe ‹he-himself-pick up-'ness-know how-caused› *he is good at dancing* (HS); -**ne** –·-**a?ne** = **wyęhw** –: nehra?newyę́hę ‹apart-he-himself-know how-caused› *he is experienced, he is used to it* (HS); **kwęhs -a'newyęhw -**: kwęhs narę'né·-wyęw ‹no two-it-itself-know how-cause› *the two of them are inconsistent, the two of them are incongruous, the two of them are incompatible* (HS); **kwęhs sawę́·te -wyęhw -**: kwęhs sawę́·te ahrawyę́hęk ‹no nothing unknown-he-know how-cause› *he is incompetent* (HS).

-wih - bog. *n.r.* n-poss., n-inc., n.sfx. -eh. yuwíheh *bog* (W 74).

-wihr - ash swamp, bog, dam, low damp place, marsh, swamp, young (lightly wooded) forest. *n.r.* n-poss., inc., n. sfx. -eh. uwíhreh *bog, dam, low damp place, marsh, swamp, young (lightly wooded) forest* (HS); **-wihrakęw**: u-wíhrakęw ‹forest-in› *ash swamp* (H 35 18), *in the forest* (W 74); **-wihręti -**: rawihrę́·tih ‹he-dam-makes› *he makes dams* (HS).

-wihręti - make dams. *v.s.-a.i.* rawihrę́·tih ‹he-dam-makes› *he makes dams* (HS).

-wihw - know how, learn. *v.s.-a.i.* wah-rà·wiw ‹fact-he-know how-caused› *he learned* (R), rawíhę ‹he-know how-caused› *he knows how* (L 49).

-winę - be virgin. *v.r.-s.i.* stat: -·, prog: -, prp: -, dst: -, caus: -, rvs: -, dat: -, n-inc. kawí·nę· *virgin* (RC 3:11).

winí·kyer vinegar (HS). *n.*

-wir - bud, embryo, infant, offspring. *n.r.* aln: nekawì·rayę' *the two of them's child* (RC 27:1), inc., n.sfx. -eh. uwì·reh *bud, embryo, infant, offspring* (HS); **-wiraraku -**: wa'ewirarakúhe' ‹fact-one-offspring-chose-going to› *one selected infant* (RC 9:2); **-wira = yęhte -**: yewirayę́hte' ‹one-offspring-lays-going to› *one was going to have a baby* (RC 3:15); **-wiręT -**: kawì·ręč ‹it-offspring-concludes› *barren* (HS);

-wiręti -: yewirę́·tih ‹one-offspring-makes› *one is prolific* (HS), kawirę́·tih ‹it-offspring-makes› *doll* (HS); -či -. **-wiraT -**: θkawí·ra·t ‹again-it-offspring-stands› *one young; a brood* (HS); **-a'nwiranę -**: ra'nwì·ranęh ‹he-himself-offspring-guards› *he nurses* (HS); **-a = 'nwiraraku -**: wa'ka'nwirará·ku' ‹fact-I-myself-offspring-chose› *I adopted child* (R); **-a'nwirarakwa' -**: yakwa'-nwirará·kwa'θ ‹we-ourselves-offspring-choose-begin› *Adoption Ceremony* (R); **-a'nwirayę(T) -**: wa'nwì·rayęhs ‹it-itself-offspring-lays› *it gives birth* (RC 7:11); **-a'nwiręčT -**: ru'-nwirę́čnę ‹he-himself-offspring-conclude-caused› *he is sterile* (HS); **-a'nwiręhaw -**: wa'nwirę́ha'w ‹it-itself-offspring-carried› *(she) took her child* (AW 102); **-a'nwiręti -**: ra'nwirę́·tih ‹he-himself-offspring-makes› *he procreates* (HS); -či -. **-a'nwiri'θ(e)r -**: nę-čę'nwirí'θe'r ‹two-prediction-again-one-oneself-offspring-drag› *the two of them will take infant home* (RC 11: 15); -ne -. **-a'nwirya'k -**: newa'nwì·-rya'ks ‹two-it-itself-off-spring-breaks› *it pups* (HS); **ha' -wir -**: ha' uwì·reh ‹the offspring› *interest, profit* (HS).

-wir - interest, profit. *n.s.* ha' uwì·reh ‹the offspring› *interest, profit* (HS).

-wirayęhte - have a baby. *v.s.-a.i.* yewi-rayę́hte' ‹one-offspring-lay-going to› *one was going to have a baby* (RC 3: 15).

-wiręT - barren. *dv.n.s.* kawì·ręč ‹it-offspring-concludes› *barren* (HS).

-wiręti - be prolific. *v.s.-a.i.* yewirę́·tih ‹one-offspring-makes› *one is prolific* (HS).

-wiręti - doll. *dv.n.s.* kawirę́·tih ‹it-offspring-makes› *doll* (HS).

wírhę apparently (RC 30:47). *part.*

-wiθ(e)r - snow. *n.r.* n-poss., inc., n.sfx.

-eh. uwí·θreh *snow* (R) [Gallatin «ow-weetsray» 'Snow']; **-wiθ(e)r** -: uwí·θrch ‹snow› *snowy owl* (R); **-wiθerhar** -: yuwiθérha'r ‹it-snow-hangs› *snow held up by reeds, etc.* (H 3518); **-wi=θrę'** -: yuwiθrę́·'ę ‹it-snow-fall-began› *frost* (H 3518); **-wiθrę'ke:** uwiθrę́·'kye ‹snow-at› *on snow* (RC 2:12); **-či-. -wiθraT** -: θkawí·θra·t ‹again-it-snow-stands› *snowflake* (R).

-wiθ(e)r - snowy owl. *n.r.* uwí·θreh ‹snow› *snowy owl* (R).

-wiθrę' - frost. *dv.n.s.* yuwiθrę́·'ę ‹it-snow-fall-began› *frost* (H 3518).

-wis - goblet, hail, ice, crystal, ice cream, glass. *n.r.* n-poss., inc., n.sfx. -eh. uwí·seh *goblet, hail* (HS), *ice, crystal: ice cream* (R), *glass* (PC) [Gallatin «oowees-seh» 'Ice']; **-wis** -.**#hči:** uwiséhči ‹ice-very› *icy* (HS); **-wisa'ne** -: wa'uwisá·'ne' ‹fact-it-ice-was present› *hail* (R); **-wisa'r** -: yuwí·sa'r ‹it-ice-is much› *icy* (HS); **-wiseθ** -: yuwí·se·θ ‹it-ice-is long› *icy* (HS); **-wisę=** 'ni -: yuwisę́·'nyęhs ‹it-ice-throws› *sleet* (HS); **-wisęy** -: yuwí·sęy ‹it-ice-hangs› *icicle* (HS); **-wiskwek** -: wa'-kawískwe·k ‹fact-it-ice-closed› *the water freezes* (AG); **-wisur** -: kawí·suč ‹it-ice-covers› *it covers with ice, it freezes* (HS), yuwisù·rę ‹it-ice-covered› *icy* (HS).

-wis -.**#hči** icy. *n.s.* uwiséhči ‹ice-very› *icy* (HS).

-wisa'ne - hail. *dv.n.s.* wa'uwisá·'ne' ‹fact-it-ice-was present› *hail* (R).

-wisa'r - icy. *dv.n.s.* yuwí·sa'r ‹it-ice-is much› *icy* (HS).

-wiseθ - icy. *dv.n.s.* yuwí·se·θ ‹it-ice-is long› *icy* (HS).

wí·sę·t strawberry *(Fragaria virginiana, Fragaria* sp.*)* (R). *n.* Also: wíhsę·t (R).

-wisę'ni - sleet. *dv.n.s.* yuwisę́·'nyęhs ‹it-ice-throws› *sleet* (HS).

-wisęy - icicle. *dv.n.s.* yuwí·sęy ‹it-ice-hangs› *icicle* (HS).

wísk five (RC 26:1) [Lawson «Ouchwhe» 'Five']. *part.* Also: wihsk (R). **wísk** -**či** -. -**(i)har** -: wísk θkáhe'r ‹five again-it-hangs› *fifteen* (R); **wísk tha+ne** -. -**hswatet'** -: wísk tha'neyuhswá·te·t ‹five unusual-apart-it-back-lines› *quintuple* (HS); **wísk ti** -. -**ahθhę** -: wísk tiwáhθhę· ‹five so-it-is ten› *fifty* (R); **wísk ti+či** -. -**hterhę** -: wísk tičuhtérhę ‹five so-again-it-X-is day› *Friday* (R); **wísk** -**kerhęte:** wísk ukyerhę́·te ‹five body-certain one› *fifth body* (AW 57).

wísk -**či** -. -**(i)har** - fifteen. *dv.n.s.* wísk θkáhe'r ‹five again-it-hangs› *fifteen* (R).

wísk tha+ne -. -**hswatet'** - quintuple. *dv. n.s.* wísk tha'neyuhswá·te·t ‹five un-usual-apart-it-back-lines› *quintuple* (HS).

wísk ti -. -**ahθhę** - fifty. *dv.n.s.* wísk ti-wáhθhę· ‹five so-it-is ten› *fifty* (R).

wísk ti+či -. -**hterhę** - Friday. *dv.n.s.* wísk tičuhtérhę ‹five so-again-it-X-is day› *Friday* (R).

-wiskwek - freeze water. *v.s.-a.i.* wa'-kawískwe·k ‹fact-it-ice-closed› *the water freezes* (AG).

-wisur - cover with ice, freeze. *v.s.-a.i.*

kawí·suč ‹it-ice-covers› *it covers with ice, it freezes* (HS).

-wisur – icy. *dv.n.s.* yuwisù·rę ‹it-ice-covered› *icy* (HS).

wí?er because, since (RC 3:2). *part.*

-wy – fan, wing; armspan, wingspan. *n.r.* n-poss., inc., n.sfx. -eh. ú·wyeh *fan, wing; armspan, wingspan* (R); -či-. **-wyaT** –: θwa?né·wya·t ‹again-it-itself-armspan-stands› *a fathom* (HS); **-ne** –. **-a'newyarahte** –: (θá·st) newa?newya-ráhte? (stá·kwi?) ‹(black squirrel) a-part-it-itself-wing-is in-going to (up high)› *(black squirrel) jumping to another tree & so on* (AG); ti-. **-a'newya = ke** –: tiwa?newyá·kye· ‹so-it-itself-armspan-is in number› *it is so many armspans* (RC 30:60); ti-. **-a'newyaT** –: thwa?né·wya·t ‹so-it-itself-armspan-stands› *measure as long as the arms extend from tip of one hand to the other* (AG); ti-. **-a'newyeθ** –: tihsa?-né·wye·θ ‹so-you-yourself-armspan-is long› *as long as both your arms extend* (R).

-wyahs – cross. *n.r.* n-poss., inc., n.sfx. -eh. uwyáhseh *cross* (HS); **-wyah = sęhawi** –: rawyahęhà·wi? ‹he-cross-bears› *he carries cross* (HS); **-wyah = sęhT** –: na?newyahsęhtha? ‹one=another-cross-fall-causes› *one crucifies another* (HS).

-wyahsęhT – crucify. *v.s.-t.* na?newyah-sęhtha? ‹one=an-other-cross-fall-causes› *one crucifies another* (HS).

-wyesT – be appropriate, be seemly. *v.r.-s.i.* stat: -ę, prog: -, prp: -, dst: -, caus: -, rvs: -, dat: -, inc.-ɸ-ag. yuwyésnę *it is appropriate, it is seemly* (RC 30:48); **-kerhawyesT** –: rukyerhawyésnę ‹he-body-is seemly› *he has grace of body* (HS); kwęhs **-wyesT** –: kwęhs aryuwyésnęk ‹no unknown-it-is seemly› *it is indecorous, it is unbecoming*

(HS); kwęhs **-ya?tawyęsT** –: kwęhs aryuya?tawyésnęk ‹no unknown-it-body-be seemly› *unseemly* (HS).

-wyęhw – learn. *v.s.-a.i.* rá·wyęws ‹he-know how-causes› *he learns* (HS).

-wy(ęn) – mixture, preparation; craft, manner, skill. *n.r.* n-poss., inc., n.sfx. -eh. The form **-wyęn** – occurs when the root is incorporated and precedes a verb root beginning with a vowel. The form **-wy** – occurs elsewhere. However, note that there are distinct elicitation forms, with very different meanings for both forms. ú·wyeh *mixture, preparation* (R), uwyę·neh *craft, manner, skill* (R); **-ne** –. **-wyatekę** –: wa?thrawya-té·kę? ‹fact-two-he-preparation-joined› *he put two preparations together* (RC 14:3); **-wyęnah = wihsT** –: kawyęnahwíhsne? ‹it-preparation-is strong› *it is a strong preparation* (RC 17:5); **-wyęnaks** –: rawyęná·ksę· ‹he-preparation-is bad› *he is uncivil* (HS); **-a'newyęnęT** –: wah-ra?newyęnę́·?na? ‹fact-he-himself-pre-paration-concluded› *he finished his preparations* (RC 12:3); **-a'newyę = nęti** –: ra?newyęnę́·tih ‹he-himself-pre-paration-makes› *he creates* (HS).

-wyęnaks – be uncivil. *v.s.-a.i.* rawyę-ná·ksę· ‹he-preparation-is bad› *he is uncivil* (HS).

-wyęwnahkw – be right side. *v.r.-s.i.* stat: -ę, prog: -, prp: -, dst: -, caus: -, rvs: -, dat: -, n-inc. kyewyęwnáhkę *my right side* (L 81), rawyęwnáhkę *his right side* (L 81).

Y

-ya –/ **-yak** –/ **-ye** – she, one (third person feminine/indefinite agent). *v.r.pfx.* The form –ya– occurs before certain roots and stems that begin with the vowel *i*. The form –yak– occurs before roots and stems that begin with the vowel *u* or the morphophoneme {ę°}. The form –ye– occurs before roots and stems that begin with consonants; the vowel *a* and certain cases of *i*, which vowels are dropped; the vowel *e* with which the final vowel of the prefix coalesces to yield –yę–; and the vowel *ę* which causes the final *e* of the prefix to be dropped.

–yah– thither, there (translocative). *v.pfx.* The translocative in most of its occurrences means "away from speaker and hearer". Its usual English translation is *there* and its gloss in this dictionary is the more archaic, but more accurate ‹thither›. In meaning, it is opposed to the cislocative, which generally means "away from the speaker, near the hearer." With a number of verb roots and stems, however, the meaning of the translocative is more opaque. With some of these, it adds a generalized meaning of "distance"; with others, it adds the notion of "extreme" in time, place, or state. With still others, it is impossible to determine precisely what the translocative adds to the meaning of the whole. Where the meaning of the translocative is opaque, it is a discontinuous part of the verb stem. In a few cases, the translocative is obligatory with a particular verb root or stem. In most cases, however, a root or stem occurs with the translocative with a particular meaning and with other affixes or unaffixed with other meanings. Below are listed all those cases that have been encountered in the data base from which this dictionary has been constructed where the translocative is opaque in meaning and forms part of the stem.

–yah–. –ač²ahT– go forth, hurry away. *v.s.-a.i.* yahwa²kayę́č²aht ‹thither-fact-they-themselves-exhaust-caused› *they hurried away* (RC 3:9), *they went forth* (RC 32:5), weyuč²áhnę ‹thither-it-itself-exhaust-caused› *it is all gone* (R).

–yah–. –ahk(e)T– go and return. *v.s.-a.i.* wewahknę́he² ‹thither-it-went back and forth-going to› *it was going and coming* (RC 28:5), wewáhknę ‹thither-it went back and forth› *it goes and returns* (RC 34:12).

–yah–. –ahnę²ęha'nye²– recede. *v.s.-a.i.* yahwa²uhnę²ęhá·²nye² ‹thither-fact-it-disappeared-going along› *it receded* (HS).

–yah–. –ahsthu– be the smallest. *v.s.-s.i.* wehráhsthę ‹thither-he-is small› *he is the smallest* (RC 13:1).

–yah–. –akęwhę– lie inside. *v.s.-a.i.* wehrakę́whęh ‹thither-he-lies within-much› *he lies inside it* (RC 3:73).

–yah–. –areręti– west. *dv.n.s.* wewarerę́·tyęhs ‹thither-it-(sun) sets› *west* (R), wewarerę́·tyęhs kę²náhkę ‹thither-it-(sun) sets side› *western* (HS).

Tuscarora Pronunciation Key:
/a/ l<u>a</u>w; /e/ h<u>a</u>t; /i/ p<u>i</u>zza; /u/ t<u>u</u>ne; /ę/ h<u>i</u>nt; /č/ <u>ch</u>eese; /h/ <u>h</u>oe; /m/ <u>m</u>other; /s/ <u>s</u>ame; /t/ <u>d</u>o (before a vowel y, or w), <u>t</u>oo (elsewhere); /k/ <u>g</u>ale (before a vowel y or w), <u>k</u>ale (elsewhere); /n/ i<u>n</u>hale (before a consonant or word-final), <u>n</u>ote (elsewhere), /r/ hi<u>ss</u> (before a consonant or word-final), <u>r</u>un (trilled as in Italian, elsewhere); /w/ cu<u>ff</u> (before a consonant other than y or word-final), <u>w</u>ay (elsewhere); /y/ fi<u>sh</u> (before a consonant or word-final), <u>y</u>ou (elsewhere), /θ/ <u>th</u>ing; /²/ (the sound between the vowels in unh-unh); /·/ long vowel, /´/ high pitch; /`/ low pitch.

–**yah** –. –**athaha̲kuhsi** – go directly, straighten out path. *v.s.-a.i.* wa⁷θathahakúhsi ‹thither-you!-yourself-path-take-undo› *straighten out your path there!* (RC 3: 44).

–**yah** –. –**athwe⁷nę** – rush forward. *v.s.-a.i.* yęθwathwé⁷nę⁷ ‹thither-prediction-you-yourselves-furrow-fall› *you will rush forward* (RC 33:5).

–**yah** –. –**athwe⁷nęti** – dart forth. *v.s.-a.i.* wewathwe⁷nę́·tyęhs ‹thither-it-itself-furrow-makes› *it darts forth* (HS).

–**yah** –. –**atkahrawi⁷T** – peak. *v.s.-a.i.* weyutkahrawí⁷nę ‹thither-it-itself-eye-give to-caused› *it was peaking* (RC 8: 35).

–**yah** –. –**atkaręwθę** – travel greatly. *v.s.-a.i.* yahwa⁷kayętkarę́wθę·⁷ ‹thither-fact-they-themselves-went around-much› *they traveled greatly* (RC 29:11).

–**yah** –. –**atkę⁷θahnę** – look over the place. *v.s.-a.i.* yahwa⁷nyetkę⁷θáhnę·⁷ ‹thither-fact-two-one-saw-going to-much› *the two of them look over the place* (R).

–**yah** –. –**atkę⁷θehrę** – go to look at. *v.s.-t.* weyętkę⁷θéhręhs ‹thither-one-oneself-sees-going to-much› *one went to look at it* (RC 3:27).

–**yah** –. –**atkwira'ne** – crown of tree, end of branch. *dv.n.s.* wekatkwirá·⁷ne⁷ ‹thither-it-branch is present› *crown of tree* (AG), *end of branch* (RC 4:1).

–**yah** –. –**a̲⁷na·θ(e)** – go around. *v.s.-a.i.* yahwahrakwa⁷ná·θe·⁷ ‹thither-fact-he-X-encircled› *he went around* (HS).

–**yah** –. –**(a)'ne** – summit, tip top, top. *dv. n.s.* wewá·⁷ne⁷ ‹thither-it-is present› *tip top, top, summit* (HS).

–**yah** –. –**a'nękuhT** – go beyond. *v.s.-a.i.* wehra⁷nękúhtha⁷ ‹thither-he-himself-go through-causes› *he goes beyond* (HS).

–**yah** –. –**a'nwęta̲kahT** – overhear. *v.s.-t.* we-

yę⁷nwętakáhtha⁷ ‹thither-one-oneself-word-catches sight of› *one overhears* (RC 4:3).

–**yah** –. –**čiyę** – pour. *v.s.-t.* yahwahrači·yę⁷ ‹thither-fact-he-poured› *he poured it* (RC 12:29).

–**yah** –. –**e** – eternity, forever. *dv.n.s.* ha⁷ yę·we⁷ ‹the thither-prediction-it-go› *eternity, forever* (HS).

–**yah** –. –**erihθe** – need. *v.s.-t.* yękyeríhθek ‹thither-prediction-I-want-be going to› *I will need it* (RC 30:24).

–**yah** –. –**(ę)⁷tikęhrhaw** – apprehend, solve. *v.s.-t.* wehrę⁷tikę́rhews ‹thither-he-mind-brings› *he apprehends it, he solves it* (HS).

–**yah** –. –**(ę)⁷tikęhra̲yeri** – be sane. *v.s.-s.i.* weka⁷tikęhrayè·ri⁷ ‹thither-it-mind-is correct› *it is sane* (HS).

–**yah** –. –**hnęwyęhsT** – absorb, sink in. *v.s.-a.i.* wekahnęwyę́hstha⁷ ‹thither-it-lake bed-go into-causes› *it sinks in, it is absorbed* (HS).

–**yah** –. –**hrihT** – break up. *v.s.-t.* wekáhrihč ‹thither-it-spill-causes› *it is broken up* (RC 10:2).

–**yah** –. –**hur** – grow old. *v.s.-a.i.* weθahù·rę ‹thither-you-grew old› *you are growing old* (R), yahwahráhu⁷r ‹thither-fact-he-grew old› *he grew old* (R).

–**yah** –. –**(i)hkʷa̲⁷T** – yearn for. *v.s.-t.* wehráhkwa⁷nę ‹thither-he-picked up› *he yearns for it* (RC 34:3).

–**yah** –. –**ihnęk** – send for. *v.s.-t.* weyę⁷na⁷níhnęks ‹thither-one=another-sends for› *one sends for another* (HS).

–**yah** –. –**i⁷rę** – abandon, leave. *v.s.-t.* yahwa⁷kayę⁷na⁷ní⁷rę⁷ ‹thither-fact-they=another-set› *they left (abandoned) him* (M 87).

–**yah** –. –**kę** – foresee. *v.s.-t.* wehrá·kęh ‹thither-he-sees› *he foresees* (HS).

–**yah** –. –**kęhruk** – strike. *v.s.-t.* weθkę́hruk ‹thither-you-strike› *strike it!* (R).

-yah -. -rẹhya̱ʔniha - horizon. *dv.n.s.* we-yurẹhyaʔníhẹ ‹thither-it-sky-sprained› *horizon* (HS).

-yah -. -rihwa̱rehsT - exaggerate. *v.s.-t.* wehrarihwaréhstha‹ʔ› ‹thither-he-matter-stretches› *he exaggerates it* (HS).

-yah -. -rihwa̱yẹ(T) -{dative II} become responsibility. *v.s.-a.i.* weθaríhwayẹhθ ‹thither-you-matter-laid-for› *it has become your responsibility* (RC 12: ·21).

-yah -. -tahrek - touch. *v.r.-t.* hab: -, pnt: -ɸ, stat: -, prog: -, prp: -, dst: -, caus: -, rvs: -, dat: -, n-inc. yahwaʔktáhre·k *I touched it* (R), yahwahrátahre·k *he touched it* (R), yahwahstáhre·k *you touched it* (R).

-yah -. -takwna̱kẹʔneti - transpose. *v.s.-t.* wehratakwnakẹʔné·tyẹhs ‹thither-he-place-changes› *he transposes it* (HS).

-yah -. -weh - talk over the phone. *v.s.-a.i.* wehrà·weh ‹thither-he-speaks› *he talks (as over the phone) in a distant place* (L 16).

-yah -. -yahskaht be absent, be away. *v.s.-s.i.* wekayáhskaht ‹thither-it-follows› *it is absent, it is away, it is still absent* (H-notebook).

-yah -. -yeri - be ample, be complete, be correct, be o.k., be right, be sane, be straight. *v.s.-s.i.* wekayè·riʔ ‹thither-it-is correct› *it is ample, it is complete, it is correct, it is o.k., it is right, it is sane, it is straight* (RC 6: 11).

-yah -. -yeriʔ - fit, suffice. *v.s.-a.i.* we-kayè·riʔθ ‹thither-it-be correct-begins› *it fits, it suffices* (HS).

-yah -. -ʔčiraʔnihrhẹ - sting. *v.s.-t.* weka-kuʔčiraʔnírhẹ· ‹thither-they-sting-stood up-many› *it stung them* (RC 26: 10).

-yah -. -ʔtẹʔni - attack. *v.r.-a.i.* hab: -, pnt: -ʔ, stat: -, prog: -, prp: -, dst: -ehθẹ-, caus: -, rvs: -, dat: -, n-inc. yahwaʔkakuʔtẹʔniʔ *they attacked there* (RC 31:12); -yah -. -ʔtẹʔnyehθẹ -: we-kakuʔtẹʔnyéhθẹʔ ‹thither-they-attacked-much› *they had attacked there* (RC 31:12).

-yah+či -. -yeri - return to normal. *v.s.-a.i.* yahẹθakayè·riʔ ‹thither-fact-again-it-is correct› *it returned to normal* (RC 18:4).

-yahč - be curious, be odd, be strange, be whimsical. *v.r.-s.i.* stat: -ih, prog: -, prp: -, dst: -, caus: -, rvs: -, dat: -, inc.-ɸ-pat. yuyáhčih *it is curious, it is strange* (HS), ruyáhčih *he is curious, he is odd, he is whimsical* (HS); -hehna̱yahč -: uhehnayáhčih ‹field-be curious› *it is a peculiar field; the field has strange, unique or strange qualities* (H 2484); -yahčẹti -: rayahčẹ́·tih ‹he-be curious-makes› *he is a specific person* (RC 12:1), kayahčẹ́·tih ‹it-be curious-makes› *it is certain, it has to be* (RC 3:10); -uhsta̱yahčẹti -: wuhsta-yahčẹ́·tih ‹it-year-be curious-makes› *a certain year* (RC 12:7).

-yahčẹti - be a certain one, be a particular one. *v.s.-s.i.* rayahčẹ́·tih ‹he-be curious-makes› *he is a specific person* (RC 12:1), kayahčẹ́·tih ‹it-be curious-makes› *it is certain, it has to be* (RC 3:10); -uhsta̱yahčẹti -: wuhstayahčę́·ti⁷ ‹it-year-be curious-makes› *a certain year* (RC 12:7).

yahęθa – translocative+factual+repetitive. *v.pfx.* Before pronominal prefixes that begin with the consonant *y* the final *a* of the prefix is dropped and the *θ* coalesces with the following *y* to yield **yahęč** –.

ya·hí⁷ yow! (said by the lead of three persons pushing a log to the other two to start them pushing together) (R). *part.*

–**yahkw** – girth; scrotum, bag-like form; see-saw. *n.r.* inal: kyáhkweh *my scrotum* (n-poss. in other meanings), inc., n.sfx. -eh. uyáhkweh *girth; see-saw* (HS), *scrotum, bag-like form, a dress or apron in bag-like form* (H-notebook); –**yahkwanhahsi** –: na⁷nyahkwanháhsyęhs ‹one=another-girth-be full-undoes› *one unswathes another, one unwraps another* (HS); –**yahkwan**= **hahsthę** –: na⁷nyahkwanháhsthęh ‹one=another-girth-be full-causes-much› *one swaddles another* (HS); –**a'nyahkwah**= **ninę** –: ra⁷nyahkwahnì·nęhs ‹it-itself-girth-buys› *he sells fish* (W 74) (possibly a mistake for, or a modern restructuring of ra⁷nyahkwì·nęhs, see below); –**a'nyahkwayę(T)** –: ru⁷nyáh-kwayęhs ‹he-himself-girth-lays› he exposes for sale (H-notebook); wa⁷nyáh-kwayę⁷ ‹it-itself-girth-laid› *prostitute* (HS); –**a'nyahkwayę'nahkw** –: yę⁷nyah-kwayę⁷náhkhwa⁷ ‹one-oneself-girth-lays-instrument› *market* (HS); –**a'nyah**= **kwhar** –: ra⁷nyáhkhwar ‹he-himself-girth-hangs› *he swings* (HS), yu⁷nyáh-khwar ‹it-itself-girth-hangs› *it oscillates, it swings* (HS); –**a'nyahkwiN** –: ra⁷nyahkwì·nęhs ‹he-himself-girth-proceeds› *he peddles goods* (HS).

–**yahkwanhahsi** – unswathe, unwrap. *v.s.-t.* na⁷nyahkwanháhsyęhs ‹one=anoth-er-girth-be full-undoes› *one unswathes another, one unwraps another* (HS).

–**yahkwanhahsthę** – swaddle. *v.s.-t.* na⁷-nyahkwanháhsthęh ‹one=another-girth-be full-causes-much› *one swaddles another* (HS).

–**yahkwe⁷ręk** – be stingy. *v.r.-a.i.* hab: -s, pnt: -, stat: -, prog: -, prp: -, dst: -, caus: -, rvs: -, dat: -, inc.-ɸ-pat. As in several other roots, the final *ę* of this root is pronounced *u* by some speakers of the modern language. ruyah-kwé⁷ręks *he is stingy* (HS), θayah-kwé⁷ręks *he is stingy* (R).

–**yahn** – sole of foot. *n.r.* poss. ?, inc. ?, n.sfx. -eh. uyáhneh *sole of foot* (SH 375).

–**yahsenha** – accommodate. *v.r.-t.* hab: -hs, pnt: -, stat: -, prog: -, prp: -, dst: -, caus: -hT-, rvs: -, dat: -, n-inc. na⁷-nyahsénhahs *one accommodates another* (HS); ha⁷ –**yahsenhahT** –: ha⁷ uyahsénhaht ‹the accommodate-cause› *assistance* (HS).

–**yahsenhahT** – assistance. *n.s.* ha⁷ uyah-sénhaht ‹the accommodate-cause› *assistance* (HS).

–**yahshę(T)** – lie down. *v.r.-a.i.* hab: -, pnt: -, stat: -?, prog: -, prp: -, dst: -, caus: -, rvs: -, dat: -, inc.-ɸ-pat. ka-yáhshę⁷ *it lay* (RC 7:4), rayáhshę⁷ *he is prostrate* (HS), ęhrayáhshę⁷ *he will lie down* (RC 3:70), ęhrayahshę́·⁷nak *he will prostrate himself* (HS), –**a**= **'nyahshę(T)** –: wahra⁷nyáhshę⁷ ‹fact-he-himself-lay down› *he lay down* (RC 3:73).

–**yahskaht** follow, result. *v.r.-s.i.* stat: -ɸ, prog: -, prp: -, dst: -, caus: -, rvs: -, dat: -, n-inc. kayáhskaht *it follows, it results* (RC 1:8); –**yah** –.–**yahskaht**: we-kayáhskaht ‹thither-it-follows› *it is absent, it is away, it is still absent* (H-notebook).

–**yahskenha** – aide, benefit. *v.s.-t.* rayahskyénhahs ‹he-X-strives› *he aides it* (HS), kayahskyénhahs ‹it-X-strives› *it benefits* (HS).

–**yahst** – individual; thousand. *n.r.* n-poss., inc., n.sfx. -eh. uyáhsteh *individual: thousand* (R) [Lawson «Youch se» 'Hundred']; –**yahstahnę** –: waˀkyahstáhnęˀ ‹fact-I-individual-disappeared› *I got lost* (RC 3:40); –**yahstahnęha** = **'nyeˀ** –: rayahstahnęháˑˀnyeˀθ ‹he-individual-disappears-going along› *he wanders* (HS); –**yahstahnęˀT** –: ęyęˀnaˀnyahstáhnęˀt ‹prediction-one=another-individual-disappear-cause› *one will murder another* (R); –**yahstę'ni** –: rayahstęˑˀnyęhs ‹he-individual-throws› *he abandons (person)* (HS); –**yahsti** –: kayáhstih ‹it-individual-is a group› *hundred* (RC 30:67) [Lawson «Ki you se» 'Thousand'], rayáhstih ‹he-individual-is a group› *male individual* (HS); –či –. –**yahsti** –: θkayáhstih ‹again-it-individual-is a group› *hundred* (L 13); –či –. –**yahstaT** –: θhrayáhstaˑt ‹again-he-individual-stands› *one male* (RC 1:8); –či –. –**yahstatha'nyeˀ** –: θkayeyahstatháˑˀnyeˀ ‹again-they-individual-stand-going along› *one-by-one* (RC 3:81); –**ne** –. –**yahsti** –: nekayáhstih ‹two-it-individual-is a group› *two hundred* (L 13); ti –. –**yahsti** –: tikayáhstih ‹so-it-individual-is a group› *hundreds of: multitude* (RC 4:1); áhsę ti –. –**yahsti** –: áhsę tikayáhstih ‹three so-it-individual-is a group› *three hundred*

(L 13); –**yahstiyu** – –a'nęˀ –: ruyahstíˑyuˑwáˑˀnęˀ ‹he-individual-is great it-becomes› *his decline of years, he is growing old* (HS), rayahstìˑyuh wáˑˀnęˀ ‹he-individual-is great it-becomes› *he grows old* (HS); –**yahsti** – **tha+ne** –. –**hswatetˀ** –: kayáhstih thaˀneyuhswáˑteˑt ‹it-individual-is a group unusual-apart-it-back-lines› *centuple* (HS); –**yahsti** – ti –. –ˀęhraˀnihr –: kayáhstih tikaˀęhráˀnihč ‹it-individual-is a group so-it-leaf-stands up› *centifolious* (HS); –**ahθhę** – ti –. –**yahsti** – **naˀ** –**yahst** –: wáhθhęˑ tikayáhstih naˀ uyáhsteh ‹it-ten so-it-individual-is a group much individual› *million* (HS); ę́ˑči naˀ –**yahst** – ti –. –**yahsti** –: ę́ˑči naˀ uyáhsteh tikayáhstih ‹one much individual so-it-individual-is a group› *million* (HS).

–**yahstahnę** – get lost. *v.s.-a.i.* waˀkyahstáhnęˀ ‹fact-I-individual-disappeared› *I got lost* (RC 3:40).

–**yahstahnęha'nyeˀ** – wander. *v.s.-a.i.* rayahstahnęháˑˀnyeˀθ ‹he-individual-disappears-going along› *he wanders* (HS).

–**yahstahnęˀT** – murder. *v.s.-t.* ęyęˀnaˀnyahstáhnęˀt ‹prediction-one=another-individual-disappear-cause› *one will murder another* (R).

–**yahstę'ni** – abandon. *v.s.-t.* rayahstęˑˀnyęhs ‹he-individual-throws› *he abandons (person)* (HS).

–**yahsti** – hundred. *dv.n.s.* kayáhstih ‹it-individual-is a group› *hundred* (RC 30:67) [Lawson «Ki you se» 'Thousand'].

Tuscarora Pronunciation Key:
/a/ l<u>a</u>w; /e/ h<u>a</u>t; /i/ p<u>i</u>zza; /u/ t<u>u</u>ne; /ę/ h<u>in</u>t; /č/ <u>ch</u>eese; /h/ <u>h</u>oe; /m/ <u>m</u>other; /s/ <u>s</u>ame; /t/ <u>d</u>o (before a vowel y, or w), <u>t</u>oo (elsewhere); /k/ <u>g</u>ale (before a vowel y or w), <u>k</u>ale (elsewhere); /n/ i<u>nh</u>ale (before a consonant or word-final), <u>n</u>ote (elsewhere), /r/ hi<u>ss</u> (before a consonant or word-final), <u>r</u>un (trilled as in Italian, elsewhere); /w/ cu<u>ff</u> (before a consonant other than y or word-final), <u>w</u>ay (elsewhere); /y/ fi<u>sh</u> (before a consonant or word-final), <u>y</u>ou (elsewhere), /θ/ <u>th</u>ing; /ˀ/ (the sound between the vowels in unh-unh); /ˑ/ long vowel, /ˊ/ high pitch; /ˋ/ low pitch.

-yahsti - tha+ne -. -hswatet⁷ - centuple. *dv.
n.s. kayáhstih tha⁷neyuhswá·te·t ‹it-
individual-is a group unusual-apart-it-
back-lines› *centuple* (HS).

-yahsti - ti -. -⁷ęhra⁷nihr - centifolious. *dv.*
n.s. kayáhstih tika⁷ęhrá⁷nihč ‹it-individual-is a group so-it-leaf-stands up›
centifolious (HS).

yahwa⁷ - translocative+factual. *v.pfx.* Before pronominal prefixes that begin
with the consonant *h* the final *⁷* of the
prefix is dropped. With pronominal
prefixes that begin with the sequence
wa the final *wa⁷* of the prefix coalesces with the initial sequence *wa* to
yield yahę -.

yahwa⁷nęθa - translocative+factual+dual-
ic+repetitive. *v.pfx.* Before pronominal prefixes that begin with the consonant *y* the final *a* of the prefix is
dropped and the *θ* coalesces with the
following *y* to yield yahwa⁷nęč -.

yahwa⁷T(i) - translocative+factual+cisloc-
ative. *v.pfx.* The form yahwa⁷n - occurs before pronominal prefixes that
begin with the consonants *w* or *y*. The
form yahwa⁷t - occurs before pronominal prefixes that begin with the consonants *k* or *h*. The form yahwa⁷ni -
occurs elsewhere. Occurs in word-
initial position before pronominal prefixes that begin with the consonants *k*
and *h*.

yahwa⁷T(i) - translocative+factual+dualic.
v.pfx. The form yahwa⁷n - occurs before pronominal prefixes that begin
with the consonants *w* or *y*. The form
yahwa⁷t - occurs before pronominal
prefixes that begin with the consonants *k* or *h*. The form yahwa⁷ni - occurs elsewhere. Occurs in word-initial
position before pronominal prefixes
that begin with the consonants *k* and
h.

-yakaw -/ -yaku - it (third person singular
feminine/indefinite patient). *v.r.pfx.*
The form -yakaw - before roots and
stems that begin with a vowel other
than *a*. The form -yaku - occurs elsewhere. After the factual mode, the
initial *y* of the prefix is dropped.

-yakę - exit, go out, leave. *v.r.-a.i.* hab: -,
pnt: -·⁷, stat: -, prog: -, prp: -, dst: -,
caus: -hw-, rvs: -, dat: -, n-inc.
akayá·kę·⁷ *that it leave* (RC 15:10),
wa⁷eyá·kę·⁷ *one left* (RC 3:62); -ya=
kęhw -: ęyeyá·kęw ‹prediction-one-go
out-cause› *one will extract* (RC 20:1),
wa⁷kayá·kęw ‹fact-it-go out-caused› *it
drove out* (RC 18:4), rayá·kęws ‹he-go
out-causes› *he issues, he turns out*
(HS); -yakę⁷ -: kyá·kę⁷θ ‹I-go out-begin› *I go out* (HS); -yakę⁷čruk -: ruya-
kę⁷čruks ‹he-go out-begin-'ness-blisters› *he goes to stool* (HS); -či -.
-yakę -: ęθkyá·kę·⁷ ‹prediction-again-
it-go out› *I will go back out* (RC 26:
10); -či -. -yakę⁷ -: θkyá·kę⁷θ ‹again-I-
go out-begin› *I go out again* (HS);
-t-. -yakę⁷ -: thrayá·kę⁷θ ‹hither-he-go
out-begins› *he emanates* (HS), thru-
yakę́⁷ę ‹hither-he-go out-began› *he
has emanated* (HS).

-yakęhw - extract, drive out, issue, turn
out. *v.s.-t.* ęyeyá·kęw ‹prediction-one-
go out-cause› *one will extract* (RC 20:
1), wa⁷kayá·kęw ‹fact-it-go out-
caused› *it drove out* (RC 18:4), rayá·-
kęws ‹he-go out-causes› *he issues, he
turns out* (HS).

-yakę⁷ - go out. *v.s.-a.i.* kyá·kę⁷θ ‹I-go
out-begin› *I go out* (HS).

yakT(i) -/yaky - our (his or her and mine)
(first person exclusive dual inalienable). *n.r.pfx.* The form yakn - occurs
before roots and stems that begin with
the vowel *ę* or the morphophoneme
{ⁿu}. The form yakt - occurs before

roots and stems that begin with the vowels *i*, *e*, or *u* (not from {"u}). The form **yaky**- occurs before roots and stems that begin with the vowel *a*. The form **yakti**- occurs before roots and stems that begin with a consonant.

-**yakT(i)**-/-**yaky**- the two of us (he or she and I) (first person exclusive dual agent). *v.r.pfx*. The form -**yakn**- occurs before roots and stems that begin with the vowel *ę* or the morphophoneme {"u}. The form -**yakt**- occurs before roots and stems that begin with the vowels *i*, *e*, or *u* (not from {"u}). The form -**yaky**- occurs before roots and stems that begin with the vowel *a*. The form -**yakti**- occurs before roots and stems that begin with a consonant.

yakwa- our (theirs and mine) (first person exclusive plural inalienable). *n.r. pfx*. With roots and stems that begin with the vowel *i* the final *a* of the prefix coalesces with the *i* to yield -**ya=kwę**-. Before roots and stems that begin with other vowels the final *a* of the prefix is lost.

-**yakwa**- all of us (they and I) (first person exclusive plural agent). *v.r.pfx*. With roots and stems that begin with the vowel *i* the final *a* of the prefix coalesces with the *i* to yield -**yakwę**-. Before roots and stems that begin with other vowels the final *a* of the prefix is lost.

-**yan(e)(r)**- lead, govern, rule. *v.r.-s.i.*

stat: -ɸ, prog: -, prp: -, dst: -, caus: -, rvs: -, dat: -, n-inc. This root is irregular and no rules for the occurrence of the forms -**yane**-, -**yaner**-, and -**yanr**- can be given. This is undoubtedly due to the fact that nearly all the words containing this root, like other words referring to government and religion, have been borrowed from other Northern Iroquoian languages. ruyà·ner *lord* (RC 12:1); *Confederate Chief; Jesus Christ* (R); -**ya=nerčr**-: uyanérčreh ‹rule-'ness› *government, monarchy, sovereignty* (R) (also: uyané?čreh (HS), kayané?čra? (HS)); -**yane?čhę(T)**-: rayané?čhę? ‹he-rule-'ness-lays› *he reigns, he rules* (HS); -**yane?čr**-: uyané?čreh ‹rule-'ness› *government, monarchy, sovereignty* (HS), kayané?čra? ‹rule-'ness› *government, monarchy, sovereignty* (HS); -**yanrahsT**-: yuyanráhsnę ‹it-rule-caused› *it is propitious* (HS); -**ya=nręhst**-: uyanręhsteh ‹rule-'ness› *institutes, law, statute* (HS); -**yanręhsta?ke**: uyanręhstá?kye ‹rule-'ness-at› *legal, legitimate* (HS); -**yanręhstęti**-: rayanręhstę́·tih ‹he-rule-'ness-makes› *legislator* (HS); -**yanręhstatkahT**-: rayanręhstatkáhne? ‹he-rule-'ness-chases› *he observes laws* (HS); -**yanręhsta=kęha**-: rayanręhstakę́hahs ‹he-rule-'ness-raises› *policeman* (HS); -**ya=n(e)(r)**- -**atręnayęta?črawę**-: ruyà·ner rutręnayęta?črà·węh ‹he-rules he-prayer-lay-'ness-possesses› *Lord's Prayer* (HS); -**yan(e)(r)**- -**khwah(e)r**-: ruyà·-

---

ner rakhwáher ‹he-rules he-meal-puts up› *Last Supper* (HS); **kwęhs** –ya= **n(e)(r)**– –i–: kwęhs yuyané·rę·t ará·kę·k ‹no it-rule-possesses unknown-it-is a group› *innocently* (HS); **kwęhs** –ya= **nręhsta?ke** –i–: kwęhs uyanręhstá?kye ará·kę·k ‹no rule-'ness-at unknown-it-is a group› *it is unlawful* (HS).

–**yan(e)(r)**– lord, Jesus Christ, Confederate Chief. *dv.n.s.* ruyà·ner *lord* (RC 12:1); *Confederate Chief; Jesus Christ* (R).

–**yan(e)(r)**– –**atręnayęta?črawę**– Lord's Prayer. *dv.n.s.* ruyà·ner rutręnayęta?-črà·węh ‹he-rules he-prayer-lay-'ness-possesses› *Lord's Prayer* (HS).

–**yan(e)(r)**– –**khwah(e)r**– Last Supper. *dv. n.s.* ruyà·ner rakhwáher ‹he-rules he-meal-puts up› *Last Supper* (HS).

–**yanerčr**– government, monarchy, sovereignty. *n.s.* uyanérčreh ‹rule-'ness› *government, monarchy, sovereignty* (R) (Also: uyané?čreh (HS), kayané?-čra? (HS)).

–**yane?čhę(T)**– reign, rule. *v.s.-a.i.* rayané?čhę? ‹he-rule-'ness-lays› *he reigns, he rules* (HS).

–**yane?čr**– government, monarchy, sovereignty. *n.s.* uyané?čreh ‹rule-'ness› *government, monarchy, sovereignty* (HS) (Also: uyanérčreh (R), kayané?čra? (HS)), kayané?čra? *government, monarchy, sovereignty* (HS).

–**yanrahsT**– be propitious. *v.s.-s.i.* yuyanráhsnę ‹it-rule-caused› *it is propitious* (HS).

–**yanręhst**– institutes, law, statute. *n.s.* uyanręhsteh ‹rule-'ness› *institutes, law, statute* (HS).

–**yanręhsta?ke** legal, legitimate. *n.s.* uyanręhstá?kye ‹rule-'ness-at› *legal, legitimate* (HS).

–**yanręhstęti**– legislator. *dv.n.s.* rayanręhstę́·tih ‹he-rule-'ness-makes› *legislator*

(HS).

–**yanręhstatkahT**– observe laws. *v.s.-a.i.* rayanręhstatkáhne? ‹he-rule-'ness-chases› *he observes laws* (HS).

–**yanręhstakęha**– policeman. *dv.n.s.* rayanręhstakę́hahs ‹he-rule-'ness-raises› *policeman* (HS).

–**yar**– bag, sack. *n.r.* n-poss., inc., n.sfx. -eh. uyà·reh *bag, sack* (R) [Lawson «Ooyaura» 'Basket']; –**yaręti**–: kayarę́·tih‹it-bag-makes› *wicker* (HS).

ya(r)(a)– translocative+optative. *v.pfx.* The form **yara**– occurs when the prefix receives word accent; if this form is followed by a pronominal prefix that begins with the sequence *wa*, the final vowel contracts with the sequence to give **yarę**–. The form **yar**– occurs when the prefix is unaccented before pronominal prefixes that begin with the glides *w* or *y*. The form **ya**– occurs elsewhere.

–**yaręti**– wicker. *dv.n.s.* kayarę́·tih ‹it-bag-makes› *wicker* (HS).

–**yaθ**– be called, be named. v.r.-*a.i.* hab: -s, pnt: -, stat: -ę, prog: -, prp: -, dst: -hę-, caus: -, rvs: -, dat: -, n-inc. kayá·θę *it is called* (RC 3:38), yè·yač *one is called* (RC 9:1), kayè·yač *they call it* (L 39), akayá·θęk *that it be called* (R); –**yaθęhst**–: uyaθę́hsteh ‹be called-'ness› *character, name* (R); –**ya**= **θęhstakareti**–: ruyaθęhstakaré·ti· ‹he-be called-'ness-is loud› *he is famous* (HS); –**yaθhę**–: kayá·θhęh ‹it-is called-much› *it is pronounced* (HS).

–**yaθęhst**– character, name. *n.s.* uyaθę́hsteh ‹be called-'ness› *character, name* (R).

–**yaθęhstakareti**– be famous. *v.s.-s.i.* ruyaθęhstakaré·ti· ‹he-be called-'ness-is loud› *he is famous* (HS).

–**yaθhę**– pronounce. *v.s.-t.* kayá·θhęh ‹it-is called-much› *he pronounces it* (HS).

-yat – gait. *n.r.* n-poss., inc., n.sfx. -eh. uyá·teh *gait* (HS); –yatahshay –: ruyatahshà·yę ‹he-gait-is slow› *his gait is slow* (HS).

-yatahshay – have a slow gait. *v.s.-s.i.* ruyatahshà·yę ‹he-gait-is slow› *his gait is slow* (HS).

-yataʔT – pout, sulk. *v.r.-a.i.* hab: -, pnt: -, stat: -eʔ, prog: -, prp: -, dst: -, caus: -, rvs: -, dat: -, inc.-ɸ-pat. ruyatáʔneʔ *he pouts* (HS), rayatáʔthaʔ *he sulks* (HS); –aˈnyataʔT –: yuʔnyatáʔnę ‹it-it-self-sulked› *it is poison* (RC 2:14); –a=tkęhsayataʔnahnę –: ratkęhsayataʔnáhnęh ‹he-himself-face-sulks-much› *he makes grimaces* (HS); –atkęhsaya=taʔT –: ratkęhsayatáʔthaʔ ‹he-himself-face-sulks› *he makes grimaces* (H-notebook).

-yatkay – be slow. *v.r.-s.i.* stat: -ę, prog: -, prp: -, dst: -, caus: -, rvs: -, dat: -, n-inc. ruyatkà·yę *he is slow* (R); –ya=tkayaʔT –: rayatkayáʔthaʔ ‹he-be slow-causes› *he slackens* (HS).

-yatkayaʔT – slacken. *v.s.-a.i.* rayatkayáʔthaʔ ‹he-be slow-causes› *he slackens* (HS).

-yaw –/–yu – it (third person singular neuter patient). *v.r. pfx.* The form –yaw – occurs before roots and stems that begin with the vowels *i, e, u,* or *ę.* The form –yu – occurs before roots and stems that begin with a consonant or the vowel *a.* The initial *y* of the prefix is dropped after the factual mode marker.

-yaʔk – market basket. *n.r.* n-poss., n-inc., n.sfx. -eh. uyáʔkyeh *market basket* (AW 50).

-yaʔk – break. *v.r.-t.* hab: -s, pnt: -ɸ, stat: -ę, prog: -, prp: -he-, dst: -hę-, caus: -T-, rvs: -, dat: I (-θe-/-θ-), inc.-ɸ-pat. í·kyaʔks *I am breaking it* (R), wáʔ-kyaʔk *I broke it* (R), čáʔk *break it!* (L 27); –(a)hahyaʔk –: raháhyaʔks ‹he-path-breaks› *he intercepts* (HS), *he prevents it (by cutting off its path, lit. he cuts or breaks off its road; also, he crosses the road, but this latter requires the prefixation of the dualic)* (H 2484), kaháhyaʔks ‹it-path-breaks› *it obviates it: difficulty (concrete)* (HS); –(a)hęˈnayaʔk –: rahęʔnayaʔks ‹he-clearing-breaks› *he cuts the meadow (i.e., the crop growing on the meadow)* (H 2484); –čiʔruryaʔkhe –: wahračiʔruryáʔkheʔ ‹fact-he-medicine stick-broke-going to› *he was going to break a medicine stick* (RC 30:53); –čiʔtkwaryaʔk –: yučiʔtkwaryáʔkę ‹it-bile-broke› *it is sprouting leaves (said of a forest or tree that has just burst its buds)* (HS); –(ę)traʔnyaʔk –: rętráʔ-nyaʔks ‹he-horn-breaks› *he breaks horns* (HS); –(ę)ʔtikęhryaʔkhę –: raʔti-kęhryáʔkhęh ‹he-mind-breaks-much› *he bothers it* (HS); –hehnyaʔk –: rahéhnyaʔks ‹he-field-breaks› *he cuts, divides the field in two, he cuts off a portion of the field* (H 2484); –he=ryaʔk –: rahé·ryaʔks ‹he-green-breaks› *he mows, he reaps* (HS); –heryaʔkT –: yeheryáʔkthaʔ ‹one-green-break-causes› *grass-cutter, scythe, sickle* (HS);

–hękarya?k –: rahçká·rya?ks ‹he-volunteer-breaks› *he hires it, he orders it*
(HS); –irya?k –.#áh: kęrya?k'?áh ‹it-
grain-breaks-little› *it broke in small
pieces* (RC 12:29); –karya?k –: natká·-
rya?ks ‹one=another-debt-breaks› *one
credits another* (HS); –karya?kčr –: u-
karyá?kčreh ‹debt-break-'ness› *hireage,
salary, wages* (HS); –kęhsya?k –: ę'?-
nwakęhsya?k ‹prediction-we-face-
break› *we'll eat* (R); –kęhya?khe –:
wa?kayę?natkęhyá?khe? ‹fact-they=
another-hem-broke-going to› *they
were disturbed* (RC 9:2); –rę'nya?k –:
rarę·?nya?ks ‹he-log-breaks› *he saws*
(R); –rihwya?k –{dative I}: na?rih-
wyá?kθeh ‹one=another-matter-breaks-
for› *one interrupts another* (HS);
–?ęya?k –: ra?ę̀·ya?ks ‹he-debt-breaks›
creditor (HS); –ne –. –ya?khę –: nehru-
yá?kę ‹two-he-broke› *he has broken it*
(L 27); –ne –. –či?ehnya?k –: nehrači?-
éhnya?ks ‹two-he-claw-breaks› *he
breaks the claw, he breaks its claw*
(HS); –ne –. –(ę)ta?rya?k –: newętá?-
rya?ks ‹two-it-head-breaks› *violet (Viola sp.)* (HS); –ne –. –(ę)tu?ča?k –: nehrętú?ča?ks ‹two-he-tooth-breaks› *he
breaks his tooth* (HS); –ne –. –hsu? =
θrya?k –: nehrahsú?θrya?ks ‹two-he-
point-breaks› *he breaks the point off*
(HS); –ne –. –(i)?nhahnya?k –: wa?tki?n-
háhnya?k ‹fact-two-I-branch-broke› *I
split branch in two* (R); –ne –. –nęh =
sya?khę –: nekanęhsyá?khęh ‹two-it-
house-breaks-much› *partition: the
house is divided (into two rooms)* (H-
notebook); –ne –. –rę'nya?kT –: neyerę?-
nyá?ktha? ‹two-one-log-break-causes›
saw (R); –ne –. –θręwya?k –: nehraθrę́·-
wya?ks ‹two-he-wax-breaks› *he
breaks the seal* (HS); –athriya?k –:
yuthriyá?kę ‹it-itself-spill-broke› *precipice* (HS); –athriya?k –.#ú?y: yuthri-
ya?kę?ú?y ‹it-itself-spill-broke-great›
abyss (HS), *great precipice* (RC 25:
27); –atkarya?k –: rutkaryá?ki ‹he-
himself-debt-broke› *his pension* (HS);
–a'na?wya?k –: ra?ná?wya?ks ‹he-
himself-back-breaks› *he limps* (HS);
–a'na?wya?khę –.#ú?y: ra?na?wya?-
khę?ú?y ‹he-himself-back-breaks-
much-great› *he, the big one, is going
limping* (RC 25:13); –a'nęrihstiya?k –:
ra?nęrihstì·ya?ks ‹he-himself-breathe-
'ness-breaks› *he expires* (H-notebook);
–a?rihwa?tikęhrya?khę –: ra?rihwa?ti-
kęhryá?khęh ‹he-himself-matter-mind-
breaks-much› *he inconveniences* (HS);
–ne –. –a'nya?k –: nęwá?nya?k ‹two-
prediction-it-itself-break› *I will break
it in two* (RC 24:8); –ne –. –a'nya?khę –:
newa?nyá?khę· ‹two-it-itself-broke-
much› *it broke in two* (RC 30:42);
–ne –. –a'nęnę?arya?k –: wa?nwa?nęnę?-
á·rya?k ‹fact-apart-it-itself-climbing
vine-broke› *the vine broke* (AG);
–ne –. –a'nwirya?k –: newa?nwí·rya?ks
‹two-it-itself-offspring-breaks› *it pups*
(HS); –ne –. –a?ręhsya?k –: wa?thra?-
rę́hsya?k ‹fact-two-he-himself-leg-
broke› *he broke his leg* (R); ha?
–yękwirya?k –: ha? rayękwí·rya?ks ‹the
he-wood-breaks› *wood-cutter* (HS);
ha? –athriya?k –: ha? yuthriyá?kę ‹the
it-itself-spill-broke› *extremity* (HS);
ha? čhę? –herya?k –: ha? čhę? kaheryá?kę ‹the just it-green-broke› *stubble*
(HS); ę́·či ha? hę́?tahk tha+ne –. –ya?k –:
ę́·či ha? hę́?tahk tha?nekayá?khęh ‹one
the four unusual-apart-it-breaks-much›
a quarter (HS).

–ya?kar – upper part of body. *n.r.* n-poss.,
inc., n.sfx. -eh. uyá?kareh *upper part
of body (above the waist)* (R); –ya? =
karyęti –: raya?karyę́·ti? ‹he-upper body-extends› *he is laying down supine*
(RC 3:50); –ya?karu?yehT –: ęyeya?-

karú'?yeht ‹prediction-one-upper body-bend-cause› *one will entrap upper body* (RC 24:8); ti‑. ‑ya'?kareθ‑: tika-yá'?kare·θ ‹so-it-upper body-is long› *the length of body* (AW 53); ‑a'nya'? = kar ę'ni‑: ra'?nya'?karę·'?nyęhs ‹he-him-self-upper body-throws› *he canters, he gallops* (HS); ‑ne‑. ‑a'nya'?karu'narhu‑: nę'?nya'?karu'?nárhu'? ‹apart-fact-it-it-self-upper body-hook-caused› *it hooked upper part of body* (RC 32:14).

‑ya'?karyęti‑ lay down supine. *v.s.-a.i.* raya'?karyę·ti'? ‹he-upper body-extends› *he is laying down supine* (RC 3:50).

‑ya'?karu'?yehT‑ entrap. *v.s.-t.* ęyeya'?karú'?yeht ‹prediction-one-upper body-bend-cause› *one will entrap* (RC 24:8).

‑ya'?n‑ carcass, corpse, dead body. *n.r.* n-poss., inc., n.sfx. ‑eh. uyá'?neh *carcass, corpse, dead body* (HS).

ya'?na(r)(a)‑ translocative+dualic+optative. *v.pfx.* The form ya'?nara‑ occurs whenever the prefix receives word accent; if this form is followed by a pronominal prefix that begins with the sequence *wa*, the final vowel contracts with the sequence to give ya'?narę‑. The form ya'?nar‑ occurs when the prefix is unaccented before pronominal prefixes that begin with the glides *w* or *y*. The form ya'?na‑ occurs elsewhere.

ya'?ne‑ translocative+dualic. *v.pfx.* Before pronominal prefixes that begin with the consonant *y* the final *e* is optionally dropped.

ya'?neči‑ translocative+dualic+repetitive. *v.pfx.* The form ya'?neči‑ occurs before the consonants θ or *t*, or the clusters '?*n* or '?*t*. The form ya'?neč‑ occurs before the consonant *y* and the *y* is dropped. The form ya'?neθ‑ occurs elsewhere.

ya'?nę‑ translocative+dualic+future. *v.pfx.*

ya'?nęči‑ translocative+dualic+future+repetitive. *v.pfx.* The form ya'?nęči‑ occurs before the consonants θ or *t*, or the clusters '?*n* or '?*t*. The form ya'? = nęč‑ occurs before the consonant *y* and the *y* is dropped. The form ya'? = nęθ‑ occurs elsewhere.

ya'?nęθa(r)(a)‑ translocative+dualic+optative+repetitive. *v.pfx.* The form ya'? = nęθara‑ occurs whenever the prefix receives word accent; if this form is followed by a pronominal prefix that begins with the sequence *wa*, the final vowel contracts with the sequence to give ya'?nęθarę‑. The form ya'?nęθar‑ occurs when the prefix is unaccented before pronominal prefixes that begin with the glides *w* or *y*. The form ya'?nęθa‑ occurs elsewhere.

‑ya'?r‑ bowel, entrails, intestine; hot dog, sausage. *n.r.* n-poss., inc., n.sfx. ‑eh. uyá'?reh *bowel, entrails, intestine; hot dog, sausage* (R); ‑ya'?rawihsi‑: na'?-nya'?rawíhsyęhs ‹one=another-intestine-give-undoes› *one disembowels another* (HS).

‑ya'?rawihsi‑ disembowel. *v.s.-t.* na'?-nya'?rawíhsyęhs ‹one=another-intestine-give-undoes⟩ *one disembowels another* (HS).

–yaʔθ– print, track; sole (of foot). *n.r.* n-poss., inc., n.sfx. –eh. uyáʔθeh *print, track: sole (of foot)* (HS); **–yaʔθa̱r–**: uyáʔθareh ⟨track-be in⟩ *tracks, footprints* (R), kayáʔθar ⟨it-track-is in⟩ *print* (HS); **–yaʔθa̱ra̱wę–**: kayaʔθarà·węh ⟨it-track-be in-possesses⟩ *its tracks* (RC 2:11); **–yaʔθaʔθ–**: kayáʔθaʔθ ⟨it-track-is of a size⟩ *mud sleigh* (H 3518); **–yaʔθęhawiʔ–**: rayaʔθęhà·wiʔθ ⟨he-track-bring-X-begins⟩ *he trails* (HS). ti–. **–yaʔčerih–**: tihrayaʔčeríhahs ⟨so-he-track-straightens⟩ *he is strict* (HS), tihruyaʔčeríhę· ⟨so-he-track-straightened⟩ *he is ingenious* (HS); ti+či–. **–yaʔčerih–**: tiθhrayaʔčeríhahs ⟨so-again-he-track-straightens⟩ *he rectifies* (HS); ti–. **–rihwa̱yaʔčerih–**: tihrarihwayaʔčeríhahs ⟨so-he-matter-track-straightens⟩ *he justifies* (HS); **haʔti–. –yaʔčerih–**: haʔtihruyaʔčeríhę· ⟨the so-he-track-straightened⟩ *his rectitude* (HS); **kwęhs tha–. –aʹnyaʔčerih–**: kwęhs tharyuʔnyaʔčeríhęhs ⟨no unusual-unknown-it-itself-track-straighten⟩ *it is indirect* (HS).

–yaʔθa̱r– tracks, footprints. *n.s.* uyáʔθareh ⟨track-be in⟩ *tracks, footprints* (R).

–yaʔθa̱r– print. *dv.n.s.* kayáʔθar ⟨it-track-is in⟩ *print* (HS).

–yaʔθaʔθ– mud sleigh. *n.* kayáʔθaʔθ ⟨it-track-is of a size⟩ *mud sleigh* (H 35 18).

–yaʔθ(e)r– cross, fold. *v.r.-t.* hab: ()-ɸ, pnt: -, stat: -·t, prog: -, prp: -, dst: -awę-, caus: -, rvs: -aku-, dat: -, inc.-ɸ-ag./pat. The form **–yaʔθr–** occurs whenever a morpheme beginning with a vowel follows. The form **–yaʔθer–** occurs elsewhere. **–yaʔθraʔke:** uyaʔθráʔkye ⟨cross-at⟩ *on a cross* (R); **–a̱=**

ʹnyaʔθrawę–: yuʔnyaʔθrà·węʔ ⟨it-itself-crossed-much⟩ *it is tiered* (HS); **–ne–. –rihwa̱yaʔθraku–**: waʔthrarihwayaʔθrá·kuʔ ⟨fact-two-he-matter-cross-undid⟩ *he answered* (RC 3:13), nyerihwayaʔθrá·kuʔ ⟨two-one-matter-cross-undid⟩ *one answers* (RC 3:29); **–t–. –rihwa̱yaʔθraku–**: tkrarihwayaʔθrá·kwahs ⟨hither-it-matter-cross-undoes⟩ *echo* (HS); **–ne+či–. –rihwa̱yaʔθraku–**: neθhrarihwayaʔθrá·kwahs ⟨two-again-he-matter-cross-undoes⟩ *he takes revenge: his vengeance* (HS); **–aʔrih=wa̱yaʔθrakʷahT–**: yuʔrihwayaʔθrá·kwaht ⟨it-itself-matter-cross-undo-caused⟩ *expiatory* (HS); **–ne–. –aʔrih=wa̱yaʔθraku–**: nehraʔrihwayaʔθrá·kwahs ⟨two-he-himself-matter-cross-undoes⟩ *he retorts* (HS); **tha+ne–. –atkyerha̱yaʔθ(e)r–**: thaʔneyutkyerhayáʔθer ⟨unusual-two-it-itself-body-crosses⟩ *body is crisscrossed* (RC 30:31); **–ne–. –athaha̱yaʔθ(e)r–**: neyuthahayáʔθer ⟨two-it-itself-path-crosses⟩ *crossroads* (HS); **–ne–. –aʹnyaʔθrawę–**: neyuʔnyaʔθrà·węʔ ⟨two-it-itself-crossed-much⟩ *it is crisscrossed (with markings)* (RC 32:7); **haʔ –ne–. –rihwa̱=yaʔθrakʷahT–**: haʔ neyurihwayaʔθrá·kwaht ⟨the two-it-matter-cross-undo-caused⟩ *answer* (HS); **kęʔ –athaha̱ya̱=θ(e)r–**: kęʔ yuthahayáʔθer ⟨where it-itself-path-crosses⟩ *where the roads are folded one on the other, or are tiered (this is the term applied to the four corners at the juncture of roads or where one crosses the other)* (H 24 84).

–yaʔθęhawiʔ– trail. *v.s.-t.* rayaʔθęhà·wiʔθ ⟨he-track-bring-begins⟩ *he trails* (HS).

–yaʔθraʔke on a cross. *n.s.* uyaʔθráʔkye ⟨cross-at⟩ *on a cross* (R).

–yaʔt– body. *n.r.* n-poss., inc., n.sfx. -. This root occurs only incorporated, in stems most of which have the appearance of being loan words from other Northern Iroquoian languages where -ya?t- is used, like Tuscarora -kerh- *body*, to form abstract stems. (The Tuscarora cognate of this root is -ya?n- *carcass, corpse*.) -ya?tahsteni-: akya?tahstè·ni? ‹unknown-I-body-adorn› *that I arrange it, that I put it in order, that I embellish it* (RC 3:11), raya?tahstè·nih ‹he-body-adorns› *he adorns it, he decorates it, he ornaments it* (HS); -ya?tahtir-: wa?akuyá?tahti?r ‹fact-one-body-was durable› *one walked upright* (RC 29:2); -ya?ta=kwe?niyu-: kaya?takwe?nì·yu? ‹it-body-is the main one› *principal* (HS); -ya?tanurehsT-: raya?tanuréhstha? ‹he-body-be precious-causes› *he ennobles it* (HS); -ya?tuhrarak-: yakuya?túhraraks ‹one-body-presses› *nightmare* (R); -ya?turehčraye(T)-: ruya?turéhčraye? ‹he-body-?/?-'ness-lays› *he is considerate, he is judicious* (HS); -ya?turehnahne-: raya?turehnáhneh ‹he-body-?/?-much› *he deliberates, he judges, he surveys it carefully* (HS); -ne-. -ya?ta'ne-: neyuya?tá·?ne? ‹apart-it-body-becomes› *it is becoming, it becomes it, it is appropriate, it is appropriate to it, it is seemly* (HS); -ne-. -ya?turehT-: wa?tkayeya?tù·reht ‹fact-apart-they-body-?/?› *they counseled, they studied* (RC 24:4), nekakheya?tù·reht ‹apart-I=them-body-?/?› *I will judge them* (R), wa?thruya?tù·reht ‹fact-apart-he-body-?/?› *he is convicted*

(HS), nehraya?turéhtha? ‹apart-he-body-?/?› *judge, magistrate* (HS); -ne-. -ya?turehT-.#ú?y: nehraycya?turchtha?ú?y ‹apart-he-body-?/?-great› *chancellor* (HS); tha+ne-. -ya?tiha'nye?-: tha?neycya?tihá·?nye? ‹unusual-apart-one-body-is a group-going along› *every one alone* (RC 12:18); tha+ne-. -ya?tiha?ne'nye?-: tha?nekaya?tiha?né·?nye? ‹unusual-apart-it-body-is a group-many-going along› *each one by itself* (RC 12:5); -a'nya?tahstenya?T-: ye?nya?tahstenyá?tha? ‹one-oneself-body-adorn-causes› *ornament* (HS); -a'nya?takwe?niyuhsT-: ra?nya?takwe?niyúhstha? ‹he-himself-body-be principal-causes› *he monopolizes* (HS); kwehs -ya?ta'ne-: kwehs ahruya?tá·?nek ‹no unknown-he-body-become› *he is unbecoming* (HS); kwehs -ya?tatukeht--i-: kwehs ruya?tatukéhti ará·ke·k ‹no he-body-is holy unknown-it-is a group› *he is unholy* (HS); kwehs -ya?tatukehtiha'nye?-: kwehs aryuya?tatukehtihá·?nye? ‹no unknown-it-body-be holy-going along› *it is unholy* (HS); kwehs -ya?ta=wyehsT-: kwehs aryuya?tawyéhsnek ‹no unknown-it-body-be appropriate› *unseemly* (HS); kwehs -ne-. -ya?tahT-: kwehs naryuyá?taht ‹no apart-it-body-stand› *it is unfit* (HS); kwehs -ne-. -ya?turehT-: kwehs nahraya?turéhthek ‹no apart-unknown-he-body-?/?› *he is undeliberate* (HS); -kč- -ya?tarahsT-: úkθeh yeya?taráhstha? ‹dish one-body-is sprightly› *chalice* (HS).

Tuscarora Pronunciation Key:
/a/ law; /e/ hat; /i/ pizza; /u/ tune; /e̜/ hint; /č/ cheese; /h/ hoe; /m/ mother; /s/ same; /t/ do (before a vowel y, or w), too (elsewhere); /k/ gale (before a vowel y or w), kale (elsewhere); /n/ inhale (before a consonant or word-final), note (elsewhere), /r/ hiss (before a consonant or word-final), run (trilled as in Italian, elsewhere); /w/ cuff (before a consonant other than y or word-final), way (elsewhere); /y/ fish (before a consonant or word-final), you (elsewhere), /θ/ thing; /?/ (the sound between the vowels in unh-unh); /·/ long vowel, /'/ high pitch; /`/ low pitch.

-ya?tahstẹni - adorn, arrange, decorate, ornament, put in order, embellish. *v. s.-t.* akya?tahstẹ·ni? ‹unknown-I-body-adorn› *that I arrange it, that I put it in order, that I embellish it* (RC 3:11). raya?tahstẹ·nih ‹he-body-adorns› *he adorns it, he decorates it, he ornaments it* (HS).

-ya?tahtir - walk upright. *v.s.-a.i.* wa?a-kuyá?tahti?r ‹fact-one-body-was durable› *one walked upright* (RC 29:2).

-ya?takwe?niyu - principal. *dv.n.s.* kaya?takwe?nì·yu? ‹it-body-is the main one› *principal* (HS).

-ya?tanurẹhsT - ennoble. *v.s.-t.* raya?tanurẹhstha? ‹he-body-be precious-causes› *he ennobles it* (HS).

-ya?turehčrayẹ(T) - be considerate, be judicious. *v.s.-s.i.* ruya?turéhčrayẹ? ‹he-body-?'?-'ness-lays› *he is considerate, he is judicious* (HS).

-ya?turehnahnẹ - deliberate, judge, survey carefully. *v.s.-a.i.* raya?turehnáhnẹh ‹he-body-?'?-much› *he deliberates, he judges, he surveys it carefully* (HS).

-ya?w - gaunt, an unfilled man. *n.r.* n-poss., n-inc., n.sfx. -eh. uyá?weh *gaunt, an unfilled man* (HS).

yeči - translocative+repetitive. *v.pfx.* The form yeči - occurs before the consonants θ or *t,* or the clusters ?*n* or ?*t.* The form yeč - occurs before the consonant *y* and the *y* is dropped. The form yeθ - occurs elsewhere.

-yehnẹ - allow, let. *v.r.-a.i.* hab: -, pnt: -, stat: -, prog: -, prp: -, dst: -, caus: -, rvs: -, dat: -, n-inc. Found only in the imperative. čéhnẹ *allow!, let!* (R); -yehnẹ - nẹ́h: čéhnẹ nẹ́h ‹you!-allow very› *well, let's see now* (R).

-yehnẹ - nẹ́h well, let's see now. *v.s.-a.i.* čéhnẹ nẹ́h ‹you!-allow very› *well, let's see now* (R)

-yehnu - mature squash. *n.* n-poss., n-inc., n.sfx. -?, yuyéhnu? *mature squash* (H 3518).

-yehrak - bring together *v.r.-t.* hab: -s, pnt: -ɸ, stat: -ɸ, prog: -, prp: -, dst: -θẹ-, caus: -sT-, rvs: -, dat: III (-ati-/-ẹ-), n-inc. wakyéhrak *I bring together* (AG); -ne -. -yehrak -: nẹyakwayéhrak ‹apart-prediction-we-bring together› *we will mix it in* (R), wa?thrayéhrak ‹fact-apart-he-brought together› *he mixed together* (RC 30:53), nehrayéhraks ‹apart-he-brings together› *he alloys, he mixes two things* (HS); -ne -. -yehrak -{dative III}: wa?nyẹ?-nyehrá·kẹ? ‹fact-apart-one-brought together-for› *Feast of the Dead* (AG); -ne -. -yehraksT -: neyeyehrákstha? ‹apart-one-bring together-causes› *ingredient* (HS); -ne -. -a'nyehrakθẹ -: neyu?-nyehrákθẹ? ‹two-it-itself-brought together-much› *mixture* (HS); à·wẹ? -ne -. -yehrak -: à·wẹ? nẹčéhrak ‹water two-prediction-you!-bring together› *dilute it with water!* (HS).

-yehs - appearance, manner, physiology, plan. *n.r.* n-poss., inc., n.sfx. -eh. uyéhseh *appearance, manner* (RC 30:53), *physiology, plan* (HS); -yehsa = kẹ'neti -: rayehsakẹ?né·tyẹhs ‹he-appearance-changes› *he disguises it* (HS); -yehsẹte: rayehsẹ́·te ‹he-appearance-certain one› *he is a special one* (RC 9:5); -yehsukrẹhT -: rayehsu?-krẹ́htha? ‹he-appearance-be loose-causes› *he disfigures* (HS); čwe -. -yeh = sẹte.#kẹha?nẹ?: čwekayehsẹtekẹ́ha?nẹ? ‹all kinds of-it-appearance-certain on-many› *every living creature* (RC 12:4); -ne -. -a'nyehsakẹ'neti -: newa?nyeh-sakẹ?né·tyẹhs ‹apart-it-it-self-appearance-changes› *it metamorphoses* (HS); wa?thra?nyehsakẹ?né·ti? ‹fact-apart-he-himself-appearance-changed› *he changed his appearance* (RC 26:13);

-t-. -a'nyehsayer-: naka'nyéhsaye'r ‹a-part-fact-I-myself-appearance-did› *I conduct myself* (RC 26:4); tha+či-. -yehsu'nę-: thahçθahraychsú'nę' ‹unusual-fact-again-he-appearance-was a kind of› *he transformed himself again* (RC 26:15); tha+yah-. -yehsawę-: thweθayehsà·wę' ‹unusual-thither-you-appearance-possessed› *it has happened to you* (RC 11:5); ti-. -yehsu'nę-: tikayehsú'nę· ‹so-it-appearance-is a kind of› *so its appearance is* (RC 28:9).

-yehsakę'neti – disguise. *v.s.-a.i.* rayehsakę'né·tyęhs ‹he-appearance-changes› *he disguises it* (HS).

-yehsęte special one. *n.s.* rayehsę́·te ‹he-appearance-certain one› *he is a special one* (RC 9:5).

-yehsu'kręhT – disfigure. *v.s.-t.* rayehsu'krę́htha' ‹he-appearance-floats› *he disfigures* (HS).

-yehwaT – be awake, be aware. *v.r.-s.i.* stat: -ɸ, prog: -, prp: -, dst: -θę-, caus: -, rvs: -, dat: -, n-inc. rayéhwat *he is awake, he is aware, he is an early-riser* (HS); -yehwaT-.#áh: yeyehwa·t'áh ‹one-is aware-little› *one's mind is on it* (RC 30:4).

-yehwaT-.#áh have mind on. *v.s.-t.* yeyehwa·t'áh ‹one-is aware-little› *one's mind is on it* (RC 30:4).

-yen – dead tree. *n.r.* n-poss., inc., n.sfx. -. This root occurs only incorporated. -yenęhnahnę-: rayenęhnáhnęh ‹he-tree-fall-causes-many› *he cuts down trees* (R); -yenę'-: yuyenę́'ę ‹it-dead tree-fall-began› *fallen tree* (RC 34:2),

aryuyenę́'ek ‹unknown-it-dead tree-fall-begin› *that it knock down tree* (RC 9:8).

-yenę – catch, hold. *v.r.-t.* hab: -hs, pnt: -·', stat: -·, prog: -, prp: -, dst: -θę- ~ -hrę-, caus: -, rvs: -, dat: -, inc.-ɸ-ag./pat. The completive suffix –t is optionally used to mark the stative aspect. ruyé·nę *he has caught it* (L 22), ruyé·nę·t *he has caught it* (L 22), rayè·nęhs *he retains (thing)* (HS), ruyè·nęhs *he has cramps, he has fits, he has seizures* (HS), wa'kyé·nę·' *I held it* (L 74), ęhrayé·nę·' *he will capture it* (RC 15:3), čé·nę· *catch it!, hold it!* (R); -yenę-.#aka·'?: rayenęhs'á·ka·'' ‹he-grabs-characterized by› *catcher (in a ball game)* (L 21); -či-. -yenę-: θhrayè·nęhs ‹again-he-grabs› *he retakes it, he takes back* (HS); ti+yah-. -yenę-: tyahwahruyè·nę' ‹so-thither-fact-he-grabbed› *he was grabbed* (RC 24:8); -(a)hahyenę'-: ruhahyè·nę'θ ‹he-path-grab-begins› *the road falls on him* (*this means that one's way has failed him, in fact, died by the way; so that it may be rendered as well, he died by the way*) (H 2484); -(ę)'tikęhryenę-: ra'tikęhryenę́hręh ‹he-mind-grabs-much› *he escorts it* (HS), na'tikęhryè·nęh ‹one=another-mind-grabs› *one accompanies another* (HS); -kerha=yenę-: rukyerhayè·nęhs ‹he-body-grabs› *he spasms* (HS); -a'nyenę-: ra'nyè·nęhs ‹he-himself-grabs› *he catches it; he wrestles; policeman* (R); -ne-. -a'nyenę-: nehra'nyè·nęhs ‹apart-

---

he-himself-grabs⟩ *he wrestles* (HS):
-ne-. -(ę)ʔtikęhrayenę-: neyęʔnęʔtikęh-
rayé·nę· ⟨apart-one=another-mind-
grabbed⟩ *one comforts another* (RC
29:1); húʔs -(ę)taʔrakęw -yenę-: húʔs
ratáʔrakęw ruyé·nę·t ⟨cold he-head-in
he-grabbed⟩ *he has a head cold* (HS).
-yenę-.#aka·ʔ catcher. *dv.n.s.* rayenęhs-
ʔá·ka·ʔ ⟨he-grabs-characterized by⟩
catcher (in a ball game) (L 21).
-yenęhnahnę- cut down trees. *v.s.-a.i.*
rayenęhnáhnęh ⟨he-dead tree-fall-caus-
es-many⟩ *he cuts down trees* (R).
-yenęʔ- fell tree. *v.s.-a.i.* yuyenę́ʔę ⟨it-
dead tree-fall-began⟩ *fallen tree* (RC
34:2), aryuyenę́ʔek ⟨unknown-it-dead
tree-fall-begin⟩ *that it knock down tree*
(RC 9:8).
-yenęʔ- fallen tree. *dv.n.s.* yuyenę́ʔę ⟨it-
dead tree-fall-began⟩ *fallen tree* (RC
34:2).
-yer- flesh. *n.r.* inaln: kyè·ręʔ *my flesh*
(RC 3:19), inc., n.sfx. -eh (older
n.sfx. -ęʔ). uyè·reh *flesh* (older: uyè·-
ręʔ (W 74)); -yer-.#keha·ʔ: uyeręʔ-
kyé·haʔ ⟨flesh-characterized by⟩ *carnal, sensual* (HS); -yerakha-: rayerákhę ⟨he-flesh-divided⟩ *he mingles*
(HS); -yeraraʔT-: ruyè·raraʔt ⟨he-
flesh-be in-caused⟩ *he is incarnate*
(HS); -yerawę-: yeyè·rawęhs ⟨one-
flesh-smears⟩ *goldplate, silverplate*
(HS), rayè·rawęhs ⟨he-flesh-smears⟩
he soils it, he taints it (HS); -yera=
węri-: rayerawę̀·rih ⟨one-flesh-stirs⟩ *he
begrimes it, he tarnishes it* (HS); -ye=
ręti-: kayerę́·tih ⟨it-flesh-makes⟩ *vestige: it is legible, it is obvious, it is
plain, it is perceptible, it is visible*
(HS), *it shows* (RC 2:12), *it is evident*
(L 75); -yerętihT-: rayerętíhthaʔ ⟨he-
flesh-make-causes⟩ *he marks it, he
prints (writing), he symbolizes it*
(HS); -yeрętiʔ-: rayerę́·tiʔθ ⟨he-flesh-

make-begins⟩ *he appears* (HS): -yerę=
'nakęw: eyerę́·ʔnakęw ⟨one-flesh-in⟩ *in
one's flesh* (RC 7:11); -či-. -yeręti-:
θkayerę́·tih ⟨again-it-flesh-makes⟩ *vestige* (HS); ti-. -yeręti-: thwaʔkayerę́·tiʔ
⟨so-fact-it-flesh-made⟩ *it became visible* (RC 9:7); ti-. -yeręti-.#áh: tika-
yerętiháh ⟨so-it-flesh-makes-little⟩ *indistinct* (HS); -a'nyerawęri-: raʔnyc-
rawę̀·rih ⟨he-himself-flesh-stirs⟩ *he
soils himself* (HS); -a'nyerętihnahkw-:
yuʔnyerętihnáhkę ⟨it-itself-flesh-make-
caused-instrument⟩ *sign, symbol* (HS);
-a'nyerętihnęha'nyeʔ-: yuʔnyerętihnę-
háʔnyeʔ ⟨it-itself-flesh-make-caused-
going along⟩ *apparently* (HS); -a'nye=
rę'narahkw-: waʔnyeręʔnaráhkhwaʔ
⟨it-itself-flesh-collects⟩ *it assimilates*
(HS); -či-. -a'nyeręt: θwaʔnyé·rę·t ⟨a-
gain-it-itself-flesh-possesses⟩ *it resembles* (HS); -či-. -a'nyerętihnahkw-:
čuʔnyerętihnáhkę ⟨again-it-itself-flesh-
make-caused-instrument⟩ *vestige* (HS);
-yer- -iheyęʔ-: rayè·ręʔ kęhè·yęʔθ
⟨he-flesh it-die-begins⟩ *paralytic* (HS);
kwęhs -yeręti-: kwęhs akayerę́·tihk
⟨no unknown-it-flesh-make⟩ *it is imperceptible* (HS).
-yer- do. *v.r.-t.* hab: -haʔ ~ -φ, pnt: -ʔ,
stat: -ę, prog: -, prp: -he-, dst: -hę-,
caus: -aʔT-, rvs: -, dat: I (-aʔθe-/-aʔθ-
), inc.-φ-pat. The habitual aspect is
marked by the suffix -haʔ whenever
the verb has the simple meaning *do*.
In other constructions, e.g., those
meaning *wonder, happen*, the -φ habitual suffix is used. kyérhaʔ *I am
doing it* (R), wáʔkycʔr *I did it* (R),
čé·r *do it!: o.k., alright* (RC 30:52);
-yeraʔT-: waʔeyè·raʔt ⟨fact-one-do-
caused⟩ *one made it happen* (RC 6:6);
ti-. -yer-: tyuyè·rę ⟨so-it-did⟩ *it happened* (RC 30:8), tikà·yer ⟨so-it-does⟩
it happens (RC 25:9), nękà·yeʔr ⟨so-

prediction-it-do› *it must be done* (RC 25:16); ti -. -yer -.#áh: tyuyerȩháh ‹so-it-did-little› *lightly* (HS); ti -. -yer -{dative I}: tikayerá'ᵠeh ‹so-it-does-for› *it goes a certain way* (RC 26:26); ti -. -yera?T -: tikakuyerá'nȩ ‹so-they-do-caused› *they used it* (R); ti -. -yer = hȩ -: thwa'kayérhȩ·' ‹so-fact-it-did-much› *it happened over and over* (RC 3:85); ti+t -. -yer -: nȩtkayè·rȩk ‹so-prediction-hither-it-do› *it will continue to do it* (RC 16:2); ti -. -ȩ'nyer -: tiwȩ́·'-nyer ‹so-it-day-does› *weather* (R); ti -. -a'nyer -: tikayȩ́·'nyer ‹so-they-themselves-do› *they wonder* (R); -ne -. -a'nyehsayer -: naka'nyéhsaye'r ‹apart-fact-it-itself-appearance-did› *that I conduct myself in such a way* (RC 26: 4); -ne -. -a'rȩhyayerȩ'nye -: newa'rȩhyayerȩ́·'nye' ‹apart-it-itself-sky-does-going along› *Aurora Borealis, Northern Lights* (R); ha? -t -. -yer -: ha' thruyè·rȩ ‹the hither-he-did› *he is dil-igent* (HS), ha' nakà·yer ‹the hither-it-does› *Amen* (HS); ha? -a'nyerȩ? -: ha' yu'nyerȩ́'ȩ ‹the it-itself-do-began› *happening, incident* (HS); kwȩhs -t -. -yer -: kwȩhs ȩ'nahruyé·rȩ·k ‹no un-known-hither-he-do› *he is inconstant* (HS).

–yer - –iheyȩ? - paralytic. *dv.n.s.* rayè·rȩ' kȩhè·yȩ'ᵠ ‹he-flesh it-die-begins› *paralytic* (HS).

–yer -.#keha·? carnal, sensual. *n.s.* uyerȩ́'kyé·ha' ‹flesh-characterized by› *carnal, sensual* (HS).

–yerakha - mingle. *v.s.-a.i.* rayerákhȩ ‹he-flesh-released› *he mingles* (HS).

–yerara?T - be incarnate. *v.s.-s.i.* ruyè·ra-ra'?t ‹he-flesh-be in-caused› *he is incarnate* (HS).

–yeraT - go in a specific direction, tack. *v.r.-a.i.* hab: -ha', pnt: -φ, stat: -ȩ, prog: -ȩha'nye'-, prp: -, dst: -, caus: -, rvs: -, dat: -, n-inc. rayerá·tha' *he tacks (nautical)* (HS); ti -. -yeraT -: tyuyerá·'nȩ ‹so-it-went in a specific di-rection› *toward* (HS), thwa'kayé·ra·t ‹so-fact-it-went in a specific direction› *the direction taken* (AW 102), nȩkaye-yé·ra·t ‹so-prediction-they-go in a spe-cific direction› *it will be their direc-tion* (AW 99); ti+či -. -yeraT -: nȩᵠaka-yeyé·ra·t ‹so-unknown-again-they-go in a specific direction› *that they turn back* (MP); ti -. -yera'nȩha'nye -: tikaku-yera'nȩhá·'nye' ‹so-they-went in a specific direction-going along› *they went in every direction* (AW 57); ha? ti -. -yeraT -: ha' tyuyerá·'nȩ ‹the so-it-went in a specific direction› *direction* (HS).

–yerawȩ - goldplate, silverplate. *dv.n.s.* yeyè·rawȩhs ‹one-flesh-smears› *gold-plate, silverplate* (R).

–yerawȩ - soil, taint. *v.s.-t.* rayè·rawȩhs ‹he-flesh-smears› *he soils it, he taints it* (HS).

–yerawȩri - begrime, tarnish. *v.s.-t.* raye-rawȩ̀·rih ‹one-flesh-stirs› *he begrimes it, he tarnishes it* (HS).

–yera?T - make happen. *v.s.-t.* wa'eyè·-ra'?t ‹fact-one-do-caused› *one made it happen* (RC 6:6).

-**yerẹti** – vestige. *dv.n.s.* kayerẹ·tih ‹it-flesh-makes› *vestige* (HS).

-**yerẹti** – be evident, be legible, be obvious, be perceptible, be plain, be visible, show. *v.s.-a.i.* kayerẹ·tih ‹it-flesh-makes› *it is legible, it is obvious, it is plain, it is perceptible, it is visible* (HS), *it shows* (RC 2:12), *it is evident* (L 75).

-**yerẹtihT** – mark, print, symbolize. *v.s.-t.* rayerẹtíhtha' ‹he-flesh-make-causes› *he marks it, he prints (writing), he symbolizes it* (HS).

-**yerẹti'** – appear. *v.s.-a.i.* rayerẹ·ti'θ ‹he-flesh-make-begins› *he appears* (HS).

-**yeri** – be complete, be fit, be just, be perfect; be ample, be complete, be correct, be o.k., be right, be sane, be straight. *v.r.-s.i.* stat: -', prog: -, prp: -, dst: -, caus: -, rvs: -, dat: -, inc.-φ-pat. Requires a locative prefix unless an incorporated noun is present. With the cislocative, the root has the meanings indicated by those glosses above that precede the semicolon; with the translocative, it has the meanings indicated by those glosses that follow the semicolon. -**t**-.-**yeri**-: tkayè·ri' ‹hither-it-is correct› *it is complete, it is fit, it is just, it is perfect* (HS); -**yah**-.-**yeri**-: wekayè·ri' ‹thither-it-is correct› *it is ample, it is complete, it is correct, it is o.k., it is right, it is sane, it is straight* (RC 6:11); -**yah**-.-**yeri'**-: wekayè·ri'θ ‹thither-it-be correct-begins› *it fits, it suffices* (HS); **tha+ne**-.-**yeri**-.#**ha'nẹ'**: tha'neyuyerihá'nẹ' ‹unusual-apart-it-is correct-much› *it is equidistant away from* (RC 31:10), *it is opposite* (HS); -**yah+či**-.-**yeri**-: yahẹθakayè·ri' ‹thither-fact-again-it-is correct› *it returned to normal* (RC 18:4); -**(a)hahạyeri**-: kahahayè·ri' ‹it-path-is correct› *a straight*

road (L 78); -**t**-.-**(ẹ)'tikẹhrạyeri**-: thra'tikẹhrayè·ri' ‹hither-he-mind-is correct› *he is right-minded* (HS); -**yah**-.-**(ẹ)'tikẹhrayeri**-: weka'tikẹhrayè·ri' ‹thither-it-mind-is correct› *it is sane* (HS); -**t**-.-**rihwạyeri**-: tkarihwayè·ri' ‹hither-it-matter-is correct› *correct, right* (HS); -**yah+či**-.-**ẹnhạyeri**-: wečakẹnhayè·ri' ‹thither-again-one-be alive-is correct› *one is in good health again* (RC 18:4); **íhskah** -**t**-.-**yeri**-: íhskah ẹ'nakayè·rik ‹not unknown-hither-it-be correct› *it is abnormal* (R); **kwẹhs** -**t**-.-**yeri**-: kwẹhs ẹ'nakayè·rik ‹no unknown-hither-it-be correct› *it is imperfect* (HS); **kwẹhs** -**yah**-.-**yeri**-: kwẹhs yakayè·rik ‹no thither-unknown-it-be correct› *it is incomplete, it is insufficient* (HS).

-**yeriha** – scatter, spread out, straighten. *v.r.-t.* hab: -hs, pnt: -', stat: -ẹ·, prog: -, prp: -, dst: -, caus: -, rvs: -, dat: I (-'θe-/-'θ-), inc.-φ-pat. kayeríhahs *it is scattered, it is spread about* (HS); **tha**-.-**yeriha**-: thahrayeríha' ‹unusual-fact-he-straightened› *he goes straight* (RC 31:2); **ti**-.-**yeriha**-: tihruyeríhẹ· ‹so-he-straightened› *in his direction* (RC 31:3); **ti**-.-**yeriha**-{dative I}: tihrayerihá'θeh ‹so-he-straightens-for› *he puts them in order, he levels it* (HS); **ti+či**-.-**yeriha**-{dative I}: tiθhrayerihá'θeh ‹so-again-he-straightens-for› *he adjusts* (HS); **ti+yah**-.-**yeriha**-: tyahwa'eyeríha' ‹so-thither-fact-one-straightened› *one went straight there* (RC 30:6); -**či'čihstyeriha**-: rači'čihstyeríhahs ‹he-flowers-straightens› *he strews flowers* (HS); -**(ẹ)tahsnyeriha**-: kakutahsnyeríhẹ· ‹they-pole-straightened› *they spread sticks* (RC 24:9); -**'čharyeriha**-: wa'kaye'čharyeríha' ‹fact-they-branch-straightened› *they spread out branches* (RC 24:7); -**'te**=

hyeriha –: wa'ktehyeríha' ‹fact-I-sand-straightened› *I have spread sand over* (AG): ti –. -ya'čeriha –: tihraya'čeríhahs ‹so-he-path-straightens› *he is strict* (HS). tihruya'čeríhẹ· ‹so-he-path-straightened› *he is ingenious* (HS); ti+či –. -ya'čeriha –: tiθhraya'čeríhahs ‹so-again-he-path-straightens› *he rectifies* (HS): tha –. -a'nyeriha –: thyu'nyeríhẹ· ‹unusual-it-itself-straightened› *it is straight* (HS); tha –. -a'nya'čeriha –: thyu'nya'čeríhẹ ‹unusual-it-itself-path-straightened› it is equitable (H-notebook): ti –. -a'nyeriha –: tyu'nyeríhẹ· ‹so-it-itself-straightened› *straight* (L 82); ha' ti –. -ya'čeriha –: ha' tihruya'čeríhẹ· ‹the so-he-path-straightened› *his rectitude* (HS); kwẹhs ti –. -a'nya'čeriha –: kwẹhs tharyu'nya'čeríha' ‹no so-unknown-it-itself-path-straighten› *it is indirect* (HS).

-yerik – fill up. *v.r.-t.* hab: -s, pnt: -ɸ, stat: -ɸ, prog: -, prp: -, dst: -, caus: -T-, rvs: -, dat: -, inc.-ɸ-pat. –či –. -ye = rik –: θhrayè·riks ‹again-he-fills up› *he fills it back up, he restores it* (HS): –či –. -yerikT –: ẹθhrayè·rikt ‹prediction-again-he-fill up-cause› *he will fill it back up, he will restore it* (HS), θhruyeríknẹ ‹again-he-fill up-caused› *he filled it back up, he restored it* (HS); -(ẹ)'tikẹhrayerik –: na'tikẹhrayè·riks ‹one=another-mind-fills up› *one satisfies another* (HS): -t –. -rihwayerik –: tkarihwayè·rik ‹hither-it-matter-filled up› *it is trustable* (HS); -a'nwẹta = yerik –: ra'wẹtayè·riks ‹he-himself-word-fills up› *he fulfills his promise, he realizes his promise* (HS); kwẹhs -yah –. -yerik –: kwẹhs yakayè·rik ‹no thither-unknown-it-fill up› *it is insufficient* (HS); kwẹhs -(ẹ)'tikẹhrayerik –: kwẹhs ahra'tikẹhrayè·rik ‹no unknown-he-mind-fill up› *he is an imbecile* (HS): kwẹhs -t –. -rihwayerik –: kwẹhs ẹ'nakarihwayè·rik ‹no unknown-hither-it-matter-fill up› *it is unjust* (HS), kwẹhs ẹ'nahrarihwayè·rik ‹no unknown-hither-he-matter-fill up› *he is unjust* (HS).

-yeθa – she, one…you alone (third person singular feminine/indefinite agent= second person singular patient). *v.r. pfx.* The final *a* of the prefix coalesces with a following root or stem-initial *i* to yield -yeθẹ –. Before other root or stem-initial vowels, the final *a* of the prefix is dropped. This initial *y* of the prefix is dropped following the factual mode marker.

yeθa(r)(a) – translocative+repetitive+optative. *v.pfx.* The form yeθara – occurs whenever the prefix receives word accent; if this form is followed by a pronominal prefix that begins with the sequence *wa*, the final vowel contracts with the sequence to give yeθarẹ –. The form yeθar – occurs when the prefix is unaccented before pronominal prefixes that begin with the glides *w* or *y*. The form yeθa – occurs elsewhere.

-yeθa'T – banter, curse, revile, swear. *v.r.-a.i.* hab: -ha', pnt: -, stat: -, prog:

-, prp: -, dst: -hę-, caus: -, rvs: -, dat:
-, inc.-φ-pat. rayeθá'tha' *he banters,
he curses, he reviles, he swears* (HS);
−yeθa²na²T −: rayeθa²ná²nch ‹he-cur-
ses-moving› *he banters, he rails at*
(HS); −yeθa²thę −: uyeθá²thę· ‹curse-
much› *blaspheme* (HS); −hsęnaye =
θa²T −: náchęnayeθá²tha' ‹one=anoth-
er-name-curses› *one denounces another* (HS); −a'nyeθa²T −: ra²nyeθá²-
tha' ‹he-himself-curses› *he curses
himself, he is profligate, he squanders*
(HS).
−yeθa²na²t − banter, rail. *v.s.-t.* rayeθa²-
ná²nch ‹he-banters-moving› *he banters, he rails at* (HS).
−yeθa²thę − blaspheme. *n.s.* uyeθá²thę·
‹curse-much› *blaspheme* (HS).
Yé·suhs Jesus (MP). *n.*
−yet − grease. *n.r.* n-poss., inc., n.sfx. -eh.
uyé·teh *grease* (R); −yetarhu −: rayetárhuhs ‹he-grease-mixes in› *he lards
it* (HS); −yetarihę² −: yuyetaríhę²θ ‹it-
grease-boil-begins› *grease has been
boiling* (RC 15:10); −yetatukęht −: uye-
tatukę́hti ‹grease-be holy› *chrism, holy
oil* (HS); −yetaw −: rayetà·węhs ‹he-
grease-gives› *he greases it, he oils it*
(HS); −yetawa²k −: ruyetawá²kę ‹he-
grease-held› *he holds it* (HS); −yeta =
wihsi −: ęyeyetawíhsi' ‹prediction-one-
grease-give-undo› *one will extract
grease* (RC 11:23); −ne −. −yetawa²k −:
nekayetawá²kę ‹apart-it-grease-held›
accessory (HS); −a'nyetawa²k −: yu²-
nyetawá²kę ‹it-itself-grease-grabbed›
receipt (HS); −a'nyethar −: wa²nyé·ther
‹it-itself-grease-hangs› *cream* (HS).
−yetarhu − lard. *v.s.-t.* rayetárhuhs ‹he-
grease-mixes in› *he lards it* (HS).
−yetatukęht − chrism, holy oil. *dv.n.s.*
uyetatukę́hti ‹grease-be holy› *chrism,
holy oil* (HS).
−yetaw − grease, oil. *v.s.-t.* rayetà·węhs

‹he-grease-gives› *he greases it, he oils
it* (HS).
−yetawaT − bond. *v.r.-a.i.* hab: -, pnt: -,
stat: -ę, prog: -, prp: -, dst: -, caus: -,
rvs: -, dat: -, n-inc. yuyetawá·²nę *it
bonds* (HS).
yeyęwę́·tih goldenrod *(Solidago* sp.*)*
(R). *n.*
yę − translocative+future. *v.pfx.*
−yę − enter, go into. *v.r.-a.i.* hab: -h, pnt:
-², stat: -· ~ -², prog: -, prp: -, dst: -,
caus: -hsT- ~ -hT-, rvs: -, dat: -, inc.-
φ-pat. −yęhst −: uyę́hsteh ‹go into-'ness›
home, residence (HS); −yęhT −: yeyę́h-
tha' ‹one-go into-causes› *ambuscade*
(RC 10:8); −či −. −yę −: θkà·yęh ‹again-
it-goes into› *it goes into eclipse, it is
wont to eclipse: eclipse* (H-notebook),
čú·yę· ‹again-it-went into› *it is in
eclipse* (H-notebook), θhrà·yę² ‹again-
he-went into› *he reenters* (HS); −či −.
−yęhT −: θhrayę́hnę ‹again-it-go into-
caused› *he takes one or something
back* (HS); −t −. −yęhT −: thrayę́htha'
‹hither-he-go into-causes› *he brings in,
he introduces* (HS); −yah −. −yę −: yę́h-
syę' ‹thither-prediction-you-go into›
you will go into there (RC 11:3), yah-
wahrà·yę' ‹thither-fact-he-went into›
he went into there (RC 11:3), yah-
wá²kyę' ‹thither-fact-I-went into› *I
came in* (R); −hęhsyę −: wa²kakuhę́h-
syę' ‹fact-they-ear-went into› *they
heard* (RC 10:4), ękahę́hsyę' ‹prediction-it-ear-go into› *one will hear* (RC
17:3); −hęhsyęhT −: wa²kayę²nathę́h-
syęht ‹fact-they=another-ear-go into-
caused› *one made them hear it* (RC
12:5), nathęhsyę́htha' ‹one=another-
ear-go into-causes› *one notifies another* (HS); −hnęwyę −: yuhnę́·wyę ‹it-
lake bottom-went into› *it is sunken*
(HS); −rha'nayę −: wahrarhá·²nayę'
‹fact-he-forest-went into› *he entered*

forest (RC 26:15); –**rihwayę** –: karíhwayęhs ‹it-matter-goes into› *causal* (HS), raríhwayęhs ‹he-matter-goes into› *agent: he causes* (HS), ękaríhwayę⁊ ‹prediction-it-matter-go into› *it will result* (HS); –**či** –. –**ta'nyę** –: θhratá·⁊nyę⁊ ‹again-he-village-went into› *he revisits* (HS); –**t** –. –**ra⁊narye** –: tkara⁊ná·ryę⁊ ‹hither-it-hollow tree-went into› *in the hollow tree* (RC 10:19); –**t** –. –**rihwayę** –: tkaríhwayę⁊ ‹hither-it-matter-went into› *it is difficult* (RC 25:7); –**yah** –. –**hnęwyęhsT** –: wekahnęwyę́hstha⁊ ‹thither-it-lake bottom-go into-causes› *it sinks in, it is absorbed* (HS); ti+**yah** –. –**hnęwyę** –: thwehrahnę́·wyę· ‹so-thither-he-lake bottom-went into› *he sinks* (HS); ti+**yah** –. –**(ę)ta⁊** = **rahnęwyę** –: tyahwa⁊kata⁊rahnę́·wyę⁊ ‹so-thither-fact-it-head-lake bottom-went into› *its head disappeared from sight into the mud* (HS); –**a'nwęta** = **yęhT** –: u⁊nwę́tayęht ‹self-word-go into-cause› *invective* (HS), ra⁊nwętayę́htha⁊ ‹he-himself-word-go into-causes› *he speaks ill of it* (HS); **ha⁊** –**t** –. –**yę** –: ha⁊ tkà·yę⁊ ‹the hither-it-went into› *entry(way), ingress; income* (HS); **ha⁊** –**rihwayę** –: ha⁊ karíhwayęhs ‹the it-matter-goes into› *agency* (HS); **kwęhs** –**hęhsyę** –: kwęhs ahruhęhsyę́hek ‹no unknown-he-ear-go into› *it is intractable (to him)* (HS); **tha** –. –**yę** – –**rę⁊nha** –: thikà·yę⁊ ahrarę́⁊nha⁊ ‹unusual-it-went into unknown-he-frequent› *he learns easily* (HS).

–**yęči(y)** – they...you alone; all of you...

him, her, one (third person non-singular feminine/indefinite agent=second person patient, second person non-singular agent=third person feminine/indefinite patient). *v.r. pfx.* The form –**yęčhiy** – occurs before roots or stems that begin with a vowel. The form –**yęčhi** – occurs before roots or stems that begin with a consonant. The initial *y* of the prefix is dropped following the factual mode marker.

yęči – translocative+future+repetitive. *v. pfx.* The form **yęči** – occurs before the consonants θ or *t*, or the clusters ⁊*n* or ⁊*t*. The form **yęč** – occurs before the consonant *y* and the *y* is dropped. The form **yęθ** – occurs elsewhere.

–**yęhakre** – be slovenly. *v.r.-s.i.* stat: -⁊, prog: -, prp: -, dst: -hnę-, caus: -, rvs: -, dat: -, n-inc. As is usual for stative intransitive verbs, Hewitt & Smith give a "past" formed with the decessive enclitic (**ruyękáhre⁊ kę́he⁊**) and a "future" formed with the particle meaning *it will be* (**ruyęhá-kre⁊ ę́·= kę·k**). **ruyęhákre⁊** *it is slovenly* (HS).

–**yęhkwatat** – bluster, storm, whirl. *v.r.-a.i.* hab: -s, pnt: -, stat: -, prog: -, prp: -, dst: -, caus: -, rvs: -, dat: -, n-inc. **kayę́hkwatač** *it blusters, it storms, it whirls* (HS).

–**yęhsaw** – rubbish. *n.r.*, n-poss., inc., n.s. -eh. **uyę́hsaweh** *rubbish* (H-notebook); –**yęhsawanh** –: **kayęhsawánhę** ‹it-rubbish-filled› *it is full of rubbish; discord* (H-notebook).

–**yęhsawanh** – discord. *dv.n.s.* **kayęhsa**-

wánhę ‹it-rubbish-filled› *discord* (H-notebook).

-**yęhskwe** – laugh at. *v.r.-t.* hab: -h, pnt: -', stat: -·, prog: -, prp: -, dst: -hnę-, caus: -, rvs: -, dat: -, n-inc. čę́hskwe *laugh!* (R), wa'kyę́hskwe' *I laughed* (R), wa'kayę'na'nyę́hskwe' *they laughed at another* (R): -**yęhskwe?T** –: ruyę́hskwe'̓t ‹he-laugh-caused› *he is laughable* (HS); -**yęhskwe?T** –: ruyęhskwé'ne' ‹he-laughed-moving› *he giggles* (HS); -**a'nyęhskwe?T** –: ru'̓nyęhskwé'nę ‹he-himself-laugh at-caused› *he smiles* (HS), ru'̓nyęhskwe'néhe' ‹he-himself-laugh at-caused-remote› *he had smiled* (HS).

-**yęhskwe?T** – be laughable. *v.s.-s.i.* ruyę́hskwe'̓t ‹he-laugh-caused› *he is laughable* (HS).

-**yęhskwe?T** – giggle. *v.s.-a.i.* ruyęhskwé'ne' ‹he-laughed-moving› *he giggles* (HS).

-**yęhst** – home, residence. *n.s.* uyę́hsteh ‹go into-'ness› *home, residence* (HS).

-**yęhT** – ambuscade. *dv.n.s.* yeyę́htha' ‹one-go into-causes› *ambuscade* (RC 10:8).

-**yęhw** – fail. *v.r.-a.i.* hab: -, pnt: -', stat: -, prog: -, prp: -, dst: -, caus: -, rvs: -, dat: -, n-inc. wa'ù·yęw *it failed* (RC 12:9).

-**yęhwan** – leafless tree. *n.r.* n-poss., inc., n.sfx. -eh. uyęhwà·neh *leafless tree* (HS); -**yęhwanęti** –: kayęhwané·tih ‹it-leafless tree-makes› *it decays* (HS).

-**yęhwanęti** – decay. *v.s.-a.i.* kayęhwané·tih ‹it-leafless tree-makes› *it decays* (HS).

-**yęhwiθ(n)** – wing. *n.r.* inaln: nekayęhwí·θnę·t *its two wings* (RC 28:3), inc., n.sfx. -eh. The form -**yęhwiθ** – is found only in the construction for *spotted wing*, cited below. The form -**yęhwiθn** – occurs elsewhere. uyęhwí·θnęh *wing* (RC 12:15); -**yęhwiθkwę?** = rar –: uyęhwiθkwę́'ra'r ‹wing-be spotted› *spotted wing* (H-notebook); -**yęhwiθna?nihr** –: yuyęhwiθna'níhrę ‹it-wing-stood up› *it wing stands* (M 87); -**yęhwiθnęt**: yuyęhwí·θnę·t ‹it-wing-possesses› *winged* (HS).

-**yękęhst** – fen, salt-lick. *n.r.* n-poss., n-inc., n.sfx. -eh. uyękę́hsteh *fen, salt-lick* (HS).

-**yękhi(y)** – she, one...all of us; all of us...her, one (third person feminine/indefinite agent=first person non-singular patient, first person non-singular agent=third person feminine/indefinite patient). *v.r.pfx.* The form -**yękhiy** – occurs before roots and stems that begin with a vowel. The form -**yękhi** – occurs before roots and stems that begin with a consonant. The initial *y* of the prefix is dropped following the factual mode marker.

yękT(i) –/**yęky** – our (his or hers and mine) (first person exclusive dual alienable). *n.r.pfx.* The form **yękn** – occurs before roots and stems that begin with the vowel ę or the morphophoneme {"u}. The form **yękt** – occurs before roots and stems that begin with the vowels *i, e,* or *u* (not from {"u}). The form **yęky** – occurs before roots and stems that begin with the vowel *a.* The form **yękti** – occurs before roots and stems that begin with a consonant.

-**yękT(i)** –/-**yęky** – the two of us (he or she and I) (first person exclusive dual patient). *v.r.pfx.* The form -**yękn** – occurs before roots and stems that begin with the vowel ę or the morphophoneme {"u}. The form -**yękt** – occurs before roots and stems that begin with the vowels *i, e,* or *u* (not from {"u}). The form -**yęky** – occurs before roots and stems that begin with the vowel *a*. The form –yękti– occurs before roots and stems that begin with a consonant.

yękwa– our (theirs and mine) (first person exclusive plural alienable). *n.r. pfx.* With roots and stems that begin with the vowel *i* the final *a* of the prefix coalesces with the *i* to yield yękwę–. Before roots and stems that begin with other vowels the final *a* of the prefix is lost.

–yękwa– all of us (they and I) (first person exclusive plural patient). *v.r.pfx.* With roots and stems that begin with the vowel *i* the final *a* of the prefix coalesces with the *i* to yield –yękwę–. Before roots and stems that begin with other vowels the final *a* of the prefix is lost.

–yękwir– wood. *n.r.* n-poss., inc., n.sfx. -eh. uyękwì·reh *wood* (RC 7:4) [Lawson «Ouyunkgue» 'Wood']; –yękwi=rahru?T–: yuyękwirahrú'nę ‹it-wood-is soft› *softwood* (PC); –yękwirahtir–: yuyękwirahtì·rę ‹it-wood-is hard› *hardwood* (PC); –yękwiraruhčrę–: kakuyękwirarúhčrę· ‹they-wood-gathered› *they gathered wood* (RC 6:15); –yękwirayę'nahkw–: yeyękwirayę'náhkhwa' ‹one-wood-lays-instrument› *woodshed* (HS); –yękwirihsak–: wa'kayeyękwiríhsa·k ‹fact-they-wood-sought› *they look for wood* (AW 55); –yękwirya?k–: rayękwí·rya'ks ‹he-wood-breaks› *he cuts wood, he saws* (HS); –a'nyękwirukar–: yu'nyękwi-

ruká·rę· ‹it-it-self-wood-is broken up› *split wood* (HS).

–yękwirahru?T– softwood. *dv.n.s.* yuyękwirahrú'nę ‹it-wood-is soft› *softwood* (PC).

–yękwirahtir– hardwood. *dv.n.s.* yuyękwirahtì·rę ‹it-wood-is hard› *hardwood* (PC).

–yękwirayę'nahkw– woodshed. *dv.n.s.* yeyękwirayę'náhkhwa' ‹one-wood-lays-instrument› *woodshed* (HS).

–yękwirya?k– cut wood, saw. *v.s.-a.i.* rayękwí·rya'ks ‹he-wood-breaks› *he cuts wood, he saws* (HS).

–yęr– odor, scent, smell. *n.r.* n-poss., inc., n.sfx. -eh. uyę̀·reh *odor* (L 76), *scent, smell* (HS); –yęrakwahs(T)– {dative I}: wakyęrakwáhsθeh ‹I-odor-is good-for› *I like the smell of it* (L 76); –yęranurę–: kayęranù·rę' ‹it-odor-is precious› *perfume* (HS); ti–.–yę=raks–: tikayęrá·ksę· ‹so-it-odor-is bad› *it smells bad* (RC 33:11); *stench* (HS).

–yęranurę– perfume. *dv.n.s.* kayęranù·rę' ‹it-odor-is precious› *perfume* (HS).

–yęθ(e)r– flay, skin, take hide off. *v.r.-t.* hab: -ęhs, pnt: -', stat: -ę, prog: -, prp: -, dst: -, caus: -, rvs: -ęku-, dat: -, inc.-ɸ-pat. The form –yęθr– occurs whenever a morpheme beginning with a vowel follows. The form –yęθer– occurs elsewhere. With this verb root, the reversive suffix serves to intensify rather than "undo" the action of the root. ruyę́·θrę *he flayed* (HS), rayę́·θręhs *he flays* (HS), wahrayę́·θe'r *he skinned it* (RC 8:13); –yęθ(e)r–: uyę́·θreh ‹flay› *skin* (HS); –yęθręku –: wahrayęθrę́·ku’ ‹fact-he-flay-undid› *he skinned it* (RC 30:32); –yęθrękuhę –: rayęθrękúhçh ‹he-flay-undoes-much› *he removes skin* (RC 8:21); –hehna= yęθ(e)r –: rahehnayę́·θręhs ‹he-field-flays› *he is skinning the field (said of one who is taking all of the substance from the field without giving back to it any return in the shape of manure)* (H 2484).

–yęθ(e)r – skin. *n.s.* uyę́·θreh ‹flay› *skin* (HS).

–yęθręku – skin. *v.s.-t.* wahrayęθrę́·ku’ ‹fact-he-flay-undid› *he skinned it* (RC 30:32).

–yęθrękuhę – remove skin. *v.s.-a.i.* rayęθrękúhęh ‹he-flay-undoes-much› *he removes skin* (RC 8:21).

–yę(T) – lay. *v.r.-t.* hab: -hs, pnt: -’, stat: -’, prog: -a'nye’-, prp: -, dst: -hnę-, caus: -’T-, rvs: -, dat: I (-’θ-/-’θ-) ~ II (-hθ-/-ę-) ~ III (-ati-/-ę-), inc.-ϕ- ag./pat. This verb has several different functions. Besides its basic meaning of *lay*, it often appears in constructions similar to French idioms built on "en avoir" and "y avoir" to express possession (e.g., **rù·yę’** *he has* [lit., *it lays with him*]) and existence in a location (e.g., **kanę́hsayę’** *there is (a) house* (lit., *house lays*). This root also takes on idiomatic meanings with certain affixes. With the semireflexive it means *sit* and with the dualic it means *bet, wager*. Note also the specialized meaning of *beget* with masculine agent pronouns, with or without the addition of the inchoative suffix. The form –yęT – occurs before certain suffixes beginning with a vowel, specifically, the inchoative, the instrumental, and the modal stative marker (–ahk). The form –yę – occurs else-where. rù·yę’ *he has* (RC 34:1), rà·yęhs *he lays it, he puts it down* (HS), wa’è·yę’ *one laid it* (RC 3:41), aryu-yę́·’nahk *that it possess* (RC 28:11); –yę(T)–: rà·yęhs ‹he-lays› *he begets* (HS), rù·yę’ ‹he-laid› *he begot* (HS), ęhrá·yę·’ ‹prediction-he-lay› *he will beget* (HS); –yę(T)–: ę’tì·yę’ ‹prediction-we two-lay› *you and I will bet* (RC 25:6); –yę'na’–: rayę́·’na’θ ‹he-lay-begins› *he begets* (HS), ruyę’ná·’ę ‹he-lay-began› *he begot* (HS), ęhra-yę́·’na’ ‹prediction-he-lay-begins› *he will beget* (HS), ruyę́·’na’θ ‹he-lay-begins› *he inherits* (HS); –(a)hę'na= yę(T)–: kahę́’nayę’ ‹it-clearing-laid› *the meadow lies, is, exists: there is a meadow* (H 2484), wahę́’nayę’ ‹it-clearing-laid› *grotto* (HS); –(a)hkara= yę(T)–{dative III}: ruhkarayę́·ti· ‹he-bark-laid-for› *he laid bark for* (RC 12:2); –a’nahkwa’rayę(T)–: yu’nah-ka’rà·yę’ ‹it-affray-laid› *affray, tumult* (HS); –a’nahkwa’rayę'na'nye’–: yu’-nahka’rayę’ná·’nye’ ‹it-affray-laid-going along› *tumultuously* (HS); –a’wnayę(T)–: wá’wnayę’ ‹it-earth-laid› *there is land* (RC 3:38); –čę= hayę(T)–: yečę́hayę’ ‹one-fire-laid› *family* (RC 16:1); –čisnayę(T)–: ka-čí·snayę’ ‹it-ember-laid› *court of justice* (HS); –činę’therayę(T)–: račinę’-therà·yę’ ‹he-curl-laid› *he has, possesses a curl, or a curly-headed person* (H 2484); –e’θayę(T)–{dative II}: re’θayę́·’nahθ ‹he-be in a location-laid-for› *he settles* (HS); –(ę)nęhra= yęhnę –: Kunęhrayę́hnęh ‹o!-scalp-lays-much› *Flying Head (mythic creature)* (RC 28:title), Kwęnęhrayę́hnęh ‹o!-scalp-lays-much› *Flying Head* (AG), Unęhrayę́hnęh ‹scalp-lay-much› *Flying Head (jumped on two legs like grasshopper, 4 foot tall)* (AG); –(ę)’ti=

kȩhrayȩ(T) –: na'tikȩ́hrayȩhs ‹one=an-other-mind-lays› *one comforts another* (HS), ra'tikȩ́hrayȩ' ‹he-mind-laid› *he has confidence* (HS); –(ȩ)'tikȩhra=yȩ'na' –: ȩktikȩhrayȩ́·'na' ‹fact-I-mind-lay-began› *I understood* (R), ru'tikȩh-rayȩ́·'na'θ ‹he-mind-lay-begins› *he discerns* (HS); –hehnayȩ(T) –: kahéhnayȩ' ‹it-field-laid› *the field lies, is lying* (H 2484), rahéhnayȩ' ‹he-field-laid› *he has a field, he owns a field or lot* (H 2484), rahéhnayȩhs ‹he-field-lays› *he is laying out a field, he is acquiring a field* (H 2484); –hehna=yȩhnȩ –: kahehnayȩ́hnȩh ‹it-field-laid-many› *the fields lie in groups* (H 24 84); –heruhkwayȩ'nahkw –: yeheruh-kwayȩ'náhkhwa' ‹one-green-cover-in-strument-lays-instrument› *hayloft* (HS); –hnawayȩ(T) –: yuhnà·wayȩ' ‹it-stream of water-laid› *there is a swamp* (RC 2:13); –hnekayȩ(T) –: kahné·kayȩ' ‹it-liquor-laid› *body of water (laying there)* (H-notebook); –hnȩwayȩ'T –: kahnȩ̀·wayȩ't ‹he-mark-lay-caused› *commerce* (HS); –hse'wayȩ(T) –: kah-sé'wayȩ' ‹it-pox-laid› *it has pox* (RC 16:1); –hskȩnȩ'nayȩ(T) –: rahskȩnȩ́'na-yȩhs ‹he-be at peace-cause-lays› *he is peaceful* (HS); –hswayȩ(T) –: ráhswa-yȩ' ‹he-back-laid› *he sits (or lies) bent low forward* (H-notebook); –hya=tȩhstayȩ'nahkw –: yehyatȩhstayȩ'náh-khwa' ‹one-book-lays-instrument› *library* (HS); –i'nyuhkwayȩ(T) –: ya-kwȩ'nyúhkwayȩ' ‹we-group-laid› *our organization: Temperance Society*

(i.e., 6-Nations Temperance Soc(iety) over 100 yrs. old—Seneca, Onondaga and Tuscarora (L 37–[yakwa·nyúh-kwayā·]); –(i)'θhaθnȩhčrayȩ(T) –: wa-kye'θhaθnȩ́hčrayȩ' ‹I-power-be heav-y-'ness-laid› *I am strong* (R); –kahra=yȩ(T) –{dative I}: ȩhskáhrayȩ'θ ‹pre-diction-you-eye-lay-for› *you must leave a trap (leave something (as bait) to catch the eye* (HS); –ka'nayȩ(T) –: wahraká'nayȩ' ‹fact-he-ring-laid› *he went in circles* (RC 31:3); –kerha=yȩ(T) –: kakyérhayȩ' ‹it-body-laid› *there is body* (RC 8:32); –kȩheyȩ'=nayȩ(T) –: rakȩheyȩ́'nayȩ' ‹he-die-cause-laid› *he is lying there dying* (HS); –kwatihčayȩ(T) –: rakwatíhčayȩ' ‹he-boldness-lays› *he is bold* (HS); –kwatihčayȩhčr –: ukwatihčayȩ́hčreh ‹boldness-lay-'ness› *audacity, bravery* (HS); –kwenyȩhčrayȩ(T) –: rukwenyȩ́h-črayȩ' ‹he-be able-'ness-lays› *he has ability* (HS); –nȩhsayȩ(T) –: kanȩ́hsa-yȩ' ‹it-house-lays› *the house lies, is established, stands* (H 2484); –nȩhsna=yȩ(T) –: ranȩ́hsnayȩ' ‹he-seed-lays› *he lays grain down* (H 2484); –nȩhsna=yȩhnȩ –: ranȩhsnayȩ́hnȩhs ‹he-seed-lays-much› *he goes habitually to leave grain (said of a person taking grain to market or other depot)* (H 2484); –nȩhsnayȩ'nahkw –: yenȩhsnayȩ'náh-khwa' ‹one-seed-lay-instrument› *gran-ary* (HS); –nȩ'arayȩ(T) –: unȩ'à·rayȩ' ‹climbing vine-lay› *wild grape* (R); –rharahčrayȩ(T) –: rarharáhčrayȩ' ‹he-be confident-'ness-laid› *he has hope*

Tuscarora Pronunciation Key:

/a/ l<u>a</u>w; /e/ h<u>a</u>t; /i/ p<u>i</u>zza; /u/ t<u>u</u>ne; /ȩ/ h<u>i</u>nt; /č/ <u>ch</u>eese; /h/ <u>h</u>oe; /m/ <u>m</u>other; /s/ <u>s</u>ame; /t/ <u>d</u>o (before a vowel y, or w), <u>t</u>oo (elsewhere); /k/ <u>g</u>ale (before a vowel y or w), <u>k</u>ale (elsewhere); /n/ i<u>n</u>hale (before a consonant or word-final), <u>n</u>ote (elsewhere), /r/ hi<u>ss</u> (before a consonant or word-final), <u>r</u>un (trilled as in Italian, elsewhere); /w/ c<u>u</u>ff (before a consonant other than y or word-final), <u>w</u>ay (elsewhere); /y/ fi<u>sh</u> (before a consonant or word-final), <u>y</u>ou (elsewhere), /θ/ <u>th</u>ing; /'/ (the sound between the vowels in unh-unh); /·/ long vowel, /'/ high pitch; /`/ low pitch.

(HS); -rihwayę(T) -: raríhwayęhs ‹he-matter-lays› *he obliges* (HS); -θuh=ra?tayę(T) -: yuθuhrá?tayę? ‹it-flat-leafed cedar-laid› *there is a flat-leafed cedar* (RC 2:13); -wirayęhte -: yewirayęhte? ‹one-offspring-laid-going to› *one was going to have a baby* (RC 3:15); -yękwirayę'nahkw -: yeyękwirayę?náhkhwa? ‹one-wood-lay-instrument› *woodshed* (HS); -?ęwarayę(T) -. #ú?y: ka?ęwarayę?ú?y ‹it-coil-lay-great› *great coil lays* (RC 7:1); -?ę=yayę(T) -: yu?ę·yayę? ‹it-debt-lays› *it costs* (HS); -ne -. -yę(T) -: nehrà·yęhs ‹apart-he-lays› *he bets* (HS); -t -. -yę(T) -: ká·čę ‹hither-you-lay› *give it!* (R) [Lawson «Cotshau» 'Give it to me']; ti -. -yę(T) -: tikà·yę? ‹so-it-laid› *it is easy* (R); ti+yah+či -. -yę(T) -: thweθkà·yę? ‹so-thither-again-it-laid› *it abandoned it, it left it there* (HS); -či -. -tahskwayę(T) -: θkakutahskwayę́·?-nahk ‹again-they-domestic animal-laid› *they had a pet again* (RC 22:11); -ne -. -(a)hkarayę'nahkw -: neyęhkarayę?náhkhwa? ‹apart-one-bark-lays-instrument› *draughthead* (HS); -ne -. -ah=θę?nayę'na? -: wa?nwahθę?nayę́·na? ‹fact-apart-it-be dark-lay-began› *it got dark* (RC 3:65); -ne -. -čha'nayę(T) -: neyučhá·?nayę? ‹apart-it-fog-laid› *it is foggy, it is misty* (R); -ne -. -ę'nayę='na? -: wa?nwę?nayę́·?na? ‹fact-apart-it-day-lay-began› *the full day* (HS); -ne -. -hak"ayę(T) -: nehrahá·kwayę? ‹two-he-bow-leg-laid› *he is bow-legged* (HS); -ne -. -hęwayę'nahkw -: neyuhęwayę?náhkę ‹apart-it-boat-laid-instrument› *concave* (HS); -ne -. -hskę=nę?nayę(T) -: nehrahskęnę́?nayęhs ‹two-he-be at peace-cause-lays› *he arbitrates* (HS); -ne -. -hyatęhstayę='nahkw -: neyehyatęhstayę?náhkhwa? ‹two-one-book-lays-instrument› *play-

ing cards (HS); -ne -. -ręhyayę(T) -.#áh: neyuręhyayę?áh ‹apart-it-sky-lays-little› *watermelon (Citrullus vulgaris)* (R); -ne -. -rihwayę(T) -{dative I}: wa?-tkakurihwayę́·?na?θ ‹fact-apart-they-matter-laid-for› *they resolved* (RC 12:17); -t -. -yęwayę(T) -.#áh: Nyuyęwayę?áh ‹hither-it-treeless tract of ground-lays-little› *Four Mile Creek* (H 3518); ti -. -(a)hkarači?tkwahnayę(T) -: tiwahkarači?tkwáhnayę? ‹so-it-bark-yellow-laid› *yellow oak (Quercus sp.)* (H-notebook); ti -. -či?tkwahnayę(T) -: tikači?tkwáhnayę? ‹so-it-yellow-laid› *gold* (R) [Gallatin «ticot-tcheet kwaunaugeh» 'Yellow']; ti -. -či?tkwahna=yę(T) -.#ętíh: tikači?tkwahnayę?ętíh ‹so-it-yellow-laid-many little› *yellow jackets, hornets (Vespa maculata)* (R); ti -. -hshęwayę(T) -: tihrahshę̀·wayę? ‹so-he-hollow-lays› *he is light* (HS); ti -. -hshęwayę?T -: tihrahshęwayę́?tha? ‹so-he-hollow-lay-causes› *he lightens it* (HS); -yah -. -rihwayę(T) -{dative II}: weθaríhwayęhθ ‹thither-you-matter-laid-for› *it has become your responsibility* (RC 12:21); -ne+či -. -hskęnę?=nayę(T) -: neθhrahskęnę́?nayę? ‹apart-again-he-be at peace-cause-laid› *he reconciles* (HS); -yah+ne -. -ahsa=yę(T) -: yahwa?thráhsayę? ‹thither-fact-two-he-foot-laid› *his two feet lay there* (RC 3:50); -a'nyę(T) -: ęyę́·?nyę? ‹prediction-one-oneself-lay› *one will sit* (RC 3:70); -arahsayę(T) -: ruráhsayę? ‹he-himself-foot-laid› *his shoe* (HS); -athahayę'na'nye? -: ruthahayę?ná·?nye? ‹he-himself-path-laid-going along› *he is traveling along* (H 2484); -atkarayę'nahkw -: ratkarayę?náhkhwa? ‹he-himself-debt-lays-instrument› *he pledges* (HS); -atkęheyę?nayę'nahkw -: yętkęheyę?nayę?náhkhwa? ‹one-oneself-die-cause-lays-instrument› *hospi-

tal. infirmary (HS); -at²ęy̲ayę(T) -: wat²ę·yayę² ‹it-itself-enclosed area-laid› *fort* (HS). rat²ę·yayęhs ‹he-himself-enclosed area-lays› *he fortifies* (HS); -a'nekay̲ę(T) -{dative III}: yaku²nekayę́·tih ‹one-oneself-liquid-laid-for› *dropsy* (RC 18:title); -a'nekhwa̲ = yę(T) -: wa²nékhwayę² ‹it-itself-food-laid› *there is food* (RC 17:5); -a'nę = nawayę'nahkw -: yę²nęnawayę²náhkhwa² ‹one-oneself-??-lays-instrument› *storehouse* (HS); -a'nwira̲ = yę(T) -: wa²nwì·rayęhs ‹it-itself-infant-lays› *it gives birth* (RC 7:11); -a'nwę = tay̲ę²T -: ra²nwętayę́²tha² ‹he-himself-word-lays› *he speaks ill of it* (HS); -a'nyahkwa̲yę(T) -: wa²nyáhkwayę² ‹it-itself-girth-lays› *prostitute* (HS); -a'nyahkwa̲yę'nahkw -: yę²nyahkwayę²náhkhwa² ‹one-oneself-girth-lays-instrument› *market* (HS); -či -. -a = 'nyę(T) -: θhrá·²yęhs ‹again-he-himself-lays› *he abdicates* (HS); ti+yah -. -ačkę²ra̲yę(T) -: thweyęčkę́²rayęhs ‹so-thither-one-oneself-bone-lays› *consumption, tuberculosis* (HS); ha² -yę(T) -: ha² rù·yę² ‹the he-laid› *his property* (HS); ha² -ne -. -yę(T) -: ha² nekà·yęhs ‹the apart-it-lays› *wager* (HS); kę² -hyatęhsta̲yę'nahkw -: kę² yehyatęhstayę²náhkhwa² ‹where one-book-lays-instrument› *bookcase, desk* (HS); kwęhs -(ę)²tikęhra̲yę'nahsT -: kwęhs u²tikęhrayę́·²nahst ‹no mind-lay-cause› *inexplicable* (HS); ti+yah -. -ačkę²ra̲yę(T) - -thwę -: thweyęčkę́²rayęhs yú·thwę· ‹so-thither-one-one-

self-bone-lays it-is good for› *boneset (Eupatorium perfoiatum)* (H-notebook); **kuráhku·** -a'nyę'nahkw -: kuráhku· yę²nyę²náhkhwa² ‹British one-oneself-lays-instrument› *throne* (HS). -yę(T) - property. *dv.n.s.* ha² rù·yę² ‹the he-laid› *his property* (HS). -yę(T) - beget. *v.s.-a.i.* rà·yęhs ‹he-lays› *he begets* (HS), rù·yę² ‹he-laid› *he begot* (HS), ęhrá·yę·² ‹prediction-he-lay› *he will beget* (HS). -yęt - brick pile, stone pile, wood pile. *n.r.* n-poss., inc., n.sfx. -eh. uyę́·tch *brick pile, stone pile, wood pile* (HS); -yęta²nihr -: rayętá²nihč ‹he-pile-stands up› *he piles it up* (HS); -t -. -yęta²nihr -: nahrayęta²níhrę ‹hither-fact-he-pile-stood up› *he stood up brush* (RC 7:4). -yęthu - plant. *v.r.-t.* stat: -ę, hab: -hs, pnt: -², prog: -ęha'nye²-, prp: -hθc-, dst: -, caus: -hT-, rvs: -aku-, dat: -, inc.-ɸ-pat. ruyę́·thwę *he has planted* (R), rayę́·thuhs *he is planting* (R), wa²kyę́·thu² *I planted* (R); -yęthu -. #aka·²: rayęthuhs²á·ka·² ‹he-plants-characterized by› *farmer, tiller* (HS); -yęthuhθe -: rayęthúhθe² ‹he-plants-going to› *he is going to plant: he vaccinates* (HS); -yęthwaku -: ruyęthwá·kwę ‹he-plant-undid› *he has harvested* (R), wahrayęthwá·ku² ‹fact-he-plant-undid› *he harvested* (R); -yęthwę = ha'nye² -: ruyęthwęhá·²nye² ‹he-planted-going along› *he is going along planting* (R); -či -. -yęthu -: θhrayę́·thwahs ‹again-he-plants› *he replants it*

(HS); -ę°hrayęthu -: yawǫhrayę́·thwę ‹it-dirt-planted› *alluvium* (HS); -nęh-
-yęthuhT -: unę́heh kayęthúhtha'' ‹corn it-plant-causes› *corn planter* (L 60).

-yęthu -.#aka·'' farmer, tiller. *dv.n.s.* rayęthuhs''á·ka·'' ‹he-plants-characterized by› *farmer, tiller* (HS).

-yęthuhθe - vaccinate. *v.s.-a.i.* rayęthúh-θe'' ‹he-plants-going to› *he vaccinates* (HS).

-yęthwaku - harvest. *v.s.-t.* ruyęthwá·kwę ‹he-plant-undid› *he has harvested* (R), wahrayęthwá·ku'' ‹fact-he-plant-undid› *he harvested* (R).

-yęti - extend. *v.r.-t.* hab: -h, pnt: -, stat: -'', prog: -ha'nye''-, prp: -, dst: -hę-, caus: -''T- ~ -hsT-, rvs: -, dat: -, inc.-ɸ-pat. -(a)hahyęti -: wahahyę́·ti'' ‹it-path-extends› *the path, road lies extended away* (H 2484); -(a)hahyęti=ha'nye'' -: wahahyętihá·''nye'' ‹it-path-extends-going along› *the road extends along, meanders* (H 2484); -(a)hah=yętihę -: wahahyętíhęh ‹it-path-extends-much› *the rows extend away lengthwise (said of rows of hills of corn, etc., trees, or cocks of grain, etc.* (H 2484); -(a)hę'nyęti -: wahę''nyę́·ti'' ‹it-clearing-extends› *the meadow lies, extending hence* (H 2484); -hehnyęti -: kahehnyę́·ti'' ‹it-field-extends› *the field, plot, lot lies extending away lengthwise* (H 2484); -hnęwyęti''T -: rahnęwyętí''tha'' ‹he-mark-extend-causes› *he streaks it* (HS); -hsnę=wyętihę -: kahsnęwyętíhęh ‹it-stream-extends-many› *they are brooks extending along, running in many directions* (H-notebook); -nęhsyęti -: ranęhsyę́·tih ‹he-house-extends› *he extends house, he builds an addition* (HS), *he extends the house lengthwise* (H 2484), kanęhsyę́·ti'' ‹it-house-extends› *it is an extended house, one lengthened*

by making an addition to its end (H 2484); -nęhsyęti''T -: ękęnęhsyę́·ti''t ‹prediction-I=you-house-extend-cause› *I will confederate you* (AG), kakhenęhsyętí''tha'' ‹I=them-house-extend-cause› *I am confederating them* (AG), kakhenęhsyętí''nę ‹I=them-house-extend-caused› *I have confederated them* (AG); -nę'nyęti -: yunę''nyę́·ti'' ‹it-mountain-extends› *ridge* (HS); -rih=wayęti -: rarihwayę́·tih ‹he-matter-extends› *he idolizes it, he worships it* (HS); -wenę'nayętihsT -: yewenę''na-yętíhstha'' ‹one-metal-extend-causes› *trap* (HS); -ya''karyęti -: raya''karyę́·ti'' ‹he-upper body-extends› *he was lying down* (RC 3:50); ha'' -rihwayęti -: ha'' rarihwayę́·tih ‹the he-matter-extends› *his adoration* (HS); kwęhs -ya''čęti -: kwęhs akaya''čę́·tik ‹no unknown-it-track-extend› *it is indefinite* (HS).

-yęw - treeless plot of ground in the woods. *n.r.* inc., n-poss., n.sfx. -eh. uyę̀·weh *treeless plot of ground in the woods* (R); -yęwakraθ -: kayęwá·kra·θ ‹it-treeless plot of ground-smells› *horsemint, monarda (Monarda* sp.) (R); -yęwa''ke: uyęwá''kye ‹treeless plot of ground-at› *a treeless tract at times surrounded by woods* (H 3518); -t -.-yęwayę(T) -.#áh: Nyuyęwayę''áh ‹hither-it-treeless tract of ground-lays-little› *Four Mile Creek* (H 3518).

-yęwahnęhčr - benevolence, glory. *n.s.* kayęwahnę́hčra'' ‹it-bless-'ness› *benevolence, glory* (HS).

-yęwahT - bless. *v.r.-t.* hab: -ha'', pnt: -ę·'', stat: -ę, prog: -, prp: -, dst: -, caus: -, rvs: -, dat: III (-ti-/-ę-), n-inc. na''nyęwáhtha'' *one blesses another* (HS); -yęwahnęhčr -: kayęwahnę́hčra'' ‹it-bless-'ness› *benevolence, glory* (HS); -či -.-yęwahT -: čę́''na''nyęwáh-tha'' ‹again-one=another-blesses› *one*

blesses another again (HS); –a'**nyę** =
wahT –: ru'ʔnyęwáhnę'ʔ ‹he-himself-
blessed› *he sacrificed, he immolated*
(HS), ęhra'ʔnyęwáhnę·'ʔ ‹prediction-he-
himself-bless› *he will immolate* (HS);
–a'**na'nyęwahT** –: ra'ʔna'ʔnyęwáhtha'ʔ
‹he-himself-blesses› *he is lavish, he
spends foolishly* (HS); –a'**nyęwahT** –
{dative III}: ra'ʔnyęwahnę́·ti· ‹he-him-
self-blessed-for› *he made votive offerings* (RC 12:6); ha'ʔ –a'**nyęwah** =
nęhkw –: ha'ʔ yę'ʔnyęwahnę́hkhwa'ʔ ‹the
one-oneself-bless-instrument› *altar*
(HS); kwęhs –**yęwahT** –: kwęhs ahruyęwáhnęk ‹no unknown-he-bless› *he
is unblest* (HS); –**węniyu** – –**yęwah** =
nęhčrawę –: rawęni·yu'ʔ ruyęwahnę́h-
črawęh ‹he-is God he-bless-'ness-possesses› *glory of God* (HS).

–**yęwakraθ** – horsemint, monarda. *dv.n.s.*
kayęwá·kra·θ ‹it-treeless plot of
ground-smells› *horsemint, monarda*
(*Monarda* sp.) (R).

–**yęwaksta'ʔkyeha·'ʔ** dandelion. *n.r.* n-
poss., n-inc., n.sfx. -. uyęwaksta'ʔkyé-
ha·'ʔ *dandelion* (*Taraxacum officinale*)
(R).

–**yęwarę** – splint. *v.r.-t.* hab: -, pnt: -'ʔ,
stat: -, prog: -, prp: -, dst: -, caus: -,
rvs: -, dat: -, n-inc. wa'ʔeyęwà·rę'ʔ *one
splinted it* (R).

–**yęwn** – right hand. *n.r. West.* inaln., inc.
-'ʔ, n.sfx. -. Found only in the Western
dialect. See: –**wyęwnahkw** –. kyeyęw-
nę́'ʔkye *my right hand* (PC).

–**yę'ʔ** –.#**ú'ʔy** snow a great deal. *v.r.-s.i.*
stat: -ę, prog: -, prp: -, dst: -, caus: -,
rvs: -, dat: -, n-inc. yuyę'ʔęhú'ʔy *it
snowed a great deal* (SH 375); ti –.
–**yę'ʔ** –.#**ú'ʔy**: tyuyę'ʔęhú'ʔy ‹so-it-snowed
a great deal› *it snowed a great deal*
(SH 375).

–**yę'ʔkʷ** – shoot. *v.s.-t.* See: –i'ʔa(k) –/
–**yę'ʔkʷ** –.

–**yę'ʔkw(ar)** – smoke. *n.r.* n-poss., inc.,
n.sfx. -eh. uyę'ʔkweh *smoke* (R), u-
yę'ʔkwareh *smoke* (PC); –**yę'ʔkwaku'ʔ** =
čęri –: ruyę'ʔkwaku'ʔčę́·ryę ‹he-smoke-
found› *he found smoke* (RC 12:23);
–**yę'ʔkwararhu** –: wahrayę'ʔkwarárhu'ʔ
‹fact-he-smoke-mixed in› *he smoked
it (i.e., preserved it by smoking)* (RC
8:18); –**yę'ʔkwaraθhu** –: wa'ʔuyę'ʔkwa-
ráθhu'ʔ ‹fact-it-smoke-smelled› *it
smelled of smoke* (RC 32:11); –**yę'ʔ** =
kwarhar –: yuyę'ʔkwárhar ‹it-smoke-
hangs› *mold* (R); –**yę'ʔkwarihsak** –:
wahrayę'ʔkwarihsá·khe'ʔ ‹fact-he-
smoke-sought-going to› *he went looking for smoke* (RC 12:22); –t –. –**yę'ʔ** =
kwhar –: nakayę'ʔkhwà·ra'ʔ ‹hither-fact-
it-smoke-hung› *a swarm* (RC 26:10);
–a'**nyę'ʔkwa'ʔnihr** –: yu'ʔnyę'ʔkwa'ʔníhrę
‹it-itself-smoke-stood up› *it smokes
(e.g., a gun)* (HS), *it is smoking* (PC);
–**yę'ʔkwararhu** – –'ʔ**wahr** –: kayę'ʔkwarárhę u'ʔwáhreh ‹it-smoke-mixed in
meat› *bacon* (HS).

–**yę'ʔkwararhu** – smoke. *v.s.-t.* wahrayę'ʔ-
kwarárhu'ʔ ‹fact-he-smoke-mixed in›
*he smoked it (i.e., preserved it by
smoking)* (RC 8:18).

–**yę'ʔkwararhu** – –'ʔ**wahr** – bacon. *dv.n.s.*
kayę'ʔkwarárhę u'ʔwáhreh ‹it-smoke-

mixed in meat› *bacon* (HS).

–yę**ʔkwarhar** – mold. *dv.n.s.* yuyę·ʔkwárhar ‹it-smoke-hangs› *mold* (R).

–yę**ʔkwih** – gird. *v.r.-t.* hab: -, pnt: -, stat: -, prog: -, prp: -, dst: -, caus: -, rvs: -si-, dat: -, n-inc. –yę**ʔkwihčr** –: uyę·ʔkwíhčreh ‹gird-'ness› *belt* (R); –yę**ʔ**=**kwihsi** –: rayę·ʔkwíhsyęhs ‹he-gird-undoes› *he ungirds* (HS); –a**ʔnyęʔkwih** –: raʔnyę́·ʔkwihs ‹he-himself-girds› *he belts himself, he puts on his belt* (HS), ruʔnyę́·ʔkwih ‹he-himself-girded› *it encircles him* (RC 32:10); –yę**ʔ**=**kwihst** – –at**ʔahsęhnahkw** –: uyę·ʔkwíhsteh yętʔahsęhnáhkhwaʔ ‹gird-'ness one-oneself-breast-fall-causes-instrument› *bandolier* (HS).

–yę**ʔkwihčr** – belt. *n.s.* uyę·ʔkwíhčreh ‹gird-'ness› *belt* (R).

–yę**ʔkwihsi** – ungird. *v.s.-t.* rayę·ʔkwíhsyęhs ‹he-gird-undoes› *he ungirds* (HS).

–yę**ʔkwihst** – –at**ʔahsęhnahkw** – bandolier, bra. *dv.n.s.* uyę·ʔkwíhsteh yętʔahsęhnáhkhwaʔ ‹gird-'ness one-oneself-breast-fall-causes-instrument› *bandolier* (HS), *bra* (R).

–yę**ʔn** – splint; mat made of corn husks. *n.r.* n-poss., n-inc., n.sfx. -eh. uyę́ʔneh *splint* (SH 375); *mat made of corn husks* (R) [Lawson «Ooyethne» 'A Mat'].

–yę**ʼnaT(e)** – she, one...him, her, one (third person singular feminine/indefinite agent=third person feminine/indefinite patient). *v.r.pfx.* The form –yę**ʼnat**- occurs before roots and stems that begin with the consonants *k*, ʔ, or *h*; when the root or stem begins with the cluster *hs*, this cluster coalesces with the final *t* of the prefix to yield –yę**ʼnač** –. The form –yę**ʼnaʼn** – occurs before roots and stems that begin with a vowel. The form –yę**ʼnaʔ** – occurs before roots and stems that begin with the consonants *t, č, r* or, sometimes, *n*. The form –yę**ʼnaʼnę** – occurs before certain roots and stems that begin with the consonant *n* or the consonant clusters *hn* or *ht*. The form –yę**ʼnaʼne** – occurs before roots and stems that begin with clusters that condition the appearance of "epenthetic" e. The initial *y* of the prefix is dropped following the factual mode marker.

–yę**ʼnaʔ** – beget. *v.s.-a.i.* rayę́·ʔnaʔθ ‹he-lay-begins› *he begets* (HS), ruyęʔná·ʔę ‹he-lay-began› *he begot* (HS), ęhrayę́·ʔnaʔ ‹prediction-he-lay-begins› *he will beget* (HS).

–yę**ʼnaʔ** – inherit. *v.s.-a.i.* ruyę́·ʔnaʔθ ‹he-lay-begins› *he inherits* (HS).

yę**ʔnekhriʔnuharáhkhwaʔ** sycamore, buttonwood *(Platanus* sp.*)* (R). *n.*

–yę**ʼner** – know. *v.r.-t.* hab: -ɸ, pnt: -ʔ, stat: -ih ~ -ę, prog: -, prp: -, dst: -, caus: -T- ~ -hu-, rvs: -, dat: -, inc.-ɸ pat. The rare stative form –**ih** found with the unmodified root is replaced by the more common form –**ę** in certain derived forms. kyęʔnè·rih *I know* (RC 11:27), kyęʔneríhahk *I used to know* (HS), wahrayę́·ʔneʔr *he knew* (RC 26:1), akayeyęʔnè·rik *that they have known* (RC 3:21); –yę=**ʼnerhuku** –{dative III}: naʔnyęʔnerhukwá·tih ‹one=another-know-cause-undoes-for› *one notifies another* (HS); –(a)**hahayęʼner** –: kayehahayęʔnè·rih ‹they-path-know› *they know the path* (RC 32:2); –**hyatęhstayęʼner** –: rahyatęhstayęʔnè·rih ‹he-book-knows› *he learned: scholar* (HS); –**či** –. –yę**ʼner** –: θhrayę́·ʔner ‹again-he-knows› *he recognizes* (HS), θhruyęʔnè·rę ‹again-he-knew› *he recognized* (HS); kwęhs –yę**ʼnerT** –: kwęhs aryuyęʔnérnęk ‹no unknown-it-know-cause› *it is un-*

known (HS); **kwęhs -ʔnihahstayę'ner -**: kwęhs aryeʔnihahstayęʔnè·rihk ‹no un-known-it-know-cause› *it is unknown* (HS); **kwęhs -ʔnihahstayę'ner -**: kwęhs aryeʔnihahstayęʔnè·rihk ‹no unknown-one-be young male-'ness-know› *chaste woman, maidenhood* (HS).

-yę'nerhuku -{dative III} notify. *v.s.-t.* naʔnyęʔnerhukwá·tih ‹one=another-know-cause-undoes-for› *one notifies another* (HS).

-yęʔtu - rat. *n.r.* n-poss., inc., n.sfx. -ʔ. ruyęʔtuʔ *rat* (R); **-yęʔtuhrahT -**: ruyęʔ-túhraht ‹he-rat-put up-cause› *mythic strong creature* (AW 53).

-yęʔtuhrahT - mythic strong creature. *dv. n.s.* ruyęʔtúhraht ‹he-rat-put up-cause› *mythic strong creature* (AW 53).

-yhih - blueberry, huckleberry. *n.r.* n-poss., n-inc., n.sfx. -aʔ. uyhíhaʔ *blueberry (Vaccininum sp.), huckleberry (Gaylusacia baccata)* (H-notebook).

-yuhkuhčr - lace. *n.s.* uyuhkúhčreh ‹border-cover-'ness› *lace* (HS).

-yuhkur - border, make a border, rim. *v.s.-a.i.* yeyúhkuč ‹one-border-covers› *one borders it, one makes a border* (HS), rayúhkuč ‹he-border-covers› *he rims it* (HS).

-yuhkw - border, rim. *n.r.* n-poss., inc., n.sfx. -eh. uyúhkweh *border, rim* (HS); **-yuhkuhčr -**: uyuhkúhčreh ‹border-cover-'ness› *lace* (HS); **-yuhkur -**: yeyúhkuč ‹one-border-covers› *one borders it, one makes a border* (HS), rayúhkuč ‹he-border-covers› *he rims it* (HS).

-yuhr - be abreast of. *v.r.-t.* hab: -, pnt: -, stat: -, prog: -a'nyeʔ-, prp: -, dst: -, caus: -, rvs: -, dat: -, n-inc. Encoun-tered only in the construction cited below. **tha+ne -. -yuhra'nyeʔ -**: thaʔne-yeyuhrá·ʔnyeʔ ‹unusual-apart-one-is abreast of-going along› *abreast (with verbs of motion)* (R).

-yuraʔkw - accuse, taunt. *v.r.-t.* hab: -haʔ, pnt: -ɸ, stat: -ę̊, prog: -a'nyeʔ-, prp: -, dst: -, caus: -, rvs: -, dat: -, n-inc. ru-yurá·ʔkę *he taunts it* (HS), rayurá·ʔ-khwaʔ *he accuses it, he taunts it* (HS), ęhrayù·raʔkw *he will taunt it* (HS); **haʔ -yuraʔkw -**: haʔ ruyurá·ʔkhwaʔ ‹the he-accuses› *reproach* (HS).

-yuraʔkw - reproach. *dv.n.s.* haʔ ruyurá·ʔ-khwaʔ ‹the he-accuses› *reproach* (HS).

Yuyęčhanęʔná·kę Fore Paw-Pressed-A-gainst-Breast (Chief of the Bear Clan) (H-Handbook). *n.*

-yuʔn(e) - work; ferment. *v.r.-a.i.* hab: ()-ʔ, pnt: -, stat: -ę, prog: -a'nyeʔ-, prp: -ęhθre-, dst: ()-tyę-, caus: -ęhT-, rvs: -, dat: ?, inc.-ɸ-ag. Lounsbury (p. 60) cites two dative forms that do not fit either of the three established da-tive series for the language. These forms are **rakyuʔnęhθeh** *he works for me* and **rakyuʔnęhθatíhahk** *he has worked for me.* θayúʔnę *you worked* (RC 3:52), kayúʔneʔ *it works* (RC 3:52), yuyúʔneʔ *it ferments* (HS); **-yuʔnetyę -**: yuyuʔné·tyęʔ ‹it-worked-much› *machinery, manufacturer* (HS); **-yuʔnęhčr -**: uyuʔnę́hčreh ‹work-'ness› *craft, labor, work* (HS); **-yuʔnęhθre -**:

Tuscarora Pronunciation Key:
/a/ law; /e/ hat; /i/ pizza; /u/ tune; /ę/ hint; /č/ cheese; /h/ hoe; /m/ mother; /s/ same; /t/ do (before a vowel y, or w), too (elsewhere); /k/ gale (before a vowel y or w), kale (elsewhere); /n/ inhale (before a consonant or word-final), note (elsewhere), /r/ hiss (before a consonant or word-final), run (trilled as in Italian, elsewhere); /w/ cuff (before a consonant other than y or word-final), way (elsewhere); /y/ fish (before a consonant or word-final), you (elsewhere), /θ/ thing; /ʔ/ (the sound between the vowels in unh-unh); /·/ long vowel, /´/ high pitch; /`/ low pitch.

wahruyu·'nḗhθre·' ‹fact-he-worked-went to› *he's going to work* (L 60); **-yu'nęhčratak(e)r** –: ękayu·'nęhčratá·krę·' ‹prediction-it-work-'ness-be plentiful› *work will become abundant* (H 2892), akayu·'nęhčratá·krę·' ‹unknown-it-work-'ness-be plentiful› *work would become abundant* (H 2892); **-yu'nęh = stačha'nur** –: yuyu·'nęhstačhá·'nur ‹it-work-'ness-is difficult› *it is laborious* (HS); **-yu'nęhT** –: kayu·'nḗhtha·' ‹it-work-causes› *workshop* (HS), rayu·'nḗhtha·' ‹he-work-causes› *he exercises* (HS); **-rihwayu'n(e)** –: rurihwayú·'ne·' ‹he-matter-worked› *he plots* (HS); **ti** –. **-yu'nehkw** –: tihruyu·'nḗhkę ‹so-he-worked-instrument› *he works for* (RC 12:1); **-ahsę – -yu'nehkw** –: wáhsęh ruyu·'nḗhkę ‹it-is evil he-worked-instrument› *malefactor* (HS); **kę' -yu' = nęhT** –: kę·' kayu·'nḗhtha·' ‹where it-work-causes› *laboratory* (HS).

-yu'netyę – machinery, manufacturer. *dv. n.s.* yuyu·'né·tyę·' ‹it-worked-much› *machinery, manufacturer* (HS).

-yu'nęhčr – craft, labor, work. *n.s.* uyu·'nḗhčreh ‹work-'ness› *craft, labor, work* (HS).

-yu'nęhstačha'nur – be laborious. *v.s.-s.i.* yuyu·'nęhstačhá·'nur ‹it-work-'ness-is difficult› *it is laborious* (HS).

-yu'nęhT – workshop. *dv.n.s.* kayu·'nḗhtha·' ‹it-work-causes› *workshop* (HS).

-yu'nęhT – exercise. *v.s.-a.i.* rayu·'nḗhtha·' ‹he-work-causes› *he exercises* (HS).

'

-'ahn – rib. *n.r. West.* aln: k·'ahnę́'kye *my rib* (PC), inc. ?, n.sfx. -ę·'. u·'-áhnę·' *rib* (PC).

-'ahθr – basket. *n.r.* aln: ak·'áhθrawęh *my basket* (R), inc., n.sfx. -eh. u·'áhθreh *basket* (R); **-'ahθraw** –: wa·'nat·'áhθrę·' ‹fact-one=another-basket-gave to› *one gave another a basket* (R); **-'ahθra = werhu** –: wahra·'aθrawérhu·' ‹fact-he-basket-covered› *he fastened the basket shut* (RC 30:14); **-yah** –. **-'ahθruha** –: yahwa·'kaye·'ahθrúha·' ‹thither-fact-they-basket-put in water› *they put basket in water* (RC 10:1).

-'ahs – bosom, breast. *n.r.* inaln: k·'ahsę́'kye *(on) my breast* (R), inc., n.sfx. -eh. u·'áhseh *bosom, breast* (R); **-ne** –. **-at'ahstrę** –: wa·'thrat·'áhstrę·' ‹fact-a-part-he-himself-breast-tied› *he tied it on breast* (RC 30:58); **-t** –. **-at'ahsę = ya'T** –.**#ú'y**: nwat·'ahsęya'nęhú·'y ‹hither-it-itself-breast-hang down-caused-great› *giantess* (RC 11:5); **-yę'kwihst – -at'ahsęhnahkw** –: uyę·'kwíhsteh yęt·'ahsęhnáhkhwa·' ‹gird-'ness one-oneself-breast-fall-causes-instrument› *bandolier* (HS), *bra* (R).

-'ar – lower lip. *n.r.* poss. ?, inc., n.sfx. -eh. u·'à·reh *lower lip* (HS); **-'a = ru'čir** –: ra·'aru·'čírha·' ‹he-lower lip-sucks› *he kisses* (HS); **-'tihsn – -'a = ręT** –: u·'tíhsneh yu·'á·rę·t ‹cup it-lower lip-possesses› *pitcher* (HS).

-'aru'čir – kiss. *v.s.-t.* ra·'aru·'čírha·' ‹he-lower lip-sucks› *he kisses* (HS).

-'awy – dew. *n.r.* n-poss., inc., n.sfx. -eh. u·'á·wyeh *dew* (HS); **-'awyir** –: ra·'a-wyì·ręhs ‹he-dew-wanders› *he rambles through the dew* (H-notebook).

-'čaka'ręw – urethra. *n.r.* n-poss., inc., n.sfx. -eh. u·'čaka·'rę̀·weh *urethra* (HS).

-'čękahr – nostril. *n.r.* inaln: ka·'čękahrę́·'nę·' *its nostril* (RC 28:8), inc., n. sfx. -eh. Possibly an old compound of **-'tyęhs** – *nose* plus **-kahr** – *eye.* u·'čękáhreh *nostril* (R).

-ʔčę̧w - swindle. *v.r.-a.i.* hab: -ahs, pnt: -ʔ, stat: -ę̧ʔ, prog: -, prp: -, dst: -, caus: -, rvs: -, dat: -, n-inc. ruʔčę̧·wę̧ʔ *he swindled* (HS), raʔčę̧·wahs *he swindles* (HS), ę̧hráʔčę̧ʔw *he will swindle* (HS).

-ʔčha̱r - branch. *n.r.* n-poss., inc., n.sfx. -eh. úʔchareh *branch* (RC 20:1); -ʔcha̱ra̱kʷahT -: wahraʔchà·rakwaht ‹fact-he-branch-cut off› *he cut up branch* (RC 26:6); -ʔcha̱ryeriha -: waʔ-kayeʔcharyeríhaʔ ‹fact-they-branch-straightened› *they spread out branches* (RC 24:7); -(ę)tiʔcha̱rihrę̧ -: wahrę̧tiʔcharíhrę̧ʔ ‹fact-he-himself-branch-put up› *he lifted twig* (RC 26:8); -ʔcha̱ruhsku -: ruʔcharúhskę̧ ‹he-branch-picked off› *he has lots of humor* (R).

-ʔčih(e)r - aim (a gun), sight. *v.r.-a.i.* hab: ()-ɸ, pnt: -ę̧ʔ, stat: -, prog: -, prp: -, dst: -, caus: -, rvs: -, dat: -, n-inc. wahraʔčíhrę̧ʔ *he aimed* (RC 24:2), raʔčíher *he sights, he aims a gun* (HS).

-ʔčir - sting. *n.r.* n-poss., inc., n.sfx. -eh. uʔčì·reh *sting* (HS); -ʔčiraʔnihr -: raʔčiráʔnihč ‹he-sting-stands up› *he stings* (HS); -ʔčirukʷ -: ruʔčirú·kwahs ‹he-sting-spreads out› *he smarts, it stings him* (HS); -yah -. -ʔčiraʔnihr = hę̧ -: wekakuʔčiraʔnírhę̧ ‹thither-they-sting-stood up-much› *it stung them* (RC 26:10).

-ʔčirawę̧ - gesticulate. *v.r.-a.i.* hab: -h, pnt: -, stat: -, prog: -, prp: -, dst: -, caus: -, rvs: -, dat: -, n-inc. raʔči-rà·wę̧h *he gesticulates* (HS).

-ʔčiraʔnihr - sting. *v.s.-a.i.* raʔčiráʔnihč ‹he-sting-stands up› *he stings* (HS).

-ʔčirukʷ - sting. *v.s.-t.* ruʔčirú·kwahs ‹he-sting-spreads out› *he smarts, it stings him* (HS).

-ʔčuhn - fishhook, hook. *n.r.* n-poss., inc. ?, n.sfx. -eh. Mithun (1984) cites the form uttsúhneh (= utčúhneh). This may be an archaic form since everywhere else in the language, the cluster *tč* has shifted to *ʔč*. uʔčúhneh *fishhook, hook* (R).

-ʔehn - hand. *n.r.* inaln: kʔéhneh *my hand* (R), inc., n.sfx. -eh. uʔéhneh *hand* (RC 12:27) [Gallatin «uhehneh» 'Hand']; -ʔehna̱kęw: uʔéhnakęw ‹hand-in› *palm of hand* (SH 375); -ʔehnaʔ = ke: sʔehnáʔkye ‹you-hand-at› *on your hand* (RC 30:28); -ʔehnę̧T -: raʔéhnę̧·t ‹he-hand-possesses› *he has a hand, as a part of his body* (H 2892); -ʔeh = nuha -: wahraʔehnúhaʔ ‹fact-he-hand-put in water› *he put his hand in water* (RC 12:29); -t -. -ʔehnitkę̧ -: nakaʔehní·tkę̧ʔ ‹hither-it-hand-came forth› *hand came down* (RC 10:5); -atʔeh = na̱kwę̧ʔnar -: rutʔehnakwę̧ʔnà·rę̧ ‹he-himself-hand-turned down› *he slapped* (HS), ratʔehnakwę̧́ʔnar ‹he-himself-hand-turns down› *he slaps* (HS), ę̧hratʔehnakwę̧́ʔnaʔr ‹prediction-he-himself-hand-turn down› *he will slap* (HS); haʔ -atʔehnakewahT -: haʔ yę̧tʔehnakyewáhthaʔ ‹the one-oneself-hand-wipe-causes› *towel* (HS).

-ʔehna̱kęw palm of hand. *n.s.* uʔéhnakęw

‹hand-in› *palm of hand* (SH 375).

-ʔę̄ mother. *n.r.* aln: kakúʔ̇ę *their mother* (RC 27:3), n-inc., n.sfx. -ɸ. See: ę̇·nę̄ʔ *my mother.* θáʔę *your mother* (R); -ʔę̄.#áh: akuʔę̄háh ‹one-mother-little› *one's paternal aunt* (R); -ʔę̄hst -: uʔę̄hsteh ‹mother-'ness› *maternity, motherhood* (R).

-ʔę̄.#áh maternal aunt. *n.s.* akuʔę̄háh ‹one-mother-little› *one's maternal aunt* (R).

-ʔę̄hr- leaf. *n.r.* n-poss., inc., n.sfx. -eh. uʔę̄hreh *leaf* (R) [Gallatin «ohuhreh» 'Leaf']; -ʔę̄hračiwakę -: kaʔę̄hrači·wakę ‹it-leaf-is bitter› *smartweed* (R), yuʔę̄hrači·wakę ‹it-leaf-is bitter› *smartweed* (R) *sorrel* (HS); -ʔę̄hra= huk -: yuʔę̄hráhuks ‹it-leaf-lights up› *brilliant, gorgeous (leaves are lighted–in primitive times a fire that would light up the leaves to any considerable distance about was considered extraordinary & only on great occasions was it seen)* (HS); -ʔę̄hrę= θkarahkw -: kaʔę̄hrę̄θkaráhkhwaʔ ‹it-leaf-spreads out› *Virginia water plant* (R); -ʔę̄hruʔθkar -: raʔę̄hrúʔθkarhę̄hs ‹he-leaf-clips› *he strips off leaves* (HS); -ʔę̄hrʔe(k) -: raʔę̄hrʔehs ‹he-leaf-strikes› *he strikes leaf (archaic method of signaling one's lover in the woods by cupping a leaf and striking it like a drum)* (HS); -atʔę̄hrę̄ʔyT -: watʔę̄h-rę̄ʔythaʔ ‹it-itself-leaf-hang down-causes› *quaking aspen (Populus sp.)* (R); áhsę̄ ti -.-ʔę̄hrę̄t: áhsę̄ tyuʔę̄hrę̄·t ‹three so-it-leaf-possesses› *clover* (HS); tá·ku·θ -ʔę̄hrak -: tá·ku·θ kaʔę̄h-ra·ks ‹cat it-leaf-eats› *catnip* (H-notebook); haʔ -ʔę̄hrak -: haʔ yeʔę̄hra·ks ‹the one-leaf-eats› *salad* (HS); -yahsti - ti -.-ʔę̄hraʔnihr -: kayáhsti tikaʔę̄háʔ-nihč ‹it-individual-is a group so-it-leaf-stands up› *centifolious* (HS).

-ʔę̄hračiwakę - smartweed, sorrel. *dv.n.* yuʔę̄hrači·wakę ‹it-leaf-is bitter› *sorrel* (HS), kaʔę̄hrači·wakę ‹it-leaf-is bitter› *smartweed* (R).

-ʔę̄hrahuk - brilliant, gorgeous. *dv.n.s.* yuʔę̄hráhuks ‹it-leaf-lights up› *brilliant, gorgeous (leaves are lighted–in primitive times a fire that would light up the leaves to any considerable distance about was considered extra-ordinary & only on great occasions was it seen)* (HS).

-ʔę̄hrak - salad. *dv.n.s.* haʔ ye ʔę̄hra·ks ‹the one-leaf-eats› *salad* (HS).

-ʔę̄hrę̄θkarahkw - Virginia water plant. *n.s.* kaʔę̄hrę̄θkaráhkhwaʔ ‹it-leaf-spreads out› *Virginia water plant* (R);

-ʔę̄hst - maternity, motherhood. *n.s.* uʔ-ę̄hsteh ‹mother-'ness› *maternity, motherhood* (R).

-ʔę̄w - tray, trough, wooden bowl. *n.r.* n-poss., inc., n.sfx. -eh. uʔę̄·weh *tray, trough, wooden bowl* (R); -ʔę̄waʔr -: kaʔę̄·waʔr ‹it-tray-is much› *small "hill" of plants* (H 3518).

-ʔę̄waʔr - small hill of plants. *dv.n.s.* kaʔę̄·waʔr ‹it-tray-is much› *small "hill" of plants* (H 3518).

-ʔę̄war - coil, spiral. *n.r.* n-poss., inc., n.sfx. -eh. uʔę̄·wareh *coil, spiral* (R); -ʔę̄warayę(T)-.#úʔy: kaʔę̄warayę̄ʔúʔy ‹it-coil-lays-great› *great coil lays* (RC 7:1).

-ʔę̄y - cost, debt, pay, price, value. *n.r.* n-poss., inc., n.sfx. -eh. uʔę̄·yeh *cost, debt, pay, price, value* (HS); -ʔę̄yah= sthuʔT -: raʔę̄yahsthúʔthaʔ ‹he-cost-be small-causes› *he depreciates it* (HS); -ʔę̄yakwahsnaʔ -: yuʔę̄yakwáhsnaʔθ ‹it-cost-be good-begins› *it is cheap, the price falls, the price becomes good* (HS); -ʔę̄yayę(T)-: yuʔę̄·yayę̄ʔ ‹it-cost-lays› *it costs* (HS); -ʔę̄yaʔk -: raʔę̄·yaʔks ‹he-cost-breaks› *creditor*

(HS); -ʔeyaʔtyę'nę -: raʔeyaʔtyę́·ʔnęh ‹he-cost-measures› *he appraises* (HS), *he measures price* (H-notebook); -ʔę = yeθ -: yuʔę̀·ye·θ ‹it-cost-is long› *it is dear, it is expensive* (HS); -ʔeyeθ - {dative I}: ęyeθáʔθeh ‹cost-is long-for› *appreciation* (HS), natʔeyeθáʔθeh ‹one=another-cost-is long-for› *one appreciates another* (HS); -ʔeyeθT -: raʔeyéθthaʔ ‹he-cost-be long-causes› *he raises the price* (HS); -ʔeytęʔr -: ruʔeytę́ʔrę ‹he-cost-??› *he is in debt* (HS); -ʔeyuhar -: raʔeyúhar ‹he-cost-washes› *he pays* (HS); -ʔeyuhrarakT -: yeʔeyuhraráktha ʔ‹one-cost-press-causes› *stake* (HS); -či -. -ʔeyuhar -: θhraʔę-yúhar ‹again-he-cost-washes› *he reimburses, he repays, he revenges* (HS); -t -. -ʔeyeθę -: nyuʔeyé·θę ‹hither-it-cost-is long-much› *high prices* (R); -atʔeyaʔnęr -: yutʔeyaʔnę̀·rę ‹it-itself-cost-self-left behind› *arrears* (HS); -atʔeyityęʔT -: ratʔeyityę́ʔthaʔ ‹he-himself-cost-go to-causes› *he runs into debt* (HS); haʔ ti -. -ʔeyaʔθ -: haʔ tyuʔę̀·yaʔθ ‹the so-it-cost-is of a size› *cost, the price of it* (HS); haʔ -či -. -atʔeyuhar -: haʔ θwatʔeyúhar ‹the again-it-itself-cost-washes› *retaliation* (HS); íhsʔę ti+yah -. -ʔeyuhar -{dative I}: íhsʔę thweyęʔnatʔeyuhárθeh ‹more so-thither-one=another-cost-washes-for› *one overpays* (HS); séʔči kwà·nę -ʔeyuhar -: séʔči kwà·nę natʔeyúhar ‹because much one=another-cost-washes› *one overpays* (HS).

-ʔey - enclosed area, fence, prison. *n.r.* n-poss., inc., n.sfx. -ch. uʔę̀·yeh *enclosed area, fence, prison* (R); -ʔę = yakęw: uʔę̀·yakęw ‹enclosed area-in› *in barricade* (RC 33:11); -ʔęyuhT -: yeʔeyúhthaʔ ‹one-enclosed area-cover-causes› *pasture* (HS); -ne -. -ʔeyę = kuhT -: waʔtkayeʔeyę́·kuht ‹fact-apart-they-enclosed area-go through-caused› *they caused it to go out of barricade* (RC 33:11); -atʔeyayę(T) -: watʔę̀·ya-yęʔ ‹it-itself-enclosed area-lay› *fort* (HS), ratʔę̀·yayęhs ‹he-himself-enclosed area-lays› *he fortifies himself* (HS); -atʔeyaʔnihθT -: kakutʔeyaʔnih-θnę́heʔ ‹they-themselves-enclosed area-stand up-cause-were going to› *they were setting up enclosure* (RC 24:11); -ne -. -atʔeyaʔnęʔ -: nekakutʔę-yáʔnęʔ ‹apart-they-themselves-enclosed area-became› *they had enclosed in barricade* (RC 33: 11).

-ʔeyahsthuʔT - depreciate. *v.s.-t.* raʔeyah-sthúʔthaʔ ‹he-cost-be small-causes› *he depreciates it* (HS).

-ʔeyakwahsnaʔ - be cheap, be a good price. *v.s.-a.i.* yuʔeyakwáhsnaʔθ ‹it-cost-be good-begins› *it is cheap, the price falls, the price becomes good* (HS).

-ʔeyayę(T) - cost. *v.s.-a.i.* yuʔę̀·yayęʔ ‹it-cost-lays› *it costs* (HS).

-ʔeyaʔk - creditor. *dv.n.s.* raʔę̀·yaʔks ‹he-cost-breaks› *creditor* (HS).

-ʔeyaʔtyę'nę - appraise. *v.s.-t.* raʔeyaʔ-tyę́·ʔnęh ‹he-cost-measures› *he appraises* (HS), *he measures price* (H-notebook).

Tuscarora Pronunciation Key:
/a/ law; /e/ hat; /i/ pizza; /u/ tune; /ę/ hint; /č/ cheese; /h/ hoe; /m/ mother; /s/ same; /t/ do (before a vowel y, or w), too (elsewhere); /k/ gale (before a vowel y or w), kale (elsewhere); /n/ inhale (before a consonant or word-final), note (elsewhere), /r/ hiss (before a consonant or word-final), run (trilled as in Italian, elsewhere); /w/ cuff (before a consonant other than y or word-final), way (elsewhere); /y/ fish (before a consonant or word-final), you (elsewhere), /θ/ thing; /ʔ/ (the sound between the vowels in unh-unh); /·/ long vowel, /´/ high pitch; /`/ low pitch.

-ʔęyeθ- be dear, be expensive. *v.s.-s.i.* yuʔ$\acute{e}$·ye·θ ‹it-cost-is long› *it is dear, it is expensive* (HS).

-ʔęyeθ-{dative I} appreciate. *v.s.-t.* nat-ʔęyeθáʔθeh ‹one=another-cost-is long-for› *one appreciates another* (HS).

-ʔęyeθ-{dative I} appreciation. *n.s.* ęye-θáʔθeh ‹cost-is long-for› *appreciation* (HS).

-ʔęyeθT – raise the price. *v.s.-a.i.* raʔęyé-θthaʔ ‹he-cost-be long-causes› *he raises the price* (HS).

-ʔęytęʔr – be in debt. *v.s.-a.i.* ruʔęytę́ʔrę ‹he-cost-??› *he is in debt* (HS).

-ʔęyuhar – pay. *v.s.-t.* raʔęyúhar ‹he-cost-washes› *he pays* (HS).

-ʔęyuhrarakT – stake. *dv.n.s.* yeʔęyuhra-rákthaʔ ‹one-cost-press-causes› *stake* (HS).

-ʔęyuhT – pasture. *dv.n.s.* yeʔęyúhthaʔ ‹one-enclosed area-cover-causes› *pasture* (HS).

-ʔę'n – bow. *n.s. West.* inc. ?, poss. ?, n.sfx. uʔę́·ʔneh *bow* (PC).

-ʔkęh be younger sibling. *v.r.-k.* khéʔkęh *my younger sibling: my younger brother, my younger sister* (R), nátkęh *one's younger sibling* (R) [Lawson «Caunotka» 'Brother'], yękhíʔkęh *our younger sibling* (RC 29:9), kayę́tkęh *they are younger brothers* (AW 55); -atkęhst –: utkę́hsteh ‹self-be younger sibling-'ness› *brother (very rare)* (HS).

-ʔnahkw – barrel, bowl, box, case, cask, drum, pail, pulpit. *n.r.* n-poss., inc. uʔnáhkweh *barrel, bowl, box, case, cask, drum, pail, pulpit* (HS); -ʔnah=kwaʔnihrhę –: kaʔnahkwaʔnírhęh ‹it-box-stands up-much› *boxes standing upright* (RC 11:16); -ʔnahkwęt –: yuʔ-náhkwę·t ‹it-box-possesses› *drawer* (HS); -ʔnahkwęti –: raʔnahkwę́·tih ‹he-box-makes› *cooper* (HS); -ʔnahkw=ʔe(k) –: raʔnáhkwʔehs ‹he-box-strikes›

he beats drum (HS).

-ʔnahkwęt – drawer. *dv.n.s.* yuʔnáhkwę·t ‹it-box-possesses› *drawer* (HS).

-ʔnahkwęti – cooper. *dv.n.s.* raʔnahkwę́·tih ‹he-box-makes› *cooper* (HS).

-ʔnahkwʔe(k) – beat drum. *v.s.-a.i.* raʔ-náhkwʔehs ‹he-box-strikes› *he beats drum* (HS).

-ʔnahsęr – poison hemlock. *n.r.* n-poss., n-inc. uʔnahsę̀·reh *poison hemlock* (H-notebook).

-ʔnar – peak (of a cap). *n.r.* n-poss., n-inc. úʔnareh *peak (of a cap)* (HS).

-ʔnaręw – mastic, mud, plaster, putty. *n.r.* n-poss., inc., n.sfx. -eh. uʔnà·ręweh *mastic, mud, plaster, putty* (R); -ʔna=ręw–.#hči: uʔnaręwéhči ‹he-mud-gives› *muddy* (HS); -ʔnaręwawę –: raʔ-narę̀·wawęhs ‹he-mud-gives› *he limes, he plasters* (HS); -ʔnaręwayę(T) –. #úʔy: yuʔnaręwayęʔúʔy ‹it-mud-lays-great› *there is much mud* (RC 24:7); -ʔnaręwęti –: yuʔnaręwę́·ti· ‹it-mud-made› *mud puddle* (RC 24:7); -ʔna=ręwhar –: wahraʔnaręwhà·raʔ ‹fact-he-mud-hung› *he got muddy* (RC 24:9); haʔ –t –. -ʔnaręwar –: haʔ nyuʔnarę̀·war ‹the hither-it-mud-is in› *ceiling* (HS).

-ʔnaręw–.#hči muddy. *n.s.* uʔnaręwéhči ‹he-mud-gives› *muddy* (HS).

-ʔnaręwawę – lime, plaster. *v.s.-a.i.* raʔ-narę̀·wawęhs ‹he-mud-gives› *he limes, he plasters* (HS).

-ʔnaręwęti – mud puddle. *dv.n.s.* yuʔna-ręwę́·ti· ‹it-mud-made› *mud puddle* (RC 24:7).

-ʔnaręwhar – get muddy. *v.s.-a.i.* wahraʔ-naręwhà·raʔ ‹fact-he-mud-hung› *he got muddy* (RC 24:9).

-ʔnehahčr – ignominy, shame. *n.s.* uʔ-neháhčreh ‹shame-'ness› *ignominy, shame* (HS).

-ʔnehahčrukęʔ be immodest, be shame-less, loose all shame. *dv.n.s.* ruʔnehahčrú·kę^ʔ ‹he-shame-less› *he has lost all shame* (HS).

-ʔnehahT – shame. *v.r.-t.* hab: -ha^ʔ, pnt: -, stat: -ɸ, prog: -, prp: -, dst: -, caus: -, rvs: -, dat: -, n-inc. na^ʔna^ʔneháhtha^ʔ *one shames another* (HS), yu^ʔnéhaht *it is shameful* (R); **-ʔnehahT-**: u^ʔnéhaht ‹shame› *reproach, shame* (HS); **-ʔnehahčr-**: u^ʔneháhčreh ‹shame-'ness› *ignominy, shame* (HS); **-ʔnehahčrukę^ʔ**: ru^ʔnehahčrú·kę^ʔ ‹he-shame-less› *he is immodest, he is shameless, he has lost all shame* (HS); **-nh- -ʔnehahT-**: kánhę u^ʔnéhaht ‹it-is full shame› *shameful* (HS).

-ʔnehahT – reproach, shame. *n.s.* u^ʔnéhaht ‹shame› *reproach, shame* (HS).

-ʔnehkw – conceal. *v.r.-t.* hab: -ahs, pnt: -ɸ, stat: -, prog: -, prp: -, dst: -, caus: -, rvs: -, dat: -, n-inc. wa^ʔnyé^ʔnehkw *one concealed* (RC 6:19); **-a^ʔrihwa^ʔ=nehkw-**: ra^ʔrihwa^ʔnéhkwahs ‹he-himself-matter-conceals› *he dissembles* (HS).

-ʔnehr-{dative II} tire out. *v.s.-t.* ra^ʔnehrę́·tih ‹he-be tired-for› *he tires it out* (HS).

-ʔnehr(e) – be tired. *v.r.-s.i.* stat: ()-ę, prog: -, prp: -, dst: ()-khrę-, caus: ()-T-, rvs: -, dat: III (-ti-/-hθ-), n-inc. This final (e) of the root occurs before derivational suffixes such as the causative and inchoative. waknéhrę *I am tired* (R), ru^ʔnéhrę *he is tired* (R); **-ʔnehre^ʔ-**: ru^ʔnehré^ʔę ‹he-be tired-began› *he is tired* (HS), ra^ʔnéhre^ʔθ ‹he-be tired-begins› *he grows weary*

(HS), ęhra^ʔnéhre^ʔ ‹prediction-he-be tired-begin› *he will grow weary* (HS); **-ʔnehr-{dative II}**: ra^ʔnehrę́·tih ‹he-be tired-for› *he tires it out* (HS); **-ʔneh=re^ʔT-**: yu^ʔnéhre^ʔt ‹it-be tired-caused› *it is tedious, it is tiresome* (HS); ti-. **-ʔnehre^ʔkhrę'nye^ʔ-**:tyu^ʔnehre^ʔkhrę́·^ʔnye^ʔ ‹so-he-be tired-began-much-going along› *he is having a bad dream* (R).

-ʔnehre^ʔ – be tired, grow weary. *v.s.-a.i.* ru^ʔnehré^ʔę ‹he-be tired-began› *he is tired* (HS), ra^ʔnéhre^ʔθ ‹he-be tired-begins› *he grows weary* (HS), ęhra^ʔnéhre^ʔ ‹prediction-he-be tired-begin› *he will grow weary* (HS).

-ʔnehre^ʔT – be tedious, be tiresome. *v.s.-s.i.* yu^ʔnéhre^ʔt ‹it-be tired-caused› *it is tedious, it is tiresome* (HS).

-ʔnehs – crust. *n.r.* n-poss., n-inc., n.sfx. -eh. u^ʔnéhseh *crust (of bread, of snow)* (R).

-'nek – burn. *v.r.-a.i.* hab: -s, pnt: -ɸ, stat: -, prog: -, prp: -, dst: -, caus: -a^ʔT-, rvs: -, dat: -, inc.-ɸ-pat. yú·^ʔneks *it burns, it is lit* (R), wa^ʔú·^ʔnek *it burned* (R); **-'neka^ʔnahkw-**: yę^ʔneka^ʔnáhkhwa^ʔ ‹one-burn-causes-instrument› *lighter, match* (R); **-'neka^ʔT-**: kaku^ʔneká^ʔnę ‹they-burn-caused› *they kindled* (RC 12:22), ra^ʔneká^ʔtha^ʔ ‹he-burn-causes› *he lights it* (HS); **-'neksk-**: yu^ʔnékskę· ‹it-burned-easily› *it is inflammable* (HS); **-(ę)tahsna='nek-**: yutáhsna^ʔneks ‹it-stick-burns› *burning stick* (AW 56); **-nęhsa'nek-**: yunę́hsa^ʔneks ‹it-house-burns› *burning*

---

house (PC); **kwęhs –'nek –**: kwęhs a-
ryuʔnékshek ‹no unknown-it-burn› *it
is incombustible* (HS); **kwęhs
–'neksk –**: kwęhs aryuʔnékskę·k ‹no unknown-it-burn-easily› *it is incombustible* (HS).

–'neka ʔnahkw – lighter, match. *dv.n.s.*
yęʔnekaʔnáhkhwaʔ ‹one-burn-causes-
instrument› *lighter, match* (R).

–'neka ʔT – kindle, light. *v.s.-t.* kakuʔne-
káʔnę ‹they-burn-caused› *they kindled*
(RC 12:22), raʔnekáʔthaʔ ‹he-burn-
causes› *he lights it* (HS).

–'neksk – be inflammable. *v.s.-s.i.* yuʔ-
nékskę· ‹it-burned-easily› *it is inflammable* (HS).

–ʔnęn – bottom. *n.r.* poss. ʔ, n-inc., n.sfx.
–eh. uʔnę̀·neh *bottom (of pails, baskets)* (HS).

–ʔnenę – dwell, reside; make a fire. *v.r.-
a.i.* hab: -, pnt: -ʔ, stat: -ʔ, prog: -,
prp: -, dst: -, caus: -, rvs: -, dat: -, n-
inc. yuʔnè·nęʔ *it dwells* (RC 11:6),
wahraʔnè·nęʔ *he dwelt* (RC 26:26),
waʔkayeʔnè·nęʔ *they made a fire* (AW
55), ęhsnè·nęʔ *you will make a fire*
(AW 58), yęktiʔnè·nęʔ *my husband
(the one I live with)* (L 34), yęktiʔ-
nè·nęhk *my former husband* (L 33);
ti –. –ʔnenę –: tiwaknè·nęʔ ‹so-I-dwell› *I
dwell* (RC 25:9); **–ʔnenęʔna'nyeʔ –**
{dative I}: ęyękwaʔnenęʔnaʔnyéʔθek
‹prediction-we-dwell-cause-going a-
long-for› *wherever we will be living*
(RC 30:67); **–ʔnenęhkw –**: waʔkayeʔ-
nè·nęhkw‹fact-they-dwelt-instrument›
they used it to live by (RC 6:14).

–ʔnenę – husband. *dv.n.s.* yęktiʔnè·nęʔ
‹we two-dwell› *my husband (the one
I live with)* (L 34), yęktiʔnè·nęhk ‹we
two-dwelt› *my former husband* (L 33).

–ʔnewak ghost. *n.r.* n-poss., n-inc., n.sfx.
–φ. uʔné·wa·k *ghost* (R); **–ʔnewak.
#keha·ʔ**: uʔnewa·kkyéha·ʔ ‹ghost-cus-

tomarily› *ghost-like* (H-notebook);
–ʔnewak – –a'nuri –: uʔné·wa·k waʔnù·-
rih ‹ghost it-itself-stirs› *pussytoes (Antennaria* sp.) (R).

–ʔnewak – –a'nuri – *dv.n.s.* uʔné·wa·k waʔ-
nù·rih ‹ghost it-itself-stirs› *pussytoes
(Antennaria* sp.) (R).

–ʔnewak.#keha·ʔ ghost-like. *n.s.* uʔne-
wa·kkyéha·ʔ ‹ghost-customarily›
ghost-like (H-notebook).

–'nęhT – bury. *v.r.-t.* hab: -φ, pnt: -, stat: -
, prog: -, prp: -, dst: -, caus: -, rvs:
-aku-, dat: -, n-inc. This is a highly
irregular root in that the unsuffixed
form has only been encountered in
noun compounds, the inchoative form
is missing an expected *a* (i.e., * –'nęh =
naʔ –), and the words for *cemetery* and
burial ground contain an unidentified
suffix. **–'nęhnaku –**: raʔnęhná·kwahs
‹he-bury-undoes› *he exhumes* (HS);
–'nęhnary –: yeʔnęhná·ryę ‹one-bury-
??› *cemetery* (HS), yeʔnęhná·ryeh
‹one-bury-??› *burial ground* (HS);
–'nęhtʔ –: yeʔnę́htʔahs ‹one-bury-be-
gins› *burial* (HS), raʔnę́htʔahs ‹he-
bury-begins› *he buries, he entombs,
he inters* (HS); **–at'nęhtʔahsT –**: yęt-
ʔnęhtʔáhsthaʔ ‹one-oneself-bury-be-
gin-causes› *womb* (?) (SH 375);
kwęhs –'nęhtʔ –: kwęhs ahraʔnę́htʔak
‹no unknown-he-bury-begin› *he is
unburied* (HS); **haʔ kęʔ –'nęhT –**: haʔ
kęʔ rá·ʔnęht ‹the where he-buries›
grave, tomb (HS).

–'nęhnaku – exhume. *v.s.-t.* raʔnęhná·
kwahs ‹he-bury-undoes› *he exhumes*
(HS).

–'nęhnary – burial ground, cemetery. *dv.
n.s.* yeʔnęhná·ryę ‹one-bury-??› *cemetery* (HS), yeʔnęhná·ryeh ‹one-bury-
??› *burial ground* (HS).

–'nęhtʔ – burial. *dv.n.s.* yeʔnę́htʔahs ‹one-
bury-begins› *burial* (HS).

-'nęhtʔ - bury, entomb, inter. *v.s.-t.* raʔ-nę́htʔahs ⟨he-bury-begins⟩ *he buries, he entombs, he inters* (HS).

-ʔnęnaw - bundle, belongings, pack. *n.r.* poss. ʔ, inc., n.sfx. -. Found only in the construction cited below. -ʔnęna = węhawi -: raʔnęnawęhà·wiʔ ⟨he-bundle-brings-X⟩ *he carries bundle* (RC 8:3).

-'nęθ - be thick. *v.r.-s.i.* stat: -ɸ, prog: -, prp: -, dst: -, caus: -, rvs: -, dat: -, inc.-ɸ-pat. ká·ʔnę·θ *it is thick* (HS); -(ę)taʔra'nęθ -: ratáʔra'nę·θ ⟨he-head-is thick⟩ *he is dull* (HS); -nęhsa'nęθ -: kanę́hsaʔnę·θ ⟨it-house-is thick⟩ *the house is thick, that is, its sides are: the sides of the house are thick* (H 2484), *(the walls of) the house are thick* (HS); ti -. -'nęθ -: tiká·ʔnę·θ ⟨so-it-is thick⟩ *it is so thick* (RC 30:44); ti -. -'nęθ -.#áh: tikaʔnę·θʔáh ⟨so-it-is thick-little⟩ *thin* (L 78); ti -. -'nęθ -. #úʔy: tikaʔnę·θʔúʔy ⟨so-it-is thick-great⟩ *it is thick* (R).

-ʔnęthiʔ be relatives of one's father. *n.r.*, aln: ru·ʔnę́·thiʔ *his father's relations* (HS), n-inc., n.sfx. -ɸ. ruʔnę́·thiʔ *his father's relations* (HS); -ʔnęthiʔke. #aka·ʔ: ruʔnęthiʔkyehá·ka·ʔ ⟨he-father's relatives-at-characterized by⟩ *people of his father's relations* (HS).

-ʔnęthiʔke.#aka·ʔ people of one's father's relations, one's father's nation. *n.s.* Since the Tuscarora are a matrilineal culture, a child of a Tuscarora mother is by birth a member of the Tuscarora Nation. If one's father is not Tus-

carora, this term refers to the ethnic or political group from which he comes. ruʔnęthiʔkyehá·ka·ʔ ⟨he-be father's relatives-at-characterized by⟩ *people of his father's relations* (HS).

-ʔnęw - bucket, kettle, pot; tobacco pipe. *n.r.* n-poss., inc., n.sfx. -eh. uʔnę̀·weh *bucket, bucket, pot* (R); *tobacco pipe* (HS); -ʔnęw -.#ęwe: uʔnęwehę̀·we ⟨pot-genuine⟩ *brass, copper* (HS); -ʔnęw -.#ęwe.#hči: uʔnęwehęwéhči ⟨pot-genuine-very⟩ *brassy* (HS); -ʔnę = wawęhte -: yuʔnęwawę́hteʔ ⟨it-pot-is between two things⟩ *a small kettle put in the space made by two larger and the back log* (H-notebook); -ʔnęwę = haw -: waʔkayeʔnęwę́haʔw ⟨fact-they-pot-carried⟩ *they carried kettle* (RC 24:6); -ʔnęwhar -{dative III}: ęyeʔ-nęwhà·ręʔ ⟨prediction-one-pot-hang-for⟩ *one will hang pot* (RC 15:4), waʔkayeʔnęwhà·ręʔ ⟨fact-they-pot-hung-for⟩ *they hung pot* (RC 12:13); -ʔnęwharahkw -: yeʔnęwharáhkhwaʔ ⟨one-pot-hangs-instrument⟩ *pothanger* (HS); -ʔnęw -.#ęwe kwę́: uʔnęwehę̀·we kwę́ ⟨pot-genuine like⟩ *copperish* (HS).

-ʔnęw -.#ęwe brass, copper. *n.s.* uʔnę-wehę̀·we ⟨pot-genuine⟩ *brass, copper* (HS).

-ʔnęw -.#ęwe kwę́ copperish. *n.s.* uʔnę-wehę̀·we kwę́ ⟨pot-genuine like⟩ *copperish* (HS).

-ʔnęw -.#ęwe.#hči brassy. *n.s.* uʔnęwehę-wéhči ⟨pot-genuine-very⟩ *brassy* (HS).

-ʔnęwawęhte - small kettle. *dv.n.s.* yuʔ-

nęwawę́htcʔ ‹it-pot-is between two things› *a small kettle put in the space made by two larger and the back log* (H-notebook).

-ʔnęwharahkw - pothanger. *dv.n.s.* yeʔnęwharáhkhwaʔ ‹one-pot-hangs-instrument› *pothanger* (HS).

-'nęʔθ-.#aka·ʔ writer. *dv.n.s.* raʔnęʔθhaʔ-á·ka·ʔ ‹he-writes-characterized by› *writer* (L 23–[rɑ·ʔ'nɔ̃ʔθɑhɑ́·ka·']).

-'nęʔθęhst - writing. *n.s.* uʔnęʔθę́hsteh ‹write-'ness› *writing* (HS).

-ʔnhęh - bladder, urine. *n.r.* poss. ʔ, inc., n.sfx. -eh. uʔnhę́heh *bladder, urine* (R); -ʔnhęhahsthu -: raʔnhęháhsthę ‹he-urine-is small› *his urine is scanty, he makes but a small quantity of urine* (H 2484); -ʔnhęhakʷek -: ruʔnhę́hakweks ‹he-urine-closes› *he has the strangury (lit., it closes or shuts up his urine)* (H 2484); -ʔnhęhakęw: uʔnhę́hakęw ‹urine-in› *in urine, in the midst of urine* (H 2484); -ʔnhęha=tyaʔkwahT -: ruʔnhęhatyáʔkwaht ‹he-urine-is nasty› *his urine is disgusting, nauseating (said of one who is so dirty as to have an offensive effluvia from his person)* (H 2484); -ʔnhę=haʔke: uʔnhęháʔkye ‹urine-at› *on urine, on the top of urine* (H 2484); -ʔnhęhehke: uʔnhęhéhkye ‹urine-at› *at the place of urine, at the urine* (H 24 84); -ʔnhęheθ -: raʔnhęhe·θ ‹he-urine-is long› *his membrum virile is long* (H 2484); -ʔnhęhę -.#hči: yeʔnhęhę́hči ‹one-urine-falls-much› *one urinates often* (H-notebook); -ʔnhęhitkęʔ -: rä·ʔnhęhí·tkęʔθ ‹he-urine-come forth-begins› *the urine he voids* (H 2484); -ʔnhęhiyu -: raʔnhęhí·yu· ‹he-urine-is great› *his urine is plentiful, abundant* (H 2484); -ʔnhęhuk -: ruʔnhę́huks ‹he-urine-blisters› *he desires to urinate (lit., his urine chafes or blisters him)*

(H 2484); ti -. -ʔnhęhaʔθ -.#áh: tihraʔnhęhaʔθʔáh ‹so-he-urine-is of a size-little› *his urine is small in quantity* (H 2484); -ʔnhęh- -teʔkwawę -: uʔnhęheh utéʔkwawęh ‹urine bag-possess› *bladder* (HS).

-ʔnhęh- -teʔkwawę - bladder. *n.s.* uʔnhę́heh utéʔkwawęh ‹urine bag-possess› *bladder* (HS).

-ʔnhęhakʷek - have strangury. *v.s.-a.i.* ruʔnhę́hakweks ‹he-urine-closes› *he has the strangury (lit., it closes or shuts up his urine)* (H 2484).

-ʔnhęhs - egg, testicle. *n.r.* n-poss., inc., n.sfx. -eh. uʔnhę́hseh *egg, testicle* (R); -ʔnhęhsawihsi -: raʔnhęhsawíhsyęhs ‹he-egg-give-undoes› *he castrates* (HS); -ʔnhęhsę -: waʔnhęhsęh ‹it-egg-falls› *it lays eggs* (HS); -ʔnhęhsęh =ra·heʔ -: kaʔnhęhsęhrá·heʔ ‹it-egg-fries-going to› *fried eggs* (R); -ʔnhęh=sukęʔ: ruʔnhęhsú·kęʔ ‹he-egg-less› *eunuch* (HS); -ʔnhęhsukr -: uʔnhęhsú·kreh ‹egg-rubbish› *urine (disgusting), foul or disgusting urine: a slovenly or slatternly person so filthy as to emit an odor of urine* (H 2484), uʔnhęhsú·kriʔ ‹egg-rubbish› *what is exuded from eggs or testicles, semen, sperm* (H 2484); -ʔnhęhsukrakęw: uʔnhęhsú·krakęw ‹egg-rubbish-in› *in, amidst urine (that is offensive)* (H 2484); -ʔnhęhsukraθ -: kaʔnhęhsú·kra·θ ‹it-egg-rubbish-smells› *it emits a foul odor of urine (said of an animal)* (H 2484); -ʔnhęhsukraθhu -: ruʔnhęhsukráθhwahs ‹he-egg-rubbish-smell-causes› *he smells (filthy) urine* (H 24 84); -ʔnhęhsukratetʔ -: ruʔnhęhsú·krate·ʔt ‹he-egg-rubbish-lined› *he has beside him a slatternly woman, a woman disgustingly filthy* (H 2484); -ʔnhęhsukrayę(T) -: raʔnhęhsú·krayęʔ ‹he-egg-rubbish-lays› *he lies in offen-*

sive urine; his garments emit the disgusting odor of urine (H 2484); –ʔnhęhsukraʔke: uʔnhęhsukráʔkye ‹egg-rubbish-at› *on foul urine* (H 2484); –ʔnhęhsukryęti –: kaʔnhęhsukryę́·tiʔ ‹it-egg-rubbish-extends› *he lies extended in (foul) urine, its urine lies spanned out* (H 2484); –ʔnhęh = suri –: raʔnhęhsù·rih ‹he-egg-stirs› *intruder* (HS).

–ʔnhęhsawihsi – castrate. *v.s.-t.* raʔnhęhsawíhsyęhs ‹he-testicle-give-undoes› *he castrates* (HS).

–ʔnhęhsę – lay eggs. *v.s.-a.i.* This stem behaves as if it began with *a.* waʔnhę́hsęh ‹it-egg-falls› *it lays eggs* (HS).

–ʔnhęhsęhra·heʔ – fried eggs. *dv.n.s.* kaʔnhęhsęhrá·heʔ ‹it-egg-fries-going to› *fried eggs* (R).

–ʔnhęhsukęʔ eunuch. *dv.n.s.* ruʔnhęhsú·kęʔ ‹he-egg-less› *eunuch* (HS).

–ʔnhęhsukr – urine; slovenly person; semen, sperm. *n.s.* uʔnhęhsú·kreh ‹egg-rubbish› *urine (disgusting), foul or disgusting urine; a slovenly or slatternly person so filthy as to emit an odor of urine* (H 2484), uʔnhęhsú··kriʔ ‹egg-rubbish› *what is exuded from eggs or testicles, semen, sperm* (H 2484).

–ʔnhęhsukrayę(T) – lie in urine, smell of urine. *v.s.-a.i.* raʔnhęhsú·krayęʔ ‹he-egg-rubbish-lays› *he lies in offensive urine; his garments emit the disgusting odor of urine* (H 2484).

–ʔnhęhsuri – intruder. *dv.n.s.* raʔnhęhsù·rih ‹he-egg-drives› *intruder* (HS).

–ʔnhękuhči – hatch. *v.r.-t.* hab: -ęhs, pnt: -ʔ, stat: -ę, prog: -, prp: -, dst: -, caus: -, rvs: -, dat: -, n-inc. The habitual form shows the **w-** form of the neuter singular pronominal prefix, rather than expected **ka-**, and an "epenthetic" e. aryuʔnhękúhčęk *that it be hatched* (RC 8:12), waʔkaʔnhękúhčiʔ *it hatched it* (R), weʔnhękúhčęhs *it hatches* (HS), yuʔnhękúhčę *it hatched* (HS).

–ʔnhęθt – dumplings, lump of dough; pill. *n.r.* n-poss. (but see note), n-inc., n.sfx. -eh. With pronominal prefixes marking inalienable possession this root takes on the meaning *chubbiness*. uʔnhę́θteh *dumplings, lump of dough; pill* (HS); –ʔnhęθt –: raʔnhę́θteh ‹he-lump of dough› *he is chubby* (HS).

–ʔnhęθt – chubbiness. *n.s.* raʔnhę́θteh ‹he-lump of dough› *he is chubby* (HS).

–ʔnhuhskwar – lower part of face, mouthful. *n.r.* See: –(ę)ʔnhuhskwar –.

–ʔniha – sprain. *v.r.-t.* hab: -hs, pnt: -ʔ, stat: -ę, prog: -, prp: -, dst: -, caus: -, rvs: -, dat: -, inc.-ɸ-pat. ruʔníhahs *he sprains it, he is sprained* (HS); –kwe = raʔniha –: wahrukweraʔníhahk ‹fact-he-ankle-sprained› *he twisted his ankle* (RC 25:13); –nęchaʔniha –: ranęchaʔníhahs ‹he-arm-sprains› *he sprains his arm* (HS); –ne –.–ʔniha –: nehraʔníhahs ‹two-he-sprains› *he discriminates, he varies the two* (HS); –ne –.–atʔniha –: newatʔníhahs ‹two-it-itself-sprains› *it changes, it varies* (HS), nęwatʔníhaʔ ‹two-prediction-it-itself-sprains› *it will change, it will vary* (HS), neyut'ʔníhę ‹two-it-it-self-sprained› *dissimilar, the two of them differ* (HS); -yah-. -ręh = yaʔniha-: weyuręhyaʔníhę ‹thither-it-sky-sprained› *horizon* (HS).

-ʔniha· maleness, masculinity. *n.r.* inaln: kayeʔníha· *the men* (L 34), n.sfx. -φ. Hewitt and Smith cite an unusual form, raʔnihá· *manly*, with accent shift. Such accent shift to the final syllable, in the absence of the addition of an enclitic, is otherwise unknown in the language. raʔníha· *he is male: male* (RC 3:14), kaʔníha· *male animal* (R), raʔnihá· *manly* (HS), eʔníha· *one is male: male* (RC 3:17); -ʔniha·-.#áh: raʔniha·háh ‹he-masculinity-little› *young man* (RC 27:1); -ʔniha·-.#ke = ha·ʔ: yeʔniha·kyéha·ʔ ‹one-masculinity-customarily› *masculine* (HS); -at = ʔnihahsT-: watʔniháhsnę ‹it-itself-masculinity-caused› *tom-boy* (HS); kwęhs -ʔnihahstayę'ner-: kwęhs aryeʔ-nihahstayęʔnè·rik ‹unknown-one-masculinity-'ness-know› *chaste woman, maidenhood* (HS).

-ʔniha·-.#áh young maleness. *n.s.* raʔ-niha·háh ‹he-masculinity-little› *young man* (RC 27:1).

-ʔniha·-.#keha·ʔ masculine. *n.s.* yeʔni-ha·kyéha·ʔ ‹one-masculinity-customarily› *masculine* (HS).

-ʔnihsęr- planet, star; navel. *n.r.* n-poss., inc., n.sfx. -eh. uʔnihsę̀·reh *planet, star: navel* (R); -ʔnihsęrarawę-: yuʔ-nihsęrarà·węʔ ‹it-star-is in-much› *it is starred* (HS); -ʔnihsęr- -ręryuhkwęT-: uʔnihsę̀·reh yuręryúhkwę·t ‹star it-ray-possesses› *comet* (HS).

-ʔnihsęr- -ręryuhkwęT- comet. *dv.n.s.* uʔnihsę̀·reh yuręryúhkwę·t ‹star it-ray-possesses› *comet* (HS).

-ʔnihsn- stem. *n.r.* n-poss., n-inc., n.sfx. -ch. uʔníhsneh *stem* (HS).

-ʔnihtyar- nipples. *n.r.* poss. ʔ, inc. ʔ, n.sfx. -aʔ. uʔníhtyaraʔ *nipples* (SH 375).

-ʔnikęhkari- be uncomfortable. *v.s.-s.i.* See: -(ę)ʔnikęhkari-.

-ʔnikęhkaryaʔt agony. *dv.n.s.* See: -(ę)ʔ = nikęhkaryaʔt.

-ʔnikęhryaʔk- despair. *v.s.-a.i.* See: -(ę)ʔnikęhryaʔk-.

-ʔnikwey- long, non-slopping kettle. *n.r.* n-poss., n-inc., n.sfx. -eh. uʔnikwè·yeh *a long, non-sloping kettle* (H-notebook).

-ʔnwiy- bat, club (hewn). *n.r.* n-poss., inc., n.sfx. -eh. uʔnwì·yeh *bat, club (hewn)* (HS).

-ʔnyehr- chimney. *n.r.* n-poss., n-inc., n.sfx. -eh. uʔnyéhreh *chimney* (R).

-ʔnyeruruθ- kidney. *n.r.* poss. ʔ, n-inc., n.sfx. -φ. uʔnyè·ruru·θ *kidney* (HS).

-ʔrhuhkw- cultiver. *n.r.* n-poss., inc., n.sfx. -eh. uʔrhúhkweh *cultiver* (HS); -ʔrhuhkwar-: uʔrhúhkwareh ‹cultiver-be in› *plot of land* (R); -ne-. -ʔrhuh = kwarurę-: nehraʔrhuhkwarù·ręh ‹apart-he-cultiver-be in-stirs› *he harrows it* (HS); -ne+či-. -ʔrhuhkwarurę-: nęčuʔr-huhkwarù·ręʔ ‹apart-fact-again-it-cultiver-be in-stirred› *it stirred, divided, poked up through land* (RC 5:22).

-ʔrhuhkwar- plot of land. *n.s.* uʔrhúh-kwareh ‹cultiver-be in› *plot of land* (R).

-ʔriye- entangle. *v.r.-t.* hab: -, pnt: -·ʔ, stat: -, prog: -, prp: -, dst: -, caus: -, rvs: -, dat: -, n-inc. Found only with incorporated noun roots. -(a)haha ʔ = riye-: yuhahaʔrì·yeʔ ‹it-path-entangled› *(it is) a blind-road, a road overgrown by weeds or shrubs from non-use (this term is applied to a road which is lost in a forest or to one that is no longer in use and has become overgrown by weeds or shrubs)* (H

2484); -athahaʔriye -: wathahaʔrì·yehs ‹it-itself-path-entangled› *it wears away the road* (HS).

-ʔru - grind. *v.r.-t.* hab: -, pnt: -·ʔ, stat: -, prog: -, prp: -, dst: -, caus: -, rvs: -, dat: -, n-inc. waʔéʔru·ʔ *one ground it* (RC 3:53).

-ʔθharar - be prickly. *v.r.-s.i.* stat: -ʔ, prog: -, prp: -, dst: -, caus: -, rvs: -, dat: -, inc.-ɸ-pat. Found only nominalized. -ʔθharar -: yúʔθharaʔr ‹it-is prickly› *cucumber* (HS), *Indian cucumber root (Medeola virginiana)* (H-notebook); -(a)hyaʔθharar -: yuhyáʔ-θharaʔr ‹it-fruit-is prickly› *gooseberry (Ribes sp.), wild gooseberry (Grosularia cynosbati)* (H-notebook).

-ʔθharar - cucumber, Indian cucumber root. *dv.n.s.* yúʔθharaʔr ‹it-is prickly› *cucumber* (HS), *Indian cucumber root (Medeola virginiana)* (H-notebook).

-ʔθkar - flow. *v.r.-a.i.* hab: -ahs, pnt: -, stat: -, prog: -, prp: -, dst: -, caus: -, rvs: -, dat: -, n-inc. yúʔθkarahs *it flows* (R), aryuʔθkaráhshek *that it flow, that it cover over* (RC 2:13); -t -.-ʔθkar -: nyúʔθkarahs ‹hither-it-spreads out› *it is covered there* (RC 8:11).

-ʔθkęw - roast. *n.r.* n-poss., inc., n.sfx. -eh. uʔθkwę̀·weh *roast (of any kind of meat)* (HS); -ʔθkęwęti -: raʔθkęwę́·tih ‹he-roast-makes› *he broils it* (HS).

-ʔθkęwęti - broil. *v.s.-t.* raʔθkęwę́·tih ‹he-roast-makes› *he broils it* (HS).

-ʔθkwehs - bench, chair, seat, stool; cutting block, chair, round block of wood, piece of a log. *n.r.* n-poss., inc., n.sfx. -eh. uʔθkwéhseh *bench, chair, seat, stool* (R); *round block of wood, piece of log* (AG), *cutting block* (R); -ʔθkwehsaʔke: uʔθkwehsáʔkye ‹cutting block-at› *on cutting block* (RC 30:28); -ʔθkwehsayę(T): kaʔθkwéhsayęʔ ‹it-cutting block-lays› *there is a cutting block* (RC 25:17); -ne -. -ʔθkwehsukwahT -{dative III}: neyuʔθkwehsukwahná·ti· ‹apart-it-round block of wood-spread out-caused-for› *cylinder* (AG); -atkaręhrę - -ʔθkwehs -: ęhsatkaréhręʔ uʔθkwéhseh ‹prediction-you-yourself-go around-much chair› *rocking chair* (R).

-ʔθnar - pork; pork rind. *n.r.* n-poss., n-inc., n.sfx. -eh. uʔθnà·reh *pork; pork rind* (R).

-ʔθrahrehsT - be immoderate, be intemperate. *v.r.-a.i.* hab: -ɸ, pnt: -, stat: -ę, prog: -, prp: -, dst: -, caus: -, rvs: -, dat: -, n-inc. ruʔθráhrehst *he is immoderate, he is intemperate* (HS), yuʔθrahréhnsę *immoderately* (HS).

-ʔθrahrehsT - immoderately. *dv.n.s.* yuʔ-θrahréhsnę *immoderately* (HS).

-ʔθriʔčr - sawdust, wood chips. *n.r.* n-poss., n-inc., n.sfx. -eh. uʔθríʔčreh *sawdust, wood chips* (RC 14:7).

-ʔθwahsT - be a good shot. *v.r.-s.i.* stat: -ɸ, prog: -, prp: -, dst: -, caus: -, rvs: -, dat: -, n-inc. ráʔθwahst *he is a good shot* (R).

-ʔθwętahrahT - be severe, be vigorous. *v.r.-s.i.* stat: -ɸ, prog: -, prp: -, dst: -, caus: -, rvs: -, dat: -, n-inc. ruʔθwę-

---

Tuscarora Pronunciation Key:
/a/ law; /e/ hat; /i/ pizza; /u/ tune; /ę/ hint; /č/ cheese; /h/ hoe; /m/ mother; /s/ same; /t/ do (before a vowel y, or w), too (elsewhere); /k/ gale (before a vowel y or w), kale (elsewhere); /n/ inhale (before a consonant or word-final), note (elsewhere), /r/ hiss (before a consonant or word-final), run (trilled as in Italian, elsewhere); /w/ cuff (before a consonant other than y or word-final), way (elsewhere); /y/ fish (before a consonant or word-final), you (elsewhere), /θ/ thing; /ʔ/ (the sound between the vowels in unh-unh); /·/ long vowel, /ˊ/ high pitch; /ˋ/ low pitch.

táhraht *he is severe, he is vigorous, his power is awful* (HS).

-ʔT- moving (ambulative). *v.r.sfx.* pnt: -aʔ, stat: -eʔ, prog: -, prp: -, dst: -, caus: -, rvs: -, dat: -, n-inc. A relatively infrequent suffix that has several meanings. Most often it is used to indicate that the activity described by the verb is accomplished while the agent is in motion (e.g., tikakuyeráʔneʔ ‹so-they-did-moving› *they had done it while on their way*). More rarely, it is used to add an iterative sense to the verb (e.g., ruyęhskwéʔneʔ ‹he-laughed-moving› *he giggles*).

-ʔtahs- tongue. *n.r.* See: -(ę)ʔtahs-.

-ʔtahsę- bee swarm. *dv.n.s.* See: -(ę)ʔ= tahsę-.

-ʔtahsarahkw- gossip, joke. *v.s.-a.i.* See: -(ę)ʔtahsarahkw-.

-ʔtare- touch. *v.r.-t.* hab: -hs, pnt: -, stat: -ʔ, prog: -, prp: -, dst: -, caus: -, rvs: -, dat: -, n-inc. raʔtà·rehs *he touches it* (HS), yuʔtà·reʔ *touching* (HS).

-ʔteh- gravel, hail, sand. *n.r.* n-poss., inc., n.sfx. -eh. See: -ʔtehar-. uʔtéheh *sand* (RC 30:56), *gravel, hail* (HS); -ʔteh-.#hči: uʔtehéhči ‹sand-very› *sandy, mixed with sand* (HS); -ʔtehaʔ= kye: uʔteháʔkye ‹sand-at› *it is sandy (said of a place with deep sand, or where you have put sand)* (AG); -ʔte= hahriʔ-: kaʔteháhriʔθ ‹it-sand-spill-begins› *it hails* (H-notebook); -ʔteha= kwęhnarhu-: katehakwęhnárhuhs ‹it-sand-throw down-causes› *it hails* (HS), yuʔtehakwęhnárhę ‹it-sand-throw down-caused› *sandy country, plains (a desert would be called so)* (AG); -ʔtehakwęhnarhu-.#úʔy: yuʔte-hakwęhnarhęʔúʔy ‹it-sand-throw down-caused-great› *desert (a vast spread of sand)* (HS); -ʔtehaʔke: uʔ-teháʔkye ‹sand-at› *on sand, sandy*

(HS); -ʔtehyeriha-: waʔktehyeríhaʔ ‹fact-I-sand-straightened› *I have spread sand over* (AG); haʔ -ʔtehah= riʔ-: haʔ yuʔtehahríʔę ‹the it-sand-spill-began› *hail* (HS); haʔ -ne-. -ʔte= hiθaʔT-: haʔ neyuʔtehiθáʔnę ‹the a-part-it-sand-join-caused› *hail* (HS).

-ʔteh-.#hči sandy, mixed with sand. *n.s.* uʔtehéhči ‹sand-very› *sandy, mixed with sand* (HS).

-ʔtehahriʔ- hail. *v.s.-a.i.* kaʔteháhriʔθ ‹it-sand-spill-be-gins› *it hails* (H-notebook).

-ʔtehahriʔ- hail. *dv.n.s.* haʔ yuʔtehahríʔę ‹the it-sand-spill-began› *hails* (HS).

-ʔtehakwęhnarhu- desert, plains, sandy country. *dv.n.s.* yuʔtehakwęhnárhę ‹it-sand-throw down-caused› *sandy country, plains (a desert would be called so)* (AG).

-ʔtehakwęhnarhę-.#úʔy desert. *dv.n.s.* yuʔtehakwęhnarhęʔúʔy ‹it-sand-throw down-caused-great› *desert (a vast spread of sand)* (HS).

-ʔtehar- sand. *n.r. West.* n-poss., n-inc., n.sfx. -eh. uʔtéhareh *sand* (PC).

-ʔtehaʔke on sand, sandy. *n.s.* uʔte-háʔkye ‹sand-at› *on sand, sandy* (HS).

-ʔtehęw- loam. *n.r.* n-poss., n-inc., n.sfx. -eh. uʔtehę̀·weh *loam* (HS); -ʔtehę= waʔke: uʔtehęwáʔkye ‹loam-at› *loam* (HS).

-ʔtehęwaʔke loam. *n.s.* uʔtehęwáʔkye ‹loam-at› *loam* (HS).

-ʔtehsnakt back, backward, behind, reverse. *n.r.* aln: raʔtéhsnakwt *backwards, behind of him* (H-notebook), n-inc., n.sfx. -ɸ. uʔtéhsnakwt *back, backward, behind, reverse* (HS); -ʔtehsnakt naʔ-. -(a)'ni: uʔtéhsnakwt naʔú·ʔni ‹back much-it-at the edge of› *backward, reverse* (HS).

-ʔtehsnakt naʔ-. -(a)'ni backward, reverse. *n.s.* uʔtéhsnakwt naʔú·ʔni ‹back much-it-at the edge of› *backward, reverse* (HS).

–ʔtehsyę – disappear. *v.r.-a.i.* hab: -, pnt: -ʔ, stat: -, prog: -, prp: -, dst: -, caus: -, rvs: -, dat: -, n-inc. waʔeʔtéhsyęʔ *one disappeared* (RC 2:10).

–ʔtehyeriha – spread sand over. *v.s.-a.i.* waʔktehyeríhaʔ ‹fact-I-sand-straightened› *I have spread sand over* (AG).

–ʔtek – partake, share. *v.r.-a.i.* hab: -ahs, pnt: -ɸ, stat: -ę, prog: -, prp: -, dst: -, caus: -, rvs: -, dat: -, n-inc. raʔté·kahs *he partakes, he shares* (HS), ruʔté·kę *he partook, he shared* (HS), ęhráʔtek *he will partake, he will share* (HS).

–ʔterhęčh – heel. *n.r.* inaln: raʔterhęčhęʔkye *at his heels* (RC 6:9), n-inc., n.sfx. -eh. uʔterhęčheh *heel (of foot)* (R).

–ʔtey – crowd, drove, herd, team; sweet cicely. *n.r.* See: –(ę)ʔtey –.

–ʔteyanę –.#aka·ʔ shepherd. *dv.n.s.* See: –(ę)ʔteyanę –.#aka·ʔ.

–ʔteyaruhčrę – assemble, congregate. *v.s.-a.i.* See: –(ę)ʔteyaruhčrę –.

–ʔteyę – yeast bread. *dv.n.s.* See: –(ę)ʔ= teyę –.

–ʔteyęhawihT – bus. *dv.n.s.* See: –(ę)ʔte = yęhawihT –.

–ʔteyęhkw – frame, rack. *n.s.* See: –(ę)ʔ = teyęhkw –.

–ʔteyhę publicly. *n.s.* See: –(ę)ʔteyhę.

–ʔteyu – mosquito. *dv.n.s.* See: –(ę)ʔteyu –.

–ʔteyuręhT – announce, denounce. *v.s.-t.* See: –(ę)ʔteyuręhT –.

–ʔteyuʔawi – crowd, flock, swarm. *dv.n.s.* See: –(ę)ʔteyuʔawi –.

–ʔteʔti – catch up to, overtake. *v.r.-t.* hab: -ęhs, pnt: -ʔ, stat: -ę, prog: -, prp: -, dst: -, caus: -, rvs: -, dat: -, n-inc. ruʔtéʔtyę *he caught up to it* (RC 2:13), raʔtéʔtyęhs *he overtakes it* (HS), waʔakuʔtéʔtiʔ *it caught up to one* (R); -či -. –ʔteʔti –: ęčęktiʔtéʔtiʔ ‹prediction-again-we two-catch up to› *it will catch back up to the two of us* (RC 30:18).

–ʔtih – flank, side. *n.r.* n-poss., n-inc., n.sfx. -eh. uʔtíheh *flank, side (of animate things)* (HS); –ʔtihakT: kaʔtíhakwt ‹it-flank-next to› *left(side)* (HS).

–ʔtihakT left(side). *n.s.* kaʔtíhakwt ‹it-flank-next to› *left (side)* (HS).

–ʔtihsn – cup, dipper. *n.r.* n-poss., inc., n.sfx. -eh. uʔtíhsneh *cup, dipper* (R); –ʔtihsn – –ʔaręT –: uʔtíhsneh yuʔá·rę·t ‹cup it-lower lip-possesses› *pitcher* (HS).

–ʔtihsn – –ʔaręT – pitcher. *n.s.* uʔtíhsneh yuʔá·rę·t ‹cup it-lower lip-possesses› *pitcher* (HS).

–ʔtikahn – corn pounder; mortar and pestle. *n.r.* n-poss., n-inc., n.sfx. -eh. uʔtikáhneh *corn pounder; mortar and pestle* (R) [Lawson «Tic-caugh-ne» 'A Pestel'; «Ootic-caugh-ne» 'A Mortar'].

–ʔtikęh – mind, reason, temper. *n.r.* See: –(ę)ʔtikęh –/ –(ę)ʔtikęhn –/ –(ę)ʔtikęhr –.

–ʔtikęhaw – inquire. *v.s.-t.* See: –(ę)ʔti = kęhaw –.

–ʔtikęhkaręhrę – agitate. *v.s.-t.* See: –(ę)ʔ = tikęhkaręhrę –.

–ʔtikęhkaręʔrahT – commotion. *n.s.* See:

-(ę)ʔtikęhkaręʔrahT -.

-ʔtikęhkaθne - patience. *n.s.* See: -(ę)ʔti =
kęhkaθne -.

-ʔtikęhkaθne - patience. *dv.n.s.* See:
-(ę)ʔtikęhkaθne -.

-ʔtikęhkęnyęhčr - cheating. *n.s.* See:
-(ę)ʔtikęhkęnyęhčr -.

-ʔtikęhkeyaʔT - arrive at a conclusion, be
solicitous, be oppressed. *v.s.-a.i.* See:
-(ę)ʔtikęhkeyaʔT -.

-ʔtikęhkeyaʔT - uncertainty. *dv.n.s.* See:
-(ę)ʔtikęhkeyaʔT -.

-ʔtikęhn - mind, reason, temper. *n.r.* See:
-(ę)ʔtikęh -/ -(ę)ʔtikęhn -/ -(ę)ʔtikęhr -.

-ʔtikęhnę - be state of mind, calculate,
imagine, intend. *v.s.-a.i.* See: -(ę)ʔti =
kęhnę -.

-ʔtikęhnęhčr - behavior, meditation, thinking. *n.s.* See: -(ę)ʔtikęhnęhčr -.

-ʔtikęhnęhčrukęʔ be thoughtless. *v.s.-s.i.*
See: -(ę)ʔtikęhnęhčrukęʔ.

-ʔtikęhnęhkw -{dative III} be baffled, be
stumped. *v.s.-a.i.* See: -(ę)ʔtikęh =
nęhkw -{dative III}.

-ʔtikęhnętyę - meditate, project, think,
think through. *v.s.-a.i.* See: -(ę)ʔti =
kęhnętyę -.

-ʔtikęhr - mind, reason, temper. *n.r.* See:
-(ę)ʔtikęh -/ -(ę)ʔtikęhn -/ -(ę)ʔtikęhr -.

-ʔtikęhr -.#ęwe voluntarily. *n.s.* See:
-(ę)ʔtikęhr -.#ęwe.

-ʔtikęhr -.#keha·ʔ spiritual. *n.s.* See:
-(ę)ʔtikęhr -.#keha·ʔ.

-ʔtikęhrahnę - be lethargic, faint, lose
consciousness. *v.s.-a.i.* See: -(ę)ʔti =
kęhrahnę -.

-ʔtikęhrahnęʔT - stun, stupefy. *v.s.-t.* See:
-(ę)ʔtikęhrahnęʔT -.

-ʔtikęhrahręhw - anticipate. *v.s.-a.i.* See:
-(ę)ʔtikęhrahręhw -.

-ʔtikęhrahruʔT - be affable. *v.s.-s.i.* See:
-(ę)ʔtikęhrahruʔT -.

-ʔtikęhrahtirahT - confirmation. *dv.n.s.*
See: -(ę)ʔtikęhrahtirahT -.

-ʔtikęhraks - Bad Mind (one of the primordial twins); evil spirit. *dv.n.s.* See:
-(ę)ʔtikęhraks -.

-ʔtikęhraks -{dative II} be unhappy. *v.s.-
a.i.* See: -(ę)ʔtikęhraks -{dative II}.

-ʔtikęhraksaʔT - sadden, vex. *v.s.-t.* See:
-(ę)ʔtikęhraksaʔT -.

-ʔtikęhraksaʔT - grief. *dv.n.s.* See: -(ę)ʔ =
tikęhraksaʔT -.

-ʔtikęhrakwahsT - Good Mind (one of
the primordial twins); good spirit;
benevolence. *dv.n.s.* See: -(ę)ʔtikęh =
rakwahsT -.

-ʔtikęhrakweni - influence. *v.s.-t.* See:
-(ę)ʔtikęhrakweni -.

-ʔtikęhranurę - drug-free. *n.s.* See: -(ę)ʔ =
tikęhranurę -.

-ʔtikęhranę'nahsi - dissuade. *v.s.-t.* See:
-(ę)ʔtikęhranę'nahsi -.

-ʔtikęhrar - be careful, be mindful. *v.s.-
a.i.* See: -(ę)ʔtikęhrar -.

-ʔtikęhraręhyakę - be anxious. *v.s.-a.i.*
See: -(ę)ʔtikęhraręhyakę -.

-ʔtikęhraręhyakęʔT - be anxious. *v.s.-s.i.*
See: -(ę)ʔtikęhraręhyakęʔT -.

-ʔtikęhraręhyakęʔT - anxiety. *n.s.* See:
-(ę)ʔtikęhraręhyakęʔT -.

-ʔtikęhrarhaʔ - distrust. *v.s.-t.* See: -(ę)ʔ =
tikęhrarhaʔ -.

-ʔtikęhrarheryeti - be candid. *v.s.-a.i.* See:
-(ę)ʔtikęhrarheryeti -.

-ʔtikęhraT - animal (as opposed to vegetable). *dv.n.s.* See: -(ę)ʔtikęhraT -.

-ʔtikęhraT - have discretion. *v.s.-a.i.* See:
-(ę)ʔtikęhraT -.

-ʔtikęhratukęht - Great Spirit; Holy Spirit. *dv.n.s.* See: -(ę)ʔtikęhratukęht -.

-ʔtikęhratʔa - advise. *v.s.-t.* See: -(ę)ʔti =
kęhratʔa -.

-ʔtikęhrawehθayę(T) - be dark-minded. *v.
s.-s.i.* See: -(ę)ʔtikęhrawehθayę(T) -.

-ʔtikęhrawęri - bewilder. *v.s.-t.* See:
-(ę)ʔtikęhrawęri -.

-ʔtikęhrayaʔnerę - chide. *v.s.-t.* See:

-(ę)ʔtikęhraya·ʔnerę -.

-ʔtikęhrayerik - satisfy. *v.s.-t.* See: -(ę)ʔ= tikęhrayerik -.

-ʔtikęhrayę(T) - comfort. *v.s.-t.* See: -(ę)ʔtikęhrayę(T) -.

-ʔtikęhrayę(T) -{dative II} discern. *v.s.-t.* See: -(ę)ʔtikęhrayę(T) -{dative II}.

-ʔtikęhraʔnihr - sympathy. *dv.n.s.* See: -(ę)ʔtikęhraʔnihr -.

-ʔtikęhraʔtyę·ʔnę - tempt. *v.s.-t.* See: -(ę)ʔtikęhraʔtyę·ʔnę -.

-ʔtikęhreθ - be patient. *v.s.-a.i.* See: -(ę)ʔtikęhreθ -.

-ʔtikęhrę - have a thought. *v.s.-a.i.* See: -(ę)ʔtikęhrę -.

-ʔtikęhręT -{dative II} forget. *v.s.-a.i.* See: -(ę)ʔtikęhręT -{dative II}.

-ʔtikęhręthuhT - comfort, remember. *v.s.-t.* See: -(ę)ʔtikęhręthuhT -.

-ʔtikęhręti - make up mind, premeditate. *v.s.-a.i.* See: -(ę)ʔtikęhręti -.

-ʔtikęhrę·ʔ - be dejected. *v.s.-a.i.* See: -(ę)ʔtikęhrę·ʔ -.

-ʔtikęhrhęreT - be alluring. *v.s.-a.i.* See: -(ę)ʔtikęhrhęreT -.

-ʔtikęhrihsʔa - resolve. *v.s.-a.i.* See: -(ę)ʔtikęhrihsʔa -.

-ʔtikęhriyu -{dative III} please. *v.s.-t.* See: -(ę)ʔtikęhriyu -{dative III}.

-ʔtikęhriyuhT - amuse. *v.s.-t.* See: -(ę)ʔ= tikęhriyuhT -.

-ʔtikęhrukęʔ be boisterous, be mindless, be rash, be thoughtless. *n.s.* See: -(ę)ʔtikęhrukęʔ.

-ʔtikęhrut - invent. *v.s.-a.i.* See: -(ę)ʔ= tikęhrut -.

-ʔtikęhruryahT - amusement. *n.s.* See:

-(ę)ʔtikęhruryahT -.

-ʔtikęhruʔkręhT - debauch. *v.s.-t.* See: -(ę)ʔtikęhruʔkręhT -.

-ʔtikęhruʔnaku - allure, beguile, tempt. *v.s.-a.i.* See: -(ę)ʔtikęhruʔnaku -.

-ʔtikęhruʔnaku - allurer, tempter. *v.s.-a.i.* See: -(ę)ʔtikęhruʔnaku -.

-ʔtikęhruʔnakʷahT - charm, charming. *dv. n.s.* See: -(ę)ʔtikęhruʔnakʷahT -.

-ʔtikęhruʔnakʷahT - temptation. *dv.n.s.* See: -(ę)ʔtikęhruʔnakʷahT -.

-ʔtikęhryaʔkhę - bother, disconcert. *v.s.-t.* See: -(ę)ʔtikęhryaʔkhę -.

-ʔtikęhryenę - accompany, escort. *v.s.-t.* See: -(ę)ʔtikęhryenę -.

-ʔtikęhtahT - danger, dangerous, peril. *n. s.* See: -(ę)ʔtikęhtahT -.

-ʔtikęhtahT - dangerous, hazardous, perilous. *dv.n.s.* See: -(ę)ʔtikęhtahT -.

-ʔtikęhthę - have an idea. *v.s.-a.i.* See: -(ę)ʔtikęhthę -.

-ʔtikθ - skull. *n.r.* n-poss., inc., n.sfx. -eh. uʔtí·kθeh *skull* (R).

-ʔtikʷ - sew. *v.r.-t.* hab: -ahs, pnt: -ɸ, stat: -, prog: -, prp: -, dst: -ahnę, caus: -, rvs: -si-, dat: -, n-inc. Possibly in Lawson «Tic-hah» 'A Button'. θtí·kw *sew it!* (R), raʔtí·kwahs *he sews* (HS); -ʔtikʷahnę -: ruʔtikwáhnę·t ‹he-sewed-much-complete› *he had sewn some* (W 74), waʔktikwáhnę·ʔ ‹fact-I-sewed-much› *I sewed some* (W 74), Kayeʔ-tikwáhnęh ‹they-sew-much› *Sewing Society* (R); -ʔtikʷst -: uʔtíksteh ‹sew-'ness› *sewing, stitch* (HS), *beadwork* (R); -ʔtikʷsi -: raʔtí·kwsyęhs ‹he-sew-undoes› *he unrips* (HS); -ʔtikʷy -:

---

uʔtí·kwyeh ‹sew-ʔʔ› *skirt* (HS).

-ʔtikʷahnę – Sewing Society. *dv.n.s.* Kayeʔtikwáhnęh ‹they-sew-much› *Sewing Society* (R).

-ʔtikʷst – beadwork, sewing, stitch. *n.s.* uʔtíksteh ‹sew-'ness› *sewing, stitch* (HS), *beadwork* (R).

-ʔtikʷsi – unrip. *v.s.-t.* raʔtí·kwsyęhs ‹he-sew-undoes› *he unrips* (HS).

-ʔtikʷy – skirt. *n.s.* uʔtí·kwyeh ‹sew-ʔʔ› *skirt* (HS).

-ʔtiranhe – aide, assist. *v.r.-a.i.* hab: -, pnt: -ʔ, stat: -ʔ, prog: -, prp: -, dst: -, caus: -, rvs: -, dat: -, n-inc. raʔtiránheʔ *he aides, he assists* (HS), ęhsktitiránheʔ *you two must help me* (RC 30:33).

-ʔtiθkraręT – tickling, ticklish. *dv.n.s.* The root from which this stem is derived has not been found in a verbal construction. yuʔtiθkrá·ręt ‹it-tickle-possesses› *tickling* (HS), yuʔtiθkraré·ʔnę ‹it-tickle-caused› *ticklish* (HS).

-ʔtiθku – be late. *v.r.-a.i.* hab: -ahs, pnt: -ʔ, stat: -ʔ, prog: -, prp: -, dst: -, caus: -, rvs: -, dat: -, n-inc. yuʔtíθkuʔ *it is late* (R), ęhraʔtíθkuʔ *he will be late* (HS), ruʔtíθkwahs *he defers, he delays* (HS); –ʔtiθkuʔ–: yękwaʔtiθkúʔę ‹we-be late-began› *we are late* (R).

-ʔtiθkuʔ – be late. *v.s.-a.i.* yękwaʔtiθkúʔę ‹we-be late-began› *we are late* (R).

-ʔtiʔnęhkw – earthen pan, pan, pot. *n.r.* n-poss., n-inc., n.sfx. -eh. uʔtiʔnęhkweh *earthen pan, pan, pot* (R).

-ʔtuher – nestle. *v.r.-a.i.* hab: -ɸ, pnt: -, stat: -, prog: -, prp: -, dst: -, caus: -, rvs: -, dat: -, n-inc. raʔtúher *he nestles* (HS).

-ʔtuhs – clam, mollusk, oyster; clam shell. *n.r.* n-poss., inc., n.sfx. -eh. uʔtúhseh *clam, mollusk, oyster* (R); *clam shell* (RC 35:14) (also: uhtúhseh (R)); –ʔtuhsaw–: naʔtuhsà·wi ‹one=an-

other-clam-gave to› *one gave another clam(shell)* (RC 35:23).

-ʔtuhsar – markings on a milk snake. *n.r.* n-poss., n-inc., n.sfx. -eh. uʔtúhsareh *markings on a milk snake* (R).

-ʔtuhsarę adder, viper. *n.r.* n-poss., n-inc., n.sfx. -ɸ. uʔtúhsarę *adder, viper* (HS).

-ʔtuθ(e)r – itch, scurf. *n.r.* n-poss., n-inc., n.sfx. -ɸ ~ -eh. uʔtú·θer *itch* (R), uʔtú·θreh *itch, scurf* (HS); –ʔtuθ(e)r– -thwę –: uʔtú·θer yú·thwę· ‹itch it-is good for› *elecampagne (Inula helenium)* (H-notebook).

-ʔtuθ(e)r– -thwę – elecampagne *(Inula helenium).* *n.s.* uʔtú·θer yú·thwę· ‹itch it-is good for› *elecampagne (Inula helenium)* (H-notebook).

-ʔtuθh – begrudge, envy. *v.r.-t.* hab: -ahs, pnt: -aʔ, stat: -ę, prog: -, prp: -, dst: -, caus: -ʔT-, rvs: -, dat: -, n-inc. raʔtú·θhahs *he begrudges, he envies* (HS), ęhraʔtú·θhaʔ *he will envy* (HS); –ʔtuθh–: uʔtú·θhaʔ ‹envy› *jealousy* (R); –ʔtuθhaʔniyu –: ruʔtuθhaʔní·yu· ‹he-envy-cause-is great› *he is envious* (HS); –ʔtuθhę ʔ –: uʔtuθhę́ʔę ‹envy-began› *envy* (HS).

-ʔtuθh – jealousy. *n.s.* uʔtú·θhaʔ ‹envy› *jealousy* (R).

-ʔtuθhaʔniyu – be envious. *v.s.-s.i.* ruʔtuθhaʔní·yu· ‹he-envy-cause-is great› *he is envious* (HS).

-ʔtuθhęʔ – envy. *n.s.* uʔtuθhę́ʔę ‹envy-began› *envy* (HS).

-ʔty – bay. *n.r.* See: -(ę)ʔty –.

-ʔtyatih – be a long time. *v.r.-a.i.* hab: -θ, pnt: -ɸ, stat: -ę, prog: -, prp: -, dst: -, caus: -T-, rvs: -, dat: -, n-inc. waʔuʔtyá·tih *it was a long time* (RC 3:22); –ʔtyatihT –: raʔtyatíhthaʔ ‹he-be a long time-causes› *he delays it* (HS); -ne –. –ʔtyatih –.#áh: neyuʔtyatiháh ‹a-part-it-is a long time-little› *little while*

(R); **ti –. –ʔtyatih –**: tyuʔtyá·tihθ ‹so-it-is a long time› *during, as long as it lasts* (HS), tyuʔtyatíhę ‹so-it-was a long time› *during, as long as it lasted* (HS), thwaʔuʔtyá·tih ‹so-fact-it-was a long time› *in the meantime (present and past)* (HS), *it was such a long time* (RC 3:75), nęyuʔtyá·tih ‹so-prediction-it-be a long time› *in the meantime (future)* (HS); **tha+či –. –ʔtyatih –**: tha-hęθayuʔtyá·tih ‹unusual-fact-again-it-was a long time› *very long time* (RC 15:6); **–a'nęʔtyatiʔT –**: ruʔnęʔtyá·tiʔt ‹he-himself-be a long time-causes› *he is tardy* (HS); **haʔ ti –. –ʔtyatih –**: haʔ tyuʔtyá·tihθ ‹the so-it-is a long time› *duration* (HS).

–ʔtyatihT – delay. *v.s.-t.* raʔtyatíhtaʔ ‹he-be a long time-causes› *he delays it* (HS).

–ʔtyeh – be fortuitous, happen by chance, occur casually, occur spontaneously, occur with ease; conjure, exorcise. *v.r.-a.i.* hab: -θ, pnt: -, stat: -ę, prog: -, prp: -, dst: -, caus: -, rvs: -, dat: -, n-inc. yúʔtyehθ *it chances, it happens: fortuitous* (HS), raʔtyéhę *he conjures, he exorcises* (HS); **–ʔtyeh –**: uʔtyéhę ‹happen by chance› *chance* (HS); **ti –. –ʔtyeh –**: tyúʔtyehθ ‹so-it-happens by chance› *casual: it just happens* (R).

–ʔtyeh – chance. *n.s.* uʔtyéhę ‹happen by chance› *chance* (HS).

–ʔtyęhkr – phlegm, snot. *n.r.* n-poss., inc., n.sfx. -eh. This root is pronounced **–ʔčęhkr –** by some speakers. Hewitt & Smith's transcription, «u'-tce''''-kre», suggests that this alternative pronunciation is old. The root appears to be an old compound of **–ʔtyęh(s) –** *nose* and **–(a)kr –** *liquid* with loss of the parenthetical elements. uʔtyęhkreh *phlegm, snot* (HS); **–ʔtyęhkr –.#hči**: yuʔtyęhkréhči ‹it-snot-very› *snotty* (HS); **–ʔtyęhkrar –**: ruʔtyęhkrar ‹he-snot-is in› *he is soiled by snot* (HS); **–ʔtyęhkraʔnihęthu –**: wahraʔtyęhkraʔ-nihę́·thuʔ ‹fact-he-snot-pulled› *he sniffed* (R); **–ne –. –ʔtyęhkrakar –**: nehraʔ-tyęhkrakar ‹apart-he-snot-makes a noise› *he snivels* (HS).

–ʔtyęhkr –.#hči snotty. *dv.n.s.* yuʔtyęhkréhči ‹it-snot-very› *snotty* (HS).

–ʔtyęhkrar – be soiled with snot. *v.s.-s.i.* ruʔtyęhkrar ‹he-snot-is in› *he is soiled by snot* (HS).

–ʔtyęhkraʔnihęthu – *v.s.-a.i.* wahraʔtyęhkraʔnihę́·thuʔ ‹fact-he-snot-pulled› *he sniffed* (R).

–ʔtyęhs – nose; pickax, plow point. *n.r.* inaln (in meaning *nose*): ktyę́hseh *my nose* (R), n-poss. (in meaning *pickax, plow point*), inc., n.sfx. -eh. This root is pronounced **–ʔčęhs –** by some speakers. The form cited by Gallatin (see below) suggests that this pronunciation is old. uʔtyę́hseh *nose* (R), *pickax, plow point* (HS) [Gallatin «uhtchyuhsay» 'Nose']; **–ʔtyęhsatkęh –**: kaʔtyęhsá·tkęhθ ‹it-nose-is rotten› *catarrh* (HS).

–ʔtyęhsatkęh – catarrh. *dv.n.s.* kaʔtyęhsá·tkęhθ ‹it-nose-is rotten› *catarrh* (HS).

–ʔtyę'nęh – attempt, calculate, earn, ex-

Tuscarora Pronunciation Key:
/a/ law; /e/ hat; /i/ pizza; /u/ tune; /ę/ hint; /č/ cheese; /h/ hoe; /m/ mother; /s/ same; /t/ do (before a vowel y, or w), too (elsewhere); /k/ gale (before a vowel y or w), kale (elsewhere); /n/ inhale (before a consonant or word-final), note (elsewhere), /r/ hiss (before a consonant or word-final), run (trilled as in Italian, elsewhere); /w/ cuff (before a consonant other than y or word-final), way (elsewhere); /y/ fish (before a consonant or word-final), you (elsewhere), /θ/ thing; /ʔ/ (the sound between the vowels in unh-unh); /·/ long vowel, /ʹ/ high pitch; /ˎ/ low pitch.

periment. gain. intend. measure. test. try. *v.r.-t.* hab: -ɸ. pnt: -, stat: -, prog: -, prp: -, dst: -, caus: -sT-, rvs: -ku-, dat: -, inc.-ɸ-ag./pat. raʔtyę̇·ʼnęh *he attempts it. he calculates it, he earns it, he experiments, he gains it, he intends it, he measures it, he tests it, he tries it* (HS); -ʔęyaʔtyę'nęh -: raʔęyaʼ-tyę̇·ʼnęh ‹he-cost-measures› *he appraised* (HS), *he measures price* (H-notebook); -rihwaʔtyę'nęhku -: rarihwaʔtyęʼnę́hkwahs ‹he-matter-measure-undoes› *he philosophizes* (HS); -ne -. -ʔtyę'nęhsT -: nehruʼtyęʼnęhsnę ‹apart-he-measure-caused› *he measured by* (RC 12:2), neyeʼtyęʼnę́hstha' ‹apart-one-measure-causes› *model, pattern* (HS); -ne -. -ʔtyę'nęhsnahkw -: neyeʼ-tyęʼnęhsnáhkhwa' ‹apart-one-measure-causes-instrument› *model* (HS); ti -. -ʔtyę'nęhsT -: tihraʼtyęʼnę́hstha' ‹so-he-measure-causes› *he acquiesces* (HS); -a'nęʔtyę'nęh -: θaʼnęʼtyę̇·ʼnęh ‹you!-yourself-measure› *try it!* (R), wahraʔnęʼtyę̇·ʼnęh ‹fact-he-himself-measured› *he tried* (RC 27:21), ękaʼ-nęʔtyę̇·ʼnęh ‹prediction-I-myself-measure› *I will try* (RC 11:7); haʔ ti -. -ʔtyę'nęhsT -: haʔ tihruʼtyęʼnę́hsnę ‹the so-he-measure-caused› *his acquiescence* (HS).

-ʔu - show. *v.r.-t.* hab: -, pnt: -ʼ, stat: -, prog: -, prp: -, dst: -, caus: -hT-, rvs: -, dat: -, inc.-ʔʔ-pat. Encountered only in the following constructions. -ne -. -θtʔuhT -: nehraθtʼúhtha' ‹two-he-edge of teeth-show-causes› *he gnashes teeth* (HS); -t -. -atkahrʔu -: nahratkár-ʼuʼ ‹hither-he-himself-eye-showed› *he blinked, he winked* (RC 26:28).

-ʔw - potion. *n.r.* n-poss., inc., n.sfx. -. Found only incorporated. -t -. -ʔwa= yę(T) -: tkáʼwayęʼ ‹hither-it-potion-lays› *there is a potion* (RC 6:9); -ne+

či -. -ʔwahkw -: nęθahráʼwahkw ‹apart-fact-again-he-potion-picked up› *he again picked up potion* (RC 6:9); -ne+či -. -ʔwaw -: nęθahráʼwaʼw ‹apart-fact-again-he-potion-came› *he again came to potion* (RC 6:10).

-ʔwah(r) - meat. *n.r.* aln: akʼwáhrawçh *my meat* (R), inc., n.sfx. -eh. The final *r* of this root is inexplicably absent before the verb stem -(i)hey - *die.* uʼwáhreh *meat* (RC 30:65) [Gallatin «ohwaureh», «uowaugh-reh» 'Flesh, Meat']; -ʔwahkęheyęʔ -: kaʼwahkęhè·yęʼθ ‹it-meat-die-begins› *it mortifies* (HS); -ʔwahrak -: kaʼwáhra·ks ‹it-meat-eats› *cannibal; carnivore; it eats meat* (RC 10:7), yakuʼwáhra·ks ‹one-meat-eats› *cancer* (R); -ʔwahranę -: kaʼwahrá·nę· ‹it-meat-is tender› *it is tender meat* (HS); -ʔwahranęT -: wahraʼwáhranę·t ‹fact-he-meat-gave to eat› *he fed it meat* (RC 30:32); -ʔwahrarętyęku -: yuʼwahrarętyę́·kwę ‹it-meat-pick out-undid› *it picked away meat* (RC 17:3); -ʔwahraryu -: raʼwahrá·ryuhs ‹he-meat-kills› *butcher* (HS); -ʔwahratʔa -: raʼwahrá·tʼahs ‹he-meat-puts in› *he stuffs it* (HS); -ʔwahręhra·heʔ -: kaʼwahręhrá·heʼ ‹it-meat-fries-going to› *fried meat* (R); loan word from another Northern Iroquoian language containing the root -ʔwahr -: čuʼwahrù·waʼ *elk (Alces alces); wapiti (Cervus canadensis)* (R).

-ʔwahrak - cannibal, carnivore. *dv.n.s.* kaʼwáhra·ks ‹it-meat-eats› *cannibal, carnivore* (RC 10:7).

-ʔwahrak - cancer. *dv.n.s.* yakuʼwáhra·ks ‹one-meat-eats› *cancer* (R).

-ʔwahraryu - butcher. *dv.n.s.* raʼwahrá·ryuhs ‹he-meat-kills› *butcher* (HS).

-ʔwahratʔa - stuff. *v.s.-t.* raʼwahrá·tʼahs ‹he-meat-puts in› *he stuffs it* (HS).

-ʔwahręhra·heʔ - fried meat. *dv.n.s.* kaʼ-

waɂrǫhráˑheʔ ‹it-meat-fries-going to› *fried meat* (R).

-ʔwahθr – drop. *n.r.* n-poss., inc., n.sfx. -eh. uʔwáhθreh *drop* (R); -ʔwah= θrahrihr –: raʔwahθráhrihč ‹he-drop-scatters› *he sprinkles* (HS); ti–. -ʔwahθraʔθ –.#áh: tikaʔwahθraʔθʔáh ‹so-it-drop-is of a size-little› *a little drop* (RC 8:48); -ne –. -atʔwahθrukʷ –: neyutʔwahθrúˑkwę ‹apart-it-itself-drop-spread out› *drops spread out* (RC 2:14).

-ʔwahθrahrihr – sprinkle. *v.s.-a.i.* raʔwah-θráhrihč ‹he-drop-scatters› *he sprinkles* (HS).

-ʔwashar – earrings made of wampum, earrings. *n.r.* n-poss., inc., n.sfx. -eh. uʔwashàˑreh *earrings made of wampum, earrings* (R); -ʔwasharatekę –: Raʔwasharatéˑkęhs ‹he-earring-joins› *He-Puts-Earrings-Together (male proper name)* (RC 16:11).

-ʔwasharatekę – He-Puts-Earrings-Together (male proper name). *dv.n.s.*

Raʔwasharatéˑkęhs ‹he-earring-joins› *He-Puts-Earrings-Together (male proper name)* (RC 16:11).

-ʔwaʔčr – hoop & javelin game. *n.s.* uʔwáʔčreh ‹play hoop & javelin game-'ness› *hoop & javelin game* (H-notebook).

-ʔwn – brood. *n.r.* poss. ʔ, inc., n.sfx. -. Found only in the cited construction. -ne –. -ʔwnę –.#úʔy: nekaʔwnęʔúʔy ‹a-part-it-brood-possesses-great› *it is with brood, it has young (said of a large or old animal)* (H-notebook).

-ʔyhuč – chin. *n.r.* inaln: kyeʔyhúˑčeh *my chin* (R), n-inc., n.sfx. -eh. uʔyhúˑčeh *chin* (R).

●

-ˑ stative aspect. *v.r.sfx.*
-ˑk stative aspect. *v.r.sfx.*
-ˑʔ punctual aspect. *v.r.sfx.*

ENGLISH-TUSCARORA DICTIONARY

A

abandon. *v.t.* rú·ʔnyęhs *he abandons it* (-aʹni -); rayahstę́·ʔnyęhs *he abandons someone* (-yahstęʹni -).

abbreviate. *v.t.* rakwę́ʔnhrahč *he abbreviates it* (-akwę́ʔnhrahT -).

abdicate. *v.i.* θhračhęnaʔná·kʔuhs *he abdicates* (-či -.-ačhęnaʔnakʔu -); θhrá·ʔnyęhs *he abdicates* (-či -.-aʹnyę -); θhrà·yęhs *he abdicates* (-či -.-yę(T) -).

abdomen. *n.* útkweh *abdomen* (-tkw -).

abdominal. *adj.* utkwehkyéha·ʔ *abdominal* (-tkw -.#keha·ʔ).

abide. *v.i.* rę́ʔrę·ʔ *he abides* (-iʔrę -).

ability. *n.* ukwenyę́hčreh *ability* (-kwe = nyęhčr -).

able. *adj.* yukwé·nyę *it is able* (-kweni -).

able-bodied. *adj.* rukyerhahtì·rę *he is able-bodied* (-kerhahtir -).

abnormal. *adj.* nyuʔnę́·ʔnuʔkt *it is abnormal* (-t -.-aʹnęʹnuʔkT -).

abolish. *v.t.* rahnę́ʔthaʔ *he abolishes it* (-ahnęʔT -).

abortion. *n.* θkawirę́ʔę *abortion (by accident)* (-či -.-wirę́ʔ -); θwaʔnwirę́hnę *abortion (by choice)* (-či -.-aʹnwi = ręhT -).

abound. *v.i.* see: -tak(e)r - .

about. *adj.* à·rę *about* (à·rę).

about. *prep.* ukwthá·ʔnyeʔ *about* (-aktha'nyeʔ -).

above-mentioned. *adj.* nyuʔnwehrá·ʔnę *above-mentioned* (-t -.-aʹnwehraʔT -); haʔ nyuwéhrę *above-mentioned* (-t -.-wehr -).

abreast. *adv.* thaʔneyeyuhrá·ʔnyeʔ *abreast (with verbs of motion)* (-yuhr -).

abreast of. *prep.* newaʔná·ʔrar *the two of them are abreast of one another* (-a = ʹnaʔrar -).

abroad. *adv.* uʔwnayáʔkęh *abroad* (-aʔwnayaʔk -).

abrupt. *adj.* yutkwahnáhkę *it is abrupt* (-atkʷahnahkw -).

abruptly. *adv.* thwaʔkahwéʔnęht *abruptly* (ti -.-hweʔnęht -).

absent. *v.i.* wekayáhskaht *it is absent* (-yah -.-yahskaht).

absolve. *v.t.* račhęnúhar *he absolves* (-a = čhęnuhar -).

absurd. *adj.* kwęhs aryurihwakahrę́ʔnak *it is absurd* (kwęhs -rihwakahrę́ʔT -).

abundant. *adj.* yuʔnerkę́hę *it is abundant* (-aʹnerkęhw -).

abuse. *v.t.* raʔrihuryáʔthaʔ *he abuses it* (-aʔrihuryaʔT -).

abyss. *n.* yuthriyaʔkęhúʔy *abyss* (-athri = yaʔk -.#úʔy).

accept. *v.t.* rá·kwahs *he accepts it* (-ku -); raríhwakwahs *he accepts it* (-rihwaku -).

accident. *n.* haʔ yuʔnyerę́ʔę *accident* (-a = ʹnyerę́ʔ -).

accidents, have. *v.i.* thwaʔkakuʔnyerę́hθręʔ *accidents happened to them* (ti -.-aʹnyeręhθrę -).

accommodate. *v.t.* naʔnyahsénhahs *one accommodates another* (-yahsenha -).

accompany. *v.t.* naʔtikęhryè·nęh *one accompanies another* (-(ę)ʔtikęhryenę -).

accomplish. *v.t.* raθnérhuhs *he accomplishes it* (-aθnerhu -).

according to. *prep.* katká·'ne' *according to* (-tka·'T-).

account. *n.* yu'rihwá··'ne' *account* (-a'=rihwa'ne-).

accumulate. *v.t.* rarúhčręh *he accumulates it* (-ruhčrę-).

accuse. *v.t.* na'ríhwarhuhs *one accuses another* (-rihwarhu-); rayurá'khwa' *he accuses it* (-yura'kw-).

accustom. *v.t.* khe'rę'nhá'tha' *I accustom another* (-rę'nha'T-).

accustomed to, become. *v.t.* ahru-rę'nhá·'ęk *that he become accustomed to it* (-rę'nha'-).

acid. *adj.* neyu'čísne' *it is acid* (-ne-. -'čisne-).

acorn *n.* kù·reh *acorn* (kù·reh); ru'né·tuk awę' rę́·te *acorn* (ru'né·tuk -ę'ręte).

acquit. *v.t.* ktahskúhčęhs *I acquit it* (-tahskuhči-).

acrid. *adj.* yu'θhá·θneh *acrid* (-(i)'=θhaθn-); uwrę'kyéha·' *acrid* (-w(e)r-. #keha·').

acrobat. *n.* ratihyečkna'náhnęh *acrobat* (-atihyečkna'nahnę-).

act. *v.i.* nehra'nyerę́·'nye' *he is acting* (-ne-. -a'nyerę'nye'-).

active. *adj.* rawę́'wá··'neht *he is active* (-ę'wa'nęhT-).

actually. *adv.* ka'nęwehę̀·we *actually* (ka'nęwehę̀·we).

add. *v.t.* kyeríhstha' *I am adding it* (-e=rihst-); rà·ręh *he adds it* (-rę-); nakyè·rihst *I added it* (-t-.-erihst-).

add to. *v.t.* ráher *he adds to it* (-(a)=h(e)r-).

adder. *n.* u'túhsarę *adder* (-'tuhsarę).

adder's tongue, yellow. *n.* utyę'nà·ri' *yellow adder's tongue* (-tyę'nari-).

address. *v.t.* na'nwéhratih *one addresses oneself to another* (-wehr-{dative II}).

adhere. *v.i.* yurha'nę'núhskę· *it adheres* (-rha'ę'nuhsk-).

adhesive. *n.* yurhá'ne' *adhesive* (-rha'n-).

adolescent. *adj.* ruhčúhkhwe·'r *male adolescent* (-hčuhkwhar-).

adopt a child. *v.t* wa'ka'nwirará·ku' *I adopted a child* (-a'nwiraraku-).

Adoption Ceremony. *n.* yakwa'nwirará·kwa'θ *Adoption Ceremony* (-a'nwi=rarakwa'-).

adoration. *n.* ha' rarihwayę́·tih *his adoration* (-rihwayęti-).

adorn. *v.t.* raya'tahstę̀·nih *he adorns it* (-ya'tahstęni-); see: -hstęni-.

adulation. *n.* utawę́'nęht *adulation* (-ta=wę'nęhT-).

adulterer. *n.* nehrakyerháhkhwa' *adulterer* (-ne-.-kerhahkw-).

adultery. *n.* unęhwaru'yéhčreh *adultery* (-nęhwaru'yehčr-).

adulthood. *n.* u'nehyahrę́hčreh *adulthood* (-a'nehyahrę́hčr-).

advise. *v.t.* ru'tikęhrá·t'ę *he advises* (-(ę)'tikęhrat'a-).

advocate. *n.* nehrarihwakyénhahs *advocate* (-ne-.-rihwakenha-).

adze. *n.* ú'θreh *adze* (-a'θr-); yerętah-stęnyá'tha' *adze* (-rętahstęnya'T-).

aerial. *adj.* uwrę'kyéha·' *aerial* (-w(e)r-. #keha·').

aerie. *n.* węnę'yečkwráhkhwa' *aerie* (-(ę)nę'yečkwrahkw-).

affair. *n.* uríhweh *affair* (-rihw-).

affinity. *n.* unęhwíhčreh *affinity* (-nęh=wihčr-).

afflicted. *adj.* nehrutęnheká·ryę *he is afflicted* (-ne-.-tęnhekari-).

affix. *v.t.* see: -nę'na(k)-.

affluence. *n.* učhu'kuwáhčreh *affluence* (-ačhu'kuwahčr-).

afraid of, be. *v.t.* ratéhra'θ *he is afraid of it* (-tehra'-).

after. *prep.* uhta'kę́'kye *after* (uhta'=kę́'kye).

afternoon. *n.* the'nę̀·reh *afternoon* (the'=nę̀·reh).

afterwards. *adv.* sté·ʔkę·θ *afterwards* (sté·ʔkę·θ).

again. *adv.* čwé·ʔkye *again* (čwé·ʔkye); čwé·ʔn *again* (čwé·ʔn).

age. *n.* neyę·ʔnúhsner *the two of them are of the same age* (-a'nuhsner-).

agency. *n.* haʔ karihwà·yęhs *agency* (-rihwayę-).

agent. *n.* rarihwà·yęhs *agent* (-rihwayę-); kù·rah *Indian agent* (kù·rah).

aggressor. *n.* haʔ račirù·ręh *aggressor* (-čirurę-).

agile. *adj.* ruhkarí·yu· *he is agile* (-(a)h = kariyu-).

agitate. *v.t.* naʔtikęhkaręʔrę *one agitates another* (-(ę)ʔtikęhkaręhrę-); nehraka-réhręh *he agitates it* (-ne-. -karehrę-).

agony. *n.* uʔnikęhká·ryaʔt *agony* (-(ę)ʔ = nikęhkaryaʔt).

agreeable. *adj.* rawękwehstaθáʔnę *he is agreeable* (-ęˣk"ehstaθahraʔT-).

agriculture. *n.* uhehnaʔkyéha·ʔ *agriculture* (-hehn-.#keha·ʔ).

aid. *n.* ukyerhakyénhaʔt *aid* (-kerhaken = haʔT-).

aide. *v.t.* rayahskyénhahs *he aides it* (-yahskenha-); raʔtiránheʔ *he aides it* (-ʔtiranhe-).

aim. *n.* úʔθreh *aim* (-aʔθr-).

aim. *v.i.* raʔčíher *he aims (a gun)* (-ʔči = h(e)r-).

aim be off. *v.i.* ęʔnęʔtrá·kuʔ *its aim was off* (-a'nęʔtraku-).

air. *n.* ù·wereh *air* (-w(e)r-).

aisle. *n.* uháheh *aisle* (-(a)hah-).

alarm. *v.t.* natkahkwé·ksyęhs *one alarms another* (-kahk"eksi-).

alarmed. *adj.* ręhré·θręʔθ *he is alarmed* (-ęhreθręʔ-).

alcohol. *n.* uhné·kyeh *alcohol* (-hnek-); yakunęʔyáhsthaʔ *alcohol* (-nęʔ = yahsT-).

alcoholic. *n.* kakunęʔyahs *alcoholics* (-nęʔy-).

alder, spotted. *n.* nú·θriʔ *spotted alder* (nú·θriʔ).

algae. *n.* awęráhθreh *algae* (-ęrahθr-).

alight. *v.i.* yuhsharúhkwę·t *it alighted* (-hsharuhkwęt).

alive. *adj.* ręnheʔ *he is alive* (-ęˣnh(e)-).

all. *adj.* sę̀·weʔ *all* (sę̀·weʔ); thwé·ʔn *all* (thwé·ʔn); see: -i-/-ęˣ-.

all kinds of. *adj.* čwewá·kye· *all kinds of* (čwe-. -ake-).

allegory. *n.* yuʔnwętahskané·kę·t *allegory* (-a'nwętahskanekęt-).

alleviate. *v.t.* raʔθhanę́hthaʔ *he alleviates it* (-(i)ʔθhanęhT-).

alliance. *n.* nehruʔrihwí·θę *his alliance* (-ne-. -aʔrihwiθ-); unahyę́hčreh *alliance* (-(ę)na·hyęhčr-).

alliance, make an. *v.i.* rętiʔnyuhkwę́·tih *he makes an alliance* (-(ę)tiʔnyuh = kwęti-).

alligator. *n.* θríʔrar *alligator* (-θriʔrar-).

allow. *v.t.* čéhnę *allow it!* (-yehnę-); rariwhará·kwahs *he allows it* (-rihw = haraku-).

allowance. *n.* haʔ ruriwhará·kwę *his allowance* (-rihwharaku-).

alloy. *v.t.* nehrayéhraks *he alloys the two* (-ne-. -yehrak-).

ally. *n.* haʔ rawęná·hyę· *ally* (-(ę)na·h = yę-).

Tuscarora Pronunciation Key:
/a/ law; /e/ hat; /i/ pizza; /u/ tune; /ę/ hint; /č/ cheese; /h/ hoe; /m/ mother; /s/ same; /t/ do (before a vowel y, or w), too (elsewhere); /k/ gale (before a vowel y or w), kale (elsewhere); /n/ inhale (before a consonant or word-final), note (elsewhere), /r/ hiss (before a consonant or word-final), run (trilled as in Italian, elsewhere); /w/ cuff (before a consonant other than y or word-final), way (elsewhere); /y/ fish (before a consonant or word-final), you (elsewhere), /θ/ thing; /ʔ/ (the sound between the vowels in unh-unh); /·/ long vowel, /ʹ/ high pitch; /ˋ/ low pitch.

ally. *v.i.* raʾnǫnahyę́hsthaʾ *he allies* (-aˈnǫna·hyęhsT-); ranahyę́hsthaʾ *he allies* (-(ę)na·hyęhsT-); see: -(ę)na·h= yę-.

almanac. *n.* węʾnáhra·č *almanac* (-ę= ˈnạhraT-).

almighty. *adj.* raʾθhaθnęhstakwé·kę *he is almighty* (-(i)ʾθhaθnęhstạkᵂek-)

almond. *n.* yawęʾrahwà·raʾneht *almond* (-ę°ʾrahwarạˈnehT-).

almost. *adv.* čaʾúhshęʾ *almost* (čaʾúh= shęʾ); núhskę *almost* (núhskę).

aloft. *adv.* stá·kwiʾ *aloft* (stá·kwiʾ).

alone. *adj.* rukyerhúhskę *he is alone* (-kerhuhsku-).

alongside. *prep.* ukwthá·ʾnyeʾ *alongside* (-akthaˈnyeʾ-).

aloof. *adj.* inę́hah *aloof* (inę́hah); tyù·reʾ *aloof* (ti-.-re-).

already. *adv.* naʾ *already* (naʾ); náʾwak *already* (náʾwak).

also. *adv.* her *also* (her); nę́·kwer *also* (nę́·kwer); nęʾ *also* (nęʾ); séher *also* (séher).

altar. *n.* haʾ yęʾnyęwahnę́hkhwaʾ *altar* (-aˈnyęwahnęhkw-).

alternatively. *adv.* è·re *alternatively* (è·re); úʾnęʾ *alternatively* (úʾnęʾ).

although. *adv.* kaʾnehnę́ *although* (kaʾ-nehnę́).

always. *adv.* karáhkęʾ *always* (karáhkęʾ).

amazed. *adj.* ęknehrá·kuh *I was amazed* (-nehraku(h)-).

ambient. *adj.* neyuhkętíhsnę *it is ambient* (-ne-.-hkętihsT-).

ambiguous. *n.* neyuwętahskané·kę·t *ambiguous* (-ne-.-wętạhskanekęT-).

Amen. *n.* haʾ nakà·yer *Amen* (-t-.-yer-).

amend. *v.t.* raʾrihwahstę̀·nih *he amends it* (-aʾrihwahstęni-).

amicably. *adv.* uhskęnę́ʾčrakęw *amicably* (-hskęnęʾčrakęw-).

amorous. *adj.* ratahkwanę́hwaks *he is amorous* (-tahkwạnęhwak(T)-).

amount. *n.* see: -ęhr-.

ample. *adj.* wekayè·riʾ *it is ample* (-yah-.-yeri-).

amplify. *v.t.* ręyúhthaʾ *he amplifies it* (-iyuhT-).

amuse. *v.i.* yęʾnęʾtikęhruríhthaʾ *one a-muses oneself* (-aˈnęʾtikęhrurihT-); ruʾtikęhriyúhthaʾ *it amuses him* (-(ę)ʾtikęhriyuhT-).

amusement. *n.* awęʾnhékwčreh *amuse-ment* (-ęʾnhekᵂčr-); uʾtikęhrú·ryaht *a-musement* (-(ę)ʾtikęhruryahT-).

analyze. *v.t.* nehrarihwakęʾθahnę́hči *he analyzes it* (-ne-.-rihwạkęʾθahnę-. #hči).

ancestor. *n.* áksu·t *my female ancestor* (-hsut); akhryáhsu·t *my male ancestor* (-hryahsut).

ancestors. *n.* yękhihsutkę́haʾnęhk *our an-cestors* (-hsut.#kęhạʾnęʾ); yękwahsu-taʾshę́ʾnęhk *our ancestors* (-hsutaʾ= shęʾnę-).

anchor. *n.* uwenę́·ʾneh *anchor* (-wenęT-).

ancients. *n.* kakunęhaʾahkę́heʾ *ancients* (-nęha·ʾ.#áh.#kęheʾ).

and. *conj.* tíhsnęʾ *and* (tíhsnęʾ).

anemia. *n.* učíʾyeh *anemia* (-čiʾy-).

angelica. *n.* tkaré·nyę·ʾ *angelica* (tkaré·= nyę·ʾ).

angels. *n.* kayeręhyaʾkyehrù·nęʾ *angels* (-ręhyaʾkehrunęʾ).

anger. *n.* učháʾreh *anger* (-chaʾr-).

anger. *v.t.* naʾčhaʾrę́·tih *one angers an-other* (-chaʾręti-).

anger, be quick to. *v.i.* račhaʾrahęhθáh-kę *he quick to anger* (-chaʾrạhęh= θahkw-).

angle. *n.* yunhú·čęʾ *it is an angle* (-nhu= čę-).

angry. *adj.* ručhaʾuríhahk *he was angry* (-chaʾruri-).

animal. *adj.* yuʾtikę́hra·t *animal (as op-posed to vegetable)* (-(ę)ʾtikęhraT-).

animal. *n.* kačhè·nęʾ *domestic animal*

(-čhenę-); utáhskweh *domestic animal* (-tahskw-); ká·ryu·ʔ *wild animal* (-r(i)yu-).

animal droppings. *n*. uθnęʔkweh *animal droppings* (-aθnęʔkw-).

animate. *v.t*. ręnhéhthaʔ *he enlivens it, he animates it* (-ęˀnhehkT-).

animosity. *n*. úhsęht *animosity* (-ahsęhT-).

ankle. *n*. učahskwì·reh *ankle* (-čahskwir-); ukwè·reh *ankle* (-kwer-).

annex. *v.t*. nehratahθę́·thaʔ *he annexes it* (-ne-. -tahθęT-).

announce. *v.t*. nehraʔrihukwáhthaʔ *he announces it* (-ne-. -aʔrihukwaʔT-); ruʔteyurę́hthaʔ *he announces it* (-(ę)ʔ= teyuręhT-).

announcement. *n*. haʔ nehruʔrihukwáhnę· *his announcement* (-ne-. -aʔrihu= kʷahT-).

annoy. *v.t*. ratáhskwar *he annoys* (-tah= skwah(e)r-).

annoyance. *n*. utahskwáhraht *annoyance* (-tahskwahrahT-).

annul. *v.t*. rarihwahríhthaʔ *he annuls* (-rihwahrihT-).

answer. *v.i*. nehrarihwayaʔθrá·kwahs *he answers* (-ne-. -rihwayaʔθraku-).

answerable. *adj*. neyurihwayaʔθrá·kwaht *answerable* (-ne-. -rihwayaʔθrakʷahT-).

ant. *n*. ručì·nękw *ant* (ručì·nękw).

antelope. *n*. nakwę́čhaʔ *antelope* (nakwę́čhaʔ).

anterior. *adj*. uhę́ʔnę kęʔnáʔkę *anterior* (-(a)hęʔT- kęʔnáʔkę); tyuréʔkye *anterior* (ti-. -reʔke-).

anticipate. *v.t*. ruʔnęʔtikęhráhręw *he an-ticipates it* (-aˀnęʔtikęhrahręhw-); ruʔtikęhráhręw *he anticipates it* (-(ę)ʔ= tikęhrahręhw-); nehruʔnęʔtikęhráhręw *he anticipates it* (-ne-. -aˀnęʔtikęhrah= ręhw-).

antidote. *n*. yunę́hkwaʔt *antidote* (-nęh= kwaʔT-).

antiquated. *adj*. yuʔnéhskwnę *it is an-tiquated* (-aʔnchskT-).

anus. *n*. stiʔkà·rch *anus* (stiʔkà·rch); utihkęhrę̀·weh *anus* (-tihkęhręw-).

anxiety. *n*. haʔ uʔtikęhraręhyá·kęʔt *an-xiety* (-(ę)ʔtikęhraręhyakęʔT-).

anxious. *adj*. ruʔtikęhraręhyá·kę· *he is anxious* (-(ę)ʔtikęhraręhyakę-); ruʔtikęhraręhyakę́ʔthaʔ *he is anxious* (-(ę)ʔtikęhraręhyakęʔT-).

anything. *n*. tawę́·te *anything* (tawę́·te); taʔawę́·te *anything* (taʔawę́·te).

anywhere. *n*. thikawęnì·yuʔ *anywhere* (thikawęnì·yuʔ).

apart. *adv*. tyù·reʔ *apart* (ti-. -re-).

apartment. *n*. utákwneh *apartment* (-takwT-).

ape. *n*. kačihkwnaksʔúʔy *ape* (-čihkw= nak-.#úʔy).

apology. *n*. haʔ rawętathrewáʔnę *his a-pology* (-ętathrewaʔT-).

appall. *v.t*. nehrutęharę́ʔręh *it appalls him* (-ne-. -tęharęʔrę-).

apparel. *n.r*. uhkwę́·nyeh *apparel* (-hkwę= ni-).

apparently. *adv*. yuʔnyerętihnęhá·ʔnyeʔ *apparently* (-aʔnyerętihnęha'nyeʔ); wírhę *apparently* (wírhę).

appear. *v.i*. rakwę́·ryehs *he appears* (-kwęri-); rayerę́·tiʔθ *he appears* (-ye=

rȩti'⟩-); see: -itkȩ'⟩-.

appear to. *v.t.* ru'⟩nyerȩhnyȩ́·tih *it appears to him (supernatural)* (-a'nyerȩhnyȩ-{dative II}).

appearance. *n.* uyéhseh *appearance* (-yehs-).

appetite. *n.* uhá'⟩yeh *appetite* (-ha'⟩y-).

appetizing. *n.* yuha'⟩yȩ́·tyaht *appetizing* (-ha'⟩yȩtyahT-).

applaud. *v.i.* nehrarahsiθá'⟩tha'⟩ *he applauds* (-ne-.-arahsiθa'⟩T-).

apple. *n.* θwahyù·wa'⟩ *apple* (θwahyù·wa'⟩).

apply. *v.t.* rárhuhs *he applies it* (-rhu-).

appraise. *v.t.* ra'⟩eya'⟩tyȩ̀·'⟩nȩh *he appraises it* (-'⟩eya'⟩tyȩ'nȩ-).

appreciate. *v.t.* runurȩ́'⟩θeh *he appreciates it* (-nurȩ-{dative I}); nat'⟩ȩyeθá'⟩θeh *one appreciates another* (-'⟩ȩyeθ-{dative I}).

appreciation. *n.* ȩyeθá'⟩θeh *appreciation* (-'⟩ȩyeθ-{dative I}).

apprehend. *v.t.* wehrȩ'⟩tikȩ́rhews *he apprehends it* (-yah-.-(ȩ)'⟩tikȩhrhaw-).

apprehensive. *adj.* rȩhré·θrȩ'⟩θ *he is apprehensive* (-ȩhreθrȩ'⟩-); rahskwatkȩ'⟩črȩ́·tih *he is apprehensive* (-hskwatkȩ'⟩črȩti-).

approach. *v.i.* kayéhskaht *they approached* (-hskahT-).

appropriate. *adj.* yuwyésnȩ *it is appropriate* (-wyesT-).

approve. *v.t.* rarihwahtì·rahč *he approves it* (-rihwahtirahT-); raríhwakwahs *he approves it* (-rihwaku-).

approximately. *adj.* à·rȩ *approximately* (à·rȩ).

April. *n.* čuhyeθá'⟩kye *April* (-či-.-(a)h=yeθa'⟩ke); kanȩharȩ́'⟩kye *April* (-nȩ=hahrȩ'⟩ke).

apron. *n.* uhnȩyáhčreh *apron* (-hnȩ=yahčr-).

aquatic. *adj.* awȩ'⟩kyéha·'⟩ *aquatic* (awȩ'⟩.#keha·'⟩).

arbitrate. *v.t.* nehrahskȩnȩ́'⟩nayȩhs *he arbitrates it* (-ne-.-hskȩnȩ'⟩nayȩ(T)-).

arbitration. *n.* urihwahstȩ́·nya'⟩t *arbitration* (-rihwahstȩnya'⟩T-).

arc. *n.* ukwá'⟩neh *arc* (-kwa'⟩n-).

architect. *n.* ranȩhsȩ́·tih *architect* (-nȩh=sȩti-).

ardent. *adj.* rarihwa'⟩naríhȩ· *he is ardent* (-rihwa'⟩narih-).

ardor. *n.* ha'⟩ ru'⟩nahθkyénhȩ *his ardor* (-a'⟩nahθkenha-).

argue. *v.i.* nehrarihwakyénhahs *he argues* (-ne-.-rihwakenha-); *v.t.* nȩyerihwakyénha'⟩ *the two of them will argue* (-rihwakenha-).

arid. *adj.* yuhsnathá'⟩θe· *it is arid* (-hsnath-{dative I}).

arise. *v.i.* ratkȩ́hahs *he arises (from a supine position)* (-atkȩha-); thra'⟩ná'⟩-nihč *he arises (from a sitting position)* (-t-.-a'na'⟩nihr-).

arm. *n.* unȩ́čheh *arm* (-nȩčh-).

armful. *n.* θwȩhnȩ́θhara·t *armful* (-či-.-(ȩ)hnȩθharaT-); uhnȩ́hsteh *armful* (-hnȩhst-); uhnȩ́θhareh *armful* (-(ȩ)h=nȩθhar-).

armpit. *n.* uhȩhtkwí'⟩reh *armpit* (-hȩh=tkwi'⟩r-).

armspan. *n.* ú·wyeh *armspan* (-wy-).

army. *n.* u'⟩nyúhkweh *army* (-i'⟩=nyuhkw-).

aromatics. *n.* neyurhuθhwahnȩ́hkhwa'⟩ *aromatics* (-ne-.-rhuθhwahnȩhkw-).

around. *prep.* ukwthá·'⟩nye'⟩ *around* (-aktha'nye'⟩-).

around or about. *prep.* à·rȩ ukȩ́'⟩ *around or about* (à·rȩ ukȩ́'⟩).

arrange. *v.t.* račhakwahsnáhnȩh *he arranges it* (-ačhakwahsnahnȩ-); retyahčíwha'⟩ *he arranges it* (-etyahčihw-); akya'⟩tahstȩ̀·ni'⟩ *that I arrange it* (-ya'⟩=tahstȩni-).

arrears. *n.* yut'⟩ȩya'⟩nȩ̀·rȩ *arrears* (-at'⟩ȩ=ya'⟩nȩr-).

arrive. *v.i.* íhraws *he arrives* (-aw-); kakutihú᾽ę *they have arrived* (-tihu᾽-).

arrive at. *v.t.* see: -ityę-.

arrow. *n.* á᾽teh *arrow* (-a᾽t-).

artful. *adj.* rutkweru᾽nawyę́hęh *he is artful* (-atkweru᾽nawyęhę-).

artichoke. *n.* urhę́hskri᾽ *artichoke* (-rhęh=skri-).

artificial. *adj.* ha᾽ wetì·yę *artificial* (-e=ti(y)-).

as. *adv.* kunikwę́ *as* (kunikwę́); kù·ni᾽ *as* (kù·ni᾽); kwę́ *as* (kwę́); né᾽či *as* (né᾽-či).

as a result. *adv.* he᾽thúhči *as a result* (he᾽thúhči).

as a rule. *adv.* kę·θ *as a rule* (kę·θ).

as if. *adv.* né᾽či *as if* (né᾽či).

as soon as. *adv.* ha᾽ ù·nę *as soon as* (ha᾽ ù·nę); kanyú᾽ *as soon as* (kanyú᾽); tikawęnì·yu᾽ *as soon as* (tikawęnì·yu᾽).

ascend. *v.i.* ru᾽rathé᾽nę *he ascended* (-a᾽rathe᾽T-).

ash. *n.* u᾽kę́hreh *ash* (-a᾽kęhr-); uhsé-hači· *ash* (-hsehači-); *n.* uhséhareh *ash* (-hsehar-).

ash, black. *n.* kahęwè·ya᾽ *black ash* (kahęwè·ya᾽).

ash, white. *n.* wáht *white ash* (wáht).

ashen. *adj.* kahęwè·ya᾽ wetyá᾽nę *ashen* (kahęwè·ya᾽ -etya᾽T-).

ask. *v.i.* ęhsahrù·yę᾽ *you will ask* (-ah=ruyę᾽-); ra᾽nahrù·yę᾽ *he asks* (-a'nah=ruyę᾽-).

ass. *n.* áha·θ kahęhné·θęh *ass* (áha·θ -hęhneθę-).

assassinate. *v.t.* rahkwę́᾽naws *he assas-*

sinates (-hkwę᾽᾽na(w)-).

assassination. *n.* ha᾽ ruhkwę́᾽na· *assas-sination* (-hkwę᾽na(w)-).

assault. *v.t.* ra᾽nékskruh *he is assaulting it* (-a᾽nekskru-); rú·tahsę *he assaulted it* (-tahs-).

assemble. *v.i.* wę᾽teyarúhčręh *they are assembled* (-(ę)᾽teyaruhčrę-).

assembly. *n.* wa᾽rúhčręh *assembly* (-a᾽=ruhčrę-); yę᾽ruhčrę́hkhwa᾽ *assembly* (-a᾽ruhčręhkw-).

assimilate. *v.i.* wa᾽nyerę᾽naráhkhwa᾽ *it assimilates* (-a'nyerę᾽narahkw-).

assist. *v.t.* ra᾽tiránhe᾽ *he assists it* (-᾽ti=ranhe-).

assistance. *n.* ukyerhakyénha᾽t *assistance* (-kerhakenha᾽T-); ha᾽ uyahsénhaht *assistance* (-yahsenhahT-).

assistant. *n.* ha᾽ ra᾽nę᾽tiránheh *assistant* (-a'nę᾽tiranhe-).

associate. *n.* ha᾽ rawęná·hyę· *associate* (-(ę)na·hyę-).

associate. *v.i.* ra᾽nęnahyę́hstha᾽ *he associates himself* (-a'nęna·hyęhsT-); see: -(ę)na·hyę-.

association. *n.* unahyę́hčreh *association* (-(ę)na·hyęhčr-).

assure. *v.t.* wehrę᾽è̜·we rę́·tih *he assures it* (wehrę᾽è̜·we -ę°ti-).

asthma. *n.* weryáhnakweks *asthma* (-e=ryahnakʷek-); uhwéksteh *asthma* (-hwekst-).

asthma, have. *v.i.* nehrúhweks *he has asthma* (-ne-.-hwek-).

asthmatic. *adj.* neyuhwekstù·rę᾽ *asthmatic* (-ne-.-hweksturę-).

astonished. *adj.* runehrá·kwahs *he is as-*

---

tonished (-nehraku(h)-).

astonishing. *n.* yunehrá·kwaht *astonishing* (-nehrakwahT-).

astride. *adj.* ruthukę́hsnę *he is astride* (-athukęhsT-).

astronomy. *n.* yurę̨hyarà·węʔ uhyatę́hsteh *astronomy* (-rę̨hyarawę- -hyatę̨hst-).

at anchor. *adv.* yuʔnwenęʔnúhę *it is at anchor* (-aʔnwenęʔnuha-).

at most. *adv.* ęwéhruʔ *at most* (ęwéhruʔ).

at night. *adv.* ahθę́·thęʔ *at night* (ahθę́·thęʔ).

at peace. *adv.* kayehskę̀·nęʔ *they are at peace* (-hskęnęʔ-).

at that time. *adv.* aθę̨hkę́hči *at that time* (aθę̨hkę́hči); heʔthúhkye *at that time* (heʔthúhkye).

athletic. *adj.* rakwá·tihs rękwehstahtì·rę *he is athletic* (-kwati- -ękʷehstahtir-); rakwá·tihs rukwatihčrahtì·rę *he is athletic* (-kwati- -kwatihčrahtir-).

atlas. *n.* yuʔwnarà·węʔ *atlas* (-aʔwnarawę-).

atmospheric. *adj.* uwrę̨ʔkyéha·ʔ *atmospheric* (-w(e)r-.#keha·ʔ).

atrocious. *adj.* sáy wakyé·tih *it is atrocious to me* (sáy -ę̊ti-).

attach. *v.t.* waʔthrahsí·θhęʔ *he attached it* (-ne-.-hsiθhę-); see: -nę'na(k)-.

attack. *v.t.* rawę̨ʔtuhérhę *he attacked it* (-ę̨ʔtuherhu-); waʔkayetahsáhstaʔw *they attacked* (-tahsahstaw-); yahwaʔ-kakuʔtę́ʔniʔ *they attacked there* (-yah-.-ʔtę̨ʔni-).

attempt. *v.t.* raʔtyę́·ʔnęh *he attempts it* (-ʔtyę'nęh-).

attempt, make an. *v.i.* ruʔnuryáhnę· *he made an attempt* (-a'nuryahnę-).

attend to. *v.t.* waʔthráhsnyeʔ *he attended to it* (-ne-.-(i)hsnye-).

attest. *v.i.* nehranęhruhkwá·nyęh *he attests* (-ne-.-nęhruhkwanyę-).

attestation. *n.* haʔ nehrunęhruhkwá·nyęʔ *his attestation* (-ne-.-nęhruhkwanyę-).

auctioneer. *n.* haʔ rahę̀·rehθ *auctioneer* (-hęrehθ-).

audacious. *adj.* ruʔrihukwáhnę *he is audacious* (-aʔrihukʷahT-).

audacity. *n.* ukwatihčayę́hčreh *audacity* (-kwatihčayęhčr-).

audible. *n.* yuhę́hsyęht *audible* (-hęh=syęhT-).

audience. *n.* haʔ kakuthę̨hnáčthaʔ *audience* (-athę̨hnačT-); kanęhsakwé·kę *audience* (-nęhsakʷek-).

auger. *n.* yęhrarákthaʔ *auger* (-ahra=rakT-); uhsęwáʔreh *auger* (-hsęwaʔr-).

August. *n.* rahθeʔkyeháh *August* (rahθeʔkyeháh); kę̀·nęʔr *August* (-inęr-).

aunt. *n.* akuʔę̨háh *one's maternal aunt* (-ʔę̨.#áh); kúrhak *my paternal aunt* (-arhak).

aurora. *n.* nayuhúkθe· *aurora* (-t-.-huk-{dative I}).

Aurora Borealis. *n.* newaʔrę̨hyayerę́·ʔ-nyeʔ *Aurora Borealis* (-ne-.-aʔrę̨hya=yerę'nye-); yurę́hyahuks *Aurora Borealis* (-rę̨hyahuk-).

authentic. *adj.* urihwehę̀·we *authentic* (-rihw-.#ęwe).

authenticate. *v.t.* rarihwakʔúhsyęhs *he authenticates it* (-rihwakʔuhsi-).

author. *n.* haʔ nehruʔnę́ʔθę *author* (-ne-.-'nęʔθ-).

authority. *n.* uʔθhá·θneh *authority* (-(i)ʔ=θhaθn-); uʔθhaθnę́hčreh *authority* (-(i)ʔθhaθnęhčr-).

authorize. *v.t.* raʔθhaθnę́hstaws *he authorizes it* (-(i)ʔθhaθnęhstaw-).

automobile. *n.* uʔθréhčreh *automobile* (-(i)ʔθrehčr-).

autumn. *n.* rahθéʔkye *autumn* (rahθéʔ-kye).

avarice. *n.* uhθkyenháʔę *avarice* (-ah=θkenhaʔ-).

average. *n.* ahsę̀·nę *average* (ahsę̀·nę).

avoid. *v.t.* wakaʔneʔkuhéʔθę·ʔ *I avoided another* (-aʔneʔkuheʔθę-); raʔnuʔnár=

hę· *he avoids it* (-a'nu'narhę-).

awake. *adj*. rayéhwat *he is awake* (-ych =
waT-).

awake. *v.i.* wahraθręhnù·ri' *he awoke*
(-θręhnuri-).

away from. *part*. è·re *away from* (è·re).

awe. *n*. ha' neyutęharé'rę't *awe* (-ne-.
-tęharę'rę'T-).

awe. *v.t*. nehrutęharé'ręh *it awes him*
(-ne-.-tęharę'rę-).

awe-inspiring. *adj*. nehrutęharé'rę't *he is
awe-inspiring* (-ne-.-tęharę'rę'T-).

awful. *adj*. see: -(a)hrahT-.

awfulness. *n*. uhskanenáhraht *awfulness*
(-hskanenahrahT-).

awkward. *adj*. rúnhiht *he is awkward*
(-nhihT-).

ax. *n*. a'nú·kę' *ax* (a'nú·kę'); ú'θreh *ax*
(-a'θr-); uré·'neh *ax* (-ręT-).

azure. *adj*. uréhyeh tiwahθuhkú'nę· *azure*
(-ręhy- ti-.-ahθuhku'nę-).

B

baby. *n*. utkú'θreh *baby* (-tku'θr-); ut-
'ahú'y *big baby* (-t'ah-.#ú'y).

babyish. *adj*. utku'θra'kyéha·' ⟨baby-
customarily⟩ *babyish* (-tku'θr-.#ke =
ha·').

Bacchanalian. *adj*. ha' rawé·k'ę *Bacha-
nalan* (-ek'-).

bachelor. *n*. kwęhs ahrutyákshek *bachelor* (kwęhs -tyak-).

back. *adv*. u'téhsnakwt *back* (-'teh =
snakt).

back. *n*. awę́'weh *upper back* (-ę'w-);
úhsweh *lower back* (-hsw-); uθù·weh
animal's back (-θuw-).

back up. *v.i.* rętihrečhę́·'nyęhs *he backs
up* (-ętihręčhę'ni-).

backache, have a. *v.i.* wakę'wanę́hwaks
my backaches (-ę'wanęhwak(T)-).

backbiter. *n*. ha' rę́'wari·ks *backbiter*
(-ę'warik-).

backpack. *n*. uhwarí·teh *backpack* (-hwa =
rit-); uthwarí·teh *backpack* (-athwa =
rit-).

backslide. *v.i.* rurihwaθhę́·nyęhs *he backslides* (-rihwaθhęni-).

backward. *adj*. rahtyakà·yęh *he is backward* (-htyakayę-).

backward. *adv*. u'téhsnakwt *backward*
(-'tehsnakt); u'téhsnakwt na'ú·'ni
backward (-'tehsnakt na'-.-(a)'ni).

bacon. *n*. uθá'reh *bacon* (-θa'r-); kayę'-
kwarárhę u'wáhreh *bacon* (-yę'kwa =
rarhu- -'wahr-).

bad. *adj*. wá·ksę· *it is bad* (-aks-); wáh-
sę· *it is bad* (-ahsę-).

badge. *n*. učá·teh *badge* (-čaN-).

badlands. *n*. wa'wná·ksę· *badlands*
(-a'wnaks-).

baffled. *adj*. wa'u'tikęhnę́hkwę' *it was
baffled* (-(ę)'tikęhnęhkw-{dative III}).

bag. *n*. uté'kweh *bag* (-te'kw-); uyà·reh
bag (-yar-).

bag. *v.t*. kate'kwá'nihč *it bags it* (-te' =
kwa'nihr-).

bait. *n*. úhryeh *bait* (-ahry-).

bake. *v.t*. rę́hsęh *he bakes it* (-ęhsę-).

bald. *adj*. učá'weh *bald* (-ča'w-).

ball. *n*. uthnę́hsteh *ball* (-athnęhst-).

balsam. *n.* čuhkúhnę*ʔ balsam* (čuhkúhnę*ʔ*).

banks. *n.* uhθę́*ʔ*kareh *banks of river*
(-hθę*ʔ*ka̲r-).

banter. *v.i.* nehrarihwakę́·tih *he banters*
(-ne-.-rihwakęti-).

baptism. *n.* ha*ʔ* na*ʔ*ni*ʔ*θkúhahs *baptism*
(-(i)*ʔ*θkuha-).

baptize. *v.t.* na*ʔ*ni*ʔ*θkúhahs *one baptizes
another* (-(i)*ʔ*θkuha-); nathnekuhθráwstha*ʔ* *one baptizes another* (-hnekuh=
θrahwsT-).

barb. *n.* úhnyeh *barb* (-hny-).

barbarian. *n.* nwá*ʔ*kan *barbarian* (Nwá*ʔ*-
kan).

bare. *adj.* učù·neh *bare* (-čun-).

bare spot. *n.* učá*ʔ*weh *bare spot*
(-ča*ʔ*w-).

barefoot. *adj.* ruhsuhskęhá·*ʔ*nye*ʔ* *he is
barefoot* (-ahsuhsku-).

bareheaded. *adj.* ruta*ʔ*rúhskę*ʔ* *he is bareheaded* (-(ę)ta*ʔ*ruhskę-).

barely. *adv.* kwé*ʔ*yę·*ʔ* *barely* (kwé*ʔ*yę·*ʔ*).

bargain. *v.i.* ra*ʔ*rihwíhs*ʔ*ahs *he bargains*
(-a*ʔ*rihwihs*ʔ*a-).

bark. *n.* úhkareh *green bark* (-(a)hka̲r-);
úhsteh *inner bark* (-hsti-); awętih-
skę*ʔ*nà·reh *outer bark* (-ętihskę*ʔ*nar-);
yuhsętathúhθę· *shaggy, dried, peeling
outer bark* (-hsętathuhθę-); uhskę́*ʔ*-
nareh *tree bark* (-hskę*ʔ*na̲r-); uhsúhsneh *bark from large trees* (-hsuhsn-).

bark. *v.i.* rahtyà·nęh *he barks* (-htyanę-).

barn swallow. *n.* čutráθnakar *barn swallow* (čutráθnakar).

barrel. *n.* u*ʔ*náhkweh *barrel* (-*ʔ*nahkw-).

barren. *adj.* kawì·ręč *barren* (-wiręT-).

barter. *v.i.* nehrá·*ʔ*na*ʔ*naws *he barters*
(-ne-.-aw-).

base. *n.* kę*ʔ* neyuhré̜hthę· *base* (kę*ʔ* -ne-.
-hręhthę-).

bashful. *adj.* rucheyárhę· *he is bashful*
(-čheyarhę-); rútkuθt *he is bashful*
(-tkuθt-).

basis. *n.* ha*ʔ* yu*ʔ*nęhskę*ʔ*θráhkę *basis*
(-a*ʔ*nęhskę*ʔ*θrahkw-).

bask. *v.i.* ru*ʔ*nętenę́hsnę *he basks in the
sun* (-a'nętenęhsT-).

basket. *n.* u*ʔ*áhθreh *basket* (-*ʔ*ahθr-); yenęhuharé*ʔ*tha*ʔ* *basket for washing
corn* (-nęhuhare*ʔ*T-); uyá*ʔ*kyeh *market
basket* (-ya*ʔ*k-).

bass. *adj.* ha*ʔ* kawętì·yuh *bass (voice)*
(-wętiyu-).

bass. *n.* kęčahę́sči *black bass* (-iča̲hęsči);
naré*ʔ*re *rock bass* (naré*ʔ*re); kęθna-
kę̀·rat *white bass* (-iθna̲kęrat).

basswood. *n.* uhúhsteh *basswood* (-huh=
st-).

bastard. *n.* newętikhwáhkęh *bastard* (newętikhwáhkęh).

bat. *n.* utáhsneh *bat (unhewn)* (-(ę)=
tahsn-); u*ʔ*nwì·yeh *bat* (-*ʔ*nwiy-).

bat. *n.* krá·kra· *bat (mammal)* (krá·kra·).

bath. *n.* ha*ʔ* yę*ʔ*ni*ʔ*θkuhá*ʔ*tha*ʔ* *bath*
(-a'ni*ʔ*θkuha*ʔ*T-).

bathe. *v.i.* ra*ʔ*ni*ʔ*θkúhar *he bathes* (-a=
'ni*ʔ*θkuhar-); ka*ʔ*nà·węhs *I am bathing*
(-a*ʔ*nawę-).

batter. *v.t.* rá·kwara·č *he batters it* (-kʷa̲=
ra·θ-).

bawl. *v.i.* ručhakwara*ʔ*níhrę *he bawls*
(-ačhakʷa̲ra*ʔ*nihr-).

bay. *n.* wę́*ʔ*tyayę*ʔ* *a bay* (-(ę)*ʔ*ty-).

bay. *v.i.* rahtyà·nęh *he bays* (-htyanę-).

bayonet. *n.* uhsé·kwareh *bayonet* (-hse=
kʷa̲r-).

be. *v.i.* í·kę· *it is* (-i-/-ę̇°-).

beach. *n.* učá·takwt neyutehúharęw *beach*
(-čatakT- -ne-.-tehuha̲ręhw-).

bead. *n.* uθkwarú*ʔ*neh *bead* (-aθkwa̲=
ru*ʔ*T-).

beadwork. *n.* u*ʔ*tíksteh *beadwork* (-*ʔ*tikʷ=
st-).

beam. *n.* ú·treh *beam* (-atr-).

bean. *n.* θáhe*ʔ* *bean* (-θahe̲*ʔ*(r)-).

bear. *n.* uhčíhrę*ʔ* *bear* (-hčihrę-); thęhčí*ʔ*na· *grizzly bear* (thęhčí*ʔ*na·); yu-

tkęryá'khę· *grizzly bear* (-atkę= rya'khę-).

bear fruit. *v.i.* wahyę́·tih *it bears fruit* (-(a)hyęti-).

beard. *n.* uhsú·kareh *beard* (-hsukar-)

bearded. *adj.* rahsú·karę·t *he is bearded* (-hsukaręt).

beast. *n.* ká·ryu·' *beast* (-r(i)yu-); u-ryú'neh *beast* (-r(i)yu'T-).

beautiful. *adj.* wí·yu· *it is beautiful* (-i= yu-).

beautify. *v.i.* yętku'čęnyá'tha' *one beautifies oneself* (-atku'čęnya'T-); *v.t.* rę'na'néhstha' *he beautifies it* (-ę'na= 'nehsT-); rakwahyęhčrę́·tih *he beautifies it* (-kwahyęhčręti-).

beauty. *n.* ukwahyę́hčreh *beauty* (-kwah= yęhčr-).

beaver. *n.* čú'nakę'. *beaver* (čú'nakę').

because. *conj.* nyawè·rih *because* (nya-wè·rih); uríhwawęh *because* (-rihwa= wę-); sé'či *because* (sé'či); wí'er *because* (wí'er).

because of. *prep.* uríhwanęh *because of* (-rihwanę-).

become. *v.i.* ká·'nęh *I become* (-a'nę-); yu'nę́'ę *it became* (-a'nę'-).

bed. *n.* utákwneh *bed* (-takwT-).

bed, go to. *v.i.* ęwakit'úhe' *I will go to bed* (-(i)t'uhe-).

bedbug. *n.* ru'θé'tę *bedbug* (ru'θé'tę).

bedding. *n.* urí'weh *bedding* (-ri'w-); u-ri'wehę̀·we *bedding* (-ri'w-.#ęwe).

bedroom. *n.* kę' yetakwthráhkhwa' *bedroom* (kę' -takwthrahkw-).

bedside. *n.* utákwnakwt *bedside* (-takw= nakT).

bee. *n.* ru'táhkę *bee* (ru'táhkę).

bee swarm. *n.* yawę'táhsę' *bee swarm* (-(ę)'tahsę-).

beech. *n.* učkyérha' *beech* (-čkerh-); ruhsnè·yę'θ *blue beech* (-hsneyę'-).

beehive. *n.* ru'táhkę yawę̀·nę· *beehive* (ru'táhkę -ęnę-); ru'táhkę yetihú'-stha' *beehive* (ru'táhkę -tihu'sT-).

beeline. *n.* kahsirakę́·θnę *beeline* (-hsira= kęθT-).

beer. *n.* pì·ye' *beer* (pì·ye').

beet. *n.* tikahne'ratkwarà·yę' *beet* (ti-. -hne'ratkwarayę(T)-).

beetle. *n.* učik'ę̀·war *beetle* (-čik'ęwar-).

before. *adv.* ahθę́·the' *before* (ahθę́·the'); uhtá'kę *before* (uhtá'kę); tyà·re' *before* (tyà·re').

befriend. *v.t.* ra'nęru'črę́·tih *he befriends someone* (-a'nęru'čręti-).

beg. *v.i.* wa'kayę'nęhnyà·yę' *they begged* (-a'nęhnyayę-); θahrarihwahtì·nę' *he begged* (-či-.-rihwahtinę-); *v.t.* ę-kęrihwahtì·nę'θ *I will beg you* (-rih= wahtinę-{dative I}); rahtì·nęh *he begs for it* (-htinę-).

beget. *v.i.* rà·yęhs *he begets* (-yę(T)-); rayę́·'na'θ *he begets* (-yę'na'-).

beggar. *n.* ha' rahtì·nęh *beggar* (-htinę-).

begin. *v.i.* rahθá·w'ahs *he begins* (-ah= θaw'-).

begrudge. *v.t.* ra'tú·θhahs *he begrudges* (-'tuθh-).

behave. *v.i.* θa'nęhę̀·we'θ *behave yourself!* (-a'nę-.#ęwe.{dative I}).

behavior. *n.* u'tikęhnę́hčreh *behavior* (-(ę)'tikęhnęhčr-).

behead. *v.t.* ranęhkwáhtha' *he beheads it*

Tuscarora Pronunciation Key:
/a/ law; /e/ hat; /i/ pizza; /u/ tune; /ę/ hint; /č/ cheese; /h/ hoe; /m/ mother; /s/ same; /t/ do (before a vowel y, or w), too (elsewhere); /k/ gale (before a vowel y or w), kale (elsewhere); /n/ inhale (before a consonant or word-final), note (elsewhere), /r/ hiss (before a consonant or word-final), run (trilled as in Italian, elsewhere); /w/ cuff (before a consonant other than y or word-final), way (elsewhere); /y/ fish (before a consonant or word-final), you (elsewhere), /θ/ thing; /'/ (the sound between the vowels in unh-unh); /·/ long vowel. /´/ high pitch; /`/ low pitch.

(-nęhkʷahṪ -).

behind. *prep*. uhtáʼkę *behind* (uhtáʼkę);
uʼtéhsnakwt *behind* (uʼtéhsnakwt).

behoove. *v.i.* ruʼné·θwekt *it behooves
him* (-aʼneθwekT -).

being. *n.* ukwéhsteh *being* (-(ę°)kʷehst -).

belch. *v.i.* rutyaʼnukáʼthaʼ *he belches*
(-tyaʼnukaʼT -).

believe. *v.i.* sè·rih *you believe* (-er-).

belittle. *v.t.* nehrahsęwiré·thaʼ *he belittles
it* (-ne-. -hsęwireT -).

bell. *n.* utičkyéʼneh *bell* (-tičkeʼn -); ye-
wenętʼéhsthaʼ *bell* (-wenętʼehsT -).

bellow. *v.i.* runęhwarù·rih *he bellows*
(-nęhwaruri -).

bellows. *n.* čhaʼ warę̀·ʼna·č *bellows*
(čhaʼ -(a)rę'naT -).

belly. *n.* uhwé·θneh *belly* (-hweθn -); ú-
tkweh *belly* (-tkw-).

bellyache. *n.* katkwanę́hwaks *bellyache*
(-tkwanęhwak(T) -).

belong to. *v.t.* rù·węh *it belongs to him*
(-wę-).

belongings. *n.* uhwarí·teh *belongings*
(-hwarit -); uthwarí·teh *belongings* (-a=
thwarit -); see: -ʼnęnaw -.

below. *prep*. ehnáhkę *below* (ehnáhkę).

belt. *n.* waʼnetkwahtrę́hsthaʼ *belt* (-a'ne=
tkwahtręhsT -); yeʼnhęhθuʼnarhúh-
sthaʼ *belt* (-(i)ʼnhęhθu'narhuhst -); uh-
kwíʼsteh *beaded belt* (-hkwiʼst -);
uyęʼkwíhčreh *belt* (-yęʼkwihčr-).

belt. *v.i.* raʼnyę́ʼkwihs *he belts himself*
(-a'nyęʼkwih -).

bench. *n.* uʼθkwéhseh *bench* (-ʼθkwe=
hs -).

bend. *v.t.* nehrúʼknęhs *he bends it*
(-ne-. -uʼkT -); see: -uʼy(e)-.

beneficent. *adj.* rurihwákwahst *he is beneficent* (-rihwakwahsT -).

benefit. *v.t.* kayahskyénhahs *it benefits it*
(-yahskenha -).

benevolence. *n.* kaʼtikęhrákwahst *benevolence* (-(ę)ʼtikęhrakwahsT -).

benevolence. *n.* kayęwahnę́hčraʼ *benevolence* (-yęwahnęhčr-).

bent. *adj.* neyuʼnúʼknę *it is bent* (-ne-.
-a'nuʼkT -).

berry. *n.* úhyeh *berry* (-(a)hy-).

beseech. *v.i.* raʼnęnhę́·thaʼ *he beseeches*
(-a'nęnhęT -).

beside. *prep*. ú·kwt *beside* (-akT -).

besides. *adv*. tíʼer *besides* (tíʼer);
thweʼnhé·θuʼ *besides* (thweʼnhé·θuʼ).

besmear. *v.t.* račihskwà·węhs *he besmears it* (-čihskwaw -).

betray. *v.t.* naʼnatęhnì·nęh *one betrays
another* (-atęhninę -).

between. *prep*. ú·kęʼt *between* (ú·kęʼt).

beware. *v.i.* θaʼnęʼtikę́hrarę *beware!* (-a=
'nęʼtikęhrar -{dative III}).

bewilder. *v.t.* naʼtikęhrawę̀·rih *one bewilders another* (-(ę)ʼtikęhrawęri -).

beyond. *prep*. íhsʼę *beyond* (íhsʼę).

bib. *n.* uhnęyahčreháh *bib* (-hnęyahčr -.
#áh).

Bible. *n.* Uhyatęhstatukę́hti *Bible* (-hya=
tęhstatukęhT -).

bicep. *n.* unuhskwíʼθreh *muscle of upper
arm (bicep)* (-nuhskwiʼθr -).

bicker. *v.i.* ručiʼrę́hsę· *he bickers* (-čiʼ=
ręhsę -).

biennial. *n.* newuhstakyehá·ʼnyeʼ *biennial* (-ne-. -uhstakeha'nyeʼ -).

big. *adj.* tiwę́·θeʼr *it is so big* (-ę°θ(e)r -);
sęθrí·yu· *you are big* (-ę°θriyu -);
tiwáʼθrę· *it is so big* (ti -. -aʼθr -); see:
-ę°θ(e)r -.

bigger, make. *v.i.* waʼawęθrę́·tiʼ *it made
it bigger* (-ę°θręti -).

bile. *n.* číʼtkwar *bile* (číʼtkwar).

bilious. *adj.* ručiʼtkwáhnahs *he is bilious*
(-čiʼtkwahn -).

billion *adj./n.* ę́·či mí·ryę *billion* (ę́·či
mí·ryę); mí·ryę *billion* (mí·ryę).

billowy. *adj.* unęʼnéhči *billowy* (-nęT -.
#hči).

bind. *v.t.* nehrahtrę́hstęh *he binds it*

(-ne -. -(i)htrẹhstẹ -).

biped. *n.* ncyúhsẹ·t *biped* (-ne -. -ahsẹt).

birch. *n.* uná·kyeh *birch* (-nak -).

bird. *n.* čí'nẹ' *bird* (čí'nẹ').

birth, give. *v.i.* wa'nú'nẹh *it gives birth (animal)* (-a'nu'nẹ -); wa'nwì·rayẹhs *she gives birth (human)* (-a'nwira̱= yẹ(T) -).

birthday. *n.* thwečé·haws *birthday* (ti+ yah+či -. -(ẹ)haw -).

biscuit. *n.* píhskit *biscuit* (píhskit); u- tá'nareh *biscuit* (-ta'na̱r -).

bison. *n.* čuhstekyerhyá'kẹ *bison* (čuh- stekyerhyá'kẹ).

bite. *v.t.* rá·ri·ks *he bites it* (-rik -).

bits. *n.* awú·kri' *bits* (-ukr -).

bitter. *adj.* yuhkará·'ne' *it is bitter* (-(a)hka̱ra'ne -); yuči·wakẹ *it is bitter* (-čiwa̱k -).

bitterness. *n.* učiwákčreh *bitterness* (-či= wa̱kčr -); učiwáksteh *bitterness* (-či= wa̱kst -).

bittersweet. *n.* nekaθuwahrí'ẹ *bittersweet* (-ne -. -θuwa̱hri' -)

black. *adj.* kahẹ́sči *it is black* (-hẹsči -); učihẹ́hreh *black* (-čihẹhr -).

black, become. *v.i.* rahẹ́sči'θ *he becomes black* (-hẹsči' -).

black eye, give a. *v.t.* natkahkwirúhahs *one gives another a black eye* (-kah= kwiruh -).

blackbird, red-winged. *n.* θú'krihst *red- winged blackbird* (θú'krihst).

blacken. *v.t.* rahθẹ'nárhuhs *he blackens it* (-ahθẹ'narhu -); rahẹsčíhtha' *he blackens it* (-hẹsčihT -).

black-eyed Susan. *n.* unẹθéhwi·t *black- eyed Susan* (-nẹθehwit -).

blackhaw. *n.* rutí·kẹ *blackhaw* (-tikẹ -).

blacksnake. *n.* rurá·thẹ *blacksnake* (-rath -).

bladder. *n.* u'nhẹ́heh *bladder* (-'nhẹh -); u'nhẹ́heh uté'kwawẹh *bladder* (-'n= hẹh - -te'kwawẹ -).

blamable. *adj.* ruthré'ahs *he is blamable* (-athre' -).

blame. *v.t.* rahré'ahs *he blames it* (-hre' -); wahruríhwara' *he got blam- ed for it* (-rihwa̱ra' -); wa'na'rihwár- hu' *one blamed another* (-rihwa̱rhu -).

blanch. *v.i.* ra'nahθú·kwahs *he blanches* (-a'nahθuku -).

blanket. *n.* urí'weh *blanket* (-ri'w -); uri'wehẹ̀·we *Indian blanket* (-ri'w -. #ẹwe).

blast. *n.* wẹ'nakẹheyá'tha' *blast* (-ẹ'na̱= kẹheya'T -).

blaze. *v.i.* yu'nẹ'tahkra'níhrẹ *it blazes* (-a'nẹ'tahkra'nihr -).

bleak. *adj.* yuwrakẹ́θnẹ' *it is bleak* (-w(e)ra̱kẹθnẹ -).

bleary-eyed. *adj.* ukahkawẹ́'neh *bleary- eyed* (-kahkawẹ'n -).

bleed. *v.i.* ratkwarí·tkẹ'θ *he bleeds* (-tkwaritkẹ' -).

bless. *v.t.* na'nyẹwáhtha' *one blesses an- other* (-yẹwahT -).

blind. *adj.* nehrakahkwé·kẹ *he is blind* (-ne -. -kahkʷek -).

blindfolded. *adj.* ratkahráhtrẹhs *he is blindfolded* (-atkahra̱htrẹ -).

blink. *n.* ukahčẹ́'reh *a blink* (-kahčẹ'r -).

blink. *v.i.* nahratkár'u' *he blinked* (-t -. -atkar'u -).

---

bliss. *n.* učhęnę́·tyat *bliss* (-ačhęnę= tyaT-).

blister. *n.* nawekunę́·tyę *blister* (-t-. -ekunętyę-); awú·kę *blister* (-uk-).

blister. *v.i.* rà·wuks *he is blistered* (-uk-).

bloat. *v.i.* rathwęná·kuhs *he bloats* (-a= thwęnaku-).

bloated. *adj.* ratkúhkwe *he is bloated* (-atkuhkw-); ratkuhkwì·yuh *he is bloated* (-atkuhkwiyu-).

blood. *n.* ká·tkę *blood* (-tkę-); utkwà·reh *blood* (-tkwar-).

bloodline. *n.* urę́hseh *bloodline* (-(i)r= ęhs-).

bloodroot. *n.* newętikwęhčhaksúy *bloodroot* (newętikwęhčhaksúy); yutkwehθętíh *little bloodroot* (-tkweh= θętíh).

bloodsucker. *n.* rutéhwęh *bloodsucker* (-tehwę-).

bloom. *v.i.* kačičíhskęws *it is blooming* (-čičihskęhw-).

blossoms. *n.* yučičíhskę́he *blossoms* (-čičihskę-).

blot out. *v.t.* rahnę́tha *he blots it out* (-ahnęT-); yutíyheh *it blotted it out* (-tiyheh-).

blow. *v.i.* wahú·na·t *it (the wind) blew* (-u'n<u>a</u>T-); *v.t.* rarę́na·č *he blows air on it* (-(a)ręnaT-).

blubber. *n.* utkrę́hneh *blubber* (-a= tkręhT-).

blue. *adj.* utihę́·ryeh *blue* (-tihęry-); katihęryahę́sči *dark blue* (-tihęry<u>a</u>hęsči-); utihęryahwaryá·kę *light blue* (-tihę= ry<u>a</u>hwaryakę-).

blueberry. *n.* uyhíha *blueberry* (-yhih-); runáwher *high bush blueberry* (runáwher).

bluebird. *n.* čurù·ruθ *bluebird* (čurù·ruθ).

blueweed. *n.* kará·θkęws *blueweed* (-ra= θkęws).

bluffer. *n.* rahnyawíhęh *bluffer* (-hny<u>a</u>wi= hę-).

blunt. *adj.* ukwè·neh *blunt* (-kwen-).

blush. *v.i.* račiérher *he blushes* (-a= čierhar-).

boar. *n.* unahéreh *species of wild boar* (-naher-).

board. *n.* uhwę́khareh *board* (-hwę= khar-).

boast. *v.i.* ranwętahsę́htha *he boasts* (-a'nwętahsęhT-).

boastful. *adj.* rurihukwáhnę *he is boastful* (-arihuk^wahT-).

boat. *n.* uhę̀·weh *boat* (-hęw-); uhęwehúy *steam boat* (-hęw-.#úy); uhęwéhuy uhsęryúhkweh warekwáhtha *steam boat* (-hęw-.#úy -hsęryuhkw--arekwahT-).

bobcat. *n.* tkęhwè·nuh *bobcat* (tkęhwè·nuh).

body. *n.* ukyérheh *body* (-kerh-); uthwarí·teh *body (as a physical container for the non-corporal spirit)* (-athwarit-); uhwarí·teh *body (as a physical container for the non-corporal spirit)* (-hwarit-); uyákareh *upper body (above the waist)* (-yak<u>ar</u>-); see: -yat-.

bog. *n.* yuwíheh *bog* (-wih-).

boil. *n.* náku *boil (sore)* (náku).

boil. *v.i.* yuríhęθ *it boils* (-rihę-); wakà·rih *it boiled* (-rih-); waučanaríhat *it boiled* (-čanarihaT-); yučanaríhęθ *it is boiling* (-čanari= hę-); yučanarihęhθéhahk *it has boiled* (-čanarih-); *v.t.* wakkáhnę· *I boil it* (-kahnę-); θríht *boil it!* (-rih= T-).

boisterous. *adj.* rutikęhrú·kę *he is boisterous* (-(ę)tikęhrukę).

bold. *adj.* rukwatíhčayę *he is bold* (-kwatihčayę-).

bolt. *n.* uhsęwáreh *bolt* (-hsęwar-).

bond. *v.i.* yuyetawá·nę *it bonds* (-ye= tawaT-).

bone. *n.* uhskę́reh *bone* (-hskęr-).

boneset, white. *n.* uhskę'’rakę'’náhkhwa'’ (-hskę'’ra̱kę'’nahkw-).

bony. *n.* uhskę'’réhči *bony* (-hskę'’r-. #hči).

book. *n.* uhyatę́hsteh *book* (-hyatę̧hst-).

bookcase. *n.* kę'’ yehyatę̧hstayę'’náhkhwa'’ *bookcase* (kę'’ -hyatę̧hsta̱yę = 'nahkw-).

boot. *n.* uhshę̀·weh *boot* (-hshę̧w-).

border. *n.* uyúhkweh *border* (-yuhkw-).

border, make a. *v.i.* yeyúhkuč *one makes a border* (-yuhkur-).

bore. *n.* yę̧hraráktha'’ *bore (tool)* (-ah = ra̱ra̱kT-); yę̧rę̧'’ahraráktha'’ *carpenter's (large) bore* (-rę̧'’ahra̱ra̱kT-).

bore. *v.i.* ráhrara·ks *he bores* (-ahra̱rak-).

born. *adj.* ra'’nę́·tih *he is born* (-a'nę̧ti-).

borrow. *v.t.* rahtì·nęh *he borrows it* (-hti̱ = nę̧-).

bosom. *n.* u'’áhseh *bosom* (-'ahs-).

both. *adj.* sę̧·we'’ *both* (sę̧·we'’).

bother. *v.t.* ka'’čtehríhstha'’ *it bothers me* (-a'’čtehrihsT-); ra'’rihuryá'’tha'’ *he bothers it* (-a'’rihurya'’T-); ra'’tikę̧hryá'’khę̧h *he bothers it* (-(ę̧)'’tikę̧h = rya'’khę̧-); nę̧θa'’tikę̧hkarę́'’rę'’ *you will be bothered by it* (-ne-. -(ę̧)'’ = tikę̧hkarę̧'’r-).

bottle. *n.* účheh *bottle* (-čhe'’-); uché'’weh *bottle* (-čhe'’w-).

bottom. *n.* u'’nę̧·neh *bottom (of pails, baskets)* (-'’nę̧n-); unę̧'’sę́'’kye *at the bottom* (-nę̧'’s-).

bovine. *n.* usherę̧tkyéha·'’ *bovine* (-she = rę̧t.#keha·'’); usherę̧·t'’áh *bovine* (-she = rę̧t.#áh).

bow. *n.* unáčreh *bow (for arrows)* (-načr-); á'’neh *bow (for arrows)* (-a'’n-).

bow. *v.i.* rę̧nę̧'’kyę́hstha'’ *he bows* (-inę̧'’ = kyę̧hst-); nehrę̧nę́·knę̧hs *he bows* (-ne-. -ę̧nę̧kT-).

bowel. *n.* uyá'’reh *bowel* (-ya'’r-).

bowl. *n.* uti'’nę́hkweh *bowl* (-ti'’nę̧hkw-); u'’náhkweh *bowl* (-'’nahkw-)

bow-legged. *adj.* nehrahá·kwayę'’ *he is bow-legged* (-ne-. -hakʷayę̧(T)-).

bowstring. *n.* urę́·θeh *bowstring* (-rę̧θ-).

boy. *n.* raká·θ'’ah *boy* (-kaθ'’ah); uhčúhkweh *boy* (-hčuhkw-); ručhúhkhwer *boy (10-15 years old)* (-ačhuh = kwh(e)r-).

boyfriend. *n.* wa'’nę̧rú'’čhę'’ *her boyfriend* (-a'nę̧ru'’čhę̧(T)-).

box. *n.* u'’náhkweh *box* (-'’nahkw-).

bra. *n.* uyę'’kwíhsteh yęt'’ahsę̧hnáhkhwa'’ *bra* (-yę'’kwihst- -at'’ahsę̧hnahkw-).

brace. *n.* ha'’ neyutekà·rę̧ *a brace* (-ne-. -tekar-).

brace. *v.t.* nehrutekà·rę̧ *he braced it* (-ne-. -tekar-).

bracelet. *n.* yę̧therahwanháhstha'’ *bracelet* (-atherahwanhahsT-); utyahskarí'’čreh *bracelet* (-(ę̧)tyahskari'’čr-).

braid. *n.* utáhθeh *braid* (-tahθ-).

braid. *v.t.* ratahθę́·tih *he braids it* (-tah = θę̧ti-).

brain. *n.* unę́hwareh *brain* (-nę̧hwa̱r-).

brakeman. *n.* nehraka'’núhraraks *brakeman* (-ne-. -ka'’nuhrarak-).

bramble. *n.* úhskaweh *bramble* (-hs = ka̱w-).

bran. *n.* urí'’reh *bran* (-ri'’r-).

branch. *n.* ú'’čkaweh *branch* (-(i)'’ =

Tuscarora Pronunciation Key:
/a/ law; /e/ hat; /i/ pizza; /u/ tune; /ę̧/ hint; /č/ cheese; /h/ hoe; /m/ mother; /s/ same; /t/ do (before a vowel y, or w), too (elsewhere); /k/ gale (before a vowel y or w), kale (elsewhere); /n/ inhale (before a consonant or word-final), note (elsewhere), /r/ hiss (before a consonant or word-final), run (trilled as in Italian, elsewhere); /w/ cuff (before a consonant other than y or word-final), way (elsewhere); /y/ fish (before a consonant or word-final), you (elsewhere), /θ/ thing; /'’/ (the sound between the vowels in unh-unh); /·/ long vowel, /'/ high pitch; /`/ low pitch.

čk<u>a</u>w-); utkwì·reh *branch* (-(a)tkwir-);
u'nháhneh *large branch* (-(i)'nhahT-);
ú'čhareh *branch* (-'čh<u>a</u>r-).

brandy. *n.* unęhkwa't'ę·we *brandy* (-nęhkwa'T-.#ęwe).

brass. *n.* u'nęwehę·we *brass* (-'nęw-. #ęwe).

brassy. *adj.* u'nęwehęwéhči *brassy* (-'nęw-.#ęwe.#hči).

bravery. *n.* ukwatihčayę́hčreh *bravery* (-kwatihč<u>a</u>yęhčr-).

bray. *v.i.* ratkrè·nęč *he brays* (-atkre= nęT-).

breach. *n.* ukahrę̀·weh *breach* (-kahręw-).

bread. *n.* utá'nareh *bread* (-ta'n<u>a</u>r-); kata'naręhrá·heh *fried bread* (-ta'n<u>a</u>= ręhra·he-); ka'té·yę·k *yeast bread* (-(ę)'teyę-).

breadth. *n.* uhwá·θeh *breadth* (-hwač-).

break. *v.t.* í·kya'ks *I am breaking it* (-ya'k-); wa'nyehwáhriht *one broke it* (-ne-.-hwahrihT-); nęwá'nya'k *I will break it in two* (-ne-.-a'nya'k-).

break down. *v.i.* ráhryenę'θ *he breaks down* (-hryenę'-).

break up. *v.t.* wekáhrihč *it is broken up* (-yah-.-hrihT-).

breakfast. *n.* θuhtérhę yę'nekhwáher *breakfast* (-či-.-hterhę- -a'nekhwa= h(e)r-).

breast. *n.* u'áhseh *breast* (-'ahs-).

breastplate. *n.* yę'nyętarę́hkhwa' *breastplate* (-a'nyętaręhkw-).

breath. *n.* awęríhsteh *breath* (-ę°rihst-); awęrihst'á·ka·' *breath* (-ę°rihst-.#a= ka·'); see: -eryahn-.

breath, draw a. *v.i.* thra'nęrihsta'nihę́·thuhs *he draws a breath* (-t-.-a'nęrih= sta'nihęthu-).

breathe. *v.i.* ka'nę́·ryęhs *I breathe* (-a= 'nęri-); see: -ę°ri-.

breathless. *adj.* rawęrihshú·kę' *he is breathless* (-ę°rihshukę').

breechcloth. *n.* u'khà·reh *breechcloth*

(-i'khar-).

briar. *n.* unę'à·reh *briar* (-nę'ar-).

bribe. *v.t.* na'tyá'tha' *one bribes another* (-tya'T-).

brick. *n.* unę̀·yeh *brick* (-nęy-).

bridge. *n.* úhskweh *bridge* (-ahskw-).

bridle. *n.* awęhkwarú'črch *bridle* (-ęh= kwar-).

brightness. *n.* učá·teh *brightness* (-čaN-); uhúkčreh *brightness* (-hukčr-).

brilliant. *adj.* yu'ęhráhuks *brilliant* (-'ęh= r<u>a</u>huk-).

brine. *n.* učikhe'ná·kri' *brine* (-čikhe'= nakri').

bring. *v.t.* wa'káhe'w *it brought it* (-(ę)haw-); khà·wi' *I bring it* (-(ę)= hawi-); nákha'w *I brought it back* (-t-.-(ę)haw-); thrayę́htha' *he brings it in* (-t-.-yęhT-).

brink. *n.* uhθę́'kareh *brink* (-hθę'k<u>a</u>r-).

briny. *adj.* à·wę' čikhé'či *briny* (à·wę' čikhe'.#hči).

bristle. *n.* uhsnwé'reh *bristle* (-hsn= we'r-).

brittle. *adj.* watkwáhtha' *it is brittle* (-atkʷahT-).

broach. *n.* uhskarí'čreh *broach* (-hska= ri'čr-); utyahskarí'čreh *broach* (-(ę)= tyahskari'čr-).

broad. *adj.* kahwačí·yu· *broad* (-hwa= čiyu-).

broil. *v.t.* ra'θkęwę́·tih *he broils it* (-'θkęwęti-).

broken. *adj.* neyuhwahrí'ę *it is broken* (-ne-.-hwahri'-); see: -ne-.-ukar-.

brook. *n.* uhsnę̀·weh *brook, stream* (-hsnęw-).

broom. *n.* ukyé'weh *broom* (-ke'w-).

broomstick. *n.* ukyé'weh uhtyuharę́·te *broomstick* (-ke'w- -htyuh<u>a</u>ręte).

brother-in-law. *n.* akà·ra' *my brother-in-law* (-ara'); akawé·ryuh *my brother-in-law (sister's husband)* (-awe= ryuh); akaweryuháh *my bother-in-law* *(wife's brother)* (-aweryuháh); u'nyúh-čreh *brother-in-law* (-a'nyuhčr-).

brother *n.* akhryáhči' *my older brother* (-hryahči'); khé'kęh *my younger brother* (-'kęh); khchsę́·te *my younger brother* (-hsęte).

brow. *n.* ukahré'neh *brow* (-kahre'n-); ukę́'neh *brow* (-kę'n-).

brown. *adj.* učí'ereh *brown* (-či'ęr-); wahθuhkwahę́sči *brown* (-ahθuhkwa=hęsči-); učirę́hreh *brown* (-čiręhr-).

browse. *v.i.* kakwirúhskwahs *it browses* (-kwiruhsku-); kakwí·ra·ks *it browses* (-kwirak-).

bruise. *v.t.* ęyé·kwara·θ *one will bruise it* (-kʷara·θ-).

brush. *n.* ukwì·reh *brush* (-kwir-).

brutal. *adj.* kačhenę́'kwę́ *brutal* (-čhenę-.#kwę́).

bubble. *v.i.* yuríhę́'θ *it bubbles* (-rihę'-).

buck. *n.* ręthę *buck (male deer)* (ręthę).

bucket. *n.* yęθahnę́hstha' *bucket* (-aθah=nęhst-); u'nę̀·weh *bucket* (-'nęw-).

buckle. *n.* utyahskarí'čreh *buckle* (-(ę)=tyahskari'čr-).

buckle. *v.t.* rętyahskari'čru'nárhuhs *he buckles it* (-(ę)tyahskari'čru'narhu-).

buckskin. *n.* kę́hnę' *buckskin* (-ihn-).

bud. *n.* uwì·reh *bud* (-wir-).

buffalo. *n.* čuhstekyerhyá'kę *buffalo* (čuhstekyerhyá'kę).

bug. *n.* učik'ę̀·war *bug* (-čik'ęwar-).

buggy. *n.* u'θrehčreháh *buggy* (-(i)'=θrehčr-.#áh).

building. *n.* yakę̀·nę' *building* (-ę°nę-).

bulb. *n.* unę́·θeh *bulb* (-nęč-).

bulge. *v.i.* yutkwa'níhrę *it bulges* (-tkwa'nihr-).

bulk. *n.* yuhs'áhnę *bulk* (-(i)hs'ahT-).

bull. *n.* ushé·rę·t ka'níha· *bull* (-sheręt -'niha-).

bulldog. *n.* čir'ú'y *bulldog* (čir.#ú'y).

bullet. *n.* á'teh *bullet* (-a't-).

bully. *n.* rahęhsù·rih *a bully* (-hęhsuri-).

bumblebee. *n.* ru'terhęruhú'y *bumblebee* (ru'terhęruhú'y).

bump. *v.t.* ręnęhrá'nihč *he bumps it* (-(ę)nęhra'nihr-).

bunch. *n.* unę́'kweh *bunch* (-nę'kw-); uθnę́'kweh *bunch* (-aθnę'kw-); u-thúhkweh *bunch* (-athuhku-).

bunchy. *adj.* uθnę́'kwéhči *bunchy* (-aθ=nę'kw-.#hči).

bundle. *n.* ukyé'čeh *bundle* (-ke'č-); uθnę́'kweh *bundle* (-aθnę'kw-); see: -'nęnaw-.

burden. *n.* ukyé'čeh *burden* (-ke'č-); uθnę́'kweh *burden* (-aθnę'kw-).

burden. *v.t.* natkyéhna·č *one burdens another* (-kehT(aT)-).

burdock. *n.* unę́'ahči·reh *burdock* (-nę'=ahčir-).

burglar. *n.* ranęhská·ryahs *burglar* (-nęh=skari-).

burial. *n.* ye'néht'ahs *burial* (-'nęht'-).

burial ground. *n.* ye'nęhná·ryeh *burial ground* (-'nęhnary-).

burly. *adj.* ukęθrę́hneh *burly* (-kęθręhn-).

burn. *v.i.* yú·'neks *it burns* (-'nek-); *v.t.* rę́'naws *he burns it* (-i'naw-).

burnish. *v.t.* račanę́·tih *he burnishes it* (-čanęti-).

burrow. *v.i.* ręhrá'kha' *he burrows* (-ę°h=ra'k-).

Tuscarora Pronunciation Key:
/a/ law; /e/ hat; /i/ pizza; /u/ tune; /ę/ hint; /č/ cheese; /h/ hoe; /m/ mother; /s/ same; /t/ do (before a vowel y, or w), too (elsewhere); /k/ gale (before a vowel y or w), kale (elsewhere); /n/ inhale (before a consonant or word-final), note (elsewhere), /r/ hiss (before a consonant or word-final), run (trilled as in Italian, elsewhere); /w/ cuff (before a consonant other than y or word-final), way (elsewhere); /y/ fish (before a consonant or word-final), you (elsewhere), /θ/ thing; /'/ (the sound between the vowels in unh-unh); /·/ long vowel, /´/ high pitch; /`/ low pitch.

bury. *v.t.* wahráhsa'ṇę·' *he buried it* (-(i)hsa̲'ṇę -); wa'na'níhra'̧t *one buried another* (-(i)hra'T -); ra'nę́ht'ahs *he buries it* (-'nęht' -); see: -'nęhT -.

bus. *n.* ka'teyę̧hawíhtha' *bus* (-(ę)'teyę= hawihT -); θká'teyhaws *bus* (-či -. -(ę)'teyhaw -).

bushel. *n.* ute'nyętę́hčreh *bushel* (-te'= nyętę̧hčr -).

business. *n.* uríhweh *business* (-rihw -).

business, have as. *v.i.* ru'ríhę·t *he has it as his business* (-a'rihęt).

bust. *n.* úhsweh *bust* (-hsw -).

busy. *adj.* nehruyahserhár'ę *he is busy* (-ne -. -yahserhar' -).

but. *conj.* ahá'ne' *but* (ahá'ne'); úč'aht *but* (úč'aht).

butcher. *n.* ra'wahrá·ryuhs *butcher* (-'wahra̲ryu -).

butcher. *v.t.* rá·ryuhs *he butchers it* (-r(i)yu -).

butt. *n.* uhnę̀·neh *butt (of a person)* (-hnęn -).

butt heads. *v.i.* wa'nyęnę́htri·θ *the two of them butted heads* (-anęhtriθ -).

butter. *n.* utú'θreh *butter* (-tu'θr -).

butternut. *n.* kahsu'kwé·θę *butternut* (-hsu'kweθę -).

buttery. *adj.* utu'θréhči *buttery* (-tu'θr -. #hči).

buttocks. *n.* uhéčheh *buttocks* (-hečh -).

button. *n.* uniθkú'reh *button* (-niθku'r -).

button. *v.t.* raniθku'ru'nárhuhs *he buttons it* (-niθku'ru'narhu -).

buttonwood. *n.s.* wa'rę̧'ačhęwá·tih *buttonwood* (-a'rę̧'ačhęwati -); yę̧'ne-khri'nuharáhkhwa' *buttonwood* (yę̧'-nekhri'nuharáhkhwa').

buy. *v.t.* ratyá'tha' *he buys it* (-tya'T -).

buzzard. *n.* kwę̧θnè·reh *buzzard* (kwę̧θ-nè·reh); kwę̧θnereháh *kind of buzzard* (kwę̧θnereháh).

by rights. *adv.* ha' kę́hčih *by rights* (ha' kę́hčih).

bygone. *adj.* yu'nękúhnę *bygone* (-a'nę-kuhT -).

C

cabbage. *n.* utá'reh *cabbage* (-(ę)ta'r -).

cabinet. *n.* yurętu'črę̧hnà·wę' *cabinet* (-rętu'črę̧hnawę -).

cackle. *v.i.* kahę̀·rehθ *it cackles* (-hę= rehθ -).

cage. *n.* unę́hseh *cage* (-nęhs -).

cake. *n.* urę'nakrí'či utá·'nareh *cake* (-rę'nakri -.#hči -ta'na̲r -); yurę'nakrí'-čra'r *cake* (-rę'nakri'čra'r -); utá'na-reh *cake (e.g., of yeast)* (-ta'na̲r -).

calculate. *v.i.* rę'tikę́hnęh *he calculates* (-(ę)'tikę̧hnę -)

calf. *n.* usherę·t'áh *calf* (-sheręt.#áh).

calf. *n.* uθęnè·neh *calf of leg* (-θęnęn -).

call. *v.i.* wahrahę̧réhθę' *he called* (-hę= rehθ -); *v.t.* kayè·yač *they call it* (-yaθ -).

call on. *v.t.* sahknę́hęhs *you call on someone* (-ahknę̧hę -).

calm. *adj.* tha'θa'tikę̧hrę́·'na·k *be calm!* (tha -. -(ę)'tikę̧hręT -).

calvary. *n.* yakuhsa'nę́·'nye' *calvary* (-ihsa'nę'nye' -).

calve. *v.i.* wa'nú'nęh *it calves* (-a'nu'= nę -).

camp. *n.* utá·'neh *camp* (-ta'n -).

can. *v.t.* ę̧hsθrahkwá·'nę' *you will can it* (-θrahkwa'nę -).

cancer. *n.* yaku'wáhra·ks *cancer* (-'wah= ra̲k -).

candid. *v.i.* ra'tikę̧hrarheryé·tih *he is candid* (-(ę)'-tikę̧hrarheryeti -).

candle. *n.* učí'reh *candle* (-či'r -); utú'-θreh uči'rę́·te *candle* (-tu'θr - -či'= ręte).

candle snuffer. *n.* yčči'rakwahnáhkhwa' *candle snuffer* (-či'ra̲kʷahnahkw -).

cane, walking. *n*. uhnǫhtíhčrch *walking cane* (-hnǫhtihčr -).

canine. *adj*. čirkyéha·ʼ *canine* (čir. #ké = ha·ʼ).

cannibal. *n*. ǫ·kweh raʼwáhraks *cannibal* (-ǫ°kʷe - -ʼwahrak -).

cannon. *n*. aʼnahúʼy *cannon* (aʼn -.#uʼy).

cannon ball. *n*. aʼnahúʼy úʼtawǫh *cannon ball* (aʼnahúʼy -aʼtawǫ -).

canoe. *n*. uhǫ·weh *canoe* (-hǫw -); usì·reh *canoe* (-sir -).

cape. *n*. uhnyáhθeh *cape* (-(i)hnyahθ -).

cape. *n*. yunhú·čǫʼ *cape (of land)* (-nhu = čǫ -).

capitol city. *n*. kataʼnakweʼnì·yuʼ *capitol city* (-ta'nakweʼniyu -).

capture. *v.t*. ǫhrayé·nǫ·ʼ *he will capture it* (-yenǫ -).

car. *n*. uʼθréhčreh *car* (-(i)ʼθrehčr -).

carbuncle. *n*. naʼkuʼúʼy *carbuncle* (naʼ = kuʼ.#úʼy).

carcass. *n*. uyáʼneh *carcass* (-yaʼn -).

card. *n*. uhyatǫ́hsteh *card* (-hyatǫhst -).

cardinal. *n*. čutkwará·ʼneht *cardinal* (-či -. -tkwara'nehT -).

care for. *v.t*. rúsθhar *he cares for it* (-asθhar -); raʼnwì·ranǫh *he cares for a child* (-a'nwiranǫ -).

careful. *adj*. raʼtikǫ́hrar *he is careful* (-(ǫ)ʼtikǫhrar -).

caress. *v.t*. naʼnǫθrǫtyáʼthaʼ *one caresses it* (-ǫ°θrǫtyaʼT -).

carnal. *adj*. aʼwnaʼkyéha·ʼ *carnal* (-aʼwT -.#keha·ʼ); uyerǫʼkyé·ha·ʼ *carnal* (-yer -.#keha·ʼ).

carousal. *n*. yuʼnahkaʼrà·yǫʼ *carousal* (-aʼnahka̱ʼrayǫ(T) -).

carouse. *v.i*. raʼnakhwerǫ́·tih *he carouses* (-aʼnakhwerǫti -).

carpenter. *n*. raʼnewyǫ́hǫ *carpenter* (-a = 'newyǫhw -); ranǫhsǫ́·tih *carpenter* (-nǫhsǫti -); ranǫhsawyǫ́hǫ *carpenter* (-nǫhsa̱wyǫhw -).

carry away. *v.t*. rahǫré·thaʼ *he carries it away* (-(i)hǫreT -); see: -ne -. -aʼθθku -.

carve. *v.i*. ráhču·ʼ *he carves it* (-hčuʼ -).

case. *n*. uʼnáhkweh *case* (-ʼnahkw -).

casement. *n*. newé·kanǫh *casement of a window* (-ne -. -ekanǫ -).

cash. *n*. uhwíhsteh *cash* (-hwihst -).

cashier. *n*. rahwíhstanǫh *cashier* (-hwih = stanǫ -).

cask. *n*. uʼnáhkweh *cask* (-ʼnahkw -).

cast. *v.t*. rú·ʼnyahθ *he casts (a mold)* (-a'ni -{dative II}).

cast a spell on. *v.t*. nehrurǫʼkǫ́·nyǫhs *it casts a spell on him* (-ne -. -rǫʼkǫni -).

castor oil. *n*. učiʼení·či kǫ̀·yeʼ *castor oil* (-čiʼeniči -iye -).

castrate. *v.t*. raʼnhǫhsawíhsyǫhs *he castrates* (-ʼnhǫhsawihsi -).

casual. *adj*. tyúʼtyehθ *casual* (ti -. -ʼtyeh -).

cat. *n*. tá·ku·θ *cat* (tá·ku·θ).

catch. *v.t*. ruyé·nǫ· *he has caught it* (-yenǫ -).

catch sight of. *v.t*. wáʼkkaht *I caught sight of it* (-kahT -); waʼakukáhkǫ·ʼ *it caught sight of one* (-kahkǫ -).

catch up to. *v.t*. ǫhrutáhkiʼw *it will catch up to him* (-tahkiʼw -); ruʼtéʼtyǫ *he caught up to it* (-ʼteʼti -).

catcher. *n*. rayenǫhsʼá·ka·ʼ *catcher (in a ball game)* (-yenǫ -.#aka·ʼ).

Tuscarora Pronunciation Key:

/a/ law; /e/ hat; /i/ pizza; /u/ tune; /ǫ/ hint; /č/ cheese; /h/ hoe; /m/ mother; /s/ same; /t/ do (before a vowel y, or w), too (elsewhere); /k/ gale (before a vowel y or w), kale (elsewhere); /n/ inhale (before a consonant or word-final), note (elsewhere), /r/ hiss (before a consonant or word-final), run (trilled as in Italian, elsewhere); /w/ cuff (before a consonant other than y or word-final), way (elsewhere); /y/ fish (before a consonant or word-final), you (elsewhere), /θ/ thing; /ʼ/ (the sound between the vowels in unh-unh); /·/ long vowel, /ʹ/ high pitch; /ˋ/ low pitch.

caterpillar. *n.* uhtyárhch *caterpillar* (-htyarh-); uhstwáhrarę *caterpillar* (-hstwahrar-).

catfish. *n.* čunęhwarí·yu· *catfish* (-či-. -nęhwariyu-); rukyé'nę·t *catfish* (rukyé'nę·t).

catnip. *n.* tá·ku·θ ka'ęhra·ks *catnip* (tá·ku·θ -'ęhrak-).

cattail. *n.* una'kwè·ya' *cattail* (-na'= kwey-).

cattle. *n.* usherętkę'na'nę' *cattle* (-she= ręt.#kę'na'nę').

caul. *n.* awú·θ'eh *caul* (-uθ'-).

cause. *n.* uríhwawęh *cause* (-rihwawę-).

cause. *v.t.* wa'nehá'nę *it caused it* (-a'= neha'T-); rarihwà·yęhs *he causes it* (-rihwayę-).

caution. *v.i.* rahθawęhra'č *he cautions* (-ahθawęhra'T-).

cave. *n.* yu'wnáhrarę *cave* (-a'wnah= rar-); yunhú·čę' *cave* (-nhučę-); yawętehstáhrarę· *cave* (-ętehstahrar-); yunę'náharę *cave* (-nę'nahrar-).

cavern. *n.* yunę'náharę *cavern* (-nę= 'nahrar-).

cavity. *n.* awę̀·yeh *cavity* (-ę°y-).

cedar. *n.* anę̇·'nya' *red cedar* (anę̇·'- nya'); uθuhrá'ta' *white cedar* (-θuh= ra't-).

cede. *v.t.* ra'ná·k'wahs *he cedes* (-a= 'nak'u-).

ceiling. *n.* ha' nyu'narę̀·war *ceiling* (-t-. -'naręwar-).

celebrate. *v.t.* ratawę́'nęh *he celebrates it* (-tawę'nę-).

celebrity. *n.* utawę'nę́hčreh *celebrity* (-tawę'nęhčr-).

celestial. *adj.* uręhyakęw'áh *celestial* (-ręhyakęw.#áh).

celibacy. *n.* utahkukę́'čreh *celibacy* (-tahkukę'čr-).

cell. *n.* ha' yutákwnę·t *cell (in a jail)* (-takwnęT-).

cement. *n.* wa'kęhraríhnę *cement*

cement (-a'kęhrarihT-); uθrę̀·weh *cement* (-θręw-).

cemetery. *n.* ye'nęhná·ryę *cemetery* (-'nęhnary-).

censure. *n.* yuthré'ahst *censure* (-athre'= ahst-).

censure. *v.t.* rahré'ahs *he censures it* (-hre'-).

center. *n.* ahsę̀·nę *center* (ahsę̀·nę).

central. *adv.* ahsęnęháh *central* (ahsęnę- háh); ahsęnęteháh *central* (ahsęnęte- háh).

cents. *n.* kwè·nihs *cents* (kwè·nihs).

certain. *adj.* kayahčę́·tih *it is certain* (-yahčęti-).

certain one. *n.* wa'nę́·te' *it is a certain one* (-a'nęte-); tikayakę́·te' *they are certain ones* (-ę°te-).

cervine. *adj.* akwehkyéha·' *cervine* (akʷ-. #keha·').

cessation. *n.* ha' yuhrę́whę· *cessation* (-hręwhę-).

chaff. *n.* urí'reh *chaff* (-ri'r-); utù·reh *chaff* (-tur-).

chain. *n.* urì·reh *chain* (-rir-).

chair. *n.* u'θkwéhseh *chair* (-'θkwehs-); uthečráhkweh *chair* (-athečrahkw-).

chairman. *n.* uthečráhkweh rę́'rę' *chairman* (-athečrahkw- -i'rę-).

chalice. *n.* úkθeh yeya'taráhstha' *chalice* (-kč- -ya'tarahst-).

chamber. *n.* ha' stá·kwi' *chamber* (stá·- kwi').

chance. *n.* utyé·nę· *chance* (-tyenę-); u'- tyéhę *chance* (-'tyeh-).

change. *v.i.* newat'níhahs *it changes* (-ne-. -at'niha-); nehrukę'né·tyę *he changes* (-ne-. -kę'neti-).

changeable. *adj.* yutkę'netyá'nę *it is changeable* (-atkę'netya'T-).

channel. *n.* kę' kahyęhę́·tih *channel* (kę' -(i)hyęhęti-).

character. *n.* uyaθę́hsteh *character* (-ya= θęhst-); u'nehyahrę́hčreh *character*

(-a'nehyahrẹhčr-); awẹnhe⁷ *character*
(-ẹ°nhe-).

charity. *n.* u⁷ni⁷nẹrẹhčreh *charity* (-a'ni =
'nẹrẹhčr-).

charm. *n.* yu⁷tikẹhru⁷ná·kwaht *charm*
(-(ẹ)⁷tikẹhru⁷nakʷahT-); úrhuht *charm*
(-rhuht-).

charming. *adj.* yu⁷tikẹhru⁷ná·kwaht
charming (-(ẹ)⁷tikẹhru⁷nakʷahT-).

chase. *v.t.* ratkáhne⁷ *he chases it* (-t(i) =
kahT-); ra⁷nẹtikáhne⁷ *he chases it*
(-a'nẹtikahT-).

chaste. *adj.* yú⁷θrẹn *it is chaste* (-a⁷ =
θrẹn-).

cheap. *adj.* kwáhst *cheap* (kwáhst); yu⁷-
ẹyakwáhsna⁷θ *it is cheap* (-⁷ẹyakwah =
sna⁷-).

cheat. *n.* nehru⁷nẹ⁷tikẹhkè·yẹ *he is a*
cheat (-ne-.-a'nẹ⁷tikẹhkẹy-); nehru⁷-
tikẹhkẹ·nyẹ *he is a cheat* (-ne-.
-(ẹ)⁷tikẹhkẹni-).

cheat. *v.i.* kaku⁷nẹhwá·tyẹ· *they cheated*
(-a'nẹhwati-); nehra⁷tikẹhkẹ·nyẹhs *he*
cheats (-ne-.-(ẹ)⁷tikẹhkẹni-).

cheating. *n.* u⁷tikẹhkẹnyẹhčreh *cheating*
(-(ẹ)⁷tikẹhkẹnyẹhčr-).

cheek. *n.* unhú⁷weh *cheek* (-nhu⁷w-).

cheer. *v.t.* rahsnyà·rẹ *he cheers it* (-hs =
nyar-).

cheese. *n.* čí·hs *cheese* (čí·hs).

cherry. *n.* čè·ri⁷ *wild cherry* (čè·ri⁷); è·ri⁷
wild cherry (è·ri⁷); tya⁷tarahkwáhnẹh
choke cherry (tya⁷tarahkwáhnẹh);
kwanya⁷tarahkwáhnẹh *choke cherries*
(kwanya⁷tarahkwáhnẹh).

chestnut. *n.* číhtkẹr *chestnut* (číhtkẹr).

chickadee. *n.* nekčirè·re *chickadee* (nek-

čirè·re).

chicken. *n.* tahuré·tik *chicken* (tahuré·-
tik).

chicken hawk. *n.* nwí⁷nwi⁷ *chicken*
hawk (nwí⁷nwi⁷).

chide. *v.t.* na⁷tikẹhraya⁷nè·rẹh *one*
chides another (-(ẹ)⁷tikẹhraya⁷nerẹ-).

chief. *n.* rakuwà·nẹ· *chief* (-uwan-);
ruyà·ner *confederate chief* (-ya =
n(e)(r)-).

chiefship. *n.* ukuwanẹhčreh *chiefship*
(-kuwanẹhčr-).

child. *n.* yeká·θ⁷ah *child* (-kaθ⁷ah); wa-
ka⁷nú⁷nẹ⁷ *my child* (-a'nu⁷nẹ⁷).

childish. *adj.* ekaθ⁷ahkyéha·⁷ *childish*
(-kaθ⁷ah.#keha·⁷).

chill. *n.* uhsi⁷thẹhčreh *chill* (-hsi⁷ =
thẹhčr-).

chill. *v.t.* rahsi⁷thẹhčrẹ·tih *he chills it*
(-hsi⁷thẹhčrẹti-); sáy wakyé·tih *it*
chills (scares) me (sáy -ẹ°ti-).

chilled. *adj.* ru⁷nẹnhatúhsnẹ *he is chilled*
(-a'nẹnhatuhsT-).

chimney. *n.* u⁷nyéhreh *chimney* (-⁷nye =
hr-).

chin. *n.* u⁷yhú·čeh *chin* (-⁷yhuč-).

chip. *v.t.* rahkarẹ·tih *he chips it* (-(a)h =
karẹti-).

chipmunk. n. čuhryú⁷kẹ *chipmunk* (čuhryú⁷kẹ).

chisel. *n.* úhnyeh *chisel* (-hny-).

choke. *v.i.* rúhsni⁷θ *he chokes* (-hsni⁷-);
nehrúhweks *he is choking* (-ne-.
-hwek-).

chokeberry. *n.* ruhtyéhrawik *chokeberry*
(ruhtyéhrawik).

choler. *n.* učhá⁷reh *choler* (-čha⁷r-).

Tuscarora Pronunciation Key:
/a/ law; /e/ hat; /i/ pizza; /u/ tune; /ẹ/ hint; /č/
cheese; /h/ hoe; /m/ mother; /s/ same; /t/ do
(before a vowel y, or w), too (elsewhere); /k/ gale
(before a vowel y or w), kale (elsewhere); /n/
inhale (before a consonant or word-final), note
(elsewhere), /r/ hiss (before a consonant or word-
final), run (trilled as in Italian, elsewhere); /w/ cuff
(before a consonant other than y or word-final),
way (elsewhere); /y/ fish (before a consonant or
word-final), you (elsewhere), /θ/ thing; /⁷/ (the
sound between the vowels in unh-unh); /·/ long
vowel, /´/ high pitch; /`/ low pitch.

chomp. *v.i.* rarí·khęh *he chomps* (-ri = khę-).

choose. *v.t.* rará·kwahs *he chooses it* (-raku-).

chop. *v.t.* rawé·θhęh *he chops* (-awe = θhę-).

chore. *n.* ha? yuríhwa?ne? *chore* (-rih = wa̲'ne-).

Christian. *adj.* rurihwiyúhsnę *he is Christian* (-rihwiyuhsT-).

Christianity. *n.* karihwiyúhsnahk *Christianity* (-rihwiyuhsT-); urihwiyúhčreh *Christianity* (-rihwiyuhčr-); urihwiyuhsnę́hčreh *Christianity* (-rihwiyuh = snęhčr-).

chubby. *adj.* ra?nhę́θteh *he is chubby* (-?nhęθt-).

church. *n.s.* yę?ruhčręhkhwá?kye *church* (-a?ruhčręhkw-.#ke).

church, go to. *v.i* ra?ruhčrę́hnęhs *he goes to church* (-a?ruhčręhT-).

churn. *v.i.* yenęhra?sárhuhs *one churns* (-nęhra?sarhu-); yenęhra?sarhúhstha? *one churns* (-nęhra?sarhuhsT-).

cider. *n.* sá·iter *cider* (sá·iter).

circle. *n.* uká?neh *circle* (-ka?n-).

circumstance. *n.* yuríhę·t *circumstance* (-rihęt-).

circumstantial. *adj.* yuríhwar *circumstantial* (-rihwa̲r-).

circus. *n.* kate?kwa?níhrę *circus* (-te? = kwa?nihr-).

city. *n.* utá·?neh *city* (-ta'n-).

civility. *n.* yutkwę́·nyęhst *civility* (-a = tkwęnyęhsT-).

civilization. *n.* u?nehyahrę́hčreh *civilization* (-a'nehyahręhčr-).

clabber. *n.* uθráhkweh *clabber* (-θrah = kw-).

clairvoyant. *n.* ra?rę́?na·č *clairvoyant* (-a?rę?naT-); nehrurę?kę́·nyę *clairvoyant* (-ne-.-rę?kęni-).

clam. *n.* u?túhseh *clam* (-?tuhs-).

clamor. *n.* u?náhka?reh *clamor* (-a?nah = ka?r-); uhsá·kwareh *clamor* (-hsa = k̈ar-).

clamor. *v.i.* račhakwara?níhtha? *he clamors* (-ačhak̈ara?nihT-).

clan. *n.* ur?ę́hseh *clan* (-(i)r?ęhs-).

clan mother. *n.* ukuwaná?tha? *clan mother* (-kuwana?T-).

clank. *v.i.* yú·kar *it clanks* (-kar-).

clap. *v.i.* nehrahθrár?ehs *he claps his hands* (-ne-.-hθrar?e(k)-).

clasp. *v.t.* ręhnę́θhar *he clasps it* (-(ę)hnęθha̲r-).

class. *n.* u?nyúhkweh *class* (-i?nyuhkw-).

classify. *v.t.* rę?nyuhkwę́·tih *he classifies it* (-i?nyuhkwęti-).

claw. *n.* učihskę́hkareh *claw* (-čihskęh = ka̲r-); uči?éhneh *claw* (-či?ehn-); utihtyúhčreh *claw* (-tihtyuhčr-).

claw. *v.i.* rahθharętyę́·kwahs *he claws* (-ahθha̲rętyęku-); *v.t.* raθkwehthará·kwahs *he claws it* (-θkwehtharaku-).

clay. *n.* utáwneh *clay* (-tawn-).

clean. *adj.* yú?θręn *it is clean* (-a?θręn-).

clean. *v.t.* rá·θręhs *he cleans it* (-θ(e)r-); nayu?θrę̀·nęht *it cleaned it* (-t-.-a?θręnęhT-).

clear. *adj.* awúhskę *clear* (-uhsk-).

clearing. *n.* uhę́?neh *clearing* (-(a)hę?n-).

cliff. *n.* yučtę́hreh *cliff on land or in water* (-čtęhr-).

climb. *v.i.* wa?kará·thę? *it climbed* (-rath-).

cling. *v.i.* rutkętyęyá?nę *he clung* (-atkę = tyęya?T-).

clip. *v.t.* rú?θkarhęhs *he clips it* (-u? = θka̲rh-).

clock. *n.* kawenę́·t?ehs *clock* (-wenęt = ?c(k)-).

clod. *n.* unęnyúhreh *clod (lump of earth)* (-nęnyuhr-).

close. *adj.* yawęhkwá·thę *it is close (as of trees)* (-ęhkwath-).

close. *v.t.* kayekwé·kę *they closed it* (-k̈ek-); see: -ęT-; see: -k̈ek-.

close a door. *v.i.* ručárhę *he has closed door* (-čarhu-).

cloth. *n.* úhneh *cloth* (-ihn-); úhskareh *cloth* (-hskar-); yęθkaręhkhwa' *cloth* (-iθkaręhkw-).

clothes. *n.* ukyerhúhčreh *clothes* (-ker=huhčr-); u'khà·reh *clothes* (-i'khar-); u'netyáhčreh *clothes* (-a'netyahčr-); u'netyáhsteh *clothes* (-a'netyahst-).

cloud. *n.* urá'θeh *cloud* (-ra'θ-); urá'θreh *cloud* (-ra'θr-); u'nęrhweh *cumulus cloud* (-a'nęrhw-).

clouded. *adj.* yura'θrú·tyę' *it is clouded (dotted with clouds)* (-ra'θrutyę-).

cloudy, get. *v.i.* ę'nęrhwa·t *it got cloudy* (-a'nęrhw-).

clover. *n.* áhsę tyu'ęhrę·t *clover* (áhsę ti-.-'ęhręT-).

clown. *n.* učisnuhkwehú'y *clown* (-čis=nuhkw-.#ú'y).

club. *n.* učíhkweh *club* (-čihkw-); utáhsneh *club (unhewn)* (-(ę)tahsn-); u'nwì·yeh *club (hewn)* (-'nwiy-); yenęhwar'éhstha' *war club* (-nęhwar='ehsT-).

clump. *n.* uthúhkweh *clump* (-athuhku-).

cluster. *n.* węti'nyuhkwę́·tih *cluster* (-(ę)ti'nyuhkwęti-); uθnę́'kweh *cluster* (-aθnę'kw-).

coach. *n.* utyá'neh *coach* (-tya'T-).

coagulate. *v.i.* kaθrahkwę́·tih *it coagulates* (-θrahkwęti-).

coagulation. *n.* uθráhkweh *coagulation* (-θrahkw-).

coal. *n.* učihę́hreh *coal* (-čihęhr-).

coalesce. *v.i.* ę́·či wá·'nę' *it coalesces* (ę́·či -a'nę-).

coarse. *adj.* à·wur *coarse* (-ur-).

coast. *n.* ha' tiwakę́hya·t *the coast* (ti-.-akę́hyaT-); kę' tiwakęhya'ná·'nyc' *the coast* (kę' ti-.-akęhya'na'nyc'-).

coat. *n.* ukyerhúhčreh *coat* (-kerhuhčr-).

cobweb. *n.* unę́'rch *cobweb* (-nę'r-).

cock. *n.* tahuré·tik ka'níha· *cock* (tahuré·tik -'niha-).

cock's comb. *n.* ukyé'θrch *cock's comb* (-ke'θr-); ukú'čeh *cock's comb* (-ku'č-).

coffee. *n.* káhwih *coffee* (káhwih).

coffin. *n.* urętú'čreh *coffin* (-rętu'čr-).

coil. *n.* u'ę̀·wareh *coil* (-'ęwar-).

colander. *n.* yakękuhnáhkhwa' *colander* (-ę̊kuhnahkw-).

cold. *adj.* á·thu' *cold* (á·thu'); ka'čá'tuh *I am cold* (-a'ča'tuh-); á·thu' wakrì·yuhs *I am cold* (á·thu' -r(i)yu-).

cold. *n.* hú's *cold (disease)* (-hu's-).

cold, have a. *v.i.* ruthu'seryé'θe· *he has a cold* (-athu'seryę(T)-{dative I}); hú's ratá'rakęw ruyé·nę·t *he has a head cold* (-hu's- -(ę)ta'rakęw -ye=nę-).

collar. *n.* uhá'θeh *collar* (-ha'(č)-).

collect. *v.t.* rarúhčręh *he collects it* (-ruhčrę-).

cologne. *n.* neyurhuθhwahnę́hkhwa' *cologne* (-ne-.-rhuθhwahnęhkw-).

colonel. *n.* rahsęnuwà·nę *colonel* (-hsę=nuwan-).

color. *n.* uhθúhkweh *color* (-ahθuhkw-).

colored. *adj.* yúhθuhθ *it is colored* (-ahθuh-).

colt. *n.* aha·θ'áh *colt* (aha·θ.#áh).

column. *n.* ú·treh *column* (-atr-).

Tuscarora Pronunciation Key:
/a/ law; /e/ hat; /i/ pizza; /u/ tune; /ę/ hint; /č/ cheese; /h/ hoe; /m/ mother; /s/ same; /t/ do (before a vowel y, or w), too (elsewhere); /k/ gale (before a vowel y or w), kale (elsewhere); /n/ inhale (before a consonant or word-final), note (elsewhere), /r/ hiss (before a consonant or word-final), run (trilled as in Italian, elsewhere); /w/ cuff (before a consonant other than y or word-final), way (elsewhere); /y/ fish (before a consonant or word-final), you (elsewhere), /θ/ thing; /'/ (the sound between the vowels in unh-unh); /·/ long vowel, /́/ high pitch; /̀/ low pitch.

comb. *n.* unę'yúhčreh *comb* (-nę' = yuhčr -).

come. *v.i.* íhraws *he comes* (-aw -); náhre' *he is coming* (-t -. -e -).

come down. *v.i.* nęčnęhsná'či *it came down* (-t -. -ačnęhsT -. #hči).

come forth. *v.i.* see: -itkę' -.

come from. *v.i.* nwaré·kwę· *it comes from* (-t -. -ar(e)ku -); thrawenę'nę *he came from* (-t -. -enę'T -).

come off. *v.i.* ę'ranę'náhsi' *it came off* (-a'ranę'nahsi -).

come to. *v.t.* rawú'θch *it comes to him* (-aw -{dative I}).

come to an end. *v.i.* yú·'nu'kt *it came to an end* (-a'nu'kT -).

comet. *n.* u'nihsę̀·reh yuręryúhkwę·t *comet* (-'nihsęr - -ręryuhkwęT -).

comfort. *v.t.* aryę'na'tikęhrę́·thuht *that one comfort another* (-(ę)'tikęh = ręthuhT -); neyę'nę'tikęhrayé·nę· *one comforts another* (-ne -. -(ę)'tikęhra = yenę -); na'tikę́hrayęhs *one comforts another* (-(ę)'tikęhrayę(T) -).

comic. *adj.* yutérhya't *it is comic* (-ter = hya'T -).

comma. *n.* učísnuhkweh *comma* (-čis = nuhkw -).

command. *n.* uwę́·teh *command* (-węt -).

command. *v.i.* ra'nénha'θ *he commands* (-a'nenha' -).

commemorate. *v.t.* θhręnehyarhuhkwá·tih *he commemorates it* (-či -. -ęnehyahr = huhkw -{dative III}).

commend. *v.t.* rakyerhę́·'ne' *he commends it* (-kerhęT -).

commerce. *n.* kahnę̀·wayę't *commerce* (-hnęwayę'T -).

commit cruelty. *v.i.* wa'tkayę'na'na'tę-hękaryá'thahθ *they committed cruelty* (-ne -. -a'tęhękarya'T -{dative II}).

common. *adj.* awéhsayę' *common* (-eh = sayę -).

commonly. *adv.* kwè·ni' *commonly* (kwè·ni'); yutká'ne' *commonly* (-tka'T -).

commotion. *n.* u'tikęhkarę́'raht *commotion* (-(ę)'tikęhkarę'rahT -).

companionship. *n.* unahyę́hčreh *companionship* (-(ę)na·hyęhčr -).

company. *n.* u'nyúhkweh *company* (-i' = nyuhkw -).

compare. *v.t.* nehrá·'na·č *he compares it* (-ne -. -a'naT -).

compassion. *n.* čí'nęhs *compassion* (čí'-nęhs).

compassionate. *adj.* ru'ni'nę̀·rę *he is compassionate* (-a'ni'nęr -).

compete for. *v.t.* rahθkyénha' *he is competing for it* (-ahθkenha -); nehra-tkę́·nyęhs *he competes for it* (-ne -. -atkęni -).

competitor. *n.* ha' rahθkyénhahs *competitor* (-ahθkenha -).

complain. *v.i.* ra'nęnhę́·tha' *he complains* (-a'nęnhęT -); kayę'na'rihwa'-tyę'ná·ti· *they complained* (-rihwa' = tyęT -{dative III}).

complete. *adj.* tkayè·ri' *it is complete* (-t -. -yeri -); wekayè·ri' *it is complete* (-yah -. -yeri -).

complexion. *n.* uhskaté·teh *complexion* (-hskatet -).

compliment. *v.t.* na'tawę́'nęh *one compliments another* (-tawę'nę -).

concave. *adj.* neyuhęwayę'náhkę *concave* (-ne -. -hęwayę'nahkw -).

conceal. *v.t.* wa'nyé'nehkw *one concealed it* (-'nehkw -).

conception. *n.* utè·reh *conception* (-(ę) = ter -).

concerning. *prep.* na' urihwá'kye *concerning* (na' -rihwa'ke).

conclude. *v.i.* wahru'tikęhkyè·ya't *he concluded* (-(ę)'tikęhkeya'T -); see: -ęT -.

condemn. *v.t.* raríhwakę'č *he condemns* (-rihwakę'T -).

condemnation. *n.* kahrewa'nę́hčra' *condemnation* (-hrewa'nęhčr-).

condense. *v.t.* raθnę́htha' *he condenses it* (-aθnęhT-).

Condolence Ceremony. *n.* Kayę'nę́·ta'θ *Condolence Ceremony* (-a'nęt(a')-).

conduct oneself. *v.i.* naka'nyéhsaye'r *I conduct myself* (-t-.-a'nyehsayer-).

cone. *n.* uhsè·yeh *cone of a tree* (-hsey-); uhsú'θreh *cone (shape)* (-hsu'θr-)

confederate. *v.t.* kakhenęhsyętí'nę *I have confederated them* (-nęhsyęti'T-).

confide in. *v.t.* ękayetiheθę́hek *they shall confide in it* (-tiheθ-{dative III}).

confidence. *n.* urharáhčreh *confidence* (-rharahčr-).

confident. *adj.* rurhà·re' *he is confident* (-rhar-).

confirmation. *n.* u'tikęhrahtiráhtha' *confirmation* (-(ę)'tikęhrahtirahT-).

confusion. *n.* u'náhka'reh *confusion* (-a'nahka'r-).

congregate. *v.i.* kayę'teyarúhčręh *they congregate* (-(ę)'teyaruhčrę-).

congregation. *n.* kę'nyuhkwí·yu· *congregation* (-i'nyuhkwiyu-).

congress. *n.* kahwenę́·tih *congress* (-hwe=nęti-); uhwenętíhsteh *congress* (-hwe=nętihst-).

conifer. *n.* kahseyę́·tih *conifer* (-hse=yęti-).

conjure. *v.i.* ra'tyéhę *he conjures* (-'tyeh-).

conquer. *v.t.* wa'kakhe'θhę̀·ni' *I conquer them* (-(i)'θhęni-).

conquered. *adj.* kakawękwé'ę *they are*

conquered (-ę°kʷe'-).

conscience. *n.* u'nchyahrę́hčreh *conscience* (-a'nchyahręhčr-).

considerate. *adj.* ruya'turéhčrayę' *he is considerate* (-ya'turehčrayę(T)-).

contemptible. *adj.* yukęhrę́·tyaht *it is contemptible* (-kęhretyahT-).

continent. *n.* uhwenętíhsteh *continent* (-hwenętihst-).

continuous. *adj.* tičunuwéhnę *continuous* (tičunuwéhnę).

contract. *v.i.* ra'rihwíhs'ahs *he contracts* (-a'rihwihs'a-).

contribute to. *v.t.* rarù·ręh *he contributes to it* (-rurę-).

control. *v.t.* thrawę'tikę́hnę' *he controls it* (-t-.-(ę)'tikęhnę-).

converse. *v.i.* ráhtharę *he conversed* (-hthar-).

convex. *adj.* yutkwa'níhrę *it is convex* (-tkwa'nihr-).

convey. *v.t.* ra'nętiyé·tha' *he conveys* (-aT-.-ętiyeT-).

coo-coo. *n.* narú'naru' *coo-coo* (narú'-naru').

cook. *v.i.* ratkáhnęh *he cooks* (-atkah=nę-); aryù·rihk *that it be cooked* (-rih-).

cook. *v.t.* wa'ekáhnę·' *one cooked it* (-kahnę-); raríhtha' *he cooks it* (-rihT-).

cook a meal. *v.i.* wa'kyekhwę́·ti' *I cook a meal* (-khwęti-).

cool. *adj.* yučá'tuh *it is cool* (-ča'tuh-).

cool. *v.t.* rača'túhstha' *he cools it* (-ča'=tuhsT-).

copper. *n.* kwè·ni' *copper* (kwè·ni');

---

kwè·nihs *copper* (kwè·nihs); uʔnęwe-
hę̀·we *copper* (-ʔnęw-.#ęwe).

copperish. *adj.* uʔnęwehę̀·we kwę́ *copperish* (-ʔnęw-.#ęwe kwę́).

copulate. *v.t.* wahratíʔka·t *he copulates*
(-tiʔk-).

copy. *n.* nekahswaʔteʔnáhkwę *copy*
(-ne-.-hswaʔte'nahkw-); utáhskweh
copy (-tahskw-).

cord. *n.* uhsì·reh *cord* (-hsir-).

core. *n.s.* awęnhéʔčreh *core* (-ę̓nheʔčr-).

cork. *n.* uhseʔyúhčreh *cork* (-hseʔyu-).

corkscrew. *n.* yehseʔyuhčráhthaʔ *corkscrew* (-hseʔyuhčrahT-).

corn. *n.* unę́heh *corn* (-nęh-); kanę́hačiʔ
black corn (-nęha̲či-); unù·reh *braided
string of corn* (-nur-); kanęhakáθneʔ
flint corn (-nęhakaθne-); kanęhakę̀·rat
flour corn (-nęha̲kęrat-); uhskę̀·neh
unę́heh *ghost corn* (-hskęn- -nęh-);
utyú·θer *green corn* (-tyuθ(e)r-); unę-
hatyú·θer *green corn* (-nęha̲tyuθer-);
unęháhskwariʔ *the mother-corn, that
is, the corn from which a certain kind
may have been derived* (-nęhahskwa̲=
ri-); unęhaθríʔreh *sweet corn* (-nęha̲=
θriʔr-); kanú·ta·ʔ *white corn* (-nuta-);
unęhahwaryá·kęʔ *white corn* (-nęhah=
waryakę-); kanęhakę̀·rat *white corn*
(-nęhakęrat-); neyuthahahkwáʔthaʔ
ground, baked, white corn (-ne-.-atha=
hahkwaʔT-); kanúʔči·t *calico corn*
(-nuʔčit).

corn bread. *n.* kanęhúčhęʔ *corn bread*
(-nęhučhę(T)-).

corn cob. *n.* ukawéhseh *corn cob* (-ka=
wehs-).

corn pounder. *n.* uʔtikáhneh *corn pounder* (-ʔtikahn-).

corn roaster. *n.* yutáʔche·θ *corn roaster*
(-taʔcheθ-).

corn shuck. *n.* uhtyè·reh *corn shuck*
(-htyer-).

corn silk. *n.* ukrúʔrch *corn silk* (-kruʔr-).

corn soup. *n.* urà·nch *corn soup* (-ran-).

corner. *n.* yunhú·čęʔ *it is a corner*
(-nhučę-).

corner. *v.t.* wahranhučę́ʔthahθ *he cornered it* (-nhučęʔT-{dative I}).

corner, be in a. *v.i.* see: -hsuʔθhę-.

cornhusk. *n.* utù·reh *cornhusk* (-tur-).

cornplanter. *n.* yenęhakwaʔnáhkhwaʔ
cornplanter (-nęhakwaʔnahkw-).

corpse. *n.* uyáʔneh *corpse* (-yaʔn-).

corpulence. *n.* ukęθrę́hneh *corpulence*
(-kęθręhn-).

correct. *adj.* tkarihwayè·riʔ *correct* (-t-.
-rihwa̲yeri-); wekayè·riʔ *it is correct*
(-yah-.-yeri-).

corrode. *v.i.* wahčaʔnáhkhwaʔ *it corrodes*
(-ahčaʔnahkw-).

cost. *n.* ú·kareh *cost* (-ka̲r-); uʔę̀·yeh *cost*
(-ʔęy-).

cost. *v.i.* yuʔę̀·yayęʔ *it costs* (-ʔęya̲=
yę(T)-).

cottage. *n.* unę́hseh *cottage* (-nęhs-).

cotton. *n.* uhsirehę̣tíh *cotton* (-hsir-.
#ętíh); ukrì·reh *cotton* (-krir-).

cottonwood tree. *n.* kahskęʔnaraʔθʔúʔy
cottonwood tree (-hskęʔna̲raʔθ-.#uʔy).

cough. *v.i.* wahrahskrá·θaʔ *he coughed*
(-hskraθ-).

council. *n.* uhwenętíhsteh *council* (-hwe=
nętihst-).

council house. *n.* yętkęnihsʔáʔthaʔ *council house* (-atkęnihsʔaʔT-).

councilman. *n.* ratkęníhsʔahs *councilman*
(-atkęnihsʔa-).

counsel. *v.i.* kakutkęníhsʔę *they counseled* (-atkęnihsʔa-); kakučisnę́·ti· *they
counsel* (-čisnęti-).

count. *v.i.* ráhra·č *he counts* (-hraT-).

countenance. *n.* uhskaté·teh *countenance*
(-hskatet-).

country. *n.* kęʔ ratá·kreʔ *his country* (kęʔ
-tak(e)r-).

course. *n.* naʔ tyuhahúʔnę· *course (e.g.,
for a race)* (naʔ ti-.-(a)hahuʔnę-).

court. *n.* kačí·snayę⁷ *court of justice*
(-čisnayę(T)-).

court. *v.t.* sahknę́hęhs *you court someone*
(-ahknęhę-).

courteous. *adj.* rawętahrú⁷nę *he is courteous* (-wętahru⁷T-).

cousin. *n.* rurá⁷θe⁷ *cousin* (-ara⁷θe⁷);
akyará⁷se⁷ *the two of us are cousins,
my cousin* (-ara⁷se⁷); ákči⁷ *my older
older maternal female cousin* (-hči⁷);
akhryáhči⁷ *my older maternal male
cousin* (-hryahči⁷).

cousin's husband. *n.* akà·ra⁷ *my cousin's
husband* (-ara⁷).

cousin's wife. *n.* akara⁷áh *my cousin's
wife* (-ara⁷áh).

cover. *n.* uwerhúhčreh *cover* (-awer=
huhčr-).

cover. *v.t.* rawérhuhs *he covers it*
(-awerhu-); íhruč *he covers it* (-ur-);
rù·ruks *he covers it* (-uruk-); see:
-ur-.

cover over. *v.i.* yutíyheh *it covered over
it* (-tiyheh-).

cover with ice. *v.i.* kawí·suč *it covers
with ice* (-wisur-).

covering. *n.* awú·θ⁷eh *covering* (-uθ⁷-);
urí⁷weh *covering* (-ri⁷w-).

covet. *v.t.* ratkwè·rihθ *he covets* (-a=
tkwerih-).

covetousness. *n.* uhθkyenhá⁷ę *covetousness* (-ahθkenha⁷-).

cow. *n.* yunęhrá⁷sa·t *cow* (-nęhra⁷saT-);
kanęhra⁷sá·ku⁷ *cow* (-nęhra⁷saku-); u-
shé·rę·t *cow* (-sheręt).

coward. *n.* ratihčayę́hah *he was a coward*
(-tihčayęhah-).

cowardly. *adj.* tihčayę́hah *cowardly* (tih-
čayę́hah).

coy. *adj.* ručheyà·rę *he is coy* (-čheyar-).

crab. *n.* ruhsè·nu⁷ *crab* (ruhsè·nu⁷).

crab apple. *n.* kwę⁷ráhsi⁷ *crab apple*
(kwę⁷ráhsi⁷).

crack. *n.* neyu⁷nú·rę· *crack* (-ne-.
-a'nurę-).

cradle board. *n.* urháhsteh *cradle board*
(-rhahst-).

craft. *n.* uwyę̀·neh *craft* (-wy(ęn)-);
uyu⁷nę́hčreh *craft* (-yu⁷nęhčr-).

crafty. *adj.* rutkweru⁷nawyę́hęh *he is
crafty* (-atkweru⁷nawyęhę-); ra⁷ne-
wyę́hę *he is crafty* (-a'newyęhw-).

cramps, have. *v.i.* ruyè·nęhs *he has
cramps* (-yenę-).

cranberry. *n.* tú⁷ks *cranberry* (tú⁷ks);
tú⁷ks wá·⁷nęh *cranberry* (tú⁷ks
-a'nę-).

crane, white. *n.* ruhákwaręt *white crane*
(ruhákwaręt).

craziness. *n.* uręhya⁷náhčreh *craziness*
(-ręhya⁷nahčr-).

crazy. *adj.* ruręhyá⁷nahs *he is crazy*
(-ręhya⁷T-).

crazy, drive. *v.t.* nehręhya⁷nahčrę́·tih *he
drives another crazy* (-ne-.-ęhya⁷=
nahčręti-).

cream. *n.* wa⁷nyé·ther *cream* (-a'nye=
thar-).

create. *v.i.* ra⁷newyęnę́·tih *he creates*
(-a'newyęnęti-).

credible. *adj.* kwęhs aryutuwę́hnęk *it is
credible* (kwęhs -tuwęhT-).

credit. *v.t.* natká·rya⁷ks *one credits another* (-karya⁷k-).

---

creditor. *n.* ra'ę̀·ya'ks *creditor* (-'ę = ya'k -).

creek. *n.* kì·nę' *creek* (kì·nę').

creep. *v.i.* ęhrę'tiθrę́·θę' *he will creep* (-ę'tiθrę́θę -).

crescent. *n.* yuhihte'črahù·rę'θ *crescent* (-hihte'čr<u>a</u>hurę' -).

crevice. *n.* neyu'nú·rę· *crevice* (-ne-. -a'nurę -).

cricket. *n.* kanę́hsanęh *cricket* (-nęh = s<u>a</u>nę -); nekčihę́hrę·t *cricket* (nekči- hę́hrę·t).

crime. *n.* urihwáhraht *crime* (-rihwah = rahT -).

cripple. *n.* rata'yúhkwayę' *he is a cripple* (-ta'yuhkw<u>a</u>yę(T) -).

crispness. *n.* učę́'weh *crispness* (-čę'w -).

criticize. *v.t.* na'rihwakę́θheh *one criticizes another* (-rihw<u>ak</u>ę́θhe -); nyę'- na'rihu'kná·tih *one criticizes another* (-t -. -rihu'kT -{dative III}).

crock. *n.* uti'nę́hkweh *crock* (-ti' = nęhkw -).

crocodile. *n.* suká·we·θ *crocodile* (suká· we·θ).

crooked. *adj.* neyu'nú'knę· *it is crooked* (-ne-. -a'nu'kT -); neyu'nu'knę́·kwę *it is crooked* (-ne-. -a'nu'knęku -).

crop hair. *v.i.* na'ne'rakwáhtha' *one crops another's hair* (-e'r<u>ak</u>ʷahT -).

cross. *adj.* ručha'rá·ksę· *he is cross* (-čha'raks -).

cross. *n.* uwyáhseh *cross* (-wyahs -).

cross. *v.t.* see: -ya'θ(e)r -.

cross over. *v.t.* wahrę́hya'k *he crossed over it* (-(i)hya'k -).

crossroads. *n.* yuthaharúhčrę' *crossroads* (-ath<u>a</u>h<u>a</u>ruhčrę -); kę' yuthaharúhčrę' *crossroads* (kę' -ath<u>a</u>h<u>a</u>ruhčrę -).

crosswise. *adj.* neyúthręw *crosswise* (-ne-. -athręhw -).

crow. *n.* á·'a·' *crow* (á·'a·').

crowd. *n.* u'tè·yeh *crowd* (-(ę)'tey -); yu'teyu'à·wi' *crowd* (-(ę)'teyu'awi -).

crown. *n.* učihskęnyá'čreh *crown of the head* (-čihskęnya'čr -).

crucify. *v.t.* na'newyahsę́htha' *one crucifies another* (-wyahsęhT -).

crumb. *n.* učę́'weh *crumb* (-čę'w -).

crush. *v.t.* rahwačí'ehs *he crushes it* (-hwači'e(k) -); wa'thrahwár'ek *he crushed it* (-ne-. -hwar'e(k) -).

crust. *n.* učę́'weh *crust* (-čę'w -); u'- néhseh *crust* (-'nehs -).

cry. *v.i.* neká·θnar *I am crying* (-aθnar -).

crystal. *n.* uwí·seh *crystal* (-wis -).

cucumber. *n.* učhé'weh *cucumber* (-čhe'w -).

cucumber root, Indian. *n.* yú'θhara'r *Indian cucumber root* (-'θh<u>a</u>rar -).

cull. *v.t.* rarę́·kwahs *he culls it* (-ręku -).

cultivate. *v.i.* nehręhra'né·tyęhs *he cultivates* (-ne-. -ęhr<u>a</u>'netyę -).

cultiver. *n.* u'rhúhkweh *cultiver* (-'rhuh = kw -).

culture. *n.* urihwakà·yę' *culture* (-rih = wakayę -).

cup. *n.* úkθeh *cup* (-kč -); u'tíhsneh *cup* (-'tihsn -).

cupboard. *n.* utí'θreh *cupboard* (-ti' = θ(e)r -).

curable. *adj.* yu'tyá·kęwst *curable* (-a' = tyakęhwsT -).

cure. *v.i.* yú·thwę· *it cures* (-thwę -); *v.t.* ahru'tyá·kęw *that it cure him* (-a' = tyakęhw -); ę́θkakawęnę́hkwa't *it will cure them* (-či -. -ęnęhkwa'T -).

curiosity. *n.* uhskwatkę́'čreh *curiosity* (-hskwatkę'čr -); neyurihwahskané·kę·t *curiosity* (-ne-. -rihw<u>a</u>hskanekęT -).

curious. *adj.* yuyáhčih *it is curious* (-yahč -).

curl of hair. *n.* učinę́'thereh *curl of hair* (-činę'ther -); unęčí'thereh *a curl of hair* (-nęči'th<u>e</u>r -).

currant, wild black. *n.* θkahę́'θkahę' *wild black currant* (θkahę́'θkahę').

current. *n.* úhtaweh *current of water*

(-ht<u>a</u>w-).

curse. *v.i.* rayeθá'tha' *he curses* (-ye = θa'T-).

cursing. *n.* kahrewa'néhčra' *cursing* (-hrewa'nehčr-).

curtain. *n.* yuhskareyá'tha' *curtain* (-hs = k<u>a</u>reya'T-).

curve. *n.* ukwá'neh *curve* (-kwa'n-).

curved. *adj.* neyu'nú'kne· *it is curved* (-ne-.-a'nu'kT-).

cushion. *n.* uté'kweh *cushion* (-te'kw-).

custard. *n.* uθráhkweh *custard* (-θrah = kw-).

customarily. *adv.* ke·θ *customarily* (ke·θ).

cut. *v.t.* rahrè·nahs *he cuts it* (-hren-); ranéhkarehs *he cuts hair* (-nehk<u>a</u>r-); wa'kyé·tiht *I cut it into pieces* (-e̜° = tihT-); rakwáhtha' *he cuts it off* (-k^wahT-); ruhará·kwahs *he cuts off the end* (-uh<u>a</u>raku-); ráhču·' *he cuts it up* (-hču'-).

cute. *adj.* yekwáhye *she is cute* (-kwahy-).

cutting block. *n.* u'θkwéhseh *cutting block* (-'θkwehs-).

cylinder. *n.* neyu'θkwehsukwahná·ti· *cylinder* (-ne-.-'θkwehsukwahT-{dative III}).

cymbal. *n.* úkθeh *cymbal* (-kč-).

D

dagger. *n.* uhsá'ke'neh *dagger* (-hsa'= ke̜'n-).

daily. *n.* wa'úrhe' *daily* (-rhe'-); ur-he'ekyéha·' *daily* (-rhe'-.#keha·').

daisy. *n.* uθehrú'ne' *field daisy* (-θeh = ru'n-).

damage. *v.t.* rakare̜·nih *he damages it* (-kare̜ni-).

damn. *v.t.* na'rihwaksa'á·tih *one damns another* (-rihwaksa'T-{dative III}).

damp. *adj.* yawù·re' *it is damp* (-ure-).

dams, make. *v.i.* rawihré·tih *he makes dams* (-wihre̜ti-).

damsel. *n.* yeθrà·yeh *damsel* (-θray-).

dance. *n.* utkwáhčreh *dance* (-atkwah = čr-).

dance. *v.i.* nehrátkhwa' *he dances* (-ne-.-atkw-).

dandelion. *n.* ká·ra· *dandelion* (ká·ra·); uyewaksta'kyéha·' *dandelion* (-ye = waksta'kyeha·').

danger. *n.* u'tiké̜htaht *danger* (-(e̜)'= tike̜htahT-).

dangerous. *adj.* yu'tiké̜htaht *dangerous* (-(e̜)'tike̜htahT-).

dangle. *v.t.* see: -kehsT-.

dare. *v.i.* ra'ne̜htirá'tha' *he dares* (-a = 'ne̜htira'T-).

dark. *adj.* yuhθá·the̜ *it is dark* (-ah = θathu-); e̜'nyuhθé̜·'nara' *it will be dark* (-t-.-ahθe̜'n<u>a</u>r-); yawéhθaye̜' *it is dark* (-ehθ<u>a</u>ye̜-).

dark, get. *v.i.* wa'nwahθé̜'nayé̜·'na' *it got dark* (-t-.-ahθe̜'n<u>a</u>ye̜(T)-); see: -ahθe̜T-.

darken. *v.t.* rahθé̜'nárhuhs *he darkens it* (-ahθe̜'narhu-); rehθayé̜hstha' *he darkens it* (-ehθ<u>a</u>ye̜hsT-).

darken out. *v.i.* yutíyheh *it darkened it*

---

out (-tiyheh-).

darkness. *n.* uhθǫ́·ʔneh *darkness* (-ah=θęT-).

dart. *n.* áʔteh *dart* (-aʔt-).

dart forth. *v.i.* wewathweʔnę́·tyęhs *it darts forth* (-yah-.-athweʔnęti-).

date. *v.t.* rę́·ʔnar *he dates it* (-ęʹnar-).

daughter. *n.* wakaʔnúʔnęʔ *my daughter* (-aʹnuʔnęʔ); khehsę́·te *my daughter* (-hsęte).

daughter-in-law. *n.* ákθaʔw *my daughter-in-law* (-θaʔw-).

dawn. *n.* nyawę́·ʔnu·t *dawn* (-t-.-ęʹnut); nawęʔnahrę́hwę *dawn* (-t-.-ęʹnah=ręhw-); nayúrhęʔ *very early dawn* (-t-.-rhęʔ-); nayurhęʔúʔy *very early dawn* (-t-.-rhęʔ-.#úʔy).

day. *n.* awę́·ʔneh *day* (-ęT-); see: -rhę-.

day after tomorrow. *n.* íhsʔę yęčúrhęʔ *day after tomorrow* (íhsʔę -yah+či-.-rhęʔ-).

daybreak. *n.* nayúrhęʔ *daybreak* (-t-.-rhęʔ-); nayurhęʔúʔy *daybreak* (-t-.-rhęʔ-.#úʔy).

daylight. *n.* waʔúrhęʔ *daylight* (-rhęʔ-).

daytime. *n.* awę́·ʔneh *daytime* (-ęT-).

dazzle. *v.i.* nehrukahkweθrá·theʔ *it dazzles him* (-ne-.-kahkweθrathe-).

dead. *n.* haʔ kakúčʔę *the dead* (-ačʔa-).

deaf. *adj.* nehrahęhnakwé·kę *he is deaf* (-ne-.-hęhnakʷek-).

dearth. *n.* wakę̀·reʔ *dearth* (-akęre-).

death. *n.* kanęhsatarí·nę·ʔ *death* (-nęhsa=tarinę-).

debate. *v.i.* nehrurihwakyénhę *he debates* (-ne-.-rihwakenha-).

debt. *n.* ú·kareh *debt* (-kar-); uʔę̀·yeh *debt* (-ʔęy-).

debt, in. *adj.* ruʔęytę́ʔrę *he is in debt* (-ʔęytęʔr-).

debt, run into. *v.i.* ratʔęyityę́ʔthaʔ *he runs into debt* (-atʔęyityęʔT-).

decanter. *n.* haʔ yakyekarahkwáhthaʔ wekanù·ręh *decanter* (-ekarahkwahT-

-ekanurę-).

decay. *v.i.* wúhriʔθ *it decays* (-uhriʔ-); kayęhwanę́·tih *it decays* (-yęhwanęti-).

December. *n.* kuhserhęhé·θuʔ *December* (kuhserhęhé·θuʔ).

decency. *n.* yutkwę́·nyęhst *decency* (-a=tkwęnyęhsT-).

decently. *adv.* yutkwęnyęhsnęhá·ʔnyeʔ *decently* (-atkwęnyęhsnęhaʹnyeʔ-).

decide. *v.i.* nehrurihwayęʔná·θe· *he decides* (-ne-.-rihwayęT-{dative I}); nyakuʔtikęhrá·ʔnęʔ *one has decided* (-t-.-(ę)ʔtikęhraʹnę-).

decide for. *v.t.* ętkęʔtikéhnęʔ *I will decide for you* (-t-.-(ę)ʔtikęhnę-).

decisive. *adj.* neyurihwayę́·ʔnaht *it is decisive* (-ne-.-rihwayęʹnahT-); karihwakʔúhsyęhs *decisive* (-rihwakʔuh=si-).

declaration. *n.* haʔ neyuʔrihukwáhnę· *declaration* (-ne-.-aʔrihukʷahT-).

decorate. *v.t.* rayaʔtahstę̀·nih *he decorates it* (-yaʔtahstęni-).

decrepit. *adj.* raʔnáwsteʔ *he is decrepit* (-aʹnawst-).

dedicate. *v.t.* ranęhsúhar *he dedicates it* (-nęhsuhar-).

deduct. *v.t.* thrará·kwahs *he deducts* (-t-.-raku-).

deduction. *n.* yurá·kwę *deduction* (-ra=ku-).

deer. *n.* á·kweh *deer* (akʷ-).

deface. *v.t.* rukrę́ʔthaʔ *he defaces it* (-u=kręʔT-).

defame. *v.t.* raręhsarę́·kwahs *he defames* (-ręhsaręku-).

defeat. *v.t. I defeated another* (-(i)ʔθhę=ni-).

defecate. *v.i.* rahtkíʔyę· *he defecated* (-ahtkiʔyę-).

defend. *v.t.* ruʔnahθkyénhę *he defends it* (-aʹnahθkenha-); nakkyerhuʔnárhęhk *defend me from it!* (-kerhuʔnarhu-).

defender. *n.* yęʔnęʔneʔnáhkhwaʔ *defend-*

er (-a'nę'ne'nahkw-).

defer. *v.i.* ru'tíθkwahs *he defers* (-'tiθ= ku-).

definitely. *adv.* utukę́'ę *definitely* (-tu= kę'-).

deflower. *v.i.* rači'čihstúhskwahs *he deflowers it* (-či'čihstuhsku-).

deformed. *adj.* nehru'nyerę́hnyę' *he is deformed* (-ne-.-a'nyeręhnyę-).

degrade. *v.t.* rahsęwiré·tha' *he degrades it* (-hsęwireT-).

dejected. *adj.* ru'tikęhrę́'ę *he is dejected* (-(ę)'tikęhrę'-).

delay. *v.i.* račhayá'tha' *he delays* (-a= čhaya'T-); ru'tíθkwahs *he delays* (-'tiθku-); *v.t.* ra'tyatíhtha' *he delays it* (-'tyatihT-).

delegate. *n.* uhę́·kareh *delegate* (-hękar-).

delegate. *v.i.* ru'rihę'ná·'nye' *he delegates* (-a'rihę'na'nye'-).

deliberate. *v.i.* kakučisnę́·ti· *they deliberate* (-čisnęti-); raya'turehnáhnęh *he deliberates it* (-ya'turehnahnę-).

delicious. *adj.* yawé·k'ę *it is delicious* (-ek'-).

delight. *n.* učhęnętyá'čreh *delight* (-a= čhęnętya'čr-).

deluge. *n.* uθrú'nę· *deluge* (-θru'T-).

demolish. *v.t.* ruhríhtha' *he demolishes it* (-hrihT-).

denounce. *v.t.* načhęnayeθá'tha' *one denounces another* (-hsęnayeθa'T-); ru'-teyurę́htha' *he denounces someone* (-(ę)'teyuręhT-).

deny. *v.i.* rahθawę́hra'č *he denies* (-ah= θawęhra'T-); ręti'nę̀·wahs *he denies* (-ęti'nęw-).

deny. *v.t.* ranę́snač *he denies it* (-nęs= naT-).

depend on. *v.t.* ra'rá'kar *he depends on it* (-a'ra'kar-); wa'kętihé·θę' *I depend on you* (-tiheθ-{dative III}).

dependable. *adj.* rutihé·θa'ť *he is dependable* (-tiheθa'T-).

dependent. *adj.* rutíhe·θ *he is dependent* (-tiheθ-).

deplore. *v.t.* ranhá'nę *he deplores it* (-nha'nę-).

depreciate. *v.t.* ra'ęyahsthú'tha' *he depreciates it* (-'ęyahsthu'T-).

depression. *n.* see: -ę̊'y-.

depth. *n.* see: -ę̊'y-.

deride. *v.t.* rahkwéhęh *he derides it* (-hkwehę-).

derision. *n.* ukęhrá·'nę *derision* (-kęh= raT-).

descent. *n.* yučnę́hnę *descent* (-ačnęhT-).

describe. *v.t.* rehu'nà·węh *he describes it* (-ehu'nawę-).

desert. *n.* u'wnayá'kęh *desert* (-a'w= naya'k-); urha'nakęw'ú'y *desert* (-rha'nakęw.#ú'y); yu'tehakwęhnárhę *desert* (-'tehakwęhnarhu-); yu'teha-kwęhnárhę *desert* (-'tehakwęhnarhu-); yu'tehakwęhnarhę'ú'y *desert* (-'teha= kwęhnarhę-.#ú'y).

desert. *v.i.* rá·t'wa'θ *he deserts* (-at'wa-{dative I}).

deserve. *v.t.* rathwę́·re·θ *he deserves it* (-athwęr-).

desire. *v.t.* wahθawę́hre' *it desires it* (-ahθawęhr-); ratkwè·rihθ *he desires it* (-atkwerih-); wa'enęhnyè·yę' *one desired it* (-nęhnyeyę-).

---

desk. *n.* kę^ʔ ychyatęhstayę^ʔnáhkhwa^ʔ *desk* (kę^ʔ -hyatęhsta̱yę'nahkw -).

despair. *v.i.* rę^ʔnikę́hrya^ʔks *he despairs* (-(ę)^ʔnikęhrya^ʔk -).

despise. *v.t.* rahsęnyę́^ʔθeh *he despises it* (-hsęnyę -{dative I}).

destroy. *v.t.* rahčę́^ʔwáhtha^ʔ *he destroys it* (-ahčę́^ʔwahT -); wahča^ʔnahkwáhnęh *it destroys it* (-ahča^ʔnahkwahnę -); rahnę́^ʔtha^ʔ *he destroys it* (-ahnę́^ʔT -).

detain. *v.t.* na^ʔtúhrar *one detains another* (-tuhrar -).

deteriorate. *v.i.* wáhsę^ʔθ *it deteriorates* (-ahsę^ʔ -); rękwehstá·ksę^ʔθ *he deteriorates* (-ę́k^wehstaksę^ʔ -).

detestable. *adj.* yuhsę́·nyęht *it is detestable* (-ahsęnyęhT -).

devil. *n.* uneshęhrù·nę^ʔ *devil* (-neshęh = runę^ʔ).

devil's darning needle. *n.* ná^ʔku^ʔ *devil's darning needle* (ná^ʔku^ʔ).

devine. *v.i.* wahra^ʔrę́^ʔna·t *he devined* (-a^ʔrę^ʔnaT -).

devour. *v.t.* raká·ryahs *he devours it* (-kari -).

dew. *n.* u^ʔá·wyeh *dew* (-^ʔawy -).

dewberry. *n.* ku^ʔte^ʔtù·rę^ʔ *dewberry* (ku^ʔte^ʔtù·rę^ʔ).

diabetes. *n.* urę^ʔná·kri^ʔ kakunę́hwaks *diabetes* (-rę^ʔnakri - -nęhwak -).

diabetic. *n.* urę^ʔná·kri^ʔ kakunę́hwaks *they are diabetics* (-rę^ʔnakri - -nęh = wak -).

dial. *n.* kawenę́·t^ʔehs ukę́hsawęh *dial (of a clock)* (-wenę̱t^ʔe(k) - -kęhsa̱wę -).

diarrhea. *n.* newę́·kuhθ *diarrhea* (-ne -. -ę°kuh -).

dictionary. *n.* uwętáhčreh *dictionary* (-wętahčr -).

die. *v.i.* rahè·yęhs *he is dying* (-ihey -); kayę́č^ʔahs *they are dying* (-ač^ʔa -).

differ. *v.i.* neyut^ʔníhę *the two of them differ* (-at'niha -).

differently. *adv.* ú·^ʔyči *differently* (ú·^ʔy.

#hči).

difficult. *adj.* yúčha^ʔnur *it is difficult* (-čha̱^ʔnur -); tkarihwà·yę^ʔ *it is difficult* (-t -. -rihwa̱yę -).

difficulty. *n.* učha^ʔnú·rę·^ʔ *difficulty* (-čha̱^ʔnur -); wa^ʔriwhárhuhs *difficulty (abstract)* (-a^ʔrihwharhu -); kaháhya^ʔks *difficulty (concrete)* (-(a)hahya^ʔk -); yu^ʔriwhárhę *it is a difficulty* (-a^ʔrihw = harhu -).

dig. *v.t.* ratá^ʔkha^ʔ *he is digging* (-a^ʔk -).

digit. *n.* uhsú^ʔkweh *digit* (-hsu^ʔku -).

diligence. *n.* uθnyarę́^ʔčreh *diligence* (-θnyarę^ʔčr -).

diligent. *adj.* ruθnyà·rę^ʔ *he is diligent* (-θnyarę -); ha^ʔ thruyè·rę *he is diligent* (-t -. -yer -).

din. *n.* yu^ʔnęrihstúhar *din* (-a'nęrih = stuhar -).

dinosaur. *n.* ka^ʔtárhwaht *dinosaur* (ka^ʔtárhwaht); uya^ʔkwáher *dinosaur* (uya^ʔkwáher).

dip for water. *v.i.* rá·čęhs *he dips for water* (-čę -).

dipper. *n.* kačę́^ʔtha^ʔ *dipper* (-čę^ʔT -); u^ʔtíhsneh *dipper* (-^ʔtihsn -).

direction. *n.* ha^ʔ tyuyerá·^ʔnę *direction* (ti -. -yeraT -).

directly. *adv.* kę *directly* (kę).

dirt. *n.* u^ʔnę́hrareh *dirt* (-a'nęhra̱r -); a-wę́hreh *dirt* (-ę°hr -).

dirty. *adj.* yu^ʔnę́hra^ʔr *it is dirty* (-a = 'nęhrar -); u^ʔnęhraréhči *dirty* (-a'nęh = ra̱r -.#hči); rutyá^ʔkwaht *he is dirty (in speech, in conduct)* (-tya^ʔk^wahT -).

dirty. *v.t.* ra^ʔnęhrarawę̀·rih *he dirties it* (-a'nęhra̱rawęri -).

disagree. *v.t.* neyakurihwákhahs *the two of them disagree* (-rihwa̱kha -).

disagreeable. *adj.* yawę^ʔnę́·ti· *it is disagreeable* (-ę'nęti -).

disappear. *v.i.* wáhnęh *it disappears* (-ah = nę -); wa^ʔe^ʔtéhsyę^ʔ *one disappeared* (-^ʔtehsyę -).

disappointed. *adj.* runęθhú'ʔę *he is disappointed* (-nęθhuʔ-).

disaster, come to. *v.i.* ru'ʔnyę́wnarę'ʔθ *he comes to disaster* (-a'nyęwnarę'ʔ-).

disastrous. *adj.* yutra'ʔθwá·ksa'ʔt *it is disastrous* (-atra'ʔθwaksaʔT-).

disbelieve. *v.t.* ratuwę́htha'ʔ *he disbelieves it* (-tuwęhT-).

discern. *v.i.* ru'ʔtikęhrayę́·'ʔnahθ *he discerns* (-(ę)'ʔtikęhrayę(T)-{dative II}).

disconcert. *v.t.* na'ʔtikęhryá'ʔkhęh *one disconcerts another* (-(ę)'ʔtikęhrya'ʔkhę-).

discontented. *adj.* kwęhs ahru'ʔtikęhriyu'ʔθéhek *he is discontented* (kwęhs -(ę)'ʔtikęhriyu-{dative I}).

discord. *n.* yurihwákhę *discord* (-rihwa̱=kha̱-); kayęhsawánhę *discord* (-yęhsa=wanh-).

discourage. *v.i.* na'ʔtikęhkęheyá'ʔtha'ʔ ‹one=another-mind-agitates› *one discourages another* (-(ę)'ʔtikęhkeyaʔT-).

discover. *v.t.* rakahkę́·nyęhs *he discovers* (-kahkęni-).

discredit. *v.t.* načhęnaksá'ʔtha'ʔ *one discredits another* (-hsęnaksaʔT-).

discretion, have. *v.i.* ru'ʔtikę́hra·t *he has discretion* (-(ę)'ʔtikęhraT-).

discriminate. *v.i.* nehra'ʔníhar *he discriminates (makes unequal)* (-ne-.-a'ni=har-).

discussion. *n.* neyurihwakyénhę *discussion* (-ne-.-rihwa̱kenha-).

disdain. *v.t.* rukęhra'ʔná·tih *he disdains it* (-kęhraT-{dative II}); rahsę́htih *he disdains it* (-hsęhti-).

disease. *n.* kanęhsatarí·nę·'ʔ *disease* (-nęhsatarinę-); unhù·reh *disease (with visible symptoms)* (-nhur-).

disembark. *v.i.* ra'ʔra'ʔná·kwahs *he disembarks* (-a'ʔra'ʔnaku-); rahęwanę'ʔnáhsyęhs *he disembarks* (-hęwanę='nahsi-).

disembowel. *v.t.* na'ʔnya'ʔrawíhsyęhs *one disembowels another* (-ya'ʔrawihsi-).

disengage. *v.i.* ra'ʔnu'ʔnaríhsyęhs *he disengages himself* (-a'nu'narihsi-).

disentangle. *v.t.* nehranę'ʔriyéhsyęhs *he disentangles it* (-ne-.-nę'ʔriyehsi-).

disfigure. *v.t.* rayehsu'ʔkrę́htha'ʔ *he disfigures it* (-yehsu'ʔkręhT-).

disguise. *v.t.* rayehsakę'ʔné·tyęhs *he disguises it* (-yehsa̱kę'neti-); ú·'ʔy rakęhsę́·tha'ʔ *he disguises it* (ú·'ʔy -kęhsęT-).

disgusting. *adj.* yúθtka'ʔt *it is disgusting* (-aθtkaʔT-); sti'ʔkà·reh *disgusting* (sti'ʔkà·reh).

dish. *n.* úkθeh *dish* (-kč-).

dishonest. *adj.* nehru'ʔnę'ʔtikęhkę́·nyę *he is dishonest* (-ne-.-a'nę'ʔtikęhkęni-); nehru'ʔtikęhkę́·nyę *he is dishonest* (-ne-.-(ę)'ʔtikęhkęni-).

dishonor. *v.t.* na'ʔręhsarę́·kwahs *one dishonors another* (-ręhsa̱ręku-).

dishwater. *n.* kakθuhárnę *dishwater* (-kθuharT-).

dislocate. *v.i.* wat'ʔnáhkwahs *it dislocates* (-at'ʔnahkw-).

dislodge. *v.t.* rata'ʔnuríhtha'ʔ *he dislodges it* (-ta'nurihT-).

dismount. *v.i.* račhe'ʔná·kwahs *he dismounts* (-ačhe'ʔnaku-).

disobedient. *adj.* kwęhs ahru'ʔnwętaráhkęk *he is disobedient* (kwęhs -a=nwęta̱rahkw-).

Tuscarora Pronunciation Key:
/a/ law; /e/ hat; /i/ pizza; /u/ tune; /ę/ hint; /č/ cheese; /h/ hoe; /m/ mother; /s/ same; /t/ do (before a vowel y, or w), too (elsewhere); /k/ gale (before a vowel y or w), kale (elsewhere); /n/ inhale (before a consonant or word-final), note (elsewhere), /r/ hiss (before a consonant or word-final), run (trilled as in Italian, elsewhere); /w/ cuff (before a consonant other than y or word-final), way (elsewhere); /y/ fish (before a consonant or word-final), you (elsewhere), /θ/ thing; /ʔ/ (the sound between the vowels in unh-unh); /·/ long vowel, /'ʔ/ high pitch; /'/ low pitch.

disorganize. *v.t.* rarurȩ́·kwahs *he disorganizes it* (-rurȩku -).

disown. *v.t.* naʔnȩnhíhthaʔ *one disowns another* (-ȩnhihT -).

disperse. *v.t.* nehraretyáʔthaʔ *he disperses it* (-ne -. -aretyaʔT -).

disproportionate. *adj.* neyutʔníhȩ *disproportionate* (-at'niha -).

dissect. *v.t.* rȩtíhthaʔ *he dissects it* (-ȩ°= tihT -).

dissolve. *v.t.* waʔktaʔtà·wȩʔ *I dissolved it* (-taʔtawȩ -).

distant. *adj.* tyù·reʔ *it is distant* (ti -. -re -).

distill. *v.i.* wekí·tkȩʔθ *it distills* (-eki= tkȩʔ -).

distress. *v.t.* wahruhráwhȩʔ *he was distraught* (-hrawhȩ -); natkȩ́hyaʔks *one distresses another* (-kȩhyaʔk -).

distrust. *v.t.* naʔtikȩhrárhaʔθ *one distrusts another* (-(ȩ)ʔtikȩhrarhaʔ -).

distrustful. *adj.* rawerí·θkȩ *he is distrustful* (-eriθk -).

disturbed. *adj.* rathȩhsù·rih *he disturbed* (-athȩhsuri -).

ditch. *n.* kahyȩhȩ́·tih *ditch* (-(i)hyȩhȩti -).

dive. *v.i.* raʔnȩhrúhahs *he dives in* (-a= 'nȩhruha -).

diver. *n.* raʔnȩhrúhahs *diver* (-a'nȩh= ruha -).

diverted. *adj.* ruʔnȩhrúhar *he is diverted* (-a'nȩhruhar -).

divide. *v.t.* nehrá·khahs *he divides it* (-ne -. -kha -); see: -ukenȩ -.

divorce. *n.* uríʔreh *divorce* (-riʔr -).

divorce. *v.t.* ratahkwahríhthaʔ *he divorces it* (-tahkwahrihT -).

divulge. *v.t.* rarihwí·tkȩws *he divulges it* (-rihwitkȩhw -).

dizzy. *adj.* nehrarȩʔné·tyȩhs *he is dizzy* (-ne -. -rȩʔneti -).

do. *v.t.* kyérhaʔ *I am doing it* (-yer -).

docile. *adj.* ruthȩhnáčkȩ· *he is docile* (-a= thȩhnačk -).

dock. *n.* wathȩwaʔnéhthaʔ *dock* (-athȩ= waʔnehT -).

doctor. *n.* tá·kteh *doctor* (tá·kteh).

doe. *n.* áhkwir *doe* (áhkwir).

dog. *n.* čír *dog* (čír).

dogfish. *n.* θkȩ́·čanȩh *dogfish* (-či -. -iča̲= nȩ -).

dogwood. *n.* runȩká̲ʔnȩt *dogwood* (runȩ= ká̲ʔnȩt); núhiʔ *white-flowering dogwood* (núhiʔ).

doll. *n.* kawirȩ́·tih *doll* (-wirȩti -).

donate to. *v.t.* rarù·rȩh *he donates to it* (-rurȩ -).

door. *n.* ú·čareh *door* (-ča̲r -).

doorman. *n.* račarà·nȩh *doorman* (-ča̲ra̲= nȩ -).

doorway. *n.* utakȩ́hsteh *doorway* (-ta= kȩhst -).

dose. *n.* θwé·ka·t *dose* (-či -. -ekaT -).

double. *v.t.* nehrúhstʔahs *he doubles it* (-ne -. -uhstʔ -); ruhsná·ryȩ *he doubles them* (-uhsnari -).

doubt. *n.* utù·wȩht *doubt* (-tuwȩhT -).

doubt. *v.t.* ratuwȩ́hthaʔ *he doubts it* (-tuwȩhT -).

doubtful. *adj.* yutuwȩhnù·rȩ *doubtful* (-tuwȩhnur -).

dough. *n.* ukyéʔčeh *dough* (-keʔč -).

doughy. *adj.* ukyeʔčéhči *doughy* (-keʔč -. #hči).

dove. *n.* urí·ʔneh *dove* (-ri'n -).

down. *n.* uhstwáhreh *bird down* (-hs= twahr -); utíhkweh *bird down* (-(ȩ)= tihkw -).

downhill. *adv.* ukarȩ́ʔreh *downhill* (-(a)= karȩʔr -).

dozen. *n.* táhsȩ *dozen* (táhsȩ).

draft. *n.* yuʔnewrȩkúhnȩ *draft of air* (-a'newrȩkuhT -).

drag. *v.t.* ráʔθrȩhs *he drags it* (-(i)ʔ= θ(e)r -).

dragon fly. *n.* kahahstì·nȩhs *dragon fly* (-hahstiN -).

draw. *v.i.* waʔkatkyerhà·rȩʔ *I drew myself* (-atkerha̲ -{dative III}); *v.t.* waʔ-

khekyerhà·rẹˀ *I drew someone* (-ker=
haṟ-{dative III}).
drawer. *n.* yuˀnáhkwẹ·t *drawer* (-ˀnah=
kwẹT-).
dream. *n.* uθrẹ́hneh *dream* (-θrẹhn-).
dream. *v.i.* raθrẹhná·ksẹˀθ *he dreams*
(-θrẹhnaksẹˀ-).
dregs. *n.* uˀnekẹ̀·reh *dregs* (-aˈnekẹr-).
dress. *n.* ukyerhúhčreh *dress* (-ker=
huhčr-).
dress. *v.t.* natkyérhuč *one dresses another* (-kerhur-).
dressed, get. *v.i.* waˀẹ́ˀné·tiˀ *one got
dressed* (-aˈneti(y)-).
drift. *v.i.* katéˀkwiks *it (snow) is drifting*
(-teˀkwik-).
driftwood, wet. *n.* awehnúˀẹ *wet driftwood* (awehnúˀẹ).
drink. *v.i.* rérhaˀ *he drinks* (-ïhr-).
drip. *v.i.* wačˀáhnẹ *it drips* (-ačˀahT-).
drive. *v.t.* raˀnù·rih *he drives it* (-a=
ˈnuri-); θhraknáˀthaˀ *he drives it back*
(-či-.-aknaˀT-); waˀkayá·kẹw *it drove
it out* (-yakẹhw-).
drivel. *n.* yúθkrẹy *drivel* (-θkrẹy-).
drop. *n.* uˀwáhθreh *drop* (-ˀwahθr-).
drop. *v.t.* raˀθẹ́hthaˀ *he drops it* (-aˀ=
θẹhT-).
dropsy. *n.* yakuˀnekayẹ́·tih *dropsy* (-a=
ˈnekayẹ(T)-{dative II}).
drought. *n.* haˀ yawẹtakarháˀnẹˀ *drought*
(-(ẹ)takaṟ-.#haˀnẹˀ).
drove. *n.* uˀtè·yeh *drove* (-(ẹ)ˀtey-).
drown. *v.i.* ráˀθkuˀθ *he drowns* (-(i)ˀ=
θkuˀ-); *v.t.* ranẹwẹthúhthaˀ *he drowns
it* (-nẹwẹthuhT-).
drug. *n.* ẹnẹ́hkwaˀt *drug* (ẹnẹ́hkwaˀt);

yunẹ́hkwaˀt *drug* (-nẹhkwaˀT-).
drug-free. *adj.* kaˀtikẹhranù·rẹˀ *drug-free*
(-(ẹ)ˀtikẹhraṇurẹ-).
drum. *n.* uˀnáhkweh *drum* (-ˀnahkw-).
drumming of partridges. *n.* wahkwé·θaˀθ
drumming of partridges (-ahkwe=
θaˀθ-).
drunk. *adj.* runẹ́ˀyahs *he is drunk*
(-nẹˀy-).
drunk, get. *v.i.* raˀnẹnẹ́ˀyáhsthaˀ *he gets
drunk* (-aˈnẹnẹˀyahsT-).
drunkard. *n.* rawé·kˀẹ *he is a drunkard*
(-ekˀ-).
drunkenness. *n.* unẹ́ˀyeh *drunkenness*
(-nẹˀy-).
dry. *adj.* yuhsná·thẹ *it is dry* (-ath-).
dry. *v.t.* kahsnatháˀnẹ *they were dried*
(-hsnathaˀT-); raθnẹ́hthaˀ *he dries it*
(-aθnẹhT-).
dry up. *v.i.* wáθnẹhs *it dries up* (-aθnẹ-).
dry-rot. *n.* uhswẹ́ˀneh *dry-rot* (-hs=
wẹˀn-).
dubious. *adj.* nehruˀtikẹ́hkye· *he is
dubious* (-ne-.-(ẹ)ˀtikẹhke-).
duck. *n.* kwéˀkwek *duck* (kwéˀkwek);
θúˀyẹ·t *duck* (θúˀyẹ·t); rurẹ̀·narẹ *mallard duck* (rurẹ̀·narẹ).
dull. *adj.* ukwè·neh *dull* (-kwen-).
dumb. *adj.* tihruθkwé·kẹ *he is dumb*
(-θkʷek-).
dumplings. *n.* uθnẹ́ˀkweh *dumplings*
(-aθnẹˀkw-); uˀnhẹ́θteh *dumplings*
(-ˀnhẹθt-).
duplicate. *n.* nekahswaˀteˀnáhkwẹ *duplicate* (-ne-.-hswaˀteˈnahkw-).
durable. *adj.* yuhtì·rẹ *it is durable*
(-htir-).

Tuscarora Pronunciation Key:
/a/ la̱w; /e/ ha̱t; /i/ pi̱zza; /u/ tu̱ne; /ẹ/ hi̱nt; /č/
cheese; /h/ ho̱e; /m/ mo̱ther; /s/ s̱ame; /t/ do̱
(before a vowel y, or w), to̱o (elsewhere); /k/ gale
(before a vowel y or w), ḵale (elsewhere); /n/
inhale (before a consonant or word-final), note
(elsewhere), /r/ hiss (before a consonant or word-

final), run (trilled as in Italian, elsewhere); /w/ cuff
(before a consonant other than y or word-final),
way (elsewhere); /y/ fish (before a consonant or
word-final), you (elsewhere), /θ/ thing; /ˀ/ (the
sound between the vowels in unh-unh); /·/ long
vowel, /́/ high pitch; /̀/ low pitch.

duration. *n.* ha⁷ tyu⁷tyá·tihθ *duration* (ti -. -⁷tyatih -).

during. *prep.* tyu⁷tyá·tihθ *during* (ti -. -⁷tyatih -).

dust. *n.* u⁷ḱ̨ehreh *dust* (-a⁷ḱ̨ehr -); awę́- hę⁷ *dust* (-ęh -).

dust. *v.i.* ra⁷ḱ̨ehrę́htha⁷ *he dusts* (-a⁷= ḱ̨ehręhT -).

dusty. *adj.* u⁷ḱ̨ehréhči *dusty* (-a⁷ḱ̨ehr -. #hči); yu⁷na⁷ḱ̨ehra⁷níhrę *it is dusty (e.g., a road)* (-a⁷na⁷ḱ̨ehra⁷nihr -).

dwarf. *n.* ękwéhsayę⁷ *dwarf* (-ę°kʷeh = sayę -).

dwell. *v.i.* wahra⁷nè·nę⁷ *he dwelt* (-⁷nenę -); yetá·kre⁷ *one dwells* (-ta = k(e)r -).

dynasty. *n.* ur⁷ę́hseh *dynasty* (-(i)r⁷ęhs -).

E

eagle. *n.* stakwi⁷áh *eagle* (stá·kwi⁷.#áh).

ear. *n.* uhę́hneh *ear* (-hęhs -/ -hęhT -).

ear of corn. *n.* uhsè·yeh *ear of corn* (-hsey -); uhsè·yur *ear of corn* (-hse = yur -); kahsè·yuhk *boiled ear of corn* (-hseyu -).

earache, have an. *v.i.* wakhę́hnari·ks *I have an earache* (-hęhnarik -).

earlobe. *n.* uhsà·wareh *earlobe* (-hsa = war -).

early riser. *n.* nekčirè·re *an early riser* (nekčirè·re); rayéhwat *he is an early riser* (-yehwaT -).

earn. *v.t.* ra⁷tyę́·⁷nęh *he earns it* (-⁷tyę = ⁷nęh -).

earrings. *n.* u⁷washà·reh *earrings* (-⁷wa = shar -).

earth. *n.* ú⁷wneh *earth* (-a⁷wT -).

earthquake. *n.* wa⁷wnakahrę́hrę⁷ *earthquake* (-a⁷wnakaręhrę -); wa⁷nyu⁷wna- kwaríhę⁷ *earthquake* (-ne -. -a⁷wna = kwarihę⁷ -).

east. *n.* nwa⁷né·tkę⁷θ *east* (-t -. -a⁷ne = tkę⁷ -).

easy. *adj.* tikà·yę⁷ *it is easy* (ti -. -yę(T) -).

eat. *v.i.* račhù·rih *he eats* (-ačhuri -); ę⁷nwakę́hsya⁷k *we'll eat* (-kęhsya⁷k -); *v.t.* see: -k -.

eat up. *v.i.* kíhs⁷ahs *I eat up* (-(i)hs⁷a -).

eatable. *adj.* ačhù·rih *eatable* (-ačhuri -).

eater, great. *n.* rakhwí·yu· *he is a great eater* (-khwiyu -).

ecclesiastic. *adj.* urihwatukę́htikyéha·⁷ *ecclesiastic* (-rihwatukęht -.#keha·⁷).

echo. *n.* nwa⁷nwętáhtha⁷ *echo* (-t -. -a = 'nwętahT -); tkarihwaya⁷θrá·kwahs *echo* (-t -. -rihwaya⁷θraku -); tkaríh- wahs *echo* (-t -. -rihwara -).

eclipse. *n.* θkà·yęh *eclipse* (-či -. -yę -).

eddy. *n.* nekahtawakwá⁷nahč *eddy* (-ne -. -htawakwa⁷nahT -).

eddy. *v.i.* newekáhkwa⁷nahč *it eddies* (-ne -. -ekahkwa⁷nahT -).

edge. *n.* uhθę́⁷kareh *edge* (-hθę⁷kar -); u- tá·kareh *edge* (-(ę)takar -); tiwakę́hya·t *its edge* (ti -. -akęhyaT -); kę⁷ tiwakęh- ya⁷ná·⁷nye⁷ *edge* (kę⁷ ti -. -akęhya = 'na'nye⁷ -); see: -heskw -.

eel. *n.* kę́·⁷neh *eel* (-i'n -); θwará·ŗ̨e·k *lamprey eel* (θwará·ŗ̨e·k).

effervescence. *n.* uhwáhsteh *effervescence* (-hwahst -).

egg. *n.* u⁷nhę́hseh *egg* (-⁷nhęhs -).

eggs, fried. *n.* ka⁷nhęhsęhrá·he⁷ *fried eggs* (-⁷nhęhsęhra·he⁷ -).

eggs, lay *v.i.* wa⁷nhę́hsęh *it lays eggs* (-⁷nhęhsę -).

eggshell. *n.* utičkę̀·reh *eggshell* (-tičkęr -).

egotism. *n.* ha⁷ rat⁷íhstha⁷ *his egotism* (-at⁷ihsT -).

egotistic. *adj.* rat⁷íhstha⁷ *he is egotistic* (-at⁷ihsT -).

eight. *adj./n.* né·krę⁷ *eight* (né·krę⁷).

eighteen. *adj./n.* né·krę⁷ θkáhe·⁷r *eighteen* (né·krę⁷ -či -. -(i)har -).

eighty. *adj./n.* né·krę⁷ tiwáhθhę· *eighty*

(né·krę⁷ ti -. -ahθhę -).

elastic. *n.* newa⁷ne⁷nihę́·thuhs *elastic* (-ne -. -a'ne'nihęthu -).

elbow. *n.* uhkyúhseh *elbow* (-hkyuhs -).

elbow. *v.t.* rahkyúhskwahs *he elbows it* (-hkyuhsku -).

elbows, lean upon. *v.i.* rahkyúhsiher *he leans upon his elbows* (-hkyuhsihar -).

elderberry. *n.* čaweryahskáhrę *elderberry* (čaweryahskáhrę).

eldest. *n.* yęthuráhtha⁷ *eldest* (-athu = rahT -).

elecampagne. *n.* u⁷tú·θer yú·thwę· *elecampagne* (-⁷tuθ(e)r - -thwę -).

elect. *v.t.* natkyé·θkwahs *one elects another* (-keθku -).

elegant. *adj.* yuthéhtrak *it is elegant* (-athehtrak -).

elephant. *n.* uθri⁷rehú⁷y *elephant* (-θri⁷r -.#ú⁷y).

elevate. *v.t.* nehrahkwá⁷tha⁷ *he elevates it* (-ne -. -(i)hkʷa⁷T -).

eleven. *adj./n.* ę́·či θkáhe⁷r *eleven* (ę́·či -či -. -(i)har -).

eligible. *adj.* yakyéhwaya⁷č *eligible (for marriage) male* (-ehwaya⁷θ -).

elk. *n.* ču⁷wahrù·wa⁷ *elk* (ču⁷wahrù·wa⁷).

elm. *n.* karátkwar *elm* (karátkwar); u-kęhré⁷wa⁷ *a kind of elm* (-kęhre⁷w -); hú⁷ks *slippery elm* (hú⁷ks).

elsewhere. *adv.* è·re *elsewhere* (è·re); uwá⁷čeh *elsewhere* (uwá⁷čeh); he⁷skęhę·we è·re *elsewhere* (he⁷skęhę·we è·re).

elude. *v.t.* na⁷nat⁷wá⁷θeh *one eludes another* (-at⁷wa -{dative I}).

emaciate. *v.t.* rahsneyę́·tih *he emaciates it* (-hsneyę -{dative II}).

emanate. *v.i.* thrayá·kę⁷θ *he emanates* (-t -. -yakę⁷ -).

embarrass. *v.t.* nathe⁷nę⁷nę́·tih *one embarrasses another* (-he⁷nę⁷nęti -).

embarrassed. *adj.* ru⁷nęnhihná·ti· *he is embarrassed* (-a'nęnhihT -{dative II}).

embarrassing. *adj.* yúnhiht *it is embarrassing* (-nhihT -).

embellish. *v.t.* akya⁷tahstę̀·ni⁷ *that I embellish it* (-ya⁷tahstęni -).

ember. *n.* učí⁷reh *ember* (-či⁷r -); učí·sneh *ember* (-či·sn -).

emblem. *n.* neyawętahkyerá⁷nę *emblem* (-ne -. -ętahkera⁷T -).

embolden. *v.i.* ratkwatihčayę́hstha⁷ *he emboldens himself* (-atkwatihča = yęhst -).

embrace. *n.* uhnę́θhareh *embrace* (-(ę)h = nęθhar -).

embrace. *v.t.* ręhnę́θhar *he embraces it* (-(ę)hnęθhar -).

embroider. *v.i.* nehraθkwaru⁷nárhęh *he embroiders* (-ne -. -aθkwaru'narhę -).

embryo. *n.* utè·reh *embryo* (-(ę)ter -); uwì·reh *embryo* (-wir -).

emetic. *n.* yęθtka⁷náhkhwa⁷ *emetic* (-aθ = tka⁷nahkw -).

emissary. *n.* unhá⁷čreh *emissary* (-nha⁷ = čr -).

employ. *v.t.* ráhstha⁷ *he employs it* (-(i)hsT -); ęyénha⁷ *one will be employed* (-nha⁷ -).

empty. *v.t.* rakę̀·yaws *he empties it* (-kęyaw -).

emulate. *v.t.* nehrutkę́·nyę *he emulates it*

(-ne-.-atkęni-).

enchain. *v.t.* nehrahtrę́hstęh *he enchains it* (-ne-.-(i)htrę̨hstę-).

enchantment, put in a state of. *v.t.* wa²kayę²ręnę́·ti² *they put it in a state of enchantment* (-a²ręnęti-).

enclosed. *adj.* yu²nečárhę *it is enclosed* (-a'nečarhu-).

enclosed area. *n.* u²ę̀·yeh *enclosed area* (-²ęy-)

end. *n.* yú·²nu²kt *the end* (-a'nu²kT-).

end. *v.i.* see: -u²kT-; *v.t.* rahčę²wáhtha² *he ends it* (-ahčę²wahT-); nę²nú²knę² *it ended* (-t-.-a'nu²kT-).

enduring. *adj.* we²θhá·θne² *it is enduring* (-(i)²θhaθn-).

enemies. *n.* neyęčhę́²θeh *the two of them are enemies* (-ačhę-{dative I}).

enemy. *n.* nwá²kan *enemy* (nwá²kan).

enervate. *v.t.* rači²yuhčrę́·tih *he enervates it* (-či²yuhčręti-).

enervated by women. *adj.* θhra²núhsar *he is enervated by women* (-či-.-a='nuhsar-).

engrave. *v.i.* nehra²nę́²θha² *he engraves* (-ne-.-'nę²θ-).

enigma. *n.* yurihwawéhθayę² *enigma* (-rihwawehθayę-).

enjoy oneself. *v.i.* ra²nę²na²néhstha² *he enjoys himself* (-a'nę'na'nehsT-).

enliven. *v.t.* ręnhéhktha² *he enlivens it, he animates it* (-ę̈́nhehkT-).

ennoble. *v.t.* raya²tanurę́hstha² *he ennobles it* (-ya²tanuręhsT-).

enough. *adj.* hè·wi *enough* (hè·wi); hé²thu *enough* (hé²thu).

enrich. *v.t.* račhu²kuwahčrę́·tih *he enriches it* (-ačhu²kuwahčręti-).

enroll. *v.t.* wa²khehà·rę² *I enrolled someone (on the tribal rolls)* (-(i)har-{dative III}).

enslave. *v.t.* ratáhskwar *he enslaves* (-tahskwah(e)r-).

entangled. *adj.* nehranę²rì·yehs *he is en-*
tangled (-ne-.-nę²riye-).

enter. *v.i.* see: -yę-.

entertain. *v.i.* wa²tkayę́·²nę·t *they entertained* (-ne-.-a'nęt-).

entity. *n.* ukwéhsteh *entity* (-(ę̈́)kʷehst-).

entomb. *v.t.* ra²nę́ht²ahs *he entombs it* (-'nęht²-).

entrails. *n.* uyá²reh *entrails* (-ya²r-).

entrap. *v.t.* ęyeya²karú²yeht *one will entrap it* (-ya²karu²yehT-).

entry. *n.* ha² tkà·yę² *entry* (-t-.-yę-).

envious. *adj.* ru²tuθha²ní·yu· *he is envious* (-²tuθha²niyu-).

envy. *n.* u²tuθhę́²ę *envy* (-²tuθhę²-).

envy. *v.t.* ra²tú·θhahs *he envies it* (-²tu=θh-).

epidemic. *n.* kanhurá²na²r *epidemic* (-nhura²na²r-).

epidermis. *n.* urí²reh *epidermis* (-ri²r-).

equidistant. *adj.* tha²neyuyerihá²nę² *it is equidistant away from* (tha+ne-.-yeri-.#ha²nę²).

equitable. *adj.* thyu²nya²čeríhę *it is equitable* (tha-.-a'nya²čeriha-).

erect. *v.t.* rakę́hahs *he erects it* (-kęha-).

escape. *v.i.* nyá·t²wa·² *you and I escape* (-at²wa-); wa²kayę²nękuhnáhnę² *they escaped* (-a'nękuhnahnę-).

escort. *v.t.* ra²tikęhryenę́hreh *he escorts it* (-(ę)²tikęhryenę-).

especially. *adv.* ha² kę́hčih *especially* (ha² kę́hčih).

esteem. *n.* anęnù·ręk *esteem* (anęnù·ręk).

et cetera. *n.* te²té² *et alia* (te²té²).

eternity. *n.* ha² yę̀·we² *eternity* (-yah-.-e-).

eunuch. *n.* ru²nhęhsú·kę² *eunuch* (-²nhę=hsukę²).

evade. *v.t.* ra²nęnhíhtha² *he evades it* (-a'nęnhihT-).

evaporate. *v.i.* wáθnęhs *it evaporates* (-aθnę-).

even though. *adv.* ka²nehnę́ *even though* (ka²nehnę́).

evening. *n.* wa⁷uhθá·thu⁷ *evening* (-ah = θathu -); the⁷nę̀·reh *evening* (the⁷-nę̀·reh).

event. *n.* uríhweh *event* (-rihw -).

evergreen. *n.* ukhrę̀·weh *evergreen* (-khręw -).

everywhere. *adv.* hęweté⁷ *everywhere* (hęweté⁷); u⁷níhska⁷ *everywhere* (u⁷-níhska⁷).

evident. *adj.* hę́⁷te⁷ *evident* (hę́⁷te⁷); ka-yerę́·tih *it is evident* (-yeręti -).

evil. *adj.* wáhsę· *it is evil* (-ahsę -).

exactly that. *adv.* ka⁷nę́ kyè·nę· *exactly that* (ka⁷nę́ kyè·nę·); ka⁷nę́ hà·ne⁷ *exactly that* (ka⁷nę́ hà·ne⁷).

exaggerate. *v.t.* wehrarihwaréhstha⁷ *he exaggerates it* (-yah -. -rihwarehsT -).

exalt. *v.t.* rakuwaná⁷tha⁷ *he exalts it* (-kuwana⁷T -).

examine. *v.t.* ratkę́⁷θeh *he examines* (-atkę⁷θe -); nehrakę⁷θáhnęh *he examines it* (-ne -. -kę⁷θahnę -).

excel at. *v.t.* nehrakę́·nyęhs *he excels at it* (-ne -. -kęni -).

except. *prep.* úč⁷aht *except* (úč⁷aht).

exception. *n.* θhra⁷ná·⁷nęr *he was the exception* (-či -. -a'na'nęr -).

excessive. *adj.* ru⁷θraréhstha⁷ *he is excessive* (-a⁷θrarehsT -).

excessively. *adv.* yu⁷θrà·rehst *excessively* (-a⁷θrarehsT -).

exchange. *v.t.* nehrakę⁷né·tyęhs *he exchanges it* (-ne -. -kę⁷neti -).

excite. *v.t.* rahsnyà·rę *he excites it* (-hs = nyar -).

excluded. *adj.* è·re yuráhkhwa⁷ *it is excluded* (è·re -rahkw -).

excrete. *v.i.* rahtkí⁷yę· *he excreted* (-ah = tki⁷yę -).

executioner. *n.* rahà·ręh *executioner* (-(i) = har -{dative III}).

exempt. *adj.* rura⁷náhkwahs *he is exempt* (-ra⁷nahkw -); etírher *one is exempt from work* (-tirher -).

exercise. *v.i.* rayu⁷nę́htha⁷ *he exercises* (-yu⁷nęhT -).

exhale. *v.i.* wačhęryuhkwá⁷nihč *it exhales* (-ačhęryuhkwa⁷nihr -); nekačha⁷-núhtha⁷ *it exhales* (-ne -. -čha⁷nuhT -).

exhaust. *v.t.* ráhs⁷ahs *he exhausts it* (-(i)hs⁷a -).

exhaustion from lack of food. *n.* yuθnę́⁷ę *exhaustion from lack of food* (-aθ = nę⁷ -).

exhibit. *v.t.* rehú·tha⁷ *he exhibits it* (-e = huT -).

exhort. *v.t.* rahsnyà·rę *he exhorts it* (-hsnyar -).

exhume. *v.t.* ra⁷nęhná·kwahs *he exhumes it* (-'nęhnaku -).

exist. *v.i.* katíhu⁷θ *it exists* (-tíhu⁷ -); see: -i -/-ę° -.

exit. *n.* tka⁷teyitkęhnáhkhwa⁷ *exit* (-t -. -(ę)⁷teyitkęhnahkw -).

exorcise. *v.i.* ra⁷tyéhę *he exorcises* (-⁷tyeh -).

expense. *n.* ú·kareh *expense* (-kar -).

expensive. *adj.* kanù·rę⁷ *it is expensive* (-nurę -); yu⁷ę̀·ye·θ *it is expensive* (-⁷ęyeθ -).

experience, have an unexpected. *v.i.* see: -a'nyerę -.

experiment. *v.i.* ra⁷tyę́·⁷nęh *he experiments* (-⁷tyę'nęh -).

Tuscarora Pronunciation Key:
/a/ law; /e/ hat; /i/ pizza; /u/ tune; /ę/ hint; /č/ cheese; /h/ hoe; /m/ mother; /s/ same; /t/ do (before a vowel y, or w), too (elsewhere); /k/ gale (before a vowel y or w), kale (elsewhere); /n/ inhale (before a consonant or word-final), note (elsewhere), /r/ hiss (before a consonant or word-final), run (trilled as in Italian, elsewhere); /w/ cuff (before a consonant other than y or word-final), way (elsewhere); /y/ fish (before a consonant or word-final), you (elsewhere), /θ/ thing; /⁷/ (the sound between the vowels in unh-unh); /·/ long vowel, /́/ high pitch; /̀/ low pitch.

expire. *v.i.* ra'nẹrihstì·ya'ks *he expires*
(-a'nẹrihstiya'k-).

expose. *v.t.* ru'náhsẹhs *he exposes it*
(-a'nahsi-).

expressive. *adj.* wẹhnáhkhwa' *expressive*
(-ẹhnahkw-).

exquisite. *adj.* yúhskataht *it is exquisite*
(-hskatahT-).

exterior. *n.* aθnéhte *exterior* (aθnéhte).

exterminate. *v.t.* wa'kayakẹčí'waht *they
exterminated it* (-ẹ̆či'wahT-); tikaku'-
ta'wẹthuhsthẹ́he' *they went along exterminating it* (ti-.-a'ta'wẹthuhst-).

extinguish. *v.t.* ra'θwáhtha' *he extinguishes it* (-a'θwahT-); θwá'θwa'θ *it
is extinguished* (-či-.-a'θwa'-).

extra one. *n.* yu'na'nẹ̀·rẹ *extra one*
(-a'na'nẹr-).

extract. *v.t.* ẹwawíhsi' *it will extract* (-a=
wihsi-); ẹyeyá·kẹw *one will extract it*
(-yakẹhw-).

extraordinary. *n.* yunehrá·kwaht *extraordinary* (-nehrakwahT-).

extravagant. *adj.* yu'θrà·rehst *extravagant*
(-a'θrarehsT-).

extreme. *adj.* kẹ' weyú·'nu'kt *extreme*
(kẹ' -yah-.-a'nu'kT-).

extremity. *n.* ha' yuthriyá'kẹ *extremity*
(-athriya'k-); kẹ' weyú·'nu'kt *extremity* (kẹ' -yah-.-a'nu'kT-).

eye. *n.* ukáhreh *eye* (-kah(r)-).

eyebrow. *n.* ukahré'neh *eyebrow* (-kah=
re'n-).

eyelash. *n.* ukahčú'neh *eyelash* (-kah=
ču'n-).

eyelid. *n.* utihsé'yeh *eyelid* (-tihse'y-).

F

fabulous. *adj.* neyawẹkhwyú·rẹ· *fabulous*
(-ne-.-ẹkhwyurẹ-).

face. *n.* ukẹ́hseh *face* (-kẹhs-); ukẹ́h-
skwareh *big face* (-kẹhskwar-); uhẹ́h-
skaweh *dirty face* (-hẹhskaw-); u'n-
húhskwareh *lower part of face (from
nose to chin)* (-(ẹ)'nhuhskwar-).

facetious. *adj.* awé·ha·k *facetious* (-e=
hak-).

fade. *v.t.* wáhθkwahs *it fades it* (-ah=
θkw-).

fail. *v.i.* ratù·rẹh *he fails (to do it)*
(-turẹ-); wa'ù·yẹw *it failed* (-yẹhw-).

faint. *v.i.* wa'nwakahθẹ́hnẹ'θ *I fainted*
(-ne-.-ahθẹhT-{dative I}); wahra'ti-
kẹhráhnẹ' *he fainted* (-(ẹ)'tikẹhrah=
nẹ-).

fair. *adj.* ru'nahwà·ra'neht *he is fair*
(-a'nahwara'nehT-).

fair. *n.* neyẹtkẹ́·nyẹhs *fair* (-ne-.-atkẹni-).

faith, have. *v.i.* thrawe'náhkẹ *he has
faith* (-t-.-e'nahkw-).

fall. *n.* rahθé'kye *fall (season)* (rahθé'kye); sá'thu *fall (season)* (sá'thu).

fall. *v.i.* ráhsha'na'θ *he falls backward*
(-hsha'na'-); wa'káhsha·' *it fell on
its back* (-hsha-); wúhri'θ *it falls to
pieces* (-uhri'-); see: -ẹ-.

fallow. *adj.* yawẹhrá·tkẹh *fallow* (-ẹ̆'h=
ratkẹh-).

false Solomon's seal. *n.* θkẹhná·ksẹ'
wáhyaks *false Solomon's seal* (-či-.
-ihnaks- -(a)hyak-).

false face. *n.* utkẹhsù·rẹ *false face*
(-atkẹhsurẹ-); učíhseh *false face*
(-čihs-).

falsehood. *n.* utuwẹ́hneh *falsehood* (-tu=
wẹhT-).

falsify. *v.t.* ratuwẹhnẹ́·tih *he falsifies it*
(-tuwẹhnẹti-).

familiar with, become. *v.t.* rarẹ́'nha'θ *he
becomes familiar with it* (-rẹ'nha'-).

familiarize. *v.t.* khe'rẹ'nhá'tha' *I familiarize another* (-rẹ'nha'T-).

family. *n.* kčẹ́heh *my family* (-(a)čẹh-);
uhwačì·reh *extended family* (-hwa=
čir-).

family line. *n.* ur'ę́hseh *family line* (‑(i)r'ęhs‑).

famine. *n.* u'nęhkaryá'kę *famine* (‑a='nęhkarya'k‑).

famous. *adj.* ruyaθęhstakaré·ti· *he is famous* (‑yaθęhstakareti‑).

fan. *n.* yę'ča'tuhsnáhkhwa' *fan* (‑a'ča'=tuhsnahkw‑); ú·wyeh *fan* (‑wy‑).

fan. *v.t.* ka'rhè·wahs *I fan it* (‑a'rhew‑).

fan with. *v.t.* yerhewáhtha' *one fans with it* (‑rhewahT‑).

far. *adv.* ì·nę *far* (ì·nę).

farm. *n.* ú'wneh *farm* (‑a'wT‑).

farm. *v.i.* nehręhra'né·tyęhs *he farms* (‑ne‑.‑ęhra'netyę‑).

farmer. *n.* rayęthuhs'á·ka·' *farmer* (‑yę=thu‑.#aka·').

farrier. *n.* áha·θ ręnęhkwá'tha' *farrier* (áha·θ ‑ęnęhkwa'T‑).

fart. *n.* utí'neh *fart* (‑ti'n‑).

farther. *adv.* hésnę· ì·nę *farther* (hésnę· ì·nę).

fast. *adj.* kwaríha't *fast* (kwaríha't); yuhstù·re' *it is fast* (‑hstur‑).

fast. *v.i.* raruráhshęh *he fasts* (‑rurah=shę(T)‑).

fasten. *v.t.* né·kw rę́·tih *he fastens it* (né·kw ‑ę́·ti‑); weθnú·'nari' *you two fastened it* (‑ⁿu'nari‑); nęhrahθę́'rę' *he will fasten end to end* (‑ne‑.‑hθę'n(e)r‑); rúhar *he fastens it to the end* (‑uhar‑); see: ‑nę‑'na(k)‑.

fastened. *adj.* né·kw yú'nę· *it is fastened* (né·kw ‑a'nę‑).

fat. *adj.* rúsθę· *he is fat* (‑asθę‑); ratkrę́hne' *he is fat* (‑atkręhT‑).

fat. *n.* utkrę́hneh *fat* (‑atkręhT‑).

fat back. *n.* uθá'reh *fat back* (‑θa'r‑).

father. *n.* akhrí'ę *my father* (‑hri'ę); rahθkwaríhtha' *father* (‑ahθkwarihT‑).

father-in-law. *n.* yaktihę́·θhu' *my father-in-law* (‑hęθhu‑); yé·θa'w *my father-in-law* (‑θa'w‑); uhę́·θę *father-in-law* (‑hęθę).

fatherhood. *n.* uhri'ę́hsteh *fatherhood* (‑hri'ęhst‑).

fathom. *n.* θwa'né·wya·t *one fathom* (‑či‑.‑a'newyat‑).

fatigued. *adj.* nehruhwihshęhé·yę· *he is fatigued* (‑ne‑.‑(a)hwihshęhey‑).

fatiguing. *adj.* neyuhwihshęhè·yaht *it is fatiguing* (‑ne‑.‑(a)hwihshęheyahT‑); yurę́hyakę't *it is fatiguing* (‑ręhya=kę'T‑).

fauna. *n.* ha' katá·kre' *fauna* (‑tak(e)r‑).

favor. *n.* ukyerhakyénha't *favor* (‑kerha=kenha'T‑).

fawn. *n.* čí'raręh *fawn* (čí'raręh); neyuna'kwéyher *fawn* (neyuna'kwéyher).

fear. *n.* awęhreθrę́'neh *fear* (‑ęhre=θrę'T‑).

fear. *v.i.* ráhraw'θ *he fears* (‑hraw'‑).

fearful. *adj.* ręhré·θrę'θ *he is fearful* (‑ęhreθrę'‑).

feasible. *adj.* yukwé·nya't *feasible* (‑kwenya'T‑).

feast, make a. *v.i.* yakwakhwáher *we make a feast* (‑khwah(e)r‑).

Feast of the Dead. *n.* Wa'nyę'nyehrá·kę' *Feast of the Dead* (‑ne‑.‑yehrak‑{dative III}).

feather. *n.* uhrá'neh *feather* (‑hra'n‑); uhsnú'kreh *feather* (‑hsnu'kr‑); uθnù·reh *feather* (‑θnur‑); yuhrá'kwa'r *tail* *feather* (-hrakwar-).

feathers, make. *v.i.* kahranę́·tih *it makes feathers (said of a birdling just starting to grow feathers)* (-hranęti-).

feathers, put on. *v.i.* rahránęh *he puts feathers on (e.g., arrows)* (-hranę-).

feathers, shed. *v.i.* wathranę́htha *it sheds its feathers* (-athranęhT-).

February. *n.* kęnę́hti *February* (-inęht-); čuhyeθákye *February* (-či-.-(a)hye=θake).

feces. *n.* utkwéhreh *feces* (-tkwehr-).

feeble. *adj.* ručíyu· *he is feeble* (-či=yu-); kihskwà·rih *I am feeble* (-(i)h=skwari-).

feebly. *adv.* učiyúhčrakęw *feebly* (-či=yuhčrakęw).

feed. *v.t.* nanę́·nę *one feeds another* (-nęT-).

feel. *v.i.* rę́ner *he feels* (-iner-); *v.t.* rahskwá·tkęθ *he feels it* (-hskwa=tkę-).

feel bad. *v.i.* wakatkyè·yu *I don't feel well* (-atkeyu-).

fell. *v.t.* načweníehs *one fells another* (-hswenie(k)-).

female. *adj.* kanę̀·wę *female* (-nęwę-).

fence. *n.* uę̀·yeh *fence* (-ęy-)

ferment. *v.i.* yuyúne *it ferments* (-yu=n(e)-).

ferocious. *adj.* uhskanenáhraht *ferocious* (-hskanenahrahT-).

fervent. *adj.* thrawenáhkę *he is fervent* (-t-.-enahkw-).

fetid. *n.* watkę́hθraθ *fetid* (-atkęh=θraθ-).

fetus. *n.* utè·reh *fetus* (-(ę)ter-).

fever. *n.* unarhwékčreh *fever* (-a'nar=hwekčr-).

fever, have a. *v.i.* runárhweks *he has a fever* (-a'narhwek-); wakanaríhę· *I have a fever* (-anarih-).

few. *adj.* nú·kah *few* (nú·kah).

few. *n.* narà·west *a few* (narà·west).

fiddle. *n.* učikę̀·weh *fiddle* (-čikęw-).

field. *n.* uhéhneh *field* (-hehn-); uhę́neh *field* (-(a)hęn-).

fife. *n.* yehęwarahthaáh *fife* (-hęwa̲=rahT-.#áh).

fifteen. *n.* wísk θkáher *fifteen* (wísk -či-.-(i)har-).

fifty. *n.* wísk tiwáhθhę· *fifty* (wísk ti-.-ahθhę-).

fight. *v.t.* wakarì·yu *I fought it* (-a=riyu-); nekayętawę́·thuhs *they fight each other* (-ne-.-tawęthu-).

fight for. *v.t.* rahθkyénha *he is fighting for it* (-ahθkenha-).

fighter. *n.* wakariyúne *I am a (professional) fighter* (-ariyuT-).

fighting. *n.* uriyúčreh *fighting* (-ari=yučr-).

fill. *v.t.* ránhahs *he fills it* (-(a)nha-).

fill back up. *v.t.* θhrayè·riks *he fills it back up* (-či-.-yerik(T)-).

fill up. *v.t.* see: -yerik-.

film. *n.* unéhseh *film (for a camera)* (-nehs-).

film. *v.t.* runéhsuh *he films it* (-nehsur-).

filter. *v.t.* ręhkęráhtha *he filters it* (-ęh=kęrahT-).

filth. *n.* unę́hrareh *filth* (-a'nęhra̲r-); a=wę́·taweh *filth* (-ęta̲w-).

filthy. *adj.* yúθtkat *it is filthy* (-aθ=tkaT-).

fin. *n.* utúhneh *fin* (-tuhn-).

finally. *adv.* áθę hà·ne *finally* (áθę hà·ne); ù·nę séher *finally* (ù·nę séher).

find. *v.t.* wahrakučę̀·ri *he found it* (-kučęri-).

finger. *n.* uhsúkweh *finger* (-hsuku-).

finger span. *n.* see: -ręka̲r-.

fingernail. *n.* učihskę́hkareh *fingernail* (-čihskęhka̲r-); uhskękwà·reh *fingernail* (-hskękwar-).

finish. *v.t.* raθnérhuhs *he finishes it* (-aθnerhu-).

finish eating. *v.i.* ráhs⁷ahs *he finishes eating* (-(i)hs⁷a-); rukhwí⁷ę *he finished eating* (-khwi⁷-).

finish speaking. *v.i.* wa⁷erihú⁷knę⁷ *she had finished speaking* (see: -rihu⁷ = kT-).

fire. *n.* učę́heh *fire* (-(a)čę̧h-).

fire, build. *v.i.* wa⁷ętkahnę́·tyę⁷ *one built a fire* (-atkahnęti-{dative III}); wa⁷ = kaye⁷nè·nę⁷ *they built a fire* (-⁷ne = nę-).

fire, put in. *v.t.* see -ę̊T-.

fire, set on. *v.i.* rači⁷rá⁷nihč *he sets it on fire* (-či⁷ra⁷nihr-).

fire, take off the. *v.t.* wa⁷ekahnę́·ku⁷ *one took it off the fire* (-kahnęku-).

fire extinguisher. *n.* ra⁷θwahnáhkhwa⁷ *fire extinguisher* (-a⁷θwahnahkw-).

firefly. *n.* uhsnuká⁷nęh *firefly* (-hsnu = ka⁷T-).

first. *adv.* tyà·re⁷ *first* (tyà·re⁷); ikę́hči *first* (-i-.#hči); nyu⁷nyeręhnáhkę *first* (-ne-.-a'nyeręhnahkw-).

first time. *n.* nę⁷nyè·ręht *first time* (-t-. -a'nyeręhT-).

fish. *n.* kę́·čęh *fish* (-ič-).

fish. *v.i.* ráhryuh *he fishes* (-ahryu-).

fish net. *n.* unę́⁷reh yečihsáktha⁷ *fish net* (-nę⁷r- -ičihsakT-).

fishhook. *n.* u⁷čúhneh *fishhook* (-⁷ču = hn-).

fishing, go. *v.i.* ęhsičíhsa·k *you will go fishing* (-ičihsak-).

fishing gear. *n.* úhryeh *fishing gear* (-ahry-).

fishing line. *n.* úhryeh *fishing line* (-ahry-).

fishline. *n.* yęhryúhkweh *fishline* (-ah = ryuhkw-).

fishy. *n.* kęčę́hči *fishy* (-ič-.#hči).

fissure. *n.* ukahrę̀·weh *fissure* (-kahręw-).

fist. *n.* úhčeh *fist* (-ahč-); učíhkweh *fist* (-čihkw-).

fit. *adj.* tkayè·ri⁷ *it is fit* (-t-.-yeri-); he⁷thúhči *fit* (he⁷thúhči).

fit. *v.i.* wekayè·ri⁷θ *it fits* (-yah-.-ye = ri⁷-).

five. *adj./n.* wísk *five* (wísk).

fix. *v.t.* ęhsačhákwahst *you will fix it* (-ačhakwahsT-).

fixed in place. *adj.* yu⁷ní⁷rę⁷ *it is fixed in place* (-a'ni⁷rę-).

flab. *n.* utkrę́hneh *flab* (-atkręhT-).

flame. *n.* awę⁷táhkreh *flame* (-ę⁷tahkr-); uręryúhkweh *flame* (-ręryuhkw-).

flame. *v.i.* yu⁷nę⁷tahkra⁷níhrę *it flames* (-a'nę⁷tahkra⁷nihr-).

flank. *n.* u⁷tíheh *flank* (-⁷tih-).

flannel, red. *n.* uči⁷nè·wareh *red flannel* (-či⁷newar-).

flash. *n.* učí⁷reh *flash of light* (-či⁷r-).

flatness. *n.* uhwá·θeh *flatness* (-hwač-).

flax. *n.* yehskará·kwara·č *flax* (-hskara = kʷaraθ-); yehskarakwará·θ⁷ę *flax* (-hskarakʷaraθ⁷-).

flay. *v.t.* rayę́·θręhs *he flays it* (-yę = θ(e)r-).

flea. *n.* nà·werk *flea* (nà·werk).

flee. *v.i.* ra⁷né⁷kwahs *he flees* (-a⁷ = ne⁷ku-); nehrutihárhę *he has fled* (-ne-.-tihar-); nakayéhs⁷aht *they fled* (-t-.-(i)hs⁷ahT-).

flesh. *n.* uhčúhkweh *flesh* (-hčuhkw-); uyè·reh *flesh* (-yer-).

---

flexible. *adj.* yuhrú⁷nę *it is flexible* (-hru⁷T-).

flicker. *n.* katí⁷nęh *flicker* (-ti⁷nę-).

flint. *n.* úhnareh *flint* (-hnar-).

float. *v.i.* ra⁷nu⁷kráhkhwa⁷ *he floats* (-a='nu⁷krahkw-); yá·wu·⁷ *it floats* (-u-); yawú⁷kyer *it floats (on water)* (-u⁷=k(e)r-); yutíyheh *it floated over* (-tiyheh-); newętáhkruč *it floats to the top* (-ne-.-ętahkruT-); wa⁷nu⁷krakwáhte⁷ *it is floating up* (-a'nu⁷=krakwahte⁷-); see: -u⁷awi-.

flock. *n.* yu⁷teyu⁷à·wi⁷ *flock* (-(ę)⁷te=yu⁷awi-).

flood. *n.* à·wę⁷ wa⁷wnawérhę *flood* (à·wę⁷ -a⁷wnawerhu-).

flood. *v.i.* yuθrú⁷nę· *it floods* (-θru⁷T-); węθrúhnęh *it floods* (-ęθruhnę-).

floor. *n.* kahwę⁷kharęθka⁷r *floor* (-hwę⁷=kharęθkar-); awętéhsteh *dirt floor* (-ę=téhst-).

flour. *n.* uthé⁷čreh *flour* (-athe⁷čr-).

flourish. *v.i.* wa⁷ka⁷ner⁷ęhsę́·ti⁷ *I flourish* (-a'ner⁷ęhsęti-).

flow. *v.i.* yú⁷θkarahs *it flows* (-⁷θkar-).

flow copiously. *v.i.* yuθrú⁷nę· *it is flowing copiously* (-θru⁷T-).

flower. *n.* uči⁷číhsteh *flower* (-či⁷čih=s(t)-).

flute. *n.* uhę̀·wareh *flute* (-hęwar-).

flutter. *v.i.* yuθrárha⁷ *it flutters* (-θrar-).

fly. *v.i.* neká·⁷nę⁷ *it flies* (-ne-.-'nę-).

foal. *n.* utè·reh *foal* (-(ę)ter-).

foam. *n.* uhwá⁷reh *thick foam* (-hwa⁷r-); uhwáhsteh *thin foam* (-hwahst-).

foam over. *v.i.* newásθręhs *it foams over* (-ne-.-asθr-).

fog. *n.* učhá·⁷neh *fog, mist* (-čha'n-).

foggy. *adj.* neyučhá·⁷nayę⁷ *it is foggy* (-ne-.-čha'nayę(T)-).

fold. *v.t.* nehrúhknęhs *he folds it* (-ne-.-ahk(e)T-); see: -ya⁷θ(e)r-.

follow. *v.i.* katká⁷ne⁷ *it follows* (-tka⁷T-); kayáhskaht *it follows* (-yahskaht); *v.t.* nehra⁷nahθę̨⁷rá·kwahs *he follows it* (-ne-.-a'nah=θę⁷raku-).

follow an example. *v.i.* ruta⁷kyè·rę *he followed an example* (-(ę)ta⁷ker-).

following. *adj.* uhta⁷kę́⁷kye *following* (uhta⁷kę́⁷kye).

fondle. *v.t.* ra⁷nęθrętyá⁷tha⁷ *he fondles it* (-a'nęθrętya⁷T-).

food. *n.* úkhweh *food* (-khw-); unęnhù·reh *food* (-nęnhur-).

foot. *n.* úhseh *foot* (-ahs-).

footprint. *n.* uyá⁷θeh *footprint* (-ya⁷θ-); uyá⁷θareh *footprint* (-ya⁷θar-).

for instance. *adv.* né⁷či *for instance* (né⁷-či).

for nothing *adv.* kwęhs kwè·ni⁷ *for nothing* (kwęhs kwè·ni⁷).

for sure. *adv.* ka⁷nę́ utukę́⁷ę *for sure* (ka⁷nę́ -tukę⁷-).

for the sake of. *prep.* hà·ne⁷ nyawè·rih *for the sake of* (hà·ne⁷ nyawè·rih).

forage. *n.* unęnhù·reh *forage* (-nęnhur-).

forbid. *v.t.* rahθawę́hra⁷č *he forbids it* (-ahθawęhra⁷T-); wa⁷ęhθawęhrá⁷nę⁷ *one forbade it* (-ahθawęhra⁷T-{dative III}); wa⁷khenę́sna⁷nę⁷ *I forbid another* (-nęsnaT-).

force. *n.* ú⁷θheh *force* (-(i)⁷θh-).

force. *v.t.* rathwihshę́·tih *he forces it* (-athwihshęti-).

forceps. *n.* yetu⁷θawihsyá⁷tha⁷ *forceps* (-(ę)tu⁷θawihsya⁷T-).

ford. *n.* yehyá⁷ktha⁷ *ford* (-(i)hya⁷kT-).

forefathers. *n.* ruhryahsutkę́he⁷ *forefathers* (-hryahsut.#kęhe⁷); ruhsučrayę́·⁷nęhk *his forefathers* (-hsučra=yę(T)-).

forehead. *n.* ukę́⁷neh *forehead* (-kę⁷n-).

forenoon. *n.* θuhterhę́·kye *forenoon* (-či-.-hterhę.#ke).

foresee. *v.t.* wehrá·kęh *he foresees* (-yah-.-kę-).

foresee the future. *v.t.* nehrurę⁷kę́·nyę *he*

foresaw the future (-ne-.-rę˛'kęni-).

forest. *n.* úrha˛'neh *forest* (-rha˛'n-); uwíhreh *young, lightly wooded forest* (-wihr-).

foretell a bad experience. *v.i.* wa˛'thru˛'nyerę˛hnyę˛'θ *he foretold a bad experience* (-ne-.-a'nyerę˛hnyę˛-{dative I}).

forethought. *n.* thrawę˛'tikę˛hnę˛' *his forethought* (-t-.-(ę˛)'tikę˛hnę˛-).

forever. *adv.* ha˛' yę˛·we˛' *forever* (-yah-. -e-).

forget. *v.i.* ru˛'tikę˛hrę˛·'nę˛hθ *he forgets* (-(ę˛)'tikę˛hrę˛T-{dative II}).

forgive. *v.t* nakwa˛'rihwanę˛·ta˛'θ *forgive us!* (-a˛'rihwanę˛t(a˛')-).

fork. *n.* uhsę˛wá˛'reh *fork* (-hsę˛wa˛'r-).

forked. *adj.* neyawú·kę˛' *it is forked* (-ne-.-ukę˛-).

forlorn. *adj.* ru˛'ná˛'čwe˛'n *he is forlorn* (-a˛'na˛'čwen-).

fornicate. *v.i.* ra˛'nę˛nę˛hwaru˛'yéhstha˛' *he fornicates* (-a'nę˛nę˛hwaru˛'yehsT-).

fort. *n.* wa˛'tę˛·yayę˛' *fort* (-at'ę˛yayę˛(T)-).

fortify. *v.i.* ra˛t'ę˛·yayę˛hs *he fortifies himself* (-at'ę˛yayę˛(T)-).

fortuitous. *adj.* yú˛'tyehθ *fortuitous* (-'tyeh-).

fortune teller. *n.* ra˛'rę˛'na·č *fortune teller* (-a˛'rę˛'naT-).

forty. *adj./n.* hę˛'tahk tiwáhθhę˛· *forty* (hę˛'tahk ti-.-ahθhę˛-).

found out. *adj.* rahswakwę˛·ri˛'θ *he is found out* (-hswakwę˛ri˛'-).

foundation. *n.* yu˛'nę˛nę˛hstáhkę˛ *foundation* (-a'nę˛nę˛hstahkw-); yu˛'nę˛hstáhkę˛ *foundation* (-a'nę˛hstahkw-); kę˛' káher

foundation (kę˛' -(i)har-).

foundry. *n.* kę˛' nyewenę˛'na˛'tawę˛'tha˛' *foundry* (kę˛' -t-.-wenę˛'na˛'tawę˛'T-).

four. *adj./n.* hę˛'tahk.

fourteen. *adj./n.* hę˛'tahk θkáhe˛'r *fourteen* (hę˛'tahk -či-.-(i)har-).

fox. *n.* θkę˛hná·ksę˛ *fox* (-či-.-ihnaks-), číčhu *small fox* (číčhu).

foyer. *n.* utakę˛hsteh *foyer* (-takę˛hst-).

fragile. *adj.* neyuhwa˛'rí˛'ne˛' *it is fragile* (-ne-.-hwa˛'ri˛'ne-).

fragments. *n.* awú·kri˛' *fragments* (-ukr-).

frame. *n.* u˛'teyę˛hkweh *frame* (-(ę˛)'te=yę˛hkw-).

frame a picture. *v.i.* rarę˛·war *he frames a picture* (-rę˛war-).

free. *adj.* kwè·ni˛' *free (of charge)* (kwè·ni˛'); ka˛'nwę˛nì·yu˛' *I am free (from slavery)* (-a'nwę˛niyu-).

freed. *adj.* ra˛'nwę˛nì·yu˛'θ *he is freed* (-a'nwę˛niyu˛'-).

freeze. *v.i.* nakáhratuhst *it froze* (-t-. -hratuhsT-); kawí·suč *it freezes* (-wi=sur-).

freeze water. *v.i.* wa˛'kawískwe·k *the water freezes* (-wiskwek-).

frenzy. *n.* urę˛hya˛'náhčreh *frenzy* (-rę˛h=ya˛'nahčr-).

frequent. *v.t.* rarę˛'nhę˛hs *he frequents it* (-rę˛'nh-).

frequently. *adv.* tyure˛'áh *frequently* (ti-. -re-.#áh).

fresh. *adj.* uθrà·yeh *fresh* (-θray-).

freshen. *v.t.* račikhe˛'núhar *he freshens it* (-čikhe˛'nuhar-); račikhe˛'nú·kwahs *he freshens it* (-čikhe˛'nuku-).

Friday. *n.* wísk tičuhtérhę˛ *Friday* (wísk

ti+či-. -hterhę-).

friend. *n.* raʔnę̀·nur *his friend* (-a'nęnur); waʔnęrúʔčhę *her close friend* (-a'nę=ruʔčhę(T)-); raʔnę̀·ruʔ *his good friend* (-a'nęruʔ).

friends with, become. *v.t.* waʔčhaʔnę-ná·hyęhst *you became friends with someone* (-ne-. -a'nęna·hyęhsT-).

fringe. *n.* učíʔčeh *fringe* (-čiʔči-).

fritter. *n.* uθrahwíʔreh *fritter* (-θrah=wiʔr-).

frivolous. *adj.* yurihwáhsthę *frivolous* (-rihwahsthu-); yurihwéhsayę *frivolous* (-rihwehsayę-).

frog. *n.* warè·reh *bull frog* (warè·reh); né·kre· *early spring frog* (né·kre·); ruté·krar *green frog* (ruté·krar); kwà·ręʔr *northern tree frog* (kwà·ręʔr).

frolicsome. *adj.* rawęʔnhékwskę *he is frolicsome* (-ęʔnhekʷsk-).

front of, in. *prep.* uhę́ʔnę *in front of* (-(a)hęʔT-).

frontward. *n.* uhęʔnęhá·ʔnyeʔ *frontward* (-(a)hęʔnęha'nyeʔ-).

frost. *n.* yuwiθrę́ʔę *frost* (-wiθręʔ-).

froth. *n.* uhwáhsteh *froth* (-hwahst-).

frown. *n.* ukyéʔθreh *frown* (-keʔθr-).

fruit. *n.* úhyeh *fruit* (-(a)hy-).

fruitful. *adj.* yuhyętyáhneʔ *it is fruitful* (-(a)hyętyahnę-).

fry. *v.i.* węhrá·heʔ *it is frying* (-ęhra·-); *v.t.* rę́hraws *he fries it* (-ęhrahw-).

frying pan. *n.* utkwę́hneh *frying pan* (-tkwęhn-).

full. *adj.* waká·tʔę *I am full* (-(a)tʔa-).

fullness. *n.* unháhčreh *fullness* (-(a)n=hahčr-).

fumble. *v.t.* ruθkrì·ręhs *he fumbles it* (-uθkrir-).

fun of, make. *v.t.* θakayęʔnaʔrihú·ryeʔ *they made fun of him* (-či-. -rihuri-).

fundament. *n.* utiʔnę̀·weh *fundament* (-tiʔnęw-).

fungus. *n.* utráhseh *fungus* (-trahs-).

funnel. *n.* yeθerhuhnáhkhwaʔ *funnel* (-θerhuhnahkw-).

fur. *n.* awéʔreh *fur* (-eʔr-); utíhkweh *fur* (-(ę)tihkw-); uhstwáhreh *light fur* (-hstwahr-).

furious. *adj.* rętichaʔrę́·tih *he is furious* (-ętichaʔręti-); rętičháʔrakweks *he is furious* (-ętičhaʔrak̲ʷek-).

furniture. *n.* ę́·kyeʔ yęčnáhkhwaʔ *furniture* (ę́·kyeʔ -ačnahkw-).

furrow. *n.* uhwéʔneh *furrow* (-hweʔn-); kęʔ neyawęhruręhá·ʔnyeʔ *furrow* (kęʔ -ne-. -ę̇ʔhruręha'nyeʔ-).

furry. *adj.* aweʔrę́ʔči *furry* (-eʔr-.#hči).

further. *adv.* héʔnęʔ *further* (héʔnęʔ).

future. *n.* haʔ nà·weʔ *future* (-t-. -e-).

fuzz. *n.* uhstwáhreh *fuzz* (-hstwahr-).

G

gag. *v.i.* rutyáʔkwrę· *he gags* (-tyaʔ=kʷhrę-); rutyaʔkwahná·ti· *he gags* (-tyaʔk̲ʷahT-{dative III}).

gain. *v.t.* raʔtyę́·ʔnęh *he gains it* (-ʔtyę='nęh-).

gait. *n.* uyá·teh *gait* (-yat-).

gall. *n.* učháʔneh *gall* (-čhaʔn-).

gallon. *n.* uwenę́·ʔneh *gallon* (-wenęT-).

gallop. *v.i.* raʔnyaʔkarę́·ʔnyęhs *he gallops* (-a'nyaʔk̲arę̇'ni-).

game. *n.* awęʔnhé·kwęʔ *game* (-ęʔn=hekʷ-); awęʔnhékwčreh *game* (-ęʔn=hekʷčr-).

gander. *n.* katúʔθę·t kaʔníha· *gander* (-(ę)tuʔθęT- -ʔniha-).

gangrene. *n.* yuhwéθtkę· *gangrene* (-hweθtkę-).

gape. *v.i.* nehruhskahręwáhthaʔ *he gapes* (-ne-. -(i)hskahręwahT-).

garden. *n.* uhéhneh *garden* (-hehn-).

gargle. *v.i.* račkahręwúhar *he gargles* (-ačkahręwuhar-).

garrulous. *adj.* awé·ha·k *garrulous* (-e = ha<u>k</u>-).

gasp for air. *v.i.* wa^ʔthranhę^ʔnará^ʔθrę^ʔ *he gasped for breath* (-ne-.-nhę'n<u>a</u>ra^ʔ = θrę-).

gather. *v.t.* rarúhčręh *he gathers it* (-ruhčrę-).

gay. *adj.* warásči· *it is gay* (-arasči-).

gelding. *n.* áha·θ u^ʔnhęhsú·kę^ʔ *gelding* (áha·θ -^ʔnhęhsukę^ʔ).

generous. *adj.* rá·nę· *he is generous* (-(a)nę-).

genitals, female. *n.* učí^ʔnę^ʔ *female genitals* (-či^ʔnę^ʔ).

genteel. *adj.* ruthéhtrak *he is genteel* (-athehtrak-).

geranium, wild. *n.* neyuhkarúθ^ʔne^ʔ *wild geranium* (-ne-.-(a)hk<u>a</u>ruθT-).

gesticulate. *v.i.* ra^ʔčirà·węh *he gesticulates* (-^ʔčirawę-).

get. *v.t.* wá·kkwę *I have gotten it* (-ku-); *v.i.* θáčnęht *get down!* (-ačnęhT-/ -ačnęhsT-); ra^ʔrá·t'ahs *he gets in* (-a^ʔrat^ʔa-); *v.t.* yù·ra^ʔθ *it gets into things* (-ra^ʔ-); yuhrá^ʔę *it has gotten on it* (-(a)hra^ʔ-); *v.i.* ra^ʔra^ʔná·kwahs *he gets out* (-a^ʔra^ʔnaku-); ratkęhahs *he gets out of bed* (-atkęha-); thru·tkęhá^ʔnę *as soon as he got up* (-t-.-atkęha^ʔn-).

get over. *v.i.* ręryę́·^ʔna^ʔθ *he gets over an attack of sickness or a spasm* (-ę°ryę = 'na^ʔ-).

ghost. *n.* uhskę̀·neh *ghost* (-hskęn-); u^ʔné·wa·k *ghost* (-^ʔnewak).

ghost-skeleton. *n.* uhskę́^ʔrarih *ghost-skeleton (departed spirit)* (-hskę́^ʔr<u>a</u> = rih-).

ghostly. *n.* u^ʔnewa·kkyéha·^ʔ *ghostly* (-^ʔnewak.#keha·^ʔ).

giantess. *n.* nwat^ʔahsęya^ʔnęhú^ʔy *giantess* (-at^ʔahsęya^ʔT-.#ú^ʔy).

giddy. *adj.* nehrarę^ʔné·tyęhs *he is giddy* (-ne-.-rę^ʔneti-).

giggle. *v.i.* ruyęhskwé·^ʔne^ʔ *he giggles* (-yęhskweT-).

gild. *v.t.* rarihstárhahs *he gilds it* (-rih = starh-).

gills. *n.* wa^ʔnęryéhtha^ʔ *gills* (-a'nę = ryehT-); ukęhúhseh *gills* (-kęhuhs-).

ginger, wild. *n.* uhskwarí^ʔna^ʔ *wild ginger* (uhskwarí^ʔna^ʔ).

ginseng. *n.* karętú·kę^ʔ *ginseng* (-rętukę^ʔ).

girl. *n.* yeká·θ^ʔah *girl* (-kaθ^ʔah); eθrà·yeh *young girl* (-θray-); etyáčhayę^ʔ *adolescent girl (10-15 years old)* (-tyačhayę-).

girth. *n.* uyáhkweh *girth* (-yahkw-).

give. *v.t.* ráws *he gives* (-aw-); tkę̀·yaws *I give it to you* (-t-.-aw-); ra^ʔná·k-^ʔwahs *he gives up* (-a'nak^ʔu-).

gizzard. *n.* utkwęnúhθreh *gizzard* (-tkwęnuhθr-).

glass. *n.* uwí·seh *glass (object)* (-wis-); awé·kyeh *glass (material)* (-ek-).

glasses. *n.* ukáhreh *glasses* (-kah(r)-).

glimmer. *v.i.* rahsnuká^ʔtha^ʔ *he glimmers* (-hsnuka^ʔT-).

globular. *adj.* tha^ʔneyutkwe^ʔné·ti· hané^ʔ·či uthnę́hsteh *globular* (tha+ne-.-atkwe^ʔnęti- hané^ʔči -athnęhst-).

gloomy. *adj.* yawę^ʔné·ti· *it is gloomy* (-ę'nęti-); rawę^ʔnętyá^ʔθe· *he is gloomy* (-ę'nęti-{dative I}).

Tuscarora Pronunciation Key:
/a/ l<u>a</u>w; /e/ h<u>a</u>t; /i/ p<u>i</u>zza; /u/ t<u>u</u>ne; /ę/ h<u>i</u>nt; /č/ <u>ch</u>eese; /h/ <u>h</u>oe; /m/ <u>m</u>other; /s/ <u>s</u>ame; /t/ <u>d</u>o (before a vowel y, or w), <u>t</u>oo (elsewhere); /k/ <u>g</u>ale (before a vowel y or w), <u>k</u>ale (elsewhere); /n/ i<u>nh</u>ale (before a consonant or word-final), <u>n</u>ote (elsewhere), /r/ hi<u>ss</u> (before a consonant or word-final), <u>r</u>un (trilled as in Italian, elsewhere); /w/ cu<u>ff</u> (before a consonant other than y or word-final), <u>w</u>ay (elsewhere); /y/ fi<u>sh</u> (before a consonant or word-final), <u>y</u>ou (elsewhere), /θ/ <u>th</u>ing; /ʔ/ (the sound between the vowels in unh-unh); /·/ long vowel, /ˊ/ high pitch; /ˋ/ low pitch.

glory. *n*. kayęwahnęhčra⁷ *glory* (-yę=
wahnęhčr-).

glossy. *adj*. kačatuká⁷tha⁷ *it is glossy*
(-čatuka⁷T-).

glottis. *n*. uhęhkweh *glottis* (-hęhkw-).

glove. *n*. uhčúhčreh *glove* (-ahčuhčr-).

gloves, wear. *v.i*. ruhčúhčrę⁷ *he is wearing gloves* (-ahčuhčrę-).

glue. *n*. učíhskwa⁷ *glue* (-čihskw-); uh-
snahrę·weh *glue* (-hsnahręw-); uθrę·-
weh *glue* (-θręw-).

glutton. *n*. rawęnhe⁷neht *he is a glutton*
(-ę̊nhe̲⁷nehT-).

gluttonous. *adj*. rawęnhe⁷neht *he is gluttonous* (-ę̊nhe̲⁷nehT-).

gnash teeth. *v.i*. nehraθčúhčha⁷ *he
gnashes his teeth* (-ne-.-θčuhčha-).

gnat. *n*. ruhsnyáhrę *gnat* (ruhsnyáhrę);
ru⁷kę·rarahs *gnat* (ru⁷kę·rarahs).

gnaw. *v.t*. rakęθhęh *he gnaws at it*
(-kęθhę-); rahsniyáhnęh *he gnaws it
to the bone* (-hsniy-).

go. *v.i*. ę́·kye⁷ *I will go* (-e-); yę̀·nęhs
one goes (-enę-); wewáhknę *it goes
and returns* (-yah-.-ahk(e)T-); ę⁷nwa-
kà·ręw *we will go around* (-ka=
rę(hw)-); yahwahrakwa⁷ná·θe·⁷ *he
went around* (-yah-.-a̲⁷na·θ(e)-); yah-
wahrakwa⁷ná·θe·⁷ *he went around*
(-a̲⁷naθ(e)-); ruré·kwę· *he has gone
away* (-ar(e)ku-); nehra⁷níhar *he goes
beyond* (-ne-.-a'nihar-); wehra⁷nękúhtha⁷ *he goes beyond* (-yah-.-a'nę=
kuhT-); rathęwúhahs *he goes by boat*
(-athęwuha-); rahęwí·te⁷ *he goes by
boat* (-hęwiN-); yahwa⁷kayęč⁷aht *they
went forth* (-yah-.-ač⁷ahT-); wahra-
ká⁷nayę⁷ *he went in circle* (-ka⁷na̲=
yę(T)-); kyá·kę⁷θ *I go out* (-yakę⁷-);
nehra⁷níhar *he goes over* (-ne-.-a=
'nihar-); nahráhs⁷aht *he went rapidly*
(-t-.--(i)hs⁷ahT-); nęyehahakháhsi⁷
they two will go separate ways (-(a)=
haha̲khahsi-); see: -iN-; *v.t*. see: -i=

go into. *v.i*. see: -yę-.

goat. *n*. kakyerhá·kra·θ *goat* (-kerha=
kraθ-).

goblet. *n*. uwí·seh *goblet* (-wis-).

gold. *n*. tikači⁷tkwáhnayę⁷ *gold* (ti-.
-či⁷tkwahna̲yę(T)-).

goldenrod. *n*. rahθé⁷kye *goldenrod* (rahθé⁷kye) yeyęwę́·tih *goldenrod* (yeyę-
wę́·tih).

goldplate. *n*. yeyè·rawęhs *goldplate* (-ye=
ra̲wę-).

gonorrhea. *n*. účkreh *gonorrhea* (-čkr-).

good. *adj*. wákwahst *it is good* (-a=
kwahsT-).

good again, make. *v.i*. ęhsačhákwahst
you will make it good again (-ačha=
kwahsT-).

goods. *n*. uthahkwę̀·yeh *goods* (-thah=
kwęy-).

goose. *n*. uhę́⁷rę⁷ *Canadian goose* (u-
hę́⁷rę⁷); katú⁷θę·t *domestic goose*
(-(ę)tu⁷θęT-).

gooseberry. *n*. yuhyá⁷θhara⁷r *gooseberry*
(-(a)hya̲⁷θha̲rar-).

gopher. *n*. aθneháh *gopher* (aθneháh).

gore. *n*. ká·tkę⁷ *gore* (-tkę-).

gorgeous. *adj*. yu⁷ęhráhuks *gorgeous*
(-⁷ęhra̲huk-).

gossip. *v.i*. yę⁷tahsaráhkhwa⁷ *one is gossiping* (-(ę)⁷tahsa̲rahkw-).

gourd. *n*. účheh *gourd* (-čhe⁷-); učhé⁷-
weh *gourd* (-čhe⁷w-).

gourd bowl. *n*. čhé⁷ru⁷r *gourd bowl*
(čhé⁷ru⁷r).

govern. *v.t*. thrę⁷tikę́hnęh *he governs*
(-t-.-(ę)⁷tikę́hnę-); see: -yan(e)(r)-.

government. *n*. uyané⁷čreh *government*
(-yane⁷čr-).

governor. *n*. kà·winar *governor* (kà·wi-
nar); kuráhkuwa⁷ *governor* (kuráhkuwa⁷).

grace. *n*. u⁷ni⁷nęrę́hčreh *grace* (-a'ni'nę=
rę̆hčr-).

gracious. *adj.* ru⁷ni⁷ṇ̀·rẹ *he is gracious* (-a'ni'nẹr-).

graft. *n.* uhθẹ́⁷reh *graft* (-(a)hθẹ⁷r-).

graft. *v.t.* nehrahθẹ́⁷ner *he grafts it* (-ne-.-hθẹ'n(e)r-).

grain. *n.* unẹ́hsneh *grain of wheat, corn, etc.* (-nẹhsn-).

grain meal. *n.* awẹ́hẹ⁷ *fine grain meal* (-ẹh-).

granary. *n.* yenẹhsnayẹ⁷náhkhwa⁷ *granary* (-nẹhsnayẹ'nahkw-).

grandchild. *n.* kẹyá·⁷reh *my grandchild* (-a⁷reh).

grandfather. *n.* akhryáhsu·t *my grandfather* (-hryahsut).

grandmother. *n.* áksu·t *my grandmother* (-hsut).

grandnephew. *n.* kẹyá·⁷reh *my grandnephew* (-a⁷reh).

grandniece. *n.* kẹyá·⁷reh *my grandniece* (-a⁷reh).

grape. *n.* kwẹnẹ⁷rurá·yẹ·θ *grape* (kwẹnẹ⁷rurá·yẹ·θ); unẹ⁷à·rayẹ⁷ *wild grape* (-nẹ⁷arayẹ(T)-).

grasp. *v.t.* see: -wa⁷k-.

grass. *n.* uherúhkweh *grass* (-heruhkw-); unẹ́hsakwt kater⁷ahθẹ́·tih *grass* (-nẹh=sakT -ter⁷ahθẹti-).

grasscutter. *n.* yeheryá⁷ktha⁷ *grasscutter* (-herya⁷kT-).

grasshopper. *n.* čihkwé·kẹh *grasshopper* (čihkwé·kẹh).

gratis. *adj.* kwè·ni⁷ *gratis* (kwè·ni⁷).

grave. *adj.* nehrukyé⁷θru⁷ *he is grave* (-ne-.-ke⁷θrur-).

grave. *n.* ha⁷ kẹ⁷ rá·⁷nẹht *grave* (kẹ⁷ -'nẹhT-).

gravel. *n.* u⁷téheh *gravel* (-⁷teh-).

gray. *n.* u⁷kẹ́hreh *gray* (-a⁷kẹhr-).

grease. *n.* kẹ̀·ye⁷ *grease* (-iye-); uyé·teh *grease* (-yet-).

grease. *v.t.* rayetà·wẹhs *he greases it* (-yetaw-).

great. *adj.* kwà·nẹ *great* (kwà·nẹ); wí·yu· *it is great* (-iyu-).

great grandchild. *n.* kẹyá·⁷reh *my great grandchild* (-a⁷reh).

great grandfather. *n.* akhryáhsu·t *my great grandfather* (-hryahsut); a-khryahsu·t⁷ú⁷y *my great grandfather* (-hryahsut.#ú⁷y).

great grandmother. *n.* áksu·t *my great grandmother* (-hsut); aksu·t⁷ú⁷y *my great grandfather* (-ahsut.#ú⁷y).

greediness. *n.* uhθkyenhá⁷ẹ *greediness* (-ahθkenha⁷-).

greedy. *adj.* rawẹ́nhe⁷neht *he is greedy* (-ẹ⁷nhe⁷nehT-); ruhθkyenhá⁷θe· *he is greedy* (-ahθkenha-{dative I}).

green. *n.* uhè·reh *green (color)* (-her-); á·θe·⁷ *green (unripe)* (á·θe·⁷).

grief. *n.* ha⁷ yu⁷tikẹhrá·ksa⁷t *grief* (-(ẹ)⁷tikẹhraksa⁷T-).

grimace. *v.i.* ratkẹhsayatá⁷tha⁷ *he makes grimaces* (-atkẹhsayata⁷T-).

grin. *v.i.* nehrẹnú⁷kẹws *he grins* (-ne-.-ẹnu⁷kẹhw-).

grind. *v.t.* rará·tih *he grinds it* (-rati-); wa⁷é⁷ru·⁷ *one ground it* (-⁷ru-).

grind stone. *n.* uhrẹ́⁷neh *grind stone* (-hrẹ⁷n-).

grip. *n.* úhsyu⁷ *grip* (-hsyur-).

groan. *v.i.* rẹ́nhẹ⁷θ *he groans* (-ẹnhẹ⁷-); nẹ⁷nwẹθkẹ́·rye⁷ *it groaned* (-ẹθkẹri-).

Tuscarora Pronunciation Key:

/a/ law; /e/ hat; /i/ pizza; /u/ tune; /ẹ/ hint; /č/ cheese; /h/ hoe; /m/ mother; /s/ same; /t/ do (before a vowel y, or w), too (elsewhere); /k/ gale (before a vowel y or w), kale (elsewhere); /n/ inhale (before a consonant or word-final), note (elsewhere), /r/ hiss (before a consonant or word-final), run (trilled as in Italian, elsewhere); /w/ cuff (before a consonant other than y or word-final), way (elsewhere); /y/ fish (before a consonant or word-final), you (elsewhere), /θ/ thing; /⁷/ (the sound between the vowels in unh-unh); /·/ long vowel, /´/ high pitch; /`/ low pitch.

grocery store. *n.* krú·si⁷ *grocery store* (krú·si⁷).

groin. *n.* útkweh *groin* (-tkw-).

groove in, make a. *v.t.* see: -tet⁷-.

grotto. *n.* wahę́⁷nayę⁷ *grotto* (-ahę⁷na̲= yę(T)-).

ground. *n.* úhskweh *hard ground* (-ah= skw-); awętéhsteh *solid ground* (-ę= tehst-).

ground hog. *n.* runá⁷kę·t *ground hog* (ru- ná⁷kę·t).

group. *n.* u⁷nyúhkweh *group* (-i⁷= nyuhkw-); see: -i-/ -ę°-.

grow fast. *v.i.* yu⁷niθtù·re⁷ *it was grow- ing fast* (-a'niθtur-).

growl. *v.i.* wačętráhtha⁷ *it growls* (-ačę= trahT-).

grumble. *v.i.* ruhskrú·ri· *he grumbles* (-hskruri-).

guard. *v.t.* ná⁷nęh *one guards another* (-nę-); kayę⁷na⁷nęnę́nhyar *they guard another* (-ęnęnhyar-).

guess. *v.i.* thwehráhews *he guesses* (ti+ yah-. -(ę)haw-).

guide. *n.* utačí·teh *guide* (-tačit-); raha- hęhà·wi⁷ *guide* (-(a)hahęhawi-).

guild. *v.t.* rahwihstaθerhú⁷θeh *he guilds it* (-hwihstaθerhu-{dative I}).

guilty. *adj.* nehrurihù·ręh *he is guilty* (-ne-. -rihurę-).

guinea hen. *n.* túhkwak *guinea hen* (túh- kwak).

gull. *n.* čuha⁷θ⁷á·ka·⁷ *gull* (čuha⁷θ⁷á·- ka·⁷).

gum. *n.* učíhskwa⁷ *gum* (-čihskw-); uθrę̀·weh *gum* (-θręw-).

gums. *n.* utkęwá⁷θeh *gums (in the mouth)* (-tkęwa⁷θ-).

gum. *v.t.* raθręwawę́hsthęh *he gums them* (-θręwa̲węhsthę-).

gummy. *adj.* uθręwéhči *gummy* (-θręw-. #hči).

gun. *n.* á⁷neh *gun* (-a⁷n-).

gunpowder. *n.* awę́hę⁷ *gunpowder* (-ęh-).

H

habit. *n.* uríhweh *habit* (-rihw-).

hail. *n.* uwí·seh *hail* (-wis-); wa⁷uwi- sá·⁷ne⁷ *hail* (-wisa'ne-); u⁷téheh *hail* (-⁷teh-); ha⁷ yu⁷tehahrí⁷ę *hail* (-⁷te= hahri⁷-).

hail. *v.i.* ka⁷teháhri⁷θ *it hails* (-⁷te= hahri⁷-).

hair. *n.* ukyé⁷weh *hair* (-ke⁷w-); uh- sú·kareh *facial hair* (-hsuka̲r-); unéθ- twa⁷reh *pubic hair* (-neθtwa̲⁷r-).

hairy. *adj.* ukye⁷wéhči *hairy* (-ke⁷w-. #hči); awe⁷ŕę́⁷či *hairy* (-e⁷r-.#hči).

half. *n.* ahsę̀·nę *half* (ahsę̀·nę); tha⁷- ahsę̀·nę *half* (tha⁷ahsę̀·nę).

halfway. *n.* tha⁷ahsę̀·nę *halfway* (tha⁷- ahsę̀·nę); unę́·thę *halfway* (-nęthę).

halo. *n.* uręryúhkweh *halo* (-ręryuhkw-).

halter. *n.* watkęhsu⁷narhúhstha⁷ *halter* (-atkęhsu'nar-huhsT-).

ham. *n.* uhá·θareh *ham (inside of thigh)* (-haθa̲r-).

hamburger. *n.* neka⁷wahrahríhnę *ham- burger* (-ne-. -⁷wahra̲hrihT-).

hammer. *n.* učíhkweh *hammer* (-čihkw-).

hammer. *v.t.* rahsęwa⁷rá⁷nihč *he ham- mers it* (-hsęwa⁷ra⁷nihr-); rakę́⁷čręh *he hammers it* (-kę⁷črę-); rá·kę⁷č *he hammers it* (-kę⁷T-).

hand. *n.* u⁷éhneh *hand* (-⁷ehn-).

hand to. *v.t.* na⁷ná·⁷nę⁷ *one handed it to another* (-aw-).

handful. *n.* úhθheh *handful* (-ahθh-).

handkerchief. *n.* uhskareháh *handkerchief* (-hska̲r-.#áh).

handle. *n.* uhtyúhareh *handle* (-htyuha̲r-).

handle. *v.t.* rahsyawę̀·rih *he handles it* (-hsyawęri-).

handsome. *adj.* rakwà·nihst *he is hand- some* (-kwanihst-); rakwáhyę *he is handsome* (-kwahy-).

hang. *v.t.* ráha⁷r *he has hung it* (-(i)=

har-).

hang down. *v.i.* kahθę́ʔrhaʔ *it hangs down* (-(a)hθę'n(e)r-); see: -ę°y-.

hanger. *n.* yeharáhkhwaʔ *hanger* (-(i)= harahkw-).

hangman. *n.* rahà·ręh *executioner* (-(i)= har-{dative III}).

happen. *v.i.* tikà·yer *it happens* (ti-. -yer-).

happen, make. *v.t.* waʔeyè·raʔt *one made it happen* (-yeraʔT-); nahraʔnyè·ręht *he made it happen* (-t-. -a'nyeręhT-).

happen by chance. *v.i.* yúʔtyehθ *it happens by chance* (-ʔtyeh-).

happening. *n.* haʔ yuʔnyerę́ʔę *happening* (-a'nyerę́ʔ-).

happiness. *n.* učhęnę́·tyaʔt *happiness* (-a= čhęnętyaʔT-).

happy. *adj.* warásči· *it is happy* (-aras= či-); waʔęčhęnę́·tiʔ *one was happy* (-ačhęnęti-).

hard. *adj.* waká·θneʔ *it is hard* (-aθn-); yuhtì·rę *it is hard* (-htir-).

harden. *v.t.* rahtì·rahč *he hardens it* (-htirahT-).

hardly. *adv.* θrę́ʔkye *hardly* (θrę́ʔkye).

hardness. *n.* haʔ uhtì·rę *hardness* (-htir-).

hardwood. *n.* yuyękwirahtì·rę *hardwood* (-yękwirahtir-).

hardy. *adj.* ęʔnęhtì·ręʔ *it was hardy* (-a'nęhtir-{dative III}).

harm. *n.* uyaʔné·rę·t *harm* (-ayaʔnerę-); ukaré·nyaht *harm* (-karęnyahT-).

harm. *v.t.* rayaʔnè·ręh *he harms it* (-a= yaʔnerę-).

harness. *n.* uʔnetyáhsteh *harness* (-a'ne= tyahst-); áha·θ yuʔnetyahstà·węh *hor-*

se's harness (áha·θ -aʔnetyahstawę-).

harvest. *v.t.* ruyęthwá·kwę *he has harvested it* (-yęthwaku-).

haste. *n.* ukwarihę́ʔneh *haste* (-kwari= hę́ʔT-).

hasten. *v.i.* ruʔnahθkyénhę *he hastens* (-a'nahθkenha-); *v.t.* khekwariháʔthaʔ *I hasten another* (-kwarihaʔT-); see: -kwarih-.

hasten on. *v.i.* raʔnyatù·rahč *he hastens on* (-a'nyaturahT-).

hat. *n.* unęhrúhčreh *hat* (-(ę)nęhruhčr-).

hatch. *v.t.* waʔkaʔnhękúhčiʔ *it hatched it* (-ʔnhękuhči-).

hatchet. *n.* úʔθreh *hatchet* (-aʔθr-).

hate. *n.* sę́·nyęʔ *hate* (sę́·nyęʔ); úhsęht *hate* (-ahsęhT-).

hate. *v.t.* ruhsaʔrę́·ti· *he hates it* (-hsaʔ= rę-{dative III}); neyęčhę́ʔθeh *the two of them hate each other* (-ačhę-{dative I}); rahséheʔ *he hates it* (-ah= sęheʔ-); načhę́ʔθeh *one hates another* (-(i)hsę-{dative I}).

hateful. *adj.* ruhsaʔrę́·tyaht *he is hateful* (-hsaʔrę-{dative III}-ahT-).

hatter. *n.* ranęhruhčrę́·tih *hatter* (-(ę)nęh= ruhčręti-).

haughty. *adj.* raʔrihú·kwaht *he is haughty* (-aʔrihukʷahT-).

haunting. *adj.* newaʔnyerę́hnyęʔ *it is haunting* (-ne-. -a'nyeręhnyę-).

have. *v.t.* rù·yęʔ *he has it* (-yę(T)-).

hay. *n.* uherúhkweh *hay* (-heruhkw-).

hayloft. *n.* yeheruhkwayęʔnáhkhwaʔ *hayloft* (-heruhkwayę'nahkw-).

hazard. *v.i.* raʔnęhtiráʔthaʔ *he hazards (e.g., a guess)* (-a'nęhtiraʔT-).

---

hazardous. *adj.* yu'tikę́htaht *hazardous* (-(ę)'tikę́htahT-).

head. *n.* utá'reh *head* (-(ę)ta'r-).

head man. *n.* uhę́'nę ru'nę́'nę *the head man* (-(a)hę'T- -a'nę'T-).

head of family. *n.* rahwačirakwe'nì·yu' *he is head of family* (-hwačirakwe'=niyu-).

headache, have a. *v.i.* ruta'ranę́hwaks *he has a headache* (ę)ta'ranęhwak(T)-).

heal. *v.i.* čuthwęhę́·tyę· *it had healed* (-či-.-thwęhętyę-).

healer. *n.* ranęhkwa'črayę'nè·rih *healer* (-nęhkwa'črayę'ner-).

health. *n.* awę́nhe' *health* (-ę°nhe-).

heap. *n.* unę́'kweh *heap* (-nę'kw-); uta'čúhkweh *heap (of corn, earth, wheat)* (-(ta)'čuhkw-).

heap. *v.t.* rakyéhręhs *he heaps it* (-ke=hr-).

hear. *v.t.* ękahę́hsyę' *one will hear it* (-hęhsyę-).

heart. *n.* aweryáhseh *heart* (-eryahs-); awęnhé'čreh *heart* (-ę°nhe'čr-).

heart attack, have a. *v.i.* wa'nyakuti-hù·rę' *one had a heart attack* (-ne-.-tihurę-).

hearth. *n.* učę́hakwt *hearth* (-(a)čę́hakT-).

heat. *n.* u'narihę́hsteh *heat* (-a'nari=hęhst-).

heat up. *v.t.* see: -tawę-.

heaven. *n.* urę́hyakęw *heaven* (-ręhya=kęw).

heavy. *adj.* wahwíhsne' *it is heavy* (-(a)hwihsT-); raká·θne' *he is heavy* (-aθn-).

heel. u'terhę́čheh *heel* (-'terhęčh-).

height. *adj.* see: -hsure-.

hell. *n.* unéshę' *hell* (-neshę-).

hello. *interj.* čwé·'n ahskę̀·nę hę *hello* (čwé·'n ahskę̀·nę hę).

helmet. *n.* una'čúhkweh *helmet* (-na'=čuhkw-).

help. *v.t.* ękękyerhakyénha' *I will help you* (-kerhakenha-).

helper. *n.* ha' ra'nę'tiránheh *helper* (-a=nę'tiranhe-).

hem. *n.* ukę́heh *hem* (-kęh-).

hem. *v.t.* neyakú'knęhs *one hems it* (-ne-.-u'k(e)T-); yekę́huč *one hems it* (-kęhur-).

hemlock. *n.* unę́'teh *hemlock* (-nę't-); u'nahsę̀·reh *poison hemlock* (-'nah=sęr-); neyukuyaná·tręhs *ground hemlock* (neyukuyaná·tręhs).

hemorrhage. *n.* yutkwararáhkę *hemorrhage* (-tkwararahkw-).

hemp. *n.* ruhskyé·'nę *wild hemp* (-hs=keT-).

hen harrier. *n.* nwí'nwi' *hen harrier* (nwí'nwi').

hen hawk. *n.* nyę́·nyę *hen hawk* (nyę́·nyę).

hence. *adv.* tyuh *hence* (tyuh).

henceforth. *adv.* uhę́'nę yękahá·wi·t *henceforth* (-(a)hę'T- -yah-.-(ę)ha=wi-).

herald. *n.* rarihwaretyá'tha' *herald* (-rih=waretya'T-).

herd. *n.* u'tè·yeh *herd* (-(ę)'tey-).

here. *adv.* kę̀·nę' *here* (kę̀·nę'); yé'-θhahk *one had been here* (-e'θ-).

here and there. *adv.* thu'níhskah *here and there* (thu'níhskah); u'níhska' *here and there* (u'níhska').

herring. *n.* čúnhę *herring* (-či-.-(a)nha-).

herring tooth. *n.* uhsú'kweh *herring tooth (pattern)* (-hsu'ku-).

hibernate. *v.i.* ra'núhstęh *he hibernates* (-a'nuhstę-).

hiccough. *v.i.* ruhę́hθ'ehs *he hiccoughed* (-hęhθ'e(k)-).

hickory. *n.* rú'ta'rw *hickory* (rú'ta'rw); yukyerhačiwá·kę *bitter hickory* (-ker=hačiwak-).

hide. *n.* utéhweh *hide* (-tehw-).

hide. *v.i.* wahra'nęnà·yę' *he hid himself* (-a'nęnayę-); ru'nihsúhe'r *he was hid-*

ing (-a'nihsuh(e)r-); *v.t.* kahθéhtha' *I
am hiding it* (-ahθehT-); ẹhsihsá'nẹ·'
you will hide it* (-(i)hsa̲'nẹ-); ra'nẹ'-
né·tha' *he hides behind it* (-aT-.
-ẹ'neT-).

hide & seek. *n.* yẹ'nihsúher *hide & seek
(game)* (-a'nihsuh(e)r-).

hiding place. *n.* yẹ'nihsuhráhkhwa' *hiding place* (-a'nihsuhrahkw-).

high. *adj.* hé'tkẹh.

higher, make. *v.t.* nehrahkwá'tha' *he
makes it higher* (-ne-.-hkwa'T-).

highway. *n.* wahahakwẹ'nì·yu' *highway*
(-(a)hahakwe'niyu-); stá·kwi' è·nẹ't
highway (stá·kwi' -enẹ'T-).

hill. *n.* unẹ·'neh *hill* (-nẹT-); yunẹ́·ther
hill (-nẹth(e)r-); ka'ẹ̀·wa'r *small hill
of plants* (-'ẹwa'r-).

hinge. *n.* yučaratiharáhkẹ *hinge* (-čạrati=
harahkw-).

hip. *n.* uhtíčheh *hip* (-htič-); uhtyà·weh
hip (-htyaw-).

hire. *v.t.* rahẹká·rya'ks *he hires it* (-hẹ=
kạrya'k-); wa'khénha' *I hired him*
(-nha'-).

hire out. *v.i.* ra'nénha'θ *he hires out*
(-a'nenha'-).

hitch up. *v.t.* ratahskúhar *he hitches up
(the horse)* (-tahskuhạr-).

hither. *adv.* kà·ru' *hither* (kà·ru').

hoarfrost. *n.* neyurẹharà·yẹ' *hoarfrost*
(-ne-.-rẹharayẹ-).

hoarse. *adj.* ra'nwẹtúhnẹh *he is hoarse*
(-a'nwẹtuhnẹ-).

hoe. *n.* uhtikarí'neh *hoe* (-htikari'n-).

hoe. *v.i.* rẹhè·wahs *he hoes* (-ẹhew-).

hoggish. *adj.* kwískwis né'či *hoggish*
(kwískwis né'či).

hoist. *v.t.* rahkyerhúhtha' *he hoists it*
(-hkyerhuhT-); rari'wá'nihč *he hoists
sail* (-ri'wa'nihr-).

hold. *v.t.* íkha'w *I am holding it* (-(ẹ)=
haw-); čé·nẹ· *hold it!* (-yenẹ-); see:
-wa'k-.

hold in high regard. *v.t.* na'nẹkwehsta'-
ẹyeθá'θeh *he has high regard for another* (-ẹ°kʷehsta'ẹyeθ-{dative I}).

hold up. *v.t.* nehrú'kẹh *he holds it up*
(-ne-.-u'kẹ-).

hole. *n.* awẹ̀·yeh *hole* (-ẹ°y-); ukahrẹ̀·weh
hole (-kahrẹw-); yúhrarẹ *it is a hole*
(-ahrạr-).

holiday season. *n.* ukẹnhatukẹ́hti *holiday
season* (-kẹnhatukẹht-).

holler. *v.i.* wa'ehẹréhθẹ' *one hollered*
(-hẹrehθ-).

hollow. *adj.* uhshẹ̀·weh *hollow* (-hshẹ=
w-).

hollow out. *v.t.* kate'ná·kwahs *it hollows
it out* (-te'naku-).

holy. *adj.* rurihwatukẹ́hti *he is holy*
(-rihwạtukẹht-); see: -tukẹht-.

home. *n.* uyẹ́hsteh *home* (-yẹhst-).

home, be at. *v.i.* kakutihú'ẹ *they are at
home* (-tíhu'-).

homeless shelter. *n.* yakú·tẹht wásθhar
homeless shelter (-(i)tẹhT- -asθhar-).

homely. *adj.* ráhsẹh *he is homely* (-(i)h=
sẹ-).

hominy. *n.* katkù·ri' *hominy* (-tkuri-).

honey. *n.* ru'táhkẹ uθrẹ̀·weh *honey* (ru'-
táhkẹ -θrẹw-).

honeysuckle, wild. *n.* čawekẹ́·tye' *wild
honeysuckle* (-či-.-ekẹti-).

---

honor. *n.* anenù·rek.

honor. *v.t.* rakwenyéhsthaʔ *he honors it* (-kwenyehsT-).

hood. *n.* unaʔčúhkweh *hood* (-naʔ= čuhkw-).

hoof. *n.* učikúhseh *hoof* (-čikuhs-).

hook. *n.* uʔčúhneh *hook* (-ʔčuhn-).

hook. *v.t.* see: -ⁿu'narhu-.

hoop. *n.* ukáʔneh *hoop* (-kaʔn-).

hoop snake. *n.* tiʔkarè·weh *hoop snake (mythic, turns into a hoop by biting its sharp-boned tail)* (-tiʔkarewe-).

hoop & javelin game. *n.* uʔwáʔčreh *hoop & javelin game* (-ʔwaʔčr-).

hoop & javelin game, play. *v.i.* nehraʔ-wáʔthaʔ *he plays hoop & javelin game* (-ne-.-ʔwaʔT-).

hop. *v.i.* nehratkyeʔčáhkhwaʔ *he hops* (-ne-.-atkeʔčahkw-).

hope. *n.* urharáhčreh *hope* (-rharahčr-).

horizon. *n.* weyurehyaʔníhe *horizon* (-yah-.-rehyaʔniha-); keʔ kwé weyurehyaʔníhe *horizon* (keʔ kwé -yah-.-rehyaʔniha-).

horizontal. *adj.* neyúthrew *horizontal* (-ne-.-athrehw-).

horn. *n.* awetráʔneh *horn* (-(e)traʔn-).

hornbeam. *n.* né·kuʔ *hornbeam* (né·kuʔ); čiráhsaʔ *hornbeam* (čiráhsaʔ).

hornet. *n.* ruʔtáhke *hornet* (ruʔtáhke); tikačiʔtkwahnayeʔetíh *hornets* (ti-.-čiʔtkwahnaye(T)-.#etíh).

horrible. *adj.* neyuthunehyaníʔne *it is horrible* (-ne-.-thunehyaniʔn-).

horse. *n.* áha·θ *horse* (áha·θ).

horse's harness. *n.* áha·θ yuʔnetyahstà·weh *horse's harness* (áha·θ -aʔnetyah=stawe-).

horsemint. *n.* kayewá·kra·θ *horsemint* (-yewakraθ-).

hospital. *n.* yetkeheyeʔnayeʔnáhkhwaʔ *hospital* (-atkeheyeʔnaye'nahkw-).

hot. *adj.* yuʔnaríhe· *it is hot* (-aʔnarih-).

hot dog. *n.* uyáʔreh *hot dog* (-yaʔr-).

house. *n.* unéhseh *house* (-nehs-); unéhsehè·we *ancient bark-house* (-nehs-.#ewe).

house, log. *n.* nekaré·ʔnaʔneʔ *log house* (-ne-.-reʔna'ne-).

housefly. *n.* rutihstéʔreʔ *housefly* (-tih=steʔre-).

hover. *v.i.* rutíheh *he hovers* (-tihe-).

however. *adv.* séher *however* (séher).

howl. *v.i.* waθhéʔruh *it howls* (-aθheʔ=ru-); rarhérhuh *he howls* (-rherhu-).

huckleberry. *n.* uyhíhaʔ *huckleberry* (-yhih-).

hug. *v.t.* see: -taʔkwar-.

hum. *v.i.* yuʔnwé·taʔneʔ *it hums* (-a='nwetaT-); ruwetù·rih *he hums* (-wetu=ri-).

human being. *n.* é·kweh *human being* (-eᵒkʷe-).

humble. *v.i.* raʔnenitéhthaʔ *he humbles himself* (-a'nenitehT-); runitéhne *he humbles himself* (-(e)nitehT-).

humid. *adj.* yutaʔtá·we· *humid* (-taʔ=tawe-).

humiliate. *v.t.* naʔraʔnyé·thaʔ *one humiliates another* (-ne-.-raʔnyeT-); rakehré·tih *he humiliates it* (-kehreti-).

humiliating. *adj.* neyuchewí·re·t *it is humiliating* (-ne-.-ačhewireT-).

humility. *n.* ukehrá·ʔne *humility* (-keh=raT-).

hummingbird. *n.* čuteθewará·θe (čuteθewará·θe).

humor, have lots of. *v.i.* ruʔčharúhske *he has lots of humor* (-ʔčharuhsku-).

hump. *n.* ukyeʔyéhsteh *hump* (-keʔ=yehst-); see: -kety-.

hump-backed. *adj.* rawéʔwakyéʔyeʔ *he is hump-backed* (-eʔwakeʔy-).

humped. *adj.* see: -keʔy-.

hundred. *adj./n.* kayáhstih *hundred* (-yahsti-).

hunger. *n.* uʔnehkaryáʔke *hunger* (-a='nehkaryaʔk-).

hungry. *adj.* rawęhré·tihs *he is hungry*
(-ę°hretihs -); nwakęhré·tihs *I am hun-*
gry (-t -. -ę°hretihs -); rúkhwa[?]neht *he is*
hungry (-khwa̲[?]nehT -).

hunt. *v.i.* ratú·ra·č *he hunts* (-aturaT -).

hunter. *n.* ratú·ra·č *hunter* (-aturaT -); ra-
turá·the[?] *amateur hunter* (-aturathe[?] -);
računa[?]tí·yu· *he is a great hunter*
(-čuna[?]tiyu -); raturač[?]á·ka·[?] *profes-*
sional hunter (-aturaT -.#aka·[?]).

hurricane. *n.* wa[?]katyę́[?]kwi[?]n *hurricane*
(-tyę[?]kwiN -).

hurry. *v.i.* rutkwarihá[?]nę *he is hurrying*
(-atkwariha[?]T -); yu[?]nyatù·rę *it hurries*
(-a'nyatur -); ru[?]nahθkyénhę *he hurries*
(-a'nahθkenha -); ručtù·re[?] *he hurries*
(-ačtur -); θkwaríha[?]t *hurry up!* (-kwa =
riha[?]T -); *v.t.* rahstù·ra[?]č *he hurries it*
(-hstura[?]T -).

hurry away. *v.i.* yahwa[?]kayę́č[?]aht *they*
hurried away (-yah -. -ač[?]ahT -).

hurt. *n.* uya[?]né·rę·t *hurt* (-aya[?]nerę -).

hurt. *v.i.* ra[?]neθnę́·ryęhs *he hurts himself*
(-a[?]neθnęri -); ra[?]nékskruh *he is hur-*
ting it (-a[?]nekskru -).

husband. *n.* yękti[?]nè·nę[?] *my husband*
(-[?]nenę -); katyá·kę *husband* (-tyak -).

husband and wife. *n.* newa[?]netyá·kę *hus-*
band and wife (-ne -. -a'netyak -).

husband of a cousin. *n.* aka[?]nyuháh *my*
cousin's (of a clan other than my own)
husband (-a'nyuháh).

husk. *n.* utù·reh *husk* (-tur -).

hut. *n.* unę́hseh *hut* (-nęhs -).

hymnal. *n.* neyę[?]rihwahkwáhtha[?] *hymnal*
(-ne -. -a[?]rihwa̲hkwahT -).

hypocrite. *n.* nehru[?]tikęhkę́·nyę *hypocrite*
(-ne -. -(ę)[?]tikęhkęni -); nehru[?]nę[?]tikęh-
kę́·nyę *hypocrite* (-ne -. -a'nę[?]tikęh =
kęni -).

I

I. *pro.* í·[?] *I* (í·[?]); í·[?]i· *I* (í·[?]i·); hé[?]i·[?] *I!*
(hé[?]i·[?]).

ice. *n.* uwí·seh *ice* (-wis -).

ice cream. *n.* uwí·seh *ice cream* (-wis -).

ice skates. *n.* yę[?]nwenę[?]nanę[?]naknáh-
khwa[?] *ice skates* (-a'nwenę'nanę'na =
knahkw -).

icicle. *n.* yuwí·sęy *icicle* (-wisęy -).

icy. *adj.* yuwisù·rę *icy* (-wisur -); yu-
wí·sa[?]r *icy* (-wisa[?]r -); yuwí·se·θ *icy*
(-wiseθ -); uwiséhči *icy* (-wis -.#hči).

idea, give an idea. *v.t.* cęktikęhrá·[?]nę[?]
one gives me an idea (-či -. -(ę)[?]tikęh =
raT -{dative III}).

idea, have an. *v.i.* wa[?]ka[?]tikę́hthę[?] *it had*
an idea (-(ę)[?]tikęhthę -).

idleness. *n.* utaturé[?]weh *idleness* (-tatu =
re[?]w -).

idol. *n.* kawęniyuhčrę́·tih *idol* (-węniyuh =
čręti -).

idolater. *n.* kakyerhętyáhnęh rawęniyuh =
črę́·tih *idolater* (-kerhętyahnę - -weni =
yuhčręti -).

idolize. *v.t.* rarihwayę́·tih *he idolizes it*
(-rihwa̲yęti -).

if. *adv.* ne[?] *if* (ne[?]); nę *if (subjunctive*
marker) (nę).

ignore. *v.t.* íhskah wa[?]kačtéhriht *I ig-*
nored it (íhskah -a[?]čtehrihsT -); *see:*

-ę̓nhi -.

ill. *adj.* ranę́hwaks *he is ill* (-nęh=
wak(T)-); wačtkę́·ʾneʾ *it is deathly ill*
(-ačtkę'ne-).

ill-luck. *n.* uθrę́shayęʾ *ill-luck* (-θrę=
shạy-).

illicit. *adj.* kwęhs aryuʾriwhará·kwęk *it is
illicit* (kwęhs -aʾrihwharaku-).

illness. *n.* unęhwaknę́hčreh *illness* (-nęh=
waknęčr-); unęhwákčreh *illness* (-nęh=
wakčr-); úrhweht *witch-induced illness* (-rhweht-).

illusory. *adj.* yuʾnęʾtikęhkę́·nya·t *it is
illusory* (-a'nęʾtikęhkęni-).

illustrious. *adj.* runehrá·kwaht *he is illustrious* (-nehrakwahT-).

imagine. *v.i.* rè·rih *he imagines* (-er-);
rę́ʾtikę́hnęh *he imagines* (-(ę)ʾtikęh=
nę-).

imbecile. *n.* kwęhs ahraʾtikęhrayè·rik *imbecile* (kwęhs -(ę)ʾtikęhrạyerik-).

imbedded. *adj.* yuhwíhstuʾ *metal is imbedded (most commonly used of gold,
silver, copper, etc.)* (-hwihstur-).

imitate. *v.t.* rutaʾkyè·rę *he imitated it*
(-(ę)taʾker-).

immaculate. *adj.* yurihstuhθérhę· *immaculate* (-rihstuhθerhę-).

immediately. *adv.* thuʾù·nę *immediately*
(thuʾù·nę); ù·nę haʾ *immediately* (ù·nę
haʾ).

immerse. *v.t.* naʾniʾθkúhahs *one immerses another* (-(i)ʾθkuha-).

immoderate. *adj.* ruʾθráhrehst *he is immoderate* (-ʾθrahrehsT-).

immoderately. *adv.* yuʾθrahréhsnę *immoderately* (-ʾθrahrehsT-).

immolate. *v.t.* ruʾnyęwáhnę *he immolated it* (-a'nyęwahT-).

immortal. *adj.* kwęhs ahręheyę́hθek *he is
immortal* (kwęhs -iheyęhθe-).

immortalize. *v.t.* načhęnęnhehktha'ę̀·we
one immortalizes another (-hsęnęn=
hehkT-.#ęwe).

immovable. *adj.* kwęhs arę́ʾnuryahnę́hek
it is immovable (kwęhs -a'nuryahnę-);
kwęhs arętkwíʾthek *it is immovable*
(kwęhs -atkwiʾT-).

immutable. *adj.* kwęhs arętkwíʾthek *it is
immutable* (kwęhs -atkwiʾT-).

impair. *v.t.* rukrę́ʾthaʾ *he impairs it* (-u=
kręʾT-).

impatiens. *n.* wawahúʾy *impatiens* (wawahúʾy).

impatiently. *adv.* ukwarihę́ʾčreh *impatiently* (-kwarihęʾčr-).

impenetrable. *adj.* kwęhs yaʾnaręʾnę-
kúhthek *it is impenetrable* (kwęhs
-yah+ne-.-ę'nękuhT-).

imperceptible. *adj.* kwęhs aryawęʾnéh-
snęk *imperceptibly* (kwęhs -ę'nehsT-).

imperious. *adj.* ruʾnęnháhnę· *he is imperious* (-a'nęnhahnę-).

impertinent. *adj.* raʾrihú·kwaht *he is impertinent* (-aʾrihukʷahT-).

impetuous. *adj.* ruθráhrehst *he is impetuous* (-θrahrehst-).

implore. *v.i.* rahtinęhè·we *he implores*
(-htinę-.#ęwe).

impolite. *adj.* kwęhs ahruʾnękwehsta-
kwęnyę́hsnęk *he is impolite* (kwęhs
-a'nękwehstạkwęnyęhsT-).

impose. *v.i.* ráher *he imposes* (-(a)=
h(e)r-).

impossible. *adj.* kwęhs aryukwenyáʾnęk
it is impossible (kwęhs -kwenyaʾT-).

impotent. *adj.* ruhwihstú·kęʾ *he is impotent* (-hwihstukęʾ).

impoverish. *v.t.* naʾtęhtheʾčrę́·tih *one im-
poverishes another* (-(i)tęhtheʾčręti-).

impracticable. *adj.* kwęhs arékwahst *it is
impracticable* (kwęhs -akwahsT-).

impregnable. *adj.* kwęhs aryuʾnihθkwáʾ-
nęk *it is impregnable* (kwęhs -aʾnih=
θkwaʾT-).

imprison. *v.t.* naʾnečárhuhs *one imprisons another* (-čarhu-).

improbable. *adj.* urihwatukę́ʾę *it is im-

probable (-rihwątukę́ˀ-).

impudent. *adj*. raˀrihú·kwaht *he is impudent* (-aˀrihukʷahT-).

impunity *n*. kwęhs kwè·niˀ *impunity* (kwęhs kwè·niˀ).

impute. *v.i*. naˀríhwaws *one imputes* (-rihwaw-).

in. *prep*. ì·wa·t *it is in* (-aT-); see: -r-.

in charge of. *adj*. raríhę·t *he is in charge of* (-rihęt-).

in distress. *adj*. nehrutęnheká·ryę *he is in distress* (-ne-.-tęnhekari-).

in motion. *adj*. yukyérwęˀθ *it is in motion* (-kerwęˀ-).

in order that. *part*. her *in order that* (her).

in peace. *adv*. uhskęnę́ˀčrakęw *in peace* (-hskęnęˀčrakęw-).

in regard to. *prep*. urihwáˀkye *in regard to* (-rihwaˀke).

in spite of. *prep*. tuhtíˀ *in spite of* (tuhtíˀ).

in the first place. *adv*. ikę́hči *in the first place* (-i-.#hči).

in the middle of. *prep*. wahę́ˀthę *in the middle of* (-(a)hęˀthę-); see: -(i)hę.

in the midst. *adv*. kaharawę́·ˀnyeˀ *it is in the midst* (-(i)harawę'nyeˀ-).

in the morning. *adv*. θuhterhę́·kye *in the morning* (-či-.-hterhę.#ke).

in-laws. *n*. ráhnęw *his in-laws (wife's relations)* (-hnęw-).

inactive. *adj*. kwęhs ahraˀnuryahnę́hek *he is inactive* (kwęhs -a'nuryahnę-).

incapable. *adj*. kwęhs ahrakwenyę́hshek *he is incapable* (kwęhs -kweni-).

incense. *v.t*. račhaˀrę́·tih *he incenses* (-čhaˀręti-).

incident. *n*. haˀˀ yuˀnyerę́ˀę *incident* (-a='nyeręˀ-).

incipient. *adj*. nwaˀrihę́·tih *incipient* (-t-. -aˀrihęti-).

incite. *v.t*. račirù·ręh *he incites it* (-či=rurę-).

inclination. *n*. wakarę́ˀreh *inclination* (-(a)karęˀr-).

incline. *n*. ukarę́ˀreh *incline* (-(a)ka=ręˀr-).

incline. *v.t*. rakarę́ˀrahč *he inclines it* (-(a)karęˀrahT-).

inclined. *adj*. wakarę́ˀreˀ *it is inclined* (-(a)karęˀr-).

inclusively. *adv*. kakwékthaˀ *inclusively* (-kʷekT-).

incombustible. *adj*. kwęhs aryuˀnékshek *it is incombustible* (kwęhs -'nek-); kwęhs aryuˀnékskę·k *it is incombustible* (kwęhs -'neksk-).

income. *n*. haˀ tkà·yęˀ *income* (-t-.-yę-).

incomparable. *adj*. kwęhs ęθętkuˀčęryę́hshek *it is incomparable* (kwęhs -či-.-atkuˀčęri-).

incompatible. *adj*. kwęhs narę́ˀné·wyęw *the two of them are incompatible* (kwęhs -ne-.-a'newyęhw-).

incompetent. *adj*. kwęhs sawę́·te ahrawyę́hęk *he is incompetent* (kwęhs sawę́·te -wyęhw-); kwęhs ahrakwè·niˀ *he is incompetent* (kwęhs -kwe=ni-).

incomprehensible. *adj*. kwęhs yaˀnaryúhek *it is incomprehensible* (kwęhs -yah+ne-.-(i)he-).

incongruous. *adj*. kwęhs narę́ˀné·wyęw *the two of them are incongruous*

(kwęhs -ne-.-a'newyęhw-).

inconsistent. *adj.* kwęhs narę'né·wyęw *the two of them are inconsistent* (kwęhs -ne-.-a'newyęhw-).

inconvenience. *v.t.* ra'rihwa'tikęhryá'khęh *he inconveniences it* (-a'rihwa'= tikęhrya'khę-).

inconvenient. *adj.* yúnhiht *it is inconvenient* (-nhihT-).

incorporeal. *n.* yukyerhú·kę' *incorporeal* (-kerhukę').

incorrigible. *adj.* kwęhs ęθayučhakwáhsnęk *it is incorrigible* (kwęhs -či-.-a=čhakwahsT-).

incorruptible. *adj.* kwęhs arę'na'čha'náhkhwek *it is incorruptible* (kwęhs -čha'nahkw-).

increase. *v.t.* thráher *he increases it* (-t-. -(i)har-).

incredible. *adj.* yutù·węht *incredible* (-tu= węhT-).

incredulous. *adj.* yutù·węht *incredulous* (-tuwęhT-).

indecent. *adj.* kwęhs aryutkwęnyéhsnęk *it is indecent* (kwęhs -atkwęnyęhsT-).

indeed. *adv.* wehrę'ę̀·we *indeed* (wehrę'ę̀·we).

indefinite. *adj.* kwęhs akaya'čę́·tik *it is indefinite* (kwęhs -ya'čęti-).

indemnity. *n.* yutkaruhárnę *indemnity* (-atkaruharT-).

indentation in, make an. *v.t.* see: -tet'-.

indented. *adj.* yutú·karar *it is indented* (-tukarar-).

independent. *adj.* ru'natkwé·nyę *he is independent* (-a'natkweni-).

Indian. *n.* ękwehę̀·we *Indian* (-ę̊kʷe-.#ę=we).

indicate. *v.i.* ręhnáhkhwa' *he indicates* (-ęhnahkw-); ratukę́htha' *he indicates* (-tukęhT-).

indifferent. *adj.* kwęhs thahréhsthek *he is indifferent* (kwęhs tha-.-ehsT-).

indigence. *n.* utęhtá'ę *indigence* (-(i)tęh=ta'-).

indigent. *adj.* rú·tęht *he is indigent* (-(i)=tęhT-).

indigestion, have. *v.i.* kwęhs nahrutkwarihnatíhek *he has indigestion* (kwęhs -ne-.-tkwarihT-{dative III}).

indirect. *adj.* kwęhs tharyu'nya'čeríhęhs *it is indirect* (kwęhs tha-.-a'nya'=čerih-).

indistinct. *adj.* tikayerętiháh *indistinct* (ti-.-yeręti-.#áh).

individual. *n.* uyáhsteh *individual* (-yahst-).

indivisible. *adj.* kwęhs narę'nekhahsyę́hshek *it is indivisible* (kwęhs -ne-.-a='nekhahsi-).

indoors. *adv.* ę́·kye' *indoors* (ę́·kye').

induce. *v.t.* natkwé·nyęhs *one induces another* (-kweni-).

induct. *v.t.* na'nihstrá'nihč *one inducts another* (-(i)hstra'nihr-).

industrious. *adj.* ručáhniht *he is industrious* (-čahnihT-); ruθte'nyà·rę' *he is industrious* (-θte'nyarę-); ruθnyà·rę' *he is industrious* (-θnyarę-).

inestimable. *adj.* kwęhs yaryéha'w tikanú·rę· *it is inestimable* (kwęhs -yah-.-(ę)haw- ti-.-nurę-).

inexcusable. *adj.* kwęhs arę'rihwahnę́'= thek *it is inexcusable* (kwęhs -a'rih=wahnę'T-).

inexhaustible. *adj.* kwęhs aręč'áhthek *it is inexhaustible* (kwęhs -ač'ahT-).

inexplicable. *adj.* kwęhs u'tikęhrayę́·'nahst *inexplicable* (kwęhs -(ę)'tikęh=rayę'nahsT-); kwęhs ęθę'rihwahnę́'thek *it is inexplicable* (kwęhs -či-.-a'=rihwahnę'T-); kwęhs narę'rihuká'thek *it is inexplicable* (kwęhs -ne-.-a'rihu=ka'T-).

inexpressible. *adj.* kwęhs aryutkahryé'nek *it is inexpressible* (kwęhs -atkah=rye'T-).

infallible. *adj.* kwęhs ahrarihwater'áh-

shek *he is infallible* (kwęhs -rihw<u>a</u>=
ter^ꞌ(ak)-); kwęhs ahratꞌwáhthek *he is
infallible* (kwęhs -atꞌwahT-).

infamous. *adj.* nehruꞌraꞌnyéhnę· *he is infamous* (-ne-.-aꞌra'nyehnę-).

infant. *n.* uwì·reh *infant* (-wir-).

infect. *v.t.* naꞌnà·węhs *one infects another* (-aw-); rù·raꞌθ *it infects him* (-raꞌ-).

inferior. *adj.* rahsęnáhsthę *he is inferior in rank* (-hsęnahsthu-).

infinite. *adj.* kwęhs aryuꞌnúꞌknak *it is infinite* (kwęhs -a'nuꞌkT-).

infirmary. *n.* yętkęheyęꞌnayęꞌnáhkhwaꞌ *infirmary* (-atkęheyęꞌn<u>a</u>yę'nahkw-).

inflame. *v.i.* waꞌnukáꞌthaꞌ *it inflames, it ulcerates* (-a'nukaꞌT-); see: -ukaꞌT-.

inflammable. *adj.* yawęꞌtahkraꞌníhθkę· *inflammable* (-ęꞌtahkraꞌnihθk-); yuꞌnékskę· *it is inflammable* (-'neksk-).

influence. *v.t.* naꞌtikęhrakwé·nyęhs *one influences another* (-(ę)ꞌtikęhr<u>a</u>kwe=ni-).

influence, have. *v.i.* rahsęnakaré·tih *he has influence* (-hsęn<u>a</u>kareti-).

infrequent. *adj.* tiwahereθthaꞌáh *infrequent* (ti-.-ahereθT-.#áh); ì·nę yúꞌręꞌ *infrequent* (ì·nę -(i)ꞌrę-).

infuse. *v.t.* rataꞌtawę́hthaꞌ *he infuses it* (-taꞌtawęhT-).

ingenious. *adj.* raꞌnewyę́hę *he is ingenious* (-a'newyęhw-).

ingredient. *n.* neyeyehráksthaꞌ *ingredient* (-ne-.-yehraksT-).

inhabit. *v.i.* yetá·kreꞌ *one inhabits* (-ta=k(e)r-).

inhabitant. *n.* ratá·kreꞌ *inhabitant* (-ta=

k(e)r-).

inhale. *v.i.* kwer04ká·ryahs *I am inhaling* (-w(e)r<u>a</u>kari-).

inherit. *v.t.* ruyę́·ꞌnaꞌθ *he inherits it* (-yę 'naꞌ-).

inhospitable. *adj.* kwęhs ahruꞌniꞌnęráhskęk *he is inhospitable* (kwęhs -a'ni='nęrahsk-).

injure. *v.t.* rayaꞌnè·ręh *he injures it* (-a=yaꞌnerę-); rakarę̀·nih *he injures it* (-karęni-).

injury. *n.* ukarę́·nyaht *injury* (-karę=nyahT-).

inn. *n.* yęthnekahnì·nęh *inn* (-athne=k<u>a</u>hninę-).

innocent. *adj.* kwęhs ahruꞌrihwáꞌęk taꞌawę́·te *he is innocent* (kwęhs -a'=rihw<u>a</u>raꞌ- taꞌawę́·te).

innocently. *adj.* kwęhs yuyané·ręt a-rá·kę·k *innocently* (kwęhs -yan(e)(r)--i-).

innovation. *n.* urihwá·θe·ꞌ *innovation* (-rihwaθe·ꞌ).

innumerable. *adj.* kwęhs aryuthrá·ꞌnęk *it is innumerable* (kwęhs -athraT-).

inoculate. *v.t.* naꞌnęčháhrara·ks *one inoculates another* (-nęčhahr<u>a</u>rak-).

inquire of. *v.t.* waꞌkayęꞌnaꞌtikę́hę·ꞌ *they inquired of another* (-(ę)ꞌtikęhaw-).

insatiable. *adj.* kwęhs ahruhewíhsthek *he is insatiable* (kwęhs -hewihsT-).

insensitive. *adj.* rawerihkáθneꞌ *he is insensitive to pain* (-erihkaθne-).

inseparable. *adj.* kayekwarì·yeꞌ *they are inseparable* (-kwari(y)-); kwęhs na-ręꞌnekhahsyáꞌnęk *it is inseparable* (kwęhs -ne-.-a'nekhahsyaꞌT-).

Tuscarora Pronunciation Key:
/a/ l<u>a</u>w; /e/ h<u>a</u>t; /i/ p<u>i</u>zza; /u/ t<u>u</u>ne; /ę/ h<u>i</u>nt; /č/ <u>ch</u>eese; /h/ <u>h</u>oe; /m/ <u>m</u>other; /s/ <u>s</u>ame; /t/ <u>d</u>o (before a vowel y, or w), <u>t</u>oo (elsewhere); /k/ <u>g</u>ale (before a vowel y or w), <u>k</u>ale (elsewhere); /n/ i<u>nh</u>ale (before a consonant or word-final), <u>n</u>ote (elsewhere), /r/ hi<u>ss</u> (before a consonant or word-final), <u>r</u>un (trilled as in Italian, elsewhere); /w/ cu<u>ff</u> (before a consonant other than y or word-final), <u>w</u>ay (elsewhere); /y/ fi<u>sh</u> (before a consonant or word-final), <u>y</u>ou (elsewhere), /θ/ <u>th</u>ing; /ꞌ/ (the sound between the vowels in u<u>nh-u</u>nh); /·/ long vowel, /ˊ/ high pitch; /ˋ/ low pitch.

insert. *v.t.* rawí'tha' *he inserts* (-a = wi'T -).

inside. *adv.* ę́·kye' *inside* (ę́·kye').

inside, lie. *v.t.* wehrakę́whęh *he lies inside it* (-yah -. -ak̲ę̲whę -).

insinuate. *v.i.* re'náhkhwa' *he insinuates* (-e'nahkw -).

insipid. *adj.* yawę̨θritkę́'ę *insipid* (-ę̨θri = tkę' -).

insolvent. *adj.* rahryenę́'ę *he is insolvent* (-hry̲e̲nę' -); ruhwihstú·kę' *he is insolvent* (-hwihstukę').

inspire. *v.t.* rahsnyà·rę *he inspires it* (-hsnyar -).

instead. *adv.* heríhsę' *instead* (heríhsę'); stí·yu· *instead* (stí·yu·).

insubordinate. *adj.* kwę̨hs ahru'nwę̨taráhkęk *he is insubordinate* (kwę̨hs -a = 'nwę̲ta̲rahkw -).

insufficient. *adj.* hé'thu ará·kę·k *it is insufficient* (hé'thu -i -); kwę̨hs hé'thu ará·kę·k *it is insufficient* (kwę̨hs hé'thu -i -).

insult. *v.t.* na'ra'nyé·tha' *one insults another* (-ne -. -ra'nyeT -); na'nahčira'θéhręh *one insults another* (-ahčir -{dative I} -hrę -).

intelligent. *adj.* rę'nakáhrę· *he is intelligent* (-ę'n̲a̲kahrę -).

intemperate. *adj.* ručha'rá·ksę· *he is intemperate* (-čha'raks -); ru'θráhrehst *he is intemperate* (-'θrahrehsT -).

intend. *v.i.* rę'tikę́hnęh *he intends* (-(ę)' = tikę̨hnę -); ra'tyę́·'nęh *he intends it* (-'tyę̨'nęh -).

intention. *n.* hà·ne' rè·rih *his intention* (-er -).

inter. *v.t.* ra'nę́ht'ahs *he inters it* (-'nę̨= ht' -).

intercede for. *v.t.* na'rihwakyenhá'θeh *one intercedes for another* (-rihw̲a̲= kenha -{dative I}).

interest. *n.* ha' uwì·reh *interest (on borrowed money)* (-wir -); ha' wa'nú'nę'

interest (on borrowed money) (-a'nu' = nę').

interested. *adj.* ráha'r *he is interested* (-(i)har -).

interfere. *v.i.* nehru'nę̨nihárhę *he interferes* (-ne -. -a'nę̨niharhu -).

interpret. *v.i.* ra'nwę̨takará'na·č *he interprets* (-a'nwę̲ta̲kara'naT -).

interrogate. *v.t.* ra'nahrù·yę' *he interrogates it* (-a'nahruyę' -).

interrupt. *v.t.* na'rihwyá'kθeh *one interrupts another* (-rihwya'k -{dative I}).

intersection. *n.* kę' yuthahayáhθe'r *intersection* (kę' -athah̲a̲yahθ(e)r -).

interval. *n.* ha' yutákwnu·t *interval* (-takwnut).

intestine. *n.* uyá'reh *intestine* (-ya'r -).

intimidate. *v.t.* na'tehra'ná·tih *one intimidates another* (-tehra'T -{dative II}).

intoxicate. *v.t.* na'nę́'yahs *one intoxicates another* (-nę'y -).

intractable. *adj.* kwę̨hs ahruhę̨hsyę́hek *it is intractable* (kwę̨hs -hę̨hsyę -).

intricate. *adj.* neyunę̨'rì·ye' *it is intricate* (-ne -. -nę'riye -).

introduce. *v.t.* thrayę́htha' *he introduces it* (-t -. -yęhT -).

intruder. *n.* ra'nhę̨hsù·rih *intruder* (-'n = hę̨hsuri -).

inundate. *v.i.* kę̨θrúhnęh *it inundates* (-ę = θruhnę -).

inure. *v.t.* rurę̨'nháhstha' *it inures him* (-rę'nhahsT -).

invade. *v.t.* rú·tahsę *he invaded it* (-t̲a̲hs -); rata'naká·ryahs *he invades it* (-ta'n̲a̲kari -).

invalid. *adj.* kwę̨hs akarihwę́nhek *it is invalid* (kwę̨hs -rihwę̨nhe -).

invariable. *adj.* kwę̨hs narę̨tkę'né·ti' *it is invariable* (kwę̨hs -ne -. -atkę'neti -).

invent. *v.t.* rę'tikę̨hrú·tha' *he invents it* (-(ę)'tikę̨hrut -).

invert. *v.t.* rakarhá·thuhs *he inverts it* (-karhathu -).

investigate. *v.t.* ratkę́^ʔθeh *he investigates* (-atkę^ʔθe-).

invisible. *adj.* kwę̨hs ú·kę^ʔt ará·kęk *it is invisible* (kwę̨hs -kę^ʔT- -i-); kwę̨hs aryukę́^ʔnęk *it is invisible* (kwę̨hs -kę^ʔT-).

invoke. *v.t.* ra^ʔnęnhę́·tha^ʔ *he invokes it* (-a'nęnhęT-).

involved with, become. *v.i.* wa^ʔkačtéhriht *I got involved* (-(a)čtehrihT-).

invulnerable. *adj.* kwę̨hs aryu^ʔnihθkwá^ʔnęk *it is invulnerable* (kwę̨hs -a^ʔnih= θkwa^ʔT-).

inward. *adv.* ukyérhakęw kę^ʔná^ʔkę *inward* (-kerhakęw kę^ʔná^ʔkę).

iris. *n.* uturúhkweh *flag iris* (-turuhkw-).

iron. *n.* uwè·nę^ʔ *iron* (-wenę-); uweńę́·^ʔneh *iron* (-wenęT-).

ironwood. *n.* čiráhsa^ʔ.

ironworks. *n.* uwè·nę^ʔ yu^ʔnáčnę *ironworks* (-wenę- -a-'načT-); uwè·nę^ʔ yu^ʔnačnáhnę· *ironworks* (-wenę- -a= 'načnahnę-).

irremediable. *adj.* kwę̨hs ęθayunęhkwá·^ʔnę^ʔk *it is irremediable* (kwę̨hs -či-. -nęhkwa'nę^ʔ-).

irreparable. *adj.* kwę̨hs ęθayučhakwáhsnęk *it is irreparable* (kwę̨hs -či-. -ačhakwahsT-).

irresponsible. *adj.* kwę̨hs ahru^ʔnwę́·tanhęk *he is irresponsible* (kwę̨hs -a'nwę= tanh-).

irritate. *v.t.* račirù·ręh *he irritates it* (-či= rurę-).

island. *n.* yuhwè·nu^ʔ *island* (-hwenu-).

islander. *n.* uhwena^ʔkyehrù·nę^ʔ *islander* (-hwena^ʔkehrunę^ʔ).

issue. *v.i.* see: -itkę^ʔ-.

it is said *adv.* ì·ya·k *it is said* (ì·ya·k).

itch. *n.* u^ʔtú·θer *itch* (-^ʔtuθ(e)r-); awé·hareh *itch* (-ehar-).

itch. *v.i.* yuręhkwáhnę· *it itches* (-ręh= kwahnę-).

itchy, feel. *v.i.* rarę́hkhwa^ʔ *he feels itchy* (-ręhkw-).

ivy. *n.* yakunę^ʔà·rara^ʔθ *ivy* (-nę^ʔarara^ʔ-).

J

jack o' lantern. n. nekačęhuhkwáhkhwa^ʔ *jack o' lantern* (-ne-. -(a)čęhuh= kwahkw-).

jack-in-the-pulpit. *n.* urháhsteh *jack-in-the-pulpit* (-rhahst-); ná^ʔku^ʔ *jack-in-the-pulpit* (ná^ʔku^ʔ).

jam. *n.* uθrę̀·weh *jan* (-θręw-).

jam. *v.t.* rahwačí^ʔehs *he jams it* (-hwa= či^ʔe(k)-).

January. *n.* θkawé^ʔrkye *January* (-či-. -we^ʔrke).

jaundice. *n.* či^ʔtkwar^ʔú^ʔy *jaundice* (či^ʔ-tkwar.#ú^ʔy).

javelin. *n.* uhsé·kwareh *javelin* (-hse= kʷar-); uhsekwarúhar *javelin* (-hsekʷa= ruhar-).

jay. *n.* ní^ʔni^ʔ *jay* (ní^ʔni^ʔ).

jealous. *adj.* ruhskà·rę *he is jealous* (-hskar-).

jealousy. *n.* u^ʔtú·θha^ʔ *jealousy* (-^ʔtuθh-).

jelly. *n.* uθrę̀·weh *jelly* (-θręw-).

jelly, make. *v.i.* yeθręwętyáhnęh *one makes jelly* (-θręwętyahnę-).

---

jest. *v.i.* raterhya⁷črę̇·tih *he jests* (-ter=
hya⁷črę̇ti-).

jester. *n.* awé·ha·k *jester* (-eha̱k-).

jewelry. *n.* kahwihstanù·rę⁷ yę⁷nya⁷tah-
stę̱nyá⁷tha⁷ *jewelry* (-hwihsta̱nurę-
-a'nya⁷ta̱hstę̱nya⁷T-).

jilt. *v.t.* na⁷níhstkę⁷θ *one jilts another*
(-(i)hstkę⁷-).

join. *v.t.* akatháhrę⁷ *that I join it* (-a=
thaha̱r-{dative III}); wa⁷thratahθę̇·⁷-
nę⁷ *he joined it* (-ne-.-tahθę̱T-); neh-
rahsí·θahs *he joins two things* (-ne-.
-hsiθ-); nehrahθę̇⁷ner *he joins it*
(-ne-.-(a)hθę̇⁷n(e)r-); see: -ne-.-tekę-.

join together. *v.i.* neyu⁷nę̱tahθę̇·⁷nę *it is
joined together* (-ne-.-a'nę̱tahθę̱T-);
see: -ne-.-iθ-.

joined in marriage. *adj.* nehrara⁷té·kę̱hs
he is joined in marriage (-ne-.-ra⁷=
tekę-).

joint. *n.* uhθę̇⁷reh *joint (of pipes)* (-(a)=
hθę̇⁷r-); neyuhθę̇⁷ner *joint (of bones)*
(-ne-.-(a)hθę̇⁷n(e)r-).

joist. *n.* neyerę̱⁷arę̱hwáhkhwa⁷ *joist*
(-ne-.-rę̱⁷a̱rę̱hwahkw-).

joke. *v.i.* yę̱⁷tahsaráhkhwa⁷ *one is joking*
(-(ę̱)⁷tahsa̱rahkw-).

journey. *n.* uháheh *journey* (-(a)hah-).

jovial. *adj.* warásči· *it is jovial* (-arasči-).

jowls. *n.* ukę̇hskwareh *jowls* (-kę̱h=
skwa̱r-); uhská⁷yeh *jowls* (-hska⁷y-).

judge. *v.t.* wa⁷ka⁷θhę̇·ti⁷ *it judged it*
(-(i)⁷θhę̱ti-); raya⁷turehnáhnę̱h *he
judges it* (-ya⁷turehnahnę-).

judicious. *adj.* ruya⁷turéhčrayę̱⁷ *he is judicious* (-ya⁷turehč̱ra̱yę̱(T)-).

jug. *n.* účheh *jug* (-čhe⁷-).

juggle. *v.i.* nehračkanekę̇·tha⁷ *he juggles*
(-ne-.-ačkane-kę̱T-).

juice. *n.* yawekitkę̇⁷ę̱ *juice* (-ekitkę̱⁷-);
uhné·kyeh *juice* (-hnek-).

July. *n.* kę̱nhyehé·θu⁷ *July* (kę̱nhyehé·-
θu⁷).

jump. *v.i.* nehratkye⁷čáhkhwa⁷ *he jumps*

(-ne-.-atke⁷čahkw-).

June. *n.* kę̱nhyeháh *June* (kę̱nhyeháh).

juniper. *n.* unę̱⁷takwę̇·te *juniper* (-nę̱⁷ta=
kwę̱te).

just. *adj.* tkayè·ri⁷ *it is just* (-t-.-yeri-).

just. *adv.* čhę̱⁷ *just* (čhę̱⁷); kwè·ni⁷ *just*
(kwè·ni⁷); ka⁷nę̇ *just!* (ka⁷nę̇).

just as soon as. *part.* netyá⁷kiw *just as
soon as* (netyá⁷kiw).

just at the right time. *adv.* uhsę̱nę̇·thę̱⁷
just at the right time (uhsę̱nę̇·thę̱⁷).

just like. *adv.* né⁷či *just like* (né⁷či).

just now. *adv.* čhę̱⁷ *just now* (čhę̱⁷).

justify. *v.t.* rarihwak⁷úhsyę̱hs *he justifies
it* (-rihwak⁷uhsi-).

K

kangaroo. *n.* uhstrù·ri⁷ *kangaroo* (-hstru=
ri-).

katydid. *n.* čihskę̇·kę̱· *katydid* (čihskę̇·-
kę̱·).

keel. *n.* utúhna⁷ *keel of a ship* (-tuhn-).

keep to oneself. *v.i.* ra⁷rá·kwahs *he
keeps to himself* (-a⁷raku-).

keep watch. *v.i.* rutháha⁷r *he keeps
watch* (-athaha̱r-).

kestrel. *n.* nekanę̱θnahkwáhshayę̱⁷ *kestrel* (-ne-.-nę̱θnahkwahshayę-).

kettle. *n.* u⁷nę̇·weh *kettle* (-⁷nę̱w-);
kwè·ni⁷ *kettle* (kwè·ni⁷); unikhwéhθeh
long, non-slopping kettle (-ni=
khwehθ-); u⁷nikwè·yeh *long, non-
sloping kettle* (-⁷nikwey-); yu⁷nę̱wa-
wę̇hte⁷ *small kettle* (-⁷nę̱wawę̱hte-).

key. *n.* uhsę̱wá⁷reh *key* (-hsę̱wa⁷r-).

kick. *v.t.* ra⁷nahsuhčę̇hę̱h *he is going
kicking it* (-a'nahsuhči-); wa⁷karah-
sę̇·thu⁷ *I kicked it* (-arahsę̱thu-).

kidney. *n.* u⁷nyè·ruru·θ *kidney* (-⁷nye=
ruruθ-).

kill. *v.t.* wa⁷na⁷rì·yu⁷ *one killed another*

(-r(i)yu -); ahratiháhkwaʔ *that he kill it*
(-tihahku -).

kin. *n.* sheyaʔreʔkę́haʔnę̨ʔ *your kin* (aʔ =
reʔ.#kęhaʔnę̨).

kind. *n.* see: -ę̨hr-, -uʔnę̨-.

kindle. *v.t.* kakuʔnekáʔnę̨ *they kindled it*
(-'nekaʔT -).

kindling. *n.* úʔčkaweh *kindling* (-(i)ʔ =
čk<u>a</u>w-); yuhsnè·yę̨ʔθ *kindling* (-hsne =
yę̨ʔ -).

kindred. *n.* unę̨hwíhčreh *kindred* (-nę̨h =
wihčr -).

king. *n.* kuráhkuwaʔ *king* (kuráhkuwaʔ);
ratírher *king* (-tirher -).

kingfisher. *n.* θučá·kʔu *kingfisher* (θu-
čá·kʔu).

kiss. *v.t.* raʔaruʔčírhaʔ *he kisses it* (-ʔa =
ruʔčir -).

kitchen. *n.* yę̨čhuryáʔthaʔ *kitchen* (-a =
čhuryaʔT -); yekhwę̨tyáʔthaʔ *kitchen*
(-khwę̨tyaʔT -).

knead. *v.t.* ę̨yekyeʔčę́·tiʔ *one will knead
it* (-keʔčę̨ti -); rakyeʔčačí·rwę̨hs *he
kneads it* (-keʔč<u>a</u>čirwę̨ -).

knee. *n.* awę̨tkwé·θeh *knee* (-ę̨tkweθ -).

knife. *n.* uhsáʔkę̨ʔneh *knife* (-hsaʔkę̨'n -).

knob. *n.* uhskúʔkwareh *knob* (-hskuʔ =
kw<u>a</u>r -).

knock at a door. *v.i.* waʔkayę̨ʔčarakę́h-
črę̨·ʔ *they knocked at the door* (-aʔ =
kayę̨ʔčarakę̨hčrę̨ -).

knock off. *v.t.* raʔθę́hthaʔ *he knocks it
off* (-aʔθę̨hT -).

knock the evil out of. *v.t.* ruʔnatkę̨ʔ-
črę̨ʔnahkę́heʔ *it had knocked the evil
out of him* (-a'natkę̨ʔčrę̨ʔnahkw -).

knot. *n.* učíhkweh *knot of a tree* (-čih =

kw -).

knotty. *adj.* učihkwéhči *knotty* (-čihkw -.
#hči).

know. *v.t.* kyę̨ʔnè·rih *I know it* (-yę̨ =
'ner -); ę́hskwi·t *you will know me*
(-wi -).

know how. *v.i.* rawíhę̨ *he knows how*
(-wihw -).

knowledge. *n.* uʔnehyahrę́hčreh *knowledge* (-a'nehyahrę̨hčr -).

knuckle. *n.* uhθę́ʔreh *knuckle* (-(a)h =
θę̨ʔr -).

L

labor. *n.* uyuʔnę́hčreh *labor* (-yuʔnę̨hčr -).

laboratory. *n.* kę̨ʔ kayuʔnę́hthaʔ *laboratory* (kę̨ʔ -yuʔnę̨hT -).

laborious. *adj.* yuyuʔnę̨hstačháʔnur *it is
laborious* (-yuʔnę̨hst<u>a</u>čhaʔnur -).

lace. *n.* unę́ʔreh *lace* (-nę̨ʔr -); uyuhkúhčreh *lace* (-yuhkuhčr -).

lacrosse. *n.* yunę̨hrúhaʔr *lacrosse* (-(ę̨) =
nę̨hruh<u>a</u>r -).

ladder. *n.* urę̨ʔnáhrareh *ladder* (-rę̨'nah =
r<u>a</u>r -).

lady. *n.* akuthéhtrak *she is a lady* (-a =
thehtrak -).

lady's slipper. *n.* úrhuht *lady's slipper*
(-rhuht -); kweʔkú·ryeʔ uʔnáhkweh
yellow lady's slipper (kweʔkú·ryeʔ
uʔnáhkweh).

lake. *n.* unyá·tareh *lake* (-nyat<u>a</u>r -).

lake bed. *n.* uhnę̀·weh *lake bed* (-hnę̨w -).

lamb. *n.* weʔrá·ksę̨· *lamb* (-eʔraks -).

---

lament. *v.i.* yęˀnę́·ˀnę *one lamented* (-a=
'nęt(aˀ)-).

lamp. *n.* učíˀreh *lamp* (-čiˀr-).

lance. *n.* uhsé·kwareh *lance* (-hsekʷar-).

land. *n.* úˀwneh *land* (-aˀwT-).

land a boat. *v.i.* waˀakyathęwanę́·ˀnakt
the two of us landed a boat (-athę=
wanę'nakT-).

language. *n.* uwę́·teh *language* (-węt-).

lantern. *n.* yečiˀriˀθréhthaˀ *lantern* (-čiˀ=
riˀθrehT-).

larch. *n.* unę́ˀteh *larch* (-nęˀt-).

lard. *v.t.* rayetárhuhs *he lards it* (-ye=
tarhu-).

large. *adj.* ratkuhkwì·yuh *he is large* (-a=
tkuhkwiyu-); tì·waˀθ *it is large*
(-aˀθ-); ratkúhkweˀ *he is large* (-a=
tkuhkw-).

lark. *n.* tkurehči·yu *lark* (tkurehči·yu).

last. *n.* učˀáhči *the last* (učˀáhči).

last. *v.i.* weˀθhá·θneˀ *it lasts* (-(i)ˀ=
θhaθn-).

last night. *adv.* ahθę́·ˀnyeˀ *last night* (ah-
θę́·ˀnyeˀ).

lastly. *adv.* učˀahná·te·t *lastly* (učˀahná·-
te·t).

late. *adj.* yuˀtíθkuˀ *it is late* (-ˀtiθku-).

lately. *adv.* kyewęhę̀·we *lately* (kyewę.
#ęwe).

lateral. *adj.* ukwtkęˀnáˀkę *lateral* (-akT-.
#kęˀnaˀkę).

laugh at. *v.t.* waˀkayęˀnaˀnyę́hskweˀ *they
laughed at another* (-yęhskwe-).

laugh immoderately. *v.i.* ruterhyaˀna-
tihúˀy *he laughs immoderately* (-ter=
hyaˀT-{dative III}.#úˀy).

laughable. *adj.* ruyę́hskweˀt *he is
laughable* (-yęhskweˀT-).

lavish. *adj.* raˀnaˀnyęwáhthaˀ *he is lavish* (-a'na'nyęwahT-).

law. *n.* uyanŕ̥ęhsteh *law* (-yanŕ̥ęhst-).

law, observe the. *v.i.* rayanŕ̥ęhstatkáhneˀ
he observes the law (-yanŕ̥ęhsta=
tkahT-).

lawnmower. *n.* yeheryáˀkthaˀ *lawnmower* (-heryaˀkT-).

lawyer. *n.* nehrarihwakyénhahs *lawyer*
(-ne-.-rihwakenha-).

lax. *adj.* tyawú·krę· *it is lax* (ti-.-ukr-).

laxative. *n.* neyawękúhnę *laxative* (-ne-.
-ę˚kuhT-).

lay. *v.t.* rà·yęhs *he lays it* (-yę(T)-).

lay down. *v.t.* waˀkiθká·rę·t *I laid it
down* (-iθkar-).

lay eggs. *v.i.* waˀnhę́hsęh *it lays eggs*
(-ˀnhęhsę-).

lay in wait. *v.i.* rutháhaˀr *he lays in wait*
(-athahar-).

layman. *n.* kwè·niˀ ę́·kweh *layman*
(kwè·niˀ ę́·kweh).

laziness. *n.* utaturéˀweh *laziness* (-tatu=
·reˀw-).

lazy. *adj.* see: -tatur-.

lead. *n.* unawáˀčteh *lead* (-nawaˀčt-).

lead. *v.i.* see: -iN-, -yan(e)(r)-.

leader. *n.* uhę́ˀnę ruˀnę́ˀnę *leader* (-(a)=
hęˀT- -a'nęˀT-).

leaf. *n.* uˀę́hreh *leaf* (-ˀęhr-).

league. *n.* uˀnyúhkweh *league* (-iˀ=
nyuhkw-); wętiˀnyuhkwę́·tih *league*
(-(ę)tiˀnyuhkwęti-).

leak. *v.i.* kači·yęˀθ *it leaks* (-čiyęˀ-).

lean. *adj.* nęθahsnè·yęˀ *you will be lean*
(-ne-.-hsneyę-); rahsné·yę· *he is lean*
(-hsneyę-).

lean. *v.i.* raˀráˀkaraˀč *he leans* (-aˀ=
raˀkaraˀT-); káhręw *it leans* (-hrę=
hw-); *v.t.* rakarę́ˀrahč *he leans it*
(-(a)karęˀrahT-); raˀráˀkar *he leans
against it* (-aˀ'raˀkar-); kahręhwáhkę *it
leans toward it* (-hręhwahkw-).

leap. *v.i.* rętíˀθhar *he leaps* (-ętiˀθhar-).

learn. *v.i.* wahrà·wiw *he learned* (-wi=
hw-); rá·wyęws *he learns* (-wyęhw-);
rahyatęhstayęˀnè·rih *he learned* (-hya=
tęhstayę'ner-); *v.t.* waˀurihę́·tyęˀ *it
learned it* (-rihęti-{dative III}); wah-
rarę́ˀnhaˀ *he learned it* (-ręˀnhaˀ-).

leather wood. *n.* utkę́hθri⁷ *leather wood* (-atkę́hθr-).

leave. *v.i.* waré·kwę· *it has left* (-ar(e)= ku-); wa⁷eyá·kę·⁷ *one left* (-yakę-); *v.t.* rú·⁷nyahθ *he leaves it* (-a'ni- {dative II}); yahwa⁷kayę⁷na⁷ní⁷rę⁷ *they left him* (-yah-.-i⁷rę-).

leave alone. *v.t.* thęθahstá·wi·k *you will leave it alone* (tha-.-ahstaw-); íhskah wa⁷kheyačtéhriht *I left another alone* (íhskah -a⁷čtehrihsT-).

leave behind. *v.t.* see: -ęr-.

leaven. *v.t.* yekye⁷čatkęhnáhkhwa⁷ *one leavens it* (-ke⁷čatkęhnahkw-).

leavings. *n.* ha⁷ yu⁷na⁷nę̀·rę *leavings* (-a'na'nęr-).

leech. *n.* rutéhwęh *leech* (-tehwę-).

left-handed. *adj.* ra⁷θwa⁷níhę *he is left-handed* (-(i)⁷θwa⁷nihu-).

leftover. *n.* yu⁷na⁷nę̀·rę *leftover* (-a'na= 'nęr-).

leftside. *n.* yu⁷na⁷nę̀·rę *leftside* (-a'na= 'nęr-); ka⁷tíhakwt *leftside* (-⁷tihakT); ra⁷θwa⁷níhę *his leftside* (-(i)⁷θwa⁷ni= hu-).

leg. *n.* urę́hseh *leg* (-ręhs-); see: -ręhθ-.

legal. *adj.* uyanręhstá⁷kye *legal* (-ya= nręhsta⁷ke).

legend. *n.* awę́khwyaht *legend* (-ę= khwyahT-).

legends, tell. *v.i.* rę́khwih *he tells legends* (-ękhwi-).

leggings. *n.* uríhsteh *leggings* (-rihst-).

legible. *adj.* kayerę́·tih *it is legible* (-ye= ręti-); yu⁷nwętahθá·w⁷ahst *it is legible* (-a'nwętahθaw⁷ahsT-).

legislator. *n.* rayanręhstę́·tih *legislator* (-yanręhstęti-).

legislature. *n.* kahwenę́·tih *congress, legislature* (-hwenęti-); uhwenętíhsteh *legislature* (-hwenętihst-).

legitimate. *adj.* uyanręhstá⁷kye *legitimate* (-yanręhsta⁷ke).

lemon. *n.* lè·mun *lemon* (lè·mun).

lemonade. *n.* lè·mun wekę́·tih *lemonade* (lè·mun -ekęti-).

lend. *v.i.* ra⁷nęhníhahs *he lends it* (-a= 'nęhniha-).

lengthen. *v.t.* ré·θtha⁷ *he lengthens it* (-eθT-).

lengthwise. *adv.* weθnáhkę *lengthwise* (-eθnahkw-).

leopard. *n.* kę́hreks učísnuhkweh *leopard* (-ihreks -čisnuhkw-).

less. *n.* áhči⁷ *less* (áhči⁷); see: -ukę⁷.

less than. *conj.* kà·ru⁷ *less than* (kà·ru⁷).

lessen. *v.t.* rahsthú⁷tha⁷ *he lessens it* (-ahsthu⁷T-).

lest. *conj.* kwęhs her *lest* (kwęhs her).

let. *v.i.* čéhnę *let!* (-yehnę-).

let go. *v.i.* ra⁷ná·k⁷wahs *he lets go* (-a= 'nak⁷u-); *v.t.* θhra⁷ná·k⁷uhs *he lets it go* (-či-.-a'nak⁷u-).

lethargic. *adj.* ra⁷tikęhráhnęh *he is lethargic* (-(ę)⁷tikęhrahnę-).

letter. *n.* uwę́·teh *letter (postal)* (-węt-); ukyérheh *letter (of the alphabet)* (-kerh-).

lettuce. *n.* katá⁷re·θ *lettuce* (-(ę)ta⁷reθ-).

level. *n.* yehskweyahčrihráhkhwa⁷ *level (tool)* (-hskweyahčri̯hrahkw-).

lever. *n.* učę̀·weh *lever* (-čęw-).

lexicon. *n.* uwętáhčreh *lexicon* (-wę= tahčr-).

---

liberal. *adj.* rá·nę· *he is liberal* (-(a)nę-).
library. *n.* yehyatęhstayę'náhkhwa' *library* (-hyatęhsta̲yę'nahkw-).
licentious. *adj.* ra'nęnęhwaru'yéhstha' *he is licentious* (-a'nęnęhwa̲ru'=yehsT-); ruhsú'ye' *he is licentious* (-hsu'ye-).
lick. *v.t.* wa'nyakuká·nę·t *the two of them licked it* (-kanęT-).
lid. *n.* uwerhúhčreh *lid* (-awerhuhčr-).
lie. *n.* utù·węht *lie* (-tuwęhT-).
lie down. *v.i.* í·kra·t *I lie down* (-rat-); rayáhshę' *he lies down* (-yahshę(T)-); rá·ta'č *he lies down* (-ta'T-).
lie on back. *v.i.* ráhsha·t *he lies on his back* (-hshaT).
lie, tell a. *v.i.* ratù·węh *he tells a lie* (-tu=wę-); ęka'tù·węht *I will tell a lie* (-a'tuwęhT-).
life. *n.* awę́nhe' *life* (-ę°nhe-); u'nęnhéhkčreh *life* (-a'nęnhehkčr-); u'nę́nhehkt *life* (-a'nęnhehkT-).
lifeless. *adj.* u'nęnhehkčrú·kę' *lifeless* (-a'nęnhehkčrukę').
lift. *v.t.* nehráhkhwa' *he lifts it* (-ne-. -hkw-); nehrahkwá'tha' *he lifts it* (-ne-. -hkwa'T-).
light. *n.* učí'reh *light* (-či'r-); yú·huks *light* (-huk-); uhúkčreh *light* (-huk=čr-).
light. *v.i.* kači'ra'níhrę *it is lit* (-či'=ra'nihr-); *v.t.* ra'neká'tha' *he lights it* (-'neka'T-).
light up. *v.i.* yú·huks *it lights up* (-huk-).
light-skinned. *adj.* ru'nahwà·ra'neht *he is light-skinned* (-a'nahwa̲ra'nehT-).
lighter. *n.* yę'neka'náhkhwa' *lighter* (-'neka'nahkw-).
lightly. *adv.* tyuyeręháh *lightly* (ti-. -yer-. #áh).
lightning. *n.* newatkahréhnari·ks *lightning* (-ne-. -atkahrehna̲rik-).
like. *adv.* né'či *like* (né'či); kunikwę́ *like* (kunikwę́); kwę́ *like* (kwę́); kù·ni' *like* (kù·ni'); see: -u'nę-.

like. *v.t.* knurę́hkhwa' *I like it* (-nu=ręhkw-); runę́sne' *it likes him* (-nęs=ne-)
like to. *v.i.* rawęθrę́·ti· *he liked to* (-ę°=θręti-).
lily. *n.* lí·li· *lily* (lí·li·); tú'θeh *meadow lily* (tú'θeh).
limb. *n.* awętráhreh *limb (of body)* (-ę=trahr-); u'nháhneh *limb (of tree)* (-(i)'nhahT-).
limber. *adj.* tyawú·krę· *it is limber* (ti-. -ukr-); ruhkarí·yu· *he is limber* (-(a)h=ka̲riyu-).
lime. *n.* wa'kęhraríhnę *lime* (-a'kęh=ra̲rihT-).
lime. *v.t.* ra'narę̀·wawęhs *he limes it* (-'naręwawę-).
lime kiln. *n.* yę'kęhrarihnáhkhwa' *lime kiln* (-a'kęhrarihnahkw-).
limit. *n.* ha' tiwakę́hya·t *the limit* (ti-. -akęhyaT-).
limp. *v.i.* ra'ná'wya'ks *he limps* (-a='na'wya'k-).
line. *n.* uhnę̀·weh *line* (-hnęw-).
line in, make a. *v.t.* see: -tet'-.
lineage. *n.* ur'ę́hseh *lineage* (-(i)r'ęhs-).
linen. *n.* uhsirehętíh *linen* (-hsir-.#ętíh); úhskareh *linen* (-hska̲r-).
liniment. *n.* yętihtawę́hstha' *liniment* (-(ę)tihta̲węhsT-).
link. *n.* uhθę́'reh *link* (-(a)hθę'r-).
lip. *n.* uhsúhkweh *lip* (-hsuhkw-); u'-à·reh *lower lip* (-'ar-); uhskwé'neh *upper lip* (-hskwe'n-); úθkwareh *lips* (-aθkwa̲r-).
liquid. *n.* awé·kyeh *liquid* (-ek-); see: -akri'.
liquid, be in. *v.i.* see: -u-.
liquid, put. *v.t.* see: -uha-.
liquify. *v.t.* awé·kę' rę́·tih *he liquifies it* (-ek- -ę°ti-).
liquor. *n.* uhné·kyeh *liquor* (-hnek-); unę́'yeh *liquor* (-nę'y-).

list. *n.* kayehsęnarà·węh *list* (-hsęnara =
wę -).

listen. *v.i.* rathę́hna·č *he listens* (-athęh =
naT -); *v.t.* wa⁷kayę⁷nahrę́⁷na·t *they
listened to another* (-ahrę⁷n -).

litter. *n.* yekyerhęhawíhtha⁷ *litter* (-ker =
hęhawihT -).

little. *adj.* yú·t⁷ah *it is little* (-t⁷ah -);
awéha⁷ *little* (-eh -).

little. *n.* ahči⁷áh *little* (áhči·⁷.#áh); áhči⁷
little (áhči⁷); narà·we⁷st *a little* (na =
rà·we⁷st).

little one. *n.* ú·t⁷ah *little one* (-t⁷ah -).

live in peace. *v.i.* ahskę̀·nę⁷ tha⁷neyé⁷rę⁷
the two of them live in peace (-hskę =
nę⁷ - tha -. -i⁷rę -).

liveforever. *n.* čawęnhéhkę *liveforever*
(-či -. -ę̨̊nhehkw -).

liver. *n.* uthwę́hseh *liver* (-athwęhs -).

liverwort. *n.* karę́⁷anęh *liverwort* (-rę⁷a =
nę -).

liverwort flower. *n.* učí⁷či⁷ *liverwort
flower* (-či⁷či -).

lizard. *n.* rukwéhu⁷y *lizard* (rukwéhu⁷y);
arekwéhu⁷y *lizard* (arekwéhu⁷y); ru-
kwé⁷kwe⁷ *common lizard* (rukwé⁷-
kwe⁷); kwé⁷kwe⁷ *female green lizard*
(kwé⁷kwe⁷); rurakwnyę́hre⁷ *red-spotted lizard* (rurakwnyę́hre⁷); ru⁷túrher
yellow-spotted lizard (ru⁷túrher).

load. *n.* uhwarí·⁷neh *load* (-hwari'n -).

load. *v.t.* raráhkhwa⁷ *he loads it* (-rah =
kw -).

loam. *n.* u⁷tehę̀·weh *loam* (-⁷tehęw -);
u⁷tehęwá⁷kye *loam* (-⁷tehęwa⁷ke).

loathe. *v.t.* rawe⁷θrá⁷θeh *he loathes it*
(-we⁷θra⁷θe -).

lobby. *n.* uháheh *lobby* (-(a)hah -).

lobelia, great. *n.* thyakyekatha⁷áh *great
lobelia* (tha -. -ekat -.#áh).

lobster. *n.* či⁷erá·kwę *lobster* (-či⁷ę =
raku -).

lock. *n.* učik⁷ę̀·war *lock* (-čik⁷ęwar -).

locomotive. *n.* učíhkweh *locomotive*
(-čihkw -).

locust. *n.* wáyway *locust* (wáyway); ę̀·-
re⁷w *locust* (ę̀·re⁷w); kanęharíhtha⁷
locust (-nęharihT -).

lodge. *n.* unę́hseh *lodge of an animal
such as a beaver or muskrat* (-nęhs -).

log. *n.* urę́·⁷neh *log* (-ręT -); awéhseh *log*
(-ehs -).

loin. *n.* u⁷nyeruruhčę́⁷kye *loin* (-a'nyeru =
ruhčę⁷ke).

lonely. *adj.* uhráw⁷aht *lonely* (-hraw =
⁷ahT -).

lonesome. *adj.* uhráw⁷aht *lonesome*
(-hraw⁷ahT -).

long. *adj.* ì·we·θ *it is long* (-eθ -), tiwe·θ-
⁷ú⁷y *it is long* (ti -. -eθ -.#ú⁷y).

long ago. *adv.* unę́ha·⁷ *long ago* (-nę =
ha·⁷ -).

long for. *v.t.* na⁷ná⁷ręr *one longs for
another* (-a⁷ręr -).

long time. *n.* wa⁷u⁷tyá·tih *it was a long
time* (-⁷tyatih -).

longball. *n.* kayehswaí⁷aks *longball
(game)* (-hswai⁷a(k) -).

look. *v.i.* ka⁷nehwá·tyę *I have looked*
(-a'nehwati -).

look at. *v.t.* ratkáhthuhs *he looks at it*
(-atkahthu -); nehskné⁷yar *you are
looking at me* (-ne -. -nę⁷yar -).

look for. *v.t.* réhsaks *he looks for it* (-ïh =

sak -).

loon. *n.* a'ù·wę' *loon* (a'ù·wę').

loop. *n.* ukahkyé'neh *loop* (-kahke'n -); ukahkaríhneh *loop* (-kahkarihn -).

loose. *adj.* tyawú·krę· *it is loose* (ti -. -ukr -).

loosen. *v.t.* tihrukráhkhwa' *he loosens it* (ti -. -ukrahkw -); rú·'nyahθ *he loosens it* (-a'ni-{dative II}); rahtrę́hsyęhs *he loosens it* (-(i)htręhsi -); rahsu'ranęh-tha' *he loosens it* (-hsu'ranęhT -).

lop off. *v.t.* ra'nhahnú'θkarhahs *he lops it off* (-(i)'nhahnu'θkarh -).

lord. *n.* ruyà·ner *lord* (-yan(e)(r) -).

lose. *v.t.* ęwakwá·'ni' *I will lose it* (-a='ni -).

lose consciousness. *v.i.* wahra'tikęhráh-nę' *he lost consciousness* (-(ę)'tikęh=rahnę -).

lost, get. *v.i.* wa'kyahstáhnę' *I got lost* (-yahstahnę -).

lot. *n.* uhéhneh *lot* (-hehn -).

loud. *adj.* yurakaré·ti· *it is loud* (-ra=kar(e)-{dative II}).

louse. *n.* číhkw *louse* (číhkw); učik'ę̀·war *wood louse* (-čik'ęwar -).

lousy. *adj.* číhkwči *lousy* (číhkw.#hči); račinę́hnuh *he is lousy* (-činęhnu -).

lout, be a filthy. *n.* kihstkú·kre' *I am a filthy lout* (-(i)hstkukr -).

love. *n.* unuręhkwáhčreh *love* (-nuręh=kwahčr -).

love. *v.t.* knurę́hkhwa' *I love it* (-nu=ręhkw -); runę́sne' *it loves him* (-nęs=ne -)

lover. *n.* natkwà·rihθ *one is another's lover* (-kwari(y)-{dative II}); wa'nę-rú'čhę' *her lover* (-a'nęru'čhę(T) -); neyę'nę̀·nur *lovers* (-a'nęnur).

lovesick. *adj.* rahstrè·nę'θ *he is lovesick* (-hstrenę' -).

low. *adj.* awéhsayę' *low* (-ehsayę -).

lower. *adj.* ehnáhkę *lower* (ehnáhkę).

luck, have bad. *v.i.* ahrukęhsawęrę́hthahθ *that he have bad luck* (-kęhsawę=ręhT -{dative II}); θatra'θwá·ksę· *you have bad luck* (-atra'θwaks -).

luck, have good. *v.i.* θatra'θwí·yu· *you have good luck* (-atra'θwiyu -).

lucrative. *adj.* yuhwíhstu' *it is lucrative* (-hwihstur -).

ludicrous. *adj.* yutérhya't *it is ludicrous* (-terhya'T -).

lump. *n.* ukyé'čeh *lump* (-ke'č -); uθ-nę́'kweh *lump* (-aθnę'kw -); utkyéh-reh *lump* (-atkehr -); uhwarí·'neh *lump* (-hwari'n -); u'nhę́θteh *lump of dough* (-'nhęθt -).

lunatic. *n.* ruręhyá'nahs *lunatic* (-ręh=ya'T -).

lung. *n.* uthwę́'reh *lung* (-athwę'r -).

lurch. *v.i.* ru'rę'kúhę *he lurches* (-a'=rę'kuhw -).

lust. *n.* utkę́hyeh *lust* (-atkęhy -); uh-su'yé'ę *lust* (-hsu'ye' -).

luxury. *n.* utkanę́·nyaht *luxury* (-atkanę=nyaht).

lye. *n.* uhséhareh *lye* (-hsehar -).

lying face down. *adj.* rahswakwę́'na·t *he is lying face down* (-hswakwę'n -).

lynx. *n.* číčhu *lynx* (číčhu).

M

macerate. *v.t.* rę'nikęhkarya'ná·tih *he macerates it* (-ę'nikęhkarya'n -{dative III}).

machinery. *n.* yuyu'né·tyę' *machinery* (-yu'netyę -).

mad. *adj.* wakčha'rú·ri· *I am mad* (-čha'ruri -).

mad, get. *v.i.* wahruhsá'rę'θ *he got mad* (-hsa'rę -{dative III}).

maggot. *n.* awętihsé'yeh *maggot* (-ętih=se'y -).

magic. *n.* urę́·teh *magic* (-ręN -); uhęčí'reh *black magic* (-hęči'r-).

magic, make. *v.i.* wa'ę'ręnę́·ti' *one made magic* (-a'ręnęti-).

magician. *n.* ru'ręnę́·ti· *magician* (-a'ręnęti-).

magnificent. *adj.* ručhu'kuwahčratkę́hę *he is magnificent* (-ačhu'kuwahčra=tkęha-); rawękwehstanehrá·kwahst *he is magnificent* (-ę°k\u1d42ehstanehrakwah=sT-).

magnolia. *n.* nú·θri' *magnolia* (nú·θri').

maidenhood. *adj.* kwęhs arye'nihahstayę'nè·rihk *maidenhood* (kwęhs -'nihahstayę'ner-).

main. *adj.* ha' kę́hčih *main* (ha' kę́hčih); see: -kwe'niyu-.

majestic. *adj.* rawękwehstanehrá·kwahst *he is majestic* (-ę°k\u1d42ehstanehrakwah=sT-).

majesty. *n.* uthehtrákčreh *majesty* (-a=thehtrakčr-).

make. *v.t.* retì·yahs *he makes it* (-e=ti(y)-); ęhrę́·ti' *he will make it* (-ę'ti-).

male. *adj.* ra'níha· *he is male* (-'niha·).

malefactor. *n.* wáhsę· ruyu'néhkę *malefactor* (-ahsę- -yu'nehkw-).

malice. *n.* uhsę́hčreh *malice* (-ahsęhčr-).

mallet. *n.* učíhkweh *mallet* (-čihkw-).

maltreat. *v.t.* ra'nékskruh *he is maltreating it* (-a'nekskru-).

man. *n.* ra'níha· *man* (-'niha·); rę́·kweh *man* (-ę°k\u1d42e-); rakwá·tihs *young man* (-kwati-); ra'niha·háh *young man* (-'niha·-.#áh).

manage. račtehríhstha' *he manages it* (-(a)čtehrihsT-)

mandrake. *n.* ruhsù·warę *mandrake* (ruh-

sù·warę).

mane. *n.* ukę́heh *mane* (-kęh-).

manger. *n.* wačhuryá'tha' kačhè·nę' *manger* (-ačhurya'T- -čhenę-).

mankind. *n.* ehnú·kęw *mankind* (ehnú·kęw).

manly. *adj.* ra'nihá· *manly* (-'niha·).

mannequin. *n.* ękweháh *mannequin* (-ę°=k\u1d42e-.#áh).

manner. *n.* uwyę̀·neh *manner* (-wy(ęn)-); uyéhseh *manner* (-yehs-).

manners, good. *n.* u'nehyahrę́hčreh *good manners* (-a'nehyahręhčr-).

manufacturer. *n.* yuyu'né·tyę' *manufacturer* (-yu'netyę-).

many. *adj.* kwà·nę *many* (kwà·nę); yawęhrí·yu· *there are many* (-ęhriyu-).

many, have. *v.i.* ruká'ne' *he has many* (-ka'ne-).

maple. *n.* akę́·su'r *red maple* (akę́·su'r); učikhé'ta' *sugar maple* (-čikhe'ta-).

maple sap. *n.* karę'nahrarękę́he' *maple sap* (-rę'nahrar-.#kę́he').

march. *v.i.* kayenęhrahstę̀·nih *they march* (-(ę)nęhrahstęni-).

March. *n.* kanęharę́'kye *March* (-nęhah=rę'ke).

mare. *n.* áha·θ unę̀·we' *mare* (áha·θ -nę=we-).

maritime. *n.* unyatara'kyéha·' *maritime* (-nyatar-.#keha·').

mark. *n.* uhnę̀·weh *mark* (-hnęw-).

mark. *v.t.* rayerętíhtha' *he marks it* (-ye=rętihT-).

market. *n.* neyętkę́·nyęhs *market* (-ne-.-atkęni-); yę'nyahkwayę'náhkhwa' *market* (-a'nyahkwayę'nahkw-).

---

marksmanship. *n*. úʔθreh *marksmanship* (-aʔθr-).

maroon. *adj*. katkwęʔnahrahę́sči *maroon* (-tkwęʔnahraha̱hęsči-).

marrow. *n*. uhsnahrę̀·weh *marrow* (-hs=nahręw-); uθnahrę̀·weh *marrow* (-θnahręw-).

marry. *v.t*. ęyęktí·tya·k *the two of us will marry one another* (-tyak-); nekheya-tręnayę́·tih *I marry him to her* (-atrę=na̱yę-{dative II}).

marsh. *n*. uhryúhkweh *marsh* (-hryuh=kw-); uwíhreh *marsh* (-wihr-).

marten. *n*. čuranuháh *marten* (čura-nuháh).

martyr. *n*. karihwiyúhsnahk rawęheyaʔ-náhkę *martyr* (-rihwiyuhsT- -ęhe=yaʔnahkw-).

masculine. *adj*. yeʔniha·kyéha·ʔ *masculine* (-ʔniha·-.#keha·ʔ).

mask. *n*. utkęhsù·rę *mask* (-atkęhsurę-).

mason. *n*. račtę́hranęh *mason* (-čtęh=ra̱nę-).

mass. *n*. ukyéʔčeh *mass* (-keʔč-); uh-waríʔneh *mass* (-hwari'n-); uθnę́ʔ-kweh *mass* (-aθnęʔkw-).

massacre. *v.t.* ˙rarę́ʔkęʔč *he massacres it* (-ręʔkęʔr-); kakutiháhkuh *it massacres them* (-tihahku-).

master. *n*. rarihwakweʔnì·yuʔ *master* (-rihwa̱kweʔniyu-).

master. *v.t*. raʔniʔθhę́·nyęhs *he masters it* (-a'niʔθhęni-).

mastic. *n*. uʔnà·ręweh *mastic* (-ʔnaręw-).

mat. *n*. učíhseh *mat* (-čihs-); uyę́ʔneh *mat made of corn husks* (-yęʔn-).

match. *n*. yęʔnekaʔnáhkhwaʔ *match* (-'nekaʔnahkw-).

material. *n*. yakyetyáʔthaʔ *material* (-e=tyaʔT-).

materials. *n*. yehsnahnę́hkhwaʔ *materials* (-(i)hsnahnęhkw-).

maternity. *n*. uʔę́hsteh *maternity* (-ʔęh=st-).

mathematics. *n*. haʔ káhra·č *mathematics* (-hraT-).

matter. *n*. uríhweh *matter* (-rihw-); yakyetyáʔthaʔ *matter* (-etyaʔT-).

mattress. *n*. utéʔkweh *mattress* (-teʔkw-).

mature. *v.i*. raʔnękwehstíhsʔahs *he matures* (-a'nękʷehstihsʔa-).

may apple. *n*. ruhsù·warę *may apple* (ruhsù·warę).

maybe. *adv*. tehčíhęʔ *maybe* (tehčíhęʔ); kę́hčih *maybe* (kę́hčih).

mayor. *n*. haʔ rataʔnakweʔnì·yuʔ *mayor* (-ta'na̱kweʔniyu-).

meadow. *n*. uhę́ʔneh *meadow* (-(a)=hęʔn-).

meagre. *n*. áhčiʔ *meagre* (áhčiʔ).

meal. *n*. úkhweh *meal* (-khw-).

meal, take a. *v.i*. raʔnekhwáher *he takes his meal* (-a'nekhwah(e)r-).

mean. *adj*. ruʔnęnéʔner *he is mean* (-aʔnęneʔner-); kahsyá·ksę· *it is mean* (-hsyaks-).

mean. *v.i*. ręhnáhkhwaʔ *he means* (-ęh=nahkw-); rę́hteʔ *he means* (-ihteʔ-).

meanly. *adv*. uʔnęneʔnerčrá·kęw *meanly* (-aʔnęneʔne̱rčrakęw).

meanness. *n*. haʔ yuʔnęnéʔner *meanness* (-aʔnęneʔner-).

measure. *v.t*. raʔtyę́·ʔnęh *he measures it* (-ʔtyę'nęh-).

measure by. *v.t*. nehruʔtyęʔnę́hsnę *he measured by* (-ne-.-ʔtyęʔnęhsT-).

meat. *n*. uʔwáhreh *meat* (-ʔwah(r)-); kaʔwahręhrá·heʔ *fried meat* (-ʔwah=ręhra·heʔ-); uhčúʔkweh *piece of meat* (-hčuʔkw-).

mediator. *n*. rarihwahstę̀·nih *mediator* (-rihwa̱hstęni-).

medicine. *n*. yunę́hkwaʔt *medicine* (-nęhkwaʔT-); ęnę́hkwaʔt *medicine* (ęnę́hkwaʔt).

medicine man. *n*. ranęhkwaʔčrayęʔnè·rih *medicine man* (-nęhkwaʔčra̱yęʔner-).

medicine stick. *n*. učíʔrureh *medicine*

stick (-či⁷r<u>u</u>r-).

meditate. *v.i.* rę⁷tikęhnę́·tyęh *he meditates* (-(ę)⁷tikęhnętyę-).

meditation. *n.* u⁷tikęhnę́hčreh *meditation* (-(ę)⁷tikęhnęhčr-).

meet. *v.t.* nehručhí·θę *he met it* (-ne-.-ačhiθ-); nehrahahí·θahs *he meets it* (-ne-.-(a)hahiθ-).

meeting room. *n.* yę⁷ruhčrę́hkhwa⁷ *meeting room* (-a⁷ruhčręhkw-).

mellow. *adj.* ká·nę· *it is mellow* (-(a)=nę-); yù·rih *it is mellow* (-rih-); yuhsu⁷rá·nę· *mellow* (-hsu⁷ranę-).

mellowness. *n.* yuhyà·rih *mellowness* (-(a)hy<u>a</u>rih-).

melon. *n.r.* učhé⁷weh *melon* (-čhe⁷w-).

melt. *v.i.* kata⁷tà·wę⁷θ *it melts* (-ta⁷=tawę⁷-); wa⁷kata⁷tà·wę⁷ *it melted* (-ta⁷tawę-); yunyataná·wę· *it is melted* (-nyatanawę-).

member. *n.* ráha⁷r *he is a member* (-(i)=har-).

memorize. *v.t.* θhrawehyarhuhkwá·tih *he memorizes it* (-či-.-ehyahrhuhkw-{dative III}).

memory. *n.* ha⁷rehyahráhstha⁷ *his memory* (-ehyahr-).

menstration. *n.* kakunęhwakčrà·węh *menstration* (-nęhwakčrawę-).

mention. *v.t.* rawehrá⁷tha⁷ *he mentions it* (-wehra⁷T-).

merciful. *adj.* ru⁷ni⁷nęráhskę *he is merciful* (-a'ni'nęrahsk-).

mercy. *n.* u⁷ni⁷nęrę́hčreh *mercy* (-a'ni='nęręhčr-); čí⁷nęhs *mercy* (čí⁷nęhs).

meritorious. *adj.* yu⁷nęnęherá·tęht *meritorious* (-a'nęnęheratęhT-).

merry, make. *v.i.* ra⁷nęnę⁷yáhstha⁷ *he makes merry* (-a'nęnę⁷yahsT-).

message. *n.* uwę́·teh *message* (-węt-).

messenger cane. *n.* uhnęhtíhčreh *messenger cane* (-hnęhtihčr-).

metal. *n.* uhwíhsteh *metal* (-hwihst-); see: -rihst-.

metamorphose. *v.i.* newa⁷nyehsakę⁷né·tyęhs *it metamorphoses* (-ne-.-a'nyeh=sakę⁷neti-).

meteor. *n.* yuči⁷rę́·⁷nyęhs *meteor* (-či⁷=rę'ni-).

middle. *n.* ahsę̀·nę *middle* (ahsę̀·nę); see: -(i)hę.

might. *n.* ukwenyę́hčreh *might* (-kwe=nyęhčr-).

mild. *adj.* ruhrú⁷nę *he is mild* (-hru⁷T-).

milk. *n.* unęhrá⁷seh *milk* (-nęhra⁷s-).

milk. *v.t.* ranęhra⁷sa⁷náhkhwa⁷ *he milks it* (-nęhra⁷sa⁷nahkw-).

milkweed. *n.* čunęwahskrì·yu⁷ *common milkweed* (čunęwahskrì·yu⁷).

Milky Way. *dv.n.s.* yurę́hyahuks *Milky Way* (-rę̨hy<u>a</u>huk-).

million. *adj./n.* wáhθhę· tikayáhstih na⁷ uyáhsteh *million* (-ahθhę-ti-.-yahsti-na⁷-yahst-); ę́·či na⁷ uyáhsteh tikayáhstih *million* (ę́·či na⁷ -yahst-ti-.-yahsti-).

millipede. *n.* ruhtkę̀·ye·⁷ *millipede* (ruhtkę̀·ye·⁷).

mince. *v.t.* raθkrawę̀·rih *he minces it* (-θkrawęri-).

mind. *n.* u⁷tikę́hreh *mind* (-(ę)⁷tikęh-).

mind. *v.t.* ęhskwę́·tarahkw *you will mind me* (-węt<u>a</u>rahkw-).

mindful. *adj.* ra⁷tikę́hrar *he is mindful*

(-(ę)ʾtikęhrar-).

mindless. *adj.* ruʾtikęhrú·kęʾ *he is mind-less* (-(ę)ʾtikęhrukęʾ).

mingle. *v.i.* rayerákhę *he mingles* (-yera=kha-).

minister. *n.* račihę́hstačih *minister* (-či=hęhstači-).

mink. *n.* θenę́·ku·t *mink* (θenę́·ku·t).

minnow. *n.* rukayę́heh *minnow* (ruka-yę́heh); kunúhθraks *minnow* (kunúh-θraks).

minor. *n.* kwęhs ahruʾnuhstíhsʾęk *a min-or* (kwęhs -aʾnuhstihsʾa-).

minute. *n.* mę̀·nit *minute* (mę̀·nit).

mirror. *n.* awé·kyeh *mirror* (-ek-).

mirthful. *adj.* wà·rahst *it is mirthful* (-arahsT-); θhuhtyerúhskęʾ *mirthful* (θhuhtyerúhskęʾ).

miscarriage. *n.* θkawirę́ʾę *miscarriage* (-či-.-wiręʾ-).

miscarry. *v.i.* čewì·ręʾθ *one miscarries* (-či-.-wiręʾ-).

mischief. *n.* uhtyę́·kweh *mischief* (-htyę=kʷ-).

mischievous. *adj.* ruhtyę́·kwę· *he is mis-chievous* (-htyękʷ-).

misfortune. *n.* yutraʾθwaksę́ʾę *misfor-tune* (-atraʾθwaksęʾ-); kanęhsatarí·-nę·ʾ *misfortune that brings death* (-nęhsatarinę-); uθrę́shayęʾ *misfortune* (-θręshay-).

mist. *n.* neyuręʾnę́ʾę *mist* (neyuręʾnę́ʾę); učhá·ʾneh *mist* (-čha̱ʾn-).

mistake, make. *v.i.* rúnhiks *he is making a mistake* (-unhik-); runhíhthręh *he makes mistakes* (-nhihthrę-).

mistaken. *adj.* nehruʾtikęhkę́·nyę *he is mistaken* (-ne-.-(ę)ʾtikęhkęni-).

mistreat. *v.t.* rukę́hčręh *he is mistreated* (-kęhčrę-).

mistress. *n.* uʾnęrúʾčreh *mistress* (-aʾnę=ruʾčr-).

mistrust. *v.t.* naʾtuwę́htha ʾ*one mistrusts another* (-tuwęhT-).

mitten. *n.* uhčúhčreh *mitten* (-ahčuhčr-).

mix. *v.t.* rárhuhs *he mixes it* (-rhu-); nehrárhuhs *he mixes it* (-ne-.-rhu-); nehrayéhraks *he mixes two things to-gether* (-ne-.-yehrak-).

mixture. *n.* ú·wyeh *mixture* (-wy(ęn)-); neyuʾnyehrákθęʾ *mixture* (-ne-.-a=ʾnyehrakθę-).

moan. *v.i.* ruwętù·rih *he moans* (-wę=turi-).

moccasin. *n.* uhnáhkwaʾ *moccasin* (-ah=nahkw-); uhnahkwehę̀·we *moccasins* (-ahnahkw-.#ęwe); máʾmaʾ *moccasin* (máʾmaʾ).

model. *n.* neyeʾtyęʾnę́hsthaʾ *model* (-ne-.-ʾtyęʾnęhsT-).

moderate. *adj.* kwéʾyę·ʾ *moderate* (kwéʾyę·ʾ).

moderate. *v.t.* raʾθhanę́htha ʾ*he mod-erates it* (-(i)ʾθhanęhT-).

moderately. *adv.* kweʾyęhá·ʾnyeʾ *mod-erately* (kweʾyęhá·ʾnyeʾ).

modern. *adj.* urihwá·θe·ʾ *modern* (-rih=waθe·ʾ).

modest. *adj.* ručheyà·rę *he is modest* (-čheyar-).

modesty. *n.* učhè·yaʾr *modesty* (-čhe=yar-).

modify. *v.t.* nehrakęʾné·tyęhs *he modi-fies it* (-ne-.-kęʾneti-).

moist. *adj.* yawù·ręʾ *it is moist* (-urę-).

molasses. *n.* uθrę̀·weh *molasses* (-θrę=w-).

mold. *n.* yuyęʾkwárhar *mold (fungus)* (-yęʾkwa̱rhar-).

mole. *n.* čunaʾtáhčre·θ *mole* (čunaʾ-táhčre·θ); aθneháh *mole* (aθneháh); čę́htkwęʾ *flower-nosed mole* (čę́h-tkwęʾ).

mollusk. *n.* uʾtúhseh *mollusk* (-ʾtuhs-).

molt. *v.i.* wačnyuʾθrę́hthaʾ *it (animal, reptile) molts* (-ačnyuʾθręhT-).

monarchy. *n.* uyanéʾčreh *monarchy* (-ya=neʾčr-).

monarda. *n.* kayęwá·kra·θ *monarda* (-yę = wakraθ-).

Monday. *n.* mę́·teh *Monday* (mę́·teh).

money. *n.* uhwíhsteh *money* (-hwihst-).

monkey. *n.* kačíhkwna·ks *monkey* (-čihkwnak-).

monopolize. *v.t.* ra'nya'takwe'niyúhstha' *he monopolizes it* (-a'nya' = takwe'niyuhsT-).

monotonous. *adj.* ru'nwętahsá'nę' *he is monotonous* (-a'nwętahsa'nę-).

monster. *n.* neyu'nyeré·nyę· *monster* (-ne-. -a'nyeręnyę-).

monstrous. *adj.* neyu'nyeré·nyę· *monstrous* (-ne-. -a'nyeręnyę-).

month. *n.* uhihté'čreh *month* (-hih = te'čr-).

moon. *n.* í·ka'r *moon* (-r-); ahθę'nyéha·' *moon* (-ahθę'nyeha·'); čęčúhner *first quarter of moon* (čęčúhner); čúhner *first half of moon* (čúhner); kahihté'črih *second half of moon* (-hih = te'čri-); yuhihte'črá·θe·' *new moon* (-hihte'čraθe·'-); tha'uhihte'čríhę *second quarter of moon* (tha-. -hih = te'črihę); ča'úhshę' nyutkwáhnę *third quarter of moon* (ča'úhshę' -t-. -a = tkwahT-).

moon dog. *n.* nyuwętú·the' *moon dog* (-t-. -ętuthe'-).

moor boat. *v.i.* rahęwáhtręhs *he moors boat* (-hęwahtrę-).

moose. *n.* θka'nyę́hseh *moose* (θka'-nyę́hseh).

more. *adj.* íhs'ę *more* (íhs'ę); na' *more* (na').

moreover. *adv.* čwé·'n ha' íhs'ę *more-over* (čwé·'n ha' íhs'ę).

morning. *n.* θuhtérhę *morning* (-či-. -hterhę-); θuhterhę'áh *morning* (-či-. -hterhę.#áh).

mortality. *n.* yękwęhè·yaht *our mortality* (-iheyahT-).

mortar. *n.* a'nahú'y *mortar* (a'nahú'y).

mortar and pestle. *n.* u'tikáhneh *mortar and pestle* (-'tikahn-).

mortise. *v.t.* rarę'áhrara·ks *he mortises it* (-rę'ahrarak-).

mosquito. *n.* ru'té·yu·' *mosquito* (-(ę)'= teyu-).

moss. *n.* awęráhθreh *moss* (-ęrahθr-).

mossy. *n.* yawęrahθrù·rę *it is mossy* (-ę = rahθrurę-).

most. *adj.* tha'awę̀·ruh *most* (tha-. -ęruh-).

moth. *n.* rá'θ *moth* (rá'θ).

mother. *n.* rú'ę *his mother* (-'ę); yęhθkwaríhtha' *mother* (-ahθkwarihT-); ę́·nę' *my mother* (ę́·nę').

mother-in-law. *n.* uhę́·θę *mother-in-law* (-hęθę); yé·θa'w *my mother-in-law* (-θa'w-); yaktihę́·θhu' *my mother-in-law* (-hęθhu-).

motherhood. *n.* u'ę́hsteh *motherhood* (-'ęhst-).

motion, be in. *v.i.* yukyérwę'θ *it is in motion* (-kerwę'-).

mount. *v.i.* račhé'tha' *he mounts* (-a = čhe'T-).

mountain. *n.* unę́·'neh *mountain* (-nęT-); yunęther'úy' *mountain* (-nęth(e)r-. #ú'y).

mountain lion. *n.* kę́hreks *mountain lion* (-ihreks); tkę́hwè·nuh *mountain lion*

(tkęhwè·nuh).

mountainous. *n.* yunęthrawę'ú'y *mountainous* (-nęthrawę-.#ú'y).

mourn. *v.i.* ra'nę́·ta'θ *he mourns* (-a='nęt(a')-); ęθa'nęnhá'nę'θ *you will mourn* (-a'nęnha'nę'-{dative I}); *v.t.* ranhá'nę *he mourns for it* (-nha'nę-); ranhá'nę *he mourns the loss of it* (-nha'nę-).

mouse. *n.* ruskwè·nę' *mouse* (-skwenę-); čuna'táhčre·θ *field mouse* (čuna'táhčre·θ).

mouth. *n.* uhskahrę̀·weh *mouth* (-(i)h=skahręw-); uhská'yeh *big mouth* (-hs=ka'y-); nyawé·kę' *mouth of a river* (-t-.-ekę-).

mouth, have around. *v.t.* nehrukę́hę *he has it all around his mouth* (-ne-.-kęhu-).

mouth, have in the. *v.t.* see: -nhęT-.

mouthful. *n.* awęhúhskwareh *mouthful* (-ęhuhskwar-); u'nhúhskwareh *mouthful* (-(ę)'nhuhskwar-).

move. *v.i.* ratkwe'nę́·tyę *he moved* (-a=tkwe'nęti-); *v.t.* ruryáhnęh *he moves it* (-ⁿuryahnę-).

move away. *v.i.* ęwátkwi'tⁱ *it will move away* (-atkwi'T-).

move away from. *v.t.* ęyéhkwi'tⁱ *one will move away from it* (-hkwi'T-).

movement. *n.* ukwé'neh *movement* (-kwe'n-).

mow. *v.t.* rahé·rya'ks *he mows it* (-he=rya'k-).

much. *adj.* kwà·nę *much* (kwà·nę); na' *much* (na'); tiwá·θręk *it will be that much* (ti-.-aθrę-).

much, have. *v.i.* ruká'ne' *he has much* (-ka'ne-).

mucilage. *n.* uhú'kreh *mucilage* (-hu'=kr-).

muck. *n.* węhrahę́sči *muck* (-ę°hrahęsči-); uhryúhkweh *black muck* (-hryuhkw-).

mud. *n.* u'nà·ręweh *mud* (-'naręw-); učíhskwa' *mud* (-čihskw-).

mud hen. *n.* kę́'kahwa' *mud hen* (kę́'kahwa').

mud puddle. *n.* yu'naręwę́·ti· *mud puddle* (-'naręwęti-).

muddy. *adj.* awę́·te kęrá·'ne' *muddy* (a-wę́·te -ira'ne-); u'naręwéhči *muddy* (-'naręw-.#hči).

muddy, get. *v.i.* wahra'naręwhà·ra' *he got muddy* (-'naręwhar-).

mulberry. *n.* θhúhye·θ *mulberry* (-či-.-(a)hyeθ-).

mule. *n.* kahęhné·θęh áha·θ *mule* (-hęh=neθę- áha·θ).

mullein. *n.* urí'weh *mullein* (-ri'w-).

mullet. *n.* θkarihstù·wa' *mullet* (θkarihstù·wa').

multiply. *v.t.* nehrahswa'te'nárhyę *he multiplies it* (-ne-.-hswa'te'narhy-).

multitude. *n.* u'nyuhkwáhraht *multitude* (-i'nyuhkwahrahT-).

mumble. *v.i.* ra'nwęθkę̀·rih *he mumbles* (-a'nwęθkęri-).

murder. *v.t.* ęyę'na'nyahstáhnę'tⁱ *one will murder another* (-yahstahnę'T-); rahkwę́'naws *he murders someone* (-hkwę'na(w)-).

muscle. *n.* unęhyaθe'kę́ha'nę' *muscle* (-nęhyaθ-.#kęha'nę'); unuhskwí'θreh *muscle of upper arm (bicep)* (-nuh=skwi'θr-).

mush. *n.* učíhskweh *mush* (-čihskw-).

mushroom. *n.* utráhseh *fungus* (-trahs-).

music. *n.* uwę́·teh *music* (-węt-); u'nwę'erę́'čreh *music* (-a'nwę'erę'čr-).

musk. *n.* utká'neh *musk* (-tka'n-).

muskmelon. *n.* warę́'krę'θ *muskmelon* (warę́'krę'θ).

muskrat. *n.* anú'kwyę *muskrat* (anú'kwyę).

mutilate. *v.t.* rahča'náhkhwa' *he mutilates it* (-ahča'nahkw-).

mutiny. *v.i.* ręti'nyuhkwę́·tih *he mutinies* (-(ę)ti'nyuhkwęti-).

mutter. *v.i.* ruwętù·rih *he mutters* (-wę= turi-); rarihwaríkhęh *he mutters* (-rihwarikhę-).

mutton. *n.* we⁷rá·ksę· *mutton* (-e⁷raks-).

mystery. *n.* yurihwahθéhnę *it is a mystery* (-rihwahθehT-).

myth. *n.* ękhwyaht *myth* (-ękhwyahT-).

N

nail. *n.* uhsęwá⁷reh *nail* (-hsęwa⁷r-).

naked. *adj.* učù·neh *naked* (-čun-).

name. *n.* uhsę̀·neh *name* (-hsęn-); uyaθéhsteh *name* (-yaθęhst-).

name. *v.t.* kayè·yač *they name it* (-yaθ-).

nape. *n.* uhnęhwéčheh *nape of neck* (-hnęhwečh-).

napkin. *n.* úhneh yęhčakyewá⁷tha⁷ *napkin* (-ihn- -ahčakewa⁷T-).

narrow. *n.* yunhú·čę⁷ *it is narrow* (-nhu= čę-).

nation. *n.* utá·kre⁷ *nation* (-tak(e)r-); ru⁷nęthi⁷kyehá·ka·⁷ *father's nation* (-⁷nę= thi⁷ke.#aka·⁷).

national. *adj.* utakrę⁷kyéha·⁷ *national* (-tak(e)r-.#keha·⁷).

native. *adj.* ha⁷ ratá·kre⁷ *native* (-ta= k(e)r-).

nausea. *n.* učí⁷yeh *nausea* (-či⁷y-).

nauseous. *adj.* rutya⁷kwahná·ti· *he is nauseous* (-tya⁷kʷahT-{dative III}); rutyá⁷kwrę· *he is nauseous* (-tya⁷= kʷhrę-).

navel. *n.* u⁷nihsę̀·reh *navel* (-⁷nihsęr-).

near. *adv.* núhskę *near* (núhskę); ú·kwt *near* (-akT-); kwè·ni⁷ *near* (kwè·ni⁷).

nearby. *adv.* kyé·⁷nyę⁷ *nearby* (kyé·⁷- nyę⁷).

nearly. *adv.* ča⁷úhshę⁷ *nearly* (ča⁷úh- shę⁷).

necessary. *adj.* yu⁷né·θwekt *it is necessary* (-a⁷neθwekT-); neyutahwęčúhę *it is necessary* (-ne-.-tahwęčuhu-).

neck. *n.* uhá⁷θeh *neck* (-ha⁷(č)-).

neck, have a stiff. *v.i.* ruhnęhwečhah- rená·thę· *he has a stiff neck* (-hnęhwe= čhahrenathę-).

necklace. *n.* uhnyáhsteh *necklace* (-(i)h= nyahst-).

need. *v.t.* yękyeríhθek *I will need it* (-yah-.-erihθe-).

needle. *n.* uhsęwá⁷reh *needle* (-hsę= wa⁷r-).

neigh. *v.i.* kahę̀·rehθ *it neighs* (-hęrehθ-).

neighbor. *n.* neyękyačęhaté·kę· *my neighbor* (-ne-.-(a)čęhatekę-).

nephew. *n.* ka⁷nu⁷nę⁷áh *my nephew* (-a= 'nu⁷nę⁷-.#áh); rawęhwá⁷nę⁷ *his nephew* (-ę̌hwa⁷nę⁷); kheyahwá⁷nę⁷ *my nephew* (-ahwa⁷nę⁷); khehsę́·te *my nephew* (-hsęte).

nerve. *n.* rę⁷nérstha⁷ *his nerve(s)* (-i⁷= nersT-).

nest. *n.* unę⁷yéčkweh *nest* (-(ę)nę⁷= yečkw-); yutyá⁷nęy *hornet's nest* (-tya⁷nęy-); katyá⁷thar *hornet's nest* (-tya⁷thar-).

nest, build. *v.i.* kanę⁷yéčkhwar *it builds nest* (-(ę)nę⁷yečkwhar-).

nestle. *v.i.* ra⁷túher *he nestles* (-⁷tuher-).

net. *n.* unę⁷reh *net* (-nę⁷r-).

nettle. *n.* yuherará·⁷ne⁷ *nettle* (-hera=

ra'ne -).

neutral. *adj.* kwęhs ę·'nahrurihwaráhkęk *he is neutral* (kwęhs -t-.-rihw̲a= rahkw -).

never. *adv.* sè·nę·' *never* (sè·nę·').

nevertheless. *adv.* séher *nevertheless* (séher); tuhtí' *nevertheless* (tuhtí').

New Year's Day. *n.* Nyú·ya· *New Year's Day* (Nyú·ya·); awuhstá·θe·' *New Year's Day* (-uhstaθe·').

new. *adj.* á·θe·' *new* (á·θe·').

newly. *adv.* aθé'či *newly* (aθe·'.#hči); čhę' *newly* (čhę').

news. *n.* uríhweh *news* (-rihw -); úhnyeh *news* (-hny-).

newspaper. *n.* uhyatę́hsteh *newspaper* (-hyatęhst -).

newt. *n.* rukwéhu *newt* (rukwéhu); ná'w-nę' *newt* (ná'wnę').

next. *adj.* ha' čwé·'kye *the next* (čwé·'-kye).

niece. *n.* waka'nú'nę' *my niece* (-a= 'nu'nę'); rawęhwá'nę' *his niece* (-ę°hwa'nę'); ka'nu'nę'áh *my niece* (-a'nu'nę'-.#áh); kheyahwá'nę' *my niece* (-ahwa'nę'); khehsę́·te *my niece* (-hsęte).

night. *n.* yuhθá·thę *night* (-ahθathu -); θwahθę́·'na·t *night* (-či -.-ahθę'nat).

nightmare. *n.* neyakuya'túhraraks *nightmare* (-ne-.-ya'tuhr̲arak -).

nightshade. *n.* čír wáhyaks *nightshade* (čír -(a)hy̲ak -).

nine. *adj./n.* níhrę' *nine* (níhrę').

nineteen. *adj./n.* níhrę' θkáhe'r *nineteen* (níhrę' -či -.-(i)har -).

ninety. *adj./n.* níhrę' tiwáhθhę· *ninety* (níhrę' ti -.-ahθhę -).

nipple. *n.* uhsú'neh *nipple* (-hsu'n -); u'-níhtyara' *nipple* (-'nihty̲ar -).

no. *adv.* the' *no* (the'); kwęhs *no* (kwęhs); ę̀·ru *no* (ę̀·ru).

no one. *pro.* kwęhs káhne·' *no one* (kwęhs káhne·').

nobody. *n.* sękwéh *nobody* (sękwéh).

nocturnal. *adj.* ahθę·'nyéha·' *nocturnal* (ahθę·'nyéha·').

nod. *v.i.* ręnę'kyę́hstha' *he nods* (-i= nę'kyęhst -).

noise. *n.* yurá·kar *noise* (-rakar(e)-); nyu= rá·kar *a noise* (-t-.-rakar -); wa'račę́·kwahs *the tearing, ripping noise of thunder* (-a'račęku -).

noise, make a. *v.i.* yú·kar *it makes a noise* (-kar -).

noisemaker. *n.* yę'rakareráhstha' *noisemaker* (-a'rakarerahsT -).

none. *n.* úhshęh *none* (-hshę -).

nook. *n.* yunhú·čę' *nook* (-nhučę -).

noon. *n.* ę'nyéhči *noon* (ę'nyéhči); tha'-nyawę'níhę *noon* (tha+ne -.-ę'nihę).

north. *n.* athú'kye *north* (athu'.#ke).

northerly. *adv.* athu'áh *northerly* (athu'.#áh).

Northern Lights. *n.* newa'ręhyayerę́·'-nye' *Northern Lights* (-ne -.-a'ręhy̲a= yerę'nye -).

nose. *n.* u'tyę́hseh *nose* (-'tyęhs -).

nose, blow. *v.i.* ręti'tyę́'θręhs *he blows his nose* (-(ę)ti'tyę'θ(e)r -).

nose bleed, have a. *v.i.* newáktyęhk *I have a nose bleed* (-ne -.-'tyęhk -).

nostril. *n.* u'čękáhreh *nostril* (-'čękahr -).

not. *adv.* íhskah *not* (íhskah); kwęhs *not* (kwęhs); the' *not* (the'); ę̀·ru *not* (ę̀·ru).

not too much. *adv.* nà·re'θ *not too much* (nà·re'θ).

not yet. *adv.* áθę the' *not yet* (áθę the').

notary. *n.* ra'rihwaté·t'ahs *notary* (-a'= rihw̲atet' -).

note. *n.* yučisnúhkwa'r *note (of music)* (-čisn̲uhkw̲ar -).

nothing. *n.* sawę́·te *nothing* (sawę́·te).

notice. *n.* yuhyatęhstanę'ná·kę *notice* (-hyatęhstan̲ę-'nak -).

notice. *v.t.* wahrahskwá·tkę·' *he noticed it* (-hskwatkę -); rahnú·kę'w *he no-*

ticed it (-hnukęw -).

notify. *v.t.* nathęhsyęhtha⁷ *one notifies
another* (-hęhsyęhT -); na⁷nyę⁷nerhu-
kwá·tih *one notifies another* (-yę'ner=
huku -{dative III}).

notorious. *adj.* nehratá·⁷nih *he is notorious* (-ne -. -ta'ni -).

notwithstanding. *adv.* sę́·r à·rę *notwithstanding* (sę́·r à·rę).

nourish. *v.t.* rá·nę·č *he nourishes it*
(-nęT -).

novelty. *n.* urihwá·θe·⁷ *novelty* (-rihwa=
θe·⁷).

November. *n.* kuhserhęháh *November*
(kuhserhęháh).

now. *adv.* ù·nę *now* (ù·nę); kyè·wę *now*
(kyè·wę).

now-a-days. *adv.* ha⁷ kyè·wę tyurhę́⁷θrę⁷
now-a-days (kyè·wę ti -. -rhę⁷θrę -).

number, be of such. *v.i.* see: -ake -.

numbness. *n.* uhsi⁷thę́hčreh *numbness*
(-hsi⁷thęhčr -).

nurse. *v.t.* runę⁷kyè·rę *he nursed it*
(-nę⁷ker -); ra⁷nwì·ranęh *he nurses it*
(-a'nwiranę -); yenę⁷kyerá⁷tha⁷ *one
nurses it* (-nę⁷kera⁷T -).

nut. *n.* awę́⁷reh *nut* (-ę°⁷r -).

nutcracker. *n.* neyakę⁷rahrihnáhkhwa⁷
nutcracker (-ne -. -ę°⁷rahrihnahkw -).

nutshell. *n.* utkę́⁷reh *nutshell* (-tkę⁷r -).

O

o that. *adv.* ne⁷ *o that* (ne⁷).

o.k. *interj.* wekayè·ri⁷ *it is o.k.* (-yah -.

-yeri -).

o' clock. *n.* tiwę⁷nę́·te⁷ *o' clock* (ti -.
-ę'nęte -).

oak. *n.* rà·ruh *black oak* (rà·ruh); čúhe⁷
pin oak (čúhe⁷); kù·reh *red oak* (kù·-
reh); ru⁷né·tuk *red oak* (ru⁷né·tuk);
unęhnù·rę⁷ *swamp oak* (-nęhnur -);
runęhnù·rę⁷ *white oak* (runęhnù·rę⁷);
tiwahkarači⁷tkwáhnayę⁷ *yellow oak*
(ti -. -(a)hkarači⁷tkwahnayę(T) -).

oar. *n.* ukawéhčreh *oar* (-kawehčr -).

oats. *n.* ú·č *oats* (ú·č); unawę́hkri⁷ *oats*
(-nawęhkr -).

obedient. *adj.* ru⁷nwę́·tarahkw *he is o-
bedient* (-a'nwętarahkw -).

obesity. *n.* utkrę́hneh *obesity* (-atkręhT -).

obey. *v.i.* ra⁷nwętaráhkhwa⁷ *he obeys*
(-a'nwętarahkw -); yuthę́hne⁷ *it obeys*
(-athęhn -).

obliging. *adj.* ru⁷nwę́·tarahkw *he is o-
bliging* (-a'nwętarahkw -).

oblique. *adj.* kahska⁷yáhręw *oblique*
(-hska⁷yahręhw -).

obscene. *adj.* yutyá⁷kwaht *it is obscene*
(-tya⁷kʷahT -).

obstinate. *v.i.* ruta⁷rahtì·ręh *he is obstinate* (-(ę)ta⁷rahtir -).

obtain. *v.t.* ratyè·nęh *he obtains it* (-tye=
nę -).

obviate. *v.t.* kaháhya⁷ks *it obviates it*
(-(a)hahya⁷k -).

obvious. *adj.* kayerę́·tih *it is obvious*
(-yeręti -).

occasion. *n.* uríhwawęh *occasion* (-rih=
wawę -); thwáhę· *occasion* (ti -. -i -).

occasionally. *adv.* ihskáhkye *occasionally*
(ihskáhkye); tyu⁷rę́⁷nhę *occasionally*

(ti‑. ‑aʔręʔnh‑).

occupant. *n.* rá·ra·t *occupant (of a vehicle)* (‑rat‑); rà·nęh *occupant (of a building)* (‑nę‑).

occupation. *n.* yęʔnęnhihsákthaʔ *occupation* (‑a'nęnhihsakT‑).

ocean. *n.* čikhéʔkye *ocean* (čikhéʔkye).

ocher. *n.* ukwę́hčreh *ocher* (‑kwęhčr‑).

October. *n.* rahθeʔkyehé·θuʔ *October* (rahθeʔkyehé·θuʔ).

odd. *adj.* ruyáhčih *he is odd* (‑yahč‑).

odor. *n.* uyę̀·reh *odor* (‑yęr‑); uhsęryúhkweh *odor* (hsęryuhkw‑).

odor, have body. *v.i.* skyerhá·kra·θ *you have body odor* (‑kerhakraθ‑); skyerhá·kse· *you have body odor* (‑ker=haks‑).

off and on. *adv.* yutkáʔneʔ *off and on* (‑tkaʔT‑).

offend. *v.t.* račhaʔrę́·tih *he offends* (‑čhaʔręti‑).

offense, take. *v.i.* ruhsaʔrę́·ti· *he takes offense* (‑hsaʔrę‑{dative III}); ruhsę́·θeʔ *he takes offense* (‑(i)hsę‑{dative I}).

offensive. *adj.* yučhaʔrę́·tyaht *offensive* (‑čhaʔrętyahT‑).

offer. *v.i.* raʔnéhthaʔ *he offers* (‑(a)='nehT‑).

officer. *n.* ruʔríhę·t *officer* (‑aʔrihęt); rahsęnuwà·nę *officer* (‑hsęnuwan‑).

official. *adj.* urihwáʔkye *official* (‑rih=waʔke).

officiate. *v.i.* rurihwarekwáʔnę *he officiates* (‑rihwarekwaʔT‑).

offspring. *n.* uwì·reh *offspring* (‑wir‑).

often. *adv.* yutkáʔneʔ *often* (‑tkaʔT‑).

oil. *n.* kę̀·yeʔ *oil* (‑iye‑).

oil. *v.t.* rayetà·węhs *he oils it* (‑yetaw‑).

oily. *adj.* kęyéʔči *oily* (‑iye‑.#hči).

ointment. *n.* ukyéʔčeh *ointment* (‑keʔč‑).

old. *adj.* yunę́ha·ʔ *it is old* (‑nęha·ʔ‑); waká·yę·ʔ *it is old* (‑akayę‑); kihskwà·rih *I am old (female)* (‑(i)h=skwari‑).

old, grow. *v.i.* yuhù·ręʔθ *it grows old* (‑huręʔ‑); yahwahráhuʔr *he grew old* (‑yah‑.‑hur‑).

old man. *n.* rúhur *old man* (‑hur‑).

old timers. *n.* kakunęhaʔkę́haʔnęʔ *old timers* (‑nęha·ʔ.#kęhaʔnęʔ).

old woman. *n.* káhskwariʔ *old woman* (‑(i)hskwari‑).

omit. *v.t.* nehraʔníhar *he omits it* (‑ne‑.‑a'nihar‑).

on the other side. *adv.* à·rę naʔ úʔnęʔ *on the other side* (à·rę naʔ úʔnęʔ).

on top. *adv.* héʔtkęh *on top* (héʔtkęh).

once again. *adv.* čwé·ʔkye *once again* (čwé·ʔkye).

once upon a time. *adv.* unęha·ʔáh *once upon a time* (‑nęha·ʔ.#áh); ę́·či tikahà·wiʔ *once upon a time* (ę́·či ti‑.‑(ę)hawi‑).

one. *adj./n.* ę́·či *one* (ę́·či).

one-by-one. *adv.* ęčihá·ʔnyeʔ *one-by-one* (ęčihá·ʔnyeʔ); θkayeyahstathá·ʔnyeʔ *one-by-one* (‑či‑.‑yahstatha'nye‑).

onerous. *adj.* wahwíhsneʔ *it is onerous* (‑(a)hwihsT‑).

onion. *n.* awęʔnè·waht *onion* (‑ęʔne=waht‑).

only. *adv.* účʔaht *only* (účʔaht); čhęʔ *only* (čhęʔ).

only one. *v.i.* see: ‑i‑/‑ę̊·‑.

onward. *adv.* uhęʔnęhá·ʔnyeʔ *onward* (‑(a)hęʔnęha'nyeʔ‑).

open. *v.i.* waʔnečá·ryęhs *it opens* (‑a='nečari‑); newaʔnętá·kę *it opens* (‑ne‑.‑a'nętak‑); *v.t.* nehratá·kęhs *he opens it* (‑ne‑.‑tak‑); račá·ryęhs *he opens the door* (‑čari‑); nehráθkwaraws *he opens his mouth* (‑ne‑.‑aθkwaraw‑).

opening. *n.* ukahrę̀·weh *opening* (‑kah=ręw‑).

opiate. *n.* yutʔúhneʔ *opiate* (‑(i)tʔuhT‑).

opium. *n.* yakutʔúhthaʔ *opium* (‑(i)t=ʔuhT‑).

opossum. *n.* číˀreˀ *opossum* (číˀreˀ);
čiˀreˀáh *opossum* (čiˀreˀ.#áh).

oppose. *v.t.* nęhrathréhweˀ *he will oppose it* (-ne-.-athręhw-).

opposite. *adj.* è·re *opposite* (è·re); thaˀ-
neyuyerihẃˀnęˀ *it is opposite* (tha+
ne-.-yeri-.#haˀnęˀ).

opposite sides, be on. *v.i.* see: -hrut.

oppress. *v.t.* naˀturí·yę· *one oppressed
another* (-turiyę-).

oppressed. *adj.* ruˀtikęhkyeyáˀthaˀ ‹he-
mind-agitates› *he is oppressed* (-(ę)ˀ=
tikęhkeyaˀT-).

or. *conj.* ukẹ́ˀ *or* (ukẹ́ˀ).

orchard. *n.* karhaˀnę́·tih *orchard* (-rha=
'nęti-).

order. *n.* uwę́·teh *order* (-węt-).

order. *v.t.* waˀeθarihwahtì·nęˀθ *one ordered you* (-rihwahtinę-{dative I}); ra-
hęká·ryaˀks *he orders it* (-hękarya ˀk-)

orderly. *n.* unháˀčreh *orderly* (-nhaˀčr-).

ordinarily. *adv.* haˀ karáhkęˀ kwę́ tì·yuht
ordinarily (haˀ karáhkęˀ kwę́ tì·yuht).

ordinary. *adv.* haˀ karáhkęˀ tì·yuht *ordinary* (haˀ karáhkęˀ tì·yuht).

organ. *n.* yęˀnwęˀeréhkhwaˀ *organ
(musical instrument)* (-a'nwęˀe=
ręhkw-).

organization. *n.* uˀnyúhkweh *organization* (-iˀnyuhkw-).

origin. *n.* waˀrihętyáˀthaˀ *origin* (-aˀri=
hętyaˀT-).

oriole, Baltimore. *n.* ruhnyárhar *Baltimore oriole* (ruhnyárhar).

ornament. *n.* yęˀnyaˀtahstęnyáˀthaˀ *ornament* (-a'nyaˀtahstęnyaˀT-).

ornament. *v.t.* rayaˀtahstę̀·nih *he orna-*

ments it (-yaˀtahstęni-).

orphan. *n.* waˀnęnhú·θnę *orphan* (-a'nęn=
huθnę).

oscillate. *v.i.* yuˀnyáhkhwar *it oscillates*
(-a'nyahkwhar-).

ossify. *v.i.* kahskęˀrę́·tih *it ossifies* (-hs=
kęˀręti-).

ostensibly. *adv.* sáˀrkęˀ *ostensibly* (sáˀrkęˀ).

ostrich. *n.* uhstrù·riˀ *ostrich* (-hstruri-).

other. *adj.* ú·ˀy *other* (ú·ˀy).

otter. *n.* čaˀkawì·nę *otter* (čaˀkawì·nę).

out do. *v.t.* nehraké·nyęhs *he out does it*
(-ne-.-kęni-).

out of the way. *prep.* yuthaharáhkwę *it is
out of the way* (-athaharahkw-).

out of sight. *adv.* waˀekahnę́ˀnakuˀ *one
is out of sight* (-kahnęˀnaku-).

outhouse. *n.* unęhseháh yęhtkiˀę́hkhwaˀ
outhouse (-nęhs-.#áh -ahtkiˀęhkw-).

outrageous. *adj.* yuˀθrà·rehst *outrageous*
(-aˀθrarehsT-).

outrun. *v.t.* ratahkíˀwahs *he outruns it*
(-tahkiˀw-).

outside. *adv.* áθneh *outside* (áθneh); aθnéhte *outside* (aθnéhte).

outward. *adv.* aθnéhte *outward* (aθnéhte).

outwit. *v.i.* nehraˀtikęhkę́·nyęhs *he outwits* (-ne-.-(ę)ˀtikęhkęni-).

oven. *n.* stúw *oven* (stúw).

over and over again. *adv.* nę́·ˀnyuht *over
and over again* (nę́·ˀnyuht).

over there. *adv.* héˀnęˀ *over there* (héˀnęˀ).

overcome. *v.t.* raˀniˀθhę́·nyęhs *he overcomes it* (-a'niˀθhęni-); rakwaná·-

kwahs *he overcomes (a difficulty)* (-kwanaku-).

overhang. *n*. utí'ʔθreh *overhang* (-ti'ʔ= θ(e)r-).

overhear. *v.t.* weyę'ʔnwętakáhtha'ʔ *one overhears* (-yah-. -a'nwętakahT-).

overload. *v.t.* rahwihsháʔtha'ʔ *he overloads it* (-(a)hwihsha'ʔT-).

overpay. *v.i.* íhs'ʔę thweyę'ʔnat'ʔęyúharθeh *one overpays* (íhs'ʔę ti+yah-. -'ʔęyu= har-{dative I}).

overpower. *v.t.* ra'ʔni'ʔθhę́·nyęhs *he overpowers it* (-a'ni'ʔθhęni-).

overshadow. *v.t.* yuti'ʔθrę́hstara'ʔθ *it overshadows it* (-ti'ʔθręhstara'ʔ-); kati'ʔθrę́hstha'ʔ *it overshadows it* (-ti'ʔ= θręhsT-).

overtake. *v.t.* ra'ʔté'ʔtyęhs *he overtakes it* (-'ʔte'ʔti-).

owe. *v.t.* yękyátkaru·t *I owe another or you, another or you owe me* (-atka= rut); yękwarihwahríhnę ‹we-matter-spill-cause› *we owe (e.g., a debt)* (-rihwahrihT-).

owl. *n*. ù·wa'ʔ *owl* (ù·wa'ʔ); uhsné·krik *hoot owl* (uhsné·krik); ruhsné·kri'ʔ *horned owl* (ruhsné·kri'ʔ); kwarù·wak *screech owl* (kwarù·wak), uwí·θreh *snowy owl* (-wiθ(e)r-).

ox. *n*. wętra'ʔné·θę *ox* (-(ę)tra'ʔneθ-).

oyster. *n*. u'ʔtúhseh *oyster* (-'ʔtuhs-).

P

pace. *n*. ú'ʔθheh *pace* (-(i)'ʔθh-); θkáhθa·t *one pace (of 3 feet)* (-či-. -hθaT-).

pack. *n*. see: -'ʔnęnaw-.

pack up. *v.i.* rathwari'ʔnę́·tih *he packs up* (-athwari'nęti-).

package. *n*. awęhskwí'ʔneh *package* (-ęh= skwi'ʔT-); uθnę́'ʔkweh *package* (-aθ= nę'ʔkw-).

paddle. *n*. utkuryá'ʔčreh *paddle* (-tku= rya'ʔčr-); utúhneh *paddle* (-tuhn-).

pail. *n*. uná'ʔča'ʔ *pail* (-na'ʔč-); u'ʔnáh-kweh *pail* (-'ʔnahkw-).

painful. *adj*. yunęhwá·kne'ʔ *it is painful* (-nęhwak(T)-).

paint. *n*. uhθúhkweh *paint* (-ahθuhkw-); kwę́ht *face paint* (-kwęhT-); ukwę́h-čreh *red paint* (-kwęhčr-).

paint. *v.i.* rahθúhahs *he paints* (-ah= θu(h)-).

painter. *n*. rahθúhahs *painter* (-ahθuh-).

pair. *n*. né·kę· *pair* (-ne-. -i-); yutíhstę'ʔ *a pair* (-tihstę-).

palate. *n*. yewéhstha'ʔ *palate* (-wehsT-).

pale. *adj*. yutehwitkę́'ʔę *it is pale* (-teh= witkę'ʔ-); yuhwà·ra'ʔneht *it is pale* (-ahwara'nehT-); ru'ʔnahwà·ra'ʔneht *he is pale* (-a'nahwara'ʔnehT-).

pale, grow. *v.i.* rutéhwęh *he grew pale* (-tehwę-); ratehwitkę́'ʔę'ʔθ *he grows pale* (-tehwitkę'ʔę'ʔ-).

pallid. *adj*. rahskatetá·ksę· *he is pallid* (-hskatetaks-).

palm. *n*. uhθrá'ʔreh *palm of hand* (-hθra'ʔr-); u'ʔéhnakęw *palm of hand* (-'ʔehnakęw); úhsyeh *palm of the hand* (-hsy-).

pamper. *v.t.* rahsyúhčręh *he pampers it* (-hsyuhčrę-).

pan. *n*. u'ʔti'ʔnę́hkweh *pan* (-'ʔti'ʔnęhkw-).

pancake. *n*. uθrahwí'ʔreh *pancake* (-θrah= wi'ʔr-); učá'ʔreh *pancake* (-ča'ʔr-).

panel. *v.t.* ráhkaruč *he panels it* (-(a)h= karur-).

paneling. *n*. yu'ʔnehkarù·rę *paneling* (-a= 'nehkarur-).

pant. *v.i.* rawęríhshę'ʔθ *he pants* (-ę°rih= shę'ʔ-).

panther. *n*. tkęhwè·nuh *panther* (tkęhwè·-nuh).

pants. *n*. uta'ʔčhúhčreh *pants* (-ta'ʔčhuh= čr-).

pap. *n*. unęhrá'ʔseh *pap* (-nęhra'ʔs-).

papaw. *n.* nyę'ę̀·we *papaw* (nyę'ę̀·we).

paper. *n.* uhyatę́hsteh *paper* (-hyatęhst-).

parable. n. neyetakyera'náhkhwa' *parable* (-ne-. -takera'nahkw-).

parade. *v.i.* kayenęhrahstę̀·nih *they parade* (-(ę)nęhrahstęni-).

paralysis. *n.* rayè·rę' kęhè·yę'θ *paralysis* (-yer- -iheyę'-).

parcel out. *v.t.* rakhahsyę́·kwahs *he parcels it out* (-khahsyęku-).

parch. *v.t.* rę́hsęh *he parches it* (-ęhsę-); aryę'θkę́hsę' *that one parch it* (-a'=θkęhsę-).

parchment. *n.* úhneh *parchment* (-ihn-).

pardon. *v.t.* rarihwahnę́'tha' *he pardons it* (-rihwahnę'T-).

pardonable. *adj.* yu'rihwáhnę't *pardonable* (-a'rihwahnę'T-).

parent. *n.* kahθkwaríhtha' *I am parent* (-ahθkwarihT-).

parley. *v.i.* nehrà·weh *he parleys* (-ne-. -weh-); rahtharę́·tyęh *he parleys* (-htharętyę-).

parlor. *n.* kanęhsákwahst *parlor* (-nęh=sakwahsT-); kanęhsanú·rę· *parlor* (-nęhsanurę-).

parrot. *n.* trí'tri' *parrot* (trí'tri').

partake. *v.i.* ra'té·kahs *he partakes* (-'tek-).

partition. *n.* yu'nuwhárhę· *partition* (-a='nuwharhę-); nekanęhsyá'khęh *partition* (-ne-. -nęhsya'khę-).

partridge. *n.* uhkwé·θę *partridge* (-ah=kweθ-).

partridge vine. *n.* úhskwa'neh wáhya·ks *partridge vine* (-hsk^wa'n- -(a)hyak-).

pass through. *v.i.* ęwa'nę́·kuht *it will pass through* (-a'nękuhT-).

pass time. *v.i.* nęyú·ter *so many days will pass* (-tehr-).

passage. *n.* è·nę'T *passage* (-enę'T-); yę'nękuhnáhkhwa' *passage* (-a'nękuh=nahkw-).

passionate. *adj.* račha'rahęhθáhkę *he is passionate* (-čha'rahęhθahkw-).

past. *n.* ha' yu'nękúhnę *the past* (-a='nękuhT-).

pasturage. *n.* wa'nekhwihsáktha' *pasturage* (-a'nekhwihsakT-).

pasture. *n.* uhę́'neh *pasture* (-(a)hę'n-); ye'ęyúhtha' *pasture* (-'ęyuhT-).

pasture land. *n.* wačhurya'náhkhwa' *pasture land* (-ačhurya'nahkw-).

patch. *n.* úhneh *patch (of cloth or leather)* (-ihn-).

patch. *v.t.* rę́hnar *he patches it* (-ihnar-).

path. *n.* uháheh *path* (-(a)hah-); yęnę́hstha' *path* (-enęhsT-); wá'u· *path* (-a'u-).

patience. *n.* u'tikęhká·θne' *patience* (-(ę)'tikęhkaθne-); ha'rawerihká'θne' *his patience* (-erihkaθne-).

patient. *adj.* ra'tikę́hre·θ *he is patient* (-(ę)'tikęhreθ-); rawerihká'θne' *he is patient* (-erihkaθne-).

patrol. *v.i.* rutháha'r *he patrols* (-atha=har-).

pattern. *n.* utáhskweh *pattern* (-tahskw-); neye'tyę'nę́hstha' *pattern* (-ne-. -'tyę='nęhsT-).

paucity. *n.* ha' tikakawęhráhsthę *paucity* (ti-. -ęhrahsthu-).

pave. *v.i.* račtęhrę́θkar *he paves* (-čtęh=ręθkar-).

---

pavement. *n.* kačtęhréθkar *pavement* (-čtęhręθkar-).

paw. *n.* uči⁷éhneh *paw* (-či⁷ehn-); uhsę̇·⁷neh *paw* (-ahsęT-).

paw. *v.i.* warahskà·ręws *it paws* (-arah= skaręhw-).

pay. *n.* u⁷ę̇·yeh *pay* (-⁷ęy-).

pay. *v.i.* θhra⁷núhčęhs *he pays* (-či-. -a'nuhči-); *v.t.* ra⁷ęyúhar *he pays it* (-⁷ęyuhar-).

peace. *n.* ahskę̀·nę⁷ *peace* (-hskęnę⁷-); uhskęnę́⁷čreh *peace* (-hskęnę⁷čr-).

peace, make. *v.i.* wa⁷kayerihwahstę̀·ni⁷ *they make peace* (-rihwahstęni-).

peaceably. *adv.* uhskęnę́⁷črakęw *peaceably* (-hskęnę⁷črakęw-).

peaceful. *adj.* rahskęnę́⁷nayęhs *he is peaceful* (-hskęnę⁷nayę(T)-); rahskęnę⁷črę́·tih *he is peaceful* (-hskęnę⁷= čręti-).

peach. *n.* kwáhrak *peach* (kwáhrak).

peak. *n.* yunę́·ther *peak (mountain top)* (-nęth(e)r-); ú⁷nareh *peak (of a cap)* (-⁷nar-).

peak. *v.i.* weyutkahrawí⁷nę *it was peaking* (-yah-.-atkahrawi⁷T-).

peak at. *v.t.* wahrakahranę́hsku⁷ *he peaked at it* (-kahranęhsku-).

peanut. *n.* unahé⁷reh *peanut* (-nahe⁷r-).

pear. *n.* uhčíhrę⁷ *pear* (-hčihrę-).

peas. *n.* θáhe⁷ u⁷nekrirù·rę⁷ *peas* (θáhe⁷ -a'nekrirurę-).

peasant. *n.* ruhehna⁷kyéha·⁷ *peasant* (-hehn-.#keha·⁷).

pebble. *n.* uhrę́⁷neh *pebble* (-hrę⁷n-).

peck. *v.i.* wanęwhę́rhęh *it pecks* (-anęw= hęrhę-).

peculiar. *adj.* neyuhskané·kę·t *it is peculiar* (-ne-.-hskanekęT-).

peel. *n.* urí⁷reh *peel* (-ri⁷r-).

peel. *v.t.* rari⁷rúhčęhs *he peels it* (-ri⁷= ruhči-); rúhčęhs *he peels it* (-uhči-).

peel off. *v.i.* ęwa⁷ri⁷rúhči⁷ *it will peel off* (-a⁷ri⁷ruhči-); rutéhrę· *he had peeled off bark* (-tehr-).

peevish. *adj.* ručha⁷rá·ksę· *he is peevish* (-čha⁷raks-).

pen. *n.* neye⁷nę⁷θáhkhwa⁷ *pen* (-ne-. -'nę⁷θahkw-).

penance, do. *v.i.* ra⁷nęnhwì·yęh *he does penance* (-a'nęnhwiyę-).

pencil. *n.* neye⁷nę⁷θáhkhwa⁷ *pencil* (-ne-.-'nę⁷θahkw-).

pendant. *n.* yúhθęy *pendant* (-hθęy-).

penetrate. *v.t.* ratyè·nęh *he penetrates it* (-tyenę-).

peninsula. *n.* kahę⁷nú·či⁷ *peninsula* (-(a)= hę⁷nuči-).

penis. *n.* úhtreh *penis* (-htr-).

penknife. *n.* uhsa⁷kę⁷neháh *penknife* (-hsa⁷kę'n-.#áh).

pennyroyal. *n.* hačhíharahst *pennyroyal* (hačhíharahst).

penny. *n.* kwè·ni⁷ *penny* (kwè·ni⁷); kwè·nihs *pennies* (kwè·nihs).

pension. *n.* ratkaryá⁷ki *his pension* (-a= tkarya⁷k-).

people. *n.* nehratá·kyer *his own people* (-ne-.-tak(e)r-).

pepper, black. *n.* yunęhsnačì·wakę *black pepper* (-nęhsnačiwak-).

peppermint. *n.* yučá⁷tuhθ *peppermint* (-ča⁷tuh-).

perceive. *v.t.* rahskwá·tkę⁷θ *he perceives it* (-hskwatkę-); rahnú·kę⁷w *he perceived it* (-hnukęw-); wakyek⁷ę̀·yę⁷ *I am perceived* (-k⁷ęyę-).

perch. *n.* kahstrá⁷nihč urę⁷á⁷kye *perch (seat)* (-hstra⁷nihr-rę⁷a⁷ke); ruté·ru·⁷ *perch (fish)* (-(ę)teru-).

perfect. *adj.* tkayè·ri⁷ *it is perfect* (-t-. -yeri-).

perfect. *v.t.* raθnerhuhs⁷ę̀·we *he perfects it* (-aθnerhu-.#ęwe).

perfume. *n.* neyurhuθhwahnę́hkhwa⁷ *perfume* (-ne-.-rhuθhwahnęhkw-); kayęranù·rę⁷ *perfume* (-yęranurę-).

perhaps. *adv.* kutí⁷ *perhaps* (kutí⁷); kę́hčih *perhaps* (kę́hčih).

peril. *n.* uˀtikę́htaht *peril* (-(ę)ˀtikę̨h = tahT -).

perilous. *adj.* yuˀtikę́htaht *perilous* (-(ę)ˀtikę́htahT -).

permit. *v.t.* ękà·yę̨ˀ *it permitted it* (-ka = yę -); rariwhará·kwahs *he permits it* (-rihwharaku -).

perpendicular. *v.i.* tyuhweˀnę́ˀnę *it is perpendicular* (ti -. -hweˀnę̨ˀn -).

perpetually. *adv.* karahkę̨ˀé·θuˀ *perpetually* (karahkę̨ˀ.#eθuˀ).

perpetuity. *n.* haˀ karáhkę̨ˀ ęhraˀná·ˀ-nyeˀ *perpetuity* (haˀ karáhkę̨ˀ ęhraˀná·ˀnyeˀ).

perplexed. *adj.* nehranę̨ˀrì·yehs *he is perplexed* (-ne -. -nę̨ˀriye -).

person, young. *n.* yeθrayeháh *young person* (-θray -.#áh).

perspiration. *n.* ú·thekw *perspiration* (-thekw -).

perspire. *v.i.* rathekwní·tkę̨ˀθ *he perspires* (-thekwnitkę̨ˀ -); ú·thekw yú·-ryuhs *one perspires* (-thekw- -r(i)yu -).

pervade. *v.t.* newękúhthaˀ *it pervades it* (-ne -. -ę̨°kuhT -).

pervert. *v.t.* rahčaˀnáhkhwaˀ *he perverts it* (-ahčaˀnahkw -); rukrę̨ˀthaˀ *he perverts it* (-ukrę̨ˀT -).

perverted, be. *v.i.* rutyáˀkwaht (-tyaˀkʷ -).

pestilence. *n.* kanęhsatarí·nę̨·ˀ *pestilence* (-nęhsatarinę -).

pestle. *n.* uhráˀneh *pestle* (-hraˀn -).

pet. *n.* utáhskweh *pet* (-tahskw -); kačhè·nę̨ˀ *pet* (-čhenę -).

petitioner. *n.* rarihwahtì·nęh *petitioner* (-rihwahtinę -).

petrify. *v.i.* kačtęhrę́·tih *it petrifies* (-čtę̨hrę̨ti -).

petty. *adj.* wáhsthę̨ *it is petty* (-ahsthu -).

pewter. *n.* unawáˀčteh *pewter* (-na = waˀčt -).

phantom. *n.* uhskę̨·neh *phantom* (-hs = kęn -).

pheasant. *n.* tahuré·tik aˀwthę́ha·ˀ *pheasant* (tahuré·tik aˀwthę́ha·ˀ).

phial. *n.s.* učheˀweháh *phial* (-čheˀw -. #ah).

philosophize. *v.i.* rarihwaˀtyę̨ˀnę́hkwahs *he philosophizes* (-rihwaˀtyę̨'nęhku -).

philosophy. *n.* yękwaˀtikęhrúˀnę· *(our) philosophy* (-(ę)ˀtikęhruˀnę -).

phlegm. *n.* uhúˀkreh *phlegm* (-huˀkr -); uˀtyę́hkreh *phlegm* (-ˀtyę̨hkr -).

photograph. *v.t.* waˀkhekyerhà·rę̨ˀ *I photographed someone* (-kerhar -{dative III}).

physiology. *n.* uyéhseh *physiology* (-ye = hs -).

pick. *v.t.* rà·ręh *he picks it* (-rę -); wahraˀníhθkuˀ *he picked it (a flower)* (-aˀnihθku -); rúhskwahs *he picks them (plural objects)* (-uhsku -).

pick away. *v.t.* see: -ręti -.

pick flowers. *v.i.* waˀkčiˀčihstúhskę̨ˀ *I picked flowers* (-čiˀčihstuhsku -).

pick fruit. *v.i.* rahyáˀtyęh *he picks fruit* (-(a)hyaˀtyę -).

pick on. *v.t.* waˀetahskę́·tiˀ *one picked on* (-tahskęti -).

pick out. *v.t.* rarę́·kwahs *he picks it out* (-ręku -); see: -ręti -.

pick up. *v.t.* waˀkíhkwaˀt *I picked it up* (-(i)hkʷa̱ˀT -); nehrahkwáˀthaˀ *he* *picks it up* (-ne-.-(i)hk^wa̱ʔT-); wá·-kkwę *I have picked it up* (-ku-).

pickax. *n.* uʔtyę́hseh *pickax* (-ʔtyęhs-); yakę̱hrakáhthaʔ *pickax* (-ę°hra̱k^wahT-).

pickerel. *n.* θkakahrá·ksęʔ *pickerel* (-či-.-kahraks-).

picture of, paint a. *v.t.* natkyérhar *one paints a picture of someone* (-ker=ha̱r-).

picture of, take a. *v.t.* natkyérhar *one takes another's picture* (-kerha̱r-).

pie. *n.* katkwá·tʔę *pie* (-tkwatʔa-).

piece. *n.* úhneh *piece (of cloth or leather)* (-ihn-).

pieces. *n.* see: -ahnahn-.

piece together. *v.t.* rę́hnar *he pieces it together* (-ihna̱r-).

pier. *n.* wathęwaʔnéhthaʔ *pier* (-athę=wa̱'nehT-).

pierce. *v.t.* θčú·ʔri·θ *pierce it!* (-čuʔriθ-); newękúhthaʔ *it pierces it* (-ne-.-ę°=kuhT-).

pig. *n.* kwískwis *pig* (kwískwis).

pigeon. *n.* urí·ʔneh *pigeon* (-ri'n-).

pigweed. *n.* θkanatanę́hweʔ *pigweed* (θkanatanę́hweʔ).

pike. *n.* kù·wahk *pike (fish)* (kù·wahk); katúʔθę·t *yellow pike* (-(ę)tuʔθę́T-).

pile. *n.* utaʔčúhkweh *pile* (-(ta)ʔčuhkw-); ukyehrę́hsteh *pile* (-kehrę̱hst-); unę́ʔ-kweh *pile* (-nęʔkw-); uyę́·teh *brick pile, stone pile, wood pile* (-yęt-); čutkyéhreʔ *it is a pile* (-či-.-atkehr-).

pile. *v.t.* rakyéhrę̱hs *he piles it* (-kehr-).

pill. *n.* uʔnhę́θteh *pill* (-ʔnhę̱θt-).

pillage. *v.t.* rataʔnaká·ryahs *he pillages it* (-ta'na̱kari-).

pillow. *n.* ukę́ʔθreh *pillow* (-kę́ʔθr-).

pillow case. *n.* ukęʔθrúhčreh *pillow case* (-kęʔθruhčr-).

pilot a ship. *v.i.* raʔnyarutárhuhs *he pilots a ship* (-a'nyarutarhu-).

pimple. *n.* unę́·θkareh *pimple* (-nęθka̱r-).

pin. *n.* yunękwarúʔnę·t *pin* (-nękwaruʔ=nęt).

pincers. *n.* nekaʔtúhrara·ks *pincers* (-ne-.-ʔtuhra̱rak-).

pinch. *v.t.* nehrę̱hnúhraraks *he pinches* (-ne-.-ihnuhra̱rak-); nehrúhraraks *he pinches it* (-ne-.-uhra̱rak-); waʔtkheyaʔčihskę̱hkaráʔnir *I pinched someone* (-ne-.-aʔčihskę̱hka̱raʔnihr-).

pine. *n.* háhteh *pine* (háhteh); uhtéhneh *loblolly pine* (-htehn-).

pine. *v.i.* rahstrè·nęʔθ *he pines* (-hstre=nęʔ-).

pint. *n.* uwenę́·ʔneh *pint* (-wenęT-).

pip. *n.* unę́ha·t *pip* (-nęhaT-).

pipe. *n.* uhę̀·wareh *pipe (e.g. for sewer or water)* (-hęwa̱r-); yečarhúhthaʔ *pipe (for smoking)* (-čarhuhT-); uʔ-nę̀·weh *tobacco pipe* (-ʔnęw-).

piquant. *adj.* yúhsęt *it is piquant* (-hsęT-).

pistol. *n.* tiwaʔne·θʔáh *pistol* (ti-.-aʔ=neθ-.#áh).

pit. *n.* awę̀·yeh *pit (hole)* (-ę°y-); unę́hsneh *pit (of a fruit)* (-nęhsn-).

pitch. *n.* háhteh uθrę̱wę́·te *pitch* (háhteh -θrę̱węte).

pitch. *v.t.* ęhrú·ʔniʔ *he will pitch it (ball)* (-a'ni-).

pitcher. *n.* uʔtíhsneh yuʔá·rę·t *pitcher* (-ʔtihsn- -ʔarę̱T-).

pitchfork. *n.* uhsęwáʔreh *pitchfork* (-hsę=waʔr-); yeheruhkuriθáʔthaʔ *pitchfork* (-heruhkuriθaʔT-).

pith. *n.* uhsnahrè·weh *pith* (-hsnahrę̱w-).

pitiable. *adj.* yuʔniʔnę̀·raht *it is pitiable* (-a'ni'nę̱rahT-); yuʔnę̀·raht *it is pitiable* (-i'nę̱rahT-).

pitiful. *adj.* ruʔniʔnę̀·rę *he is pitiful* (-a='ni'nę̱r-); yunháʔnęʔt *it is pitiful* (-nhaʔnęʔT-).

pitiless. *n.* ruʔniʔnę̱rę̱hčrú·kęʔ *he is pitiless* (-a'ni'nę̱rę̱hčrukęʔ).

pity. *n.* uʔniʔnęrę́hčreh *pity* (-a'ni'nę=rę̱hčr-).

pity. *v.t.* ręꞏ'nęr *he pities it* (-i'nęr -).

place. *v.t.* yukyéhrę' *it is placed* (-ke= hr -).

plague. *n.* úrhweht *plague* (-rhweht -).

plain. *adj.* kayerę́ꞏtih *it is plain* (-yeręti -).

plain. *n.* kahkwá'kye *plain* (-hkw -.#ke).

plains. *n.* yu'tehakwęhnárhę *plains* (-'te= hakwęhnarhu -).

plan. *n.* utáhskweh *plan* (-tahskw -); u-yéhseh *plan* (-yehs -).

plane. *n.* yehsęwatíhtha' *plane (smoothing instrument)* (-hsęwatihT -).

plane. *v.t.* rahsęwáꞏtih *he planes it* (-hsę= wati -).

planet. *n.* u'nihsę̀ꞏreh *planet* (-'nihsęr -).

plank. *n.* uhwę́'khareh *plank* (-hwę'= khar -).

plant. *n.* uhtwę́heh *plant* (-htwęh -); u-tráhneh *plant* (-trahn -).

plant. *v.t.* rayę́ꞏthuhs *he is planting it* (-yęthu -); ranęháhrę *he plants corn* (-nęhah(e)r -); ranę́har *he plants corn* (-nęhar -).

plantain. *n.* uhaha'kyéhaꞏ' *plantain* (-(a)= hah -.#kehaꞏ'); unęhyáꞏθeh *plantain* (-nęhyaθ -).

plaster. *n.* u'nàꞏręweh *plaster* (-'naręw -).

plaster. *v.t.* ra'narę̀ꞏwawęhs *he plasters it* (-'naręwawę -).

plate. *n.* utráhθneh *plate* (-trahθn -); úk-θeh *plate* (-kč -).

play. *n.* awę'nhékwčreh *play* (-ę'n= hek"čr -).

play. *v.i.* ra'nwę'èꞏręh *he plays a musical instrument* (-a'nwę'ęrę -); ra'nék-skruh *he is playing a trick on it* (-a'nekskru -); wakę'nhéꞏkwę *I am playing a game* (-ę'nhek" -); nehrá-thnęꞏ *he plays ball* (-ne -.-athnę -); ra-čikęwakàꞏratih *he is playing the fiddle* (-čikęwakarati -).

play, child's. *n.* ekáꞏθ'ah yę'nhékwtha' *child's play* (-kaθ'ah -ę°'nhek"T -).

playful. *adj.* rawę'nhékwskę *he is playful* (-ę'nhek"sk -).

playing cards. *n.* neyehyatęhstayę'náh-khwa' *playing cards* (-ne -.-hyatęhsta= yę'nahkw -).

plaything. *n.* yę'nhékwstha' *plaything* (-ę'nhek"sT -).

playthings. *n.* yę'nhekwsnahnę́hkhwa' *playthings* (-ę'nhek"snahnęhkw -).

plentiful. *adj.* see: -tak(e)r -.

please. *interj.* nyàꞏwę *please* (nyàꞏwę).

please. *v.t.* ękheyačhętyá'thahθ *I will please them* (-ačhętya'T -{dative II}); ru'tikęhriyú'θeh *it pleases him* (-(ę)'= tikęhriyu -{dative III}).

pleasant, make. *v.t.* rę'na'néhstha' *he makes it pleasant* (-ę'na'nehsT -).

pleased. *adj.* wa'thračhę́ꞏnya't *he was pleased* (-ačhęnya'T -).

pledge. *v.i.* ratkarayę'náhkhwa' *he pledges* (-atkarayę'nahkw -).

plentiful. *v.i.* yu'nyé'ti *it is plentiful* (-a= 'nye't -).

plenty, have. *v.i.* wakrkę́hę *I have plenty* (-rkęhw -).

plot. *n.* u'rhúhkwareh *plot of land* (-'rhuhkwar -); uyę̀ꞏweh *treeless plot of ground in the woods* (-yęw -).

plot. *v.i.* rurihwayú'ne' *he plots* (-rih= wayu'n(ę) -); kaku'rihwíhs'ę *they plotted* (-a'rihwihs'a -).

Tuscarora Pronunciation Key:

/a/ law; /e/ hat; /i/ pizza; /u/ tune; /ę/ hint; /č/ cheese; /h/ hoe; /m/ mother; /s/ same; /t/ do (before a vowel y, or w), too (elsewhere); /k/ gale (before a vowel y or w), kale (elsewhere); /n/ inhale (before a consonant or word-final), note (elsewhere), /r/ hiss (before a consonant or word-final), run (trilled as in Italian, elsewhere); /w/ cuff (before a consonant other than y or word-final), way (elsewhere); /y/ fish (before a consonant or word-final), you (elsewhere), /θ/ thing; /'/ (the sound between the vowels in unh-unh); /ꞏ/ long vowel, /´/ high pitch; /`/ low pitch.

plover. *n.* tawistawis'ú'y *plover* (tawis-tawis'ú'y).

plow. *v.i.* nehrᶒhrù·rᶒhs *he plows* (-ne-. -ᶒhrurᶒ-).

plow point. *n.* u'tyᶒ́hseh *plow point* (-'tyᶒhs-).

pluck. *v.t.* rará'karᶒhs *he plucks it (feathers)* (-ra'kar-).

plumb. *adj.* tyu'nahkwrᶒ́'či *it is plumb* (ti-. -a'nahkwrᶒ-.#hči).

plunge. *v.i.* ra'nᶒhrúhahs *he plunges* (-a='nᶒhruha-).

pocket. *n.* uté'kweh *pocket* (-te'kw-); rate'khwárhuhs *he pockets it* (-te'=khwarhu-).

pod. *n.* unᶒhkwíhsteh *pod* (-nᶒhkwihst-); utyà·neh *pod* (-tyan-).

poet. *v.i.* rᶒ́khwih *poet* (-ᶒkhwi-).

point. *n.* utá·kareh *point* (-(ᶒ)takar-); uhsú'θreh *point* (-hsu'θr-); utú·kareh *point* (-tukar-).

point out. *v.i.* ᶒyᶒhčá·thahθ *one will point out* (-ahčaT-{dative II}).

pointed. *adj.* yutá·karᶒ·t *pointed* (-(ᶒ)ta=karᶒt).

pointless. *n.* uhsu'θrú·kᶒ' *pointless* (-hsu'θrukᶒ').

poison. *n.* utíhseh *poison* (-tihs-); yu'-nyatá'nᶒ *it is poison* (-a'nyata'T-).

poison. *v.t.* ratihsanhᶒ́·thuhs *he poisons it* (-tihsanhᶒthu-).

poke along. *v.i.* rᶒnᶒča'nᶒ́'teh *he pokes along* (-ᶒnᶒča'nᶒ'N(e)-).

poke fun at. *v.t.* rakᶒhrᶒ́·tih *he pokes fun at it* (-kᶒhrᶒti-).

pole. *n.* utáhsneh *pole* (-(ᶒ)tahsn-); ú·treh *pole* (-atr-); učᶒ̀·weh *burial pole* (-čᶒw-).

policeman. *n.* ra'nyè·nᶒhs *policeman* (-a'nyenᶒ-); rayanrᶒhstakᶒ́hahs *policeman* (-yanrᶒhstakᶒha-).

polish. *v.t.* račanᶒ́htha' *he polishes it* (-čanᶒhT-); račanᶒ́·tih *he polishes it* (-čanᶒti-).

politeness. *n.* yutkwᶒ́·nyᶒhst *politeness* (-atkwᶒnyᶒhsT-).

pollute. *v.t.* ranᶒ'rarawᶒ̀·rih *he pollutes it* (-nᶒ'rarawᶒri-).

pollution. *n.* unᶒ'raratyá'kwaht *pollution* (-nᶒ'raratya'kʷahT-).

pond. *n.* utyᶒ̀·wareh *pond* (-tyᶒwar-).

pony-tail. *n.* uhsnéhweh *pony-tail* (-hs=nehw-).

poor. *adj.* rú·tᶒht *he is poor* (-(i)tᶒhT-).

poor, get. *v.i.* rutᶒhtá'ᶒ *he got poor* (-(i)tᶒhta'-).

poor house. *n.* yakú·tᶒht wásθhar *poor house* (-(i)tᶒhT- -asθhar-).

poplar. *n.* wat'ᶒhrᶒ́'ytha' *poplar* (-at='ᶒhrᶒy'T-).

populace. *n.* kayetá·krᶒ' *populace* (-ta=k(e)r-).

porcelain. *n.* kakθanú·rᶒ· yakyetyá'tha' *porcelain* (-kθanurᶒ- -ᶒtya'T-).

porch. *n.* utakᶒ́hsteh *enclosed porch* (-ta=kᶒhst-).

porcupine. *n.* u'nhé·ta' *porcupine* (u'n=hé·ta').

pork. *n.* u'θnà·reh *pork* (-'θnar-).

porridge. *n.* newᶒhú·ryeh *porridge* (-ne-. -ᶒhuri-).

port. *n.* wathᶒwa'néhtha' *port* (-athᶒ=wa'nehT-).

portal. *n.* utakᶒ́hsteh *portal* (-takᶒhst-); yučaraktíhar *portal* (-čaraktihar-).

portrait. *n.* yukyérhar *portrait* (-kerhar-).

portulaca. *n.* unᶒθkwarù·rih *portulaca* (-nᶒθkwaruri-).

position. *n.* utákwneh *position* (-takwT-).

possess. *v.t.* ru'nà·wᶒh *he possesses it* (-a'nawᶒ-); see: -ᶒ'T-.

possible. *adj.* yukwé·nyᶒ *it is possible* (-kweni-).

poster. *n.* yuhyatᶒhstanᶒ'ná·kᶒ *poster* (-hyatᶒhstanᶒ'nak-).

posterity. *n.* kar'ᶒhsa'ná·'nye' *posterity* (-(i)r'ᶒhsa'na'nyc'-).

posture. *n.* tihrutakwnayè·rᶒ *his posture*

posture. *n.* tihrutakwnayè·rę *his posture* (ti-.-takwnayer-).

pot. *n.* u⁷nę̀·weh *pot* (-⁷nęw-); neyuhča⁷nírhę· *pot* (-ne-.-ahča⁷nihrhę-); u⁷ti⁷nę́hkweh *pot* (-⁷ti⁷nęhkw-).

potato. *n.* unę́·θeh *potato* (-nęč-); nę́·tu·⁷ *wild potato* (nę́·tu·⁷).

potent. *adj.* ka⁷θá·θne⁷ *it is potent* (-(i)⁷θhaθn-).

pothanger. *n.* ye⁷nęwharáhkhwa⁷ *pothanger* (-⁷nęwharahkw-).

potion. *n.* tká⁷wayę⁷ *there is a potion* (-⁷w-); úrhuht *love potion* (-rhuht-).

potter. *n.* rakθę́·tih *potter* (-kθęti-).

poultice. *n.* yę⁷nihtrę́hstha⁷ *poultice* (-a⁷nihtręhsT-).

pound. *n.* ukwę́⁷čreh *pound* (-akwę⁷čr-).

pound. *v.t.* wa⁷ká·the⁷ *I pounded it* (-a=the⁷-); kyéshwę *I pound corn to flour* (-eshu-).

pour. *v.t.* ęyeθérhu⁷ *one will pour it* (-θerhu-); yahwahračì·yę⁷ *he poured it* (-yah-.-čiyę-).

pout. *v.i.* ruyatá⁷ne⁷ *he pouts* (-yata⁷T-).

poverty. *n.* utęhtá⁷ę *poverty* (-(i)tęhta⁷-).

powder. *n.* uthé⁷čre *powder* (-athe⁷čr-).

powdery. *adj.* yuthé⁷čra⁷r *powdery* (-a=the⁷črar-).

power. *n.* ú⁷θheh *power* (-(i)⁷θh-); u⁷θhá·θneh *power* (-(i)⁷θhaθn-); u⁷θhaθnę́hčreh *power* (-(i)⁷θhaθnęh=čr-); útkę⁷ *inherent power* (-atkę-).

powerful. *adj.* rahwíhsne⁷ *he is powerful* (-(a)hwihsT-); ka⁷θhá·θne⁷ *it is powerful* (-(i)⁷θhaθn-).

pox. *n.* uhsé⁷weh *pox* (-hse⁷w-); účkreh *pox* (-čkr(ę⁷n)-).

praise. *n.* utawę́⁷nęht *praise* (-tawę⁷=nęhT-).

praise. *v.t.* ratawę́⁷nęh *he praises it* (-ta=wę⁷nę-).

praiseworthy. *adj.* yutawę́⁷nęht *praiseworthy* (-tawę⁷nęhT-).

pray. *v.i.* wahratrę̀·nayę⁷ *he prayed* (-a=tręnayę-).

prayer. *n.* utręnayętá⁷čreh *prayer* (-atrę=nayęta⁷čr-).

preach. *v.i.* rarihuwaná⁷tha⁷ *he preaches* (-rihuwana⁷T-).

precipice. *n.* yuthriyá⁷kę *precipice* (-a=thriya⁷k-).

precisely. *adv.* ka⁷nę́ hà·ne⁷ *precisely* (ka⁷nę́ hà·ne⁷); ka⁷nę́ kyè·nę· *precisely* (ka⁷nę́ kyè·nę·).

precocious. *adj.* karihθkáhnęh *it is precocious* (-rihθkahnę-).

prefer. *v.t.* rará·kwahs *he prefers it* (-raku-).

pregnant. *adj.* katè·rih *she is pregnant* (-(ę)teri-); yetè·ręh *she is pregnant* (-(ę)terę-).

prejudice. *adj.* thru⁷tikęhríhs⁷ę *he is prejudice* (-t-.-(ę)⁷tikęhrihs⁷a-).

premonition. *n.* wa⁷nwá⁷kwih *it is a premonition* (-a'nwa⁷kw-).

preoccupied. *adj.* thruča⁷uryá⁷tha⁷ *he is preoccupied* (-t-.-ča⁷urya⁷T-).

preparation. *n.* ú·wyeh *preparation* (-wy(ęn)-).

prepare. *v.t.* ękayęčhákwahst *they will prepare it* (-ačhakwahsT-); retyahčíwha⁷ *he prepares it* (-etyahčihw-).

prerogative. *n.* u⁷θhaθnę́hsteh *prerogative* (-(i)⁷θhaθnęhst-).

present. *v.t.* ráws *he presents* (-aw-).

preserve. *v.t.* yeθręwętyáhnęh *one preserves it* (-θręwętyahnę-); ęhsθrahkwá·ʔnęʔ *you will preserve it* (-θrah= kwa'nę-); ratù·ręh *he preserves it* (-tu= rę-)

preside. *v.i.* uhęʔnę rá·ʔnęh *he presides* (-(a)hęʔT- -a'nę-).

president. *n.* haʔ ranętaká·ryahs *president* (-nętakaryahs).

press. *n.* wekí·tkęws *press (e.g., for wine, cider)* (-ekitkęhw-).

press. *v.t.* nehraʔtúhrara·ks *he presses (a thing together)* (-ne-.-ʔtuhrarak-).

press close to. *v.t.* see: -taʔkwar-.

press down on. *v.t.* ęhsturì·yęʔ *you will press down on it* (-turiyę-).

presumptuous. *adj.* raʔnaʔnè·rih *he is presumptuous* (-a'na'ner-).

pretence. *n.* sáʔrkęʔ *pretence* (sáʔrkęʔ).

pretend to be sick. *v.i.* ruʔnęnęhwá·knę *he pretended to be sick* (-a'nęnęh= wakT-).

pretext. *n.* rarihwáwsthaʔ *his pretext* (-rihwawsT-).

pretty. *adj.* kakwà·nihst *it is pretty* (-kwanihst-).

prevail over. *v.t.* raʔniʔθhę́·nyęhs *he prevails over it* (-a'niʔθhęni-).

prevent. *v.t.* raháhyaʔks *he prevents it* (-(a)hahyaʔk-).

previously. *adj.* tyuréʔkye *previously* (ti-. -reʔke-).

prey. *n.* ká·ryu·ʔ *prey* (-r(i)yu-).

price. *n.* ú·kareh *price* (-kar-); uʔę̀·yeh *price* (-ʔęy-); nyuʔęyé·θę *high prices* (-t-.-ʔęyeθ-).

prick. *v.t.* račuʔríθahs *he pricks it* (-čuʔ= riθ-).

prickly ash. *n.* aʔnahę̀·we *prickly ash* (aʔnahę̀·we).

prickly pear. *n.* unę̀ʔà·reh *prickly pear* (-nęʔar-).

pride. *n.* unayéʔčreh *pride* (-nayeʔčr-);

unayéʔę *pride* (-nayeʔ-).

priest. *n.* račihę́hstačih *priest* (-čihęh= stači-).

prince. *n.* kurahkuháh *prince* (kurahkuháh).

princess. *n.* kurahkuháh *princess* (kurahkuháh).

principal. *n.* kayaʔtakweʔnì·yuʔ *principal* (-yaʔtakweʔniyu-); see: -kweʔniyu-.

principle. *n.* nyurihwaʔníhθnę *principle* (-t-.-rihwaʔnihθt-).

print. *v.t.* rayerętíhthaʔ *he prints it (as opposed to writing in cursive)* (-ye= rętihT-); nehrarihstúhraraks *he prints it (on a printing press)* (-ne-.-rih= stuhrarak-).

printing. *n.* neyuʔrihstuhrará·kę *printing* (-ne-.-aʔrihstuhrarak-).

printing press. *n.* nekarihstúhraraks *printing press* (-ne-.-rihstuhrarak-).

priority. *n.* yuthęʔnéʔnę *priority* (-athęʔ= neʔT-).

prison. *n.* uʔę̀·yeh *prison* (-ʔęy-); yęʔ= nečarhúhsthaʔ *prison* (-a'nečarhuhsT-).

prisoner. *n.* utáhskweh *prisoner* (-tah= skw-); naʔtahskę́·tih *prisoner* (-tah= skęti-).

privy. *n.* unęhseháh yęhtkiʔę́hkhwaʔ *privy* (-nęhs-.#áh -ahtkiʔęhkw-).

proceed. *v.i.* see: -iN-.

procession. *n.* urì·reh kakunęhrahstę= ní·ʔnyeʔ *procession* (-rir- -nęhrahstę= ni'nyeʔ-).

proclamation. *n.* neyuʔrihukwáʔthaʔ *proclamation* (-ne-.-aʔrihukwaʔT-).

procreate. *v.i.* raʔnwirę́·tih *he procreates* (-a'nwiręti-).

procure. *v.t.* ratyè·nęh *he procures it* (-tyenę-).

prodigy. *n.* nehruʔnyerę́hnyęʔ *he is a prodigy* (-ne-.-a'nyeręhnyę-).

produce. *v.t.* wetì·yahs *it produces it* (-e= ti(y)-).

profane. *v.i.* rarihwaksáʔthaʔ *he profanes*

(-rihwaksa'?T -).

profit. *n.* ha'? uwì·reh *profit* (-wir -).

profitable. *adj.* yuthwihstę́·tyaht *profit-able* (-athwihstętyahT -).

profligate. *adj.* ra'?nyeθá'?tha'? *he is profligate* (-a'nyeθa'?T -).

progress, make. *v.i.* rurekwęhá·'?nye'? *he makes progress* (-ar(e)kwęha'nye'? -).

progressively. *adv.* yurekwęhá·'?nye'? *progressively* (-ar(e)kwęha'nye'? -).

prohibit. *v.t.* ranę́snač *he prohibits it* (-nęsnaT -).

project. *v.i.* nwá·'?ne'? *it projects* (-t-. -(a)'ne -).

projectile. *n.* á'?teh *projectile* (-a'?t -).

prolific. *adj.* yewirę́·tih *one is prolific* (-wiręti -).

prolong. *v.t.* ré·θtha'? *he prolongs it* (-eθT -).

promiscuity. *n.* yu'?nihθkawę́hsnę *promiscuity* (-a'nihθkawęhsT -).

promise. *n.* ha'? rurihwíhs'?ę *his promise* (-rihwihs'?a -).

promise. *v.i.* kaku'?rihwíhs'?ę *they promised* (-a'?rihwihs'?a -); rarhà·rahč *he promises* (-rharahT -).

promote. *v.t.* nehrarihwáhčar *he promotes it* (-ne-. -rihwahčar -).

prompt. *adj.* rahę'?θáhkęh *he is prompt* (-hę'?θahkę -).

promptly. *adv.* thu'?ù·nę *promptly* (thu'?-ù·nę).

pronounce. *v.t.* kayá·θhęh *he pronounces it* (-yaθhę -).

prop. *n.* ha'? neyutekà·rę *a prop* (-ne-. -tekar -).

propagate. *v.i.* wa'?ka'?ner'?ęhsę́·ti'? *I propagate* (-a'ner'?ęhsęti -).

proper. *adj.* he'?thúhči *proper* (hc'?thúhči).

property. *n.* unękwì·reh *property* (-(ę)nę=kwir -); ha'? rù·yę'? *his property* (-yę(T) -).

prophecy. *n.* ha'? ru'?rę'?ná·'?nę *his prophecy* (-a'?rę'?naT -).

prophesy. *v.i.* ra'?rę́'?na·č *he prophesies* (-a'?rę'?naT -).

prophet. *n.* ra'?rę́'?na·č *prophet* (-a'?=rę'?naT -); retà·yę'? *prophet* (-etayę -).

propose. *v.i.* raríhwa'?na·č *he proposed* (-rihwa'naT -); ra'?nwętáhę'?č *he proposes* (-a'nwętahę'?T -).

proprietor. *n.* ranęhsakwe'?nì·yu'? *proprietor* (-nęhsakwe'?niyu -).

prosper. *v.i.* ratkwa'?ná·kwahs *he prospers* (-atkwa'?naku -); wakatra'?θwí·yu· *I prosper* (-atra'?θwiyu -).

prosperity. *n.* unękwì·reh *prosperity* (-(ę)nękwir -).

prostitute. *n.* wa'?nyáhkwayę'? *prostitute* (-a'nyahkwayę(T) -).

protect. *v.i.* aryętkyérhanę·t *that one protect oneself* (-atkerhanę -).

protest. *v.i.* raríhwayę'?kws *he protests* (-rihwayę'?k^w -).

protrude. *v.i.* wá·'?ne'? *it protrudes* (-(a)='ne -); nwá·'?ne'? *it protrudes* (-t-. -(a)='ne -).

proud. *adj.* ranà·ye'? *he is proud* (-na=ye'? -).

prove. *v.t.* ę'?nehú·'?nę'? *it proved it* (-a='nehuT -).

provide. *v.t.* rús̱θhar *he provides for it* (-as̱θhar -).

provided that. *conj.* kanyú'? *provided that*

Tuscarora Pronunciation Key:

/a/ l̲aw; /e/ h̲at; /i/ pi̲zza; /u/ t̲une; /ę/ h̲int; /č/ cheese; /h/ h̲oe; /m/ m̲other; /s/ s̲ame; /t/ d̲o (before a vowel y, or w), t̲oo (elsewhere); /k/ gale (before a vowel y or w), k̲ale (elsewhere); /n/ inh̲ale (before a consonant or word-final), n̲ote (elsewhere), /r/ hi̲s̲s̲ (before a consonant or word-final), r̲un (trilled as in Italian, elsewhere); /w/ cu̲f̲f̲ (before a consonant other than y or word-final), w̲ay (elsewhere); /y/ fi̲s̲h (before a consonant or word-final), y̲ou (elsewhere), /θ/ t̲h̲ing; /'?/ (the sound between the vowels in unh-unh); /·/ long vowel, /'/ high pitch; /ˋ/ low pitch.

(kanyúʔ).

provident. *adj.* ręnękwirawyę́hę *he is provident* (-(ę)nękwirawyęhw-).

provisions. *n.* utíʔreh *provisions* (-tiʔr-); uʔnętáhčreh *provisions* (-a'nętahčr-).

provoke. *v.t.* račirù·ręh *he provokes it* (-čirurę-).

prowl about. *v.i.* raθhukwyę́hteʔθ *he prowls about* (-θhukwyęhteʔ-).

prudent. *adj.* raʔnęʔtikę́hrar *he is prudent* (-a'nęʔtikęhrar-).

prune. *v.t.* raré̜·kwahs *he prunes it* (- rę̜=ku-).

psalms. *n.* neyerihwahkwáʔthaʔ *psalms* (-ne-.-rihwahkwaʔT-).

public. *n.* haʔ yetá·kreʔ *the public* (-ta=k(e)r-).

publicly. *adv.* héʔtkęh *publicly* (héʔtkęh); uʔtéyhę *publicly* (-(ę)ʔteyhę).

publisher. *v.t.* nehrarihstúhraraks *publisher* (-ne-.-rihstuhrarak-).

pucker. *v.i.* rakwéhčręh *he puckers* (-kwehčrę-); ratéθkwihs *he puckers it* (-teθkwi(k)-).

pudding. *n.* katkwá·tʔę *pudding* (-tkwat=ʔa-).

puddle. *n.* utyę̜·wareh *puddle* (-tyę̜war-).

pull. *v.t.* waʔkaʔnihę́·thuʔ *I pulled it* (-a='nihęthu-); ęhsatkyerhaʔnéʔkuʔ *you will pull back* (-atkerhaʔneʔku-); ruhríhthaʔ *he pulls it down* (-hrihT-); rarurę́·kwahs *he pulls it in pieces* (-ru=ręku-); rúhθręhs *he pulls it off* (-uh=θ(e)r-).

pulpit. *n.* uʔnáhkweh *pulpit* (-ʔnahkw-); haʔ kęʔ yerihuwanaʔnáhkhwaʔ *pulpit* (kęʔ -rihuwanaʔnahkw-).

pulsate. *v.i.* newę́·tkhwaʔ *it pulsates* (-ne-.-ętkʷ-).

pulse. *v.i.* newę́·tkhwaʔ *it pulses* (-ne-.-ętkʷ-).

pumpkin. *n.* katéčraʔθ *pumpkin* (katéčraʔθ); učhéʔweh *pumpkin* (-čheʔw-).

punch. *v.t.* waʔnatkę́hruk *one punched*

another (-kęhruk-).

punish. *v.t.* nathrewáʔthaʔ *one punishes another* (-hrewaʔT-).

punishment. *n.* kahrewaʔnę́hčraʔ *punishment* (-hrewaʔnęhčr-).

pup. *v.i.* newaʔnwì·ryaʔks *it pups* (-ne-.-a'nwiryaʔk-).

pupil. *n.* haʔ raʔrihętyá·tih *pupil (student)* (-aʔrihęti-{dative III}); yučisnúhkuʔ ukáhrakęw *pupil (of the eye)* (-čisnuhku- -kahrakęw).

puppet. *n.* kakyerhę́·tih *puppet* (-ker=hęti-).

pure. *adj.* yúʔθręn *it is pure* (-aʔθręn-); awúhkęʔ *pure* (-uhk-); awúhskę *pure* (-uhsk-).

purge. *v.t.* neyawękúhnę *it purges it* (-ne-.-ę̊kuhT-).

purify. *v.t.* rá·θręhs *he purifies it* (-θ(e)r-).

purloin. *v.t.* rahnę́ʔthaʔ *he purloins it* (-ahnęʔT-).

purple. *adj.* čutakę́hkuʔ *purple* (-či-.-takęhku-); θwaʔnahθúhkwahst *purple* (-či-.-a'nahθuhkwahsT-); wahθuhkwákwahst *purple* (-ahθuhkwakwahsT-); katihęryahę́sči *purple* (-tihęryahęsči-).

purpose. *n.* uríhwawęh *purpose* (-rih=wawę-).

purse. *n.* yehwihstaráhkhwaʔ *purse* (-hwihstarahkw-); utéʔkweh *purse* (-teʔkw-).

pursue. *v.t.* ratkáhneʔ *he pursues it* (-t(i)kahT-)

pus. *n.* utkę́hθreh *pus* (-atkęhθr-).

pussytoes. *n.* uʔné·wa·k waʔnù·rih ‹ghost it-itself-stirs› *pussytoes* (-ʔnewak- -a='nuri-)

push. *v.i.* waʔnyę́hčaręʔ *they two pushed* (-ahčarę-).

put. *v.t.* rà·ręh *he puts it among others* (-rę-); kahrà·węh *it puts it around* (-(a)hrawę-); wahrakyéhręʔ *he put it around* (-kehr-); rutú·rę· *he put it*

away (-turę-); rà·yęhs *he puts it down*
(-yę(T)-); nęyé·t²a·² *the two of them
will put it in* (-(a)t²a-); ęyakúha² *one
will put it in water* (-uha-); na²nen-
hę́·thuhs *one puts it in another's
mouth* (-nhęthu-); rárhuhs *he puts it
on* (-rhu-); rúhe· *he put it on* (-(i)he-);
ráher *he puts it on top* (-(a)h(e)r-);
ra²θwáhtha² *he puts it (fire) out* (-a²=
θwahT-); ęθwáhrę² *you will put it up*
(-hrę-).

putty. *n.* u²nà·ręweh *putty* (-²naręw-).
putty. *v.t.* račihskwà·węhs *he putties it*
(-čihskwaw-).
puzzled, become. *v.i.* thwahru²ríhwa-
kwekθ *he becomes puzzled* (ti-.-a²=
rihwak^wek-{dative I}); thwahrahθę²-
nę́·²nyę² *he becomes puzzled* (ti-.
-ahθę'nę'ni-{dative III}).

Q

quail. *n.* kúhkwih *quail* (kúhkwih).
quake. *v.i.* neyukwaríhę²θ *it quakes*
(-ne-.-kwarihę²-).
quaking aspen. *n.* wat²ęhrę́²ytha² *quaking aspen* (-at²ęhręy²T-).
quarrel. *n.* ha² ru²rihwaksę́²ę *his quarrel*
(-a²rihwaksę²-).
quarrel. *v.i.* ra²rihwaksę́²tha² *he quarrels*
(-a²rihwaksę²T-).
quarrelsome. *adj.* ru²rihwaksę²ná²ne² *he
is quarrelsome* (-a²rihwaksę²na²T-).
quart. *n.* uwenę́·²neh *quart* (-wenę́T-).
quarter. *n.* ę́·či ha² hę́²tahk tha²neka-

yá²khęh *a quarter* (ę́·či ha² hę́²tahk
tha+ne-.-ya²k-).
quay. *n.* wathęwa²néhtha² *quay* (-athę=
wa'nehT-).
queen. *n.* etírher *queen* (-tirher-).
queer. *adj.* uyá²či *it is queer* (uyá²či);
neyuhskané·kę·t *it is queer* (-ne-.
-hskanekęT-).
quench thirst. *v.i.* ra²nęta²nuráhstha² *he
quenches his thirst* (-a'nęta²nurahst-).
quick. *adj.* kwaríha²t *quick* (kwaríha²t);
rahę²θáhkęh *he is quick* (-hę²θahkę-).
quickly. *adv.* thwa²kahwé²nęht *quickly*
(ti-.-hwe²nęht-).
quill. *n.* uhrá²kweh *quill* (-hra²kw-).
quilt. *n.* uhθa²kę́hsteh *quilt* (-hθa²=
kęhst-); urí²weh *quilt* (-ri²w-).
quit. *v.i.* ahruhsná²ku² *that he quit*
(-hsna²ku-); rahčę²wáhtha² *he quits*
(-ahčę²wahT-).
quiver. *v.i.* ruθrárha² *he quivers* (-θrar-);
see: -kya²w-.

R

rabbit. *n.* kwè·ru² *rabbit* (kwè·ru²).
rabble. *n.* θatiwéhek *rabble* (θatiwéhek).
raccoon. *n.* ruhsá·tu·² *raccoon* (ruhsá·-
tu·²).
race. *n.* ur²ę́hseh *race* (-(i)r²ęhs-).
rack. *n.* u²teyę́hkweh *rack* (-(ę)²te=
yęhkw-).
radiance. *n.* uhúkčreh *radiance* (-hukčr-).
radiant. *adj.* kahsnuká²tha² *it is radiant*
(-hsnuka²T-).

---

radiate. *v.i.* newaré·tyęhs *it radiates* (-ne-.-areti-).

raft. *n.* úhskaweh *raft* (-hska̲w-); ú·tkaweh *raft* (-tka̲w-).

rags. *n.* ukrí'?reh *rags* (-kri'?r-); ehnú·kęw *rags* (ehnú·kęw).

ragweed. *n.* uti'?néhθreh *ragweed* (-ti'?= nehθr-).

rail. *n.* uháhsteh *rail* (-hahst-).

railroad. *n.* rahahahkwí'?tha'? *railroad* (-(a)haha̲hkwi'?T-).

rain. *n.* wę́·tu·č *rain* (-ętuT-).

rain shower. *n.* úhtaweh *rain shower* (-htaw-).

rainbow. *n.* yuwè·nę'? *rainbow* (-wenę-); yurę́hyahuks *rainbow* (-rę̲hya̲huk-).

rainwater. *n.* awętú·'?nę *rainwater* (-ę= tuT-).

rainy. *n.* yawętúčkę *rainy* (-ętučk-).

raise. *v.i.* wa'?né·k'?uhs *it is raising* (-a= 'nek'?u-); nehráhkhwa'? *he raises it* (-ne-.-hkw-); rakę́hahs *he raises it* (-kęha-); wa'?kkyé·θku'? *I raised it* (-keθku-).

raise the dead. *v.t.* θhrę́nhahkt *he raises the dead* (-či-.-ę̊nhahkT-); čę'?natkę́hahs wę̨hè·yę *one raises the dead* (-či-.-atkęha- -(i)hey-).

raise the price. *v.i.* ra'?ęyéθtha'? *he raises the price* (-'?ęyeθT-).

raise voice. *v.i.* ra'?nwętakyé·θkwahs *he raises his voice* (-a'nwęta̲keθku-).

raisin. *n.* réhse·n *raisin* (réhse·n).

rake. *n.* uhsú'?kweh *rake* (-hsu'?ku-).

rake. *v.t.* raherarúhčręh *he rakes it* (-he= ra̲ruhčrę-).

rally. *v.t.* rarúhčręh *he rallies it* (-ruh= črę-).

ramble about. *v.i.* ra'?nawę̀·rih *he rambles about* (-a'nawęri-).

ramrod. *n.* u'?nú'?yeh *ramrod* (-a'?nu'?= y(e)-).

rancid. *v.i.* yučì·wakę *it is rancid* (-či= wa̲k-).

rancor. *n.* úhsęht *rancor* (-ahsę̨hT-).

rap. *v.t.* rá·kę'?č *he raps it* (-kę'?T-).

rapids. *n.* yuhtawakarerú'?nę *rapids* (-hta̲= wakareru'?T-).

rare. *adj.* thu'?níhskah *rare* (thu'?níhskah); tiwahereθtha'?áh *it is rare* (ti-.-ahe= reθT-.#áh); ì·nę yú'?rę'? *rare* (ì·nę -(i)'?rę-).

rarely. *adv.* ihskáhkye *rarely* (ihskáhkye).

rash. *adj.* ru'?tikęhrú·kę'? *he is rash* (-(ę)'?tikę̨hrukę'?).

raspberry. *n.* takwaká·yę· *raspberry* (takwaká·yę·); watkahna'?náhkwahs *raspberry* (-atkahna'?nahkw-); tka'?ne'?náhkwahs *black raspberry* (tka'?ne'?náhkwahs); tahkwà·yę'? *red raspberry* (tahkwà·yę'?); tahkwayę'?ú'?y *red-flowering raspberry* (tahkwayę'?.#ú'?y).

rat. *n.* ruyę́'?tu'? *rat* (-yę'?tu-); ruhskwé·'?nę'? *rat* (ruhskwé·'?nę'?).

rattle. *n.* yę'?rakareráhstha'? *rattle* (-a'?ra= karerahsT-); ustawę́'?čreh *rattle* (-sta= wę'?čr-); uθę̀·reh *rattle of a snake* (-θęr-).

rattlesnake. *n.* ruθę́·rę·t *rattlesnake* (-θę= ręt).

ravage. *v.t.* rata'?naká·ryahs *he ravages it* (-ta'na̲kari-).

rave. *v.i.* ručha'?rú·ri· *he raves* (-čha'?= ruri-).

raven. *n.* ká·hka·h *raven* (ká·hka·h); kwę́hkwęh *raven* (kwę́hkwęh).

ravish. *v.i.* rathwihstaráhkhwa'? *he ravishes* (-athwihsta̲rahkw-).

raw. *adj.* á·θe·'? *raw* (á·θe·'?).

rawhide strip. *n.* u'?nhę́hθeh *rawhide strip* (-(i)'?nhę̨hθ-).

ray. *n.* uręryúhkweh *ray* (-ręryuhkw-).

raze. *v.t.* ruhríhtha'? *he razes it* (-hrihT-).

razor. *n.* yęčhukarę̨hnáhkhwa'? *razor* (-a= čhukarę̨hnahkw-); uhsá'?kę'?neh *razor* (-hsa'?kę'n-).

reach. *v.t.* ra'?téwna'?t *he reaches it* (-a'?= tewna'?-).

read. *v.i.* ra'rihętyá·tih *he reads* (-a' =
rihęti -{dative III}).

readjust. *v.t.* θhrę́'ręhs *he readjusts it*
(-či-. -i'rę-).

ready. *adj.* ru'netyahčíhę· *he is ready*
(-a'netyahčihę-).

ready, make. *v.t.* ękayęčhákwahst *they
will make it ready* (-ačhakwahsT-)

realize. *v.t.* rahskwá·tkę'θ *he realizes it*
(-hskwatkę-).

really. *adv.* utukę'ę́hči *really* (-tukę'-.
#hči); ha' kę́hčih *really* (ha' kę́hčih).

realm. *n.* uhwenętíhsteh *realm* (-hwenę =
tihst-).

reap. *v.t.* rahé·rya'ks *he reaps it* (-he =
rya'k-).

rear. *n.* u'téhsnakwt *rear* (u'téhsnakwt).

rear. *v.i.* wa'ręwá'nihč *it rears (e.g.,
horse)* (-a'ręwa'nihr-).

reason. *n.* u'tikę́hreh *reason* (-(ę)'ti =
kęh-); uríhwawęh *reason* (-rihwawę-).

rebel. *n.* ra'nwęniyúhstha' *rebel* (-a =
'nwęniyuhsT-).

recapitulate. *v.i.* ra'rihwatukę́htha' *he recapitulates* (-a'rihwatukęhT-).

recede. *v.i.* yahwa'uhnę'ęhá·'nye' *it receded* (-yah-.-ahnę'ęha'nye'-).

receipt. *n.* yu'nyetawá'kę *receipt* (-a =
'nyetawa'k-).

receive. *v.t.* rawú'θeh *he receives it*
(-aw-{dative I}); see: -u'na-.

recently. *adv.* čhę' *recently* (čhę').

receptacle. *n.* urętú'čreh *receptacle* (-rę =
tu'čr-).

reciprocate. *v.i.* nehrá·'na'naws *he reciprocates* (-ne-.-aw-).

reckon. *v.i.* thwehráhews *he reckons* (ti+

yah-.-(ę)haw-).

recline. *v.i.* see: -tekwęnarę-.

recognize. *v.t.* θhrayę́·'ner *he recognizes
it* (-či-.-yę'ner-).

recoil. *v.i.* ncθwa'náhwyar *it recoils*
(-ne+či-.-a'nahwyar-).

reconquer. *v.t.* θhra'ni'θhę́·nyęhs *he reconquers* (-či-.-a'ni'θhęni-).

recover. *v.i.* θhratkyé·θkwahs *he recovers* (-či-.-atkeθku-); θhra'tyá·kę'θ *he
recovers* (-či-.-'tyakę'-); *v.t.* θhraku'-
čę́·ryęhs *he recovers it* (-či-.-ku' =
čęri-).

recreation. *n.* wà·rahst yawę́·tyaht *recreation* (-arahsT- -ętyahT-).

red. *adj.* katkwarà·yę' *it is red* (-tkwa =
rayę(T)-); tikatkwará·yę·t *it is red* (ti-.
-tkwarayę(T)-); čutakę́hku *deep red*
(čutakę́hku).

redden. *v.t.* rakwęhčrárhuhs *he reddens it*
(-kwęhčrarhu-).

redeemer. *n.* čękhi'θkęhnakúhę' *redeemer* (-či-.-'θkęhnakuhę-).

reed. *n.* uherúhkweh *reed* (-heruhkw-);
urháhkweh *reed* (-rhahkw-); utihθù·-
reh *reed* (-tihθur-).

reembrace. *v.t.* θhręhnę́θhar *he reembraces it* (-či-.-ęhnęθhar-).

reenter. *v.i.* θhrà·yę' *he reenters* (-či-.
-yę-).

refectory. *n.* yęčhurya'náhkhwa'. *refectory* (-ačhurya'nahkw-).

reform. *v.i.* θhračhekwáhstha' *he re-
forms* (-či-.-ačhekwahsT-).

refresh. *v.i.* wà·rahst rawę́·ti· *he refreshes*
(-arahsT- -ęti-).

refreshed. *adj.* θhrawę́·'nahtič *he is re-*

---

freshed (-či-. -ę'na̲htir-).

refuge. *n.* yę'ʔnihsuhráhkhwaʔ *refuge* (-a=
'nihsuhrahkw-); yę'ʔneʔkwahshę'ʔnáh-
khwaʔ *refuge* (-a'ʔneʔkwahshę=
'nahkw-).

refuge, take. *v.i.* raʔneʔkwáhshęhs *he
takes refuge* (-aʔneʔkwahshę(T)-).

refuse. *n.* haʔ yuhsęhtíʔę *refuse* (-hsęh=
tiʔ-).

refuse. *v.t.* rahsę́htih *he refuses it* (-hsęh=
ti-).

regard. *v.t.* nehranę́ʔyar *he regards it*
(-ne-. -nęʔyar-).

regret. *v.t.* ranháʔnę *he regrets it* (-nhaʔ=
nę-).

reheat. *v.t.* θhraʔnariháʔthaʔ *he reheats it*
(-či-. -a'nariha ʔT-).

reign. *n.* uhwenętíhsteh *reign* (-hwenę=
tihst-).

reign. *v.i.* rayanéʔčhęʔ *he reigns* (-ya=
neʔčhę(T)-).

reimburse. *v.i.* θhraʔęyúhar *he reimburses* (-či-. -ʔęyuhar-).

rein. *n.* uʔnhę́hθeh *rein* (-(i)ʔnhęhθ-).

reindeer. *n.* θkaʔnyę́hsaʔ *reindeer* (θkaʔ-
nyę́hsaʔ).

reinforce. *v.t.* ęhstì·raht *you will reinforce it* (-htirahT-).

reject. *v.t.* ráhstkęʔθ *he rejects it* (-(i)h=
stkęʔ-).

rejoin. *v.t.* nehraraʔté·kęhs *he rejoins it*
(-ne-. -raʔtekę-).

relapse of sickness, cause a. *v.i.* raʔnu-
kwá·tyęh *he causes a relapse of sickness* (-a'nukʷatyę-).

relation. *n.* unęhwíhčreh *relation* (-nęh=
wihčr-); ruʔnę́·thiʔ *his father's relations* (-ʔnęthiʔ).

relationship. *n.* unęhwíhčreh *relationship*
(-nęhwihčr-).

relatives. *n.* ranę́hwih *his relative* (-nęh=
wih); nyęʔnę̀·nur *one's close relatives*
(-a'nęnur).

release. *v.t.* θhraʔná·kʔuhs *he releases it*
(-či-. -a'nakʔu-).

relent. *v.i.* raʔniʔθhahnę́hthaʔ *he relents*
(-a'niʔθhahnęhT-).

relieve. *v.t.* naʔnęrihshęʔná·kwahs *one
relieves another* (-ę̊rihshę'naku-).

religion. *n.* urihwiyúhčreh *religion* (-rih=
wiyuhčr-).

religious. *adj.* rurihwiyúhsnę *he is religious* (-rihwiyuhsT-).

relish. *n.* awę́·θreh *relish* (-ę̊θr-).

relish. *v.t.* ręθrakʔúʔθrę· *he relishes it*
(-ę̊θrakʔuʔθrę-).

remain. *v.i.* rę́ʔręʔ *he remains* (-iʔrę-).

remainder. *n.* haʔ yuʔnaʔnę̀·rę *remainder*
(-a'na'nęr-).

remains. *n.* haʔ yuʔnaʔnę̀·rę *remains* (-a=
'na'nęr-).

remedy. *v.t.* ręnęhkwáʔthaʔ *he remedies
it* (-ęnęhkwaʔT-).

remember. *v.t.* réhyar *he remembers it*
(-ehyahr-); θahrehyáhraʔ *he remembered it* (-či-. -ehyahraʔ-); aryęʔnaʔ-
tikęhrę́·thuht *that one remember another* (-(ę)ʔtikęhręthuhT-).

remorse. *n.* haʔ θhrawúʔθeʔ *remorse*
(-či-. -awʔθeʔ-).

remove. *v.t.* raʔθę́hthaʔ *he removes it*
(-aʔθęhT-); rahkwíʔthaʔ *he removes it*
(-hkwiʔT-).

rend. *v.t.* raračę́·kwahs *he rends it* (-ra=
čęku-).

renounce. *v.t.* raʔnęnhíhthaʔ *he renounces it* (-a'nęnhihT-).

rent. *n.* haʔ yuʔrá·čęʔ *rent* (-aʔračę-).

rent. *v.t.* raʔnęhníhahs *he rents it* (-a=
'nęhniha-).

renumerate. *v.t.* θhráhra·č *he renumerates*
(-či-. -hraT-).

reopen. *v.t.* θhračá·ryęhs *he reopens it*
(-či-. -čari-).

repair. *v.y.* θhračhakwáhsthaʔ *he repairs
it* (-či-. -ačhakwahsT-).

reparable. *adj.* čučhákwahst *reparable*
(-či-. -ačhakwahsT-).

repay. *v.i.* θhraʔnúhčẹhs *he repays* (-či-.
-aˈnuhči-); θhraʔẹyúhar *he repays*
(-či-.-ʔẹyuhar-).

repeat. *v.i.* čaíhrẹ·ʔ *one repeated it (said
it again)* (-či-.-ihrẹ-); θhrurihwáhθaʔw
he repeats it (does it again) (-či-.
-rihwahθawʔ-).

repent. *v.i.* rẹtathrewáʔthaʔ *he repents*
(-ẹtathrewaʔT-).

replace. *v.t.* naʔá·ktakwt *that I replace
another* (-t-.-akT-); θhrà·yẹhs *he replaces it* (-či-.-yẹ(T)-); nehrakẹʔ-
né·tyẹhs *he replaces it* (-ne-.-kẹʔ=
neti-).

reply. *v.i.* θhrarihwayahθrá·kwahs *he
replies* (-či-.-rihwayahθraku-); nahrá·
wẹ· *he replied* (-t-.-ẹ-); nahrà·raʔ *he
replies* (-t-.-raʔ-).

report. *v.i.* θhrahnyẹhà·wiʔ *he reports*
(-či-.-hnyẹhawi-); waʔthrathnyaré·
tyaʔt *he reported* (-ne-.-athnyare=
tyaʔT-).

reproach. *n.* uʔnéhaht *reproach* (-ʔne=
hahT-); haʔ ruyuráʔkhwaʔ *reproach*
(-yuraʔkw-).

reproach. *v.t.* nehrahsẹwiré·thaʔ *he reproaches it* (-ne-.-hsẹwireT-).

require. *v.t.* nehrutahwẹčù·nih *he requires
it* (-ne-.-tahweču-{dative II}).

rescue. *v.t.* ratahskúhčẹhs *he rescues it*
(-tahskuhči-).

research. *v.t.* rarihwíhsʔahs *he researches
it* (-rihwihsʔa-); nehrarihwakẹʔθáhnẹh
he researches it (-ne-.-rihwakẹʔ=
θahnẹ-).

reseat. *v.t.* θhrahstráʔnihč *he reseats it*
·(-či-.-hstraʔnihr-).

resell. *v.t.* θhratẹhnì·nẹh *he resells it*
(-či-.-atẹhninẹ-).

resemble. *v.t.* θwaʔnyé·rẹ· *it resembles*
(-či-.-aˈnyerẹ-); see: -uʔnẹ-.

resentment. *n.* úhsẹht *resentment* (-ah=
sẹhT-).

reserved. *adj.* rutkuwíhsnẹ *he is reserved*
(-atkuwihsT-).

reset. *v.t.* θhrẹ́ʔrẹhs *he resets it* (-či-.
-iʔrẹ-).

reside. *v.i.* yetá·kreʔ *one resides* (-ta=
k(e)r-).

residence. *n.* uyẹ́hsteh *residence* (-yẹh=
st-).

residue. *n.* uʔnekẹ̀·reh *residue* (-aˈne=
kẹr-).

resin. *n.* uθrẹ̀·weh *resin* (-θrẹw-).

resinous. *adj.* uθrẹwéhči *resinous*
(-θrẹw-.#hči).

resolution, alter. *v.i.* θhrarihwakẹʔné·
tyẹhs *he alters his resolution* (-či-.
-rihwakẹʔneti-).

resolution, make a. *v.i.* raʔrihwihsʔá·tih
he makes a resolution (-aʔrihwihsʔa-
{dative III}).

resolve. *v.i.* rẹʔtikẹhríhsʔahs *he resolves*
(-(ẹ)ʔtikẹhrihsʔa-).

resonant. *adj.* yuwẹtú·ri· *resonant* (-wẹtu=
ri-).

resound. *v.i.* čurá·kar *it resounds* (-či-.
-rakar(e)-).

respect. *v.i.* raʔnatkwẹnyẹ́hsthaʔ *he respects himself* (-aˈnatkwẹnyẹhsT-);
v.t. rakwẹnyẹ́hsthaʔ *he respects it*
(-kwẹnyẹhsT-).

respectability. *n.* haʔ yutkwẹ́·nyẹhst *respectability* (-atkwẹnyẹhsT-).

---

resplendent. *adj.* neyurẹryuhkwitkẹ́ʔẹ *it is resplendent* (-ne-.-rẹryuhkwitkẹʔ-).

respond. *v.i.* rà·raʔθ *he responds* (-raʔ-).

responsibility. *n.* haʔ ruʔnwẹtánhẹ *his responsibility* (-aʔnwẹtanh-).

responsibility, become. *v.i.* weθaríhwayẹhθ *it has become your responsibility* (-yah-.-rihwayẹ(T)-{dative II}).

responsible. *adj.* wahsaʔnwẹtánhek *you are responsible* (-aʔnwẹtanh-).

rest. *v.i.* raʔnẹríhshẹh *he is resting* (-a= ʔnẹrihshẹ(T)-).

resting place. *n.* yẹʔnẹrihshẹʔnáhkhwaʔ *resting place* (-aʔnẹrihshẹʔnahkw-).

restive. *adj.* yuʔnẹ́ʔθrẹ *it is restive* (-aʔ= nẹʔθr-).

restore. *v.t.* θhrayè·riks *he restores it* (-či-.-yerik(T)-).

result. *v.i.* kayáhskaht *it results* (-yah= skaht); yunhučẹ́ʔthaʔ *it results* (-nhu= čẹʔT-); ẹkarihwà·yẹʔ *it will result* (-rihwayẹ-).

resume. *v.i.* θhrahθá·wʔahs *he resumes* (-či-.-ahθawʔ-); θhraʔnyatakʔúhsyẹhs *he resumes* (-či-.-aʔnyaʔtakʔuhsi-).

resurrection. *n.* haʔ ẹčẹtkẹháʔθeʔ *resurrection* (-či-.-atkẹhaʔθe-).

retain. *v.t.* rayè·nẹhs *he retains (thing)* (-yenẹ-).

retain knowledge. *v.i.* raʔnewyẹ́hsthaʔ *he retains knowledge* (-aʔnewyẹhsT-).

retaliate. *v.i.* θhraʔnúhčẹhs *he retaliates* (-či-.-aʔnuhči-).

retarded. *adj.* nyuʔnẹ́·ʔnuʔkt *it is retarded* (-t-.-aʔnẹʔnuʔkT-).

retch. *v.i.* ratyáʔkwrẹh *he retches* (-tyaʔkʷhrẹ-).

retort. *v.i.* nehraʔrihwayaʔθrá·kwahs *he retorts* (-ne-.-aʔrihwayaʔθraku-).

retrace steps. *v.i.* θhraʔnyáʔθrẹh *he retraces his steps* (-či-.-aʔnyaʔθrẹ-).

retrace way. *v.i.* rahahakà·rẹws *he retraces his way* (-(a)hahakarẹhw-).

retract. *v.t.* θhraʔnwẹ́·ta·ks *he retracts it*

(-či-.-aʔnwẹtak-).

retreat. *v.i.* θhrẹtihrečhẹ́·ʔnyẹhs *he retreats* (-či-.-ẹtihrečhẹʔni-).

return. *v.i.* θhrá·wu· *he returns* (-či-. -aw-); íθhreʔθ *he returned* (-či-.-eʔ-); θakayẹthahakà·rẹw *they returned* (-či-. -athahakarẹ(w)-); θẹ́rkuʔ *it returned home* (-či-.-ar(e)ku-).

reveal. *v.t.* rahswakwẹríhthaʔ *he revealed it* (-hswakwẹrihT-).

revenge. *v.i.* θhraʔẹyúhar *he revenges* (-či-.-ʔẹyuhar-).

reverse. *n.* uʔtéhsnakwt *reverse* (-ʔteh= snakt); uʔtéhsnakwt naʔú·ʔni *reverse* (-ʔtehsnakt naʔ-.-(a)ʔni).

revert. *v.i.* θwáhknẹhs *it reverts* (-či-. -ahk(e)T-).

revisit. *v.t.* θhratá·ʔnyẹʔ *he revisits it* (-či-.-taʔnyẹ-).

revive. *v.i.* θhraʔtikẹhrí·tkẹhθ *he revives* (-či-.-(ẹ)ʔtikẹhritkẹʔ-); θhrẹ́nhahkt *he revives it* (-či-.-ẹ́ʔnhahkT-).

revocable. *adj.* yuʔrihwarurẹ́·kwaht *revocable* (-aʔrihwarurẹkʷahT-).

revoke. *v.t.* θhrarihwaʔnihẹ́·thuhs *he revokes it* (-či-.-rihwaʔnihẹthu-).

revolve. *v.i.* wathrẹhwakúhẹh *it revolves* (-athrẹhwakuhẹ-).

rib. *n.* uturáhčreh *rib* (-turahčr-).

ribbon. *n.* ukẹhúhčreh *ribbon* (-kẹ= huhčr-).

rice. *n.* uná·čaʔ *rice* (-nač-).

rice pudding. *n.* uná·čaʔ utkuriʔnẹ́·te *rice pudding* (-nač- -tkuriʔnẹte).

rich. *adj.* arẹkwačhúʔku·k *that I were rich* (-ačhuʔkuw-).

riches. *n.* unẹkwì·reh *riches* (-(ẹ)nẹ= kwir-); učhuʔkuwáhčreh *riches* (-a= čhuʔkuwahčr-).

ride. *v.i.* rúʔθre·ʔ *he rode* (-(i)ʔθ(e)r-).

ride bareback. *v.t.* waʔnaʔnihsáʔnẹʔ *one rode another bareback* (-ihsaʔnẹʔ-).

ridge. *n.* yunẹʔnyẹ́·tiʔ *ridge* (-nẹʔnyẹti-).

ridicule. *v.t.* rakẹhrẹ́·tih *he ridicules it*

(-kǫhrǫti -).

ridiculous. *adj.* yutérhya'ʔt *it is ridiculous* (-terhya'ʔT -).

right. *adj.* he'ʔthúhči *right* (he'ʔthúhči); wekayè·ri'ʔ *it is right* (-yah -. -yeri -).

right. *adv.* kǫ *right* (kǫ).

right. *n.* u'ʔθhaθnǫ́hsteh *right* (-(i)'ʔ = θhaθnǫhst -); tkarihwayè·ri'ʔ *right* (-t -. -rihwayeri -).

right away. *adv.* thu'ʔù·nǫ *right away* (thu'ʔù·nǫ).

right side. *n.* rawyǫwnáhkǫ *his right side* (-wyǫwnahkw -).

rigid. *adj.* tyurhenáthǫ· *it is rigid* (-rhe = nathǫ -).

rigidity. *n.* ha'ʔ uhtì·rǫ *rigidity* (-htir -).

rim. *n.* uyúhkweh *rim* (-yuhkw -).

rim. *v.t.* rayúhkuč *he rims it* (-yuhkur -).

rind. *n.* urí'ʔreh *rind* (-ri'ʔr -).

ring. *n.* uhsu'ʔkwéhčreh *ring (on finger)* (-hsu'ʔkwehčr -); uká'ʔneh *ring (circle)* (-ka'ʔn -).

ring bell. *v.i.* rawenǫ́·t'ʔehs *he rings bell* (-wenǫt'ʔe(k) -).

ringlet. *n.* uka'ʔneháh *ringlet* (-ka'ʔn -. #áh).

ringworm, have. *v.i.* runǫ̀·yǫhθ *he has ringworm* (-nǫyǫhθ -).

rip. *v.t.* rará·čǫhs *he rips it* (-račǫ -).

ripe. *adj.* yù·rih *it is ripe* (-rih -).

ripen. *v.i.* kà·rihθ *it ripens* (-rih -); karíhtha'ʔ *it ripens it* (-rihT -).

rise. *v.i.* yu'ʔnétkǫ'ʔ *it has risen (of bread)* (-a'ʔnetkǫ'ʔ -).

rival. *n.* nehru'ʔna'ʔnírhǫh *rival* (-ne -. -aˈna'ʔnihrhǫ -).

river. *n.* kahyǫháhrǫ *river* (-(i)hyǫha = h(e)r -); kéyhnu·'ʔ *river* (-(i)yhnu -); uyhǫ́heh *river* (-(i)yh(ǫh) -).

rivet. *v.i.* rahsǫwa'ʔrá'ʔnihč *he rivets* (-hsǫwa'ʔra'ʔnihr -).

road. *n.* uháheh *road* (-(a)hah -); è·nǫ'ʔt *road* (-enǫ'ʔT -); yǫnǫ́hstha'ʔ *road* (-e = nǫhsT -).

roadscraper. *n.* kahahahsǫwá·tih *roadscraper* (-(a)hahahsǫwati -).

roam. *v.i.* rì·rǫhs *he roams* (-ir -).

roar. *v.i.* runǫhwarù·rih *he roars* (-nǫh = waruri -); kahǫ̀·rehθ *it roars* (-hǫrehθ -).

roast. *n.* u'ʔθkwǫ̀·weh *roast (of any kind of meat)* (-'ʔθkǫw -).

roast. *v.t.* rǫ́hsǫh *he roasts it* (-ǫhsǫ -).

rob. *v.i.* rá·tkwahs *he robs* (-atku -).

robin. *n.* čihskú'ʔu'ʔ *robin* (čihskú'ʔu'ʔ); runyá'ʔrha'ʔr *golden robin* (runyá'ʔrha'ʔr).

rock. *n.* učtǫ́hreh *rock* (-čtǫhr -).

rocking chair. *n.* ǫhsatkarǫ́hrǫ'ʔ u'ʔθkwéhseh *rocking chair* (-atkarǫhrǫ - -'ʔθ = kwehs -).

rod. *n.* utáhsneh *rod* (-(ǫ)tahsn -).

roe. *n.* utè·reh *roe* (-(ǫ)ter -); uθrà·yeh *roe* (-θray -).

roll. *n.* uhǫ̀·wareh *roll (e.g., of wrapping paper)* (-hǫwar -); píhskit *roll (bread)* (píhskit).

roll around. *v.i.* ka'ʔrakǫ̀·rih *I roll around* (-a'ʔrakǫri -).

rolling, be. *v.i.* see: -kareru -.

roof. *n.* unǫhsá'ʔkye *roof* (-nǫhsa'ʔke); unǫhsúhareh *roof* (-nǫhsuhar -); uhsè·reh *bark roof* (-hser -).

room. *n.* utákwneh *room* (-takwT -).

roost. *n.* rǫnǫhwe'ʔnáhkhwa'ʔ *his roost* (-ǫnǫhwe'ʔnahkw -).

---

roost. *v.i.* ręnęhwé·tha⁷ *he roosts* (-ęnęh= weT-).

root. *n.* uhné⁷reh *root* (-hne⁷r-).

root. *v.i.* ręhrá⁷kha⁷ *he roots* (-ę°hra⁷k-).

root, take. *v.i.* kahne⁷rę́·tih *it takes root* (-hne⁷ręti-).

rope. *n.* uhsì·reh *rope* (-hsir-).

rot. *n.* utkę́hθreh *rot* (-atkęhθr-).

rotten. *adj.* yú·tkęh *it is rotten* (-atkęh-).

rough. *adj.* yutkará⁷wę *it is rough* (-a= tkara⁷w-).

round. *adj.* ęyehwé·⁷nu⁷ *one will be round* (-hwe'nu-); tha⁷neyuthwęhnę́·ti· *it is round* (tha+ne-.-athwęhnęti-).

round. *v.t.* nehrakwa⁷nę́·tih *he rounds it* (-ne-.-kwa⁷nęti-).

row. *n.* urì·reh *row* (-rir-).

row. *v.i* rahęwí·te⁷ *he rows* (-hęwiN-); wa⁷kká·we·⁷ *I rowed* (-kawe-).

rub. *v.t.* rará·tih *he rubs it* (-rati-); ęyeh- tà·wę⁷ *one will rub it* (-(i)htawę-); ra- kará·tih *he rubs it against it* (-karati-).

rubbish. *n.* awú·kri⁷ *rubbish* (-ukr-).

rude. *adj.* ruθwętáhraht *he is rude* (-θwętahrahT-).

rudiments. *n.* nyu⁷rihwáhθa⁷w *rudiments* (-t-.-a⁷rihwahθaw⁷-).

ruffle. *n.* učí⁷čeh *ruffle* (-či⁷či-).

ruffled grouse. *n.* uhkwé·θę *ruffled grouse* (-ahkweθ-).

rug. *n.* yęθkarę́hkhwa⁷ *rug* (-iθkaręh= kw-).

ruin. *n.* ha⁷ yawuhrí⁷ę *ruin* (-uhri⁷-).

ruin. *v.t.* rahča⁷náhkhwa⁷ *he ruins it* (-ahča⁷nahkw-); rahskawę́htha⁷ *he ruins it* (-hskawęhT-).

ruin, come to. *v.i.* ru⁷nyę́wnarę⁷θ *he comes to ruin* (-a'nyęwnarę⁷-).

rule. *v.i.* rayané⁷čhę⁷ *he rules* (-yane⁷= čhę(T)-); see: -yan(e)(r)-.

ruler. *n.* ruthéhtrak *he is ruler* (-atheh= trak-).

rumble. *v.i.* yurakarè·re⁷ *it rumbles* (-ra= karere-).

rumor. *n.* úhnyeh *rumor* (-hny-).

rump. *n.* uti⁷nę̀·weh *rump* (-ti⁷nęw-); uti⁷θę̀·yeh *rump* (-ti⁷θęy-); uhtyù·weh *rump* (-htyuw-); uθę̀·yeh *rump* (-θęy-).

run. *v.i.* karerúha⁷ *I am running* (-are= ru-); yu⁷né⁷kwę *it had run away* (-a⁷ne⁷ku-); *v.t.* rahkwéhęh *he runs it down* (-hkwehę-); wa⁷kayę⁷nú⁷knę⁷ *they ran out of it* (-a'nu⁷kT-).

run-down. *n.* učí⁷yeh *run-down* (-či⁷y-).

runt. *n.* è·rihs *runt* (è·rihs).

rupture, have a. *v.i.* rutkwę́⁷ę *he has a rupture* (-tkwę⁷-).

rush. *n.* úhskaweh *rush* (-hskaw-); utéh- θeh *rush* (-tehθ-); utihθù·reh *rush* (-tihθur-).

rush forward. *v.i.* yęθwathwé⁷nę⁷ *you will rush forward* (-yah-.-athwe⁷nę-).

rust. *n.* ukwę́hneh *rust* (-kwęhT-).

rustic. *adj.* kwęhs uta⁷nakęw⁷áh *rustic* (kwęhs -ta'nakęw.#áh).

rut. *n.* yuhaháhkwę· *rut* (-(a)hahahkw-).

S

Sabbath. *n.* yawę⁷natukę́htha⁷ *Sabbath* (-ę'natukęhT-).

sachem. *n.* rahsęnuwà·nę *sachem* (-hsę= nuwan-).

sack. *n.* uyà·reh *sack* (-yar-).

sacred. *adj.* see: -tukęht-.

sacrifice. *v.t.* ru⁷nyęwáhnę *he sacrificed it (by fire)* (-a'nyęwahT-).

saddening. *adj.* yu⁷tikęhrá·ksa⁷t *saddening* (-(ę)⁷tikęhraksa⁷T-).

saddle. *n.* awe⁷wíhseh *saddle* (-e⁷wihs-).

saddle. *v.t.* re⁷wíhsher *he saddles it* (-e⁷= wihsher-).

sail. *v.i.* rari⁷wa⁷nírhęh *he sails* (-ri⁷= wa⁷nihrhę-).

sailor. *n.* ruhęwa⁷kyéha·⁷ *sailor* (-hęw-.

#keha·ʔ).

salary. *n.* ukaryáʔkčreh *salary* (-k<u>a</u>ryaʔ= kčr-).

saliva. *n.* utúʔkreh *saliva* (-tuʔkr-).

salmon. *n.* úyhęhst *salmon* (-(i)yhęhsT-).

salt. *n.* číkheʔ *salt* (číkheʔ).

salt pork. *n.* uθáʔreh *salt pork* (-θaʔr-).

salty. *n.* čikhéʔkye *salty* (čikhéʔkye).

samp. *n.* unęhsnúhkweh *samp* (-nęh= snuhkw-).

sample. *n.* utáhskweh *sample* (-tahskw-).

sanctify. *v.t.* ratukęhtíhsthaʔ *he sanctifies* (-tukęhtihsT-).

sanction. *v.t.* rariwhará·kwahs *he sanctions it* (-rihwharaku-).

sanctuary. *n.* unęhsatukęhti *sanctuary* (-nęhs<u>a</u>tukęhT-).

sand. *n.* uʔtéheh *sand* (-ʔteh-).

sandy. *adj.* uʔtehéhči *sandy* (-ʔteh-.#hči); uʔteháʔkye *sandy* (-ʔtehaʔke).

sane. *adj.* wekaʔtikęhrayè·riʔ *it is sane* (-yah-.-(ę)ʔtikęhr<u>a</u>yeri-); wekayè·riʔ *it is sane* (-yah-.-yeri-).

sap. *n.* uhné·kyeh *sap* (-hnek-).

sarsaparilla. *n.* čuhneʔre·θʔáh *sarsaparilla* (-či-.-hneʔreθ-.#áh); čuhneʔre·θʔúʔy *wild sarsaparilla* (-či-.-hneʔreθ-. #úʔy).

sash. *n.* uhkwíʔsteh *sash* (-hkwiʔst-).

sassafras. *n.* anéhsnači *sassafras* (anéhsnači).

satisfaction. *n.* nyuʔtikęhrì·yuht *satisfaction* (-t-.-(ę)ʔtikęhriyuhT-).

satisfy. *v.t.* rahewíhsthaʔ *he satisfies it* (-hewihsT-); naʔtikęhrayè·riks *up› one satisfies another* (-(ę)ʔtikęhr<u>a</u>yerik-).

Saturday. *n.* awę́·ʔnakwt *Saturday* (-ę= 'nakT-).

sausage. *n.* uyáʔreh *sausage* (-yaʔr-).

save. *v.t.* nahskrihwatú·rę· *you save me* (-t-.-rihw<u>a</u>turę-).

save up. *v.t.* ęčaʔnętíhyęʔ *that you save up some* (-a'nętihyę-).

saw. *n.* neyeręʔnyáʔkthaʔ *saw* (-ne-.-rę= 'nyaʔkT-); yehwęʔkharakwahnáhkhwaʔ *saw* (-hwęʔkh<u>a</u>rak^wahnahkw-); sáw *saw* (sáw).

saw. *v.i.* raré·ʔnyaʔks *he saws* (-rę= 'nyaʔk-); sáw ré·tih *he saws* (sáw -ę°ti-); waʔkkyé·thę·ʔ *I sawed it* (-ke= thę-).

sawdust. *n.* uʔθríʔčreh *sawdust* (-ʔθriʔ= čr-).

sawmill. *n.* nekahwęʔkharurę́hshahk *sawmill* (-ne-.-hwęʔkh<u>a</u>rurę-).

scab. *n.* úθneh *scab* (-iθn-).

scald. *v.t.* raʔθkaríhthaʔ *he scalds it* (-aʔθk<u>a</u>rihT-).

scale. *n.* úθneh *scale (of a fish)* (-iθn-).

scale. *v.t.* ręθnę́hthaʔ *he scales it (e.g., the fish)* (-iθnęhT-).

scallop. *v.t.* ratukarętyáhnęh *he scallops (the edges)* (-tukarętyahnę-).

scalp. *n.* unę́hreh *scalp* (-(ę)nęhr-); utičkę̀·reh *scalp* (-tičkęr-).

scalp. *v.t.* waʔkayęʔnaʔnęhrúhčiʔ *they scalped another* (-(ę)nęhruhči-).

scaly. *adj.* uθnéhči *scaly* (-iθn-.#hči).

scant. *adj.* áhčiʔ *scant* (áhčiʔ).

scar. *n.* úθneh *scar* (-iθn-); uhwè·neh *scar* (-hwen-).

scar. *v.t.* rahwè·nar *he scars it* (-hwe= nar-).

scarce. *adj.* úhshęh *scarce* (-hshę-); wa-

Tuscarora Pronunciation Key:
/a/ l<u>a</u>w; /e/ h<u>a</u>t; /i/ p<u>i</u>zza; /u/ t<u>u</u>ne; /ę/ h<u>i</u>nt; /č/ <u>ch</u>eese; /h/ <u>h</u>oe; /m/ <u>m</u>other; /s/ <u>s</u>ame; /t/ <u>d</u>o (before a vowel y, or w), <u>t</u>oo (elsewhere); /k/ <u>g</u>ale (before a vowel y or w), <u>k</u>ale (elsewhere); /n/ i<u>n</u>hale (before a consonant or word-final), <u>n</u>ote (elsewhere); /r/ hi<u>ss</u> (before a consonant or word-final), <u>r</u>un (trilled as in Italian, elsewhere); /w/ cu<u>ff</u> (before a consonant other than y or word-final), <u>w</u>ay (elsewhere); /y/ fi<u>sh</u> (before a consonant or word-final), <u>y</u>ou (elsewhere), /θ/ <u>th</u>ing; /ʔ/ (the sound between the vowels in unh-<u>u</u>nh); /·/ long vowel, /́/ high pitch; /̀/ low pitch.

kę̀·rc^ʔ *it is scarce* (-akę̨re-).

scare. *v.t.* na^ʔtehwáhkhwa^ʔ *one scares another* (-tehwa̱hkw-).

scarecrow. *n.* rathehnù·rih *scarecrow* (-a= thehnuri-).

scarlet. *adj.* učí^ʔereh *scarlet* (-či^ʔe̱r-); katkwę̨^ʔnahrahę́sči *scarlet* (-tkwę̨^ʔnah= raha̱hę̨sči-); čutakę́hku *scarlet* (čuta- kę́hku).

scarlet fever, have. *v.i.* rakwę̨hčrę́θhaʔk *he has scarlet fever* (-kwę̨hčrę̨θhaʔk-).

scatter. *v.i.* kayeríhahs *it is scattered* (-yeriha-); *v.t.* yuhwačerihę̨hú^ʔy *it is scattered around a lot* (-hwačeriha-. #ú^ʔy); nehra^ʔnukwáhtha^ʔ *he scatters it* (-ne-. -a'nukʷahT-); nehraretyá^ʔtha^ʔ *he scatters it* (-ne-. -aretyaʔT-).

scent. *v.t.* ra^ʔrę̨θhwáhtha^ʔ *he scents it* (-a^ʔrę̨θhwahT-).

scepter. *n.* uhnę̨htíhčreh *scepter* (-hnę̨h= tihčr-).

schism. *n.* ha^ʔ neyu^ʔnekháhsyę̨ *schism* (-ne-. -a'nekhahsi-).

scholar. *n.* rahyatę̨hstayę̨^ʔnè·rih *scholar* (-hyatę̨hsta̱yę'ner-).

school. *n.* yerihę̨tyá^ʔtha^ʔ *school* (-rihę̨= tya^ʔT-); yę̨^ʔna^ʔrihę̨tyá·tih *school* (-ri= hę̨ti-{dative III}).

scissors. *n.* yunę̨hkaráhčreh *scissors* (-nę̨hka̱rahčr-).

scoff at. *v.t.* natkę̨hrę̨tyáhnę̨h *one scoffs at another* (-kę̨hrę̨tyahnę̨-).

scold. *v.t.* wa^ʔkę̨yathráhtha^ʔr *I scolded you* (-athrahthar-); rarì·raws *he scolds it* (-riraw-).

scoop. *n.* yakučę́^ʔtha^ʔ *scoop* (-čę̨^ʔT-).

scour. *v.t.* račanę́·tih *he scours it* (-ča= nę̨ti-).

scowl. *n.* ukyé^ʔθreh *scowl* (-ke^ʔθr-).

scowl. *v.i.* ratkye^ʔθrarù·rę̨h *he scowls* (-atke^ʔθra̱rurę̨-); ratkye^ʔθrę́·tih *he scowls* (-atke^ʔθrę̨ti-).

scrape. *v.t.* wá^ʔkkye·t *I scraped it* (-keT-); wahstyú·θe^ʔr *you scrape corn* (-tyuθ(e)r-).

scraper. *n.* yekyethę́hkhwa^ʔ *scraper* (-ke= thę̨hkw-).

scratch. *v.i.* rahθharę̨tyę́·kwahs *he scratches* (-ahθha̱rę̨tyę̨ku-); tyawuhka- ráhsne^ʔ *it scratches* (ti-. -uhkarahsT-); raθkwéhthar *he scratches* (-θkweh= thar-); *v.t.* raθkwehthará·kwahs *he scratches it (with his nails)* (-θkweh= tharaku-); wa^ʔkkyé·thę̨·^ʔ *I scratched it* (-kethę̨-).

screech. *n.* uhsá·kwareh *screech* (-hsa= kʷa̱r-).

scrotum. *n.* uyáhkweh *scrotum* (-yah= kw-).

scruff. *n.* see: -hsnyu^ʔθr-.

sculptor. *n.* račtę̨hrę́·tih *sculptor* (-čtę̨h= rę̨ti-).

scum. *n.* uhwáhsteh *scum* (-hwahst-); a- wę̨ráhθreh *scum on stagnant water* (-ę̨rahθr-).

scythe. *n.* yeheryá^ʔktha^ʔ *scythe* (-he= rya^ʔkT-).

sea. *n.* unyá·tareh *sea* (-nyata̱r-); kanya- tarehú^ʔy *sea* (-nyata̱r-.#ú^ʔy).

sea gull. *n.* čuha^ʔθ^ʔá·ka·^ʔ *sea gull* (ču- ha^ʔθ^ʔá·ka·^ʔ).

seal. *v.t.* raθrę̀·wawę̨hs *he seals it* (-θrę̨= wa̱wę̨-); raθrę̨wanę̨^ʔnáktha^ʔ *he seals it* (-θrę̨wa̱nę̨'nakT-).

seam. *n.* ukę́heh *seam* (-kę̨h-).

seaman. *n.* ruhę̨wa^ʔkyéha·^ʔ *seaman* (-hę̨w-.#keha·^ʔ).

sear. *v.t.* ruhsù·rę̨ *he sears it* (-hsur-).

search. *v.i.* ka^ʔnę̨hwá·tyę̨ *I searched* (-a= 'nę̨hwati-).

search for. *v.t.* réhsaks *he searches for it* (-ïhsak-).

seaside. *n.* učá·takwt *seaside* (-čatakT-).

season. *n.* sá^ʔthu *season* (sá^ʔthu); ukę́n- heh *season* (-kę̨nh-).

season. *v.t.* neyerhúhθę̨h *one seasons it* (-ne-. -rhuhθę̨-); neyerhúhstha^ʔ *one is seasoning it* (-ne-. -rhuhsT-).

seasoning. *n.* neyerhúhstha⁷ *seasoning* (-ne-.-rhuhsT-).

seat. *n.* u⁷θkwéhseh *seat* (-⁷θkwehs-); uthečráhkweh *seat* (-athečrahkw-).

seat. *v.t.* na⁷nihstra⁷níhθneh *one seats another* (-hstra⁷nihθne-).

seated. *adj.* rę́⁷rę⁷ *he is placed* (-i⁷rę-).

secede. *v.i.* ra⁷rá·kwahs *he secedes* (-a⁷= raku-).

secret. *n.* yurihwahθéhnę *it is a secret* (-rihwahθehT-).

secretion. *n.* ha⁷ yunháhkę *secretion* (-(a)nhahkw-).

secretly. *adj.* u⁷nahθehnę́⁷kye *secretly* (-a'nahθehnę⁷ke).

sedentary. *adj.* ękyéhah *sedentary* (ękyé-hah).

see. *v.t.* rú·kę· *he has seen it* (-kę-).

see-saw. *n.* uyáhkweh *see-saw* (-yah= kw-).

seed. *n.* unę́hsneh *seed* (-nęhsn-).

seek. *v.t.* réhsaks *he seeks it* (-ïhsak-).

seemly. *v.i.* neyuya⁷tá·⁷nę⁷ *it is seemly* (-ne-.-ya⁷ta'nę⁷-).

seethe. *v.i.* rarihá⁷tha⁷ *he seethes* (-ri= ha⁷T-).

seizures, have. *v.i.* ruyè·nęhs *he has seizures* (-yenę-).

seldom. *adv.* ihskáhkye *seldom* (ihskáh-kye).

select. *v.t.* rará·kwahs *he selects it* (-ra= ku-).

self. *pro.* rawę̀·ruh *himself* (-ęruh-).

self-respect. *n.* u⁷nehyahrę́hčreh *self-respect* (-a'nehyahrę̨hčr-).

sell. *v.t.* ratę̨hnì·nęh *he sells it* (-atę̨h= ninę-).

semen. *n.* u⁷nhę̨hsú·kri⁷ *semen* (-⁷nhęh= sukr-).

senator. *n.* rahwenętihú⁷y *senator* (-hwe= nęti-.#ú⁷y).

send. *v.t.* nakayę⁷náthre·k *they sent someone* (-hrek-); ra⁷nętiyé·tha⁷ *he sends it* (-aT-.-ętiyeT-).

send for. *v.t.* ráhnęks *he sends for it* (-(i)hnęk-); weyę⁷na⁷níhnęks *one sends for another* (-yah-.-ihnęk-).

senile. *adj.* ka⁷néhsktha⁷ *I am senile* (-a⁷nehskT-).

senior. *n.* rathuráhtha⁷ *senior* (-athu= rahT-).

sensual. *n.* uyerę⁷kyé·ha⁷ *sensual* (-yer-. #keha·⁷).

separate. *adj.* neyu⁷né·khę *they are separate* (-ne-.-a'nekha-).

separate from. *v.t.* nekakukháhsyę *they were separated from it* (-ne-.-khahsi-).

separately. *adv.* awęruhá·⁷nye⁷ *separately* (-ęruha'nye⁷-).

sequester. *v.t.* kahθéhtha⁷ *I am hiding it, I am sequestering it* (-ahθehT-).

serious. *adj.* rukęhsahtí·rę· *he is serious* (-kęhsahtir-).

servant. *n.* unhá⁷čreh *servant* (-nha⁷čr-).

serve. *v.i.* ra⁷nénha⁷θ *he serves* (-a'nen= ha⁷-).

set. *v.t.* θhrę́ *set it down!* (-hrę-); rà·ręh *he sets it on* (-rę-); rà·ręh *he sets it out* (-rę-).

set the table. *v.i.* ęhsekθrà·wę⁷ *you will set the table* (-kθhrawę-).

settle. *v.i.* re⁷θayę́·⁷nahθ *he settles* (-e⁷= θayę(T)-{dative II}).

settled. *adj.* aki⁷rę́⁷nak *that I be settled*

(-iʔrę·ʔT-).

settlement. *n.* utá·ʔneh *settlement* (-ta='n-).

seven. *adj./n.* čá·ʔnahk *seven* (čá·ʔnahk).

seventeen. *adj./n.* čá·ʔnahk θkáheʔr *seventeen* (čá·ʔnahk -či-.-(i)har-).

seventy. *adj./n.* čá·ʔnahk tiwáhθhę· *seventy* (čá·ʔnahk ti-.-ahθhę-).

several. *adj.* steʔ tiwá·kye· *several* (steʔ ti-.-ake-).

severe. *adj.* ruθrà·rahst *he is severe* (-θrarahsT-); ruʔθwętáhraht *he is severe* (-ʔθwętahrahT-).

sex with spouse, have. *v.t.* wahratíʔka·t *he has sex with his spouse* (-tiʔk-).

shad. *n.* uθnahwaryá·kęʔ *shad* (-iθnah=waryakę-).

shade. *n.* utiʔθręhsteh *shade* (-tiʔθręhst-).

shade. *v.i.* yutíʔθręʔ *it shades* (-tiʔθrę-); *v.t.* ratiʔθręh-thaʔ *he shades it* (-tiʔ=θręhT-).

shadow. *n.* utiʔθręhsteh *shadow* (-tiʔ=θręhst-).

shaggy. *adj.* ukyeʔwehúʔy *shaggy* (-keʔw-.#úʔy).

shake. *v.t.* rà·waks *he shakes it* (-awak-); nehraneʔkęθnáhnęh *he shakes it* (-ne-.-neʔkęθnahnę-); ęwuryáhnę·ʔ *it will shake it up* (-ⁿuryahnę-).

sham. *n.* sáʔrkęʔ *sham* (sáʔrkęʔ).

shame. *v.t.* raʔneháʔthaʔ *he shames it* (-aʔnehaʔT-).

shameful. *adj.* kánhę uʔnéhaht *shameful* (-(a)nha- -ʔnehahT-).

shank. *n.* utáʔneh *shank* (-taʔn-).

shape, take. *v.i.* ętkyehná·we·k *it took shape* (-atkehnawek).

share. *v.t.* rá·nę· *he shares it* (-(a)nę-); naʔrurę·tih *one shares with another* (-rurę-{dative II}); raʔté·kahs *he shares it* (-ʔtek-).

shark. *n.* waʔnewakstaksʔúʔy *shark* (waʔnewakstaksʔúʔy).

sharp. *adj.* yutú·karę·t *it is sharp* (-tu=

karęt); yú·ʔneht *it is sharp* (-(a)='nehT-).

sharpen. *v.t.* waʔktukaráʔnir *I sharpened it* (-tukaraʔnihr-); ratakarę·tih *he sharpens it* (-(ę)takaręti-); waʔktukarę·tiʔ *I sharpened it* (-tukaręti-); see: -uʔ=thiy-.

shatter. *v.t.* rahsuryę·thuhs *he shatters it* (-hsuryęthu-).

shave. *v.t.* yęčhuhkwę·tiht *one shaves it* (-ačhuhkwętihT-).

sheaf. *n.* uthúhkweh *sheaf* (-athuhku-).

shear. *v.t.* ranęhrù·rę *he shears it* (-(ę)=nęhrur-).

shed tears. *v.i.* nehrakahθrarúhθręh *he sheds tears* (-ne-.-kahθraruhθrę-).

sheep. *n.* weʔrá·ksę· *sheep* (-eʔraks-).

sheepish. *adj.* rętiʔrhwęθawíhthaʔ *he is sheepish* (-(ę)tiʔrhwęθawihT-).

sheet. *n.* uríʔreh *sheet (of paper)* (-riʔr-); yęθkaręhkhwaʔ *sheet (of a bed)* (-i=θkaręhkw-); uriʔwehę̀·we *sheet (of a bed)* (-riʔw-.#ęwe); uhθaʔkęhsteh *sheet (of a bed)* (-hθaʔkęhst-); úθkareh *sheet (of a bed)* (-iθkar-).

shelf. *n.* utíʔθreh *shelf* (-tiʔθ(e)r-).

shell. *n.* utyà·neh *shell* (-tyan-).

shell. *v.t.* rukę̀·yahs *he shells it (e.g., nuts)* (-ukęy-); wahrahtí·teʔ *he shelled it (e.g., crab)* (-htite-).

shepherd. *n.* raʔteyanęʔá·ka·ʔ *shepherd* (-(ę)ʔteyanę-.#aka·ʔ).

shield. *n.* yęʔnęʔneʔnáhkhwaʔ *shield* (-a='nęʔne'nahkw-).

shine. *v.i.* kačatukáʔthaʔ *it shines* (-čatu=kaʔT-); yú·huks *it shines* (-huk-); kahsnukáʔthaʔ *it shines* (-hsnukaʔT-).

shingle. *n.* uháhsteh *shingle* (-hahst-); yehahstihráhkhwaʔ *shingle* (-hahstih=rahkw-).

shingle. *v.t.* rahahstíher *he shingles it* (-hahstihar-).

shiny. *adj.* yučáʔtaʔneht *it is shiny* (-ča=ta'nehT-).

ship. *n*. uhę·weh *ship* (-hęw -); uhęwe-
hú⁷y *ship* (-hęw -.#ú⁷y).

ship. *v.t*. raráhkhwa⁷ *he ships it* (-rah =
kw -).

shirt. *n*. węhtá⁷θrę· *shirt* (-ęhta⁷θrę -);
úhskareh *shirt* (-hskar -).

shit. *n*. utkwéhreh *shit* (-tkwehr -).

shiver. *v.i*. ru⁷nęnhatúhsnę *he shivers
(from cold)* (-a'nęnhatuhsT -); ruθrárha⁷ *he shivers (for any reason)*
(-θrar -).

shoal. *n*. yuhtawakaré·ru· *shoal* (-htawa =
kareru -).

shoe. *n*. uráhsu⁷ *shoe* (-arahsu -); učhikú⁷reh *manufactured shoe* (-čhiku⁷r -);
uhnáhkwa⁷ *Indian shoe* (-ahnahkw -).

shoe. *v.i*. áha·θ nehrarahsú·θe⁷ *he shoes
a horse* (áha·θ -ne -.-arahsuθ -).

shoe polish. *n*. yečhiku⁷rahθuháhtha⁷
shoe polish (-čhiku⁷rahθuhahT -).

shoelace. *n*. učhikú⁷reh yehtręhstha⁷
shoelace (-čhiku⁷r - -(i)htręhst -).

shoemaker. *n*. račhiku⁷rę́·tih *shoemaker*
(-čhiku⁷ręti -); rahnahkwę́·tih *shoemaker* (-ahnahkwęti -).

shoot. *n*. yu⁷nhahnu·t⁷áh *shoot (of a
plant)* (-(i)⁷nhahnut.#áh).

shoot. *v.t*. ratì·yę⁷kws *he shoots it* (-i⁷ =
a(k) -/-yę⁷kʷ -).

shoot arrows. *v.i*. ru⁷tę́·⁷nyęhs *he shoots
arrows* (-a⁷tę'ni -).

shop. *n*. utęhninę́hsteh *a shop* (-atęhni =
nęhst -).

shore. *n*. uhθę́⁷kareh *shore* (-hθę⁷kar -);
učá·teh *shore* (-čaN -).

short. *adj*. wakwę́⁷nhe⁷r *it is too short*
(-akwę⁷nh(e)r -).

shorten. *v.t*. rakwę́⁷nhrahč *he shortens it*
(-akwę⁷nhrahT -).

shortly. *adv*. narà·we⁷st *shortly* (narà·-
we⁷st).

shoulder blade. *n*. awętráhreh *shoulder
blade* (-ętrahr -); utkuryá⁷čreh *shoulder
blade* (-tkurya⁷čr -).

shoulder. *n*. uhnę́hweh *upper shoulder*
(-hnęhu -).

shout. *v.i*. raθkwár⁷ehs *he shouts* (-aθ =
kwar⁷e(k) -); rahę̀·rehθ *he shouts* (-hę =
rehθ -).

shovel. *n*. uterhyá⁷čreh *shovel* (-ter =
hya⁷čr -).

show. *v.t*. rehú·tha⁷ *he shows it* (-e =
huT -).

shred. *n*. úhneh *shred (of cloth or leather)* (-ihn -).

shrill. *adj*. yú·⁷neht *it is shrill* (-(a) =
'nehT -).

shrink. *v.i*. yu⁷nú⁷rę *it shrank* (-a'nu⁷r -).

shrivel. *v.i*. wáθnęhs *it shrivels* (-aθnę -);
wačri⁷rarù·ręh *it shrivels* (-ačri⁷ra =
rurę -).

shroud. *n.s*. uhkwáčreh *shroud* (-hkwa =
čr -).

shrub. *n*. ukwì·reh *shrub* (-kwir -).

shuck. *n*. urí⁷reh *shuck* (-ri⁷r -); uhtyúhkweh *shuck* (-htyuhkw -).

shudder. *v.i*. ruθrárha⁷ *he shudders*
(-θrar -).

shutters. *n*. yehse⁷yuθnahnę́hkhwa⁷ *shutters* (-hse⁷yuθnahnęhkw -).

shy. *adj*. ručheyárhę· *he is shy* (-čhe =
yarhę -); rútkuθt *he is shy* (-tkuθt -).

sick. *adj*. runę́hwaks *he is sick* (-nęh =
wak(T) -).

---

sick by witchcraft, make. *v.t.* wa'na'-nerhuhčrà·wę' *one made someone else sick by witchcraft* (-rhuhčrawę-).

sickle. *n.* yeheryá'ktha' *sickle* (-he=rya'kT-); yenęhakwa'náhkhwa' *sickle* (-nęhakwa'nahkw-).

sickly. *adj.* runęhwákskhę· *he is sickly* (-nęhwakskhę-).

sickness. *n.* unęhwákčreh *sickness* (-nęh=wakčr-).

side. *n.* kę'ná'kę *side* (#kę'na'kę).

sidelong. *adv.* ukwthá·'nye' *sidelong* (-aktha'nye'-).

sieve. *n.* unę́'reh *sieve* (-nę'r-); yakękuhnáhkhwa' *sieve* (-ę̊kuhnahkw-).

sift. *v.t.* ka'rhè·wahs *I sift it* (-a'rhew-); rękúhtha' *he sifts it* (-ę̊kuhT-).

sifter. *n.* kękúhstha' *sifter* (-ę̊kuhsT-).

sigh. *v.i.* ra'nęryęhs'ú'y *he sighs* (-a='nęri-.#ú'y).

sight. *n.* rakę́hstha' *his sight* (-kęhsT-).

sight, be out of. *v.i.* wa'ekahnę́'naku' *one is out of sight* (-kahnę'naku-).

sign. *n.* yu'nyerętihnáhkę *sign* (-a'nye=rętihnahkw-); yu'nehu'náhkę *sign* (-a'nehu'nahkw-).

sign. *v.t.* račhę̀·nar *he signs it* (-a=čhęnar-).

signature. *n.* ha' kahsę̀·nar *signature* (-hsęnar-).

signify. *v.i.* ęhrę́hte·θ *he will signify* (-ihteθ-).

silk. *n.* ukęhúhčreh *silk* (-kęhuhčr-).

silver. *n.* kahwihstanù·rę' *silver* (-hwih=stanurę-); kahwihstanù·rę' uhwaryá·kę' *silver* (-hwihstanurę- -ahwarya=kę-).

silverplate. *n.* yeyerà·węhs *silverplate* (-yeraw-).

simmer. *v.t.* raθnę́htha' *he simmers it* (-aθnęhT-).

simply. *adv.* kwè·ni' *simply* (kwè·ni').

sin. *n.* kakurihwater'ę́hčrawęh *their sins* (-rihwater'ęhčrawę-); yurihwater'ak-čra'nyerę́hnę *original sin* (-rihwater='akčra'nyeręhT-).

sin. *v.i.* rurihwatér'ahs *he sins* (-rihwa=ter'(ak)-).

since. *conj.* sé'či *since* (sé'či); wí'er *since* (wí'er); karú'kye *since* (karú'-kye).

sinew. *n.* unęhyá·θeh *sinew* (-nęhyaθ-).

sing. *v.i.* wa'thra'ríhwahkw *he sang* (-ne-.-a'rihwahkw-); ra'nwę'è·ręh *he sings* (-a'nwę'erę-); *v.t.* wa'nyę'na'-rihwáhkę'θ *one sang about another* (-ne-.-a'rihwahkw-{dative I}).

singe. *v.t.* rahęčí'naws *he singes it* (-hę=či'naw-).

single. *adj.* rukyerhúhskę *he is single* (-kerhuhsku-); wahréhwaya'θ *he was single* (-ehwaya'θ-).

sink. *v.i.* yuhnę́·wyę· *it is sunken* (-hnę=wyę-); wekahnęwyę́hstha' *it sinks* (-yah-.-hnęwyęhsT-); wa'katérhu' *it sunk* (-terhu-); *v.t.* runęwę́·thuhs *it sinks him* (-nęwęthu-).

sip. *v.i.* raθkwarúhahs *he sips* (-aθkwa=ruha-).

sister-in-law. *n.* akyá·ryeh *my sister's-in-law* (-aryeh); akara'áh *my sister-in-law* (-ara'áh); akaweryuháh *my sister-in-law* (-aweryuháh); u'nyúhčreh *sister-in-law* (-a'nyuhčr-).

sister. *n.* u'nęnúrcreh *sister* (-a'nęnurčr-); ákči' *my older sister* (-hči'); khehsę́·te *my younger sister* (-hsęte); khé'kęh *my younger sister* (-'kęh).

sisterhood. *n.* uhčí'čreh *sisterhood* (-hči'čr-); u'nęnúrcreh *sisterhood* (-a='nęnurčr-).

sit bent forward. *v.i.* ráhswayę' *he sits bent low forward* (-hswayę(T)-).

sit up. *v.i.* kahstra'níhrę *it is sitting up* (-hstra'nihr-).

situated. *adj.* kę'rę́'nahk *it is situated* (-i'rę'T-).

six. *adj./n.* úhya'k *six* (-(i)hya'k-).

sixteen. *adj./n.* úhya⁷k θkáha⁷r *sixteen* (-(i)hya⁷k - -či -. -(i)har -).

sixty. *adj./n.* úhya⁷k tiwáhθhę· *sixty* (-(i)hya⁷k - ti -. -ahθhę -).

size. *n.* tì·wa⁷θ *it is of a size* (-a⁷θ -).

skein. *n.* uθnę⁷kweh *skein* (-aθnę⁷kw -).

skeleton. *n.* uhskę́⁷reh *skeleton* (-hs = kę⁷r -); učkę́⁷reh *skeleton* (-ačkę⁷r -).

skepticism. *n.* utù·węht *skepticism* (-tu = węhT -).

skill. *n.* uwyę̀·neh *skill* (-wy(ęn) -).

skillful. *adj.* ruręhá⁷ę *he is skillful* (-rę = ha⁷ -); ra⁷newyę́hę *he is skillful* (-a = 'newyęhw -).

skim. *v.t.* rúhθręhs *he skims it* (-uh = θ(e)r -).

skin. *n.* utéhweh *skin* (-tehw -); urí⁷reh *skin* (-ri⁷r -); uθnáhreh *human skin* (-θnahr -); uhčúhkweh *raw skin* (-hčuhkw -).

skin lesion. *n.* uhsé⁷weh *skin lesion* (-hse⁷w -).

skip. *v.t.* nehra⁷níhar *he skips it* (-ne -. -a'nihar -).

skirt. *n.* u⁷khà·reh *skirt* (-i⁷khar -).

skittish. *adj.* rutéhwaręhs *he is skittish* (-tehwarę -).

skunk. *n.* nér⁷ę *skunk* (nér⁷ę).

skunk cabbage. *n.* čirá·kare·θ *skunk cabbage* (čirá·kare·θ).

sky. *n.* urę́hyeh *sky* (-ręhy -).

slabber. *v.i.* rúθkręy *he slabbers* (-θkręy -).

slack. *adj.* tyawú·krę· *it is slack* (ti -. -ukr -).

slander. *v.t.* nehrahsęwiré·tha⁷ *he slanders it* (-ne -. -hsęwireT -).

slap. *v.t.* rat⁷ehnakwę́hnar *he slaps it* (-at⁷ehnakwęhnar -); natkę́hsakę⁷č *one slaps another's face* (-kęhsakę⁷T -).

slaughter. *v.t.* rarę́⁷kę⁷č *he slaughters it* (-rę⁷kę⁷r -); ęhrarę⁷ké⁷rhuk *he will slaughter* (-rę⁷kę⁷rhu -); wa⁷kayę⁷na⁷·ta⁷wę́·thu⁷ *they slaughtered them* (-ta⁷węthu -).

slave. *n.* kačhè·nę⁷ *slave* (-čhenę -); utáhskweh *slave* (-tahskw -).

slay. *v.t.* načwení⁷ehs *one slays another* (-hsweni⁷e(k) -).

sleep. *n.* uθrę́hneh *sleep* (-θręhn -).

sleep. *v.i.* ęwakí·t⁷uh *I will go to sleep* (-(i)t⁷uh -); rat⁷uhná·tih *he puts it to sleep* (-(i)t⁷uhT -{dative II}); ęčì·natę⁷ *it slept with its spouse* (-ačinatę -).

sleepless. *adj.* ruθręhnú·kę⁷ *he is sleepless* (-θręhnukę⁷).

sleepy. *adj.* ruθrę́hnara⁷θ *he is sleepy* (-θręhnara⁷ -).

sleet. *n.* yuwisę́·⁷nyęhs *sleet* (-wisę'ni -).

sleeve. *n.* unę́čheh *sleeve* (-nęčh -).

sleeveless. *adj.* unęčhú·kę⁷ *sleeveless* (-nęčhukę⁷).

sleigh. *n.* newathwačí⁷θręhs *sleigh* (-ne -. -athwači⁷θ(e)r -).

slender. *adj.* wáhsthę *it is slender* (-ah = sthu -); rahsnerę̀·weh *he is slender* (-hsneręwe -).

slice. *n.* úhkareh *slice* (-(a)hkar -).

slices, cut. *v.i.* rahkarętíhtha⁷ *he cuts slices* (-(a)hkarętihT -).

slide. *v.i.* nehratharu⁷činé·tha⁷ *he slides* (-ne -. -atharu⁷činet -).

slight. *adj.* ra⁷nę̀·rih *he is slight (small in stature)* (-a'nęr -).

Tuscarora Pronunciation Key:
/a/ law; /e/ hat; /i/ pizza; /u/ tune; /ę/ hint; /č/ cheese; /h/ hoe; /m/ mother; /s/ same; /t/ do (before a vowel y, or w), too (elsewhere); /k/ gale (before a vowel y or w), kale (elsewhere); /n/ inhale (before a consonant or word-final), note (elsewhere), /r/ hiss (before a consonant or word-final), run (trilled as in Italian, elsewhere); /w/ cuff (before a consonant other than y or word-final), way (elsewhere); /y/ fish (before a consonant or word-final), you (elsewhere), /θ/ thing; /⁷/ (the sound between the vowels in unh-unh); /·/ long vowel, /´/ high pitch; /`/ low pitch.

slime. *n*. uhú⁊kreh *slime* (-hu⁊kr-); u-tkę́hθreh *slime* (-atkęhθr-).

slip. *v.i*. nehruháhskwahs *he slips* (-ne-.-hahskw-).

slipper. *n*. yę⁊nahsawi⁊náhkhwa⁊ *slipper* (-a'nahsawi⁊nahkw-).

slippery. *adj*. neyuthahskwáhnę⁊ *it is slippery* (-ne-.-athahskwahnę-).

sliver. *n*. uháhsteh *sliver* (-hahst-).

slope. *n*. yunę⁊nakyéhę *slope of a mountain* (-nę'na⁊kehę).

sloped. *adj*. wakarę́⁊re⁊ *it is a slope* (-(a)karę⁊r-).

slovenly. *adj*. ruyęhákre⁊ *he is slovenly* (-yęhakre-).

slow. *adj*. ruhshà·yę *he is slow* (-hshay-); rahtyakà·yęh *he is slow* (-htyakayę-); ruyatkà·yę *he is slow* (-yatkay-).

slow. *v.t*. rahshayá⁊tha⁊ *he slows it* (-hshaya⁊T-).

slowly. *adv*. ahskę̀·nę⁊ *slowly* (-hskę= nę⁊-); ahskę̀·nę⁊ kę́hči *slowly* (-hskę= nę⁊- kę́hči).

slug. *n*. čihskęhrè·weh *slug* (čihskęhrè·weh).

slush. *n*. yunyataná·wę· *slush* (-nyata= nawę-).

small. *adj*. áhči⁊ *small* (áhči⁊); awęháh *small* (awęháh); wáhsthę *it is small* (-ahsthu-).

smallest. *adj*. wehráhsthę *he is the smallest* (-yah-.-ahsthu-).

smallpox. *n*. uhsé⁊weh *smallpox* (-hse⁊= w-).

smart. *adj*. ručáhniht *he is smart* (-čahnihT-); ruθte⁊nyà·rę⁊ *he is smart* (-θte⁊nyarę-); ruθnyà·rę⁊ *he is smart* (-θnyarę-).

smartness. *n*. učahníhčreh *smartness* (-čahnihčr-).

smartweed. *n*. rukyé·kę⁊ *smartweed* (rukyé·kę⁊), ka⁊ęhračì·wakę *smartweed* (-⁊ęhračiwak-).

smear. *v.t*. wa⁊kayakú·ka⁊w *they smeared it* (-ukaw-); rà·węhs *he smears it* (-wę-).

smell. *n*. uhsę̀·reh *smell* (-hsęri-).

smell. *v.i*. raręθhwáhtha⁊ *he smells* (-rę= θhwahT-); *v.t*. ękrę́θhu⁊ *I smelled it* (-rę́θhu-); ękrę́θhu⁊ *I smelled it* (-a= θhu-);

smell, make. *v.t*. ra⁊ręθhwáhtha⁊ *he makes it smell* (-a⁊ręθhwahT-).

smell of death. *v.i*. yehskęná·kraθ *one smells of death* (-hskęnakraθ-).

smile. *v.i*. ru⁊nyęhskwé⁊nę *he smiles* (-a'nyęhskwe⁊T-).

smoke. *v.i*. yu⁊nyę⁊kwa⁊níhrę *it smokes (e.g., a gun)* (-a'nyę⁊kwa⁊nihr-); sčárhuhs *you smoke tobacco* (-čarhu-).

smoky. *adj*. yú·kyęr *it is smoky* (-kyęr-).

smolder. *v.i*. yu⁊nę⁊kwé·kę *it smolders* (-a'nę⁊kʷek-).

smooth. *adj*. yučhęwá·tye⁊ *it is smooth* (-ačhęwati-); yuθahrú⁊nę *it is smooth* (-θahru⁊T-).

smooth. *v.t*. rahsęwá·tih *he smoothes it* (-hsęwati-); račanę́·tih *he smoothes it* (-čanęti-).

smoothness. *n*. učá·teh *smoothness* (-čaN-).

smother. *v.t*. rę́⁊kweks *he smothers it* (-ę⁊kʷek-).

smutty. *adj*. učkrę⁊néhči *smutty* (-čkre⁊n-.#hči).

snail. *n*. čihskęhrè·weh *snail* (čihskęhrè·weh); uθrí⁊ra⁊ *snail* (-θri⁊r-).

snake. *n*. rúhskwa⁊neh *snake* (-hskʷa'n-); rutkwe⁊núhę⁊ *copperhead snake* (rutkwe⁊núhę⁊); rú⁊ta⁊w *male milk snake* (rú⁊ta⁊w); ru⁊túhsarę *milk snake* (ru⁊túhsarę).

snatch. *v.t*. rahθhará·kwahs *he snatches it* (-ahθharaku-).

sneeze. *v.i*. hehčę́ rawę́·ti· *he sneezes* (hehčę́ -ę̊ti-).

sniff. *v.i*. wahra⁊tyęhkra⁊nihę́·thu⁊ *he*

sniffed (-ˀtyęhkraˀnihęthu -); ŗętyę-
kwéhnęh *he sniffs* (-ętyękwęhnę -).
snipe. *n.* tawístawis *snipe* (tawístawis).
snivel. *v.i.* nehraˀtyéhkrakar ‹apart-he-
snot-makes a noise› *he snivels* (-ne -.
-ˀtyęhkrakar -).
snore. *v.i.* ruθŗęhnakaré·tih *he snores*
(-θŗęhnakareti -); raˀnyę́·kwakar *he
snores* (-a'nyękʷakar -).
snort. *v.i.* raŗę́ˀnęws *he snorts* (-arę́ˀ =
nęw -).
snow. *n.* uwí·θreh *snow* (-wiθ(e)r -).
snow, start to. *v.i.* waˀká·tkwęˀ *it started
snowing* (-tkwęˀ -).
snowflake. *n.* θkawí·θra·t *snowflake*
(-či -. -wiθraT -).
snowsnake. *n.* utrahwę́hteˀ *snowsnake*
(-trahwęhte -).
snuff out a candle. *v.i.* račiˀrakwáhthaˀ
he snuffs out a candle (-čiˀrakʷahT -).
so. *adv.* tyuh *so* (tyuh).
so that. *part.* her *so that* (her).
soak. *v.t.* rataˀtawę́hthaˀ *he soaks it*
(-taˀtawęhT -).
soaked. *adj.* kataˀtà·węˀθ *it is soaked*
(-taˀtawęˀ -).
soap. *n.* utuháˀčreh *soap* (-tuhaˀčr -);
utuháˀstaˀ *soap* (-tuhaˀst -).
soap. *v.t.* ratuharéhčrawęhs *he soaps it*
(-tuharehčrawę -).
sob. *v.i.* newaθnárčrakar *it sobs* (-ne -.
-aθnarčrakar -).
sod. *n.* uhníˀruˀ *sod* (-hniˀru -); uter-
ˀę́hθeh *sod* (-terˀęhθ -).
soft. *adj.* yuθahrúˀnę *it is soft* (-θah =
ruˀT -); ká·nę· *it is soft* (-(a)nę -);
yuhrúˀnę *it is soft to the touch*

(-hruˀT -).
soften. *v.t.* rahruˀnę́hsthaˀ *he softens it*
(-hruˀnęhsT -); ranę́ˀthaˀ *he softens it*
(-(a)nęˀT -); rahsuˀranę́hthaˀ *he softens it* (-hsuˀranęhT -).
softly. *adv.* yuhruˀnęhá·ˀnyeˀ *softly*
(-hruˀnęha'nyeˀ -).
soggy. *adj.* yukyéˀčeh *soggy* (-keˀč -).
soil. *n.* à·wiˀr *soil* (-ir -); awę́hreh *soil*
(-ę°hr -).
soil. *v.t.* rayerà·węhs *he soils it* (-ye =
raw -); raˀnęhrarawę̀·rih *he soils it*
(-a'nęhrarawęri -).
soiled. *adj.* awę́·te kęrá·ˀneˀ *soiled*
(awę́·te -ira'ne -).
solder. *v.t.* ranawaˀčtárhuhs *he solders it*
(-nawaˀčtarhu -).
soldier. *n.* raθútahs *he is a soldier* (-θu =
tahs).
sole. *n.* uyáˀθeh *sole of foot* (-yaˀθ -);
uyáhneh *sole of foot* (-yahn -).
solely. *adv.* učˀahná·te·t *solely* (učˀah-
ná·te·t).
solicitous. *adj.* raˀtikęhkyeyáˀthaˀ *he is
solicitous* (-(ę)ˀtikęhkeyaˀT -).
solid. *adj.* yuhtì·rę *it is solid* (-htir -).
solidify. *v.t.* rahtì·rahč *he solidifies it*
(-htirahT -).
solve. *v.t.* wehręˀtikę́rhews *he solves it*
(-yah -. -(ę)ˀtikęhrhaw -).
some. *adj.* steˀ *some* (steˀ); syà·wę *some*
(syà·wę).
some specific. *adj.* steˀ *some specific*
(steˀ).
somebody. *n.* saˀkáhne·ˀ *somebody* (saˀ-
káhne·ˀ).
someday. *adv.* ihskáhkye *someday* (ih-

---

skáhkye).

someone. *n*. káhne·ˀ *someone* (káhne·ˀ); saˀkáhne·ˀ *someone* (saˀkáhne·ˀ).

somersault. *v.i*. ręnęhyéčknęhs *he somersaults* (-ęnęhyečkT-).

something. *n*. sawę́·te *something* (sawę́·te); sawętawę́·te *something* (sawętawę́·te).

sometimes. *adv*. tyúˀrę̨ˀ *sometimes* (tyúˀrę̨ˀ).

somewhere. *adv*. heˀskęhę̀·we *somewhere* (heˀskęhę̀·we).

son. *n*. wakaˀnúˀnę̨ˀ *my son* (-a'nuˀnę̨ˀ); khehsę́·te *son* (-hsęte).

son-in-law. *n*. yaktihę́·θę *my son-in-law* (-hę̨θę); uhę́·θeh *son-in-law* (-hę̨θ-).

song. *n*. uríhweh *song* (-rihw-).

song book. *n*. neyę̨ˀrihwahkwáhthaˀ *song book* (-ne-.-aˀrihwahkwahT-).

sonorous. *adj*. kawętì·yuh *it is sonorous* (-wętiyu-).

soon. *adv*. kyewę̨hę̀·we *soon* (kyewę̨.#ęwe).

soot. *n*. uhtyéhseh *soot* (-htyehs-)

soothsayer. *n*. rurę́·taˀr *soothsayer* (-rę̨·taˀr-).

sorcerer. *n*. rútkę̨ˀ *sorcerer* (-atkę̨-); raˀnékskruh *sorcerer* (-aˀnekskru-).

sore. *n*. utihtwę̀·yeh *sore* (-tihtwęy-).

sorrel. *n*. yuˀęhračì·wakę *sorrel* (-ˀęhra̱čiwak-); kwačì·rah *wood sorrel* (kwačì·rah); kwačirahúˀy *red sorrel* (kwačirahúˀy).

sort. *n*. see: -ęhr-.

sort. *v.t*. rarę́·kwahs *he sorts it* (-ręku-).

soul. *n*. uˀnę́nhehkt *soul* (-a'nęnhehkT-).

sound. *n*. yurá·kar *sound* (-rakar(e)-).

sound. *v.i*. yurá·kar *it sounds* (-rakar(e)-).

soup. *n*. úkhę̨h *soup* (-khę̨-).

sour. *adj*. yučì·wakę *it is sour* (-čiwak-); neyuˀčísneˀ *it is sour* (-ne-.-ˀčisne-).

sourness. *n*. učiwáksteh *sourness* (-čiwakst-).

south. *n*. uhskú·tkye *south* (-hskut-.#ke).

southward. *adv*. uhsku·tˀáh *southward* (-hskut-.#áh).

sovereignty. *n*. uyanéˀčreh *sovereignty* (-yaneˀčr-).

sow. *v.t*. ráhrihč *he sows* (-ahrihr-).

space. *n*. utákwneh *space* (-takwT-).

spade. *n*. uterhyáˀčreh *spade* (-terhyaˀčr-).

spare. *v.t*. raˀnwętéˀthaˀ *he spares it* (-a'nwęteˀT-).

spark. *n*. učíˀreh *spark* (-čiˀr-); učí·sneh *spark* (-či·sn-).

sparkle. *v.i*. kačisnukáˀthaˀ *it sparkles* (-čisnukaˀT-); kahsnukáˀthaˀ *it sparkles* (-hsnukaˀT-).

sparrow hawk. *n*. wathnęhwaˀníhahs *sparrow hawk* (-athnęhwa'niha-).

sparse. *adj*. nú·kˀah *sparse* (nú·kˀah).

spawn. *v.i*. węterà·waks *it spawns·* (-(ę)=terawak-).

speak. *v.i*. kà·weh *it speaks* (-weh-); ruwéhrę *he spoke* (-wehr-); rawętí·tkę̨ˀθ *he speaks* (-wętitkę̨ˀ-); nehrawętí·tkę̨ˀ *he spoke out* (-ne-.-wętitkę̨ˀ-); *v.t*. rawehráˀthaˀ *he speaks (a language); he speaks about it* (-wehraˀT-); raˀnwętayę́ˀthaˀ *he speaks ill of it* (-a'nwętayęˀT-); aθahshewę̀·naraˀ *that you speak to someone* (-wę̨nar-); ęyewérhahθ *one will speak to it* (-wehr-{dative II}).

spear. *n*. uhsé·kwareh *spear* (-hsekʷa̱r-).; úhnyeh *spear* (-hny-).

species. *n*. urˀęhsę́·te *species* (-(i)rˀęhsęte).

specific. *adj*. rayahčę́·tih *he is a specific person* (-yahčęti-).

specify. *v.i*. rarihwatukę́hthaˀ *he specifies* (-rihwatukęhT-).

speck. *n*. uhθę́·ˀneh *a speck* (-ahθęT-).

speckle. *v.t*. račisnuhkwahrà·węh *he speckles it* (-čisnuhkwa̱hrawę-).

spectator. *n*. haˀratkę́ˀθeh *spectator* (-a=

tkę^ʔθe-).

speech. *n.* uwę́·teh *speech* (-węt-); uwehrę́hčreh *speech* (-wehrę̄hčr-).

speed. *v.i.* ru^ʔnyatù·rę *he speeds* (-a'nya= tur-).

spellbind. *v.t.* wa^ʔkayenęhyu^ʔná·ri·k *they spellbound it* (-nęhyu'narik-).

spend. *v.t.* rahnę́^ʔtha^ʔ *he spends it* (-ah= nę^ʔT-).

spend foolishly. *v.i.* ra^ʔna^ʔnyęwáhtha^ʔ *he spends foolishly* (-a^ʔna^ʔnyęwahT-)

spend the night. *v.i.* ęhsęnę́hwe·t *you will spend the night* (-ęnęhweT-); nę^ʔnęnęhwé·či^ʔ *it spent so many nights* (-a'nęnęhweči-).

sperm. *n.* u^ʔnhęhsú·kri^ʔ *sperm* (-^ʔnhęh= sukr-).

spicebush. *n.* newęta^ʔę́·nya^ʔks *spicebush* (newęta^ʔę́·nya^ʔks).

spider. *n.* ruki^ʔyáhskę *spider* (ruki^ʔyáhskę).

spider web. *n.* ruki^ʔyáhskę unę́^ʔreh *spider web* (ruki^ʔyáhskę -nę^ʔr-).

spikenard. *n.* čuhné^ʔre·θ *spikenard* (-či-. -hne^ʔreθ-).

spill. *v.i.* wa^ʔkáhri^ʔ *it spilled (of solids or semisolids)* (-hri-); kači·yę^ʔθ *it spills (of liquids)* (-čiyę^ʔ-); rači·yęws *he spills (a liquid)* (-čiyęhw-); ękahrí^ʔθrę^ʔ *it will spill over* (-hri^ʔθrę-).

spin. *v.i.* rahsirę́·tih *he spins (thread)* (-hsiręti-).

spindle. *n.* kahsirę́·tih *spindle* (-hsiręti-).

spine. *n.* uhsnyę́hθreh *spine* (-hsnyęh= θr-); awę́^ʔweh yuhsnahrę́·wa·t *spine* (-ę^ʔw- -hsnahręw-).

spiral. *adj.* neyęthwa^ʔnaθéhęh *it is spiral* (-ne-. -athwa̲^ʔnaθehę-).

spiral. *n.* u^ʔę̀·wareh *spiral* (-^ʔęwa̲r-).

spirit, evil. *n.* ka^ʔtikęhrá·ksę· *evil spirit* (-(ę)^ʔtikęhraks-); utkęhčrá·ksę· *evil spirit from whom all witches get their power* (-atkęhčraks-).

spirit, good. *n.* ka^ʔtikęhrákwahst *good spirit* (-(ę)^ʔtikęhrakwahsT-).

spiritual. *adj.* u^ʔnęnhehktkyéha·^ʔ *spiritual* (-a'nęnhehkT-.#keha·^ʔ); u^ʔtikęhrę́^ʔkyéha·^ʔ *spiritual* (-(ę)^ʔtikęhr-.#ke= ha·^ʔ).

spit. *n.* utú^ʔkreh *spit* (-tu^ʔkr-).

spit. *v.i.* wa^ʔktu^ʔkrę́·^ʔni^ʔ *I spit* (-tu^ʔ= krę'ni-).

spite. *n.* úhsęht *spite* (-ahsęhT-).

spittle. *n.* úθkreh *spittle* (-θkr-).

spittoon. *n.* yeθkrarahkwáhtha^ʔ *spittoon* (-θkra̲rahkwahT-).

splatter. *v.i.* kahrí^ʔθręh *it splatters* (-hri^ʔθrę-); newa^ʔnukwahnáhnęh *it splatters* (-ne-. -a'nuk^wahnahnę-).

spleen. *n.* urá^ʔθreh *spleen* (-ra^ʔθr-).

splice. *v.t.* nehrahθę́^ʔner *he splices it* (-ne-. -(a)hθę^ʔn(e)r-).

splint. *n.* uyę́^ʔneh *splint* (-yę^ʔn-).

splint. *v.t.* wa^ʔeyęwà·rę^ʔ *one splinted it* (-yęwarę-); rahahstanę^ʔnáktha^ʔ *he splints it* (-hahsta̲nę'nakT-); nęhrahθę́^ʔrę^ʔ *he will splint it* (-ne-. -hθę= 'n(e)r-).

split. *adj.* neyu^ʔnú·rę· *it is split* (-ne-. -a'nurę-).

split. *v.t.* nehrù·ręhs *he splits it* (-ne-. -ⁿurę-).

spoil. *v.t.* rahča^ʔnáhkhwa^ʔ *he spoils it* (-ahča^ʔnahkw-); rukrę́^ʔtha^ʔ *he spoils*

Tuscarora Pronunciation Key:
/a/ la̲w; /e/ ha̲t; /i/ pi̲zza; /u/ tu̲ne; /ę/ hi̲nt; /č/ cheese; /h/ ho̲e; /m/ mo̲ther; /s/ sa̲me; /t/ do̲ (before a vowel y, or w), to̲o (elsewhere); /k/ ga̲le (before a vowel y or w), ka̲le (elsewhere); /n/ inha̲le (before a consonant or word-final), no̲te (elsewhere), /r/ hi̲ss (before a consonant or word- final), ru̲n (trilled as in Italian, elsewhere); /w/ cu̲ff (before a consonant other than y or word-final), wa̲y (elsewhere); /y/ fi̲sh (before a consonant or word-final), yo̲u (elsewhere), /θ/ thi̲ng; /ʔ/ (the sound between the vowels in unh̲-unh̲); /·/ long vowel, /´/ high pitch; /`/ low pitch.

it (-ukrę̂ʔT-).

spoon. *n.* uhtkwì·reh *spoon* (-htkwir-).

spot. *n.* učísnuhkweh *spot* (-čisnuhkw-).

spot. *v.t.* račisnuhkwahrà·węh *he spots it* (-čisnuhkwahrawę-).

spotted. *adj.* see: -kwęʔrar-.

spouse. *n.* katyá·kę *spouse* (-tyak-); utáhkweh *spouse* (-tahkw-).

sprain. *v.t.* ruʔníhahs *he sprains it* (-ʔni=ha-).

spread out. *v.i.* kayeríhahs *it is spread out* (-yeriha-); ręθkà·ręhs *he spreads it out* (-iθkar-); see: -hiθ-, -ukʷ-.

spread the news. *v.i.* waʔthraʔrihwaré·tyaʔt *he spread the news* (-ne-.-aʔrih=waretyaʔT-).

sprightly. *adj.* wà·rahst *it is sprightly* (-arahsT-).

spring. *n.* učaʔtuhstaʔkyéha·ʔ *spring (of water)* (-čaʔtuhst-.#keha·ʔ).

springtime. *n.* nęwúhstahkw *springtime* (-ne-.-uhstahkw-).

sprinkle. *v.t.* rahnekúhθraws *he sprinkles it* (-hnekuhθrahw-); raʔwahθráhrihč *he sprinkles it* (-ʔwahθrahrihr-).

sprout. *n.* uhtwę́heh *sprout* (-htwęh-); utráhneh *sprout* (-trahn-); kahsętá·thuhs *sprout* (-hsętathu-).

sprout. *v.i.* yuhsętá·thę *it sprouts (a branch)* (-hsętathu-); rahtyú·thaʔ *he is sprouting it (grain, corn, etc.)* (-htyuT-).

sprout leaves. *v.i.* yučiʔtkwaryáʔkę *it is sprouting leaves* (-čiʔtkwaryaʔk-).

spruce. *n.* unęhkwíhskriʔ *spruce* (-nęh=kwihskri-); hahtehę̀·we *Norway spruce* (hahte.#ęwe).

spry. *adj.* ruhkarí·yu· *he is spry* (-(a)h=kariyu-).

spur. *n.* utihtyúhčreh *spur of bird's leg* (-tihtyuhčr-).

sputter. *v.i.* yutkuriʔnaríhęʔθ *it sputters* (-tkuriʔnarihęʔ-).

squall. *n.* kahawrúhsthaʔ *squall* (-haw=

ruhsT-).

squander. *v.i.* raʔnyeθáʔthaʔ *he squanders* (-aʹnyeθaʔT-).

square. *adj.* neyuhkaręhnáhnę· *it is square* (-ne-.-(a)hkaręhnahnę-).

square. *n.* uhskweyáhčreh *square* (-hs=kweyahčr-).

squash. *n.* učéʔweh *squash* (-čheʔw-); yuyéhnuʔ *mature squash* (-yehnu-); utáʔθruh *young squash* (-taʔθru-).

squat. *v.i.* rutaʔyaʔníhrę *he is squatting* (-taʔyaʔnihr-).

squeamish. *adj.* ruhrę́hčihst *he is squeamish* (-hręhčihsT-).

squeeze. *v.t.* ęyakę́hskwik *one will squeeze it* (-ę̊hskwi(k)-); nęyečirwę́hstęʔ *one will squeeze it out* (ti-.-čirwęhsthę-).

squint. *v.i.* ratkahčiʔraʔníhahs *he squints* (-atkahčiʔraʔniha-).

squirm. *v.i.* račkwaʔnetyę́·kwahs *he squirms* (-ačkʷaʔnetyęku-).

squirrel. *n.* θá·st *black squirrel* (θá·st); θá·st tiwaʔkę́hrayęʔ *gray squirrel* (θá·st ti-.-aʔkęhrayę(T)-); čuhsuʔ-kwaká·nę·t *red squirrel* (-či-.-hsuʔ=kwakanęt-).

squirt. *v.t.* rakyeʔnuθérhuhs *he squirts it* (-keʔnuθerhu-).

stab. *v.t.* waʔkčú·ʔri·θ *I stabbed it* (-čuʔ=riθ-).

stack. *n.* utaʔčúhkweh *stack* (-(ta)ʔ=čuhkw-).

stack. *v.t.* rataʔčuhkwę́·tih *he stacks it* (-(ta)ʔčuhkwęti-).

stage. *n.* utákwneh *stage* (-takwĨ`-); utíʔ-θreh *stage* (-tiʔθ(e)r-).

stagger. *v.i.* ruręhkuhę́hteh *he staggers* (-ręhkuhęhte-); ruʔręʔkúhę *he staggers* (-aʔręʔkuhw-).

stained. *adj.* yúhθuhθ *it is stained* (-ah=θuh-).

staircase. *n.* yerathahsnáhkhwaʔ *staircase* (-rathahsnahkw-).

stairs. *n.* stá·kwiˀ è·nęˀt *stairs* (stá·kwiˀ -enęˀT-).

stairway. *n.* yuhahakyérhę *stairway* (-(a)= hahakerhu-); stá·kwiˀ è·nęˀt *stairway* (stá·kwiˀ -enęˀT-).

stake. *n.* učę̀·weh *stake (pole)* (-čęw-); neyeˀęyuhraráktháˀ *stake (pole)* (-ne-. -ˀęyuhrarakT-); yeˀęyuhraráktháˀ *stake (in a game of chance)* (-ˀęyuh= rarakT-).

stalk. *n.* utù·reh *stalk* (-tur-).

stammer. *v.i.* raˀnwakanyę́·kwahs *he stammers* (-a'nwakanyęku-).

stamp. *v.i.* nehrarahstáhkhwaˀ *he stamps (his feet)* (-ne-.-arahstahkw-).

stand. *v.i.* ì·wa·t *it stands* (-aT-); yuˀrę= waˀníhrę *it stands on end* (-aˀrę= waˀnihr-); wahraˀnáˀnir *he stood up* (-aˀnih(r)-); see: -hT-, -aˀnih(r)-, -ut.

star. *n.* uˀnihsę̀·reh *star* (-ˀnihsęr-); ne- kačisnahkwáˀnęˀ *falling star* (-ne-. -čisnahkwa'nę-).

starch. *n.* stá·č *starch* (-hstač-).

stare. *v.i.* nehranęˀyarˀúˀy *he stares* (-ne-.-nęˀyar-.#úˀy); *v.t.* nehsknę́ˀyar *you are staring at me* (-ne-.-nęˀyar-).

starlit. *adj.* yukyéhę *it is starlit* (-kehu-).

startling. *adj.* yutehwáhkwaht *startling* (-tehwahkwahT-).

starvation. *n.* uˀnęhkaryáˀkę *starvation* (-a'nęhkaryaˀk-).

starve. *v.i.* kayęˀnęhká·ryaˀks *they starve* (-a'nęhkaryaˀk-); raˀnikęhká·ryahs *he starves* (-a'nikęhkari-); naˀnęhretih- sná·tih *one starves another* (-ę°hre= tihsn-{dative III}).

state. *v.i.* nyewętí·tkęˀ *one stated* (-t-. -wętitkęˀ-).

stationary. *n.* uhyatęhstaˀkę́haˀnęˀ *stationary* (-hyatęhst-.#kęhaˀnęˀ).

stationer. *n.* rathyatęhstatęhnì·nęh *stationer* (-athyatęhstatęhninę-).

statue. *n.* haˀ kakyerhę́·tih *puppet* (-ker= hęti-).

stature. *n.* úhstreh *stature* (-(i)hstr-); urę̀·weh *stature* (-ręw-).

statute. *n.* uyanrę́hsteh *statute* (-ya= nręhst-).

stay all day. *v.i.* ręˀniré·thaˀ *he stays all day* (-ę°nireT-).

stay overnight. *v.i.* nehrarhę́hthaˀ *he stays overnight* (-ne-.-rhęhT-); ręnęh- wé·čęhs *he stays overnight* (-ęnęh= weči-).

steal. *v.i.* ranę́hskwahs *he steals* (-nęh= sku-).

stealth. *n.* uˀnęnęhskwáhčrakęw *stealth* (-a'nęnęhskwahčrakęw); uˀnęnę́h- skwaht *stealth* (-a'nęnęhskwahT-).

steam. *n.* uhsęryúhkweh *steam* (-hsę= ryuhkw-).

steel. *n.* yuwenęˀnahtì·rę *steel* (-wenę= 'nahtir-).

steel. *v.t.* rawenęˀnahtì·raˀč *he steels it* (-wenę'nahtiraˀT-).

steep. *adj.* yuhθęˀkará·ˀneht *it is steep* (-hθęˀkara'nehT-); yuhθęˀkare·θˀúˀy *it is steep* (-hθęˀkareθ-.#úˀy).

steep. *v.t.* aryakyekę́·tiˀ *that one steep it* (-ekęti-).

steeple. *n.* utá·kareh *steeple* (-(ę)takar-).

steer. *v.i.* runyarutárhę *he steered (a vessel)* (-nyarutarhu-).

Tuscarora Pronunciation Key:

/a/ l<u>a</u>w; /e/ h<u>a</u>t; /i/ p<u>i</u>zza; /u/ t<u>u</u>ne; /ę/ h<u>i</u>nt; /č/ <u>ch</u>eese; /h/ <u>h</u>oe; /m/ <u>m</u>other; /s/ <u>s</u>ame; /t/ <u>d</u>o (before a vowel y, or w), <u>t</u>oo (elsewhere); /k/ ga<u>l</u>e (before a vowel y or w), <u>k</u>ale (elsewhere); /n/ i<u>nh</u>ale (before a consonant or word-final), <u>n</u>ote (elsewhere), /r/ hi<u>ss</u> (before a consonant or word- final), <u>r</u>un (trilled as in Italian, elsewhere); /w/ cu<u>ff</u> (before a consonant other than y or word-final), <u>w</u>ay (elsewhere); /y/ fi<u>sh</u> (before a consonant or word-final), <u>y</u>ou (elsewhere), /θ/ <u>th</u>ing; /ˀ/ (the sound between the vowels in unh-unh); /·/ long vowel, /´/ high pitch; /`/ low pitch.

stem. *n.* uʔníhsneh *stem* (-ʔnihsn-).

stench. *n.* uhsę̇·reh *stench* (-hsęri-).

step. *n.* úʔθheh *step* (-(i)ʔθh-).

step. *v.i.* yéʔθhahk *one had stepped* (-eʔθ-); waʔtkaʔníhyaʔkt *I stepped* (-ne-. -aʹnihyaʔkT-); rętiʔθháhkhwaʔ *he steps* (-(ę)tiʔθhahkw-); *v.t.* waʔ-kturì·yęʔ *I stepped on it* (-turiyę-).

step-brother. *n.* akhryahčiʔáh *my older step-brother* (-hryahčiʔ.#áh).

step-sister. *n.* akčiʔáh *my older step-sister* (-hčiʔ.#áh).

steps, take. *v.i.* θéʔθę *take steps!* (-eʔθ- {dative III}).

sterile. *adj.* ruʔnwirę́čnę *he is sterile* (-aʹnwiręčT-).

stew. *n.* yekahnę́hteʔ *stew* (-kahnęhte-).

stew. *v.t.* ękayekáhnę·ʔ *they will stew it* (-kahnę-).

stick. *n.* utáhsneh *stick* (-(ę)tahsn-).

stick. *v.i.* yuθrę̇·waraʔθ *it sticks* (-θrę=waraʔ-); yurhaʔnęʔnúhskę· *it sticks* (-rhaʔęʔnuhsk-); wá·ʔneʔ *it sticks out* (-(a)ʹne-); *v.t.* waʔakučú·ʔri·θ *one was stuck by it* (-čuʔriθ-).

stiff. *adj.* tyurhenáthę· *it is stiff* (-rhe=nathę-).

stiffen. *v.t.* rarhenatháʔthaʔ *he stiffens it* (-rhenathaʔT-).

still. *adv.* čwé·ʔn *still* (čwé·ʔn); sę́·r à·rę *still* (sę́·r à·rę).

still. *adj.* ęθwahrę́hwaʔ *you will be perfectly still* (-hręhw-).

sting. *n.* uʔčì·reh *sting* (-ʔčir-).

sting. *v.i.* raʔčiráʔnihč *he stings* (-ʔči=raʔnihr-); *v.t.* ruʔčirú·kwahs *it stings him* (-ʔčirukʷ-); wekakuʔčiraʔnírhę· *it stung them* (-yah-.-ʔčiraʔnihrhę-).

stingy. *adj.* ruyahkwéʔręks *he is stingy* (-yahkweʔ ręk-).

stink. *n.* uhskwáʔneh *stink* (-hskwaʔn-).

stink. *v.i.* katéhskrahs *it stinks* (-tehskr-).

stipulate. *v.i.* raʔrihwíhsʔahs *he stipulates* (-aʔrihwihsʔa-).

stir. *v.t.* nekawę̇·rih *I stir it* (-awęri-); wcθnù·riʔ *you two stirred it* (-ⁿuri-); nehruhkwanę́·ʔnę *he stirs it* (-ne-.-uh=kwanęT-).

stirrup. *n.* yęʔnahsawiʔnáhkhwaʔ aweʔ-wihsę́ʔkye *stirrup* (-aʔnahsawiʔnahkw--eʔwihsę́ʔke).

stitch. *n.* uʔtíksteh *stitch* (-ʔtikʷst-).

stocking. *n.* wahsę́·ʔneh *stocking* (-ah=sęT-).

stole. *n.* yęʔnihnyáhsthaʔ *stole* (-aʹnih=nyahsT-).

stomach. *n.* útkweh *stomach* (-tkw-); uhwę́ʔneh *distended stomach* (-hwęʔ=n-); utkúhkweh *fat stomach* (-tkuh=kw-); katkwanę́hwaks *upset stomach* (-tkwa̲nęhwak(T)-).

stomachache, have a. *v.i.* ruʔnarę́ʔneʔ *he has a stomachache from overeating* (-aʔnaręʔT-).

stone. *n.* uctę́hreh *stone* (-čtęhr-); uh-rę́ʔneh *stone* (-hręʔn-); unę́hsneh ·*stone (of a fruit)* (-nęhsn-).

stone. *v.t.* račtę́hrayęʔkws *he stones it* (-čtęhra̲yęʔkʷ-); rahrę́ʔnayęʔkws *he stones it* (-hręʔna̲yęʔkʷ-).

stoniness. *n.* uctęhráʔkye *stoniness* (-čtęhraʔke).

stony. *adj.* uctęhréhči *stony* (-čtęhr-.#hči).

stool. *n.* uʔθkwéhseh *stool* (-ʔθkwehs-); uthečráhkweh *stool* (-athečrahkw-).

stop. *v.i.* rahčęʔwáhthaʔ *he stops* (-ah=čęʔwahT-); rahrę́wsthaʔ *he stops it* (-hręhwsT-).

stopper. *n.* uhseʔyúhčreh *stopper* (-hseʔ=yu-).

store. *v.t.* waʔnętíhyęhs *it stores it* (-a=ʹnętihyę-); rutú·rę· *he stored it* (-turę-).

storehouse. *n.* yęʔnęnawayęʔnáhkhwaʔ *storehouse* (-aʹnęnawayęʹnahkw-).

storm. *n.* wę́ʔnaksáʔthaʔ *storm* (-ę́ʹnak=saʔT-); katyęʔkwí·theʔ *storm* (-tyęʔ=kwithe-).

storm. *v.i.* katyęˀkwì·nęhs *it storms* (-tyęˀkwiN-); kayę́hkwatač *it storms* (-yęhkwatat-).

stormy. *adj.* węˀná·ksę· *stormy* (-ę='naks-).

story. *n.* utkahryéˀčreh *story (tale)* (-atkahryeˀčr-); ę́khwyaht *story (tale)* (-ękhwyahT-); urihwátkęˀ *medicine story* (-rihwatkę-); yutákwnę·t *story (of a building)* (-takwnęT-).

stove. *n.* stúw *stove* (stúw).

stow. *v.t.* ratù·ręh *he stows it* (-turę-).

straight. *adj.* tyuˀnyeríhę· *straight* (ti-.-a'nyeriha-); wekayè·riˀ *it is straight* (-yah-.-yeri-).

straight, go. *v.i.* thahrayeríhaˀ *he goes straight* (tha-.-yeriha-).

straighten. *v.t.* see: -yeriha-.

strain. *v.t.* ręhkęráhthaˀ *he strains it* (-ęhkęrahT-).

strand. *n.* učá·takwt *strand* (-čatakT-).

strange. *adj.* neyuhskané·kę·t *it is strange* (-ne-.-hskanekęT-); yuyáhčih *it is strange* (-yahč-).

strangle. *v.t.* waˀkęhaˀčí·rwęˀ *I strangled you* (-haˀčirwę-); ęyečí·rwęˀ *one will strangle it* (-čirwę-).

strap. *n.* uˀnhę́hθeh *strap* (-(i)ˀnhęhθ-).

strawberry. *n.* wí·sę·t *strawberry* (wí·sę·t).

streak. *v.t.* rahnęwyętiˀthaˀ *it streaks it* (-hnęwyętiˀT-).

stream. *n.* uhsnę̀·weh *stream* (-hsnęw-); úhtaweh *stream of water* (-htaw-).

street. *n.* yutaˀnakáhręˀ *street* (-ta'na=kahrę(w)-).

strength. *n.* uˀθhaθnę́hčreh *strength*

(-(i)ˀθhaθnęhčr-); uˀθhá·θneh *strength* (-(i)ˀθhaθn-).

strengthen. *v.t.* naktiráhthahθ *strengthen me!* (-htirahT-{dative II}).

stretch. *v.t.* raθráˀnęh *he stretches it* (-θraˀnę-); raréhsthaˀ *he stretches it* (-rehsT-).

stretcher. *n.* yekyerhęhawíhthaˀ *stretcher* (-kerhęhawihT-); yętkęheyęˀnęhawiˀ-náhkhwaˀ *stretcher* (-atkęheyęˀnęha=wiˀnahkw-).

strew. *v.t.* nehraretyáˀthaˀ *he strews it* (-ne-.-aretyaˀT-).

stride. *n.* úˀθheh *stride* (-(i)ˀθh-).

strike. *v.t.* rá·kęˀč *he strikes it* (-kęˀT-); wahrúhsnaˀt *it struck him* (-hsnaˀT-); ráˀ ehs *he strikes it* (-(i)ˀe(k)-); ęh-rakę́hruk *he will strike it* (-kęhruk-); raréˀkęˀč *he strikes it down* (- ręˀ=kęˀr-); rakwęhnárhuhs *he strikes it down flat* (-kwęhnarhu-).

string. *n.* uhsì·reh *string* (-hsir-).

string beads. *v.i.* wáθkwaruh *string of beads* (-aθkwarur-).

strip. *v.i.* waˀ ęˀčuné·tiˀ *one stripped* (-aˀčunęti-); nathwá·θ ręhs *one strips another's clothes off* (-hwaθr-).

striped. *adj.* učiˀnè·wareh *striped* (-čiˀ=newar-).

strive. *v.i.* nehruˀnaˀníhrę *he strives* (-ne-.-a'naˀnihr-); ruˀnahθkyénhę *he strives for it* (-a'nahθkenha-); see: -kenha-.

stroke, have a. *v.i.* waˀnyakutihù·ręˀ *one had a stroke* (-ne-.-tihurę-).

strong. *adj.* waká·θneˀ *it is strong* (-aθn-); khwíhsneˀ *I am strong*

(-(a)hwihsT-); wakye'ᵔθhaθnę́hčrayę'ᵔ
I am strong (-(i)'ᵔθhaθnęhčra̲yę(T)-).
struggle. *v.i.* wahra'ᵔnuryáhnę'ᵔ *he strug-*
gled (-a'nuryahnę-).
strut. *v.i.* ru'ᵔnahkna'ᵔná·'ᵔnye'ᵔ *he struts*
(-a'nahkna'ᵔna'nye'ᵔ-).
stubble. *n.* ha'ᵔ čhę'ᵔ kaheryá'ᵔkę *stubble*
(čhę'ᵔ -herya'ᵔk-); kę'ᵔ čhę'ᵔ kaheryá'ᵔkę
stubble (kę'ᵔ čhę'ᵔ -herya'ᵔk-).
student. *n.* ha'ᵔ ra'ᵔrihętyá·tih *student*
(-a'ᵔrihęti-{dative III}).
studious. *adj.* ru'ᵔrihętyatí'ᵔne'ᵔ *he is stud-*
ious (-a'ᵔrihęti-{dative III}-'ᵔT-).
study. *v.t.* wa'ᵔkayę'ᵔna'ᵔnęnęnhyà·rę'ᵔ
they studied one another (-ęnęnhyar-);
nehranę́'ᵔyar *he studies it* (-ne-.-nę'ᵔ=
yar-).
stuff. *n.* awehčrú·kri'ᵔ *stuff* (-ehčrukr-).
stuff. *v.t.* ra'ᵔwahrá·t'ᵔahs *he stuffs it*
(e.g., a turkey) (-'ᵔwahrat'ᵔa-).
stumble. *v.i.* rúht'ᵔehs *he stumbles* (-aht=
'ᵔe(k)-).
stumbling block. *n.* yakuht'ᵔéhstha'ᵔ *stum-*
bling block (-aht'ᵔehsT-).
stump. *n.* uhskwéhteh *tree stump* (-hs=
kweht-).
stumped. *adj.* wa'ᵔu'ᵔtikęhnę́hkwę'ᵔ *it was*
stumped (-(ę)'ᵔtikęhnęhkw-{dative
III}).
stun. *v.t.* na'ᵔtikęhrahnę́'ᵔtha'ᵔ *one stuns*
another (-(ę)'ᵔtikęhrahnę'ᵔT-).
stupefy. *v.t.* ra'ᵔtikęhrahnę́'ᵔtha'ᵔ *he stup-*
efies it (-(ę)'ᵔtikęhrahnę'ᵔT-).
stupid. *adj.* thahrawę'ᵔnehę̀·we *he is*
stupid (tha-.-ęT-.#ęwe).
sturgeon. *n.* kà·ra'ᵔ *sturgeon* (kà·ra'ᵔ).
subdue. *v.t.* rękwé'ᵔtha'ᵔ *he subdues it*
(-ę̊kʷe'ᵔT-).
submerge. *v.t.* ranęwęthúhtha'ᵔ *he sub-*
merges it (-nęwęthuhT-).
submit to. *v.t.* ręnęhwé·tha'ᵔ *he submits*
to it (-ęnęhweT-).
subscribe to. *v.t.* račhę̀·nar *he subscribes*
to it (-ačhęnar-); rahsęnyę́'ᵔθeh *he*

subscribes to it (-hsęnyę-{dative I}).
substitute. *v.t.* nehrukę'ᵔné·tyę *he sub-*
stitutes it (-ne-.-kę'ᵔneti-).
subterfuge. *n.* neyurihwa'ᵔtikęhkę́·nyę
subterfuge (-ne-.-rihwa̲'ᵔtikęhkęni-).
subterranean. *adj.* ú'ᵔwnakęw *subter-*
ranean (-a'ᵔwna̲kęw).
succeed. *v.t.* nehra'ᵔnahθę'ᵔrá·kwahs *he*
succeeds it (-ne-.-a'nahθę'ᵔraku-).
success. *n.* utkwaná·kwę·'ᵔ *success*
(-tkwanakʷę-).
succinct. *adj.* thwahrahéhskwaht *wah-*
rę́hrę·'ᵔ he is succinct (ti-.-heh=
skwahT- -ihrę-).
succomb. *v.i.* rę́·kwe'ᵔθ *he succombs*
(-ę̊kʷe'ᵔ-); rarękrú'ᵔri·θ *he succombs*
(-rękru'ᵔriθ-).
suck. *v.i.* ru'ᵔčírha'ᵔ *he sucks* (-u'ᵔčir-);
kanę'ᵔkyérha'ᵔ *it sucks* (-nę'ᵔker-); *v.t.*
wu'ᵔčirá'ᵔtha'ᵔ *it sucks it* (-u'ᵔčira'ᵔT-).
sucker. *n.* čunęhwarí·yu· *sucker (fish)*
(-či-.-nęhwa̲riyu-).
suckle. *v.t.* yenę'ᵔkyerá'ᵔtha'ᵔ *one suckles*
it (-nę'ᵔkera'ᵔT-).
suddenly. *adv.* thwa'ᵔkahwé'ᵔnęht *sudden-*
ly (ti-.-hwe'ᵔnęht-).
suffer. *v.i.* kayę'ᵔnę́·ta'ᵔθ *they suffer to-*
gether (-a'nęt(a'ᵔ)-); wa'ᵔerę́hyakę'ᵔ *one*
suffered (-ręhya̲kę-); newaka'ᵔtęhę-
ká·ryę *I suffer* (-ne-.-a'ᵔtęhękari-);
rawerihkáθne'ᵔ *he suffers patiently*
(-erihkaθne-).
suffering. *n.* urę́hyakę'ᵔt *suffering* (-ręh=
ya̲kę'ᵔT-); uręhyakę́'ᵔčreh *suffering*
(-ręhya̲kę'ᵔčr-).
suffice. *v.i.* wekayè·ri'ᵔθ *it suffices*
(-yah-.-yeri'ᵔ-).
suffocate. *v.i.* ra'ᵔnę́hkweks *he is suf-*
focating (-a'nęhkʷek-).
suffocating. *adj.* yawęryę́hkwekt *suffo-*
cating (-ę̊ryęhkʷek-).
sugar. *n.* urę'ᵔná·kri'ᵔ *sugar* (-rę'nakri-).
sulk. *v.i.* rayatá'ᵔtha'ᵔ *he sulks* (-yata'ᵔT-).
sullen. *adj.* nehručhá'ᵔrhu'ᵔ *he is sullen*

(-ne-.-čha'rhu-).

sum up. *v.i.* rarihwarúhčrẹh *he sums up* (-rihwaruhčrẹ-).

sumac. *n.* nará·kwi' *sumac* (nará·kwi').

summer. *n.* kẹnhá'kye *summer* (-kẹn=ha'ke).

summit. *n.* wewá·'ne' *summit* (-yah-.-(a)'ne-); ha' wá·'ne' *summit* (-(a)='ne-).

summon. *v.t.* ráhnẹks *he summons it* (-(i)hnẹk-).

sun. *n.* híhte' *sun* (híhte'); uthnẹ́hsteh *setting sun* (-athnẹhst-).

Sunday. *n.* yawẹtatukẹ́htẹ *Sunday* (-ẹta=tukẹht-); tatukẹ́hti *Sunday* (tatukẹ́hti).

sunfish. *n.* naré're *sunfish* (naré're); čikahkwarè·reh *sunfish* (čikahkwarè·reh).

sunflower. *n.* uru'wẹhsa'ẹtíh *wild sunflower* (-ru'wẹhs-.#ẹtíh).

sunny. *adj.* yutè·nẹ' *it is sunny* (-tenẹ-); yutenẹhstá·'neht *sunny* (-tenẹhsta='nehT-).

sunset. *n.* yurerẹ́·tyẹ· *sunset* (-arerẹti-); sawá·thu' *sunset* (sawá·thu').

sunshine. *n.* utenẹ́hsteh *sunshine* (-te=nẹhst-).

supple. *adj.* ruhkarí·yu· *he is supple* (-(a)hkariyu-).

support. *n.* ukẹ́'θreh *support* (-kẹ'θr-).

support. *v.t.* rúsθhar *he supports it* (-asθhar-); kkẹ'θráhkhwa' *I support it* (-kẹ'θrahkw-); rahtíθtha' *he supports it* (-htiθT-).

supposedly. *adv.* tehčíhẹ' *supposedly* (tehčíhẹ').

sure. *adj.* urihwí·yu· *it is sure* (-rih=wiyu-); yutukẹ́'ẹ *it is sure* (-tukẹ'-)

surge. *v.i.* wẹnéhkwrẹh *it surges* (-ẹ=nehkwr-).

surgeon. *n.* rahrè·nahs *surgeon* (-hren-); rẹnéhkwa't ráhču·' awẹ́·te *surgeon* (-ẹnẹhkwa'T--hču·'-awẹ́·te).

surpass. *v.t.* ra'nẹkúhtha' *he surpasses it* (-a'nẹkuhT-).

surprised. *adj.* wa'kakunehrá·kuh *they were surprised* (-nehraku(h)-); thwahra'nyerẹ́hči' *he was quite surprised* (ti-.-a'nyerẹ-.#hči).

surrender. *v.i.* ruwẹná'tha' *he surrenders* (-wẹna'T-).

surreptitious. *v.i.* yu'nẹhsku'yé·'nẹ *it is surreptitious* (-a'nẹhsku'yeT-).

surround. *v.i.* neyuhkẹtíhsnẹ *it surrounds* (-ne-.-hkẹtihsT-); *v.t.* nehráhweks *he surrounds it* (-ne-.-hwek-).

survey. *v.i.* rarihstí'θrẹhs *he surveys* (-rihsti'θ(e)r-); *v.t.* raya'turehnáhnẹh *he surveys it carefully* (-ya'tureh=nahnẹ-).

survive. *v.i.* nehra'nẹkúhtha' *he survives* (-ne-.-a'nẹkuhT-).

suspenders. *n.* rathnẹhu'narhúhstha' *his suspenders* (-athnẹhu'narhuhst-).

suspicion. *n.* uhskwatkẹ́'čreh *suspicion* (-hskwatkẹ'čr-).

sustain. *v.t.* nehrú'kẹh *he sustains it* (-ne-.-u'kẹ-).

swallow. *v.t.* nyẹwé·thẹk *one swallowed it* (-awethu-).

swamp. *n.* uhnà·weh *swamp* (-hnaw-); uhnà·wakẹw *swamp* (-hnawakẹw); yuhnà·wayẹ' *there is a swamp* (-hna=wayẹ(T)-); uwíhreh *swamp* (-wihr-);

uhryúhkweh *tamarack swamp* (-hryu = hkw -).

swan. *n.* úrhwareh *swan* (-rhwa̱r -); katu⁹θę·t⁹ú⁹y *swan* (-(ę)tu⁹θęT - .#u⁹y).

swarm. *n.* yu⁹teyu⁹à·wi⁹ *swarm* (-(ę)⁹ = teyu⁹awi -); nakayę⁹khwà·ra⁹ *a swarm* (-t - . -yę⁹khwar -).

swarm. *v.i.* neyu⁹teyahsihár⁹ę *crowd swarms* (-ne - . -hsihar⁹ -).

sway. *v.i.* ru⁹rę⁹kúhę *he sways* (-a⁹ = rę⁹kuhw -); rarę⁹kúhę *he sways* (-rę⁹ = kuhw -); rarę⁹krú⁹ri⁹θ *he sways* (-rę⁹ = kru⁹ri⁹ -); rahręhwá⁹θręh *he sways* (-hręhwa⁹θrę -).

swear. *v.i.* rarihwaksá⁹tha⁹ *he swears* (-rihwaksa⁹T -); rayeθá⁹tha⁹ *he swears* (-yeθa⁹T -).

sweat. *n.* ú·thekw *sweat* (-thekw -).

sweat. *v.i.* rathekwní·tkę⁹θ *he sweats* (-thekwnitkę⁹ -); nekačha⁹núhtha⁹ *it sweats* (-ne - . -čha⁹nuhT -); ú·thekw rú·ryuhs *he sweats* (-thekw - -r(i)yu -).

sweaty. *adj.* uthékwnakęw *sweaty* (-thekwna̱kęw).

sweep. *v.i.* rętawanęhkwih *he sweeps* (-ętawa̱nęhkwi -).

sweet cicely. *n.* u⁹tè·ya⁹ *sweet cicely* (-(ę)⁹tey -).

sweetflag. *n.* urahú⁹ta⁹ *sweetflag* (-ra = hu⁹t -).

sweetmeat. *n.* karę⁹nakri⁹črarhú⁹θeh *sweetmeat* (-rę'nakri⁹črarhu -{dative I}); kaθręwętyáhnęh *sweetmeat* (-θrę = wętyahnę -).

swell. *v.i.* wa⁹núhnęh *it swells (as of a bruise, a sore, or a part of the body)* (-a'nuhnę -); newásθręhs *it swells (as of something boiling)* (-ne - . -asθr -); wa⁹né·k⁹uhs *it is swelling (of dough)* (-a'nek⁹u -).

swift. *n.* náwnę⁹ *swift* (náwnę⁹).

swill. *n.* kwískwis úkhwawęh *swill* (kwískwis -khwa̱wę -).

swim. *v.i.* ka⁹nà·węhs *I am swimming*

(as an amusement) (-a⁹nawę -); ratyù·re⁹ *he's swimming (as a means of locomotion)* (-tyur -).

swindle. *v.t.* ra⁹čę̀·wahs *he swindles it* (-⁹čęw -).

swine. *n.* waθkwà·reh *swine* (-aθkwa = re -).

swing. *v.i.* yu⁹nyáhkhwar *it swings* (-a = 'nyahkwhar -).

sword. *n.* uti⁹ré·θhreh *sword* (-ti⁹re = θh(e)r -).

sycamore. *n.* wa⁹rę⁹ačhęwá·tih *sycamore* (-a⁹rę⁹ačhęwati -); yę⁹nekhri⁹nuharáhkhwa⁹ *sycamore* (yę⁹nekhri⁹nuharáhkhwa⁹).

symbol. *n.* yu⁹nyerętihnáhkę *symbol* (-a = 'nyerętihnahkw -).

symbolize. *v.t.* rayerętíhtha⁹ *he symbolizes it* (-yerętihT -).

sympathy. *n.* ru⁹tikęhra⁹níhrę *his sympathy* (-(ę)⁹tikęhra⁹nihr -).

syphilis. *n.* účkreh *syphilis* (-čkr(ę⁹n) -).

syrup. *n.* uθrę̀·weh *syrup* (-θręw -); urę⁹ná·kri⁹ uθrę̀·weh *syrup* (-rę'nakri - -θręw -).

T

table. *n.* u⁹nekhwahráhčreh *table* (-a'ne = khwahrahčr -).

tablecloth. *n.* yę⁹nekhwahrúhtha⁹ *tablecloth* (-a'nekhwahruhT -).

taboo. *adj.* yuhré⁹ę *it is taboo* (-hre⁹ -).

tackle. *n.* úhryeh *tackle* (-ahry -).

tacks. *n.* té·ks *tacks* (té·ks); uhsęwa⁹rehętíh *tacks* (-hsęwa⁹r - .#ętíh).

tadpole. *n.* warereháh *tadpole* (warereh. #ah).

tag alder. *n.* či⁹rarę́hkwaht *tag alder* (či⁹raręh. -kʷahT -).

tail. *n.* u⁹rhwę́·θeh *tail (of an animal)* (-(i)⁹rhwęθ -); utréhneh *tail (of a bird* *or fish)* (-trehn -).

tailless. *adj.* urhwęθú·kę *tailless* (-(i)rhwęθukę).

tailor. *n.* rakyerhuhčrę́·tih *tailor* (-ker= huhčręti -).

taint. *v.t.* rayerà·węhs *he taints it* (-ye= raw -).

take. *v.t.* ęhrahà·wi *he will take it* (-(ę)hawi -); rà·ręh *he takes it* (-rę -); rá·kwahs *he takes it* (-ku -); wá·khaw *I take it* (-(ę)haw -); rá·tkwahs *he takes it away* (-atku -); ruhríhtha *he takes it down* (-hrihT -); rahará·kwahs *he takes it down* (-(i)haraku -); θwah-rawę́·kuh *you take it down* (-(a)hra= węku -); rahrá·kwahs *he takes it off* (-(a)hraku -); ranáhkwahs *he takes it out* (-a'nahku -).

take from. *v.t.* see: -tekar -.

take up space. *v.i.* nehrahehnawęrę́htha *he takes up unnecessarily needed space or ground* (-ne -. -hehnawę= ręhT -).

tale. *n.* úhnyeh *tale* (-hny -); ę́khwyaht *tale* (-ękhwyahT -).

talk. *v.i.* rawéhahk *he talked* (-weh -); runwehá·ksę·*he talks nonsense* (-a= 'nwehaks -); wehrà·weh *he talks over the phone* (-yah -. -weh -); ráhtharę *he talked* (-hthar -).

talkative. *adj.* ruwátkę· *he is talkative* (-watkę -).

tall. *adj.* krę́·we·θ *I am tall* (-ręweθ -).

tallow. *n.* ushé· rę·t kę̀·ye *tallow* (-sheręt -iye -).

talon. *n.* učiéhneh *talon* (-čiehn -).

tamable. *adj.* yurihwaráθkę· *it is tam-*

able (-rihwaraθk -).

tamarack. *n.* kanę́tęhs *tamarack* (-nę= tęhs).

tame. *v.t.* rarihwaráhstha *he tamed it* (-rihwarahsT -).

tangle. *v.t.* nehranęrì·yehs *he tangles it* (-ne -. -nęriye -).

tangled. *adj.* neyunęrì·ye *it is tangled* (-ne -. -nęriye -).

tannery. *n.* kę yehnę́·tih *tannery* (kę -ihnęti -).

tantalize. *v.t.* rutáhskwar *he tantalizes it* (-tahskwah(e)r -).

tap a tree. *v.i.* rahkaránihč *he taps a tree* (-(a)hkaranihr -).

taper. *n.* učireh *taper* (-čir -); uhsúθreh *tapered thing* (-hsuθr -).

taper. *v.i.* wú·či *it tapers* (-uči -).

tapeworm. *n.* te tì·we·θ *tapeworm* (te ti -. -eθ -).

tar. *n.* uθrę̀·weh *tar* (-θręw -); yeθreh-črawę́hshtha *tar* (-(i)θrehčrawęh= sT -).

tar. *v.i.* raθrę̀·wawęhs *he tars it* (-θrę= wawę -).

tardy. *adj.* runętyá·tit *he is tardy* (-a'nętyatiT -).

tarnish. *v.i.* wanáhθkwahs *it tarnishes* (-a'nahθkw -); *v.t.* rayerawę̀·rih *he tarnishes it* (-yerawęri -).

taste. *n.* awę́·θreh *taste* (-ę̨θr -).

taste, have good. *v.i.* rahsyákwahst *he has good taste* (-hsyakwahsT -).

taste. *v.i.* yawé·kę *it tastes good* (-ek -); *v.t.* ranęθratyę́nę *he tastes it* (-a'nęθratyęnę -).

tasteful. *adj.* yawę́·θrar *tasteful* (-ę̨=

θraˀr–).

tasteless. *adj*. awęθrú·kęˀ *tasteless* (–ę= θrukęˀ).

tattered. *adj*. ukahθaríˀneh *tattered* (–kahθariˀn–).

tatters. *n*. ukríˀreh *tatters* (–kriˀr–).

tattle. *v.i*. nehrahnyakará·tih *he tattles* (–ne–.–hnyakarati–).

tattoo. *n*. watkęhsaˀnęˀθáhnęh *tattoo marks* (–atkęhsa'nęˀθahnę–).

taunt. *v.t*. rayuráˀkhwaˀ *he taunts it* (–yuraˀkw–).

tax. *n*. té·ks *tax* (té·ks).

taxes, collect. *v.i*. té·ks rarù·ręh *he collects taxes* (té·ks –rurę–).

taxes, pay. *v.i*. té·ks raˀęyúhar *he pays taxes* (té·ks –ˀęyuhar–).

tea. *n*. thí· *tea* (thí·).

teach. *v.i*. rarihę́·tih *he teaches* (–rihęti–); *v.t*. naˀrihę́·tyęˀ *one taught another* (–rihęti–{dative III}).

teacher. *n*. yerihę́·tih *teacher* (–rihęti–).

team. *n*. uˀtè·yeh *team* (–(ę)ˀtey–).

tear. *n*. ukáhθreh *tear (in the eye)* (–kah= θr–); haˀ yuˀrá·čęˀ *tear (in cloth)* (–aˀračę–).

tear. *v.t*. rará·čęhs *he tears it* (–račę–); raračę́·kwahs *he tears it* (–račęku–).

tease. *v.t*. naˀnaˀnaˀrihuryáˀthaˀ *one is teasing another* (–aˀrihuryaˀT–).

teasing. *n*. uhtyę́·kweh *teasing* (–htyękʷ–).

tedious. *adj*. yuˀnéhreˀt *it is tedious* (–aˀnehreˀT–).

teeth, gnash. *v.i*. nehraθčúhčhaˀ *he gnashes his teeth* (–ne–.–θčuhčha–).

teeth, pull. *v.i*. ratuˀθawíhsyęhs *he pulls teeth* (–(ę)tuˀθawihsi–).

teethe. *v.i*. rętuˀθę́·tih *he teethes* (–(ę)= tuˀθęti–); raˀnętuˀθę́·tih *he teethes* (–a'nętuˀθęti–).

telephone. *v.t*. ękhehsęwaˀrakę́hruk *I will telephone someone* (–hsęwaˀra= kęhruk–).

telescope. *n*. yętkahratˀáhsthaˀ *telescope*

(–atkahratˀahsT–).

tell. *v.i*. ratkáhryeh *he tells* (–atkahri–); wahrę́hte·θ *he told* (–ihteθ–).

temper. *n*. uˀtikę́hreh *temper* (–(ę)ˀti= kęh–).

temperate. *adv*. kwéˀyę·ˀ *temperate* (kwéˀyę·ˀ).

temperature. *n*. haˀ tyuˀnaríhę· *temperature* (ti–.–aˀnarih–).

temple. *n*. utahwę́hneh *temple* (–tah= węhn–).

tempt. *v.t*. raˀtikęhruˀná·kwahs *he tempts it* (–(ę)ˀtikęhruˀnaku–); raˀti= kęhraˀtyę́ˀnęh *he tempts it* (–(ę)ˀti= kęhraˀtyęˀnę–).

temptation. *n*. haˀ yuˀtikęhruˀná·kwaht *temptation* (–(ę)ˀtikęhruˀnakʷahT–).

temptor. *n*. raˀtikęhruˀná·kwahs *temptor* (–(ę)ˀtikęhruˀnaku–).

ten. *adj./n*. wáhθhę· *ten* (–ahθhę–).

tend. *v.t*. rà·nęh *he tends it* (–nę–).

tendency. *n*. káhręw *tendency* (–hręhw–).

tender. *adj*. ká·nę· *it is tender* (–(a)nę–).

tenth. *adj*. wahθhęháˀnęˀt *tenth* (–ah= θhę–.#haˀnęˀt).

tepid. *adj*. kwéˀyę·ˀ tyuˀnaríhę· *tepid* (kwéˀyę·ˀ ti–.–a'narih–).

terminate. *v.i*. waˀnúˀkthaˀ *it terminates* (–a'nuˀkT–).

terrible. *adj*. yawęˀnę́·ti· *it is terrible* (–ę= 'nęti–); see: –(a)hrahT–.

test. *v.t*. raˀtyę́·ˀnęh *he tests it* (–ˀtyę= 'nęh–).

testament. *n*. théhstemęt *testament* (théh- stement).

testicle. *n*. uˀnhę́hseh *testicle* (–ˀnhęhs–).

testimony. *n*. haˀ rutkáhryeˀ *testimony* (–atkahri–).

thank. *v.t*. naˀnęherá·tęhs *one thanks another* (–nęheratę–).

thank you. *interj*. nyà·wę *thank you* (nyà·wę).

thankful. *adj*. nekaˀnęneherá·tęh *I am thankful* (–ne–.–a'nęnęheratę–).

thanks, give. *v.i.* waʔtkayęʔnęnęheratę́·nyęʔ *they gave thanks* (-ne-. -a'nę= nęheratęnyę-).

that. *adj.* haʔ *that* (haʔ); hé *that!* (hé); hení·kę· *that is* (hení·kę); hà·neʔ *that is* (hà·neʔ).

that one. *pro.* héʔkye *that one* (héʔkye).

thaw. *v.i.* yunyataná·wę· *it (snow) is thawed* (-nyatanawę-); kataʔtà·węhs *it thaws* (-taʔtawę-).

the. *adj.* haʔ *the* (haʔ).

theft. *n.* haʔ yenę́hskwahs *theft* (-nęh= sku-); unęhskuʔyéhčreh *theft* (-nęh= skuʔyehčr-).

theme. *n.* uríhweh *theme* (-rihw-).

then. *adv.* hésnę· *then* (hésnę·); henę́ʔkye *then* (henę́ʔkye).

there. *adv.* thúh *there* (thúh); héʔthu *there* (héʔthu).

there at. *adv.* čhaʔ *there at* (čhaʔ).

therefore. *adv.* tyuh *therefore* (tyuh).

thick. *adj.* ká·ʔnę·θ *it is thick* (-'nęθ-); yawęhkwá·thę *it is thick with* (-ęh= kwath-).

thicken. *v.i.* ręhkwatháʔthaʔ *he thickens it* (-ęhkwathaʔT-).

thief. *n.* runęhskúʔye· *thief* (-nęhskuʔ= ye-).

thigh. *n.* urę́ʔéʔčreh *thigh* (-ręʔeʔčr-).

thimble. *n.* uhsúʔkweh *thimble* (-hsuʔ= ku-).

thimbleberry. *n.* ù·waʔ *thimbleberry* (ù·waʔ).

thin. *adj.* karáhrę· *it is thin* (-rahr-).

thin. *v.t.* rarahráʔthaʔ *he thins it* (-rah= raʔT-).

thing. *n.* awę́·te *thing* (awę́·te).

think. *v.i.* sè·rih *you think* (-er-); ŗęʔ-tikęhnę́·tyęh *he thinks* (-(ę)ʔtikęh= nętyę-); *v.t.* kęyehyahrá·ʔnyeʔ *I am thinking about you* (-ehyahr-).

thinking. *n.* uʔtikęhnę́hčreh *thinking* (-(ę)ʔtikęhnęhčr-).

thirst. *n.* yakuʔtaʔnatháʔthaʔ *thirst* (-iʔ= taʔnathaʔT-); uʔtaʔnathę́ʔę *thirst* (-iʔ= taʔnathę·ʔ-).

thirsty. *adj.* kiʔtaʔná·thę·ʔθ *I am thirsty* (-iʔtaʔnathęʔ-).

thirteen. *adj./n.* áhsę θkáheʔr *thirteen* (áhsę -či-. -(i)har-).

thirty. *adj./n.* áhsę tiwáhθhę· *thirty* (áhsę ti-. -ahθhę-).

this. *adj.* kyé·nę· *this* (kyé·nę·); kyení·kę· *this is* (kyení·kę·).

thistle. *n.* uhsnéʔθareh *thistle* (-hsneʔ= θar-); unihkyéhweh *Canada thistle* (-nihkyehw-).

thorn. *n.* uhsnéʔθareh *thorn* (-hsneʔθar-).

thorn apple. *n.* háʔθruʔ *thorn apple* (háʔ-θruʔ).

thoughtless. *adj.* ruʔtikęhrú·kęʔ *he is thoughtless* (-(ę)ʔtikęhrukęʔ); ruʔti-kęhnęhčrú·kęʔ *he is thoughtless* (-(ę)ʔtikęhnęhčrukęʔ).

thousand. *adj./n.* uyáhsteh *thousand* (-yahst-).

thread. *n.* uhsì·reh *thread* (-hsir-).

thread. *v.t.* rahsirúhar *he threads a needle* (-hsiruhar-).

three. *adj./n.* áhsę *three* (áhsę).

thresh. *v.t.* rahérʔehs *he threshes it* (-her= ʔe(k)-).

thrift. *n.* unękwì·reh *thrift* (-(ę)nękwir-); utkwaná·kwę·ʔ *thrift* (-tkwanakʷę-).

Tuscarora Pronunciation Key:
/a/ l<u>a</u>w; /e/ h<u>a</u>t; /i/ p<u>i</u>zza; /u/ t<u>u</u>ne; /ę/ h<u>i</u>nt; /č/ <u>ch</u>eese; /h/ <u>h</u>oe; /m/ <u>m</u>other; /s/ <u>s</u>ame; /t/ <u>d</u>o (before a vowel y, or w), <u>t</u>oo (elsewhere); /k/ <u>g</u>ale (before a vowel y or w), <u>k</u>ale (elsewhere); /n/ i<u>n</u>hale (before a consonant or word-final), <u>n</u>ote (elsewhere), /r/ hi<u>ss</u> (before a consonant or word-final), <u>r</u>un (trilled as in Italian, elsewhere); /w/ c<u>u</u>ff (before a consonant other than y or word-final), <u>w</u>ay (elsewhere); /y/ fi<u>sh</u> (before a consonant or word-final), <u>y</u>ou (elsewhere), /θ/ <u>th</u>ing; /ʔ/ (the sound between the vowels in unh-unh); /·/ long vowel, /ˊ/ high pitch; /ˋ/ low pitch.

throat. *n.* uháhkwareh *throat* (-hah=
kwar-); uhę́hkweh *throat* (-hęhkw-);
uhę́hθeh *throat* (-hęhθ-).

throne. *n.* kuráhku· yę²nyę²náhkhwa²
throne (kuráhku· -a'nyę'nahkw-).

throw. *v.t.* ęhrú·²ni² *he will throw it*
(-a'ni-); kaθá·²ni *throw it to me!* (-t-.
-a'ni-); rę́hrayę²kws *he throws it on
the ground* (-ehra̲yę²k ͧ -).

thumb. *n.* uhsú²kweh wì·yuh *thumb*
(-hsu²ku- -iyu-).

thunder. *n.* hí²nę² *thunder* (hí²nę²).

thunder. *v.i.* hí²nę² kà·weh *it thunders*
(hí²nę² -weh-).

thundercap. *n.* u²nę́rhweh *thundercap*
(-a²nęrhw-).

Thursday. *n.* hę́²tahk tičuhtérhę *Thursday*
(hę́²tahk ti+či-. -hterhę-).

tick. *n.* ruθè·rę *tick* (ruθè·rę)

tickle. *v.t.* nehra²tiθkrà·ręh *he tickles it*
(-ne-. -²tiθkrarę-).

tickling. *adj.* yu²tiθkrá·rę·t *tickling* (-²ti=
θkraręT-).

ticklish. *adj.* yu²tiθkrarę́·²nę *ticklish*
(-²tiθkraręT-).

tie. *v.t.* wahráhtrę·² *he tied it* (-(i)htrę-).

tight. *adj.* né·kw *tight* (né·kw).

tighten. *v.t.* né·kw rę́·tih *he tightens it*
(né·kw -ę°ti-).

till. *v.i.* ręhra²netì·yęhs *he tills* (-ę°hra²=
neti(y)-).

timber. *n.* úhkareh *timber* (-(a)hka̲r-);
uhwę́²khareh *timber* (-hwę²kha̲r-).

time. *n.* nyawę²nę́·tehk *time* (-t-. -ę=
'nęte-); tikahà·wi² *time* (ti-. -(ę)hawi-).

timid. *adj.* tihčayę́hah *timid* (tihčayę́hah);
rutéhwaręhs *he is timid* (-tehwa̲rę-);
rutehwarę́hskę· *he is timid* (-tehwa̲=
ręhsk-).

timothy. *n.* uherehè·we *timothy (grass)*
(-her-.#ęwe).

tiny. *adj.* wáhsthę *it is tiny* (-ahsthu-).

tip. *v.t.* rúhar *he fastens it to the end*
(-uha̲r-).

tire out. *v.t.* ra²nehrę́·tih *he tires it out*
(-²nehr-{dative II}).

tire. *v.t.* nathwihshęheyáhtha² *one tires
another* (-(a)hwihshęheyahT-); rah-
wihshá²tha² *he tires it* (-(a)hwih=
sha²T-).

tired. *adj.* rawę́rihshę²θ *he is tired*
(-ę°rihshę²-); nehruhwihshęhé·yę· *he is
tired* (-ne-. -(a)hwihshęhey-); ru²néhrę
he is tired (-²nehre²-); ru²nehré²ę *he
is tired* (-²nehre²-).

tired, become. *v.i.* ruhsęritkę́²ę *he has
become tired* (-hsęritkę²-).

tiresome. *adj.* yu²néhre²t *it is tiresome*
(-²nehre²T-).

title. *v.t.* rahsę̀·naws *he titles it* (-hsę=
naw-).

toad. *n.* runę́hθkwarę² *toad* (runę́h-
θkwarę²).

toast. *v.t.* rę́hsęh *he toasts it* (-ęhsę-).

tobacco. *n.* čárhu² *tobacco* (čárhu²).

today. *adv.* kyè·wę *today* (kyè·wę); kyè·-
wę yurhę́²ę *today* (kyè·wę -rhę²-).

toe. *n.* uhsú²kweh *toe* (-hsu²ku-).

together. *adv.* ęyakyahríhskę² *the two of
us must be together* (-ahrihskę-).

together, bring. *v.t.* wakyéhrak *I bring
(them) together* (-yehrak-).

together, put. *v.t.* wa²thrahsí·θhę² *he put
it together* (-ne-. -hsiθhę-).

toil. *v.i.* ra²ręhyakę́²tha² *he toils* (-a²=
ręhyakę²T-).

tomahawk. *n.* ú²θreh *tomahawk* (-a²θr-);
yę²θriharhúhstha² *tomahawk* (-a²θri=
harhuhsT-).

tomato. *n.* thumé·tuhs *tomato* (thumé·-
tuhs).

tomb. *n.* ha² kę² rá·²nęht *tomb* (kę²
-'nęhT-).

tomboy. *n.* wat²niháhsnę *tomboy* (-at=
²nihahsT-).

tombstone. *n.* kačtęhra²níhrę *tombstone*
(-čtęhra²nihr-).

tomorrow. *n.* ęyúrhę² *tomorrow* (-rhę²-).

tongue. *n.* awętáhseh *tongue* (-(ę)^ʼ = tahs -).

too. *adv.* se^ʼčí *too* (se^ʼčí).

too bad. *adj.* yawę^ʼnę́·ti· *it is too bad* (-ę'nęti -).

tooth. *n.* utú^ʼθeh *tooth* (-(ę)tu^ʼθ -).

tooth, break. *v.i.* nehrętú^ʼča^ʼks *he breaks his tooth* (-ne -. -(ę)tu^ʼča^ʼk -).

tooth decay. *n.* yuhskę^ʼrá·tkęhθ *tooth decay* (-hskę^ʼratkęh -).

toothache, have a. *v.i.* rutú^ʼθariks *he has a toothache* (-(ę)tu^ʼθarik -); waktu^ʼθanę́hwaks *I have a toothache* (-(ę) = tu^ʼθanęhwak(T) -).

top. *n.* wewá·^ʼne^ʼ *top* (-yah -. -(a)'ne -); unę́htreh *top of head* (-anęhtr -).

topple over. *v.i.* ráhryenę^ʼθ *he topples over* (-hryenę^ʼ -).

torment. *v.t.* rahtyękwę́hsthęh *he torments it* (-htyęk^węhsthę -).

torso. *n.* učù·neh *torso* (-čun -).

torture. *v.t.* rę^ʼnikęhkarya^ʼná·tih *he tortures it* (-ę^ʼnikęhkarya^ʼn -{dative III}).

totality. *n.* yuhs^ʼáhnę *totality* (-(i)hs = ^ʼahT -).

totter. *v.i.* ru^ʼrę^ʼkúhę *he totters* (-a^ʼ = rę^ʼkuhw -).

touch. *v.t.* ra^ʼtà·rehs *he touches it* (-^ʼtare -); akatáhre·k *that it touch it* (-tahrek -); yahwahrátahre·k *he touched it* (-yah -. -tahrek -); wa^ʼù·ra^ʼ *it touched upon it* (-ra^ʼ -).

touch-me-not. *n.* tawę́·nya^ʼks *touch-me-not* (tawę́·nya^ʼks).

toward. *prep.* tyuyerá·^ʼnę *toward* (ti -. -yeraT -).

towel. *n.* ha^ʼ yęt^ʼehnakyewáhtha^ʼ *towel* (-at^ʼehnakewahT -).

tower. *n.* uhsú^ʼθreh *tower* (-hsu^ʼθr -).

toy. *n.* awę^ʼnhékwčreh *toy* (-ę^ʼn = hek^wčr -).

trace. *v.t.* rahnęwí^ʼθręhs *he traces it* (-hnęwi^ʼθ(e)r -).

track. *n.* uháheh *track* (-(a)hah -).

tracks. *n.* uyá^ʼθeh *tracks* (-ya^ʼθ -); uyá^ʼθareh *tracks* (-ya^ʼθar -).

tract. *n.* yu^ʼwnakwę́^ʼnhe^ʼr *tract (a spot of ground)* (-a^ʼwnakwę^ʼnh(e)r -).

trade. *n.* yę^ʼnęnhihsáktha^ʼ *a trade* (-a = 'nęnhihsakT -).

tradition. *n.* ę́khwyaht *tradition* (-ę = khwyahT -).

traditions. *n.* urihwakà·yę^ʼ *traditions* (-rihwakayę -).

trail. *v.t.* raya^ʼθęhà·wi^ʼθ *he trails it* (-ya^ʼθęhawi^ʼ -).

train. *v.t.* na^ʼrihę́·tyę^ʼ *one trained another* (-rihęti -{dative III}).

tranquil. *adj.* ahskę̀·nę^ʼ *tranquil* (-hskę = nę^ʼ -).

transform into. *v.t.* wa^ʼnwatkę^ʼnetyę́·ku^ʼ *it transformed into it* (-ne -. -atkę^ʼ = netyęku -).

transgress. *v.i.* nehrarihwahríhtha^ʼ *he transgresses* (-ne -. -rihwahrihT -).

translator. *n.* nehrawętakę^ʼné·tyęhs *translator* (-ne -. -wętakę^ʼneti -).

translucent. *n.* newathukstękúhtha^ʼ *translucent* (-ne -. -athukstękuhT -).

transpose. *v.t.* wehratakwnakę^ʼné·tyęhs *he transposes it* (-yah -. -takwnakę^ʼ = neti -).

trap. *n.* yewenę^ʼnayętíhstha^ʼ *trap* (-we = nę'nayętihsT -); see: -hθer -.

Tuscarora Pronunciation Key:
/a/ law; /e/ hat; /i/ pizza; /u/ tune; /ę/ hint; /č/ cheese; /h/ hoe; /m/ mother; /s/ same; /t/ do (before a vowel y, or w), too (elsewhere); /k/ gale (before a vowel y or w), kale (elsewhere); /n/ inhale (before a consonant or word-final), note (elsewhere), /r/ hiss (before a consonant or word-final), run (trilled as in Italian, elsewhere); /w/ cuff (before a consonant other than y or word-final), way (elsewhere); /y/ fish (before a consonant or word-final), you (elsewhere), /θ/ thing; /^ʼ/ (the sound between the vowels in unh-unh); /·/ long vowel, /ˊ/ high pitch; /ˋ/ low pitch.

trap. *v.i.* ruhθérhar *he traps* (-hθerhar-).

trap, leave a. *v.i.* ęhskáhrayę⁷θ *you must leave a trap* (-kahra̲yę(T)-{dative I}).

travel. *v.i.* yę̀·nęhs *one travels* (-enę-); rathahì·nęhs *he travels* (-athahiN-); ra⁷nawę̀·rih *he travels around* (-a'na=węri-).

traverse. *v.i.* ru⁷nękuhnáhnę· *he traversed* (-a'nękuhnahnę-).

tray. *n.* u⁷ę̀·weh *tray* (-⁷ęw-).

treasure. *n.* utí⁷reh *treasure* (-ti⁷r-).

treasure. *v.t.* ratù·ręh *he treasures it* (-tu=rę-).

treasurer. *n.* rahwíhstanęh *treasurer* (-hwihsta̲nę-).

treat. *v.t.* na⁷nęhrukwá·nyęh *one treats another* (-ęhrukʷanyę-).

tree. *n.* urę́⁷eh *tree* (-rę⁷-); ukwì·reh *tree (standing)* (-kwir-); yuyenę́⁷ę *fallen (dead) tree* (-yenę⁷-); uyęhwà·neh *leafless tree* (-yęhwan-); kyérhi⁷ *standing tree* (kyérhi⁷); see: -ręt-, -yen-.

tree. *v.t.* rará·⁷nęh *he trees it* (-ra'nę-).

tremble. *v.i.* ruθrárha⁷ *he trembles* (-θrar-).

trench. *n.* kata⁷kęhá·⁷nye⁷ *trench* (-ta⁷=kęha'nye⁷-).

tribe. *n.* nehratakrę́·te *his tribe* (-ne-.-takręte).

trickle. *v.i.* wukyę⁷né·tha⁷ *it trickles* (-u=kyę⁷neT-).

trifle with. *v.t.* ra⁷rihuryá⁷tha⁷ *he trifles with it* (-a⁷rihurya⁷T-).

trigger. *n.* urę́·θeh *trigger* (-rę̲θ-).

trillium, red. *n.* utuhá⁷sta⁷ *red trillium* (-tuha⁷st-).

trip. *v.i.* rúht⁷ehs *he trips* (-aht⁷e(k)-).

troop. *n.* u⁷nyúhkweh *troop* (-i⁷=nyuhkw-).

trough. *n.* uhę̀·weh *trough* (-hęw-).

trout. *n.* rutyá·ktę⁷ *speckled trout* (rutyá·ktę⁷).

true. *adj.* yutukę́⁷ę *it is true* (-tukę⁷-); wáhi⁷r *it is true* (wáhi⁷r).

truly. *adv.* utukę́⁷ę *truly* (-tukę⁷-); wehrę⁷ę̀·we *truly* (wehrę⁷ę̀·we).

trunk. *n.* uhnę̀·neh *trunk (of a tree)* (-hnęn-); urętú⁷čreh *trunk (suitcase)* (-rętu⁷čr-).

trust. *v.t.* ękayetiheθę́hek *they shall trust it* (-tiheθ-{dative III}).

trustable. *adj.* tkarihwayè·rik *it is trustable* (-t-.-rihwa̲yerik-).

trusting. *adj.* wa⁷ka⁷rihwatihé·θę⁷ *I am trusting* (-a⁷rihwatiheθ-{dative III}).

try. *v.i.* wahra⁷nę⁷tyę́·⁷nęh *he tried* (-a⁼'nę⁷tyę'nęh-); *v.t.* ra⁷tyę́·⁷nęh *he tries it* (-⁷tyę'nęh-).

tube. *n.* uhę̀·wareh *tube* (-hęwa̲r-).

tuber. *n.* unę́·θeh *tuber* (-nęč-); nę́·tu·⁷ *tuber* (nę́·tu·⁷).

tuberculosis. *n.* yęčrayayę́⁷θkę· *tuberculosis* (-ačraya̲yę⁷θk-).

Tuesday. *n.* né·kti· tičuhtérhę *Tuesday* (né·kti· ti+či-.-hterhę-).

tuft. *n.* uthúhkweh *tuft* (-athuhku-).

tulip tree. *n.* runęhru·⁷ *tulip tree* (-(ę)=nęhru-).

tumor. *n.* utihtwę̀·yeh *tumor* (-tihtwęy-); utkyéhreh *tumor* (-atkehr-).

tumult. *n.* yu⁷nahka⁷rà·yę⁷ *tumult* (-a⁷=nahka̲⁷rayę(T)-).

tumultuously. *adv.* yu⁷nahka⁷rayę⁷ná·⁷·nye⁷ *tumultuously* (-a⁷nahka⁷rayę⁷=na⁷nye⁷-).

tune. *n.* uríhweh *tune* (-rihw-); neyerihwahkwá⁷tha⁷ *tune* (-ne-.-rihwah=kwa⁷T-).

turbid. *adj.* awę́·te kęrá·⁷ne⁷ *turbid* (a-wę́·te -ira'ne-).

turd. *n.* utkwéhreh *turd* (-tkwehr-).

turf. *n.* uter⁷ę́hθeh *turf* (-ter⁷ęhθ-).

turkey. *n.* kę̀·nę⁷ *turkey* (-inę-).

turn. *n.* yutkarę́hę *turn* (-atkaręhw-).

turn. *v.i.* ratkà·ręws *he turns* (-atka=ręhw-); rathręhwá·kwahs *he turns around* (-athręhwaku-); rahahakà·ręws *he turns back* (-(a)haha̲karęhw-); θahráhkye·t *he turned back* (či-.-ah=k(e)T-); θči⁷rá⁷nir *turn on the lights!* (-či⁷ra⁷nihr-); *v.t.* rakarhá·thuhs *he turns it over* (-karhathu-); rakwę́·ryehs *he turns it up* (-kwęri-).

turn upward. *v.t.* see: -karhaT-.

turnip. *n.* učíhkwa⁷ *turnip* (-čihkw-).

turpitude. *n.* ha⁷ wáhsę· *turpitude* (-ah=sę-).

turtle. *n.* rá⁷kwihs *turtle* (rá⁷kwihs); čihkù·weh *mud turtle* (čihkù·weh); kaθrí⁷kwe·θ *sand turtle* (-θri⁷kweθ-).

turtledove. *n.* runehúhu *turtledove* (runehúhu).

tutor. *n.* rarihę́·tih *tutor* (-rihęti-).

twelve. *adj./n.* né·kti· θkáhe⁷r *twelve* (né·kti· -či-.-(i)har-).

twig. *n.* ukwì·reh *twig* (-kwir-); ú⁷čkaweh *twig* (-(i)⁷čkaw-).

twilight. *n.* wa⁷uhθathu⁷áh *twilight* (-ah=θathu-.#ah).

twinkle. *v.i.* rahsnuká⁷tha⁷ *he twinkles* (-hsnuka⁷T-).

twins. *n.* neyé·khę *twins* (-ne-.-kha-); neyę⁷núhsner *twins* (-a'nuhsner-).

twist. *v.t.* rahwanhá⁷θehs *he twists it* (-hwanha⁷θe-).

twitter. *v.i.* kačihę́·tyęh *they twitter (of birds)* (-čihętyę-).

two. *adj./n.* né·kti· *two* (né·kti·).

U

udder. *n.* unęhrá⁷seh *udder* (-nęhra⁷s-).

ugly. *adj.* ráhsęh *he is ugly* (-(i)hsę-);

wáhsę· *it is ugly* (-ahsę-).

ulcer. *n.* utihtwę̀·yeh *ulcer* (-tihtwęy-).

ulcerate. *v.i.* wa⁷nuká⁷tha⁷ *it ulcerates* (-a'nuka⁷T-).

ultimate. *adj.* u⁷nu⁷knakę́wkye *ultimate* (-a'nu⁷knakęwke).

ultimately. *adv.* uč⁷ahná·te·t *ultimately* (uč⁷ahná·te·t).

umbrella. *n.* unę́hseh *umbrella* (-nęhs-); yenęhsa⁷níhθtha⁷ *umbrella* (-nęhsa⁷=nihθT-).

unaccustomed. *adj.* kwęhs ahrurę⁷nhá⁷ęk *he is unaccustomed to it* (kwęhs -rę⁷nha⁷-).

unalterable. *adj.* kwęhs naryutkę⁷netyá⁷nęk *it is unalterable* (kwęhs -ne-.-atkę⁷netya⁷T-); kwęhs narętkę⁷netyę́hshek *it is unalterable* (kwęhs -ne-.-atkę⁷neti-{dative III}).

unapproachable. *adj.* kwęhs ahruríhwarak *he is unapproachable* (kwęhs -rih=war-).

unbecoming. *adj.* kwęhs aryuwyésnęk *it is unbecoming* (kwęhs -wyesT-); kwęhs ahruya⁷tá·⁷nęk *he is unbecoming* (kwęhs -ya⁷ta'nę-).

unbridle. *v.t.* ra⁷nęhkwaru⁷naríhsyęhs *he unbridles it* (-a'nęhkwaru'narihsi-).

unbuckle. *v.t.* ratyahskari⁷čru⁷naríhsyęhs *he unbuckles* (-(ę)tyahskari⁷čru'na=rihsi-).

unbutton. *v.t.* newakniθku⁷ru⁷naríhsyę *I have unbuttoned it* (-ne-.-niθku⁷ru='narihsi-).

uncertain. *adj.* neyu⁷tikę́hkye· *uncertain* (-ne-.-(ę)⁷tikęhke-).

uncertainty. *n.* yu⁷tikęhkyè·ya⁷t *uncer-*

tainty (-(ę)ʔtikęhkeyaʔT -).

unchristian. *adj.* kwęhs ahrurihwiyúhsnęk *he is unchristian* (kwęhs -rihwi=yuhsT -).

uncivil. *v.i.* rawyęná·ksę· *he is uncivil* (-wyęnaks -).

uncivilized. *adj.* aʔwthę́haʔ *uncivilized* (aʔwthę́haʔ).

uncle. *n.* akhryá·tu·ʔ *my maternal uncle* (-hryatuʔ); akhriʔęháh *my paternal uncle* (-hriʔę.#áh).

unclog. *v.t.* ranhęʔná·kwahs *he unclogs it* (-nhęʹnaku -).

unclouded. *adj.* yukyéhę *it is unclouded* (-kehu -).

uncomfortable. *adj.* rawęʔnętyáʔθe· *he is uncomfortable* (-ęʹnęti -{dative I}); ruʔnikęhká·ryę *he is uncomfortable* (-(ę)ʔnikęhkari -).

uncover. *v.t.* rawerhúhsyęhs *he uncovers it* (-awerhuhsi -).

undated. *adj.* kwęhs aryawę́·ʔnarak *it is undated* (kwęhs -ę̨ʹnar -).

undecided. *adj.* kwęhs naryuʔrihúhθręk *it is undecided* (kwęhs -ne -. -aʔrihuh=θ(e)r -).

underbelly. *n.* uhwé·θneh *underbelly* (-hweθn -).

underside. *n.* uhwé·θneh *underside* (-hweθn -).

understand a language. *v.t.* θahę́hsyęʔ hę skarù·ręʔ ? *do you understand Tuscarora?* (-hęhsyę -).

underwear. *n.* węhtáʔθrę· *underwear* (-ęhtaʔθrę -).

undeserving. *adj.* kwęhs ahruthwę̀·ręk *he is undeserving* (kwęhs -athwęr -).

undue. *adj.* kwęhs yaryúhek *undue* (kwęhs -yah -. -(i)he -).

undulate. *v.i.* węnéhkwręh *it undulates* (-ęnehkwr -).

undying. *adj.* kwęhs akęheyę́hθek *it is undying* (kwęhs -iheyęhθe -).

uneven. *adj.* kwęhs tharyuʔnaʔwnyeríhęk

it is uneven (kwęhs tha -. -aʹnaʔw=nyeriha -); kwęhs aryučhęwá·tyek *it is uneven* (kwęhs -ačhęwati -).

unexpected. *adj.* kwęhs aryurharáhnęk *it is unexpected* (kwęhs -rharahT -).

unfaithful. *adj.* kwęhs ęʔnahrawehnáhkęk *he is unfaithful* (kwęhs -t -. -eh=nahkw -).

unfeeling. *adj.* kwęhs ahraʔtikę́hranę·k *he is unfeeling* (kwęhs -(ę)ʔtikęhranę -).

unfit. *adj.* kwęhs naryuyáʔtaht *it is unfit* (kwęhs -ne -. -yaʔtahT -); kwęhs heʔthúhči ará·kę·k *it is unfit* (kwęhs heʔthúhči -i -).

unfold. *v.t.* rakʔúhsyęhs *he unfolds it* (-akʔuhsi -).

unfruitful. *adj.* kwęhs aręhyętíhek *it is unfruitful* (kwęhs -(a)hyęti -).

unfurl. *v.t.* rariʔwakʔúhsyęhs *he unfurls it* (-riʔwakʔuhsi -).

ungrateful. *adj.* kwęhs ahrunęheratę́hnek *he is ungrateful* (kwęhs -nęheratęhT -).

ungulate. *adj.* neyuhsú·kęʔ *it is ungulate* (-ne -. -ahsukę -).

unhappy. *adj.* waktikęhrá·ksęhθ *I am unhappy* (-(ę)ʔtikęhraks -{dative II}); kwęhs ahrawęʔnaʔnéhsnęk *he is unhappy* (kwęhs -ęʹnaʹnehsT -).

unhealthy. *n.* yunhurętyáʔneʔ *unhealthy* (-nhurętyaʔT -); kanhurę́·tih *unhealthy* (-nhuręti -).

unheard of. *adj.* kwęhs aryurihwakaréʔęk *it is unheard of* (kwęhs -rihwakareʔ -).

unholy. *adj.* kwęhs ruyaʔtatukę́hti ará·kę·k *he is unholy* (kwęhs -yaʔta=tukęhT - -i -); kwęhs aryuyaʔtatukęhtihá·ʔnyeʔ *it is unholy* (kwęhs -yaʔta=tukęhtihaʹnyeʔ -).

unhoped for. *adj.* kwęhs aryurharáhnęk *it is unhoped for* (kwęhs -rharahT -).

uninhabitable. *adj.* kwęhs hè·wi arę́ʔręʔ aryęʔtakyé·ra·t *it is uninhabitable* (kwęhs hè·wi -iʔrę- -aʔtak(e)r -).

uninhabited. *adj.* kwęhs arę́ʔręʔ aryęʔ-

takyé·ra·t *it is uninhabited* (kwęhs -i'rę- -a'tak(e)r-); kwęhs aryetá·krek *it is uninhabited* (kwęhs -tak(e)r-).

unique. *adj.* kwęhs aryukęwá·'nęk *it is unique* (kwęhs -akęwaT-).

unjust. *adj.* kwęhs ę'nakarihwayè·rik *it is unjust* (kwęhs -t-.-rihwayerik-).

unkind. *adj.* rahsyá·ksę· *he is unkind* (-hsyaks-).

unknowable. *n.* kwęhs aryu'tikęrháwsnęk *it is unknowable* (kwęhs -(ę)'tikęhr= hawsT-).

unknown. *adj.* kwęhs aryuyę'nérnęk *it is unknown* (kwęhs -yę'nerT-).

unlace. *v.t.* rahtréhsyęhs *he unlaces it* (-(i)htręhsi-).

unlawful. *adj.* kwęhs uyanręhstá'kye ará·kę·k *it is unlawful* (kwęhs -ya= nręhsta'ke -i-).

unleavened. *adj.* kwęhs aryukye'čatkę́hęk *it is unleavened* (kwęhs -ke'ča= tkęh-).

unless. *adv.* ne' the' *unless* (ne' the'); ha' the' *unless* (ha' the').

unlimited. *adj.* kwęhs aryu'nú'knak *it is unlimited* (kwęhs -a'nu'kT-).

unload. *v.t.* rará·kwahs *he unloads it* (-raku-).

unloosen. *v.t.* ru'naríhsyęhs *he unloosens it* (-ⁿu'narihsi-).

unnecessary. *adj.* nehrahehnawęréhtha' *he is an unnecessary person* (-ne-. -hehnawęręhT-).

unpalatable. *adj.* yuha'yá·ryu't *unpalatable* (-ha'yaryu'T-).

unpleasant. *adj.* yawę'nę́·ti· *it is unpleasant* (-ę'nęti-).

unproductive. *adj.* kwęhs arwetiyáhshek *unproductive* (kwęhs -eti(y)-).

unquenchable. *adj.* kwęhs aryu'θwáhnęk *it is unquenchable* (kwęhs -a'= θwahT-).

unravel. *v.i.* wa'rurę́·kwahs *it unravels* (-a'ruręku-); *v.t.* rahwanháhsyęhs *he unravels it* (-hwanhahsi-).

unreal. *adj.* kwęhs wehre'ę̀·we ará·kę·k *unreal* (kwęhs wehre'ę̀·we -i-).

unreasonable. *adj.* kwęhs aryurihwakahrę́'nak *it is unreasonable* (kwęhs -rih= wakahrę'T-).

unrelated. *adj.* kwęhs ahra'nęnęhwíhek *he is unrelated* (kwęhs -a'nęnęhwih-).

unrelenting. *adj.* kwęhs ahru'θhęnyę́'thek *he is unrelenting* (kwęhs -(i)'= θhęnyę'T-).

unrepenting. *adj.* kwęhs ahrętathrewá'thek *he is unrepenting* (kwęhs -ęta= threwa'T-).

unrip. *v.t.* ra'tí·kwsyęhs *he unrips it* (-'tikʷsi-).

unripe. *n.* á·θe·' *unripe* (á·θe·').

unruly. *adj.* ra'nęnę'yaksę́'tha' *he is unruly* (-a'nęnę'yaksę'T-).

unsatisfactory. *adj.* kwęhs ę'nayu'tikęhriyúhnęk *unsatisfactory* (kwęhs -t-. -(ę)'tikęhriyuhT-); kwęhs aryu'tikęhriyú'nęk *unsatisfactory* (kwęhs -(ę)'ti= kęhriyu'T-).

unseemly. *adj.* kwęhs aryuya'tawyésnęk *unseemly* (kwęhs -ya'tawyesT-).

unsocial. *adj.* kwęhs ahruríhwarak *he is unsocial* (kwęhs -rihwar-).

unspoiled. *adj.* kwęhs aryu'nahča'náhkęk *unspoiled* (kwęhs -a'nahča=

'nahkw -).

unstring. *v.t.* rúhθręhs *he unstrings it* (-uhθ(e)r -).

unswerving. *adj.* thrawe⁷náhkę *he is unswerving* (-t-. -e⁷nahkw -).

untamed. *adj.* a⁷wthę́ha⁷ *untamed* (a⁷wthę́ha⁷).

untie. *v.t.* rahtrę́hsyęhs *he unties it* (-(i)htręhsi -).

until. *prep.* θhę́⁷ru⁷ *until* (θhę́⁷ru⁷); uθę́·the⁷ *until* (uθę́·the⁷).

untimely. *adj.* kwęhs aryúhek *untimely* (kwęhs -(i)he -).

untwist. *v.t.* nehrahwanhatíhsyęhs *he untwists it* (-ne-. -hwanhatihsi -).

unwind. *v.t.* nehrahwanhatíhsyęhs *he unwinds it* (-ne-. -hwanhatihsi -).

unwrap. *v.t.* na⁷nyahkwanháhsyęhs *one unwraps another* (-yahkwanhahsi -).

up high. *adv.* stá·kwi⁷ *up high* (stá·kwi⁷).

up-so-quick-none-so-pretty. *n.* kanú·ta·⁷ *up-so-quick-none-so-pretty* (-nuta -).

uphold. *v.t.* nehrúhkwa⁷nę *he upholds it* (-ne-. -(i)hkʷa⁷T -).

upright. *adj.* tihru⁷náhkwrę· *he is upright* (ti-. -aT-. -ahkwrę -); see: -ut.

uproar. *n.* yu⁷nahka⁷rà·yę⁷ *uproar* (-a⁷= nahka⁷rayę(T) -); u⁷náhka⁷reh *uproar* (-a⁷nahka⁷r -).

uproot. *v.t.* rahne⁷rawíhsyęhs *he uproots it* (-hne⁷rawihsi -).

upside down. *adj.* kahswakwę́⁷nar *it is upside down* (-hswakwę⁷nar -).

upstart. *n.* raθhuhwáhkę *he is an upstart* (-θhuhwahkw -).

urbane. *adj.* uta⁷nakęw⁷áh *urbane* (-ta= 'nakęw.#áh).

urethra. *n.* u⁷čaka⁷rę̀·weh *urethra* (-⁷ča= ka⁷ręw -).

urge. *v.t.* račirù·ręh *he urges it* (-čirurę -); rahsnyà·rę *he urges it* (-hsnyar -).

urgent. *adj.* yu⁷né·θwekt *it is urgent* (-a⁷neθwekT -).

urinate. *v.i.* ru⁷nyá·kye· *he urinated* (-a= 'nyake -).

urine. *n.* u⁷nhę́heh *urine* (-⁷nhęh -); u⁷nhęhsú·kreh *foul or disgusting urine* (-⁷nhęhsukr -).

use. *v.t.* ráhstha⁷ *he uses it* (-(i)hsT -); wáčtha⁷ *it uses it* (-ačT -); ęyęčnáhkwa⁷ *one will use it for* (-ačnahkw -); nakahs⁷áhnahk *it used it up* (-t-. -(i)hs⁷a -).

used to, get. *v.t.* rarę́⁷nha⁷θ *he gets used to it* (-rę⁷nha⁷ -).

useful. *adj.* ráhsa⁷k *he is useful* (-hsa̲⁷k -).

usher. *n.* račarà·nęh *usher* (-č̲a̲r̲a̲nę -).

usurp. *v.i.* rá·tkwahs *he usurps* (-atku -).

usurpation. *n.* ha⁷ rú·tkwę *usurpation* (-atku -).

uvula. *n.* uháhkwareh *uvula* (-hahkwar -).

V

vacancy. *n.* ha⁷ yutákwnu·t *vacancy* (-takwnut).

vaccinate. *v.i.* rayęthúhθe⁷ *he vaccinates* (-yęthuhθe -).

vagina. *n.* učísneh *vagina* (-čisn -).

vaguely. *part.* kwení⁷sayę⁷ *vaguely* (kwení⁷sayę⁷).

value. *n.* u⁷ę̀·yeh *value* (-⁷ęy -).

value, little. *n.* see: -čayę(T) -.

value, assign a. *v.t.* rakara⁷tyè·nęh *he assigns a value to it* (-k̲a̲r̲a̲⁷tyenę -).

vanity. *n.* unayé⁷čreh *vanity* (-naye⁷čr -); unayé⁷ę *vanity* (-naye⁷ -).

vanquish. *v.t.* rękwé⁷tha⁷ *he vanquishes it* (-ę̊kʷe⁷T -).

vanquished. *adj.* rawękwé⁷ę *he is vanquished* (-ę̊kʷe⁷ -).

vary. *v.i.* newat⁷níhahs *it varies* (-ne-. -at⁷niha -).

vegetable. *n.* uhné⁷reh *vegetable* (-hne⁷=

r-).

vehicle. *n.* u'θréhčreh *vehicle* (-(i)' = θrehčr-).

veil. *n.* uné'reh *veil* (-ne'r-).

vein. *n.* unehyá·θeh *vein* (-nehyaθ-).

venereal disease. *n.* účkreh *venereal disease* (-čkr(e'n)-).

vermillion. *n.* ukwéhčreh *vermillion* (-kwehčr-); kwéht *vermillion* (-kweh= T-).

vertical. *adj.* tihru'náhkwre· *he is vertical* (ti-.-aT-.-ahkwre-).

very. *adv.* weyúhre· *very* (weyúhre·); ka'né *very* (ka'né); tha'awè·ruh *very* (tha-.-eruh-); néh *very (emphatic)* (néh).

vest. *n.* úhsweh *vest* (-hsw-).

vestige. *n.* ču'nyeretihnáhke *vestige* (-či-.-a'nyeretihnahkw-); kayeré·tih *vestige* (-yereti-).

vex. *v.t.* na'tikehraksá'tha' *one vexes another* (-(e)'tikehraksa'T-).

vice. *n.* wáhse· *vice* (-ahse-).

view. *v.t.* ratké'θeh *he views* (-a= tke'θe-).

vigorous. *adj.* ru'θwetáhraht *he is vigorous* (-'θwetahrahT-).

vile. *adj.* yu'nené'ner *it is vile* (-a' = nene'ner-).

vilify. *v.t.* na'rihwaksa'á·tih *one vilifies another* (-rihwaksa'T-{dative III}).

village. *n.* utá·'neh *village* (-ta'n-); yetá·kre' *village* (-tak(e)r-).

villagers. *n.* kayetá·kre' *villagers* (-ta= k(e)r-).

vine. *n.* une'à·reh *climbing vine* (-ne' = ar-).

vinegar. *n.* winí·kyer *vinegar* (winí·kyer).

violate. *v.t.* wa'kayethwíhstrarahk *they violated them* (-athwihstarahkw-); keyathwihstrarahkwá·tih *I am violating you* (-athwihstarahkw-{dative III}).

violent. *adj.* ru'θháhraht *he is violent* (-(i)'θhahrahT-).

violet. *adj.* čí'či' tiwahθuhkú'ne· *violet* (-či'či- ti-.-ahθuhku'ne-).

violet. *n.* newetá'rya'ks *violet* (-ne-. -(e)ta'rya'k-); newenéhrya'ks uhwaryá·ke' *Canada violet* (-ne-.-(e)= nehrya'k- -ahwaryake-); utye'nà·ri' *dogtooth violet* (-tye'nari-).

violin. *n.* učike·weh *violin* (-čikew-); yerehskaratíhtha' *violin* (-rehskara= tihT-).

viper. *n.* u'túhsare *viper* (-'tuhsare).

virgin. *n.* kawí·ne· *virgin* (-wine-).

virtue. *n.* u'nehyahréhčreh *virtue* (-a= 'nehyahrehčr-).

virtuous. *adj.* ra'nehyáhre *he is virtuous* (-a'nehyahr-).

visible. *adj.* yú·ke'·t *it is visible* (-ke'T-); neyuhketíhsne *it is visible* (-ne-.-hke= tihsT-); kayeré·tih *it is visible* (-ye= reti-).

vision, have good. *v.i.* rakahká·θne' *he has good vision* (-kahkaθn-).

vision, share a. *v.t.* nakwakahratáhči *share our vision* (-kahrat-.#hči).

visions, have. *v.i.* ru'nyeretyá·tih *he has visions* (-a'nyereti-{dative II}); rukera'ná'θeh *he has visions* (-keraT-{dative I}).

visit. *v.i.* ratá·'nyeh *he visits* (-ta'nye-); *v.t.* wa'ktá·'nye'θ *one visited me*

(-ta'nyę-{dative I}).
visit, go to. *v.i.* ratkyé'ther *he goes to visit* (-atke'th(e)r-).
vocabulary. *n.* uwętáhčreh *vocabulary* (-wętahčr-).
voice. *n.* uwę́·teh *voice* (-węt-).
voluntarily. *adv.* na'tikęhrehę̀·we *voluntarily* (-(ę)'tikęhr-.#ęwe).
volunteer. *n.* uhę́·kareh *volunteer* (-hę=kar-); rathęká·rya'ks *volunteer* (-athę=karya'k-).
volunteer. *v.i.* ruthękaryá'kę *he volunteered* (-athękarya'k-).
vomit. *n.* wáθtkęhs *vomit* (-aθT(e)k-); uθtká'čreh *vomit* (-aθtka'čr-).
vomit. *v.i.* yę́θtkęhs *one vomits* (-aθ=T(e)k-).
votive offerings, make. *v.i.* ra'nyęwahnę́·ti· *he made votive offerings* (-a='nyęwahnęti-).
vulgar. *adj.* awéhsayę' *vulgar* (-ehsayę-).

W

wages. *n.* ukaryá'kčreh *wages* (-karya'=kčr-).
waist. *n.* úhsweh *waist* (-hsw-).
wait. *v.i.* wa'khrę́hwa' *I waited* (-hrę=hw-); *v.t.* kęhręhwá'θeh *I am waiting for you* (-hręhw-{dative I}).
wake up. *v.i.* nęθkayętkáhnęw *they will wake up again* (-atkahnęhw-).
walk. *v.i.* kakuthahahkę́he' *they had been walking* (-athahahkw-); nehruthaháhkę *he is walking* (-ne-.-atha=hahkw-); í·kye' *I am walking* (-e-); ę́θawé'θhek *that it be walking around* (-či-.-e'θ-); wa'akuyá'tahti'r *one walked upright* (-ya'tahtir-).
walnut. *n.* ru'ta'rw'ú'y *walnut* (ru'-ta'rw'ú'y); ču'kwakwe'nę́·ni· *black walnut* (ču'kwakwe'nę́·ni·).

wampum. *n.* čuhtíche·θ *wampum* (čuhtí-che·θ); unękwì·reh *wampum* (-(ę)nę=kwir-).
wand. *n.* utáhsneh *wand* (-(ę)tahsn-).
wander. *v.i.* rayahstahnęhá·'nye'θ *he wanders* (-yahstahnęha'nye'-).
want. *v.i.* ru'neθwé·kih *he wants* (-a'=neθwek-); kakawerę́he' *they wanted to* (-er-).
war. *n.* u'riyú'čreh *war* (-a'riyu'čr-).
war. *v.i.* ra'riyu'črarę́'nha'θ *he wars* (-a'riyu'črarę'nha'-).
war whoop, make a. *v.i.* wahraθkwarakará·tyę' *he made the whoop (war whoop)* (-aθkwarakaratyę-).
warm. *adj.* yu'naríhę· *it is warm* (-a'=narih-); yuhnatá·wę·t *it is warm* (-hnatawę-).
warm. *v.t.* rahnatawę́hstha' *he warms it* (-hnatawęhsT-); see: -tawę-.
warm, become. *v.i.* ruhnatà·wę'θ *he becomes warm* (-hnatawę'-).
warrior. *n.* ruhskę'rakyéhne' *warrior* (-hskę'rakehT-).
wart. *n.* runę́hθkwarę' *wart* (runę́hθkwarę').
wash. *v.t.* ratúhar *he washes it* (-uhar-).
washcloth. *n.* yekθakyewá'tha' *washcloth* (-kθakewa'T-).
washer. *n.* wa'katuharę́he' *washer* (-tu=haręhe'-).
wasp. *n.* kahéche·θ *wasp* (-hecheθ-); ru'táhkę *wasp* (ru'táhkę).
watch. *v.t.* kayętkę́'θeh *they are watching it* (-atkę'θe-); rawę́nę́nhyar *he watches it* (-ęnęnhyar-).
water. *n.* à·wę' *water* (à·wę'); kahné·kayę'θ *a body of water* (-hnekayę(T)-{dative I}); yaweká·tkęhθ *stagnant water* (-ekatkęh-); aweká·θe' *fresh water* (-ekaθe').
water. *v.t.* rehrá'tha' *he waters (e.g., the animals)* (-ïhra'T-).
water, be in. *v.i.* see: -u-.

water, put in. *v.t.* see: -uha-.

water hemlock. *n.* nę·tu·ʔ *water hemlock* (nę·tu·ʔ).

water lily. *n.* ruhséhkwrę *water lily* (ruhséhkwrę).

water moccasin. *n.* tyaweryahnatkwarà·yęʔ *water moccasin* (ti-.-eryahna=tkwarayę(T)-).

waterfall. *n.* yuhtawę́ʔę *waterfall* (-hta=węʔ-).

watermelon. *n.* neyuręhyayęʔáh *watermelon* (-ne-.-ręhyayę(T)-.#áh).

watery. *adj.* awę́ʔči *watery (of food)* (awę́ʔ.#hči); awę́ʔkye *watery (of roads)* (awę́ʔ.#ke).

wave. *n.* utúʔtaʔ *wave* (-tuʔt-).

wave. *v.i.* węnéhkwręh *it waves (e.g. water)* (-ęnehkwr-).

waver. *v.i.* nehruʔtikę́hkye· *he wavers* (-ne-.-(ę)ʔtikęhke-).

wax. *n.* uθrę̀·weh *wax* (-θręw-).

we. *pro.* í·ʔ *we* (í·ʔ); í·ʔi· *we* (í·ʔi·); héʔ-i·ʔ *we!* (héʔi·ʔ).

weaken. *v.t.* račiʔyuhčrę́·tih *he weakens it* (-čiʔyuhčręti-).

wealth. *n.* unękwì·reh *wealth* (-(ę)nę=kwir-).

wean. *v.t.* naʔrù·rahs *one weans another* (-rur-); naʔnęhraʔsáhkwahs *one weans another* (-nęhraʔsahkw-).

weapon. *n.* yę́čthaʔ *weapon* (-ačT-).

wear. *v.t.* rú·θnę *he's wearing it* (-θn-); rúhnyę *he wore it* (-(i)hnya-).

weary, grow. *v.i.* raʔnéhreʔθ *he grows weary* (-aʔnehr(eʔ)-).

weasel. *n.* tyaʔnuhθrę́hę· *weasel* (tyaʔnuhθrę́hę·).

weather. *n.* tiwę́·ʔnyer *weather* (ti-.-ęʹnyer-).

web. *n.* yunę́ʔraʔr *web* (-nęʔraʔr-).

Wednesday. *n.* áhsę tičuhtérhę *Wednesday* (áhsę ti+či-.-hterhę-).

weed. *n.* uherúhkweh *weed* (-heruhkw-).

weed. *v.i.* raherúhskwahs *he weeds* (-he=ruhskw-).

welcome. *n.* haʔ kanęherá·tęht *welcome* (-nęheratehT-); nyà·wę *you're welcome* (nyà·wę).

well. *adv.* ahskę̀·nęʔ *well* (-hskęnęʔ-).

well. *n.* učaʔtúhsteh *well* (-čaʔtuhst-).

west. *n.* wewarerę́·tyęhs *west* (-yah-.-areręti-).

wet. *adj.* učáʔkraʔ *wet* (-čaʔkr-).

wet. *v.t.* račaʔkrę́·tih *he wets it* (-čaʔ=kręti-).

wet, get. *v.i.* ęktyaʔkrę́·tiʔ *I got wet* (-tyaʔkręti-).

wetness. *n.* učáʔkraʔ *wetness* (-čaʔkr-).

whale. *n.* uhsú·kawe·θ *whale* (uhsú·ka-we·θ).

what. *n.* teʔ *what* (teʔ).

wheat. *n.* ú·tuhs *wheat* (-tuhs).

wheel. *n.* ukáʔneh *wheel* (-kaʔn-); ukaʔnę́·te *wheel* (-kaʔnęte).

wheelbarrow. *n.* yakęhraʔθkwáhthaʔ *wheelbarrow* (-ęʰhraʔθkʷahT-); uʔθréhčreh neyęhčaráhkhwaʔ *wheelborrow* (-(i)ʔθrehčr- -ne-.-ahčarahkw-).

when. *adv.* áθę *when* (áθę); kahnę́ʔkye *when* (kahnę́ʔkye); neʔ *when* (neʔ); ù·nę hésnę· *when* (ù·nę hésnę·); haʔ ù·nę *when* (haʔ ù·nę).

whenever. *adv.* tikawęnì·yuʔ *whenever* (tikawęnì·yuʔ).

---

where. *adv.* kę^ʔ *where* (kę^ʔ); hę̀·we *where* (hę̀·we).

whimsical. *adj.* yutérhya^ʔt *it is whimsical* (-terhya^ʔT-); ruyáhčih *he is whimsical* (-yahč-).

whip. *n.* učí^ʔrureh *whip* (-či^ʔr<u>u</u>r-).

whip. *v.t.* wa^ʔna^ʔtehę́hčrę·^ʔ *one whipped another* (-tehę̧hčrę-); na^ʔtéhę̧č *one whips another* (-tehę̧r(uk)-).

whippoorwill. *n.* kwa^ʔkúrhyeh *whippoorwill* (kwa^ʔkúrhyeh).

whirl. *v.i.* kayę́hkwatač *it whirls* (-yę̧h=kw<u>a</u>tat-).

whirlpool. *n.* nekahtawakwá^ʔnahč *whirlpool* (-ne-.-htaw<u>a</u>kwa^ʔnahT-).

whirlwind. *n.* yu^ʔθkurę́·^ʔnye^ʔ *whirlwind* (-(i)^ʔθkurę'nye^ʔ-).

whisper. *v.i.* račíhę̧h *he whispers* (-či=hę̧-).

whistle. *v.i.* ratá·kar *he is whistling* (-ta=k<u>a</u>r-); nyetá·kare^ʔ *one whistles* (-t-.-tak<u>a</u>r-).

white. *adj.* uhwaryá·kę^ʔ *white* (-ahwa=ryakę-); see: -kę̧rat.

whitefish. *n.* kę̧čahwaryá·kę^ʔ *whitefish* (-ičahwaryakę-).

whiteman. *n.* krirù·rę^ʔ *whiteman* (krirù·-rę^ʔ).

whiteness. *n.* uhwá^ʔneh *whiteness* (-hwa^ʔn-).

whitish. *adj.* yuhwà·ra^ʔneht *it is whitish* (-ahw<u>a</u>r<u>a</u>'nehT-).

whittle. *v.i.* rahrenhę́·tyę̧h *he is whittling* (-hrenhę̧tyę̧-).

who. *pro.* káhne·^ʔ *who* (káhne·^ʔ).

whoever. *pro.* káhne·^ʔ *whoever* (káhne·^ʔ).

whole. *adj.* à·wur *whole (of things)* (-ur-).

whole, make. *v.t.* see: -k^wek-.

whoop. *v.i.* raθkwár^ʔehs *he whoops* (-aθkw<u>a</u>r^ʔe(k)-).

whooping cough. *n.* ha^ʔ wa^ʔnihę́·thuhs *whooping cough* (-a'nihę̧thu-).

whooping crane. *n.* ruhákwarę̧t *whooping crane* (ruhákwarę̧t).

why. *adv.* téher *why* (téher).

wick. *n.* uhsì·reh *wick* (-hsir-).

wicked. *adj.* rurihwatér^ʔahs *he is wicked* (-rihw<u>a</u>ter^ʔ(ak)-).

wicker. *n.* kayarę́·tih *wicker* (-yarę̧ti-).

wicket. *n.* učareháh *wicket* (-č<u>a</u>r-.#ah).

wide. *adj.* kahwačí·yu· *wide* (-hwačiyu-); neyuhčí·yu· *it is wide* (-ne-.-hčiyu-).

widen. *v.t.* rahwačiyúhtha^ʔ *he widens it* (-hwačiyuhT-).

widower. *n.* rúsθę̧r *he is a widower* (-as=θ<u>ę</u>r).

wife. *n.* yéhnę̧w *wife* (-hnę̧w-); katyá·kę̧ *wife* (-tyak-); yè·nę̧h *wife* (-nę̧-).

wig. *n.* yę̧tkye^ʔwrákhwa^ʔ *wig* (-a=tke^ʔwraku-).

wiggle. *v.i.* ratkwáhnę̧h *he wiggles* (-a=tkwahnę̧-).

wild. *adj.* a^ʔwthę́ha^ʔ *wild* (a^ʔwthę́ha^ʔ).

wildcat. *n.* tkę̧hwè·nuh *wildcat* (tkę̧h-wè·nuh).

willing. *adj.* rurhà·re^ʔ *he is willing* (-rhar-).

willow. *n.* krę́rhyu *weeping willow* (krę́r-hyu); tikači^ʔruratkwarà·yę^ʔ *rose willow* (ti-.-či^ʔr<u>u</u>ratkw<u>a</u>rayę(T)-).

wilted flower. *n.* yuči^ʔčihstuhrí^ʔę̧ *wilted flower* (-či^ʔčihstuhri^ʔ-).

win. *v.i.* ratkwé·nyę̧hs *he wins* (-atkwe=ni-); *v.t.* wáhskhwę̧^ʔr *you won from me* (-hwę̧r-).

wind. *n.* wú·^ʔna·č *wind* (-u'n<u>a</u>T-); ù·wereh *wind* (-w(e)r-).

wind. *v.t.* rahwanhá^ʔθehs *he winds it* (-hwanha^ʔθe-); rahwánhahs *he winds it* (-hwanh-); rathnę̧hstę́·tih *he winds it into a ball* (-athnę̧hstęti-).

winding. *adj.* neyu^ʔnu^ʔknę́·kwę̧ *it is winding* (-ne-.-a'nu^ʔknę̧ku-).

window. *n.* yunę̧hsáhrarę̧ *window* (-nę̧h=sahr<u>a</u>r-); awé·kyeh *window* (-ek-); yawekanę̧^ʔná·kę̧ *window* (-ek<u>a</u>nę̧'nak-).

window sash. *n*. θwé·ka·t *window sash* (-či-. -ekaT-).

wine. *n*. wekę́·tih *wine* (-ekęti-).

wing. *n*. ú·wyeh *wing* (-wy-); uyęh-wí·θneh *wing* (-yęhwiθ(n)-).

wingspan. *n*. ú·wyeh *wingspan* (-wy-).

wink. *v.i.* nahratkár[?]u[?] *he winked* (-t-. -atkar[?]u-); nehratkahčira[?]níhahs *he winks* (-ne-. -atkahčira[?]niha-).

winnow. *v.t.* waka[?]rhè·wę *I winnow it* (-a[?]rhew-).

winter. *n*. kuhsérhę *winter* (kuhsérhę).

winter. *v.i.* ra[?]núhstęh *he winters* (-a='nuhstę-).

wipe. *v.t.* rarakyè·wahs *he wipes it* (-akew-).

wire. *n*. uhsì·reh *wire* (-hsir-).

wit. *n*. awé·ha·k *a wit* (-ehak-).

witch. *n*. kakútkę[?] *witches* (-atkę-); yetihsayę[?]nè·rih *witch* (-tihsayę'ner-); ucę́húhkweh *flickering-light witch* (-(a)čęhuhkw-); čuhkwá·tę·t *witch* (čuhkwá·tę·t).

witch hazel. *n*. súhwe[?]t *witch hazel* (súhwe[?]t).

witchcraft. *n*. útkęht *witchcraft* (-a=tkęhT-); urę́·teh *witchcraft* (-ręN-); ha[?] yetihsayę[?]nè·rih *witchcraft* (-tih=sayę'ner-).

withdraw. *v.i.* ęhsatkyerha[?]né[?]ku[?] *you will withdraw* (-atkerha[?]ne[?]ku-); thra[?]nihę́·thuhs *he withdraws* (-t-. -a'nihęthu-).

wizard. *n*. ru[?]ręnę́·ti· *wizard* (-a[?]ręneti-).

wolf. *n*. θkwarì·nę *wolf* (θkwarì·nę).

woman. *n*. akę́·kweh *woman* (-ę°kʷe-); yeθrà·yeh *young woman* (-θray-);

yéhnęw *woman of the house* (-hnęw-).

womb. *n*. yęt[?]nęht[?]áhstha[?] *womb* (-at='nęht[?]ahsT-).

wonder. *n*. ha[?] yunehrá·kwaht *a wonder* (-nehrakwahT-).

wonder. *v.i.* tikayę́·[?]nyer *they wonder* (ti-. -a'nyer-).

wonderfully. *adv*. yunęhrakwahnęhá·[?]nye[?] *wonderfully* (-nehrakwahnęha='nye[?]-).

wood. *n*. úhkareh *wood* (-(a)hkar-); uhwę́[?]khareh *wood* (-hwę[?]khar-); uyękwì·reh *wood* (-yękwir-).

wood betony. *n*. runęhkwrę̀·rę *wood betony* (runęhkwrę̀·rę).

woodchuck. *n*. runá[?]kę·t *woodchuck* (runá[?]kę·t).

woodcock. *n*. rutihkę·t[?]ú[?]y *woodcock* (rutihkę·t[?]ú[?]y).

woodpecker. *n*. nà·ra[?]r *red-headed woodpecker* (nà·ra[?]r); tá[?]kwnę[?] *small gray woodpecker* (tá[?]kwnę[?]); ní[?]sni[?]s *speckled woodpecker* (ní[?]sni[?]s).

woods. *n*. úrha[?]neh *woods* (-rha'n-).

woodshed. *n*. yeyękwirayę[?]náhkhwa[?] *woodshed* (-yękwirayę'nahkw-).

wool. *n*. ukrì·reh *wool* (-krir-); utíhkweh *wool* (-(ę)tihkw-).

word. *n*. uwę́·teh *word* (-węt-).

wordy. *adj*. yuwętaká[?]ne[?] *wordy* (-węta=ka[?]ne-).

work. *v.i.* rayú[?]ne[?] *he works* (-yu[?]=n(e)-).

workshop. *n*. kayu[?]nę́htha[?] *workshop* (-yu[?]nęhT-).

worldly. *adj*. a[?]wna[?]kyéha·[?] *worldly*

(-a'wT-.#keha·').

worm. *n.* uhtyárheh *worm* (-htyarh-).

worms, have. *v.i.* runré̜hahs *he has worms* (-nré̜h-).

worn out. *v.i.* the' nakahsnáhkȩk *it is worn out* (the' t-.-(i)hsnahkw-).

worship. *v.t.* rarihwayé̜·tih *he worships it* (-rihwa̲yȩti-).

worst. *adj.* ratkiwá·tha' *he is the worst* (-atkiwaT-).

worthless. *adj.* the' nakahsnáhkȩk *it is worthless* (the' t-.-(i)hsnahkw-).

worthy. *adj.* ruthwȩ̀·rȩ *he is worthy* (-a= thwȩr-).

wound. *v.t.* raya'nè·rȩh *he wounds it* (-aya'nerȩ-); wahrú·thȩ' *he wounded it* (-uthȩ-).

wrap. *v.t.* yuhkwá·θȩ *it is wrapped* (-hkwaθ-); rahwánhahs *he wraps it up* (-hwanh-); wa'aké̜hskwik *one wrapped it up* (-ȩ̊hskwi(k)-); rahwanhá'θehs *he wraps it up* (-hwan= ha'θe-).

wrapper. *n.* yehwanháhstha' *wrapper* (-hwanhahsT-).

wrath. *n.* učhá'reh *wrath* (-čha'r-).

wreath. *n.* yȩ'ta'rahwanháhstha' *wreath* (-a'ta'ra̲hwanhahsT-); yȩ'ta'rahtré̜hstha' *wreath* (-a'ta'ra̲htrȩhsT-).

wreckage. *n.* yuhskawé̜hnȩ *wreckage* (-hska̲wȩhT-).

wrestle. *v.i.* nehra'nyè·nȩhs *he wrestles* (-ne-.-a'nyenȩ-).

wrinkle. *n.* uθrí'reh *wrinkle* (-θri'r-).

wrinkle. *v.i.* wačri'rarù·rȩh *it wrinkles* (-ačri'rarurȩ-).

wring out. *v.t.* wahračirwé̜hstȩ·' *he wrings it out* (-čirwȩhsthȩ-).

wrist. *n.* uθè·reh *wrist* (-θer-).

wristwatch. *n.* yȩthahsȩhnáhkhwa' *wristwatch* (-athahsȩhnahkw-).

write. *v.i.* nehra'né̜'θha' *he writes* (-ne-.-'nȩ'θ-).

writer. *n.* ra'nȩ'θha'á·ka·' *writer* (-'nȩ'θ-.#keha·').

writing. *n.* u'nȩ'θé̜hsteh *writing* (-'nȩ'= θȩhst-).

wrong, do. *v.i.* thahsa'rihwá·twaht *you did wrong* (tha-.-a'rihwatwahT-).

Y

yam. *n.* učhé'weh *yam* (-čhe'w-).

yard. *n.* uhéhneh *yard (lawn)* (-hehn-); θkáhθa·t *yard (unit of measure)* (-či-.-hθaT-).

yarrow, common. *n.* ukhrȩ̀·weh utráhneh *common yarrow* (-khrȩw- -trahn-).

yawn. *v.i.* newakska'yakwáhtha' *I am yawning* (-ne-.-hska'ya̲kʷahT-); nehruhskahrȩwáhtha' *he yawns* (-ne-.-(i)hskahrȩwahT-).

yawner. *n.* nehruhskahrȩwahthá'θkȩ· *yawner* (-ne-.-(i)hskahrȩwahT-.-hsk-).

year. *n.* awúhsteh *year* (-uhst-).

yearly. *adv.* θwuhstathá·'nye' *yearly* (-či-.-uhstatha'nye-).

yearn for. *v.t.* wehráhkwa'nȩ *he yearns for it* (-yah-.-(i)hkʷa̲'T-).

yelling. *n.* uhsá·kwareh *yelling* (-hsa= kʷar-).

yellow. *adj.* uči'tkwáhneh *yellow* (-či'= tkwahn-).

yellow, grow. *v.i.* kači'tkwáhnu·č *it grows yellow* (-či'tkwahnut).

yellow dock *n.* í·tyate' *yellow dock* (í·tyate').

yellow jackets. *n.* tikači'tkwahnayȩ'ȩtíh *yellow jackets* (ti-.-či'tkwahna̲yȩ(T)-.#ȩtíh).

yes. *interj.* ȩ̀·hȩ· *yes* (ȩ̀·hȩ·).

yesterday. *n.* thé·'nȩ' *yesterday* (thé·'-nȩ').

yet. *adv.* séher *yet* (séher).

yoke. *n.* úhkareh *yoke* (-(a)hka̲r-); utáhsneh *yoke* (-(ȩ)tahsn-).

you. *pro.* í·θ *you* (í·θ); hé'²i·θ *you!* (hé'²-
 i·θ).
young. *adj.* kkaθ'²ahkę́he'² *I was young*
 (-kaθ'²ah.#kęhe'²).
youth. *n.* awękwehstá·θe·'² *youth* (-ę°=
 k"ehstaθe·'²).

Z

zeal. *n.* urharáhčreh *zeal* (-rharahčr-).
zigzag. *adj.* neyu'²nu'²knę́·kwę *it is zigzag* (-ne-.-a'nu'²knęku-).

INDEX OF PROPER NAMES

A

Ahkwesasne Reservation residents. *n.* Wahkweθa⁷θkyehá·ka·⁷ *residents of the Ahkwesasne Mohawk Reservation* (-ahkweθa⁷θ-.#ke.#aka·⁷).

Akutrę̀·we. *n.* Akutrę̀·we *Akutrę̀·we (mythic creature)* (Akutrę̀·we).

Albany, New York. *n.* Θkahnéhtati *Albany, New York* (Θkahnéhtati).

Algonquian. *n.* Nwá⁷kan *Algonquian* (Nwá⁷kan).

Alleghanean. *n.* Uhiyu⁷á·ka·⁷ *resident of the Alleghany Seneca Reservation* (-hiyu-.#aka·⁷).

Alleghany Reservation. *n.* Uhì·yu⁷ *Alleghany Seneca Reservation* (-hiyu-).

America. *n.* Ha⁷ Kę̀·ne⁷ Yuhwè·nu⁷ *America* (kę̀·ne⁷ -hwenu-).

Americans. *n.* Wahstęhá·ka·⁷ *Americans* (Wahstęhá·ka·⁷), Kę̀·ne⁷ Kahwena⁷kyehá·ka·⁷ *Americans* (kę̀·ne⁷ -hwe=na⁷ke.#aka·⁷).

Andaste. *n.* Čunahstí·yu· *Andaste* (Čunahstí·yu·).

Asia. *n.* U⁷wnanę́ha⁷ *Asia* (-a⁷wna=nęha⁷-).

Auburn, New York. *n.* Áhsku·⁷ (-ah=sku-).

Á·kuks. *n.* Á·kuks *Á·kuks (mythic creature)* (Á·kuks).

B

Bad Mind. *n.* Ka⁷tikęhrá·ksę· *Bad Mind* *(one of the primordial twins)* (-(ę)⁷ti=kęhraks-).

Bear Clan. *n.* Uhčíhrę⁷ *Bear Clan* (-hčihrę-), Tihréčha⁷ks *White Bear Clan* (-tihrečha⁷k-).

Beaver Clan. *n.* Rakinęhá·ka·⁷ *he is of the Beaver Clan* (kì·nę⁷.#aka·⁷).

Boston, Massachusetts. *n.* Wáhstę *Boston, Massachusetts* (Wáhstę).

British. *n.* Kuráhku· *British* (Kuráhku·).

Brotherton, New York. *n.* Nyę́·tkye *Brotherton, New York (eighteen century community of New England Algonquian refugees on Oneida territory)* (Nyę́·tkye).

Buffalo, New York. *n.* Nyuθrù·rę⁷ *Buffalo, New York* (Nyuθrù·rę⁷).

C

Canada. *n.* Swé·kę⁷ *Canada* (Swé·kę⁷).

Canandaigua, New York. *n.* Uta⁷naráhkhwa⁷ *Canandaigua, New York* (-ta'narahkw-).

Cattaraugus Seneca. *n.* Katarakraθ⁷á·ka·⁷ *residents of the Cattaraugus Seneca Reservation* (Katarakraθ⁷á·ka·⁷).

Cauteghna. *n.* Kahtéhnu·⁷ *Cauteghna (Tuscarora village in colonial North Carolina, occupied until the eighteenth century)* (-htehnu-).

Cayuga. *n.* Kwęyukwęhá·ka·⁷ *Cayuga* (Kwęyukwęhá·ka·⁷); Čuhkwá·tę·t *Cayuga* (čuhkwá·tę·t).

Celandine. *n.* Wawahú⁷y *mythic tree that*

marked the home of He-Holds-The-Earth (wawahúʔy).

Cherokee. *n.* Uyá·taʔ *Cherokee* (Uyá·taʔ).

Chief of the Bear Clan. *n.* Nekayę́·tęʔ *Chief of the Bear Clan* (Nekayę́·tęʔ), Utekwahtęʔáh *The-Bear-Cub (Chief of the Bear Clan)* (Utekwahtęʔáh).

Chief of the Beaver Clan. *n.* Nihnuhkà·weʔ *He-Anoints-The-Hide (Chief of the Beaver Clan)* (Nihnuhkà·weʔ), Karihę́·tyeʔ *It-Goes-Along-Teaching (Chief of the Beaver Clan)* (-rihęti-), Nekahęwáhθhę· *Twenty-Canoes (Chief of the Beaver Clan)* (-ne-.-hęwahθhę-).

Chief of the Snipe Clan. *n.* Thanetáhkhwaʔ *Chief of the Snipe Clan* (Thanetáhkhwaʔ), Karętawáʔkę *One-Is-Holding-The-Tree (Chief of the Snipe Clan)* (-rętawaʔk-).

Chief of the Turtle Clan. *n.* Hutyuhkwawáʔkę *He-Holds-The-Multitude (Chief of the Turtle Clan)* (Hutyuhkwawáʔkę), Nihawęnáʔah *His-Voice-Is-Small (Chief of the Turtle Clan)* (Nihawęnáʔah), Sekwaríʔθre· *Spear-Carrier (Chief of the Turtle Clan)* (-hsekʷariʔθ(e)r-).

Chief of the Wolf Clan. *n.* Neyučháʔktę *It-Is-Bent (Chief of the Wolf Clan)* (Neyučháʔktę), Nayuhkawéʔah *Chief of the Wolf Clan* (Nayuhkawéʔah).

Creator. *n.* Tharęhyawáʔkę *Creator* (tha-.-ręhyawaʔk-).

D

Delaware Indians. *n.* Čhakyéha·ʔ *Delaware Indians* (Čhakyéha·ʔ).

Door-Keepers. *n.* Kayęʔčarà·nęh *Door-Keepers (Seneca Nation)* (-aʔčaranę-).

E

Eel Clan. *n.* Akunęhukwatíha·ʔ *Eel Clan* (-nęhuku-{dative III}.#ha·ʔ).

English. *n.* Kurahkuháh *English* (Kurahkuháh), Nyurhęʔθʔá·ka·ʔ *English* (-t-.-rhęʔ-.#aka·ʔ).

Erie. *n.* Skwakíhahs *Erie* (Skwakíhahs); Káhkwahs *Erie* (Káhkwahs).

Europeans. *n.* Θkanyataratiʔkuʔá·ka·ʔ *Europeans* (-či-.-nyataratiʔku-.#a=ka·ʔ).

F

Fire Dragon of the White Body. *n.* Kahahstì·nęhs *Fire Dragon of the White Body (mythic creature)* (-hahstiN-).

Flying Head. *n.* Kunęhrayę́hnęh *Flying Head (mythic creature)* (-(ę)nęhrayęh=nę-).

Fort Neoheroka. *n.* Neyuherú·kęʔ *Fort Neoheroka (a fortified Tuscarora village in colonial North Carolina)* (-ne-.-herukę-).

France. *n.* Tkayekurárhę *France* (-t-.-ku=rarhu-), Nyuʔtyáʔkye *France* (-t-.-(ę)ʔtyaʔke).

G

Genesee River. *n.* Čunehstí·yu· *Genesee River* (Čunehstí·yu·).

God. *n.* Rawęnì·yuʔ *God* (-węniyu-).

Good Mind. *n.* Kaʔtikęhrákwahst *Good Mind (one of the primordial twins)* (-(ę)ʔtikęhrakwahsT-).

Grand River Indians. *n.* Swekęʔá·ka·ʔ *Grand River Indians* (Swekęʔá·ka·ʔ).

Great-Long-Vine. *n.* Kanęʔare·θʔúʔy

Great-Long-Vine (name of a Tuscarora chief in 1727 (-nę·ʔar-.#úʔy).
Great Spirit. *n.* Uʔtikęhratukę́hti *Great Spirit* (-(ę)ʔtikęhratukęht-).

H

Ha-ha. *n.* Héheʔ *Ha-ha (female nickname)* (Héheʔ).
Half-Body. *n.* Utáʔčheh *Half-Body (mythic creature that affixes itself to promiscuous persons)* (-taʔčh-).
Handsome Lake. *n.* Ɵkanyatarí·yu· *Handsome Lake (Seneca prophet)* (-či-.-nyatariyu-).
He-Holds-The-Earth. *n.* Ruʔwnawáʔkę *He-Holds-The-Earth (mythic proto-human)* (-aʔwnawaʔk-).
He-Anoints-The-Hide. *n.* Nihnuhkà·weʔ *He-Anoints-The-Hide (Chief of the Beaver Clan)* (Nihnuhkà·weʔ).
He-Has-Plenty-Of-Beans. *n.* Ruɵaheʔrakáʔneʔ *He-Has-Plenty-Of-Beans (male proper name)* (-ɵaheʔrakaʔne-).
He-Holds-The-Heavens. *n.* Tharęhyawáʔkę *He-Holds-The-Heavens (mythic proto-human)* (tha-.-ręhyawaʔk-).
He-Holds-The-Multitude. *n.* Hutyuhkwawáʔkę *He-Holds-The-Multitude (Chief of the Turtle Clan)* (Hutyuhkwawáʔkę).
His-Voice-Is-Small. *n.* Nihawęnáʔah *His-Voice-Is-Small (Chief of the Turtle Clan)* (Nihawęnáʔah).
Holy Spirit. *n.* Uʔtikęhratukę́hti *Holy Spirit* (-(ę)ʔtikęhratukęht-).
House-In-Between. *n.* Kanęhsawę́hteʔ *House-In-Between (male proper name)* (-nęhsawęhte-).
Hudson River. *n.* Ɵkahnéhtati *Hudson River* (Ɵkahnéhtati).

I

Irish. *n.* Runáʔkę·t *Irish* (runáʔkę·t).
Iroquois Confederacy. *n.* Akunęhsyę̀·niʔ *Iroquois Confederacy* (Akunęhsyę̀·niʔ).
It-Goes-Along-Teaching. *n.* Karihę́·tyeʔ *It-Goes-Along-Teaching (Chief of the Beaver Clan)* (-rihęti-).
It-Is-Bent. *n.* Neyučháʔktę *It-Is-Bent (Chief of the Wolf Clan)* (Neyučháʔktę).

J

Jesuit. *adj.* račihę́hstačih nehraʔnewyaʔréhthaʔ *Jesuit* (-čihęhstači- -ne-.-aʔne=wyaʔręht-).
Jesus Christ. *n.* Yé·suhs *Jesus Christ* (Yé·suhs), Ruyà·ner *Jesus Christ* (-ya=n(e)(r)-).

K

Kahnawake Reserve. *n.* Kahnawáʔkye

Kahnawake Mohawk Reserve (-hna= wa^ʔke).

Kanhato, New York. *n*. Ka^ʔnháhnu·^ʔ *Kanhato, New York (an old Tuscarora village in south central New York)* (-(i)^ʔnhahnu-).

Keepers-Of-The-Fire. *n*. Kayečisnakwe^ʔnì·yu^ʔ *Keepers-Of-The-Fire (Onondaga chiefs)* (-čisnakwe^ʔniyu-).

King Blunt's Town. *n*. Rahsutá^ʔkye *King Blunt's Town (a village on the Tuscarora Reservation of 1717 in North Carolina)* (-hsuta^ʔke).

L

Last Supper. *n*. Ruyà·ner Rakhwáher *Last Supper* (-yan(e)(r)- -khwah(e)r-).

League of the Iroquois. *n*. Akunęhsyę̀·ni^ʔ *League of the Iroquois* (Akunęhsyę̀·ni^ʔ).

Lewiston, New York. *n*. Uyhę́ha·kwt *Lewiston, New York* (-(i)yhę́hakT).

Little Wolf Clan. *n*. Unę^ʔtakęw^ʔáh *Little Wolf Clan* (-nę^ʔtakęw.#áh).

Little People. *n*. ękwéhsayę^ʔ *Little People (mythic creatures)* (-ę°k^wehsayę-).

Live-House. *n*. Kanęhsę́nhe^ʔ *Live-House (male proper name)* (-nęhsęnhe-).

Lord's Prayer. *n*. Ruyà·ner Rutręnayęta^ʔčrà·węh *Lord's Prayer* (-ya= n(e)(r)- -atręnayęta^ʔcrawę-).

Lucifer. *n*. Rači^ʔręhà·wi^ʔ *Lucifer* (-či^ʔrę= haw-).

M

Meherrin. *n*. Akawę̌č^ʔá·ka·^ʔ *Meherrin* (Akawę̌č^ʔá·ka·^ʔ).

Mischief-Maker. *n*. Ɵhuhtyerę́hskę^ʔ *Mischief-Maker (mythic creature)* (Ɵhuh-

tyerę́hskę^ʔ).

Mississippi River. *n*. Uhtawiyú^ʔkye *Mississippi River* (-htawiyu^ʔke).

Mohawk. *n*. Kanyę^ʔkyehá·ka·^ʔ *Mohawk* (-nyę^ʔke.#aka·^ʔ).

Mohawk Valley. *n*. Yenę^ʔná·^ʔna·č *Mohawk Valley* (-nę^ʔna^ʔna·ɵ-).

Move-Through-House. *n*. Kanęhsiréhtha^ʔ *Move-Through-House (female proper name)* (-nęhsirehT-).

Muncytown, Ontario. *n*. Ętíhę *Muncytown, Ontario* (Ętíhę).

N

Naked-Bodies-Floating. *n*. Čunu^ʔawíhɵę^ʔ. *Naked-Bodies-Floating (female proper name)* (-čunu^ʔawi-).

Nanticokes. *n*. Ɵkanyataratihá·ka·^ʔ *Nanticokes* (-či-. -nyatarati.#aka·^ʔ).

Nativity. *n*. Kę^ʔ Tihra^ʔnę́·tih *Nativity* (kę^ʔ ti-. -a'nęti-).

Neuse River. *n*. Neyuherú·kę^ʔ Kì·nę^ʔ *Neuse River* (-ne-. -herukę- kì·nę^ʔ).

New York City. *n*. Kanę́·^ʔnu·^ʔ *New York City* (-nę'nu-).

New York State. *n*. Kanę^ʔnu·^ʔá·ka·^ʔ *New York State* (-nę'nu-.#aka·^ʔ).

Niagara Falls. *n*. Nyuhtawę́^ʔę *Niagara Falls* (-t-. -htawę^ʔ-).

Niagara Landing, New York. *n*. Yehęwakwá^ʔtha^ʔ *Niagara Landing, New York (former name of Lewiston, New York)* (-hęwak^wa^ʔT-).

Nottoway. *n*. Čiru^ʔęhá·ka·^ʔ *Nottoway* (Čiru^ʔęhá·ka·^ʔ).

O

Ojibwe. *n*. Nwá^ʔkan *Ojibwe* (Nwá^ʔkan).

Old World. *n*. u^ʔwnanę́ha^ʔ *Old World*

(-aʔwnanɛhaʔ -).

One-Is-Holding-The-Tree. *n.* Karɛtawáʔ-kɛ *One-Is-Holding-The-Tree (Chief of the Snipe Clan)* (-rɛtawaʔk -).

Oneida. *n.* Thwahrù·nɛ̨ʔ *Oneida* (Thwahrù·nɛ̨ʔ).

Onondaga. *n.* Unɛtaʔkyehá·ka·ʔ *Onondaga* (Unɛtaʔkyehá·ka·ʔ).

Ottawa, Ontario. *n.* Kuhyá·kɛ *Ottawa, Ontario* (Kuhyá·kɛ).

P

Penobscot. *n.* Nwáʔkan *Penobscot* (Nwáʔkan).

Philadelphia, Pennsylvania. *n.* Kanɛtayɛ́ʔku *Philadelphia, Pennsylvania* (Kanɛtayɛ́ʔku).

Pope. *n.* Račihɛhstačihúʔy *Pope* (-čihɛh=stači -.#úʔy).

R

Rabbit. *n.* Číhstuh *Rabbit (male proper name)* (Číhstuh).

S

Sandusky, Ohio. *n.* Čaʔnúhskye *Sandusky, Ohio* (Čaʔnúhskye).

Satan. *n.* Utkɛhčraksɛhúʔy *Satan* (-a=tkɛhčraks -.#úʔy).

Sault St. Louis. *n.* Kahnawáʔkyc *Sault St. Louis* (-hnawaʔke).

Schenectady, New York. *n.* Θkahnéhtati *Schenectady, New York* (Θkahnéhtati).

Seneca. *n.* Twaʔá·ka·ʔ *Seneca* (Twaʔá·ka·ʔ).

Shawnee. *n.* Sawà·nu *Shawnee* (Sawà·nu), Sawanuʔá·ka·ʔ *Shawnee* (Sawanu.#aka·ʔ).

Shawnee chief. *n.* Sukuhɛté·thaʔ *Shawnee chief on the Tuscarora Chiefs Council, responsible for the descendants of adopted Shawnee* (Sukuhɛté·thaʔ).

Six Nations. *n.* Akunɛhsyɛ̀·niʔ *Six Nations* (Akunɛhsyɛ̀·niʔ).

Sky Land. *n.* Urɛ́hyakɛw *Sky Land (celestial abode of the premordial protohumans)* (-rɛhyakɛw).

Small Turtle Clan. *n.* Kaθríʔkwe·θ *Small Turtle Clan* (-θriʔkweθ -).

Snipe Clan. *n.* Tawístawis *Snipe Clan* (tawístawis).

Spear-Carrier. *n.* Sekwaríʔθre· *Spear-Carrier (Chief of the Turtle Clan)* (-hsekʷariʔθ(e)r -).

Spirit of the North Wind. *n.* Kaʔtárhwaht *Spirit of the North Wind* (Kaʔtárhwaht).

St. Regis residents. *n.* Wahkweθaʔθkyehá·ka·ʔ *residents of the St. Regis Mohawk Reserve* (-ahkweθaʔθ -.#ke.#aka·ʔ).

St. Lawrence River. *n.* Kahnawáʔkye *St. Lawrence River* (-hnawaʔke).

Stone Giant. *n.* Thunɛhyárhɛ̨ʔ *Stone Gi-*

Tuscarora Pronunciation Key:
/a/ law; /e/ hat; /i/ pizza; /u/ tune; /ɛ̨/ hint; /č/ cheese; /h/ hoe; /m/ mother; /s/ same; /t/ do (before a vowel y, or w), too (elsewhere); /k/ gale (before a vowel y or w), kale (elsewhere); /n/ inhale (before a consonant or word-final), note (elsewhere), /r/ hiss (before a consonant or word-final), run (trilled as in Italian, elsewhere); /w/ cuff (before a consonant other than y or word-final), way (elsewhere); /y/ fish (before a consonant or word-final), you (elsewhere), /θ/ thing; /ʔ/ (the sound between the vowels in unh-unh); /·/ long vowel, /ʹ/ high pitch; /ˋ/ low pitch.

ant (mythic creature) (thunęhyárhęˀ).
Susquehannock. *n.* Čunahstí·yu· *Susquehannock* (Čunahstí·yu·).

T

Temperance Society. *n.* Yakwęˀnyúhkwayęˀ *Temperance Society* (-iˀnyuh=kwa̱yę(T)-).
Ten Commandments. *n.* Wáhθhę· Tyurihwá·kye· *Ten Commandments* (-ah=θhę- ti-.-rihwake-).
The-Bear-Cub. *n.* Utekwahtęˀáh *The-Bear-Cub (Chief of the Bear Clan)* (Utekwahtęˀáh).
Thunders. *n.* Híˀnęˀ *the Thunders (legendary personifications of thunder)* (híˀnęˀ).
Tonawanda Reservation Senecas. *n.* Tahnawatehá·ka·ˀ *Tonawanda Reservation Senecas* (Tahnawateh.#aka·ˀ).
Tonawanda Seneca Reservation. *n.* Tahnawá·teh *Tonawanda Seneca Reservation* (Tahnawá·teh).
Tonawanda, New York. *n.* Tahnawá·teh *Tonawanda, New York* (Tahnawá·teh).
Toronto, Ontario. *n.* Tharę́·tu·ˀ *Toronto, Ontario* (Tharę́·tu·ˀ).
Turtle Clan. *n.* Ráˀkwihs *Turtle Clan* (ráˀkwihs), Akunętheríha·ˀ *Turtle Clan* (-nęth(e)r-.#ha·ˀ).

Tuscarora. *adj.* raskarù·ręˀ *he is Tuscarora* (-skarurę-), kayę́čkarù·ręˀ *they are Tuscarora* (-ačkaruręˀ).
Tuscarora. *n.* Skarù·ręˀ *Tuscarora* (Skarù·ręˀ).
Tuscarora Reservation in New York State. *n.* Nyučirhéˀ ę *Tuscarora Reservation (archaic)* (Nyučirhéˀ ę).
Twelve Mystical Bugs. *n.* Kanęhę́·twaht *Twelve Mystical Bugs (mythic creatures)* (-nęhętwahT-).
Twenty-Canoes. *n.* Nekahęwáhθhę· *Twenty-Canoes (Chief of the Beaver Clan)* (-ne-.-hęwahθhę-).

U

United States of America. *n.* Haˀ Kę̀·neˀ Yuhwè·nuˀ *United States of America* (kę̀·neˀ -hwenu-).
Utica, New York. *n.* Yunę́·ˀnare·θ *Utica, New York* (-nę'na̱reθ-).

W

Washington, District of Columbia. *n.* Kanętakaryáhskye *Washington, District of Columbia* (kanętakaryahs.#ke).
Wolf Clan. *n.* Θkwarì·nę *Wolf Clan* (Θkwarì·nę).

INDEX OF INTERJECTIONS AND EXPRESSIVE VOCABULARY

A

ah. *interj.* á· *ah* (á·).

alas! *interj.* haháh *alas!* (haháh).

and what did you expect? *interj.* téher hę í·θ *and what did you expect?* (téher hę í·θ).

arrgh. *interj.* kwa·ʔáh *arrgh (wail of mourning said when a chief dies)* (kwa·ʔáh).

atchoo! *interj.* hehčę́ *atchoo! (sound of a sneeze)* (hehčę́).

aw. *interj.* á· *aw* (á·); kú *aw* (kú).

awful, isn't that. *interj.* ù·nę séʔči hę̀·we *isn't that awful* (ù·nę séʔči hę̀·we).

B

barf. *interj.* weʔ *barf (sound of vomiting)* (weʔ).

be it so. *interj.* háuʔ *be it so* (háuʔ).

behold! *interj.* hę́ʔę *behold!* (hę́ʔę).

blah, blah, blah. *interj.* waʔwaʔwaʔ *blah, blah, blah (sound of people talking too much)* (waʔwaʔwaʔ).

boo! *interj.* čé··n *boo! (said with hands splayed like lion's claws)* (čé··n).

bzzz. *interj.* tí··· *bzzz (sound of a mosquito)* (tí···).

C

caw. *interj.* á·ʔ, á·ʔ, á·ʔ *caw* (á·ʔ, á·ʔ, á·ʔ).

clomp, clomp

clomp, clomp. *interj.* tikętéh, tikętéh *clomp, clomp (sound of a horse running)* (tikętéh, tikętéh).

cluck. *interj.* ka·kakáh *cluck (sound of a chicken)* (ka·kakáh).

come! *v.i.* ká·či *come!* (ká·či).

come now! *interj.* čé *come now!* (čé).

crow. *interj.* kaʔiʔíʔi· *crow (morning call of a rooster)* (kaʔiʔíʔi·).

G

good enough. *interj.* thuh hè·wi *good enough* (thuh hè·wi).

gulp. *interj.* kúʔr *gulp (sound of liquid being swallowed)* (kúʔr).

H

hallelujah. *interj.* háy. *hallelujah* (háy).

Happy New Year's! *interj.* nyuyaʔáh! *Happy New Year's! (cry yelled out when arriving at someone's house on New Year's Day)* (nyú·ya·.#áh).

hello. *interj.* čwé·ʔn ahskę̀·nę hę *hello* (čwé·ʔn ahskę̀·nę hę).

hel-lo! is anybody there? *interj.* čá··hu *hel-lo! is anybody there? (yelled in the woods to see if anyone else is there)* (čá··hu).

how awful. *interj.* uhskanenáhraht *how awful* (-hskanenahrahT-); hé hà·neʔ *how awful* (hé hà·neʔ).

hush! *interj.* sy·· *hush!* (sy··).

I

isn't it? *interj.* wáhi⁷r *isn't it* (wáhi⁷r).
isn't that so? *interj.* hé hà·ne⁷ hę *isn't that so* (hé hà·ne⁷ hę).
isn't that awful? *interj.* ù·nę sé⁷či hę̀·we *isn't that awful?* (ù·nę sé⁷či hę̀·we).
it has a mind of its own. *interj.* kęrha⁷nę̀·we *it has a mind of its own (said when something refuses to stay put, like a broom that falls over each time that it is stood in a corner)* (kęrha⁷nę̀·we).

J

just a minute! *interj.* kę̀·we⁷ θhę́⁷ru⁷ *just a minute!* (kę̀·we⁷ θhę́⁷ru⁷).

K

knock knock knock. *interj.* ta⁷ta⁷tá⁷ *knock knock knock* (ta⁷ta⁷tá⁷).

L

listen! *interj.* kí⁷ah *listen!* (kí⁷ah).
look! *interj.* hę́⁷ę *look!* (hę́⁷ę).
look here! *interj.* kę⁷ sá⁷ *look here!* (kę⁷ sá⁷); sa⁷áh *look (here)!* (sa⁷áh).
look there! *interj.* sá⁷ *look (there)!* (sá⁷).

N

no wonder. *interj.* kayhá·ya· *no wonder* (kayhá·ya·).
now-now. *interj.* kú *now-now (expres-*

sion of sympathy) (kú).

O

o come now. *interj.* wah sè·nę⁷ *o come now, that's not true* (wah sè·nę⁷).
oh! *interj.* wah *oh! (and expression of surprise or emphasis)* (wah).
oh nuts! *interj.* syah *oh nuts!* (syah).
o.k. *interj.* háu⁷ *o.k.* (háu⁷).
ouch! *interj.* akyá *ouch!* (akyá).

P

phlat. *interj.* pú·ks *phlat! (sound of a noisy fart)* (pú·ks).
please. *interj.* nyà·wę *please* (nyà·wę).
plop. *interj.* plúks *plop (sound of something mushy, like mashed potatoes, hitting the floor)* (plúks).
pop. *interj.* tá⁷ks *pop* (tá⁷ks).
pow. *interj.* kwá⁷ks *pow (sound of hitting someone in the head)* (kwá⁷ks).
pshaw! *interj.* wéthnya⁷ *pshaw! (and expression of disbelieve)* (wéthnya⁷).
putt putt putt. *interj.* čitipátpat *putt putt putt (sound of the engine of an old car)* (čitipátpat).

R

run fast! *interj.* kwíhstet *run fast!* (kwíhstet).

Q

quiet! *interj.* náhst *quiet!* (náhst).

S

see! *interj.* hę́ʔę *see!* (hę́ʔę); sáʔ *see!* (sáʔ).

shiver. *interj.* sáy *shiver (of fear)* (sáy).

shucks. *interj.* wáthnyu· *shucks (an expression of disappointment)* (wáthnyu·).

squeek. *interj.* kwí·ks *squeek* (kwí·ks).

stop it! *interj.* á *stop it! (used only with children)* (á).

stop it now! *interj.* áhči *stop it now!* (áhči).

T

thank God! *interj.* háy *thank God!* (háy).

thanks. *interj.* nyà·wę *thanks* (nyà·wę).

that's too bad. *interj.* nę́h séʔči hę̀·we *that's too bad* (nę́h séʔči hę̀·we).

that's that. *interj.* hé hà·neʔ *that's that* (hé hà·neʔ).

thwuck. *interj.* pó·ks *thwuck (sound of an arrow hitting a deer or other animal in a fleshy part)* (pó·ks).

thwump. *interj.* čà·wak *thwump (sound of a spear or other projectile entering water* (čà·wak).

U

uh. *interj.* eʔ *uh (sound of hesitation in conversation)* (eʔ).

W

welcome, you're. *interj.* nyà·wę *you're welcome* (nyà·wę).

well, let's see now. *interj.* čéhnę nę́h *well, let's see now* (-yehnę- nę́h).

what'd you expect? *interj.* téher úʔnęʔ *what'd you expect?* (téher úʔnęʔ).

who knows? *interj.* tihčaryéhsteh *who knows?* (tihčaryéhsteh).

woof. *interj.* wąwąwą *woof (bark of a dog)* (wąwąwą).

Y

yeah. *interj.* è·hę· *yeah* (è·hę·).

yes, I have. *interj.* náhwęr *yes, I have* (náhwęr).

yow! *interj.* ya·híʔ *yow (said by the lead of three persons pushing a log to start them all pushing together)* (ya·híʔ).

yuk! *interj.* e·ʔ *yuk! (said of something that tastes awful)* (e·ʔ).

Z

zzzzz. *interj.* kwà·rerar *zzzzz (sound of snoring)* (kwà·rerar).

uh! *interj.* ę́h *uh! (said when lifting something heavy)* (ę́h).

Tuscarora Pronunciation Key:
/a/ law; /e/ hat; /i/ pizza; /u/ tune; /ę/ hint; /č/ cheese; /h/ hoe; /m/ mother; /s/ same; /t/ do (before a vowel y, or w), too (elsewhere); /k/ gale (before a vowel y or w), kale (elsewhere); /n/ inhale (before a consonant or word-final), note (elsewhere), /r/ hiss (before a consonant or word-final), run (trilled as in Italian, elsewhere); /w/ cuff (before a consonant other than y or word-final), way (elsewhere); /y/ fish (before a consonant or word-final), you (elsewhere), /θ/ thing; /ʔ/ (the sound between the vowels in unh-unh); /·/ long vowel, /́/ high pitch; /̀/ low pitch.

INDEX OF GRAMMATICAL MORPHEMES

A

ambulative. *sfx.* -(a)T-.
augmentative. *enc.* #ú'y.
augmentative distributive. *enc.* #eθu'.
authenticative. *enc.* #ęwe.

C

causative. *sfx.* -(a)hsT-, -(a)hT-, -(a)'T-,
  -hu-.
characterizer. *enc.* #aka·'.
cislocative. *pfx.* -t-, ka-.
completive. *sfx.* -(a)·t.
contrastive. *pfx.* tha'-, tha-.
contrastive+cislocative+factual. *pfx.*
  thwa'T(i)-.
contrastive+dualic. *pfx.* tha'ne-.
contrastive+dualic+optative. *pfx.* thę'=
  na(r)(a)-.
contrastive+dualic+factual. *pfx.* thwa'=
  T(i)-.
contrastive+factual. *pfx.* thwa'-.
contrastive+future. *pfx.* thę-.
contrastive+optative. *pfx.* tha(r)(a)-.
contrastive+repetitive+factual. *pfx.* tha=
  hęθa-.
contrastive+translocative. *pfx.* tha'we-.
customary. *enc.* #ha·', #keha·'.

D

dative. *sfx.* -(a)ti-, -(a)hθ-, -(a)'θ),
  -(a)'θe-, -ę-.

Tuscarora Pronunciation Key:
/a/ law; /e/ hat; /i/ pizza; /u/ tune; /ę/ hint; /č/
cheese; /h/ hoe; /m/ mother; /s/ same; /t/ do
(before a vowel y, or w), too (elsewhere); /k/ gale
(before a vowel y or w), kale (elsewhere); /n/
inhale (before a consonant or word-final), note
(elsewhere), /r/ hiss (before a consonant or word-

---

decessive. *enc.* #kęhe'.
diminutive. *enc.* #áh.
diminutive distributive. *enc.* #ętíh.
distributive. *sfx.* -(a)hę-, -(a)hnę-, -(a)=
  hθę-, -(a)hθrę-, -(a)tyę-, -(a)wę-,
  -(a)'θrę-, -hrę-, *enc.* #ha'nę', #kę=
  ha'nę'.
dualic. *pfx.* -ne-.
dualic+cislocative+optative. *pfx.* nę'na=
  (r)(a)-.
dualic+future. *pfx.* nę-.
dualic+future+cislocative. *pfx.* nęt-.
dualic+future+repetitive. *pfx.* nęči-.
dualic+optative. *pfx.* nę-.
dualic+optative. *pfx.* na(r)(a)-.
dualic+optative+third person singular
  agent. *pfx.* nę-.
dualic+repetitive+optative. *pfx.* nęθa=
  (r)(a)-.

E

external locative. *enc.* #ke.

F

facilatative. *sfx.* -hsk-.
factual mode. *pfx.* wa'-.
factual mode+cislocative. *pfx.* wa'T(i)-.
factual mode+dualic. *pfx.* wa'T(i)-.
factual mode+third person singular neuter agent. *pfx.* wah-.
first person dual agent=third person singular patient. *pfx.* -ne-.-khe(y)-.

---

final), run (trilled as in Italian, elsewhere); /w/ cuff
(before a consonant other than y or word-final),
way (elsewhere); /y/ fish (before a consonant or
word-final), you (elsewhere), /θ/ thing; /'/ (the
sound between the vowels in unh-unh); /·/ long
vowel, /´/ high pitch; /`/ low pitch.

first person exclusive dual agent. *pfx.*
  -yakT(i)-/-yaky-.
first person exclusive dual agent=second
  person patient. *pfx.* -kekT(i)-/-keky-.
first person exclusive dual alienable. *pfx.*
  yękT(i)-/yęky-.
first person exclusive dual inalienable.
  pfx. yakT(i)-/ yaky-.
first person exclusive dual patient. *pfx.*
  -yękT(i)-/-yęky-.
first person exclusive plural agent. *pfx.*
  -yakwa-.
first person exclusive plural agent=sec-
  ond person patient. *pfx.* -kekwa-.
first person exclusive plural alienable.
  pfx. yękwa-.
first person exclusive plural inalienable.
  pfx. yakwa-.
first person exclusive plural patient. *pfx.*
  -yękwa-.
first person inclusive dual inalienable.
  pfx. T(i)-/ny-.
first person inclusive plural inalienable.
  pfx. nwa-.
first person non-singular agent=third person feminine/ indefinite patient. *pfx.*
  -yękhi(y)-.
first person singular agent. *pfx.* -k-.
first person singular agent=second person
  singular patient. *pfx.* -kę(y)-.
first person singular agent=second person
  dual patient. *pfx.* -kekT(i)-/-keky-.
first person singular agent=second person
  plural patient. *pfx.* -kekwa-.
first person singular agent=third person
  dual patient. *pfx.* -ne-.-khe(y)-.
first person singular agent=third person
  plural patient. *pfx.* -kakhe(y)-.
first person singular agent=third person
  singular patient. *pfx.* -khe(y)-.
first person singular alienable. *pfx.* ak-/
  akʷ-.
first person singular inalienable. *pfx.* k-.
first person singular patient. *pfx.* -wak-/

-wakʷ-.
first person singular vocative. *pfx.* ku-.
future mode. *pfx.* ę-.
future mode+cislocative. *pfx.* ęT-.
future mode+repetitive. *pfx.* ęči-.

G

generic. *pfx.* čwe-.

H

habitual aspect. *sfx.* -(a)hs, -(a)hshek,
  -ęhs, -h, -hahk, -ha'?, -hk, -k.

I

inchoative. *sfx.* -(a)'?-.
instrumental. *sfx.* -(a)hkw-.
intensive. *enc.* #hči.
internal locative. -akęw.
internal locative+intensive. *sfx.* -akęw=
  'ahči.

L

lateral locative. *enc.* -akT.

M

medial locative. *sfx.* -(i)hę.

N

nominalizer. *sfx.* -(a)hčh-, -(a)hčr-,

-(a)hsh-, -(a)hst-, -(a)'čh-, -(a)'čr-.
noun prefix. *pfx.* aw-/u-.
noun suffix. *sfx.* -a', -eh, -ę', -i'.

O

optative mode. *pfx.* a(r)(a)-.
optative mode+cislocative. *pfx.* ę'na-.
optative mode+repetitive. *pfx.* ęθa-.
ordinal suffix. *enc.* #ha'nę't.

P

particularizer. *sfx.* -ę°te.
partitive. *pfx.* ti-.
partitive+cislocative. *pfx.* tit-.
partitive+dualic. *pfx.* ta'ne-.
partitive+dualic+future. *pfx.* ta'nę-.
partitive+dualic+optative. *pfx.* ta'na=(r)(a)-.
partitive+future. *pfx.* nę-.
partitive+repetitive. *pfx.* tiči-.
partitive+translocative. *pfx.* thwe-.
partitive+translocative+cislocative+factual. *pfx.* tyahwa'ʔT(i)-.
partitive+translocative+dualic+factual. *pfx.* tyahwa'ʔT(i)-.
partitive+translocative+factual. *pfx.* tyah=wa'-.
partitive+translocative+future. *pfx.* nyę-.
partitive+translocative+optative. *pfx.* tya=(r)(a)-.
partitive+translocative+repetitive+factual. *pfx.* tyahęθa-.

peripheral locative. *sfx.* -(a)'ni.
populative. *enc.* #hrunę'.
progressive. *sfx.* -(h)(a)'nye'-.
punctual aspect. *sfx.* -(a)', -', -·'.
purposive. *sfx.* -(a)hθe'-, -(a)hθre'-, -(a)hte'-, -(a)'-θre'-, -he'-.

Q

question marker. *enc.* hę.

R

reflexive. *pfx.* -a'naT(e)-.
remote. *sfx.* -he'.
repetitive. *pfx.* -či-.
reversive. *sfx.* -(a)hsi-, -(a)ku-, -ęku-, -hkwi-.

S

second person agent=first person dual patient. *pfx.* -h-skT(i)-.
second person dual actor. *pfx.* -θT(i)-/-č-.
second person dual agent=first person singular patient. *pfx.* -hskT(i)-.
second person dual agent=third person singular patient. *pfx.* -ne-.-hshe(y)-.
second person dual possessor. *pfx.* θT(i)-/č-.
second person nonsingular agent=third

Tuscarora Pronunciation Key:
/a/ law; /e/ hat; /i/ pizza; /u/ tune; /ę/ hint; /č/ cheese; /h/ hoe; /m/ mother; /s/ same; /t/ do (before a vowel y, or w), too (elsewhere); /k/ gale (before a vowel y or w), kale (elsewhere); /n/ inhale (before a consonant or word-final), note (elsewhere), /r/ hiss (before a consonant or word-final), run (trilled as in Italian, elsewhere); /w/ cuff (before a consonant other than y or word-final), way (elsewhere); /y/ fish (before a consonant or word-final), you (elsewhere), /θ/ thing; /'/ (the sound between the vowels in unh-unh); /·/ long vowel, /'/ high pitch; /`/ low pitch.

person patient. *pfx.* -kahshe(y)-.
second person nonsingular imperative. *pfx.* -čhi(y)-.
second person plural actor. *pfx.* -θwa-.
second person plural possessor. *pfx.* θwa-.
second person singular agent. *pfx.* -hs-.
second person singular agent=first person singular patient. *pfx.* -hsk-/-hsk^w-.
second person singular agent=third person singular patient. *pfx.* -hshe(y)-.
second person singular agent=third person dual patient. *pfx.* -ne-.-hshe(y)-.
second person singular agent=third person plural patient. *pfx.* -kahshe(y)-.
second person singular alienable. *pfx.* θa-.
second person singular imperative. *pfx.* θ-/č-.
second person singular imperative=first person singular patient. *pfx.* nak-/nak^w-.
second person singular imperative=first person dual patient. *pfx.* nak=T(i)-/naky-.
second person singular imperative=first person plural patient. *pfx.* nakwa-.
second person singular inalienable. *pfx.* s-.
second person singular patient. *pfx.* -θa-.
semireflexive. *pfx.* -ar-, -aT(e)-, -(ę)ni-, -(ę)ti-.
simple noun suffix. -aʔ, -eh, -eʔ, -ęʔ.
simple noun suffix+external locative. *sfx.* -aʔke, -ehke, -ęʔke.
stative aspect. *sfx.* -(a)·k, -eʔ, -ę, -ę°, -ih, -i, -k, -·, -·k.
stative factual. *sfx.* -(a)hk.

T

third person agent=third person plural patient. *pfx.* kayę'naT(ę)-.

third person dual feminine/indefinite agent. *pfx.* -ne-. -ka-, -ne-.-w-, -ne-.-ya-/-ne-.-yak-/-ne-.-ye-.
third person dual feminine/indefinite agent=first person singular patient. *pfx.* ne-.-wak-/-ne-.-wak^w-.
third person dual feminine/indefinite agent=first person nonsingular patient. *pfx.* -ne-.-yęk-/-ne-.-yęk^w-.
third person dual feminine/indefinite agent=second person singular patient. *pfx.* -ne-.-θa-.
third person dual feminine/indefinite agent=second person nonsingular patient. *pfx.* -ne-.-yeθa-.
third person dual feminine/indefinite agent=third person feminine/indefinite patient. *pfx.* -ne-.-yę'naT(e)-.
third person dual feminine/indefinite alienable. *pfx.* -ne-.-yakaw-/-ne-.-yaku-.
third person dual feminine/indefinite inalienable. *pfx.* -ne-.-ka-, -ne-.-w-, -ne-.-ya-/-ne-.-yak-/-ne-.-ye-.
third person dual masculine agent. *pfx.* -ne-.-hra-.
third person dual masculine alienable. *pfx.* -ne-. -hraw-/-ne-.-hru-.
third person dual masculine inalienable. *pfx.* -ne-.-hra-.
third person dual masculine patient. *pfx.* -ne-. -hraw-/-ne-.-hru-.
third person nonsingular feminine/indefinite agent=second person patient. *pfx.* -yęčhi(y)-.
third person plural agent. *pfx.* -kaya-/-kayak-/-kaye-.
third person plural agent=second person singular patient. *pfx.* -kayeθa-.
third person plural agent=first person singular patient. *pfx.* -kayęk-/-ka=yęk^w-.
third person plural alienable. *pfx.* ka=kaw-/kaku-.

third person plural inalienable. *pfx.* ka=
ya-/kayak-/kaye-.
third person plural patient. *pfx.* -kakaw-/
-kaku-.
third person singular feminine/indefinite
agent. *pfx.* -ya-/-yak-/-ye-.
third person singular feminine/indefinite
agent=first person nonsingular patient.
pfx. -yękhi(y)-.
third person singular feminine/indefinite
agent=second person singular patient.
pfx. -yeθa-.
third person singular feminine/indefinite
agent=third person dual feminine/in-
definite patient. *pfx.* -ne-.-yę'naT(e)-.
third person singular feminine/indefinite
agent=third person plural patient. *pfx.*
-yę'naT(e)-.
third person singular feminine/indefinite
inalienable. ak-/e-.
third person singular feminine/indefinite
patient. *pfx.* -yakaw-/-yaku-.
third person singular masculine agent.
pfx. -hra-.
third person singular masculine agent=
first person singular patient. *pfx.*
-hrak-/-hrakʷ-.
third person singular masculine alienable. *pfx.* raw-/ru-.
third person singular masculine inalienable. *pfx.* ra-.
third person singular masculine patient.
pfx. -hraw-/ -hru-.
third person singular neuter agent. *pfx.*
-ka-, w-.

third person singular neuter alienable.
aw-/u-.
third person singular neuter inalienable.
pfx. ka-/w-.
third person singular neuter patient. *pfx.*
-yaw-/ -yu-.
translocative. *pfx.* -yah-, wa'-, we-.
translocative+dualic. *pfx.* ya'ne-, wa'=
ne-.
translocative+dualic+future. *pfx.* ya'nę-.
translocative+dualic+future+repetitive.
pfx. ya'nęči-.
translocative+dualic+optative. *pfx.* ya'=
na(r)(a)-.
translocative+dualic+optative+repetitive.
pfx. ya'nęθa(r)(a)-.
translocative+dualic+repetitive. *pfx.* ya'=
neči-.
translocative+factual. *pfx.* yahwa'-.
translocative+factual+cislocative. *pfx.*
yahwa'T(i)-.
translocative+factual+dualic. *pfx.* yah=
wa'T(i)-.
translocative+factual+dualic+repetitive.
pfx. yahwa'nęθa-.
translocative+factual+repetitive. *pfx.* ya=
hęθa-.
translocative+future. *pfx.* yę-.
translocative+future+repetitive. *pfx.* yę=
či-.
translocative+optative. *pfx.* ya(r)(a)-.
translocative+repetitive. *pfx.* yeči-, we=
či-.
translocative+repetitive+optative. *pfx.*
yeθa(r)(a)-.

Tuscarora Pronunciation Key:
/a/ law; /e/ hat; /i/ pizza; /u/ tune; /ę/ hint; /č/
cheese; /h/ hoe; /m/ mother; /s/ same; /t/ do
(before a vowel y, or w), too (elsewhere); /k/ gale
(before a vowel y or w), kale (elsewhere); /n/
inhale (before a consonant or word-final), note
(elsewhere), /r/ hiss (before a consonant or word-

final), run (trilled as in Italian, elsewhere); /w/ cuff
(before a consonant other than y or word-final),
way (elsewhere); /y/ fish (before a consonant or
word-final), you (elsewhere), /θ/ thing; /'/ (the
sound between the vowels in unh-unh); /·/ long
vowel, /´/ high pitch; /`/ low pitch.

Bibliography

Cayuga, Percy. 1972. Canadian Tuscarora Vocabulary and Texts. Recorded by Michael K. Foster at the Six Nations Reserve. Hull, Quebec: Canadian Ethnological Service, Canadian Museum of Civilization.

Chafe, Wallace. 1967. *Seneca Morphology and Dictionary*. Smithsonian Contributions to Anthropology no. 4. Washington, D.C.: Smithsonian Institution.

Christjohn, Amos, and Maria Hinton. 1996. *An Oneida Dictionary*. Clifford Abbott (ed.). Oneida, Wisc.: Authors.

Feeling, Durban. 1978. *Cherokee-English Dictionary*. Tahlequah, Okla.: Cherokee Nation of Oklahoma.

Fickett, Joan G. 1967. The Phonology of Tuscarora. *Studies in Linguistics* 19: 33-57.

Foster, Michael, Karin Michelson, and Hanni Woodbury. 1988. Base and Affix Dictionary for Iroquoian. Rensselaerville, N.Y.: Conference on Iroquois Research.

Gallatin, Albert. 1836. A Synopsis of Indian Tribes within the United States East of the Rocky Mountains, and in the British and Russian Possessions in North America. *Transactions and Collections of the American Antiquarian Society* 2:1-422.

Hewitt, J.N.B. 1903. Iroquoian Cosmology, First Part. *Twenty-first Annual Report of the Bureau of American Ethnology for the Year 1901-2*, pp. 127-339. Washington, D.C.: Government Printing Office.

Hewitt, J.N.B. 1928. Iroquoian Cosmology, Second Part. *Forty-third Annual Report of the Bureau of American Ethnology for the Year 1925-26*, pp. 449-819. Washington, D.C.: Government Printing Office.

Jefferson, Thomas. 1817. A Manuscript Comparative Vocabulary of Several Indian Languages. Ms. no. 497/J35. Philadelphia, Penn.: American Philosophical Society.

Landy, David. 1978. Tuscarora among the Iroquois. *Handbook of North American Indians*. Vol. 15: 518-524. Washington, D.C.: Smithsonian Institution.

Lawson, John. 1709. *A New Voyage to Carolina*. Originally published as part of *A New Collection of Voyages and Travels: With Historical Accounts of Discoveries and Conquests in All Parts of the World,* collected by John Stevens. London: 1708-1711. [1714 edition reprinted as *Lawson's History of North Carolina,* 1937, edited by F. L. Hariss, the North Carolina Society of the Colonial Dames of America. Richmond, Va.: Garrett and Massie.]

Lounsbury, Floyd G. 1953. *Oneida Verb Morphology.* Yale University Publications in Anthropology no. 48. New Haven, Conn.: Yale University.

Lounsbury, Floyd G. 1961. Iroquois-Cherokee Linguistic Relationships. *Bureau of American Ethnology Bulletin* no. 180:11-17. Washington, D.C.: Smithsonian Institution.

Michelson, Gunther. 1974. *A Thousand Words of Mohawk.* Mercury Series Paper No. 5. Ottawa, Ontario: National Museum of Man, National Museums of Canada.

Michelson, Gunther. 1995. Notes for a Mohawk Dictionary. Ottawa, Ont.: Author.

Mithun, Marianne. 1981. Stalking the Susquehannock. *International Journal of American Linguistics* 47:1-26.

Morgan, Lewis Henry. 1851. *League of the Ho-de´-no-sau-nee, or Iroquois.* Rochester, N.Y.: Sage & Brother.

Morgan, Lewis Henry. 1870. *Systems of Consanguinity and Affinity of the Human Family.* Smithsonian Contributions to Knowledge no. 17. Washington, D.C.: Smithsonian Institution.

Rudes, Blair A. 1976. Historical Phonology and the Development of the Tuscarora Sound System. Unpublished PhD Dissertation. Buffalo: State University of New York.

Rudes, Blair A. 1981. A Sketch of the Nottoway Language from a Historical-Comparative Perspective. *International Journal of American Linguistics* 47: 28-51.

Rudes, Blair A. 1984. Cowinchahakon/ Akawęč'á·ka·': The Meherrin in the Nineteenth Century. *Algonquian and Iroquoian Linguistics* 6.3: 5-7.

Rudes, Blair A. 1987. *Tuscarora Roots, Stems, and Particles: Toward a Dictionary of Tuscarora.* Memoir No. 3. Winnipeg, Manitoba: Algonquian and Iroquoian Linguistics.

Rudes, Blair A. 1992. The Status of Affricates and Fricatives in the Northern and Southern Iroquoian Languages. Ms. Washington, D.C.: Author.

Rudes, Blair A. 1995. Iroquoian Vowels. *Anthropological Linguistics* 37: 16-69.

Rudes, Blair A., and Dorothy Crouse. 1987. *The Tuscarora Legacy of J.N. B. Hewitt: Materials for the Study of the Tuscarora Language and Culture.* 2 Vols. Mercury Series Paper No. 108. Hull, Quebec: Canadian Museum of Civilization.

Saunders, William L. (ed.). 1886-1980. *The Colonial Records of North Carolina.* 10 Vols. Raleigh, N.C.

Schoolcraft, Henry Rowe. 1846. *Notes on the Iroquois or Contributions to the American History, Antiquities, and General Ethnography.* New York: Bartlett & Welford.

Williams, Marianne Mithun. 1974. A Grammar of Tuscarora. Unpublished PhD dissertation. New Haven, Conn.: Yale University. [New York: Garland, 1975]

Williams, Ted. 1976. *The Reservation.* Syracuse, N.Y.: Syracuse University.